Rapidex®

English *to* English & Hindi DICTIONARY

with usage in English

अंग्रेज़ी से अंग्रेज़ी-हिन्दी डिक्शनरी

Rapidex®
PUBLICATIONS

Published by:

Rapidex PUBLICATIONS

An Imprint of

Pustak Mahal®

Administrative office and sale centre

J-3/16 , Daryaganj, New Delhi-110002

☎ 011-23276539, 23272783, 23272784, 23260518

E-mail: info@pustakmahal.com • *Website:* www.pustakmahal.com

Branches

Bengaluru: ☎ 080-22234025, 40912845

E-mail: pustakmahalblr@gmail.com

Mumbai: ☎ 022-22010941, 22053387

E-mail: unicornbooksmumbai@gmail.com

Rapidex Trade Mark Registration No. 318345//dt. 6.9.76

ISBN 978-81-223-1452-6

Edition: 2022

Printed at : Radha Offset, Delhi

Aa

Aa *(n.)* ए–अंग्रेज़ी वर्णमाला का पहला अक्षर, सर्वोच्च, बहुत अच्छा The first letter of the English alphabet. Anita begins with 'A'.

a/an *(Indefinite articles)* अ/ऐन–one, any, some एक, प्रत्येक, कोई 1. Do you have *a* book of short stories? I drink milk twice *a* day. He drove eighty miles in *an* hour.
2. *A* & *An* as indefinite articles are used before a single countable noun. *A* is used before a consonant sound and *An* before a vowel sound: Seema is *a* teacher. Rahul is *an* engineer.

aback *(adv.)* अबैक–surprised, startled चकित, भौचक्का I was taken *aback* by his rudeness.

abacus *(n.)* ऐबकस–a frame with beads sliding on rods for mathematical calculations गिनतारा The Japanese prefer to use *abacus* for calculations.

abandon *(v.)* अबैन्डन–to give up entirely त्यागना, जाने देना Why did you *abandon* your studies?

abase *(v.)* अबेस–to lower in reputation अपमानित करना A policeman was *abasing* a gentleman.

abashed *(adj.)* अबैशड–to make embarrassed लज्जित Her teacher's criticism left her feeling rather *abashed.*

abate *(v.)* अबेट–to reduce in intensity प्रभाव कम करना Hardships could not *abate* his zest for life.

abatement *(n.)* अबेटमण्ट– decrease, deduction घटाव, कमी This trend shows no sign of *abatement.*

abbess *(n.)* ऐबेस– a female superior of a convent of nuns धार्मिक समाज की प्रमुख महिला, महंतिन Mother Teresa was the *abbess* of Nirmal Hriday in Kolkata.

abbey *(n.)* ऐबि– a convent of monastery ईसाइयों का मठ Wordsworth has written many poems on *abbey.*

abbot *(n.)* ऐबॅट्– head of an abbey or monastery साधु-समाज का प्रमुख पुरुष, मठाधिपति The Dalai Lama is the *abbot* of the Tibetan monastery.

abbreviation *(n.)* अब्रीविएशन– short form of a word संक्षेप, संक्षिप्त रूप U.N.O. is the *abbreviation* of United Nations Organisation.

abdicate *(v.)* ऐब्डिकेट– renounce formally (throne, etc.) पद का त्याग करना The Queen *abdicated* in favour of her stepson.

abdomen *(n.)* ऐब्डमन– belly, the part between diaphragm and pelvis उदर, पेट He had severe pain in his *abdomen.*

abdominal *(adj)* ऐब्डॉमिनल– relating to the abdomen उदरीय Pilates greatly benefits the lower *abdominals.*

abduct *(v.)* ऐब्डक्ट– kidnap अपहरण करना Sarita was *abducted* by gangsters.

abduction *(n.)* ऐब्डक्शन– kidnapping अपहरण *Abduction* is a crime.

aberrant *(adj.)* ऐबॅरन्ट– departing or deviating from right course गुमराह, पथभ्रष्ट He has *aberrant* ideas on social issues.

abhor *(v.)* अब्हॉर– to regard with hatred अत्यधिक घृणा करना I *abhor* terrorism.

abhorrence *(n.)* अबहॉरन्स– something which is hated घृणा की प्रबल भावना Anna is known for his *abhorrence* of corruption.

abhorrent *(adj.)* अब्हॉरंट– repugnant; loathsome घृणित Violence is *abhorrent* to my nature.

abide *(v.)* अबाइड्– to accept without opposition or question क़ानून आदि का

पालन करना We should *abide* by the laws of the country.

ability *(n.)* अबिलटि– talent, capacity or power योग्यता, किसी कार्य को पूरा करने की शक्ति एवं क्षमता She has an *ability* to make decisions.

ablaze *(adj.)* अब्लेज़–1. on fire दहकता हुआ The fireman rushed to the house, which was set *ablaze*.
2. radiantly bright उज्ज्वल, प्रदीप्त The auditorium was *ablaze* with lights.

able *(adj.)* एबूल– talented, capable योग्य, समर्थ They would never be *able* to afford such a big house.

abnormal *(adj.)* ऐब्नॉर्मल– different from what is normal असामान्य Karan's *abnormal* behaviour made his parents worried.

aboard *(adv.)* अबॉर्ड– on board; in or into a ship, train, airplane, etc. हवाई जहाज़ या रेलगाड़ी में सवार The plane crashed, killing all 158 people *aboard*.

abode *(n.)* अबोड– house, dwelling place निवास स्थान, आवास, घर I do not know his place of *abode*.

abolish *(v.)* ऐबॉलिश– to put an end to the existence समाप्त करना, हटा देना Evil practices should be *abolished* by society.

abolition *(n.)* ऐबॉलिशन– being abolished उन्मूलन, समापन, अन्त Gandhiji worked very hard for the *abolition* of the Sati Pratha.

abominable *(adj.)* अबॉमिनबल– unpleasent, bad घिनौना, बहुत बुरा I do not like her *abominable* behaviour.

abomination *(n.)* अबॉमिनेशन– something that invokes complete dislike घृणित वस्तु या बात Her behaviour is an *abomination* for me.

aboriginal *(adj.)* ऐबरिजनल– pertaining to those who have been at a place since the earliest unknown times आदिवासी, आदिम Some people were the *aboriginal* inhabitants of Australia.

abort *(v.)* अबॉर्ट्– to miscarry, to end prematurely किसी कार्य को पूरा होने से पहले ही समाप्त कर देना The peace talks had to be *aborted*. She *aborted* her pregnancy and lost the baby.

abortion *(n.)* अबॉर्शन– the deliberate termination of a human pregnancy, a person or thing that is deformed गर्भपात, भ्रूणहत्या *Abortion* is a crime.

abortive *(adj.)* अबॉर्टिव– futile, fruitless निष्फल, बेकार He made two *abortive* attempts to rescue the passengers.

about *(prep.)* अबाउट–1. concerned with (के) विषय में, I am reading a book *about* birds.
2. here and there चारों ओर, यहां-वहां The children walked *about* the zoo.
3. near, close निकट, समीप He came here at *about* ten o'clock.
4. almost equal क़रीब उतना ही Sudha is *about* as tall as Meena.

above *(prep.)* अबव– at a higher point ऊपर The plane flies *above* the clouds.

abrade *(v.)* अब्रेड– rub, erase घिसना, मिटाना, हटाना She *abraded* her jeans so hard that it tore.

abrasion *(n.)* अब्रेशन– rubbing, scrapping खरोंच, रगड़ The area with *abrasion* has become red.

abrasive *(adj.)* अब्रेसिव– rough, harsh खुरदरा, खरोंचदार Do not use *abrasive* cleaners on the basin.

abreast *(adv.)* अब्रेस्ट– alongside in progress एक क़तार में The soldiers marched forward *abreast*.

abridge *(v.)* अब्रिज– to cut short काँट-छाँट करना, संक्षिप्त करना We cannot *abridge* this book.

abridged *(adj.)* अब्रिजूड्– curtailed, reduced संक्षिप्त किया हुआ This is the *abridged* edition of Jane Austen's 'Pride and Prejudice'.

abroach *(adj.)* अब्रोच– opened, tapped खुला, खुले मुंह वाला The can was set *abroach.*

abroad *(adv.)* अब्रॉड– away from one's own country विदेश में I spent four years *abroad.*

abrogate *(v.)* ऐबूरोगेट– to abolish by authority, nullify निरस्त करना, रद्द करना I *abrogated* my plan to visit Hyderabad.

abrupt *(adj.)* अब्रप्ट–1. sudden, unexpected अचानक, आकस्मिक The music competition came to an *abrupt* end when the lights went out.

2. rough behaviour रूखा व्यवहार Her *abrupt* behaviour came as a shock to me.

abscess *(n.)* ऍब्सेस– sore, ulcer फोड़ा (मवाद भरा) The doctor removed the *abscess* from Dinesh's foot.

abscond *(v.)* अब्स्कान्ड–to depart in a sudden or secret manner फ़रार होना The cashier *absconded* from the city with a lot of money.

absence *(n.)* ऐब्सन्स–being away from अनुपस्थिति, ग़ैरहाज़िरी I have to make all the decisions in my boss's *absence.*

absent *(adj.)* ऐब्सन्ट–not present अनुपस्थित Four boys were *absent* from school today.

absent-minded *(adj.)* ऐबूसन्ट्-माइनूडड्– inattentive, lost in thoughts भुलक्कड़, खोया-खोया रहने वाला He is always *absent-minded* in the class.

absent-mindedly *(adv.)* ऐबूसन्ट्-माइनूडड्लि–inattentively अनमनेपन से The student replied to the teacher *absent-mindedly.*

absolute *(adj.)* ऐबसलूट्–1. perfect, complete समूचा, पूरा He must know the *absolute* truth.

2. unlimited पक्का, असीमित I am the *absolute* owner of this property.

3. real, undoubted वास्तविक It is an *absolute* fact.

4. unconditional बिना शर्त, पूर्णरूप से An *absolute* promise must be kept.

absolutely *(adv.)* ऐब्सलूट्लि–completely and definitely सर्वथा, बिल्कुल He *absolutely* adores that car.

absolution *(n.)* ऐब्सलूशन–a formal release from guilt, obligation or punishment पाप-क्षमा, पाप से क्षमादान की घोषणा The priest granted him full *absolution* for his sins.

absolve *(v.)* अब्ज़ॉल्व्–declare free from sin अपराध या पाप से मुक्त करना We *absolved* you from moral blame.

absorb *(v.)* अब्ज़ॉर्ब–1. take or suck in सोखना या चूसना Blotting paper *absorbs* ink.

2. engross, engage attention wholly लीन होना, तल्लीन हो जाना The cricket match *absorbed* Rakesh.

absorbed *(adj.)* अबज़ार्बड–engrossed निमग्न, तल्लीन The family firm was *absorbed* into a larger group.

abstain *(v.)* अबूस्टेन–to keep away from परहेज़ करना I *abstained* myself from smoking.

abstemious *(adj.)* ऐबस्टीमियस–not taking much food or drink संयमी Shyam is an *abstemious* person.

abstract *(adj.)* ऐबस्ट्रैक्ट– 1. considered apart from concrete existence अव्यावहारिक It is an *abstract* idea.

2. *(n.)* precis, summary संक्षेप, सारांश This book is an *abstract* of the Mahabharata.

3. *(v.)* separate, take out from निकालना, अलग करना Applications to *abstract* more water from streams

absurd *(adj.)* अब्सर्ड–unreasonable, foolish, ridiculous मूर्खतापूर्ण, निरर्थक, हास्यास्पद Ramesh's *absurd* talk showed his foolishness.

abundance *(n.)* अबन्डन्स–over sufficient quantity, fullness अधिकता, बहुतायत The fruits are found in *abundance* in Himachal Pradesh.

abundant *(adj.)* अबन्डन्ट–more than enough, pleantiful प्रचुर, अधिक This library has an *abundant* stock of books. Rice is *abundant* in Kerala.

abuse *(v.)* अब्यूज़–1. speak insultingly गाली देना, दुर्वचन कहना We should never *abuse* anybody.
2. wrong use दुरुपयोग करना Riders who *abuse* their horses should be prosecuted.
3. *(n.)* misuse अनुचित उपयोग These people have suffered sexual *abuse*.

abusive *(adj.)* अब्यूज़िव–insulting अश्लील, अपमानजनक We should not use *abusive* language.

abut *(v.)* ॲबट्–to touch at one end or side of something लगा हुआ होना, समीप होना My house *abuts* on a street.

abuzz *(adj.)* ॲबज़–filled with a buzzing sound भिनभिनाता हुआ, शोरगुल से भरा The conference hall was *abuzz* with students and teachers.

abyss *(n.)* ॲबिस–deep bottomless hole अत्यधिक गहरा गड्ढा An *abyss* seems to have no bottom.

acacia *(n.)* अकेशिआ–a tropical tree बबूल, कीकर Glue can be made of *acacia.*

academic *(adj.)* ऐकडेमिक–scholarly शैक्षिक Shyam has an *academic* background.

academy *(n.)* अकैडमि–school for higher learning पाठशाला, विद्योपार्जन का स्थान, विद्वत् परिषद्, ज्ञान समाज He was educated privately at *academies* in Margate.

accede *(v.)* ॲक्सीड–assent or agree to a request or a proposal किसी अनुरोध या मांग को मान लेना They will lightly *accede* to his request.

accelerate *(v.)* अक्सेलरेट–to increase the speed of गति बढ़ाना Inflation started to *accelerate*.

accent *(n.)* ऐक्सन्ट–prominence or stress given to a syllable बोलने की या उच्चारण की पद्धति Raman speaks English with a South Indian *accent.*

accentuate *(v.)* अक्सेनचुएट्–to give emphasis to महत्त्व बढ़ाना She uses make-up to *accentuate* her beauty.

accept *(v.)* अक्सेप्ट–1. to approve of लेना, स्वीकार करना The beggar *accepted* alms from the rich man.
2. believe विश्वास करना I am sorry I cannot *accept* what you say.

acceptable *(adj.)* अक्सेपटब्ल्–approvable स्वीकार करने योग्य A cup of coffee is *acceptable* to me.

acceptance *(n.)* अक्सेपटन्स– approval स्वीकृति I got his *acceptance.*

access *(n.)* ऐक्सेस– 1. ability to use किसी वस्तु को प्रयोग में लाने का अवसर I do not have *access* to the Internet.
2. *(v.)* to make available कंप्यूटर में विशिष्ट जानकारी तक पहुंचना Information can be *accessed* from several files.

accessary *(n.)* अक्सेसरि– person who helps in any criminal act किसी अपराध में शामिल होने वाला व्यक्ति He was made an *accessary* to the crime.

accessory *(n.)* अक्सेसरि– something extra that adds attractiveness सहायक उपकरण (सुन्दरता लाने में) She wore the suit with perfectly matching *accessories.*

accident *(n.)* ऐक्सिडन्ट–something that happens without a cause दुर्घटना, आकस्मिक घटना Gopal met with a car *accident* yesterday.

accidental *(adj.)* ऐक्सिडेन्टल–unexpected and by chance आकस्मिक The inspector made an *accidental* inspection of the school.

accidentally *(adv.)* ऐक्सिडेनटलि–happening unexpectedly and by chance संयोगवश, जानबूझकर नहीं I met him *accidentally* in a fair.

acclaim *(n.)* अक्लेम– 1. applause प्रशंसा In spite of an average business, the movie won critical *acclaim.*

2. *(v.)* welcome with shouts of approval अभिनंदन करना, जय-जयकार करना The book, the shadow lines was *acclaimed* by the readers.

accolade *(n.)* ऐकलेड– any award, honour पुरस्कार, प्रशंसात्मक उल्लेख The film received *accolades* from the public and the press.

accommodation *(n.)* अकॉमडेशन–lodging or board and lodging रहने की जगह अथवा सुविधा She is looking for *accommodation* these days.

accompany *(v.)* अकम्पनि–1. go with साथ देना या चलना Sudhir was *accompanied* by his wife to the musical concert.

2. play or sing an accompaniment to साथ गाना या बजाना The musician played the Sitar and his young son *accompanied* him on the Tabla.

accomplice *(n.)* अकमप्लिस– helper in a wrong deed सहअपराधी The police arrested him and his *accomplice*.

accomplish *(v.)* अकमप्लिश– to complete पूर्ण करना, सिद्ध करना Congratulations on *accomplishing* such a difficult task!

accord *(n.)* अकॉर्ड– 1. everybody consenting औपचारिक समझौता Israel and Palestine signed a peace *accord*.

2. *(v.)* to agree with or match sth किसी के साथ मेल खाना Her thoughts and actions do not *accord*.

accordingly *(adv.)* अकॉर्डिंगली– correspondingly इसी तरह से, तदनुसार We have to discover what his plans are and act accordingly.

according to *(prep.)* अकॉर्डिंग टू– as stated by के अनुसार We must act *according to* our strategy.

accordion *(n.)* अकॉर्डिअन्– a portable musical instrument एक प्रकार का बाजा, वाद्ययंत्र Varun plays the *accordion* very well.

accost *(v.)* अकॉस्ट–to approach (with a greeting remark) पास आना (अभिवादन के लिए) I was *accosted* on the road by a complete stranger.

account *(n.)* अकाउंट–1. a narrative or record of events वर्णन, कथन His *account* of the event was very interesting.

2. counting गणना, आय-व्यय का लेखा I do not know how to keep *accounts*.

3. *(v.)* to be the cause of कारण बतलाना How did Kamal *account* for being late today?

accountable *(adj.)* अकाउंटबल– responsible जवाबदेह I am not *accountable* for what happened yesterday.

accountant *(n.)* अकाउन्टन्ट– person whose profession is to keep accounts लेखाकार He is a loyal *accountant* of the company.

accredit *(v.)* अक्रैडिट– to recognize and approve officially मान्यता देना He was *accredited* as an ambassador to Malaysia.

accumulate *(v.)* ॲक्यूम्यलेट्– to pile up, collect इकट्ठा करना या होना Dust will *accumulate* in the room if you do not clean it daily.

accurate *(adj.)* ऐक्यूरेट– careful and correct अचूक, सही, ठीक My wrist-watch always shows the *accurate* time.

accusation *(n.)* ऐक्युज़ेशन– being accused of doing wrong आरोप A clear conscience fears no *accusation*.

accusatory *(adj.)* ऐक्युज़ेटरि– containing or implying blame or strong criticism अभियोगात्मक His tone is *accusatory*.

accuse *(v.)* अक्यूज़– to bring charge against दोष लगाना, दोषी या अपराधी ठहराना The servant was *accused* of stealing a golden ring.

accuser *(n.)* ऐक्युज़र– person who impute blame on someone अभियोक्ता The *accuser* was the main culprit.

accusing *(adj.)* अक्यूज़िंग– to blame आरोप लगाने का संकेत करते हुए She gave me an *accusing* look.

accustom *(v.)* अकस्टम– to get used to अभ्यास डालना, परिचय कराना We should *accustom* ourselves to the idea of space travel.

accustomed *(adj.)* अकस्टम्ड– habituated लती, आदी, अभ्यस्त We are not *accustomed* to very cold weather.

ace *(n.)* एस– person who is expert at something कुशल व्यक्ति He is an *ace* rifleman.

ache *(n.)* एक्– 1. pain दर्द, पीड़ा If you have a tooth-*ache,* you should go to a dentist.
2. *(v.)* have continuous pain पीड़ा होना My leg is *aching.*

achieve *(v.)* अचीव– to bring to a successful end कार्य पूर्ण करना, अन्त करना, जीतना He *achieved* his ambition to become a photographer.

achievement *(n.)* अचीव्मेन्ट– something that has been accomplished उपलब्धि, प्राप्ति To reach this stage is a great *achievement.*

acid *(n.)* ऐसिड– a substance with a sour taste तेज़ाब HCL is an *acid.*

acidity *(n.)* असिडटि– 1. the quality or state of being acid तेज़ाबी, खट्टापन I am suffering from *acidity* in the stomach.
2. ill-natured in mood, manner कटु, चुभने वाला, तीखा I found a certain *acidity* in his comments.

acknowledge *(v.)* अक्नॉलिज–1. confess to मान लेना, सत्यता स्वीकार करना The plight of refugees was *acknowledged* by the authorities. 2. to indicate or make known the receipt of रसीद लिखकर स्वीकार करना I *acknowledged* the receipt of his letter.

acne *(n.)* ऐकनि– a disease which causes pimples and blackheads on the face and neck मुंहासे She has *acnes* on her face.

acquaintance *(n.)* अक्वेण्टन्स– state of being known to someone परिचय, जान-पहचान, परिचित व्यक्ति Harish has many *acquaintances* but very few friends.

acquire *(v.)* अक्वाअर्– to gain कमाना, प्राप्त करना The businessman *acquired* a lot of money by hard work.

acquisitive *(adj.)* ऐक्विज़िटिव– seeking to acquire and possess प्राप्त करने को लालायित He has an *acquisitive* mind.

acquit *(v.)* अक्विट– to relieve from a charge of fault or crime निर्दोष ठहराना, रिहा करना He was *acquitted* of murder.

acquittal *(n.)* अक्विटल– a discharge or release from an obligation दोष से छुटकारा, बरी करने की क्रिया Lack of evidence resulted in his *acquittal.*

acre *(n.)* ऐकर– measure of land एकड़ (लगभग डेढ़ बीघा ज़मीन) The institute has acquired 54 *acres* of land.

acrid *(adj.)* ऐकरिड– bitter, sharp or biting to the taste or smell कड़वा, तीखा, कटु Sushila is not liked because of her *acrid* nature.

acrimony *(n.)* ऐक्रिमनि– hardhness, sharpness or bitterness of nature, speech, disposition कटु भावनाएं, रूखापन In his speech he attacked him with great *acrimony.*

acrobat *(n.)* ऐक्रबैट– skilled performer of gymnastic feats बाज़ीगर, नट, क़लाबाज़ The street girl was a good *acrobat.*

across *(prep.)* अक्रॉस– 1. so as to cross over एक ओर से दूसरी ओर, के पार There are many bridges *across* the Yamuna in Delhi.
2. (*adv.*) from one side to the other of आरपार, सम्मुख, सामने I came *across* an old school friend in the market today.

act *(n.)* ऐक्ट–1. something done कार्य, व्यवहार A boy-scout does an *act* of kindness every day.
2. law कानून There are many *acts* in the Indian Penal Code.

3. a division of a play नाटक का अंक The last *act* of the play is about to begin.
4. *(v.)* do something कार्य करना, व्यवहार करना One should never *act* in haste.

action *(n.)* ऐक्शन– process of doing things क्रिया, गतिविधि You will be judged by your *actions*.

actionable *(adj.)* ऐक्शनअबल– giving first cause for legal अनुयोज्य, क़ानूनी कार्यवाही करने योग्य Some illegal acts may be *actionable*.

activate *(v.)* ऐक्टिवेट– be active सक्रिय रहना A slight movement can *activate* the fan.

active *(adj.)* ऐक्टिव– constantly engaged in action सक्रिय, चुस्त A balanced diet makes you more *active*.

actively *(adv.)* ऐक्टिवलि– acting quickly फुर्ती से He climbed up the stairs *actively*.

activist *(n.)* ऐक्टिविस्ट– person acting militant action कर्मठ व्यक्ति, क्रियावादी His father is a social *activist*.

activity *(n.)* ऐक्टिवटि– the state or quality of being active सक्रियता, क्रियाशीलता The hotel offers a range of leisure *activities*.

actor *(n.)* ऐक्टर– a person who acts अभिनेता Amitabh Bachchan is a good *actor*.

actress *(n.)* ऐक्ट्रस– a female actor अभिनेत्री Madhubala was a famous *actress*.

actual *(adj.)* ऐक्चुअल– real, existing in act or fact निश्चित, यथार्थ The *actual* cost of the laptop was so high but I bargained.

actually *(adv.)* एक्चुअलि– in fact, really दरअसल He *actually* wanted to stay with his friend.

actuate *(v.)* ऐक्चुएट– to incite to action गति देना, चालू करना, उकसाना Electricity *actuates* the bulb.

acuity *(n.)* ऐक्युटि– sharpness, acuteness तीव्रता, कुशाग्रता The *acuity* of his thoughts impressed me.

acumen *(n.)* ऐक्यूमन– sharpness and accuracy of judgement कुशाग्रबुद्धि She hides a shrewd business *acumen*.

acupuncture *(n.)* ऐक्युपंक्चर– the insertion of the tips of needles into the skin at specific points for the purpose of treating various disorders शरीर में बारीक सूइयों से छेद करके रोग ठीक करने की चिकित्सा, एक चीनी पद्धति *Acupuncture* is very effective in controlling some types of pain.

acute *(adj.)* एक्यूट–1. severe बहुत अधिक She complained of an *acute* pain in her stomach last night.
2. brief and severe बीमारी जो ख़तरनाक बन जाए He is a patient of *acute* bronchitis.
3. state of being~तीक्ष्ण Animals have an *acute* sense of hearing.

adage *(n.)* ऐडेज– an old and wise saying कहावत *Adages* express the general truth.

adamant *(adj.)* एडमन्ट– utterly unyielding or firm in opinion अड़ियल, दृढ़ In spite of all appeals she was *adamant* on this point.

adapt *(v.)* अडैप्ट– to make suitable to requirements or conditions अनुकूल करना We should try to *adapt* ourselves to changing circumstances.

adaptable *(adj.)* अडैप्टबल– able to adjust oneself readily to different conditions नई परिस्थिति के अनुकूल परिवर्तनीय, बदलने योग्य Dinosaurs were not *adaptable* animals.

adaptation *(n.)* अडैप्टेशन– to make it suitable for different use रूपांतर The *adaptation* of movie was based on Tagore's novel.

add *(v.)* ऐड– to join, so as to increase the number जोड़ना, बढ़ाना You have made a mistake in *adding* these figures.

addict *(n.)* ऐडिक्ट– fall into habit व्यसनी, लत I encountered a drug *addict* in the subway.

addicted *(adj.)* ऐडिक्टड– habituated आदी, आसक्त He is *addicted* to smoking.

addition *(n.)* अडिशन–1. process of adding जोड़ने की क्रिया, संयोजन The children are learning *addition* and division. 2. something added किसी अन्य के साथ जोड़ी गई वस्तु या व्यक्ति This equipment is the latest *addition* to our office.

additional *(adj.)* अडिशनल– extra अतिरिक्त While handling this case we need an *additional* security.

addle *(v.)* ऐडल– to spoil, rotten सड़ाना, दिमाग़ ख़राब होना His brain is *addled* by whisky.

address *(n.)* ॲड्रैस–1. details of where a person can be found पता, पत्र का सिरनामा He wrote down my *address* in his notebook. 2. spech
3. *(v.)* to make a formal speech व्याख्यान देना News channels televised presidential *address*. The headmaster *addressed* the students.

ademption *(n.)* अडैम्पशन– cancellation of a will विखंडन They did not like the *ademption* of legacy.

adept *(adj.)* अडेप्ट– skilled कुशल He is *adept* at public speaking.

adequate *(adj.)* ऐडिक्वट– satisfactory पर्याप्त, योग्य The amount of money I have is not *adequate* for buying a car.

adhere *(v.)* अड्हियर्–1. to stick fast मज़बूती से चिपक जाना Make sure the paper is *adhered* to the cardboard properly.
2. remain faithful किसी नियम का पालन करना It is better you *adhere* to the company rules.

adhesive *(n.)* अड्हीसिव– a substance that makes things stick together दो वस्तुओं को चिपकाने वाला पदार्थ, गोंद Always use quick dry *adhesive* for your project work.

ad hoc *(adj.)* ऐड हॉक– for a particular purpose only तदर्थ The university appointed him on an *ad hoc* basis.

adjacent *(adj.)* अजेसन्ट्– next, lying near किसी के निकट My house is *adjacent* to the school.

adjective *(n)* ऐजिक्टिव– one that defines or limits a noun विशेषण Notorious is the *adjective* that best describes him.

adjoin *(v.)* एडजॉइन– to be close to or in contact with मिलना/मिलाना, जुड़ना/जोड़ना The officer's residence *adjoins* his office.

adjoining *(adj.)* एडजॉइनिंग– bordering सटा हुआ, निकटवर्ती Rama and Uma live in *adjoining* houses.

adjourn *(v.)* अडजर्न– to suspend the meeting स्थगित करना The meeting was *adjourned* till the next day.

adjure *(v.)* आजूर– to charge earnestly and solemnly शपथपूर्वक कहना, आग्रहपूर्वक प्रार्थना करना I *adjure* you to tell the truth.

adjust *(v.)* अड्जस्ट– to set right, to settle ठीक करना, व्यवस्थित करना He *adjusted* the lamp so that he could read better.

adjustable *(adj.)* अड्जस्टबल– that can be adjusted समायोजनीय, जिसे अनुकूल बनाया जा सके My car has *adjustable* seats.

adjustment *(n.)* अड्जस्टमण्ट– a settlement of something तालमेल, निपटारा The room needs a slight *adjustment* in seating arrangement.

administer *(v.)* अडमिनिस्टर्– control, manage प्रबंध करना, शासन करना The headmaster *administers* the school.

administration *(n.)* अडमिनिस्ट्रेशन– government प्रबंध, शासन The university *administration* took their demands seriously.

admire *(v.)* ऐडमायर– acknowledge प्रशंसा करना, स्तुति करना All of Smita's friends *admired* her beautiful sari.

admirable *(adj.)* ऐडमरबल– praiseworthy प्रशंसनीय Courage is an *admirable* quality.

admiration *(n.)* ऐडमरेशन– a feeling of wonder प्रशंसा We all felt *admiration* for his great strength.

admissibility *(n.)* अड्मिसबिलटि– acceptability ग्राह्यता We do not give *admissibility* to indecency.

admissible *(adj.)* अड्मिसबल– that can be allowed as judicial proof स्वीकृत A careless attitude is not *admissible.*

admission *(n.)* अड्मिशन–1. act of being admitted to a school प्रवेश, भर्ती I got *admission* in an engineering college.

2. confession or acknowledgment ग्रहण, स्वीकरण He made an *admission* that he had lied before.

admit *(v.)* अड्मिट–1. to accept, confess मान लेना, स्वीकार करना The boy *admitted* that he had broken the windowpane.

2. to allow to enter, let in प्रवेश देना, (अंदर) आने देना The headmaster *admitted* the new boy to his school.

admonish *(v.)* अडमॉनिश– to give a mind warning or a gentle reproof डांटना, फटकारना The teacher *admonished* the boy for being lazy.

admonition *(n.)* अडमॉनिशन– to warn फटकार, भर्त्सना She was given an *admonition* not to fight with Reema.

adobe *(n.)* अडोबि– a sun-dried brick used for building कच्ची ईंट Many houses in the village have *adobe* walls.

adolescence *(n.)* ऐडोलसन्स– the traditional period between puberty and adulthood किशोरावस्था During *adolescence* teenagers often experience mood swings.

adolescent *(n.)* ऐडोलसण्ट– growing to manhood or womenhood किशोर/किशोरी *Adolescents* often seek the advice of their parents.

adopt *(v.)* अडॉप्ट–1. to accept स्वीकार करना, पारित करना The Lok Sabha *adopted* the annual budget for discussion.

2. to take into one's family as son or daughter गोद लेना The childless couple *adopted* a boy.

adorable *(adj.)* अडॉरबल– admirable, honourable मनमोहक, पूज्य, प्यारा Sulekha is a very *adorable* child.

adore *(v.)* अडॉर्– to regard with the utmost love and respect बहुत प्यार करना, बहुत पसन्द करना Every mother *adores* her child.

adorn *(v.)* ॲडार्न– to decorate, beautify सजाना, सुन्दर बनाना The bride was *adorned* with silken clothes and jewellery.

adrift *(adj.)* अड्रिफ़्ट– not under control इधर-उधर बहता हुआ The small boat was *adrift* on the high seas for four days.

adroit *(adj.)* अड्राइट– clever, skilful, expert चतुर, दक्ष Soniya is an *adroit* debator.

adroitness *(n.)* अड्राइटनस– cleverness कुशलता, दक्षता Charlie Chaplin had both intelligence and *adroitness.*

adulation *(n.)* ऐड्युलेशन– excessive flattery ख़ुशामद, अत्यधिक तारीफ़ The leader was expert in *adulation* of his supporters.

adult *(n.)* ऐडल्ट– grown to full size or strength वयस्क, बालिग़ *Adults* have the right to marry as per their will.

adulterate *(v.)* अडल्टरेट्– to make impure by adding inferior material खाद्य पदार्थ में मिलावट करना Some merchants do not hesitate to *adulterate* even baby food.

adulterous *(adj.)* अडल्टरस– marked by adultery व्यभिचारी Sona is involved in an *adulterous* relationship with him.

adultery *(n.)* अडलटरी– voluntary sexual intercourse between two persons who are not lawfully each others spouse व्यभिचार Today *adultery* is not considered a sin.

advance *(v.)* अड्वान्स–1. forward movement, progress आगे बढ़ना, उन्नति करना The army *advanced* towards the enemy's fort.
2. *(n.)* money paid before it is due पेशगी The author was paid a £250,000 *advance.*
3. something done before time अग्रिम There was no *advance* warning of the earthquake.

advantage *(n.)* अड्वाण्टेज– something of benefit लाभ, फ़ायदा Knowledge of English is a great *advantage.*

advantageous *(adj.)* ऐडवाण्टेजस– profitable लाभदायक, सहायक The situation proved *advantageous* to us.

advent *(n.)* ऐडवेण्ट– arrival आगमन The *advent* of the Mughals into Delhi changed the culture of India.

adventure *(n.)* अड्वेन्चर्–an exciting or very unusual experience साहसिक कार्य I like to read the stories of *adventure.*

adverse *(adj.)* ऐड्वर्स– antagonistic in purpose or effect प्रतिकूल Deserts offer *adverse* living conditions.

adversity *(n.)* ऐड्वर्सटी–a condition marked by misfortune बदनसीबी, परेशानियाँ He smiles even in grave *adversities.*

advertise *(v.)* ऐड्वर्टाइज़्– to give information विज्ञापन देना, विख्यात कराना This book is widely *advertised.*

advertisement *(n.)* ऐड्वटिज़्मन्ट– any public notice, as a printed display in a newspaper, short film on television, announcement on radio, etc. designed to sell goods, publicize an event, etc. विज्ञापन Advertisements for alcoholic drinks is required.

advice *(n.)* अड्वाइस– 1. an opinion offered as a guide सलाह या परामर्श You must follow the doctor's *advice* to take rest for a week.
2. *(v.)* to guide someone सलाह देना He *advised* me to consult a doctor.

advise *(v.)* ऐडवाइज़्– to give counsel to सलाह देना, नसीहत देना He did what the doctor *advised.*

advocate *(n.)* ऐडवॅकेट– 1. one who pleads cause of somebody वकील, अधिवक्ता His father is an *advocate* in the Supreme Court.
2. *(v.)* to support sth publicly समर्थन करना I *advocated* the plan suggested by him.

aerobics *(n.)* एअरोबिक्स– any system of sustained exercises designed to increase the amount of oxygen in the blood and strengthen the heart and lungs संगीत पर किया जाने वाला व्यायाम I do *aerobics* twice a week to keep fit.

aeronautics *(n.)* एरोनॉटिक्स– design and construction of aircraft विमान विज्ञान He is a master in the field of *aeronautics.*

aesthetic *(adj.)* ईसथेटिक– concerned with beauty सौंदर्यपरक He has a very good *aesthetic* sense.

affair *(n.)* अफ़ेयर्–1. any work done or to be done काम, कार्य Cooking is largely considered a woman's *affair.*
2. a particular matter मामला, घटना After the *affair* was over, everyone went home.

affect *(v.)* अफ़ेक्ट– to have an influence on असर करना, प्रभाव डालना His chest was *affected* by constant smoking.

affected *(adj.)* अफ़ेक्टेड– assumed artificially, pretended दिखावटी, बनावटी She showed *affected* feelings when I was sad.

affection *(n.)* अफ़ेक्शन– kindly feeling, love स्नेह, अनुराग There was great *affection* between Ram and Laxman.

affectionate *(adj.)* अफ़ेक्शनेट– characterized by love or affection प्यार करने वाला, स्नेही My brother is a very *affectionate* person.

affidavit *(n.)* ऐफ़डेविट– written statement हलफ़नामा I submitted my *affidavit* in the court.

affiliate *(v.)* अफ़िलिएट– to bring into close association किसी बड़ी संस्था से संबंधित होना Our local club is *affiliated* to the national association.

affinity *(n.)* अफ़िनिटी– strong liking or attraction लगाव, पसंद I always had an *affinity* for wild and lonely places.

affirm *(v.)* अफ़र्म– to maintain as true सच बतलाना He *affirmed* that he was innocent.

affirmative *(adj.)* अफ़र्मेटिव– expressing agreement सकारात्मक He gave an *affirmative* answer.

affirmation *(n.)* अफ़र्मेशन– a statement of the existence or truth of something दृढ़ कथन, पुष्टि He was asked to give an *affirmation* letter.

affix *(v.)* अफ़िक्स– to attach चिपकाना The label should be firmly *affixed* to the package.

afflict *(v.)* अफ़्लिक्ट– to distress with bodily or mental pain दुःख देना The poor are always *afflicted* with troubles.

affluence *(n.)* ऐफ़्लुअन्स– wealth अमीरी, समृद्धि She often boasts of her *affluence*.

affluent *(adj.)* ऐफ़्लुअण्ट– wealthy धनवान, अमीर She belongs to an *affluent* family of businessmen.

afford *(v.)* अफ़र्ड–to be able to (ख़र्च) दे सकना, समर्थ होना The best that I could *afford* was a first-floor room.

afforestation *(n.)* अफ़ॉरिस्टेशन– conversion of bare land into forest वृक्षारोपण *Afforestation* is the only alternative left.

affront *(n.)* अफ़्रण्ट– to insult खुलेआम अपमान, तिरस्कार Her words were an *affront* to all the family members.

afloat *(adj.)* अफ़लोट– floating on the water पानी पर तैरता हुआ A life jacket helps you stay *afloat* if you fall in the water.

aforementioned *(adj.)* अफ़ोर्मेनशंड– mentioned earlier पूर्वकथित The *aforementioned* person was seen acting suspiciously.

afraid *(adj.)* अफ़्रेड–1. full of fear भयभीत, डरा हुआ Little children are *afraid* of dogs.

2. filled with apprehension खेद प्रकट करने की शिष्टाचार-पद्धति I am *afraid* I cannot accept your invitation.

afresh *(adv.)* अफ़्रेश– in a new way नये सिरे से, दोबारा Let's start *afresh.*

after *(prep.)* आफ़्टर्– 1. later, following बाद में The boys played cricket *after* the school was over.

2. *(adv.)* पीछे The horses galloped one *after* another.

afterlife *(n.)* आफ़टर्लाइफ़– life after death मरने के बाद का जीवन The Egyptians had firm belief in *afterlife.*

aftermath *(n.)* आफ़टर्मॉथ– a consequence किसी ख़ास घटना का परिणाम A new building was built in the *aftermath* of the earthquake.

afternoon *(n.)* आफ़्टरनून– time between noon and evening तीसरा पहर I usually go for a walk in the *afternoon.*

aftershock *(n.)* आफ़्टरशॉक– one of a series of minor tremors occurring after the main shock of an earthquake भूकम्प के बाद का छोटा झटका The *aftershock* was so disastrous.

afterthought *(n.)* आफ़्टरथॉट– a comment, reply, etc, that occurs to one after the opportunity to deliver it has passed अनुबोध As an *afterthought*, I sent a greeting to him.

afterwards *(adv.)* आफ़्टरवर्ड्ज़– later on बाद में, फिर, पश्चात् He was taken to hospital and died shortly *afterwards*.

again *(adv.)* अगेन– once more दुबारा, फिर Please sing that song once *again*.

against *(prep.)* अगेन्स्ट–1. indicating opposition विरुद्ध, ख़िलाफ़ He fought bravely *against* the enemy.
2. indicating support पास, के सहारे Keep you bicycle *against* the wall.

age *(n.)* एज– length of time a person has lived or thing has existed वय, उम्र, अवस्था What is your *age*?

aged *(adj.)* एज्ड– old बूढ़ा, वयोवृद्ध It is difficult to change the habits of *aged* people.

agency *(n.)* एजन्सी– place of business कोई विशेष सेवा प्रदान करने वाला व्यवसाय We contacted an advertising *agency* to promote our brand.

agenda *(n.)* अजेण्डा– business to be discussed by a committee कार्यसूची Reducing terrorism is the first thing in the *agenda*.

agent *(n.)* एजण्ट– a person who acts for another or others अभिकर्ता, प्रतिनिधि Rahul is a travelling *agent*.

aggravate *(v.)* ऐग्रवेट– to make worse or more severe गंभीर बनाना, बदतर कर देना Going out into the cold will *aggravate* your illness.

aggregate *(n.)* ऐग्रिगट– bring or come together in a mass कुल जोड़ In the India-Pakistan match, the *aggregate* score of both the teams crossed 500.

aggressive *(adj.)* अग्रेसिव– characterized by unprovoked attacks झगड़ालू Nobody expected such an *aggressive* behaviour from her.

aggression *(n.)* अग्रेशन– beginning a quarrel or war उद्दंडतापूर्ण व्यवहार *Aggression* in children is a matter of concern for the parents.

aghast *(adj.)* अगास्ट– struck with overwhelming shock or amazement भौचक्का He stood *aghast* at the sight of so much blood.

agile *(adj.)* ऐजाइल– active, quick moving फुर्तीला A rabbit is an *agile* animal.

agility *(n.)* अजिलिटि– nimbleness फुर्ती, तेज़ी Running requires a lot of *agility* from both the batsmen.

agitate *(v.)* ऐजिटेट– to cause to move vigorously आंदोलन करना The workers *agitated* when forced to stay late in the office.

agitated *(adj.)* ऐजिटेटिड– excited परेशान, उत्तेजित The *agitated* students boycotted the exams.

agitation *(n.)* ऐजिटेशन– excitement of the mind and feeling अशांति, आंदोलन The policy of reservation led to *agitation* among the doctors.

aglow *(adj.)* अग्लो– bright with colour चमकता हुआ The children's faces were *aglow* with excitement.

agnostic *(n.)* ऐग्नास्टिक– person who believes that nothing can be known about God संशयवादी, अनीश्वरवादी Deep knowledge of science made him *agnostic*.

ago *(adv.)* अगो– past, gone by पहले He left this city four years *ago*.

agonized (ised) *(adj.)* ऐगनाइज़्ड– expressing pain वेदनापूर्ण, दर्द से भरी We heard an *agonized* cry from the street.

agonize (ise) *(v.)* ऐगनाइज़– to suffer intensely किसी कठिन समस्या पर लम्बे समय तक सोचना I *agonized* over a difficult decision.

agony *(n.)* ऐगनी– great pain घोर व्यथा I was in great *agony* when I broke my arm.

agree *(v.)* एग्री– to consent सहमत होना, बात मान लेना He did not *agree* to my proposal.

agreement *(n.)* एग्रीमण्ट– a contract or a promise समझौता An *agreement* should be signed before starting any business.

agreeable *(adj.)* एग्रीएबल– pleasing, giving pleasure प्रिय लगने वाली Lata has an *agreeable* (pleasant) personality.

agriculture *(n.)* एग्रीकल्चर्– cultivation of the soil खेती-बाड़ी, कृषि Indian people depend upon *agriculture* for their livelihood.

ahead *(adv.)* अहेड– in front, in advance आगे Please go *ahead;* I will follow you.

aid *(n.)* एड्– 1. help, assist सहायता, मदद When the tiger attacked me, the hunter came to my *aid.*
2. *(v.)* to help मदद करना I *aided* my mother in cooking the food.

AIDS *(n.)* ऐड्स (also aids) एड्ज़, acquired immune (or immuno-) deficiency syndrome: a condition, resulting in loss of the body's ability to protect itself against disease एक घातक बीमारी जो प्रायः असुरक्षित यौन संबंध एवं दूषित रक्त व इंजेक्शन की सुई से फैलता है The government has opened an *AIDS* research centre in Delhi.

ailment *(n.)* एलमेंट– illness बीमारी जो गंभीर न हो, छोटी-मोटी तकलीफ़ She will soon recover from her *ailment.*

aim *(v.)* एम– 1. to point towards निशाना बांधना या लगाना The hunter *aimed* his gun at the tiger.
2. *(n.)* act of aiming लक्ष्य, उद्देश्य My *aim* is to become an engineer.

aimless *(adj.)* एमलस्– having no aim or purpose लक्ष्यहीन One should not have an *aimless* life.

air *(n.)* एअर्– mixture of gases that we breathe वायु, हवा Without *air,* we would not be able to live.

airborne *(adj.)* एअरबॉर्न– carried by or through the air आकाश में उड़ते हुए Ten minutes after getting on the plane I was *airborne.*

air brake *(n)* एअर्ब्रेक– a break operated by compression of air हवा के दबाव से काम करने वाली ब्रेक Her car doesn't have an *air brake.*

air-conditioned *(adj.)* एअर्कंडीशंड– air chiller वातानुकूलित Javed has an *air-conditioned* office.

aircraft *(n.)* एअर्क्राफ़्ट– an airplane विमान, हवाई जहाज़ Mukesh Ambani has his private *aircraft.*

aircrew *(n.)* एअरक्रु– the staff of an aircraft विमानकर्मी, दल All the *aircrew* on board escaped the aircrash.

airfield *(n.)* एअर्फ़ील्ड– a level area with runways हवाईपट्टी The *airfield* is the key parameter in designing of an airport.

air hostess *(n.)* एअर्हास्टेस– female crew member of the airplane विमान-परिचारिका She joined Frankfinn Institute to work as an *air hostess.*

airless *(adj.)* एअरलस– without air घुटनभरा, निर्वात The room was hot and *airless.*

airlift *(v.)* एअर्लिफ़्ट– to transport by an airlift आपातस्थिति में विमान द्वारा वहन करना Two casualties were *airlifted* to safety.

airline *(n.)* एअर्लाइन– a regular route travelled by an aircraft हवाई कम्पनी Air India is a government *airline* company.

airlock *(n.)* एअरलॉक– an airtight chamber एक वायुरोधक यंत्र (जिससे हवा का दबाव कम या अधिक किया जा सकता है) All submarines are equipped with an *airlock.*

airmail *(n.)* एअरमेल– mail conveyed by aircraft हवाई डाक सेवा I sent the parcel by *airmail.*

air pocket *(n.)* एअर पॉकेट– an airtight chamber एक बंद क्षेत्र जिसमें हवा भर जाए

Make sure there are no *air pockets* around the roots of the plant.

airship *(n.)* एअरशिप– self-propelled lighter than air aircraft with means of controlling the direction of flight एक प्रकार का वायुपोत An *airship* show was held in France recently.

airsick *(adj.)* एअरसिक– sick or nauseated from travelling in an aircraft विमान यात्रा के दौरान जी मचलाना *Airsick* people should take precautions before boarding.

airspace *(n.)* एअरस्पेस– the atmosphere above the earth or part of the earth हवाई क्षेत्र There are laws against violating another nation's *airspace*.

airstrip *(n.)* एअरस्ट्रिप– runway हवाई पट्टी *Airstrip* should be cleared to facilitate safe landing of aircrafts.

airtight *(adj.)* एअरटाईट– not allowing air to enter or escape वायुरुद्ध It was an *airtight* container.

airworthy *(adj.)* एअरवर्दि– safe to fly उड़ने योग्य Go Aircrafts are no more considered *airworthy*.

airy *(adj.)* एअरि– having plenty of fresh air हवादार My room is very *airy*.

aisle *(n.)* आइल– passage गलियारा It was difficult to find the way through the *aisle*.

ajar *(adj.)* अजॉर– slightly open अधखुला The servant left the door *ajar*.

akin *(adj.)* अकिन– allied by nature, having the same properties एक जैसा, समान She felt something *akin* to danger.

alarm *(n.)* अलार्म– 1. signal giving a warning of danger चेतावनी, ख़तरे का संकेत, संकट-सूचना When the plane began to dive, the passengers were filled with *alarm*. The silence of the night was suddenly broken by a fire *alarm*.

2. *(v.)* to warn डरा देना You really *alarmed* me by screaming so loudly.

alarmed *(adj.)* अलार्मड– frightened भयभीत I am *alarmed* by the increasing incidents of kidnapping.

alarming *(adj.)* अलार्मिंग– scary चिंताजनक Last year the onion prices were so *alarming*.

alas *(Interj.)* अलास– cry of sorrow हाय! We wanted to go for a walk, but *alas*, it rained.

albeit *(conj.)* ऑलबीइट्– although हालांकि, यद्यपि Manish finally agreed to come, *albeit* unwillingly.

album *(n.)* ऐलूबम– a blank book in which a collection of stamps, photographs, etc. can be kept एलबम, संग्रह पुस्तक He has pasted the stamps of many countries in his *album*.

alchemist *(n.)* ऐलकमिस्ट– one well-versed in alchemy कीमियागर My grandfather is an *alchemist*.

alchemy *(n.)* ऐलकमि– art of turning baser metals into gold (घटिया धातु को स्वर्ण में बदलने की कला) कीमिया My father has the knowledge of *alchemy*.

alcohol *(n.)* ऐलूकहॉल्– pure, colourless liquid present in wine, beer, brandy, whisky मादक पेय, मद्यसार Don't drive after consuming *alcohol*.

alcoholic *(adj.)* ऐलकहॉलिक– containing alcohol मद्यसार संबंधी, मादक It is an *alcoholic* drug. *(n.)* one who drinks daily too much alcohol शराबी Ashok is an *alcoholic* man.

alcove *(n.)* ऐलकोव– a recess in the wall of a room or garden दीवार में बना हुआ मेहराबदार ताख़ I have an *alcove* in my bedroom.

alert *(adj.)* अलर्ट– watchful, fully awake, lively सतर्क, चौकस The *alert* engine driver averted a major accident of his train.

algae *(n.)* ऐलगी– unicellular or multicellular organisms formerly classified as plants, occurring in fresh or salt water or moist ground, that have chlorophyll and other pigments पानी में उगने वाले पौधे, शैवाल I enjoy seeing blue-green shades on *algae.*

algebra *(n.)* ऐलजिब्रा– branch of mathematics in which signs and letters are used to represent quantities बीजगणित She is not interested in *algebra.*

alias *(n.)* एलिअस– an assumed name, other name उर्फ़, उपनाम Kareena Kapoor *alias* Bebo is a famous actress.

alien *(n.)* एलिअन– 1. a foreigner who is not a subject of the country in which he lives किसी दूसरे लोक का वासी The hero in the movie was fighting against a group of *aliens.*
2. *(adj.)* पूरी तरह से अनजान, अपरिचित I am completely *alien* to baseball.

alienate *(v.)* एलिअनेट– to cause to become unfriendly अपने से दूर कर देना New policies on defence have *alienated* many of his supporters.

alight *(v.)* अलाइट– 1. to land बस, रेलगाड़ी आदि से उतरना The driver opened the door and his master *alighted* from the car.
2. *(adj.)* on fire, illuminated, bright प्रज्वलित The whole building was *alight.*

align *(v.)* अलाइन– to arrange in a straight line सीध मिलाना She *aligned* her books in the shelf.

alignment *(n.)* अलाइनमेण्ट– arrangement in a straight line सीध में होना The tiles in the bathroom were not in *alignment.*

alike *(adv.)* अलाइक– 1. similar सदृश The twin brothers look *alike.*
2. *(adj.) like each other or one another* एक ही तरह The mother and the daughter are *alike* in their looks.

alimony *(n.)* ऐलिमनी– money allowance paid by a man to his former wife after legal seperation गुज़ारा भत्ता The *alimony* that she is getting is not sufficient for her.

alive *(adj.)* अलाइव– living ज़िन्दा, जीवित Some people were still *alive* under the collapsed building.

alkaloid *(n.)* ऐलकलॉइड– an organic compound having some resemblance with alkali क्षार से मिलता- जुलता पदार्थ, क्षारोद Some *alkaloids* are used in drugs.

all *(pron.)* ऑल– 1. entirely, totally सबकुछ, सारा Very few people come forward to sacrifice their *all* for the country.
2. *(adv.)* सभी I have read *all* the books on this subject.

allege *(v.)* अलेज्– to declare, to put forward बिना प्रमाण के आरोप लगाना The lady *alleged* that he had attacked her.

allegation *(n.)* एलिगेशन– a statement, esp. one made without proof आरोप The lady put the *allegation* of an attack on him.

allegedly *(adv.)* अलेजिडलि– reportedly, supposedly आरोपानुसार The lady was *allegedly* attacked by him.

allergic *(adj.)* ऐलर्जिक– concerning hypersensitivity to certain things नापसंद करने वाला I'm *allergic* to dust.

allergy *(n.)* ऐलर्जि– a state of hypersensitivity to certain things ऐलर्जी रोग, प्रत्यूर्जता Are you suffering from dust *allergy*?

alleviate *(v.)* अलीविएट– to make pain less or easier to bear (दर्द को) कम करना The doctor gave me an injection to *alleviate* the pain.

alliance *(n.)* अलायअन्स– union or assosiation between two मैत्री, संबंध, संधि The two groups formed an *alliance* to oppose the government.

allied *(adj.)* ऐलाइड– joined or united in a close relationship सहबद्ध, उसी वर्ग का The newspaper is closely *allied* to the government.

allocate *(v.)* ऐलकेट– to set apart for a particular purpose हिस्से के रूप में बांटना The government has *allocated* half the budget for education.

allot *(v.)* अलॉट– to divide or distribute by lot बाँटना, बाँट देना We entered the room *allotted* to us.

allotment *(n.)* अलॉटमेण्ट– the act of alloting विभाजन, वितरण The *allotment* of funds for the project will be done tomorrow.

allow *(v.)* अलाउ– to permit अनुमति देना, होने देना Please *allow* me to help you.

allowance *(n.)* अलाउअन्स– amount given भत्ता I give my son a monthly *allowance* for sundry expenses.

all right *(adj., adv.)* ऑल-राईट– 1. satisfactory ठीक Is everything *all right*?
2. reliable, safe सकुशल, सुरक्षित Do you feel *all right*?

all-round *(adj.)* ऑल-राउण्ड– including all aspects सर्वतोमुखी, चौतरफा Yuvraj Singh is an *all-round* cricket player.

all-time *(adj.)* ऑल-टाइम– unsurpassed in some respect at a particular time सदैव This is my *all-time* favourite movie.

allude *(v.)* अलूड– to refer to किसी बात की ओर इशारा करना He *alluded* to the problem but did not mention it.

allure *(n.)* अलुअर्– 1. fascination, charm प्रलोभन, आकर्षण The *allure* of working in a foreign country can never fade.
2. *(v.)* to tempt, entice मोहित करना, मुग्ध करना Big cities always *allure* people of small towns.

alluvial *(adj.)* अलूविअल– pertaining to sedimentary material like sand, etc. (बाढ़ द्वारा आई मिट्टी या रेत से बनी भूमि) जलोढ़, कछारी *Alluvial* soil is not considered very fertile.

ally *(n.)* ऐलाइ– unite formally by treaty सखा, सहायक, मित्र England and America were *allies* in the Second World War.

almighty *(adj.)* ऑलमाइटी– having unlimited power सर्वशक्तिमान Have faith in *Almighty* God and do your best.

almond *(n.)* आमण्ड– the nut like stone or kernel of the fruit of a tree बादाम *Almond* is good for skin and hair.

almost *(adv.)* ऑल्मोस्ट– nearly, all but लगभग, क़रीब-क़रीब The little boy walked *almost* four miles to reach home.

alms *(n.)* आमूज़– money, clothes, etc. given to a poor भीख, भिक्षा The rich lady distributed *alms* among the beggars.

alone *(adv.)* अलोन– 1. only, solely सिर्फ़, केवल She was afraid to go out *alone* in the dark.
2. *(adj.)* lonely, by oneself अकेला, एकाकी The general *alone* could give the order to attack.

along *(prep.)* अलॉन्ग– by the side of साथ-साथ, समानान्तर He followed the path *along* the river.

aloof *(adj.)* अलूफ़– away from, reserved अलग, मेल-जोल न बढ़ाने वाला I find her rather *aloof.*

aloud *(adv.)* अलाउड– in a spoken voice; not silently ज़ोर से, ऊंचे स्वर में He spoke *aloud* so that I could hear him.

alphabetical *(adj.)* ऐलफ़बेटिकल– in the order the alphabets वर्णमाला के क्रम से, वर्णात्मक The names are listed in *alphabetical* order.

already *(adv.)* ऑलरेडी– by this or that time, previously पहले, पहले से ही Our guests have *already* arrived.

also *(adv., conj.)* ऑल्सो– in addition, as well भी When Anil came, Anita *also* came. She not only plays piano, but *also* writes songs.

alter *(v.)* ऑल्टर्– to make or become different, change in appearance बदल देना, हेर-फेर करना The tailor *altered* David's old coat to fit him.

alteration *(n.)* ऑलटरेशन– act of changing परिवर्तन, हेर-फेर Few *alterations* to the house is required before we move in.

alternate *(adj.)* ऑल्टर्नेट– interchange repeatedly one for another एक छोड़कर एक, हर तीसरा We have our classes on *alternate* days.

alternative *(n.)* ऑलटर्नेटिव– 1. a possibility of choice, esp between two things, courses of action, etc. विकल्प Is there any *alternative* to this plan? 2. *(adj.)* presenting a choice, esp between two possibilities only कोई दूसरा, वैकल्पिक These days, people have little faith on *alternative* medicine.

although *(conj.)* ऑलूदो– inspite of the fact that हालांकि, यद्यपि He ran fast *although* his leg was injured.

altitude *(n.)* ऐलटिट्यूड– height above sea-level समुद्रतल से ऊँचाई, ऊँचा स्थान, उच्चता Oxygen is required when you are climbing at high *altitude.*

altogether *(adv.)* ऑलटुगेदर्– entirely, wholly पूर्णरूप से, पूर्णतया *Altogether,* at home and in the bank, I have five thousand rupees.

altruism *(n.)* ऐलट्रूइज़म्– the principle of unselfish concern for the welfare of the others परोपकार की भावना, परोपकारिता Social workers practice *altruism.*

aluminium *(n.)* ऐलमिनिअम्– a light white metal used for making lightweight utensils एक प्रकार की सफेद धातु, ऐलुमिनियम *Aluminium* foils are used for wrapping food.

alumna *(n.)* अलम्ना– a girl or womam who is graduate or former student of a school collage or university किसी शिक्षण संस्था की भूतपूर्व छात्रा, स्नातिका She is an *alumna* of Ramjas College.

always *(adv.)* ऑल्वेज़– everytime हमेशा, सर्वदा He is *always* busy.

amass *(v.)* अमैस्– to pile or heap up ढेर लगाना, संचित करना He *amassed* a fortune after the war.

amateur *(n.)* ऐमट्युअर– a person who engages in an activity, esp a sport, as a pastime rather than professionally or for gain नौसिखिया, शौकिया कलाकार या खिलाड़ी, अव्यवसायी The *amateur* athletes surprisingly performed well.

amaze *(v.)* अमेज़– to fill with great suprise or wonder चकित या विस्मित करना The child wrestler's great strength *amazed* everybody.

amazement *(n.)* अमेज़मेण्ट– a state of extreme surprise or astonishment अचंभा, विस्मय He looked at me in *amazement.*

ambassador *(n.)* ऐम्बैसडर्– a diplomat of the highest rank sent by one state to another as its resident representative राजदूत He was later appointed the first British ambassador to Greece.

ambience *(n.)* ऐम्बिअन्स– environment वातावरण, आस-पास का क्षेत्र Dim lights and soft music were providing a romantic *ambience.*

ambiguity *(n.)* ऐम्बिग्यूअटी– doubtfulness of meaning or intension अस्पष्टता There was an *ambiguity* in his expression.

ambiguous *(adj.)* ऐमबिग्युअस– open to various interpretations अनेक अर्थ प्रकट करने वाला, संदिग्ध His writings are often *ambiguous.*

ambition *(n.)* ऐम्बिशन– an earnest desire for some type of achievement or distinction महत्त्वाकांक्षा My son's *ambition* is to be a doctor.

ambitious *(adj.)* ऐम्बिशस– full of ambition, desirous of superiority महत्त्वाकांक्षी India has set itself a number of *ambitious* goals.

amble *(v.)* ऐम्बूल– to move along leisurely टहलना, रहवाल चलना The weary traveller *ambled* along the street.

ambulance *(n.)* ऐम्ब्युलन्स– a vehicle equipped for carrying people who are ill अस्पताल-गाड़ी The wounded man was taken to the hospital in an *ambulance.*

ambush *(n.)* ऐमबुश– the act or an instance of lying concealed as to attack by surprise घात, घात-स्थान The robbers were waiting in *ambush.*

ameliorate *(v.)* अमीलिअरेट– to make or become better स्थिति सुधारना या सुधरना Steps have been taken to *ameliorate* the situation.

amenable *(adj.)* अमीनबल– ready or willing to answer, agree or yield आज्ञाकारी, अधीन, विनम्र Bahadur is an *amenable* servant.

amend *(v.)* अमेण्ड– to make or become better संशोधन करना, सुधारना, सुधरना Our Constitution has been *amended* many times.

amendment *(n.)* अमेण्डमेण्ट– the act of amending; correction संशोधन, सुधार Certain clauses in this agreement need *amendment.*

amenity *(n.)* अमेनिटी– things/ circumstances that make life easy or pleasant सुविधाएं Big cities offer good civic *amenities.*

amiable *(adj.)* एमिअबल– having or showing agreeable personal qualities मिलनसार My mother is an *amiable* lady.

amid *(prep.)* अमिड– in the middle of में, बीच में In India, we often see honesty *amid* poverty.

amiss *(adv.)* अमिस– 1. be offended by something बुरा मानना I did not mean to hurt his feelings, but he took it *amiss.* 2. *(adj.)* out of the proper course, order or condition ग़लत, ख़राब There is nothing *amiss* in this plan.

ammunition *(n.)* ऐमयुनिशन्– all material including explosives, shells, bombs, etc. to be used against enemies गोला-बारूद The troops surrendered because they had run out of *ammunition.*

among(st) *(prep.)* अमंग(स्ट)– in association with में, में से, बीच में, मिलकर She distributed the sweets *among* her children.

amorous *(adj.)* ऐमरस्– inclined to love कामुक, प्रेमी At the first look, Neha became *amorous* of him.

amount *(n.)* अमाउंट–1. money रकम, धनराशि It is risky to carry a large *amount* in cash. 2. quantity, result मात्रा, परिणाम What is the *amount* of flour needed to prepare a small cake?

amphibian *(n.)* ऐमफ़िबिअन्– an animal which can live both on land and in water (जल और थल दोनों में रहने वाला प्राणी) उभयचर Frogs, tortoises and crocodiles are *amphibians.*

ample *(adj.)* ऐम्पल– large sized, with plenty of space पर्याप्त, प्रचुर The little boy has an *ample* stock of story books.

amplify *(v.)* ऐम्प्लिफ़ाई–1. to make larger or fuller बढ़ाना He *amplified* the tone of the radio.
2. to expand in stating or describing विस्तार से कहना The author did not *amplify* his statements.

amputate *(v.)* एम्प्यूटेट– to cut off, (parts of the body) as by surgery रोगी का हाथ, पैर काट डालना He has gangrene on his leg, we must *amputate* it.

amuse *(v.)* अम्यूज़– to entertain or divert in a pleasant or cheerful manner मन बहलाना, मनोरंजन करना The clown in the circus *amused* the children with his antics.

amusement *(n.)* अम्यूज़मन्ट– state of being amused दिल बहलाव, मनोरंजन Much to the pupils' *amusement*, the teacher fell off his chair.

analyse (ze) *(v.)* ऐनलाइज़– to examine विश्लेषण करना Let us *analyse* the situation well and come up with an appropriate solution.

analysis *(n.)* अनैलसिस– the process of analysing विश्लेषण The situation needs an in-depth *analysis*.

anarchy *(n.)* ऐनकि– absence of government control अराजकता The death of the Chief Minister led to *anarchy* in the city.

anatomy *(n.)* अनैटमी– science dealing with the structure of animals and plants शरीर-रचना विज्ञान He is a professor of *anatomy*.

ancestor *(n.)* ऐनुसेस्टर्– forefather पूर्वज, पुरखा Monkeys were the *ancestors* of human beings.

anchor *(n.)* ऐन्कर्– 1. heavy piece of iron with a ring at one end to which a cable is fastened लंगर A large ship was at *anchor* in the harbour. 2. *(v.)* to let an anchor down from a boat or ship लंगर डालना The ship was *anchored* when it arrived at the port.

ancient *(adj.)* एन्शण्ट्– belonging to times long past प्राचीन, पुरातन, पुराना *Ancient* India was a land of glory.

anecdotal *(adj.)* ऐनेकडोटल्– short amusing story about real person or event क़िस्सों पर आधारित The story was based on *anecdotal* evidence.

angel *(n.)* एन्जल– messenger esp. of God देवदूत, फ़रिश्ता *Angels* come to take the soul of saints when they die.

anger *(n.)* ऐंगर्– the strong feeling that is aroused when one is wrong गुस्सा, क्रोध Good people do not get filled with *anger* for others' lapses.

angina *(n.)* ऐनजाइना– a disease marked by inflammatory condition of throat कंठशूल He had high blood pressure and he suffered from *angina*.

angle *(n.)* ऐन्गल– space between two lines or surfaces that meet कोण A triangle has three *angles*.

angry *(adj.)* ऐंग्री– filled with anger क्रोधित, नाराज़ My brother will be *angry* with me if I lose his pen.

anguish *(n.)* ऐंग्विश– severe distress वेदना, व्यथा Three consecutive defeats caused *anguish* to the captain.

angular *(adj.)* ऐंग्यूलर– having angles of sharp corner कोणीय The *angular* blocks of stones fell from the top.

animal *(n.)* ऐनिमल– any living thing having certain characteristics which set it apart from a plant जानवर, पशु The zoo has some rare wild *animals*.

animate *(v.)* ऐनिमेट्– to give life to जान डाल देना Ravi *animated* her life with his few encouraging words.

animation *(n.)* ऐनिमेशन्– animated quality जोश और उत्साह से भरपूर *Animation* films can be made these days with the help of computers.

animosity *(n.)* ऐनिमॉसिटी– enmity, strong dislike शत्रुता, घृणा There is still *animosity* between these two teams after last year's match.

aniseed *(n.)* ऐनिसीड्– the liquorice-flavoured aromatic seeds of the anise plant, used medicinally for expelling intestinal gas and in cookery as a flavouring सौंफ़ He sowed some *aniseeds* in his garden.

ankle *(n.)* ऐन्कल– joint connecting the foot with the leg टख़ना I sprained my *ankle* this morning.

annals *(n.)* ऐनूल्ज़्– a periodical publication containing the formal reports of an organisation इतिहास, इतिवृत्त, आख्यान The battles went down in the *annals* of Indian history.

annex *(v.)* ऐनेक्स्– to take possession of कब्जे में करना Polish areas were *annexed* by Nazi Germany.

annexation *(n.)* ऐनेक्सेशन्– the act of annexing, esp territory, or the condition of being annexed दूसरे देश को अपने से मिलाने की गतिविधि, समामेलन *Annexation* of a country is not so easy in today's world.

annexe *(n.)* ऐनेक्सी– an extension to a main building उपभवन, मकान का बढ़ाया हुआ भाग This wing is an *annexe* of the main building.

annihilate *(v.)* अनाइअलेट– to destroy completely नष्ट/विनाश करना The fire *annihilated* the whole forest.

annihilation *(n.)* अनाइअलेशन– complete destruction विनाश, विध्वंस The sages guided the path from *annihilation* to resurrection.

anniversary *(n.)* ऐनिवर्सरी– the yearly return of the date of a past event वर्षगाँठ, बरसी This is the 5th wedding *anniversary* of Rahul.

annotate *(v.)* ऐनटेट– to give remark टिप्पणियां देना, व्याख्या करना The translator *annotated* the poem to make it easy to understand.

annotation *(n.)* ऐनटेशन– a note added in explanation, etc. esp of some literary work टीका, व्याख्या *Annotations* are provided at the end of the book.

announce *(v.)* अनाउन्स– to make known publicly or officially बतलाना, सूचित/घोषित करना The Principal *announced* that the school will remain close tomorrow.

announcement *(n.)* अनाउन्समण्ट– something said to make known what has happened or what will happen ऐलान, घोषणा Ladies and gentlemen, I'd like to make an *announcement.*

announcer *(n.)* अनाउन्सर– one who announces उद्घोषक The *announcer* reads out the news on the radio.

annoy *(v.)* अनॉइ– to irritate, make angry चिढ़ाना, परेशान करना The student's carelessness *annoyed* the teacher.

annoyance *(n.)* अनॉइअन्स– vexation, irritation चिढ़, खीझ, छेड़खानी A loud music is often an *annoyance.*

annoying *(adj.)* अनॉइंग– causing annoyance चिढ़ या कष्ट पैदा करने वाला, कष्टप्रद It is *annoying* to miss a bus when you are in a hurry.

annual *(adj.)* ऐन्युअल– 1. coming or happening every year वार्षिक, सालाना The *annual* gathering of our club will be held next month.
2. *(n.)* (पत्रिका का) a book, report, etc. published once a year वार्षिक विशेषांक The *annual* of a magazine is bigger than its regular issue.

annul *(v.)* अनल्– to put an end to an agreement or a law, etc. रद्द कर देना, मिटा देना Their marriage was *annulled* after just six months.

annulment *(n.)* अनलमण्ट– cancel, nullify निरस्तीकरण, निराकरण *Annulment* of the agreement was decided after discussion.

anoint *(v.)* अनाइंट– to apply oil or ointment to तेल या मरहम लगाना The mother *anointed* the baby's head.

anomalous *(adj.)* अनॉमलस्– irregular, abnormal अनियमित, असामान्य, असंगत He has an *anomalous* position in the company.

anomaly *(n.)* अनॉमली– something anomalous अनियमितता, असंगतता We discovered an *anomaly* in the sales figures for August.

anonymous *(adj.)* अनॉनिमस– without any name as that of author, contributor, etc. अज्ञात, गुमनाम, अनाम The story was submitted by an *anonymous* writer.

anorak *(n.)* ऐनरैक– a warm waterproof hip-length jacket usually with a hood वर्षा आदि से बचाव करने वाला छोटा टोपीयुक्त कोट I couldn't recognize him because he wore an *anorak.*

another *(adj.)* अनदर्– 1. one more एक और, दूसरा May I have *another* cup of tea? 2. *(pron.)* an additional one दूसरा, कोई दूसरा One man was walking, *another* was running.

answer *(v.)* आन्सर्–1. to reply, something done in return उत्तर, जवाब देना He could not *answer* my question. 2.*(n.)* solution हल, समाधान The bright boy quickly found out the *answer* of the sum. 3. respond जवाब, उत्तर I am waiting for your *answer.*

answerable *(adj.)* आन्सरबल– that can be answered जवाबदेह, उत्तरदायी You are *answerable* for this act.

ant *(n.)* ऐण्ट– small insect चींटी I saw a long line of *ants* carrying granules of sugar.

antagonize (ise) *(v.)* ऐण्टैगनाइज़्– to make an enemy of (somebody) विरोधी बनाना I advise you not to *antagonize* him.

antecedent *(n.)* ऐनटिसीडण्ट– ancestors पूर्वज, पुरखे Before marriage I would like to know about his *antecedents.*

antelope *(n.)* ऐनटिलोप– Asian or African animal like a deer बारहसिंगा There are many *antelopes* in the forest of Africa.

anthem *(n.)* ऐन्थम– musical composition used for choir स्तोत्र, वंदना, गान We sing our national *anthem* at all national festivals.

anthology *(n.)* ऐंथॉलजी– collection of poems, stories, etc. संग्रह The book is an *anthology* of stories written by famous writers.

anthropology *(n.)* ऐंथ्रपॉलजि– science of map, esp. of the beginning of mankind मानव-विज्ञान, नृविज्ञान She is a professor in *anthropology.*

antibiotic *(n.)* ऐन्टिबाइऑटिक– substance capable of preventing the growth of bacteria प्रतिजीव, प्रतिजीवाणु An *antibiotic* might cure your headache.

antibody *(n.)* ऐन्टिबॉडि– protein in blood serum which neutralises the toxic effects of antigens रोगप्रतिकारक *Antibodies* are given to the patients to fight against disease.

anticipate *(v.)* ऐन्टिसिपेट– to realize beforehand पूर्वानुमान करना, पहले से जान लेना I *anticipated* that the situation would get worse.

anticipation *(n.)* ऐन्टिसिपेशन– realization in advance पूर्वानुमान, पूर्वाभास They queued outside the stadium in excited *anticipation.*

anticlockwise *(adj., adv.)* ऐन्टिक्लॉकवाइज़्– counterclockwise वामावर्त Turn the lid in an *anticlockwise* direction.

antics *(n.)* एन्टिक्स– absurd or grotesque acts or postures दूसरों को हंसाने वाली हरकतें, मसखरापन They laughed at the clown's *antics.*

antique *(adj.)* ऐन्टिक– made in or in the style of an earlier period प्राचीन, पुरातन My mother is fond of collecting *antique* pieces of art.

antiquity *(n.)* ऐन्टिक्वटि– the quality of being ancient or very old प्राचीनकाल, पुराकाल The trade flourished until last classical *antiquity.*

antiseptic *(n.)* ऐन्टिसेप्टिक्– entirely free from contamination रोगाणुरोधक Put an *antiseptic* cream on that scratch.

antisocial *(adj.)* ऐन्टिसोशल– avoiding the company of other people; unsociable असामाजिक, समाज-विरोधी Children's *antisocial* behaviour is a matter of concern.

antithesis *(n.)* ऐन्टिथीसिस– the exact opposite विपरीतता, विरोध The aged wrestler now looks an *antithesis* of what he was earlier.

antonym *(n.)* ऐन्टनिम– a word that means the opposite of another word विलोम शब्द I told him to write the *antonym* of big.

anus *(n.)* एनस्– the excretory opening at the end of the alimentary canal मलद्वार, गुदा He has some infection in his *anus.*

anvil *(n.)* ऐनूविल– a heavy iron or steel block on which metals are hammered during forging अरहन, सन्दान, निहाई The blacksmith was shaping a hot piece of iron on his *anvil.*

anxiety *(n.)* ऐंग्ज़ाइटि– a state of uneasiness or tension चिंता, फिक्र The mother was full of *anxiety* about her infant's health.

anxious *(adj.)* ऐन्क्शस–1. intensely desirous; eager उत्सुक He was *anxious* to see her.
2. worried and tense चिंतित, चिंताग्रस्त Students were *anxious* about their examination result.

any *(pron., adv.)* एनी–1. one, some, or several कोई, कुछ Have you *any* stamps?
2. whatever or whichever कोई भी You can buy pastries from *any* bakery.

anybody *(pron.)* एनिबडि– any person; anyone कोई भी *(also anyone)* Would *anybody* else like to come with me?

anyhow *(adv.)* एनिहाउ– in any case; at any rate हर हालत में, चाहे जैसे *(also anyway)* *Anyhow* he managed to escape the police.

anything *(pron.)* एनिथिंग– any object, event, action, etc. whatever कुछ भी I could not see *anything* interesting in the magazine.

anywhere *(adv.)* एनिवेअर– in, at, or to any place कहीं भी, कहीं पर भी, सब जगह I could not find my letters *anywhere.*

apart *(adv.)* अपार्ट–1. placed or kept separately or to one side for a particular purpose, reason, etc.; aside अलावा *Apart* from movies, Ramesh is also fond of good food.
2. to pieces or in pieces पृथक्, अलग The child tore the book *apart.*

apartheid *(n.)* अपार्थाइड– the official government policy of racial segregation रंगभेद Nelson Mandela struggled a lot against *apartheid.*

apartment *(n.)* अपार्टमन्ट– any room in a building कमरा, फ्लैट Beach-side *apartments* are very costly.

apathetic *(adj.)* ऐपथेटिक्– showing no interest उदासीन, निरुत्साह They are totally *apathetic* towards world affairs.

apathy *(n.)* ऐपथि– feeling of not being interested or emotions; indifferent उदासीनता, भावशून्यता There is certain *apathy* among the public.

ape *(n.)* एप– 1. any of various primates, esp those of the family Pongidae, in which the tail is very short or absent वानर, बंदर I saw an *ape* in the zoo.
2. *(v.)* to imitate नक़ल करना We should not *ape* Western manners.

aperture *(n.)* ऐपचर्– a hole, gap, crack, slit, or other opening छेद, छिद्र, सूराख Scientists say that there are lot of *apertures* on the moon.

apex *(n.)* एपेक्स्– the highest point; vertex चोटी, शिखर At only 40, he reached the *apex* of his career.

apologize (ise) *(v.)* अपॉलजाइज़– to express or make an apology; acknowledge failings or faults क्षमा मांगना, खेद प्रकट करना The minister *apologized* for arriving late.

apology *(n.)* अपॉलजि– an oral or written expression of regret or contrition for a fault or failing क्षमायाचना, क्षमाप्रार्थना He sent an *apology* for not being able to attend the wedding.

apostle *(n.)* अपॉसल– an ardent early supporter of a cause, reform movement, etc. धर्मप्रचारक, प्रचारक,

समर्थक Gandhiji is known as an *apostle* of non-violence.

appal *(v.)* अपॉल– to fill with horror; to shock or dismay भयभीत करना His ignorance *appals* me.

appalled *(adj.)* अपाल्ड– feeling horror or disgust दहला देने वाला The city was *appalled* at the news of a likely bomb blast.

appalling *(adj.)* अपालिंग– shocking भयानक, डरावना The news of the bomb blast was *appalling.*

apparatus *(n.)* ऐपरेटस्– a collection of instruments, machines, tools, parts, or other equipment used for a particular purpose उपकरण, यंत्र, संयंत्र The patient's life was supported by the breathing *apparatus.*

apparent *(adj.)* अपैरन्ट– readily seen or understood; evident; obvious प्रकट, स्पष्ट, प्रत्यक्ष It was *apparent* from Arun's face that he didn't like the food.

apparently *(adv.)* अपैरन्टलि– it appears that; as far as one knows; seemingly स्पष्ट रूप से, स्पष्टतया The traveller was *apparently* lost, for he was not sure which way to proceed.

apparition *(n.)* ऐपरिश्न्– an appearance, esp of a ghost or ghostlike figure भूत-प्रेत He told us stories of *apparitions* which frightened us.

appeal *(v.)* अपील– 1. to make an earnest request for relief, support, etc. अनुरोध/आग्रह/निवेदन करना The politician *appealed* to the people to vote for his party.

2. *(n.)* a request for relief, aid, etc. आग्रह, निवेदन The labourers made an *appeal* for an increase in their salaries.

appear *(v.)* अपिअर्–1. to come into sight or view दिखाई देना, प्रकट होना The paperback edition didn't *appear* for another two years.

2. to seem or look लगना, प्रतीत होना It *appears* that he wants to avoid me.

3. to perform or act (परीक्षा में) बैठना, उपस्थित होना Geeta has *appeared* for I.A.S. examination this year.

appearance *(n.)* अपिअरन्स– the act or an instance of appearing, as to the eye, before the public, etc. बाहरी रूप-रंग A different hairstyle can change your *appearance.*

appease *(v.)* अपीज़– to calm, pacify, or soothe, esp by acceding to the demands of शांत/तुष्ट करना Shopkeepers try their best to *appease* their customer.

appeasement *(n.)* अपीज़मन्ट– the policy of acceding to the demands of a potentially hostile nation in the hope of maintaining peace तुष्टीकरण The opponents criticized the policy of *appeasement.*

appendix *(n.)* अपेन्डिक्स्– any part that is dependent or supplementary in nature or function; appendage परिशिष्ट, पुस्तक के अन्त में जोड़ा गया भाग The *appendix is given* at the end of the book.

appetite *(n.)* ऐपिटाइट– a desire to satisfy a bodily craving भूख, क्षुधा During illness, patients often lose their *appetite.*

appetizing (ising) *(adj.)* ऐपिटाइज़िंग– pleasing or stimulating to the appetite; delicious; tasty स्वादिष्ट, क्षुधावर्धक I am very fond of *appetizing* Mughlai dishes.

applaud *(v.)* अप्लॉड– to indicate approval of (a person, performance, etc.) by clapping the hands वाह-वाह करना, तालियां बजाना The entire gathering *applauded* the little boy's fine acting.

applause *(n.)* अप्लॉज़– appreciation or praise, esp as shown by clapping the hands शाबाशी, करतल-ध्वनि They gave him a round of *applause.*

appliance *(n.)* अप्लाइअन्स– a machine or device, esp an electrical one used domestically उपकरण, यंत्र The *appliance* of science could increase crop yields.

applicable *(adj.)* ऐप्लिकेबल– being appropriate or relevant; able to be applied; fitting उपयुक्त, लागू This offer is *applicable* only to married women.

applicant *(n.)* ऐप्लिकेन्ट– a person who applies, as for a job, grant, support, etc.; candidate उम्मीदवार, आवेदक, प्रार्थी There are over 500 *applicants* for the job.

application *(n.)* ऐप्लिकेश्नन– a verbal or written request, as for a job, etc. आवेदन-पत्र, प्रार्थना-पत्र I have filled the *application* form to get admission.

apply *(v.)* अप्लाइ–1. to put in an application or request आवेदन करना, दरख़्वास्त देना Shikha and Juhi *applied* for a job in the same firm.

2. to put to practical use; utilize; employ लगाना It will take a week to *apply* paint to our house.

3. to bring into operation or use लागू होना या करना Laws of the land *apply* to everyone.

appoint *(v.)* अपॉइंट– to prescribe or ordain नियुक्त करना, नौकरी पर रखना My brother is *appointed* as the manager in a good company.

appointment *(n.)* अपॉइंटमेण्ट– an arrangement to meet a person or be at a place at a certain time नियोजित भेंट Today my father has got an *appointment* with the dentist.

apportion *(v.)* अपॉर्श्नन्– to divide, distribute, or assign appropriate shares of; to allot proportionally बांटना The land was *apportioned* between members of the family.

appraisal *(n.)* अप्रेज़ल– an assessment or estimation of the worth, value, or quality of a person or thing मूल्यांकन, मूल्य-निर्धारण She carried out a thorough *appraisal*.

appraise *(v.)* अप्रेज़– to assess the worth, value, or quality of (किसी वस्तु आदि का) मूल्य निर्धारण करना, मूल्यांकन करना Teachers should *appraise* the work of individual students.

appreciate *(v.)* अप्रीशिएट– to value highly दाद देना, क़द्र करना, गुण पहचानना He *appreciates* classical music.

appreciation *(n.)* अप्रीशिएशन– assessment of the true worth or value of persons or things सराहना, प्रशंसा They would be the first to show their *appreciation*.

appreciative *(adj.)* अप्रीशिएटिव– feeling, expressing, or capable of appreciation प्रशंसापूर्ण He was very *appreciative* of our efforts to help.

apprehend *(v.)* ऐप्रिहेण्ड– to arrest and escort into custody; to seize गिरफ़्तार करना The servant was *apprehended* for the theft in the house.

apprehensive *(adj.)* ऐप्रिहेन्सिव– fearful or anxious आशंकित, सशंक I'm feeling *apprehensive* that something would go wrong.

apprentice *(n.)* अप्रेण्टिस– someone who works for a skilled or qualified person in order to learn a trade or profession प्रशिक्षार्थी, प्रशिक्षु He is working as an *apprentice* with a carpenter.

approach *(v.)* अप्रोच– to come nearer in position, time, quality, character, etc. to पास जाना, पहुंचना The thief *approached* the locker silently.

appropriate *(adj.)* अप्रोप्रिअट–1. right or suitable; fitting उचित, समुचित, उपयुक्त The guest of honour gave an *appropriate* brief speech.

2. *(v.)* to take for one's own use, esp illegally or without permission बिना अनुमति के रुपया अपने लिए प्रयोग करना The accused had *appropriated* the property.

3. to put aside (funds, etc.) for a particular purpose or person किसी

ख़ास काम के लिए अलग रखना My mother *appropriated* some money for our school uniform.

approval *(n.)* अप्रूवल– a favourable opinion; commendation स्वीकृति His proposal could not get anybody's *approval.*

approve *(v.)* अप्रूव– to consider that sb/sth is fair, good or right; to commend मंज़ूर करना, स्वीकृति देना, पसंद करना, अच्छा समझना No one can *approve* of such misbehaviour.

approximate *(adj.)* अप्रॉक्सिमट– almost accurate or exact लगभग, क़रीब What is the *approximate* number of students in your school?

approximately *(adv.)* अप्रॉक्सिमेटलि– close to; around; roughly or in the region of अंदाज़न, लगभग The distance is *approximately* hundred miles.

apropos *(prep.)* एप्रपोस– with regard किसी विषय पर She made a number of telling observations *apropos* the current political situation.

apt *(adj.)* ऐप्ट–1. suitable for the circumstance or purpose; appropriate योग्य, संगत, उपयुक्त The accomplished speaker made an *apt* speech.
2. having a natural tendency to do sth संभावना या प्रवृत्ति होना I am *apt* to doze if I sit in an easy chair.

aptitude *(n.)* ऐपूटिट्यूड्– inherent or acquired ability विशेष रुझान, अभिरुचि She has an *aptitude* for literature.

aptly *(adv.)* ऐप्टलि– suitable for the circumstance or purpose; appropriate योग्य रूप से, उपयुक्त ढंग से The winner of the race was *aptly* named Suman Speedy.

aquatic *(adj.)* अक्वैटिक्– growing, living, or found in water जलचर, जलीय The crocodile is an *aquatic* animal.

arbitrary *(adj.)* आबिट्रिर– despotic or dictatorial मनमाना और स्वेच्छाचारी Their decision of shifting to Dwarka was *arbitrary.*

arch *(n.)* आच– curved pointed structure चाप, तोरण Many *arches* were erected to welcome the visiting leader.

archaeology *(n.)* आकिऑलजि– the study of man's past by scientific analysis of the material remains of his cultures पुरातत्त्व विज्ञान *Archaeology* is my favourite subject.

archbishop *(n.)* आच्बिशप– a bishop of the highest rank प्रधान धर्माध्यक्ष The *archbishop* of Rome will visit India next summer.

architect *(n.)* आकिटेक्ट– a person qualified to design buildings and to superintend their erection वास्तुकार, निर्माता Your beautiful house is obviously designed by an able *architect.*

architecture *(n.)* आकिटेक्चर– the art and science of designing and superintending the erection of buildings and similar structures वास्तुकला, वास्तुशिल्प The *architecture* of the building was modern.

ardent *(adj.)* आडन्ट– expressive of or characterized by intense desire or emotion; passionate तीव्र, प्रबल, उत्कट The kids are *ardent* admirers of Harry Potter.

ardour *(n.)* आडर– feelings of great intensity and warmth; fervour जोश, उत्साह The new employees were full of zeal and *ardour.*

arduous *(adj.)* आड्युअस– requiring great physical or mental effort; difficult to accomplish; strenuous कठिन, दुष्कर The journey from Shimla to Nainital was *arduous.*

area *(n.)* एरिआ– a section, portion, or part इलाका, क्षेत्र The Chambal ravines are known as an *area* of dacoits.

arguable *(adj.)* आर्ग्युएबल– capable of being disputed; doubtful तर्कणीय, विवादास्पद King Lear is *arguably* Shakespeare's best play.

argue *(v.)* आर्ग्यू– to quarrel; wrangle वाद-विवाद करना, तर्क-वितर्क करना, आपत्ति करना The critics *argued* a lot about the good and bad points of the painting.

argument *(n.)* आर्ग्युमन्ट– a quarrel; altercation दलील, तर्क Today, the *argument* that all politicians are after power seems true.

arise *(v.)* अराइज़–1. to get or stand up उठना, उठ खड़ा होना *Arise,* awake, and stop not till the goal is reached.
2. to come into being; originate उत्पन्न होना A quarrel on a small issue *arose* among the students.

aristocrat *(n.)* ऐरिस्टक्रैट– a person who has the manners or qualities of a member of a privileged or superior class अभिजात, कुलीन His forefathers belonged to the class of *aristocrats.*

arm *(n.)* आर्म्– either of the upper limbs from the shoulder to the wrist बांह, बाहु, भुजा I have hurt my *arm.*

armament *(n.)* आर्ममेण्ट– the weapon equipment of a military vehicle, ship, or aircraft युद्ध सामग्री The barn was full of *armaments.*

armband *(n.)* आर्मबैंड– a band of material worn round the arm बाजू पर बांधी जाने वाली पट्टी The captain of the team wears an *armband.*

armed *(adj.)* आर्म्ड्– equipped with or supported by arms, armour, etc. सशस्त्र, हथियारबंद Four *armed* men committed the robbery in the house.

armful *(n.)* आर्मफुल्– the amount that can be held by one or both arms बांह भरकर She walked down the stairs carrying an *armful* of clothes.

armour *(n.)* आर्मर्– the protective metal plates on a tank, warship, etc. कवच The *armour* protects a warrior.

armpit *(n.)* आर्मपिट– the small depression beneath the arm where it joins the shoulder बग़ल, काँख The doctor placed the thermometer in the child's *armpit.*

arms *(n.)* आर्म्ज़– weapons collectively हथियार, शस्त्रास्त्र More *arms* are required to win the race of the world.

army *(n.)* आर्मी–1. a military unit usually consisting of two or more corps with supporting arms and services फ़ौज, सेना The Indian *Army* fights bravely at the times of wars.
2. the military land forces of a nation दल, भीड़ There was a huge *army* of ants in the garden.

aroma *(n.)* अरोमा– a distinctive usually pleasant smell, esp of spices, wines, and plants सुगंध An *aroma* of various delicacies was surrounding the kitchen.

around *(adv.)* अराउण्ड– surrounding, encircling, or enclosing चारों ओर People gathered *around* the famous film star.

arouse *(v.)* अराउज़– to evoke or elicit (a reaction, emotion, or response); to stimulate जगाना, सचेत करना, उत्तेजित करना She *aroused* her sleeping son.

arrange *(v.)* अरेंज–1. to put into a proper, systematic, or decorative order व्यवस्थित करना, सजाना, संजोना She *arranged* the furniture in her sitting room.
2. to arrive at an agreement or understanding about; settle निश्चित करना Rupa *arranged* to meet Shikha.

arrangement *(n.)* अरेंजमेण्ट– the act of arranging or being arranged प्रबंध, व्यवस्था, संयोजन They are making *arrangements* for his funeral.

array *(n.)* अरे– an impressive display or collection वस्तुओं का बड़ा संग्रह The lower shelf had an *array* of books on various subjects.

arrears *(n.)* अरिअर्ज– something outstanding or owed बकाया धनराशि I received my *arrears* before the festival.

arrest *(v.)* अरेस्ट– 1. to deprive (a person) of liberty by taking him into custody, esp under lawful authority गिरफ़्तार करना, हिरासत में लेना The policeman *arrested* the thief.
2. *(n.)* the act of taking a person into custody, esp under lawful authority गिरफ़्तारी, बंदीकरण The *arrest* of the notorious smuggler caused a great sensation.

arrival *(n.)* अराइवल– a person or thing that arrives or has arrived आगमन Delay in the *arrival* of the train is not unusual.

arrive *(v.)* अराइव– to come to a certain place during or after a journey; to reach a destination पहुंचना, आना The Rajdhani Express *arrives* in the morning.

arrogant *(adj.)* ऐरॅगण्ट– having or showing an exaggerated opinion of one's own importance, merit, ability, etc; conceited; overbearingly proud घमंडी, अक्खड़ Being the only son of a rich industrialist, he is very *arrogant.*

arrow *(n.)* ऐरो–1. a long slender pointed weapon तीर The hunter shot an *arrow* at the deer.
2. sign indicating direction or position संकेत Follow the *arrows* to reach the venue.

art *(n.)* आर्ट– creation or expression of what is beautiful कला, कौशल, निपुणता Painting is a fine *art.*

artefact *(n.)* आर्टिफ़ेक्ट– anything man-made, such as a spurious experimental result मानवीय कलाकृति My house is full of rare *artefacts.*

artery *(n.)* आर्टरि– any of the tubular thick-walled muscular vessels that convey oxygenated blood from the heart to various parts of the body रक्तवाहिनी, धमनी His mother's *artery* was blocked.

artful *(adj.)* आर्टफुल– cunning or tricky धूर्त, चालाक She escaped the teacher's anger through her *artful* behaviour.

arthritis *(n.)* आर्थ्राइटिस, an inflammation of a joint or joints characterized by pain and stiffness of the affected parts गठिया का रोग She is suffering from *arthritis.*

arthropod *(n.)* आर्थ्रपाड– any invertebrate of the phylum Arthropoda, having jointed limbs संधिपाद Spider, insects and crustaceans are *arthropods.*

article *(n.)* आर्टिकल–1. a written composition on a subject लेख, निबंध The *articles* in India Today give a good coverage of current topics.
2. one of a class of objects; item सामान, पदार्थ She put all the *articles* in her shopping bag.

articulate *(v.)* आर्टिक्यूलेट– to express coherently in words स्पष्ट उच्चारण करना, साफ़ बोलना She *articulated* her opinions in the meeting.

articulated *(adj.)* आर्टिक्यूलेटड– (of a vehicle) with two or more sections joined together in a way जुड़ा हुआ, संयुक्त They have designed a new truck with *articulated* lorries.

artificial *(adj.)* आर्टिफ़िशल– produced by man; not occurring naturally नक़ली, कृत्रिम Nowadays we can buy pullovers made of *artificial* wool.

artillery *(n.)* आर्टिलरी– large, heavy guns, big guns mounted on wheels तोप, तोपखाना Indian *artillery* fought excellently in 1857.

artisan *(n.)* आर्टिज़न– a skilled workman; craftsman दस्तकार, कारीगर This furniture was made by *artisans.*

artist *(n.)* आर्टिस्ट– a person who practises or is skilled in an art, esp painting, drawing, or sculpture

कलाकार She is a famous *artist* in nature painting.

artistic *(adj.)* आर्टिस्टिक– of or characteristic of art or artists कलात्मक This building is very *artistic.*

as *(adv., conj., prep.)* ऐज़–1. used correlatively before an adjective or adverb and before a noun phrase or a clause to indicate identity of extent, amount, etc. जिस समय, ज्यों ही The phone rang just *as* I was leaving the house.
2. in the way that जैसा, जैसा कि Please do *as* I told you.
3. in the role of; being क्योंकि I could not buy the dress *as* it was very expensive.

ascend *(v.)* असेण्ड– to go or move up (a ladder, hill, slope, etc.); to mount, climb चढ़ना, आरोहण करना The old man *ascended* the steep staircase with great difficulty.

ascent *(n.)* असेण्ट– act of ascending; climb or upward movement चढ़ाव, आरोहण, उत्थान There was a steep *ascent* before the path became flat again.

ascertain *(v.)* ऐसर्टेन– to determine or discover definitely पता लगाना We need to *ascertain* the practicality of this plan.

ascetic *(n.)* असेटिक– hermit, monk संन्यासी, तपस्वी The *ascetic* did penance for several years.

ascribe *(v.)* अस्क्राइब्– to credit or assign, as to a particular origin or period आरोपण करना, उत्तरदायी ठहराना Anjana *ascribed* her success to good luck.

asexual *(adj.)* असैक्शुअल– having no apparent sex or sex organs यौन-क्रिया से वंचित, अलैंगिक Plants have *asexual* reproduction.

ash *(n.)* ऐश– the non-volatile products and residue formed when matter is burnt राख, भस्म A major fire reduced the house to *ashes.*

ashamed *(adj.)* अशेम्ड– overcome with shame, guilt, or remorse लज्जित Are you not *ashamed* of being seen in the company of such vagabonds?

ashore *(adv.)* अशोर्– towards or onto land from the water तट पर, स्थल पर When the ship anchored at the harbour, the sailors came *ashore.*

aside *(adv.)* असाइड– 1. on or to one side एक ओर, अलग He took me *aside* to tell something confidential.
2. *(n.)* something spoken by an actor, intended to be heard by the audience, but not by the others on stage (नाटक में पात्रों का स्वागत करना) स्वगत One could understand Hamlet's mind by his *asides.*

ask *(v.)* आस्क्–1. to say sth in the form of a question (to) पूछना, कहना "How are you?" he *asked* me.
2. to make a request or demand मांगना, निवेदन करना The beggar *asked* him for money.
3. to request (a person) politely to come or go to a place बुलाना, निमंत्रण देना Please *ask* Anil to see me this evening.

asleep *(adv.)* अस्लीप– in or into a state of sleep सोता हुआ The tired man fell *asleep* immediately.

aspect *(n.)* ऐस्पेक्ट– the way in which a problem, idea, etc. may be considered पहलू, पक्ष Consider all the *aspects* before taking any decision.

asphyxiate *(v.)* असफ़िक्सिअट– to cause asphyxia in or undergo asphyxia; to suffocate किसी की सांस रोक देना या सांस का रुक जाना He was *asphyxiated* by the smoke while he was asleep.

aspire *(v.)* अस्पाइअर– to yearn (for) or have a powerful or ambitious plan, desire, or hope (to do or be something) कुछ पाने की प्रबल इच्छा

रखना, आकांक्षा करना She *aspires* to become a great writer.

ass *(n.)* ऑस–1. donkey (mammals of the horse family) गधा A man used an *ass* to carry bricks.
2. a foolish or fool मूर्ख, बेवक़ूफ़ Karim is a pompous *ass*.

assassin *(n.)* असैसिन– a murderer, esp one who kills a prominent political figure हत्यारा, वधिक Nathu Ram Godse was the *assassin* of Mahatma Gandhi.

assault *(v.)* असॉल्ट– 1. to make an assault upon हमला करना, प्रहार करना He was arrested for *assaulting* his neighbour.
2. *(n.)* a violent attack, either physical or verbal आक्रमण, हमला The mountaineers launched an *assault* on the high peak.

assemble *(v.)* असेम्बल– to come or bring together; collect or congregate एकत्र होना या करना, जुटना, (पुरजे) जोड़ना The students were to *assemble* in the courtyard of the school.

assembly *(n.)* असेम्बली– a number of people gathered together, esp for a formal meeting held at regular intervals सभा, जमावड़ा The *assembly* passed the resolution unanimously.

assent *(v.)* असेण्ट– to agree or express agreement सहमति प्रकट करना Nobody would *assent* to the terms he proposed.

assert *(v.)* असर्ट– to insist upon (rights, claims, etc.) बलपूर्वक कहना, दावा करना He kept *asserting* that he was not wrong.

assertive *(adj.)* असर्टिव– confident and direct in claiming one's rights or putting forward one's views हठी, आग्रही She is *assertive* by nature.

assess *(v.)* असेस– to judge the worth, importance, etc. of; evaluate आंकना The causes of failure must be *assessed* soon.

assessment *(n.)* असेसमन्ट– the act of assessing मूल्यांकन, निर्धारण It is important to make an *assessment* of the expenditure involved.

asset *(n.)* ऐसेट– anything valuable or useful सम्पत्ति, पूँजी She is a great *asset* to the organisation.

assiduous *(adj.)* असिडयुअस– hard-working; persevering मेहनती, उद्यमी, श्रमशील His success was due to his *assiduous* nature.

assign *(v.)* असाइन– to select for and appoint to a post, etc. कार्यभार सौंपना I was *assigned* the job of collecting funds.

assignment *(n.)* असाइनमन्ट– something that has been assigned, such as a mission or task नियुक्ति, कार्यभार The reporter disappeared while on *assignment* in the war zone.

assimilate *(v.)* असिमूलेट– to learn (information, a procedure, etc.) and understand it thoroughly पचाना, आत्मसात करना I cannot *assimilate* all this knowledge.

assist *(v.)* असिस्ट– to give help or support to (a person, cause, etc.); to aid सहायता करना, सहयोग देना He *assisted* the blind man to cross the street.

assistance *(n.)* असिसटन्स– help; support सहायता, सहयोग Can I be of any *assistance* to you?

assistant *(n.)* असिस्टण्ट– a person who assists, esp in a subordinate position सहायक, सहयोगी There are half a dozen *assistant* working in the project.

association *(n.)* असोसिएशन–1. a group of people having a common purpose or interest; a society or club संस्था, सभा, समाज They have formed an *association* called Friends of Freedom.

2. friendship or companionship संबंध, साहचर्य He warned his son against his *association* with bad boys.

assorted *(adj.)* असॉर्टिड– arranged in sorts; classified फुटकर, वर्गीकृत Please give me 2 kg of *assorted* dry fruits.

assume *(v.)* अस्यूम–1. to take or put on; to adopt मान लेना, कल्पना करना Why do you *assume* that you are never wrong?

2. to take for granted; to accept without proof; to suppose ग्रहण करना, धारण करना The prince *assumed* sovereign power on the death of the king.

assure *(v.)* अशॉर्– to cause to feel sure or certain; convince आश्वासन देना, विश्वास दिलाना, संदेह दूर करना He *assured* me of his full co-operation.

assurance *(n.)* अशॉरन्स– a promise or pledge of support भरोसा, यकीन, आश्वासन I give you my *assurance* that he will not harm you.

asthma *(n.)* ऐस्ट्मा– a respiratory disorder, दमा (रोग) He cannot climb the hill as he is suffering from *asthma*.

asthmatic *(adj.)* ऐसथमेटिक– of, relating to, or having asthma दमा संबंधित He had an *asthmatic* attack.

astonish *(v.)* अस्टॉनिश– to fill with amazement; to surprise greatly चकित होना या करना, अचंभे में पड़ना या डालना I was *astonished* to hear him say such a foolish thing.

astonishment *(n.)* अस्टॉनिशमण्ट– extreme surprise; amazement आश्चर्य, अचंभा He dropped his book in *astonishment*.

astound *(v.)* अस्टाउंड– to overwhelm with amazement and wonder; to bewilder भौचक्का या आश्चर्यचकित करना We were *astounded* by how well he performed.

astride *(adv., prep.)* अस्ट्राइड– with a leg on either side टाँगें फैलाकर He was sitting *astride* on the motorcycle.

astringent *(adj.)* अस्ट्रिनजण्ट–1. severe; harsh कठोर, सख़्त It was an *astringent* decision.

2. *(n.)* an astringent drug or lotion रक्त प्रवाह रोधी (द्रव या क्रीम) Rita applied *astringent* on the burn.

astrology *(n.)* एस्ट्रॉलजि-- the primitive study of celestial bodies, which formed the basis of astronomy ज्योतिषशास्त्र Not everyone believes in *astrology*.

astronomy *(n.)* एस्ट्रॉनमि– the branch of science which deals with celestial objects, space, and the physical universe as a whole खगोल-विज्ञान India is making huge progress in the field of *astronomy*.

astute *(adj.)* अस्ट्यूट– very clever, shrewd चतुर, चालाक, घाघ, धूर्त He was an *astute* man who gave an idea.

asylum *(n.)* असाइलम– shelter or protection from danger आश्रम, शरण-स्थान An *asylum* is now called a mental hospital.

at *(prep.)* ऐट– in, near, towards, on पर, में, से I reached *at* the railway station on time.

atheism *(n.)* एथिइज़्म– disbelief or lack of belief in the existence of God or gods नास्तिकता He has strong belief in *atheism*.

athlete *(n.)* ऐथलीट– a person who is proficient in sports and other forms of physical exercise खेल-कूद में भाग लेने वाला व्यक्ति, कसरती He jumps like an *athlete*.

athletic *(adj.)* ऐथलेटिक– physically strong, fit and active बलिष्ठ, खेल-संबंधी Ram has an *athletic* ability.

atlas *(n.)* ऐट्लस– a bound collection of maps एटलस, भू-चित्रावली You cannot learn Geography without an *atlas*.

at last *(adv.)* ऐट-लास्ट– in the end; after much delay अंत में *At last* India won the world cup.

at least *(adv.)* ऐट-लीस्ट– not less than; at the minimum कम से कम *At least* you should go to meet him.

atmosphere *(n.)* ऐट्मसॣफ़िअर्– the envelope of gases surrounding the earth or another planet वायुमण्डल, वातावरण Pollution in the *atmosphere* is a serious problem.

atomic *(adj.)* अटॉमिक– relating to an atom or atoms परमाणु-संबंधी, परमाणविक Oxygen has an *atomic* mass of 16.

atrocity *(n.)* एट्रॉसटि– an extremely wicked or cruel act, typically one involving physical violence or injury अत्याचार, नृशंसता The institute committed *atrocity* by abolishing the scholarship.

attach *(v.)* अटैच– to join or fasten (some-thing) to something else लगाना, जोड़ना Babu *attached* a nice new chain to his puppy's collar.

attached *(adj.)* अटैचड– joined, fastened, or connected to something लगा हुआ, संलग्न, आसक्त होना Babu is very *attached* to his uncle.

attachment *(n.)* अटैचमेण्ट– affection, fondness, or sympathy for someone or something लगाव, आसक्ति, मोह I have an emotional *attachment* with him.

attack *(v.)* अटैक 1. to take aggressive military action against (a place or enemy forces) with weapons or armed force हमला करना, आक्रमण करना The tiger *attacked* the deer.

2. to criticize or oppose fiercely and publicly आक्षेप करना The newspapers *attacked* the new policy of the government.

3.*(n.)* an aggressive and violent act against a person or place हमला, आक्रमण *Attack* is the best form of defence.

4. a sudden short bout of an illness or stress दौरा He is recovering from an *attack* of 'flu'.

attain *(v.)* अटेन– to succeed in achieving (something that one has worked for) प्राप्त करना, लाभ होना I *attained* success after strong efforts.

attempt *(n.)* अटेम्प्ट्– 1. an effort to achieve or complete a difficult task or action प्रयत्न, प्रयास Deepak passed the tough examination at the first *attempt*.

2.*(v.)* to make an effort to achieve or complete (something difficult) प्रयत्न/ कोशिश करना Dilip *attempted* to climb the tall tree, but it was too steep.

attend *(v.)* अटेण्ड–1. to be present at (an event, meeting, or function) उपस्थित या हाज़िर होना Do you *attend* school regularly?

2. to pay attention to ध्यान देना Please *attend* to what I say.

3. to give practical help and care to; to look after सेवा करना, परिचर्या करना This nurse has to *attend* to many patients.

attendance *(n.)* अटेण्डण्स– the action or state of going regularly to or being present at a place or event उपस्थिति, हाजिरी Your teacher must certify your *attendance*.

attendant *(n.)* अटेण्डण्ट– a person employed to provide a service to the public in a particular place नौकर, परिचारक The *attendant* in the cinema hall showed me my seat.

attention *(n.)* अटेन्शन–1. take notice of someone or something ध्यान, सावधान They listened to the leader's speech with great *attention*.

2. a position assumed by a soldier, standing very straight with the feet together and the arms straight down the sides of the body सीधा, निश्चल मुद्रा The soldiers stood in *attention*.

attentive *(adj.)* अटेण्टिव– paying close attention to something सावधान, सतर्क, चौकस I am very *attentive* to what he had to say.

attentively *(adv.)* अटेण्टिवली– paying close attention to something ध्यानपूर्वक I listened *attentively* to what he had to say.

attest *(v.)* अटेस्ट– to provide or serve as clear evidence of अनुप्रमाणित करना The copies of the documents need to be *attested* for admission.

attire *(n.)* अटाइअर्– clothes, especially fine or formal ones पोशाक, वस्त्र She looked beautiful in the bridal *attire.*

attitude *(n.)* ऐटिट्यूड– a settled way of thinking or feeling about something रवैया, व्यवहार The societies *attitude* towards women has changed a lot.

attract *(v.)* अट्रैक्ट– to cause (someone) to have a liking for or interest in something आकर्षित करना, मोहित करना Nature *attracts* one and all.

attraction *(n.)* अट्रैक्शन– a quality or feature that evokes interest, liking, or desire खिंचाव, आकर्षण Movies have great *attraction* for the youth today.

attractive *(adj.)* अट्रैक्टिव– pleasing or appealing to the senses लुभावना, आकर्षक She has *attractive* features.

attribute *(v.)* अट्रिब्यूट– to regard something as being caused by श्रेय देना He *attributed* his success to hard work.

attrition *(n.)* अट्रिशन– wearing away by friction; abrasion रगड़, घिसाई It was a war of *attrition* between the forces and the terrorists.

auction *(n.)* ऑक्शन– 1. a public sale in which goods or property are sold to the highest bidder नीलामी The *auction* of the land is scheduled to take place next week. 2. *(v.)* to sell sth at an auction नीलाम करना The land was *auctioned* last week.

audacity *(n.)* ऑडैसटी– a willingness to take bold risks साहसिकता He had the *audacity* to answer back to the teacher.

audible *(adj.)* ऑडिबल– able to be heard सुनाई देने योग्य, श्रवणीय Her voice was hardly *audible.*

audience *(n.)* ऑडिअन्स– the assembled spectators or listeners at a public event such as a play, film, concert, or meeting श्रोतागण, दर्शकगण, सभा A good speaker always attracts a large *audience.*

audition *(v.)* ऑडिशन– 1. to perform an audition ध्वनि एवं कला-प्रदर्शन करना या देखना I *auditioned* for a part in the play. 2. *(n.)* the power of hearing or listening गायक की ध्वनि-परीक्षण He has an *audition* on Monday.

au fait *(adj.)* ओ फ़े– having a good or detailed knowledge of निपुण, जानकार Are you an *au fait* with this type of computer system?

augment *(v.)* ऑगमेण्ट– to make (something) greater by adding to it; to increase वृद्धि होना या करना His part-time job *augmented* his income.

aura *(n.)* ऑरा– the distinctive atmosphere or quality that seems to surround and be generated by a person, thing, or place वातावरण These hills have a magical *aura.*

aunt *(n.)* आन्ट– the sister of one's father or mother or the wife of one's uncle चाची, मौसी, बुआ She has gone to stay with her *aunt* for a week.

auspicious *(adj.)* ऑसपिशस्– conducive to success; favourable शुभ, सौभाग्यशाली Her birth is considered *auspicious* in the family.

austere *(adj.)* ऑस्टिअर्– severe or strict in manner or attitud संयमी, मिताहारी Our teacher is simple and *austere.*

authentic *(adj.)* ऑथेन्टिक– of undisputed origin and not a copy; genuine प्रामाणिक, असली This is an *authentic* painting of M. F. Hussain.

author *(n.)* ऑथर्– a writer of a book, article, or document: लेखक, ग्रन्थकार A best-seller book makes its *author* famous.

authority *(n.)* ऑथॉरटि– the power or right to give orders, make decisions, and enforce obedience अधिकार, सत्ता, सत्ताधारी In any company, the *authority* to sign cheques is normally given to trustworthy persons.

authorization *(n.)* ऑथराइज़ेशन– the action of authorizing प्राधिकार He gave him *authorization* to sign documents.

authorize (ise) *(v.)* ऑथराइज़– to give official permission for or approval to (an undertaking or agent) अधिकार देना, प्राधिकृत करना My father has *authorized* my brother to act in his absence.

autobiography *(n.)* ऑटबाइआग्रफ़ी– an account of a person's life written by that person आत्मकथा Mahatma Gandhi's *autobiography* is the bestseller.

autocracy *(n.)* ऑटॉक्रसी– a system of government by one person with absolute power तानाशाही, एकतंत्र, निरंकुशता *Autocracy* leads society to destruction.

autograph *(v.)* ऑटग्राफ़– to write one's signature on (something); to sign अपने हाथ से हस्ताक्षर करना The whole team have *autographed* the football.

automatic *(adj.)* ऑटोमैटिक– working by itself with little or no direct human control स्वचालित *Automatic* machines save us a lot of manual labour.

autonomy *(n.)* ऑटॉनमी– the right or condition of self-government स्वायत्तता, स्वतंत्रता *Autonomy* is necessary for success.

autumn *(n.)* ऑटम– the season after summer and before winter पतझड़ In *autumn*, the leaves on the trees begin to fall.

availability *(n.)* अवेलबिलटी– able to be used or obtained; at someone's disposal प्राप्यता, उपलब्धता It depends on the *availability* of electricity.

available *(adj.)* अवेलबल– able to be used or obtained; at someone's disposal उपलब्ध, प्राप्त For some days, cooking oil was not *available* in the market.

avalanche *(n.)* ऐवलान्श– a mass of snow, ice, and rocks falling rapidly down a mountainside हिमस्खलन, हिमधाव Mountaineers must always guard themselves against *avalanches.*

avenge *(v.)* अवेन्ज– to inflict harm in return for (an injury or wrong done to oneself or another) बदला लेना He *avenged* his brother's death.

avenue *(n.)* ऐवन्यू– a broad road in a town or city, typically having trees at regular intervals along its sides मार्ग, रास्ता, वृक्षवीथि New Delhi is full of tree-lined *avenues.*

average *(adj.)* ऐवरिज– an amount, standard, level, or rate regarded as usual or ordinary औसत, साधारण, सामान्य स्तर What is the *average* attendance in your class?

averse *(adj.)* अवर्स्– having a strong dislike of or opposition to something विपरीत, प्रतिकूल He is not *averse* to trying out new ideas.

aversion *(n.)* अवर्श्न– a strong dislike or disinclination द्वेष, विमुखता, विरुचि Most people have an *aversion* to lizards.

avert *(v.)* अवर्ट्– to turn away (one's eyes or thoughts) फेर लेना, हटाना She *averted* her eyes from the dreadful scene.

avoid *(v.)* अवॉइड–1. to keep away from or stop oneself from doing (something) टालना, दूर रहना He tries to *avoid* me because he owes me some money.
2. to contrive not to meet (someone): बचना, बचकर रहना You should try to *avoid* catching a cold.

await *(v.)* अवेट्– to wait for (an event) राह देखना, प्रतीक्षा करना The whole assembly *awaited* the chief guest's arrival.

awake *(adj.)* अवेक– 1. aware of जाग्रत, जागरूक, सतर्क Yesterday I was *awake* till midnight.
2. *(v.)* to wake from sleep, to wake up जगाना, जागरूक करना, जागना I was *awakened* by a loud noise.

award *(v.)* अवॉर्ड– 1. give or order the giving of (something) as an official payment, compensation, or prize to (someone) पुरस्कार या इनाम देना Rekha was *awarded* a stereo tape recorder for winning the first prize in the music competition.
2. *(n.)* a prize or other mark of recognition given in honour of an achievement इनाम, पुरस्कार Our company has won an *award* for export promotion.

aware *(adj.)* अवेअर्– having knowledge or perception of a situation or fact अवगत, जानकार Satish was not *aware* of this fact.

awareness *(n.)* अवेअर्नस्– knowledge or perception of a situation or fact जानकारी We should create *awareness* on healthy eating and lifestyle.

awash *(adj.)* अवाश– covered or flooded with water, especially seawater or rain प्लावित, बहता हुआ All the pavements were *awash* with rubbish.

away *(adv.)* अवे– 1. to or at a distance from a particular place or person दूर, अलग, परे How long will he be *away*?
2. *(adj.)* at a specified distance दूर स्थित The child threw *away* the broken toy.
➢ **right away**– immediately तुरंत, फ़ौरन, Please call the doctor *right away*.

awe *(n.)* ऑ– a feeling of reverential respect mixed with fear or wonder डर, ख़ौफ़, भय The boy looked in *awe*.

awesome *(adj.)* ऑसम– extremely impressive or daunting; inspiring awe विस्मयकारी Hari's strength was *awesome*.

awful *(adj.)* ऑफ़ल– very bad or unpleasant.बहुत बुरा, भद्दा What an *awful* thing to say!

awfully *(adv.)* ऑफ़ली– very; extremely बहुत अधिक, अत्यधिक I am *awfully* sorry to keep you waiting so long.

awkward *(adj.)* ऑक्वड– causing difficulty; hard to do or deal with भद्दा, कुरूप I feel *awkward* while facing a large audience.

axe *(n.)* ऐक्स– a tool used for chopping wood, typically of iron with a steel edge and wooden handle कुल्हाड़ी, कुठार The wood-cutter cut the tree with his *axe*.

axis *(n.)* ऐक्सिस– an imaginary line about which a body rotates.धुरी, केन्द्र The earth rotates on its *axis*.

axle *(n.)* एक्सल– a rod or spindle (either fixed or rotating) passing through the centre of a wheel or group of wheels कीली, धुरी North American railways operate cars at much higher *axle* loads.

azure *(adj.)* ऐज़्युअर– bright blue in colour like a cloudless sky आसमानी, नीला I have a dress of *azure* silk.

Bb

Bb *(n.)*– बी अंग्रेज़ी वर्णमाला का दूसरा अक्षर The second letter of the English alphabet Banana begins with *'B'*.

babble *(v.)* बैबल– talk rapidly and continuously in a foolish, excited, or incomprehensible way बड़बड़ाना, बुदबुदाना They *babbled* on about their holiday.

baby *(n.)* बेबी– a very young child बच्चा, शिशु She took her *baby* into the lap.

bachelor *(n.)* बैचलर्– a man who is not married अविवाहित, कुँवारा Bhishma Pitamah remained a *bachelor* all his life.

back *(v.)* बैक– 1. to walk or drive backwards पीछे करना I *backed* my car before taking the turn.

2. to walk or drive backwards पीछे हटना The bus stopped and then *backed up.*

3.*(adj.)* of or at the back of something पिछला The servant entered the house through the *back* door.

4.*(adv.)* return वापस, पहले स्थान पर Please come *back* quickly.

5.*(n.)* the rear surface of the human body from the shoulders to the hips पीठ, पृष्ठ There is a mole on my *back.*

6. the position directly behind someone or something पिछवाड़ा, पृष्ठभाग The little boy had blotches of ink at the *back* of his hand. He ran to the *back* of the house.

- **back away** run away of the fear of loosing something डर के मारे पीछे हटना The child *backed away* from the menacing look on his face.
- **look back** to see behind पीछे देखना she launched her own company in 1981 and has never *looked back.*
- **move back** to walk backwards पीछे की ओर Please *move back* a bit.
- **hold back** hesitate to act or speak नियंत्रण में I was trying to *hold back* my toes.
- **back down** withdraw a claim or assertion in the face of opposition दावा करके पीछे हटना Don't *back down* now. It's too late.
- **back out** withdraw from a commitment वादे से मुकरना I have signed the contract, it is impossible to *back out.*
- **back up** to support sb/sth किसी का समर्थन करना There is no evidence to *back up* his accusation.

backache *(n.)* बैकएक– prolonged pain in one's back पीठ या कमर का दर्द I have got a cure for *backache.*

backbone *(n.)* बैकबॉन– the series of vertebrae extending from the skull to the pelvis; the spine रीढ़ की हड्डी Agriculture is the *backbone* of the economy of India.

backbite *(v.)* बैकबाईट– to talk about someone who is not present, to slander चुगली करना/लगाना He told me that Reena was *backbiting* me.

backdate *(v.)* बैकडेट– to make (something, especially a pay increase) retrospectively valid पिछली तारीख़ डालना The pay rise will be *backdated* to 1 April.

background *(n.)* बैकग्राउंड– the part of a picture, scene, or design that forms a setting for the main figures or objects, or appears furthest from the viewer पृष्ठभूमि You can see a house in the *background* of the picture.

backpack *(n.)* बैकपैक– (also **rucksack**) a large bag, carrying one's belongings on the back पीठ पर लटकाकर ले

जाया जाने वाला बैग I have a *backpack* to go climbing mountains.

backslide *(v.)* बैकस्लाइड्– to relapse into bad ways or error फिर बिगड़ जाना, नैतिक पतन होना One should not *backslide* from one's improved behaviour.

backstroke *(n.)* बैकस्ट्रॉक– a swimming stroke performed on the back with the arms lifted alternately out of the water in a backward circular motion and the legs extended and kicking पीठ के बल तैरने की कला Can you do *backstroke*?

backtrack *(v.)* बैकट्रैक– to retrace one's steps जिस रास्ते से आए उसी रास्ते से वापस जाना Marilyn *backtracked* and went down into the basement.

backup *(n.)* बैकअप– Computing make a spare copy of data or a disk. प्रतिलिपि Always keep a *backup* of your files.

backward *(adj.)* बैकवर्ड– having made less progress than is normal or expected पिछड़ा, फिसड्डी Many of the Indian villages are still *backward* with no electricity.

backwards *(adv.)* बैकवर्ड्ज़– directed behind or to the rear पीछे की ओर On seeing the lion in the forest, everyone ran *backwards.*

backyard *(n.)* बैकयार्ड– a yard at the back of a house or other building घर का पिछवाड़ा/पिछला आंगन She grows vegetables in her *backyard.*

bacteria *(n.)* बैक्टीरिया– plural form of bacterium जीवाणु Some *bacteria* causes diseases and infections.

bad *(adj.)* बैड– 1. lacking or failing to conform to moral virtue बुरा, ख़राब Do not keep company with *bad* boys.
2. of poor quality or a low standard दूषित, घटिया We cannot eat this fish, as it has gone *bad.*

badge *(n.)* बैज्– a small piece of metal, plastic, or cloth bearing a design or words, typically worn to identify a person or to indicate membership of an organization or support for a cause बिल्ला Every student is required to wear the school *badge.*

badly *(adv.)* बैडलि– used to emphasize the seriousness of an unpleasant event or action बुरी तरह से, अत्यधिक The driver was *badly* injured.

bad-tempered *(adj.)* बैड-टेम्परड– easily annoyed or made angry चिड़चिड़ा, बदमिज़ाज Neetu is very *bad-tempered* girl.

baffle *(v.)* बैफ़ल– to bewilder or perplex चकरा देना, निष्फल कर देना Students were *baffled* by the difficult question paper.

bag *(n.)* बैग– 1. a flexible container with an opening at the top, used for carrying things थैला, झोला, बोरा He put all the books in his school *bag.*
2. *(v.)* to succeed in killing or catching (an animal) हस्तगत करना, जीतना Dinesh *bagged* the first prize in the essay competition.

baggage *(n.)* बैगेज– suitcases and bags containing personal belongings packed for travelling; luggage सामान I put all my *baggage* in the brake van.

bail *(n.)* बेल– money paid by or for someone in order to secure their release on bail जमानत The accused was released on *bail.*

bait *(n.)* बेट– 1. something intended to entice someone to do something प्रलोभन He put a piece of cheese in the mouse-trap as a *bait.*
2. *(v.)* to put bait on (a hook) or in (a trap, net, or fishing area) to entice fish or animals चारा डालना Rahul *baited* his hook to catch the fish.

bake *(v.)* बेक– to cook (food) by dry heat without direct exposure to a flame, typically in an oven पकाना,

सेंकना She *baked* bread for her family.

balance *(v.)* बैलन्स– 1. to put (something) in a steady position so that it does not fall संतुलित होना/करना या रखना She *balanced* the mug on her knee.

2.*(n.)* an apparatus for weighing, especially one with a central pivot, beam, and two scales तराज़ू, कांटा, तुला An honest shopkeeper keeps an accurate *balance.*

3. the amount of money held in an account शेष, बाकी, बकाया I want to know the *balance* in my bank account.

balanced *(adj.)* बैलनस्ड– keeping or showing a balance; in good proportions संतुलित, स्थायी *Balanced* diet is very essential for healthy body.

balcony *(n.)* बाल्कनी– a platform enclosed by a wall or balustrade on the outside of a building, with access from an upper-floor window or door छज्जा, बारजा The glass doors opened on to a *balcony* with a view of the park.

bald *(adj.)* बॉल्ड– 1. having a scalp wholly or partly lacking hair गंजा *He was starting to go bald.*

2. without any extra detail or explanation; plain or blunt नीरस, रूखा The *bald* truth was that Sonam didn't love her husband anymore.

baldly *(adv.)* बाल्डली– without any extra detail or explanation नपे-तुले शब्दों में He told us *baldly* that he was leaving.

bale *(n.)* बेल– a large wrapped or bound bundle of paper, hay, or cotton गट्ठा, गठरी *Bales* of cotton were lying in the compound of the textile mill.

ball *(n.)* बॉल– 1. a solid or hollow spherical or egg-shaped object that is kicked, thrown, or hit in a game गेंद The children were playing with a *ball.*

2. dance नाच We were invited to a *ball.*

balloon *(n.)* बलून– a small coloured rubber bag which is inflated with air and then sealed at the neck, used as a child's toy or a decoration गुब्बारा Children like to play with *balloons.*

ballot *(n.)* बैलट– 1. a system of voting secretly and in writing on a particular issue गुप्त मतदान The new chairman was chosen through a *ballot.*

2. (also~paper) a piece of paper on which sb marks who they are voting for मतपत्र He won 54 per cent of the *ballot.*

balm *(n.)* बाम्– a fragrant cream or liquid used to heal or soothe the skin मरहम She applied *balm* on her forehead to get rid of headache.

ban *(n.)* बैन्– 1. an official or legal prohibition प्रतिबंध, रोक The government put a *ban* on sale of liquor in the city.

2. *(v.)* (officially or legally) to prohibit प्रतिबंध लगाना The screening of the movie was *banned* in Gujarat.

banal *(adj.)* बनाल्– so lacking in originality as to be obvious and boring, very ordinary तुच्छ, सामान्य He passed *banal* comments on her.

banana *(n.)* बनाना– a long curved fruit which grows in clusters and has soft pulpy flesh and yellow skin when ripe केला Eating *bananas* with milk is a nutritious breakfast.

band *(n.)* बैंड–1. a small group of musicians and vocalists who play pop, jazz, or rock music मंडली We had a big *band* at my sister's wedding.

2. a group of people who have a common interest or purpose or who share a common feature दल, समूह A *band* of devoted workers helps in popularising a political party.

3. a flat, thin strip or loop of material, used as a fastener, for reinforcement, or as decoration

फ़ीता The clerk put a rubber *band* round the file.

bandage *(n.)* बैन्डेज– 1. a strip of woven material used to bind up a wound or to protect an injured part of the body पट्टी The doctor put a *bandage* round a wound on Deepak's foot.
2. *(v.)* to bind (a wound or a part of the body) with a protective strip of material पट्टी बांधना Don't keep the wound open, better get it *bandaged*.

Bandit *(n.)* बैन्डिट– a robber or outlaw belonging to a gang and typically operating in an isolated or lawless area डाकू, दस्यु *Bandits* live in the forest.

bang *(v.)* बैंग– 1. to strike or put down (something) forcefully and noisily किसी पर ज़ोर से प्रहार करना He angrily *banged* the table.
2. *(n.)* a sudden loud, sharp noise धूम-धड़ाका, धमाका The Indian hockey team is back with a *bang*.

bangle *(n.)* बैंगल– a rigid ornamental band worn round the arm or occasionally the ankle चूड़ी The bride was wearing *bangles* made of gold.

banish *(v.)* बैनिश– to send (someone) away from a country or place as an official punishment निर्वासित करना, देश निकाला देना, निकाल देना The king *banished* his rebellious son from the kingdom.

banister *(n.)* बैनिस्टर– a single upright at the side of a staircase जंगला The children loved sliding down the *banister* at the new house.

bank *(n.)* बैंक–1. a financial establishment that uses money deposited by customers for investment, pays it out when required, makes loans at interest, and exchanges currency बैंक It is safe to keep money in the *bank*.
2. the land alongside or sloping down to a river or lake किनारा, तीर, तट I walked along the *bank* of the river.
3. *(v.)* to trust भरोसा रखना Can I *bank* upon your help?

bankrupt *(adj.)* बैंकरप्ट– 1. declared in law as unable to pay their debts: दिवालिया His increasing losses and growing debts eventually made him *bankrupt*.
2. *(v.)* to reduce (a person or organization) to bankruptcy दिवाला निकलना The increasing losses *bankrupted* him.

banner *(n.)* बैनर्– a long strip of cloth bearing a slogan or design, carried in a demonstration or procession or hung in a public place झंडा, ध्वजा During elections, *banners* of various political parties are seen everywhere.

banquet *(n.)* बैन्क्वेट– an elaborate and formal evening meal for many people दावत, भोज, प्रीतिभोज The visiting head of state was given a grand *banquet*.

banter *(n.)* बैन्टर– the playful and friendly exchange of teasing remarks मज़ाक़, हँसी-दिल्लगी We saw the friendly *banter* at the marriage party.

banyan *(n.)* बैनयन– an Indian fig tree बरगद का पेड़, वट Some branches of a *Banyan* tree grow downwards and become roots.

baptize (ise) *(v.)* बैपटाईज़– to administer baptism to (someone); christen ईसाई बनाना She was *baptized* a Catholic.

bar *(n.)* बार्–1. a long rigid piece of wood, metal, or similar material, typically used as an obstruction, fastening, or weapon डण्डा, छड़, सलाख़ The wooden *bars* erected in a row divided the courtyard into two parts.

2. counter in a pub, restaurant, or cafe across which drinks or refreshments are served मधुशाला, पानागार, शराब-घर Among the Indian middle class people, going to the *bar* daily is not considered good.

3.*(v.)* to stop रोकना, रोक लगाना, The policeman *barred* the entry of traffic into the procession route.

barb *(n.)* बार्ब– a sharp projection near the end of an arrow, fish hook, or similar object, which is angled away from the main point so as to make extraction difficult तीर, भाले आदि का मुड़ा हुआ नुकीला सिरा, काँटा, कंटक There was a *barbed* wire on all sides of the field.

barbarian *(n.)* बार्बेअरिअन– an uncultured or brutish person जंगली लोग, बर्बर The *barbarians* attacked our village.

barbarous *(adj.)* बार्बरस– extremely brutal क्रूर, असभ्य Many early child-rearing practices were *barbarous* by modern standards.

barbecue *(n.)* बार्बिक्यू– a meal or gathering at which meat, fish, or other food is cooked out of doors on a rack over an open fire or on a special appliance बाहर आयोजित प्रतिभोज Let's have a *barbecue* on the beach.

barber *(n.)* बार्बर्– a person who cuts men's hair and shaves or trims beards as an occupation नाई, हज्जाम I went to the *barber's* shop to have a haircut.

bard *(n.)* बाड– a poet, traditionally one reciting epics and associated with a particular oral tradition कवि, शायर Wordsworth was a famous *bard* of nature.

bare *(adj.)* बेअर्– (of a person or part of the body) not clothed or covered नंगा, अनावृत, अरक्षित, ख़ाली The poor man walked *bare* foot in the hot sun.

barefoot *(adj., adv.)* बेअर्फ़ूट– wearing nothing on the feet नंगे पांव She walked *barefoot* along the beach.

barely *(adv.)* बेअर्लि– only just; almost not कठिनाई से, मुश्किल से I could *barely* hear her voice from there.

bargain *(n.)* बार्गेन– 1. an agreement between two or more people or groups as to what each will do for the other सौदा, समझौता For fifty rupees, this chair is a good *bargain.*

2. *(v.)* to negotiate the terms and conditions of a transaction सौदा/समझौता करना, मोल-तोल करना The customer *bargained* hard with the shopkeeper.

barge *(n.)* बार्ज–1. a long ornamental boat used for pleasure or ceremony संकरी नौका We saw an ancient *barge* in the museum.

2. *(v.)* to move forcefully or roughly ज़बरदस्ती घुसना The thieves *barged* into the house at night.

bark *(v.)* बार्क्–1. to utter a short loud sound भौंकना A dog *barked* at her.

2. *(n.)* a part of tree; stem छाल, बक्कल The *barks* of some trees have medicinal values.

barn *(n.)* बार्न– a large farm building used for storing grain, hay, or straw or for housing livestock भुसौरा, बखार We have a huge *barn* in the village.

baron *(n.)* बैरन– a member of the lowest order of the British nobility नवाब, सामंत His father is a printing *baron.*

barracks *(n.)* बैरक्स– a large building or group of buildings used to house soldiers बैरक, बारक Soldiers live in *barracks.*

barrage *(n.)* बैराज– an overwhelming number of questions, criticisms, or complaints delivered simultaneously or in rapid succession प्रश्नों की बौछार He started a *barrage* of questions at somebody.

barrel *(n.)* बैरल–1. a cylindrical tube forming part of an object such as a gun or a pen नली, नाल The hunter pointed the *barrel* of his gun at the tiger.

2. a cylindrical container bulging out in the middle, traditionally made of wooden staves with metal hoops round them पीपा He poured the oil into the *barrel.*

barren *(adj.)* बैरन–1. too poor to produce much or any vegetation बंजर, ऊसर You cannot grow any crop in this *barren* land.

2. infertile बांझ, निष्फल A *barren* woman cannot bear a child.

barrier *(n.)* बैरिअर्– a fence or other obstacle that prevents movement or access रोक, अवरोध, घेरा The police put up a *barrier* to stop all cars.

barrister *(n.)* बैरिस्टर– a person called to the bar and entitled to practise as an advocate, particularly in the higher courts बैरिस्टर, विधिवक्ता Mahatma Gandhi went to London to train as a *barrister.*

barter *(v.)* बार्ट्र– 1. to exchange (goods or services) for other goods or services without using money (सामान की) अदला-बदली करना They *barted* their grain for machinery.

2. *(n.)* the action or system of bartering वस्तु-विनिमय, अदला-बदली Trading was carried out under a *barter* system.

base *(n.)* बेस–1. the lowest part or edge of something, especially the part on which it rests or is supported तल, तह, आधार Some dirt was sticking to the *base* of the glass.

2. (*adj.*) not having moral principles नीच, अधम She acted from *base* motives.

basement *(n.)* बेसमण्ट– the floor of a building which is partly or entirely below ground level तहख़ाना His house has a large *basement.*

bash *(v.)* बैश– 1. to strike hard and violently प्रहार करना, चोट करना He *bashed* his car in the tree.

2. *(n.)* a party or social event उत्सव, पार्टी A huge birthday *bash* awaited me at home.

bashful *(adj.)* बैशफुल– reluctant to draw attention to oneself; shy झेंपू, शर्मीला Don't be *bashful* now.

basic *(adj.)* बेसिक– fundamental, at the base बुनियादी, आधारभूत, मौलिक I have gathered the *basic* information about the place.

basin *(n.)* बेसिन– a wide open container used for preparing food or for holding liquid हौज़, कुंड The doctor asked for hot water in the *basin.*

basis *(n.)* बेसिस–1. the underlying support or foundation for an idea, argument, or process आधार, मूलाधार Trust is the only *basis* for a good working relationship.

2. an essential principle रीति-विशेष I play cricket on a regular *basis.*

bask *(v.)* बास्क– to lie exposed to warmth and light, typically from the sun, for relaxation and pleasure धूप सेंकना *Basking* in the winter sun is a soothing experience.

basket *(n.)* बास्किट–a container used to hold or carry things, typically made from interwoven strips of cane or wire टोकरी, डलिया She put the flowers in a *basket.*

bass *(n.)* बेस– the lowest adult male singing voice निम्नतम तान का पुरुष स्वर, मंद स्वर Can you sing the *bass* part in this song?

bastard *(n.)* बास्टर्ड– a person born of parents not married to each other नाजायज़ संतान, जारज, दोगला Children teased the orphan as a *bastard.*

bat *(n.)* बैट–1. a cricket bat बल्ला Rahul was presented a cricket *bat* by his father on his birthday.

2. a mainly nocturnal mammal capable of sustained flight, with membranous wings that extend between the fingers and limbs. चमगादड़ *Bats* can fly at night.

batch *(n.)* बैच– a number of things or people regarded as a group or set टोली, जत्था The company undertakes thirty-six separate quality control checks on every *batch*.

bath *(n.)* बाथ– washing of the body स्नान I was taking a *bath* when he came to see me.

bathe *(v.)* बाथ– to apply water to नहाना, नहलाना In summer, I *bathe* twice a day.

baton *(n.)* बैटन– policeman's short thick stick छड़ी A policeman carrying a *baton* walked towards him.

battalion *(n.)* बटैलिअन– army unit made up of several companies सैनिकों की टुकड़ी, वाहिनी The commander called another *battalion* for the war.

batter *(v.)* बैटर्– to beat heavily and repeatedly मारना, कूटना, चकनाचूर करना A prisoner was *battered* to death with a table leg.

battered *(adj.)* बैटर्ड– damaged, rough घिसा हुआ That old man is wearing a *battered* old hat.

battery *(n.)* बैटरी–1. portable cell for supplying electricity बैटरी I put a new *battery* in my car.

2. an army unit of big guns तोपख़ाना They could not hold out before the enemy's *battery*.

battle *(n.)* बैटल– 1. fight against someone लड़ाई, युद्ध There was a fierce *battle* between the two armies.

2. *(v.)* to struggle युद्ध / लड़ाई करना Both the armies *battled* fiercely.

be *(v.)* बी– to exist in actuality, to occupy a given position, to take place, to occur, to go होना Don't *be* late for the meeting.

beach *(n.)* बीच– shore, coast समुद्र-तट, किनारा Kerala has many lovely *beaches*.

bead *(n.)* बीड– small ball of wood or glass pierced for threading मनका, दाना The girl wore a string of colourful *beads*.

beak *(n.)* बीक– a hard, cone-shaped or poined part or structure चोंच The parrot has a curved *beak*.

beam *(n.)* बीम–1. ray or stream of light किरण, किरणपुंज The diamond sparkled in the *beams* of sunlight.

2. long horizontal piece of iron or timber used to carry the weight of a building कड़ी, कांड़ी The roof was supported by a thick *beam* in the centre.

bean *(n.)* बीन– plant bearing seeds in a long pods सेम, फली Among vegetables, I like French *beans* the most.

bear *(n.)* बेअर्–1. large, heavy animal with thick fur रीछ, भालू There are white *bears* in Siberia.

2. *(v.)* to endure, to tolerate सहन करना, बर्दाश्त करना She could not *bear* the pain.

3. to give birth जन्म देना, उपजाना, फलना To *bear* children is a natural function of women.

bearable *(adj.)* बेअॅरबल– that can be endured or borne सहने योग्य The pain was *bearable* after taking medicine.

bearer *(n.)* बेअॅरर्–1. a person who brings a letter or message धारक, वाहक Rehman received an urgent note from the *bearer* sent by his father.

2. one who carries, upholds or brings बैरा Ramesh ordered the *bearer* to bring him a cup of coffee.

beard *(n.)* बिअर्ड– hair on the lower part of the face दाढ़ी He had a black *beard*.

beast *(n.)* बीस्ट– four-footed animal पशु, जानवर Tiger is a ferocious *beast.*

beat *(v.)* बीट– 1. to hit repeatedly मारना, पीटना He *beat* the table with his hand.
2. to defeat हराना, पराजित करना Our team was *beaten* in the match.
3. a throb or pulsation धड़कना My heart was *beating* loudly before my result was announced.

beautiful *(adj.)* ब्यूटिफुल– giving delight to the mind or to the senses सुंदर, रमणीय, ख़ूबसूरत *Beautiful* girls mostly take up modelling as a career.

beauty *(n.)* ब्यूटी– loveliness, fineness ख़ूबसूरती, सुन्दरता I was struck by her *beauty.*

because *(conj.)* बिकॉज़– 1. for the reason that क्योंकि I did not go to work yesterday *because* I was not well.
2. *(prep.)* reason being इसलिए कि *Because* of the rain, we could not go for a walk.

beckon *(v.)* बेकन– to call someone's attention by a gesture इशारा करना, इशारे से बुलाना I *beckoned* the waiter to come to my table.

become *(v.)* बिकम–1. to begin to be, to grow to be हो जाना Mr. Rao *became* the headmaster last year.
2. to be well-suited to शोभा देना, जंचना This sari *becomes* you.

bed *(n.)* बेड– a piece of furniture on which to sleep पलंग, शय्या When did you go to *bed* last night?

bedraggled *(adj.)* बिड्रैगलड्– soiled by rain or dirt बहुत गंदा, मैला और गीला The poor man had *bedraggled* hair.

bedridden *(adj.)* बैडरिडन– confined to bed by sickness or old age शय्याग्रस्त His father is *bedridden* due to his old age.

bedrock *(n.)* बेडरॉक– solid rock at the bottom सुदृढ़ आधार Marriage and children are the *bedrock* of family life.

bee *(n.)* बी– small, four-winged, stinging insect that produces wax and honey after gathering nectar from flowers मधुमक्खी, भौंरा *Bees* gather nectar to produce honey.

beef *(n.)* बीफ़– the flesh of an ox, bull or cow गोमांस Hindus do not eat *beef.*

beehive *(n.)* बीहाइव– a box-like or dome-shaped structure in which bees are kept मधुमक्खी का छत्ता The boy threw a stone at the *beehive.*

beer *(n.)* बिअर्– an alcoholic drink made from malt बियर He ordered for a bottle of *beer.*

beetle *(n.)* बीटल– insect with hard, shining wing-covers भृंग I saw many *beetles* in the garden.

beetroot *(n.)* बीट्रूट– the edible dark-red spherical root of a kind of beet, eaten as a vegetable चुक़ंदर We purchased some *beetroots* from the market.

before *(prep., conj.)* बिफ़ॉर्–1. earlier than पहले, पूर्व Sunil reached office *before* time.
2. *(adv.)* at an earlier time, in the past पहले ही, अतीत में I have seen him *before,* but I cannot remember where.
3. infront of सामने, सम्मुख Ram stood *before* the house where he had lived twenty years ago.

beforehand *(adv.)* बिफ़ोर्हैंड– earlier, before पहले से I knew it *beforehand.*

befriend *(v.)* बिफ्रैंड– to make friends or become friendly with किसी का मित्र बन जाना, मित्रवत् व्यवहार करना He makes a point of *befriending* newcomers to Parliament.

beg *(v.)* बेग–1. to ask for something भीख मांगना The hungry man *begged* for food.
2. to take the liberty of doing or saying something प्रार्थना करना, विनय

करना Uma *begged* her husband not to consume liquor.

beggar *(n.)* बेगर्– one who begs esp. for livelihood भिखारी, भिक्षुक I met an old *beggar* at the stairs of the temple.

beggary *(n.)* बेगरी– living by begging भिक्षावृत्ति *Beggary* is a curse on humanity.

begin *(v.)* बिगिन– to start आरंभ करना या होना The match will *begin* after five minutes.

behalf *(n.)* बिहाफ़– as the representative of की तरफ़ से, के पक्ष में He had to attend the funeral on Mama's *behalf.*

behave *(v.)* बिहेव– to act, conduct oneself व्यवहार करना, पेश आना Every mother teaches her children to *behave* properly.

behaviour *(n.)* बिहेवयर– a way of behaving आचरण, व्यवहार Everyone praised Amit's courteous *behaviour.*

behead *(v.)* बिहेड– to cut off the head of somebody as a punishment (दण्ड के तौर पर) सिर काट देना He was *beheaded* mercilessly.

behind *(prep., adv.)* बिहाइन्ड–1. in the rear के पीछे, पीछे की ओर The ball fell *behind* the wall.
2. stay after others देर से, विलम्ब से The train was running *behind* time.

being *(n.)* बीइंग– existence अस्तित्व Bangladesh came into *being* in 1971.

belch *(v.)* बेल्च– to emit wind noisily from the throat डकार लेना He *belched* loudly.

belief *(n.)* बिलीफ़– trust, confidence विश्वास, यक़ीन We're prepared to fight for our *beliefs.*

believe *(v.)* बिलीव– to accept the statement of somebody as true विश्वास करना I strongly *believe* in the existence of God.

belittle *(v.)* बिलिट्ल– to cause to seem less important महत्त्व घटाना, छोटा करना She *belittled* my riding skills whenever she could.

bell *(n.)* बेल– hollow vessel of metal घण्टा, घण्टी There are many *bells* in the temple.

bellow *(v.)* बेलो– to make a loud noise, shout गरजना, चीख़ना He *bellowed* in agony.

belly *(n.)* बेली– the front part of the human trunk below the ribs, containing the stomach and bowels पेट, उदर These days she is exercising to get her *belly* in shape.

belong *(v.)* बिलॉन्ग–1. to be the property of का होना, की संपत्ति होना This book *belongs* to me.
2. to be a member of का सदस्य होना We *belong* to the same club.

belongings *(n.)* बिलॉन्गिंग्स– person's movable possessions सम्पत्ति, सामान He put all his *belongings* in the room.

beloved *(adj.)* बिलविड– 1. dearly loved परम प्रिय At last, I reached my *beloved* grandmother's place.
2. *(n.)* much loved person प्रेमिका He introduced her as his *beloved.*

below *(prep.)* बिलो– 1. at a lower level or layer than नीचे The boy hid the novel *below* the desk.
2. *(adv.)* at a lower level or layer निचले स्तर पर He jumped from the window into the moat *below.*

belt *(n.)* बेल्ट– a strip of leather or other material worn, typically round the waist, to support or hold in clothes or to carry weapons पेटी, कमरबंद, पट्टा Broad *belts* are in fashion among the young people.

bemused *(adj.)* बिम्यूज़्ड– confused or bewildered हक्का-वक्का, किंकर्तव्यविमूढ़ He was *bemused* after the meeting.

bench *(n.)* बेंच– a long seat for several people, typically made of wood or stone बेंच, तख़्त Many patients sat on the *bench* outside the doctor's cabin.

benchmark *(n.)* बैंचमॉर्क्– a standard or point of reference against which things may be compared कसौटी These new safety features set a *benchmark* for other manufacturers to follow.

bend *(v.)* बेण्ड– 1. to curve or to be curved झुकाना, मोड़ना It is not easy to *bend* a steel rod.
2. *(n.)* curve or turn मोड़, घुमाव His house is round the *bend* on the main road.

beneath *(adv.)* बिनीथ– 1. extending or directly underneath something नीचे, तले The mountaineer looked *beneath* from the top of the hill.
2. (prep.) at a lower level or layer than के नीचे, के तले The tired shepherd sat down to take rest *beneath* the tree.

benefactor *(n.)* बेनिफ़ैक्टर– a person who gives money or other help to a person or cause दानी, उपकार या भला करने वाला A low-interest loan from a *benefactor* allowed them to build a floor for the exhibition hall.

beneficial *(adj.)* बेनिफ़िशल– resulting in good; favourable or advantageous फ़ायदेमंद His financial support is *beneficial* for me.

benefit *(n.)* बेनिफ़िट– 1. an advantage or profit gained from something हित His wise advice was of great *benefit* to me.
2. *(v.)* receive an advantage; profit लाभ उठाना या पहुंचाना I *benefited* greatly from his advice.

benevolent *(adj.)* बनेवलण्ट– well meaning and kindly दयालु God is believed to be very *benevolent.*

benign *(adj.)* बिनाईन– gentle and kind भद्र, सौम्य She shook her head in *benign* amusement.

bent *(n.)* बेण्ट–1. a natural talent or inclination झुकाव, रुझान She has a *bent* for music.
2. *(adj.) sharply curved or having an angle* टेड़ा, मुड़ा हुआ It was so funny we were *bent* double with laughter.
3. dishonest, corrupt बेईमान, भ्रष्ट He was a *bent* policeman who sold secrets to drug dealer.

bequeath *(v.)* बिक्वीथ– to leave (property) to a person or other beneficiary by a will वसीयत में देना, वसीयत करना He *bequeathed* one lakh rupees to charity.

bequest *(n.)* बिक्वेस्ट– the action of bequeathing something वसीयत, रिक्थदान He left a *bequest* to each of his grandchildren.

bereavement *(n.)* बिरीवमेण्ट– the action or condition of being bereaved शोक, ग़मी There has been a *bereavement* in his family.

bereft *(adj.)* बिरेफ़्ट– deprived of or lacking (something) महरूम, दुःख में पड़ा हुआ My brother was utterly *bereft* when his wife died.

berserk *(adj.)* बर्ज़र्क– out of control with anger or excitement; wild or frenzied (क्रोध में) आपे से बाहर A man went *berserk* with an arsenal of guns.

berth *(n.)* बर्थ–1. a place to sleep on a train or ship शायिका I reserved a *berth* for the night train journey.
2. a place where a ship or boat can stay or stop लंगरगाह, गोदी, घाट The huge ship by the *berth* was an oil tanker.

beseech *(v.)* बिसीच– to ask someone urgently and fervently to do or give something विनती करना They *beseeched* him to stay.

beset *(v.)* बिसेट– to affect (someone or something) persistently बुरा असर डालना She was *beset* with self-doubt.

beside *(prep.)* बिसाइड– at the side of; next to पास, बग़ल में He stood *beside* his brother.

besides *(prep., adv.)* बिसाइड्ज़्– in addition to; apart from इसके सिवाय, इसके अतिरिक्त *Besides* your raincoat, you should also bring an umbrella.

besiege *(v.)* बिसीज– to surround (a place) with armed forces in order to capture it or force its surrender घेरा डालना, घेर लेना The king marched north to *besiege* Berwick.

best *(adj.)* बेस्ट– of the most excellent or desirable type or quality सर्वोत्तम, श्रेष्ठ It is *best* to consider various aspects before starting a new venture.

bestow *(v.)* बिस्टो– to confer or present (an honour, right, or gift) अर्पित / प्रदान करना The office was *bestowed* on him by the monarch of this realm.

best-seller *(n.)* बेस्ट-सेलर्– a book or other product that sells in very large numbers बड़ी संख्या में बिकने वाली किताब All her novels have turned out to be *best-sellers.*

bet *(v.)* बेट्– 1. to risk a sum of money or valued item against someone else's on the basis of the outcome of an unpredictable event such as a race or game शर्त लगाना, बाज़ी लगाना I *bet* you'll miss the flight.
2. *(n.)* an act of betting a sum of money दाँव, शर्त, बाज़ी My *bet* is that you'll miss the flight.

better *(adj.)* बेटर्– more desirable, satisfactory, or effective किसी अन्य से बेहतर, अधिक अच्छा We're hoping for *better* weather tomorrow.

betray *(v.)* बिट्रे– to be gravely disloyal to विश्वासघात करना, धोखा देना Jesus Christ was *betrayed* by one of his disciples.

between *(prep.)* बिट्वीन– 1. at, into, or across the space separating (two objects or regions) के बीच में She divided the sweets *between* her two sons.
2. *(adv.)* in the period separating two points in time बीच में, मध्य में Please see me *between* two and three o'clock.

beverage *(n.)* बेवरेज–a drink other than water पेय We need to decide upon the food and *beverage* for the party.

beware *(v.)* बिवेअर्– to be cautious and alert to risks or dangers सतर्क, सावधान रहना या होना *Beware* of pickpockets.

bewilder *(v.)* बिविल्डर्– to cause (someone) to become perplexed and confused उलझन या अचरज में डालना, घबरा देना She was *bewildered* by his sudden change of mood.

bewitch *(v.)* बिविच– to enchant (someone) जादू डालना, मोहित करना The beautiful interiors of the building *bewitched* us.

beyond *(prep.)* बियॉन्ड– at or to the further side of परे, पार There was a temple *beyond* the mountains.

bias *(n.)* बाइअस– 1. inclination or prejudice for or against one person or group, especially in a way considered to be unfair पक्षपात, झुकाव A *bias* against aged workers is visible in most companies.
2. *(v.)* to cause to feel or show inclination or prejudice for or against someone or something पक्षपात करना Editors were *biased* against authors from provincial universities.

bib *(n.)* बिब– a piece of cloth or plastic fastened round a child's neck to keep its clothes clean while eating एक प्रकार की कपड़े की गद्दी (जो बच्चों के गले में खाते समय बांधी जाती है) The mother tied a *bib* under the child's chin.

bibliography *(n.)* बिबलिऑग्रफ़ी– list of the books referred to in a scholarly work, typically printed as an appendix पुस्तक-सूची, ग्रंथ-सूची There is a *bibliography* at the end of this book.

biceps *(n.)* बाइसेप्स– the main muscles at the top part of the arm बाज़ू के ऊपरी भाग में सामने वाले हिस्से की बड़ी मांसपेशी Sahil has good *biceps* as he goes to the gym everyday.

bid *(v.)* बिड– to offer (a certain price) for something, especially at an auction: बोली लगाना Guests will *bid* for pieces of fine jewellery.

bifurcate *(v.)* बाइफ़रकेट– to divide into two branches or forks: दो फाँकों या खण्ड में विभाजित करना The state government *bifurcated* the road.

big *(adj.)* बिग– of considerable size or extent बड़ा, लंबा-चौड़ा, विशाल They bought a *big* cake for their son's birthday.

bigamy *(n.)* बिगूअॅमी– the offence of marrying someone while already married to another person एक समय में दो पति या पत्नी रखने की नीति, द्विविवाह *Bigamy* is not permitted in the Hindu religion.

bike *(n.)* बाइक्– a bicycle or motorcycle मोटरसाइकिल Afnan wants to ride a *bike.*

bilateral *(adj.)* बाइलैटरल– having or relating to two sides; affecting both sides दुतरफ़ा, द्विपक्षी They signed on *bilateral* agreement.

bilingual *(adj.)* बाइलिंगवल– speaking two languages fluently द्विभाषी I am *bilingual* in English and Hindi.

bill *(n.)* बिल–1. statement of money owned for goods or services supplied बिल, प्राप्यक The shopkeeper gave me the *bill* and I paid the money.
2. horny part of the mouth of some birds, beak चोंच A stork has a long *bill.*

billion *(n.)* बिलियन– the number equivalent to the product of one thousand million एक अरब There are about one *billion* Hindu followers all over the world.

billow *(n.)* बिलो– a large undulating mass of something, typically cloud, smoke, or steam like a wave लहर Her dress *billowed* out around her.

bin *(n.)* बिन– a receptacle in which to deposit rubbish खत्ती, कूड़ा आदि डालने का डिब्बा I threw the scraps of paper into the dust *bin.*

bind *(v.)* बाइन्ड– to tie or fasten (something) tightly together: बांधना They *bound* her hands and feet.

binding *(adj.)* बाइंडिंग– involving an obligation that cannot be broken अनिवार्य, बाह्यकारी My contract is legally *binding* with him.

binoculars *(n.)* बाइनॉक्युलर्स– an optical instrument with a lens for each eye, used for viewing distant objects. दूरबीन The sailor looked through his *binoculars* to find the seashore.

biography *(n.)* बाइऑग्रफ़ी– an account of someone's life written by someone else. जीवनी Although their individual *biographies* are different, both are motivated by a similar ambition.

biology *(n.)* बाइऑलजी– the study of living organisms, जीव-विज्ञान He has deep interest in *biology.*

biopsy *(n.)* बाइऑपसी– an examination of tissue removed from a living body to discover the presence, cause, or extent of a disease जीवोतिपरीक्षा She has to go for *biopsy.*

birch *(n.)* बर्च– a slender hardy tree which has thin peeling bark and bears catkins भोज वृक्ष, भूर्ज I have a *birch* tree in my garden.

bird *(n.)* बर्ड– a warm-blooded egg-laying vertebrate animal distinguished by the possession of feathers, wings, a beak, and typically by being able to fly पक्षी, चिड़िया *Birds* lay eggs in the nests.

birth *(n.)* बर्थ– the emergence of a baby or other young from the body of its mother; the start of life as a physically separate being जन्म Mrs. Kapoor gave *birth* to a son this morning.

birthplace *(n.)* बर्थप्लेस– the place where a person was born जन्म-स्थान Lucknow is my *birthplace.*

bisect *(v.)* बाइसेक्ट– to divide into two parts दो बराबर के टुकड़े करना, द्विभाजित करना Draw a line of 10 cm and *bisect* it.

bishop *(n.)* बिशप– a senior member of the Christian clergy, usually in charge of a diocese and empowered to confer holy orders पादरियों का अध्यक्ष, धर्माध्यक्ष It is a *bishop's* cap.

bit *(n.)* बिट– a small piece, part, or quantity of something टुकड़ा, अंश The glass was broken into many *bits.*

bitch *(v.)* बिच–1. to make spitefully critical comments किसी के पीठ पीछे उसकी बुराई करना She was *bitching* about her close friend.

2. *(n.)* a female dog कुतिया The *bitch* won the first place in the dog show.

bitter *(adj.)* बिटर्–1. having a sharp, pungent taste or smell; not sweet स्वाद में कड़ुवा, कटु This medicine is very *bitter.*

2. feeling or showing anger, hurt, or resentment because of bad experiences or a sense of unjust treatment दु:खी, संतप्त I don't feel jealous or *bitter.*

bitterly *(adv.)* बिटर्लि– (of wind or weather) intensely cold अत्यधिक ठंडा It was *bitterly* cold.

bizarre *(adj.)* बिज़ार– very strange or unusual: विचित्र, अनोखा The story had a more *bizarre* ending.

black *(adj.)* ब्लैक– of the very darkest colour owing to the absence of or complete absorption of light; the opposite of white काला Please give me a bottle of *black* ink.

blacken *(v.)* ब्लैकन– to make or become black or dark; to defame काला करना या होना, कलंक लगाना She *blackened* her parents reputation.

blacklist *(n.)* ब्लैकलिस्ट– a list of people or groups regarded as unacceptable or untrustworthy and often marked down for punishment or exclusion काली सूची Workers were *blacklisted* after being quoted in the newspaper.

blackmail *(n.)* ब्लैकमेल– the use of threats or the manipulation of someone's feelings to force them to do something भयादोहन Piyush was *blackmailing* her since long.

black mark*(n.)* ब्लैक मॉर्क– a note or record of a person's misdemeanour or discreditable action कलंक का टीका He earned a *black mark* for coming late to meetings.

black market *(n.)* ब्लैक मॉर्किट– an illegal traffic or trade in officially controlled or scarce commodities काला बाज़ार, चोर बाज़ार Stolen things are sold in the *black market.*

blade *(n.)* ब्लेड–1. the flat cutting edge of a knife, saw, or other tool or weapon: धार This knife has a sharp *blade.*

2. a long, narrow leaf of grass or another similar plant पत्ती Not even a *blade* of grass grows in this field.

blame *(n.)* ब्लेम– 1. responsibility for a fault or wrong निन्दा, दोष Everybody put the *blame* on him.

2. *(v.)* to feel or declare that (someone or something) is responsible for a fault or wrong दोष मढ़ना, इल्ज़ाम लगाना The bus driver was *blamed* for the accident.

bland *(adj.)* ब्लैण्ड– lacking strong features or characteristics and therefore uninteresting मामूली, अनाकर्षक She has a *bland* style of writing.

blank *(adj.)* ब्लैंक– unrelieved by decorative or other features; bare, empty, or plain कोरा, ख़ाली *A blank* sheet of paper.

blanket *(n.)* ब्लैंकिट– a large piece of woollen or similar material used as a covering on a bed or elsewhere for warmth कम्बल As winter is arriving, I must buy a *blanket.*

blare *(v.)* ब्लेअर्– to make or cause to make a loud, harsh sound गरजना, चिल्लाना During the traffic jam, the car horns *blared* full blast.

blast *(n.)* ब्लास्ट–1. a single loud note of a horn, whistle, or similar वाद्य यंत्र की ऊँची ध्वनि, तूर्यनाद They were thrown backwards by the *blast.*
2. an explosion or explosive firing धमाका, विस्फ़ोट The *blast* of the explosion shook the whole building.
3. a strong gust of wind or air झोंका, झकोरा As Arun opened the door, he was thrown back by a *blast* of wind.
4. *(v.)* to blow up or break apart (something solid) with explosives धमाके से फटना A bomb *blasted* in the market this morning.

blatant *(adj.)* ब्लैटेण्ट– (of bad behaviour) done openly and unashamedly साफ़, खुला She forced herself to resist his *blatant* charm.

blaze *(n.)* ब्लेज़– 1. a very large or fiercely burning fire चमक, ज्वाला The decorated hall was a *blaze* of light.
2. *(v.)* to burn fiercely or brightly धधकना, भड़कना The bonfire *blazed* brightly in the dark winter night.

blazer *(n.)* ब्लेज़र्– a coloured jacket worn by schoolchildren or sports players as part of a uniform रंगीन जाकेट All the members of the cricket team wore *blazers.*

bleach *(v.)* ब्लीच– to cause (a material such as cloth, paper, or hair) to become white or much lighter by a chemical process or by exposure to sunlight रंगहीन करना, साफ़ करना We found a new formula to *bleach* and brighten clothing.

bleak *(adj.)* ब्लीक–1. cold and miserable: उजाड़, ठंडा A *bleak* wind blew over the mountain top.
2. not hopeful or encouraging; unlikely to have a favourable outcome निराशापूर्ण, रूखा Geeta's *bleak* face indicated that something was wrong with her.

bleary *(adj.)* ब्लियरी– looking or feeling dull and unfocused from sleep or tiredness थकी हुई लाल आंखों वाला He looked *bleary*-eyed after drinking.

bleat *(v.)* ब्लीट– (of a sheep, or goat) make a characteristic weak, wavering cry मिमियाना The sheep *bleated* in the field.

bleed *(v.)* ब्लीड– to lose blood from the body as a result of injury or illness रक्त निकलना या निकालना His wound was *bleeding.*

bleep *(v.)* ब्लीप– to make a short high-pitched sound or sounds as a signal or to attract attention ऊँची ध्वनि निकालना या निकलना The cooker started to *bleep.*

blemish *(n.)* ब्लेमिश– 1. a small mark or flaw which spoils the appearance of something धब्बा, ऐब The pimple left a *blemish* on her face.
2. *(v.)* to spoil the appearance or quality of (something) रूप बिगाड़ देना, बदनाम करना His reign as world champion has been *blemished* by controversy.

blend *(v.)* ब्लेण्ड– 1. to mix (a substance) with another substance so that they combine together मिलाना, मिश्रण करना, मिल जाना *Blend* the cornflour with a tablespoon of water.
2. *(n.)* a mixture of different substances or other things मिश्रण, मेल In the evening, the sky appeared a beautiful *blend* of colours.

bless *(v.)* ब्लेस– to pronounce words in a religious rite in order to confer or invoke divine favour upon आशीर्वाद देना The temple priest *blessed* the devotees.

blessing *(n.)* ब्लेसिंग– God's favour and protection आशीर्वाद, वरदान Adversity can prove a *blessing* in disguise.

blind *(adj.)* ब्लाइण्ड– 1. unable to see because of injury, disease, or a congenital condition अंधा, नेत्रहीन She felt pity for the *blind* beggar.
2. *(n.)* cause (someone) to be unable to see, permanently or temporarily परदा She pulled down the *blinds* to avoid the light.

blink *(v.)* ब्लिंक– to shut and open the eyes quickly: पलक मारना, आंखें झपकाना The strong light made him *blink.*

blister *(n.)* ब्लिस्टर्– 1. a small bubble on the skin filled with serum and caused by friction, burning, or other damage छाला, फफोला The intense heat caused *blisters* on the baby's tender skin.
2. *(v.)* to form blisters on the skin or other surface छाला पड़ना The boiling water fell on Amit's hand and *blistered* it.

blistering *(adj.)* ब्लिस्टरिंग– expressed with great vehemence प्रचंड, घोर The runners set off at a *blistering* pace.

bloated *(adj.)* ब्लोटिड्– swollen with fluid or gas: फूला हुआ He felt *bloated* atter the heavy lunch.

block *(n.)* ब्लॉक–1. a large solid piece of hard material, especially rock, stone, or wood, typically with flat surfaces on each side: खंड, कुन्दा, शिलाखण्ड This house was built with the *blocks* of cement.
2. a large single building subdivided into separate rooms, flats, or offices एक बड़ी इमारत का हिस्सा I have rented a three-room *block.*
3. *(v.)* to prevent access to or the use of रोक देना, बाधा डालना The demonstrators *blocked* the road.

blockade *(v.)* ब्लॉकेड– to seal off (a place) to prevent goods or people from entering or leaving नाक़ाबंदी करना The police *blockaded* the road.

blockage *(n.)* ब्लॉकिज– an obstruction which makes movement or flow difficult or impossible गतिरोध The pumps are prone to *blockage.*

blockbuster *(n.)* ब्लॉकबस्टर्– a thing of great power or size, in particular a film, book, or other product that is a great commercial success अति सफ़ल Sholay was a *blockbuster* film.

bloke *(n.)* ब्लोक– a man आदमी, पुरुष He's a nice *bloke.*

blonde *(n.)* ब्लॉण्ड– (of hair) pale gold in colour सुनहरे बाल या सुनहरे बालों वाली महिला I met a *blonde* near the railway station.

blood *(n.)* ब्लड्– the fluid circulating in the vascular system of men and other vertebrates रक्त, लहू, ख़ून It is a misconception that we become weak after donating *blood.*

blood-pressure *(n.)* ब्लड्-प्रेशअर्– the pressure of the blood in the circulatory system रक्तचाप Her mother-in-law has high *blood-pressure.*

bloodshed *(n.)* ब्लड्शेड– the killing or wounding of people, typically on a large scale during a conflict ख़ून-ख़राबा, रक्तपात The king wanted to avoid further *bloodshed.*

bloody *(adj.)* ब्लडी– covered, smeared, or running with blood ख़ून से भरी हुई, ख़ूनी, रक्तरंजित It was a *bloody* war.

bloom *(v.)* ब्लूम्– 1. to become radiant and glowing फूलना, खिलना Many flowers *bloom* in my garden.
2. *(n.)* a flower, especially one cultivated for its beauty फूल, बहार The apple trees were in *bloom.*

blossom *(v.)* ब्लॉसम– 1. to mature or develop in a promising or healthy way (फूल) खिलना, फलना-फूलना The rose plant is *blossoming.*

2. *(n.)* the state or period of flowering कली I saw a new *blossom* in the rose plant.

blot *(n.)* ब्लॉट–1. a dark mark or stain made by ink, paint, dirt, etc. धब्बा, दाग़ There was a large *blot* of ink on the clean sheet of paper.

2. a shameful act or quality that damages an otherwise good character or reputation कलंक Ram's misconduct is a *blot* on his family's name.

3. *(v.)* to mark or stain (something) दाग़ या धब्बा लगाना Ram's behaviour has *blotted* the good image of his parents.

blotch *(n.)* ब्लॉच– large irregular patch or unsightly mark on the skin or another surface दाग़ या धब्बा Sweat left *blotches* on his shirt.

blouse *(n.)* ब्लाउज़– a woman's upper garment resembling a shirt, typically with a collar, buttons, and sleeves कुरती, चोली I bought a new *blouse* for my sari.

blow *(n.)* ब्लो–1. an act of blowing an instrument प्रहार, घूँसा, चोट They had a fight and exchanged *blows.*

2. *(v.)* to move creating an air current बहना Cool air was *blowing* gently.

3. to expel air through pursed lips फूँकना, बुझाना Please *blow out* (extinguish) the candle.

4. to displace violently or send flying विस्फ़ोट में नष्ट करना Terrorists *blew up* (destroyed) the bridge with dynamite.

blue *(n.)* ब्लू–1. blue colour or pigment नीला रंग *Blue* is my favourite colour.

2. of a colour intermediate between green and violet, as of the sky or sea on a sunny day आसमानी नीला She is wearing a dark *blue* jeans.

bluff *(v.)* ब्लफ़– 1. to try to deceive someone as to one's abilities or intentions झांसा देना He tried to *bluff* people but failed.

2. *(adj.)* (of people) very direct and cheerful मुंहफट He is known for his *bluff* behaviour.

blunder *(n.)* ब्लण्डर्– 1. a stupid or careless mistake भारी भूल, चूक Your refusal to go with him was a *blunder.*

2. (v.) to make a stupid or careless mistake; act or speak clumsily भारी भूल करना He knew he'd *blundered.*

blunt *(adj.)* ब्लण्ट–1. not having a sharp edge or point कुंद, भोथरा This knife is of no use, its edge is *blunt.*

2. uncompromisingly forthright स्पष्ट, रूखा Your *blunt* speech hurt his feelings.

blur *(v.)* ब्लर्– to make or become unclear or less distinct धुंधला करना The dust storm *blurred* my vision.

blurt *(v.)* ब्लर्ट– to say (something) suddenly and without careful consideration बिना सोच-समझे अचानक बोलना She *blurted* out the truth.

blush *(v.)* ब्लश्– to show shyness, embarrassment, or shame by becoming red in the face शरमाना, लज्जित होना She *blushed* at the sight of her lover.

bluster *(v.)* ब्लस्टर्– to talk in a loud, aggressive, or indignant way with little effect उग्र होना, गरजकर बोलना He *blustered* all day.

blustery *(adj.)* ब्लस्टरी– (of weather) characterized by strong winds तूफ़ानी We met on a cold and *blustery* day.

boar *(n.)* बॉर्– a tusked Eurasian wild pig from which domestic pigs are descended जंगली सूअर The hunter killed a wild *boar.*

board *(n.)* बॉर्ड्–1. a long, thin, flat piece of wood or other hard material, used for floors or other building purposes तख़्ता That wooden house has walls made of *boards.*

2. the provision of regular meals when one stays somewhere, in return for payment or services नियमित भुगतान पर ख़रीदा भोजन What does your hotel charge for bed and *board*?

3. *(v.)* to get on or into (a ship, aircraft, or other vehicle) चढ़ना, सवार होना The train started only a couple of minutes after he *boarded* it.

boast *(v.)* बोस्ट– 1. to talk with excessive pride and self-satisfaction about one's achievements, possessions, or abilities डींग हांकना, शेख़ी मारना she boasted about her many conquests.

2. *(n.)* an act of talking with excessive pride and self-satisfaction डींग, शेख़ी His *boast* that he could fight with a lion impressed nobody.

boastful *(adj.)* बोस्टफुल– showing excessive pride and self-satisfaction in one's achievements, possessions, or abilities शेखीबाज़, डींग मारने वाला We don't like her *boastful* nature.

boat *(n.)* बोट– a small vessel for travelling over water, propelled by oars, sails, or an engine नाव, किश्ती He went to England by *boat.*

bob *(v.)* बॉब– to move quickly up and down esp in water डूबना-उतराना He *bobbed* up again on the otherside of swimming pool.

body *(n.)* बॉडी– the physical structure, including the bones, flesh and organs of a person or an animal शरीर, बदन The police found the dead *body* of a man in the lake.

➢ **somebody**– a human being कोई व्यक्ति, *Somebody* (some person) informed the police about the road accident.

bodyguard *(n.)* बॉडिगार्ड– a person or group of people employed to escort and protect an important or famous person अंगरक्षक His *bodyguard* informed the police about the road accident.

bog *(n.)* बॉग– an area of wet muddy ground that is too soft to support a heavy body दलदल The wild buffalo got stuck in the *bog.*

bogey, bogy *(n.)* बोगी– a thing that causes fear हौआ, जूजू, भूत He did not fear of a *bogey.*

bogus *(adj.)* बोगस– not genuine or true (used in a disapproving manner when deception has been attempted) जाली, खोटा, बनावटी These papers are not original, but *bogus.*

boil *(v.)* बॉइल– 1. to reach or cause to reach the temperature at which it bubbles and turns to vapour उबलना She *boiled* the milk.

2. *(n.)* an inflamed pus-filled swelling on the skin फोड़ा, व्रण He has a big *boil* on his arm.

boisterous *(adj.)* बॉइसटरस– noisy, energetic, and cheerful ऊधमी, शोर मचाने वाला *a group of boisterous lads.*

bold *(adj.)* बोल्ड– showing a willingness to take risks; confident and courageous निडर, निर्भीक The *bold* man refused to tell a lie to save himself.

boldly *(adv.)* बोल्डली– a daring action or initiative: दिलेरी से, हिम्मत से The young man *boldly* faced the angry bull.

bolster *(v.)* बोल्स्टर्– to support or strengthen सहारा देना, संभालना The fall in interest rates is starting to *bolster* confidence.

bolt *(v.)* बोल्ट–1. to fasten (a door or window) with a bar that slides into a socket चटख़नी लगाना Did you *bolt* the door?

2. (of a horse or other animal) to run away suddenly, typically from fear छलाँग मारकर भागना The horse *bolted* down the lane.

3. *(n.)* a bar that slides into a socket to fasten a door or window सिटकिनी Please open the *bolt.*

bomb *(n.)* बॉम्ब– 1. a container filled with explosive or incendiary material, designed to explode बम, गोला A bomb attack.

2. *(v.)* to attack (a place or object) with a bomb or bombs बम बरसाना या गिराना The air force planes *bombed* the enemy's camps.

bombard *(v.)* बॉमबॉड– to attack (a place or person) continuously with bombs, shells, or other missiles गोलीबारी करना They will be *bombarded* with complaints.

bona fide *(adj.)* बोना-फाइड– genuine; real नेकनीयती, प्रामाणिक, सच्चा His *bona fide* is not doubted.

bond *(n.)* बॉन्ड– 1. a force or feeling that unites people; a shared emotion or interest संबंध, बंधन They share an emotional *bond* between themselves.

2. *(v.)* to tie something or to fasten things together बांधकर रखना, जोड़कर रखना I always *bonded* well with her.

bone *(n.)* बोन– any of the pieces of hard whitish tissue making up the skeleton in humans and other vertebrates हड्डी, अस्थि The broken *bones* of his leg took a long time to heal.

bonfire *(n.)* बानफाइअर्– a large open-air fire used for burning rubbish or as part of a celebration होली, उत्सवाग्नि The children danced happily round the *bonfire* for a long time.

bonnet *(n.)* बॉनिट–1. the hinged metal canopy covering the engine of a motor vehicle ढक्कन, बोनेट He opened the *bonnet* of his car.

2. a woman's or child's hat tied under the chin and with a brim framing the face टोपी Western ladies wear *bonnets* to protect their head.

bonus *(n.)* बोनस्– a sum of money added to a person's wages as a reward for good performance अधिलाभांश, बोनस Good weather is an added *bonus* but the real appeal is the landscape.

bony *(adj.)* बोनि– of or like bone: दुबला-पतला The small *bony* child begged for food.

book *(n.)* बुक–1. a written or printed work consisting of pages glued or sewn together along one side and bound in covers पुस्तक, ग्रंथ This is an interesting *book.*

2. *(v.)* to reserve (accommodation, a place, etc.); to buy (a ticket) in advance टिकट लेना I have *booked* a ticket for the evening show.

3. to reserve accommodation for आरक्षण की व्यवस्था करना Have you *booked* your ticket for Mumbai?

booking *(n.)* बुकिंग– an act of reserving accommodation, a ticket, etc. in advance अग्रिम आरक्षण The hotel does not handle group *bookings.*

bookworm *(n.)* बुक्वम्– a person who enjoys reading किताबी कीड़ा She is a *bookworm.*

boom *(n.)* बूम– sudden increase in trade तेजी, गरम बाज़ारी Last month, there was a major *boom* in the stock market.

boon *(n.)* बून– a thing that is helpful or beneficial वरदान The route will be a *boon* to many travellers.

boost *(v.)* बूस्ट– to help or encourage (something) to increase or improve बढ़ाना, वृद्धि करना या होना The unexpected increase in share market helped to *boost* the market.

boot *(n.)* बूट–1. a sturdy item of footwear covering the foot and ankle जूता, बूट Soldiers wear heavy *boots.*

2. an enclosed space at the back of a car for carrying luggage or other goods डिक्की, सामानदानी He put the bag in the *boot* of his car.

booth *(n.)* बूथ– an enclosed compartment that allows privacy, for example when telephoning, voting, or sitting in a restaurant दुकान, प्रकोष्ठ Voters crowded the voting *booth.*

booty *(n.)* बूटी– valuable stolen goods, especially those seized in war. लूट का माल The robbers shared the *booty* among themselves.

booze *(v.)* बूज़– to drink alcohol, especially in large quantities अत्यधिक शराब पीना He likes to go out *boozing* with his friends.

border *(n.)* बॉर्डर्–1. a line separating two countries, administrative divisions, or other areas सीमा The *border* between the two countries is heavily guarded.

2. the edge or boundary of something, or the part near it किनारा She wore a yellow sari with a black *border.*

bore *(v.)* बॉर्–1. to make (a hole) in something with a tool or by digging छेद करना, बेधना *Bore* a hole in the wall to pass the cable through.

2. *(n.)* a person whose talk or behaviour is dull and uninteresting: कानखाऊ, उबाने वाला व्यक्ति Everybody avoids a *bore.*

3. the hollow part inside a gun barrel or other tube नली, छेद He drilled a deep *bore* in the ground.

boring *(adj.)* बोरिंग– not interesting; tedious नीरस, उबाऊ I've got a *boring* job in an office.

born *(v.)* बॉर्न– 1. to come out of your mother's body at the beginning of your life जन्म लेना I was *born* in Delhi.

2. *(adj.)* having a specific nationality जन्मजात He is a *born* athlete.

borrow *(v.)* बॉरो– to take and use (something belonging to someone else) with the intention of returning it उधार लेना May I *borrow* your pen for a few minutes?

boss *(n.)* बॉस– 1. a person who is in charge of a worker or organization मालिक, नियोक्ता Her *boss* offered her promotion.

2. (v.) to give (someone) orders in a domineering manner: रोब जमाना, हुक्म चलाना No one likes to be *bossed* around.

bossy *(adj.)* बॉसि– fond of giving people orders; domineering रोब जमाने वाला Stop behaving so *bossy.*

botany *(n.)* बॉटनी– the scientific study of the physiology वनस्पति विज्ञान Theophrastus who was a student of Aristotle, was the father of *Botany.*

botch *(v.)* बॉच– to carry out (a task) badly or carelessly लापरवाही से काम बिगाड़ देना, कच्चा काम करना He was accused of *botching* the job.

both *(pron., adv.)* बोथ– used for emphasis to refer to two people or things, regarded and identified together दोनों *Both* my brothers are elder than me. I put *both* the apples on the table.

bother *(v.)* बॉदर–1. to worry, disturb, or upset (someone) तंग करना, परेशान करना या होना Please do not *bother* me when I am working.

2. to take the trouble to do something कुछ करने का प्रयास या कष्ट करना Please do not *bother* to come personally.

bottle *(n.)* बॉट्ल– a glass or plastic container with a narrow neck, used for storing drinks or other liquids बोतल, शीशी she managed to get through a *bottle* of wine.

bottom *(n.)* बॉटम– the lowest point or part of something तल, तह, निचला भाग The ship sank to the *bottom* of the sea.

bough *(n.)* बाउ– a main branch of a tree शाखा, डाल The *bough* of the tree was laden with fruits.

boulder *(n.)* बोल्डर्– a large rock, typically one that has been worn smooth by erosion. शिलाखंड, गोल पत्थर The seashore was strewn with *boulders.*

bounce *(v.)* बाउन्स–1. to move quickly up, back, or away from a surface after hitting it उछालना, उछलना The ball *bounced* back after hitting the wall.

2. (of a cheque) to be returned by a bank to the payee when there are not enough funds in the drawer's account to meet it चेक वापस आना The bank *bounced* the cheque.

bound *(v.)* बाउण्ड–1. to walk or run with leaping strides कूदना, छलाँग मारना The dog *bounded* after the rabbit.

2. *(adj.)* of bind आबद्ध, बाँधा हुआ He is *bound* to win the race.

3. limit सीमा, हद This area is out of *bounds* for civilians.

boundary *(n.)* बाउण्डरी– a line which marks the limits of an area; a dividing line: सीमा, मर्यादा a community without class or political *boundaries.*

boundless *(adj.)* बाउंडलस– unlimited or immense असीम, बेपनाह, बेहद He has *boundless* energy to travel a long journey in the day.

bounty *(n.)* बॉउंटी– generosity in giving उदारता, दानशीलता *Bounties* were paid to colonial producers of indigo dye.

bouquet *(n.)* बुके– an attractively arranged bunch of flowers गुलदस्ता, गुच्छा He presented a lovely *bouquet* on her birthday.

boutique *(n.)* बुटीक– a small shop selling fashionable clothes or accessories एक छोटी दुकान (जो नये ज़माने के कपड़े और फैशन के अन्य छोटे-मोटे सामान बेचती है) Sonam runs a *boutique* near my house.

bow *(n.)* बो–1. a weapon for shooting arrows धनुष, चाप Arjun attached an arrow to his *bow.*

2. a knot tied with two loops and two loose ends, used especially for tying shoelaces and decorative ribbons सरकफ़न्दा She tied the ribbon into a *bow.*

3. an act of bending the head or upper body as a sign of respect or greeting आदर के लिए झुकने की प्रवृत्ति, नमस्कार The servant welcomed his master with a *bow.*

4. *(v.)* to bend the head or upper part of the body as a sign of respect, greeting, or shame झुक जाना, नमस्कार करना He *bowed* respectfully to the old man.

bowl *(v.)* बोल्–1. to roll (a ball or other round object) along the ground गेंद चलाना, आउट करना The batsman was *bowled* out.

2. *(n.)* a round, deep dish or basin used for food or liquid कटोरा They ate huge *bowls* of steaming spaghetti.

bowling *(n.)* बॉलिंग– the game of bowls as a sport or recreation गेंदबाजी He likes *bowling* rather than batting.

bowman *(n.)* बौमैन– an archer तीरंदाज़ Arjun was a great *bowman.*

box *(n.)* बॉक्स–1. a container with a flat base and sides, typically square or rectangular and having a lid: संदूक, बक्सा, डिब्बा Tinku put his toys in a *box.*

2. *v.* to fight an opponent using one's fists; compete in the sport of boxing मुक्केबाज़ी/मुष्टि युद्ध करना He *boxed* his opponent.

boy *(n.)* बॉय– a male child or youth लड़का, बालक The survey showed that both *boys* and girls smoked regularly

boycott *(v.)* बॉइकॉट– to withdraw from commercial or social relations with (a country, organization, or person) as a punishment or protest बहिष्कार करना The opposition *boycotted* the proposal of the ruling party.

brace *(n.)* ब्रेस– 1. a device fitted to something, in particular a weak or injured part of the body, to give support दांतों में पहनी जाने वाली धातु की तार The use of *braces* shaped his teeth.
2. *(v.)* to make (a structure) stronger or firmer with wood, iron, or other forms of support किसी परिस्थिति के लिए तैयार करना/होना *Brace* yourself for a termination.

bracelet *(n.)* ब्रेस्लट– an ornamental band, hoop, or chain worn on the wrist or arm. कंगन, कंकण Anil presented a *bracelet* to Neera on her birthday.

bracket *(n.)* ब्रैकिट– 1. each of a pair of marks ( ) [ ] { } used to enclose words or figures कोष्ठक *Symbols are given in brackets.*
2. a category of people वर्ग Editors too fall in the *bracket* of journalists.
3. *(v.)* to place (one or more people or things) in the same category or group एक ही वर्ग में रखना The relevant data is included as *bracketed* points.

brackish *(adj.)* ब्रैकिश– (of water) slightly salty, as in river estuaries खारा, नमकीन The drinking water of his house was bit *brackish.*

brag *(v.)* ब्रैग– to say something in a boastful manner डींग हांकना Stop *bragging* about your high contacts.

braid *(n.)* ब्रेड– a length of hair made up of three or more interlaced strands वेणी, चोटी She coiled her hair into a *braid.*

brain *(n.)* ब्रेन– an organ of soft nervous tissue contained in the skull of vertebrates दिमाग, भेजा, बुद्धि Arun used his *brain* to solve a complex Maths problem.

brainchild *(n.)* ब्रेनचाइल्ड– an idea or invention which is considered to be a particular person's creation: आविष्कार, विचार This book is a *brainchild* of a famous painter.

brainstorm *(n.)* ब्रेनस्टॉर्म– a moment in which one is suddenly unable to think clearly or act sensibly विक्षिप्ति We can only assume that someone simply had a *brainstorm* and left the important bits out.

brainwash *(v.)* ब्रेनवॉश–to pressurize (someone) into adopting radically different beliefs मत-आरोपण करना People are *brainwashed* into believing family life is the best.

brake *(n.)* ब्रेक– a device for slowing or stopping a moving vehicle ब्रेक, रोक He applied the *brake* to stop the car when he saw a pit in the middle of the road.

bramble *(n.)* बैम्ब्ल– a prickly scrambling shrub of the rose family कांटेदार झाड़ी This area is full of *brambles.*

branch *(n.)* ब्रांच–1. a part of a tree which grows out from the trunk or from a bough पेड़ की डाल या डाली, शाखा The nimble boy climbed a high *branch* of the tree.
2. a division or office of a large business or organization (किसी कार्यालय की) शाखा The big banks have *branches* in all major cities and towns.

brand *(n.)* ब्रैंड– a particular identity or image regarded as an asset छाप Which *brand* of toothpaste do you use? *(~**new**)* completely new

नवीनतम, एकदम नया Today he came to office in a *brand* new car.

brandish *(v.)* ब्रैंडिश– to wave or flourish (something, especially a weapon) as a threat or in anger or excitement घुमाना, भाँजना The thief was *brandishing* a staff.

brash *(adj.)* ब्रैश– self-assertive in a rude, noisy, or overbearing way ढीठ, धृष्ट She was a *brash* young woman.

brass *(n.)* ब्रास– a yellow alloy of copper and zinc पीतल Indian housewives use utensils of *brass.*

brat *(n.)* ब्रैट– a child, typically one that is badly behaved ढीठ बच्चा His elder son is a *brat* and annoys everyone.

brave *(adj.)* ब्रेव– ready to face and endure danger or pain; showing courage साहसी, वीर, बहादुर She was very *brave* about the whole thing.

bravery *(n.)* ब्रेवरी– courageous behaviour or character साहस, दिलेरी, वीरता Rani Laxmibai was famous for her *bravery.*

brawl *(n.)* ब्रॉल– a rough or noisy fight or quarrel झड़प, झगड़ा Children had a *brawl* while playing.

brawn *(n.)* ब्रान– physical strength in contrast to intelligence बाहुबल, शक्ति You need more *brawn* than brain to get this job.

breach *(n.)* ब्रीच–1. an act of breaking or failing to observe a law, agreement, or code of conduct नियम-भंग, (क़ानून का) उल्लंघन I sued for *breach* of contract.

2. a gap in a wall, barrier, or defence, दरार Hunger for power created a *breach* between the politician brothers.

3. *(v.)* to make a gap in and breakthrough (a wall, barrier, or defence) कानून अथवा समझौते का उल्लंघन करना I do not intend to *breach* the contract in the middle.

bread *(n.)* ब्रेड–1. food made of flour, water, and yeast mixed together and baked रोटी I eat *bread* and butter for breakfast.

2. the food that one needs in order to live जीविका Labourers toil whole day to earn their *bread.*

breadth *(n.)* ब्रेड्‌थ– the distance or measurement from side to side of something, width चौड़ाई Area is defined as length into *breadth.*

break *(n.)* ब्रेक–1. an interruption of continuity or uniformity (पढ़ाई या काम के बीच में) मध्यांतर School children came out to play during the *break.*

2. *(v.)* to separate into pieces as a result of a blow, shock, or strain stoper तोड़ना, टूटना The boy *broke* the window-pane with a stone.

➢ **break down**– to fail a relationship, vechile, machine, etc. खराब/विफल होना The talks *broke down* without any solution.

➢ **break into**– to enter or open (a place, vehicle, or container) forcibly, especially for the purposes of theft ज़बरदस्ती घुसना या प्रवेश करना The thieves *broke into* the house at night.

➢ **break out**– (of war, fighting, or similarly undesirable things) to start suddenly अचानक शुरू होना, Fire *broke out* in the kitchen of the house.

breakage *(n.)* ब्रेकिज़– the action of breaking something, or the fact of being broken टूट-फूट They are responsible for this *breakage.*

breakfast *(n.)* ब्रेकफ़ास्ट– a meal eaten in the morning, the first of the day कलेवा, सुबह का नाश्ता I don't eat *breakfast*

breakneck *(adj.)* ब्रेकनेक– dangerously or extremely fast अंधाधुंध, बहुत तेज़ Ranjan drove his mother to the hospital at *breakneck* speed.

breakthrough *(n.)* ब्रेकथ्रू– a sudden and important development or success कोई महत्त्वपूर्ण सफलता Introduction of colour was a major *breakthrough* in cinema.

break-up *(n.)* ब्रेकअप– disintegrate or disperse विघटन, टुकड़े हो जाना Please *break-up* the sentence into clauses.

breast *(n.)* ब्रेस्ट– either of the two soft, protruding organs on the upper front of a woman's body which secrete milk after childbirth सीना, छाती He beat his *breast* in anger.

breath *(n.)* ब्रेथ– the air taken into or expelled from the lungs साँस, श्वास I was gasping for *breath.*

breathe *(v.)* ब्रीद– to take air into the lungs and then expel it श्वास/साँस लेना He was finding it difficult to *breathe.*

breathless *(adj.)* ब्रेथलस– gasping for breath, typically due to exertion; lifeless हांफ़ता हुआ, निर्जीव, बेदम She was *breathless* with shock.

breed *(n.)* ब्रीड– 1. a stock of animals or plants within a species having a distinctive appearance नस्ल Dobberman is a *breed* of dogs.
2. *(v.)* to mate and then produce offspring जनना, जन्म देना, पैदा करना Mosquitoes *breed* and multiply very fast.

breeding *(n.)* ब्रीडिंग– the mating and production of offspring by animals; good manners प्रजनन; शिष्टाचार, सौजन्य A girl of good *breeding.*

breeze *(n.)* ब्रीज़– a gentle wind हल्की हवा, समीर He sat in the garden to enjoy the cool *breeze.*

brevity *(n.)* ब्रेवटि– concise and exact use of words in writing or speech संक्षिप्तता, अल्पता, लघुता *Brevity* is the soul of wit.

brew *(v.)* ब्रू– to make beer शराब बनाना या खींचना The beer is *brewed* in the village.

bribe *(n.)* ब्राइब– 1. a sum of money or other inducement offered or given to *bribe* someone रिश्वत, घूस Lawmakers were caught accepting *bribes* to bring in legalized gambling.
2. *(v.)* to give sb money or a gift esp by doing sth dishonest घूस या रिश्वत देना He *bribed* the clerk to get his work done.

bribery *(n.)* ब्राइबरी– the giving or offering of a bribe रिश्वतख़ोरी His opponent had been guilty of *bribery* and corruption.

brick *(n.)* ब्रिक– rectangular block of clay baked by fire used in building ईंट Houses are built with *bricks.*

bride *(n.)* ब्राइड– a woman on her wedding day or just before and after the event दुलहन, नववधु The *bride* wore a gorgeous sari.

bridegroom *(n.)* ब्राइडग्रूम– a man on his wedding day or just before and after the event वर, दूल्हा The *bridegroom* was dressed in a sherwani at the wedding.

bridge *(n.)* ब्रिज– 1. a structure carrying a road, path, railway, etc. across a river, road, or other obstacle पुल, सेतु There is a *bridge* across the River Thames.
2. *(v.)* to be or make a *bridge* over (something) पुल बाँधना The valley was *bridged* by the government

bridle *(n.)* ब्राइडल्– 1. the headgear used to control a horse लगाम You cannot control a horse without a *bridle.*
2. *(v.)* to put a bridle on (a horse) लगाम लगाना/कसना He *bridled* his horse and started on his journey.

brief *(adj.)* ब्रीफ़– concise in expression; using few words संक्षिप्त, अल्पकालीन He gave me a *brief* description of the accident.

briefing *(n.)* ब्रीफ़िंग– a meeting for giving information or instructions; such information or instructions कोई

सूचना या निर्देश देने के लिए एक मुलाकात; सूचना या निर्देश He was *briefing* the news.

brigade *(n.)* ब्रिगेड– an organization with a military or quasi-military structure ब्रिगेड, वाहिनी He commanded a *brigade* of 3,000 men.

bright *(adj.)* ब्राइट–1. giving out or reflecting much light; shining चमकीला, दीप्त A *bright* light was shining in the room.
2. full of light चटकीला Children like toys of *bright* colours.
3. intelligent and quick-witted तेज़, होनहार He is one of the *bright* boys in the class.

brighten *(v.)* ब्राइटन– to make or become happier and more cheerful प्रसन्नता से चमकना Her face *brightened* when she saw me.

brilliant *(adj.)* ब्रिलिअण्ट्–1. (of light or colour) very bright चमकीला, प्रकाशमान *Brilliant* sunshine illuminated the scene.
2. exceptionally clever or talented होशियार, कुशाग्र बुद्धि Neeraj is a *brilliant* student.

brim *(n.)* ब्रिम–1. the upper edge or lip of a cup, bowl, or other container किनारा, मुंह The glass was full upto the *brim* with tea.
2. the projecting edge around the bottom of a hat टोपी का निचला भाग He pulled down the *brim* of his hat.

bring *(v.)* ब्रिंग– to take or go with (someone or something) to a place लाना, ले आना Please *bring* me a glass of water.
- **bring back**– to return something पुनः वापस करना, लौटाना We can't *bring back* the days of our childhood.
- **bring down**– to cause to fall क़ीमतों में गिरावट आना The government is trying to *bring down* the prices of petrol.
- **bring forward**– to bring in view पेश करना Can you *bring forward* any witness against him?
- **bring in**– to yield, produce as profit लाभ पहुंचाना Her new job doesn't *bring in* much.
- **bring out**– to expose, to bring to light किसी चीज़ को सामने लाना प्रकट करना They will *bring out* some secret facts.
- **bring round**– to restore someone to consciousness होश में लाना, I *brought* him *round* to unconsciousness.
- **bring up**– to look after a child until it is an adult पालन-पोषण करना She is *bringing up* her children well.

brink *(n.)* ब्रिंक– the extreme edge of land before a steep slope or a body or water किनारा The club has come close to the *brink*, surviving winding-up orders.

brisk *(adj.)* ब्रिस्क– active and energetic तेज़, फुर्तीला I go for a good *brisk* walk daily.

bristle *(n.)* ब्रिस्ल– a short, stiff hair on an animal's skin or a man's face कड़ा बाल My toothbrush is made of plastic *bristles.*

brittle *(adj.)* ब्रिट्ल– hard but liable to break easily भुरभुरा, भंगुर Glass is a *brittle* substance.

broad *(adj.)* ब्रॉड– having a distance larger than usual from side to side; wide चौड़ा, व्यापक, विस्तृत In Old Delhi, it is rare to find a *broad* avenue.

broadcast *(n.)* ब्रॉडकास्ट– 1. a radio or television programme or transmission प्रसारण, प्रोग्राम The announcement was *broadcast* live.
2. *(v.)* to transmit (a programme or some information) by radio or television प्रसारण करना They regularly *broadcast* on Radio Mirchi

broaden *(v.)* ब्रॉडन– to become larger in distance from side to side; widen चौड़ा करना, विस्तृत करना Travelling *broadened* his mind.

broadly *(adv.)* ब्रॉडली– in general and without considering minor details मोटे तौर पर I will explain you the situation *broadly.*

broad-minded *(adj.)* ब्रॉड-माइन्डिड– tolerant or liberal in one's views and reactions; not easily offended खुले विचारों वाला, उदार I have a *broad-minded* approach to religion.

brochure *(n.)* ब्रोशर्– a small book or magazine containing pictures and information about a product or service विवरणिका, पुस्तिका Get me the *brochures* of the companies.

broken *(adj.)* ब्रोकन– having been broken टूटा हुआ, खंडित Do you know how my camera got *broken*?

broker *(n.)* ब्रोकर्– a person who buys and sells goods or assets for others दलाल I called the *broker* to know about some good investment plans.

bronchitis *(n.)* ब्रॉनकाइटिस– inflammation of the mucous membrane in the bronchial tubes श्वासनली-शोथ He is suffering from *bronchitis* since long.

brooch *(n.)* ब्रोच– an ornament fastened to clothing with a hinged pin and catch जड़ाऊ पिन She pinned a diamond *brooch* on her blouse.

brood *(v.)* ब्रूड– 1. to think deeply about something that makes one unhappy, angry, or worried चिंता करना, विचार करना Why are you *brooding* over the past?
2. *(n.)* a family of birds or other young animals produced at one hatching or birth बच्चे, संतान The mother goose waddled across the street with her *brood.*

brook *(n.)* ब्रुक– 1. a small stream नाला, छोटी नदी The Lake District boasts lovely lakes and babbling *brooks.*
2. *(v.)* to tolerate or allow (something, typically dissent or opposition) सहना, बर्दाश्त करना He *brooks* no interference in his work.

broom *(n.)* ब्रूम– a long-handled brush of bristles or twigs, used for sweeping झाड़ू, कूँचा, बुहारी The municipal sweepers were given new *brooms.*

brother *(n.)* ब्रदर्– a man or boy in relation to other sons and daughters of his parents भाई, बन्धु How many *brothers* do you have?

brotherly *(adj.)* ब्रदर्लि– typical of how brothers behave towards each other; fraternal भाई जैसा, भ्रातृवत् I have given him a *brotherly* advice.

brow *(n.)* ब्राउ– an eyebrow भौंह, भ्रू His *brows* lifted in surprise.

brown *(n., adj.)* ब्राउन– of a colour produced by mixing red, yellow, and blue, as of dark wood or rich soil भूरा *Brown* is my favourite colour.

browse *(v.)* ब्राउज़–1. to survey goods for sale in a leisurely and casual way घूमना, समय बिताना I *browsed* in the bookshop for half an hour.
2. to act a casual looking or reading सरसरी नज़र डालना I *browsed* the Internet for information on the latest cars.

bruise *(v.)* ब्रूज़– 1. to inflict a bruise on (someone or something) चोट पहुंचाना I *bruised* my leg when I fell down.
2. *(n.)* an injury appearing as an area of discoloured skin on the body चोट My *bruise* is not healing.

brunch *(n.)* ब्रंच– a late morning meal eaten instead of breakfast and lunch नाश्ता एवं लंच दोनों का मिश्रित भोजन He prefers to take *brunch* on Sunday.

brush *(n.)* ब्रश– 1. an implement with a handle and a block of bristle hair or wire, used especially for cleaning, कूँची, बुरुश I have lost my tooth-*brush.*
2. *(v.)* to remove (dust or dirt) by sweeping or scrubbing झाड़ना,

पोंछना We should *brush* our teeth regularly.

brute *(n.)* ब्रूट– a savagely violent man or animal क्रूर, निर्दय (व्यक्ति), पशु The big *brute* rushed towards us.

bubble *(n.)* बबल– 1. a thin sphere of liquid enclosing air or another gas बुलबुला Children are fond of blowing soap *bubbles. Bubbles* rose on the boiling water.
2. *(v.)* to be filled with an irrepressible positive feeling बुदबुदाना The bride *bubbled* with happiness on the wedding day.

buck *(n.)* बक्– 1. a dollar एक अमरीकी डॉलर Can you give me some *bucks*?
2. *(v.)* to oppose sth किसी का विरोध करना She admired him willingness to *buck* the system.

bucket *(n.)* बकेट– a roughly cylindrical open container with a handle बालटी, डोल Please bring me a *bucket* of hot water.

buckle *(n.)* बक्ल– 1. a flat, typically rectangular frame with a hinged pin, used for joining the ends of a belt or strap बकसुआ, बकलस He bought a fashionable new *buckle* for his belt.
2. *(v.)* to fasten or decorate with a buckle बकसुए से बन्द करना, कसना He *buckled* his shoes and left for work.

bud *(n.)* बड– a compact knob-like growth on a plant which develops into a leaf, flower, or shoot कली, कलिका, मुकुल These *buds* will bloom by tomorrow morning.

buddy *(n.)* बडि– a close friend मित्र, दोस्त He is an old college *buddy* of mine.

budge *(v.)* बज– to make or cause to make the slightest movement हिलना/हिलाना, सरकना The queue in the bank hasn't *budged*

budget *(n.)* बजट– 1. an estimate of income and expenditure for a set period of time आय-व्यय पत्र, बजट We might go over-*budget* in this project.
2. *(v.)* to allow or provide a particular amount of money in a budget बजट तैयार करना The government *budgeted* a huge amount for an amusement park.

buffalo *(n.)* बफलो– a heavily built wild ox with backward-curving horns, भैंस In India, we normally drink the milk of *buffalo.*

buffet *(n.)* बुफ़े–1. a meal consisting of several dishes from which guests serve themselves खाने का प्रबंध (जहां मेहमान स्वयं भोजन परोसते हैं) We will follow *buffet* system in the party.
2. *(v.)* बफ़िट्– to strike repeatedly and violently धकेलना The car was *buffeted* by the truck.

bug *(n.)* बग– a harmful microorganism, typically a bacterium खटमल I could not sleep last night because of *bugs.*

bugle *(n.)* ब्यूगल– a brass instrument like a small trumpet बिगुल At the call of the *bugle,* the soldiers hurried out of their barracks.

build *(v.)* बिल्ड– to construct (something) by putting parts or material together बनाना, निर्माण करना The ironworks were *built* in 1736.

bulb *(n.)* बल्ब– a glass bulb inserted into a lamp or a socket in a ceiling, which provides light by passing an electric current बल्ब, लट्टू There was just one electric *bulb* in the big room.

bulge *(n.)* बल्ज– 1. rounded swelling which distorts an otherwise flat surface उभार The thick wallet in his pocket made a *bulge* in his coat.
2. *(v.)* to swell or protrude to an incongruous extent उभरना, फूलना His eyes *bulged* out as he tried to lift the heavy box.

bulging *(adj.)* बल्जिंग– be full of and distended with (बाहर की तरफ)

उभरी हुई या फूली हुई He stared with *bulging* eyes.

bulk *(n.)* बल्क– the mass or size of something large भारी मात्रा We ordered the raw material in *bulk.*

bulky *(adj.)* बल्की– taking up much space; large and unwieldy भारी-भरकम A *bulky* carrier bag.

bull *(n.)* बुल– an uncastrated male bovine animal सांड़, वृषभ An angry *bull* is a fearsome animal.

bullet *(n.)* बुलेट– a metal projectile for firing from a rifle गोली A revolver contains six *bullets.*

bulletin *(n.)* बुलेटिन– a short official statement or broadcast summary of news. प्रसारित समाचार I'll watch the news *bulletin* at 8 pm.

bullock *(n.)* बुलक– a male domestic bovine animal that has been castrated बैल The farmer yoked the *bullocks* to the plough.

bully *(n.)* बुली– 1. a person who uses strength or influence to harm or intimidate those who are weaker दबंग, धौंसिया Everyone dislikes a *bully.*
2. *(v.)* to use superior strength or influence to intimidate (someone), धमकाना, सताना The robber *bullied* the bus passengers to surrender their valuables.

bump *(n.)* बम्प– 1. a swelling on the body caused by blow गूमड़ा, गुमटा He had a nasty *bump* on the head.
2. *(v.)* to knock or run into someone or something with a jolt धक्का या टक्कर खाना While walking hurriedly, Arun *bumped* into a stranger.

bumper *(n.)* बम्पर– a horizontal bar fixed across the front or back of a motor vehicle to reduce damage in a collision (बस या कार में बचाव के लिए आगे वाला भाग जिसके कारण दुर्घटना का प्रभाव कम हो जाता है) टक्कर-रोक The cars moved *bumper* to bumper on the road.

bumpy *(adj.)* बम्पी– uneven, with many patches raised above the rest ऊबड़-खाबड़ The car jolted on the *bumpy* road.

bun *(n.)* बन–1. a small cake, typically containing dried fruit मीठी रोटी I went to the bakery to buy a *bun.*
2. a hairstyle in which the hair is drawn back into a tight coil at the back of the head जूड़ा She coiled her hair into a *bun.*

bunch *(n.)* बंच– a number of things, typically of the same kind, growing or fastened together गुच्छा She put the *bunch* of fresh flowers in a flower-vase.

bundle *(n.)* बन्ड्ल– 1. a collection of things or quantity of material tied or wrapped up together पोटली, गठरी He gave the *bundle* of soiled clothes to the washerman.
2. *(v.)* to tie or roll up (a number of things) together as though into a parcel गठरी बाँधना, एक साथ कुछ बाँधना Please *bundle* up the old newspapers.

bung *(v.)* बंग– to block something डाट/डट्टा लगाना The drains of my house are *bunged* up with plastic bags.

bungling *(n.)* बंगूलिंग– a mistake or badly carried out action गोलमाल, घपला She had *bungled* every attempt to help.

bungalow *(n.)* बंगलो– a low house having only one storey बंगला, मकान There was a beautiful *bungalow* on the top of the hill.

bunk *(v.)* बंक–1. to run away or play truant from school or work चुपके से सरक जाना, नाग़ा करना Some children tried to do a *bunk* from the school.
2. *(n.)* a narrow bed that is fixed to a wall, esp on a train or ship bed, typically in shared quarters जहाज या रेलगाड़ी में दीवार से लगी शय्या, शायिका The children were provided with a *bunk* bed.

Buoy *(v.)* बॉइ– to make (someone) cheerful and confident साहस को दृढ़ रखना He *buoyed* her up during her difficult time.

burden *(n.)* बर्डन– 1. a load, typically a heavy one भार, बोझ The old man was carrying a heavy *burden* on his frail shoulders.

2. *(v.)* to load heavily बोझ लादना या डालना Do not *burden* yourself with unnecessary work.

bureaucracy *(n.)* ब्यूअरॉक्रेसी– a system of government in which most of the important decisions are taken by state officials नौकरशाही We are living in a modern *bureaucracy.*

burglar *(n.)* बर्गलर्– a person who commits burglary चोर, सेंधमार The *burglar* broke open the safe but was caught before he could escape with the valuables.

burial *(n.)* बेरिअल– the action or practice of burying a dead body दफ़न His remains were sent home for *burial.*

burn *(n.)* बर्न–1. an injury caused by exposure to heat or flame जलने का घाव, जला, जलन, छाला Apply a soothing ointment on the *burn.*

2. *(v.)* to become red and painful through exposure to the heat जलना, जलाना The fire *burned* brightly.

3. to be or cause to be destroyed by fire नष्ट करना, जलाकर राख कर देना या हो जाना She *burnt* all the letters her lover had written to her.

burning *(adj.)* बर्निंग– very keenly or deeply felt; intense अत्यंत प्रबल, तीव्र My *burning* desire is to go on world tour.

burp *(v.)* बप्– to release air from the stomach through the mouth डकार लेना या मारना He *burps* loudly after meal.

burrow *(n.)* बरो– 1. a hole or tunnel dug by a small animal, especially a rabbit, as a dwelling बिल The rabbit jumped into its *burrow* when it saw a dog.

2. *(v.)* to make a hole or tunnel, typically for use as a dwelling बिल खोदना The rabbit *burrowed* a deep hole under a tree.

burst *(v.)* बर्स्ट–1. to break open or apart suddenly and violently फटना, फूटना, फट पड़ना The tyre of the car *burst* with a bang.

2. to feel a very strong or irrepressible emotion or impulse ज़ोर से हँसी फूटना They *burst* out laughing at the funny story.

3. *(n.)* an explosion धमाका, विस्फ़ोट We heard a sharp *burst* of car tire.

Bury *(v.)* बरी– to put or hide underground दफ़नाना, गाड़ना He *buried* the box in the back garden.

bus *(n.)* बस– a large motor vehicle carrying passengers by road बस My son goes to school by *bus.*

bush *(n.)* बुश– a shrub or clump of shrubs झाड़ी, झाड़ There are no big trees here, only *bushes.*

business *(n.)* बिज़नस– a person's regular occupation, profession, or trade व्यापार, व्यवसाय, कारोबार Ram joined his father's *business* after completing his education.

bust *(v.)* बस्ट्– 1. to break, split, or burst बुरी तरह तोड़ना Uma *busted* his cell phone in anger.

2. (n.) statue of a person, head and shoulders अर्धप्रतिमा, आवक्ष मूर्ति The *bust* of Bhagat Singh is situated at my school.

bustle *(n.)* बसल– 1. excited activity and movement हलचल, चहल-पहल There was a lot of *bustle* in the market.

2. *(v.)* to move in an energetic and busy manner दौड़-धूप करना The market was *bustling* with people.

busy *(adj.)* बिज़ी–1. occupied with or concentrating on a particular activity or object of attention व्यस्त Are you *busy* this evening?

2. full of activity भीड़भाड़ The street was so *busy* that I could not move.

butcher *(n.)* बुचर्– a person whose trade is cutting up and selling meat in a shop. क़साई I went to the *butcher's* shop to buy some meat.

butler *(n.)* बटलर्– the chief manservant of a house. ख़ानसामाँ Raheem is a famous *butler*.

butter *(n.)* बटर्– a pale yellow edible fatty substance made by churning cream मक्खन Lily *buttered* a slice of toast.

butterfly *(n.)* बटर्फ़्लाइ– a nectar-feeding insect with two pairs of large, typically brightly coloured wings that are covered with microscopic scales तितली *Butterflies* are beautiful to look at.

buttermilk *(n.)* बटरमिल्क– the slightly sour liquid left after butter has been churned छाछ, मट्ठा *Buttermilk* is a protein-rich drink.

buttock *(n.)* बटक– either of the two round fleshy parts of the human body that form the bottom. नितंब, चूतड़ He had pain in his left *buttock*.

buy *(v.)* बाइ– to obtain in exchange for payment ख़रीदना, मोल लेना He had been able to *buy* up hundreds of acres.

buyer *(n.)* बाइअर– a person who makes a purchase ख़रीदार, क्रेता We could not find a good *buyer* for our flat.

buzz *(n.)* बज़– 1. a low, continuous humming or murmuring sound भनभनाहट, गुंजन In the summer, the garden is full of the *buzz* of insects.
2. *(v.)* to make a low, continuous humming sound भिनभिनाना, गुंजारना This bee is constantly *buzzing* and disturbing me.

by *(prep., adv.)* बाइ–1. beside क़रीब, पास I saw a couple walking *by* the river.
2. near समीप A policeman was standing *by* the police jeep
3. through the means द्वारा, के ज़रिये से The letter was delivered *by* hand (not by post).

bygone *(adj.)* बाइगॉन– past, gone by विगत, बीता हुआ The museum consists of a fascinating collection of rural *bygones*.

bypass *(n.)* बाइपास– 1. surgical operation in which the flow of blood is redirected बाह्य-पथ (हृदय की शल्य-क्रिया जिसमें रक्त प्रवाह के लिए भिन्न मार्ग बनाया जाता है) He has to go for heart *bypass* surgery.
2. *(v.)* to go past or round उपमार्ग से निकलना, बाहरी रास्ते से निकलना Let's try to *bypass* for Noida City.

by-product *(n.)* बाइप्रॉडक्ट– substance obtained during the manufacture of some other substance उपोत्पादन, गौण उत्पादन Pollution is a *by-product* of growing number of vehicles in the city.

Cc

Cc *(n.)* सी–अंग्रेज़ी वर्णमाला का तीसरा अक्षर–The third letter of the English alphabet. Camera begins with a *'C'*.

cab *(n.)* कैब– a taxi घोड़ागाड़ी, टैक्सी I hired a *cab* to go to the railway station.

cabbage *(n.)* कैबिज– a cultivated plant eaten as a vegetable, having thick green or purple leaves बंदगोभी *Cabbage* is my favourite vegetable.

cabin *(n.)* कैबिन–1. a cubicle or individual work space within a larger office कमरा, कोठरी Which is the General Manager's *cabin?*
2. a small wooden shelter or house in a wild or remote area कुटी, कुटीर The poor family lived in a *cabin* on the edge of the town.

cabinet *(n.)* कैबिनट–1. a cupboard with drawers or shelves for storing or displaying articles अलमारी, पेटिका Uma arranged the new crockery on the shelves of the *cabinet.*
2. the committee of senior ministers responsible for controlling government policy मंत्रिमंडल Mostly decisions are taken unanimously by the *cabinet.*

cable *(n.)* केबल– 1. a thick rope of wire or hemp used for construction, mooring ships, and towing vehicles रस्सा, समुद्री तार The workmen dug the ground to repair the telephone *cables.*
2. *(v.)* to send a message to (someone) by cablegram तार भेजना My brother *cabled* from London that he was coming to India.

cackle *(v.)* कैकल– to laugh in a loud, harsh way भद्दे ढँग से हँसना She *cackled* with delight.

cafe *(n.)* कैफ़े– a small restaurant selling light meal; a drinks कॉफ़ी हाउस; कॉफी, क़हवा A South Indian *cafe* usually serves a nice cup of filter coffee.

cafeteria *(n.)* कैफ़टिअरिआ– a restaurant in which customers serve themselves from a counter and pay before eating अल्पाहार-गृह Loveena is an open *cafeteria* near my office.

caffeine *(n.)* कैफ़ीन– an alkaloid compound which is found especially in tea and coffee plants (कॉफ़ी और चाय में पाया जाने वाला उत्तेजक पदार्थ) कैफ़ीन *Caffeine,* when consumed moderately, is not harmful.

cage *(n.)* केज– 1. a structure of bars or wires in which birds or other animals are confined पिंजरा, कटघरा The little girl brought a *cage* for her pet parrot.
2. *(v.)* to confine in a cage पिंजरे में बंद करना Rahul *caged* his pet rabbits before going out.

cajole *(v.)* कजोल– to persuade (someone) to do something by sustained coaxing or flattery फुसलाना We can't *cajole* him into being a part of our team.

cake *(n.)* केक– an item of soft sweet food made from a mixture of flour, fat, eggs, sugar, and other ingredients, baked and sometimes iced or decorated केक, मीठी रोटी My father bought a big *cake* on my birthday.

calamity *(n.)* कलैमिटी– an event causing great and often sudden damage or distress; a disaster विपत्ति, संकट It is always difficult to deal with a natural *calamity.*

calcium *(n.)* कैल्शियम– the chemical element of atomic number 20, a soft grey metal चूना *Calcium* is good for bones.

calculate *(v.)* कैल्क्युलेट– to determine (the amount or number of something) mathematically हिसाब लगाना, गणना करना Harish knows well how to *calculate.*

calculation *(n.)* कैलक्युलेशन– a mathematical determination of the amount or number of something हिसाब, गणना His *calculation* was not correct.

calendar *(n.)* कैलेण्डर– a chart or series of pages showing the days, weeks, and months of a particular year, or giving particular seasonal information तिथिपत्र, पंचांग, जंत्री, पत्रा Companies use *calendars* for their publicity.

calf *(n.)* काफ़–1. a young bovine animal, especially a domestic cow or bull in its first year बछड़ा (गाय का बच्चा) The *calf* walked behind the cow.
2. the fleshy part at the back of a person's leg below the knee पिण्डली, पिण्डिका The doctor dressed the wound on the labourer's *calf.*

calibre *(n.)* कैलिबर्– the quality of someone's character or the level of their ability चरित्रबल, योग्यता They could ill afford to lose a man of his *calibre.*

call *(v.)* कॉल–1. to cry out to (someone) in order to summon them or attract their attention बुलाना, पुकारना I *called* out loudly when I saw Ram.
2. to give sb/sth a name नाम रखना A heart specialist is *called* the cardiologist.
3. to fix a date or time for (a meeting, strike, or election) मिलने जाना The Prime Minister *called* on the President.
4. *(n.)* message through telephone टेलीफ़ोन कॉल I have a phone *call* to make.

caller *(n.)* कॉलर– a person who pays a brief visit; one who makes a telephone call भेंट करने वाला व्यक्ति; फोन करने वाला व्यक्ति Sunil had many *callers* yesterday.

callous *(adj.)* कैलस– showing or having an insensitive and cruel disregard for others बेदर्द, निर्दय, कठोरहृदय The master was *callous* enough to make his ill servant work.

calm *(adj.)* काम– not showing or feeling nervousness, anger, or other strong emotions शांत One should always be *calm* and composed.

calorie *(n.)* कैलरी– either of two units of heat energy ऊर्जा की इकाई कैलोरी (जो भोजन से मिलती है) One tea spoon of sugar contains 15 *calories.*

camel *(n.)* कैमल– a large, long-necked mammal of arid country ऊँट *Camel* is called the ship of the desert.

camera *(n.)* कैमरा– a device for recording visual images in the form of photographs, film, or video signals कैमरा (फोटो लेने का उपकरण) A professional photographer requires a good *camera.*

camp *(n.)* कैम्प– 1. a place with temporary accommodation of huts, tents, or other structures, typically used by soldiers, refugees, or travelling people शिविर, पड़ाव The boy-scout's summer *camp* was a great success.
2. *(v.)* to live for a time in a tent, especially while on holiday पड़ाव डालना The soldiers *camped* by the side of the river.

campaign *(n.)* कैम्पेन– 1. a series of military operations intended to achieve a goal अभियान, मुहिम The government launched a *campaign* against smugglers.
2. *(v.)* to work in an organized and active way towards a goal आंदोलन करना He spent his life *campaigning* for the rights of the poor.

campus *(n.)* कैम्पस– the grounds and buildings of a university or college

परिसर I've lost my purse in the school *campus* itself.

can *(n.)* कैन– 1. a cylindrical metal container पात्र, डिब्बा I bought a *can* of apple juice.
2. *(v.)* to be able to सकना, समर्थ होना *Can* you drive a car?

canal *(n.)* कनैल– an artificial waterway constructed to allow the passage of boats or ships inland or to convey water for irrigation नहर, नाल Punjab is a land of *canals.*

cancel *(n.)* कैन्सूल– to neutralize or negate the force or effect of रद्द करना, हटा देना He *cancelled* all his appointments as he was not feeling well.

cancellation *(n.)* कैनसलेशन– the action of cancelling something रद्द, निरस्त Bad weather led to the *cancellation* of the journey.

candid *(adj.)* कैण्डिड– truthful and straightforward; frank स्पष्टवादी; निष्पक्ष She gave a *candid* reply when asked why she was still single.

candidate *(n.)* कैण्डिडेट– a person seeking or nominated for election to a position of authority or honour or selection for a job, promotion, etc. उम्मीदवार, प्रत्याशी, परीक्षार्थी My elder brother was a *candidate* in the last municipal election.

candle *(n.)* कैण्डल– a cylindrical piece of wax, tallow, or other fatty substance surrounding a wick, which is burned to produce light मोमबत्ती She bought a box of *candles* for Diwali.

cane *(n.)* केन– 1. the long jointed pithy or hollow flexible stem of the bamboo, rattan, or any similar plant गन्ना, ईख, बेंत Sugar is made from *cane.*
2. *(v.)* to make or repair with cane बेंत बुनना, बेंत-प्रहार करना The unruly mob was *caned* by the police.

cannibal *(n.)* कैनिबूल– a person who eats the flesh of other human beings नरभक्षी Power-hungry politicians have really turned into a race of *cannibals.*

cannon *(n.)* कैनन– 1. an automatic aircraft gun of large calibre तोप The fort was protected by *cannons* mounted on its turrets.
2. *(v.)* to make a cannon गोलाबारी करना The fort was *cannoned* by the enemy.

canoe *(n.)* कनू– a light narrow open boat, propelled by one or more paddles डोंगी, बनहटी The adventurous young man crossed the sea in a *canoe.*

canteen *(n.)* कैण्टीन– a restaurant attached to a factory, school, etc. providing meals for large numbers of people जलपान-गृह We have a good *canteen* in our office premises.

cantonment *(n.)* कैन्टॉनमन्ट– a permanent military camp in British India सैन्य छावनी No outsiders were allowed in the *cantonment* area.

canvas *(n.)* कैन्वस– a heavy durable cloth made of cotton, hemp, or jute, used for sails, tents, etc. किरमिच, कैन्वस Sportsmen wear shoes of *canvas.*

cap *(n.)* कैप–1. a covering for the head, esp a small close-fitting one made of cloth or knitted टोपी The *cap* provides protection from the sun.
2. *(v.)* to outdo; excel मात कर देना, से बढ़कर होना The batsman *capped* his brilliant century with a sixer.

capability *(n.)* केपबिलटि– the quality of being capable; ability सामर्थ्य, क्षमता, योग्यता Do you have the *capability* to translate it into French?

capable *(adj.)* केपबूल्–1. having ability, esp in many different fields; competent प्रतिभाशाली, योग्य, समर्थ, सक्षम A *capable* executive always rises in his organisation. Are you *capable* of handling office independently?

capacity *(n.)* कपैसिटी–1. the ability or power to contain, absorb, or hold सामर्थ्य, समर्थता The theatre was filled to its *capacity.*

2. the ability to understand or learn; aptitude क्षमता, योग्यता He has great *capacity* for work.

capital *(n.)* कैपिट्ल–1. the most important city of a country राजधानी Delhi is the *capital* of India.

2. material wealth owned by an individual or business enterprise पूँजी He invested his *capital* in business.

3. *(adj.)* primary, chief, or principal उत्तम, प्रमुख Our *capital* concern is that everyone be fed.

4. a capital letter अंग्रेज़ी का बड़ा अक्षर Write the address in *capital* letters.

capitalism *(n.)* कैपिटलिज़्म– economic structure in a country's trade and industry organised and controlled by capitalists पूंजीवाद Our social system is based on *capitalism.*

capricious *(adj.)* कप्रिशस्– whimsical, indicative of caprice सनकी, झक्की He is as *capricious* as his father had been.

capsicum *(n.)* कैप्सिकम– a tropical plant of the genus शिमला मिर्च My mother prepared stuffed *capsicums* for lunch.

capsize *(v.)* कैपसाइज़्– (of a boat) to overturn into the water उलट जाना The sea storm *capsized* the boat.

capsule *(n.)* कैप्स्यूल– a gelatinous case containing a dose of medicine पुटी, संपुटिका The doctor prescribed some *capsules* to my mother.

captain *(n.)* कैप्टॅन–1. leader or chief commander कप्तान, अधिपति Balraj is a *captain* in the Army.

2. a leading figure (खिलाड़ियों की टीम का) नायक Anil was selected as the *captain* of the football team of his school.

caption *(n.)* कैप्शन– short title ot heading of an article in a magazine अनुशीर्षक Please write an interesting *caption* for this picture.

captivate *(v.)* कैप्टिवेट– to capture the fancy of, charm मोहित/मुग्ध करना, लुभाना He was *captivated* by her voice.

captive *(n.)* कैप्टिव– a person, animal taken prisoner, kept as a prisoner बन्दी, क़ैदी The *captive* was put in a dark cell.

capture *(v.)* कैप्चर– to make a prisoner of बन्दी बनाना, गिरफ़्तार करना The thief was *captured* by the policeman after a chase.

caravan *(n.)* कैरवैन– a company of persons such as pilgrims कारवां, क़ाफ़िला The *caravan* slowly travelled across the desert.

carbon dioxide *(n.)* कार्बन डाइऑक्साइड– gas breathed out from lungs (एक गंधहीन गैस जो मनुष्य एवं पशु सांस से बाहर फेंकते हैं) कार्बन डाइऑक्साइड *Carbon dioxide* is a heavier gas than oxygen.

carcass *(n.)* कार्कस– dead body of an animal लाश, लोथ The *carcass* of a pig was found floating in a canal.

card *(n.)* काड– a piece of stiff paper or thin cardboard कार्ड, पत्र, पत्रक

1. Do you have your visiting *card*?

2. Please bring this invitation *card* with you.

cardamom *(n.)* कार्डमम– a kind of aromatic spice इलायची The porridge became tastier with the flavour of *cardamom.*

cardboard *(n.)* कार्डबॉर्ड– a thick, stiff kind of paper for making boxes or binding books, etc. गत्ता, दफ्ती The shopkeeper packed my glasses in a *cardboard* box.

cardiac *(adj.)* कार्डिऐक– of heart हृदय-संबंधी, हृदय का She died of a *cardiac* attack.

cardigan *(n.)* कार्डिगन– a knitted woollen jacket बुनी हुई ऊनी जाकेट Uma wore a matching *cardigan* over her sari.

care *(v.)* केअर–1. to be concerned परवाह करना, ध्यान रखना Take *care* when you cross the road.
2. to look after देखभाल करना There was no one to *care* for the child after its parents died.
3. to have a taste for, like रुचि रखना, पसंद करना The only thing she seems to *care* about is money.
4. *(n.)* serious attention देखभाल, चिंता Now the patient needs a proper *care.*

career *(n.)* करियर्– progress through life जीविका, पेशा, जीवन-वृत्ति Journalism offers good *career* opportunities.

carefree *(adj.)* केअरफ़्री– without worry or responsibility बेफ़िक्र, निश्चिंत He is a very *carefree* person.

careful *(adj.)* केअरफुल्– cautious in attitude or action; prudent सतर्क, होशियार I have to take this task in a very *careful* manner.

carefully *(adv.)* केअर्फुली– full of care सावधानीपूर्वक Operate the computer system *carefully.*

careless *(adj.)* केअरलस्– done with or acting with insufficient attention; negligent लापरवाह, बेपरवाह Rohit failed in his exams due to his *careless* attitude.

carelessly *(adv.)* केअर्लेसली– unconcerned in attitude or action; heedless; indifferent (to) लापरवाही से Kanchan deals with the customers *carelessly.*

caress *(v.)* करेस– a gentle touch or embrace, esp one given to show affection दुलार, लाड़ The mother *caressed* the sleeping child.

caretaker *(n.)* केअरटेकर्– a person who is in charge of a place or thing, esp in the owner's absence रखवाला, प्रभारी The *caretaker* of the old bungalow opened the gate for us.

cargo *(n.)* कार्गो– goods carried by a ship, aircraft, or other vehicle जहाज़ी माल, पोतभार A ship can carry a lot of *cargo.*

caricature *(n.)* कैरिकैचर– a pictorial, written, or acted representation of a person, which exaggerates his characteristic traits for comic effect व्यंग्यचित्र She raised objection against her *caricature* in the magazine.

carnage *(n.)* कार्नेज– extensive slaughter, esp of human beings in battle हत्याकांड The film has a scene of *carnage.*

carnival *(n.)* कार्निवल– a festive occasion or period marked by merrymaking, processions, etc. मनोरंजन मेला, आंनदोत्सव Visiting Goa at the time of *carnival* was an exciting experience.

carnivore *(n.)* कार्निवोर्– any animal that feeds on animals मांसभक्षी A lion is a *carnivore.*

carpenter *(n.)* कार्पेण्टर– a person skilled in woodwork, esp in buildings, ships, etc. बढ़ई Some *carpenters* specialize in making artistic furniture.

carpet *(n.)* कार्पेट– a heavy fabric for covering floors क़ालीन, ग़लीचा, दरी The rich man bought an expensive *carpet* for his sitting room.

carriage *(n.)* कैरियेज– a railway coach for passengers रेलगाड़ी का डिब्बा They always travel by the first-class *carriage.*

carrier *(n.)* कैरिअर्–1. a person, thing, or organization employed to carry goods, passengers, etc. सामान ढोने वाला वाहन We need a *carrier* to transport our goods to the other city.
2. a person or animal that carries disease from one place to another

रोग संवाहक Insects are the *carriers* of germs.

carrot *(n.)* कैरट– an umbelliferous plant, with finely divided leaves and flat clusters of small white flowers गाजर It is good to eat *carrots* in winter.

carry *(v.)* कैरि– to move from place to place ढोना, वहन करना The porter *carried* Ram's luggage.

➢ **carry on**– to continue जारी रखना Please *carry on* your work.

➢ **carry out**– to perform, conduct आदेश को पूरा करना, आज्ञापालन करना The soldiers *carried* out (obeyed) the General's orders.

cart *(n.)* कार्ट– any small vehicle drawn or pushed by , such as a trolley छकड़ा, ठेला, गाड़ी The farmer bought a pair of bullocks for his *cart.*

cartography *(n.)* कार्टगरफ़ि– the art, technique, or practice of compiling or drawing maps or charts नक़्शानवीसी, मानचित्रकला His father was skilled in *cartography.*

carton *(n.)* कार्टन– a cardboard box for containing goods गत्ते का डिब्बा Arun bought a *carton* of ice-cream on his son's birthday.

cartoon *(n.)* कॉटून– a humorous or satirical drawing, esp one in a newspaper or magazine, concerning a topical event हास्यचित्र, व्यंग्यचित्र, कार्टून The *cartoon* of Shahrukh Khan was very funny.

cartrldge *(n.)* कार्टरिज– a cylindrical, usually metal casing containing an explosive charge and often a bullet, for a rifle or other small arms कारतूस, गोली He put a *cartridge* into a gun when he wanted to fire.

carve *(v.)* कार्व– to cut or chip in order to form something काटना, तराशना The sculptor *carved* a beautiful statue out of the rock.

carving *(n.)* कार्विंग– a figure or design produced by carving stone, wood, etc. उत्कीर्णन, नक़्क़ाशी There are beautiful *carvings* on the walls of the Taj Mahal.

case *(n.)* केस–1. a container, such as a box or chest सन्दूक, मंजूषा, पेटी The carpenter made a book-*case* for me.

2. a question or matter for discussion in court मुक़दमा Ram filed a *case* against his employer.

➢ **in case**– in order to allow for eventualities यदि, Please call me *in case* you need money.

➢ **in any case**– no matter what; anyhow बहरहाल, जो भी हो, I don't know how much tickets for the movie cost, but I would buy *in any case.*

➢ **In case of**– in the event of की अवस्था में, *In case of* recession what should MNCs do?

cash *(n.)* कैश–1. banknotes and coins, esp in hand or readily available; money or ready money नक़द, रोकड़, नक़दी It is safe to make large payments through cheque instead of *cash.*

2. *(v.)* to obtain or pay ready money for चेक भुनाना, नकदी देना I have to go to the bank to *cash* a cheque.

cashier *(n.)* कैशियर– a person responsible for receiving and pay out money ख़ज़ांची, रोकड़िया He received the payment from the *cashier.*

cashew *(n.)* कैशू– a tropical American cashew tree, bearing kidney-shaped nuts काजू *Cashew* is good for kidneys.

casserole *(n.)* कैसरोल– a covered dish of earthenware, glass, etc. in which food is cooked and served हाँडी, हँडिया Food stored in a *casserole* remains warm for a long time.

cassette *(n.)* कसेट– a plastic container for magnetic tape, as one inserted into a tape deck कैसेट Today CDs have replaced the *cassettes.*

cast *(v.)* कास्ट– 1. to throw or expel with violence or force फेंकना, डालना The fisherman *cast* his net into the sea.
2. *(n.)* a set of actors in a play भूमिका, अभिनेतावृंद Some films flop despite their big star *cast.*

castle *(n.)* कासल– a fortified building or set of buildings, usually permanently garrisoned, as in medieval Europe दुर्ग, गढ़, महल Akbar built many *castles.*

casual *(adj.)* कैश्ज़ुअल– happening by accident or chance आकस्मिक, अनियत His question was only a *casual* inquiry.

casually *(adv.)* कैश्ज़ुअली–1. unexpectedly अकस्मात्, संयोग से She *casually* completed her responsibility.
2. not extraordinarily सादा Raju was *casually* dressed.

casualty *(n.)* कैश्युअल्टी– a person who is injured or killed in an accident हताहत, घायल, मृत The *casualties* of the blast were admitted to the hospital.

cat *(n.)* कैट– a small domesticated feline mammal बिल्ली My sister is very fond of *cats.*

catalogue *(n.)* कैटलॉग– a complete, usually alphabetical list of items, often with notes giving details सूचीपत्र, सूची, तालिका At the book fair, one can collect *catalogues* of many publishers.

catalyst *(n.)* कैटलिस्ट्– a person or thing that causes a change आवेजक, (ऐसा व्यक्ति या वस्तु जो परिस्थितियों को बदल दे) उत्प्रेरक He gave me a role as being a *catalyst* for change.

catapult *(n.)* कैटपल्ट– 1. a Y-shaped implement with a loop of elastic fastened to the ends of the two prongs गुलेल, शिलाप्रक्षेपक Boys used *catapults* to hit the birds with stones.
2. *(v.)* to shoot forth from or as if from a catapult गुलेल से मारना He was *catapulted* out of the bus as it hit the wall.

cataract *(n.)* कैटरैक्ट–1. a disease of the eye मोतियाबिंद He has *cataract* in his left eye.
2. a large waterfall or rapids जलप्रपात The water fell down the hillside in a roaring *cataract.*

catastrophe *(n.)* कटैस्ट्रफ़ी– a sudden, extensive, or notable disaster or misfortune आकस्मिक महाविपत्ति Tsunami proved to be a major *catastrophe.*

catastrophic *(adj.)* कैटस्ट्रॉफ़िक– pertaining to catastrophe तबाही लाने वाला The earthquake was *catastrophic* to the whole city.

catch *(n.)* कैच–1. a device used for fastening sth (खिड़की-दरवाज़ों में लगाने के लिए लकड़ी की रोक) अड़ानी There is no *catch* on this window.
2. *(v.)* to stop by holding with the hand पकड़ना He could not *catch* the ball.
3. to reach with a blow बराबर आ पहुंचना He ran fast but I *caught* up with him.
4. to be infected with लग जाना The baby has *caught* (got) a cold.

➢ **catch on**– to understand sth समझना It took a long time before the police *caught on* to what he was doing.

➢ **catch out**– to trap (a person), esp in an error or doing something reprehensible फंसाना, The interviewer may try to *catch* me *out.*

➢ **catch up**– to seize and take up (something) quickly जा पकड़ना, You go ahead. I'll *catch* you *up.*

categorical *(adj.)* कैटगॉरिकल– expressed clearly सुस्पष्ट The minister made a *categorical* statement.

category *(n.)* कैटगरी– a class or group of things, people, etc. possessing some quality or qualities in common संवर्ग, वर्ग, कोटि, श्रेणी The garments shop were divided into different *categories*.

cater *(v.)* केटर्– to provide food and drinks for a social events खान-पान का प्रबंध करना We *cater* to the overseas markets only.

catering *(n.)* कैटरिंग– the trade of a professional caterer खान-पान सेवाएं प्रदान करने का कार्य या प्रबंध He is the owner of a hotel and *catering* company.

caterpillar *(n.)* कैटर्पिलर्– the wormlike larva of butterflies and moths इल्ली, सूँड़ी A *caterpillar* grows into a butterfly.

cathedral *(n.)* कैथीड्रल– the principal church of a diocese, containing the bishop's official throne बड़ा गिरजाघर Is the *cathedral* really a centre of worship?

cattle *(n.)* कैटल्– bovid mammals of the tribe ढोर, मवेशी, गाय-बैल The *cattle* grazed in the shade of the tree.

cause *(n.)* कॉज़– 1. a person, thing, event, state, or action that produces an effect कारण, हेतु An inquiry is going on to find out the *cause* of the rail accident.

2. *(v.) to be the cause of; bring about; precipitate; be the reason for* कारण बनना, उत्पन्न करना The accident *caused* the traffic jam.

causeway *(n.)* कॉज़वे– a raised path or road crossing water, marshland, sand, etc. सेतुपथ, पक्का जलपथ Mumbai has many *causeways.*

caution *(n.)* कॉशन– 1. care, forethought, or prudence, esp in the face of danger; wariness सावधानी, सतर्कता You must take due *caution* while crossing a busy street.

2. *(v.)* to urge or warn (a person) to be careful सचेत करना Advisers have *cautioned* against tax increases.

cautious *(adj.)* कॉशस– showing or having caution; wary; prudent सावधान, सतर्क, चौकस I am very *cautious* while travelling in night.

cavalry *(n.)* कैवल्री– (esp formerly) the part of an army composed of mounted troops घुड़सवार फ़ौज, अश्वारोही सेना Shivaji was famous for his *cavalry.*

cave *(n.)* केव– an underground hollow with access from the ground surface or from the sea, गुफ़ा, गुहा, कंदरा The hermit lived in a *cave* high in the hills.

cavern *(n.)* कैवर्न– a cave, esp a large one बड़ी गुफ़ा The wounded tiger hid in a *cavern.*

cavity *(n.)* कैवटि– any empty or hollow space within the body खोखलापन My elder son got a *cavity* in his teeth.

caw *(n.)* कॉ– the harsh cry of a rook or crow काँव-काँव या काँय काँय I was disturbed by the *cawing* of a crow.

cease *(v.)* सीज़– to may take a gerund or an infinitive as object to bring or come to an end; to desist from; to stop बन्द/समाप्त होना या करना They were asked to *cease* all military activity.

ceaselessly *(adv.)* सीज़लेसली– without stop or pause; incessant निरंतरतापूर्वक The rain came down *ceaselessly.*

ceiling *(n.)* सीलिंग– the inner upper surface of a room (भीतरी) छत This room has a high *ceiling.*

celebrate *(v.)* सेलिब्रेट– to rejoice in or have special festivities to mark (a happy day, event, etc.) उत्सव मनाना We *celebrate* Diwali with great joy. The young couple *celebrated* the first birthday of their child.

celebrated *(adj.)* सेलिब्रेटिड– famous प्रख्यात, यशस्वी Kalidas was a *celebrated* poet.

celebrity *(n.)* सलेब्रिटी– a famous person जाना-माना व्यक्ति These days everyone wants to be a *celebrity.*

celestial *(adj.)* सलेसटिअल– heavenly; divine; spiritual खगोलीय, स्वर्गीय, दिव्य We saw a movie of *celestial* bodies.

celibacy *(n.)* सेलिबसी– living in an unmarried state and not having sex अविवाहित जीवन, ब्रह्मचर्य Nuns use to practice *celibacy.*

cell *(n.)* सेल्–1. a small simple room, as in a prison, convent, monastery, or asylum कोठरी, कक्ष The prisoner was kept in a dark *cell.*
2. any small compartment विभाग The police department set up a separate *cell* for car thieves.

cellar *(n.)* सेलर– an underground room, rooms, or storey of a building, usually used for storage तहख़ाना Residential houses are usually without a *cellar.*

celsius *(adj.)* सेल्सिअस– denoting a measurement on the Celsius scale C तापमान मापने की पद्धति Last light, the temperature was 17^0 *celsius.*

cement *(v.)* सिमेंट– to make a relationship friendship, etc. or joins; bond (किसी संबंध, दोस्ती आदि को) दृढ़ता से पक्का करना The two firms are expected to *cement* an agreement soon.

cemetery *(n.)* सेमेट्री– a place where the dead are buried, esp one not attached to a church क़ब्रिस्तान There is a *cemetery* just outside the village.

censor *(n.)* सेन्सर्– a person authorized to examine books, films, movies, etc. सेंसर, नियंत्रक, निरीक्षक His movie was banned by the *censor* for immoral scenes.

censure *(v.)* सेन्शर्– to criticize sb severely निंदा करना The revolutionary was *censured* for misleading the masses.

centenary *(n.)* सेण्टिनरी– a 100th anniversary or its celebration सौवीं वर्षगांठ, शताब्दी Our organisation is celebrating its *centenary* this year.

central *(adj.)* सेन्ट्रल्– main, principal, or chief; most important मुख्य, प्रमुख, प्रधान Her mother is a *central* figure in her family.

centre *(n.)* सेन्टर–1. a point, area, or part that is approximately in the middle of a larger area or volume केन्द्र, मध्य, मध्यबिंदु The office of the municipal corporation is in the *centre* of the city.
2. a hub of activity or influence संस्था India International *Centre* is famous among intellectuals.

century *(n.)* सेंचुरी–1. one of the successive periods of 100 years dated before or after an epoch or event, esp the birth of Christ सदी, शताब्दी We are living in the twenty-first *century.*
2. a score or grouping of 100 शतक Scoring a *century* at the Lord's in London is a dream of every batsman.

cereal *(n.)* सिअरिअल– any grass that produces an edible grain, such as oat, rye, wheat, rice, maize, sorghum and millet अनाज, अन्न, धान्य Rice and wheat are *cereals.*

ceremony *(n.)* सेरमनी– a formal act or ritual, often set by custom or tradition धर्मक्रिया, शिष्टाचार The marriage *ceremony* will begin after the pandit arrives.

certain *(adj.)* सर्टन्–1. definite, fixed, inevitable निश्चित, पक्का, अवश्यंभावी Prakash is *certain* to pass the I.I.T. exam.
2. known but not specified or named कोई, कुछ *Certain* people are very fond of bragging.

certainly *(adv.)* सर्टनली– definitely without doubt निश्चित रूप से, अवश्य

I think the students will *certainly* improve their efforts.

certainty *(n.)* सर्टनटी– the condition of being certain निश्चितता, निश्चय There is no *certainty* of his coming tonight.

certificate *(n.)* सर्टिफ़िकट– an official document attesting the truth of the facts stated प्रमाणपत्र Doctor's *certificate* is required to avail the medical leaves.

certify *(v.)* सर्टिफ़ाई– to confirm or attest (to), usually in writing प्रमाणित करना, प्रमाण देना It need to *certify* that this is his signature.

chain *(n.)* चेन–1. a flexible length of metal links, used for confining, connecting, pulling, etc. or in jewellery ज़ंजीर, माला, कड़ी Uma wore a beautiful golden *chain* round her neck.

2. a series of related or connected facts, events, etc. पर्वतमाला, शृंखला The Himalayas is a *chain* of mountains.

3. *(v.)* to confine, tie, or make fast with or as if with a chain ज़ंजीर से बांधना We *chain* our door at night.

chair *(n.)* चेअर्–1. a seat with a back on which one person sits, typically having four legs and often having arms कुर्सी, आसन Please sit in this *chair.*

2. an official position of authority पद The *chair* of Prime Minister is not a bed of roses.

chairman *(n.)* चेअर्मैन– a person who presides over a company's board of directors, a committee, a debate, an administrative department, etc. सभापति, अध्यक्ष The *chairman* presented the annual report of the company.

chalk *(n.)* चॉक– a soft fine-grained white sedimentary rock consisting of nearly pure calcium carbonate खड़िया The teacher wrote on the blackboard with a piece of *chalk.*

challenge *(n.)* चैलेंज– 1. a call to engage in a fight, argument, or contest चुनौती देना, ललकार He looked upon the difficult task as a *challenge* to his capability.

2. *(v.)* to invite or summon (someone to do something, esp to take part in a contest) चुनौती देना, ललकारना Mike Tyson *challenged* Evander Holyfield for a boxing match.

challenging *(adj.)* चैलेंजिंग– demanding or stimulating चुनौतीभरा Shan is doing a *challenging* job.

chamber *(n.)* चेम्बर्–1. an enclosed space; compartment कमरा, कक्ष After the verdict was given, the judge retired to his *chamber.*

2. one of the parts of a Parliament सदन I saw the *chamber* of deputies in Indian Parliament

chameleon *(n.)* कमीलिअन– a small lizard that can change its colour गिरगिट I saw a *chameleon* in the garden.

champion *(n.)* चैम्पिअन्–1. a person who has defeated all others in a competition विजेता, सर्वश्रेष्ठ He was declared the *champion* batsman of the year.

2. a person who defends a person or cause समर्थक, हिमायती Gandhiji was a *champion* of the downtrodden.

championship *(n.)* चैम्पिअन्शिप– any of various contests held to determine a champion सर्वश्रेष्ठ खिलाड़ी का स्थान Khali won world heavy weight wrestling *championship.*

chance *(v.)* चान्स–1. to happen sth by chance संयोग से होना If you *chance* to meet Vishal, please give him my regards.

2. *(n.)* an opportunity or occasion अवसर, मौक़ा Arun was given three *chances* to give the right answer.

3. fortune; luck; fate संयोग, दैवयोग We met at a common friend's place by *chance*.

➢ **by chance**– accidentally संयोगवश, I met him *by chace* in the market.

➢ **no chance**– hopeless कोई संभावना नहीं, There is *no chance* of his coming back to India.

➢ **take chance**– to behave in a risky manner जोखिम उठाना, She will *take* another *chance* after losing 50 thousand on her last business venture.

change *(v.)* चेंज–1. to make or become different; alter बदल जाना या बदल देना The boss *changed* his travelling plan at the last moment.

2. *(n.)* coins of a small denomination रेज़गारी, खुदरा Do you have some *change*?

3. the act or fact of changing or being changed कपड़े बदलने की क्रिया The guest wished to have a wash and a *change*.

channel *(n.)* चैनल– a broad strait connecting two areas of sea नहर, जलमार्ग, मार्ग, माध्यम The river is confined in a narrow *channel*.

chant *(n.)* चाण्ट– 1. a simple song or melody गीत A holy *chant* was echoing the temple.

2. *(v.)* to sing or recite (a psalm, prayer, etc.) as a chant लय से गाना The priests were *chanting* hymns in the temple.

chaos *(n.)* केऑस– complete disorder; utter confusion अव्यवस्था Heavy rains caused a *chaos* on the roads.

chaotic *(adj.)* केऑटिक– in a state of complete confusion and disorder अस्त-व्यस्त, अव्यवस्थित No one was there to take care, so situation became *chaotic*.

chapter *(n.)* चैप्टर्– a division of a written work, esp a narrative, usually titled or numbered अध्याय The textbooks have many *chapters*.

character *(n.)* कैरक्टर्–1. a summary or account of a person's qualities and achievements; testimonial गुण, स्वभाव, चरित्र Good *character* is a man's most precious possession.

2. a person represented in a play, film, story, etc.; role पात्र, चरित्र How many *characters* are there in this play?

characteristic *(n.)* कैरक्टरिस्टिक्– 1. a distinguishing quality, attribute, or trait विशिष्ट लक्षण, विशिष्टता, विशेषता A round dome is a major *characteristic* of Muslim architecture.

2. *(adj.)* indicative of a distinctive quality, etc; typical विशिष्टतासूचक, विशिष्ट She laughed at her *characteristic* sarcastic laugh.

characterize (ise) *(v.)* कैरक्टराइज़्– to distinguish or mark as a characteristic किसी का चरित्र-चित्रण करना, विशेषता बताना She *characterized* the period as the decade of revolution.

charcoal *(n.)* चार्कोल– a black amorphous form of carbon made by heating wood or other organic matter काठकोयला *Charcoal* is commonly used as a fuel in India.

charge *(n.)* चार्ज–1. accusation or allegation, आरोप, अभियोग The police arrested the servant on a *charge* of theft.

2. a price charged for some article or service; cost भाड़ा, शुल्क What will be your *charge* for repairing my watch?

3. place a burden upon or assign responsibility to निगरानी, देखरेख, उत्तरदायित्व I would like to see an honest person in *charge* of this office.

4. *(v.)* to make a rush at or sudden attack upon हमला करना The soldiers *charged* the enemy.

5. to hold financially liable; enter a debit against दाम माँगना They

charged Rs. 2000 per day for a single room.

6. to accuse or impute a fault to (a person, etc.), as formally in a court of law अभियोग लगाना He has been *charged* with attemped murder.

chariot *(n.)* चैरिअट– a light four-wheeled horse-drawn ceremonial carriage रथ The king stopped his *chariot* outside the castle.

charisma *(n.)* करिज़्मा– a special personal quality or power of an individual making him capable of influencing or inspiring large numbers of people विशिष्ट गुण We were instantly charmed by her *charisma.*

charitable *(adj.)* चैरिटेबल–1. concerned with or involving charity ख़ैराती, धर्मार्थ Homeopathy dispensaries are mostly *charitable.*

2. generous in giving to the needy दयालु, उदार Ram has a *charitable* (kind) disposition.

charity *(n.)* चैरटी– the giving of help, money, food, etc. to those in need सद्‌भाव, दान, भिक्षादान The rich man gave away his wealth in *charity.*

charm *(n.)* चार्म–1. a small object worn or kept for supposed magical powers of protection तावीज़ Arun wears a *charm* round his wrist.

2. a pleasing or attractive feature आकर्षण, सौजन्य Rekha is a lady with great *charm.*

3. *(v.)* to attract or fascinate; delight greatly मोहित/मुग्ध करना Rakhi will *charm* you with her sunny smile.

charming *(adj.)* चार्मिंग– delightful; pleasant; attractive मोहक, मनोहर She is a very *charming* lady.

chart *(n.)* चार्ट–1. an outline map, esp one on which weather information is plotted नक्शा, मानचित्र We prepared a *chart* on environmental problems.

2. *(v.)* to record the progress किसी घटना के विकास का विस्तारपूर्वक वर्णन करना The book *charts* the growth and development of Indian cinema.

charter *(n.)* चार्टर्– 1. a formal document granting or demanding from the sovereign power घोषणापत्र, अधिकारपत्र The textile workers presented a *charter* of demands to the Government.

2. *(v.)* to lease or hire by charter party किराए पर लेना The millionaire *chartered* a plane for his business tours.

chase *(v.)* चेस– 1. to follow or run after (a person, animal, or goal) persistently or quickly पीछा करना, पीछे पड़ना The policeman *chased* the thief.

2. *(n.)* the act of chasing; pursuit पीछा The policeman gave the thief a good *chase.*

chaste *(adj.)* चेस्ट्– (of a woman) not having sex with anyone except her husband पतिव्रता, सती, साध्वी A woman is expected to be always *chaste.*

chastity *(n.)* चेस्‌टटी– the state of being chaste; purity पवित्रता, सतीत्व, शुद्धता Nobody can doubt about her *chastity.*

chastise *(v.)* चैस्टाइज़– to discipline or punish, esp by beating डांटना व पीटना, दंड/सजा देना The teacher *chastised* Gaurav for his misbehaviour.

chat *(v.)* चैट– 1. to talk in an easy familiar way गपशप करना The two friends sat *chatting* for a long time.

2. *(n.)* informal conversation or talk बातचीत, गपशप The *chat* of two old friends was quite long.

chatter *(v.)* चैटर्– to speak (about unimportant matters) rapidly and incessantly; to prattle चहकना, बकबक करना The talkative little girl *chattered* continuously.

chauffeur *(n.)* शोफ़र्– a person employed to drive a car कार का ड्राइवर The *chauffeur* took us to the venue within an hour.

cheap *(adj.)* चीप–1. charging low prices सस्ता Nothing is *cheap* these days.
2. not worthy of respect; vulgar अनुदार, तुच्छ Amit played a *cheap* trick on me.
3. worth relatively little हल्के दर्जे की His taste in clothes is rather *cheap.*

cheaply *(adv.)* चीपली– costing relatively little; inexpensive सस्ते दाम का, सस्ते में It will produce electricity more *cheaply* than nuclear plant.

cheat *(v.)* चीट– 1. to deceive or practise deceit धोखा देना, बेईमानी करना A dishonest shopkeeper *cheats* his customers.
2. *(n.)* a person who cheats धोखेबाज़ Beware! He is a *cheat.*

check *(v.)* चेक–1. to examine, investigate, or make an inquiry into जाँच-पड़ताल, परीक्षण करना Have you *checked* the air pressure in your car tyres?
2. to restrain or control रोकना The policemen *checked* people before going in.
3. *(n.)* a pattern of squares or crossed lines चारख़ाना Shaloo wore a shirt with *checks.*

check-up *(n.)* चैक-अप– an examination of sth to see if something is in order परीक्षण I will go for a routine *check-up.*

cheek *(n.)* चीक–1. either side of the face, esp that part below the eye गाल, कपोल The teacher slapped him on his *cheek.*
2. impudence; effrontery आदरहीनता She's got a *cheek,* coming late to the office every day!

cheeky *(adj.)* चीकी– disrespectful in speech or behaviour; impudent गुस्ताख, ढीठ She is a *cheeky* little girl.

cheer *(n.)* चिअर्–1. happiness; good spirits ख़ुशी, प्रसन्नता *Cheers* for the holiday.
2. *(v.)* to make or become happy or hopeful प्रसन्न करना My visit *cheered* the sick man.
3. to applaud with shouts जयध्वनि करना, ताली बजाना The school boys *cheered* when their team won the match.

cheerful *(adj.)* चिअरफुल– having a happy disposition; in good spirits ख़ुशदिल, प्रफुल्लित, प्रसन्न He has a *cheerful* temperament.

cheery *(adj.)* चिअरि– happy and cheerful प्रसन्न, प्रफुल्ल, हँसमुख She gave a *cheery* smile.

cheese *(n.)* चीज़– the curd of milk separated from the whey and variously prepared as a food पनीर Rahul ordered for a plate of *cheese* pakoras.

chemical *(adj.)* केमिकल– of, made from, or using chemicals रासायनिक Sulphuric acid is used for *chemical* weapons.

chemist *(n.)* केमिस्ट– a shop selling medicines, cosmetics, etc. औषधि-विक्रेता At the *chemist's* shop, we can buy medicines.

chemistry *(n.)* केमिस्ट्री– the composition, properties, and reactions of a particular substance रसायनशास्त्र *Chemistry* is an interesting subject for her.

cheque *(n.)* चेक– a bill of exchange drawn on a bank by the holder of a current account; चेक, हुण्डी, धनादेश It's safe to make payments by *cheque.*

cherish *(v.)* चेरिश– to show great tenderness for; treasure सँजोए रखना Sita *cherished* her as if she was her own daughter.

cherry *(n.)* चेरी– any of several trees of the rosaceous genus Prunus, such as P. avium (sweet cherry), having a small fleshy rounded fruit एक प्रकार का छोटा गोल लाल फल, चेरी *Cherries* are good for health.

chess *(n.)* चेस– a game of skill for two players using a chessboard on which chessmen are moved. शतरंज The game of *chess* originated in India.

chest *(n.)* चेस्ट–1. the front part of the trunk from the neck to the belly छाती, सीना A wrestler has a broad *chest.* 2. a box, usually large and sturdy, used for storage or shipping तिजोरी, संदूक़ The jeweller locked his valuables in a strong *chest.*

chew *(v.)* चू– to work the jaws and teeth in order to grind (food); to masticate चबाना, चबाकर खाना Young children should be taught to *chew* their food well.

chewy *(adj.)* चूइ– of a consistency requiring chewing; somewhat firm and sticky चर्वणीय, चबाने वाला Cadbury Eclairs is a very *chewy* toffee.

chick(en) *(n.)* चिक्, चिकेन–1. the young of a bird, esp of a domestic fowl चूज़ा, चिंगना He bought a dozen *chicks* for his poultry farm.
2. a domestic fowl bred for its flesh or eggs, पकी हुई मुर्ग़ी I had *chicken* for lunch.

chickenpox *(n.)* चिकिनपॉक्स– a highly communicable viral disease most commonly affecting children, छोटी चेचक, छोटी माता The child was suffering from *chickenpox.*

chide *(v.)* चाइड– to rebuke or scold डांटना, फटकारना The boss *chided* the peon on his negligence.

chief *(n.)* चीफ़– 1. the head, leader, or most important individual in a group or body of people प्रमुख, प्रधान The Army head is called the *Chief* of Staff. 2. *(adj.)* most important; principal सर्वोच्च *Chief* among her concerns is working alone at night.

chiefly *(adv.)* चीफ़ली– especially or essentially; above all मुख्यतः We eat *chiefly* rice and wheat.

child *(n.)* चाइल्ड– a boy or girl between birth and puberty बच्चा, बालक Mr. and Mrs. Sen brought their *child* with them to the party.

childbirth *(n.)* चाइल्डबर्थ– the act of giving birth to a child प्रसव, प्रसूति The poor lady died in *childbirth.*

childhood *(n.)* चाइल्डहुड– the condition of being a child; the period of life before puberty बचपन Her *childhood* was very unhappy.

childish *(adj.)* चाइल्डिश– in the manner of, belonging to, or suitable to a child बचकाना She has a very *childish* handwriting.

chill *(n.)* चिल– a moderate coldness सर्दी, कँपकँपी Infants quickly catch a *chill.*

chilly *(adj.)* चिली– causing or feeling cool or moderately cold ठण्डा A *chilly* wind was blowing.

chime *(n.)* चाइम– 1. an individual bell or the sound it makes when struck घण्टानाद The *chime* of the church bell could be heard from a distance.
2. *(v.)* to sound (a bell) or (of a bell) to be sounded by a clapper or hammer घंटा बजाना The wall clock *chimes* every hour.

chimney *(n.)* चिम्नी– a vertical structure of brick, masonry, or steel that carries smoke or steam away from a fire, engine, etc. चिमनी, धुआँरा, धुआँदान The *chimney* smoke pollutes the atmosphere.

chimpanzee *(n.)* चिम्पैन्ज़ी– a gregarious and intelligent anthropoid ape, वनमानुष Human beings evolved from *chimpanzees.*

chin *(n.)* चिन– the protruding part of the lower jaw ठोढ़ी He nicked his *chin* while shaving.

china *(n.)* चाइना– ceramic ware of a type originally from China चीनी मिट्टी

(के बरतन) I went to the crockery store to buy *china.*

chink *(n.)* चिंक–1. a small narrow opening, such as a fissure or crack दरार, झरोखा I looked through a *chink* between the curtains.

2. to make or cause to make a light ringing sound, as by the striking of glasses or coins खनकना, खनखनाना I could hear the *chink* of crockery.

chip *(n.)* चिप– 1. a small piece removed by chopping, cutting, or breaking चिप्पड़, टुकड़ा *Chips* of wood catch fire quickly.

2. *(v.)* to break or cut into small pieces छोटा टुकड़ा तोड़ना, चिप्पड़ उतारना This tea cup is old and *chipped.*

chirp *(v.)* चर्प्– to make a short high-pitched sound चीं-चीं करना Sparrows *chirp* together at the time of sunrise.

chisel *(n.)* चिज़ल– a hand tool for working wood, consisting of a flat steel blade with a cutting edge attached to a handle of wood, plastic, etc. छेनी The sculptor worked on the block of stone with a *chisel.*

chit *(n.)* चिट– a requisition or receipt परची I left the note for him on a *chit.*

chivalry *(n.)* शिवल्री– the medieval system and principles of knighthood (स्त्रियों के प्रति पुरुषों का) नम्र आचरण, क्षात्रधर्म The days of *chivalry* are now gone.

chocolate *(n.)* चॉकलेट– a food preparation made from roasted ground cacao seeds, usually sweetened and flavoured चॉकलेट The child cried for a *chocolate.*

choice *(n.)* चॉइस– the act or an instance of choosing or selecting चुनाव, वरण I had no *choice* but to shift to Mumbai.

choir *(n.)* क्वाइयर्– an organized group of singers, esp for singing in church services गायक-मंडली, गायक-वृंद She was a part of musical *choir* in the church.

choke *(v.)* चोक–1. to hinder or stop the breathing of (a person or animal), दम घुटना, गला घोंटना In the Bhopal gas leakage tragedy, hundreds of people were *choked* to death.

2. to block or clog up बंद करना या होना The tube was *choked* with dirt.

choose *(v.)* चूज़्– to select चुनना, पसंद करना Usha *chose* a black sari.

chop *(v.)* चॉप– to cut (something) with a blow from an axe or other sharp tool काटना, चीरना The woodcutter *chopped* down the tree with an axe.

choral *(adj.)* कोरल– relating to, sung by, or designed for a chorus or choir गायक-दल का वृंदगान संबंधी, समवेत They sang a *choral* on the stage.

chore *(n.)* चॉर– a tedious but necessary task अरुचिकर परंतु अनिवार्य काम I always get bored of the household *chores.*

choreograph *(v.)* कॉरिअग्राफ़्– to compose the sequence of steps and moves for dancers in a ballet or a show नृत्य-रचना का संयोजन करना Farha Khan *choreographed* the song.

choreographer *(n.)* कॉरिअग्राफ़र–a person who teaches the art of dancing नृत्य- निर्देशक Saroj Khan is a veteran *choreographer.*

choreography *(n.)* कॉरिऑग्रफ़ी– the composition of dance steps and sequences for ballet and stage dancing नृत्य रचना या निर्देशन *The choreography* of Farah Khan is praiseworthy.

chorus *(n.)* कोरस– 1. a large choir of singers; a piece of music composed for such a choir गायक-वृन्द; वृन्दगान Some plays end with a *chorus.*

2. *(v.)* to speak, sing, or utter

(words, etc.) in unison एक साथ गाना या कुछ कहना "We want to play cricket," the children *chorused*.

christianity *(n.)* क्रिसटिऐनटी– the Christian religion ईसाई धर्म He has firm belief in *Christianity*.

chronic *(adj.)* क्रॉनिक– (esp of a disease) continuing for a long time; constantly recurring पुरानी (बीमारी), पुराना (रोग) She is suffering from a *chronic* disease.

chubby *(adj.)* चबी– (esp of the human form) plump and round मोटा-ताजा, मांसल Reema was very *chubby* while she was a child.

chuck *(v.)* चक– to throw फेंक देना, त्याग देना I am going to *chuck* my old socks.

chuckle *(v.)* चकल्– to laugh softly or quietly धीरे-धीरे/मुँह बंद करके हँसना The old man *chuckled* at his own joke.

chug *(v.)* चग– to operate while making such sounds (धीरे-धीरे इंजन चलने की आवाज़ करना) छुक-छुक करना The boat *chugged* along the river.

chum *(n.)* चम– a close friend लंगोटिया यार, घनिष्ठ मित्र We were *chums* in the college.

chunk *(n.)* चंक– a thick solid piece, as of meat, wood, etc. (किसी वस्तु का) बड़ा टुकड़ा He took a large *chunk* of meat.

church *(n.)* चर्च– a building designed for public forms of worship, esp Christian worship गिरजाघर The *church* was decorated beautifully for Christmas.

churn *(v.)* चर्न– to turn and stir milk in a container in order to produce butter मथना, बिलोना The cyclone *churned* the sea completely.

cinder(s) *(n.)* सिन्डर्ज़– a piece of charred material that burns without flames; ember, अंगार, अंगारा She tried to light a fire with the *cinders*.

cigar *(n.)* सिगार– a cylindrical roll of dried tobacco leaves, for smoking सिगार, चुरुट His uncle is having a *cigar* in his hand.

cigarette *(n.)* सिगरेट– a short tightly rolled cylinder of tobacco, wrapped in thin paper and often having a filter tip सिगरेट *Cigarette* smoking is injurious to health.

cinema *(n.)* सिनेमा– a place designed for the exhibition of films सिनेमाघर Let's watch a movie in a *cinema* hall.

cinnamon *(n.)* सिनमन– the inner bark of tropical Asian tree used in cooking as a spice दालचीनी Rice tasted better with the aroma of *cinnamon*.

circle *(n.)* सर्कल्– 1. a closed plane curve every point of which is equidistant from a given fixed point वृत्त, चक्कर, चक्र, घेरा The geometry teacher taught the students to draw a *circle*.

2. *(v.)* to move in a circle (around) चक्कर लगाना, घेरना The dancers *circled* the tree as they danced.

circuit *(n.)* सर्किट– a complete route or course, esp one that is curved or circular or that lies around an object (विद्युत धारा का) परिपथ, सर्किट The factory caught fire because of the short *circuit*.

circular *(adj.)* सर्क्युलर्– 1. of, involving, resembling, or shaped like a circle गोल, गोलाकार, वर्तुल The Parliament House is a *circular* building.

2. *(n.)* a printed or duplicated advertisement or notice for mass distribution परिपत्र, सूचना-पत्र The company sent a *circular* to all its clients about its new product.

circulate *(v.)* सर्क्युलेट–1. to send, go, or pass from place to place or person to person प्रचारित करना, फैलाना, चक्कर लगाना, The rumour of her marriage was *circulated* in her locality.

2. to distribute or be distributed over a wide area वितरण करना The pamphlets were *circulated* to the members of the society.

circulation *(n.)* सर्क्युलेशन– the spreading or transmission of something to a wider group of people or area संचरण, वितरण The Times of India claims to have the largest *circulation.*

circumstances *(n.)* सर्कम्स्टान्सस्– a condition of time, place, etc. that accompanies or influences an event or condition घटना, बात, परिस्थिति We wanted to marry but *circumstances* didn't permit.

circus *(n.)* सर्कस– a travelling company of entertainers such as acrobats, clowns, trapeze artistes, and trained animals सर्कस Children laughed at the clown in the *circus.*

cite *(v.)* साइट– to quote or refer to उद्धरण देना, उद्धृत/उल्लेख करना Can you *cite* an example to prove your point?

citizen *(n.)* सिटिज़न– a native registered or naturalized member of a state, nation, or other political community नागरिक We are responsible *citizens* of the country.

city *(n.)* सिटी– any large town or populous place नगर, शहर Tokyo is the biggest *city* in the world.

civil *(adj.)* सिविल– of the ordinary life of citizens as distinguished from military, legal, or ecclesiastical affairs सभ्य, शिष्ट, नागरिक This law is for every *civil* man.

civilian *(n.)* सिविल्यन– a person whose primary occupation is civil or nonmilitary असैनिक, असैनिक पदाधिकारी Rehman has retired from the Army, now he is a *civilian.*

civilization (-isation) *(n.)* सिविलाइज़ेशन – a human society that has highly developed material and spiritual resources and a complex cultural, political, and legal organization सभ्यता Cleopatra was a powerful empress of the Roman *civilization.*

civilized (ised) *(adj.)* सिविलाइज़्ड– having a high state of culture and social development सभ्य His behaviour was highly *civilized* and sophisticated.

claim *(v.)* क्लेम– 1. to demand as being due or as one's property दावा करना Daughters can also *claim* a share in their father's property.

2. *(n.)* an assertion of a right; a demand for something as due दावा, अधिकार A son's *claim* to his father's property is universally accepted.

claimant *(n.)* क्लेमण्ट– a person who makes a claim दावेदार, वादी The insurance company refused to pay the *claimant* any money.

clammy *(adj.)* क्लैमी– unpleasantly sticky; moist गीला एवं चिपचिपा My shirt was *clammy* with sweat.

clamp *(v.)* क्लैम्प– 1. to fix or fasten with or as if with a clamp कसना, जकड़ना The labourers *clamped* the iron rods together.

2. *(n.)* a tool for holding things tightly together शिकंजा Bind it with a *clamp.*

clan *(n.)* क्लैन– a group of people interrelated by ancestry or marriage वंश, कुल Chanakya vowed to destroy the whole Nand *clan.*

clandestine *(adj.)* क्लैन्डेस्टिन– secret and concealed, often for illicit reasons; furtive गुप्त, प्रच्छन्न A *clandestine* marriage can no longer go on smoothly.

clang *(v.)* क्लैंग– to make or cause to make a loud resounding noise, as metal when struck टनटनाना, झनझनाना The *clang* of the ambulance alarmed the passers-by.

clank *(v.)* क्लैंक– to make or cause to make such a sound झनझनाना

The lift *clanked* it up to the 5th floor.

clap *(v.)* क्लैप– to applaud (someone or something) by striking the palms of the hands together sharply ताली बजाना Everyone *clapped* when the political leader rose to speak.

clarification *(n.)* क्लैरफ़िकेशन– the action of making a statement or situation less confused and more comprehensible स्पष्टीकरण I don't want any *clarification* for the mistakes you committed.

clarify *(v.)* क्लैरिफ़ाई– to make or become clear or easy to understand स्पष्ट करना Let me *clarify* my point.

clarity *(n.)* क्लैरटी– clearness, as of expression स्पष्टता Your essay lacks *clarity* of thought.

clash *(n.)* क्लैश–1. a collision or conflict भिड़न्त, संघर्ष, टकराव Some people were injured during the *clash*.
2. a loud harsh noise शोर, खटाखट With a *clash* of cymbals, the band began to play.
3. *(v.)* to make or cause to make a loud harsh sound, esp by striking together टकराना, झगड़ा करना The two groups *clashed* and many people were injured.

clasp *(v.)* क्लास्प– 1. to hold in a firm grasp पकड़ना, जकड़ना, गले लगाना He *clasped* my hand warmly.
2. *(n.)* a bar or insignia on a medal ribbon, बकलस, बकसुआ She bought a beautitul golden *clasp.*

class *(n.)* क्लास–1. group of pupils or students who are taught and study together कक्षा I was late for a *class.*
2. a collection or division of people or things sharing a common characteristic, attribute, quality, or property वर्ग, श्रेणी Rail journey in the first *class* is quite comfortable. Cats and tigers belong to the same *class* of animals.

classic *(adj.)* क्लासिक– of the highest class, esp in art or literature उत्कृष्ट, आदर्श Mrs. Dalloway is a *classic* novel.

classical *(adj.)* क्लासिकल– of, relating to, or characteristic of the ancient Greeks and Romans or their civilization, esp in the period of their ascendancy उच्चकोटि का, शास्त्रीय, प्रतिष्ठित He is good at *classical* music.

classification *(n.)* क्लॉसिफ़िकेशन– systematic placement in categories वर्गीकरण The *classification* makes it easier to browse through.

classify *(v.)* क्लासिफ़ाइ– to arrange or order by classes; categorize वर्गीकृत करना The books were *classified* into various subjects.

clatter *(n.)* क्लैटर्– 1. a rattling sound or noise खड़खड़ाहट The plate fell down from Usha's hand with a *clatter.*
2. *(v.)* to make or cause to make a rattling noise, esp as a result of movement खड़खड़ाना Open doors and windows *clattered* in the storm.

clause *(n.)* क्लॉज़– a section of a legal document such as a contract, will, or draft statute (क़ानूनी दस्तावेज़ की) धारा, दफ़ा She raised an objection against the *clause* of three-year bond.

claw *(n.)* क्लॉ– a curved pointed horny process on the end of each digit in birds, some reptiles, and certain mammals पंजा, चंगुल The eagle flew away with the serpent in its *claws.*

clay *(n.)* क्ले– earth or mud in general चिकनी मिट्टी Crockery is made of *clay.*

clean *(v.)* क्लीन–1. to make or become free of dirt, filth, etc. साफ़ करना Sheela *cleaned* out the cupboard.
2. *(adj.)* without dirt or other impurities; unsoiled साफ़, स्वच्छ We should wear *clean* clothes.

3. pure; morally sound शुद्ध, दोषमुक्त People with *clean* reputation get respect from all.

cleanliness *(n.)* क्लीनलिनस– habitually clean and careful to avoid dirt: सफ़ाई, स्वच्छता *Cleanliness* is next to godliness.

cleanse *(v.)* क्लेन्ज़– to remove dirt, filth, etc. from skin त्वचा या किसी धातु को साफ़ करना Always *cleanse* the blade after use.

clear *(adj.)* क्लिअर्–1. (of weather) free from dullness or clouds स्वच्छ, निर्मल The sky was *clear* and cloudless.

2. easy to see or hear; distinct स्पष्ट, साफ़ What you say is not quite *clear* to me.

3. *(v.)* to remove sth that is not needed साफ/स्वच्छ करना I had *cleared* my drawer before I left.

clearance *(n.)* क्लिअरन्स– the process or an instance of clearing जाने की अनुमति, छुट्टी, निकासी The students got the *clearance* from the hostel to go home.

clear-cut *(adj.)* क्लिअर-कट– definite; not vague सुनिश्चित एवं स्पष्ट She always give *clear-cut* replies.

clearly *(adv.)* क्लिअर्लि– distinctly, obviously साफ़, स्पष्टतया I could *clearly* see him going out.

clench *(v.)* क्लेन्च– to grip, press firmly together भींचना, जकड़ना He *clenched* his fists in anger.

clerk *(n.)* क्लर्क– person employed in a bank, office, shop, etc. to keep records and accounts लिपिक, क्लर्क, मुंशी It is not easy to get even a *clerk's* job.

clever *(adj.)* क्लेवर्–1. quick in learing and understanding things चतुर, होशियार, धूर्त *Clever* students generally score good marks.

2. skilful प्रवीण, निपुण Reena is *clever* at embroidery.

cliché *(n.)* क्लीशे– a word or expression that has lost much of its force through overexposure, घिसी-पिटी उक्ति You must avoid *clichés* in your writings.

click *(v.)* क्लिक–1. to make a slight sharp sound खटखट करना She *clicked* her fingers to call the driver.

2. (n.) an act of pressing and releasing a button on a mouse माउस का बटन दबाने की क्रिया Sending e-mails is just a matter of a *click*.

client *(n.)* क्लायण्ट्– a person, company, etc. uses the services or that seeks the advice of a professional person ग्राहक, मुवक्किल The *clients* were impressed by the quality of work.

cliff *(n.)* क्लिफ़– steep rock खड़ी चट्टान A coast path along the top of rugged *cliffs*.

climate *(n.)* क्लाइमट्–1. weather conditions of a place जलवायु, आबोहवा In summer, Delhi's *climate* is extremely hot.

2. prevailing condition वातावरण How is the political *climate* in the capital these days?

climax *(n.)* क्लाइमैक्स्– the highest or most intense point in the development of something, story, drama, etc. (पुस्तक, नाटक, फ़िल्म, घटना आदि की) चरमावस्था, चरम सीमा The movie reached a tragic *climax*.

climb *(v.)* क्लाइम्–1. to incline or slope upward चढ़ना, आरोहण करना You require special training to *climb* a mountain.

2. to go up or ascend (stairs, a mountain, etc.) ऊपर चढ़ना The old man *climbed* the staircase with great difficulty.

3. *(n.)* an act of climbing up a mountain चढ़ाई, आरोहण *Climb* to success is hard.

cling *(v.)* क्लिंग– to hold on tightly to sb/sth चिपकना, लिपटना Small children *cling* to their mother while sleeping.

clinic *(n.)* क्लिनिक्– hospital or institution where the medical treatment is given एक छोटा दवाख़ाना, क्लीनिक I was looking for a dental *clinic.*

clink *(v.)* क्लिंक– to make a sharp ringing sound झनझनाना They *clinked* the keys together.

clip *(n.)* क्लिप– 1. metal clasp for holding things क्लिप, चुटकी, पंजा The loose sheets are put together with a paper *clip.*

2. *(v.)* to cut with scissors कतरना, काटना Little boys like to *clip* pictures out of newspapers.

cloak *(n.)* क्लोक़– loose outer garment without sleeves लबादा The judge wore a long black *cloak.*

clock *(n.)* क्लॉक– instrument for measuring time घड़ी Some wall *clocks* chime every hour.

clog *(v.)* क्लॉग– to hinder बाधा डालना, अवरुद्ध या बन्द हो जाना The sewer was *clogged* with dirt.

close *(v.)* क्लोज़–1. to shut बन्द करना Please *close* the door.

2. *(adj.)* near in space or time निकट, पास The children sat *close* together.

3. thorough सूक्ष्म On a good day the climate in LA is *close* to perfection.

➢ **close by**– near बहुत पास, She lives *close by* my house.

closely *(adv.)* क्लोज़ली– carefully ध्यानपूर्वक I watched the situation *closely.*

closing *(adj.)* क्लोज़िंग– coming at the end of a speech अंतिम The President gave her *closing* remarks.

clot *(n.)* क्लॉट–1. a semisolid mass, as of coagluated blood ख़ून का थक्का A blood *clot* formed inside his brain.

2. *(v.)* to form or cause to form into a soft thick lump or clot ख़ून का थक्का जमना The blood inside his brain began to *clot.*

cloth *(n.)* क्लॉथ– a fabric formed by weaving, felting or knitting wool, cotton, etc. कपड़ा, वस्त्र Nowadays shirts are made of synthetic *cloth.*

clothes *(n.)* क्लोद्ज़– articles of dress पोशाक, पहनावा Youngsters like fashionable *clothes.*

cloud *(n.)* क्लाउड–1. a mass of water or ice particles visible in the sky, usually white or grey बादल There were black *clouds* all over the sky.

2. *(v.)* to make or become cloudy, overcast, or indistinct बादल घिरना, धुंधला करना या हो जाना Her judgement was *clouded* by jealousy.

cloudy *(adj.)* क्लाउडी– covered with cloud or clouds बादलों से भरा, धुँधला On a *cloudy* day, we cannot see the sun.

clove *(n.)* क्लोव– the dried flower of a tropical tree, used in cooking as a spice लौंग, लवंग Oil of *cloves* is good for toothache.

clown *(n.)* क्लाउन– a comic entertainer, usually grotesquely costumed and made up, appearing in the circus विदूषक, मसख़रा The children laughed at the circus *clown's* antics.

club *(n.)* क्लब–1. a group or association of people with common aims or interests क्लब, सभा *The club* is a place for recreation.

2. a heavy stick, usually with one end thicker than the other, डण्डा, लाठी, मुद्गर He defended himself with his *club.*

cluck *(v.)* क्लक– to make a clicking sound (चूज़े जैसी आवाज़ में) कुट-कुट करना She was *clucking* like a hen.

clue *(n.)* क्लू– something that helps to solve a problem or unravel a mystery संकेत, इशारा, सूत्र The detectives looked for *clues* that could lead them to the murderer.

clumsy *(adj.)* क्लम्ज़ी– lacking in skill or physical coordination भद्दा, भोंडा,

बेडोल, बेढंगा The cold made his fingers *clumsy*.

cluster *(n.)* क्लस्टर्– 1. number of things growing, fastened, or occurring close together गुच्छा, झुण्ड, समूह The rabbit ran to the *cluster* of bushes to hide from the hound.

2. *(v.)* to gather or be gathered in clusters जमा होना या करना The children *clustered* round the ice cream vendor.

clutch *(v.)* क्लच– to seize with or as if with hands or claws जकड़ना/पकड़ना The frightened child *clutched* his mother's hand.

clutter *(n.)* क्लटर्– 1. a disordered heap or mass of objects गड्डमड्ड, अस्त-व्यस्त (वस्तुएँ) There was a lot of *clutter* on the table.

2. *(v.)* to strew or amass (objects) in a disorderly manner (वस्तुएं) गड्डमड्ड/अस्त-व्यस्त करना She *cluttered* the table with cosmetics.

cluttered *(adj.)* क्लटरड– a disordered heap or mass of objects अस्त-व्यस्त, गड्डमड्ड Her desk is always *cluttered.*

coach *(n.)* कोच– a vehicle for several passengers, used for transport over long distances, sightseeing, etc. कोच, सवारी डिब्बा The Rajdhani Express has air-conditioned *coaches* only.

coal *(n.)* कोल– a combustible compact black or dark-brown carbonaceous rock formed from compaction of layers of partially decomposed vegetation कोयला Most industries in India run on *coal* energy.

coalition *(n.)* कोअलिशन– an alliance or union between groups, factions, or parties, esp for some temporary and specific reason गठबंधन, सम्मिलन A *coalition* government always faces problems.

coarse *(adj.)* कॉर्स–1. rough in texture, structure, etc.; not fine मोटा, खुरदरा, रुक्ष The poor woman wore a sari of *coarse* cloth.

2. lacking refinement or taste; indelicate; vulgar असभ्य, गंवार *Coarse* manners are disliked by all.

coast *(n.)* कोस्ट– the line or zone where the land meets the sea or some other large expanse of water तट, समुद्रतट We could see the *coast* from the deck of the ship.

coat *(n.)* कोट–1. an outdoor garment with sleeves, covering the body from the shoulder to waist, knee, or foot कोट, कुरता, अंगरखा The poor man had no *coat* to wear.

2. a layer that covers or conceals a surface तह, परत, लेप This door needs a fresh *coat* of paint.

3. *(v.)* to cover (with) a layer or covering लेपना, परत चढ़ाना She *coated* the dough with fine flour before rolling it.

coax *(v.)* कोक्स– to seek to manipulate or persuade (someone) by tenderness, flattery, pleading, etc. फुसलाना Don't *coax* him to cook today.

cobbler *(n.)* कॉब्लर्– a person who makes or mends shoes मोची The *cobbler* repairs and polishes the shoes.

cobweb *(n.)* कॉबवेब– a web spun by certain spiders, often found in the corners of disused rooms मकड़ी का जाला The unused room was dusty and full of *cobwebs.*

cock *(n.)* कॉक– the male of the domestic fowl मुर्गा The *cock* crows at the daybreak.

cockroach *(n.)* कॉक्रोच– an insect that lives in houses तिलचट्टा Lizards eat the *cockroaches.*

cocktail *(n.)* काक्टेल्– any mixed drink with a spirit base, usually drunk before meals एक मिश्रित मदिरा It was a *cocktail* party.

coconut *(n.)* कोकोनट– the fruit of the coconut palm नारियल The *coconut* is considered a sacred fruit in India.

code *(n.)* कोड–1. a conventionalized set of principles, rules, or expectations संहिता, नियमावली There is a *code* of conduct for Government servants.
2. a system of letters or symbols, and rules for their association by means of which information can be represented or communicated for reasons of secrecy, brevity, etc. कूट, संकेत-पद्धति The spy sent his secret message in *code.*

coerce *(v.)* कोअर्स– to compel or restrain by force or authority without regard to individual wishes or desires मजबूर/बाध्य करना He was *coerced* into signing the document.

coffee *(n.)* कॉफ़ी– a drink consisting of an infusion of the roasted and ground or crushed seeds of the coffee tree क़हवा, काफ़ी Over consumption of *coffee* is not good for health.

coffin *(n.)* कॉफ़िन– a box in which a corpse is buried or cremated शवपेटी, ताबूत The departed leader's *coffin* was ready for its last journey.

coherent *(adj.)* कोहिरण्ट– capable of logical and consistent speech, thought, etc. समझने में सरल, स्पष्ट Sameer gave a *coherent* account of the incident.

coil *(n.)* कॉइल– 1. something wound in a connected series of loops कुण्डली, कुण्डल The fan motor has a *coil* of wire.
2. *(v.)* to wind or gather (ropes, hair, etc.) into loops or (of rope, hair, etc.) to be formed in such loops कुण्डल बनाना, लपेटना Nisha got her hair *coiled* from a beauty parlour.

coin *(n.)* कॉइन– a metal disc or piece used as money सिक्का, मुद्रा *Coins* last longer than paper currency.

coincide *(v.)* कोइन्साइड– to occur or exist simultaneously एक ही समय में या समान होना Their views *coincide* completely.

coincidence *(n.)* कोइन्सिडन्स– a chance occurrence of events remarkable either for being simultaneous or for apparently being connected संयोग, समानता, अनुरूपता I met him in the market by a sheer *coincidence.*

cold *(adj.)* कोल्ड–1. without sufficient or proper warmth ठण्डा, शीतल I like *cold* coffee.
2. lacking in affection, enthusiasm, or warmth of feeling तटस्थ, उदासीन, भावशून्य Ram was upset by Gita's *cold* behaviour.
3. having relatively little warmth; of a rather low temperature ठण्डक, सर्दी Anil got wet in the rain and caught a *cold.*

cold-blooded *(adj.)* कोल्ड-ब्लडड्– having or showing a lack of feeling or pity निष्ठुर, नृशंस It was a *cold-blooded* murder.

cold-hearted *(adj.)* कोल्ड-हॉटेड– lacking in feeling or warmth; unkind बेदर्द, हृदयहीन, निर्दयी He is such a *cold-hearted* man.

collaborate *(v.)* कलैबरेट– to work with another or others on a joint project सहयोग देना She *collaborated* with a colleague to complete the project.

collaboration *(n.)* कलैबरेशन– the act of working with another or others on a joint project सहयोग She has written this book in *collaboration* with a friend.

collapse *(v.)* कोलैप्स–1. to fall down in suddenly ढह जाना, ढेर हो जाना The old house *collapsed* in the storm.
2. to break down or fail completely समाप्त हो जाना Talks between two friends have *collapsed.*

collar *(n.)* कॉलर्– the part of a garment around the neck and shoulders कालर, गरदनी, गरेबान Shirts with short *collars* are no more in fashion.

colleague *(n.)* कलीग– a fellow worker or member of a staff, department, profession, etc. सहकर्मी, सहयोगी She is my *colleague* in the office.

collect *(v.)* कलेक्ट– to gather together or be gathered together जमा करना या होना, एकत्र/संग्रह करना Children love to *collect* coloured pebbles on the seashore.

collection *(n.)* कलेक्शन– the act or process of collecting संग्रह, संचय I have a good *collection* of old coins.

collective *(adj.)* कलेक्‌टिव– formed or assembled by collection सामूहिक It is our *collective* responsibility to save the environment.

college *(n.)* कॉलिज– an institution of higher education; part of a university कॉलेज, महाविद्यालय The *college* was shocked by his death.

collide *(v.)* कलाइड– to crash together with a violent impact टकराना, टक्कर लगना When a taxi *collided* with a bus, all the traffic came to a halt.

collision *(n.)* कोलिश़न– a violent impact of moving objects; crash टक्कर The taxi was smashed in the *collision.*

colloquial *(adj.)* कलोक्विअल– of or relating to conversation बोलचाल की (भाषा) Avoid *colloquial* words in your essays.

collusion *(n.)* कलूश़न– secret agreement for a fraudulent purpose; connivance; conspiracy साँठ-साँठ, दुरभिसंधि They did a *collusion* with criminals.

colonial *(adj.)* कलोनिअल– of, characteristic of, relating to, possessing, or inhabiting a colony or colonies उपनिवेशीय, औपनिवेशिक France was once a *colonial* power country.

colony *(n.)* कॉलनी– a body of people who settle in a country distant from their homeland but maintain ties with it बस्ती, उपनिवेश The traveller came across a *colony* of tribal people.

colour *(n.)* कलर्– an attribute of things that results from the light they reflect, transmit, or emit in so far as this light causes a visual sensation that depends on its wavelengths वर्ण, रंग The white *colour* is a combination of seven *colours.*

colourful *(adj.)* कलर्फ़ुल– having intense colour or richly varied colours रंगीन, रंगबिरंगा She was wearing a very *colourful* dress.

colouring *(n.)* कलरिंग– the process or art of applying colour रंजन, रँगाई का रंग Katreena has fair *colouring.*

colourless *(adj.)* कलर्लैस– without colour रंगहीन, फीका She is a *colourless* character.

column *(n.)* कॉलम–1. an upright post or pillar usually having a cylindrical shaft, a base, and a capital स्तम्भ, खम्भा The old palace had huge *columns.*

2. any of two or more vertical sections of type on a printed page, esp on a newspaper page कॉलम, स्तम्भ I've been reading your *column* for five years.

3. a row, line, or file, as of people in a queue दस्ता, सैन्यदल The soldiers marched in a *column.*

comb *(v.)* कोम–1. to use a comb on कंघी करना The mother *combed* her daughter's hair.

2. to search or inspect with great care छान डालना The police *combed* the town for the thief.

3. *(n.)* a toothed device of metal, plastic, wood, etc., used for disentangling or arranging hair कंघा I want to buy a new *comb.*

combat *(n.)* कॉम्बैट– 1. an action fought between two military forces लड़ाई, संघर्ष, भिड़ंत A *combat* took place between the police and the protestors.

2. *(v.)* to fight or defy लड़ना, संघर्ष करना The government is taking measures to *combat* poverty.

combination *(n.)* कॉम्बिनेशन– the act of combining or state of being combined मेल, साथ, संगत, संयोजन Her dress was a good *combination* of red and black colours.

combine *(v.)* कमूबाइन– to integrate or cause to be integrated; join together मिलाना, जोड़ना The two companies *combined* to form one big corporation.

combustion *(n.)* कम्बस्चन– the process of burning आग से जलने की प्रक्रिया, दहन A chamber in an engine where *combustion* occurs.

come *(v.)* कम्– to arrive, to reach आना, पहुंचना Ram *came* to see me as I was ill.

➢ **come about**– to happen, occur, take place कुछ घटित होना या आना, The opportunity *came about* quite by accident.

➢ **come across**–1. to provide what is expected अपना प्रभाव या छाप छोड़ना, Prema *comes across* as being rather arrogant.
2. to meet or find by chance: संयोग से किसी का मिलना I *came across* an old book in her almirah.

➢ **come along**– to arrive, appear सामने आना, ज़ाहिर होना, पता चलना, Your English language is *coming along* really well.

➢ **come apart**– to break or fall into pieces टुकड़े-टुकड़े हो जाना, Ravi picked an old book and it *came apart* in his hands.

➢ **come away**– to become detatched किसी से अलग हो जाना, One of the wires in the plug had *come away*.

➢ **come back**–1. to return वापस आना, लौटकर आना, He never persuaded her to *come back* home.
2. to remind याद आना, स्मरण आना, I can't remember her name, but it'll *come back* to my mind.

➢ **come before**– to be presented to sb/sth किसी के सामने उपस्थित होना He *comes before* the court tomorrow.

➢ **come between**– to interfere with a relationship फूट डालना Sarita doesn't want to *come between* the husband and wife.

➢ **come by**– to obtain (something) प्राप्त करना How did you *come by* these precious jewellery?

➢ **come down**– to collapse उतरना, कम होना, Prices of onion are *coming down*.

➢ **come forward**– to offer one's services सहायता के लिए आगे आना, Arun *came forward* and gave us an important information.

➢ **come from**– to originate in; to have as its source किसी ख़ास स्थान का निवासी होना, Veer Sawarkar *came from* Mumbai.

➢ **come in**– to enter घुसना, प्रवेश करना, आना, What time does your bus *come in*?

➢ **come in on**– to join, take part in शामिल होना, I have a chance to *come in on* the deal he proposed.

➢ **come of**– to be the result of sth परिणाम निकलना/होना You made all efforts, but nothing *come of* it in the end.

➢ **come off**– to take place; to happen किसी घटना का पूरा होना, My efforts to meet the minister didn't *come off*.

➢ **come on**– to follow बाद में आना, पीछे आना The rain *came on* just before departure.

➢ **come out**– to appear, become visible प्रकट होना The truth finally *came out*.

➢ **come over**– *see*–come across.

➢ **come round** (also **come around**) –1. to regain consciousness फिर से

होश में आना, The fainting girl *came round.*

2. to happen again पुनः होना Her birthday seems to *come around* every year.

➢ **come through**– (of a message or news) to arrive by radio, TV, etc. कोई संदेश या समाचार आना A message is *coming through* radio.

➢ **come to**– to reach or be brought to a specified situation or result संबद्ध होना, When it *comes to* politics, I say nothing.

➢ **come up with**– to produce an answer especially when pressured or challenged समस्या का समाधान पा लेना, Bhanu *came up with* great ideas and solutions.

comedy *(n.)* कॉमेडी– a branch of drama that deals with humorous events मनोरंजन प्रधान नाटक I like to watch *comedy* movie.

comfort *(n.)* कम्फ़र्ट– 1. state of being free from pain and anxiety आराम, सुख-चैन Rich men live in great *comfort.*

2. *(v.)* to console दिलासा देना I *comforted* the weeping child.

comfortable *(adj.)* कम्फ़र्टबूल– give comfort to the body आरामदेह, सुखद Please sit here and make yourself *comfortable.*

comfortably *(adv.)* कम्फ़र्टबली– act of being comfortable आराम के साथ I am sitting *comfortably* in the arm chair.

comic *(adj.)* कॉमिक– causing laughter हास्यजनक, विनोदपूर्ण The drama is both *comic* and tragedy.

command *(n.)* कमाण्ड–1. an order; mandate आदेश, हुक्म The General gave the *command* to march.

2. the act of commanding प्रभुत्व, प्रभाव A captain is in *command* of a company of soldiers.

3. *(v.)* to order, require, or compel आज्ञा देना The king *commanded* his army to attack.

commence *(v.)* कमेन्स– to start or begin; come or cause to come into being, operation, etc. प्रारंभ करना या होना When does the show *commence*?

commendable *(adj.)* कमेन्डबूल– deserving praise प्रशंसनीय She has really done a *commendable* job.

comment *(n.)* कॉमेण्ट– 1. a remark, criticism, or observation टिप्पणी, आलोचना She ignored the *comment* he made about her dress.

2. *(v.)* to takes a clause as object to remark or express an opinion टीका-टिप्पणी करना He *commented* on her dress.

commentary *(n.)* कॉमेण्ट्री– an explanatory series of notes or comments (रेडियो एवं टेलीविज़न पर घटित होते खेल एवं उत्सव का आंखों देखा हाल) वर्णन The reporter was giving a running *commentary.*

commentator *(n.)* कॉमेंटेटर्– a person who provides a spoken commentary for a broadcast, film, etc. esp of a sporting event विवरणकार, आँखों देखा हाल सुनाने वाला व्यक्ति Narottam Puri was a good *commentator.*

commerce *(n.)* कॉमर्स– the activity embracing all forms of the purchase and sale of goods and services वाणिज्य, व्यापार Mumbai is a big centre of *commerce.*

commercial *(adj.)* कमर्शल्– of, connected with, or engaged in commerce; mercantile वाणिज्य संबंधी, व्यापारिक Radio Taxy is a commercial vechicle.

commercialize (ise) *(v.)* कर्मशलाइज़– to make commercial in aim, methods, or character व्यापारिक बनाना Festivals have become very *commercialized.*

commission *(n.)* कमिशन–1. a duty or task committed to a person or group to perform आयोग A *Commission* was appointed to investigate the causes of the accident.

2. the fee allotted to an agent for services rendered आढ़त, दलाली He earned Rs 500 on *commission* last week.

commit *(v.)* कमिट– to do sth wrong (कुछ गलत) करना या कर डालना He *committed* many thefts before being caught.

commitment *(n.)* कमिटमन्ट– the act of committing or pledging वचनबद्धता, वायदा I always stick on my *commitment.*

committee *(n.)* कमिटी– a group of people chosen or appointed to perform a specified service or function कमेटी, समिति A *committee* was set up to go into the affairs of the company.

commodity *(n.)* कमॉडटी– an article or product उपयोगी वस्तु, माल Gold is a precious *commodity.*

common *(adj.)* कॉमन–1. widely known or frequently encountered; ordinary सामान्य, आम The crow is a *common* bird in India.

2. of ordinary standard; average सामान्य, सहज Fools have no *common* sense.

commotion *(n.)* कमोशन– violent disturbance; upheaval हुल्लड़, शोरगुल The crowd was creating a lot of *commotion.*

community *(n.)* कम्यूनटी–1. the people living in one locality समुदाय, समाज, समूह There is a large *community* of shoemakers in this locality.

communal *(adj.)* कम्यूनल– belonging or relating to a community as a whole सामुदायिक, सांप्रदायिक There was *communal* tension in the city.

communicate *(v.)* कम्युनिकेट– to exchange (thoughts, feelings, or ideas) by speech, writing, gestures, etc. विचारों एवं भावनाओं का आदान-प्रदान करना Parents should *communicate* freely with their children.

communication *(n.)* कम्युनिकेशन– the act or an instance of communicating; the imparting or exchange of information, ideas, or feelings संवाद, पत्र-व्यवहार, संचार Radio is still the only means of *communication* in villages.

communicative *(adj.)* कम्युनिकेटिव– inclined or able to communicate readily; talkative समाचार एवं सूचना देने में सक्षम Sharon has excellent *communicative* skill.

commute *(v.)* कम्यूट– to travel some distance regularly दैनिक यात्रा करना I *commute* from my home to office by bus.

commuter *(n.)* कम्यूटर– a person who travels to work over an appreciable distance दैनिक यात्री The strike of buses created a problem for the *commuters.*

compact *(n.)* कम्पैक्ट– 1. an official contract or agreement संविदा, समझौता They made a *compact* to meet on the demands.

2. *(adj.)* closely packed together; dense पूरा भरा हुआ My house was very *compact.*

companion *(n.)* कम्पैनिअन– 1. a person who is an associate of another or others; comrade साथी, सखा, सहचर Without a *companion,* one feels lonely on a long journey.

2. *(adj.)* one of a pair of things that go together संबद्ध, साथ का This is a *companion* volume to the previous publication.

company *(n.)* कम्पनी–1. a business enterprise कम्पनी, समवाय At last, the *company* started making profits.

2. a number of people gathered together; assembly दल, मंडली, टोली A Captain commands a *company* of soldiers.

3. the fact of being with someone; companionship संगति, मित्र, साथी A

man is known by the *company* he keeps.

comparatively *(adj.)* कम्पैरेटिवली– denoting or involving comparison तुलनात्मक, आपेक्षिक The last question was *comparatively* easy.

compare *(v.)* कम्पेअर्– to regard or represent as analogous or similar; liken तुलना करना, मिलाना, बराबर समझना या होना We must *compare* the price and performance both.

comparison *(n.)* कम्पैरिज़न– the act or process of comparing तुलना There is no *comparison* between the lifestyles of rich and poor.

compass *(n.)* कम्पस्–1. an instrument for finding direction, कम्पास, दिक्सूचक A ship cannot be kept on its course without a *compass.*
2. an instrument used for drawing circles, परकार The math teacher asked the students to buy a *compass* box.

compassion *(n.)* कम्पैश्न– a feeling of distress and pity for the suffering or misfortune of another, often including the desire to alleviate it सहानुभूति, करुणा He has no *compassion* for the poor.

compatible *(adj.)* कम्पैटब्ल– able to exist together harmoniously अनुकूल, संगत, माफिक They were not *compatible* with the fast lifestyle abroad.

compel *(v.)* कम्पेल– to force sb to do sth लाचार/मजबूर करना, बाध्य करना, विवश करना It's not good to *compel* a person to do something against his wish.

compensate *(v.)* कॉम्पेन्सेट्– to make amends to (someone), esp for loss or injury क्षतिपूर्ति करना, मुआवजा देना I had to *compensate* for the damage I caused to their car.

compensation *(n.)* कॉम्पेन्सेशन– the act or process of making amends for something मुआवज़ा, क्षतिपूर्ति, हरजाना She did not ask for any *compensation* after her divorce.

compère *(v.)* कॉमपेअर– to act as a compere for a show (कार्यक्रम) प्रस्तुत करना Who *compered* the filmfare award show?

competent *(adj.)* कॉम्पिटन्ट– having sufficient skill, knowledge, etc.; capable सक्षम, समर्थ, सुयोग्य She is one of the most *competent* workers of her company.

competition *(n.)* कॉम्पटिशन– the act of competing; rivalry प्रतियोगिता, प्रतिस्पर्द्धा, मुकाबला Ramesh won the first prize in the painting *competition.*

competitor *(n.)* कॉम्पेटिटर– a person, group, team, firm, etc. that vies or competes; rival प्रतिद्वंद्वी, प्रतियोगी, प्रतिस्पर्द्धी There were more than twenty *competitors* in the field.

compile *(v.)* कम्पाइल– to make or compose from other materials or sources संकलित/एकत्र करना, बनाना He *compiled* a book of short stories written by Indian writers.

complacency *(n.)* कम्प्लेसन्सि– a feeling of satisfaction, esp extreme self-satisfaction; smugness आत्म-संतुष्टि, संतोष We lost that match because of *complacency.*

complacent *(adj.)* कम्प्लेसन्ट– pleased or satisfied, esp extremely self-satisfied आत्म-संतुष्ट He was *complacent* that he would win the elections.

complain *(v.)* कम्प्लेन्– to express resentment, displeasure, etc. esp habitually; grumble शिकायत करना, दुखड़ा रोना The guests in the hotel *complained* about the bad food.

complaint *(n.)* कम्प्लेन्ट– the act of complaining; an expression of grievance शिकायत, परिवाद He lodged a *complaint* about the theft in his house.

complement *(n.)* कॉम्प्लिमेंट– 1. a person or thing that completes something संपूरक, पूरक This scarf is a perfect *complement* to that dress.
2. *(v.)* to add to, make complete, or form a complement to अनुकूल/पूरक होना This scarf *complements* that dress very well.

complementary *(adj.)* कॉम्प्लिमेंटरी– acting as or forming a complement; completing अनुपूरक, पूरक They gave us *complementary* tickets for the show.

complete *(adj.)* कम्प्लीट– 1. total, whole, entire पूर्ण, संपूर्ण, पूरा My work here is not yet *complete.*
2. *(v.)* to make whole or perfect पूरा करना *Complete* your homework before you go to play.

completely *(adv.)* कम्प्लीटली– totally; absolutely पूर्णतया, संपूर्ण रूप से The building was *completely* destroyed in the fire.

complex *(adj.)* कॉम्प्लेक्स–1. made up of various interconnected parts; composite जटिल, पेचीदा This is a *complex* problem, but we need to find a solution to it.
2. *(n.)* a group of buildings in one place भवनों की संयुक्त श्रेणी I shall see you in the shopping *complex.*
3. an obsession or excessive fear हीन भावना She has developed a *complex* about her looks.

complexion *(n.)* कम्प्लेक्शन– the colour and general appearance of a person's skin, esp of the face (चेहरे की त्वचा का) रूप-रंग, स्वरूप She has a dusky *complexion,* but still looks good.

complexity *(n.)* कॉम्प्लेक्सटी– the state or quality of being intricate or complex पेचीदगी, जटिलता I was surprised to see the *complexity* of the problem.

complicated *(adj.)* कॉम्प्लिकेटड– made up of intricate parts or aspects that are difficult to understand or analyse जटिल, पेचीदा The Maths problem was too *complicated* to solve.

complication *(n.)* कॉम्प्लिकेशन– a condition, event, etc. that is complex or confused उलझन, समस्या There is no *complication* after the surgery.

compliment *(n.)* कॉम्प्लिमण्ट– 1. a remark or act expressing respect, admiration, etc. प्रशंसोक्ति, प्रशंसा I paid her a *compliment* for organising the party so well.
2. *(v.)* to express admiration of; congratulate or commend प्रशंसा करना, बधाई देना I *complimented* her for organising the party so well.

component *(n.)* कम्पोनन्ट– a constituent part or aspect of something more complex अवयव, घटक The *components* of this machine have rusted.

composed *(adj.)* कम्पोज़्ड– (of people) calm; tranquil; serene शांत He looked *composed* at the funeral of his son.

composition *(n.)* कॉम्पज़िश्न्–1. the act of putting together or making up by combining parts or ingredients रचना, सृजन Arun's essay on Gandhiji was a fine piece of *composition.*
2. the arrangement of objects or people in photography or painting संयोजन, संघटन, बनावट The balanced *composition* of the new Cabinet was praised alot.

compound *(n.)* कॉम्पाउंड– 1. an enclosure, esp on the mines, containing the living quarters for Black workers घेरा, अहाता Her dead body was found in the *compound* of the building.
2. *(v.)* to intensify by an added element स्थिति को बिगाड़ना The controversy *compounded* the problem further.

comprehend *(v.)* कॉम्प्रिहेन्ड– to perceive or understand समझना I could not *comprehend* what he wanted to say.

comprehensible *(adj.)* कॉम्प्रिहेन्सिबल– capable of being comprehended आसानी से समझ में आने वाला, बोधगम्य Illustrations and diagrams make the book more *comprehensible.*

comprehension *(n.)* कॉम्प्रिहेन्शन– the act or capacity of understanding बोध, समझ Her excuses for arriving late are beyond my *comprehension.*

comprehensive *(adj.)* कॉम्प्रिहेन्सिव– of broad scope or content; including all or much विस्तृत, व्यापक This dictionary is quite *comprehensive.*

comprise *(v.)* कम्प्राइज़्– to constitute the whole of; consist of समाविष्ट करना Our family *comprises* four members in all.

compromise *(n.)* कॉम्प्रमाइज् – 1. settlement of a dispute by concessions on both or all sides समझौता We made a *compromise* to bring the situation under control.
2. *(v.)* to settle (a dispute) by making concessions समझौता करना With no other option left, we *compromised* with the situation.

compulsion *(n.)* कम्पल्श्न्– the act of compelling or the state of being compelled मजबूरी, विवशता There is no *compulsion* on either side, I can go abroad.

compulsory *(adj.)* कम्पल्सरी– required by regulations or laws; obligatory अनिवार्य It is *compulsory* to wear a helmet while riding a bike.

comrade *(n.)* कॉम्रेड– a friend, associate or companion मित्र, सखा, सहचर, साथी He has been my *comrade* for many years.

conceal *(v.)* कन्सील– to hide, to cover छिपाना, गुप्त रखना The stolen necklace was *concealed* in the cupboard.

conceit *(n.)* कन्सीट– a high, often exaggerated, opinion of oneself or one's accomplishments; vanity घमंड, अहंकार She is full of *conceit* about her beauty.

conceited *(adj.)* कन्सीटेड– having a high or exaggerated opinion of oneself or one's accomplishments अहंकारी, घमंडी He is so *conceited* and thinks he is the best player of his team.

conceive *(v.)* कन्सीव–1. to have an idea (of); to imagine; to think नया विचार आना या कल्पना करना She *conceived* the idea to play cards during her journey.
2. to become pregnant with (young) गर्भ धारण करना Rozy *conceived* after a long time.

concentrate *(v.)* कॉन्सन्ट्रेट्– to come or cause to come to a single purpose or aim ध्यान लगाना, चित्त एकाग्र करना You need to *concentrate* on your studies to pass the exams.

concentration *(n.)* कॉन्सन्ट्रेशन– intense mental application; complete attention ध्यान, एकाग्रता I lost my *concentration* and hit my bike against a car.

concept *(n.)* कॉन्सेप्ट– a theoretical construct within some theory मूल सिद्धांत Unless your *concepts* are clear, you won't understand it.

conception *(n.)* कन्सेप्शन्– something conceived; notion, idea, design, or plan (दिमाग़ में आने वाला) विचार या योजना, संकल्पना She is not able to grasp the basic *conception* of Mathematics.

concern *(v.)* कन्सर्न– to relate to; be of importance or interest to; affect संबंध रखना This order *concerns* all government employees.

concerned *(adj.)* कन्सर्न्ड– worried, troubled, or solicitous चिंतित Amit is *concerned* about his health.

concerning *(prep.)* कन्सर्निंग– about; regarding; on the subject of के विषय

पर, से संबंधित Books *concerning* crime detection are very popular.

concert *(n.)* कॉन्सर्ट– a performance of music by players or singers that does not involve theatrical staging संगीत समारोह Last year I attended a music *concert.*

concerted *(adj.)* कन्सर्टिड– mutually contrived, planned, or arranged आयोजित, संगठित We have to make a *concerted* effort to fight against terrorism.

concession *(n.)* कन्सेशन– the act of yielding or conceding, as to a demand or argument छूट The poor students were granted half fee *concession.*

conciliation *(n.)* कन्सिलिएशन्– the act or process of conciliating सुलह, समझौता All attempts at *conciliation* failed and the fight began.

conclude *(v.)* कन्क्लूड– to come or cause to come to an end or conclusion समाप्त करना या होना, ख़त्म करना, निष्कर्ष निकालना The leader *concluded* his speech with an appeal for unity.

conclusion *(n.)* कन्क्लूशन– the outcome or result of an act, process, event, etc. नतीजा, निष्कर्ष The judge came to the *conclusion* that the accused was not guilty.

concoct *(v.)* कन्कॉक्ट– to make by combining different ingredients मनगढ़ंत कहानी कहना, असत्य बातें बताना My sister *concocted* a story for being late.

concord *(n.)* कन्कॉर्ड– agreement or harmony between people or nations; amity सहमति एवं मेल Some Asian countries live in *concord.*

concrete *(n.)* कॉन्क्रीट– 1. construction material made of a mixture of cement, sand, small stones and water that hardens to a stonelike mass कंकरीट, रोड़ी Lot of *concrete* is required to build a durable house.

2. *(adj.)* formed by the coalescence of particles; condensed; solid मूर्त, ठोस, निश्चित They gave some *concrete* proposals to the management.

condemn *(v.)* कन्डेम– to express strong disapproval of; to censure निंदा करना Arya Samaj *condemned* idol worship.

condense *(v.)* कन्डेन्स– to increase the density of; to compress गाढ़ा करना, संक्षिप्त करना The long report was *condense* into one paragraph.

condescend *(v.)* कन्डिसेण्ड– to act graciously towards another or others regarded as being on a lower level; to behave patronizingly बड़प्पन छोड़कर झुक जाना, नम्र हो जाना She *condescends* to me when she wants me to do something.

condition *(n.)* कन्डिशन–1. a particular state of being or existence दशा, स्थिति, अवस्था This house is not in a good *condition.*

2. something that limits or restricts something else; शर्त What is your *condition* for joining us?

3. external or existing circumstances परिस्थिति Under the stormy *conditions,* it is better to stay indoors.

conditional *(adj.)* कन्डिशनल– depending on other factors; not certain शर्तबंद, सप्रतिबंध The thief was found guilty but given a *conditional* discharge.

condolence *(n.)* कण्डोलंस– an expression of sympathy with someone in grief, etc. संवेदना I sent a letter of *condolence* to him.

conducive *(adj.)* कण्ड्यूसिव– on tributing, leading, or tending सहायक, प्रेरक The hot weather is not *conducive* to me to work hard.

conduct *(n.)* कण्डक्ट–1. the manner in which a person behaves; behaviour

आचरण, व्यवहार या बरताव His *conduct* is always under watch.

2. *(v.)* to lead or direct नेतृत्व करना The doorkeeper *conducted* me to my seat in the cinema hall.

3. to do or carry out संचालन करना He presided over the conference and *conducted* it ably.

conference *(n.)* कॉन्फ़रन्स– a meeting for consultation, exchange of information, or discussion, esp one with a formal agenda सम्मेलन A *conference* of leaders was held to discuss budget.

confess *(v.)* कन्फ़ेस– to make an acknowledgment or admission (of faults, misdeeds, crimes, etc.) ग़लती मानना, अपराध क़बूल करना, स्वीकार करना The boy *confessed* that he broke the windowpane.

confession *(n.)* कन्फ़ेशन– the act of confessing अपराध-स्वीकरण, स्वीकारोक्ति The thief made a full *confession* of his crimes before the judge.

confide *(v.)* कन्फ़ाइड– to disclose (secret or personal matters) in confidence (to); to reveal in private (to) किसी को गोपनीय बात बताना I *confided* my feelings to my best friend.

confidence *(n.)* कॉन्फ़िडन्स– a feeling of trust in a person or thing भरोसा, विश्वास The *confidence* on a friend is tested in a crisis.

confident *(adj.)* कॉन्फ़िडन्ट– sure of oneself; bold आत्मविश्वासी, आश्वस्त Ram was very *confident* of scoring good marks in the exams.

confine *(v.)* कन्फ़ाइन– to keep or close within bounds; limit; restrict सीमित करना या रखना, बंद करना A fracture in the leg kept Ram *confined* to his home for a month.

confinement *(n.)* कन्फ़ाइन्मन्ट– the act of confining or the state of being confined कारावास, क़ैद The murderer was kept in a solitary *confinement.*

confirm *(v.)* कन्फ़र्म– to prove to be true or valid; corroborate; verify पुष्टि/समर्थन करना The India-Pakistan cricket tournament has been *confirmed.*

confirmation *(n.)* कन्फ़र्मेशन– the act of confirming पुष्टि, समर्थन You need to send me a *confirmation* before coming.

confiscate *(v.)* कॉन्फ़िस्केट– to seize (property), esp for public use and esp by way of a penalty (दंडस्वरूप कोई वस्तु) ज़ब्त कर लेना Any mobile found in school will be *confiscated.*

conflict *(n.)* कॉन्फ़्लिक्ट– 1. a struggle or clash between opposing forces; battle संघर्ष, युद्ध Pakistan and India have witnessed three *conflicts.*

2. *(v.)* to come into opposition; clash किसी दूसरे से असहमत होना, भिन्न होना Young generation's ideas *conflict* with those of their parents.

conform *(v.)* कन्फ़ॉर्म– to comply in actions, behaviour, etc. with accepted standards or norms के अनुकूल बनाना, सदृश करना The young girl refused to *conform* to the local custom of marriage.

confront *(v.)* कन्फ़्रन्ट– to present or face (with something), esp in order to accuse or criticize का सामना करना The man screamed when it *confronted* a lion.

confuse *(v.)* कन्फ़्यूज़–1. to bewilder; perplex चकरा देना, उलझाना The lawyer's question *confused* the witness.

2. to fail to recognize the difference between; mistake (one thing) for another एक को दूसरा समझना Between the twins, it is usual to *confuse* one with the other.

confusion *(n.)* कन्फ़्यूशन– the act of confusing or the state of being confused, disorder; jumble गड़बड़, घपला, उलझन A great *confusion* ensued with the arrival of train.

congenial *(adj.)* कन्जीनिअल– friendly, pleasant, or agreeable अनुकूल, अनुरूप I spent a pleasant evening with him. It was a *congenial* climate.

congested *(adj.)* कन्जस्टेड– crowded to excess; overfull भीड़-भाड़ वाला, घना The roads in Old Delhi are very *congested.*

congratulate *(v.)* कनग्रैचुलेट्– to communicate pleasure, approval, or praise to (a person or persons); compliment बधाई देना He *congratulated* him on his success in the examination.

congratulation *(n.)* कनग्रैचुलेशन– the state or an instance of congratulating or being pleased with oneself बधाई, मुबारकबाद He received a telegram of *congratulations* on his birthday.

congregate *(v.)* कन्ग्रिगेट– to collect together in a body or crowd; assemble एकत्रित होना या करना The visitors *congregated* round the tourist guide.

conjecture *(v.)* कन्जेक्चर– 1. to infer or arrive at (an opinion, conclusion, etc.) from incomplete evidence अंदाज़ा लगाना Sometimes, when we *conjecture* about the weather it becomes true.

2. *(n.)* the formation of conclusions from incomplete evidence; guess अटकल, अंदाज़, अनुमान It was just a *conjecture.*

connect *(v.)* कनेक्ट–1. to relate or associate संबंध या स्थापित करना/होना He is well *connected* in Delhi's political circle.

2. to link or be linked together; join; fasten जोड़ना, मिलाना This lane *connects* two busy streets.

connection *(n.)* कनेक्शन– the act or state of connecting; union मेल-मिलाप, संबंध There is no *connection* between the two incidents.

conquer *(v.)* कॉन्कर्–1. to overcome (an enemy, army, etc.); to defeat जीतना, हराना, अधीन करना Hitler *conquered* a large part of Europe.

2. to overcome (an obstacle, feeling, desire, etc); surmount सफ़ल होना Tenzing *conquered* Mount Everest.

conquest *(n.)* कांक्वेस्ट– the act or an instance of conquering or the state of having been conquered; victory जीत, विजय It was a glorious *conquest.*

conscience *(n.)* कॉन्शन्स– the sense of right and wrong that governs a person's thoughts and actions विवेक, अंतःकरण He has a *conscience* about his unkind action.

conscientious *(adj.)* कॉनशिएनशस– involving or taking great care; painstaking; diligent ईमानदार, कर्तव्यनिष्ठ He is too *conscientious* to neglect his duties.

conscious *(n.)* कॉन्शस–1. alert and awake; not sleeping or comatose सचेतन, चेतन The victim was *conscious* to give his address to the policeman.

2. aware of one's surroundings, one's own thoughts and motivations, etc. से अभिज्ञ Are you *conscious* of the serious consequences of your deeds?

consciousness *(n.)* कॉन्शसनस– the state of being aware of and responsive to one's surroundings चेतना, होश Ajay gained *consciousness* after two hours.

consecutive *(adj.)* कन्सेक्यूटिव– following chronological sequence क्रमिक, क्रमागत She was absent for three *consecutive* days.

consent *(v.)* कन्सेन्ट– 1. to give assent or permission (to do something);

agree; accede राज़ी होना, स्वीकृति देना I felt bad that he would do such a thing without my *consent*.

2. *(n.)* acquiescence to or acceptance of something done or planned by another; permission स्वीकृति You should have your parent's *consent* for a tour to Agra.

consequence *(n.)* कॉन्सिक्वॅन्स– a result or effect of some previous occurrence परिणाम, नतीजा Often, thoughtless acts lead to serious *consequences*.

consequently *(adv.)* कॉन्सिक्वंटली– as a result or effect; therefore; hence फलतः, परिणामतः I missed the bus and *consequently* (as a result) was late for office.

conservation *(n.)* कॉन्ज़वेशन– the act or an instance of conserving or keeping from change, loss, injury, etc. संरक्षण We must take steps towards environmental *conservation*.

consider *(v.)* कन्सिडर्–1. to think carefully about or ponder on (a problem, decision, etc.); contemplate सोचना, विचार करना Please *consider* this matter carefully.

2. to judge, deem, or have as an opinion मानना, समझना I do not *consider* it an important matter.

considerable *(adj.)* कन्सिडरबल्– large enough to reckon with बहुत, काफ़ी Dhanraj has a *considerable* amount of money in the bank.

considerate *(adj.)* कन्सिडरट– thoughtful towards other people; kind विचारवान, दूसरों के प्रति चिंतनशील It was very *considerate* of you to offer to drive me home.

consist *(v.)* कन्सिस्ट– to be composed (of); be formed (of) में होना, (से, का) बना होना Our colony's welfare committee *consists* of five members.

consistent *(adj.)* कन्सिस्टन्ट– showing consistency; not self-contradictory संगत, अनुकूल She is not very *consistent* in the way she treats her students.

consolation *(n.)* कॉन्सलेशन– the act of consoling or state of being consoled; solace सांत्वना, दिलासा, तसल्ली My children were a great *consolation* for me.

console *(v.)* कॉन्सोल– to serve as a source of comfort to (someone) in disappointment, loss, sadness, etc. सांत्वना/दिलासा देना It was hard to *console* her after her dog's death.

consolidate *(v.)* कन्सॉलिडेट– to form or cause to form into a solid mass or whole; unite or be united पक्का करना, मज़बूत करना He *consolidated* his position after a new movie.

conspire *(v.)* कन्स्पाइअर्– to plan or agree on (a crime or harmful act) together in secret षड्यंत्र रचना The commander was *conspiring* against his own country.

conspiracy *(n.)* कन्स्पिरसी– a secret plan or agreement to carry out an illegal or harmful act, esp with political motivation; plot षड्यंत्र, साज़िश The commander was hatching a *conspiracy*.

constable *(n.)* कन्स्टबल्– a police officer of the lowest rank सिपाही The traffic police *constable* signalled the speeding car to stop.

constant *(adj.)* कॉन्स्टन्ट–1. fixed and invariable; unchanging नियत, स्थिर, अटल I drive my car at a *constant* speed.

constantly *(adv.)* कॉन्स्टंटली– continuously over a period of time; always बराबर, निरंतर She is *constantly* reading novels.

constipation *(n.)* कॉन्स्टिपेशन– infrequent or difficult evacuation of the bowels, with hard faeces,

क़ब्ज़, क़ब्ज़ियत He is suffering from *constipation* since last few weeks.

constitution *(n.)* कॉन्स्टिट्यूशन–1. the fundamental political principles on which a state is governed, संविधान, नियम-संग्रह Students of law have to study the Indian *Constitution.*

2. a person's state of health शरीर गठन Meena has a delicate *constitution.*

constrain *(v.)* कन्स्ट्रेन– to restrain by or as if by force; confine मजबूर करना, रोकना Lack of funds *constrained* the expansion of our business.

constraint *(n.)* कन्स्ट्रेण्ट– restriction, force or restraint जबर्दस्ती, प्रतिबंध, रोक We left that project because of financial *constraints.*

constrict *(v.)* कन्स्ट्रिक्ट– to make smaller or narrower, esp by contracting at one place संकुचित करना, सिकोड़ना Her face *constricted* with fear.

construct *(v.)* कन्स्ट्रक्ट– to put together substances or parts, esp systematically, in order to make or build (a building, bridge, etc.); assemble बनाना, निर्माण करना The company has *constructed* flats for its employees.

consult *(v.)* कन्सल्ट– to ask advice from (someone); confer with (someone) परामर्श लेना या करना The rich lady *consulted* many specialists about her illness.

consultation *(n.)* कन्सल्टेशन– a conference for discussion or the seeking of advice, esp from doctors or lawyers परामर्श, सलाह-मशविरा, राय She took the decision without her parents *consultation.*

consume *(v.)* कन्ज़्यूम– to eat or drink sth कुछ खाना या पीना He *consumed* several cups of tea.

contact *(n.)* कॉण्टैक्ट– 1. the act or state of touching physically संपर्क, स्पर्श I don't have his *contact* details.

2. *(v.)* to communicate with sb संपर्क स्थापित करना You can *contact* me at this number.

contagious *(adj.)* कन्टेजस– harbouring or spreading the causative agent of a transmissible disease संक्रामक, छूत (का) Tuberculosis is a *contagious* disease.

contain *(v.)* कण्टेन– to consist of; comprise रखना, के बराबर होना Textbooks *contain* many chapters.

contaminate *(v.)* कण्टैमिनेट– to make impure, esp by touching or mixing; pollute किसी वस्तु को दूषित कर देना The drinking water was *contaminated* with chemicals.

contemplate *(v.)* कॉण्टम्प्लेट– to think about intently and at length; consider calmly विचार/चिंतन करना I am *contemplating* taking a long leave.

contemporary *(adj.)* कण्टेम्प्ररी– belonging to the same age; living or occurring in the same period of time समकालीन, समसामयिक या वस्तु *Contemporary* trends in dress designing are very much popular.

contempt *(n.)* कन्टेम्प्ट– wilful disregard of or disrespect for अवमानना, तिरस्कार, अवज्ञा I was filled with *contempt* for the family who killed their son.

contend *(v.)* कन्टेण्ड–1. to struggle in rivalry, battle, etc. संघर्ष करना I have my own problems to *contend* with.

2. to argue earnestly; debate तर्क-वितर्क करना Several companies were *contending* for the tender.

3. to assert or maintain दावा करना The servant *contended* that he did not commit the theft.

content *(adj.)* कण्टेण्ट– mentally or emotionally satisfied with things as they are संतुष्ट, सहमत The guest was *content* with the arrangements made for him.

contented *(adj.)* कॉन्टेन्टिड– accepting one's situation or life with equanimity and satisfaction संतुष्ट एवं प्रसन्न It was a *contented* smile on her face.

contents *(v.)* कण्टेण्ट्स– all that is contained or dealt with in a discussion, piece of writing, etc. substance विषय-सूची, विषय-वस्तु It is better to go through the *contents* of the book.

contentious *(adj.)* कॉन्टेन्शस– tending to argue or quarrel विवादास्पद, झगड़ालू Their views were highly *contentious.*

contest *(n.)* कॉन्टेस्ट– a formal game or match in which two or more people, teams, etc. compete and attempt to win प्रतियोगिता, विवाद Rajendra won the first prize in the essay *contest.*

continent *(n.)* कॉन्टिनन्ट– one of the earth's large land masses महाद्वीप India is in the *continent* of Asia.

continual *(adj.)* कन्टिन्युअल– recurring frequently, esp at regular intervals लगातार, निरंतर Her *continual* interruption made him angry.

continually *(adv.)* कन्टिन्युअली– repeated frequently in the same way; regularly बारंबार, लगातार It is raining *continually.*

continue *(v.)* कन्टिन्यू– to remain or cause to remain in a particular condition, capacity, or place जारी रहना/रखना, करते रहना Many TV serials *continue* even after their 100th episodes.

continuous *(adj.)* कन्टिन्युअस– prolonged without interruption; unceasing अविराम, लगातार, निरंतर The boss was very happy with his *continuous* performance.

continuously *(adv.)* कन्टिन्युअसली– without interruption निरंतर, लगातार The labourers *continuously* worked in the suger field.

contort *(v.)* कनटॉर्ट– to twist or bend severely out of place or shape, esp in a strained manner मरोड़ना, ऐंठना, टेढ़ा करना Her face was *contorted* with pain.

contract *(n.)* कॉन्ट्रैक्ट– 1. a formal agreement between two or more parties ठेका, संविदा, इक़रारनामा The two friends entered into a *contract* to set up a company.
2. *(v.)* to make or become smaller, narrower, shorter, etc. सिकुड़ना, संकुचित होना Metals *contract* as they grow colder.

contraction *(n.)* कॉन्ट्रैक्शन– an instance of contracting or the state of being contracted सिकुड़न, संकुचन की प्रतिक्रिया, संक्षिप्तीकरण The *contraction* of his muscle was worth-seeing.

contractor *(n.)* कॉन्ट्रैक्टर– a person or firm that contracts to supply materials or labour, esp for building ठेकेदार Some firms prefer to give their various jobs to *contractors.*

contradict *(v.)* कॉन्ट्रडिक्ट– to affirm the opposite of (a proposition, statement, etc) खण्डन करना, विरोधी होना The minister *contradicted* the statement attributed to him by the press.

contradiction *(n.)* कॉन्ट्रडिक्शन– the act of going against; opposition; denial खण्डन, विरोध, अंतर्विरोध There was a *contradiction* between them.

contrary *(adj.)* कॉन्ट्ररी–1. opposed in nature, position, etc. विरुद्ध, विपरीत, प्रतिकूल What Ram had done was *contrary* to the rules of his company.
2. in an opposite or unexpected way के विपरीत, के विरुद्ध *Contrary* to my expectations, Ramesh declined my invitation.

contrast *(n.)* कॉन्ट्रास्ट– 1. distinction or emphasis of difference by comparison of opposite or dissimilar things, qualities, etc. विषमता, विरोध There is a remarkable *contrast* between the looks of both.

2. *(v.)* to distinguish or be distinguished by comparison of unlike or opposite qualities भेद दिखलाना Bright lights *contrasted* beautifully with the dark night.

contribute *(v.)* कॉन्ट्रिब्यूट–1. to give (support, money, etc.) for a common purpose or fund चन्दा देना, अंशदान करना People *contributed* generously to the flood relief fund.

2. to write (articles) for a publication सहयोग या लेख देना I *contribute* articles to many journals.

contribution *(n.)* कॉन्ट्रिब्यूशन– something contributed, such as money or ideas योगदान, अंशदान Gandhiji's *contribution* for freedom will be remembered.

contrived *(adj.)* कन्ट्राइव्ड– obviously planned, artificial, or lacking in spontaneity; forced; unnatural अविश्वसनीय The happy ending of the movie seemed *contrived*.

control *(n.)* कन्ट्रोल–1. power to direct or determine नियंत्रण, क़ाबू The truck suddenly got out of *control*.

2. a means of regulation or restraint; curb; check नियंत्रित The police brought the law and order situation in the riot-torn city under *control*.

3. *(v.)* to command, direct, or rule वश में रखना, नियंत्रण में करना The jockey *controlled* the untamed horse skilfully.

controversy *(n.)* कॉन्ट्रॉवर्सि– dispute, argument, or debate, esp one concerning a matter about which there is strong disagreement विवाद, वाद-विवाद There was a bitter *controversy* before they agreed.

convenient *(adj.)* कन्वीनिअन्ट– suitable for one's purpose or needs; opportune सुविधाजनक, आरामदेह When will it be *convenient* to you to come to my place?

conventional *(adj.)* कन्वेन्शनल– following the accepted customs and proprieties, esp in a way that lacks originality परंपरागत, रूढ़िगत I never liked the *conventional* 9 to 5 job.

conversant *(adj.)* कन्वर्सण्ट– experienced (in), familiar (with), or acquainted (with) जानकार, सुपरिचित We should be fully *conversant* with the company's policies.

conversation *(n.)* कॉन्वसेशन– the interchange through speech of information, ideas, etc. spoken communication वार्तालाप, बातचीत, संवाद Geeta had a long *conversation* with her friend over the phone.

convert *(v.)* कन्वर्ट– 1. to change or adapt the form, character, or function of; transform परिवर्तित करना Her very presence *converted* a dull party into a lively one.

2. *(n.)* a person who has been converted to another belief, religion, etc. धर्मांतरित व्यक्ति After reading so many books on Islam, I almost feel like a *convert* now.

convey *(v.)* कन्वे– to communicate (a message, information, etc.) बतलाना, सूचित करना Did you *convey* my message to Ram?

conveyance *(n.)* कनवेअन्स– a means of transport वाहन, सवारी I go to office in my own *conveyance*.

convict *(n.)* कन्विक्ट– 1. a person found guilty of an offence against the law, अपराधी, दोषी The *convict* was arrested soon.

2. *(v.)* to pronounce (someone) guilty of an offence दोषी ठहराना He was *convicted* of a theft.

conviction *(n.)* कन्विक्शन– a fixed or firmly held belief, opinion, etc. पक्का विश्वास It was with great *conviction* that I contacted him.

convince *(v.)* कन्विन्स– to make (someone) agree, understand, or realize the truth or validity of something; persuade मनवाना, स्वीकार कराना The judge was *convinced* of the guilt of the accused.

convivial *(adj.)* कन्विवअल– sociable; jovial or festive मिलनसार, प्रफुल्ल I enjoy in his *convivial* company.

convulse *(v.)* कनवल्स– to shake or agitate violently (शरीर को अचानक ज़ोर से) झकझोर देना, हिला देना, मरोड़ना Ram was *convulsed* with pain.

cook *(v.)* कुक– 1. to prepare (food) पकाना, भोजन बनाना Sita's mother *cooks* very tasty food.

2. *(n.)* a person who prepares food for eating, esp as an occupation रसोइया, बावर्ची She is an excellent *cook.*

cooking *(n.)* कुकिंग– the process of preparing food by heating खाना बनाने की क्रिया Her roommate knows *cooking* at a very young age.

cool *(adj.)* कूल–1. moderately cold, neither warm nor cold शीतल, ठण्डा The weather became quite *cool* after the rain.

2. calm, unexcited शांत, धीर Arun's behaviour is always *cool* and composed.

cooperate *(v.)* कोऑपरेट– to work or act together; to be helpful मिलकर काम करना, सहयोग देना All the villagers *cooperated* in building the village school.

cooperative *(adj.)* कोऑपरेटिव– willing to cooperate; helpful मिलकर किया गया, सहकारी Asim is a very *cooperative* boy.

coordinate *(v.)* कोऑर्डिनेट– to work or act together efficiently मिलकर काम करना I'll have to *coordinate* with her to get this project completed.

cope *(v.)* कोप– to deal successfully with or handle a situation; manage कठिन स्थिति से सफलतापूर्वक निपटना It's difficult to *cope* with the ever-changing technology.

copy *(n.)* कॉपि– 1. an imitation or reproduction of an original नक़ल, प्रतिकृति, प्रतिलिपि Usha asked for a *copy* of Sita's picture in the bridal make-up.

2. *(v.)* to make a copy or reproduction of (an original) नक़ल/अनुकरण करना I *copied* down some booksellers' phone numbers from the directory.

copious *(adj.)* कोपिअस– abundant; extensive in quantity भरपूर मात्रा में, प्रचुर Some plants need *copious* sunshine.

cord *(n.)* कॉर्ड्– string or thin rope made of several twisted strands रस्सी, डोरी He tied his bedding with a *cord.*

cordial *(adj.)* कॉर्डिअल– warm and friendly मैत्रीपूर्ण, हार्दिक I have a *cordial* relationship with her.

core *(n.)* कोर्– central or most important part of something बीजकोष, सारभाग, अभ्यन्तर One must first understand the *core* of a problem to solve it.

cork *(n.)* कॉर्क– the thick light porous outer bark of the cork oak, used widely as an insulator and for stoppers for bottles, casks, etc. डाट, डट्टा, कॉर्क He closed the bottle with a *cork.*

corn *(n.)* कॉर्न्– any of various cereal plants, अनाज, धान्य The farmers were busy harvesting the *corn.*

corny *(adj.)* कॉर्नि– trite or banal घिसा-पिटा, बहुत मामूली, पिटा-पिटाया Sofia made a *corny* joke.

corner *(n.)* कॉर्नर्–1. the place where two streets meet नुक्कड़ The chemist's shop at the street *corner* had the entrance from two sides.

2. the place, position, or angle formed by the meeting of two converging lines or surfaces कोना Old papers were stacked in a *corner* of the room.

3. *(v.)* to manoeuvre (a person or animal) into a position from which escape is difficult or impossible घेरना, घेर लेना The cat *cornered* the mouse and killed it.

corporal *(adj.)* कॉर्पूरल– of or relating to the body; bodily शारीरिक, दैहिक Gandhiji was against *corporal* punishment.

corporate *(adj.)* कार्पोरेट– forming a corporation; incorporated निगम से संबंधित, संगठित The BBC is a *corporate* body.

corpse *(n.)* कॉर्प्स– a dead human body, cadaver शव, लाश He took away the unclaimed *corpse* lying on the roadside.

correct *(v.)* करेक्ट– 1. to make free from errors ठीक करना, सही करना Please *correct* all these mistakes.

2. *(adj.)* free from error; true; accurate शुद्ध, सही, ठीक Only Ramesh gave the *correct* answer.

correlate *(v.)* कॉरलेट– to place or be placed in a mutual, complementary, or reciprocal relationship परस्पर संबंध होना Her decision in this issue does not *correlate* with mine.

correspondence *(n.)* कॉरसपॉण्डन्स– communication by the exchange of letters पत्र-व्यवहार *Correspondence* plays a significant role in business dealings.

corridor *(n.)* कॉरिडोर्– a hallway or passage connecting parts of a building गलियारा The building had a long *corridor* leading to the servants quarter.

corrupt *(adj.)* करप्ट– 1. lacking in integrity; open to or involving bribery or other dishonest practices भ्रष्ट, बेईमान *Corrupt* officers have spoiled the image of police department.

2. *(v.)* to become or cause to become dishonest or disloyal भ्रष्ट करना या बनना, बेईमान बनाना There are few who are not *corrupted* by money and power.

corruption *(n.)* करप्शन– the act of corrupting or state of being corrupt भ्रष्टाचार *Corruption* has spread like a disease in India.

cosmetic *(adj.)* कॉज़्मेटिक– 1. serving or designed to beautify the body, कांतिवर्धक She did *cosmetic* surgery last month.

2. *(n.)* any preparation designed with the intention of beautifying the body शृंगार का सामान, अंगराग I avoid using *cosmetics*.

cost *(v.)* कॉस्ट– 1. to be obtained or obtainable in exchange for (money or something equivalent); be priced at दाम लगाना, ख़र्च होना How much does this book *cost*?

2. *(n.)* the price paid or required for acquiring, producing, or maintaining something क़ीमत, मूल्य For job interview, you must reach in time at all *costs*.

costly *(adj.)* कॉस्टलि– of great price or value; expensive क़ीमती, महंगी A necklace of diamonds is very *costly* (expensive).

costume *(n.)* कॉस्ट्यूम– a complete style of dressing, including all the clothes, accessories, etc. worn at one time, as in a particular country or period; dress पोशाक This *costume* suits your role well.

cosy *(adj.)* कोजी– warm and snug आरामदेह Homeless people dreamed of a *cosy* home.

cot *(n.)* कॉट– light portable bed खाट, चारपाई The child was sleeping on the *cot*.

cottage *(n.)* कॉटेज– a small simple house, esp in a rural area झोंपड़ी, कुटीर The poor family lived in a *cottage* outside the town.

cotton *(n.)* कॉटन– soft, white fibrous substance कपास, रूई, सूती कपड़ा *Cotton* clothes are the best in a hot country like India.

couch *(n.)* काउच– a piece of upholstered furniture, usually having a back and armrests, for seating more than one person बाजुओं वाली लम्बी आरामदेह कुर्सी, सोफ़ा He is sitting on a *couch* and watching TV.

cough *(n.)* कॉफ़– 1. a condition of the lungs or throat that causes frequent coughing खांसी He was suffering from cold and *cough.*

2. *(v.)* to expel air or solid matter from the lungs abruptly and explosively through the partially closed vocal chords खांसना The patient *coughed* constantly.

council *(n.)* काउन्सल– an assembly of people meeting for discussion, consultation, etc. परिषद, समिति, सभा Our association has a General *Council* and a Committee.

counsel *(v.)* काउनसल– 1. to give advice or guidance to सलाह/परामर्श देना She *counsels* drug addicts as she is a psychiatrist.

2. *(n.)* advice or guidance on conduct, behaviour, etc. सलाह, परामर्श You must listen to the *counsel* for the defence.

count *(n.)* काउंट–1. the number reached by counting; sum गिनती, गणना The little child was taught to *count.*

2. notice; regard; account अभियोग का विषय On what *count* was he charged?

3. *(v.)* to add up or check (each unit in a collection) in order to ascertain the sum; to enumerate गणना करना The teacher *counted* the papers before distributing them.

4. *(n.)* to have a certain specified value or importance काउंट/(सामंत) His uncle was Polish *Count.*

countenance *(n.)* काउन्टनन्स–1. the face, esp when considered as expressing a person's character or mood मुखड़ा, चेहरा, मुखाकृति She has a pleasant *countenance.*

2. *(v.)* to support , to consent समर्थन/अनुमोदन करना His boss will never give her *countenance* to such a plan.

counter *(n.)* काउन्टर्– a horizontal surface, as in a shop or bank, over which business is transacted काउन्टर, पटल People queued up before the cashier's *counter.*

counter-attack *(n.)* काउंटर-अटैक– an attack in response to an attack जवाबी हमला, प्रत्याक्रमण Indian forces thought to *counter-attack* the enemy.

countless *(adj.)* काउन्टलस– innumerable; myriad अनगिनत, अंसख्य The function was attended by *countless* people.

country *(n.)* कण्ट्री– a territory distinguished by its people, culture, language, geography, etc. देश, प्रदेश India is a very big *country.*

couple *(n.)* कपल–1. two people considered as a pair, वर-वधु, दम्पत्ति The old man blessed the newly married *couple.*

2. two person or things that are seen together or associated जोड़ा, युगल Please give me a *couple* of oranges.

coupon *(n.)* कूपॅन– a detachable slip usable as a commercial order form कूपन The boys sold *coupons* for the school fete.

courage *(n.)* करेज्– the power or quality of dealing with or facing danger, fear, pain, etc. साहस, हिम्मत The soldier was awarded a medal for his extraordinary *courage.*

courier *(n.)* कुरिअर्– a special messenger, esp one carrying diplomatic correspondence कुरिअर, संदेशवाहक I'll send you the documents by *courier.*

course *(n.)* कॉर्स–1. a route or direction followed पथ, मार्ग The river changed its *course* during the flood.

2. a prescribed number of lessons, lectures, etc. in an educational curriculum पाठ्यक्रम, विषय Have you completed your *course* for the examination?

court *(n.)* कोर्ट–1. the room or building in which such a tribunal sits to adjudicate in civil, criminal, military, or ecclesiastical matters अदालत, न्यायालय The culprit was produced in a *court* of law.

2. a mansion or country house राजदरबार, राजसभा The noblemen took their appointed places in the royal *court*.

3. *(v.)* to attempt to gain the love of (someone); woo चाहना, पीछे लगना, प्रेम जताना, लुभाना The Satyagrahis *courted* arrest.

courteous *(adj.)* कर्टिअस–1. polite and considerate in manner विनम्र, भद्र His behaviour is very *courteous*.

courtesy *(n.)* कर्टसी–1. politeness; good manners शिष्टाचार, भद्रता *Courtesy* costs nothing.

2. favour or consent सौजन्य This documentry is presented by the *courtesy* of Channel x.

court martial *(n.)* कोर्ट-मॉशल– a military court that tries persons subject to military law फ़ौजी अदालत His case will be heard by a *court martial*.

courtship *(n.)* कोर्टशिप– the act, period, or art of seeking the love of someone with intent to marry विवाहपूर्व प्रेम-संबंध After a long *courtship* they got married.

courtyard *(n.)* कॉर्टयार्ड– an open area of ground surrounded by walls or buildings आँगन, प्रांगण The children were playing in the *courtyard*.

cousin *(n.)* कज़न्– the child of one's aunt or uncle चचेरा, फुफेरा, ममेरा, मौसेरा भाई या बहन I visited my *cousin* in Mumbai last week.

covenant *(v.)* कवनन्ट– to give (one's) word लिखित वचन देना All profits are *covenanted* to local charity.

cover *(v.)* कवर्– 1. to provide with a covering; clothe ढकना, आच्छादित करना The mother *covered* her sleeping child with a blanket.

2. *(n.)* anything that covers, spreads over, protects, or conceals आवरण, आच्छादन The thief approached the house under the *cover* of darkness.

coverage *(n.)* कवरेज– the amount and quality of reporting or analysis given to a particular subject or event समाचारों का घटना-विवरण The *coverage* of election reports on TV was excellent.

covert *(adj.)* कवर्ट्– concealed or secret छिपा हुआ, गुप्त The *covert* operations of intelligence was carried out.

covetous *(adj.)* कवटस– having a strong desire for the possession of something लालची, लोभी, लोलुप Rohan has *covetous* plans to grab his father's wealth.

cow *(n.)* काउ– the mature female of any species of cattle, esp domesticated cattle गाय *Cow's* milk is good for babies.

coward *(n.)* कॉवर्ड्– a person who shrinks from or avoids danger, pain, or difficulty कायर, डरपोक A *coward* cannot be a soldier.

cowardice *(n.)* कॉवर्ड्इस– lack of courage in facing danger, pain, or difficulty कायरता, डरपोकपन He was accused of *cowardice*.

cowl *(n.)* काउल– a hood, esp a loose one टोप, शिरोवेष्टन They cover their head with *cowl* and go to pray.

coy *(adj.)* काई– shy; modest शर्मीला, लज्जाशील, संकोची She lifted her head a little and gave him a *coy* smile.

crack *(n.)* क्रैक–1. a break or fracture without complete separation of the two parts दरक, दरार Many *cracks* appeared in the building following the earthquake.

2. a sudden sharp noise कड़क, चटाका The *crack* of a gun startled everybody in the market.

3. *(v.)* to make or cause to make a sudden sharp sound चटकना The egg *cracked* and the chick came out.

cracked *(adj.)* क्रैक्ड– damaged by cracking चटका/फूटा हुआ The *cracked* cup should be discarded.

crackdown *(n.)* क्रैकडाउन– severe action taken to restrict the crime अपराध रोकने की कार्रवाई Some people have been arrested in a police *crackdown.*

crackle *(v.)* क्रैकल– to make or cause to make a series of slight sharp noises चटचटाना, चरचराना The TV started to *crackle* and then stopped.

cradle *(n.)* क्रेडल–1. a baby's bed with enclosed sides, often with a hood and rockers पालना She put her baby in the *cradle.*

2. a place where something originates or is nurtured during its early life उद्गम India is the *cradle* of ancient civilisations.

craft *(n.)* क्राफ़्ट–1. skill or ability, esp in handiwork कारीगरी, शिल्प-कौशल Wood carving is a *craft* of skill.

2. a single vessel, aircraft, or spacecraft जलयान, वायुयान The *craft* took off on schedule.

crafty *(adj.)* क्राफ़्टी– skilled in deception; shrewd; cunning धूर्त, चालाक, चालबाज़ Never trust a *crafty* person.

craggy *(adj.)* क्रेगि– having many crags चट्टानी, पथरीला There were lot of *craggy* rocks on the beach of Mumbai.

cram *(v.)* क्रैम–1. to force (people, material, etc.) into (a room, container, etc.) with more than it can hold; stuff ठूंसना She *crammed* all her cosmetics in a small bag.

2. to study or cause to study (facts, etc.), esp for an examination, by hastily memorizing रटना I *crammed* the whole essay for the exams.

crammed *(adj.)* क्रैम्ड– completly filled ठसाठस भरा The bus was *crammed* with passengers.

cramp *(n.)* क्रैम्प– a painful involuntary contraction of a muscle, typically caused by overexertion, heat, or chill ऐंठन, मरोड़ I had terrible *cramps* in my stomach last night.

cramped *(adj.)* क्रैम्प्ड– closed in; restricted ठसाठस भरा होना The room was too *cramped* to accommodate more people.

crane *(n.)* क्रेन–1. a device for lifting and moving heavy objects भारी वजन उठाने वाली मशीन, क्रेन The car was picked up by a *crane.*

2. any large long-necked long-legged wading bird सारस I saw two *cranes* near the lake.

3. *(v.)* to stretch out (esp the neck), as to see over other people's heads गरदन बाहर निकालना She *craned* her neck out of the window to see the weather.

crank *(n.)* क्रैंक– an eccentric or odd person, esp someone who stubbornly maintains unusual views सनकी व्यक्ति, झक्की Her husband is such a *crank.*

cranny *(n.)* क्रैनि– a narrow opening, as in a wall or rock face; दीवार आदि में छोटा-सा छेद, दरार There is a *cranny* in my living room.

crap *(n.)* क्रैप– nonsense बकवास My mother got fed up with the *crap* of my sister.

crash *(n.)* क्रैश–1. an act or instance of breaking and falling to pieces धमाका, धड़ाका The building came down with a *crash.*

2. *(v.)* to move or cause to move violently or noisily धमाके से टक्कर खाना या मारना The motor-car *crashed* against a wall.

3. *(adj.)* requiring or using intensive effort and all possible resources in order to accomplish something quickly लघु अवधि में किया गया She joined a *crash* course in cooking.

crass *(adj.)* क्रैस– stupid; gross अत्यंत मूर्ख, ठस दिमाग़ वाला Don't waste my time on *crass* questioning.

crate *(v.)* क्रेट– to pack or place in a crate पेटी में बांधना The set of glasses has been *crated* safely.

crater *(n.)* क्रेटर– the bowl-shaped opening at the top or side of a volcano or top of a geyser through which lava and gases are emitted ज्वालामुखी का मुंह, गह्वर, गड्ढा A big *crater* can be seen at the top of the volcano.

crave *(v.)* क्रेव– to desire intensely; long (for) लालायित होना I am *craving* for a chocolate since morning.

crawl *(v.)* क्रॉल– to move slowly, either by dragging the body along the ground or on the hands and knees रेंगना The little baby *crawls* on its hands and feet.

crazy *(adj.)* क्रेज़ी– insane पागल, सनकी Sameer is *crazy* about watching cricket match.

creak *(v.)* क्रीक– to make or cause to make a harsh squeaking sound चरचराना, चरमराना I have wooden staircase in my old house which *creaks*.

creaky *(adj.)* क्रीकी– harsh squeaking sound चरमराता हुआ I have a *creaky* staircase in my house.

cream *(n.)* क्रीम– the fatty part of milk, which rises to the top if the milk is allowed to stand मलाई, क्रीम I like coffee with *cream*.

creamy *(adj.)* क्रीमी– resembling cream in colour, taste, or consistency मलाईदार, Reema has a glowy & *creamy* skin.

crease *(n.)* क्रीज़– 1. a line or mark produced by folding, pressing, or wrinkling सिलवट The sari was full of *creases*.

2. *(v.)* to make or become wrinkled or furrowed सिलवटें पड़ना She *creased* the paper in the middle.

create *(v.)* क्रिएट– to cause to come into existence उत्पन्न करना, बनाना God *created* the world.

creation *(n.)* क्रिएशन– something that has been brought into existence or created, सृजन, रचना, उत्पत्ति *Creation* of a new government brought a drastic change.

creative *(adj.)* क्रिएटिव– having the ability to create रचनात्मक, मौलिक She is so *creative* in her field.

creativity *(n.)* क्रिएटिवटि– a creative person, esp one who devises advertising campaigns सृजन-क्षमता, रचनात्मकता The teacher encouraged the *creativity* of the students.

creature *(n.)* क्रीचर– a living being, esp an animal जीव, प्राणी All living things are God's *creatures*.

credibility *(n.)* क्रेडबिलटी– the quality of being believed or trusted विश्वसनीयता Sohan had lost all the *credibility*.

credible *(adj.)* क्रेडब्ल– capable of being believed विश्वसनीय It was hardly *credible* that India lost a this match.

credit *(n.)* क्रेडिट–1. commendation or approval, as for an act or quality गौरव He passed the examination with *credit*.

2. on the promise of payment at a future time उधार, ऋण Some shopkeepers give no *credit*.

3. the quality of being believable or trustworthy विश्वास Nobody placed *credit* in Rahul's story.

4. *(v.)* to ascribe (to); give credit (for) श्रेय देना, मानना Only the brave are *credited* with success.

creditable *(adj.)* क्रेडिटेबल– deserving credit, honour, etc. praiseworthy प्रशंसा के योग्य, श्रेयस्कर They gave a very *creditable* performance in the drama.

creditor *(n.)* क्रेडिटर– a person or commercial enterprise to whom money is owed लेनदार, ऋणदाता, साहूकार His *creditor* is demanding his money to be paid.

creek *(n.)* क्रीक– a narrow inlet or bay, esp of the sea छोटी नदी A *creek* flows near my uncle's house.

creep *(v.)* क्रीप– to crawl with the body near to or touching the ground रेंगना, सरकना, खिसकना The thief *crept* into the house without making a sound.

creeper *(n.)* क्रीपर्– a plant, such as the ivy or periwinkle, that grows by creeping लता, वल्लरी The wall of the garden was covered with *creepers.*

cremate *(v.)* क्रमेट– to burn up (something, esp a corpse) and reduce to ash अंतिम संस्कार करना, दाह संस्कार करना My grandfather always wanted his dead body to be *cremated* at Haridwar.

crescent *(n.)* क्रेसुन्ट– the biconcave shape of the moon in its first or last quarters बालचन्द्र, अर्धचंद्र, अर्धचन्द्राकार The *crescent* of the new moon could be seen in the clear sky.

crest *(n.)* क्रेस्ट– the top, highest point, or highest stage of something शिखा, चोटी The ship was thrown up on the *crest* of a huge wave.

crevice *(n.)* क्रेविस– a narrow fissure or crack; split; cleft दरार, तरेड़ There was a *crevice* in a wall of the fort.

crew *(n.)* क्रू– the men working on a ship, boat, aircraft, etc. कर्मीदल, मल्लाहों का जत्था The plane has a *crew* of six.

crib *(n.)* क्रिब– a fodder rack or manger भूसा रखने की नांद, टोकरी Goats usually eat its fodder from the *crib.*

crick *(n.)* क्रिक– a painful muscle spasm or cramp, esp in the neck or back ऐंठन, अकड़न (मांसपेशियों में) I got a *crick* in my neck last night.

cricket *(n.)* क्रिकिट–1. ball game of two teams of eleven players each with bats and wickets क्रिकेट, गेंद-बल्ला Indians love to watch *cricket.*

2. small brown jumping insect झींगुर I saw *crickets* flying about in the garden.

crime *(n.)* क्राइम– an act or omission prohibited and punished by law अपराध It is a *crime* to steal.

criminal *(n.)* क्रिमिनल– a person charged with and convicted of crime अपराधी, मुजरिम The *criminal* was sent to jail.

criminology *(n.)* क्रिमिनॉलजी– the scientific study of crime, criminal behaviour, law enforcement, etc. अपराध-विज्ञान She is doing research on *criminology.*

crimson *(n.)* क्रिमज़न– dark red in colour किरमिज़ी, गहरे लाल रंग का At sunset, the clouds in the west become *crimson* in colour.

crinkle *(v.)* क्रिंकल–1. to form or cause to form wrinkles, twists, or folds किसी चीज़ में सिलवटें डालना या पड़ना I *crinkled* my uniform while lying.

2. *(n.)* a wrinkle, twist, or fold झुर्री, सिकुड़न His father has *crinkles* on his face.

crippled *(n.)* क्रिपुल्ड– 1. a person who is or seems disabled or deficient in some way अपंग, विकलांग The *crippled* hobbled down the street.

2. *(v.)* to make a cripple of; disable बिगाड़ना, अपंग करना The spinner's absence *crippled* the team's bowling.

crisis *(n.)* क्राइसिस– a crucial stage or turning point in the course of something संकट, संकटावस्था She always supports me in the times of a *crisis.*

crisp *(adj.)* क्रिस्प–1. dry and brittle कुरकुरा We enjoyed the *crisp* potato chips with tea.

2. clear; sharp स्पष्ट और रूखा She gave a *crisp* reply to my question.

criterion *(n.)* क्राइटिअरिअन– a standard by which something can be judged or decided मापदंड Entrance test score is the sole *criterion* to get the admission.

critic *(n.)* क्रिटिक– a professional judge of art, music, literature, etc. आलोचक, समालोचक, समीक्षक The art *critic* of the newspaper praised the exhibition.

critical *(adj.)* क्रिटिकल–1. containing or making severe or negative judgments आलोचनात्मक, छिद्रान्वेषी Father was *critical* of his son's rude manners.

2. so seriously injured or ill as to be in danger of dying संकटपूर्ण, नाज़ुक The man was taken to the hospital in a *critical* condition.

criticism *(n.)* क्रिटिसिज़्म– the act or an instance of making an unfavourable or severe judgment, comment, etc. निंदा, आलोचना The government's new education policy came in for a lot of *criticism.*

criticize (ise) *(v.)* क्रिटिसाइज़– to judge (something) with disapproval; censure आलोचना करना The players were *criticized* for poor performance.

critique *(n.)* क्रिटिक– a critical essay or commentary, esp on artistic work समीक्षा He wrote a *critique* of capitalism.

croak *(v.)* क्रॉक– to make a low, hoarse cry टर्र-टर्र करना Frogs are *croaking* in the pond.

crockery *(n.)* क्रॉकरी– china dishes, earthen vessels, etc. collectively चीनी मिट्टी के बर्तन I have a very expensive China *crockery.*

crony *(n.)* क्रॉनि– a friend or companion यार, साथी, पक्का दोस्त Mohan spends most of his time with his *crony.*

crocodile *(n.)* क्रॉकडाइल– any large tropical reptile मगर, घड़ियाल I saw a very big *crocodile* in the zoo.

crook *(n.)* क्रुक– a dishonest person, esp a swindler or thief धोखेबाज़ *Crooks* are quick to cheat the innocent.

crooked *(adj.)* क्रूकिड–1. bent, angled or winding टेढ़ा The boy drew a *crooked* line on his slate.

2. dishonest or illegal कुटिल, धूर्त It is not good to keep company with *crooked* people.

crop *(n.)* क्रॉप–1. the produce of cultivated plants, esp cereals, vegetables, and fruit फ़सल Rain destroyed the whole *crop* of wheat.

2. *(v.)* to cut (hair, grass, etc) very short काटकर छोटा करना He *cropped* his hair very short.

3. *crop up* to appear or arise अप्रत्याशित रूप से प्रकट हो जाना A fight *cropped* up between the two neighbours.

cross *(n.)* क्रॉस–1. a structure or symbol consisting essentially of two intersecting lines or pieces at right angles to one another क्रूस, सूली Jesus Christ died on the *cross.*

2. *(v.)* to move or go across (something); पार करना We must use subways to *cross* the busy roads.

3. to cancel with a cross or with lines; delete काटना, काटा लगाना The teacher *crossed* out the wrongly spelt words.

4. *(adj.)* angry; ill-humoured; vexed अप्रसन्न, क्रुद्ध Why do you look so *cross*?

cross-examine *(v.)* क्रॉस-एग्ज़ामिन– to examine closely or relentlessly जिरह करना, बारीकी से सवाल पूछना The advocate *cross-examined* the case in the court.

cross-eyed *(n.)* क्रॉस-आइड– having one or both eyes turning inwards towards the nose भेंगा One of his son is *cross-eyed.*

crossing *(n.)* क्रॉसिंग– a place, often shown by markings, lights, or poles, where a street, railway, etc. may be crossed चौराहा, पारगमन We should always use zebra *crossing.*

cross-legged *(adv., adj.)* क्रॉस-लैग्ड– sitting with the legs bent and the knees pointing outwards पालथी मारे हुए She always sits *cross-legged* on the floor.

crossroads *(n.)* क्रॉसरोड्ज़– an area or the point at which two or more roads cross each other चौराहा, चौक You have to turn your car to the next *crossroads.*

crossword *(n.)* क्रॉसवर्ड– a puzzle in which the solver deduces words suggested by numbered clues and writes them into corresponding boxes वर्ग-पहेली I like to play *cross-words* whenever I get free time.

crouch *(v.)* क्राउच– to bend low with the limbs pulled up close together, उकड़ूँ बैठना The cat *crouched* on the ground before jumping on the mouse.

crow *(n.)* क्रो– 1. a large, black bird with a harsh cry कौआ The *crow* is a bird commonly found in India.
2. *(v.)* to utter the characteristic cry of a rooster बाँग देना Cock *crows* early in the morning.

crowd *(n.)* क्राउड– a large number of things or people gathered or considered together भीड़, जनसमूह, भीड़भाड़ A large *crowd* gathered at the airport to greet the leader.
2. *(v.)* to fill to excess; to fill by pushing into ठसाठस भर देना The journalists *crowded* around the chief minister.

crowded *(adj.)* क्राउडेड– having a large number of people भीड़ भरा In Delhi, the buses are mostly *crowded.*

crown *(n.)* क्राउन– 1. an ornamental headdress denoting sovereignty, मुकुट The king wore a glittering *crown.*
2. *(v.)* to put a crown on the head of, मुकुट पहनाना, राज्याभिषेक करना He was *crowned* as the king.

crucial *(adj.)* क्रूश्यल– involving a final or supremely important decision or event; decisive; critical निर्णायक, कठिन Deciding between the two was a *crucial* choice to make.

crucify *(v.)* क्रूसिफ़ाई– to put to death by crucifixion किसी को सूली पर लटकाना Jesus Christ was badly *crucified* on the cross by Jews.

crude *(adj.)* क्रूड– lacking taste, tact, or refinement; vulgar कच्चा, अपक्व, अशिष्ट, गंवार, उजड्ड Rohan talked in a very *crude* manner.

cruel *(adj.)* क्रूअल– causing or inflicting pain without pity क्रूर, निर्दय, निष्ठुर *Cruel* Kans put Devaki and Vasudev into prison.

cruelty *(n.)* क्रूअलटी– deliberate infliction of pain or suffering क्रूरता, निर्दयता, निष्ठुरता Never show *cruelty* to animals.

cruise *(n.)* क्रूज़– an act or instance of cruising, esp a trip by sea समुद्री यात्रा या पर्यटन We went on a *cruise* during the holidays.

crumb *(n.)* क्रम– a small fragment of bread, cake, or other baked foods टुकड़ा, कण I threw a *crumb* of bread to the dog.

crumble *(v.)* क्रम्बल– to break or be broken into crumbs or fragments टुकड़े-टुकड़े हो जाना/कर देना The old building is about to *crumble.*

crumple *(v.)* क्रम्पल– to crush or cause to be crushed so as to form wrinkles or creases दबाकर मोड़-तोड़ करना, सिलवट पड़ना या मुड़-तुड़ जाना Veena *crumpled* the letter and threw it into the dustbin.

crusade *(n.)* क्रूसेड– any holy war undertaken on behalf of a religious cause धर्मयुद्ध/जिहाद Anna Hazare is leading a moral *crusade* against corruption.

crush *(v.)* क्रश– to press, mash, or squeeze so as to injure, break, crease, etc. रौंदना, कुचलना The unfortunate cyclist was *crushed* under the bus.

crust *(n.)* क्रस्ट– the hard outer part of bread पपड़ी There was a thick *crust* on the surface of the old paint.

crutch *(n.)* क्रच– a long staff of wood or metal having a rest for the armpit, for supporting the weight of the body बैसाखी That lame man is on the *crutches* after an accident.

crux *(n.)* क्रक्स– a vital or decisive stage or point; nub सबसे महत्त्वपूर्ण अंश The Kurukshetra war forms the *crux* of Mahabharata.

cry *(v.)* क्राइ– 1. to shed tears; to weep रोना, पुकारना The little boy was *crying* for his mother.
2. *(n.)* the act or sound of crying; a shout, exclamation, scream, or wail चीख़ He gave a *cry* of surprise after seeing Suresh.

crystallize (ise) *(v.)* क्रिस्टलाइज़– to give a definite form or expression to (विचार या विश्वास आदि को) स्पष्ट और सुनिश्चित होना We *crystallized* our ideas and then proceeded to a final step.

cub *(n.)* कब– the young of certain animals, such as the lion, bear, etc. शावक The lioness in the zoo gave birth to two *cubs.*

cuckoo *(n.)* कुकू– a bird having pointed wings, a long tail पपीहा A *cuckoo* sings everyday in the morning near my house.

cucumber *(n.)* क्यूकमूबर– a creeping plant, cultivated in many forms for its edible fruit खीरा, ककड़ी We should eat lot of *cucumber* in salad.

cuddle *(v.)* कडल– to hold (another person or thing) close or (of two people, etc) to hold each other close, as for affection, comfort, or warmth; embrace; hug गले लगाना, छाती से लगाना The small children *cuddled* up to each other while playing.

cuisine *(n.)* क्विज़ीन– a style or manner of cooking खाना पकाने की विधि, पाकविद्या Indian *cuisines* are famous in the whole world.

culprit *(n.)* कल्प्रिट– a person awaiting trial, esp one who has pleaded not guilty दोषी, अपराधी The *culprit* was sent to the jail.

culminate *(v.)* कल्मिनेट– to end or cause to end, esp to reach or bring to a final or climatic stage चरम-सीमा पर पहुंचना, ऊपर तक जाना The team's efforts *culminated* in the world championship.

cultivate *(v.)* कल्टिवेट–1. to till and prepare (land or soil) for the growth of crops खेती करना, जोतना The farmer *cultivates* his land.
2. to give special attention to परिचय बढ़ाना Some people *cultivate* others to get their things done.

culture *(n.)* कल्चर– the total of the inherited ideas, beliefs, values, and knowledge, which constitute the shared bases of social action संस्कृति Our scriptures reflect the richness of the Indian *culture.*

cultured *(adj.)* कल्चर्ड– showing or having good taste, manners, upbringing and education सुसंस्कृत He belongs to a very *cultured* family.

cunning *(adj.)* कनिंग– crafty and shrewd, esp in deception; sly चालाक, धूर्त The fox is a *cunning* animal.

cup *(n.)* कप– a small open container, usually having one handle, used for drinking from प्याला, कटोरा Can I have a *cup* of tea?

curb *(v.)* क़र्ब्– to control with or as if with a curb; restrain रोकना, नियंत्रण करना Vaibhav needs to *curb* his anger.

cure *(n.)* क्युअर– 1. any course of medical therapy, esp one proved effective in combating a disease उपचार There is no *cure* for the common cold.
2. *(v.)* to get rid of (an ailment, fault, or problem); to heal निरोग करना, उपचार करना The doctor *cured* the poor man free of charge.

curiosity *(n.)* क्युअरिऑसटी– an eager desire to know; inquisitiveness जिज्ञासा, उत्सुकता, जानने की अभिलाषा To satisfy my *curiosity*, I peeped into the room.

curious *(adj.)* क्यूरिअस्–1. eager to learn; inquisitive जिज्ञासु, कुतूहली Father was *curious* to see his daughter's dance performance.
2. interesting because of oddness or novelty; strange; unexpected विलक्षण, विचित्र The archaeologists found some *curious* marks on the articles.

curl *(v.)* कर्ल– 1. to roll (something, esp hair) into coils or ringlets घुँघराला बनाना, मोड़ना Her hair *curls* naturally.
2. *(n.)* a curve or coil of hair छल्ला, घूँघर Zarah's head is full of lovely *curls*.

curly *(adj.)* कर्ली– having curls छल्लेदार, घुँघराले Zarah has *curly* hair.

current *(n.)* करन्ट–1. a steady usually natural flow धारा, प्रवाह The river flows with a swift *current*.
2. a flow of electric charge through a conductor बिजली का प्रवाह Turn off the *current* before you change the bulb.
3. a general trend or drift चालू, प्रचलित Youngsters are quick to follow the *current* trends in dressing.

curry *(n.)* करी– curry seasoning or sauce कढ़ी, सालन He is very fond of chicken *curry*.

curse *(v.)* कर्स्– 1. to utter obscenities or oaths शाप देना, कोसना My ill-natured neighbour is always *cursing* the world.
2. *(n.)* a profane or obscene expression of anger, disgust, surprise, etc. oath अभिशाप, शाप, दुर्वचन Poverty is a *curse*.

cursory *(adj.)* कर्सरी– hasty and usually superficial; quick सरसरी, जल्दबाज़ी में किया गया The teacher took a *cursory* glance at the class.

curtail *(v.)* कर्टेल– to cut short; abridge छोटा करना, कम करना, संक्षिप्त करना I have to *curtail* my expenses this year.

curtain *(n.)* कर्ट्न्– a piece of material that can be drawn across an opening or window, to shut out light or to provide privacy परदा, आवरण *Curtains* help in keeping out the summer heat.

curve *(n.)* कर्व्– a continuously bending line that has no straight parts घुमाव, मोड़, वक्र, वक्र रेखा Rahul's home is round the *curve*.

cushion *(n.)* कुशन– a bag made of cloth, leather, plastic, etc. filled with feathers, air, or other yielding substance, used for sitting on, leaning against, etc. गद्दा, तोशक I bought *cushions* for my sofa set.

custody *(n.)* कस्टडी– 1. the act of keeping safe or guarding, esp the right of guardianship of a minor अभिरक्षा The *custody* of the child was granted to the mother.

2. the state of being in prison हिरासत, हवालात After dispute, three people were taken into pulice *custody*

custom *(n.)* कस्टम– a usual or habitual practice; typical mode of behaviour रिवाज़, प्रथा Some Indian *customs* are quite old.

customs *(n.)* कस्टम्ज़– the government department that collects duty on imports or exports सीमा-शुल्क विभाग Dinesh is an officer in the *customs.*

customer *(n.)* कस्टमर्– a person who buys ग्राहक A good shopkeeper tries to please his *customers.*

cut *(v.)* कट–1. to divide or be divided with or as if with a sharp instrument काटना, कतरना Uma *cut* her finger while slicing the apple.

2. *(n.)* a stroke or incision made by cutting; gash काट, कटाव The doctor cleaned the *cut* on finger with an antiseptic lotion.

3. a piece or part cut off, टुकड़ा Please give me a *cut* of the meat.

cute *(adj.)* क्यूट– appealing or attractive, esp in a pretty way आकर्षक, मनोहर She looks *cute* with her dimpled cheeks.

cutlery *(n.)* कटलरी– implements used for eating, such as knives, forks and spoons छुरी-काँटा My friend brought good *cutlery* set from China.

cycle *(n.)* साइकल– 1. a biycle; a recurring period of time in which certain events or phenomena occur साइकिल; चक्र, कालचक्र *Cycle* of seasons is an important phenomenon of Nature.

2. *(v.)* to ride a bicycle, साइकिल चलाना He *cycles* to office every day.

cylinder *(n.)* सिलिंडर्– a solid consisting of two parallel planes bounded by identical closed curves सिलिंडर, बेलन The house caught fire when the gas *cylinder* burst.

cynic *(n.)* सिनिक्– a person who believes the worst about people or the outcome of events दोषदर्शी, निंदक Stay away from him; he is a *cynic.*

cynical *(adj.)* सिनिकल– sarcastic; mocking मानव-द्वेषी Don't be discouraged with his *cynical* remarks.

cyst *(n.)* सिस्ट– a membranous sac or cavity of abnormal character in the body, containing fluid पुटी, पूयकोष Poonam's mother got a *cyst* in her breast.

Dd

Dd *(n.)* डी–अंग्रेज़ी वर्णमाला का चौथा अक्षर The fourth letter of the English alphabet. Dehradun begins with *'D'*.

dab *(v.)* डैब– to touch lightly and quickly हाथ से थपकना, थपथपाना Deepa *dabbed* her cheeks with a powder puff.

dacoit *(n.)* डैकॉइट– a member of a gang of armed robbers डकैत *Dacoits* lived in the Chambal Valley many years ago.

dagger *(n.)* डैगर्– a short stabbing weapon with a pointed blade छुरा, कटार A collection of *daggers* was on display in the museum.

daily *(adv.)* डेली– 1. every day प्रतिदिन He was advised to take a walk *daily* in the morning.

2. *(n.)* a daily publication, esp a news-paper दैनिक अख़बार Reena is employed as a reporter in a local *daily*.

3. *(adj.)* of or occurring every day or every weekday दैनिक Exercise is an essential part of *daily* routine.

dainty *(adj.)* डेण्टी– delicate or elegant सुकुमार, रुचिकर We were all charmed by the dancer's *dainty* performance.

dairy *(n.)* डेअरि– 1. a company that supplies milk and milk products डेरी, दुग्धशाला From which *dairy* do you get your milk supply?

2. *adj.) food containing milk or milk products* दुग्ध-निर्मित *Dairy* products are a good source of calcium.

dam *(n.)* डैम्– a barrier of concrete, earth, etc. built across a river to create a body of water for a hydroelectric power station, domestic water supply, etc. बाँध I am going to visit Bhakhra *Dam*.

damage *(v.)* डैमेज्– 1. to cause damage to नुक़सान पहुँचाना You will *damage* the apples if you let them fall on the ground.

2. *(n.)* injury or harm impairing the function or condition of a person or thing क्षति, नुक़सान The storm caused a lot of *damage* to the garden.

damages *(n.)* डैमेजस– money to be paid as compensation to a person for injury, loss, etc. हरजाना, क्षतिपूर्ति They were asked to pay the *damages* for the windowpanes.

damn *(adj.)* डैम– 1. an exclamation of surprise or pleasure निंदनीय एवं क्रोधव्यंजक शब्द This is none of your *damn* business.

2. *(v.)* to condemn as bad, worthless, etc. कटु आलोचना करना, निंदा करना Satanic Verses was *damned* by many critics.

damp *(adv.)* डैम्प– slightly wet, as from dew, steam, etc. गीला, आर्द्र We shall catch a cold if we wear *damp* clothes.

damson *(n.)* डैमज़न– an edible purple fruit like a plum आलूबुख़ारा *Damson* is a healthy fruit of the summer season.

dance *(n.)* डान्स– 1. a series of rhythmic steps and movements, usually in time to music नाच, नृत्य Radha became famous after her first *dance* performance.

2. *(v.)* to move the feet and body rhythmically, esp in time to music नाच/नृत्य करना It was my pleasure to *dance* with her.

danger *(n.)* डेंजर्– the state of being vulnerable to injury, loss, or evil; risk ख़तरा, संकट Roma was seriously ill last week, but now she is out of *danger*.

dangerous *(adj.)* डेंजरस– causing danger; perilous ख़तरनाक, भयंकर Cobra is a *dangerous* snake.

dangle *(v.)* डैंगूल– to hang or cause to hang freely झूलना, झुलाना, लटकना, लटकाना The boy saw a kite *dangling* from the tree.

dare *(v.)* डेअर्– to challenge (a person to do something) as proof of courage साहस/हिम्मत करना, सामना करना How *dare* he say such a nasty thing about you!

dark *(adj.)* डार्क्–1. having little or no light अंधकारपूर्ण Are you not afraid to go out in a *dark* night?
2. not fair or blond; swarthy; brunette गहरा, साँवला Some people dye their hair to make them *dark* black.
3. *(n.)* absence of light; darkness अँधेरा, अंधकार Don't go out in the *dark.*

darkness *(n.)* डार्कनस्– without light, in dark अंधकार, अँधेरा We were sitting in a complete *darkness* when he reached.

darling *(adj.)* डार्लिंग– 1. much loved परमप्रिय I want my *darling* daughter to be a famous singer.
2. *(n.) beloved* प्रियतम, प्रेयसी It was a gift from her *darling.*

darn *(v.)* डान– to mend (a hole or a garment) with a series of crossing or interwoven stitches रफ़ू करना The man was *darning* the old shirt.

dart *(v.)* डार्ट– to move or throw swiftly and suddenly; to look at sb suddenly झपटना, चौंककर देखना she *darted* an impatient look at mother.

dash *(v.)* डैश–1. to move hastily or recklessly; rush झपटना, तेज़ दौड़ना Suresh *dashed* into my room to give me the latest news.
2. to throw sth पटक देना, फेंक देना The boat was *dashed* against a big stone.
3. *(n.)* a sudden quick movement; dart जोश, तेज़ दौड़ The waiting passengers made a *dash* for the bus.

data *(n.)* डेटा– a series of observations, measurements, or facts; information आँकड़े, सूचना संग्रह The *data* stored in the computer was lost.

database *(n.)* डेटबेस– a systematized collection of data that can be accessed immediately सूचना सामग्री Prepare a *database* of all our customers.

date *(n.)* डेट–1. a specified day of the month तारीख़, दिनांक What will be the *date* next Monday?
2. the fruit of the date palm खजूर The *dates* are commonly grown in Saudi Arabia.
3. *(v.)* to mark (a letter, coin, etc.) with the day, month, or year तारीख़ डालना, दिनांकित करना Always *date* the official letters and job applications.

> **out of date**– old fashioned पुराना, अप्रचलित This medicine is *out of date.*

> **up to date**– the present moment; modern पूर्णतया नया, आधुनिक This dress is *up to date.*

daughter *(n.)* डॉटर– a female offspring; a girl or woman in relation to her parents बेटी, पुत्री My *daughter* scored 90% in her board exams.

dawdle *(v.)* डॉडल– to be slow or lag behind मटरगश्ती करना, समय गंवाना, सुस्ती से चलना She was *dwadling* as she was so tired.

dawn *(n.)* डॉन– daybreak; sunrise प्रभात, भोर, उषाकाल The villagers usually get up at *dawn.*

day *(n.)* डे– the period of time, the calendar day दिन, दिवस I had a wonderful *day* in office today.

> **day by day**– gradually समय बीतने के साथ, दिन-ब-दिन His health is improving *day by day.*

> **day to day**– occuring each day, daily थोड़े समय के अंदर, His mood swings from *day to day.*

daydream *(n.)* डेड्रीम– a pleasant dreamlike fantasy indulged in while awake; idle reverie दिवास्वप्न Sheikh Chilli was always lost in *daydreaming.*

daylight *(n.)* डेलाइट– light from the sun सूरज की रोशनी, दिन का उजाला, दिवालोक We have to go to the temple in *daylight.*

daytime *(n.)* डेटाइम– the time between dawn and dusk; the day as distinct from evening or night दिन का समय We can meet up in the *daytime.*

daze *(n.)* डेज़– to stun or stupefy, esp by a blow or shock चकित या भौचक्का करना, सुन्न कर देना I was so *dazed* by the accident that I did not know what to do.

dazzle *(v.)* डैज़ल– 1. to blind or be blinded partially and temporarily by sudden excessive light चौंधियाना, चकाचौंध होना The sun will *dazzle* you if you look at it.

2. *(n.)* bewilderment caused by glamour, brilliance, etc. चकाचौंध The *dazzle* of money attracts everybody.

dead *(adj.)* डेड– no longer alive मृत, मरा हुआ He was *dead* in the car accident.

dead end *(n.)* डेड ऐंड– a situation in which further progress is impossible अंतिम बिंदु, (जहां से आगे न जाया जा सके), बंद गली When they reached to a *dead end,* they returned back.

deadline *(n.)* डेड्लाइन– a time limit for any activity (किसी कार्य को पूरा करने के लिए) निर्धारित अंतिम तिथि The boss was happy when we met the unrealistic *deadline.*

deadlock *(n.)* डेडलॉक– a state of affairs in which further action between two opposing forces is impossible; stalemate गतिरोध Their talks had reached a *deadlock which caused this issue.*

deadly *(adj.)* डेडलि– likely to cause death घातक, जानलेवा She is suffering from a *deadly* disease.

deaf *(adj.)* डेफ़– partially or totally unable to hear बहरा, बधिर The accident has made him *deaf* in one ear.

deafen *(v.)* डेफ़न– to make deaf, esp momentarily, as by a loud noise बहरा कर देना, शोर मचाकर कान फोड़ना The loud music of loudspeaker *deafened* us.

deal *(v.)* डील–1. to work upon संबंध रखना Ram's job is to *deal* with routine correspondence in his office.

2. to engage (in) commercially लेन-देन करना, व्यापार करना We *deal* with M/s. Pustak Mahal and we have no complaint.

3. *(n.)* quite a lot, a large quantity मात्रा, परिमाण Rats destroy a great *deal* of foodgrain.

dealer *(n.)* डीलर– a person or firm engaged in commercial purchase and sale; trader व्यापारी The *dealer* ran away after selling the property.

dealing *(n.)* डीलिंग– business transaction लेन-देन, व्यापारिक संबंध She is famous for her fair *dealing.*

dean *(n.)* डीन– the chief administrative official of a college or university faculty अध्यक्ष, संकायाध्यक्ष You need to take the permission from the *dean* for it.

dear *(adj.)* डिअर्– beloved; precious प्रिय, प्यारा Ramesh is a *dear* friend of mine.

dearly *(adv.)* डिअर्लि– very much अत्यधिक, बहुत ज़्यादा Hari loves her sister *dearly.*

dearth *(n.)* डर्थ– an inadequate amount, esp of food; scarcity अपर्याप्तता, कमी, अभाव There is a *dearth* of talented professionals in this industry.

death *(n.)* डेथ– the permanent end of all functions of life in an organism or some of its cellular components

मृत्यु, मौत *Death* of all living beings is certain.

deathly *(adj.)* डेथलि– resembling death मृत्युवश, मृत्युतुल्य There was a *deathly* silence when she entered.

death penalty *(n.)* डेथ पेनल्टी– sentence to death मृत्युदंड The terrorist is facing the *death penalty.*

debate *(n.)* डिबेट– 1. a formal discussion, as in a legislative body, in which opposing arguments are put forward विवाद, बहस I participated in the *debate* competition held last week.

2. *(v.)* to discuss (a motion), esp in a formal assembly बहस करना Stop *debating,* it's better we should work on the solution.

debilitate *(v.)* डिबिलिटेट– to make feeble; weaken कमज़ोर या निर्बल कर देना Arthritis *debilitates* the joints of the spine, hands, hips and knees.

debit *(v.)* डेबिट– to remove (money) from a customer's account बैंक के खाते से पैसे की निकासी करना The instalment of the loan was *debited* directly from my bank account.

debris *(n.)* डेब्री– fragments or remnants of something destroyed or broken; rubble मलबा Many people are feared to be buried beneath the *debris.*

debt *(n.)* डेट– something that is owed, such as money, goods, or services क़र्ज़, ऋण you will be penalized if you could not clear your *debt* in time.

decade *(n.)* डेकेड– a period of ten consecutive years दशक Bollywood has undergone a dramatic change over the past one *decade.*

decay *(v.)* डिके– 1. to decline or cause to decline gradually in health, prosperity, excellence, etc. deteriorate; waste away सड़ना, बिगड़ना Fruits *decay* fast if not kept in the refrigerator.

2. *(n.)* the process of decline, as in health, mentality, beauty, etc. क्षय, सड़न, सड़ाव Eating chocolates causes tooth *decay.*

deceitful *(adj.)* डिसीटफ़ुल– full of deceit कपटी, बहकाने वाला, धोखेबाज़, छली Natwar Lal was known for his *deceitful* behaviour.

deceive *(v.)* डिसीव्– to mislead by deliberate misrepresentation or lies ठगना, धोखा देना The cheat could not *deceive* the wise trader.

December *(n.)* डिसेम्बर– the twelfth and last month of the year, (वर्ष का बारहवां महीना) दिसंबर X-max falls in the month of *December.*

decency *(n.)* डीसनसि– conformity to the prevailing standards of propriety, morality, modesty, etc. मर्यादापन, शालीनता, अच्छा आचरण *Decency* in a person is always appreciated.

decent *(adj.)* डीसन्ट– polite or respectable शालीन, उचित, मर्यादित Your friend is a *decent* fellow.

deception *(n.)* डिसेप्शन– the act of deceiving or the state of being deceived धोखा, छल, कपट It was a deliberate *deception* by the management.

deceptive *(adj.)* डिसेप्टिव– likely or designed to deceive; misleading छलपूर्ण, भ्रामक Looks are often *deceptive.*

decide *(v.)* डिसाइड– to reach a decision निर्णय करना I couldn't *decide* whether to go to Shimla or Mumbai.

decided *(adj.)* डिसाइडिड– unmistakable सुनिश्चित, स्पष्ट, दृढ़ Please tell me your *decided* operations.

decimal *(adj.)* डेसिमल– a fraction that has a denominator of a power of ten दशमलव The figure is accurate to two *decimal* places.

decipher *(v.)* डिसाइफ़र्– to determine the meaning of (something obscure or illegible) कूटवाचन करना, गूढ़ लिपि का

अर्थ निकालना Can you *decipher the* medicine doctor has prescribed?

decision *(n.)* डिसिज़न– a judgment, conclusion, or resolution reached or given; verdict फ़ैसला, निर्णय, निश्चय The prime minister's *decision* to surprised the journalists.

decisive *(adj.)* डिसाइसिव– influential; conclusive निर्णायक, अंतिम The First Battle of Panipat was a *decisive* battle that established Mughal rule in India.

declaration *(n.)* डेकलरेशन– a formal statement or announcement; proclamation घोषणा, ऐलान The company's *declaration* of a bonus was a pleasant surprise.

declare *(v.)* डिकलेअर्–1. to make clearly known or announce officially प्रकट करना, घोषित करना, बताना Morality demands that all politicians must *declare* their assets.

2. to close an innings voluntarily before all ten wickets have fallen क्रिकेट में पारी-समाप्ति की घोषणा करना The captain *declared* the innings when the total score reached 450.

decline *(v.)* डिक्लाइन– 1. to refuse to do or accept (something), esp politely अस्वीकार करना Ramesh *declined* Rahul's invitation to dinner.

2. *(n.)* gradual deterioration or loss क्षय, ह्रास, पतन Moral values are in *decline* these days.

decode *(v.)* डिकोड– to convert (a message, text, etc.) from code into ordinary language गुप्त संदेश का अर्थ निकालना This is a secret message; we need to *decode* it.

decompose *(v.)* डीकम्पोज़– to break down (organic matter) or (of organic matter) to be broken down physically and chemically by bacterial or fungal action; to rot विघटित होना, सड़ना The body was *decomposed* when it was found in the forest.

décor *(n.)* डेकॉर्– a style or scheme of interior decoration, furnishings, etc. as in a room or house सजावट, सज्जा The interior *décor* of the building was praiseworthy.

decorate *(v.)* डेकरेट– to make more attractive by adding ornament, colour, etc. सजाना, अलंकृत करना, पदक देना, सम्मानित करना Sita has *decorated* her drawing room very beautifully.

decoration *(n.)* डेकरेशन– the act, process, or art of decorating सज्जा, सजावट, सजावट की प्रक्रिया The *decoration* of the marriage hall was worth-seeing.

decorative *(adj.)* डेकरटिव– serving to decorate or adorn; ornamental सजावटी, आलंकारिक It was a very *decorative* and beautiful glass painting.

decrease *(v.)* डिक्रीज़– to diminish or cause to diminish in size, number, strength, etc. घटना या घटाना The manager will *decrease* your pay if you do not come.

decree *(n.)* डिक्री– 1. an order or judgment of a court made after hearing a suit, सरकारी आदेश, निर्णय, डिगरी He was expelled from the services on the royal *decree.*

2. *(v.)* to order, adjudge, or ordain by decree आधिकारिक आदेश जारी करना We thought we would win the competition, but fate *decreed* otherwise.

dedicate *(v.)* डेडिकेट– to devote (oneself, one's time, etc.) wholly to a special purpose or cause समर्पित/समर्पण करना Mother Teresa *dedicated* her whole life to serving the poor.

dedicated *(adj.)* डेडिकेटिड– devoted to a particular purpose or cause समर्पित To achieve the goal we require *dediated* force.

dedication *(n.)* डेडिकेशन– complete and wholehearted devotion, esp to a career, ideal, etc. समर्पण Her *dedication* to work is praiseworthy.

deduct *(v.)* डिडक्ट– to take away or subtract (a number, quantity, part, etc.) घटाना The teacher *deducted* his marks for bad handwriting.

deed *(n.)* डीड–1. something that is done or performed; act काम, कार्य Raju has done a good *deed* by saving a drowning child.

2. a formal legal document signed, witnessed, and delivered to effect a conveyance or transfer of property or to create a legal obligation or contract दस्तावेज़ Two businessmen signed a *deed* of partnership.

deem *(v.)* डीम– to judge or consider समझना, मानना The airplane was *deemed* unsuitable for flying.

deep *(adj.)* डीप–1. extending or situated relatively far down from a surface गहरा (सतह में) Why have you dug such a *deep* hole in your garden?

2. of great intensity; extreme प्रगाढ़, गहरा (भाव में) Death of a dear son is a cause of *deep* sorrow for his parents.

3. having an intense or dark hue गहरा (रंग में) My car is *deep* blue in colour.

deepen *(v.)* डीपन– become stronger अधिक गहरा या प्रगाढ़ होना Our friendship soon *deepened* into love.

deeply *(adv.)* डीपलि– greatly, keenly गहराई से Think *deeply* before deciding to resign from your present job?

deep-rooted *(adj.)* डीप-रूटेड– firmly fixed, implanted, or held; ingrained गहरी जड़ों वाला, गहराई में जमा हुआ His fears are *deep-rooted* into his heart.

deer *(n.)* डिअर्– a hoofed grazing animal हिरन, मृग I saw a *deer* and elephant in the zoo.

defame *(v.)* डिफ़ेम– to attack the good name or reputation of; slander; libel बदनाम करना, बुराई करना, अपयश फैलाना Don't *defame* her, she is an innocent girl.

default *(n.)* डिफ़ॉल्ट– a failure to act, esp a failure to meet a financial obligation or to appear in a court of law at a time specified चूक, अनुपस्थिति They won the championship by *default.*

defeat *(n.)* डिफ़ीट– 1. the act of defeating or state of being defeated हार, पराजय The Indian cricket team suffered *defeat.*

2. *(v.)* to overcome in a contest or competition; to win a victory over हराना, विफल कर देना How could a good player like you be *defeated* so easily?

defect *(n.)* डिफ़ेक्ट– a lack of something necessary for completeness or perfection; shortcoming; deficiency कमी, त्रुटि, खराबी She has a slight *defect* in her eye.

defence *(n.)* डिफ़ेन्स–1. resistance against danger, attack, or harm; protection बचाव, रक्षा, प्रतिरक्षा US comes to India's *defence* on the issue of terrorism.

2. a plea, essay, speech, etc. in support of something; vindication; justification सफाई, रक्षा What do you want to say in your *defence*?

defend *(v.)* डिफ़ेन्ड–1. to protect (a person, place, etc.) from harm or danger; ward off an attack on रक्षा/बचाव करना Father did not *defend* his son's bad conduct in the school.

2. to say sth in support समर्थन करना How can I *defend* such behaiour?

defendant *(n.)* डिफ़ेंडन्ट– a person against whom an action or claim is brought in a court of law प्रतिवादी Asha was not having any *defendant* in a court.

defensive *(adj.)* डिफ़ेन्सिव– intended, suitable, or done for defence, as opposed to offence रक्षात्मक, सुरक्षा- America is *defensive* on the nuclear issue.

deficiency *(n.)* डिफ़िशियन्सि– a lack or insufficiency; shortage कमी, अभाव *Deficiency* of Vitamin A can cause night blindness.

deficient *(adj.)* डिफ़िशण्ट– lacking some essential; incomplete; defective अपूर्ण, त्रुटिपूर्ण Junk food is *deficient* in nutrients.

deficit *(n.)* डेफ़िसिट– the amount by which an actual sum is lower than that expected or required कमी, अभाव, घाटा The trade balance has been in *deficit* for past two years.

define *(v.)* डिफ़ाइन– to state precisely the meaning of (words, terms, etc.) किसी बात को ठीक से समझना, परिभाषित करना He had to *define* the theory of relativity.

definite *(adj.)* डेफ़िनट– clearly defined; exact; explicit निश्चित, सुस्पष्ट It is *definite* that she will not come.

definitely *(adv.)* डेफ़िनटली– in a definite manner निश्चित रूप से I shall *definitely* call you tonight.

definition *(n.)* डेफ़िनिशन– a formal and concise statement of the meaning of a word, phrase, etc. परिभाषा What is the *definition* of personality?

deform *(v.)* डिफ़ॉर्म– to make or become misshapen or distorted बिगाड़ना, विकृत करना Badly fitted shoes can *deform* our feet.

deformity *(n.)* डिफ़ॉर्मिटी– a deformed condition; disfigurement विरूपता, विकृति The doctor recorded no *deformity* in the child.

defrost *(v.)* डिफ़्रॉस्ट– to make or become free of frost or ice बर्फ़ पिघलाकर हटाना, सामान्य तापमान पर लाना *Defrost* the fridge before cleaning.

defuse *(v.)* डिफ़्यूज़– to remove the triggering device of (a bomb, etc.) बम को निष्क्रिय करना It was difficult to *defuse* the bombs.

defy *(v.)* डिफ़ाइ– to resist (a powerful person, authority, etc.) openly and boldly अवज्ञा करना, चुनौती देना An obedient son does not *defy* his parents.

degenerate *(v.)* डिजेनरेट– to become less specialized or functionally useless किसी स्थिति में गिरावट करना या आना Corruption has *degenerated* our society.

degradation *(n.)* डिग्रेडेशन– the act of degrading or the state of being degraded अवनति, निम्नीकरण Pollution is the major cause of environmental *degradation*.

degrade *(v.)* डिग्रेड– to reduce in worth, character, etc. disgrace; dishonour किसी की स्थिति को बिगाड़ना या सम्मान घटाना Growing urbanisation *degrades* the natural habitats of animals.

degree *(n.)* डिग्री–1. an academic award conferred by a university or college on successful completion of a course उपाधि Has your son taken the *degree* in Physics?
2. a stage in a scale of relative amount or intensity मात्रा, अंश I agree with you to some *degree* (to some extent).

deity *(n.)* डेअटी– a god or goddess देवता The devotee prostrated himself before the *deity*.

dejected *(adj.)* डिजेक्टिड– miserable; despondent; downhearted हताश, उदास He felt *dejected* with his marks.

delay *(v.)* डिले– 1. to put off to a later time; defer विलंब करना , देर होना/लगाना I got stuck in a jam due to which the work got *delayed*.
2. *(n.)* the act or an instance of *delaying* or being delayed देरी, देर Do your homework without *delay*.

delegate *(n.)* डेलिगेट– 1. a person chosen or elected to act for or represent another or others, esp at a conference or meeting प्रतिनिधि Some foreign *delegates* are coming next week.

2. *(v.)* to give or commit (duties, powers, etc.) to another as agent or representative; depute दायित्व सौंपना *Delegate* your work to your juniors.

delegation *(n.)* डेलिगेशन– a person or group chosen to represent another or others प्रतिनिधिमंडल *Delegation* of authority is an important principle of management.

delete *(v.)* डिलीट– to remove (something printed or written); erase; cancel; strike out लिखे शब्दों को हटाने की क्रिया, काट देना *Delete* this sentence; it is not required.

deliberate *(adj.)* डिलिबरट– intentional, planned जान-बूझकर किया हुआ It was not a *deliberate* act to break the windowpanes of her drawing room.

deliberately *(adv.)* डिलिबरटली– consciously and intentionally; on purpose जान-बूझकर, सोच-समझकर Some students *deliberately* make their teacher angry.

delicacy *(n.)* डेलिकसी– refinement of feeling, manner, or appreciation भद्रता, उत्कृष्टता It was a matter of great *delicacy.*

delicate *(adj.)* डेलिकट– 1. exquisite, fine, or subtle in quality, character, construction, etc. कोमल, सुकुमार Let us not argue over this *delicate* point.

2. easily damaged or injured; lacking robustness, esp in health; fragile बार-बार रोगी हो जाना, नाजुक (कमज़ोर) Your son's health is *delicate,* you should give him a good tonic.

delicious *(adj.)* डिलिशस– very appealing to the senses, esp to the taste or smell स्वादिष्ट, सुस्वादु One tends to overeat if food is *delicious.*

delight *(v.)* डिलाइट– 1. to please greatly हर्षित/आनन्दित होना I was *delighted* to receive the news of my son succeeding in the IAS exam.

2. *(n.)* extreme pleasure or satisfaction; joy आनन्द, हर्ष Suresh was filled with *delight* to see his old friend.

delirious *(adj.)* डिलिरिअस–1. affected with delirium बावला, उन्मादी The beggar was *delirious* and could not move properly.

2. wildly excited, esp with joy or enthusiasm खुशी से पागल, बहुत खुश Rani was *delirious* while opening her birthday gifts.

deliver *(v.)* डिलिवर्–1. to carry (goods, etc.) to a destination, esp to carry and distribute (goods, mail, etc.) to several places पहुँचाना, सौंपना The postman *delivered* a parcel to Ramesh.

2. to utter or present (a speech, oration, idea, etc.) (भाषण) देना, प्रदान करना You *delivered* your speech very well.

3. to give birth to (offspring) जन्म देना She *delivered* a healthy baby boy.

delivery *(n.)* डिलिवरी– the process of giving birth to प्रसूति, प्रसव She was very critical at the time of her *delivery.*

deluge *(n.)* डेल्यूज– a great flood of water बाढ़, जलप्रलय The village was in a great *deluge* after heavy rains.

delusion *(n.)* डिलूश़न– a mistaken or misleading opinion, idea, belief, etc. भ्रम, भ्रांति Mahesh is under the *delusion* that he is a good actor.

deluxe *(adj.)* डिलक्स– luxurious or sumptuous; of a superior kind:a deluxe hotel उच्चकोटि का, ठाठदार,

राजसी We stayed in a *deluxe* hotel of Agra.

demand *(v.)* डिमान्ड– 1. to request peremptorily or urgently मांग या दावा करना Have you *demanded* the compensation for your losses in the flood?
2. *(n.)* an urgent or peremptory requirement or request मांग, दावा This soap is not at all in *demand* these days.

demanding *(adj.)* डिमानडिंग– requiring a lot of skill, patience, etc. अत्याधिक मांग Her boss is very *demanding* at times.

demise *(n.)* डिमाइज़– death मृत्यु, निधन, देहांत The sudden *demise* of the president shocked the whole nation.

democracy *(n.)* डिमॉक्रसी– government by the people or their elected representatives लोकतंत्र India is the largest *democracy* in the world.

democratic *(adj.)* डैमॉक्रेटिक– of, characterized by, derived from, or relating to the principles of democracy, popular with or for the benefit of all लोकतांत्रिक We have a *democratic* system of government.

demolish *(v.)* डिमॉलिश– to tear down or break up (buildings, etc.) गिरा देना, नष्ट करना We decided to *demolish* the wall between our two houses.

demon *(n.)* डीमन– an evil spirit or devil राक्षस Anger is a *demon* we must fight against.

demonstrate *(v.)* डेमॉन्स्ट्रेट– to show, manifest, or prove, esp by reasoning, evidence, etc. प्रदर्शित करना, दिखाना, सिद्ध करना, स्पष्ट करना Please *demonstrate* the right way of using this machine.

demonstration *(n.)* डेमॉन्स्ट्रेशन– an explanation, display, illustration, or experiment showing how something works प्रदर्शन There was a *demonstration* against Obama in Chicago.

demoralize (ise) *(v.)* डिमॉरलाइज़– to undermine the morale of; dishearten मनोबल गिराना, उत्साह कम करना Continuous defeats *demoralized* the team.

den *(n.)* डेन– the habitat or retreat of a lion or similar wild animal; lair गुफ़ा I saw him hiding in the *den.*

denial *(n.)* डिनाइअल– a refusal to agree or comply with a statement; contradiction नकार, अस्वीकृति How do we change his *denial* to affirmation?

denounce *(v.)* डिनाउंस– to condemn openly or vehemently निंदा करना, सार्वजनिक रूप से किसी को दोषी ठहराना We should not *denounce* our government for its economic policies.

dense *(adj.)* डेन्स–1. thickly crowded or closely set घना, सघन In some *dense* forests, there is darkness throughout the day.
2. stupid; dull; obtuse मन्दबुद्धि I am sure he is not as *dense* as he looks.

density *(n.)* डेन्सिटी– the degree to which something is filled, crowded, or occupied घनत्व, सघनता There is a high *density* of wildlife in Corbet National Park.

dent *(n.)* डे'न्ट– a hollow or dip in a surface, as one made by pressure or a blow छेद, गड्ढा When did your car get this *dent*?

dentist *(n.)* डेन्टिस्ट– a person qualified to practise dentistry दन्त चिकित्सक The *dentist* looks after our teeth.

denunciation *(n.)* डिनन्सिएशन– open condemnation; censure; denouncing बुराई, निंदा, आरोप There was an angry *denunciation* of the government's policies.

deny *(v.)* डिनाइ– to declare (an assertion, statement, etc.) to be untrue इनकार करना, नकारना No one can *deny* with the fact that future is unpridictable.

depart *(v.)* डिपार्ट्– to go away; leave चले जाना, प्रस्थान करना The train *departed* at its scheduled time.

departure *(n.)* डिपार्चर– the act or an instance of departing प्रस्थान, रवानगी What is the *departure* time of your train?

department *(n.)* डिपार्टमन्ट– a specialized division of a large concern, such as a business, store, or university विभाग, क्षेत्र There was a seperate *department* of clothing.

depend *(v.)* डिपेन्ड– to rely (on) निर्भर/आश्रित Villagers *depend* on agriculture for thier livelihood.

dependant *(n.)* डिपेनडन्ट– a person who depends on another person, organization, etc. for support, aid, or sustenance, esp financial support आश्रित व्यक्ति How many *dependants* are there in your family?

dependence *(n.)* डिपेनडन्स– the state or fact of being dependent, esp for support or help निर्भरता, आश्रय His *dependence* on his son worries him.

dependent *(adj.)* depending on a person or thing for aid, support, life, etc. निर्भर, आश्रित His pay is *dependent* on how much he works and produces.

depict *(v.)* डिपिक्ट– to represent by or as by drawing, sculpture, painting, etc. delineate; portray चित्रांकन करना There was a chart *depicting* the effects of pollution.

deplete *(v.)* डिप्लीट– to use up (supplies, money, energy, etc.); reduce or exhaust कम करना, खाली करना Harmful gases are *depleting* the ozone layer.

deport *(v.)* डिपॉट– to remove (an alien) forcibly from a country; expel निर्वासित/तड़ीपार करना The country *deported* all the illegal immigrants immediately.

deposit *(v.)* डिपॉज़िट– 1. to put money into a bank account जमा करना It is safe to *deposit* the valuables in bank locker.

2. *(n.)* an instance of entrusting money or valuables to a bank or similar institution जमा, धरोहर The loan is granted only against any compulsory *deposit*.

depot *(n.)* डे'पो– a storehouse or warehouse डिपो, गोदाम, भंडार The ordnance *depot* supplies weapons to the armed forces.

depravity *(n.)* डिप्रेवटी– the state or an instance of moral corruption, wickedness चरित्रहीनता, भ्रष्टता Smitha was leading a life of *depravity.*

depress *(v.)* डिप्रेस– to lower in spirits; make gloomy; deject उदास करना Poverty and human suffering *depress* me very much.

depression *(n.)* डिप्रेशन–1. slump in business मंदी *Depression* causes unemployment.

2. without hope, feelings of inadequacy, and inability to concentrate उदासी Failure causes *depression.*

deprive *(v.)* डिप्राइव– to prevent from possessing or enjoying; dispossess (of) वंचित करना He was deprived from food that made him ill.

deprived *(adj.)* डिप्राइव्ड– lacking adequate food, shelter, education, etc. (सुविधाओं से) वंचित She came from a *deprived* section of the society.

depth *(n.)* डेप्थ– the extent, measurement, or distance downwards, backwards, or inwards गहराई Before stepping into a lake, you must be aware of its *depth.*

deputy *(n.)* डेप्युटी– a person appointed to act on behalf of or represent another उप-प्रमुख, प्रतिनिधि He was promoted to the post of *deputy* superintendent.

derelict *(adj.)* डेरलिक्ट– (esp of land or buildings) deserted or abandoned, as by an owner, occupant, etc. वीरान, उजड़ा हुआ, अप्रयुक्त The old man was living in a *derelict* house near the river.

derision *(n.)* डिरिशन– the act of deriding; mockery; scorn उपहास, हास्यप्रद His father's comment was met with *derision.*

derive *(v.)* डिराइव– to obtain by reasoning; deduce; infer व्युत्पन्न होना, से उत्पन्न होना The name of this place is *derived* from the temple of Shiva.

dermatology *(n.)* डर्मटॉलजी– the branch of medicine concerned with the skin and its diseases चर्मरोग विज्ञान, त्वचा-विज्ञान *Dermatology* is a science dealing with the skin, hair and nails.

descend *(v.)* डिसेन्ड–1. to move, pass, or go down (a hill, slope, staircase, etc.) उतरना, नीचे आना The sick old man was unable to *descend* the staircase.

2. have as ancestors से उत्पन्न होना, का वंशज होना Do you believe that man has *descended* from monkey?

descendant *(n.)* डिसेनडन्ट– a person, animal, or plant when described as descended from an individual, race, species, etc. वंशज He is a *descendants* of a royal family.

descent *(n.)* डिसेन्ट– a downward slope or inclination उतार, अवरोहण, ढलान We saw there was a gradual *descent* to the sea.

describe *(v.)* डिस्क्राइब– to give an account or representation of in words वर्णन करना, बनाना Arun *described* the accident in detail.

description *(n.)* डिस्क्रिप्शन– a statement or account that describes; representation in words वर्णन The *description* was clearly given in the book.

descriptive *(adj.)* डिस्क्रिप्टिव– characterized by or containing description; serving to describe वर्णनात्मक There is some excellent *descriptive* writing in that novels.

desert *(n.)* डेज़र्ट– 1. a region that is devoid or almost devoid of vegetation, esp because of low rainfall रेगिस्तान, मरुभूमि, मरुस्थल It's difficult to stay in a *desert* without any stock of water.

2. *(v.)* to leave or abandon (a person, place, etc.) without intending to return, esp in violation of a duty, promise, or obligation छोड़ भागना, त्याग देना We should not *desert* our friends just when they need us.

deserted *(adj.)* डिज़र्टिड– (of a place) empty वीरान, सुनसान, उजड़ा हुआ The house became *deserted* since the day people have left.

deserve *(v.)* डिज़र्व– to be entitled to or worthy of; merit पात्र/योग्य होना He *deserves* first prize for his wonderful performance.

deserving *(adj.)* डिज़र्विंग– worthy, esp of praise or reward योग्य, सुपात्र, अधिकारी I give one forth of my annual income to the *deserving* cause.

design *(n.)* डिज़ाइन– 1. a plan, sketch, or preliminary drawing आकृति, रूपरेखा I appreciated the *design* of the building.

2. *(v.)* to work out the structure or form of (something), as by making a sketch, outline, pattern, or plans किसी चीज़ की रूपरेखा बनाना He *designed* the interiors well.

designate *(v.)* डेज़िग्नेट– to give a name to; style; entitle पदनाम देना She was *designated* as the Marketing Executive.

designation *(n.)* डैज़िग्नेशन– something that designates, such as a name or distinctive mark पद, ओहदा She holds the *designation* of a Marketing Executive in the company.

designer *(n.)* डिज़ाइनर– a person who devises and executes designs, as for works of art, clothes, machines, etc. अभिकल्पक, रूपांकक, वेश-भूषाकार Rohit Bahl is a famous fashion *designer* of India.

desirable *(adj.)* डिज़ाइअरबल– worthy of desire or recommendation वांछनीय, अभीष्ट An applicant for a job must have all the *desirable* qualifications.

desire *(v.)* डिज़ायर्– 1. to wish or long for; crave; want इच्छा करना, माँगना Humans always *desire* to live a happy and peaceful life.

2. *(n.)* a wish or longing; craving चाह, इच्छा All the *desires* can't be fulfilled.

desk *(n.)* डेस्क– a piece of furniture with a writing surface and usually drawers or other compartments डेस्क, मेज़ Please clean the *desk* before I reach office.

desktop *(n.)* डेस्कूटॉप– the main screen display on a personal computer, from which windows may be opened and programs run कम्प्यूटर स्क्रीन (जिस पर संकेत अंकित होते हैं) Suddenly, all the icons vanished from my computer *desktop.*

desolate *(adj.)* डेसलट–1. uninhabited; deserted सुनसान, निर्जन It is risky to live in a *desolate* place.

2. without friends, hope, or encouragement; forlorn, wretched, or abandoned अकेला, उदास I felt so *desolated* after the fight.

despair *(v.)* डिस्पेअर– to lose or give up hope निराश होना Never let *despair* overcome you.

desperate *(adj.)* डेसपरट– extermely serious (निराशा के कारण) चिंतित, गंभीर Don't get *desperate;* keep calm.

despise *(v.)* डिस्पाइज़– to look down on with contempt; scorn तिरस्कार करना We *despise* Ravana because he was an evil man.

despite *(prep.)* डिस्पाइट– in spite of; undeterred by के बावजूद, के होने पर भी We enjoy life *despite* having very little money.

despondency *(n.)* डिस्पानडन्सी– a feeling of hopelessness and unhappiness about a seemingly insurmountable problem; dejection विषाद, निराशा, खिन्नता Life should not be spent on gloom and *despondency.*

despotic *(adj.)* डेस्पॉटिक– unfair and cruel in the exercise of power निरंकुश, अन्यायी, स्वेच्छाचारी The people revolted against the *despotic* rule.

dessert *(n.)* डिज़र्ट– the sweet, usually last course of a meal (खाने के बाद परोसी जाने वाली) मीठी चीज, दही-चीनी *Desserts* served were the best of the whole dinner.

destination *(n.)* डेस्टिनेशन– the predetermined end of a journey or voyage लक्ष्य, मंज़िल, गन्तव्य स्थान I will reach my *destination* in two days.

destiny *(n.)* डेस्टनि– the future destined for a person or thing; fate; fortune; lot क़िस्मत, भाग्य Don't curse the *destiny* for what happened.

destitute *(adj.)* डेस्टिट्यूट– lacking the means of subsistence; totally impoverished बेसहारा, दीनहीन After the death of her mother she was left completely *destitute.*

destroy *(v.)* डिस्ट्रॉइ–1. to ruin; spoil; render useless नष्ट/बर्बाद करना The children often *destroy* their books by using them carelessly.

2. to tear down or demolish; break up; raze बिगाड़ना, टुकड़े-टुकड़े करना Children should not do anything that would *destroy* their parents' confidence in them.

destruction *(n.)* डिस्ट्रक्शन– the act of destroying or state of being destroyed; demolition तोड़-फोड़, विनाश Have you seen what *destruction* an earthquake can cause?

detach *(v.)* डिटैच– to disengage and separate or remove, as by pulling; unfasten; disconnect से अलग करना, काटना He *detached* the hood from his coat and folded it.

detachment *(n.)* डिटैचमन्ट– indifference to other people or to one's surroundings; aloofness पृथक, निर्लिप्तता, अनासक्ति Umesh felt a sense of *detachment* from his friend.

detail *(n.)* डीटेल– an item or smaller part that is considered separately; particular ब्योरा, विस्तृत वर्णन Please narrate the incident in *detail.*

detailed *(adj.)* डीटेल्ड– having many details or giving careful attention to details विस्तृत, विस्तारपूर्वक Give me a *detailed* account of the incident.

detain *(n.)* डिटेन–1. to delay; hold back; stop रोकना *Detain* him in this class to polish his subject knowledge.
2. to confine or hold in custody; restrain हवालात में रखना Many fighters were *detained* in the jails during freedom struggle.

detect *(v.)* डिटेक्ट– to discover the existence or presence of (esp something likely to elude observation) पता लगाना, ढूँढ़ निकालना It was *detected* that these is some fault in the connection.

detective *(n.)* डिटेक्टिव– a police officer who investigates crimes जासूस, गुप्तचर 'Karamchand Jasoos' was a famous *detective* serial on TV.

detention *(n.)* डिटेंशन– custody or confinement, esp of a suspect awaiting trial नज़रबंदी, क़ैद, कारावास Anarkali was kept in *detention* for many weeks.

deteriorate *(v.)* डिटिअरिअरेट– to make or become worse or lower in quality, value, character, etc. depreciate स्थिति को बिगाड़ना His health started *deteriorating* after the injection was given.

determine *(v.)* डिटरमिन्– to settle or decide (an argument, question, etc.) conclusively, as by referring to an authority तय करना, निर्धारित करना My son is *determined* to become a pilot.

determination *(n.)* डिटरमिनेशन– a decision or opinion reached, rendered, or settled upon संकल्प, दृढ़निश्चय Strong *determination* is needed to succeed in life.

detest *(v.)* डिटेस्ट– to dislike intensely; loathe घृणा/नफरत करना I *detest* boastful talk.

detract *(v.)* डिट्रैक्ट– to take away a part (of); diminish घटाना या कम करना One mistake is not going to *detract* from your achievement.

detriment *(n.)* डेट्रिमेण्ट– disadvantage or damage; harm; loss हानि, नुक़सान Prem is indulged in drinking wine to the *detriment* of his health.

devastate *(v.)* डेवस्टेट– to lay waste or make desolate; ravage; destroy सर्वनाश/विध्वंस करना The nuclear bomb *devastated* Hiroshima completely.

devastated *(adj.)* डिवस्टेटेड– extremely shocked स्तब्ध, अत्यधिक परेशान, घबराया हुआ He was *devastated* when he failed in exams.

devastation *(n.)* डिवस्टेशन– severe and widespread destruction or damage तबाही, सर्वनाश The city faced a total *devastation* because of the earthquake.

develop *(v.)* डिवेलप–1. to progress or cause to progress from simple to complex stages in the growth of an individual or the evolution of a species प्रगति/विकास करना या होना Your son has *developed* into a healthy young man.

2. to come or bring into existence; generate or be generated विकसित होना/करना Amit has *developed* a liking for coffee.

3. to process (photographic material) in order to produce negatives and prints फोटो को साफ़ करने के लिए कैमरा फ़िल्म को रासायनिक पदार्थों में डालना I gave the negatives to the photographer to *develop* the pictures.

development *(n.)* डिवेलपमेण्ट– the act or process of growing, progressing, or developing प्रगति, विकास, उन्नति All of us should contribute for the *development* of our country.

deviate *(v.)* डिविएट– to differ or diverge or cause to differ or diverge, as in belief or thought मार्ग से हटाना, विचलित होना, हट जाना No one can *deviate* my attention towards my studies.

deviation *(n.)* डीविएशन– an act or result of deviating विचलन, परिवर्तन I have a *deviation* in my plan.

device *(n.)* डिवाइस– a machine or tool used for a specific task; contrivance उपाय, साधन The scientist came up with a new *device* to solve the problem.

devil *(n.)* डेवूल– the chief spirit of evil and enemy of God, often represented as the ruler of hell शैतान, राक्षस, नर-पिशाच This child is a naughty little *devil.*

devious *(adj.)* डीविअस– not sincere or candid; deceitful; underhand चालबाज़, छली, चक्करदार He played a *devious* trick with me.

devoid *(adj.)* डिवॉइड– destitute or void (of); free (from) विहीन, रहित She was *devoid* of words and did not know what to say.

devote *(v.)* डिवोट– to apply or dedicate (oneself, time, money, etc.) to some pursuit, cause, etc. दे देना, अर्पित करना One should *devote* complete attention while working.

devoted *(adj.)* डिवोटेड– feeling or demonstrating loyalty or devotion; ardent; devout निष्ठावान, ईमानदार, सच्चा The servant was *devoted* to his kind master.

devotion *(n.)* डिवोशन– strong attachment (to) or affection (for a cause, person, etc.) marked by dedicated loyalty निष्ठा, समर्पण The followers of the saint held him in great *devotion.*

devour *(v.)* डिवाउअर– to swallow or eat up greedily or voraciously निगल जाना, खा जाना Don't *devour* your food, chew it properly.

devout *(adj.)* डिवाउट– deeply religious; reverent श्रद्धालु, धर्मपरायण My grandmother is a *devout* Muslim lady.

dew *(n.)* ड्यू– drops of water condensed on a cool surface, esp at night, from vapour in the air ओस There were tiny drops of *dew* on the leaves in the morning.

dexterity *(n.)* डेक्स्टेरटी– physical, esp manual, skill or nimbleness दक्षता, महारत, चतुराई, कौशल She needs manual *dexterity* to be good at computer games.

diabetes *(n.)* डाइअबिटीज़– any of various disorders, esp diabetes mellitus, characterized by excretion of an abnormally large amount of urine मधुमेह He is a patient of *diabetes* since 5 years.

diagnose *(v.)* डाइअग्नोज़– to examine (a person or thing), as for a disease रोग की पहचान करना He was *diagnosed* for typhoid.

diagram *(n.)* डाइअग्रैम– a sketch, outline, or plan demonstrating the form or workings of something रेखाचित्र, आरेख The child drew a *diagram* of the water cycle.

dial *(n.)* डायल– 1. the face of a watch, clock, chronometer, sundial, etc.

marked with divisions representing units of time डायल (घड़ी का सीधा रुख जिस पर घड़ी के घंटे, मिनट आदि के निशान लगे होते हैं) She got the *dial* of her watch changed to a stylish one.

2. *(v.)* to establish or try to establish a telephone connection with (a subscriber or his number) by operating the dial on a telephone फोन करने के लिए नंबर मिलाना I *dialled* your number, but it was engaged.

dialect *(n.)* डाइअलेक्ट– a form of a language spoken in a particular geographical area or by members of a particular social class or occupational group बोली, उपभाषा My wife understands our servant's *dialect.*

dialogue *(n.)* डाइअलॉग–1. the lines spoken by characters in drama or fiction संवाद She forgot her *dialogues* on the stage.

2. conversation between two or more people वार्तालाप The *dialogue* solved the problem between both of them.

diamond *(n.)* डाइअमन्ड्– a colourless exceptionally hard mineral found in certain igneous rocks, used as a gemstone, हीरा The *diamond* ring looked very pretty on the bride's finger.

diarrhoea *(n.)* डाइअरिआ– frequent and copious discharge of abnormally liquid faeces दस्त, अतिसार He was suffering from *diarrhoea* and vomiting.

diary *(n.)* डाइअरि– a personal record of daily events, appointments, observations, etc. डायरी, दैनिकी Ever since my school days, I am fond of writing a *diary.*

dice *(n.)* डाइस– 1. cubes of wood, plastic, etc. each of whose sides has a different number of spots (1 to 6), used in games of chance पासा I threw the *dice* and moved five spaces ahead.

2. *(v.)* to cut (food, etc.) into small cubes छोटे टुकड़ों में काटना *Dice* the potatoes in small pieces.

dictate *(v.)* डिक्टेट–1. to say (messages, letters, speeches, etc.) aloud for mechanical recording or verbatim transcription by another person लिखाना, लिखवाना The teacher *dictated* a poem, and the students wrote it down.

2. to prescribe (commands) authoritatively हुक्म चलाना, आदेश देना You cannot befriend people if you *dictate* to them.

dictation *(n.)* डिक्टेशन– the act of dictating material to be recorded or taken down in writing श्रुतलेख Take this *dictation* and type it fast.

dictionary *(n.)* डिक्शनरी– a reference resource, in printed or electronic form, that consists of an alphabetical list of words with their meanings and parts of speech, शब्दकोश We can refer to any *dictionary* for its clear meaning.

die *(v.)* डाइ– (of an organism or its cells, organs, etc.) to cease all biological activity permanently, to stop living मरना, मर जाना Last evening, a man *died* in a car accident.

diet *(n.)* डाइअट–1. the food and drink that a person or animal regularly consumes आहार, भोजन, ख़ुराक Wheat is the staple *diet* of North Indians.

2. a specific allowance or selection of food, esp prescribed to control weight परहेज़ी ख़ुराक Rekha was *dieting* to get slim.

differ *(v.)* डिफ़र– to be at variance (with); disagree (with) अलग राय होना, भिन्न होना He *differs* with me on the issue of communalism.

difference *(n.)* डिफ़रन्स– the state or quality of being unlike भेद, फ़र्क़, अंतर

There should not be any *difference* between the two.

different *(adj.)* डिफ्रन्ट– part or completely unlike असमान, भिन्न His way of thinking is *different* from mine.

differentiate *(v.)* डिफ़रेनशिएट– to serve to distinguish between अन्तर/भेद करना It's important to *differentiate* between love and friendship.

difficult *(adj.)* डिफ़िकल्ट– not easy to do; requiring effort कठिन, मुश्किल Many consider Maths a *difficult* subject.

difficulty *(n.)* डिफ़िकल्टी– a task, problem, etc. that is hard to deal with कठिनाई, मुश्किल In modern times, life is full of *difficulties.*

diffidence *(n.)* डिफ़िडेन्स– lack of self-confidence; shyness आत्मसंदेह, संकोच She overcame with her natural *diffidence* and was more confident.

diffuse *(v.)* डिफ़्यूज़– to spread or cause to spread in all directions फैलना/फैलाना, बिखेरना His writing is *diffuse* and difficult to understand.

dig *(v.)* डिग– to form or excavate (a hole, tunnel, passage, etc.) by digging, usually with an implement or (of animals) with feet, claws, etc. खोदना, खोज निकालना Why are you *digging* a hole in your own garden?

digest *(v.)* डाइजेस्ट– 1. to subject (food) to a process of digestion पचाना, हज़म करना I cannot *digest* spicy food.
2. *(n.)* a comprehensive and systematic compilation of information or material, often condensed सार, संक्षेप Please prepare a *digest* of this article.

digestion *(n.)* डाइजेस्चन– the act or process in living organisms of breaking down ingested food material into easily absorbed and assimilated substances by the action of enzymes and other agents हाज़मा, पाचनक्रिया My brother has a very good *digestion.*

digestive *(adj.)* डाइजेसटिव– relating to, aiding, or subjecting to digestion पाचन- संबंधी My *digestive* sysytem is upset these days.

digit *(n.)* डिजिट– a finger or toe, any of the ten Arabic numerals from 0 to 9 अंक, संख्या, उंगली The number 786 contains three *digits.*

dignified *(adj.)* डिग्निफ़ाइड– characterized by dignity of manner or appearance; stately गौरवपूर्ण, प्रतिष्ठित Be *dignified* in your behaviour always.

dignity *(n.)* डिग्निटी–1. the state or quality of being worthy of honour मान-मर्यादा, गरिमा, प्रतिष्ठा We should accept the *dignity* of labour.
2. the state or quality of being worthy of honour सम्मान, महत्ता Always receive your guests with *dignity.*

digress *(v.)* डाइग्रेस– to depart from the main subject in speech or writing मुख्य विषय से भटकना Let's not *digress* from the main point of the discussion.

dilemma *(n.)* डाइलेमा– a situation necessitating a choice between two equal, esp equally undesirable, alternatives दुविधा, असमंजस I was in a *dilemma* for a week as to which company to join.

diligence *(n.)* डिलिजन्स– steady and careful application परिश्रम, कर्मिष्ठ He was appreciated for his *diligence* at work.

diligent *(adj.)* डिलिजन्ट– careful and persevering in carrying out tasks or duties परिश्रमी, कर्मिष्ठ Sarah is a *diligent* student and always stands first in the class.

diligently *(adv.)* डिलिजेण्टली– 1. carefully and with perseverance परिश्रमपूर्वक She works *diligently* in the office.

dilute *(v.)* डाइलूट– to make or become less concentrated, esp by adding water or a thinner पतला/हलका करना He *diluted* the wine with a little water.

dim *(adj.)* डिम– badly illuminated धुंधला, मंद, फीका It was difficult to find our way in the *dim* light.

dimension *(n.)* डाइमेन्शन–1. a measurement of the size of something in a particular direction, such as the length, width, height, or diameter परिमाप, माप Have you taken the *dimensions* of the room?
2. aspect आयाम, पहलू Her statement gave a new *dimension* to the case.

diminish *(v.)* डिमिनिश– to make or become smaller, fewer, or less घटाना/कम करना The rain *diminished* all the enthusiasm of the forthcoming match.

dimple *(n.)* डिम्पल– a small natural dent or crease in the flesh, esp on the cheeks or chin (मुस्कराते समय गाल में पड़ने वाला) गड्ढा When she smiles, *dimples* form in her cheeks.

din *(n.)* डिन– a loud discordant confused noise शोरगुल, हल्ला Sanjay made a great *din* with his drum.

dine *(v.)* डाइन– to eat dinner भोजन करना They *dined* in an exclusive Chinese restaurant.

dingy *(adj.)* डिंजी– dirty; discoloured मैला, कुचैला, गंदा It was such a *dingy* room.

dinner *(n.)* डिनर्– a meal taken in the evening रात्रि-भोज, भोजन Avoid taking *dinner* very late in the night.

dip *(v.)* डिप– to plunge or be plunged quickly or briefly into a liquid, esp to wet or coat डुबोना या डूबना Don't *dip* your finger in the curry.

diploma *(n.)* डिप्लोमा– a document conferring a qualification, recording success in examinations or successful completion of a course of study शैक्षिक उपाधि-पत्र, सनद She holds one *diploma* degree.

diplomacy *(n.)* डिप्लोमेसी– tact, skill, or cunning in dealing with people कूटनीति My friend handled the tricky situation with *diplomacy*.

direct *(v.)* डाइरेक्ट–1. to tell or show (someone) the way to a place मार्ग दिखाना, पथ-प्रदर्शन करना, भेजना He *directed* me to the place where I can sit for some time.
2. to give commands or orders with authority to (a person or group) निर्देशन करना, संचालन करना Gulzar *directed* the award-winning film 'Maachis'.
3. *(n.)* directly; straight सीधा Which is the *direct* route to your house?

direction *(n.)* डाइरेक्शन– the place towards which a person or thing is directed आदेश, निर्देश, रास्ता Which *direction* should I take to reach Janpath?

directly *(adv.)* डाइरेक्ट्ली– in a direct manner, at once; without delay सीधे, तुरन्त The speeding truck rammed *directly* into the stationary car.

directory *(n.)* डाइरेक्टरी– a book, arranged alphabetically or classified by trade listing names, addresses, telephone numbers, etc. of individuals or firms निर्देशिका The telephone *directory* is updated every year.

dirt *(n.)* डर्ट– any unclean substance, such as mud, dust, excrement, etc. filth धूल, मिट्टी, गंदगी I saw the *dirt* on my car.

dirty *(adj.)* डर्टी– covered or marked with dirt; filthy गन्दा, मैला, नीच, कुत्सित Please wash your *dirty* hands before sitting down to eat.

disabled *(n.)* डिसेबूल्ड– 1. lacking one or more physical powers, such as the ability to walk or to coordinate one's movements, अपंग The college has a separate section for the *disabled.*

2. *(v.)* to make ineffective, unfit, or incapable, as by crippling अपंग हो जाना, विकलांग कर देना The accident *disabled* his arm.

disadvantage *(n.)* डिसॅएडवान्टिज– an unfavourable circumstance, state of affairs, thing, person, etc. असुविधा, हानि, घाटा It is a *disadvantange* if you do not hold any degree.

disagree *(v.)* डिसग्री– to dissent in opinion (from another person) or dispute (about an idea, fact, etc.) असहमत होना I *disagree* with you in this regard.

disappear *(v.)* डिसअपिअर्– to cease to be visible; vanish लुप्त/गायब हो जाना I searched for him, but he *disappeared* in the crowd.

disappoint *(v.)* डिस्अपॉइन्ट– to fail to meet the expectations, hopes, desires, or standards of; let down निराश करना या होना He was *dissapointed* when he lost his job.

disappointing *(adj.)* डिसअपॉइंटिंग– failing to meet one's expectations, hopes, desires, or standards नाउम्मीदी, निराशापूर्ण Your work is *disappointing.* I think you could do better.

disappointment *(n.)* डिसअपॉइंटमन्ट– the act of disappointing or the state of being *disappointed* हताशा, निराशा He was filled with *disappointment* after the incident.

disapprove *(v.)* डिसअप्रूव– to consider wrong, bad, etc. नापसंद करना, अनुचित समझना I strongly *disapproved* of giving alms to beggars.

disarmament *(n.)* डिसआर्मामंट– he reduction of offensive or defensive fighting capability, as by a nation निरस्त्रीकरण The *disarmament* nation agreed to get rid of all their nuclear weapons of war.

disaster *(n.)* डिज़ास्टर्– an occurrence that causes great distress or destruction दुर्घटना, घोर विपत्ति या संकट Sixty persons were killed in the train *disaster.*

disbelief *(n.)* डिसबिलीफ़– refusal or reluctance to believe अविश्वास She shook her head in *disbelief.*

discharge *(v.)* डिस्चार्ज–1. to dismiss from or relieve of duty, office, employment, etc. हटा देना, बरख़ास्त करना He was *discharged* from his job when he din't submitted his report.

2. to release or allow to go (अस्पताल या जेल से) छुट्टी देना, रिहा करना, मुक्त करना Asha was *discharged* from the hospital after 3 days.

3. to perform (the duties of) or meet (the demands of an office, obligation, etc.) निबाहना, अपना काम ठीक-ठाक करना I will *discharge* my duties to the best of my abilities.

disciple *(n.)* डिसाइपल– a follower of the doctrines of a teacher or a school of thought चेला, शिष्य, अनुयायी Ananda was the most loved *disciple* of Gautam Buddha.

discipline *(n.)* डिसिप्लिन– training or conditions imposed for the improvement of physical powers, self-control, etc. अनुशासन Maintaining *discipline* at the work place is very important.

disclose *(v.)* डिस्क्लोज़– to make (information) known प्रकट करना/ अनावृत करना I tried hard, but she did not *disclose* the secret.

discolour *(v.)* डिस्कलर– to change or cause to change in colour; fade or stain बदरंग हो जाना The season of autumn *discoloured* the leaves.

discomfort *(n.)* डिस्कम्फ़र्ट– an inconvenience, distress, or mild pain कष्ट, तकलीफ़, असुविधा, बेचैनी His sudden arrival caused me considerable *discomfort.*

disconnect *(v.)* डिसकनेक्ट– to undo or break the connection of or between (something, such as a plug and a socket) काटना, अलग या पृथक करना The call got *disconnected* in the middle of the conversation.

disconsolate *(adj.)* डिस्कॉन्सलेट– sad beyond comfort; inconsolable उदास, मायूस, हताश The defeat left the team in a *disconsolate* state.

discord *(n.)* डिस्कॉर्ड– lack of agreement of harmony; strife फूट, अनबन, कलह A *discord* took place between them.

discourage *(v.)* डिस्करेज– to deprive of the will to persist in something निरुत्साहित/हतोत्साहित करना Her mother *discouraged* her from giving up her job.

discover *(v.)* डिस्कॅवर्– to be the first to find or find out about पता लगाना, खोज निकालना Columbus *discovered* America.

discovery *(n.)* डिस्कवरी– the act, process, or an instance of discovering खोज, आविष्कार It was a great *discovery*.

discretion *(n.)* डिस्क्रेशन– the quality of behaving or speaking in such a way as to avoid social embarrassment or distress विवेक, समझबूझ I left on him to use his *discretion.*

discriminate *(v.)* डिस्क्रिमिनेट– to single out a particular person, group, etc. for special favour or, esp, disfavour, often because of a characteristic such as race, colour, sex, intelligence, etc. पक्षपात/भेदभाव करना It is illegal to *discriminate* on grounds of religion, race, etc.

discrimination *(n.)* डिस्क्रिमिनेशन– unfair treatment of a person, racial group, minority, etc. action based on prejudice पक्षपात, भेदभाव There should not be religious *discrimination* in the society.

discuss *(v.)* डिस्कस्– to have a conversation about; consider by talking over; debate विचार-विमर्श करना, वाद-विवाद करना The Lok Sabha *discussed* the budget proposals.

discussion *(n.)* डिस्कशन– the examination or consideration of a matter in speech or writing परिचर्चा, विचार-विमर्श, बहस This *discussion* is really going to be fruitful.

disease *(n.)* डिज़ीज़– any impairment of normal physiological function affecting all or part of an organism, रोग, बीमारी She was suffering from so many *diseases* at the same time.

disfigure *(v.)* डिसफ़िगर– to spoil the appearance or shape of; deface बिगाड़ना, विरूपित करना She was *disfigured* after burning in the fire.

disgrace *(v.)* डिसग्रेस– to behave badly in a way that makes people feel ashamed अपमानित/कलंकित करना A society is *disgraced* by the criminal acts of its members.

disguise *(n.)* डिस्गाइज़– 1. a mask, costume, or manner that disguises छद्मवेश, बहाना, छल-कपट Sometimes adversity turns out to be a blessing in *disguise.*

2. *(v.)* to modify the appearance or manner in order to conceal the identity of (oneself, someone, or something) छिपाना Pushpa tried to smile but she could not *disguise* her anger.

disgust *(v.)* डिस्गस्ट– to sicken or fill with loathing खीझ या घृणा उत्पन्न करना The way he eats completely *disgusts* me.

disgusting *(adj.)* डिस्गस्टिंग– loathsome; repugnant घृणाजनक, अरुचिकर Rahul's rude manners were *disgusting.*

dish *(n.)* डिश–1. a container used for holding or serving food, esp an open shallow container of pottery, glass, etc. थाली, रकाबी Usha wants to buy some *dishes.*

2. a particular article or preparation of food पकवान, भोजन Sita brought a very yummy *dish* in her tiffin today.

disheartening *(adj.)* डिसहार्टनिंग– If something is disheartening, it makes you feel disappointed and less confident or less hopeful निराशाजनक, दिल तोड़ने वाला It was *disheartening* to know that she is so unwell.

dishonest *(adj.)* डिसऑनिस्ट– not honest or fair; deceiving or fraudulent बेईमान, कपटी The *dishonest* servant was fired from the job.

dishonour *(n.)* डिसऑनर– a lack of honour or respect अनादर, अपयश, अपमान His cheating has brought *dishonour* and shame to his family.

disintegrate *(v.)* डिसइन्टग्रेट– to break or be broken into fragments or constituent parts; shatter विघटित करना/होना Russia got *disintegrated* in 1991.

dislike *(v.)* डिस्लाइक– to consider unpleasant or disagreeable नापसंद करना I *dislike* reaching late to the office.

dislocate *(v.)* डिस्लोकेट– to disrupt or shift out of place or position (हड्डी का) अपने स्थान से हट जाना, जोड़ उखड़ना/उखाड़ना The accident *dislocated* his arm.

dismal *(adj.)* डिज़्मल– causing gloom or depression दुःखद, निराशाजनक The cancer patient's face was very *dismal.*

dismantle *(v.)* डिस्मैन्टल– to take apart खोल देना, पुर्ज़े-पुर्ज़े अलग करना Karan *dismantled* the machine in ten minutes.

dismay *(n.)* डिसमे– 1. consternation or agitation घबराहट, व्याकुलता I was filled with *dismay* when I was told of her resignation.

2. *(v.)* to fill with apprehension or alarm भयभीत कर देना, निराश कर देना He was *dismayed* when his salary was deducted.

dismiss *(v.)* डिस्मिस– to remove or discharge from employment or service बरखास्त/पदच्युत करना The master *dismissed* a corrupt employee.

dismount *(v.)* डिसमाउन्ट– to get off a horse, bicycle, etc. उतरना The old man could not *dismount* from the horse.

disobedient *(adj.)* डिसअबिडिअन्ट– not obedient; neglecting or refusing to obey आज्ञा न मानने वाला, अवज्ञाकारी Amit is a very *disobedient* child in his class.

disobey *(v.)* डिसअबे– to refuse to obey आज्ञा न मानना, अवज्ञा करना He *disobeyed* his father and was punished.

disorder *(n.)* डिसॉर्डर– a lack of order; disarray; confusion अव्यवस्था, गड़बड़ The political state of the country is in a complete *disorder.*

disorganized (ise) *(adj.)* डिसआर्गनाइ- Someone who is disorganized is very bad at organizing things in their life अव्यवस्थित She is very *disorganized* in her household activities.

dispatch *(v.)* डिस्पैच– 1. to send off promptly, as to a destination or to perform a task भेजना, प्रेषित करना, शीघ्रता से सम्पन्न करना Please *dispatch* this message immediately.

2. *(n.)* the act of sending off a letter, messenger, etc., प्रेषण A quick *dispatch* on train accident was sent to inform.

dispensary *(n.)* डिस्पेंसरी– a place where medicine and medical supplies are dispensed औषधालय The wounded man was taken to the *dispensary.*

dispense *(v.)* डिस्पेन्स– 1. to do away (with) or manage (without) अलग

करना, दूर करना One should *dispense* with the services of an inefficient secretary quickly.

2. to give out or issue in portions दवा तैयार करना या देना Does that chemist *dispense* good medicines?

dispersal *(n.)* डिसपर्सल– the act of dispersing or the condition of being dispersed छितराव The farmer was going to the field for *dispersal* of seeds.

display *(v.)* डिस्प्ले– 1. to show or make visible दिखाना, प्रदर्शित करना I like the sarees that were *displayed* on the window.

2. *(n.)* the act of exhibiting or displaying; show प्रदर्शन Both girls and boys participated in the acrobatic *display.*

displease *(v.)* डिसप्लीज़– to annoy, offend, or cause displeasure to (someone) अप्रसन्न/नाराज़ करना The teacher was *displeased* with the lack of progress.

disposal *(n.)* डिस्पोज़ल– the act or means of getting rid of something परित्याग, निपटान *Disposal* of waste from the house is very important.

dispose *(v.)* डि्सपोज़–1. to arrange things in a specific way व्यवस्थित करना, क्रम से रखना I have *disposed* my shoes, shirt, etc.

2. to deal with or settle निपटाना, ख़ात्मा करना I have *disposed* of my work and now I am free.

disposition *(n.)* डिसुपज़िशन– a person's usual temperament or frame of mind प्रवृत्ति, मनोवृत्ति, स्वभाव Some people have a very nervous *disposition.*

disproportionate *(adj.)* डिसप्रपोर्शनेट्– out of proportion; unequal बेमेल, असमान *Disproportinate* division of time will not give the maximum output.

dispute *(n.)* डिसुप्यूट– 1. an argument or quarrel विवाद, कलह, झगड़ा It is best to avoid taking your familial *disputes* to a court of law.

2. *(v.)* to argue, debate, or quarrel about (something) खंडन करना, प्रतिवाद करना The minister's statement was *disputed* by the members.

disregard *(v.)* डिसरिगार्ड– to give little or no attention to; ignore उपेक्षा करना, अवहेलना करना Suhail *disregarded* the feelings of her wife.

disrepute *(n.)* डिसरिप्यूट– a loss or lack of credit or repute बदनामी Her bad conduct brought the family into *disrepute.*

disrespect *(n.)* डिसरिस्पैक्ट– contempt; rudeness निरादर, बेइज़्जती I meant no *disrespect* to him.

disrupt *(v.)* डिसुरप्ट– to interrupt the progress of (a movement, meeting, etc.) विघ्न डालना Rain *disrupted* the telecast of the match.

dissatisfaction *(n.)* डिस्सैटिस्फ़ैक्शन– the state of being unsatisfied or disappointed असंतोष The students expressed their *dissatisfaction* at the exam results.

dissatisfy *(v.)* डिससैटिस्फ़ाई– to fail to satisfy; disappoint नाराज़ एवं असंतुष्ट होना The students were *dissatisfied* with the results.

dissent *(n.)* डिसेन्ट– a difference of opinion मतभेद, विसम्मति There is some *dissent* within the party on such issues.

dissimilar *(adj.)* डिसिमलर– not alike; not similar; different असमान, भिन्न His situation is not *dissimilar* to mine.

dissolve *(v.)* डिज़ॉल्व–1.to go or cause to go into solution घुलना, घोलना A small piece of ice soon *dissolves* in water.

2. to come or bring to an end समाप्त करना When was the last Lok Sabha *dissolved*?

dissuade *(v.)* डिस्वेड– to deter (someone) by persuasion from a course of action, policy, etc. रोकना,

मना करना I tried to *dissuade* him from joining the BJP.

distance *(n.)* डिस्टन्स– the intervening space between two points or things दूरी, फ़ासला What is the *distance* between your school and your home?

distant *(adj.)* डिस्टण्ट– far away or apart in space or time दूरस्थ, दूरवर्ती My new office is at a *distant* place.

distaste *(n.)* डिस्टेस्ट– an absence of pleasure (in); dislike (of); aversion (to) अरुचि, नापसंदगी, नफ़रत She was cooking food with *distaste.*

distend *(v.)* डिस्टेण्ड– to expand or be expanded by or as if by pressure from within; swell; inflate फूलना, फुलाना Children were starving with *distended* bellies.

distinct *(adj.)* डिसूटिन्क्ट– easily sensed or understood; clear; precise भिन्न, अलग, सुस्पष्ट Her *distinct* behaviour impressed me alot.

distinction *(n.)* डिस्टिंक्शून–1. special honour, recognition, or fame श्रेष्ठता, प्रतिष्ठा Suresh's son passed the examination with *distinction.*
2. the state of being different or distinguishable भिन्नता, भेदभाव Is there any *distinction* between nylon and cotton?

distinctive *(adj.)* डिस्टिंक्टिव– serving or tending to distinguish अंतर स्पष्ट करने वाला, विशिष्ट Traffic police wear a *distinctive* uniform.

distinctly *(adv.)* डिस्टिंक्टली– clearly and certainly साफ़-साफ़, स्पष्ट रूप से Write your name *distinctly.*

distinguish *(v.)* डिसूटिन्ग्विश–1. to make, show, or recognize a difference or differences (between or among); differentiate (between) भेद करना, पहचानना I could not *distinguish* the approaching truck in the fog.
2. to mark for a special honour or title प्रसिद्ध होना, ख्याति पाना He *distinguished* himself as a doctor.

distinguished *(adj.)* डिस्टिंग्विशड– noble or dignified in appearance or behaviour प्रतिष्ठित, प्रख्यात He became a *distinguished* doctor.

distinguishing *(n.)* डिस्टिंग्विशिंग– serving to distinguish विशिष्ट Striped skin is the *distinguishing* feature of zebras.

distract *(v.)* डिस्ट्रेक्ट– to draw the attention of (a person) away from something ध्यान बटा देना या दूसरी तरफ़ ले जाना The noise of loudspeaker is *distracting* me from my studies.

distracted *(adj.)* डिस्ट्रेक्टिड– bewildered; confused विचलित, व्याकुल, उद्विग्न Shreya has a *distracted* mind which indicates she is worried.

distraction *(n.)* डिस्ट्रेक्शन– an interruption; an obstacle to concentration ध्यान भंग, दुचित्तापन Too many *distractions* can disturbe the one who is studying.

distress *(n.)* डिसूट्रेस– 1. mental pain; anguish दुःख, कष्ट, संकट The poor old man was in great *distress.*
2. *(v.)* to cause mental pain to; upset badly पीड़ा देना, दुख देना The bad news *distressed* us.

distribute *(v.)* डिस्ट्रिब्यूट– to give out in shares; dispense बाँटना, वितरण करना Rahul *distributed* sweets on the birth of his daughter.

distribution *(n.)* डिस्ट्रिब्यूशन– the act of distributing or the state or manner of being distributed बांट, वितरण The map shows the *distribution* of rainfalls in India.

district *(n.)* डिस्ट्रिक्ट– an area of land marked off for administrative or other purposes ज़िला She stays in a *district* where I have never been before.

disturb *(v.)* डिस्टर्ब– to interrupt sb शांति भंग करना, बाधा डालना Do not *disturb* the people who are reading in the library.

disturbance *(n.)* डिस्टर्बन्स– an interruption बाधा, अशांति Emotional *disturbance* can harm your health.

disturbed *(adj.)* डिस्टर्बड– emotionally upset, troubled, or maladjusted अशांत, विक्षुब्ध She is very *disturbed* to learn he had brought a new car.

disturbing *(adj.)* डिस्टर्बिंग– tending to upset or agitate; troubling; worrying अशांत, परेशान करने वाला There is a *disturbing* increase in the crime rate of Delhi.

ditch *(n.)* डिच– 1. a narrow channel dug in the earth, usually used for drainage, irrigation, or as a boundary marker खाई, नाली The street leading to your house is full of *ditches.* 2. *(v.)* to abandon or discard किसी को छोड़ देना, किसी से छुटकारा पाना Naresh *ditched* her when he became famous.

ditto *(abbr. do) (n.)* डिट्टो– a duplicate यथोक्त, तथैव One dozen plates red in colour, *ditto* green colour.

dive *(v.)* डाइव– to plunge headfirst into water ग़ोता लगाना, डुबकी मारना Can you *dive* into the swimming pool?

diverse *(adj.)* डाइवर्स– having variety; assorted विविध, भिन्न, असमान India is the land of *diverse* cultures.

diversify *(v.)* डाइवर्सिफ़ाइ– to create different forms of; variegate; vary विभिन्नता लाना, विविधता उत्पन्न करना The company should *diversify* to become successful in future.

diversion *(n.)* डाइवर्श़न– the act of diverting from a specified course दिक्परिवर्तन, विपथन Take a slight right from the *diversion to* reach the place fast.

divert *(v.)* डाइवर्ट–1. to turn (a person or thing) aside from a course; deflect दूसरे मार्ग पर ले जाना, मोड़ना The police *diverted* the traffic to give way to the religious procession.

2. to distract the attention of ध्यान हटा देना Don't let your attention get *diverted* while studying.

divide *(v.)* डिवाइड– to separate or be separated into parts or groups; split up; part बाँटना, विभाजित करना Let us *divide* this amount equally between us.

divine *(adj.)* डिवाइन– of, relating to, or characterizing God or a deity दिव्य, दैवी, ईश्वरीय Her *divine* nature fascinated everyone.

divisible *(adj.)* डिविज़बल– capable of being divided, usually with no remainder भाज्य, विभाज्य Thirty five is *divisible* by five.

division *(n.)* डिविश़न–1. the act of sharing out; distribution विभाजन, बँटवारा How many *divisions* does your company have?

2. a mathematical operation, the inverse of multiplication भाग Is your child good at *division*?

divorce *(v.)* डिवॉर्स– to remove or separate, esp completely तलाक़ देना/लेना या होना She has been *divorced* after twenty years.

divulge *(v.)* डाइवल्ज– to make known (something private or secret); disclose रहस्य या भेद खोलना, प्रकट करना Police refused to *divulge* the identity of the suspect.

dizzy *(adj.)* डिज़्ज़ी– affected with a whirling or reeling sensation; giddy चक्कर से आक्रान्त, चकराया हुआ, विभ्रांत After riding the merry-go-round, I felt *dizzy.*

do *(v.)* डू–1. to perform or complete (a deed or action) पूरा करना, सम्पन्न करना *Do* your homework before going to play.

2. to engage oneself करना What are you *doing* this evening?

3. to serve the needs of; be suitable for (a person, situation, etc.); suffice लाभ पहुँचाना This medicine will *do* you good.

docile *(adj.)* डोसाइल– easy to manage, control, or discipline; submissive आज्ञाधीन, आज्ञापरायण, विनीत Her *docile* nature will win everyone's heart.

doctor *(n.)* डॉक्टर्–1. a person licensed to practise medicine डॉक्टर, चिकित्सक The *doctor* advised Shankar to take rest for a week.

2. a person who has been awarded a higher academic degree in any field of knowledge आचार्य *Doctor* Ram Lal Verma came to see the patient.

document *(n.)* डॉक्युमन्ट– a piece of paper, booklet, etc. providing information, esp of an official or legal nature दस्तावेज़ Send this *document* by courier.

documentary *(n.)* डॉक्युमेंट्री– a factual film or television programme about an event, person, etc. presenting the facts with little or no fiction वृत्तचित्र Shahrukh Khan first starred in a *documentary* named Anne.

dodge *(v.)* डॉज– to avoid or attempt to avoid (a blow, discovery, etc.), as by moving suddenly हट जाना, वार बचाना Ramu tell down while trying to *dodge* the cyclist.

dog *(n.)* डॉग– a domesticated canine mammal, occurring in many breeds that show a great variety in size and form कुत्ता Do you like a *dog* as a pet?

dogged *(adj.)* डॉगिड– obstinately determined; wilful or tenacious ज़िद्दी, धुन का पक्का, हठी He was impressed by my *dogged* determination.

dogmatic *(adj.)* डॉगमैटिक– based on assumption rather than empirical observation हठधर्मी, मतांध It is not good to become too *dogmatic* in approach.

doleful *(adj.)* डोलफुल– dreary; mournful उदास, शोकमय, दुखी The beggar was looking to me with *doleful* eyes.

doll *(n.)* डॉल– a small model or dummy of a human being, used as a toy गुड़िया Rahul bought a *doll* for his little daughter.

dollar *(n.)* डॉलर– the standard monetary unit of the US and its dependencies, divided into 100 cents (अमरीकी मुद्रा) डॉलर He earns 200 *dollars* daily.

dome *(n.)* डोम– a hemispherical roof or vault or a structure of similar form गुम्बद The *dome* of Golden Temple is plated with gold.

domestic *(adj.)* डमेस्टिक– of or involving the home or family घरेलू, पारिवारिक She is so *domestic* that she hardly feels like going out.

dominant *(adj.)* डॉमिनेंट– having primary control, authority, or influence; governing; ruling प्रभावशाली, प्रबल, प्रमुख Punjabis are the *dominant* community in Delhi.

dominate *(v.)* डॉमिनेट– to control, rule, or govern (someone or something) पर शासन करना, अधिकार में रखना The Indian cricket team *dominated* the 20-20 World Cup.

dominion *(n.)* डमिनिअन– rule; authority प्रभुसत्ता, शासनाधिकार The Mughal king Akbar held *dominion* over a vast area.

donate *(v.)* डॉनेट– to give (money, time, etc.), esp to a charity दान करना One should *donate* blood at least once in lifetime.

donation *(n.)* डॉनेशन– the act of giving, esp to a charity दान, चंदा This institute is run by *donations.*

donkey *(n.)* डॉङ्की– a long-eared domesticated member of the horse family गधा The washerman's *donkey* carried the clothes to the river.

doom *(n.)* डूम– death or a terrible fate क़यामत, विनाश We cannot avoid to meet our *doom.*

door *(n.)* डोर– a hinged or sliding panel for closing the entrance to a room, cupboard, etc. दरवाज़ा, द्वार It's safe to keep the main *door* closed.

doormat *(adj.)* डोरमैट– a mat, placed at the entrance to a building, for wiping dirt from shoes पायंदाज The *doormat* of my room is very soft.

dope *(n.)* डोप–1. an additive used to improve the properties of something मादक पदार्थ, नींद या उत्तेजना लाने वाली औषधि The man was habitual of taking *dope.*

2. a person considered to be stupid or slow-witted मूर्ख व्यक्ति He is such a *dope*?

dormitory *(n.)* डॉर्मिट्री– a large room, esp at a school or institution, containing several beds शयनशाला, शयनागार The school had a big *dormitory* for its resident students.

dosage *(n.)* डोसिज– the administration of a drug or agent in prescribed amounts and at prescribed intervals ख़ुराक, मात्रा The doctor asked to increase the *dosage* of the patient.

dose *(n.)* डोज़– a specific quantity of a therapeutic drug or agent taken at any one time or at specified intervals खुराक A *dose* after every 4 hour was mandatory for him.

dot *(n.)* डॉट– 1. a small round mark made with or as with a pen, etc. spot; speck; point बिंदु The teacher asked the children to circle the red *dot.*

2. *(v.)* to mark or form with a dot बिंदु लगाना You should *dot* the i's and cross the t's.

dote *(v.)* डोट– to love to an excessive or foolish degree किसी को बहुत प्यार देना She *dotes* on her youngest child.

double *(adj.)* डबूल– 1. as much again in size, strength, number, etc. दुगुना Ram had to do *double* work in the office these days.

2. *(v.)* to make or become twice as much दुगना करना या होना Why have the vegetable prices *doubled* in such a short time?

double-check *(v.)* डबूल-चैक– to check twice or again; verify दोबारा सावधानी से जांच करना The writer was *double-checking* the manuscript.

double-cross *(v.)* डबल-क्रॉस– to cheat or betray चाल खेलना, धोखा देकर ठगना He *double-crossed* his friends and ran away in seconds.

doubly *(adv.)* डबली– more than usual सामान्य से अधिक I am *doubly* sure that the door was locked.

doubt *(n.)* डाउट– 1. uncertainty about the truth, fact, or existence of something संशय, शंका I have *doubts* about her sincerity.

2. *(v.)* to be inclined to disbelieve संदेह करना, अविश्वास करना I *doubt* whether you are telling me the truth.

doubtful *(adj.)* डाउटफुल– unlikely; improbable संदेहास्पद I am still *doubtful* about his decision.

dough *(n.)* डो–1. a thick mixture of flour or meal and water or milk, used for making bread, pastry, etc. गुंथा आटा, लोई If you knead the *dough* well, the bread would be soft.

2. money धन I am not a rich man, I do not have a lot of *dough.*

dove *(n.)* डव– a bird of the pigeon family having a heavy body, small head, short legs, and long pointed wings पड़की, पंडुक The *dove* is considered a symbol of peace.

down *(adj.)* डाउन downwards; at or to a lower level or position नीचे Please sit *down* here.

downfall *(n.)* डाउनफ़ॉल– a sudden loss of position, health, or reputation तबाही, बर्बादी, पतन There was a *downfall* in her report due to the tragedy she faced.

downhearted *(adj.)* डाउनहार्टेड– discouraged; dejected हताश, निराश We were not *downhearted* after the bad result.

download *(v.)* डाउनलोड– to copy or transfer (data or a program) into the memory of one computer system from a larger one कम्प्यूटर से फाइल उतारना The *download* process sometimes kills lot of time.

downmarket *(adj.)* डाउनमार्केट– relating to commercial products, services, etc. that are cheap, have little prestige, or are poor in quality सस्ता, घटिया The company wanted to break away its *downmarket* image.

downstairs *(adj.,adv.)* डाउनस्टेअर्ज़– down the stairs; to or on a lower floor सीढ़ियों से नीचे Kamla fell *downstairs* and broke her leg.

down to earth *(adj.)* डाउन-टू-अर्थ– sensible; practical; realistic यथार्थवादी Despite being very rich and affluent, she is very *down-to-earth.*

downtrodden *(adj.)* डाउनट्रॉडन– subjugated; oppressed पददलित, कुचला या रौंदा हुआ The *downtrodden* people in our country are still suffering.

downward *(adj.)* डाउनवर्ड– descending from a higher to a lower level, condition, position, etc. नीचे की ओर Stock market continues *downward* trend.

downwards *(adv.)* डाउनवर्डज़– from a higher to a lower place, level, etc. नीचे की ओर She was lying with face *downwards* on the floor.

dowry *(n.)* डाउरी– the money or property brought by a woman to her husband at marriage दहेज *Dowry* is a blot on humanity.

doze *(v.)* डोज़– to sleep lightly or intermittently झपकी लेना, ऊँघना I like to *doze* for half an hour after a heavy lunch.

dozen *(n.)* डज़न– twelve or a group of twelve दर्जन I bought two *dozen* bananas.

draft *(v.)* ड्राफ्ट– 1. to write rough version of sth such as a speech, letter, etc. of something प्रारूप बनाना He will *draft* a letter for me.

2. *(n.)* a preliminary outline of a book, speech, etc. प्रारूप, पांडुलेख Several amendments were made in the *draft* of the project.

drag *(v.)* ड्रैग– to pull or be pulled with force, esp along the ground or other surface घसीटना If this load is too heavy for you to lift, you will have to *drag* it.

dragon *(n.)* ड्रैगन– a mythical monster usually represented as breathing fire and having a scaly reptilian body, wings, claws, and a long tail ड्रैगन, परदार साँप The child made a picture of a *dragon* breathing fire.

dragonfly *(n.)* ड्रैगनफ़्लाई– an insect having a large head and eyes, a long slender body, two pairs of large transparent wings एक लंबा पतला चमकीला पतंग, चिउरा There were many *dragonflies* near the pond.

drain *(n.)* ड्रेन– 1. a pipe or channel that carries off water, sewage, etc. नाली, मोरी All the *drains* in the colony were overflowing following a heavy downpour.

2. *(v.)* to draw off or remove (liquid) from बह जाना, (जल) निकालना As I cleaned the outlet, the water *drained* out.

drama *(n.)* ड्रामा– a work to be performed by actors on stage, radio, or television; play नाटक The whole *drama* left a good impact on the audience.

dramatic *(adj.)* ड्रामैटिक– of or relating to drama नाटकीय There was a *dramatic* change in the movie.

dramatize (ise) *(v.)* ड्रैमटाइज़– to express or represent (something) in a dramatic or exaggerated way नाटक का रूप देना, नाटकीय बनाना We *dramatized* the whole story and got lots of appreciation.

drape *(v.)* ड्रेप– to hang or cover with flexible material or fabric, usually in folds; adorn लपेटना Keep your belongings *draped* as it is raining outside.

draught *(n.)* ड्राफ़्ट– a current of air, esp one intruding into an enclosed space ठंडी हवा का झोंका, वात-प्रवाह A cold *draught* of air blew in my room.

draw *(v.)* ड्रॉ–1. to depict or sketch (a form, figure, picture, etc.) in lines, as with a pencil or pen, esp without the use of colour; delineate चित्र बनाना, अंकित करना Can you *draw* good pictures?

2. to cause (a person or thing) to move towards or away by pulling खींचना, घसीटना Two horses were *drawing* the carriage.

drawback *(n.)* ड्रॉबैक– a disadvantage or snag त्रुटि There were so many *drawbacks* in her performance.

drawer *(n.)* ड्रॉअर्– a boxlike container in a chest, table, etc. made for sliding in and out दराज़ In which *drawer* have you put my pen?

drawing *(n.)* ड्राइंग– the art of making drawings; draughtsmanship चित्रकारी, चित्रांकन She is good at *drawing*.

drawl *(n.)* ड्रॉल– the way of speech of someone who drawls धीरे-धीरे अटक-अटककर बोलने का ढँग She was speaking with a *drawl*.

dread *(v.)* ड्रे'ड– to fear greatly डरना, भयभीत होना A burnt child *dreads* the fire.

dreadful *(adj.)* ड्रेडफुल– extremely disagreeable, shocking, or bad डरावना, भयानक, बुरा Have you read the newspaper report of the *dreadful* accident?

dream *(n.)* ड्रीम– 1. mental activity, usually in the form of an imagined series of events, occurring during certain phases of sleep सपना, स्वप्न Do you sleep soundly or do you have *dreams*?

2. *(v.)* to have an image (of) or fantasy (about) in or as if in a dream स्वप्न देखना, कल्पना करना He always *dreams* about being rich.

dreary *(adj.)* ड्रिअरी– wearying; boring थकाऊ, उबाऊ, उदास, नीरस I faced a very *dreary* journey last time.

drench *(v.)* ड्रे'न्च– to make completely wet; soak सराबोर कर देना I was *drenched* in the rain while coming to see you.

dress *(n.)* ड्रे'स– 1. clothes for either men or women; attire पोशाक, कपड़े I'm not very particular about my *dress*.

2. *(v.)* to apply protective or therapeutic covering to (a wound, sore, etc.) मरहम-पट्टी करना Do you know how to *dress* a wound?

drift *(v.)* ड्रिफ़्ट–1. to be carried along by or as if by currents of air or water or (of a current) to carry (a vessel, etc.) along बह जाना Clouds were *drifting* in the wind.

2. to move aimlessly from place to place or from one activity to another भटकना, बेमतलब घूमना-फिरना Why are you *drifting* here and there?

3. *(n.)* the movement of the air or sea, current बहाव, धारा, प्रवाह It is easy to swim with the *drift* of the stream.

drill *(n.)* ड्रिल– 1. a tool with a pointed end for making holes बरमा I have a hand *drill*.

2. (v.) to pierce, bore, or cut (a hole) in (material) with or as if with a drill

बरमा चलाना, छेद करना Can you *drill* a hole in a very thick wall?

drink *(v.)* ड्रिन्क– 1. to swallow (a liquid) पीना *Drink* your tea before it gets cold. 2. *(n.)* liquid suitable for drinking; any beverage मदिरा, पेय, शर्बत He asked for a *drink,* but I refused.

drinking *(n.)* ड्रिंकिंग– the act of consuming alcoholic beverages शराब पीने की क्रिया Wayward youths are prone to start *drinking.*

drip *(v.)* ड्रिप– to fall or let fall in drops टपकना The tap in my bathroom has been *dripping* since yesterday.

drive *(v.)* ड्राइव–1. to control and guide the movement of (a vehicle, draught animal, etc.) चलाना, हाँकना Can you *drive* a car?
2. *(n.)* the act of driving (गाड़ी में) सैर Let us go for a *drive* round the lake.
3. a united effort, esp directed towards a common goal संयुक्त प्रयास A strong *drive* can make you reach heights in your career.

drizzle *(v.)* ड्रिज़ल– to rain lightly बूँदाबाँदी होना, फुहार पड़ना It was *drizzling* when they left for station.

drone *(v.)* ड्रोन– to make a monotonous low dull sound; buzz or hum भिनभिनाना, लगातार धीमी आवाज़ करना The scooter was *droning* in the street.

droop *(v.)* ड्रूप–1. to sag or allow to sag, as from weakness or exhaustion; hang down; sink झुकना, कुम्हलाना The flowers in the garden were *drooping* due to intense heat.
2. to lose courage; become dejected निराश या उदास हो जाना Don't let your spirits *droop.*

drop *(n.)* ड्रॉप–1. a very small quantity of liquid बूँद Even a *drop* of medicine can do a lot of good to the patient.
2. a decrease in amount or value; slump गिरावट, कमी, पतन, ह्रास There is a *drop* in petrol prices.
3. *(v.)* to allow to fall by letting go of छोड़ देना या छूट जाना Be careful, don't *drop* that glass.

droplet *(n.)* ड्रॉपलेट– a tiny drop छोटी-सी बूँद The tiny *droplets* were shining on the petals of rose.

drought *(n.)* ड्राउट– a prolonged period of scanty rainfall सूखा, अनावृष्टि The crops were spoilt by the *drought.*

drown *(v.)* ड्राउन– to die or kill by immersion in liquid डूब मरना, डुबाकर मारना Thirty persons were *drowned* in the boat tragedy.

drowning *(adj.)* ड्राउनिंग– an instance of someone's dying when submerged in water and therefore unable to breathe डूबता हुआ Do you know how to rescue a *drowning* person?

drowsy *(adj.)* ड्राउज़ि– heavy with sleepiness; sleepy निद्रालु, उनींदा After staying awake for the whole night, I was feeling *drowsy* in the morning.

drug *(n.)* ड्रग–1. any synthetic, semisynthetic, or natural chemical substance used in the treatment, prevention, or diagnosis of disease, or for other medical reasons दवा Penicillin is a wonder *drug.*
2. a chemical substance, esp a narcotic, taken for the pleasant effects it produces नशीली दवा Taking *drugs* is injurious to health.

drum *(n.)* ड्रम– a percussion instrument sounded by striking a membrane stretched across the opening of a hollow cylinder or hemisphere ढोल, मृदंग I want to buy a toy *drum* for my child.

dry *(adj.)* ड्राइ–1. lacking moisture; not damp or wet सूखा *Dry* your hands before holding that paper.
2. boring, not interesting नीरस, शुष्क You cannot make friends if you have a *dry* manner.

dry-clean *(v.)* ड्राइक्लीन– to clean (clothing, fabrics, etc.) with a solvent other than water, such as trichloroethylene बिना पानी के सूखी धुलाई करना The winter garments must be *dry-cleaned* after the season.

dub *(v.)* डब– to substitute for the soundtrack of (a film) a new soundtrack, esp in a different language एक भाषा की फ़िल्म का दूसरी भाषा में अनुवाद करना The movie Taare Zameen Par has been *dubbed* in other languages as well.

dubious *(adj.)* डयूबिअस– unsettled in mind; uncertain; doubtful संदेहास्पद, संदिग्ध, अनिश्चित He was rather *dubious* about the whole idea.

duck *(n.)* डक– a small aquatic bird having short legs, webbed feet, and a broad blunt bill बतख़ There were many *ducks* in the pond.

dude *(n.)* ड्यूड– a man; a guy (often as a form of address) छैला व्यक्ति, बांका He is such a good *dude.*

due *(adj.)* ड्यू–1. immediately payable देय, दातव्य (जो दिया जाना हो) Ram paid his insurance premium even before it became *due.*

2. expected or appointed to be present or arrive अपेक्षित, प्रत्याशित The train is *due* in half an hour.

3. because of के कारण, फलस्वरूप I met with an accident *due* to my careless driving.

4. *(n.)* something that is owed, required, or due देय, दातव्य Give the devil his *due.*

dull *(adj.)* डल–1. slow to think or understand; stupid मन्दबुद्धि *Dull* students needs to be more attentive in the class.

2. lacking in interest नीरस, उबाऊ A *dull* book mars the reputation of its author.

3. (of weather) not bright or clear; cloudy मेघाच्छादित, धुँधला Today is a cloudy and *dull* day.

dumb *(adj.)* डम– lacking the power to speak, either because of defects in the vocal organs or because of hereditary deafness गूँगा, मूक Though he is *dumb* but he is more intelligent than you.

dummy *(adj.)* डमी– 1. a copy or imitation of an object, नक़ली, दिखावटी I want to buy a *dummy* gun for my young son.

2. *(n.)* a figure representing the human form, used for displaying clothes, in a ventriloquist's act, as a target, etc. कठपुतली This *dummy* of the dancer looks real.

dump *(n.)* डंप– 1. a place or area where waste materials are dumped कूड़ा डालने का स्थान Throw this letter in the waste paper *dump.*

2. *(v.)* to dispose of (waste, esp radioactive nuclear waste) अवांछित वस्तु को फेंकना She *dumped* the rubbish in the dustbin.

duplex *(n.)* ड्यूप्लेक्स– a duplex apartment or house दोहरा, दुमंज़िला मकान We stayed in a *duplex* hotel in Shimla.

duplicate *(n.)* ड्यूप्लिकेट– 1. an exact copy; double प्रतिलिपि, अनुलिपि This key is a *duplicate* of the original one.

2. *(adj.)* copied exactly from an original दूसरा, अतिरिक्त Do you have a *duplicate* key of the car?

3. *(v.)* to make a replica of अनुलिपि/प्रतिलिपि बनाना It is unethical to *duplicate* the original album.

durable *(adj.)* ड्यूअरबल– long-lasting; enduring टिकाऊ This seems to be a *durable* plastic.

duration *(n.)* ड्यूरेशन– the length of time that something lasts or continues अवधि The *duration* of the movie was more than 3 hours.

during *(prep.)* ड्युअरिंग– all through a period of time के समय में, के दौरान, की अवधि तक You can always find me in my office *during* the working hours.

dusk *(n.)* डस्क– twilight or the darker part of twilight झुटपुटा, अँधेरा I must return home before *dusk.*

dusky *(adj.)* डस्की– dark in colour; swarthy or dark-skinned सांवला Her *dusky* complexion gave her the chance to enter the play.

dust *(n.)* डस्ट– dry fine powdery material, such as particles of dirt, earth or pollen धूल, गर्द Wipe the *dust* off your desk daily.

dusty *(adj.)* डस्टी– covered with or involving dust धूलभरा, धूल-धूसरित I cannot work in such a *dusty* room.

dutiful *(adj.)* ड्यूटिफुल– exhibiting or having a sense of duty कर्तव्यपरायण Vinay is a *dutiful* son of Mrs Vyas.

duty *(n.)* ड्यूटी– 1. a task or action that a person is bound to perform for moral or legal reasons कर्तव्य, फ़र्ज़ Do your *duty* and have faith in God.

2. a job or service allocated काम, कार्य Shyam is always late for his *duty.*

dwarf *(n.)* ड्वार्फ़– an abnormally undersized person, esp one with a large head and short arms and legs बौना He is a *dwarf* by birth.

dwell *(v.)* ड्वेल– to live as a permanent resident निवास करना, रहना, बसना Don't *dwell* on your troubles.

dwelling *(n.)* ड्वेलिंग– a place of residence निवास-स्थान, डेरा, घर This was his *dwelling* place last year.

dwindle *(v.)* ड्विन्ड्ल– to grow or cause to grow less in size, intensity, or number; diminish or shrink gradually घटना, कम होना/करना The stock has been *dwindling* alarmingly since two years.

dye *(v.)* डाइ– 1. to impart a colour or stain to (something, such as fabric or hair) by or as if by the application of a dye रंगना, रँग जाना Can you *dye* this saree deep blue?

2. *(n.)* a staining or colouring substance, such as a natural or synthetic pigment रंग, वर्ण, What is the price of this hair-*dye*?

dying *(adj.)* डाइंग– relating to or occurring at the moment of death मरते दम तक, मृत्युकालीन I will remember it to my *dying* day.

dynamic *(adj.)* डाइनैमिक– characterized by force of personality, ambition, energy, new ideas, etc. गतिशील One should come up with *dynamic* ideas in every meeting.

dynasty *(n.)* डिनस्टि– a sequence of hereditary rulers वंश, राजवंश The Mughal *Dynasty* ended with Bahadur Shah Zafar deported to Rangoon.

ꙮ

Ee

Ee *(n.)* ई—अंग्रेज़ी वर्णमाला का पाँचवाँ अक्षर The fifth letter of English alphabet. Eagle begins with '*E*'.

each *(adj.)* ईच– for, to, or from each one; apiece प्रत्येक, हरएक, एक-एक The teacher checked *each* and every student's homework.

each other *(pron.)* ईच अदर– used when the action, attribution, etc. is reciprocal एक-दूसरे से/को, परस्पर, आपस में Veer and Sonam loved *each other* very much.

eager *(adj.)* ईगर्– impatiently desirous (of); anxious or avid (for) उत्सुक, इच्छुक Why are you so *eager* to go home early?

eagerly *(adv.)* ईगर्लि– in a way that shows eagerness उत्सुकतापूर्वक, आतुरता से He was *eagerly* waiting for me.

eagerness *(n.)* ईगरनस– enthusiasm and alacrity in wanting something or in wanting to do something उत्सुकता, लालसा, आतुरता Sameer showed his *eagerness* to visit Delhi.

eagle *(n.)* ईगुल– a large bird of prey having large broad wings and strong soaring flight गरुड़ Can any other bird fly as high as the *eagle*?

ear *(n.)* इअर–1. the organ of hearing कान, कर्ण My father bought a hearing-aid for his left *ear*.

2. the part of a cereal plant, such as wheat or barley, that contains the seeds, grains, or kernels बाल, बाली, भुट्टा Look at those *ears* of corn heaped in the field.

> **be all ears**– very attentive; listening carefully ध्यानपूर्वक सुनना, As soon as I mentioned money, she was *all ears*.

> **play by ear**– to perform a musical piece on an instrument without written music स्मृति से संगीत रचना का गायन एवं वादन करना She *plays* turning music *by ear*.

> **go in one ear and out the other**– to be forgotten quickly बहुत जल्दी भूल जाना Whatever I tell he seems to *go in one ear and out the other*.

ear lobe *(n.)* इअर लॉब– the fleshy lower part of the external ear कर्णपाली (कान की लौ) Why is your right *ear lobe* so red?

early *(adv.)* अर्ली– 1. before the expected or usual time शीघ्र, पहले Please reach the venue as *early* as possible. 2. *(adj.)* before the expected or usual time प्रांरभ में, सवेरे I have my breakfast *early* in the morning.

> **at the earliest**– before the time or date specified यथाशीघ्र, समय से पूर्व, I will try to repair your TV by Tuesday *at the earliest*.

> **in the early hours**– in the morning time बहुत सवेरे, I have to get up *in the early hours*.

> **early on**– initial time शुरू में ही, She achieved success *early on* her life.

earmark *(v.)* ईअरमार्क– to set aside or mark out for a specific purpose निशान लगाना या डालना He was already *earmarked* for the next project.

earn *(v.)* अर्न्– to gain or be paid (money or other payment) in return for work or service कमाना, प्राप्त करना How much do you *earn* every month?

earnest *(adj.)* अर्नेस्ट्– serious in mind or intention उत्साही, जोशीला, गंभीर He succeded because he was so *earnest* to do this job.

earnings *(n.)* अर्निंग– money or other payment earned कमाई He works very hard so his *earnings* have increased by 10%.

earring *(n.)* इअरिंग– an ornament for the ear, usually clipped onto the lobe or fastened through a hole pierced in the lobe कुंडल, कर्पफूल Poonam is wearing golden *earrings.*

earth *(n.)* अर्थ–1. the third planet from the sun, the only planet on which life is known to exist पृथ्वी, धरती What is the shape of the *earth*?

2. the dry surface of this planet as distinguished from sea or sky; land; ground मिट्टी, ज़मीन Labourers were digging the *earth* to lay telephone cables.

earthquake *(n.)* अर्थक्वेक– a sudden shaking of the earth's surface भूकंप The *earthquake* destroyed the whole village.

earthworm *(n.)* अर्थवर्म– a long, thin worm that lives in soil, etc. केंचुआ There were a number of *earthworms* in the garden.

ease *(v.)* ईज़– 1. to relieve (a person) of worry or care; comfort आराम देना, सुख देना His words would *ease* my mind.

2. *(n.)* freedom from discomfort, worry, or anxiety आराम, सुविधा He passed his test with *ease.*

easily *(adv.)* ईज़िलि– with ease; without difficulty or exertion सरलता/आसानी से Anyone can *easily* do this task.

east *(n.)* ईस्ट– one of the four cardinal points of the compass, 90° clockwise from north and 180° from west पूर्व, पूरब दिशा In the morning, I pray facing the *east.*

eastern *(adj.)* ईस्टर्न– situated in or towards the east पूर्वी My best friend hails from *eastern* U.P.

eastward *(adj.)* ईस्टवर्ड– situated or directed towards the east पूरब की ओर, पूर्वाभिमुख We were travelling in an *eastward* direction.

easy *(adj.)* ईज़ी– not requiring much labour or effort; not difficult; simple आसान, सरल it's not that *easy* to solve this question.

➢ **go easy** *(adv.)*– to treat leniently नरमी बरतना, *Go easy* on him.

➢ **take it easy** *(adv.)*– to avoid stress or undue hurry आराम से काम करना, *Take* things *easy* for a few days and you should be all right.

easy-going *(adj.)* ईज़ी-गोईंग– relaxed in manner or attitude; inclined to be excessively tolerant बेपरवाह, तनावमुक्त He is an *easy-going* fellow.

eat *(v.)* ईट– to take into the mouth and swallow (food, etc.), esp after biting and chewing खाना Would you like something to *eat*?

eatable *(adj.)* ईटबल– fit or suitable for eating; edible खाने योग्य, खाद्य We took some *eatables* with us.

eccentric *(adj.)* इक्सेन्ट्रिक– deviating or departing from convention, esp in a bizarre manner; irregular or odd सनकी, झक्की He is an *eccentric* old man.

echo *(n.)* एको– 1. the reflection of sound or other radiation by a reflecting medium, esp a solid object प्रतिध्वनि, गूंज Your voice will *echo* if you will speak loudly in an empty hall.

2. *(v.)* to resound or cause to resound with an echo गूँजना His voice *echoed* in the empty hall.

eclipse *(n.)* इक्लिप्स– 1. the total or partial obscuring of one celestial body by another ग्रहण There will be an *eclipse* of the sun or the moon tommorow.

2. *(v.)* to overshadow or surpass in importance, power, etc. ग्रस्त होना, निस्तेज कर देना One defect in character can *eclipse* many good qualities.

eco-friendly *(adj.)* इको-फ्रेंड्ली– having a beneficial effect on the environment or at least not causing environmental damage पर्यावरण के

अनुकूल Paper bags look good and are *eco-friendly.*

ecology *(n.)* इकॉलजि– the study of the relationships between living organisms and their environment पारिस्थिति विज्ञान She is doing research in *ecology.*

economic *(adj.)* इकॉनॉमिक– of or relating to an economy, economics, or finance आर्थिक, अर्थशास्त्रीय The *economic* condition of my friend is very poor.

economical *(adj.)* इकॉनॉमिकल– using the minimum required; not wasteful of time, effort, resources, etc. किफ़ायती, मितव्ययी Maruti 800 is a very *economical* car to use.

economy *(n.)* इकॉनॉमी– the management of resources of a country अर्थव्यवस्था Indian *economy* needs to improve alot.

ecstasy *(n.)* एकस्टॅसी– a state of exalted delight, joy, etc. rapture आनंदातिरेक, हर्षोन्माद His *ecstasy* about the examination results knew no bounds.

ecstatic *(adj.)* एक्सटैटिक– very happy or delighted, enthusiastic अति प्रसन्न, उल्लसित, भावविभोर He was *ecstatic* about his examination results.

eczema *(n.)* एग्ज़्मा– a skin inflammation with lesions that scale, crust, or ooze a serous fluid, often accompanied by intense itching or burning खाज, छाजन He has *eczema* on his neck.

edge *(n.)* एज–1. the sharp cutting side of a blade धार Be careful, that knife has a sharp *edge.*
2. the border, brim, or margin of a surface, object, etc. कोर, किनारा Don't go near the *edge* of the cliff.

edgy *(adj.)* एजि– nervous, irritable, tense, or anxious चिड़चिड़ा, परेशान He has been very *edgy* lately, waiting for the election results.

edible *(adj.)* एडिबूल– fit to be eaten; eatable खाने योग्य, खाद्य, भोज्य Which is the *edible* part of a potato?

edict *(n.)* ईडिक्ट– a decree, order, or ordinance issued by a sovereign, state, or any other holder of authority फ़रमान, राजाज्ञा, आदेश-पत्र The *edict* was circulated in the city.

editor *(n.)* एडिटर्– a person who edits written material for publication संपादक The *editor* should sit at a quite place while working.

editorial *(n.)* एडिटोरियल– an article in a newspaper, etc. expressing the opinion of the editor or the publishers संपादकीय One must always read the *editorial* section of the newspaper.

educate *(v.)* एजुकेट– to impart knowledge by formal instruction to (a pupil); teach पढ़ाना-लिखाना, शिक्षा देना Good art can *educate* as well as amuse us.

educated *(adj.)* एजुकेटेड– having an education, esp a good one पढ़ा-लिखा, शिक्षित The peon of his company is an *educated* man.

education *(n.)* एजुकेशन– the act or process of acquiring knowledge, esp systematically during childhood and adolescence शिक्षा, पढ़ाई *Education* contributes a lot in building a person's career.

educational *(adj.)* एजुकेशनल– providing knowledge; instructive or informative शिक्षा-संबंधी, शैक्षिक *Educational* trips for kids have become mandatory nowdays.

effect *(n.)* इफ़ेक्ट– something that is produced by a cause or agent; result नतीजा, परिणाम, प्रभाव Her shouting had no *effect* on him.
➢ **side-effect**– any secondary effect, esp an undesirable one दुष्परिणाम, There were many *side-effects* of the medicine he had taken.

> **come into effect**– to begin, to apply लागू हो जाना, The new rules will *come into effect* from next week.
> **take effect**– to produce a result प्रभावित होना, The antibiotics *took effect* immediately.

effective *(adj.)* इफ़ैक्टिव– productive of or capable of producing a result प्रभावी, कारगर His suggestion was very *effective* to solve the problem.

effectively *(adv.)* इफ़ैक्टिवली– in an efficient and successful way प्रभावपूर्ण ढंग से, ज़ोरदार तरीक़े से I have done my work *effectively.*

efficacious *(adj.)* एफ़िकेशस– capable of or successful in producing an intended result; effective as a means प्रभावोत्पादक This painkiller will be *efficacious* in relieving headache.

efficient *(adj.)* इफ़िश्न्ट्– functioning or producing effectively and with the least waste of effort; competent कार्यकुशल, दक्ष He was very *efficient* in his work.

efficiency *(n.)* एफ़िशॅन्सी– the quality or state of being efficient; competence; effectiveness कार्यकुशलता, दक्षता Working *efficiency* of labourers reduces in summer.

effigy *(n.)* एफ़िजी– a statue of a person, esp as a monument or architectural decoration पुतला Iraqi protesters burn *effigy* of George Bush.

effort *(n.)* एफ़र्ट– physical or mental exertion, usually considerable when unqualified प्रयास, प्रयत्न, कोशिश Did you make an *effort* to contact me over the phone?

effortless *(adj.)* एफ़र्टलस– requiring or no little effort; easy बिना प्रयास के, सहज, सरल He painted the portrait with *effortless* skill.

egg *(n.)* एग– the oval or round reproductive body laid by the females of birds, reptiles, fishes, insects, and some other animals, consisting of a developing embryo, its food store, and sometimes jelly or albumen, all surrounded by an outer shell or membrane अंडा I like boiled *eggs* for breakfast.

ego *(n.)* ईगो– the self of an individual person; the conscious subject अहं, अहम् Self-pride is good, but *ego* is dangerous.

egocentric *(adj.)* ईगोसेन्ट्रिक– regarding everything only in relation to oneself; self-centred; selfish आत्म-केंद्रित He is very *egocentric* in nature.

eight *(n.)* एट– a numeral, 8, VIII, etc. representing this number आठ I need *eight* kgs of mango to prepare this shake.

either *(pron.)* आइदर्–1. one or the other of two दोनों में कोई एक I have two pens, you can use *either* of them.
2. *(adv.) either...or...* any, any one of (when the number is more than two) जब दो विकल्पों में से एक चुनना हो, Please have *either* an apple *or* an orange. I will *either* write or read.

eject *(v.)* इजेक्ट– to drive or force out; expel or emit बाहर निकालना The protestors were *ejected* from the hall.

elaborate *(v.)* इलैबरेट– 1. to add information or detail (to an account); expand (upon) विस्तार देना, फैलाना Will you please *elaborate* on this point?
2. *(adj.)* planned or executed with care and exactness; detailed परिष्कृत, विस्तृत The bride wore an *elaborate* dress.

elastic *(adj.)* इलैस्टिक– capable of returning to its original shape after compression, expansion, stretching, or other deformation लचीला, लचकदार This rubber is not *elastic* enough.

elated *(adj.)* इलेटिड– full of high spirits, exhilaration, pride or optimism; very happy प्रफुल्लित They were *elated* at the result of election.

elbow *(n.)* एल्बो– 1. the joint between the upper arm and the forearm, कोहनी, मोड़ My elbow was hurt when I fell down.
2. *(v.)* to push sb with elbow कोहनी मारकर किसी को हटाना He *elbowed* his way through the crowd.

elder *(adj.)* एल्डर्– born earlier; senior आयु में बड़ा, ज्येष्ठ Both my *elder* sisters are very beautiful.

elders *(n.)* एल्डर्स an older person; one's senior वयोवृद्ध लोग We should respect our *elders.*

elderly *(n.)* एल्डर्ली– quite old; past middle age अधेड़, प्रौढ़ वयोवृद्ध An *elderly* couple lives in front of my house.

eldest *(adj.)* एल्डिस्ट– being the oldest, esp the oldest surviving child of the same parents आयु में सबसे बड़ा, ज्येष्ठ He is the *eldest* amongst the all.

elect *(v.)* इलेक्ट– to choose (someone) to be (a representative or a public official) by voting चुनना, निर्वाचित करना The members of the company *elected* a new chairman.

election *(n.)* इलेक्शन– the act or an instance of choosing चुनाव, निर्वाचन When are the general *elections* going to be held?

electric *(adj.)* इलेक्ट्रिक– of, derived from, produced by, producing, transmitting, or powered by electricity बिजली उत्पन्न करने वाला, विद्युत-संबंधी, वैद्युत *Electric* engines move faster than the steam engine.

electrician *(n.)* इलेक्ट्रिशन– a person whose occupation is the installation, maintenance, and repair of electrical devices बिजली-मिस्त्री, बिजली-विशेषज्ञ Our *electrician* came and repaired this fan in 2 minutes.

electricity *(n.)* इलेक्ट्रिसटी– any phenomenon associated with stationary or moving electrons, ions, or other charged particles बिजली, विद्युत *Electricity* is one of the greatest inventions of science.

electronic *(adj.)* इलेक्ट्रॉनिक– of, concerned with, using, or operated by devices in which electrons are conducted through a semiconductor, free space, or gas (इलेक्ट्रॉन की क्रिया पर निर्भर साधन), इलेक्ट्रॉनिक Please keep all the *electronic* items away from water.

elegant *(adj.)* एलिगेन्ट– tasteful in dress, style, or design रमणीय, सुरुचिपूर्ण The young lady looked *elegant* in her new dress.

elegantly *(adv.)* एलिगेण्टली– in a simple and beautiful manner सुरुचिपूर्ण ढंग से Dressing up *elegantly* always leaves a good impression.

element *(n.)* एलिमेण्ट– a cause that contributes to a result; factor तत्त्व, घटक, अवयव Lot of *elements* were used to start this machine.

elementary *(adj.)* एलिमेण्ट्री– of or concerned with the first principles of a subject; introductory or fundamental प्राथमिक, प्रारंभिक Do you have at least an *elementary* knowledge of Chemistry?

elephant *(n.)* एलिफन्ट्– a very large animal with large ears and a trunk हाथी I saw an *elephant* while I was on my way to office.

elevator *(n.)* एलिवेटर्– a mechanical hoist for raising something, लिफ़्ट, उत्थापक, उठाने वाला He took the *elevator* to reach the third floor.

eleventh *(pron.)* इलेवन्थ– coming after the tenth in numbering or counting order, position, time, etc. being the ordinal number of eleven: often written 11th ग्यारहवां He is an *eleventh* standard student.

eligible *(adj.)* एलिजबूल– fit, worthy, or qualified, as for an office or function योग्य, पात्र, उपयुक्त She is not *eligible* to participate in the contest .

eligibility *(n.)* ऍलिजॅबलिटी– the quality or state of being fit, worthy, or qualified, as for an office or function पात्रता, योग्यता If you are 21 years old, you have the *eligibility* to vote.

eliminate *(v.)* इलिमिनेट्– to remove or take out; get rid of निकाल देना, हटाना Many people were *eliminated* in the second round of interview.

elongate *(v.)* इलाँगेट– to make or become longer; stretch लम्बा करना या हो जाना Her legs were *elongated* by wearing very high heels.

elongated *(adj.)* इलाँगेटेड– long and narrow; slender लंबा, खिंचा हुआ Afghani women have *elongated* faces.

else *(adj.)* एल्स– 1. other; different दूसरा, अन्य, और No one *else* knows what I am going to tell you. This isn't my book, it is someone *else's.*
2. *(IDM.)* or else if not, then अन्यथा, नहीं तो Walk carefully or *else* you may slip.

elsewhere *(adv.)* एल्सवेअर– in or to another place; somewhere else और कहीं, अन्यत्र She is looking for a job *elsewhere.*

elite *(n.)* एलीट– the most powerful, rich, gifted, or educated members of a group, community, etc. संभ्रांत वर्ग, श्रेष्ठ वर्ग He considers himself an intellectual *elite.*

email *(n.)* ईमेल– a way of sending messages and data to other people by electronic mail ई-मेल, ई-पत्र I sent him all the information by an *email.*

emancipate *(v.)* इमैन्सिपेट्– to free from restriction or restraint, esp social or legal restraint मुक्त/स्वाधीन करना Today's women are *emancipated* enough to fend for themselves.

embark *(v.)* एम्बार्क्– to board (a ship or aircraft) (जहाज़ पर) चढ़ना, चढ़ाना, प्रारंभ करना The announcer requested the passengers travelling to Mumbai to *embark* on the plane.

embarrass *(v.)* इमबैरस– to feel or cause to feel confusion or self-consciousness; disconcert; fluster घबरा देना, परेशान/व्याकुल करना Tripping on the stage *embarrassed* me a lot.

embarrassing *(adj.)* इमबैरसिंग– causing one to feel confusion or self-consciousness; disconcerting झेंपने वाला, परेशानी में डालने वाला I felt *embarrassing* when everybody started looking at me.

embarrassed *(adj.)* इमबैरस्ड– feeling confusion or self-consciousness; disconcerted; flustered शर्मिंदा, व्याकुल She gets *embarrassed* if we ask her to dance.

embarrassment *(n.)* इमबैरसमेण्ट– the state of being embarrassed लज्जा, घबराहट The defeat of cricket team came as a big *embarrassment.*

embassy *(n.)* एमबसी– the residence or place of official business of an ambassador दूतावास, राजदूतावास Her father works in a Russian *embassy.*

embellish *(v.)* इम्बेलिश– to improve or beautify by adding detail or ornament; adorn अलंकृत करना, सजाना, सँवारना The dress was *embellished* with stones and sequins.

emblem *(n.)* एमूब्लम्– a visible object or representation that symbolizes a quality, type, group, etc. esp the concrete symbol of an abstract idea प्रतीक चिह्न, निशान We should respect our national *emblem* and flag.

embrace *(v.)* इम्ब्रेस्– (of a person) to take or clasp (another person) in the arms, or (of two people) to clasp each other, as in affection, greeting, etc. hug आलिंगन करना, गले

लगाना, स्वीकार करना My grandmother *embraced* me when I went to see her.

embroidery *(n.)* इम्ब्रॉइडरी– decorative needlework done usually on loosely woven cloth or canvas, often being a picture or pattern बेल-बूटे काढ़ने की कला, कढ़ाई, कशीदाकारी She wore a very nice *embroidery* suit in the party.

emerald *(n.)* एमरल्ड्– 1. a green transparent precious stone पन्ना, मरकत *Emerald* is a precious stone.
2. *(adj.)* **emerald green** clear deep green पन्ना के समान *Emerald green* is my favourite colour.

emerge *(v.)* इमर्ज्– to come up to the surface of or rise from water or other liquid उभरना, ऊपर उठना All were waiting for the doctor to *emerge* from the operation theatre.

emergency *(n.)* इमर्जन्सी– an unforeseen or sudden occurrence, esp of a danger demanding immediate remedy or action आपातकाल, आपात, आकस्मिक संकट Will you please come fast. *Its an emergency.*

emigrate *(v.)* एमिग्रेट्– to leave one place or country, esp one's native country, in order to settle in another अपना देश छोड़कर दूसरे देश जा बसना, उत्प्रवास करना, प्रवासी होना Dr Khan *emigrated* to Dubai twenty years ago.

eminent *(adj.)* एमिनन्ट्– above others in rank, merit, or reputation; distinguished उत्कृष्ट, श्रेष्ठ, उच्च, प्रवर Dr Abdul Kalam is an *eminent* scientist.

eminently *(adv.)* एमिनेण्टली– extremely असाधारण रूप में, अत्यधिक Karan is *eminently* suitable for the job.

emotion *(n.)* इमोश्न्– any strong feeling, as of joy, sorrow, or fear भाव, मनोभाव Even animals have *emotions.*

emotional *(adj.)* इमोशनल्– of, characteristic of, or expressive of emotion भावुक Women are *emotional* by nature.

emotionally *(adv.)* इमोशनली– in a way that appeals to or arouses emotion; in a way that causes people to have strong feelings or shows that they have them भावुकता I was *emotionally* disturbed by the news of my friend's sudden death.

emperor *(n.)* एम्परर्– a monarch who rules or reigns over an empire सम्राट Julius Caesar was a great Roman *emperor.*

emphasis *(n.)* एम्फ़सिस– special importance or significance विशेष महत्त्व They have put more *emphasis* on red colour.

emphasize (ise) *(v.)* एमूफ़साइज़्– to give emphasis or prominence to; stress प्रमुखता देना, महत्त्व देना The teacher *emphasized* on the importance of healthy eating.

employ *(v.)* एम्प्लॉइ–1. to engage or make use of the services (of a person) in return for money; hire नौकर रखना, काम में लगाना Ram was *employed* in a bank.
2. to provide work or occupation for; keep busy; occupy काम में लाना, प्रयोग करना How will you *employ* your time during the vacation?

employment *(n.)* एम्प्लॉइमेंट– the work or occupation in which a person is employed रोज़गार, नौकरी It is difficult to find *employment* in government sector.

empty *(adj.)* एम्प्टी– 1. containing nothing खाली, रिक्त I am *empty* stomach since morning.
2. *(v.)* to make or become empty खाली करना या होना *Empty* this glass and clean it.

empty-handed *(adj.)* एम्पटि-हेन्डड– carrying nothing in the hands ख़ाली हाथ, बिना कुछ हाथ में लिए The thief went *empty-handed* from my house.

enable *(v.)* एनेब्ल्– to provide (someone) with adequate power, means, opportunity, or authority (to do something) समर्थ/योग्य बनाना, अधिकार देना My bonus *enabled* me to buy a TV set.

enchanting *(adj.)* एनचान्टिंग– pleasant; delightful मोहक, मनोहर The song that she sang in the concert was really *enchanting.*

encircle *(v.)* एनसर्कल्– to form a circle around; enclose within a circle; surround चारों ओर घेरा खींचना या बनाना, घेरना *Encircle* the odd one outs.

enclose *(v.)* एन्क्लोज़–1. to close; hem in; surround घेरना, बाड़ा लगाना The garden was *enclosed* with a fence to keep the animals away.
2. to put in an envelope or wrapper, esp together with a letter जोड़ देना, साथ रखना She *enclosed* a form along with her letter.

enclosure *(n.)* एनक्लोज़र– the act of enclosing or state of being enclosed संलग्नक, नत्थी किया हुआ The form was an *enclosure.*

encounter *(v.)* एनूकाउन्टर्–1. to come into conflict with (an enemy, army, etc.) in battle or contest का सामना करना Aged people often *encounter* discrimination at work.
2. to come upon or meet casually or unexpectedly से मिलना/भेंट होना I *encountered* a saint on my flight to Bangalore.
3. *(n.)* a meeting with a person or thing, esp when casual or unexpected मुठभेड़, भिड़ंत The criminal was killed in a police *encounter.*

encourage *(v.)* एनूकरेज–1. to inspire (someone) with the courage or confidence (to do something) हिम्मत/साहस बढ़ाना The students cheered loudly to *encourage* their school hockey team which was on victory path.
2. to stimulate (something or someone to do something) by approval or help; support प्रेरित करना She *encouraged* her to become a model.

encouragement *(n.)* एनूकेरजमेण्ट– the action of encouraging someone बढ़ावा, प्रोत्साहन This activity will bring lot of *encouragments* in the students.

end *(n.)* एण्ड– 1. a final state, esp death; destruction अन्त, समाप्ति The movie became very boring at the *end.*
2. *(v.)* to bring or come to a finish; conclude समाप्त करना/होना Where does this road *end*?

endanger *(v.)* एनडेंजर– to put in danger or peril; imperil संकट/ख़तरे में डालना Drinking while driving can *endanger* our life.

endangered *(adj.)* एनूडेंजर्ड– in danger: used esp of animals in danger of extinction संकटग्रस्त We must protect the *endangered* species.

endeavour *(n.)* एण्डेवर्– 1. an effort to do or attain something कठिन प्रयास, कोशिश Students *endeavour* to score good marks.
2. *(v.)* to try, very hard भरसक प्रयत्न करना Rahul *endeavoured* to win the marathon race.

ending *(n.)* एनूडिंग– the act of bringing to or reaching an end अंत, समाप्ति The film had a tragic *ending* which made me cry.

endless *(adj.)* एण्डलेस– having or seeming to have no end; eternal or infinite अनन्त, अंतहीन, बहुत लंबा I was performing an *endless* task.

endurance *(n.)* एण्ड्यूअरण्स– something endured a hardship, strain, or privation सहनशक्ति, धीरज Gandhiji was a man of *endurance.*

endure *(v.)* एण्ड्युअर– to undergo (hardship, strain, privation, etc.)

without yielding; to bear सहना, झेलना, टिकना Dr. B.R. Ambedkar *endured* many a hardship during his early education.

enemy *(n.)* एनिमी– a person hostile or opposed to a policy, cause, person, or group, esp one who actively tries to do damage; opponent दुश्मन, शत्रु It's better to stay alone rather than making people your *enemy*.

energetic *(adj.)* एनर्जेटिक– having or showing much energy or force; vigorous ओजस्वी, कर्मठ She was the most *energetic* person in the whole play.

energy *(n.)* एनर्जी–1. intensity or vitality of action or expression; forcefulness कर्मशक्ति, ऊर्जस्विता Doctor advised the patient to take some tonic to increase his *energy*.

2. capacity or tendency for intense activity; vigour ऊर्जा *Energy* is essential for the working of both the human body and the machines.

enforce *(v.)* एनफ़ॉर्स्– to ensure observance of or obedience to (a law, decision, etc.) बाध्य करना, दबाव डालना Government makes laws and the police *enforce* them.

engage *(v.)* एन्गेज–1. to be bound by a promise to marry, to be betrothed सगाई करना, वाग्दान करना She got *engaged* when she was just 19 years of age.

2. to secure the services of; to employ काम में लगाना, नौकरी पर रखना How do you find the new servant you have *engaged*?

3. to occupy self व्यस्त होना I have made myself *engaged* in many activities.

engagement *(n.)* एनगेजमेण्ट– an appointment or arrangement, esp for business or social purposes नियुक्ति, विनियोजन Do you have any *engagement* this evening?

engine *(n.)* एंजिन– any machine designed to convert energy, esp heat energy, into mechanical work इंजन My father has diesel *engine* in his car.

engineer *(n.)* इंजिनिअर्– a person trained in any branch of the profession of engineering अभियंता, इंजीनियर I called an *engineer* when my computer crashed.

engrave *(v.)* एन्ग्रेव– to inscribe (a design, writing, etc.) onto (a block, plate, or other surface used for printing) by carving, etching with acid, or other process उत्कीर्ण करना, अंकित करना My name is *engraved* on the trophy.

engrossed *(adj.)* एन्ग्रोस्ड्– completely absorbed in something to the exclusion of anything else तल्लीन When I went to her place, she was *engrossed* in playing games on computer.

enhance *(v.)* एन्हान्स– to intensify or increase in quality, value, power, etc. improve; augment बढ़ाना, बेहतर बनाना You can *enhance* this article by keeping the sentences short.

enjoy *(v.)* एन्जॉइ– to receive pleasure from; to take joy in रस लेना, भोगना, आनंद प्राप्त करना I really *enjoyed* the journey alot

➢ **enjoy yourself**– to have a good time मौज-मस्ती करना, मस्ती लेना, You *enjoy yourself* at the party.

enjoyable *(adj.)* एन्जॉयबल– that provides pleasure मज़ेदार, आनंदप्रद We had an *enjoyable* journey to Ooty.

enjoyment *(n.)* एन्जॉयमन्ट– the act or condition of receiving pleasure from something आनंद, मौज, मज़ा The day was full of *enjoyment* and excitment.

enlarge *(v.)* एन्लार्ज–1. to make or grow larger in size, scope, etc.

increase or expand बढ़ना, बढ़ाना, विस्तार देना There is a plan to *enlarge* our school by building new rooms.
2. to make (a photographic print) of a larger size than the negative बड़ा करना Please get this photograph *enlarged.*

enlighten *(v.)* एनलाइटन— to give information or understanding to; instruct; edify शिक्षा/जानकारी देना My grandfather *enlightened* my knowledge.

enlightenment *(n.)* एनलाइटनमेण्ट— the awakening to ultimate truth by which man is freed आत्मज्ञान, प्रबोधन Gautam Buddha got spiritual *enlightenment* at a very early age.

enlist *(v.)* एनलिस्ट— to engage or secure (a person, his services, or his support) for a venture, cause, etc. भरती करना/नाम लिखना या सहारा प्राप्त करना The public was being *enlisted* to help drought victims.

enmity *(n.)* एन्मटी— a feeling of hostility or ill-will, as between enemies; antagonism दुश्मनी, बैर, शत्रुता Their personal *enmity* brought conflict at home.

enormous *(adj.)* एनॉर्मस्— unusually large in size, extent, or degree; immense; vast बहुत बड़ा, विशाल Former President of India Dr. S. D. Sharma gifted his *enormous* collection of books to the Bhopal library.

enough *(adj.)* इनफ़— 1. sufficient to answer a need, demand, supposition, or requirement; adequate पर्याप्त, काफ़ी The snacks were more than *enough* for me.
2. *(adv.)* so as to be adequate or sufficient; as much as necessary पर्याप्त रूप से Is the tea hot *enough*?

enquire *(v.)* एन्क्वायर— to seek information; ask जांच करना, पूछताछ करना He *enquired* about my family.

enquiry *(n.)* एन्क्वाइअरी— a request for information; a question जांच, पूछताछ I will have to make a few *enquiries* about him.

enrage *(v.)* एनरेज्— to provoke to fury; put into a rage; anger क्रोध/गुस्सा करना My mother was *enraged* at my late coming.

enrich *(v.)* एनरिच्— to increase the wealth of धनी/सम्पन्न बना देना A country *enriched* by oil revenues

ensure *(v.)* एनशोर— to make certain or sure; guarantee निश्चित/सुनिश्चित करना I can't *ensure* her arrival.

entangled *(adj.)* एनटैंगल्ड— caught in or as if in a tangle उलझा हुआ, फंसा हुआ The bird was *entangled* in the net.

enter *(v.)* एण्टर्—1. to come or go into (a place, house, etc.) प्रवेश करना, घुसना Ram stood in the queue to *enter* the theatre.
2. to record (an item such as a commercial transaction) in a journal, account, register, etc. भाग लेना, नाम लिखना, दर्ज करना The teacher *entered* the name of the new student in the attendance register.

enterprise *(n.)* एण्टरप्राइज्— a project or undertaking, esp one that requires boldness or effort नई योजना या उपक्रम, कंपनी, उद्यम He has launched a big *enterprise* in Bangalore.

entertain *(v.)* एण्टॅर्टेन—1. to provide amusement for (a person or audience) मनोरंजन करना The elder brother *entertained* the children by telling them stories.
2. to show hospitality to (guests) सत्कार/स्वागत करना The host *entertained* the guest lavishly.

entertaining *(adj.)* एन्टर्टेनिंग— serving to entertain or give pleasure; diverting; amusing मनोरंजक, मनोरंजन करने वाला It was a very *entertaining* play, I enjoyed alot.

entertainment *(n.)* एन्टर्टेनमन्ट– the act or art of entertaining or state of being entertained मनोरंजन, दिल-बहलाव Theatre is a great source of *entertainment.*

enthusiasm *(n.)* एन्थ्यूज़िऐज़्म्– ardent and lively interest or eagerness उत्साह, उमंग Kids were filled with *enthusiasm* after hearing about the trip.

enthusiast *(n.)* एन्थ्यूज़िऐस्ट– a person filled with or motivated by enthusiasm उत्साही He is a sports *enthusiast.*

enthusiastic *(adj.)* एन्थ्यूज़िएस्टिक– filled with or motivated by enthusiasm; keen उत्साह से परिपूर्ण He is very *enthusiastic* about sports.

enthusiastically *(adv.)* एन्थ्यूज़िए- in an enthusiastic manner स्टिकली–जोश से भरकर The players embraced each other *enthusiastically* after the victory.

entire *(adj.)* एंटायर्– whole; complete सम्पूर्ण, समग्र I would like to see the *entire* script before finalizing it.

entirely *(adv.)* एण्टायर्ली– wholly; completely पूर्णतः, पूर्णरूप से I *entirely* agree with you.

entitle *(v.)* एण्टाइटल्– to give (a person) the right to do or have something; qualify; allow अधिकार देना She was *entitled* to do this work.

entrance *(n.)* एण्ट्रन्स– a door, gate etc. used for entering a place or room प्रवेश-द्वार, प्रवेश-मार्ग The police caught the robber at the *entrance* of the gate.

entry *(n.)* एंट्री– an act of going into a place प्रवेश, दाखिला The *entry* of boys was banned at the gate of girls' hostel.

envelop *(v.)* एन्वेलप्– to wrap or enclose in or as if in a covering ढकना, लपेट लेना The roads were *enveloped* in fog.

envelope *(n.)* एन्वलोप्– a flat covering of paper, usually rectangular in shape and with a flap that can be folded over and sealed, used to enclose a letter, etc. लिफ़ाफ़ा, आवरण Put this letter in an *envelope* and post it.

envious *(adj.)* एन्विअस– feeling, showing, or resulting from envy ईर्ष्यालु Neighbours were *envious* of Rahul's new car.

environment *(n.)* एनवाइरनमन्ट– 1. the external surroundings in which a plant or animal lives, which tend to influence its development and behaviour पर्यावरण We must protect our *environment* from pollution.

2. external conditions or surroundings, esp those in which people live or work वातावरण It is important to maintain a good *environment* in the office.

envy *(n.)* एन्वी– 1. a feeling of grudging or somewhat admiring discontent aroused by the possessions, achievements, or qualities of another ईर्ष्या, जलन Rakhi watched them with *envy.*

2. *(v.)* to be envious of (a person or thing) ईर्ष्या करना, जलन रखना Why do you *envy* me?

epic *(n.)* एपिक– a long narrative poem recounting in elevated style the deeds of a legendary hero, esp one originating in oral folk tradition वीरगाथा, महाकाव्य Keep all the indian *epics* at one place.

epidemic *(n.)* एपिडेमिक– a widespread occurrence of a disease महामारी There are chances of *epidemic* in the village after the flood.

episode *(n.)* एपिसोड–1.an incident, event, or series of events घटना, प्रसंग We should forget that humiliating *episode* and move on.

2. any one of the sections into which a serialized novel or radio

or television programme is divided धारावाहिक की कड़ी I missed the last *episode* of that serial.

equable *(adj.)* एकवबल्– even-tempered; placid धीर, शांत She is a lady of an *equable* temperament.

equal *(adj.)* ईक्वल्– identical in size, quantity, degree, intensity, etc. the same (as) समान, बराबर You can divide the cake in 8 *equal* parts.

equality *(n.)* ईक्वॉलटी– the state of being equal बराबरी, समानता We have the right to *equality* of expression.

equally *(adv.)* ईक्वली– fairly; evenly समान रूप से Boys and girls are still not treated *equally* in India.

equip *(v.)* एक्विप– to furnish with (necessary supplies, etc.) सज्जित करना Are you *equipped* to go on a hunting trip?

equipment *(n.)* एक्विपमेंट– a set of tools, devices, kit, etc. assembled for a specific purpose, such as a soldier's kit and weapons साज-सामग्री Dinesh wanted to equip his office with modern *equipment*.

equivalent *(adj.)* इक्विवलेण्ट– equal in value, quantity, significance, etc. बराबर, समान Do you have a qualification which is *equivalent* to a degree?

era *(n.)* ईरा– a period of time considered as being of a distinctive character; epoch युग, संवत्, काल The Qutub Minar was constructed long before the British *era*.

eradicate *(v.)* इरैडिकेट्– to obliterate; stamp out उन्मूलन करना, मिटाना The new Prime Minister promised to *eradicate* unemployment completely.

erase *(v.)* इरेज़्– to obliterate or rub out (something written, typed, etc.) मिटाना, लुप्त करना She *erased* the previous answer and wrote a new one.

erect *(adj.)* इरेक्ट्–1. upright in posture or position; not bent or leaning सीधा, खड़ा Stand *erect*!
2. *(v.)* to put up; construct; build खड़ा करना, निर्माण करना How much time does it take to *erect* a steel mill?

erotic *(adj.)* इरॉटिक– showing or involving sexual desire or pleasure कामविषयक, कामोद्दीपक He was reading an *erotic* poem.

err *(v.)* अर्– to make a mistake ग़लती/भूल करना या होना To *err* is human.

errand *(n.)* एरण्ड– a short trip undertaken to perform a necessary task or commission (सौंपा हुआ) काम The servant was tired of doing many *errands* for his master.

error *(n.)* एरर्– a mistake or inaccuracy, as in action or speech ग़लती, भूल I did not expect any *error* from your write-up.

erroneous *(adj.)* इरोनिअस्– based on or containing error; mistaken; incorrect अशुद्ध, ग़लत She has *erroneous* ideas about Hindu mythology.

escape *(v.)* एस्केप–1. to get away from (confinements, captors, etc.) भाग जाना, पलायन करना Prisoners' attempt to *escape* from the jail was foiled by alert guards.
2. to be articulated inadvertently or involuntarily बचना, बच जाना Amit *escaped* narrowly when his bike skidded.
3. *(n.) a means or way of escape* बचाव, रक्षा He had a narrow *escape* when his bike skidded suddenly on the road.

escort *(v.)* एस्कॉर्ट– to accompany or attend as an escort रक्षार्थ साथ जाना I have to *escort* my daughter to school.

especial *(adj.)* एस्पेशल– unusual; notable; exceptional ख़ास, विशेष, असाधारण Do you have *especial* interest in him?

especially *(adv.)* इस्पेशली– in particular; specifically खास तौर पर, असाधारण रूप से Uma *especially* prepared delicious dishes for her daughter's birthday party.

essay *(n.)* एसे– a short literary composition dealing with a subject analytically or speculatively निबंध My son won the first prize in an *essay* writing competition.

essential *(adj.)* एसेन्शल– vitally important; absolutely necessary अत्यावश्यक, लाज़िमी, मुख्य, मूलभूत Don't forget to pick up all the *essential* points in the meeting.

establish *(v.)* एस्टैब्लिश– to create or set up (an organization, etc.) on or as if on a permanent basis स्थापित करना, सिद्ध करना When was your business *established*?

establishment *(n.)* एस्टैब्लिशमेंट– the act of establishing or state of being established स्थापना, प्रतिष्ठान, संस्था My uncle decided to open a food *establishment* in New York city.

estate *(n.)* इस्टेट–1. a large piece of landed property, esp in the country भू-संपत्ति, जागीर, जायदाद Rohit bought a large *estate* outside the town.
2. a large area of property development, esp of new houses or (trading estate) of factories भूमि, भूभाग Rahul has a factory in the industrial *estate.*

estimate *(n.)* एस्टिमेट्– an approximate calculation अनुमानित ख़र्च/मूल्य, आकलन, अनुमान It is better to prepare an *estimate* before entering into the market.

eternal *(adj.)* एटर्नल– without an end; lasting for ever शाश्वत, अनादि, अनंत Romeo and Juliet is an *eternal* love story.

ethical *(adj.)* एथिकल–1. in accordance with principles of conduct that are considered correct, esp those of a given profession or group नैतिक, नीति-विषयक Is it *ethical* to promote wine through advertisement?
2. of or relating to ethics नैतिक दृष्टिकोण से उचित I don't think it is *ethical* for you to accept this job.

ethics *(n.)* एथिक्स– the philosophical study of the moral value of human conduct and of the rules and principles that ought to govern it; moral philosophy नीति-शास्त्र We must not violate the code of *ethics* of our profession.

ethnic *(adj.)* एथ्निक– relating to or characteristic of a human group having racial, religious, linguistic, and certain other traits in common जाति या प्रजाति संबंधी She gave an *ethnic* look to her boutique.

etiquette *(n.)* एटिकेट– the customs or rules governing behaviour regarded as correct or acceptable in social or official life शिष्टाचार We should follow the strict rules of professional *etiquette.*

eunuch *(n.)* यूनक– an impotent man हिजड़ा, नपुंसक He is a very famous *eunuch* of his locality.

evade *(v.)* इवेड– to get away from or avoid टालना, टालमटोल करना Why are you trying to *evade* the question?

evaluate *(v.)* एवैल्युएट– to assess the amount or value of मूल्यांकन करना We must *evaluate* the market demands before launching a new product.

evaporate *(v.)* इवैपरेट– to change or cause to change from a liquid or solid state to a vapour भाप बनना या बनाना The water in the bowl *evaporated* when kept in the sun.

eve *(n.)* ईव– the evening or day before some special event or festival संध्या, पूर्व संध्या They met on the *eve* of Christmas.

even *(adv.)* ईवन्–1. notwithstanding; in spite of भी, से भी, ज्यों, जिस समय *Even* if you have a good hand, you should get your letters typed.

2. *(adj.)* on the same level or in the same plane (as) समतल, बराबर Your table does not have an *even* surface.

3. equally balanced between two sides बराबर, समान The first half of the beauty contest was very *even*.

4. (of a number) divisible by two सम, दो से विभाज्य 2, 4, 6, 8 are *even* numbers.

evening *(n.)* ईवनिंग– the latter part of the day, esp from late afternoon शाम, सायंकाल I had a very bad *evening* yesterday.

evenly *(adv.)* ईवनली– in an equal manner समान रूप से The chocolates were *evenly* distributed among the children.

event *(n.)* इवेण्ट– anything that takes place or happens, esp something important; happening; incident घटना, परिणाम It was important to attend all the school *events*.

➢ **at any/all event**– regardless of cost or sacrifice involved चाहें कुछ हो जाए *At any event* I will meet you on Sunday.

eventually *(adj.)* इवेन्चुअली– at the very end; finally आख़िरकार, अन्ततः, अन्त में *Eventually,* Sheela realised her mistake.

ever *(adv.)* एवर्–1. always, all the time सदैव, सदा, हमेशा Have you *ever* travelled by air?

2. at any time जब से, तब से I have known Anil *ever* since we were children.

everlasting *(adj.)* एवरलास्टिंग– never coming to an end; eternal सदा रहने वाला, चिरस्थायी They have an *everlasting* love affair.

every *(adj.)* एव्रि– each one (of the class specified), without exception प्रत्येक, हर एक, हर कोई Students have to get up early *every* day.

everybody *(pron.)* एवरिबॉडी– every person; everyone प्रत्येक व्यक्ति, हर कोई *Everybody* enjoyed the performance alot.

everyone *(pron.)* एवरिवन– every person; everybody प्रत्येक व्यक्ति *Everyone* was looking perplexed.

everything *(pron.)* एवरिथिंग– the entirety of a specified or implied class सब कुछ *Everything* was going on perfectly.

everywhere *(adv.)* एवरिवेअर– to or in all parts or places सब जगह, सर्वत्र These kind of suits are available *everywhere* in India.

evidence *(n.)* एविडेन्स– a mark or sign that makes evident; indication सबूत, प्रमाण, गवाही You cannot accuse your servant of theft without *evidence.*

➢ **in evidence**– present and clearly seen स्पष्ट दिखाई देने वाला, The police was *in evidence* everywhere.

evident *(adj.)* एविडेण्ट– easy to see or understand; readily apparent सुस्पष्ट It was *evident* to me that he was telling white lie.

evil *(adj.)* ईविल– 1. morally wrong or bad; wicked बुरा, अशुभ, दुष्ट You will not escape the consequences of your *evil* acts.

2. *(n.)* the quality or an instance of being morally wrong; wickedness बुराई, दुष्टता Try to recognise *evil* and improve yourself.

exact *(adj.)* इग्ज़ैक्ट– correct in every detail; strictly accurate सही, सुनिश्चित What is the *exact* percentage you scored?

exactly *(adv.)* इग्ज़ैक्टलि– in an exact manner; accurately or precisely ठीक-ठीक, तथ्यतः I scored *exactly* 92.55% in my examinations.

exaggerate *(v.)* एग्ज़ैजरेट– to regard or represent as larger or greater, more important or more successful, etc. than is true बढ़ा-चढ़ाकर कहना, अतिशयोक्ति करना He *exaggerated* his performance by comparing himself to Sachin Tendulkar.

examination *(n.)* इग्ज़ैमिनेशन– written exercises, oral questions, or practical tasks, set to test a candidate's knowledge and skill परीक्षा After the *examinations,* results are eagerly awaited.

examine *(v.)* इग्ज़ैमिन– to look at, inspect, or scrutinize carefully or in detail; investigate परीक्षा लेना, परखना, जांचना The police *examined* the accident site for clues.

example *(n.)* इग्ज़ाम्पल–1. a specimen or instance that is typical of the group or set of which it forms part; sample उदाहरण, दृष्टांत Refer to the *example* if you cannot understand this question. 2. a precedent, illustration of a principle, or model नमूना, आदर्श Your conduct should be an *example* to the others.

excavate *(v.)* एक्सकवेट– to remove (soil, earth, etc.) by digging; to dig out खोदना, खोदकर कुछ निकालना A 3600-year-old ancient city was *excavated* in Egypt.

exceed *(v.)* इक्सीड– to be superior to (a person or thing), esp in size or quality; to excel से अधिक या बढ़कर होना, से आगे बढ़ जाना Never *exceed* the permissible speed limit when you drive.

excel *(v.)* एक्सेल– to be superior to (another or others); to surpass से बढ़कर होना, से उत्कृष्ट होना In her dancing, Usha *excelled* all the other performers.

excellence *(n.)* एक्सलन्स– the state or quality of excelling or being exceptionally good; extreme merit; superiority श्रेष्ठता Her performance was par *excellence.*

excellent *(adj.)* एक्सलन्ट– exceptionally good; extremely meritorious; superior अति उत्तम/श्रेष्ठ, बहुत अच्छा/बढ़िया She did an *excellent* job in her exams.

except *(prep.)* एक्सेप्ट– other than; apart from; with the exception of को छोड़कर, के सिवाय/अतिरिक्त There is nothing in my pocket *except* a handkerchief.

exception *(n.)* एक्सेप्शन– a thing or person that is not included in a general way अपवाद *Exceptions* are always there.

exceptional *(adj.)* एक्सेप्शनल– forming an exception; not ordinary अपवादात्मक, विशिष्ट, ख़ास, असाधारण Sachin was awarded for his *exceptional* performance.

exceptionally *(adv.)* एक्सेप्शनली– to an extremely and unusually high degree अपवादस्वरूप Sita was *exceptionally* good in her previous task.

excess *(n.)* एक्सेस– the state or act of going beyond normal, sufficient, or permitted limits अतिक्रमण, असंयम, अतिरेक *Excess* of flowery phrases lessens the impact of a serious article.

excessive *(adj.)* एक्सेसिव– exceeding the normal or permitted extents or limits; immoderate; inordinate अत्यधिक, अतिशय He died of *excessive* drinking.

excessively *(adv.)* एकसेसिवली– too great a degree; too बेहद, बेपनाह, अत्यधिक The man was *excessively* drunk while driving his car.

exchange *(n.)* एक्सचेंज–1. anything given or received as an equivalent, replacement, or substitute for something else आदान-प्रदान, विनिमय I can give you my pen in *exchange* of your book.
2. a switching centre in which telephone lines are interconnected

मिलान-केंद्र Where is the telephone *exchange*?

3. *(v.)* to give and receive (information, ideas, etc.); interchange अदला-बदली करना, विनिमय करना The shopkeeper refused to *exchange* the shirt for any other item.

excite *(v.)* एक्साइट– to arouse (a person) to strong feeling, esp to pleasurable anticipation or nervous agitation भड़काना, उकसाना, उत्तेजित करना It was very *exciting* to know about her.

excited *(adj.)* एक्साइटेड– emotionally aroused, esp to pleasure or agitation उत्तेजित, अधीर Students were *excited* about their educational tour to Goa.

excitement *(n.)* एक्साइट्मेंट्– the state of being excited उत्तेजना, आवेश What is all this *excitement* about?

exciting *(adj.)* एक्साइटिंग– causing excitement; stirring; stimulating उत्तेजक Mumbai is one of the most *exciting* city.

exclaim *(v.)* एक्स्क्लेम– to cry out or speak suddenly or excitedly, as from surprise, delight, horror, etc. चिल्ला उठना, चिल्लाना Ravi *exclaimed* in surprise when he saw his long lost friend.

exclude *(v.)* इक्स्क्लूड– to keep out; to prevent from entering, to reject or not consider; to leave out निकाल देना, अलग करना Lets *exclude* these items from the list to save the money.

exclusive *(adj.)* एकसक्लूसिव– excluding all else; rejecting other considerations, possibilities, events, etc. एकमात्र, अनन्य, My younger sister has *exclusive* interest in painting.

exclusively *(adv.)* एकसक्लूसिवली– involving only the things mentioned केवल, सिर्फ, मात्र This hostel has been built *exclusively* for the working women.

excursion *(n.)* इक्स्कर्श्न– a short outward and return journey, esp for relaxation, sightseeing, etc. outing सैर, भ्रमण I took my family on an *excursion* to Suraj Kund.

excuse *(v.)* एक्स्क्यूज़–1. to pardon or forgive sb for sth क्षमा/माफ़ करना Please *excuse* me for being late.

2. to dismiss or allow to leave छुटकारा देना, मुक्त करना You will have to *excuse* me from coming to the meeting, as I am not well.

3. *(n.)* an explanation offered in defence of some fault or offensive behaviour or as a reason for not fulfilling an obligation, etc. बहाना What is your *excuse* for being late?

execute *(v.)* एक्सिक्यूट–1. to carry out; complete; perform; do पूरा करना, पालन करना, निष्पन्न करना The whole play was planned and *executed* nicely.

2. to put (a condemned person) to death; inflict capital punishment upon फाँसी देना The murderer was *executed* early this morning.

executive *(n.)* एग्ज़ेक्यटिव– a person or group responsible for the administration of a project, activity, or business कार्यकारी अधिकारी, प्रबंधक Mohit is a senior *executive* in a corporate house.

exempt *(v.)* एग्ज़ेम्प्ट– to release from an obligation, liability, tax, etc. excuse छूट देना, माफ़ी देना The accused was *exempted* from all charges.

exercise *(n.)* एक्सर्साइज़–1. physical exertion, esp for the purpose of development, training, or keeping fit व्यायाम, कसरत Few hours of *exercise* everyday keeps the body fit and fine.

2. *(v.)* to take exercise or perform exercises; exert one's muscles, etc. esp in order to keep fit व्यायाम करना We should *exercise* our brain as well as the body.

3. to practise using in order to develop or train अभ्यास Most students could not do the *exercise* given by the geometry teacher.

exert *(v.)* एग्ज़ट– to make a physical or mental effort प्रयास करना You will have to *exert* yourself to pass the tough examination with good marks.

exertion *(n.)* एग्ज़र्शन– great mental or physical effort प्रयत्न, प्रयास Too much *exertion* is not good for older age.

exhaust *(v.)* एग्ज़ॉस्ट–1. to drain the energy of; tire out खाली/समाप्त होना या करना It was *exhausting* in the office today.

exhausted *(adj.)* एग्ज़ॉस्टेड– tired and deprived of energy पूरी तरह से थक जाना After a hard day's work, it's natural to feel *exhausted.*

exhibit *(v.)* एग्ज़िबिट–1. to display (something) to the public for interest or instruction प्रदर्शित करना, दिखाना At which art gallery are you going to *exhibit* your paintings?

2. *(n.) an object or collection exhibited to the public* प्रदर्शित वस्तु, प्रदर्शन Among *exhibits* at the show was a rare antique piece.

exhibition *(n.)* एग्ज़िबिशन– a public display of art, products, skills, activities, etc. नुमाइश, प्रदर्शनी I am planning to visit the painting *exibition* this week.

exile *(n.)* एक्साइल– a prolonged, usually enforced absence from one's home or country; banishment देशनिकाला, निर्वासन King Ram went into an *exile* of fourteen years.

exist *(v.)* एग्ज़िस्ट– to have being or reality; to be होना, अस्तित्व रखना या बना रहना It is impossible to *exist* without air and water.

existence *(n.)* एग्ज़िस्टन्स– the fact or state of existing; being अस्तित्व, विद्यमानता Tell me, which is the largest animal in *existence*?

existing *(adj.)* एग्ज़िस्टिंग– existing is used to describe something which is now present, available, or in operation, especially when you are contrasting it with something which is planned for the future विद्यमान, मौजूदा, प्रचलित New law will soon replace the *existing* one.

exit *(n.)* एग्ज़िट– 1. a way out; door or gate by which people may leave बाहर जाने का रास्ता, निकासी, प्रस्थान The *exit* gate was on the left hand side of the room.

2. *(v.) to go away or out; depart; leave* बाहर जाना, प्रस्थान करना We *exited* through the back door when the fire broke out.

exotic *(adj.)* एग्ज़ॉटिक– having a strange or bizarre विचित्र, असाधारण It is an *exotic* place to visit.

expand *(v.)* एक्स्पैंड– to make or become greater in extent, volume, size, or scope; increase फैलाना, बढ़ाना, विस्तार करना We can *expand* our business only if we have some more money.

expect *(v.)* एक्सपेक्ट– to regard as probable or likely; anticipate आशा/अपेक्षा करना I am so hurt. I did not *expect* this from you.

expectation *(n.)* एक्सपेक्टेशन– an attitude of expectancy or hope; anticipation आशा That was beyond my *expectation.*

expedition *(n.)* एक्सपेडिशन– an organized journey or voyage for a specific purpose, esp for exploration or for a scientific or military purpose किसी उद्देश्य से की गई यात्रा, खोजयात्रा We planned a fishing *expedition.*

expel *(v.)* एक्स्पेल– to eject or drive out with force निकाल देना, निष्कासित करना The principal *expelled* the misbehaving students from the school.

expend *(v.)* एक्स्पेन्ड– to spend; disburse ख़र्च करना, व्यय करना Some youth *expend* most of their money and energy on entertainment.

expenditure *(n.)* एक्स्पेन्डिचर– something expended, such as time or money ख़र्च, खर्चा, व्यय Why are your *expenditures* crossing your income?

expense *(n.)* एक्सपेन्स– a particular payment of money; expenditure व्यय, ख़र्च To travel in first class is a great *expense.*

expensive *(adj.)* एक्सपेन्सिव– high-priced; costly; dear क़ीमती, महंगी Your dress looks quite *expensive* (costly).

experience *(n.)* एक्स्पीरिअन्स–1. direct personal participation or observation; actual knowledge or contact अनुभव, तजुर्बा How many years of work *experience* do you have? 2. *(v.)* to participate in or undergo अनुभव करना I *experienced* many difficulties in this task.

experienced *(adj.)* एक्सपीरिअन्स्ड– having become skilful or knowledgeable from extensive contact or participation or observation तजुर्बेकार, अनुभवी Firoze is a very *experienced* driver.

experiment *(n.)* एक्स्पेरिमेंट– 1. a test or investigation, esp one planned to provide evidence for or against a hypothesis प्रयोग, परीक्षण Ram was very happy with the outcome of his *experiment* in Physics.

2. *(v.)* to make an experiment or *experiments* प्रयोग/परीक्षण करना Scientists *experimented* with a model of the space shuttle to test its power supply system.

expert *(adj.)* एक्स्पर्ट्– skilful or knowledgeable विशेषज्ञ, निपुण He was an *expert* in his field.

expertise *(n.)* एक्सपर्टीज़– special skill, knowledge, or judgment; expertness दक्षता Her *expertise* lies in her abiliy to speak well.

expire *(v.)* इक्सपाइअर्–1. to finish or run out; cease; come to an end, die श्वास छोड़ना, मरना When did the old man *expire*?

2. to end अन्त होना, समाप्त होना Our holidays *expire* next week.

expiry *(n.)* एक्सपायरी– a coming to an end, esp of a contract period; termination अंत, अवधि की समाप्ति The *expiry* date of this drug is November 2015.

explain *(v.)* एक्स्प्लेन– to make (something) comprehensible, esp by giving a clear and detailed account of the relevant structure, operation, surrounding circumstances, etc. स्पष्ट करना, समझाना Please *explain* to me the working of this machine.

explanation *(n.)* एक्स्प्लेनेशन– a clarification or statement of disputed terms or points स्पष्टीकरण, व्याख्या I don't need any *explanation* from you.

explicit *(adj.)* एक्सप्लिसिट– precisely and clearly expressed, leaving nothing to implication; fully stated सुस्पष्ट, साफ-साफ He gave me very *explicit* direction to reach his house.

explode *(v.)* एक्स्प्लोड– to burst or cause to burst with great violence as a result of internal pressure, esp through the detonation of an explosive; blow up विस्फोट होना/करना, फूट पड़ना The boiler will *explode* unless you let some steam out of it.

exploit *(v.)* एक्स्प्लॉइट– to take advantage of (a person, situation, etc.), esp unethically or unjustly for one's own ends शोषण करना The child labourer was *exploited* by being made to work the whole day for a small amount.

explore *(v.)* एक्स्प्लॉर्– to examine or investigate, esp systematically खोज करना, छानबीन करना I love to *explore* different places.

explorer *(n.)* एक्सप्लॉरर्– a member of the senior branch of the Scouts अन्वेषक Marco Polo, Ibn Battuta, Vasco Da Gama and Columbus were the great *explorers.*

explosion *(n.)* एक्सप्लोशन– a violent release of energy resulting from a rapid chemical or nuclear reaction, esp one that produces a shock wave, loud noise, heat, and light विस्फ़ोट, धमाका A huge *explosion* killed many innocent people on the way.

explosive *(n.)* एक्सप्लोसिव– a substance that decomposes rapidly under certain conditions with the production of gases, which expand by the heat of the reaction. विस्फ़ोटक, धमाके वाला The police recovered twenty kilograms of *explosives* from the terrorists.

export *(n.)* एक्स्पॉर्ट– 1. goods (visible exports) or services (invisible exports) sold to a foreign country or countries निर्यात Are you in the *export* business?
2. *(v.)* to sell (goods or services) or ship (goods) to a foreign country or countries निर्यात करना, (देश से) बाहर भेजना We *export* mangoes to the Western countries.

expose *(v.)* एक्स्पोज़– to bring to public notice; disclose; reveal खोलकर रखना, प्रकट करना The inquiry committee *exposed* all dubious deals of the corrupt minister.

exposure *(n.)* एक्सपोश़र– the act of exposing or the condition of being exposed अनावरण, प्रदर्शन Too much of media *exposure* succeeded in drawing the audience to the movie theatres.

express *(v.)* एक्स्प्रेस– 1. to transform (ideas) into words; utter; verbalize व्यक्त करना, प्रकट करना If you want to become a good speaker, you must learn to *express* yourself effectively.
2. *(adj.)* of, concerned with, or designed for rapid transportation of people, merchandise, mail, money, etc. आशुगामी, जल्द पहुंचानेवाला Is this an *express* train?

expression *(n.)* एक्सप्रेशन– a look on the face that indicates mood or emotion रुख, मुद्रा, भाव Why do you have such a sad *expression* on your face?

expressive *(adj.)* एक्सप्रेसिव– of, involving, or full of expression भावपूर्ण She has *expressive* eyes and face.

exquisite *(adj.)* एक्सक्विज़िट– extremely beautiful and pleasing अत्यंत सुन्दर The bride room was decorated in *exquisite* taste.

extend *(v.)* एक्सटेण्ड– to draw out or be drawn out; stretch फैलाना, बढ़ाना, विस्तृत करना You will have to *extend* your boundary wall to protect your garden.

extension *(n.)* एक्सटेंशन– the act of extending or the condition of being extended विस्तार, विस्तारण The *extension* of the subway will take several months.

extent *(n.)* एक्सटेण्ट– the range over which something extends; scope विस्तार, फैलाव He is true upto some *extent.*

exterior *(n.)* एक्स्टिअरिअर्– a part, surface, or region that is on the outside बाहरी स्वरूप, बहिर्भाग The *exterior* of the building was decorated with wooden carvings.

extinct *(adj.)* एकस्टिंक्ट– (of an animal or plant species) having no living representative; having died out विलुप्त, समाप्त There are many species which are nearly *extinct* in India.

extinguish *(v.)* एक्स्‌टिंग्विश– to put out (a light, flames, etc.) बुझाना My daughter tried to *extinguished* the flames.

extra *(adj.)* एक्सट्रा– being more than what is usual or expected; additional अधिक, अतिरिक्त I have got an *extra* T-shirt for evening.

extract *(v.)* एक्स्ट्रैक्ट– to withdraw, pull out, or uproot by force बाहर खींचना या निकालना The dentist *extracted* my broken teeth.

extraordinary *(adj.)* एक्स्ट्रॉर्डनरी– very unusual, remarkable, or surprising विलक्षण, असामान्य She was *extraordinarily* good in her last task.

extravagant *(adj.)* एक्स्ट्रैवगण्ट– spending money excessively or immoderately अपव्ययी, फिजूलखर्च She is very *extravagant* and often buys things she does not require.

extreme *(adj.)* एक्स्ट्रीम–1. being of a high or of the highest degree or intensity अधिकतम, नितान्त Martyrs showed *extreme* courage by sacrificing their life for the country's freedom.

2. farthest or outermost in direction सिरे का, दूरतम, अंत का I live at the *extreme* end of this street.

extremely *(adv.)* इक्स्ट्रीमली– to the extreme; exceedingly अत्यधिक I am *extremely* grateful to you for your assistance.

extremist *(n.)* एक्स्ट्रीमिस्ट– a person who hold extreme political or religious views उग्रवादी, अतिवादी Most of the politicians are *extremists* in nature.

extrovert *(n.)* एक्स्ट्रवर्ट– a person concerned more with external reality than inner feelings बहिर्मुखी He is an *extrovert,* while his brother is completely opposite.

eye *(n.)* आइ–1. the organ of sight on the face that you see with आँख, नयन, नेत्र Her daughter has got beautiful *eyes.*

2. a small hole, as at one end of a needle नाका Please put this thread through the *eye* of the needle.

➢ **before one's very eyes**– In one's very presence ठीक आँखों के सामने, The murder had taken place *before our very eyes.*

➢ **have an eye on**– to observe किसी पर कड़ी नज़र रखना, We should ***keep*** *an eye on* him.

➢ **in the eyes**– according to one's veiws की राय में, She is still a child *in my eyes.*

eyebrow *(n.)* आइब्रो– the line of hair above each eye भौंह, भृकुटि The new beautician at the salon spoiled my *eyebrows.*

eye-catching *(adj.)* आई-कैचिंग– tending to attract attention; striking चित्ताकर्षक It was an *eye-catching* advertisement on TV.

eyelash *(n.)* आई-लैश– any one of the short curved hairs that grow from the edge of the eyelids बरौनी Actresses use artificial *eyelashes* in movies.

eye-opener *(n.)* आई-ओपनर– something startling or revealing सच्चाई खोल देने वाली बात Travelling around the world was real *eye-opener* for me.

eyesight *(n.)* आई-साइट– the ability to see; faculty of sight नज़र, दृष्टिशक्ति Healthy foods can improve your *eyesight.*

eyewitness *(n.)* आईविटनस– a person present at an event who can describe what happened चश्मदीद गवाह, प्रत्यक्षदर्शी The statement of the *eyewitness* turned the case completely.

Ff

Ff *(n.)* एफ़–अंग्रेज़ी वर्णमाला का छठा अक्षर The sixth letter of the English alphabet. Fish begins with 'F'.

fable *(n.)* फ़ेबल– a short moral story, esp one with animals as characters उपदेशात्मक कहानी Give your child Aesop's *Fables* to read.

fabric *(n.)* फ़ैब्रिक– any cloth made from yarn or fibres by weaving, knitting, felting, etc. कपड़ा, वस्त्र Cotton *fabric* is good for the skin.

fabricate *(v.)* फैबरिकेटड– to devise, invent, or concoct (a story, lie, etc.) झूठी कहानी गढ़ना She was *fabricating* the story from start to finish.

fabulous *(adj.)* फ़ैब्युलस्– almost unbelievable; astounding; legendary आश्चर्यजनक, उत्कृष्ट You were looking *fabulous* in your black dress.

face *(n.)* फ़ेस– 1. the front of the head from the forehead to the lower jaw; visage चेहरा, मुख I have got wrinkles on my *face*.

2. *(v.)* to meet or be confronted by सामना करना, विरोध करना Rohit *faced* strong opposition from his parents in his inter-caste marriage.

➢ **face-to-face** *(adj.)*– direct; person-to-person आमने-सामने, We were standing *face to face* in the corridor.

facet *(n.)* फ़ैसेट– an aspect or phase, as of a subject or personality पहलू We must consider all the *facets* of this project before taking it up.

facetious *(adj.)* फ़सीशस– characterized by levity of attitude and love of joking मज़ाक़िया He kept *facetious* remarks on his friend.

facial *(adj.)* फ़ेशल– of or relating to the face चेहरे का, मुख-,आनन-Her *facial* expressions were showing that she was not happy.

facility *(n.)* फ़सिलटी– ease of action or performance; freedom from difficulty सुविधा, सहूलियत, आसानी The school provides excellent sports *facilities*.

fact *(n.)* फ़ैक्ट– an event or thing known to have happened or existed सत्य, तथ्य, सच्चाई The police recorded all the *facts* of the murder case.

➢ **as a matter of fact**– in reality or actuality वास्तव में, It's a *matter of fact* that the team have not performed well.

factor *(n.)* फ़ैक्टर–1. one of two or more integers or polynomials whose product is a given integer or polynomial गुणक, गुणनखंड find out the *factors* of this number.

2. an element or cause that contributes to a result घटक, कारण, निमित्त Corruption was the main *factor* behind the fall of the government.

factory *(n.)* फ़ैक्टरी– a building or group of buildings containing a plant assembly for the manufacture of goods कारख़ाना What articles do you manufacture in your *factory*?

faculty *(n.)* फ़ैकल्टी– a group of university department संकाय, प्रभाग Delhi University has got good *faculty*.

fade *(v.)* फ़ेड– to lose or cause to lose brightness, colour, or clarity मन्द पड़ना, मुरझाना The colour of quality cloth doesn't *fade* easily.

fail *(v.)* फ़ेल–1. to be unsuccessful in an attempt (at something or to do something) असफ़ल होना I am surly not going to *fail* in this examination.

2. to stop operating or working properly काम करना बन्द कर देना While we were having dinner, the power suddenly *failed*.

failing *(n.)* फ़ेलिंग– a weak point; flaw दोष, त्रुटि, दुर्बलता She felt sorry for her *failings.*

failure *(n.)* फ़ेलयर– a person or thing that is unsuccessful or disappointing नाकामयाबी, विफलता I have learnt many lessons from my past *failures.*

faint *(adj.)* फ़ेण्ट– 1. lacking clarity, brightness, volume, etc. मन्द, हलका/हलकी I heard *faint* noises of someone crying.

2. *(v.)* to lose consciousness, esp momentarily, as through weakness बेहोश होना When you *faint,* you look as if you are in a deep sleep.

fair *(adj.)* फ़ेअर्–1. (of the hair or complexion) light in colour गोरा, गौर, सुंदर, स्वच्छ Your daughter has a *fair* complexion.

2. free from discrimination, dishonesty, etc. just; impartial उचित, निष्पक्ष, न्यायसंगत Please be *fair* to all while judging.

3. moderately or quite good मामूली, साधारण Sheela's performance in the examination was just *fair.*

4. *(n.)* a person or thing that is beautiful or valuable, esp a woman मेला People came in large numbers to see the trade *fair.*

fairly *(adv.)* फ़ेअर्ली– honestly; justly ईमानदारीपूर्वक, उचित रूप से The teacher did not teach the children *fairly.*

fairy *(n.)* फ़ेअरि– an imaginary supernatural being, usually represented in diminutive human form and characterized as clever, playful, and having magical powers परी Alice in Wonderland is a good *fairy* tale.

faith *(n.)* फ़ेथ– strong belief in something, esp without proof or evidence विश्वास, भरोसा Have *faith* in God, you will definately succeed one day.

faithful *(adj.)* फ़ेथफुल–1. having faith; remaining true, constant, or loyal वफ़ादार, सच्चा Our servant is very *faithful.*

2. reliable or truthful सही, वास्तविक Give me a *faithful* account of what you did.

fake *(n.)* फ़ेक– 1. an object, person, or act that is not genuine; sham, counterfeit, or forgery फ़र्जी, नक़ली All these currency notes are a *fake.*

2. *(adj.)* not genuine; spurious खोटा, जाली These are *fake* currency notes.

3. *(v.)* to cause (something inferior or not genuine) to appear more valuable, desirable, or real by fraud or pretence जालसाज़ी करना, जाली बनाना He *faked* the documents.

fall *(n.)* फ़ॉल– 1. an act or instance of falling गिरावट, पतन 'Pride hath a *fall'.*

2. *(v.)* to descend by the force of gravity from a higher to a lower place पतन होना, गिरना Take care lest you *fall* down.

➢ **fall back**– to recede or retreat पीछे हटना, He yelled for his statement to *fall back.*

➢ **fall behind**– to drop back; to fail to keep up पीछे छूटना या रह जाना, Her sister was chatting and didn't notice that she had *fallen behind.*

➢ **fall down**– to drop suddenly or collapse नीचे गिरना, Naresh *fell down* and hurt his knee.

➢ **fall for**– to become infatuated with (a person) किसी के झांसे में आना, She *falls for* them everytime.

➢ **fall off**– to decrease in quality or quantity गुणवत्ता या मात्रा में कम होना Attendance at my school has *fallen off* considerably

➢ **fall out**– to quarrel or disagree झगड़ना, Krishna is always *falling out* with people.

➢ **fall through**– to miscarry or fail बेकार हो जाना, रद्द होना, He planned to start a business with his friend but the deal *fell through*.

false *(adj.)* फ़ॉल्स–1. not in accordance with the truth or facts ग़लत, असत्य He gave a *false* statement in the judge room.
2. disloyal or treacherous कपटी, निष्ठाहीन Never be a *false* friend.
3. not genuine, real, or natural; artificial; fake दिखावटी, कृत्रिम Do you wear *false* teeth?

falsely *(adv.)* फ़ाल्सली– wrongly झूठ-मूठ, धोखे या छल से She was *falsely* implicated in the murder charge.

fame *(n.)* फ़ेम– the state of being widely known or recognized; renown; celebrity ख्याति, यश, कीर्ति I think she joined this office just for name and *fame*.

familiar *(adj.)* फ़ॅमिलिअर्–1. well-known; easily recognized सुपरिचित, परिचित Your face looks *familiar*, but I don't remember your name.
2. friendly; informal अच्छा जानकार Ram is *familiar* with Rohit's entire family.

familiarity *(n.)* फ़मिलिऐरटी– reasonable knowledge or acquaintance, as with a subject or place अच्छी जानकारी, सुविज्ञता When I saw this place, I had a feeling of *familiarity*.

family *(n.)* फ़ैमली– a primary social group consisting of parents and their offspring, the principal function of which is provision for its members परिवार, घराना I am lucky to have such a caring *family*.

famine *(n.)* फ़ैमिन– a severe shortage of food, as through crop failure or overpopulation अकाल, दुर्भिक्ष, भुखमरी The *famine* killed many people in Orissa.

famished *(adj.)* फ़ैमिशड– very hungry or weak बहुत भूखा, भुखमरा I am very much *famished* today.

famous *(adj.)* फ़ेमस– known to or recognized by many people; renowned प्रसिद्ध, विख्यात A Nobel prize winner becomes *famous* worldwide.

fan *(n.)* फ़ैन–1. any device for creating a current of air by movement of a surface or number of surfaces, पंखा I would like to buy a table *fan*.
2. an ardent admirer of a pop star, film actor, football team, etc. प्रशंसक I am Amir Khan's *fan*.

fanatic *(n.)* फ़नैटिक– a person whose enthusiasm or zeal for something is extreme or beyond normal limits कट्टर धार्मिक व्यक्ति, हठधर्मी, मतांध Sardar Patel was a religious *fanatic*.

fancy *(v.)* फ़ैन्सि–1. to picture in the imagination कल्पना करना She *fancies* herself as another Madhuri Dixit.
2. to have a wish for; desire चाहना/पसंद करना I do not *fancy* gaudy clothes.
3. *(adj.)* not plain; ornamented or decorative रंग-बिरंगा, भड़कीला Youngsters like *fancy* clothes.
4. *(n.)* a sudden capricious idea; whim विचार, कल्पना A *fancy* passed through my mind.

fantastic *(adj.)* फ़ैन्टैस्टिक– extremely good उत्कृष्ट, बहुत अच्छा This is a *fantastic* book; you must read it.

fantasy *(n.)* फैण्टसी– imagination unrestricted by reality स्वप्न चित्र, स्वैरकल्पना Children live in the world of *fantasy*.

far *(adj.)* फ़ार्– 1. extending a great distance; long दूर Ram's office was not too *far* from his home.
2. *(adv.)* a long distance away दूर तक He did not go *far*.

faraway *(adj.)* फ़ारअवे– very distant; remote बहुत दूर I dreamed of flying away to exotic *faraway* places.

farce *(n.)* फ़ार्स– a broadly humorous play based on the exploitation of improbable situations ढोंग, तमाशा, हास्यास्पद The meeting was a complete *farce.*

fare *(n.)* फ़ेअर्–1. the sum charged or paid for conveyance in a bus, train, aeroplane, etc. भाड़ा, किराया Bus *fares* are still the cheapest.

2. *(v.)* to get on (as specified); manage सफ़ल या विफल होना Dolly *fared* well in the examination.

farewell *(n.)* फ़ेअर्वेल– an act of saying goodbye विदाई I enjoyed alot in my *farewell* party last year.

farm *(n.)* फ़ार्म– a tract of land, usually with house and buildings, cultivated as a unit or used to rear livestock खेत I have built a small cottage in my *farm.*

farmer *(n.)* फ़ार्मर– a person who operates or manages a farm किसान *Farmers* are facing monsoon problem.

farming *(n.)* फ़ार्मिंग– the business, art, or skill of agriculture कृषि, खेती He is trying to learn the *farming* methods.

far-sighted *(adj.)* फ़ार-साइटिड– possessing prudence and foresight दूरदर्शी It was a *far-sighted* decision to go back to home.

fart *(v.)* फ़ार्ट– to emit wind from the anus हवा छोड़ना, पादना Never *fart* in public.

farther *(adv.)* फ़ार्दर– to or at a greater distance in space or time अपेक्षाकृत दूर I cannot go any *farther.*

fascinate *(v.)* फ़ैसिनेट– to attract and delight by arousing interest or curiosity मोहित/मंत्रमुग्ध करना The Pyramids of Egypt has always *fascinated* me.

fascinating *(adj.)* फ़ॅसिनेटिंग– arousing great interest, extremely attractive आकर्षक, मोहक Wuthering Heights is a *fascinating* novel.

fashion *(n.)* फ़ैशन–1. style in clothes, cosmetics, behaviour, etc. esp the latest or most admired style फ़ैशन, भूषाचार Narrow trousers are not in *fashion* these days.

2. *(v.)* to give a particular form to बनाना, रूप देना He *fashioned* the sword and spear with great skill.

fashionable *(adj.)* फ़ैशनबल– conforming to fashion; in vogue प्रचलित The lady who I met yesterday was quite *fashionable.*

fast *(adj.)* फ़ास्ट–1. acting or moving or capable of acting or moving quickly; swift तेज़ Please do not drive *fast.*

2. *(adv.)* quickly तेज़ी से, फ़ुरती से Walk *fast,* it is too late.

3. firmly; tightly पक्का, स्थिर, मज़बूत I held *fast* to my umbrella in the gale.

4. *(n.)* an act or period of fasting उपवास, रोज़ा, अनशन My grandmother observes a *fast* every Monday.

5. *(v.)* to abstain from eating all or certain foods or meals, esp as a religious observance उपवास करना My father *fasted* for three days.

fasten *(v.)* फ़ासन– to make or become attached or joined बांधना *Fasten* your seatbelts, the plane is about to take off.

fastening *(n.)* फ़ासनिंग– something that fastens, such as a clasp or lock बंधन, कसनी The pant has a *fastening.*

fastidious *(adj.)* फ़ैस्टिडिअस– very critical; hard to please तुनकमिज़ाज, नकचढ़ा She is *fastidious* in her preparation for the big day.

fat *(adj.)* फ़ैट–1. having much or too much flesh or fat मोटा, मांसल The *fat* lady was looking very cute.

2. *(n.)* any of a class of naturally occurring soft greasy solids that are esters of glycerol and certain fatty acids. चर्बी, मेद Do you cook in *fat* or oil?

fatal *(adj.)* फ़ेटल– resulting in or capable of causing death घातक, विनाशक, प्राणहर I heard your neighbour met with a *fatal* accident.

fate *(n.)* फ़ेट– the inevitable fortune that befalls a person or thing; destiny क़िस्मत, भाग्य We can never know what our *fate* is.

fateful *(adj.)* फ़ेटफुल– having important consequences; decisively important भाग्यसूचक The day she won a trophy was a *fateful* day in her life.

father *(n.)* फ़ादर– a male parent पिता, बाप My *father* is the world's best *father*.

fatherly *(adj.)* फ़ादर्लि– of, resembling, or suitable to a father पिता के समान, पितृतुल्य Pankaj was giving me *fatherly* advice.

fatigue *(n.)* फ़ॅटीग– physical or mental exhaustion due to exertion थकान She fainted of *fatigue*.

fattening *(adj.)* फ़ैटनिंग– likely to cause to grow fat or fatter मोटा कर देने वाला Ice creams are very *fattening*.

fault *(n.)* फ़ॉल्ट–1. a mistake or error ग़लती, भूल Though it was not my *fault* but still he punished me.
2. an imperfection; failing or defect; flaw दोष, कमी, त्रुटि The mechanic quickly repaired the *fault* in the car engine.

faultless *(adj.)* फ़ॉल्टलस– without fault; perfect or blameless त्रुटिरहित, दोषमुक्त The pianist gave a *faultless* performance.

faulty *(adj.)* फ़ॉलटी– defective or imperfect दोषपूर्ण, खराब An accident caused by a *faulty* signal.

favour *(v.)* फ़ेवर्–1. an act of kindness कृपा, अनुग्रह I will be more than happy if you can do me a *favour*.
2. *(v.)* to treat with partiality or favouritism पक्षपात करना The treaty seems to *favour* the Pakistan.

favourable *(adj.)* फ़ेवरबल– advantageous, encouraging, or promising अनुकूल, फ़ायदेमंद Conditions are *favourable* for tracking.

favourably *(adv.)* फ़ेवरबली– in support or praise of someone or something अनुकूल दृष्टि से India is *favourably* inclined towards the United Kingdom.

favourite *(n.)* फ़ेऽवरिट– a person or thing regarded with especial preference or liking पसंदीदा Who is your *favourite* actor?

fax *(n.)* फ़ैक्स– a message or document sent by fax दूरपत्र They contacted us by *fax*.

fear *(n.)* फ़िअर्– 1. a feeling of distress, apprehension, or alarm caused by impending danger, pain, etc. डर, भय *Fear* is a powerful enemy.
2. *(v.)* to be afraid (to do something) or of (a person or thing); dread डरना, भयभीत होना I *fear* I might miss the train.

fearful *(adj.)* फ़िअर्फुल– having fear; afraid भयभीत, भयंकर, डरावना I saw a *fearful* railway accident.

feasible *(adj.)* फ़ीज़बल– able to be done or put into effect; possible उपयुक्त, उचित My brother made a *feasible* plan to go to Nainital.

feast *(n.)* फ़ीस्ट्– 1. a large and sumptuous meal, usually given as an entertainment for several people दावत, प्रीतिभोज पर्व Ram invited all the neighbours on his daughter's birthday *feast*.
2. *(v.)* to enjoy the eating (of), as if feasting दावत उड़ाना, छककर खाना Our friends *feasted* and sang songs.

feat *(n.)* फ़ीट– a remarkable, skilful, or daring action; exploit; achievement कमाल, करतब, असाधारण कार्य Children were thrilled on seeing the *feats* of the acrobat.

feather *(n.)* फ़ेदर्– any of the flat light waterproof epidermal structures forming the plumage of birds, each consisting of a hollow shaft having a vane of barbs on either side पंख Collecting *feathers* of different birds is my hobby.

feature *(n.)* फ़ीचर्–1. any one of the parts of the face, such as the nose, chin, or mouth चेहरा-मोहरा, नाक-नक्श She has got sharp features.

2. a prominent or distinctive part or aspect, as of a landscape, building, book, etc. विशेषता, विशिष्टता Dusty winds are a *feature* of Delhi summers.

3. a prominent story in a newspaper, etc. नियमित लेख The newspapers carry *features* on environment regularly.

federation *(n.)* फ़ेडरेशन– the union of several provinces, states, etc. to form a federal union संघ, राज्यसंघ The *federation* is headed by a reputed industrialist.

fed up *(adj.)* फ़ेड-अप– annoyed, discontented, or bored तंग, परेशान, ऊबा हुआ He looks *fed up* from his work.

fee *(n.)* फ़ी–1. a payment asked by professional people or public servants for their services फ़ीस, परीक्षा शुल्क How much is the *fee* for this program?

2. a charge made for a privilege (परामर्श आदि के लिए दिया गया) शुल्क, भुगतान We pay *fees* to doctors, tutors and lawyers.

feeble *(adj.)* फ़ीबल–1. lacking in physical or mental strength; frail; very weak कमज़ोर, अशक्त My long illness has made me *feeble.*

2. inadequate; unconvincing मंद, धुंधला I was unable to read in the *feeble* candle light.

feed *(v.)* फ़ीड– to give food to खिलाना, भोजन देना To *feed* an infant with the mother's milk is good for his health.

feedback *(n.)* फ़ीडबैक– the return of part of the output of an electronic circuit, device, or mechanical system to its input, so modifying its characteristics प्रतिपुष्टि The *feedback* helped me to improve this article.

feel *(v.)* फ़ील–1. to perceive (something) by touching स्पर्श करना, छूना The doctor *felt* the injured arm of Usha to see if there was a fracture.

2. to have a physical or emotional sensation of (something) लगना, प्रतीत होना We all *felt* happy at the good news.

feeling *(n.)* फ़ीलिंग– the sense of touch संवेदनशीलता The old woman had no *feeling* in her numb fingers.

feign *(v.)* फ़ेन– to put on a show of (a quality or emotion); pretend स्वांग भरना, बहाना करना The child *feigned* a headache to miss the school.

fellow *(n.)* फ़ेलो–1. a companion; comrade; associate साथी, संगी, मित्र He has a good reputation among her *fellows.*

2. a man or boy कोई पुरुष Don't let that *fellow* enter my room.

fellowship *(n.)* फ़ेलोशिप– an award of money to a student to allow them to continue their studies छात्रवृत्ति, अध्येतावृत्ति She is getting *fellowship* from the university.

felony *(n.)* फ़ेलनी– (formerly) a serious crime, such as murder or arson.घोर अपराध He was imprisoned in the charge of *felony.*

female *(adj.)* फ़ीमेल– 1. of, relating to, or characteristic of a woman मादा, स्त्री Let's make a seperate counter for *females* and senior citizens.

2. *(n.)* a female animal or plant स्त्री जाति The *female* of a deer is called doe.

feminine *(adj.)* फ़ेमिनिन– possessing qualities or characteristics considered typical of or appropriate to a woman स्त्री-संबंधी, स्त्री-सुलभ The boy with *feminine* looks was given a female role in the play.

fence *(n.)* फ़ेन्स– 1. a structure that serves to enclose an area such as a garden or field, usually made of posts of timber, concrete, or metal connected by wire, netting, rails, or boards बाड़ा, घेरा Can you jump over this *fence*?
2. *(v.)* to construct a fence on or around (a piece of land, etc.) बाड़ा लगाना He *fenced* his garden to protect it from animals.

ferment *(v.)* फ़र्मेण्ट– any agent or substance, such as a bacterium, mould, yeast, or enzyme, that causes fermentation ख़मीर उठना या उठाना The flour is *fermented* with yeast to make bread.

fern *(n.)* फ़र्न– plant with large leaves and no flowers पर्णांग I have a *fern* plant in my lawn.

ferocious *(adj.)* फ़रोशियस– savage or cruel हिंसक, क्रूर, उग्र The lion is a *ferocious* animal.

ferocity *(n.)* फ़रासटी– the quality of being fierce or violent खूंखारपन, क्रूरता, उग्रता The war was fought with great *ferocity* by both sides.

ferry *(n.)* फ़ेरि– 1. a vessel for transporting passengers and usually vehicles across a body of water, esp as a regular service तारण, नौघाट, नौका We crossed to the Swarga Ashram in a *ferry*.
2. *(v.)* to transport or go by ferry पार उतरना/ उतारना The pilgrims were *ferried* across the Ganges.

fertile *(adj.)* फ़र्टाइल–1. capable of producing offspring उपजाऊ, उर्वर My farm is quite *fertile.*
2. (of a person's mind) that produces a lot of new ideas कल्पनाशील You have a *fertile* brain.

fervent *(adj.)* फ़र्वण्ट– intensely passionate; ardent जोशीला, उत्साही I have a *fervent* desire to work for the deprived women.

fervour *(n.)* फ़र्वर्– great intensity of feeling or belief; ardour; zeal जोश, उत्साह Diwali was celebrated with great *fervour* in the city.

festival *(n.)* फ़ेस्टिवल– a day or period set aside for celebration or feasting, esp one of religious significance त्योहार, उत्सव Which one is your favourite *festival*?

fetch *(v.)* फ़ेच– to go after and bring back; get लाना, ले आना Please *fetch* me a glass of water.

feud *(n.)* फ़्यूड– long and bitter hostility between two families, clans, or individuals; vendetta पुश्तैनी रंजिश, कुलबैर The issue of property resulted in a *feud* between the brothers.

feudal *(adj.)* फ़्यूडल– of, resembling, relating to, or characteristic of feudalism or its institutions सामंती, सामंतवादी There was a *feudal* system in ancient India.

fever *(n.)* फ़ीवर्– an abnormally high body temperature, accompanied by a fast pulse rate, dry skin, etc. बुख़ार, ज्वर My son is suffering from *fever* since last 3 days.

feverishly *(adj.)* फ़ीवरिशली– in a state of restless excitement अत्यधिक उत्तेजना से, आवेशपूर्ण होकर He was *feverishly* waiting for his result of the election.

few *(adj.)* फ़्यू–1. a small number of गिने-चुने, कुछ A *few* of my friends know that I can paint.
2. a small number of; hardly any बहुत कम, शायद ही कोई *Few* of my friends know that I can paint.

fiance *(n.)* फ़िऑन्से– a man who is engaged to be married मंगेतर, वाग्दत्त I am so lucky that my *fiance* makes me feel so special.

fib *(n.)* फ़िब– a trivial and harmless lie गप, छोटा-मोटा झूठ Please stop telling *fibs*.

fibre *(n.)* फ़ाइबर्– a natural or synthetic filament that may be spun into yarn, such as cotton or nylon रेशा, तन्तु, सूत्र Of what *fibre* is your shirt made?

fickle *(adj.)* फ़िकल्– changeable in purpose, affections, etc. capricious अस्थिर, चंचल Don't believe him; he is very *fickle*-minded.

fiction *(n.)* फ़िक्शन– literary works invented by the imagination, such as novels or short stories कथा-साहित्य I like to read *fiction.*

fictitious *(adj.)* फ़िक्टिशस– not genuine or authentic; assumed; false मनगढ़ंत, बनावटी The film was based on a *fictitious* story of a noble man.

fiddle *(v.)* फ़िडल– to make restless or aimless movements with the hands निरुद्देश्य किसी वस्तु के साथ खिलवाड़ करना Why are you *fiddling* with my purse?

fidelity *(n.)* फ़िडेलटी– devotion to duties, obligations, etc; faithfulness कर्तव्यपराणता, निष्ठा, स्वामिभक्ति He probably doubted her *fidelity.*

fidget *(v.)* फ़िजिट– to move about restlessly बेचैन या अशांत होना You cannot concentrate on what you are reading if you keep *fidgeting.*

field *(n.)* फ़ील्ड–1. an area of land for growing crops खेत I will meet you in the *field* tommorow.

2. a sphere or division of knowledge, interest, etc. क्षेत्र Do you have any experience in the *field* of social work?

fierce *(adj.)* फ़िअर्स्– having a violent and unrestrained nature; savage ख़ूंख़ार, आक्रमणकारी, हिंस्र I assure you my dog is not a *fierce* animal.

fiercely *(adv.)* फ़िअर्सली– angrily ख़ूँखार तरीक़े से The Soldiers were *fiercely* attacking their enemies.

fiery *(adj.)* फ़ाइअरी– easily angered or aroused गुस्सैल, प्रचंड She is a *fiery* tempered lady.

fifth *(det., pron., adv.)* फ़िफ़्थ– coming after the fourth in order, position, time, etc. Often written: 5th पांचवां She stays on the *fifth* floor of this building.

fifty-fifty *(adj.)* फ़िफ्टी-फ़िफ्टी– in equal parts बराबर का There are *fifty-fifty* chances of my success in the competition.

fig *(n.)* फ़िग– a sweet fruit that is full of small seeds अंजीर There were many *fig* trees in the garden.

fight *(v.)* फ़ाइट– 1. to oppose or struggle against (an enemy) in battle लड़ाई करना, लड़ना, विरोध करना The two neighbours were *fighting* over a petty issue.

2. *(n.)* a battle, struggle, or physical combat लड़ाई, झगड़ा It was a fierce *fight* among street dogs.

fighter *(n.)* फ़ाइटर– a person who fights, esp a professional boxer लड़ाकू, योद्धा Indian *fighters* are very muscular and strong.

figure *(n.)* फ़िगर्–1. any written symbol other than a letter, esp a whole number अंक, रक़म, आँकड़ा I am good at *figures.*

2. the human form, esp as regards size or shape रूप, आकार, आकृति In the dark, I could make out a *figure* moving about in the room.

3. *(v.)* to calculate or compute (sums, amounts, etc.) हिसाब लगाना I *figured* the attendance at 95.

filament *(n.)* फ़िलमेण्ट– a single strand of a natural or synthetic fibre; fibril तंतु The *filament* of the flower was so soft and delicate.

file *(n.)* फ़ाइल–1. a folder, box, etc. used to keep documents or other items in order फ़ाइल, संचिका Maintain a seperate *file* for the office bills.

2. an orderly line or row क़तार, ताँता Boys march to your classrooms in a single *file.*

3. a hand tool consisting essentially of a steel blade with small cutting teeth on some or all of its faces रेती I bought a carpenter's *file* for some wood work in the house.

4. *(v.)* to place (a document, letter, etc.) in a file फ़ाइल में रखना *File* these papers carefully.

filling *(n.)* फ़िलिंग– the substance or thing used to fill a space or container भराव, किसी चीज़ के अंदर भरा जाने वाला भोज्य पदार्थ I ate yummy potatoes with cheese filling.

fill *(v.)* फ़िल–1. to make or become full भरना, भर देना You have to *fill* this form to apply for this job.

2. to occupy the whole of भर आना, भर जाना Students were *filled* with joy at the declaration of vacations.

film *(n.)* फ़िल्म–1. a sequence of images of moving objects photographed by a camera and providing the optical illusion of continuous movement when projected onto a screen चलचित्र, फ़िल्म Are you fond of *films*?

2. a form of entertainment, information, etc. composed of such a sequence of images and shown in a cinema, etc.फ़िल्म Is there a *film* in your camera?

3. a thin coating or layer परत, तह, पटल There is a *film* of dust on the table.

filter *(v.)* फ़िल्टर्– 1. to remove or separate (suspended particles, wavelengths of radiation, etc.) from (a liquid, gas, radiation, etc.) by the action of a filter फ़िल्टर करना, छानना *Filter* this water before you drink it.

2. *(n.)* any device containing such a porous substance for separating suspensions from fluids छन्नी, छन्ना I have bought a water *filter*.

filthy *(adj.)* फ़िल्थी– characterized by or full of filth; very dirty or obscene मैला, गन्दा, अश्लील The house had been empty for years and was *filthy* inside.

fin *(n.)* फ़िन– any of the firm appendages that are the organs of locomotion and balance in fishes and some other aquatic animals मीनपक्ष The *fin* of the fish was so soft.

final *(adj.)* फ़ाइनल– of or occurring at the end; concluding; ultimate; last आख़िरी, अन्तिम When are your *final* examinations starting?

finalist *(n.)* फ़ाइनलिस्ट– a contestant who has reached the last and decisive stage of a sports or other competition अंतिम चरण में पहुंचा खिलाड़ी He was an Olympic *finalist*.

finalize (ise) *(v.)* फ़ाइनलाइज़– to put into final form; settle अंतिम रूप देना I would like to see the content before *finalising* it.

finally *(adv.)* फ़ाइनली– after a long delay; at last; eventually आख़िरकार, अंत में Ram *finally* agreed to accompany Suresh to the trade fair.

finance *(n.)* फ़ाइनैन्स– the system of money, credit, etc. esp with respect to government revenues and expenditures वित्त, धन, निधि Please dont ask any personal questions related to *finance*.

financial *(adj.)* फ़ाइनैन्शल– of or relating to finance or finances आर्थिक, वित्तीय I cannot afford this car as my *financial* condition is not that good.

financially *(adv.)* फ़ाइनैनशली– with respect to money and financial matters आर्थिक दृष्टि से The state is becoming *financially* sound.

find *(v.)* फ़ाइण्ड–1. to meet with or discover by chance पाना, प्राप्त करना I can not *find* my watch anywhere.

2. to discover or obtain, esp by search or effort पता लगाना On

reaching home, Rahul *found* his friend waiting for him.

finding *(n.)* फ़ाइन्डिंग– a thing that is found or discovered प्राप्ति, उपलब्धि What are the *findings* of this survey?

fine *(adj.)* फ़ाइन–1. excellent or choice in quality; very good of its kind उत्तम, उत्कृष्ट The acrobats presented a *fine* show.

2. (of edges, blades, etc.) sharp; keen महीन, सूक्ष्म, पतला Sharpen your pencil and draw a *fine* line.

3. a certain amount of money exacted as a penalty जुर्माना Ramesh had to pay a *fine* of five rupees for returning the library book late.

finely *(adv.)* फ़ाइनलि– into small pieces; minutely बख़ूबी, अच्छे ढंग से She *finely* chopped the onion.

finger *(n.)* फ़िंगर्– 1. any of the digits of the hand, often excluding the thumb उँगली I got a cut on my fore*finger* last night.

2. *(v.)* to touch or manipulate with the fingers; handle अंगुलियों से छूना या महसूस करना They all *fingered* my beautiful dress.

fingernail *(n.)* फ़िंगरनेल– a thin horny translucent plate covering part of the dorsal surface of the end joint of each finger नाख़ून Rohan tried to open the knot with his *fingernail.*

fingerprint *(n.)* फ़िंगरप्रिंट– an impression of the pattern of lines on the tip of a person's finger अंगुली-छाप The police took the *fingerprints* of the criminals.

finish *(v.)* फ़िनिश– 1. to bring to an end; complete, conclude, or stop समाप्त करना, पूर्ण करना You have to *finish* up your homework first if you want to go out.

2. *(n.)* the surface texture or appearance of wood, cloth, etc. परिष्कार, परिसज्जा Your dining table has a nice *finish.*

finished *(adj.)* फ़िनिश्ड– perfected तैयार, पूरा Can you provide us the *finished* product if we provide you the raw material?

finite *(adj.)* फ़ाइनाइट– bounded in magnitude or spatial or temporal extent सीमित The resources in the world are *finite.*

fir *(n.)* फ़र– a pyramidal coniferous tree having single *needle-like* leaves and erect cones देवदारु *Fir* trees are normally found in the Himalayan regions in India.

fire *(n.)* फ़ाइअर्–1. the state of combustion in which inflammable material burns, producing heat, flames, and often smoke आग, ज्वाला I lost all my documents in that *fire.*

2. *(v.)* to discharge (a firearm or projectile) or (of a firearm, etc.) to be discharged गोली चलाना/दागना The police *fired* in the air to disperse a rioting mob.

fireplace *(n.)* फ़ाइअरप्लेस– an open recess in a wall of a room, at the base of a chimney, etc. for a fire; hearth अंगीठी, चूल्हा She was sitting near the *fireplace* in the room

firm *(n.)* फ़र्म–1. any commercial enterprise व्यवसाय-संघ, कंपनी, फ़र्म I learn you have joined a big *firm.*

2. *(adj.)* not soft or yielding to a touch or pressure; rigid; solid दृढ़, निश्चित, अटल It's my *firm* belief that God rewards hard work.

3. securely in position; stable or stationary ठोस, पक्का, मज़बूत I jumped from the boat on to the *firm* ground.

firmly *(adv.)* फ़र्मली– in a secure way दृढ़ता से He was *firmly* standing at the gate.

first *(adj.)* फ़र्स्ट–1. coming before all others; earliest, best, or foremost पहला, प्रथम He scored *first* position in the final examination.

2. *(adv.)* before anything else in order, time, preference, importance, etc. पहले Mother asked Usha to *first* take dinner and then watch TV programmes.

➢ **first and foremost**– more than anything else सबसे पहला या सबसे अधिक महत्त्वपूर्ण, I believe that *first and foremost* I am an Indian.

➢ **first of all**– before doing anything else सबसे पहले, *First of all* I'd better make sure that we have got what we need.

➢ **first off**– as a first point; firstly किसी और बात से पहले, *First off*, I'd like to decide who does what.

first-class *(n.)* फ़र्स्ट-क्लास– the class or grade of the best or highest value, quality, etc. प्रथम श्रेणी *I reserved my seat in a first class compartment.*

first-degree *(adj.)* फ़र्स्ट-डिग्री– denoting burns that affect only the surface of the skin and cause reddening. संगीन, जघन्य He will get cured soon as his burns are of *first degree*.

first-hand *(adj., adv.)* फ़र्स्ट-हैंड– from the original source or personal experience; direct: प्रत्यक्ष, आँखों-देखा The reporter gave me a *first-hand* information of the accident as he had seen it.

firstly *(adv.)* फ़र्स्टली– used to introduce a first point or reason सबसे पहले, प्रथमतः *Firstly,* they were angry with me but later on they became cool and happy.

first-rate *(adj.)* फ़र्स्ट-रेट– of the best class or quality; excellent: प्रथम श्रेणी का, सर्वश्रेष्ठ The quality of the food was of *first-rate.*

fish *(n.)* फ़िश– a limbless cold-blooded vertebrate animal with gills and fins living wholly in water मछली Would you like fried *fish* for lunch?

➢ **fish for**– to find out sth कुछ प्राप्त करने की कोशिश करना, She is always *fishing for* compliments.

fishing *(n.)* फिशिंग– the occupation of catching fish माहीगिरी, मछली पकड़ने का व्यवसाय *Fishing* is a major occupation of people in Kerala.

fishmonger *(n.)* फिशमॅन्गर– a retailer of fish मछली-विक्रेता A Bengali *fishmonger* lives in a very posh colony of South Delhi.

fishy *(adj.)* फ़िशी–1. of, involving, or suggestive of fish मछली के गंध वाली There is a *fishy* smell around here.

2. suspicious, doubtful, or questionable संदिग्ध Something *fishy* is going on in the classroom.

fist *(n.)* फ़िस्ट– a hand with the fingers clenched into the palm, as for hitting मुक्का, मुट्ठी The children were imitating a fight sequence from the film by waving their *fists* in the air.

fit *(v.)* फ़िट–1. to be appropriate or suitable for (a situation, etc.) ठीक आना, ठीक बैठ जाना This shirt *fits* me very well.

2. *(adj.)* in good health स्वस्थ, दुरुस्त I was ill last month, but now I am *fit.*

3. worthy or deserving अनुरूप, लायक, योग्य The employer asked the job applicant whether he was *fit* enough to hold a supervisor's post.

4. *(n.)* a short period of strong feeling दौरा He slapped his son in a *fit* of anger.

fitness *(n.)* फ़िटनस– the state of being fit तंदुरुस्ती, पूर्ण स्वस्थता I am not sure about my *fitness* for the sports.

fitting *(adj.)* फ़िटिंग– appropriate or proper; suitable उपयुक्त, सही, उचित India gave a *fitting* reply to Sri Lanka in cricket.

five *(n., adj.)* फ़ाइव– the cardinal number that is the sum of four and one पांच I have got *five* chocolates to prepare this dessert.

fix *(v.)* फ़िक्स–1. to settle definitely; decide तय करना, निश्चित करना What day shall we *fix* for the party?

2. to attach or place permanently लगाना Who *fixed* this frame on the wall?

fizz *(n.)* फ़िज़– sound that is made by bubbles; bubbling sound बुदबुद की आवाज़ There is a *fizz* when you open the coca cola bottle.

flabby *(adj.)* फ़्लैबी– having flabby flesh, esp through being overweight थुलथुल She has got a *flabby* body.

flag *(n.)* फ़्लैग– a piece of cloth, esp bunting, often attached to a pole or staff, decorated with a design and used as an emblem, symbol, or standard or as a means of signalling झण्डा, ध्वज The tricolour is our national *flag*.

flagrant *(adj.)* फ्लैग्रन्ट– openly outrageous अपमानजनक, शर्मनाक My neighbour showed a *flagrant* disregard for anyone else's feeling in the locality.

flair *(n.)* फ़्लेअर्– natural ability; talent; aptitude जन्मजात कौशल She has a *flair* for writing.

flake *(n.)* फ़्लेक– 1. a small thin piece or layer chipped off or detached from an object or substance; scale पपड़ी Huge *flakes* of snow covered the earth.

2. *(v.)* to peel or cause to peel off in flakes; chip पपड़ी बनकर उतारना या उतरना Plaster *flaked* off the wall.

flamboyant *(adj.)* फ्लैमबॉइअण्ट– elaborate or extravagant; florid; showy भड़कीला, चमकदार My friend always wears *flamboyant* clothes to make people notice him.

flame *(n.)* फ्लेम– a hot usually luminous body of burning gas often containing small incandescent particles, typically emanating in flickering streams from burning material or produced by a jet of ignited gas ज्वाला, लपट Before sleeping, put out the *flames* in the fireplace.

flaming *(adj.)* फ़्लैमिंग– burning with or emitting flames प्रज्वलित Today, *flaming* fragments are falling from the sky.

flank *(v.)* फ़्लैंक– to position or guard on or beside the flank of (a formation, etc) घिरा हुआ I left the room *flanked* by unknown people.

flap *(n.)* फ़्लेप–1. a piece of material, etc, attached at one edge and usually used to cover an opening, as on a tent, envelope, or pocket कपड़ा, पल्ला He sewed a *flap* on his pocket.

2. to move (wings or arms) up and down, esp in or as if in flying, or (of wings or arms) to move in this way फड़फड़ाना The pigeon *flapped* its wings to fly.

flare *(n.)* फ़्लेअर्–1. a blaze of light or fire used to illuminate, identify, alert, signal distress, etc. धधक, प्रदीप्ति In the *flare* of the match, I saw the lost ring on the floor.

2. *(v.)* to say sth in an angry way भड़कना, क्रोधित होना You must give up your habit of *flaring* up without cause.

flash *(n.)* फ़्लैश–1. a sudden short blaze of intense light or flame चमक, चौंध There was a sudden *flash* of lightning in the clouded sky.

2. *(v.)* to burst or cause to burst suddenly or intermittently into flame चमकना, कौंधना Why are your eyes *flashing* with anger?

3. to move very fast तीव्र गति से भागना The cars participating in the race *flashed* past us.

flat *(n.)* फ्लैट–1. a set of rooms comprising a residence entirely on one floor of a building फ्लैट,

कक्ष I recently bought a *flat* on 3rd floor.

2. *(adj.)* even or smooth, without projections or depressions समतल, सपाट, सीधे पीठ के बल Lie *flat* on the bed to overcome tiredness.

flatten *(v.)* फ्लैटन– to make or become flat or flatter समतल करना या होना Yoga will help you to *flatten* your stomach.

flatter *(v.)* फ्लैटर्– to praise insincerely, esp in order to win favour or reward खुशामद/चाटुकारी करना Everybody is *flattered* by a compliment.

flattery *(n.)* फ्लैटरी– excessive or insincere praise चापलूसी, खुशामद He is too intelligent to fall for his *flattery*

flaunt *(v.)* फ्लॉण्ट– to display (possessions, oneself, etc.) ostentatiously; show off इतराना, इठलाना She spends ₹1000 everyweek in the salon just to *flaunt* her body.

flavour *(n.)* फ्लेवर्– 1. taste perceived in food or liquid in the mouth सुगंध I like strawberry *flavour* more than chocolate one.

2. *(v.)* to impart a flavour, taste, or quality to स्वादिष्ट बनाना Sheela's birthday cake was *flavoured* with vanilla essence.

flaw *(n.)* फ्लॉ– an imperfection, defect, or blemish दोष, त्रुटि The advocates try to find a *flaw* in every law.

flawless *(adj.)* फ्लॉलेस्– without flaws; perfect दोषरहित, त्रुटिहीन She has got a *flawless* skin.

flea *(n.)* फ्ली– any small wingless parasitic blood-sucking insect, living on the skin of mammals and birds and noted for its power of leaping पिस्सू There were lot of *fleas* in the bed.

flee *(v.)* फ्ली– to run away from (a place, danger, etc.); fly भागना, भाग जाना They all *fled* from the house on fire.

fleet *(n.)* फ्लीट्– a number of aircraft, ships, buses, etc. operating together or under the same ownership वाहनों का समूह I dream of owning a huge *fleet* of cars.

flesh *(n.)* फ्लेश्– the soft part of the body of an animal or human, esp muscular tissue, as distinct from bone and viscera मांस, गोश्त You have put on *flesh* during your foreign trip.

flexible *(adj.)* फ्लेक्सिबल्– able to be bent easily without breaking; pliable लचकदार, लचीला She has got a *flexible* body.

flexibility *(n.)* फ्लेक्सबिलटी– ability to change or respond to new circumstances लचीलापन, नम्यता She has *flexibility* in nature.

flick *(v.)* फ्लिक्– to touch with or as if with the finger or hand in a quick jerky movement झटका देना या झाड़ना He *flicked* the dust from his jacket.

flicker *(v.)* फ्लिकर्–1. to shine with an unsteady or intermittent light टिमटिमाना, झिलमिलाना The candle flame *flickers* in the wind.

2. *(n.)* an unsteady or brief light or flame टिमटिमाहट, झिलमिलाहट The *flicker* of a candle is getting dim

flight *(n.)* फ्लाइट्– the act, skill, or manner of flying उड़ान, विमानयात्रा Let me go or else I will be late for my *flight*.

flimsy *(adj.)* फ्लिमज़ी– unconvincing or inadequate; weak अविश्वसनीय, कमज़ोर Stop making such *flimsy* excuses.

flinch *(v.)* फ्लिन्च्– to draw back suddenly, as from pain, shock, etc. wince डरकर पीछे हटना, मुंह मोड़ना I never *flinch* from telling the truth.

fling *(v.)* फ्लिंग–1. to throw, esp with force or abandon; hurl or toss फेंकना, पटकना, मारना Both the wrestlers were trying to *fling* each other on to the ground.

2. to put or send without warning or preparation छींटाकशी करना Don't *fling* baseless charges at me.

flip *(v.)* फ़्लिप– to read or look at (a book, newspaper, etc.) quickly, idly, or incompletely झटके से पलटना She *flipped* through the pages of the book to find the 10-rupee note inside it.

flippant *(adj.)* फ़्लिपन्ट्– talkative or nimble छिछोरा, चंचल He always sounds *flippant.*

flirt *(v.)* फ़्लर्ट– to behave or act amorously without emotional commitment; toy or play with another's affections; dally दिखावटी प्रेम-प्रदर्शन करना Did you see that he was trying to *flirt* with Heena.

flit *(v.)* फ़्लिट्– to move along rapidly and lightly फुदकना Bees were *fliting* from flower to flower.

float *(v.)* फ़्लोट–1. to rest or cause to rest on the surface of a fluid or in a fluid or space without sinking; be buoyant or cause to exhibit buoyancy तिरना, उतराना I *float* for a while before I begin to swim.

2. to move or cause to move buoyantly, lightly, or freely across a surface or through air, water, etc. drift तैरना, बहना People swim, wood *floats,* but a stone sinks.

floating *(adj.)* फ़्लोटिंग्– moving slowly on water तैरता या बहता हुआ It was a *floating* island.

flock *(n.)* फ़्लॉक्–1. a large number of people; crowd झुण्ड, समूह, दल Look at that *flock* of birds in the sky.

2. *(v.)* to gather together or move in a flock जमा या एकत्र हो जाना At the fair, the children *flocked* around the toy shops.

flog *(v.)* फ़्लॉग– to beat harshly, esp with a whip, strap, etc. कोड़े लगाना, डंडे बरसाना The man was publicly *flogged* for breaking the law.

flood *(n.)* फ़्लड–1. the inundation of land that is normally dry through the overflowing of a body of water, esp a river बाढ़, सैलाब, जलप्लावन Lot of people died in the *flood* last year.

2. a great outpouring or flow प्रचुरता, आधिक्य, अधिक On becoming an IAS officer, Sheela received a *flood* of greeting cards.

3. *(v.)* (of water) to inundate or submerge (land) or (of land) to be inundated or submerged बाढ़ आना The rain water *flooded* our street.

floor *(n.)* फ़्लॉर्–1. the inner lower surface of a room फ़र्श, ज़मीन Don't throw the waste paper on the *floor.*

2. a storey of a building मंजिल, तल्ला How many *floors* does your school building have?

flop *(n.)* फ़्लॉप– 1. a complete failure पूर्णतः असफ़ल (पुस्तक या फ़िल्म) The film was a big *flop.*

2. *(v.)* to fail; to be unsuccessful पूर्णतः विफल हो जाना The film *flopped* badly.

floppy *(adj.)* फ़्लॉपी– limp or hanging loosely ढीला-ढाला, झूलता हुआ My father was wearing a *floppy* hat.

floral *(adj.)* फ़्लॉरल– decorated with or consisting of flowers or patterns of flowers फूलों का, फूलों से संबद्ध The tiles of my bathroom have *floral* design.

florist *(n.)* फ़्लॉरिस्ट– a person who grows or deals in flowers फूल बेचने वाला, पुष्प-विक्रेता I bought these flowers from a nearby *florist.*

flounder *(v.)* फ़्लाउंडर– to struggle; to move with difficulty, as in mud तड़फड़ाना, लड़खड़ाना I was *floundering* when they asked me some personal questions.

flour *(n.)* फ़्लाउअर्– a powder, which may be either fine or coarse, prepared by sifting and grinding the meal of a grain, esp wheat आटा Give me some *flour* to make bread.

flourish *(v.)* फ्लरिश–1. to thrive; prosper उन्नति करना, फलना-फूलना I hear your business is *flourishing*.
2. to wave or cause to wave in the air with sweeping strokes घुमाना, हिलाना Don't *flourish* your pen in my face.

flout *(v.)* फ़्लाउट– to show contempt (for); scoff or jeer (at) आज्ञा न मानना They *flouted* my advice.

flow *(n.)* फ़्लो– 1. the act, rate, or manner of flowing प्रवाह, धारा, गति The *flow* of the river is swift in the hilly areas.
2. *(v.)* (of liquids) to move or be conveyed as in a stream बहना The river *flows* into the sea.

flower *(n.)* फ्लाउअर– a bloom or blossom on a plant फूल, पुष्प The plant has a beautiful white *flower*

flu *(n.)* फ्लू– any of various viral infections, esp a respiratory or intestinal infection इनफ़्लुएंज़ा, फ़्लू His child got *flu* last night.

fluctuate *(v.)* फ़्लक्चुएट– to change or cause to change position constantly; be or make unstable; waver or vary उतार-चढ़ाव होना The prices of shares are *fluctuating*.

fluent *(adj.)* फ़्लुअन्ट– able to speak or write a specified foreign language, easily and well धाराप्रवाह, प्रवाही Sohan is *fluent* in french.

fluently *(adv.)* फ़्लुअन्टलि– easily and gracefully धाराप्रवाह Gurmeet can speak four languages *fluently*.

fluffy *(adj.)* फ़्लफी– covered in fluff रोएंदार I am using a very *fluffy* towel.

fluid *(n.)* फ़्लूइड– 1. a substance, such as a liquid or gas, that can flow, has no fixed shape, and offers little resistance to an external stress तरल पदार्थ What is this golden-coloured *fluid* in the bottle?
2. *(adj.)* capable of flowing and easily changing shape अस्थिर, आसानी से बदला जा सकने वाला The picnic programme is still *fluid*.

fluorescent *(adj.)* फ्लुरोसेन्ट्– Producing bright light by using some forms of radiation प्रतिदीप्त The children were studying in a very *fluorescent* lamp.

flurry *(n.)* फ़्लरी– a sudden commotion or burst of activity अचानक उत्पन्न हलचल या घबराहट की स्थिति My arrival brought a *flurry* of excitement at home.

flush *(v.)* फ़्लश– to blush or cause to blush चेहरे का लाल हो जाना, झेंप जाना Mahak *flushed* and could not hide her emotions.

flushed *(adj.)* फ़्लशड– temporarily showing a rosy colour, esp in the cheeks; blushing लाल चेहरा, लाजभरा, आरक्त His face was *flushed* with hatred.

flute *(n.)* फ़्लूट– a wind instrument consisting of an open cylindrical tube of wood or metal having holes in the side stopped either by the fingers or by pads controlled by keys बांसुरी I love to play flute. *It is one of my favourite hobby.*

flutter *(v.)* फ़्लटर्– to wave or cause to wave rapidly; flap फड़फड़ाना, मंडराना I watched a sparrow *fluttering* its wings.

fly *(v.)* फ़्लाई–1. to move through the air in a controlled manner using aerodynamic forces उड़ना, उड़ाना At what speed does a jet plane *fly*?
2. to escape from (an enemy, place, etc.); flee भाग जाना It is very late, I must *fly* home.
3. *(n.)* a small flying insect, esp the housefly, मक्खी, मक्षिका Don't let *flies* sit on your food.

flying *(adj.)* फ़्लाइंग– able to fly उड़ने वाला It was a *flying* insect.

flying visit *(n.)* फ़्लाइंगविज़िट– a very short visit तूफानी यात्रा, थोड़ी देर की मुलाक़ात I was on a *flying visit* to Kolkata.

foam *(n.)* फ़ोम– a mass of small bubbles of gas formed on the surface of a liquid, such as the froth produced by agitating a solution of soap or detergent in water झाग, फेन Does this soap give a lot of *foam*?

focus *(v.)* फ़ोकस– to give attention ध्यान लगाना, एकाग्र करना Hardwork and *focus* are the essentials to be successful.

fodder *(n.)* फ़ॉडर– bulk feed for livestock, esp hay, straw, etc. चारा His father asked him to cut *fodder* for the cattle.

foe *(n.)* फ़ो– enemy दुश्मन, शत्रु You should be able to distinguish between friends and *foes.*

foetus *(n.)* फ़ीटस– the embryo of a mammal in the later stages of development, when it shows all the main recognizable features of the mature animal भ्रूण, गर्भ Human's *foetus* remains in mother's body for nine months.

fog *(n.)* फ़ॉग– a mass of droplets of condensed water vapour suspended in the air, often greatly reducing visibility, corresponding to a cloud but at a lower level कोहरा, धुंधलका Ships cannot sail safely in the *fog.*

foggy *(adj.)* फ़ॉगि– thick with fog कोहरेवाला, धुँधला Don't drive in the *foggy* weather.

foil *(n.)* फ़ॉइल– metal in the form of very thin sheets पर्ण, पर्णी, पन्नी Mother wrapped the chapattis in aluminium *foil.*

fold *(v.)* फ़ोल्ड– 1. to bend or be bent double so that one part covers another लपेटना, तह करना Do not *fold* this card or else it will be of no use.

2. *(n.)* a mark, crease, or hollow made by *folding* चुन्नट, मोड़ (वस्तु का) परत, तह The invitation card had three *folds.*

folk *(n.)* फ़ोक– people in general, esp those of a particular group or class लोक, जनता, जनसाधारण The country *folk* were very kind to me.

follow *(v.)* फ़ॉलो–1. to go or come after in the same direction पीछे-पीछे चलना Don't *follow* me please.

2. to understand (an explanation, argument, etc.) समझना Do you *follow* your professor's lectures?

follower *(n.)* फ़ॉलोअर– a person who accepts the teachings of another; disciple; adherent अनुयायी, भक्त Acharya Rajneesh has a large number of *followers.*

following *(adj.)* फ़ॉलोइंग– about to be mentioned, specified, etc. निम्नलिखित Please include the *following* names in the list.

folly *(n.)* फ़ॉली– the state or quality of being foolish; stupidity मूर्खता, बेवक़ूफ़ी It was a *folly* on Ashok's part to turn down a nice job offer.

fond *(adj.)* फ़ॉन्ड– predisposed (to); having a liking (for) शौक़ीन, प्रिय My little son is *fond* of pastries.

fondle *(v.)* फ़ॉण्डल– to touch or stroke tenderly; caress दुलारना, पुचकारना He *fondled* his pet dog.

fondness *(n.)* फ़ॉन्डनस– a fondness for sth a liking or taste for something किसी वस्तु के प्रति अति प्रेम I have a *fondness* for cars.

food *(n.)* फ़ूड– any substance containing nutrients, such as carbohydrates, proteins, and fats, that can be ingested by a living organism and metabolized into energy and body tissue अन्न, आहार, भोजन, खाना Have you taken your *food*?

food poisoning *(n.)* फ़ूड-पॉइज़निंग– an acute illness typically characterized by gastrointestinal inflammation, vomiting, and diarrhoea, caused by food that is either naturally poisonous or contaminated by pathogenic bacteria खाद्य विषाक्तता He got *food poisoning* and was admitted to hospital.

foodstuff *(n.)* फ़ूडस्टफ़– any material, substance, etc. that can be used as food खाद्य-पदार्थ We bought some *foodstuff* for our party tonight.

fool *(n.)* फ़ूल– 1. a person who lacks sense or judgement मूर्ख, मूढ़ Don't be a *fool*.
2. *(v.)* to trick or deceive मूर्ख बनाना, धोखा देना Don't *fool* me.

foolish *(adj.)* फ़ूलिश– unwise; silly मूर्ख, बेवकूफ़ I was *foolish* enough to trust my maid.

foolproof *(adj.)* फूलप्रूफ़– proof against failure; infallible सुगम, अचूक He made a *foolproof* plan to win this game.

foot *(n.)* फ़ुट–1- the part of the vertebrate leg below the ankle joint that is in contact with the ground during standing and walking पैर, पाँव I hurt my left *foot* yesterday.
2. the lowest part of something; base; bottom अधोभाग, मात्रा, पैताना Come up; don't stand at the *foot* of the staircase.
3. a unit of length equal to one third of a yard or 12 inches फुट (माप) How many inches are there in a *foot*?

> **back on your foot**– to recover बीमारी के बाद पुनः स्वस्थ होना, I need to get *back on* my *feet* again.

> **rushed off your feet**– to handle various jobs at a time हाथ में बहुत सारे काम होना, Before Diwali, most sales people are *rushed off their feet*.

> **keep one's feet**– to make a firm stand दृढ़ता से खड़े रहना, We have to *keep our feet* firmly on the ground in adverse circumstances.

> **have one foot in the grave**– to be so old or sick that death seems imminent मौत के नज़दीक होना, You *have one foot in the grave* but want to go on world tour.

> **put your foot down**– to take a firm stand दृढ़तापूर्वक अपनी बात कहना, You have to *put your foot down* and tell them you can't stay out.

> **put your foot in**– to blunder दूसरों को परेशानी में डालना, She has really *put her foot in* it this time. She didn't realise it before.

> **stand on your foot**– . to be independent अपनी देखरेख स्वयं करना, I can *stand on my foot* and take care of myself.

> **under your feet**– to disturb in a work किसी की राह में रोड़े अटकाते हुए, The kids are *under my feet* all day long during summer vacations.

footage *(n.)* फ़ुटेज– the extent of film material shot and exposed फ़िल्म का अंश They telecasted the *footage* of the assassination of Rajiv Gandhi.

footbridge *(n.)* फ़ुटब्रिज– a narrow bridge for the use of pedestrians पैदल पुल We should always use *footbridge* while crossing the road.

footnote *(n.)* फ़ुटनोट– a note printed at the bottom of a page, to which attention is drawn by means of a reference mark in the body of the text पाद-टिप्पणी The book contains *footnotes* at the bottom of the page.

footprint *(n.)* फ़ुटप्रिंट– an outline of the foot of a person or animal on a surface पद-चिह्न Police followed the *footprints* to catch the murderer.

footstep *(n.)* फ़ुटस्टेप– the action of taking a step in walking पदचाप, कदम I heard the *footsteps* of my mother on the stairs.

for *(prep.)* फ़ॉर– indicating destination, possession के लिए, के वास्ते The captain was responsible *for* the defeat.

forbid *(v.)* फ़ॉर्बिड्– to prohibit (a person) in a forceful or authoritative manner (from doing something or having something) मना करना, निषेध करना I *forbid* you to go out in the rain.

forbidden *(adj.)* फ़ॉर्बिडन– not permitted or not allowed वर्जित, निषिद्ध Smoking was *forbidden* in the museum.

force *(n.)* फ़ॉर्स–1. strength or energy; might; power बल, शक्ति, जोर, ताक़त I had to apply lot of *force* to open this door.

2. a group of persons organized for military or police functions सेना Would you like to join the Air *Force*?

3. *(v.)* to compel or cause (a person, group, etc.) to do something through effort, superior strength, etc. coerce विवश/मजबूर करना Sustained questioning *forced* the robber to disclose his accomplices' names.

forceful *(adj.)* फ़ोर्सफुल– powerful प्रभावशाली The Prime Minister gave a very *forceful* speech.

forcefully *(adv.)* फ़ॉर्सफुल्लि– persuasively or effectively जबरदस्ती, शक्ति से परिपूर्ण He tried to hit me *forcefully* but could not succeed.

forcible *(adj.)* फ़ॉर्सिबल– done by, involving, or having force जबरन, सशक्त It was really a *forcible* entry into the hall.

forebear *(n.)* फ़ॉरबेअर– an ancestor; forefather पूर्वज The *forebears* of my family belonged from Punjab.

forecast *(n.)* फ़ॉर्कास्ट– 1. a prophecy or prediction पूर्वानुमान, भविष्यवाणी As per the weather *forecast,* it might rain today.

2. *(v.)* to predict or calculate (weather, events, etc.) in advance भविष्यवाणी करना The astrologer *forecasts* huge success in his career.

forefront *(n.)* फ़ॉरफ्रन्ट– the extreme front सामने का भाग, अगवाड़ा My office is right at the *forefront* of a public school.

forehead *(n.)* फ़ॉर्हेड– the part of the face between the natural hairline and the eyes, formed skeletally by the frontal bone of the skull; brow माथा, मस्तक, ललाट She had a birthmark on her *forehead.*

foreign *(adj.)* फ़ॉरिन– of, involving, located in, or coming from another country, area, people, etc. विदेशी, परराष्ट्रीय Do you know any *foreign* language?

foreigner *(n.)* फ़ॉरनर– a person from a foreign country; alien विदेशी Would you like to meet a *foreigner*?

forest *(n.)* फ़ॉरिस्ट– a large wooded area having a thick growth of trees and plants वन, जंगल My native place is a village on the edge of the *forest.*

forever *(adv.)* फ़रेवर्– without end; everlastingly; eternally सदा के लिए, सर्वदा I feel like leaving this place *forever.*

forge *(v.)* फ़ॉर्ज– to make or produce a fraudulent imitation of (a signature, banknote, etc.) or to commit forgery जालसाज़ी करना He *forged* his father's signature on the report card.

forget *(v.)* फ़र्गेट– to fail to recall (someone or something once known); be unable to remember भूल जाना, भुला देना, बिसारना I can never *forget* this special day in my whole life.

forgive *(v.)* फ़र्गिव– to grant pardon for (a mistake, wrongdoing, etc.) माफ़ करना, क्षमा करना *Forgive* me for the last time. I promise, I won't repeat it again

fork *(n.)* फ़ॉर्क– a small usually metal implement consisting of two, three, or four long thin prongs on the end of a handle, used for lifting food to the mouth or turning it in cooking, etc. खाना-खाने का कांटा We use *forks* to eat noodles.

form *(n.)* फ़ॉर्म–1. a printed document, esp one with spaces in which to insert facts or answers फ़ॉर्म, प्रपत्र Please fill up this admission *form.*
2. the shape or configuration of something as distinct from its colour, texture, etc. रूप, आकृति A cloud in the sky had taken the *form* of an elephant.
3. *(v.)* to give shape or form to or to take shape or form, esp a specified or particular shape बनाना, रचना करना We have *formed* a literary association.

formal *(adj.)* फ़ॉर्मल– characterized by observation of conventional forms of ceremony, behaviour, dress, etc. औपचारिक, यथानियम Some clubs allow entry to their members only in the *formal* dress.

formality *(n.)* फ़ॉर्मेलटी– a requirement of rule, custom, etiquette, etc. औपचारिकता I have to fulfil certain *formalities* to get the driving licence.

formally *(adv.)* फ़ॉर्मली– officially; after following established or prescribed forms, conventions, etc. औपचारिक रूप से I *formally* informed him about the program.

formation *(n.)* फ़ॉर्मेशन– forming or shaping निर्माण, रचना The *formation* of this educational institute took place in September 1965.

formative *(adj.)* फ़ॉर्मेटिव– shaping; moulding रचनात्मक *Formative* years of her childhood were not of careful supervision.

former *(adj.)* फ़ॉर्मर्– belonging to or occurring in an earlier time भूतपूर्व, पुराना, पहला My *former* tenant was a lawyer.

formerly *(adv.)* फ़ॉर्मर्लि– at or in a former time; previously पहले, प्राचीन समय में Sharad Pawar was *formerly* with the Congress Party.

formula *(n.)* फ़ॉर्म्यूला– a method, pattern, or rule for doing or producing something, often one proved to be successful नुस्ख़ा, नियम, सूत्र Do you know the chemical *formula* of water?

formulate *(v.)* फ़ॉर्म्यूलेट– to put into or express in systematic terms; express in or as if in a formula सूत्र रूप में कहना, स्पष्ट कहना Bobby doesn't know how to *formulate* her new theory.

forsake *(v.)* फ़ॉर्सेक– to give up (something valued or enjoyed) छोड़ देना, त्याग देना I cannot *forsake* my old friends.

fort *(n.)* फ़ोर्ट– a fortified enclosure, building, or position able to be defended against an enemy किला, गढ़ On their trip to Rajasthan, students saw many historical *forts.*

forth *(adv.)* फ़ोर्थ– forward in place, time, order, or degree सामने, आगे The workers brought *forth* the problems they were facing at work.

forthcoming *(adj.)* फ़ोर्थकमिंग– approaching in time आने वाला, आगामी All our *forthcoming* titles are in great demand.

forthright *(adj.)* फ़ॉर्थराइट– direct and honest निष्कपट, स्पष्टवादी My brother is a *forthright* officer in his organisation.

fortnight *(n.)* फ़ोर्टनाइट– a period of 14 consecutive days; two weeks पखवाड़ा, पक्ष The bank manager was on leave for a *fortnight.*

fortunate *(adj.)* फ़ॉर्चुनेट– having good luck; lucky भाग्यशाली, भाग्यवान, खुशनसीब Mahak is *fortunate* enough to pass her pre-medical exam.

fortune *(n.)* फ़ॉर्चून–1. a person's lot or destiny भाग्य, क़िस्मत, तकदीर He has had the good *fortune* to work with me.

2. a large amount of wealth सम्पत्ति, ऐश्वर्य, धन Satpal made a *fortune* in the export trade.

forward *(adv.)* फ़ोर्वर्ड–1. towards the front आगे, अगला, प्रगतिशील Please move *forward.*

2. *(v.)* to send forward or pass on to an ultimate destination बढ़ावा देना, आगे बढ़ाना Have you *forwarded* my application?

forward-looking *(adj.)* फ़ोरवर्ड-लुकिंग– progressive; taking the future into account प्रगतिशील My father is a *forward-looking* man.

foster *(v.)* फ़ोस्टर– to promote the growth or development of पालना-पोसना My cousin is going to *foster* an orphan child.

foul *(adj.)* फ़ाउल– offensive in odour; stinking मैला, गन्दा, घृणित, बदबूदार I cannot tolerate this *foul* smell anymore.

found *(v.)* फ़ाउंड–1. to bring into being, set up, or establish (something, such as an institution, society, etc.) पाया, प्राप्त किया (find का भूतकाल) Have you *found* the book you had lost?

2. to build or establish the foundation or basis of स्थापित करना, नींव डालना Who *founded* your school?

foundation *(n.)* फ़ाउंडेशन– that on which something is founded; basis नींव, बुनियाद, स्थापना, आधार The *foundation* stone was laid by the prime minister.

founder *(n)* फ़ाउण्डर– a person who establishes an institution, company, society, etc. संस्थापक The *founder* of the company met with an accident last week.

fountain *(n.)* फ़ाउण्टेन्– a jet or spray of water or some other liquid झरना, फ़ौवारा, फुहारा In Delhi, many gardens have musical *fountains.*

four *(n.)* फ़ोर– the cardinal number that is the sum of three and one चार The student was learning the table of *four.*

fourth *(det.)* फ़ोर्थ– coming after the third in order, position, time, etc. Often written 4th, चौथा Mahak studies in *fourth* standard.

fowl *(n.)* फ़ाउल– a bird thought to be kept for its meat and eggs मुर्गा, मुर्गी, कुक्कुट I want to buy some *fowl* for my poultry farm.

fox *(n.)* फ़ॉक्स– a wild animal of dog family लोमड़ी Some people are as cunning as a *fox.*

fraction *(n.)* फ़्रैक्शन– a small piece; fragment अंश, टुकड़ा, भाग, खंड Rahul's father willed only a *fraction* of his huge property to him.

fracture *(n.)* फ़्रैक्चर्– 1. the breaking or cracking of a bone or the tearing of a cartilage अस्थि-भंग She had a *fracture* in her leg.

2. *(v.)* to break or crack (a bone) or (of a bone) to become broken or cracked हड्डी का टूटना She fell while running and *fractured* her leg.

fragile *(adj.)* फ़्रैजाइल– delicate; light नाजुक, भुरभुरा These glasses are very *fragile;* handle them with care.

fragment *(n.)* फ़्रैग्मेण्ट– a piece broken off or detached टुकड़ा, अंश, भाग Be careful while collecting the *fragments* of the broken glass.

fragrance *(n.)* फ़्रेग्रन्स– a pleasant or sweet odour; scent; perfume सुगंध The *fragrance* of the incense stick filled the whole room.

fragrant *(adj.)* फ़्रेग्रेन्ट– having a pleasant or sweet smell सुगंधित, खुशबूदार The rose is a *fragrant* flower.

frail *(adj.)* फ़्रेल– physically weak and delicate सुकुमार, कमज़ोर Behind the *frail* body of Mahatma Gandhi was a strong-willed man of principles.

frailty *(n.)* फ़्रेलटी– physical or moral weakness नैतिक दुर्बलता, चारित्रिक कमज़ोरी Shakespeare quoted in Hamlet, "*Frailty*, thy name is woman."

frame *(n.)* फ़्रेम–1. an open structure that gives shape and support to something, चौखट, ढाँचा The picture is looking beautiful in this *frame*.
2. a condition; state मनोदशा, मनोभाव You seem to be in an angry *frame* of mind today.
3. *(v.)* to construct by fitting parts together फ़्रेम चढ़वाना, चौखटा लगाना I want to *frame* this photograph.

framework *(n.)* फ़्रेमवर्क– a structural plan or basis of a project ढांचा, मूलभूत पद्धति We were discussing the topic in a particular *framework*.

franchise *(n.)* फ्रैनचाइज़्– any exemption, privilege, or right granted to an individual or group by a public authority, such as the right to use public property for a business विशेषाधिकार Women were not given the *franchise* in some countries until quite recently.

frank *(adj.)* फ़्रैंक– honest and straight forward in speech or attitude खरा, सच्चा I will let him know about this project as I am quite *frank* with him.

fraternal *(n.)* फ़्रटर्नल– of or suitable to a brother; brotherly भाई जैसा Ram always shows *fraternal* affection to me.

fraternity *(n.)* फ्रटर्निटी– a feeling of friendship and support भाईचारा, भ्रातृत्व Fraternity is a good virtue.

fraud *(n.)* फ़्रॉड– deliberate deception, trickery, or cheating intended to gain an advantage धोखा, कपट, छल An enquiry exposed the *fraud* played by the former bank manager.

fraught *(adj.)* फ्रॉट– causing worry, tense तनावयुक्त He looked *fraught*.

fray *(n.)* फ़्रे– a noisy quarrel, a fight झगड़ा, बहस, संघर्ष Shyam joined the *fray*.

freak *(n.)* फ़्रीक–1. a person who is considered to be unusual सनक, वहम He was treated like a *freak* because he didn't want parents.
2. *(v.)* to react strongly कठोर प्रतिक्रिया व्यक्त करना The mother *freaked* on seeing her child in dirty clothes.

freckle *(n.)* फ़्रेकल– a small brownish spot on the skin: a localized deposit of the pigment melanin, developed by exposure to sunlight चकत्ता, भूरा दाग़ Smriti has a lot of *freckles* on her face.

free *(v.)* फ़्री–1. to set at liberty; to release स्वतन्त्र करना/होना She opened the cage and *freed* the little bird. *(adj.) able to act at will; not under compulsion or restraint* आज़ाद, स्वतंत्र On what date did India become *free*?
2. not occupied or busy; without previous engagements खाली, सावकाश Why didn't you call me? I was *free* today.
3. costing nothing; provided without charge मुफ़्त, निःशुल्क I got a toothbrush *free* with a jar of face-cream.

➢ **free and easy**– relaxed तनावमुक्त The atmosphere in her office is very *free and easy*.

freedom *(n.)* फ़्रीडम– personal liberty, as from slavery, bondage, serfdom, etc. आज़ादी, स्वतंत्रता India got *freedom* after a long struggle.

➢ **freedom fighter** *(n.) a militant revolutionary* स्वतंत्रता सेनानी, Subhash Chandra Bose was a great *freedom fighter*.

freehand *(adj.)* फ्रीहैण्ड– done by hand without the use of guiding instruments हाथ से बनाया हुआ, मुक्तहस्त He drew a *freehand* sketch of Mahatma Gandhi.

freelance *(adj.)* फ्रीलान्स– a self-employed person, esp a writer or artist, who is not employed continuously but hired to do specific assignments स्वतंत्र (कलाकार, पत्रकार) Let me know if you come across any *freelance* work for me.

freely *(adv.)* फ़्रीलि– without obstruction or impediment स्वतंत्रतापर्वक, पूरी आज़ादी से You can use my books *freely.*

freeze *(v.)* फ़्रीज़– to change (a liquid) into a solid as a result of a reduction in temperature, or (of a liquid) to solidify in this way, esp to convert or be converted into ice जमकर बर्फ़ बनना, जमना, अकड़ना, कड़ा हो जाना Dal Lake *freezes* in the winter.

freezing *(adj.)* फ़्रीज़िंग–1. extremely cold अत्यंत ठंडा, सर्द I was *freezing* in the chilled night.

2. having temperatures that are below 0° celsius तापमान जिस पर पानी जम जाता है Last night the temperature fell to *freezing* point.

freight *(n.)* फ़्रेट– goods that is transported by trains, ships, etc. माल, भार, बोझा Many *freight* trains were started at the time of new railway minister.

frenzy *(n.)* फ़्रेनज़ि– violent mental derangement उन्माद, आवेश I told him about me in a state of *frenzy.*

frequent *(adj.)* फ़्रीक्वण्ट– recurring at short intervals बारंबार होने वाला, लगातार I have made *frequent* trips to Mumbai.

frequently *(adv.)* फ़्रीक्वन्टली– constantly or habitually; often प्रायः, बहुधा The chief minister visits his town quite *frequently.*

fresh *(adj.)* फ़्रेश–1. not stale or deteriorated; newly made, harvested, etc. ताज़ा, नवीन Seeing *fresh* flowers in the morning is quite refreshing.

2. not tired; alert; refreshed चुस्त, फुर्तीला Morning bed tea makes me feel so *fresh.*

fresher *(n.)* फ़्रेशर– a first-year student at college or university कॉलेज या विश्वविद्यालय का प्रथम वर्ष का छात्र They are *freshers* of this college.

fret *(v.)* फ़्रेट– to distress or be distressed; worry चिढ़ना, कुढ़ना Why do you *fret* so much about domestic difficulties?

friction *(n.)* फ़्रिक्शन– a resistance encountered when one body moves relative to another body with which it is in contact रगड़, घर्षण There is a lot of *friction* between the older and younger generations.

friday *(n.)* फ़्राइडे– the sixth day of the week; fifth day of the working week शुक्रवार Let's go for a movie this *Friday.*

friend *(n.)* फ़्रेण्ड– a person known well to another and regarded with liking, affection, and loyalty; an intimate मित्र, दोस्त I have a large circle of *friends.*

friendly *(adj.)* फ़्रेण्डली– helpful, easy, or good for the person or thing specified मित्रवत, दोस्ताना Rama has very *friendly* relation with her daughter.

friendship *(n.)* फ़्रेण्डशिप– a relationship between two or more friends दोस्ती, मित्रता A true *friendship* means alot to me.

fright *(n.)* फ़्राइट– sudden intense fear or alarm आतंक, भय, डर I had a *fright* when the dog rushed at me.

frighten *(v.)* फ़्राइटन– to cause fear in; terrify; scare दहला देना, डरा देना The horror movie really *frightened* me.

frightening *(adj.)* फ़्राइटनिंग– causing fear or anxiety ख़ौफ़ या सदमा पहुंचाने वाला I had such a *frightening* experience with him.

frightful *(n.)* फ़्राइटफुल– very alarming, distressing, or horrifying भयावह, ख़ौफ़नाक We saw a very *frightful* accident on the way.

frigid *(adj.)* फ्रिजिड– formal or stiff in behaviour or temperament; lacking in affection or warmth रूखा, भावशून्य His poetry is *frigid* and could not inspire me.

fringe *(n.)* फ्रिन्ज– an outer edge; periphery किनारा, सीमांत There was a hunting lodge on the *fringe* of the forest.

frisk *(v.)* फ्रिस्क– to leap, move about, or act in a playful manner; frolic अठखेलियां करना, उछल-कूद करना The animals were *frisking* in the zoo.

frivolity *(n.)* फ्रिवॉलटी– something not serious or sensible or the quality or state of not being serious or sensible छिछोरापन, टुच्चापन We cannot waste our time on such *frivolities.*

frivolous *(adj.)* फ्रिवलस– not serious or sensible in content, attitude, or behaviour; silly छिछोरा, ओछा Let's not get into a *frivolous* conversation now.

frock *(n.)* फ्रॉक– a girl's or woman's dress स्त्री के पहनने की एक पोशाक, फ्रॉक The girl wanted to wear a party *frock.*

frog *(n.)* फ्रॉग– a small animal that lives both on land and in water मेंढक Kids were happy to see the *frogs* jumping in the water.

frogman *(n.)* फ्रॉगमन– a swimmer equipped with a rubber suit, flippers, and breathing equipment for working underwater गोताख़ोर Some *frogmen* searched the river and found the dead body.

from *(prep.)* फ्रम्– used to indicate the original location, situation, etc. से We began our journey *from* Delhi.

front *(adj.)* फ्रण्ट– 1. on, at, or in the front अगला, अग्र, सामने का You can stand in *front* of the door and wait till he comes.

2. *(n.)* that part or side that is forward, prominent, or most often seen or used अगला हिस्सा, अग्रभाग, अगवाड़ा The *front* of my house faces a park.

frontier *(n.)* फ्रण्टिअर्– the region of a country bordering on another or a line, barrier, etc. marking such a boundary सरहद, सीमा Our *frontier* with Pakistan has been fenced in Punjab.

frost *(n.)* फ्रॉस्ट– a white deposit of ice particles, esp one formed on objects out of doors at night बर्फ़ की पतली परत, पाला The *frost* on the windscreen made it difficult to drive the car.

frosty *(adj.)* फ्रॉस्टी– lacking warmth or enthusiasm उमंगरहित, रूखा It was a cold and *frosty* morning.

froth *(n.)* फ्रॉथ– a mass of small bubbles of air or a gas in a liquid, produced by fermentation, detergent, etc. झाग, फेन The child licked at the *froth* on the shake.

frown *(v.)* फ्राउन– 1. to draw the brows together and wrinkle the forehead, esp in worry, anger, or concentration भौंहे चढ़ाना, त्योरी चढ़ाना Why are you *frowning* at me?

2. *(n.)* a show of dislike or displeasure भ्रूभंग, तेवर We could tell by her *frown* that she was angry.

frugal *(adj.)* फ्रूगल– practising economy; living without waste; thrifty मितव्ययी, किफ़ायती His wife is very *frugal* lady.

fruit *(n.)* फ्रूट–1. the ripened ovary of a flowering plant, containing one or more seeds. It may be dry, as in the poppy, or fleshy, as in the peach फल All these *fruits* are fresh.

2. the result or consequence of an action or effort परिणाम, नतीजा A good score is the *fruit* of regular study.

fruitful *(adj.)* फ्रूटफुल– productive or prolific, esp in bearing offspring सफ़ल, लाभदायक It is definately going to be a *fruitful* project.

frustrate *(v.)* फ्रस्ट्रेट– to make sb feel annoyed चिढ़ाना Don't *frustrate* me, I am not going to America.

frustration *(n.)* फ़्रस्ट्रेशन– the condition of being frustrated हताशा, निराशा, खीझ Her *frustration* took her to suicidal tendency.

fry *(v.)* फ़्राइ– to cook or be cooked in fat, oil, etc. usually over direct heat तलना, भूनना I am *frying* fish.

fuel *(n.)* फ़्यूअल– any substance burned as a source of heat or power, such as coal or petrol ईंधन, जलावन We use petroleum gas for *fuel.*

fugitive *(n.)* फ़्यूजटिव– a person who has escaped भगोड़ा, पलायक The newspapers published the picture of the *fugitive* prisoner.

fulfil *(v.)* फुल्फ़िल– to bring about the completion or achievement of (a desire, promise, etc.) पूरा करना, पालन करना The aim of my life is to *fulfil* all my dreams.

fulfilment *(n.)* फुलफ़िलमेंट– achievement; completing of प्राप्ति, उपलब्धि The *fulfilment* of my dream brought happiness in my life.

full *(adj.)* फुल–1.holding or containing as much as possible पूर्ण, पूरा This place is *full* of dust. Nobody can sit here for a second.
2. filled to capacity or near capacity भरा My stomach is *full* now. Can't eat anything else.
3. *(adv.)* exactly; directly; right सीधे Only an honest person can look you *full* in the face.

➢ **full of life**– with full excitment पूरे उत्साह के साथ, Sahar is a happy child, always *full of life.*

➢ **in full**– including the whole of sth पूरा का पूरा, संपूर्ण रूप से Can you write your name and address *in full*?

➢ **in full swing**– with maximum speed पूरे ज़ोरों पर/शबाब पर By 10:30 the party was *in full swing.*

➢ **in full view**– in front of everyone सबकी नजर तक पहुंचने वाली, The argument happened on stage *in full view* of the audience.

➢ **to the full**– as much as possible अधिक से अधिक, We should enjoy life *to the full.*

➢ **full length**– extending to or showing the complete length पैरों तक पहुंचने वाली, There was a *full-length* mirror in her bedroom.

full-fledged *(adj.)* फुल-फ्लेज्ड– developed or matured to the fullest degree पूर्ण विकसित He is now a *full-fledged* member of the society.

full-time *(adj.)* फुल-टाइम– for the entire time appropriate to an activity पूर्णकालिक काम करने वाला Tabassum is *a full-time* employee of the company.

fully *(adv.)* फुली– completely, totally; entirely पूरी तरह से, पूर्णतया The party is *fully* satisfied with the policy.

fumble *(v.)* फ़म्बल– to grope about clumsily or blindly, esp in searching टटोलना She *fumbled* with the letter to find the name of the sender.

fume *(v.)* फ़्यूम– 1. to be very anger or fury about sth; to rage क्रुद्ध होना The parents *fumed* over the poor performance of their child. *fumes.*
2. *(n.)* smoke, gas, vapour, etc. धुआँ, गैस, भाप The diesel *fumes* made it difficult to breathe.

fun *(n.)* फ़न– a source of enjoyment, amusement, etc. मज़ाक, ठठोली, आमोद-प्रमोद We had a great *fun* at the party.

function *(n.)* फ़न्क्शन–1. an official or formal social gathering or ceremony समारोह, उत्सव Will you be coming to the *function* in the evening today?.
2. *(v.)* to operate or perform as specified; work properly काम करना How does this machine *function*?

fund *(n.)* फ़न्ड– a reserve of money, etc. set aside for a certain purpose निधि, कोष We have started collecting *fund* for the school building.

fundamental *(adj.)* फ़न्डमेंटल–1. of, involving, or comprising a

foundation; basic मौलिक Right to speech is our *fundamental* right.
2. *(n.)* a principle, law, etc. that serves as the basis of an idea or system मूल सिद्धांत Understand the *fundamentals* before starting this venture.

funeral *(n.)* फ़्यूनरल– a ceremony at which a dead person is buried or cremated मृतक-क्रिया, अन्त्येष्टि Did you attend the old man's *funeral*?

funnel *(n.)* फ़नल–1. a hollow utensil with a wide mouth tapering to a small hole, used for pouring liquids, powders, etc, into a narrow-necked vessel कीप Use a *funnel* to fill kerosene in bottle.
2. a chimney for smoke and exhaust gases, as on a steamship or steam locomotive चिमनी We could see the *funnel* of the approaching ship.

funny *(adj.)* फ़नी– causing amusement or laughter; humorous; comical हास्यास्पद, मज़ाकिया He is such a *funny* man. He makes me laugh so much.

fur *(n.)* फ़र्– the dense coat of fine silky hairs on such mammals as the cat, sheep and mink लोम, लोमचर्म I bought a *fur* coat during my visit to Kashmir.

furious *(adj.)* फ़्युअरिअस– extremely angry or annoyed; raging अति क्रुद्ध, उग्र The manager became *furious* at the blunder of the clerk who sent an important letter at the wrong address.

furnace *(n.)* फ़र्नेस– an enclosed chamber in which heat is produced to generate steam, destroy refuse, smelt or refine ores, etc. भट्टी During a visit to the steel plant, the students were shown a huge *furnace*.

furnish *(v.)* फ़र्निश– to provide (a house, room, etc.) with furniture, carpets, etc फ़र्नीचर से सजाना, सामान जुटाना The room was *furnished* with antiques.

furniture *(n.)* फ़र्निचर– the movable, generally functional, articles that equip a room, house, etc. फ़र्नीचर, मेज़-कुर्सी This market is famous for secondhand *furniture*.

further *(adj.)* फ़र्दर्–1. more; additional और, अधिक, अतिरिक्त I have nothing *further* to say.

furthermore *(adv.)* फ़र्दरमोर– in addition; moreover इसके अलावा, इसके सिवाय Vijay said he had not discussed the matter with his friend. *Furthermore*, he had not even contacted him.

furthest *(adj., adv.)* फ़र्देस्ट– far thest दूरतम She is standing *furthest* from pole.

fury *(n.)* फ़्यूरी– violent or uncontrolled anger; wild rage प्रकोप, आवेश Avoid the *fury* of the storm by remaining indoors.

fuse *(n.)* फ़्यूज़– any device by which an explosive charge is ignited पलीता, बत्ती, फ़्यूज़ I want a *fuse* for my electric connection.

fuss *(n.)* फ़स– nervous activity or agitation, esp when disproportionate or unnecessary बतंगड़, शोर-शराबा Don't make a *fuss* if there is no milk.

fussy *(adj.)* फ़सी– characterized by overelaborate detail बतंगड़िया I cant tolerate her because of her *fussy* nature.

futile *(adj.)* फ़्यूटाइल– pointless; unimportant; trifling व्यर्थ, निरर्थक, असार They made a *futile* attempt to make his son join a medical college.

future *(n.)* फ़्यूचर्–1. the time yet to come भावी/आगामी समय या काल In *future*, never hesitate to call me when you need help.
2. likelihood of later improvement or advancement भविष्य, भविष्यत्काल If you work hard, your *future* will be bright.
3. *(adj.)* of or expressing time yet to come भावी, आगामी What are your *future* plans?

Gg

Gg *(n.)* जी–अंग्रेज़ी वर्णमाला का सातवां अक्षर The seventh letter of the English alphabet. Game begins with '*G*'

gabble *(v.)* गैबअल्– to utter (words, etc.) rapidly and indistinctly; jabber बड़बड़ाना, बकना Sarika was nervous and started to *gabble.*

gable *(n.)* गेबल– the triangular upper part of a wall between the sloping ends of a pitched roof तिकोना भाग, त्रिकोणिका There are two *gables* in my house.

gadget *(n.)* गैजिट– a small mechanical device or appliance औज़ार, जुगत He is aware of all the latest *gadgets* available in the market.

gag *(v.)* गैग– to stop up (a person's mouth), esp with a piece of cloth, etc. to prevent him or her from speaking or crying out ठेपी लगाना The gangster *gagged* her and tied her to a chair.

gaga *(adj.)* गागा– slightly crazy सनकी She has gone completely *gaga* over it.

gaiety *(n.)* गेअटी– the state or condition of being merry, bright, or lively उल्लास, प्रफुल्लता Puppet show added to the *gaiety* of the celebrations of marriage.

gain *(v.)* गेन–1. to acquire (something desirable); obtain प्राप्त करना You will *gain* many friends if you have a helpful nature.

2. *(n.)* the act of gaining; attainment; acquisition प्राप्ति There is no *gain* without pain.

3. something won, acquired, earned, etc. profit; advantage लाभ, नफ़ा *Gain* and loss are part of any business.

gait *(n.)* गेट– manner of walking or running चाल Broken shoe affected her *gait.*

gala *(n.)* गाला– a celebration; festive occasion उत्सव, समारोह We all had a *gala* time yesterday night.

galaxy *(n.)* गैलक्सी– any of a vast number of star systems held together by gravitational attraction in an asymmetric shape आकाशगंगा There are numerous stars in the *galaxy.*

gale *(n.)* गेल– a strong wind, आँधी, हवा का झोंका, झंझा Don't go out into the *gale.*

gallant *(adj.)* गैलण्ट– brave and high-spirited; courageous and honourable; dashing बहादुर, वीर, दिलेर A *gallant* young man saved the two drowning girls.

gallantry *(n.)* गैलण्ट्री– conspicuous courage, esp in war शौर्य, वीरता The policeman was rewarded for his *gallantry.*

gallery *(n.)* गैलरी–1. a room or building for exhibiting works of art दीर्घा, वीथी In which *gallery* are you exhibiting your picture?

gallop *(v.)* गैलप– 1. (of a horse or other quadruped) to run fast with a two-beat stride in which all four legs are off the ground at once सरपट दौड़ना या दौड़ाना The horses had to *gallop* to keep pace with the motor-car.

2. *(n.)* the fast speed at which a horse can run सरपट, छलांग The *gallop* of Rehman's horse could be heard from a distance.

gallstone *(n.)* गालस्टोन– a small hard concretion of cholesterol, bile pigments, and lime salts, formed in the gall bladder or its ducts पित्त-पथरी His grandfather had many *gallstones* in his gall bladder.

gamble *(n.)* गैम्बल–1. a bet, wager, or other risk or chance taken for possible monetary gain जुआ, द्यूत, जुआबाज़ी David's parents did not know that he had taken to *gambling.*

2. a risky act or venture जोखिम का काम Starting a business is a *gamble.*

3. *(v.)* to play games of chance to win money जुआ खेलना He *gambled* the entire night and lost everything he had.

game *(n.)* गेम–1. an amusement or pastime; diversion खेल, क्रीड़ा Basketball was my favourite *game* when I was in school.

2. wild animals, including birds and fish, hunted for sport, food, or profit शिकार I hear you are big *game* hunter.

gang *(n.)* गैन्ग– a group of people who associate together or act as an organized body, esp for criminal or illegal purposes टोली, गिरोह The police made intensive efforts to trace the *gang* of car thieves.

gangster *(n.)* गैंगस्टर– a member of an organized gang of criminals, esp one who resorts to violence डाकू, गुंडा Police could catch only two *gangster* that day.

gangway *(n.)* गैन्ग्वे– an aisle between rows of seats मार्ग, सीढ़ी I walked down the *gangway* of the theatre to reach my seat in the front row.

gap *(n.)* गैप–1. a break in a line of hills or mountains affording a route through छेद, दरार The thieves made a *gap* in the garden wall to enter the house.

2. a break in continuity; interruption; hiatus रिक्त, खाली जगह, अन्तराल, कमी The police found many *gaps* in the bank manager's account of the bank robbery.

gape *(v.)* गैप– to stare in wonder or amazement, esp with the mouth open मुंह फाड़ना He *gaped* in astonishment when he saw me wearing a short skirt.

garage *(n.)* गैरिज– a building or part of a building used to house a motor vehicle गराज Our house has a *garage.*

garbage *(n.)* गार्बेज– worthless, useless, or unwanted matter कूड़ा-कचरा *Garbage* should be thrown outside the home.

garden *(n.)* गार्डन– an area of land, usually planted with grass, trees, flowerbeds, etc. adjoining a house बाग़, बगीचा It's so refreshing to walk in this *garden.*

gardening *(n.)* गार्डनिंग– the planning and cultivation of a garden बाग़बानी I spend around one hour in *gardening* every sunday.

gargle *(v.)* गार्गल– to rinse (the mouth and throat) with a liquid, esp a medicinal fluid by slowly breathing out through the liquid ग़रारा करना His father *gargles* every morning with lukewarm water.

garish *(adj.)* गेअरिश– gay or colourful in a crude or vulgar manner; gaudy भड़कीला, चमकीला The carpets are too *garish* for my taste.

garland *(n.)* गार्लेण्ड– 1. a wreath or festoon of flowers, leaves, etc. worn round the head or neck or hung up फूलों का हार, माला We welcomed the chief guest with *garlands.*

2. *(v.)* to adorn with a garland or garlands फूलों की माला पहनाना The priest *garlanded* the deity.

garlic *(n.)* गार्लिक– a vegetable of the onion family having strong taste and *smell* लहसुन Few flakes of *garlic* can give a different flavour to your dish.

garment *(n.)* गार्मन्ट– a piece of clothing कपड़ा, वस्त्र I have to buy some new *garments* before going there.

garnish *(v.)* गार्निश– to decorate a dish of food (भोजन को) सजाना The cook *garnished* the dish with fresh coriander leaves.

gas *(n.)* गैस– any substance that is gaseous at room temperature and atmospheric pressure गैस, पैट्रोल How much does a cylinder of cooking *gas* cost?

gasp *(v.)* गास्प्– 1. to draw in the breath sharply, convulsively, or with effort, esp in expressing awe, horror, etc. हाँफना Running so fast made Rahul *gasp* for breath.

2. *(n.)* a short convulsive intake of breath हाँफी (खुले मुंह से अचानक जोर की सांस) Why did you give a *gasp* of surprise when you saw me?

gastric *(adj.)* गैस्ट्रिक– of, relating to, near, or involving the stomach पेट से संबंधित, जठरीय Do not drink Pepsi after meal. It will be harmful for your *gastric* juices.

gate *(n.)* गेट– a movable barrier, usually hinged, for closing an opening in a wall, fence, etc. फाटक, द्वार You can open the *gate* on your own with this key.

gatecrasher *(n.)* गेट-क्रैशर– a person who gains entry to a party, concert, etc. without invitation or payment अनामंत्रित अतिथि/मेहमान Girish was the *gatecrasher* of her party.

gateway *(n.)* गेटवे– an entrance that may be closed by or as by a gate प्रवेश-द्वार A good education is the *gateway* to success.

gather *(v.)* गैदर्–1. to assemble or cause to assemble एकत्र करना या होना Many people *gathered* at the meeting.

2. to collect or be collected gradually; muster वस्तुओं को इकट्ठा करना Please *gather* your books and put them in your bag.

3. to learn from information given; conclude or assume जमा करना, चुनना The reporter *gathered* enough information before writing a feature on kidnappings.

gathering *(n.)* गैदरिंग–1. a group of people, things, etc. that are gathered together; assembly सभा, जमाव I saw a huge *gathering* when I reached there.

gaudy *(adj.)* गॉडी– gay, bright, or colourful in a crude or vulgar manner; garish भड़कीला, चटकीला She was wearing a *gaudy* dress in the college.

gauge *(n.)* गेज– 1. a standard measurement, dimension, capacity, or quantity of माप, नाप, पैमाना If you fix a *gauge* on your cooking gas cylinder you will know the amount of gas inside.

2. *(v.)* to measure or determine the amount, quantity, size, condition, etc. of किसी वस्तु को मापना How do you *gauge* the amount of water in this barrel?

gaunt *(adj.)* गान्ट– bony and emaciated in appearance मरियल, दुबला She looked weak and *gaunt* after a long illness.

gawk *(v.)* गॉक– to stare in a stupid way; gape मूर्खों की तरह घूरना He was carried out on a stretcher, with everyone *gawking* at him.

gay *(adj.)* गे–1. homosexual समलैंगिक Is he *gay*?

2. brightly coloured चमकीला, भड़कीला Youngsters favour *gay* colours in their clothes.

3. *(n.)* a homosexual person, esp a man समलिंगी पुरुष He is a *gay* person.

gaze *(v.)* गेज़–1. to look long and fixedly, esp in wonder or admiration ताकना, टकटकी लगाकर देखना I *gazed* at the beautiful painting for a long time.

2. *(n.)* a fixed look; stare टकटकी He fixed his *gaze* at the object moving outside the window.

gazette *(n.)* गज़ेट– a official journal or newspaper राजपत्र, गजट What is written in the *gazette?*

gear *(n.)* गिअर– 1. a toothed wheel that engages with another toothed wheel or with a rack in order to change the speed or direction of transmitted motion (वाहन का) गियर Many cars have more than four *gears.*
2. *(v.)* to adjust or adapt (one thing) so as to fit in or work with another तैयार रहना, अनुकूल बनाना The country's economy must be *geared* to wartime requirements.

gem *(n.)* जेम–1. a precious or semiprecious stone used in jewellery as a decoration; jewel मणि, रत्न Diamond is a precious *gem.*
2. a person or thing held to be a perfect example; treasure उत्कृष्ट व्यक्ति She is a *gem* of a person.

gender *(n.)* जेण्डर– the state of being male, female, or neuter लिंग You have to mention your *gender* in the form.

gene *(n.)* जीन– a unit of heredity composed of DNA occupying a fixed position on a chromosome जीन (जो माता-पिता से उनकी संतानों तक पहुंचते हैं) My children have red hair because I have got it in my *gene.*

general *(adj.)* जेनरल–1. common; widespread आम, सार्वजनिक The *general* elections are going to take place in this week.
2. applicable or true in most cases; usual सामान्य, साधारण As a *general* rule, we are at home in the evening.
3. *(n.)* an officer of a rank senior to lieutenant general, esp one who commands a large military formation सेनापति, सेनानी, जनरल My friend's uncle is a *General* in the army.

generalize (ise) *(v.)* जैनरलाइज़– to form (general principles or conclusions) from (detailed facts, experience, etc.); infer व्यापक/लोकप्रिय बनाना These research findings cannot be *generalized.*

generally *(adv.)* जेनरली– usually; as a rule सामान्यतः Innocent people are *generally* cheated by the clever ones.

generate *(v.)* जेनरेट– to produce or bring into being; create उत्पादन/उत्पन्न करना News agencies *generate* useful information about the various events.

generation *(n.)* जेनरेशन– a successive stage in natural descent of organisms: the time between when an organism comes into being and when it reproduces पीढ़ी, पुश्त Today's *generation* is more fun-loving than their elders.

generation gap *(n.)* जेनरेशन गैप– the years separating one generation from the generation that precedes or follows it, दो पीढ़ियों का अंतर Modern education system filled the *generation gap.*

generator *(n.)* जेनरेटर– a device for producing a voltage electrostatically बिजली चलाने वाली मशीन There is a big *generator* in our office.

generic *(adj.)* जिनेरिक– applicable or referring to a whole class or group; general प्रजातीय, जातीय Citrus fruit is the *generic* term for oranges and lemons.

generosity *(n.)* जेनरॉसिटी– willingness and liberality in giving away one's money, time, etc. magnanimity उदारता He showed great *generosity* to them.

generous *(adj.)* जेनरस–1. willing and liberal in giving away one's money, time, etc. munificent उदार Her *generous* nature made her reach the heights.

2. more than is necessary प्रचुर, भरपूर The bus has a *generous* amount of space

generously *(adv.)* जेनरसली– kindly and helpfully उदारतापूर्वक She distributed the food packets *generously.*

genie *(n.)* जीनि– (in fairy tales and stories) a spirit with magic powers, djinn जिन्न I saw a *genie* show on the TV.

genius *(n.)* जीनिअस–1. great intelligence or ability, esp of a highly original kind प्रतिभा He was *genius* at his work.

2. a person considered as exerting great influence of a certain sort प्रतिभाशाली व्यक्ति Kalidas was a *genius,* who wrote "Abhigyan Shakuntalam", one of the greatest plays of the world.

genocide *(n.)* जेनोसाइड– the policy of deliberately killing a nationality or ethnic group जाति-संहार There are reports of *genocide* in many tribal areas of Africa.

genre *(n.)* ज्हानर– kind, category, or sort, esp of literary or artistic work शैली, ढँग These are the difficult *genres* of the epic poetry.

genteel *(adj.)* जेन्टील– affectedly proper or refined; excessively polite भद्र, कुलीन/विनम्र आचरण वाला The receptionist of the five-star hotel was behaving in a *genteel* way.

gentle *(adj.)* जेण्टल–1. having a mild or kindly nature or character कुलीन, भद्र Your manners should always be *gentle.*

2. soft or temperate; mild; moderate मन्द, हल्का Let us go for a walk and enjoy the *gentle* breeze.

gentleman *(n.)* जेन्ट्लमन– a man who is cultured, courteous, and well-educated सज्जन, कुलीन/भद्र पुरुष We must admit that he was a great *gentleman.*

gentry *(n.)* जेन्ट्रि– persons of high birth or social standing; aristocracy कुलीन वर्ग My friend is a member of the landed *gentry.*

genuine *(adj.)* जेन्यूइन– not fake or counterfeit; original; real; authentic असली, सच्चा Is your overcoat made of *genuine* fur?

geography *(n.)* जिऑग्रफ़ि– the study of the natural features of the earth's surface, including topography, climate, soil, vegetation, etc. and man's response to them भूगोल How much did you score in *geography?*

geology *(n.)* जिऑलजि– the scientific study of the origin, history, structure, and composition of the earth भूविज्ञान I have to go to the department of *geology.*

geometry *(n.)* जिऑमिट्रि– the branch of mathematics concerned with the properties, relationships, and measurement of points, lines, curves, and surfaces ज्यामिति, रेखागणित I hate to attend my *geometry* classes.

germ *(n.)* जर्म– a microorganism, esp one that produces disease in animals or plants जीवाणु, रोगाणु You should give your child a *germ* free soap for handwash.

germinate *(v.)* जर्मिनेट– to grow or cause to grow; develop उगना, अंकुरित होना An idea to write a novel began to *germinate* in my mind last night.

gesture *(n.)* जेस्चर– a motion of the hands, head, or body to emphasize an idea or emotion, esp while speaking चेष्टा, इशारा, संकेत If you want to be a successful public speaker, you must practise effective *gestures.*

get *(v.)* गेट्–1. to come into possession of; receive or earn पाना, प्राप्त करना How many marks did you *get* in Mathematics?

2. to succeed in going, coming, leaving, etc. हो जाना I have to go. It's *getting* dark.

➢ **get ahead**– to advance or attain success सफ़ल होना Parvez *got ahead* in his new job.

➢ **get along**– to leave a place किसी स्थान से चले जाना I have to *get along* now.

➢ **get around/about**– to move around, as when recovering from an illness एक जगह से दूसरी जगह जाना, My father needs a stick to *get around* these days.

➢ **get away**– to make an escape; leave कोई ग़लत काम करना लेकिन दंडित होने से बच जाना, The robbers *got away* in a stolen car.

➢ **get back**– to recover or retrieve उधार दी हुई चीज़ वापस लेना, She has *got back* her bag from her sister.

➢ **get behind**– to remain in a place after others have left; linger पीछे रह जाना, She *gets behind* her mother in household chores.

➢ **get down**– to attend seriously (to); concentrate (on) काम में लग जाना, I *get down* to my work after lunch.

➢ **get in**– to enter a car, train, etc. प्रविष्ट होना, घुसना *Get in* the car fast its raining heavily.

➢ **get off**– to move or cause to move to a distance (from) दूर हटने को कहना, *Get off* else I will call my father.

➢ **get out**– to leave or escape or cause to leave or escape: used in the imperative when dismissing a person बाहर निकालना, Please *get out* from my room.

➢ **get rid**– . to relieve or free oneself of (something or someone unpleasant or undesirable) छुटकारा पाना, How can I *get rid* from him?

➢ **get through**– to succeed or cause or help to succeed in an examination, test, etc. किसी को कुछ समझाने में सफ़ल होना, We could not *get through* to them easily.

➢ **get-together** – gather or assemble socially जुटना, एकत्रित होना Lets *get together* and make fun.

getaway *(n.)* गेटवे– the act of leaving a place quickly, especially after committing a crime or when trying to avoid someone रफूचक्कर, प्रस्थान Our *getaway* on the weekend was very refreshing.

ghastly *(adj.)* ग़ास्टलि– very frightening or unpleasant भयानक It was a *ghastly* dream I must say.

ghat *(n.)* गॉट– stairs or a passage leading down to a river घाट There are many *ghats* in Varanasi.

ghost *(n.)* गोस्ट– the disembodied spirit of a dead person, भूत, प्रेतात्मा Do you still believe in *ghosts*?

ghostly *(adj.)* गोस्ट्लि– looking like a ghost भूत जैसा She was looking like a *ghostly* figure in a white dress.

giant *(adj.)* जाइअन्ट– 1. remarkably or supernaturally large दैत्याकार We saw a *giant* animal in the circus.

2. *(n.)* a person or thing of exceptional size, reputation, etc. दानव, दैत्य There were so many *giants* in the circus.

gibber *(v.)* जिबूअ– to utter rapidly and unintelligibly; prattle बड़बड़ करना Monkeys *gibber* at one another.

gibberish *(n.)* जिबरिश– rapid chatter like that of monkeys बड़बड़, बकवास Why are you talking *gibberish*?

giddy *(adj.)* गिडि– affected with a reeling sensation and feeling as if about to fall; dizzy चक्कर I feel *giddy* in summer.

gift *(n.)* गिफ़्ट– something given; a present उपहार, भेंट I am going to give you a very special *gift* on your birthday.

gifted *(adj.)* गिफ्टिड– having or showing natural talent or aptitude गुणी, प्रतिभाशाली Zara is a God-*gifted* child in her family.

gigantic *(adj.)* जाइगैन्‌टिक– very large; enormous अति विशाल, विराट While in Mumbai, we went on-board a *gigantic* ship.

giggle *(v.)* गिगल्– 1. to laugh nervously or foolishly ही-ही करके हँसना The girls *giggled* at his funny outfit. 2. *(n.)* something or someone that provokes amusement हें-हें, हीं-हीं, तरह की हँसी The girls were taken by *giggles* at his funny outfit.

gilt *(n.)* गिल्ट– gold or a substance simulating it, applied in gilding मुलम्मा, कलई His aunty always wears *gilt* bangles.

ginger *(n.)* जिन्‌ज– root of the ginger plant used as a spice अदरक A cup of *ginger* tea helps to cure cold and cough.

giraffe *(n.)* जिराफ़– an African animal with long neck and legs जिराफ़ We saw a tall *giraffe* in the zoo.

girder *(n.)* गड्‌अ– a large beam, esp one made of steel, used in the construction of bridges, buildings, etc. गर्डर, धरन, शहतीर Can you count the *girders* of this bridge?

girl *(n.)* गर्ल–1. a female child from birth to young womanhood लड़की, बालिका Who is that *girl* in the pink sari?

2. a young unmarried woman; lass; maid नवयुवती These *girls* are very talkative.

girlfriend *(n.)* गर्ल्‌फ्रेन्ड– any female friend महिला मित्र, सखी My *girlfriend* always makes me feel so special.

girlish *(adj.)* गल्‌इश– of or like a girl in looks, behaviour, innocence, etc. लड़की जैसा, कन्यासुलभ His mother has a *girlish* figure.

girth *(n.)* गर्थ– the distance around something; circumference घेरा, कमरबंद He was a tall man of considerable *girth.*

gist *(n.)* जिस्ट– the essential point of an action सारांश I did not have time to go through the whole book, so I requested him to tell me the *gist* of it.

give *(v.)* गिव– to present or deliver voluntarily (something that is one's own) to the permanent possession of another or others देना, सौंपना, पहुँचाना Please *give* me your pen.

➢ **give away**– to reveal or betray किसी की छुपी हुई सच्चाई को उजागर करना, Don't worry, I won't *give you away.*

➢ **give back**– to return उधार ली गई वस्तु को उसे लौटाना, This isn't your money and you must *give* it *back.*

➢ **give sth in**– to submit or deliver (a document) समर्पण करना, You were supposed to *give* this work *in* four days ago.

➢ **give in**– to yield; admit defeat अपनी हार मान लेना, Eventually I *gave in* and accepted the job on their terms.

➢ **give off**– to discharge निकालना, छोड़ना The wood *gave off* a sweet, perfumed smell as it burned.

➢ **give out**– to hand out or distribute प्रत्येक को बांटना, Can you *give* the drinks *out*, please?

➢ **give up**– to relinquish or resign from रोकना, She *gave up* her job and started writing a book.

➢ **give yourself up**– to deliver a wanted person to authority: पुलिस को आत्मसमर्पण करना, At last, his family *gave* him *up* to the police.

➢ **give and take** – mutual concessions, shared benefits, and cooperation आदान-प्रदान One should not apply *give and take* philosophy every time.

giveaway *(n.)* गिवअवे–1. something that a company or organization gives to people, either for free or very cheaply, मुफ़्त में मिली वस्तु I got a *giveaway* when I bought a Shampoo.

2. something such as the look on a person's face or a movement he or she makes that makes you realize the truth about a particular person or situation रहस्य का प्रकटीकरण या विश्वासघात She said she was saying the truth but her face was a dead *giveaway*.

given *(adj.)* गिवन– specific or previously stated पूर्व निश्चित You must reach the venue before the *given* time.

glacier *(n.)* ग्लैसिअर– a slowly moving mass of ice originating from an accumulation of snow हिमनद No one could see the *glacier* in the ocean.

glad *(adj.)* ग्लैड– happy and pleased; contented ख़ुश, प्रसन्न Rakhi's parents were *glad* to know about her selection in the army.

gladden *(v.)* ग्लैडन– to make or become glad and joyful किसी को ख़ुश करना She was *gladdened* to see him.

gladly *(adv.)* ग्लैडलि– happily; contentedly ख़ुशी-ख़ुशी I *gladly* accepted his invitation.

glamour *(n.)* ग्लैमर्– physical beauty, charm लुभावनापन, मोहकता Forget all about the *glamour* of film industry.

glamorous *(adj.)* ग्लैमरस– possessing glamour; alluring and fascinating मोहक, लुभावना Journalism is a *glamorous* profession and attracts many.

glance *(v.)* ग्लान्स– 1. to look hastily or briefly दृष्टिपात करना, सरसरी दृष्टि डालना She has just *glanced* at his letter.
2. *(n.)* a hasty or brief look; peep एक झलक, सरसरी निगाह The doctor could see in a *glance* that the patient was anaemic.

gland *(n.)* ग्लैण्ड– a cell or organ in man and other animals that synthesizes chemical substances and secretes them for the body ग्रंथि, गिलटी Sweat *gland* is the most common *gland* in the body.

glare *(v.)* ग्लेअर्– 1. to look in an angry or fierce way: कोप-दृष्टि से देखना He *glared* at me with disgust.
2. *(n.)* very bright and dazzling light चमक, चमचमाहट, चकाचौंध We were almost blinded by the *glare* of the car's headlights.

glaring *(adj.)* ग्लेअरिंग– conspicuous स्पष्ट, साफ़ She committed a *glaring* mistake but was not punished.

glass *(n.)* ग्लास–1. a hard brittle transparent or translucent noncrystalline solid, consisting of metal silicates or similar compounds काँच, शीशा She broke the *glass* while washing it.
2. (old fashioned) a mirror दर्पण, आरसी While looking into the *glass*, I discovered a spot on my face.
3. the amount contained in a drinking glass शीशे का गिलास Please give me a *glass* of water.

glasses *(n.)* ग्लासेज़्– a pair of lenses for correcting faulty vision, in a frame that rests on the bridge of the nose and hooks behind the ears चश्मा, ऐनक My son is asked to wear *glasses* from now onwards.

glazed *(adj.)* ग्लेज़्ड– glassy and expressionless, often because you are bored, tired, or having difficulty concentrating on something भावशून्य The girl looked at me with *glazed* eyes.

gleam *(n.)* ग्लीम– 1. a small beam or glow of light, esp reflected light झलक,चमक A faint *gleam* of sunshine lit up the cloudy afternoon.
2. *(v.)* to send forth or reflect a beam of light झलकना, चमकना Your necklace *gleams* even in this faint light.

glee *(n.)* ग्ली– great merriment or delight, often caused by someone else's misfortune उल्लास, हर्ष Why are you laughing with such *glee*?

glib *(adj.)* ग्लिब– fluent and easy, often in an insincere or deceptive way बोलने में कुशल, वाकपटु You can be successful in sales if you become a *glib* salesman.

glide *(v.)* ग्लाइड– 1. to move or cause to move easily without jerks or hesitations बहना, फिसलना The skaters were *gliding* gracefully over the ice.
2. *(adv./prep.)* (of birds or aircraft) to fly without moving their wings or aircraft using the engine पक्षी का बिना पंख हिलाए उड़ना या इंजन का प्रयोग किए बिना हवाई जहाज़ का उड़ना I am a member of the *gliding* club.

glimmer *(n.)* ग्लिमर्– a glow or twinkle of light टिमटिमाहट In the *glimmer* of the distant candle light, I could not find my shoes.

glimpse *(n.)* ग्लिम्प्स– 1. a brief or incomplete view झलक, झाँकी I could see only a *glimpse* of that beautiful lady.
2. *(v.)* to catch sight of briefly or momentarily झाँकना, झलक दिखाना We *glimpsed* a figure at the window.

glint *(v.)* ग्लिण्ट– to gleam or cause to gleam brightly चमकना, झिलमिलाना Her eyes *glinted* to see him.

glisten *(v.)* ग्लिसन– to gleam by reflecting light झल-झल करना, झिलमिलाना My mother's eyes *glistened* with tears.

glitter *(n.)* ग्लिटर्– 1. sparkle or brilliance चमक-दमक The *glitter* of the princess's jewellery attracted everybody.
2. *(v.)* (of a hard, wet, or polished surface) to reflect light in bright flashes चमकना, जगमगाना All that *glitters* is not gold.

glittering *(adj.)* ग्लिटरिंग– successful, impressive प्रभावशाली My daughter gave a *glittering* performance on the stage.

gloat *(v.)* ग्लॉट– to look (on) with malevolent or smugness बुरी भावना से प्रसन्न होना She is *gloating* over our misery.

global *(adj.)* ग्लोबल– worldwide, universal विश्वव्यापी, सार्वभौम, सार्वत्रिक The teacher took a *global* view of the class.

globalize (ise) *(v.)* ग्लोबलाइज़– to put into effect or spread worldwide विश्वस्तर पर काम करना You should *globalize* your trade.

globe *(n.)* ग्लोब–1. a sphere on which a map of the world or the heavens is drawn or represented भूमण्डल, पृथ्वी Have you travelled all over the *globe*?
2. an object shaped like a sphere, such as a glass lampshade or fish-bowl गोला, गोलक I bought a *globe* to teach my son Geography.

gloom *(n.)* ग्लूम– partial or total darkness अंधकार, अँधेरा, उदासी, विषाद His life filled with *gloom* after his wife's death.

gloomy *(adj.)* ग्लूमि– despairing; sad मलिन, उदास Why are you looking so *gloomy*?

glorify *(v.)* ग्लॉरिफ़ाई– to make more splendid; adorn गुणगान/प्रशंसा करना The film maker denied that the movie *glorified* the violence in the city.

glorious *(adj.)* ग्लोरिअस– having or full of glory; illustrious शानदार, चमत्कारपूर्ण She gave such a *glorious* performance.

glory *(n.)* ग्लॉरि– exaltation, praise, or honour, as that accorded by general consent गौरव, महिमा, प्रशंसा Ram's topping the secondary school exam has brought *glory* to his school.

gloss *(n.)* ग्लॉस– lustre or sheen, as of a smooth surface बाहरी चिकनापन, मुलम्मा We selected the *gloss* paint for our bedroom.

glossary *(n.)* ग्लॉसरी– an alphabetical list of terms peculiar to a field of knowledge with definitions or explanations शब्दावली *Glossary* of foreign words is required at the end of this book.

glossy *(adj.)* ग्लॉसि– smooth and shiny; lustrous चमकदार और चिकना Good Housekeeping is a *glossy* magazine.

glove *(n.)* ग्लव– a shaped covering for the hand with individual sheaths for the fingers and thumb, made of leather, fabric, etc. दस्ताना Has anybody seen my rubber *glove*?

glow *(n.)* ग्लो– 1. light emitted by a substance or object at a high temperature दीप्ति, उज्ज्वलता, जोश We can see *glow* coming from cylinders even after the fire has been extinguished. 2. *(v.)* to look very pleased प्रफुल्लित होना My mother *glowed* with pride when I got the first prize.

glowing *(adj.)* ग्लोइंग– giving enthusiastic praise bright light without flames जोशीला Look at her *glowing* face.

glue *(n.)* ग्लू– 1. any natural or synthetic adhesive, esp a sticky gelatinous substance prepared by boiling animal products such as bones, skin, and horns गोंद, सरेस Do you have some *glue* to seal this envelope? 2. *(v.)* to join or stick together with or as if with glue चिपकाना The carpenter *glued* the two boards together to make a longer shelf.

glum *(adj.)* ग्लम– unhappy, gloomy निराश, अप्रसन्न, उदास Many *glum* faces could be seen after India's defeat by Sri Lanka.

glut *(n.)* ग्लट– an excessive amount, as in the production of a crop, often leading to a fall in price भरमार, आधिक्य There is a *glut* of China products in the Indian market.

glutton *(n.)* ग्लटन– a person devoted to eating and drinking to excess; greedy person पेटू, खाऊ Don't eat like a *glutton.*

gnarled *(adj.)* नाल्ड– (esp of hands) rough, twisted, and weather-beaten in appearance खुरदरा, गांठदार The old woman had *gnarled* feet.

gnash *(v.)* नैश– to grind (the teeth) together, as in pain or anger गुस्से में दाँत पीसना My father was *gnashing* when he heard that I lost his file.

gnaw *(v.)* नॉ– to bite (at) or chew (upon) constantly so as to wear away little by little कुतरना, सताना A rat seems to have *gnawed* a hole in this wooden box.

go *(v.)* –1. to move or proceed, esp to or from a point or in a certain direction जाना When will you *go* to your office today?

- **go about**– to busy oneself with में लगे रहना, My maidservant *goes about* her work with a smile.
- **go ahead**– to start or continue, often after obtaining permission आगे बढ़ना, You *go ahead* with the new project.
- **go back**– to return वापस लौटना, You must *go back* to your work.
- **go beyond**– outside the limits or scope of सीमा के बाहर होना, You shouldn't *go beyond* your limits.
- **go through**– to suffer सहना, Parents *go through* many difficulties to bring up their children.

goal *(n.)* गोल–1. the aim or object towards which an endeavour is directed लक्ष्य I will work hard to achieve all my *goals.*

2. (in various sports) the net, basket, etc. into or over which players try to propel the ball, puck, etc. to score फुटबॉल या हॉकी आदि में गोल We won the match by two *goals.*

goat *(n.)* गोट– an animal that is kept on farms for its milk or meat बकरी, बकरा Have you ever tasted *goat's* milk?

goatee *(n.)* गोटि– a pointed tuftlike beard on the chin ठोड़ी पर नुकीली, घनी दाढ़ी The boy who came from France was wearing a *goatee.*

gobble *(v.)* गॉबल– to eat or swallow (food) hastily and in large mouthfuls भकोसना, निगलना He *gobbled* up the food served to him.

gobbledegook *(n.)* गॉबलडिगूक– pretentious or unintelligible jargon, such as that used by officials आंडबरपूर्ण सरकारी भाषा We should not use *gobbledegook* in our spoken language.

go-between *(n.)* गो-बिटवीन– a person who acts as agent or intermediary for two people or groups in a transaction or dealing दलाल, बिचौलिया, मध्यस्थ Poonam acts as a *go-between.*

goblin *(n.)* गॉब्लिन– a small grotesque supernatural creature, regarded as malevolent towards human beings प्रेत, पिशाच, बेताल I have heard a lot of *goblin* stories from my grandmother.

God *(n.)* गॉड–1. a supernatural being, who is worshipped as the controller of some part of the universe or some aspect of life in the world or is the personification of some force ईश्वर, भगवान् Trust in *God* and do your duty.

2.an image, idol, or symbolic representation of such a deity देवता Hindus worship many *gods* and *goddesses.*

godfather *(n.)* गॉडफ़ादर– the head of a Mafia family or other organized criminal ring धर्मपिता He does not have any *godfather* in the film industry.

godforsaken *(adj.)* गॉडफ़ारसेकन– boring and ugly उदास, उबाने वाला I cannot even stand in this *godforsaken* place.

goggles *(n.)* गॉगूल्ज़– large glasses, often of coloured glass or covered with gauze धूप का चश्मा I wore *goggles* to protect my eyes from pollution and sun.

going *(n.)* गोइंग–1. current or accepted, as from past negotiations or commercial operation प्रचलित What are the *going* prices of Mangoes?

2. a departure किसी स्थान को छोड़ जाने की क्रिया, गमन, प्रस्थान We were all saddened by his *going.*

gold *(n.)* गोल्ड– a yellow precious metal, occurring in rocks and alluvial deposits सोना, स्वर्ण I am going to wear *gold* chain in her wedding.

golden *(adj.)* गोल्डन– of the yellowish or brownish-yellow metallic colour of gold सोने जैसा, सुनहरा Indian women like to wear *golden* jewellery in marriages.

golf *(n.)* गॉल्फ– a game played on a large open course, the object of which is to hit a ball using clubs, with as few strokes as possible, into each of usually 18 holes गोल्फ़ का खेल My uncle goes to the *golf* club every morning.

gone *(prep.)* गॉन– having left a place जाने वाला Don't worry! He's *gone* with the wind.

good *(adj.)* गुड–1. suitable or efficient for a purpose अच्छा, उत्तम We made *a good* deal.

2. morally excellent or admirable; virtuous; righteous भला, सच्चरित्र A *good* man is recognised by his behaviour.

3. beneficial or advantageous टिकाऊ, टिकनेवाला Is your car *good* for another two years?

4. *(n.)* moral or material advantage or use; benefit or profit भलाई, भलापन Always try to do *good* to others.

goodbye *(n.)* गुडबाई– farewell: a conventional expression used at leave-taking or parting with people and at the loss or rejection of things or ideas अलविदा Smith said *goodbye* to his friends before leaving to Hyderabad.

goodies *(n.)* गुडीज़– any objects, rewards, prizes, etc. considered particularly desirable, attractive, or pleasurable स्वादिष्ट भोजन There were lot of *goodies* on the dinning table.

good-looking *(adj.)* गुड-लुकिंग– handsome or pretty सुंदर, रूपवान Oh my God! How can she be so *good-looking.*

goodness *(n.)* गुडनस्–1. the state or quality of being good अच्छाई These vegetables have all the *goodness* boiled out of them.

2. generosity; kindness शराफ़त, नैतिकता I have a desire to see *goodness* and justice in the world.

good-natured *(adj.)* गुड-नेचर्ड– of a tolerant and kindly disposition साधु-स्वभाव, नेक My boss is a very *good-natured* person and everyone respects him.

good sense *(n.)* गुडसेंस– plain ordinary good judgment; sound practical sense सूझबूझ She has got a *good sense* of humour.

goods *(n.)* गुड्स– possessions and personal property माल, सौदा, पदार्थ What *goods* do you transport in your truck?

goodwill *(n.)* गुडविल– a feeling of benevolence, approval, and kindly interest साख, सद्‌भाव Mr Gupta has *goodwill* in his company.

goody-goody *(n.)* गुडी-गुडी– a smug or ostentatiously virtuous person. शिष्टता का दिखावा करने वाला व्यक्ति Mrs Kavita is a *goody-goody* lady and never uses her mind.

goose *(n.)* गूस– any of various web-footed long-necked birds like a large duck हंस, कलहंस Do you keep any *goose* in your poultry farm?

gore *(v.)* गॉर– to wound a person with a horn सींग मारकर घायल करना The man was *gored* by the bull.

gorge *(v.)* गोर्ज– to eat a large amount greedily; fill oneself with food: भकोसना, ख़ूब खाना खाना The child *gorged* himself on the chocolates.

gorgeous *(adj.)* गॉर्जस– strikingly beautiful or magnificent शानदार, भड़कीला, अलंकृत Your sari is indeed *gorgeous.*

gorilla *(n.)* गरिला– a very large African ape गोरिल्ला Do they have a *gorilla* in the Delhi Zoo?

gospel *(n.)* गासपल– an unquestionable truth ईसा-मसीह के उपदेश I was reading St. Matthew's *gospel.*

gossip *(v.)* गॉसिप– 1. to talk casually or maliciously (about other people) गपशप करना Don't *gossip* about others.

2. *(n.)* casual and idle chat गप, व्यर्थ की बात *Gossip* is your favourite time pass I guess?

gourd *(n.)* गार्ड– the fruit of any of various similar plants, esp the bottle gourd and some squashes, whose dried shells are used for ornament, drinking cups, etc. कद्दू, लौकी Prices of bottle *gourd* are increasing day by day.

gourmet *(n.)* गुअमे– a person who cultivates a discriminating palate for the enjoyment of good food and drink चटोरा आदमी Ramesh is a *gourmet* king and has written many books on cookery.

govern *(v.)* गवर्न–1. to direct and control the actions, affairs, policies, functions, etc. (a political unit, organization, nation, etc.); rule शासन चलाना Hong Kong is now *governed* by China.

2. to be a predominant influence on (something); decide or determine

(something) प्रभावित करना In this delicate matter, I would like to be *governed* by what you say.

governess *(n.)* गवर्नस– a woman teacher employed in a private household to teach and train the children आया She is a *governess* to our kids.

government *(n.)* गवर्नमन्ट– the system or form by which a community, etc. is ruled सरकार I am so glad that my brother is working with Indian *government*

gown *(n.)* गाउन– any of various outer garments, such as a woman's elegant or formal dress, a dressing robe, or a protective garment, esp one worn by surgeons during operations गाउन, लबादा What is the price of this night-*gown*?

grab *(v.)* ग्रैब– to seize hold of (something) पकड़ लेना, हथियाना, छीनना I want to *grab* this offer before the stock finishes up.

grace *(n.)* ग्रेस–1. the granting of a favour or the manifestation of goodwill, esp by a superior कृपा, दया By the *grace* of God, all the pilgrims were saved when their boat sank in the Ganges.

2. elegance and beauty of movement, form, expression, or proportion लालित्य, मनोहरता There is a *grace* in your gait.

3. *(v.)* to add elegance and beauty to सुशोभित करना Many celebrities *graced* the inauguration of the new departmental store.

graceful *(adj.)* ग्रेसफुल– elegance and beauty of movement, form, expression, or proportion कमनीय, आकर्षित, सुंदर She looks *graceful* in a sari.

gracious *(adj.)* ग्रेशस– characterized by or showing kindness and courtesy शिष्ट, कृपालु She was so *gracious* to attend the slumdwellers' function.

grade *(n.)* ग्रेड–1. a position or degree in a scale, as of quality, rank, size, or progression श्रेणी, कोटि, वर्ग, दर्जा Are you a B *grade* officer?

2. the quality of a specific product वस्तु की गुणवत्ता या महत्ता These are second-*grade* oranges.

3. *(v.)* to arrange according to quality, rank, etc. दर्जा या कोटि निर्धारित करना The Principal will *grade* the new pupils according to their marks.

gradual *(adj.)* ग्रैजुअल– occurring, developing, moving, etc. in small stages क्रमिक The company had a *gradual* and steady progress.

graduate *(n.)* ग्रेजुएट– 1. a person who has been awarded a first degree from a university or college स्नातक I am a *graduate* from commerce background.

2. *(v.)* to receive or cause to receive a degree or diploma स्नातक बनना She *graduated* from Princeton College.

graffiti *(n.)* ग्रफ़ीटी– drawings, messages, etc. often obscene, scribbled on the walls of public lavatories, advertising posters, etc. सार्वजनिक स्थान में दीवार पर की गई लिखावट *Graffiti* destroys the beauty of monuments.

grain *(n.)* ग्रेन–1. the small hard seedlike fruit of a grass, esp a cereal plant अनाज, धान्य Are you a *grain-merchant*?

2. a very small amount, iota कण There is not a *grain* of truth in your story.

gram *(n.)* ग्रैम– a metric unit of mass equal to one thousandth of a kilogram. तौल की इकाई, ग्राम I bought 500 *grams* of sweetcorns for you.

grammar *(n.)* ग्रामर्– the branch of linguistics that deals with syntax and morphology, sometimes also phonology and semantics व्याकरण If you want to master English, you must learn its *grammar*.

grand *(adj.)* ग्रैन्ड–1. of great distinction or pretension; dignified or haughty भव्य, वैभवशाली, उच्च, मुख्य, प्रसिद्ध We visited many *grand* palaces on our trip of Europe.

2. *(n.)* a thousand pounds or dollars एक हजार पाउंड या डालर She gave me ten *grands* for the job.

grandchild *(n.)* ग्रैनचाइल्ड– the son or daughter of one's child धेवती, पोता, पोती या नातिन His *grandchild* married to an Italian girl.

grandeur *(n.)* ग्रैनूजर– personal greatness, esp when based on dignity, character, or accomplishments विशालता, वैभव, शान The *grandeur* of the Himalayas is worth-seeing.

grandparent *(n.)* ग्रैंडपेअरेन्ट– the father or mother of either of one's parents दादा-दादी/नाना-नानी My *grandparents* live in Punjab.

granny *(n.)* ग्रैनी– informal words for grandmother नानी या दादी My *granny* loves me a lot.

grant *(n.)* ग्राण्ट–1. a sum of money provided by a government, local authority, or public fund to finance educational study, overseas aid, building repairs, etc. अनुदान Does your institution receive a *grant* from the government?

2. *(v.)* to consent to perform or fulfil मानना, स्वीकार करना I *grant* that you may be right, but I am also not wrong.

3. to bestow, esp in a formal manner कुछ प्रदान करना The employer *granted* the employee's request of drawing some advance against his salary.

granule *(n.)* ग्रैनूयूल– a small grain दाने, कण Coffee *granules* were difficult to dissolve in milk.

grape *(n.)* ग्रेप– the fruit of the grapevine, which has a purple or green skin and sweet flesh: eaten raw, dried to make raisins, currants, or used for making wine अंगूर, दाख I love *grape* juice.

graphic *(adj.)* ग्रैफ़िक– vividly or clearly described सुचित्रित, सजीव I have *graphic* details of the accident.

grapple *(v.)* ग्रैपल– to come to grips with (one or more persons), esp to struggle in hand-to-hand combat गुथना, मज़बूती से पकड़कर क़ाबू में करना Passengers *grappled* with the man who was a pickpocket.

grasp *(v.)* ग्रास्प–1. to seize and hold firmly कसकर पकड़ना A drowning man was *grasping* a branch of tree.

2. to comprehend fully समझना, जानना Can you *grasp* what your teacher says?

grass *(n.)* ग्रास– a wild plant with narrow green leaves that are eaten by cows, horses, etc. घास, तृण *Grass* grows very rapidly in the rainy season.

grassland *(n.)* ग्रासलैंड– land, such as a prairie, on which grass predominates घास से भरा क्षेत्र There use to be a huge *grassland* long time back.

grate *(v.)* ग्रेट– to reduce to small shreds by rubbing against a rough or sharp perforated surface कद्दूकस करना Mother *grated* the cheese and made balls out of it.

grateful *(adj.)* ग्रेटफुल– thankful for gifts, favours, etc.; appreciative कृतज्ञ, अहसानमन्द I am *grateful* to you for your help.

gratify *(v.)* ग्रैटिफ़ाइ– to satisfy or please संतुष्ट करना I was *gratified* to think it was all her work.

gratitude *(n.)* ग्रैटिट्यूड– a feeling of thankfulness or appreciation, as for gifts or favours कृतज्ञता, अहसानमंदी

She expressed her *gratitude* to her elder sister.

gratuity *(n.)* ग्रट्यूअटी– a gift or reward, usually of money, for services rendered; tip उपदान, सेवा-पारितोषिक My father got ₹10 lakh as a *gratuity* on his retirement.

grave *(adj.)* ग्रेव–1. serious and solemn उदास Why are you looking *grave*?
2. important; crucial गंभीर There was some *grave* news in the letter.
3. full of or suggesting danger घोर, महत्त्वपूर्ण, संगीन He made a *grave* mistake by not attempting all the questions.
4. *(n.)* a place in the ground where a dead body is buried क़ब्र, समाधि The devotees visited the *grave* of the famous Fakeer.

gravel *(n.)* ग्रैवल– an unconsolidated mixture of rock fragments that is coarser than sand कंकड़, बजरी Where can I get some *gravel* for my garden?

graveyard *(n.)* ग्रैवयार्ड– a place for graves; a burial ground, esp a small one or one in a churchyard क़ब्रिस्तान A *graveyard* near our house has been turned into a park.

gravity *(n.)* ग्रैविटी–1. seriousness or importance, esp as a consequence of an action or opinion गंभीरता You should realise the *gravity* of your offence.
2. the force that attracts objects in space towards each other गुरुत्वाकर्षण *Gravity* helps to keep everything on the ground.

gravy *(n.)* ग्रेवी– the sauce made by thickening and flavouring eatables मांस-यूष, तरी I would like to have paneer with *gravy* in dinner today.

graze *(v.)* ग्रेज़–1. to allow (animals) to consume the vegetation on (an area of land), or (of animals, esp cows and sheep) to feed thus चरना, चराना The cows were *grazing* in the field.
2. to brush or scrape (against) gently, esp in passing खरोंचना We might *graze* our arm against the wall if we run too close to it.

grease *(v.)* ग्रीज़– 1. to lubricate with grease चिकनाई लगाना *Grease* the bowl before pouring the batter into it.
2. *(n.)* animal fat in a soft or melted condition चरबी, ग्रीस, चिकनाई Amitabh rubbed some *grease* on his shoes to make the leather softer.

great *(adj.)* ग्रेट–1. of exceptional talents or achievements; remarkable महान् He was a *great* man I must say.
2. impressive or striking सुंदर You look *great* in these clothes.
3. relatively large in size or extent; big बड़ा, विशाल Mumbai is the *greatest* city I have ever visited.
4. of significant importance or consequence महत्त्वपूर्ण, ख़ास Are you and Prakash *great* friends?

greed *(n.)* ग्रीड– excessive consumption of or desire for food; gluttony लालच, लोभ Eating five pastries is just sheer *greed*.

greedily *(adv.)* ग्रीडिली– in a way that shows excessive desire or covetousness लालच से Don't swallow your food *greedily*.

greedy *(adj.)* ग्रीडी– excessively desirous of food or wealth, esp in large amounts; voracious लोभी, लालची The *greedy* dogs gobbled up their food quickly.

green *(adj.)* ग्रीन–1. any of a group of colours, such as that of fresh grass, that lie between yellow and blue in the visible spectrum हरा, हरित, हरा-भरा *Green* is one of my favourite colour.
2. a small area of grassland, esp in the centre of a village हरियाली, हरा-भरा मैदान I like some *green* around my house.

3. *(n.)* the colour green हरा रंग She was dressed in *green.*

greenery *(n.)* ग्रीनरी– green foliage or vegetation, esp when used for decoration हरियाली I like to see the *greenery* of fields in spring.

greenish *(adj.)* ग्रीनिश– slightly green in colour कुछ-कुछ हरा The jacket I saw was a little *greenish* in colour.

greet *(v.)* ग्रीट–1. to meet or receive with expressions of gladness or welcome प्रणाम करना, नमस्कार करना He *greeted* me very cordially when I called on him.

greeting *(n.)* ग्रीटिंग– the act or an instance of welcoming or saluting on meeting अभिवादन, नमस्कार, प्रणाम They exchanged *greetings.*

gregarious *(adj.)* ग्रिगेअरिअस– living together in herds or flocks, sociable सामाजिक, मिलनसार, झुंड में रहने वाला The sheeps are *gregarious* animals and like to live in groups.

grey *(adj.)* ग्रे– having the colour of smoke or ashes सलेटी, भूरा My school uniform is of *grey* colour.

greyish *(adj.)* ग्रेइश– slightly grey in colour भूरा-सा, सलेटी-सा The texture of this *greyish* pant is not of good quality.

griddle *(n.)* ग्रिडल– a thick round iron plate with a half hoop handle over the top, for making scones, etc. तवा She was cooking chapattis on *griddle.*

grief *(n.)* ग्रीफ़– deep or intense sorrow or distress, esp at the death of someone दुःख, व्यथा, शोक On the death of Anuj's father, his neighbours came to console him in his hour of *grief.*

grievance *(n.)* ग्रीवन्स– a feeling of resentment or injustice at having been unfairly treated शिकायत The manager heard the *grievances* of the workers.

grieve *(v.)* ग्रीव– to feel or cause to feel great sorrow or distress, esp at the death of someone शोक मनाना I was *grieved* for the dead.

grievous *(adj.)* ग्रीवस– very severe or painful दुखद, कष्टदायक It was a *grievous* bus accident.

grill *(n.)* ग्रिल– cooked (meat, fish, etc.) by direct heat, as under a grill लोहे की जाली, झँझरी Pop it under the *grill* for five minutes.

grim *(adj.)* ग्रिम–1. harsh or formidable in manner or appearance भयंकर, कराल, डरावना Why are you looking so *grim*?

2. stern; resolute दृढ़, कड़ा *Grim* determination will lead you to success in life.

grime *(n.)* ग्राइम– dirt, soot, or filth, esp when thickly accumulated or ingrained मैल, गंदगी या कालिख His face was covered with *grime* and sweat.

grin *(n.)* ग्रिन– 1. a broad smile खीस, मुस्कराहट He has a happy *grin* on his face.

2. *(v.)* to smile with the lips drawn back revealing the teeth or express (something) by such a smile दाँत निकालना, खीसें निपोरना She didn't answer me but only *grinned.*

grind *(v.)* ग्राइण्ड–1. to reduce or be reduced to small particles by pounding or abrading पीसना The miller *grinds* the corn into flour.

2. to smooth, sharpen, or polish by friction or abrasion रगड़ना, घिसना We *grind* a knife to sharpen it.

grinder *(n.)* ग्राइण्हडर– a machine for grinding पीसने की मशीन, चक्की I am going to buy a *grinder* today.

grip *(n.)* ग्रिप– 1. the act or an instance of grasping and holding firmly पकड़ The thief could not free himself from the firm *grip* of Ram's hand.

2. *(v.)* to take hold of firmly or tightly, as by a clutch कसकर पकड़ना

Grip the bag firmly, lest it should fall.

gripe *(v.)* ग्राइप– to complain, esp in a persistent nagging manner शिकायत करना Kumar is always *gripping* about the people at work.

gripping *(adj.)* ग्रिपिंग– able to hold the interest or attention of someone दिलचस्प, रोमांचक The film we saw today had a *gripping* plot.

grisly *(adj.)* ग्रिज़ली– causing horror or dread; gruesome डरावना, भयंकर It was a *grisly* murder.

grit *(n.)* ग्रिट– small hard particles of sand, earth, stone, etc. कंकड़ी, गिट्टी They were spreading *grits* on the road.

groan *(n.)* ग्रोन– 1. a prolonged stressed dull cry expressive of agony, pain, or disapproval कराह, आह The sick man's *groans* moved my heart.
2. *(v.)* to utter (low inarticulate sounds) expressive of pain, grief, disapproval, etc. दर्द के कारण चिल्लाना, कराहना He was *groaning* with pain.

grocer *(n.)* ग्रोसर– a dealer in foodstuffs and other household supplies पंसारी Some *grocers* keep their profits to the bare minimum.

groom *(n.)* ग्रूम–1. a man who has just been or is about to be married दूल्हा, वर Everybody stood up to look at the *groom.*
2. a person employed to clean and look after horses साईस, घोड़ों की देखभाल करने वाला व्यक्ति Have you engaged a *groom* to look after your horse?
3. *(v.)* to train or prepare for a particular task, occupation, etc. सिखाना, सँवारना It is easy to *groom* an inexperienced worker.

groove *(n.)* ग्रूव– a long narrow channel or furrow, esp one cut into wood by a tool खाँचा, नाली The door of my wardrobe slides into a *groove.*

grope *(v.)* ग्रोप– to feel or search about uncertainly (for something) with the hands टटोलना, ढूंढ़ना In the darkness, I *groped* around to find a candle.

gross *(adv.)* ग्रोस– in total कुल, सकल He earns ₹10 lakh a year *gross.*

grossly *(adv.)* ग्रोसली– to a very high degree; extremely अत्यधिक Pinky is *grossly* overweight.

grotesque *(adj.)* ग्रोटेस्क– strangely or fantastically distorted; bizarre भद्दा, भौंडा It was a *grotesque* sight when an old man was trying to flirt with a young girl.

grotty *(adj.)* ग्रॉटी– unpleasant, nasty, or unattractive अनाकर्षक, असुखद They live in a *grotty* flat.

ground *(n.)* ग्राउण्ड–1. an area of land given over to a purpose मैदान We will have our next match in the *ground* tommorow.
2. the land surface भूमि, ज़मीन My house stands on a flat *ground.*
3. a position or viewpoint, as in an argument or controversy आधार, The judge was not convinced by the *grounds* given by the lawyer for his client's bail.
4. *(v.)* the past tense and past participle of grind पीसा, पीसा गया (Grind का भूतकाल) She *ground* spices.
5. *(adj.)* reduced to fine particles by grinding पिसा हुआ Fresh *ground* coffee beans smell very pleasant.

groundless *(adj.)* ग्राउंडलस्– without reason or justification बेबुनियाद, आधारहीन Please don't talk on *groundless* issues.

group *(n.)* ग्रुप– 1. a number of persons bound together by common social standards, interests, etc. समूह, समुदाय A *group* of people were waiting to see the minister.
2. *(v.)* to arrange or place (things, people, etc.) in or into a group or (of things, etc.) to form into a group

एकत्र करना या होना The students *grouped* together to move the heavy table.

grove *(n.)* ग्रोव– a small wooded area or plantation उपवन, बाग Children like to play hide-and-seek in the *grove.*

grow *(v.)* ग्रो–1. to develop or come into existence or being gradually विकास करना, बढ़ना Your son has *grown* up into a fine young man.
2. (of an organism or part of an organism) to increase in size or develop (hair, leaves, or other structures) उगना, उगाना What flowers do you *grow* in your garden?

growing *(adj.)* ग्रोइंग– getting bigger because of natural growth बढ़ने वाला A *growing* number of people are becoming more health-conscious.

growl *(n.)* ग्राउल– 1. the act or sound of growling गुर्राहट, गड़गड़ाहट The *growl* of thunder could be heard at a distance.
2. *(v.)* to make sounds suggestive of an animal growling गुर्राना, गरजना The dog always *growls* at the cat.

grown *(adj.)* ग्राउन– developed or advanced जवान, वयस्क I have seen a fully *grown* bear in the zoo.

growth *(n.)* ग्रोथ– the process or act of growing, esp in organisms following assimilation of food विकास, वृद्धि I am hoping for some *growth* in near future.

grubby *(adj.)* ग्रबि– dirty; slovenly गंदा, मैला-कुचैला He always comes to office in *grubby* cloths.

grudge *(v.)* ग्रॅज– 1. to give sth unwillingly अनिच्छा से देना The master *grudged* every rupee that he gave to the lazy servant as wages.
2. *(n.)* a persistent feeling of resentment, esp one due to some cause, such as an insult or injury दुर्भाव, मनमुटाव, ईर्ष्या Please don't mind my words I don't have any personal *grudges* against you.

gruel *(n.)* ग्रूअल– a drink or thin porridge, made by boiling meal, esp oatmeal, in water or milk जई का दलिया *Gruel* is a food preparation consisting of some type of cereals and is good for health.

gruesome *(adj.)* ग्रूसम– very unpleasant and horror; ghastly घिनौना, घृणाजनक Rape is such a *gruesome* act.

gruff *(adj.)* ग्रफ़– rough or surly in manner, speech, etc. रूखा, कठोर Why has your voice become so *gruff*?

grumble *(v.)* ग्रम्बल– to utter (complaints) in a nagging or discontented way शिकायत करना Some people are always *grumbling.*

grumpy *(adj.)* ग्रम्पि– peevish; sulky चिड़चिड़ा, बदमिज़ाज No one likes her *grumpy* nature.

grunt *(v.)* ग्रण्ट– 1. to emit a low short gruff noise घुरघुराना Pigs *grunt* as they search for food.
2. *(n.)* the characteristic low short gruff noise of pigs, etc. or a similar sound, as of disgust घुरघुराहट He only gave a *grunt* of approval when I asked him if he liked my painting.

guarantee *(n.)* गैरन्टी– a formal assurance, esp in writing, that a product, service, etc. will meet certain standards or specifications गारंटी, ज़मानत Can you give me any *guarantee* for replacement?.

guard *(v.)* गार्ड–1. to watch over or shield (a person or thing) from danger or harm; protect रक्षा करना You should use sunglasses to *guard* your eyes.
2. *(n.)* the act or duty of protecting, restraining, or supervising संरक्षण, चौकसी We put the wire *guard* in front of the fire to keep the children from getting burnt.

3. a person or group who keeps a protecting, supervising, or restraining watch or control over people, such as prisoners, things, etc. गार्ड, कर्मचारी As soon as we boarded the train, the *guard* blew his whistle.

guardian *(n.)* गार्डिअन– one who looks after, protects, or defends संरक्षक, अभिभावक Get your report card signed by your *guardian*.

guava *(n.)* ग्वावा– the fruit of a tropical American tree with yellow skin अमरूद *Guava* has cancer-fighting antioxidant.

guess *(n.)* गेस– 1. an estimate or conclusion arrived at by guessing अनुमान, अन्दाज़ा What is your *guess* about the winner of the India-Pakistan match?

2. *(v.)* to form or express an uncertain estimate or conclusion (about something), based on insufficient information अंदाज़ा लगाना, अनुमान करना Can you *guess* how many times I tried to contact you over the phone?

guesswork *(n.)* गेसवर्क– a set of conclusions, estimates, etc. arrived at by guessing अटकलबाजी It was pure *guesswork* when I answered him.

guest *(n.)* गेस्ट– a person who receives hospitality at the home of another मेहमान, अतिथि We are expecting some *guests* at home today.

guest house *(n.)* गेस्ट हाउस– a guest at a house, esp one who stays for a comparatively long time अतिथि गृह We stayed in a *guest house* of my office.

guidance *(n.)* गाइडन्स– leadership, instruction, or direction मार्गदर्शन, परामर्श Good *guidance* is necessary for success of students.

guide *(n.)* गाइड–1.a person, animal, or thing that guides मार्गदर्शक, गाइड, नेता We should engage a *guide* when we go to Ajanta caves.

2. a book that instructs or explains the fundamentals of a subject or skill संदर्शिका, गाइड You should learn from your textbook, not from a *guide*.

3. *(v.)* to lead the way for (a person) मार्ग दिखाना Can you *guide* me to the post office?

guilt *(n.)* गिल्ट–1.the fact or state of having done wrong or committed an offence आत्मग्लानि, पश्चात्ताप The feeling of *guilt* can sometimes take a toll on your health.

2. responsibility for a criminal or moral offence deserving punishment or a penalty अपराध, नियम-भंग Your *guilt* is not proved.

guilty *(adj.)* गिल्टी– responsible for an offence or misdeed दोषी The judge found the accused *guilty* of the crime.

guise *(n.)* गाइज़– semblance or pretence वेश, बनावटी रूप He was a policeman under the *guise* of a bus passenger.

gulf *(n.)* गल्फ़– a large deep bay खाड़ी, खाई He got a lucrative job in Persian *Gulf* country.

gull *(n.)* गल– an aquatic bird with short legs and mostly white plumage बड़े पंखों वाली समुद्री चिड़िया Jonathan has written many beautiful stories on sea *gulls*.

gullible *(adj.)* गलबूल– easily taken in or tricked भोला-भाला Eve was *gullible* enough to believe the words of Satan.

gully *(n.)* गली– a channel or small valley, esp one cut by heavy rainwater खड्ड, नाली, मोरी The sewage water drained into the *gully*.

gulmohar *(n.)* गुलमोहर– name of a tree एक प्रकार का पेड़ *Gulmohar* is also known as flame tree.

gulp *(v.)* गल्प– to swallow rapidly, esp in large mouthfuls निगल जाना, गटगट

निगलना Don't *gulp* down hot tea in a haste.

gum *(n.)* गम–1. any of various sticky substances that exude from certain plants, hardening on exposure to air and dissolving or forming viscous masses in water गोंद I want to stick the pages, give me the bottle of *gum*.

2. the fleshy tissue that covers the jawbones around the bases of the teeth मसूड़ा Strong teeth require strong *gums*.

gun *(v.)* गन– 1. to shoot (someone) with a gun बन्दूक़ चलाना The hunter *gunned* down a wolf.

2. *(n.)* a weapon with a metallic tube or barrel from which a missile is discharged, usually by force of an explosion बंदूक़ The new recruits in the army were taught the use of *guns*.

gunfire *(n.)* गनफ़ाइअर– the firing of one or more guns, esp when done repeatedly गोलाबारी We could hear the *gunfire* in the street at the time of curfew.

gunpowder *(n.)* गनूपाउडर– an explosive mixture of potassium nitrate, charcoal, and sulphur used in time fuses, blasting, and fireworks बारूद Keep this *gunpowder* away from children.

gunnysack *(n.)* गनिसैक– a large bag made from jute and used for sacks, etc. टाट, बोरी The g*unnysack* was full of potatoes.

gunpoint *(n.)* गनपॉइंट– the muzzle of a gun बंदूक का नालमुख The family was robbed at *gunpoint*.

gurgle *(v.)* गर्गल– (of liquids, esp of rivers, streams, etc.) to make low bubbling noises when flowing गड़गड़ की ध्वनि निकालना The sea was *gurgling* loudly.

gust *(n.)* गस्ट– a sudden blast of wind झोंका, झकोरा A sudden *gust* of wind blew away my cap.

gut *(adj.)* गट– arising from or characterized by what is basic, essential, or natural भावना पर आधारित सोच I have a *gut* feeling that he will not come to my house.

gutter *(n.)* गॅटर्– a channel along the eaves or on the roof of a building, used to collect and carry away rainwater नाली, मोरी, परनाला Yesterday's heavy rain caused the *gutters* in our street to overflow.

guy *(n.)* गाइ– a man or youth लड़का, आदमी Can you see that guy anywhere?

guzzle *(v.)* गज़ल– to consume (food or drink) excessively or greedily लालची की तरह खाना- पीना Her kids *guzzle* soft drinks and chips all day.

gymnasium *(n.)* जिमूनेजिअम्– a large room or hall equipped with bars, weights, ropes, etc. for games or physical training व्यायामशाला Does your school have a *gymnasium*?

gymnastics *(n.)* जिमूनैस्टिक्स– practice or training in exercises that develop physical strength and agility or mental capacity व्यायाम, कसरत My son is good at *gymnastics*.

gynaecology *(n.)* गाइनकॉलजी– the study of medicine concerned with diseases in women स्त्री-रोग विज्ञान *Gynaecology* is my favourite subject.

gypsy *(n.)* जिप्सी– a member of a people scattered throughout Europe and North America, who maintain a nomadic way of life in industrialized societies. खानाबदोश जाति का व्यक्ति, जिप्सी The *gypsy* claimed to foretell the future correctly.

Hh

Hh *(n.)* एच–अंग्रेज़ी वर्णमाला का आठवां अक्षर The eight letter of English alphabet. House begins with 'H'.

habit *(n.)* हैबिट– a tendency or disposition to act in a particular way आदत, अभ्यास, स्वभाव You must leave bad *habits* and cultivate good ones.

habitat *(n.)* हैबिटैट– the environment in which an animal or plant normally lives or grows प्राकृतिक वास/आवास Zoo is not a natural *habitat* of lions.

habitual *(adj.)* हैबिचुअल– done or experienced regularly and repeatedly आदी, अभ्यस्त I won't be able to leave smoking as I am *habitual* of it now.

habitually *(adv.)* हैबिचुअली– out of habit आदतवश She wears dark glasses *habitually*.

hack *(v.)* हैक–1. to cut and clear (a way, path, etc.), as through undergrowth झाड़ी, पेड़ आदि को काटकर मार्ग साफ़ करना They *hacked* a trail through the jungle.

2. *(n.)* to manipulate a computer program skilfully, esp, to gain unauthorized access to another computer system अनाधिकारिक तौर पर कंप्यूटर से डाटा चोरी करना Sunita's email account was *hacked* by a hacker.

haemoglobin *(n.)* हीमॉग्लोबिन– a conjugated protein, consisting of haem and the protein globin, that gives red blood cells their characteristic colour रक्त में उपलब्ध वे लाल कण जिनसे खून बनता है, रक्तवर्णिका *Haemoglobin* is an iron containing compound which carries oxygen.

haemorrhage *(n.)* हेमरैज– profuse bleeding from ruptured blood vessels आंतरिक रक्तस्राव She was checked for any signs of *haemorrhage.*

haggard *(adj.)* हैगर्ड– careworn or gaunt, as from lack of sleep, anxiety, or starvation दुबला, पतला, मरियल She was so *haggard* earlier but she is absolutly fine now .

haggle *(v.)* हैगल– to bargain or wrangle (over a price, terms of an agreement, etc.); barter मोल-भाव करना, सौदा करना She always spent hours *haggling* over the prices of fruits.

hail *(n.)* हेल– 1. small pellets of ice that fall like rain, hailstone ओला Last night it rained *hailstones.*

2. *(v.)* to greet, esp enthusiastically स्वागत करना, पुकारना I saw my friend at a distance and *hailed* him.

hair *(n.)* हेअर्– any of the threadlike pigmented structures that grow from follicles beneath the skin of mammals and consist of layers of dead keratinized cells बाल, केश Some people dye their *hair* to hide their premature greying.

haircut *(n.)* हेअर्कट– the style in which hair has been cut केश-कर्तन Hey! I got a new *haircut* yesterday.

hairdresser *(n.)* हेअर्ड्रेसर– a person whose business is cutting, curling, colouring and arranging hair, esp that of women नाई, हज्जाम My *hairdresser* was not available yesterday.

hairline *(adj.)* हेअर्लाइन– a very narrow line बहुत पतली रेखा He got a *hairline* fracture of the bone.

hairpin bend *(n.)* हेअर्पिन बेन्ड– a very sharp curve or bend in a road सड़क का दोहरा तीव्र मोड़ There are 20 dangerous *hairpin bends* in our way to reach the peak in kodai kanal.

hair-raising *(adj.)* हेअर-रेज़िंग– inspiring horror; terrifying डरावना, रोंगटे खड़े कर

देने वाला She narrated a *hair-raising* real story to me.

hair-style *(n.)* हेअर-स्टाइल– a particular mode of arranging, cutting, or setting the hair केश संवारने का तरीक़ा Her *hair-style* is very old-fashioned.

hairy *(adj.)* हेअरी– having or covered with hair बालोंवाला, रोएँदार He has *hairy* hands and chest.

hajj *(n.)* हज– the pilgrimage to Mecca that every Muslim is required to make at least once in his life, मुसलमानों की मक्का की तीर्थयात्रा Thousands of Muslims perform *hajj* every year.

half *(adj.)* हाफ़– not perfect or complete; partial आधा I had *half* plate momos in lunch today.

half-baked *(adj.)* हाफ़बेकड– insufficiently baked अधपका (जो सुनियोजित न हो) I have a *half-baked* plan of going for a movie.

half-brother *(n.)* हाफ़-ब्रदर– the son of either of one's parents by another partner सौतेला भाई Sarah has two *half-brothers* and one half-sister.

half-hearted *(adj.)* हाफ़-हर्टेड– without enthusiasm or determination अधूरे मन से It was an *half-hearted* attempt to win the game.

half-time *(n.)* हाफ़-टाइम– a rest period between the two halves of a game मध्यांतर They took pepsi and pizzas in *half-time.*

halfway *(n.)* हाफ़वे– at or to half the distance; at or to the middle बीचोंबीच We met *halfway* between my house and him.

halfwitted *(adj.)* हाफ़-विटेड– foolish or inane अल्पबुद्धि, मूर्ख Mala is a *halfwitted* child of her class.

half-yearly *(n.)* हाफ़-इअरली– happening in the middle of a calendar year or a financial year अर्द्ध-वार्षिक His *half-yearly* examinations are going to be held soon.

hall *(n.)* हॉल–1. a large building or room used for assemblies, worship, concerts, dances, etc. बड़ा कमरा, हॉल The school's annual function was held in a spacious *hall.*
2. a building for public meetings सभा भवन Did you attend the meeting at the Town *Hall*?

hallmark *(n.)* हालमार्क– a mark or sign of authenticity or excellence निशानी, श्रेष्ठता- सूचक चिह्न The ability to motivate students is the *hallmark* of a good teacher.

hall of residence– a residential block in or attached to a university, college, etc. छात्रावास Thousands of students from different countries live in the *halls of residence* in AMU.

hallucination *(n.)* हैल्यूसिनेश्न– the alleged perception of an object when no object is present, occurring under hypnosis, in some mental disorders, etc. मतिभ्रम You saw your dead grandfather last night! It must be a *hallucination.*

halt *(v.)* हॉल्ट– 1. to stop रुकना, रोकना I did not *halt* till I reached the station.
2. *(n.)* an interruption or end to activity, movement, or progress विराम, रुकाव, पड़ाव A fire accident in our office brought all work to a *halt.*

halve *(v.)* हाल्व– to divide into two approximately equal parts आधा-आधा बाँटना, आधा करना He *halved* the apple.

hamburger *(n.)* हैमबर्गर– a flat fried cake of minced beef, often served in a bread roll मांस से भरी हुई डबल रोटी This restaurant is famous for delicious *hamburgers.*

hamlet *(n.)* हैम्लट– a small village or group of houses खेड़ा, बहुत छोटा गाँव My native place is a *hamlet* of a few houses.

hammer *(v.)* हैमर्– 1. to strike or beat (a nail, wood, etc.) with or as if with a hammer हथौड़ा मारना, ठोकना Have you *hammered* the nail properly?

2. *(n.)* a hand tool consisting of a heavy usually steel head held transversely on the end of a handle, used for hitting nails, beating metal, etc. हथौड़ा I need this *hammer* to fasten the nail.

hammering *(n.)* हैमरिंग– the sound of striking with a hammer हथौड़े से प्रहार की तेज़ आवाज़ Stop *hammering* the door.

hammock *(n.)* हैमक– a length of canvas, net, etc. suspended at the ends and used as a bed झूला I have fixed a *hammock* in my garden.

hamper *(v.)* हैम्पर्–1. to prevent the progress or free movement of रोड़ा अटकाना, विघ्न डालना The strikers tried to *hamper* the traffic movement.

2. a large basket, usually with a cover डलिया All the boys had brought *hampers* on the trip.

hand *(v.)* हैन्ड–1. to give or offer by the hand or hands देना, सौंपना You can *hand* over the book to him in sometime.

2. needle of clock घड़ी की सूई The *hands* of my watch are broken.

3. *(n.)* the prehensile part of the body at the end of the arm, consisting of a thumb, four fingers, and a palm हाथ Your *hands* are so beautiful.

- **at hand**– very near or close, esp in time समय के पास Help is close *at* your *hand.*
- **by hand**– by manual rather than mechanical means के द्वारा She washes clothes *by hand.*
- **first hand knowledge**– complete information प्रत्यक्ष रूप से He has *first hand knowledge* on the subject.
- **give a big hand**– to encourage उत्साह बढ़ाना The audience *gave a big hand* on his performance.
- **hand in hand**– clasping each other's hands बांह में बांह डाले हुए The couple walked *hand in hand* in the street.
- **hand to mouth**– with barely enough money or food to satisfy immediate needs जिसका गुज़ारा मुश्किल से होता हो They are living in a *hand to mouth* life.
- **hand over**– to surrender possession of; transfer अपना दायित्व किसी दूसरे को सौंपना She *handed over* all her responsibilities to her daughter-in-law.
- **hands up**– raise the hands above the level of the shoulders, an order usually given by an armed robber to a victim, etc. हाथ खड़े करने का आदेश देना *'Hands up,'* the police man said.
- **out of hands**– . no longer one's responsibility क़ाबू से बाहर I am afraid the matter is now *out of my hands.*
- **second hand information**– previously owned or used पुराना You have got *second hand information* about him.

handbag *(n.)* हैंड-बैग– a small suitcase that can be carried by hand हाथ में पकड़ने वाला छोटा थैला I am planning to gift her a *handbag.*

handbook *(n.)* हैंड-बुक– a reference book listing brief facts on a subject or place or directions for maintenance or repair, as of a car छोटी पुस्तक She always keeps a small *handbook* in her bag.

handbrake *(n.)* हैंड-ब्रेक– a brake operated by a hand lever हाथ से लगाया जाने वाला ब्रेक She seldom uses *handbrakes.*

handcuffs *(n.)* हैंडकफ़्स– 1. a pair of locking metal rings joined by a short bar or chain for securing prisoners, etc. हथकड़ी The *handcuffs* were dangling from the peg in the police station.

2. *(v.)* to put handcuffs on (a person); manacle हथकड़ी लगाना The police *handcuffed* the thief.

handgun *(n.)* हैंडगन– a firearm that can be held, carried, and fired with one hand, such as a pistol छोटी बंदूक The terrorist had two *handguns* and one AK-47.

handicap *(n.)* हैन्डिकेप– 1. something that hampers or hinders अड़चन, बाधा, असुविधा I feel *handicap* without my mobile phone.

2. *(v.) to be a hindrance or disadvantage to* बाधक होना, अड़ंगा लगाना Excess luggage *handicaps* one while travelling.

handicapped *(adj.)* हैंडिकैप्ड– physically disabled विकलांग All the *handicapped* children were treated.

handicraft *(n.)* हैंडिक्राफ्ट– skill or dexterity in working with the hands हस्तशिल्प, दस्तकारी Hey! lets go to the *handicraft* exhibition tomorrow.

handiwork *(n.)* हैंडिवर्क– work performed or produced by hand, such as embroidery or pottery दस्तकारी Everyone admired her exquisite *handiwork.*

handkerchief *(n.)* हैन्कर्चिफ़– a small square of soft absorbent material, such as linen, silk, or soft paper, carried and used to wipe the nose, etc. रूमाल I forgot to carry my *handkerchief* with me today.

handle *(v.)* हैण्डल–1. to manage successfully छूना, संभालना, चलाना I can't *handle* this job.

2. *(n.)* the part of a utensil, drawer, etc. designed to be held in order to move, use, or pick up the object मूठ, दस्ता The *handle* of my umbrella is broken.

handloom *(n.)* हैंडलूम– relating to a weaving device operated by hand हथकरघा I have brought a *handloom* sari from the Gandhi Ashram.

handmade *(adj.)* हैंडमेड– made by hand, not by machine, esp with care or craftsmanship हाथ का बनाया हुआ The designer salwar suit was totally *handmade.*

handout *(n.)* हैण्डआउट– a leaflet, free sample, etc, given out to publicize something इश्तहार Please read the *handout.*

handrail *(n.)* हैंडरेल– a rail alongside a stairway, etc. at a convenient height to be grasped to provide support सीढ़ी पर लगा पकड़ने का डंडा The child was hanging on *handrail.*

handshake *(n.)* हैंडशेक– the act of grasping and shaking a person's hand, as when being introduced or agreeing on a deal हाथ मिलाना, अभिवादन We *handshake* each other when we meet.

handsome *(adj.)* हैण्डसम–1. (of a man) good-looking, esp in having regular, pleasing, and well-defined features आकर्षक (पुरुष) He is a *handsome* young man.

2. liberal or ample बड़ी (धनराशि) We made a *handsome* profit in our business.

handwriting *(n.)* हैंडराइटिंग– writing by hand rather than by typing or printing लिखावट I cannot read this *handwriting.*

handwritten *(adj.)* हैंडरिटन– written by hand; not printed or typed हस्तलिखित (हाथ से लिखा हुआ) The whole manuscript was *handwritten.*

handy *(adj.)* हैंडी– conveniently or easily within reach सुगम, उपयोगी A basket is *handy* when we go for shopping.

hang *(v.)* हैन्ग–1. to fasten or be fastened from above, esp by a cord, chain, etc.; suspend लटकाना, टाँगना I want to *hang* this portrait in my room.

2. to suspend or be suspended by the neck until dead फाँसी देना The murderer was *hanged* to death.

➢ **hang around**– to waste time; loiter आवारा फिरना, He *hangs around* in the street.

➢ **hang back**– to be reluctant to go forward or carry on (with some activity) हिचकना, झिझकना Why are you *hanging back*.

➢ **hang down**– to feel ashamed मुंह लटकाना, The guilty man *hung down* his head with shame.

➢ **hang in**– to persist डटे रहना, I am happy to see you *hanging in*.

➢ **hang on**– to cling, grasp, or hold कसकर पकड़े रखना, I *hang on* to my child's hand when I cross the road.

➢ **hang up**– to suspend by placing on a peg or hook टाँगना Shall I *hang* your coat up?

hangar *(n.)* हैंगर्– a large workshop or building for storing and maintaining aircraft विमानों को रखने की इमारत, विमानशाला The planes were kept in the *hangar*.

hanger *(n.)* हैंगर्– any support, such as a hook, strap, peg, or loop, on or by which something may be hung अलमारी में कपड़े टांगने वाला हैंगर I hanged my shirt in a *hanger*.

hanging *(n.)* हैंगिंग– the putting of a person to death by suspending the body by the neck from a noose फांसी से दी गई मौत He was sentenced to death by *hanging*.

hangman *(n.)* हैंगमन– an official who carries out a sentence of hanging on condemned criminals जल्लाद The *hangman* was about to push the button.

hangover *(n.)* हैंगओवर– the headache and sick feeling after drinking too much alcohol शराब पीने के बाद होने वाला सिरदर्द He woke up with a terrible *hangover*.

hanker *(v.)* हैंकर्– to have a yearning (for something or to do something) लालयित होना, ललकना He is always *hankering* after money.

haphazard *(adj.)* हैपहैज़र्ड– not organized well अव्यवस्थित, गड्डमड्ड Your article is written in a *haphazard* way.

happen *(v.)* हैपन–1. (of an event in time) to come about or take place; occur घटना, घटित होना Oh God! When did this *happen?*
2. to chance (to be or do something) संयोग होना Do you *happen* to know Sudhir?

happening *(n.)* हैपनिंग– an occurrence; event घटना The *happening* was quite strange.

happily *(adv.)* हैपिली– cheerfully or contentedly; with satisfaction खुशी-खुशी The old couple are living *happily* in Dehradun.

happy *(adj.)* हैपी–1. feeling, showing, or expressing joy; pleased खुश, प्रसन्न I am so *happy* to meet you.
2. aptly expressed; appropriate अभिवादन के लिए प्रयुक्त Many *happy* returns of the day!

happy-go-lucky *(adj.)* हैप्पी-गो-लकी– carefree or easy-going बेपरवाह She is *happy-go-lucky* girl.

harass *(v.)* हैरस– to trouble, torment, or confuse by continual persistent attacks, questions, etc किसी को पीड़ा पहुंचाना, सताना Don't try to *harass* me.

harassed *(adj.)* हैरस्ड– worried, annoyed or stressed व्यथित, परेशान You look *harassed* today.

harassment *(n.)* हैरसमन्ट– the act of persistently worrying, annoying or stressing, often used in relation to law or to the act of harassing in the workplace उत्पीड़न, परेशानी I will not tolerate any sort of *harassment* in my office.

harbour *(n.)* हार्बर्– a sheltered port बन्दरगाह When we went to Mumbai, we saw many ships anchored at the *harbour.*

hard *(adj.)* हार्ड–1. firm or rigid; not easily dented, crushed, or pierced कड़ा, सख़्त I cannot sleep on a *hard* bed.
2. difficult to understand or perceive कठिन, दुर्भेद्य Do you find Physics a *hard* subject?
3. *(adv.)* with great energy, force, or vigour अधिक प्रयास, ज़ोरदार ढंग से If you work *hard,* you can score good marks in the examination.

- **hard and fast**– (esp of rules) invariable or strict कठोर, कड़ा, There is no *hard and fast* rule in our company.
- **hard feelings**– Hard feelings are feelings of anger or bitterness towards someone who you have had an argument with or who has upset you नाराज़गी, I don't have *hard feelings* for her.
- **hard on**– tough or adamant किसी के लिए मुश्किलें पैदा करना, Please, don't be too *hard on* your child.
- **hard time**– inflicting pain, sorrow, distress, or hardship मुश्किल वक़्त, They have *hard time* after the death of their elder son.
- **hard to swallow**– difficult to beleive मुश्किल से यक़ीन होना, It's *hard to swallow* that she is a bar girl.
- **hard up**– in need of money; poor जिसका हाथ तंग हो, I am very *hard-up* these days.

hard-bitten *(adj.)* हार्ड-बिटन– tough and realistic अदम्य, दुर्दमनीय This retired man has remained a *hard-bitten* school teacher.

hardboard *(n.)* हार्डबॉर्ड– a thin stiff sheet made of compressed saw-dust and wood pulp bound together with plastic adhesive or resin under heat and pressure प्लाई का तख़्ता I like to write on *hardboard* for good handwriting.

harden *(v.)* हार्डन– to make or become hard or harder; firm, stiffen, or set कठोर या कड़ा होना The varnish takes a few hours to *harden.*

hard-headed *(adj.)* हार्ड-हैडड– tough, realistic, or shrewd; not moved by sentiment सयाना, समझदार Dhirubhai Ambani was a *hard-headed* businessman.

hard-hearted *(adj.)* हार्ड-हार्टेड– unkind or intolerant कठोर दिल She has become so *hard-hearted* after her son left her alone.

hard-hitting *(adj.)* हार्ड-हिटिंग– uncompromising; tough खरी-खरी बातों वाला It was *a hard-hitting* campaign all over Delhi.

hardly *(adv.)* हार्ड्ली– scarcely; barely मुश्किल से It *hardiy* matters if she does'nt come to my party.

hardness *(n.)* हार्डनस– the quality or condition of being hard कड़ापन The diamond is used to cut the glass because of its *hardness.*

hard-nosed *(adj.)* हार्ड-नोज़्ड– tough, shrewd, and practical दुनियादार, सयाना India TV has some *hard-nosed* journalists.

hardship *(n.)* हार्डशिप– conditions of life difficult to endure तंगहाली, विपत्ति She has faced a lot of *hardships* in bringing up her children.

hardware *(n.)* हार्डवेअर्– machinery and electronic parts of a computer system कंप्यूटर की मशीनरी Buy a new monitor from the computer *hardware* shop.

hard-wearing *(adj.)* हार्ड-वियरिंग– resilient, durable, and tough मज़बूत एवं टिकाऊ I have a *hard-wearing* carpet in my bedroom.

hard-working *(adj.)* हार्ड-वर्किंग– (of a person) industrious; diligent मेहनती Her *hard-working* nature made her reach this height.

hardy *(adj.)* हार्डि– bold; courageous सशक्त, बलवान He is very *hardy*, he takes a cold shower every morning.

hare *(n.)* हेअर्– an animal like a large rabbit खरगोश Can you run as fast as a *hare*?

harm *(n.)* हार्म– 1. physical or mental injury or damage हानि, क्षति The crops suffered great *harm* due to the unseasonal rains.

2. *(v.)* to injure physically, morally, or mentally हानि या चोट पहुंचाना The strong should not *harm* the weak.

harmful *(adj.)* हार्मफुल– causing or tending to cause harm; injurious नुक़सानदेह Keep these *harmful* chemicals away from kids.

harmless *(adj.)* हार्मलस– not causing any physical or mental damage or injury नुक़सान न पहुंचाने वाला, अहानिकर Lizards are *harmless* creatures.

harmonious *(adj.)* हार्मोनिअस– tuneful, consonant, or melodious मैत्रीपूर्ण, तालमेल से I have a *harmonious* relationship with my neighbours.

harmony *(n.)* हार्मनी–1. agreeable sounds स्वरसंगति, तालमेल Let us sing in *harmony*.

2. agreement in action, opinion, feeling, etc.; accord सामंजस्य, मेल, मैत्री Two countries can progress only if they live in *harmony*.

harness *(v.)* हार्निस–1. to put harness on (a horse) साज चढ़ाना *Harness* the horse to the carriage.

2. *(n.)* an arrangement of leather straps buckled or looped together, fitted to a draught animal in order that the animal can be attached to and pull a cart घोड़े की काठी, साज Don't forget to hold the *harness* while riding on horse.

3. to control so as to employ the energy or potential power of किसी की ऊर्जा का व्यवस्थित प्रयोग करना We can *harness* the sun's rays as a source of energy.

harp *(v.)* हार्प– to speak; utter; express राग अलापना Why are you *harping* on this topic?

harpoon *(n.)* हार्पून– a barbed missile attached to a long cord and hurled or fired from a gun when hunting whales, etc. मत्स्य-भाला The fishermen were catching the fish with the help of *harpoon*.

harrowing *(adj.)* हैरोइंग– emotionally distressing or vexing तकलीफ़ देने वाला, भयावह I saw a *harrowing* program of apartheid on TV.

harsh *(adj.)* हार्श– rough or grating to the senses कठोर, निष्ठुर, कर्कश Do not speak in a *harsh* voice.

harshly *(adv.)* हार्शली– cruelly, sternly or severely निर्दयतापूर्वक Do not treat your children *harshly*.

harvest *(n.)* हार्विस्ट– 1. the gathering of a ripened crop फ़सल, पैदावार Farmers are very busy during the time of *harvest*.

2. *(adj.)* to reap or receive a crop फसल काटना या प्राप्त करना Farmers did not *harvest* their crops till March.

hassle *(n.)* हैसल– a great deal of trouble; difficulty; nuisance परेशानी Do you have any *hassle* about coming to my place tomorrow?

haste *(n.)* हेस्ट– hurry, esp in an action; swiftness; rapidity जल्दी, जल्दबाज़ी, उतावली *Haste* makes waste.

hasten *(v.)* हेसन– to hurry or cause to hurry; rush तुरन्त करना, तेज़ी से करवाना या करना We must *hasten* the preparations.

hasty *(adj.)* हैस्टी– rapid; swift; quick उतावलेपन का You should not take decision in a *hasty* manner.

hat *(n.)* हैट– any of various head coverings, esp one with a brim and a shaped crown हैट, टोपी Where is my *hat* that I bought from Goa.

hatch *(v.)* हैच–1. young birds, etc. to come out of an egg अण्डे से बाहर निकलना, अंडे सेना Don't count the chickens before they are *hatched.*
2. to contrive or devise (a scheme, plot, etc.) योजना या षड्यंत्र तैयार करना Rahul's colleagues *hatched* the plan to make an April Fool of him.

hatchet *(n.)* हैचिट– a short axe used for chopping wood, etc. कुल्हाड़ी The farmer was cutting woods with *hatchet.*

hate *(v.)* हेट– to dislike (something) intensely; detest वैर या द्वेष रखना, घृणा करना You should not *hate* anyone.

hateful *(adj.)* हेटफुल– causing or deserving hate; loathsome; detestable घृणित, अप्रिय It was such a *hateful* thing to say.

hatred *(n.)* हेटरेड– a feeling of intense dislike; enmity द्वेष, नफ़रत There should be no feeling of *hatred* in your heart.

hat-trick *(n.)* हैट्रिक– any achievement of three points, victories, awards, etc. within a given period किसी एक खिलाड़ी द्वारा तिहरी लगातार सफ़लता The player made a *hat-trick* in first half of the game.

haughty *(adj.)* हॉटी– having or showing arrogance घमंडी It is useless to argue with him; he is very *haughty.*

haul *(v.)* हॉल– to drag or draw (something) with effort घसीटना, बल लगाकर खींचना The wagon was *hauled* by the horse.

haunt *(v.)* हॉन्ट–1. to visit (a person or place) in the form of a ghost भूत-प्रेत का आना-जाना They entered the bungalow that was believed to be *haunted.*
2. to intrude upon or recur to (the memory, thoughts, etc.) दिमाग़ पर छाए रहना What happens to us after death is a question that often *haunts* me.

haunted *(adj.)* हाण्टेड– frequented or visited by ghosts भूतों से भरा हुआ, भुतहा This bungalow is *haunted* for many years.

haunting *(adj.)* हॉन्टिंग– (of memories) poignant or persistent बार-बार याद आने वाला Going abroad was a *haunting* incident of my life.

have *(v.)* हैव–1. to be in material possession of; own पास होना, रखना Can I *have* a pen?
2. to eat, drink, or partake of खाना/पीना I would like to *have* an apple.

haven *(n.)* हेवन–1. a port, harbour, or other sheltered place for shipping बन्दरगाह Despite the storm, our ship safely reached its *haven.*
2. a place of safety or sanctuary; shelter आश्रय स्थान My bedroom is my *haven.*

havoc *(n.)* हैवक– destruction; devastation; ruin बरबादी, तबाही, विध्वंस I can't see the *havoc* caused by the earthquake.

hawk *(n.)* हॉक– a strong diurnal bird of prey having short rounded wings and a long tail बाज़ How swiftly can a *hawk* fly?

hay *(n.)* हे– grass, clover, etc. cut and dried as fodder सूखी घास Make *hay* while the sun shines.

hay fever *(n.)* हे-फ़ीवर– an allergic reaction to pollen, dust, etc. characterized by sneezing, runny nose, and watery eyes due to inflammation of the mucous membranes of the eyes and nose परागज ज्वर I have *hay fever* due to cold.

haystack *(n.)* हेस्टैक– a large pile of hay, esp one built in the open air and covered with thatch घास का ढेर/अंबार Many *haystacks* were lying in the godown.

haywire *(adj.)* हेवाइअर्– (of things) not functioning properly; disorganized

अव्यवस्थित हो जाना The project started off well, but the problems between the co-workers made the whole thing go *haywire.*

hazard *(n.)* हैज़र्ड– 1. exposure or vulnerability to injury, loss, evil, etc. जोखिम, खतरा The climbers faced many *hazards* on their way to the Everest.
2. *(v.)* to chance or risk दाँव पर रखना, कल्पना करना Can you *hazard* a guess he wants to see you?

hazardous *(adj.)* हैज़र्डस– involving great risk ख़तरनाक, जोख़िमभरा I faced a very *hazardous* journey this time.

haze *(n.)* हेज़– reduced visibility in the air as a result of condensed water vapour, dust, etc., in the atmosphere धुंध There was a *haze* over the mountain this morning.

hazel *(adj.)* हेज़ल– reddish-brown in colour आँखों की लालिमा लिए भूरा रंग She has got lovely *hazel* eyes.

hazy *(adj.)* हेज़ि–1. characterized by reduced visibility; misty धुंधला Our plane could not take off because of the *hazy* weather.
2. indistinct; vague उलझन, अनिश्चय I had a *hazy* idea of the weather and surroundings of the hill station before I went there.

he *(pron.)* ही– refers to a male person or animal वह *He* might not come to office today.

head *(n.)* हे'ड–1. the upper or front part of the body in vertebrates, including man, that contains and protects the brain, eyes, mouth, and nose and ears when present सिर, मस्तक Did you see her new *head* band?
2. the position of leadership or command प्रधान, अध्यक्ष Who is the *head* of your company?
3. the most forward part of a thing; a part that juts out; front चोटी, शीर्षभाग, अग्रभाग When he called on me, I was standing at the *head* of the staircase.
4. *(v.)* to go or cause to go (towards) की ओर बढ़ना या मोड़ना To which direction are you *heading*?

headache *(n.)* हैडएक– any cause of worry, difficulty, or annoyance सरदर्द I want to get rid of my *headache.*

headline *(n.)* हैडलाइन– a phrase at the top of a newspaper or magazine article indicating the subject of the article, usually in larger and heavier type मुख्य समाचार I could read only the *headlines* in the newpaper today.

headlong *(adv., adj.)* हैडलाँग– with the head foremost; headfirst सिर के बल He fell down *headlong.*

headman *(n.)* हैडमेन– a chief or leader मुखिया Who is the *headman* of your family?

headmaster *(n.)* हैडमास्टर– a male principal of a school प्रधानाचार्य The vacancy for the post of *headmaster* is still vacant.

headmistress *(n.)* हैडमिस्ट्रस– a female principal of a school प्रधानाचार्या The *headmistress* of this school is also a warden of the girls' hostel.

headquarters *(n.)* हेडक्वाटर्ज़– any centre or building from which operations are directed, as in the military, the police, etc. मुख्यालय Where are the *headquarters* of your industry?

headstone *(n.)* हेडस्टोन– a memorial stone at the head of a grave, gravestone समाधि-शिला, क़ब्र पर लगा पत्थर Please engrave my late grandfather's name on this *headstone.*

headstrong *(adj.)* हेडस्ट्रॉन्ग– self-willed; obstinate हठी, ज़िद्दी Mohit is a *headstrong* boy, he will not take anyone's advice.

headway *(n.)* हेडवे– progress or rate of progress प्रगति, बढ़ने की क्रिया We are making little *headway* with the negotiations.

headword *(n.)* हेडवर्ड– a key word placed at the beginning of a line, paragraph, etc., as in a dictionary entry मुख्य शब्द In this dictionary a *headword* is followed by its pronunciation.

heal *(v.)* to restore or be restored to health घाव का भरना Bandage the wound; it will *heal* up quickly.

health *(n.)* हेल्थ– the state of being bodily and mentally vigorous and free from disease स्वास्थ्य, तन्दुरुस्ती Please take care of your *health*.

healthy *(adj.)* हैल्थी–1. enjoying good health तंदुरुस्त, स्वस्थ We should exercise to remain *healthy*.
2. indicating soundness of body or mind समझदार, विवेकपूर्ण It's not a *healthy* sign.

heap *(v.)* हीप– 1. to collect or be collected into or as if into a heap or pile ढेर लगाना, संचय करना Don't *heap* your plate with food.
2. *(n.)* a collection of articles or mass of material gathered together in one place ढेर Don't jump over that *heap* of stones.

hear *(v.)* हिअर्–1. to perceive (a sound) with the sense of hearing सुनना, ध्यान देना Please be little loud, I can't *hear* you.
2. to be informed (of); receive information (about) पता चलना, जानना I *hear* you have been promoted.

hearing *(adj.)* हिअरिंग– the faculty or sense by which sound is perceived सुनने की शक्ति His *hearing* is poor, you have to speak louder.

hearing aid *(n.)* हिअरिंग एड– a device for assisting the hearing of partially deaf people, बहरे लोगों के सुनने की मशीन The old man purchased a new pair of *hearing aids*.

hearsay *(n.)* हिअर्से– gossip; rumour जनश्रुति, अफ़वाह Don't go by *hearsay*, use your own judgment.

heart *(n.)* हार्ट–1. the hollow muscular organ in vertebrates whose contractions propel the blood through the circulatory system हृदय, दिल The doctor found nothing wrong with the patient's *heart*.
2. emotional mood or disposition प्रकृति, स्वभाव You have a warm *heart*.
3. the most important or vital part केन्द्र, मध्यभाग Try to go to the *heart* of the subject.

heartache *(n.)* हार्टएक– intense anguish or mental suffering मनोव्यथा, घोर चिंता का विषय The relationship caused her a great deal of *heartache*.

heartattack *(n.)* हार्टअटैक– any sudden severe instance of abnormal heart functioning, esp coronary thrombosis दिल का दौरा His father died of a severe *heartattack*.

heartbeat *(n.)* हार्टबीट– one complete pulsation of the heart दिल की धड़कन She fell down the moment her *heartbeat* stoped.

heartbreak *(n.)* हार्टब्रेक– intense and overwhelming grief, esp through disappointment in love गहरी मनोव्यथा We suffered the *heartbreak* of losing our mother.

heartbreaking *(adj.)* हार्टब्रेकिंग– extremely sad, disappointing, or pitiful अत्यंत दुखद, हृदय-विदारक It's *heartbreaking* to see her wasting her life doing nothing.

heartbroken *(adj.)* हार्टब्रोकन– suffering from intense grief विदीर्ण हृदय, उदास Shobha was *heartbroken* when Karan left her.

heartburn *(n.)* हार्टबर्न– a burning sensation beneath the breastbone caused by irritation of the oesophagus, as from regurgitation of the contents of the stomach हृद्‌दाह

I have to take some antacids for *heartburn.*

hearten *(v.)* हार्टन– to make or become cheerful ढांढस बंधाना, हिम्मत दिलाना We were greatly *heartened* by the good news.

heartening *(adj.)* हार्टनिंग– causing cheerfulness; encouraging उत्साहवर्द्धक It is *heartening* to see the determination of these young people.

heartfelt *(adj.)* हार्टफ़ेल्ट– sincerely and strongly felt हार्दिक It was an *heartfelt* apology that I could not call on time.

heartily *(adv.)* हार्टलि– thoroughly or vigorously पूरे उत्साह के साथ They laughed *heartily* at the joke.

heart-rending *(adj.)* हार्टरेंडिंग– causing great mental pain and sorrow हृदय-विदारक Yesterday I read a *heart-rending* story.

hearty *(adj.)* हार्टी– substantial and nourishing भरपेट, भरपूर We had a *hearty* meal before we set out.

hearth *(n.)* हार्थ– the floor of a fireplace, esp one that extends outwards into the room अंगीठी, चूल्हा, भट्ठी We sat near the *hearth.*

heat *(n.)* हीट–1. the energy transferred as a result of a difference in temperature गरमी, ताप I can't tolerate this *heat* anymore.

2. intensity of feeling; passion उत्तेजना, आवेग Do not speak with such *heat.*

heated *(adj.)* हीटेड– full of anger क्रुद्ध, नाराज़ The shopkeeper became very *heated* on the argument.

heath *(n.)* हीथ– a large open area, usually with sandy soil and scrubby vegetation, esp heather बंजर धरती There were many bushes and wild plants on the *heath.*

heathen *(n.)* हीदन– a person who does not acknowledge the God of Christianity, Judaism, or Islam; pagan गैर-ईसाई, गैर-मुसलमान, विधर्मी He is uncivilized; he is such a *heathen.*

heatstroke *(n.)* हीटस्ट्रॉक– a condition resulting from prolonged exposure to intense heat, characterized by high fever and in severe cases convulsions and coma लू लगना, तापाघात A foreigner tourist visited Delhi in summer and got *heatstroke.*

heave *(v.)* हीव–1. to lift or move with a great effort उठाना, उछालना I saw him *heave* a very heavy load on his head.

2. to utter (sounds, sighs, etc) or breathe noisily or unhappily भरना The parents *heaved* a sigh of relief after seeing there son.

3. *(n.)* the act or an instance of heaving ज़ोर से खींचने की क्रिया She gave one *heave* and the rock moved.

heaven *(n.)* हेवन– the abode of God and the angels स्वर्ग, परलोक, आकाश God is in the *heaven.*

heavenly *(adj.)* हेवनलि– alluring, wonderful, or sublime स्वर्गीय What a *heavenly* sight!

heavily *(adv.)* हैविली– greatly; to a large extent; by a large margin अत्यधिक The Indian batting relies *heavily* on Sachin Tendulkar

heavy *(adj.)* हेवी–1. of comparatively great weight भारी, वज़नदार Can you lift a *heavy* load?

2. great in yield, quality, or quantity भारी, तीव्र बड़ा We had *heavy* rains last night.

3. sad or dejected in spirit or mood उदास, खिन्न I bade him good-bye with a *heavy* heart.

heavy-duty *(adj.)*– made to withstand hard wear, bad weather, etc. टिकाऊ और मज़बूत Apollo Tyres company manufactures very *heavy-duty* tyres.

heavy-handed *(adj.)*– not showing sympathy कठोर, निर्दय They have a *heavy-handed* style of management.

heavyweight *(n.)*–हेविवेट– a person or thing that is heavier than average साधारण से अधिक भारी Alexander Povetkini is a world *heavyweight* boxing champion.

heckle *(v.)* हेकल– to interrupt (a public speaker, performer, etc.) by comments, questions, or taunts टोका-टाकी करना The reporter *heckled* the leader throughout his speech.

hectic *(adj.)* हेक्टिक– characterized by extreme activity or excitement उत्तेजक, खलबलीपूर्ण Oh! It was such a *hectic* trip.

hedge *(n.)* हेज– a row of shrubs, bushes, or trees forming a boundary to a field, garden, etc. बाड़ा, घेरा You should have a *hedge* around your garden.

hedgehog *(n.)* हेजहॉग– small nocturnal animal having a protective covering of spines on the back साही, काँटाचूहा *Hedgehogs* are the only British mammal with spines.

heed *(v.)* हीड– to pay close attention to (someone or something) ध्यान देना They *heeded* the advice of the teacher to recheck the answers before submitting the final sheet. *(n.)* close and careful attention; notice सावधानी He did not pay any *heed* to his mother's advice to return home early.

heel *(n.)* हील– the back part of the human foot from the instep to the lower part of the ankle एड़ी I do not like shoes with high *heels.*

hefty *(adj.)* हेफ़्टी– sizable; involving a large amount of money बड़ा या भारी How can you charge such an *hefty* amount for this?

height *(n.)* हाइट– the vertical distance from the bottom or lowest part of something to the top or apex ऊँचाई The height of both the tables is almost equal.

heighten *(v.)* हाइटन– to make or become high or higher ऊँचा करना, बढ़ाना The communal tension has *heightened* in the city after the bomb blast.

heir *(n.)* एअर्– the person legally succeeding to all property of a deceased person, उत्तराधिकारी, वारिस Rahul was the only *heir* to his father's property.

hell *(n.)* हेल– the place or state of eternal punishment of the wicked after death, with Satan as its ruler नरक Do you believe in the existence of heaven and *hell*?

hellish *(adj.)* हेलिश– very difficult or unpleasant नारकीय She was leading a *hellish* life with her husband.

helm *(n.)* हे'ल्म–1. the wheel, or handle by which a vessel is steered पतवार How can you guide a boat without a *helm*?

2. a position of leadership or control नियंत्रण, संचालन Who is at the *helm* of affairs in your firm?

helmet *(n.)* हेल्मेट– a piece of protective or defensive armour for the head worn by soldiers, policemen, firemen, divers, etc. टोप, शिरस्त्राण Don't fail to wear a *helmet* when you ride a scooter.

help *(n.)* हे'ल्प–1. the act of helping, or being helped, or a person or thing that helps सहायता या मदद I got much *help* from my friend.

2. *(v.)* to assist or aid मदद करना, सहायता देना My daughter is *helping* me in the kitchen.

helpful *(adj.)* हेल्पफुल– serving a useful function; giving help सहायक She is so generous and *helpful.*

helping *(n.)* हेलपिंग–1. a single portion of food taken at a meal खुराक, परोसने की मात्रा Would you like a second *helping*?

➢ **helping hand**– assistance सहारा, मदद, My friend is always ready to give me a *helping hand.*

helpless *(adj.)* हेल्पलस– unable to manage independently मजबूर, लाचार She is in *helpless* condition.

hen *(n.)* हेन– female chicken, esp the adult female of the domestic fowl मुर्गी I saw a dead *hen* in the garden today.

hence *(adv.)* हेन्स–1. from this time इसलिए I am late, *hence* I must rush.

2. from here or from this world; away अब से A week *hence* I shall be in Shimla.

henceforth *(adv.)* हेंसफ़ोर्थ– from this time forward; from now on अब से, आगे से You will not be allowed any leave *henceforth.*

her *(pron.)* हर– refers to a female person or animal उसको, उसी (स्त्री) को I like *her* choice.

herald *(n.)* हेरल्ड– 1. a person who announces important news अग्रदूत The death of the king was announced by the *herald.*

2. *(v.)* to announce publicly घोषणा करना The leader's call to the people *heralded* a new movement against corruption.

herb *(n.)* हर्ब– a seed-bearing plant whose aerial parts do not persist above ground at the end of the growing season; herbaceous plant जड़ी-बूटी, औषधि I was reading a book on medicinal *herbs.*

herbivore *(n.)* हर्बिवॉर– an animal that feeds on grass and other plants शाकाहारी प्राणी Goat, cow and horse are *herbivores* that eat only plants.

herd *(n.)* हर्ड– 1. a large group of mammals living and feeding together, esp a group of cattle, sheep, etc. पशुओं का झुंड A *herd* of cattle was grazing in the field.

2. *(v.)* to collect or be collected into a herd झुंड में रहना, एकत्र हो जाना In the evening, cows were *herded* into the yard.

here *(adv.)* हिअर– in, at, or to this place, point, case, or respect यहां I came *here* last night.

hereabout *(adv.)* हिअरअबाउट– in this region or neighbourhood; near this place आसपास There must be a bar *hereabouts.*

hereafter *(adv.)* हिअरआफ़्टर– in a subsequent part of this document, matter, case, etc. अब से, इसके बाद Do you believe in a life *hereafter?*

hereditary *(adj.)* हरेडिटरी– of, relating to, or denoting factors that can be transmitted genetically from one generation to another आनुवंशिक, वंशानुगत Baldness is a *hereditary* disease in their family.

heritage *(n.)* हेरिटेज– something inherited at birth, such as personal characteristics, status, and possessions पैतृक संपत्ति, परंपराएं, बपौती The national flag is the *heritage* of our country.

hermit *(n.)* हर्मिट– one who, usually for religious reasons, lives a very simple life alone मुनि, तपस्वी, वैरागी While passing through the forest, we came across a *hermit.*

hermitage *(n.)* हर्मिटेज– any place where a person may live in seclusion आश्रम, कुटीर You can live a carefree, enriched life at *hermitage.*

hero *(n.)* हीरो– a man distinguished by exceptional courage, nobility, fortitude, etc. वीर, नायक Who was the *hero* in the movie?

heroic *(adj.)* हिरोइक– of, like, or befitting a hero वीरतापूर्ण, साहसिक He was playing all the *heroic* roles in the drama.

heroine *(n.)* हेरोइन– a woman possessing heroic qualities नायिका Who was the *heroine* in the movie?

herself *(pron.)* हरसेल्फ़– the reflexive form of she or her स्वयं को I can't help her because she *herself* is so confused.

hesitate *(v.)* हेज़िटेट– to hold back or be slow in acting; be uncertain हिचकना, अटकना Once you take a decision, do not *hesitate* to act upon it.

hesitation *(n.)* हेज़िटेशन– an unwillingness to do something, or a delay in doing it, because you are uncertain, worried, or embarrassed about it हिचक, संकोच You should agree without *hesitation.*

heterogeneous *(adj.)* हेटरजीनिअस– composed of unrelated or differing parts or elements विविध प्रकार का, विषम रूप, विजातीय India has *heterogeneous* society.

hexagon *(n.)* हैक्सगन– a polygon having six sides षड्भुज Sneha was drawing a *hexagon* on his copy.

heyday *(n.)* हे डे– the time of most power, popularity, vigour, etc.; prime चरम समृद्धि का समय, स्वर्ण-काल Nameeta was very jolly in the *heyday* of her youth.

hibernate *(v.)* हाइबर्नेट– (of some mammals, reptiles, and amphibians) to pass the winter in a dormant condition with metabolism greatly slowed down शीत-स्वाप करना The polar bear *hibernates* in the winters.

hiccup *(n.)* हिकप–1. a spasm of the diaphragm producing a sudden breathing in followed by a closing of the glottis, resulting in a sharp sound हिचकी, हिक्का She started having *hiccups* on eating the spicy food.

2. a minor difficulty or problem व्यवधान After the initial *hiccup,* the work proceeded well.

hide *(v.)* हाइड– 1. to put or keep (oneself or an object) in a secret place; to conceal (oneself or an object) from view or discovery छिपना, छिपाना I expect that you won't *hide* anything from me.

2. *(n.)* the skin of an animal, esp the tough thick skin of a large mammal, either tanned or raw खाल, चमड़ी The shoes made of a superior *hide* last longer.

hideous *(adj.)* हिडिअस– extremely ugly; repulsive कुरूप, भद्दा She looks *hideous* in this dress.

hiding *(n.)* हाइडिंग–1. the state of concealment छिपने की स्थिति, छिपाव He has gone into *hiding* because he knows the police are looking for him.

2. a flogging; beating पिटाई, ठुकाई The child got a good *hiding.*

hierarchy *(n.)* हाइअराकी– a system of persons or things arranged in a graded order श्रेणीबद्ध संगठन We have a definite *hierarchy* in our department.

high *(adj.)* हाइ–1. being a relatively great distance from top to bottom; tall उत्तुंग, ऊँचा How *high* is the building in which you live?

2. of great eminence; very important श्रेष्ठ, महान्, ऊँचे I have friends in *high* places.

3. elated; cheerful असंयत, प्रबल I have nothing but *high* praise for you.

4. greater than normal in degree, intensity, or amount तूफ़ानी, घोर A *high* wind has been blowing since morning.

high-class *(adj.)* हाइक्लास– of very good quality; superior उच्च श्रेणी का, उच्चवर्ग She pretends as if she is from an *high-class* family.

highlight *(v.)* हाइलाइट–1. to bring notice or emphasis to कसी चीज़ की ओर ध्यान आकृष्ट करना The teacher *highlighted* the need to study well.
2. *(n.)* the most exciting or memorable part of an event or period of time झलकियां I could see only the *highlights* of the World Cup last night.

highly *(adv.)* हाइली– very; with great approbation or favour अत्यधिक I value the books *highly*.

highness *(n.)* हाइनस– the condition of being high or lofty (शाही ख़ानदान के आदर में प्रयुक्त) अत्रभवान, तत्रभवान् The minister said, "Welcome to the court, your *Highness*!"

high-pitched *(adj.)* हाइपिचड– pitched high in volume or tone तीव्र, तेज़ She has a *high-pitched* voice.

high-tech *(adj.)* हाइटेक– designed for or using high technology आधुनिक मशीनों का प्रयोग करने वाला *High-tech* industries are emerging very fast in modern India.

highway *(n.)* हाइवे– a main road, esp one that connects towns or cities राजमार्ग Drive carefully on the *highway*.

hijack *(v.)* हाइजैक– to rob (a person or vehicle) by force अपहरण करना The terrorists *hijacked* the plane going to Afghanistan.

hike *(n.)* हाइक– 1. a long walk पैदल सैर, पदयात्रा I like to go on *hikes* in the countyside.
2. *(v.)* to increase (a price) बढ़ना I was expecting some *hike* in my salary this year.

hilarious *(adj.)* हिलेरिअस– very funny or merry हास्यपूर्ण That was a *hilarious* joke.

hill *(n.)* हिल– a conspicuous and often rounded natural elevation of the earth's surface, less high or craggy than a mountain पहाड़ी, टीला Lets go to any *hill* station this week.

hilly *(adj.)* हिली– characterized by hills पहाड़ी The country is very *hilly* around here.

hilt *(n.)* हिल्ट– the handle of a knife, griddle, etc. मूठ, हत्था, दस्ता I will support you to the *hilt*.

him *(pron.)* हिम– refers to a male person or animal उसे I can't see *him* anywhere.

himself *(pron.)* हिमसेल्फ़– the reflexive form of he or him खुद, स्वयं He *himself* was not so keen to join this program.

hind *(adj.)* हाइण्ड– situated at the back or rear पिछला My horse fell and injured one of its *hind* legs.

hinder *(v.)* हिन्डर्– to prevent रोकना, बाधा डालना The strikers *hindered* the movement of the office-goers by putting roadblocks.

hindrance *(n.)* हिण्ड्रन्स– an obstruction or snag; impediment रुकावट, बाधा Don't be a *hindrance* in my work.

hindsight *(n.)* हाइंडसाइट– the ability to understand, after something has happened, what should have been done or what caused the event पश्च दृष्टि In *hindsight* we should have acted differently.

Hindu *(n.)* हिन्दू– a person who adheres to Hinduism हिन्दू धर्म She went to meet a *Hindu* saint.

hinge *(n.)* हिन्ज– a device for holding together two parts such that one can swing relative to the other, typically having two interlocking metal leaves held by a pin about which they pivot कब्ज़ा, चूल Oil the *hinges* of the door.

hint *(n.)* हिण्ट– 1. a suggestion or implication given in an indirect or subtle manner संकेत, इशारा The manager gave me a *hint* regarding my increment.
2. *(v.)* to suggest or imply indirectly संकेत करना I *hinted* that I would attend the meeting.

hip *(n.)* हिप– either side of the body below the waist and above the thigh, overlying the lateral part of the pelvis and its articulation with the thighbones कूल्हा, नितंब I fell down and hurt my *hip*.

hire *(n.)* हाइअर्– 1. the price paid or payable for a person's services or the temporary use of something किराया Let us take taxi on *hire*.
2. *(v.)* to acquire the temporary use of (a thing) or the services of (a person) in exchange for payment किराये पर लेना/देना I *hired* a mechanic to repair my car.

his *(pron.)* हिज़्– of, belonging to, or associated with him उसका, उसके *His* mom is unwell that is why he din't come to office.

hiss *(n.)* हिस–1. a voiceless fricative sound like that of a prolonged s फुफकार, फुँकार I heard a faint *hiss* as the metal struck the water.
2. *(v.)* to produce or utter a hiss फुफकारना I became alert when a snake *hissed*.

historic *(adj.)* हिस्टॉरिक– famous or likely to become famous in history; significant ऐतिहासिक 'It is a *historic* moment,' the leader told to reporter.

historical *(adj.)* हिस्टॉरिकल– belonging to or typical of the study of history इतिहास से संबंधित, ऐतिहासिक Lets visit some *historical* places this week.

history *(n.)* हिस्टरी– a record or account, often chronological in approach, of past events, developments, etc. इतिहास How much did you score in *history*?

hit *(v.)* हिट–1. to propel or cause to move by striking प्रहार करना, मारना I *hit* the ball straight into the net.
2. to guess correctly or find out by accident ठीक अनुमान करना, पता लगाना Have you *hit* upon any solution to the Maths problem?
3. *(n.)* an impact or collision प्रहार, आघात The boxer's powerful *hit* broke his opponent's jaw.

➢ **hit back** *(v.)*– to hit in return पलटकर वार करना, He hit me, so I *hit* him *back*.

➢ **hit out** *(v.)*– to direct blows forcefully and vigorously हमला बोलना, The injured man *hit out* blindly at the attacker.

hitch *(n.)* हिच– an impediment or obstacle, esp one that is temporary or minor छोटी-मोटी समस्या I am facing a technical *hitch* while working on my computer.

hitherto *(adv.)* हिदर्टु– until this time अब तक *Hitherto* I thought he was a fool, but now I think he is a rogue.

hive *(n.)* हाइव– a structure in which social bees live and rear their young शहद की मक्खियों का छत्ता Take care, there is a *hive* on a tree in our garden.

hoard *(n.)* हॉर्ड–1. an accumulated store hidden away for future use खज़ाना, संचय, ज़ख़ीरा A beehive is a *hoard* of honey.
2. *(v.)* to gather or accumulate (a hoard) जमा/संचय करना The miser *hoards* a lot of money.

hoarding *(n.)* हॉर्डिंग– a large board used for displaying advertising posters, as by a road सड़कों आदि पर लगे विज्ञापन हेतु बड़े-बड़े बोर्ड I saw a huge *hoarding* on the roadside.

hoarse *(adj.)* हॉर्स– gratingly harsh or raucous in tone कर्कश, फटा My voice became *hoarse* due to cold.

hobble *(v.)* हॉबल– to walk with a lame awkward movement लंगड़ाते हुए चलना, लंगड़ाना The beggar *hobbled* across the road.

hobby *(n.)* हॉबि– an activity pursued in spare time for pleasure or relaxation शौक़ Coin collection is my favourite *hobby*.

hockey *(n.)* हॉकि– a game played on a field by two opposing teams of 11 players each, who try to hit a ball into their opponents' goal using long sticks curved at the end हॉकी I have my *hockey* match tommorow.

hog *(v.)* हॉग– to take more than one's share of अपने हिस्से से अधिक हथियाना His car was *hogging* on the road so no one could overtake him.

hoist *(v.)* हॉइस्ट–1. to raise or lift up, फहराना The Prime Minister *hoists* the National Flag at Red Fort on every Independence Day.

2. to raise or lift up, esp by mechanical means उठाना, ऊपर उठाना My mother *hoisted* the baby upon her shoulder to show it a dancing monkey.

hold *(v.)* होल्ड–1. to have or keep (an object) with or within the hands, arms, etc; clasp पकड़ना *Hold* my hand while crossing the road.

2. to support or bear धारण करना, (में) स्थान होना How much milk does this bottle *hold*?

3. to have the ownership, possession, etc., of अधिकार होना, पास रखना Does he *hold* a Ph.D.?

4. to maintain or be maintained in a specified state or condition रखना, मानना I *hold* that honest men should contest the election.

5. to engage in or carry on करना, आयोजन करना When are you going to *hold* the club meeting?

6. to continue to go नियंत्रित करना *Hold* your breath and jump into the water.

7. *(n.)* something to hold on to, as for support or control पकड़ She keeps a firm *hold* of her little daughter.

➢ **hold back**– to restrain or be restrained रुकना, ठहरना, No one *held back* when danger came.

➢ **hold down**– to restrain or control कम करना, Please *hold down* the noise of your stereo.

➢ **hold off**– to keep apart or at a distance रुके रहना, The storm was *held off*.

➢ **hold on**– to maintain a firm grasp ख़तरे के समय डटे रहना, We should *hold on* for next two hours.

➢ **hold out**– to last or endure टिकना, How long can they *hold out* against these attacks!

➢ **hold up**– a delay; stoppage देरी करवाना, I was *held up* by the traffic.

holder *(n.)* होल्डर– a person, such as an owner, who has possession or control of something धारक He is a world record *holder* in the 100 metres race.

hole *(n.)* होल– an opening made in or through something छेद, कोटर There is a *hole* in my dress.

holiday *(n.)* हॉलिडे– a period in which a break is taken from work or studies for rest, travel, or recreation छुट्टी, अवकाश Where are you going to spend your *holidays*?

hollow *(adj.)* हॉलो– 1. having a sunken area; concave खोखला, पोला Bottles, pipes and tubes are *hollow*.

2. *(n.)* a depression or dip in the land घाटी, गड्ढा You can't see the farm house from here because it is in a *hollow*.

holocaust *(n.)* हालकास्ट– great destruction or loss of life or the source of such destruction, esp fire सर्वनाश There was a nuclear *holocaust* in Japan.

holy *(adj.)* होली– of, relating to, or associated with God or a deity; sacred पवित्र, पावन I took my grandmother on a pilgrimage to *holy* places.

homage *(n.)* होमेज– a public show of respect or honour towards someone or something श्रद्धांजलि I will definately go to pay my *homage* to the dead.

home *(n.)* होम–1. the place or a place where one lives घर, (स्व) गृह, निवास, परिवार *Home* is the best place to rest after a hard day's work.

2. a house or other dwelling आश्रम, केन्द्र When are returning *home* back?

3. the place where something is invented, founded, or developed मूल स्थान America is the *home* of baseball.

homeland *(n.)* होमलैंड– the country in which one lives or was born स्वदेश Immigrants often weep for their *homeland*.

homeless *(adj.)* होमलस– having no home बेघर Many people were *homeless* after the tragedy.

homely *(adj.)* होमलि– characteristic of or suited to the ordinary home; unpretentious घर जैसा, सीदा-सादा I felt very *homely* at my friend's house.

homeopathy *(n.)* होमिआपथी– a method of treating disease by the use of small amounts of a drug that, in healthy persons, produces symptoms similar to those of the disease being treated होमियोपैथी चिकित्सा *Homeopathy* is a new age medicine and have no side-effects.

homesick *(adj.)* होमसिक– depressed or melancholy at being away from home and family गृहासक्त I always feel *homesick* whenever I go back to the hostel.

homework *(n.)* होमवर्क– school work done out of lessons, esp at home गृहकार्य Why did you come to school without completing your *homework*?

homicide *(n.)* हॉमिसाइड– the killing of a human being by another person नरहत्या, मानवहत्या *Homicide* is not a crime when done in self-defence.

homogeneous *(adj.)* हॉमजीनिअस्– composed of similar or identical parts or elements सज़ातीय, एकसा It is impossible to find a perfect *homogeneous* society.

homosexual *(adj.)* होमॅसेक्शुअल– a person who is sexually attracted to members of the same sex समलैंगिक *Homosexual* relationships are increasing rapidly in the society.

honest *(adj.)* ऑनेस्ट्–1. not given to lying, cheating, stealing, etc.; trustworthy सत्यवादी, ईमानदार Just be *honest* if you want to save yourself.

2. not false or misleading; genuine सच्चा, सत्यनिष्ठ What is your *honest* opinion on the corruption in our society?

honesty *(n.)* ऑनेस्टी– sincerity or fairness ईमानदारी, सच्चाई Nobody can harm you if you maintain your *honesty*.

honestly *(adv.)* ऑनिस्टलि– in an honest manner वास्तव में, सच में *Honestly* speaking, I do not like him.

honey *(n.)* हनी– a sweet viscid substance made by bees from nectar and stored in their nests or hives as food. शहद, मधु Please give me a jar of *honey*.

honeymoon *(n.)* हनिमून– a holiday taken by a newly married couple प्रमोदकाल (विवाह के बाद) Where are you going for your *honeymoon?*

honk *(v.)* हौंक– to make or cause (something) to make such a sound भोंपू बजाना The car *honked* loudly.

honorary *(adj.)* ऑनररी– (esp of a position, title, etc.) held or given only as an honour, without the normal privileges or duties अवैतनिक Pradeep is the *honorary* president of the organisation.

honour *(n.)* ऑनर्–1. personal integrity; allegiance to moral principles प्रतिष्ठा, इज़्ज़त, ईमानदारी, सम्मान It is my *honour* to see you here.

2. a privilege or pleasure नैतिक रूप से उचित कार्य करने का गुण Will you give me your word of *honour*?

3. fame or glory उपाधि My friend's name has figured in this year's Republic Day *Honours* List.

4. *(v.)* to hold in respect or esteem सम्मान करना या देना He was *honoured* for his work with the mentally handicapped.

honourable *(adj.)* आनरबल– possessing or characterized by high principles सम्मान के योग्य, आदरणीय Lets welcome our *honourable* guest with a round of applause.

hood *(n.)* हुड–1. a loose head covering either attached to a cloak or coat or made as a separate garment टोप, शिरोवेष्टन I want to buy a raincoat with a *hood*.

2. the folding roof of a convertible car बरसाती These days you hardly see a car with a folding *hood*.

hoof *(n.)* हूफ़– the horny covering of the end of the foot in the horse, deer, and all other ungulate mammals खुर, टाप As the horseman approached, I could hear its *hoof*-beats.

hook *(v.)* हुक– 1. to catch (something, such as a fish) on a hook कंटिया से बाँधना/पकड़ना The fisherman sat all day on the river bank but *hooked* only three fish.

2. *(n.)* a piece of material, usually metal, curved or bent and used to suspend, catch, hold, or pull something काँटा, खूंटी Have you fixed a *hook* in the bathroom for hanging a towel?

hooligan *(n.)* हूलिगन– a rough lawless young person उपद्रवी The boys were behaving like *hooligans* on the Holi festival.

hoop *(n.)* हूप– a rigid circular band of metal or wood धातु या प्लास्टिक का बड़ा छल्ला Hang the towel in the metal *hoop*.

hoot *(v.)* हूट– to jeer or yell (something) contemptuously (at someone) शोर मचाना Some persons *hooted* in disgust.

hop *(v.)* हॉप–1. to make a jump forwards or upwards, esp on one foot कूदना, उछलना, फुदकना All the kids started *hoping* in the ground.

2. *(n.)* a trip, esp in an aircraft एक छोटी यात्रा, दौरा We flew from London to U.S.A. in one *hop*.

hope *(v.)* होप–1. to desire (something) with some possibility of fulfilment आशा करना I *hope* she will get well soon.

2. to trust, expect, or believe उम्मीद करना, भरोसा रखना I *hope* you will be able to come to my home this evening.

3. *(n.)* a feeling of desire for something and confidence in the possibility of its fulfilment आशा, उम्मीद *Hope* to see you tommorow.

hopeful *(adj.)* होपफुल– having or expressing hope आशापूर्ण I am quite *hopeful* that we will win.

hopefully *(adv.)* होपफुली– in a hopeful manner आशा है, उम्मीद है *Hopefully* he will come tomorrow.

hopeless *(adj.)* होपलेस– having or offering no hope निराशाजनक Your handwriting is *hopeless*.

horde *(n.)* हॉर्ड– a vast crowd; throng; mob भीड़, झुंड A *horde* of people arrived at the election booth.

horizon *(n.)* हराइज़न– the apparent line that divides the earth and the sky क्षितिज, दिगन्त, सीमा As we sat on the seashore, we saw a ship on the *horizon*.

horizontal *(adj.)* हॉरिज़ॉण्टल– parallel to the plane of the horizon; level; flat

समतल, क्षैतिज Draw a *horizontal* (as against vertical) line.

hormone *(n.)* हॉर्मोन– a chemical substance produced in an endocrine gland and transported in the blood to a certain tissue, on which it exerts a specific effect हारमोन (शरीर का विकास करने वाला तत्व) The changes in *hormone* levels occur during pregnancy.

horn *(n.)* हॉर्न–1. a device for producing a warning or signalling noise भोंपू, तुरही Don't blow your *horn* unnecessarily when you drive.
2. either of a pair of permanent outgrowths on the heads of cattle, antelopes, sheep, etc., consisting of a central bony core covered with layers of keratin सींग, शृंग The farmer painted his bullock's *horns*.

horoscope *(n.)* हॉरस्कोप– the prediction of a person's future based on a comparison of the zodiacal data for the time of birth with the data from the period under consideration जन्मकुंडली Their marriage was cancelled as the *horoscopes* did not match.

horrible *(adj.)* हॉरबल– disagreeable; unpleasant डरावना I can't forget that *horrible* incident in my whole life.

horrid *(n.)* हॉरिड– repulsive or frightening भयंकर, जघन्य, बुरा If you behave in such a *horrid* manner, no one will befriend you.

horrific *(adj.)* हॉरिफ़िक– provoking horror; horrible भयावह, अप्रिय I saw a breaking news about a *horrific* plane crash on T.V.

horrify *(v.)* हॉरिफ़ाई– to cause feelings of horror in; terrify; frighten दहला देना, भयभीत करना The train accident *horrified* the passengers.

horror *(n.)* हॉरर्– extreme fear; terror; dread डर, घृणा, वीभत्सता I stared in *horror* as the two cars collided.

horse *(n.)* हॉर्स– a large animal with four legs used for riding, pulling carriages, etc. घोड़ा I din't see any *horse* in the zoo.

hose *(n.)* होज़– a flexible pipe, for conveying a liquid or gas होज़, रबर का पाइप I require a long *hose* to water my garden.

hospitable *(adj.)* हास्पिटेबल– welcoming to guests or strangers मेहमाननवाज़, आतिथेय She is a *hospitable* lady and treats all her guests very well.

hospital *(n.)* हॉस्पिटल– an institution for the medical, surgical, obstetric, or psychiatric care and treatment of patients अस्पताल, चिकित्सालय She is admitted in which *hospital*?

hospitality *(n.)* हॉसपिटैलटी– kindness in welcoming strangers or guests अतिथि-सत्कार Thanks for your *hospitality* over the past few days.

host *(n.)* हॉस्ट–1. a person who receives or entertains guests, esp in his own home मेज़बान, मेहमानदार Our *host* at yesterday's party was very hospitable.
2. a great number; multitude झुंड, जमघट, भीड़, सेना A *host* of fan had besieged the film star.

hostel *(n.)* हॉस्टल– a building providing overnight accommodation, as for the homeless, etc. छात्रावास, सराय I am staying in this *hostel* since my childhood.

hostess *(n.)* हॉस्टस– a woman who receives and entertains patrons of a club, restaurant, etc. परिचारिका, महिला मेज़बान Frankfinn Institute provides training to air-*hostesses.*

hostile *(adj.)* होस्टाइल– antagonistic; opposed विरोधी, प्रतिकूल Why are you so *hostile* towards him?

hostility *(n.)* हॉस्टिलटी– enmity or antagonism बैर, शत्रुता, विद्वेष There is a lot of public *hostility* to the toll tax.

hot *(adj.)* हॉट–1. having a relatively high temperature गरम, उष्ण Give me a *hot* cup of tea.

2. causing or having a sensation of bodily heat चरपरा, तिक्त, तेज़ I do not like to eat *hot* things like pepper.

hotel *(n.)* होटे'ल– a commercially run establishment providing lodging and usually meals for guests, and often containing a public bar होटल I stayed for 5 nights in the *hotel*.

hound *(n.)* हाउन्ड– any of several breeds of dog used for hunting (शिकारी) कुत्ता Is your dog a *hound*?

hour *(n.)* आउर्– a period of time equal to 60 minutes, 1/24th of a calendar day घंटा I shall be back in a couple of *hours*.

hourly *(adv.)* आउर्ली– of, occurring, or done every hour प्रत्येक घंटे में This medicine has to be taken *hourly*.

house *(n.)* हाउस–1. a building used as a home; dwelling घर, मकान I will be more than happy if you come to see my new *house*.

2. an official deliberative or legislative body, such as one chamber of a bicameral legislature सदन Our Parliament has two *houses*.

household *(n.)* हाउसहोल्ड– all the people living together in one house collectively परिवार, कुटुम्ब, गृहस्थी How many people are there in this *household?*

housekeeping *(n.)* हाउसकीपिंग– the running of a household गृह-व्यवस्था The company is taking charge of the *housekeeping*.

house-to-house *(adj.)* हाउस-टू-हाउस– visiting all the houses in an area one after another घर-घर जाकर The police was making *house-to-house* enquiries.

housewife *(n.)* हाउसवाइफ़– a woman, typically a married woman, who keeps house, usually without having paid employment गृहिणी, घर में रहने वाली स्त्री She is a very responsible *housewife*.

housing *(n.)* हाउज़िंग– the people present in a house, esp its usual occupants घर, गृह These flats will provide *housing* for the immigrants.

hovel *(n.)* हॉवल– a dwelling place, made of grass and straw झोंपड़ी I was shocked to see the *hovel* in which the poor man lived.

hover *(v.)* हॉवर्–1. to remain suspended in one place मँडराना Excited children looked up as the helicopter *hovered* over our house.

2. to linger uncertainly in a nervous or solicitous way आगे-पीछे फिरना My children *hovered* around me in the expectation that I would tell them a story.

how *(adj.)* हाउ– in what way? in what manner? by what means? कैसे, किस तरह, क्यों *How* can you do this with me?

however *(conj.)* हाउएवर– still; nevertheless तथापि, फिर भी Amit will not get success *however* hard he tries.

howl *(v.)* हाउल– 1. (of the wind, etc.) to make a wailing noise चीखना The wind *howled,* so I could not hear the knock at the door.

2. *(n.)* a long plaintive cry or wail characteristic of a wolf or hound हुँआ, चीख At night, we heard the *howl* of the jackal.

hub *(n.)* हॅब–1. the central portion of a wheel, propeller, fan, etc., through which the axle passes पहिए या कार के बीच का हिस्सा I have bought decorative *hub-cups* for my car.

2. the focal point केन्द्र Mumbai is the *hub* of film industry.

hubbub *(n.)* हबब– a confused noise of many voices कोलाहल There was a real *hubbub* in the Parliament.

huddle *(v.)* हडल– 1. to crowd or cause to crowd or nestle closely together ठंड के कारण सटकर बैठना We *huddled* together under the blanket for warmth.

2. *(n.)* a heaped or crowded mass of people or things लोगों का जमघट, जमावड़ा They were standing in a *huddle* round the injured man.

hue *(n.)* ह्यू– a shade of a colour किसी रंग की विशेष छटा, वर्ण The sky was painted with bright *hues.*

hug *(n.)* हग– 1. a tight or fond embrace आलिंगन The mother gave the child a loving *hug.*

2. *(v.)* to clasp (another person or thing) tightly or (of two people) to cling close together; embrace आलिंगन करना, लिपटना I felt so relaxed the moment you *hugged* me.

huge *(adj.)* ह्यूज– extremely large in size, amount, or scope विशाल, बहुत बड़ा I have paid *huge* amount to you so I want it to be perfect now.

hull *(n.)* हल– the shell or pod of peas or beans; the outer covering of any fruit or seed; husk छिलका The *hulls* of oranges were thrown into the dustbin.

hullabaloo *(n.)* हलाबलू– loud confused noise, esp of protest; commotion शोरगुल, होहल्ला The teacher shouted to calm the *hullabaloo* in the classroom.

hum *(v.)* हम– 1. to make a low continuous vibrating sound like that of a prolonged गुनगुनाना, भिनभिनाना I *hummed* a tune while taking a bath.

2. *(n.)* a low continuous murmuring sound गुंजन, भिनभिनाहट The *hum* of the bees indicated the presence of a hive up in the tree.

human *(adj.)* ह्यूमन– 1. of, characterizing, or relating to man and mankind मानस, मानवीय, मानवोचित We are all *human* beings.

2. *(n.)* a human being; person मनुष्य, व्यक्ति The dog was so clever that he seemed almost *human.*

humanitarian *(adj.)* ह्यूमैनिटेरिअन– having the interests of mankind at heart लोकोपकारी He was released from the prison on *humanitarian* grounds.

humanity *(n.)* ह्यूमैनटी– kindness or mercy मानवता One should never leave *humanity* behind.

humble *(adj.)* हम्बल–1. unpretentious; lowly दीन-हीन, साधारण K.R. Narayanan rose from the *humble* beginnings to become the President of India.

2. conscious of one's failings विनीत, नम्र Rakhi is very *humble,* in spite of being rich.

humid *(adj.)* ह्यूमिड– moist; damp नम, सीलनभरा Kolkata is hot and *humid* in summer.

humiliate *(v.)* ह्यूमिलिएट– to lower or hurt the dignity or pride of नीचा दिखाना, अपमान करना He *humiliated* her infront of all family members.

humility *(n.)* ह्यूमिलिटी– the state or quality of being humble विनय, दीनता, नम्रता Your greatness lies in your *humility.*

humorous *(adj.)* ह्यूमरस– funny; comical; amusing विनोदी, मज़ाक़िया The columnist wrote a *humorous* piece of note for the magazine.

humour *(n.)* ह्यूमर्–1. the quality of being funny मज़ाक़, हास्य Your sense of *humour* is really good.

2. a state of mind; temper; mood मिज़ाज, मनोदशा Why are you in such a bad *humour*?

3. the ability to appreciate or express that which is humorous हास्यजनक Ramesh was so *humorous* that he had won a lottery prize.

hump *(n.)* हम्प– a rounded protuberance on the back of a camel or related animal कूबड़ The child asked, "How did the camel get that *hump*?"

hunch *(n.)* हञ्च– an intuitive guess or feeling अटकल, काल्पनिक सोच I have a *hunch* he will be late.

hunchback *(n.)* हन्चबैक– a person having an abnormal convex curvature of the thoracic spine कूबड़ निकला हुआ व्यक्ति A man who was having *hunchback* saved her life.

hundred *(adj.,n.)* हण्ड्रेड– the cardinal number that is the product of ten and ten; five score सौ Can you give me five *hundred* rupees for 2 days?

hunger *(n.)* हन्गार्–1. a feeling of pain, emptiness, or weakness induced by lack of food भूख, क्षुधा *Hunger* for food can easily be satisfied but not *hunger* for wealth.
2. *(v.)* to have or cause to have a need or craving for food भूखा होना, अत्यंत इच्छुक होना Why do you *hunger* so much for fame?

hungry *(adj.)* हंग्री– experiencing pain, weakness, or nausea through lack of food भूखा I can't resist now. I am so *hungry*.

hunk *(n.)* हंक– a large piece बड़ा टुकड़ा He gave a *hunk* of bread to the poor woman.

hunt *(v.)* हण्ट–1. to seek out and kill or capture (game or wild animals) for food or sport शिकार करना How many tigers have you *hunted*?
2. to look (for); search for खोज करना I *hunted* everywhere but could not find my book.
3. *(n.)* the act or an instance of hunting शिकार, तलाश Everyone joined in the *hunt* for the lost bag.

hunter *(n.)* हण्टर– a person or animal that seeks out and kills or captures game शिकारी There was a *hunter* in the woods.

hunting *(n.)* हण्टिंग– the pursuit and killing or capture of game and wild animals, regarded as a sport शिकार करने की क्रिया According to me *hunting* should be banned completely.

hurdle *(n.)* हर्डल– an obstacle to be overcome बाधा These are just temporary *hurdles*.

hurl *(v.)* हर्ल–1. to throw or propel with great force फेंकना, फेंककर मारना Don't *hurl* your books around carelessly.
2. to utter with force; yell जोर से चीखकर बेइज्जती करना Don't *hurl* baseless charges at me.

hurricane *(n.)* हरिकेन– a severe, often destructive storm, esp a tropical cyclone आंधी-तूफ़ान The *hurricane* broke many trees in the village.

hurried *(adj.)* हरिड– performed with great or excessive haste तुरंत, त्वरित This was a very *hurried* piece of work.

hurry *(n.)* हॅरी– 1. urgency or eagerness उतावली, जल्दी, उत्सुकता, हड़बड़ी You are always in a *hurry*.
2. *(v.)* to hasten (to do something); rush बहुत जल्दी चलना, फुर्ती करना As it was about to rain, the office goers *hurried* to their homes.

hurt *(n.)* हर्ट– 1. physical, moral, or mental pain or suffering चोट, हानि I got *hurt* when I was getting into the bus.
2. *(adj.)* injured or pained physically or emotionally दुःखी, घायल I felt *hurt* at his unkind remarks.
3. *(v.)* to produce a painful sensation in (someone) दुख देना, चोट पहुंचाना Please try not to *hurt* anybody.

husband *(n.)* हज़्बण्ड– a woman's partner in marriage पति, भर्ता My *husband* bought me this ring.

hush *(n.)* हश्– 1. stillness; silence चुप्पी, ख़ामोशी A *hush* came over the room.
2. *(v.)* to make or become silent; quieten चुप या शांत करना या कराना *Hush* now and don't wake the body.

hush-hush *(adj.)* हश-हश– a plea or demand for silence बहुत गोपनीय, गुप्त

Their wedding was a *hush-hush* affair.

husk *(n.)* हस्क– the external covering of grain, seeds, etc. भूसी, छिलका The grandmother separated *husk* from the rice grains.

husky *(adj.)* हस्कि– slightly hoarse or rasping भर्राई हुई (आवाज़) You sound *husky,* have you got cold?

hustle *(v.)* हसल– to shove or crowd (someone) roughly धकेलना People were *hustling* each other at the railway platform.

hut *(n.)* हॅट– a small house or shelter, usually made of wood or metal झोंपड़ी, कुटिया Our servant lives in a *hut* near our house.

hydrogen *(n.)* हाइड्रजन– a flammable colourless gas that is the lightest and most abundant element in the universe. एक रंगहीन गैस, हाइड्रोजन *Hydrogen* is the lightest fuel for passenger vehicle.

hygiene *(n.)* हाइजीन– the science concerned with the maintenance of health साफ़-सफ़ाई, स्वास्थ्य-विज्ञान Please take care of your health and *hygiene.*

hymn *(n.)* हिम– to express (praises, thanks, etc.) by singing hymns भजन, स्तोत्र Can you recite Sanskrit *hymns* correctly?

hype *(v.)* हाइप– 1. to stimulate artificially or excite बढ़ा-चढ़ाकर वर्णन करना The media *hyped* the movie greatly. 2. *(n.)* intensive or exaggerated publicity or sales promotion प्रचार, धुआंधार विज्ञापन Despite the media *hype,* the movie was a big flop.

hypnotize (ise) *(v.)* हिप्नटाइज़– to induce hypnosis in (a person) सम्मोहित करना The magician *hypnotized* the small girl.

hypocrisy *(n.)* हिपॉक्रसी– the practice of professing standards, beliefs, etc., contrary to one's real character or actual behaviour, esp the pretence of virtue and piety पाखंड Politicians emphasise on using Indian goods, while they themselves travel in foreign cars. This is the height of *hypocrisy*!

hypocrite *(n.)* हिपक्रिट– a person who pretends to be what he is not पाखंडी, ढोंगी Sometimes he behaves like an *hypocrite.*

hysterical *(adj.)* हिस्टेरिकल– suffering from hysteria उन्मादग्रस्त She was *hysterical* on hearing about her long lost son.

Ii

I i *(n.)* आई–अंग्रेज़ी वर्णमाला का नवां अक्षर The ninth letter of the English alphabet. Ice cream begins with 'I'.

i *(pron.)* आइ– refers to the speaker or writer मैं *I* would like to have coffee today.

ice *(n.)* आइस– water in the solid state, formed by freezing liquid water बर्फ़, हिम Please drop some *ice* cubes in my glass of water.

iceberg *(n.)* आइसबर्ग– a large mass of ice floating in the sea, esp a mass that has broken off a polar glacier पानी में तैरती हुई बर्फ़ की बड़ी चट्टान, हिमशैल B-15 is the world's largest *iceberg* which is 295 km long and 37 km wide.

ice cream *(n.)* आइसक्रीम– a kind of sweetened frozen liquid, properly made from cream and egg yolks but often made from milk or a custard base, flavoured in various ways आइसक्रीम, मलाई की बर्फ़ *Ice cream* is my favourite dessert.

icy *(adj.)* आइसि– made of, covered with, or containing ice बहुत ठंडा, बर्फ़ीला There is an *icy* wind blowing today.

icon *(n.)* आइकॉन–1. a pictorial representation of a facility available on a computer system, कंप्यूटर के स्क्रीन पर प्रोग्राम के लघुचित्र Suddenly the *icons* vanished from my computer.

2. a person or thing regarded as a symbol of a belief, nation, community, or cultural movement किसी वस्तु का प्रतीक She is the style *icon* of the college.

idea *(n.)* आइडिआ–1. the thought of something विचार, सुझाव What a good *idea*!

2. a scheme, intention, plan, etc. मत, धारणा How do you like the *idea* of going on a trip to Agra this Sunday?

3. an individual's conception of something उद्देश्य, प्रयोजन, कुछ करने का मक़सद The *idea* is to teach children to save money.

ideal *(adj.)* आइडिअल्– conforming to an ideal आदर्श, आदर्श (स्वरूप) काल्पनिक Amitabh Bachchan is my *ideal.*

idealize (ise) *(v.)* आइडीअलाइज– to portray as ideal; glorify आदर्श बनाना Children tend to *idealize* their parents.

ideally *(adv.)* आइडीअली– if you say that ideally a particular thing should happen or be done, you mean that this is what you would like to happen or be done, but you know that this may not be possible or practical आदर्श रूप से She is *ideally* suited for the job.

identical *(adj.)* आइडेन्टिकल– exactly alike, equal, or agreeing बिल्कुल समान This problem is *identical* to the one we faced last year.

identification *(n.)* आइडेण्टिफ़िकेश्न्– the act of identifying or the state of being identified पहचान, किसी चीज़ की शिनाख़्त *Identification* of these bodies is must.

identify *(v.)* आइडेण्टिफ़ाइ– to prove or recognize as being a certain person or thing; determine the identity of पहचानना, शिनाख़्त करना We want somebody who can *identify* these bodies.

identity *(n.)* आइडेंटिटी– the state of having unique identifying characteristics held by no other person or thing किसी वस्तु या व्यक्ति की पहचान I don't want to loose my own *identity.*

ideology *(n.)* आइडिऑलजि– a body of ideas that reflects the beliefs and interests of a nation, political system, etc. and underlies political action विचारधारा Different communities proclaims different *ideologies*.

idiom *(n.)* इडियम– a group of words whose meaning cannot be predicted from the meanings of the constituent words, मुहावरा Can you tell me the meaning of the *idiom* 'apple of the eye'?

idiomatic *(adj.)* इडिअमैटिक– (of language) grammatical and natural to native speakers of a language मुहावरेदार Vandana has the ability to write fluent and *idiomatic* English.

idiot *(n.)* इडिअट– a person with severe mental retardation मूर्ख, जड़बुद्धि Don't behave like an *idiot*.

idiosyncrasy *(n.)* इडिअसिन्क्रसी– a tendency, type of behaviour, mannerism, etc, of a specific person; quirk वज्रमूर्खता, सनक Drinking four glasses of warm water every morning is one of her *idiosyncrasy*.

idle *(adj.)* आइडल– unemployed or unoccupied; inactive बेकार, निकम्मा, आलसी Don't sit *idle*. Start your work if you are free.

idleness *(n.)* आइडलनस– the state of being unemployed, unoccupied, or inactive सुस्ती, ख़ालीपन Why do you waste your time in *idleness*?

idol *(n.)* आइडल– a material object, esp a carved image, that is worshipped as a God मूर्ति, बुत Who made the *idol* in this temple?

idolize (ise) *(v.)* आइडलाइज़्– to worship, admire or revere greatly की पूजा करना/आदर करना She *idolized* her elder brother.

idyllic *(adj.)* इडिलिक– charming; picturesque शांतप्रिय एवं मधुर, मनोरम Their honeymoon was *idyllic*.

if *(conj.)* इफ़–1. in case that, or on condition that अगर, यदि I will give you chocolates *if* you will come to meet me.

2. used to introduce an indirect question. In this sense, if approaches the meaning of whether कि, क्या Can you tell me the details, *if* you are taking a leave tomorrow?

3. used to introduce expressions of desire, विनम्रता के लिए प्रयुक्त Come this way, *if* you please.

ignite *(v.)* इग्नाइट्– to catch fire or set fire to; burn or cause to burn सुलगाना या सुलगना Strike a match and *ignite* the fire.

ignominious *(adj.)* इगनॉमिनिअस– humiliating नाम को बट्टा लगाने वाला, शर्मिंदा करने वाला This act was an *ignominious* end to his career.

ignorance *(n.)* इग्नरन्स– lack of knowledge, information, or education; the state of being ignorant अज्ञान, अनजानपन The reason for Amita's *ignorance* is that she pays no attention.

ignorant *(adj.)* इग्नरन्ट्– lacking in knowledge or education; unenlightened अनजान, अनभिज्ञ Don't be *ignorant*. I know you were aware of this fact.

ignore *(v.)* इग्नॉर्– to fail or refuse to notice; disregard उपेक्षा/अवहेलना करना I can't tolerate if you will *ignore* me like this.

ill *(adj.)* इल– not in good health; sick बीमार, अस्वस्थ She was seriously *ill* last week.

ill-feelling *(n.)* इल-फीलिंग– hostile feeling; animosity दुर्भावना I do hope you have no *ill-feeling* for me.

ill-treat *(v.)* इलट्रीट– to behave cruelly or harshly towards; misuse; maltreat दुर्व्यवहार करना If you *ill-treat* your servant, he will leave you soon.

illegal *(adj.)* इलीगल— forbidden by law; unlawful; illicit गैरकानूनी, अवैध It is *illegal* to possess a revolver without a licence.

illegality *(n.)* इलिगैलटी— the quality of being illegal अवैधता, ग़ैरक़ानूनी होना The court may correct an *illegality* of a sentence.

illegally *(adv.)* इलीगली— in an illegal manner गै़रकानूनी ढंग से Many Bangladeshis are living in Delhi *illegally*.

illegible *(adj.)* इलेजबल— unable to be read or deciphered अपाठ्य, अस्पष्ट The print on the old newspaper was quite *illegible*.

illegitimate *(adj.)* इल्लेजिटमेट— forbidden by law; illegal; unlawful अवैध, ग़ैरकानूनी, जारज It is *illegitimate* to use company's stationery as private.

ill-fated *(adj.)* इलफ़ेटड— doomed or unlucky अभागा, बदक़िस्मत Titanic was an *ill-fated* ship.

illicit *(adj.)* इलिसिट— not allowed or approved by common custom, rule, or standard अवैध, अनुचित She was having an *illicit* affair with her boss.

illiteracy *(n.)* इलिटॅरसी— the quality of being unable to read and write अशिक्षा India's *illiteracy* rate has improved.

illiterate *(adj.)* इलिटरट्— unable to read and write अनपढ़ Special classes are held in the nearby school for *illiterates*.

illness *(n.)* इलनस— a disease or indisposition; sickness बीमारी She is suffering from acute *illness*.

illogical *(adj.)* इलॉजिकल— characterized by lack of logic; senseless or unreasonable तर्कहीन Visiting Ladakh in the winters appeared an *illogical* idea to me.

illuminate *(v.)* इलूमिनेट— to throw light in or into; light up प्रदीप्त करना, प्रकाश डालना, समझाना The main bazaars and streets are *illuminated* on Diwali.

illumination *(n.)* इलूमिनेशन— spiritual or intellectual enlightenment; insight or understanding प्रबोधन, जगमगाहट, रोशनी Let us go to see the *illuminations* at the Rashtrapati Bhawan.

illusion *(n.)* इलूशॅन—1. a false appearance or deceptive impression of reality भ्रम, भ्रांति This line looks longer than the other, but it is an optical *illusion*.

2. a false or misleading perception or belief; delusion धोखा I was under this *illusion* that you don't know me.

illustrate *(v.)* इलस्ट्रेट— to clarify or explain by use of examples, analogy, etc. सचित्र करना, (उदाहरण देकर) स्पष्ट करना Books for children should be *illustrated* extensively.

illustrated *(adj.)* इलस्ट्रेटड— (of a book, text, etc.) decorated with or making use of pictures सचित्र, सोदाहरण I want to buy an *illustrated* storybook for my child.

illustration *(n.)* इलॅसट्रेशन— pictorial matter used to explain or decorate a text चित्र, उदाहरण I want to add some more *illustrations* in this book.

illustrious *(adj.)* इलॅसट्रिअस— of great renown; famous and distinguished प्रसिद्ध, सफ़ल Bharati has long and *illustrious* career in electronic media.

image *(n.)* इमिज—1. a representation or likeness of a person or thing, esp in sculpture चित्र, मूर्ति Have you seen the huge *image* at the Reserve Bank entrance?

2. an optically formed reproduction of an object, such as one formed by a lens or mirror प्रतिबिंब One can

see one's *image* in the clear water of a lake.

3. a person or thing that resembles another closely; double or copy प्रतिरूप, प्रतिकृति You are the very *image* of your father.

4. a mental representation or picture; idea produced by the imagination धारणा, कल्पना When we go abroad, we should always try to project a good *image* of India.

imaginable *(adj.)* इमैजिनबल— able to be imagined कल्पनीय These technologies were hardly *imaginable* twenty years ago.

imaginary *(adj.)* इमैजिनरी— existing in the imagination; unreal; illusory मनगढ़ंत, काल्पनिक Draw an *imaginary* scene in your mind and tell me how it looks.

imagination *(n.)* इमैजिनेशन— the faculty or action of producing ideas, esp mental images of what is not present or has not been experienced कल्पना, कल्पनाशक्ति He has got a very good *imagination* power.

imaginative *(adj.)* इमैजिनॅटिव— produced by or indicative of a vivid or creative imagination कल्पनाशील Kalidasa was one of India's most *imaginative* poets.

imagine *(v.)* इमैजिन—1. to form a mental image of, to think, believe, or guess कल्पना करना, सोचना She *imagines* that she is a wonderful singer.

2. to suppose; assume अनुमान करना, अटकल लगाना Can you *imagine* life without me?

imbalance *(n.)* इम्बैलन्स— a lack of balance, as in emphasis, proportion, etc. असंतुलन, विषमता An *imbalance* diet will keep you unfit .

imbecile *(n.)* इम्बसील्— an extremely stupid person; dolt मूढ़ व्यक्ति, अल्पमति My neighbour behaved like an *imbecile*.

imitate *(v.)* इमिटेट— to make a copy or reproduction of; duplicate; counterfeit अनुकरण/नकल करना She *imitates* her mother.

imitation *(n.)* इमिटेशन— an instance or product of imitating, such as a copy of the manner of a person; impression नक़ल, अनुकरण The lady was wearing a necklace of *imitation* pearls.

immaculate *(adj.)* इमैक्युलट—1. completely flawless, etc. त्रुटिहीन His *immaculate* stage performance was appreciating.

2. completely clean; extremely tidy साफ़-सुथरा, बेदाग She was wearing an *immaculate* light-blue jeans.

immaterial *(adj.)* इमटिअरिअल— of no real importance; inconsequential महत्त्वहीन When you die, it is *immaterial* what happens to your body.

immature *(adj.)* इमैच्युअर्—1. not fully grown or developed अपरिपक्व She delivered an *immature* baby.

2. deficient in maturity; lacking wisdom, insight, emotional stability, etc. नादानी भरा, बचकाना You should forgive his *immature* behaviour.

immediate *(adj.)* इमीजिअट—1. taking place or accomplished without delay तात्कालिक I want an *immediate* action to this complaint.

2. existing now निकटतम Please call the *immediate* relations of the victim fast.

immediately *(adv.)* इमीजिअटली— without delay or intervention; at once; instantly तुरंत, फ़ौरन Please look into this matter *immediately*.

immense *(adj.)* इमेन्स— unusually large; huge; vast अत्यधिक, विशाल People who travel by air spend an *immense* amount.

immensely *(adv.)* इमेंसलि— enormously or hugely बहुत ज़्यादा I liked this book *immensely*.

immerse *(v.)* इमर्स—1. to plunge or dip into liquid डुबाना The kid *immersed* the stick in water.
2. to involve deeply; engross पूरी तरह निमग्न/तल्लीन होना She is usually *immersed* in her studies.

immersion *(n.)* इमर्शन— a form of baptism in which part or the whole of a person's body is submerged in the water डुबकी, अवगाहन *Immersion* in cold water resulted in rapid loss of heat.

immigrant *(n.)* इमिग्रण्ट— a person who comes to a country in order to settle there आप्रवासी Saudi Arabia has a high *immigrant* population.

immigrate *(v.)* इमिग्रेट— to come to a place or country of which one is not a native in order to settle there आप्रवास करना, आकर बस जाना My brother *immigrated* to this country from Canada.

imminent *(adj.)* इमिनण्ट— liable to happen soon; impending शीघ्र होने वाली अप्रिय घटना, सन्निकट An Indo-Pakistan war is *imminent*.

immobile *(adj.)* इमोबाइल— not moving; motionless गतिहीन, अचल I was standing *immobile* by the window.

immobilize (ise) *(v.)* इमोबलाइज़— to make or become immobile स्थिर बना देना Heavy snowfall *immobilized* the traffic.

immoral *(adj.)* इमॉरल— transgressing accepted moral rules; corrupt अनैतिक Don't be so *immoral* that people will start disliking you.

immortal *(adj.)* इमॉर्टल— not subject to death or decay; having perpetual life अमर, अनश्वर Nobody is *immortal* except God.

immune *(adj.)* इम्यून—1. protected against a specific disease by inoculation or as the result of innate or acquired resistance अप्रभावित Naresh is *immune* to every type of criticism.
2. unsusceptible (to) or secure (against) प्रतिरक्षित, असंक्राम्य I am *immune* to measles.

immunity *(n.)* इम्यूनटी— ability of an organism to resist disease, (रोग से बचाव), प्रतिरक्षा My *immunity* is stronger than you.

immunize (ise) *(v.)* इम्युनाइज़— to make immune, esp by inoculation प्रतिरक्षित करना There is still no vaccine to *immunize* people against the dengue virus.

impact *(n.)* इम्पैक्ट— the act of one body, object, etc., striking another; collision संघात, टक्कर You can't even imagine what is going to be the *impact* of this.

impair *(v.)* इम्पेऑर— to reduce or weaken in strength, quality, etc. कमज़ोर कर देना The illness has *impaired* her ability to concentrate on studies.

impart *(v.)* इम्पार्ट— to communicate (information); relate प्रदान करना The newspapers *impart* information in detail.

impartial *(adj.)* इम्पार्शल— not prejudiced towards or against any particular side or party; fair; unbiased निष्पक्ष One should be *impartial* while judging.

impassioned *(adj.)* इम्पैशण्ड— filled with passion; fiery; inflamed भावपूर्ण, जोशीला Saba delivered an *impassioned* speech.

impatient *(adj.)* इम्पेशण्ट— lacking patience; easily irritated at delay, opposition, etc अधीर, बेचैन Have faith in God and don't be so *impatient*.

impeach *(v.)* इम्पीच— to bring a charge or accusation against लांछन लगाना, दोषारोपण करना The man was *impeached* for the charge of dowry.

impeccable *(adj.)* इम्पेकबल्— without flaw or error; faultless त्रुटिहीन Konkona Sen's performance in Page 3 was *impeccable*.

impede *(v.)* इम्पीड– to restrict or retard in action, progress, etc; hinder; obstruct रोकना, अड़ंगा लगाना He *impeded* me in an awkward situation.

imperative *(adj.)* इम्पेरॅटिव– extremely urgent or important; essential आवश्यक It is *imperative* that you file your tax returns soon.

imperfect *(adj.)* इम्परफ़िक्ट– exhibiting or characterized by faults, mistakes, etc.; defective सदोष, अधूरा I don't like *imperfect* arrangements.

impersonal *(adj.)* इम्पर्सनल– without reference to any individual person; objective अवैयक्तिक, भाववाचक Business letters should not be written in an *impersonal* tone.

impertinence *(n.)* इम्पर्टिनन्स– disrespectful behaviour or language; rudeness; insolence धृष्टता, ढिठाई He must be punished for his *impertinence.*

impertinent *(adj.)* इम्पर्टिनेण्ट– rude; insolent; impudent ढीठ, गुस्ताख़, अनुचित, धृष्ट, उद्धत You must talk to your son about his *impertinent* behaviour.

impetus *(n.)* इम्पिटस– an impelling movement or force; incentive or impulse; stimulus प्रेरक-शक्ति, संवेग The tsunami campaign gained *impetus* with the association of celebrities.

implausible *(adj.)* इम्प्लॉसिबल– not plausible; provoking disbelief; unlikely अविश्वसनीय He gave an *implausible* excuse to his boss.

implement *(n.)* इम्प्लिमेण्ट– 1. a piece of equipment; tool or utensil औज़ार, उपकरण Do you have some *implement* to open this jammed lock? 2. *(v.)* to carry out; put into action; perform कार्यान्वित करना, लागू करना When are you going to *implement* these plans.

implicate *(v.)* इम्प्लिकेट– to involve as a necessary inference; imply उलझना, फँसाना She was falsely *implicated* in the controversy.

implicit *(adj.)* इम्प्लिसिट– absolute and unreserved; unquestioning अप्रत्यक्ष, अस्पष्ट The issues that might affect the working of the company in future were *implicit* in his argument.

imply *(v.)* इम्प्लाई– to express or indicate by a hint; suggest बिना कुछ कहे संकेत करना Are you *implying* that I am a liar.

impolite *(adj.)* इम्पोलाइट– discourteous; rude; uncivil अभद्र I felt so bad that she was so *impolite* with my mom.

import *(n.)* इम्पॉर्ट– 1. goods (visible imports) or services (invisible imports) that are bought from foreign countries आयात How are you doing in your export-*import* business?
2. *(v.)* to buy or bring in (goods or services) from a foreign country आयात करना Wool is *imported* from Australia.

importance *(n.)* इम्पॉर्टन्स– the state of being important; significance अहमियत, महत्त्व When will you realize the *importance* of getting married?

important *(adj.)* इम्पॉर्टन्ट– of great significance or value; outstanding महत्त्वपूर्ण I saw many *important* personalities at the club meeting.

impose *(v.)* इम्पोज़– to establish as something to be obeyed or complied with; enforce आरोपित करना, थोपना Our boss never *imposes* himself on anyone.

impossibility *(n.)* इम्पॉसिबिलटी– something that is impossible असंभवता Is there any *impossibility* in this work?

impossible *(adj.)* इम्पॉसिबल्– incapable of being done, undertaken, or experienced असंभव Walking such a long distance is completely *impossible* for me.

impossibly *(adv.)* इम्पॉसबली— in a way which is incapable of being done, undertaken, or experienced नामुमकिन, असंभव I was caught in an *impossibly* difficult problem.

impotent *(adj.)* इम्पटन्ट— (esp of males) unable to perform sexual intercourse नामर्द, नपुंसक He could not marry because he is *impotent.*

impracticable *(adj.)* इम्प्रैक्टिकॅबल— incapable of being put into practice or accomplished; not feasible अव्यावहारिक Your plan is possible but quite *impracticable.*

impractical *(adj.)* इम्प्रैक्टिकल— not practical or workable जिस पर अमल न हो सके, असाध्य One should not be so *impracticle.*

impress *(v.)* इम्प्रेस—1. to make an impression on; have a strong, lasting, or favourable effect on छाप लगाना, प्रभावित करना I was very much *impressed* by the artist's personality. 2. to stress (something to a person); urge; emphasize प्रभाव डालना He *impressed* on me the value of learning Sanskrit.

impression *(n.)* इम्प्रेशन— an effect produced in the mind by a stimulus; sensation छाप, प्रभाव, ठप्पा First *impression* is the last *impression.*

impressive *(adj.)* इम्प्रेसिव— capable of impressing, esp by size, magnificence, etc.; awe-inspiring; commanding आकर्षक, प्रभावकारी He has a very *impressive* personality.

imprint *(n.)* इम्प्रिण्ट— a mark or impression produced by pressure, printing, or stamping निशान, चिह्न, छापा We saw an *imprint* of an animal foot in the sand.

imprison *(v.)* इम्प्रिज़न— to confine in or as if in prison क़ैद करना, बन्दी बनाना I hear the manager of your firm has been *imprisoned* on charges of misappropriation of funds.

imprisonment *(n.)* इम्प्रिज़न्मेण्ट— the state of being imprisoned क़ैद, कारावास His *imprisonment* lasted for one year.

impromptu *(adj.)* इम्प्रॉम्प्ट्यू— unrehearsed; spontaneous; extempore बिना तैयारी के किया गया, तत्काल She won the first prize in the *impromptu* debate competition.

improper *(adj.)* इम्प्रॉपर्— lacking propriety; not seemly or fitting अनुपयुक्त, अनुचित I feel it is *improper* to sign a new project until we complete the previous ones.

improve *(v.)* इम्प्रूव—1. to make or become better in quality; ameliorate सुधरना या सुधारना I think you need to *improve* on your language part. 2. to achieve a better standard or quality in comparison (with) उन्नति करना Is your son's health *improving* now?

improvement *(n.)* इम्प्रूवमेण्ट— the act of improving or the state of being improved सुधार, उन्नति, समृद्धि I can't see any *improvement* in your work since last week.

impudent *(adj.)* इम्प्यूडेण्ट— mischievous, impertinent, or disrespectful गुस्ताख़, निर्लज्ज, ढीठ She was *impudent* enough to call me an emotional fool.

impulse *(n.)* इम्पल्स— a sudden desire, whim, or inclination आवेग, आवेश On a generous *impulse,* Manoj gave his wrist watch to his friend.

impulsively *(adv.)* इमपलसिवली— in a manner based on sudden desires, whims, or inclinations rather than careful thought आवेग़पूर्वक, मौज में आकर If you act *impulsively* now, you may have to regret later.

impure *(adj.)* इम्प्युअर्— not pure; combined with something else; tainted or sullied अशुद्ध The water in this region is highly *impure.*

impurity *(n.)* इम्प्युअरटी– the quality of being impure अशुद्धता, मैलापन, गन्दगी This milk contains *impurities.*

in *(prep.)* इन–1. inside; within भीतर, अन्दर Please come *in.*
2. at a place where there is उपस्थित Is the boss *in*?
3. concerned or involved with, esp as an occupation में Is your brother *in* the Navy?
4. indicating a state, situation, or condition (स्थिति) में I don't want to go out *in* the dark. Don't talk *in* such a loud voice.

inability *(n.)* इनअबिलटी– lack of ability or means; incapacity अयोग्यता, अकुशलता I felt bad when she expressed her *inability* to do this job.

inaccessible *(adj.)* इनैक्सेसबल– not accessible; unapproachable पहुंच से परे, अगम The village was *inaccessible* in the rainy season.

inaccurate *(adj.)* इनऐकयूरट– not accurate; imprecise, inexact, or erroneous अशुद्ध, ग़लत She gave me an *inaccurate* information about him.

inactive *(adj.)* इनऐकटिव– idle or inert; not active आलसी, सुस्त, चुप I remained *inactive* the whole day due to fever.

inadequate *(adj.)* इनऐडिक्वट– not adequate; insufficient अपर्याप्त, नाकाफ़ी The poor man's clothing was *inadequate* on such a cold day.

inadvertently *(adv.)* इनडवर्टेण्टली– in a careless or inattentive manner अनजाने में, लापरवाही से Kamran's name was *inadvertently* omitted from the list.

inane *(adj.)* इनेन्– senseless, unimaginative, or empty; unintelligent निरर्थक Let's not waste our time in this *inane* discussion.

inanimate *(adj.)* इनऐनिमेट्– lacking the qualities or features of living beings; not animate निर्जीव, जड़ The stone is an *inanimate* object.

inapt *(adj.)* इनऐप्ट– not apt or fitting; inappropriate अनुपयुक्त, अनुचित What an *inapt* question has been asked by him.

inappropriate *(adj.)* इनअप्रोप्रिअट– not fitting or appropriate; unsuitable or untimely अनुचित, अनुपयुक्त I feel this dress is *inappropriate* for the occasion.

inasmuch as *(conj.)* इनएज़्मच एज़्– in view of the fact that; seeing that; since जहां तक कि, क्योंकि, चूंकि I'll help you *inasmuch as* it is within my power.

inattentive *(adj.)* इनअटेन्टिव– not paying attention; heedless; negligent असावधान, बेख़बर He was so *inattentive* in class that is why he scored less.

inaugurate *(v.)* इनॉग्यरेट– to commence officially or formally; initiate उद्घाटन करना My new house will be *inaugurated* next week.

inauspicious *(adj.)* इनॉस्पिशस्– not auspicious; unlucky अशुभ, अमंगल It would be an *inauspicious* step to go to his house.

inborn *(adj.)* इन्बॉर्न– existing from birth; congenital; innate जन्मजात Ragini has an *inborn* talent for music and dance.

incapable *(adj)* इनकेपबल– not capable (of); lacking the ability (to) असमर्थ, अयोग्य I am sorry I was *incapable* of doing your work .

incarnation *(n.)* इन्कार्नेशन– a bodily form assumed by God, etc. अवतार Krishna was an *incarnation* of Lord Vishnu.

incense *(n.)* इन्सेन्स– any of various aromatic substances burnt for their fragrant odour, esp in religious ceremonies अगरबत्ती, धूप I lighted the *incense* sticks to make the room fragrant.

incentive *(n.)* इन्सेन्टिव— a motivating influence; stimulus प्रोत्साहन देने वाली वस्तु We get separate *incentives* for working late in the office.

incessant *(adj.)* इन्सेसण्ट— not ceasing; continual निरंतर The *incessant* rainstorm made me cancel my trip.

inch *(n.)* इंच— a unit of length equal to one twelfth of a foot or 2.54 centimetres एक फुट का बारहवां भाग Amitabh Bachchan is six feet and two *inches* in height.

incident *(n.)* इन्सिडण्ट— a distinct or definite occurrence; event घटना, प्रसंग I can't forget that *incident* in my whole life.

incidental *(adj.)* इन्सिडेंटल— happening in connection with or resulting from something more important; casual or fortuitous आकस्मिक, प्रासंगिक Drinking too much is almost *incidental* to bartending.

incinerate *(v.)* इन्सिनरेट— to burn up completely; reduce to ashes भस्म कर देना, जलाकर राख कर देना We should *incinerate* rubbish.

incisive *(adj.)* इन्साइसिव— keen, penetrating, or acute तेज़, धारदार, तीक्ष्ण I was hurt at his *incisive* criticism.

incite *(v.)* इन्साइट— to stir up or provoke to action भड़काना, उकसाना He *incited* the crowd into violence.

incline *(v.)* इन्क्लाइन— to deviate or cause to deviate from a particular plane, esp a vertical or horizontal plane; slope or slant झुकाव होना, टेढ़ा होना, झुकना He *inclined* the pot to drain out the water.

inclined *(adj.)* इन्क्लाइण्ड—1. having a disposition; tending प्रवृत्त, प्रवण I am *inclined* to accept your argument. 2. sloping or slanting ढलुआ होना, ढलान होना The roof was slightly *inclined* to allow the rain to run off.

include *(v.)* इन्क्लूड— to add as part of something else; put in as part of a set, group, or category सम्मिलित करना, (में) लगा देना Don't *include* these items in the bill.

including *(prep.)* इन्क्लूडिंग— used to introduce examples of people or things that are part of the group of people or things that you are talking about समेत, इसको लेकर, इसके साथ The total bill was Rs. 750 *including* tax.

inclusive *(adj.)* इन्क्लूसिव— considered together (with) शामिल करते हुए The charges of electricity and water are *inclusive* in the rent.

incoherent *(adj.)* इन्कोहिअॅरन्ट— unable to express oneself clearly; inarticulate अंडबंड, बेमेल, असंबद्ध Amit was in a state of shock, sobbing and *incoherent.*

income *(n.)* इन्कम— the amount of monetary or other returns, either earned or unearned, accruing over a given period of time आय, आमदनी What is your monthly *income*?

income tax *(n.)* इन्कम टैक्स— a personal tax, usually progressive, levied on annual income subject to certain deductions आयकर How much *income tax* did you pay this year?

incoming *(adj.)* इन्कमिंग— coming in; entering आने वाला, आवक Both my *incoming* and outgoing calls have been blocked.

incomparable *(adj.)* इन्कॉमपरबल— beyond or above comparison; matchless; unequalled अतुलनीय, बेजोड़ At last she succeeded due to her *incomparable* patience.

incompatible *(adj.)* इन्कम्पैटबल— incapable of living or existing together in peace or harmony; conflicting or antagonistic असंगत, बेमेल I share an *incompatible* relation with Ram.

incompetent *(adj.)* इन्कॉमपिटन्ट— not possessing the necessary ability, skill, etc. to do or carry out a task;

incapable अयोग्य, अक्षम Anushka is an *incompetent* government teacher.

incomplete *(adj.)* इनकॅम्प्लीट—अधूरा, not complete or finished अपूर्ण, अधूरा Don't submit your *incomplete* homework again.

incomprehensible *(adj.)* इनकामप्रिहेन-सबल— incapable of being understood; unintelligible जो समझ में न आ सके, अबोधगम्य This book is *incomprehensible* to me, for it is too hard.

inconceivable *(adj.)* इनकनसीवबल— incapable of being conceived, imagined, or considered कल्पनातीत, अकल्पित It is *inconceivable* that you were not aware of the conflicts.

incongruous *(adj.)* इनकांग्रुअस— incompatible with (what is suitable); inappropriate बेमेल, बेतुका Such old traditions are *incongruous* in our modern lifestyle.

inconsiderate *(adj.)* इन्कंसिडरेट— lacking in care or thought for others; heedless; thoughtless निष्ठुर, बेमुख्वत, दूसरों का ख्याल न रखने वाला I am fed up of his *inconsiderate* behaviour at home.

inconsistent *(adj.)* इन्‌कंसिस्‌टन्ट— lacking in consistency, agreement, or compatibility; at variance विरोधी, बेमेल Don't give *inconsistent* staement again and again.

inconspicuous *(adj.)* इनकॉस्पिक्युअस— not easily noticed or seen; not prominent or striking अप्रत्यक्ष, जो आसानी से न दिखे Our new neighbour is trying to make himself as *inconspicuous* as possible.

inconvenience *(n.)* इनकनवीनिअन्स— the state or quality of being inconvenient कष्ट, असुविधा I am sorry for the *inconvenience* caused by the delay of flight.

inconvenient *(adj.)* इनकनवीनिअन्ट— not convenient; troublesome, awkward, or difficult असुविधाजनक, तकलीफ़देह It was so *inconvenient* to go out in such traffic jam.

incorporate *(v.)* इनकॉर्पोरेट— to include or be included as a part or member of a united whole समाविष्ट करना, मिलाना Sohan *incorporated* his friend's letter in his new book.

incorrect *(adj.)* इनकरेक्ट— false; wrong ग़लत, अशुद्ध All the answers you gave were *incorrect*.

increase *(v.)* इन्क्रीज़—1. to make or become greater in size, degree, frequency, etc.; to grow or expand वृद्धि करना, बढ़ोतरी करना I have *increased* my secretary's salary.
2. *(n.)* the amount by which something increases बढ़ोत्तरी, वृद्धि I am expecting an *increase* in my salary.

increasingly *(adv.)* इंक्रीसिंगली— to an ever increasing extent लगातार बढ़ते हुए It is becoming *increasingly* clear that he will not play the game.

incredible *(adj.)* इन्क्रेडिबल— beyond belief or understanding; unbelievable अविश्वसनीय, अतुल्य Her performance was *incredible* and outstanding.

increment *(n.)* इंक्रीमन्ट— an increase or addition, esp one of a series वेतन-वृद्धि, वृद्धि I am expecting some *increment* this month.

incurable *(adj.)* इनक्युअरबल— (esp of a disease) not curable; unresponsive to treatment लाइलाज, असाध्य She is suffering from an *incurable* disease.

indebted *(adj.)* इन्‌डेटिड्— owing gratitude for help, favours, etc.; obligated कृतज्ञ I am greatly *indebted* to you for all your help.

indecent *(adj.)* इन्डीसन्ट— offensive to standards of decency, esp in sexual matters अनुचित, अश्लील, अभद्र Her *indecent* behaviour gave her so many enemies.

indecision *(n.)* इन्डिसिश़न– inability to decide; indecisiveness अनिश्चय, असमंजस, हिचकिचाहट I am in a state of *indecision* as to resign from the job or not.

indecisive *(adj.)* इन्डिसाइसिव– (of a person) vacillating; irresolute अनिश्चित, ढुलमुल, दुविधापूर्ण His *indecisive* nature is really worrying me.

indeed *(adv.)* इन्डीड– certainly; actually सचमुच, अवश्य ही I am *indeed* very glad to see you.

indefinite *(adj.)* इन्डेफ़िनट्– not certain or determined; unsettled अनियत, असीमित The university was closed for an *indefinite* period.

indefinitely *(adv.)* इन्डेफ़िनटलि– without any limit of time or number अनिश्चित काल तक The Director cancelled the meeting *indefinitely.*

indemnify *(n.)* इन्डेम्निफ़ाई– a sum of money that is given as payment for damage or loss क्षतिपूर्ति, हरजाना Please *indemnify* us against all legal fees, damages and other expenses.

indent *(v.)* इन्डेंट– to make a dent or depression in टेढ़ा-मेढ़ा काटना या कटा होना, दाँतेदार बनाना The sea *indents* the coastline.

independence *(n.)* इन्डिपेंडन्स– the state or quality of being *independent* स्वतंत्रता, आजादी We should celebrate our *independence* with zeal and enthusiasm.

independent *(adj.)* इन्डिपेंडन्ट– 1. free from control in action, judgment, etc.; autonomous स्वतंत्र, स्वाधीन The property Rahul has inherited has made him *independent.*

2. capable of acting for oneself or on one's own स्वावलंबी I like your *independent* attitude.

indescribable *(adj.)* इन्डिस्क्राइबबल– beyond description; too intense, extreme, etc., for words अवर्णनीय, वर्णनातीत The beauty of Ajanta and Ellora is *indescribable.*

index *(n.)* इन्डेक्स– an alphabetical list of persons, places, subjects, etc., mentioned in the text of a printed work, usually at the back, and indicating where in the work they are referred to तालिका, सूची, अनुक्रमणिका I would like to see the *index* before finalizing the book.

index finger *(n.)* इन्डेक्स-फ़िंगर– the finger next to the thumb (अंगूठे के पास की उंगली) तर्जनी My *index finger* was injured while I was driving.

indian *(n.)* इंडिअन– a native, citizen or inhabitant of the Republic of India भारतीय She was looking so beautiful in her *Indian* dress.

indicate *(v.)* इन्डिकेट– to point out or show दिखाना, बताना, सूचित करना She *indicated* her consent to the marriage proposal.

indication *(n.)* इन्डिकेशन– something that serves to indicate or suggest; sign संकेत, लक्षण Dark green leaves are a good *indication* of healthy roots.

indict *(v.)* इन्डाइट– to charge (a person) with crime, esp formally in writing; accuse इल्ज़ाम लगाना, दोषी ठहराना The police *indicted* the man on the charge of rioting.

indifferenoc *(n.)* इन्डिफ़ॅरन्स– the fact or state of being indifferent; lack of care or concorn उदासीनता, विमुखता I told him the whole story but he showed complete *indifference.*

indifferent *(adj.)* इन्डिफ़रन्ट– no care or concern; uninterested उदासीन, तटस्थ, महत्त्वहीन Her *indifferent* attitude hurt him a lot.

indigestible *(adj.)* इन्डिजेसटबल्– incapable of being digested or difficult to digest अपचनीय, अपाच्य This food is *indigestible* for me.

indigestion *(n.)* इन्डिजेस्चन– difficulty in digesting food, accompanied by abdominal pain, heartburn and belching बदहज़मी, अपच She has been ill from *indigestion* since her childhood.

indignant *(adj.)* इन्डिग्नण्ट— feeling or showing indignation रुष्ट, क्रुद्ध Rohit was *indignant* when he was blamed for a mistake.

indignity *(n.)* इन्डिग्निटि— injury to one's self-esteem or dignity; humiliation अनादर, अपमान She was treated with *indignity*.

indigo *(n.)* इन्डिगो— a blue vat dye originally obtained from plants but now made synthetically नील He was using *indigo* in whitewashing of the fence.

indirect *(adj.)* इन्डरेक्ट— not straight-forward, open, or fair; devious or evasive अप्रत्यक्ष, घुमाव-फिराव वाला Neha gave an *indirect* answer to his question.

indiscretion *(n.)* इंडिस्क्रेशन— the characteristic or state of being indiscreet अविवेक, अविचार It was a moment of *indiscretion* when he slapped you.

indiscriminate *(adj.)* इंडिस्क्रिमिनट— lacking discrimination or careful choice; random or promiscuous लापरवाह, बिना सोचे-समझे Don't be *indiscriminate* while starting up any new project.

indispose *(v.)* इंडिस्पोज़— to make unwilling or opposed; disincline अनुपयुक्त बनाना The boxing match *indisposed* me for further activities.

indisposed *(adj.)* इंडिस्पोज़्ड— sick or ill अस्वस्थ, अनिच्छुक Seema will play the game tomorrow as Rama is *indisposed*.

indisputable *(adj.)* इंडिस्प्यूटबल— beyond doubt; not open to question दोषमुक्त, निर्विवाद This property is *indisputable*, so you can buy it.

indisputably *(adv.)* इंडिस्प्यूटबली— in a way that is beyond doubt; in a way that is not open to question निश्चित रूप से She is *indisputably* the best person I have ever met.

indistinct *(adj.)* इन्डिस्टिंक्ट— incapable of being clearly distinguished, as by the eyes, ears, or mind; not distinct अस्पष्ट Her writing was *indistinct* to read.

indistinguishable *(adj.)* इन्डिस्टिंग्वि- identical or very similar (to) जिसका दूसरे से अंतर न पता चले, अविवेच्य His words are *indistinguishable* to his actions.

individual *(adj.)* इन्डिविजुअल— 1. of, relating to, characteristic of, or meant for a single person or thing व्यक्तिगत Everybody has there own *individual* style of working.
2. *(n.)* a single person, esp when regarded as distinct from others व्यक्ति Isn't Mr. Prasad a pleasant *individual*?

individuality *(n.)* इन्डिविजुऐलटि— distinctive or unique character or personality व्यक्तित्व, पृथक अस्तित्व You should show your *individuality* to him.

individually *(adv.)* इन्डिविजुअलि— separately or distinctly rather than along with others of its kind एक-एक करके, व्यक्तिगत रूप से Five of us were called into the room *individually* by the principal.

indivisible *(adj.)* इन्डिविजिबल— unable to be divided अविभाज्य, जिसके टुकड़े न हो सकें Work and leisure are *indivisible* for me.

indoor *(adj.)* इन्डोर— of, situated in, or appropriate to the inside of a house or other building घर के अंदर होने वाले, घरेलू Kids enjoy *indoor* games more than outdoor ones.

induce *(v.)* इन्ड्यूस— to persuade or influence sb फुसलाना, राज़ी करना Ram could not *induce* Anwar to accompany him to the cinema.

inducement *(n.)* इन्ड्यूसमन्ट– a means of inducing; persuasion; incentive प्रलोभन, लालच What *inducement* can I offer to make you keep quiet?

induction *(n.)* इन्डक्शन– a formal introduction or entry into an office or position आगमन, अधिष्ठापन They are celebrating an *induction* day for new students.

indulge *(v.)* इन्डल्ज्– to yield to or gratify (a whim or desire for) मौज-मस्ती के लिए किसी काम में लिप्त होना I don't want you to *indulge* yourself in any sort of stupid thing.

indulgence *(n.)* इन्डलजन्स– the act of indulging or state of being indulgent लिप्त, प्रवृत्त I know about his *indulgence* in many illegal activities.

industrial *(adj.)* इन्डॅस्ट्रिअल– of, relating to, derived from, or characteristic of industry औद्योगिक I have purchased a shed in the *industrial* estate.

industrious *(adj.)* इन्डॅस्ट्रिअस– hard-working, diligent, or assiduous परिश्रम, मेहनती To succeed in you career, you should be as *industrious* as an ant.

industry *(n.)* इन्डस्ट्री– organized economic activity concerned with manufacture, extraction and processing of raw materials, or construction उद्योग, उद्योग-धंधा After agriculture, *industry* is the second largest employer of the workforce.

inedible *(adj.)* इनएडॅबल– not fit to be eaten; uneatable जो खाने योग्य न हो, अखाद्य Rotten fruits are *inedible* and injurious to health.

ineffective *(adj.)* इनिफ़ेक्टिव– having no effect बेअसर, निष्फल, बेकार The new drug was *ineffective* for the patient.

inefficient *(adj.)* इनिफ़िशन्ट– unable to perform a task or function to the best advantage; wasteful or incompetent अकुशल, अक्षम She is an *inefficient* secretary of this corporate house.

ineligible *(adj.)* इनएलिज़बल– of an infinitive, not fit or qualified अयोग्य, अपात्र, अनुपयुक्त Sahil is *ineligible* for this job because he is only graduate.

inequality *(n.)* इनिक्वॉलटि– the state or quality of being unequal; disparity असमानता, भेदभाव, पक्षपात Great *inequalities* in wealth causes social unrest.

inevitable *(adj.)* इनएविटबल– sure to happen; certain जिससे बचा न जा सके, अपरिहार्य It was an *inevitable* consequence of the decision taken by the government.

inexpensive *(adj.)* इनिक्सपेन्सिव– not expensive; cheap सस्ता We stayed in a relatively *inexpensive* hotel.

inexperience *(n.)* इनिक्सपीरिअन्स– lack of experience or of the knowledge and understanding derived from experience नातजुर्बेकार, अनाड़ी You are *inexperinced* for this responsibility.

infamous *(adj.)* इन्फ़ॅमस– having a bad reputation; notorious बदनाम This area is *infamous* for illegal activites.

infancy *(n.)* इनफ़न्सि– the state or period of being an infant; childhood शिशु की प्रारंभिक अवस्था, बचपन Many children die in *infancy*.

infant *(n.)* इन्फ़न्ट– a child at the earliest stage of its life; baby नवजात शिशु, बालक The *infants* are fed on only milk for a few months.

infatuated *(adj.)* इनफ़ै च्युएटिड– possessed by a foolish or extravagant passion, esp for another person मुग्ध, मोहित, सम्मोहित She was completely *infatuated* with an old man.

infect *(v.)* इन्फ़ेक्ट– to cause infection in; contaminate (an organism, wound, etc) with pathogenic microorganisms संदूषित/संक्रमित करना You were *infected* with typhoid by drinking polluted water.

infection *(n.)* इन्फ़ेक्शन– an agent or influence that infects संक्रमण, रोग-संचार He is suffering from throat *infection* since last 3 days.

inferior *(adj.)* इन्फ़िअरिअर्– lower in value or quality घटिया, निकृष्ट, निचला I don't want to buy the *inferior* quality rice this time also.

inferiority complex *(n.)* इन्फिअरिअरटि a disorder arising from the conflict between the desire to be noticed and the fear of being humiliated, characterized by aggressiveness or withdrawal into oneself हीन भावना Mahi is suffering from *inferiority complex* since last few years.

infertile *(adj.)* इन्फ़र्टाइल– not capable of producing offspring; sterile अनुपजाऊ, बंजर Since the land is *infertile* so I will not pay huge amount for this.

infidelity *(n.)* इन्फ़िडेलटि– lack of faith or constancy, esp sexual faithfulness विश्वासघात, बेवफ़ाई *Infidelity* in women can never be praised.

infiltrate *(v.)* इनफ़िलट्रेट– to undergo or cause to undergo the process in which a fluid passes into the pores or interstices of a solid; permeate छनकर प्रवेश करना, छनना The water *infiltrates* from the filter.

infinite *(adj.)* इन्फ़िनट– having no limits or boundaries in time, space, extent, or magnitude असीमित, अंतहीन We should seek for the God's *infinite* mercy.

infinitely *(adv.)* इन्फ़िनटलि– much; to a great degree बहुत अधिक This office is *infinitely* better than the last one.

infinity *(n.)* इनफ़िनटि– endless time, space, or quantity अनंतता, अपार The landscape seemed to stretch into *infinity*.

inflammable *(adj.)* इनफ़्लैमबल– liable to catch fire; flammable ज्वलनशील LPG is highly *inflammable*.

inflammation *(n.)* इनफ़्लमेशन्– the reaction of living tissue to injury or infection, characterized by heat, redness, swelling, and pain सूजन, शोथ This cream will help to reduce *inflammation* on your skin.

inflate *(v.)* इन्फ़्लेट– to expand or cause to expand by filling with gas or air फूलना या फुलाना, हवा भरना I *inflated* the balloons and decorated the room with them.

inflect *(v.)* इनफ़्लेक्ट– to change (the form of a word) or (of a word), to change in form by inflection शब्दों को घटा-बढ़ा कर बोलना, विभक्ति चलाना The hostess *inflected* her voice more to hold the attention of the audience.

inflict *(v.)* इन्फ़्लिक्ट– to impose (something unwelcome, such as pain, oneself, etc.) लगाना, मढ़ना, जबरदस्ती थोपना Your hasty decision has *inflicted* a big loss on the company.

influence *(n.)* इन्फ़्लुअन्स– 1. the power of a person or thing to have such an effect प्रभाव, असर Nobody can *influence* me so easily.
2. *(v.)* to have an effect upon (actions, events, etc.); affect असर डालना, प्रभावित करना My mother has *influenced* me greatly.

influential *(adj.)* इनफ़्लुएंशल– having or exerting influence असरदार, प्रभावशाली She is one of the most *influential* figures in the government.

inform *(v.)* इन्फ़ॉर्म– to give information to; tell सूचित करना, जानकारी देना Why did you not *inform* me that you were not well?

information *(n.)* इन्फ़र्मेशन— knowledge acquired through experience or study जानकारी, सूचना, इत्तला Can you give me some *information* about your company?

informal *(adj.)* इन्फ़ॉर्मल— not of a formal, official, or stiffly conventional nature अनौपचारिक Is it going to be an *informal* meeting today?

informed *(adj.)* इनफ़ॉर्मड— having much knowledge or education; learned or cultured जानकार, ज्ञाता We should be well *informed* of the current affairs.

infrastructure *(n.)* इनफ़्रस्टक्चर— the basic structure of an organization, system, etc. आवश्यक बुनियादी ढांचा The economic *infrastructure* of the industry is changed.

infringe *(v.)* इन्फ्रिंज— to violate or break (a law, an agreement, etc.) उल्लंघन करना Do not *infringe* on other's privacy.

infuriate *(v.)* इनफ़्युअरिएट— to anger; annoy किसी को बहुत गुस्सा दिला देना, भड़काना His indifferent attitude *infuriated* her more.

ingenuous *(adj.)* इन्जेनयुअस— naive, artless, or innocent निष्कपट, सच्चा, सरल One should always be *ingenuous* in nature.

ingratitude *(n.)* इन्ग्रैटिट्यूड— lack of gratitude; ungratefulness; thanklessness अकृतज्ञता, अहसान-फ़रामोशी I felt hurt by his *ingratitude*.

ingredient *(n.)* इन्ग्रीडिअन्ट— a component of a mixture, compound, etc., esp in cooking घटक, तत्व, अवयव Can you tell me the *ingredients* you have used in this dessert.

inhabit *(v.)* इनहैबिट— to live or dwell in; occupy बसना, रहना The Gorkhas *inhabit* this valley.

inhale *(v.)* इन्हेल— to draw (breath) into the lungs; breathe in सांस लेना We should *inhale* deep into the lungs.

inherent *(adj.)* इन्हिअरण्ट— existing as an inseparable part; intrinsic पैदाइशी, अंतर्निहित Dancing and singing are her *inherent* qualities.

inheritance *(n.)* इन्हेरिटन्स— hereditary succession to an estate, title, etc. विरासत, उत्तराधिकार They imposed *inheritance* tax on his property.

inherit *(v.)* इन्हेरिट—1. to receive (property, a right, title, etc.) by succession or under a will (धन-संपत्ति) उत्तराधिकार में प्राप्त करना She *inherited* a large amount of money from her rich uncle. 2. to possess (a characteristic) through genetic transmission (रक्त-संबंध से) अपने पूर्वजों पर जाना Reena is *inherited with* her mother's good looks.

inhibit *(v.)* इन्हिबिट— to restrain or hinder (an impulse, a desire, etc.) प्रतिबंध लगाना The people were *inhibited* from feeding the animals in the zoo.

inhospitable *(adj.)* इन्हॉस्पिटबल— not hospitable; unfriendly असत्कारशील We left his house because of his *inhospitable* behaviour.

inhuman *(adj.)* इनह्यूमन— lacking humane feelings, such as sympathy, understanding, etc.; cruel; brutal अमानुषिक, बर्बर The prisoners were given *Inhuman* treatment.

inhumane *(adj.)* इनह्यूमेन— treating people in a cruel way अमानवीय, दयारहित Hitler imposed many *inhumane* laws.

inhumanity *(n.)* इनह्यूमैनटि— lack of humane qualities निर्ममता, क्रूरता We can see man's *inhumanity* to man these days.

initial *(adj.)* इनिशल— 1. of, at, or concerning the beginning आरंभिक, प्राथमिक My *initial* days in this house were very bad. 2. *(n.)* the first letter of a word, esp a person's name हस्ताक्षर, प्रथम अक्षर

Put your *initials* on the cheque at the right place.

initiate *(v.)* इनिशिएट— to begin or originate आरंभ करना After remaining silent for a long time, she finally *initiated* the talk.

initiative *(n.)* इनिशएटिव— the first step or action of a matter; commencing move पहल, सूत्रपात I always take the first *initiative* to participate in these activities.

inject *(v.)* इन्जेक्ट— to introduce (a fluid) into (the body of a person or animal) by means of a syringe or similar instrumen सुई लगाना He is *injecting* himself with drugs since the age of 17.

injection *(n.)* इन्जेक्शन— fluid injected into the body, esp for medicinal purposes सुई, सिरिंज, टीकाकरण Doctor gave her 3 *injections* one after the other.

injure *(v.)* इन्जर्— to cause physical or mental harm or suffering to; hurt or wound चोट या हानि पहुंचाना I don't want to *injure* you for anything.

injured *(adj.)* इन्जर्ड— hurt or wounded घायल My left leg was *injured* while driving.

injury *(n.)* इन्जरि— physical damage or hurt चोट, घाव She fell down from the rickshaw and got serious *injury*.

injustice *(n.)* इन्जस्टिस— the condition or practice of being unjust or unfair अन्याय *Injustice* is simply not aceptable to me.

ink *(n.)* इन्क— a fluid or paste used for printing, writing, and drawing स्याही There is no *ink* in your fountain pen.

inland *(adj.)* इनलेंड— of, concerning, or located in the interior of a country or region away from a sea or border अंतर्देशी, देशीय Much of the *inland* part of India is plain.

in-laws *(n.)* इन'लॉज़— the parents of your husband or wife पति या पत्नी के संबंधी My in-laws always take care of me so well.

inmate *(n.)* इन्मेट— a person who is confined to an institution such as a prison or hospital संवासी, साथ में रहने वाला All the *inmates* were asleep when robbers entered the house.

inn *(n.)* इन्— a pub or small hotel providing food and accommodation सराय The quality of food was good in that *inn*.

innate *(adj.)* इनेट— existing in a person or animal from birth; congenital; inborn जन्मजात, स्वाभाविक She has an *innate* ability to dance.

inner *(adj.)* इनर— being or located further inside भीतरी, अंदरूनी, अंदर का The *inner* circle was decorated with lights.

innermost *(adj.)* इनर्मोस्ट— being or located furthest within; central अंतरतम We should never share our *innermost* feelings with anyone.

innings *(n.)* इनिंग्ज़— the batting turn of a player or team पारी, पाली I could see only two *innings* of the match.

innocence *(n.)* इनोसन्स— the quality or state of being innocent निर्दोष, भोला Is there any doubt about their child's *innocence*?

innocent *(adj.)* इनोसन्ट— not corrupted or tainted with evil or unpleasant emotion; sinless; pure निरपराध, निष्पाप, बेगुनाह You have nothing to fear if you are *innocent*.

innovate *(v.)* इनॅवेट— to invent or begin to apply (methods, ideas, etc.) नवीनता लाना, नया ढंग निकालना I am trying o *innovate* something new for the cover.

innovation *(n.)* इनवेशन— something newly introduced, such as a new method or device नवपरिवर्तन I could not find any *innovation* in his plan.

innumerable *(adj.)* इन्यूमरबल— so many as to be uncountable; extremely numerous असंख्य, अनगिनत *Innumerable* tiny creatures live in the ocean.

inoffensive *(adj.)* इनूफ़ेनूसिव— not giving offence; unobjectionable आपत्तिहीन The director made an *inoffensive* remark on his secretary.

input *(n.)* इनूपुट— the act of putting in निवेश I can't see any *inputs* in this project from your side .

inquiry (Enquiry) *(v.)* इनूक्वाइअरी— 1. a request for information; a question पूछताछ, दरियाफ्त Let us *inquiry* about the arrival time of the train.
2. *(n.)* an investigation, esp a formal one conducted into a matter of public concern by a body constituted for that purpose by a government, local authority, or other organization जांच, खोज, पूछताछ The police conducted an *inquiry* into the bank robbery.

inquisitive *(adj.)* इनक्विज़िटिव— excessively curious, esp about the affairs of others; prying प्रश्नशील, जानने का अति इच्छुक होने वाला Mahima is too *inquisitive* to know about my personal life.

insane *(adj.)* इन्‌सेन— mentally deranged; crazy; of unsound mind पागल The *insane* man was taken to the mental hospital.

insatiable *(adj.)* इनसेशबल— not able to be satisfied or satiated; greedy or unappeasable अतिलालची, अतिलोभी I have an *insatiable* desire to gain more knowledge.

inscribe *(v.)* इन्‌स्क्राइब— to make, carve, or engrave (writing, letters, a design, etc.) on (a surface such as wood, stone, or paper) लिखना, खोजना I *inscribed* my father's name on my book.

inscription *(n.)* इन्‌स्क्रिप्शन— something inscribed, esp words carved or engraved on a coin, tomb, etc. शिला-लेख The *inscriptions* were written on a stone outside of the gate.

insect *(n.)* इनूसेक्ट— any small creature having a body divided into head, thorax, and abdomen, three pairs of legs, and (in most species) two pairs of wings. कीड़ा-मकोड़ा I don't want to see any *insect* on my table.

insecure *(adj.)* इनसिक्योर— anxious or afraid; not confident or certain असुरक्षित, अरक्षित She felt *insecure* after her husband's death.

insecurity *(n.)* इनूसिक्योरटी— anxiety or fear; lack of confidence or certainty असुरक्षा She remains serious due to her job *insecurity.*

insensitive *(adj.)* इनूसेनूसटिव— lacking physical sensation संवेदनाशून्य Bina is *insensitive* to any type of criticism.

insert *(v.)* इनूसर्ट— to put in or between; introduce घुसेड़ना, निविष्ट करना I *inserted* a key into the lock but it did not open.

inside *(prep.)* इनसाइड— the interior; inner or enclosed part or surface अन्दर who all are there *inside* the room?.

insight *(n.)* इनूसाइट— the ability to perceive clearly or deeply; penetration गहन जानकारी The movie provides an *insight* into the lives of celebrities.

insignificant *(adj.)* इनूसिग्निफ़िकण्ट— having little or no importance; trifling निरर्थक, तुच्छ It was such an *insignificant* topic of the discussion.

insincere *(adj.)* इनूसिंसिअर— lacking sincerity; hypocritical बेवफ़ा, कपटी, अविश्वसनीय *Insincere* people can never be regarded.

insist *(v.)* इनूसिस्ट— to express a convinced belief (in) or assertion (of) आग्रह करना I really don't want to go. Please don't *insist* me.

insistent *(adj.)* इन्सिस्टन्ट– making continual and persistent demands आग्रहपूर्ण, हठी, ज़िद्दी I heard the *insistent* demand of the child for more toys.

inspect *(v.)* इन्स्पेक्ट– to examine closely, esp for faults or errors जांच करना The police *inspected* the house to get some clues.

inspection *(n.)* इन्स्पेक्शन– a close examining of something, esp for faults or errors जांच, मुआयना The *inspection* of the school was made in the morning hours.

inspiration *(n.)* इन्सपरेशन– stimulation or arousal of the mind, feelings, etc., to special or unusual activity or creativity प्रेरणा From where did you get the *inspiration* of doing this?

inspire *(v.)* इन्स्पाइअर्– to exert a stimulating or beneficial effect upon (a person); animate or invigorate प्रेरित करना He claims to be *inspired* by Sachin Tendulkar.

install *(v.)* इन्स्टॉल– to place (machinery, equipment, etc.) in position and connect and adjust for use लगाना, रखना, स्थापित करना What will it cost me to *install* an air-conditioner in my bedroom?

installation *(n.)* इन्स्टॅलेशन– the act of installing or the state of being installed प्रतिष्ठापन Have you included the *installation* charges in the bill.

instalment *(n.)* इन्स्टॉलमेण्ट– one of the portions, usually equal, into which a debt is divided for payment at specified intervals over a fixed period क़िस्त Arun bought the new car on *instalments.*

instance *(n.)* इन्स्टन्स– a case or particular example उदाहरण, मिसाल Can you relate any *instance* to this incident.

instant *(n.)* इन्स्टण्ट– 1. a very brief time; moment क्षण The *instant* I opened the window, I saw you coming slowly.
2. *(adj.)* immediate; instantaneous तुरंत That tablet gave Sheela *instant* relief from headache.

instantly *(adv.)* इन्स्टन्टलि– immediately; at once तुरंत, झटपट This mixture can make idlies *instantly.*

instead *(adv.)* इन्स्टेड– as a replacement, substitute, or alternative के स्थान पर, के बदले में Why do you take coffee all the time? Have some milk *instead.*

instigate *(v.)* इनस्टिगेट– to bring about, as by incitement or urging भड़काना, उकसाना She *instigated* me against him.

instinct *(n.)* इन्स्टिंक्ट– the innate capacity of an animal to respond to a given stimulus in a relatively fixed way स्वाभाविक/नैसर्गिक वृत्ति Just go by your *instinct,* everything will be fine.

institute *(n.)* इन्स्टिट्यूट– 1. an organization founded for particular work, such as education, promotion of the arts, or scientific research संस्थान, पीठ, संस्था, प्रतिष्ठान From which *institute* have you completed your MBA.
2. *(v.)* to organize; establish प्रारंभ करना, स्थापित करना An inquiry was *instituted* to investigate against the minister.

instruct *(v.)* इन्स्ट्रक्ट– 1. to teach (someone) how to do (something) शिक्षा देना, सिखलाना The handicraft master *instructed* the girls in weaving.
2. *(v.)* to direct to do something; order आदेश, सूचना देना Please *instruct* Vikas Varma to come to my office at 11 o'clock.

instruction *(n.)* इन्स्ट्रक्शन– a direction; order निर्देश, आदेश Have you read the *instructions* carefully.

instructor *(n.)* इन्स्ट्रक्टर– someone who instructs; teacher प्रशिक्षक,

निदेशक Who is the physical *instructor* at your school?

instrument *(n.)* इन्स्ट्रुमन्ट– a mechanical implement or tool, esp one used for precision work उपकरण, यन्त्र I lost my bag of music *instruments.*

insufficient *(adj.)* इनसफ़िशन्ट– not sufficient; inadequate or deficient नाकाफ़ी, थोड़ा, कम The rainfall was *insufficient* for the crops last year.

insult *(n.)* इन्सल्ट– 1. an offensive or contemptuous remark or action; affront; slight अपमान, अनादर Nobody will tolerate this kind of *insult* in the office.
2. *(v.)* to treat, mention, or speak to rudely; offend; affront किसी का अपमान या तिरस्कार करना How can you *insult* anybody like this?

insulted *(adj.)* इन्सल्टेड– offended बेइज़्ज़त I felt *insulted* when he did not return my greetings.

insulting *(adj.)* इन्सल्टिंग– offensive अपमानजनक It was so *insulting* that I could not stand it even for a minute.

insurance *(n.)* इन्शॉरंस– the act, system, or business of providing financial protection for property, life, health, etc. बीमा I am planning to buy a life *insurance* policy.

insure *(v.)* इन्शॉर– to guarantee or protect (against risk, loss, etc.) बीमा कराना या करना They *insured* me against accidents.

intact *(adj.)* इन्टैक्ट– untouched or unimpaired; left complete or perfect सही सलामत, साबुत, सम्पूर्ण I am going to keep my savings *intact* for future.

integrity *(n.)* इन्टेग्रटि– adherence to moral principles; honesty ईमानदारी, अखंडता, संपूर्णता All Indians should maintain unity and *integrity* of the country.

intellect *(n.)* इन्टलेक्ट– the capacity for understanding, thinking, and reasoning, as distinct from feeling or wishing बुद्धि, प्रतिभा Rabindranath Tagore was a person of great *intellect.*

intellectual *(adj.)* इन्टलेक्चुअल– 1. of or relating to the intellect, as opposed to the emotions बौद्धिक I feel happy in the company of *intellectual* people.
2. *(n.)* a person who enjoys mental activity and has highly developed tastes in art, literature, etc. चिंतक, बुद्धिजीवी *Intellectuals* think differently from the ordinary people.

intelligence *(n.)* इन्टेलिजन्स–1. the capacity for understanding; ability to perceive and comprehend meaning बुद्धि, समझ You are a man of great *intelligence.*
2. military information about enemies, spies, etc. गुप्त सूचना The police passed on the *intelligence* about the terrorist's movements to the army.

intelligent *(adj.)* इन्टेलिजन्ट– having or indicating intelligence बुद्धिमान, होशियार, अक़्लमंद I find her daughter really *intelligent.*

intend *(v.)* इन्टेन्ड– to propose or plan (something or to do something); have in mind; mean योजना बनाना, इरादा रखना Do you *intend* to spend the whole weakend there?

intense *(adj.)* इन्टेंस– of extreme force, strength, degree, or amount तीव्र, प्रचण्ड, उत्तेजित, भावप्रवण There was *intense* cold in Shimla.

intensely *(adv.)* इन्टेंसलि– extremely तीव्रता से, बहुत अधिक Rahul's grandmother dislikes non-veg food *intensely.*

intention *(n.)* इन्टेन्शन– a purpose or goal; aim इरादा, मंशा, अभिप्राय I really had no *intensions* to hurt you.

interaction *(n.)* इन्टएेक्शन– a mutual or reciprocal action or influence पारस्परिक क्रिया I had nice *interaction* with her today.

interconnect *(v.)* इन्टर्कनेक्ट– to relate well अंतःसम्बन्ध करना/होना We are *interconnected* with each-other with the help of network.

interdependent *(adj.)* इन्टर्डिपेंडन्ट– relating to two or more people or things dependent on each other एक-दूसरे पर निर्भर, अन्योन्याश्रित SAARC countries are *interdependent* nations.

interest *(n.)* इन्ट्रेस्ट–1. the sense of curiosity about or concern with something or someone रुचि, अभिरुचि, दिलचस्पी I really don't have any *interest* in this game.

2. a charge for the use of credit or borrowed money ब्याज, सूद How much *interest* are you paying to the bank?

3. *(v.)* to arouse or excite the curiosity or concern of किसी चीज़ के प्रति रुचि उत्पन्न करना I am not *interested* in gossip.

interesting *(adj.)* इन्ट्रेसटिंग– inspiring interest; absorbing दिलचस्प, रोचक The movie was *interesting* very much.

interfere *(v.)* इन्टरफ़िअर्– to interpose, esp meddlesomely or unwarrantedly; intervene दख़ल देना, बाधा डालना I will highly appretiate if you won't *interfere* in my work.

interference *(n.)* इन्टरफ़िअरन्स– the act or an instance of interfering दख़लअंदाज़ी, हस्तक्षेप I don't want any sort of *interference* in my project.

interior *(adj.)* इन्टिअरिअर्– of, situated on, or suitable for the inside; inner भीतरी, आंतरिक The *interior* walls were decorated with colourful carvings.

intern *(n.)* इंटर्न– a student or new graduate who is getting experience in a job नया स्नातक She worked in the hospital as an *intern* for six months.

internal *(adj.)* इन्टर्नल– situated within, affecting, or relating to the inside of the body अन्दरूनी, आन्तरिक Have you completed the *internal* audit of your firm?

international *(adj.)* इन्टरनैशनल– of, concerning, or involving two or more nations or nationalities अंतर्राष्ट्रीय I will be going for an *international* tour very soon.

interpret *(v.)* इंन्टर्प्रिट– to clarify or explain the meaning of; elucidate समझना, अर्थ लगाना, द्विभाषिया का काम करना Can you *interpret* Russian into Hindi?

interpretation *(n.)* इन्टर्प्रिटेशन– the act or process of interpreting or explaining; elucidation व्याख्या, भाषांतरण I could not understand the *interpretation* of the whole story.

interrogate *(v.)* इन्टेरॅगेट– to ask questions (of), esp to question (a witness in court, spy, etc.) closely सख़्ती से पूछताछ करना The police spent many hours *interrogating* the prisoner.

interrupt *(v.)* इन्टरप्ट– to break the continuity of (an action, event, etc.) or hinder (a person) by intrusion हस्तक्षेप करना, बाधा डालना Amit's illness *interrupted* his studies.

interruption *(n.)* इन्टरप्शन– something that interrupts, such as a comment, question, or action बाधा, रुकावट There was a short *interruption* in the play.

interval *(n.)* इन्टर्वल– the period of time marked off by or between two events, instants, etc. मध्यांतर, अन्तराल what are your *interval* timings?

intervene *(v.)* इन्टरवीन– to take a decisive or intrusive role (in) in order to modify or determine events or their outcome हस्तक्षेप करना She *intervened* an easy solution to the problem.

interview *(n.)* इन्टर्व्यू–1. a formal discussion, esp one in which an employer assesses an applicant for a job साक्षात्कार How was your *interview* with the manager?

2. a conversation with or questioning of a person, usually conducted for television, radio, or a newspaper मुलाक़ात, भेंट The paper carried a report on the Prime Minister's *interview.*

3. *(v.)* to conduct an interview with (someone) साक्षात्कार करना The journalist *interviewed* many celebrities together.

intimacy *(n.)* इन्टिमसी– close or warm friendship or understanding; personal relationship निकट संबंध, घनिष्ठता Arun has a close *intimacy* with Rakesh.

intimate *(adj.)* इन्टिमट– 1. characterized by a close or warm personal relationship अंतरंग, घनिष्ठ, जिगरी I saw her getting *intimate* with him.

2. *(v.)* to hint; suggest सूचना देना, संकेत करना Will you *intimate* me the time of your arrival?

intimidate *(v.)* इन्टिमिडेट्– to make timid or frightened; scare डराना या धमकाना I was *intimidated* by the unknown person following me.

into *(prep.)* इन्टू– to the interior or inner parts of अंदर, किसी ओर, किसी दिशा में We were walking *into* the garden.

intolerable *(adj.)* इन्टॉलरबल– more than can be tolerated or endured; insufferable जो सहा न जा सके, असहनीय Any sort of insult is highly *intolerable.*

intonation *(n.)* इन्टॅनेशन– the sound pattern of phrases and sentences produced by pitch variation in the voice बोलने की आवाज़ में उतार-चढ़ाव Her *intonation* was difficult to understand.

intoxicated *(adj.)* इनटॉक्सिकेटिड–1. drunk मदहोश, नशे में, मदहोशी में Rohan was *intoxicated* by her beauty.

2. excited; extremely stimulated बहुत खुश एवं रोमांचित I was *intoxicated* with my success in boards.

intricate *(adj.)* इन्ट्रिकट– difficult to understand; obscure; complex; puzzling जटिल, पेचीदा Extracting silk from a silkworm is an *intricate* process.

intrigue *(n.)* इन्ट्रीग– 1. the act or an instance of secret plotting, षड्यंत्र, साजिश The movie was full of thrill and *intrigue.*

2. *(v.)* to make interested or curious जिज्ञासा उत्पन्न करना He was quite *intrigued* by the news.

introduce *(v.)* इन्ट्रोड्यूस– to present (someone) by name (to another person) or (two or more people to each other) परिचय कराना/देना Come I will *introduce* you to my boss.

introduction *(n.)* इन्ट्रोडक्शन–1. the act of making one person formally known to another परिचय A brief *introduction* of everyone will be highly appreciated.

2. the first part of a book or speech भूमिका Mr. Sahni gave a brief *introduction* to the course.

introvert *(n.)* इन्ट्रवर्ट– a person prone to introversion अंतर्मुखी He is quite *introvert* in nature.

intrude *(v.)* इन्ट्रूड– to put forward or interpose (oneself, one's views, something) abruptly or without invitation घुसपैठ करना The media apologised for *intruding* the actor's privacy.

intruder *(n.)* इन्ट्रूडर– a person who enters a building, grounds, etc., without permission घुसपैठिया The *intruders* were sent to the jail immediately.

intrusion *(n.)* इन्ट्रूशन– the act or an instance of intruding; an unwelcome visit, interjection, etc. अनाधिकार प्रवेश, घुसपैठ The Prime Minister said that *intrusion* can not be tolerated.

intuition *(n.)* इण्टयुइशन– knowledge or belief obtained neither by reason nor by perception अंतःप्रज्ञा, सहजबुद्धि, अंतर्बोध I'm having a strong *intuition* that we will win this match.

invade *(v.)* इन्वेड– to enter (a country, territory, etc.) by military force आक्रमण करना The Mughals *invaded* the Rajput kingdoms.

invalid *(adj.)* इन्वैलिड–1. not legally अवैध, नाजायज अमान्य Without your signature, this cheque is *invalid*.
2. meaningless तर्कहीन You gave an *invalid* argument to me.
3. *(n.)* a person suffering from disablement or chronic ill health लम्बे समय से बीमार व्यक्ति, रोगी, अशक्त His father has been an *invalid* for the last five years.

invaluable *(adj.)* इन्वैल्युअबल– having great value that is impossible to calculate; priceless अनमोल The advice that you gave me was *invaluable*.

invariably *(adv.)* इनवेरिअबलि– always; without exception सदा, निरपवाद रूप से I *invariably* go for a stroll after dinner.

invent *(v.)* इन्वेण्ट–1. to create or devise (new ideas, machines, etc.) आविष्कार करना The gramophone was *invented* by Edison.
2. to make up (falsehoods); fabricate गढ़ना, कल्पना करना I could not *invent* any excuse in 2 minutes.

invention *(n.)* इन्वेन्शन– the act or process of inventing आविष्कार, खोज, ईजाद The telephone is a useful *invention*.

invert *(v.)* इन्वर्ट– to turn or cause to turn upside down or inside out रुख़ बदलना, उलटना, दिशा बदलना The theme was *inverted* in the animation movie.

invest *(v.)* इन्वेस्ट–1. to lay out (money or capital in an enterprise, esp by purchasing shares) with the expectation of profit धन का निवेश करना I would like to *invest* in property this time.
2. to devote (effort, resources, etc., to a project) समय या शक्ति लगाना Are you ready to *invest* another year in your struggle?

investigate *(v.)* इन्वेस्टिगेट– to inquire into (a situation or problem, esp a crime or death) thoroughly; examine systematically, esp in order to discover the truth अनुसंधान करना, जाँच-पड़ताल करना The police *investigated* the cause of the fire accident.

investigation *(n.)* इन्वेस्टिगेशन– the act or process of investigating; a careful search or examination in order to discover facts, etc. जांच-पड़ताल, छानबीन The *investigation* into the case is in progress.

investment *(n.)* इन्वेस्टमेण्ट– the act of investing money पूंजी-निवेश I am expecting good from my *investment*.

invisible *(adj.)* इन्विज़बल– not visible; not able to be perceived by the eye लुप्त, जो दिखाई न पड़े The kite was *invisible* to my eyes.

invite *(v.)* इन्वाइट– to ask (a person or persons) in a friendly or polite way (to do something, attend an event, etc.) निमंत्रण देना, बुलाना Is he *invited* in the party?

invitation *(n.)* इन्विटेशन– the act of inviting, such as an offer of entertainment or hospitality निमंत्रण, न्यौता Did you receive her *invitation*?

inviting *(adj.)* इन्वाइटिंग– tempting; alluring; attractive आकर्षक, मोहक The pool looked so *inviting* that we went for a swim.

invoice *(n.)* इनवॉइस– a document issued by a seller to a buyer listing the goods or services supplied and stating the sum of money due बीजक, सामान या सेवाओं का ब्यौरा या सूची I have lost the *invoice* of my expenses.

involve *(v.)* इन्वॉल्व– to include or contain as a necessary part उलझना, संबंधित होना, सहभागी होना I don't want to *involve* myself in any political activity.

involved *(adj.)* इन्वॉल्व्ड– complicated; difficult to comprehend दुर्भेद्य, जटिल, उलझा हुआ No I was not *involved* in this crime.

involvement *(n.)* इन्वॉल्वमन्ट– the fact of taking part in something उलझाव, फंसाव, ग्रस्तता My *involvement* in this project was not that important.

inward *(adj.)* इनवर्ड– going or directed towards the middle of or into something भीतरी, आंतरिक, मन के अंदर *Inward* happiness can never be hidden.

inwardly *(adv.)* इनवर्डली– within the private thoughts or feelings; secretly मन ही मन में, अंदर से She was *inwardly* happy when she got promoted.

iodine *(n.)* आइअडीन– a bluish-black element of the halogen group that sublimates into a violet irritating gas. आयोडीन *Iodine* is good for thyroid gland.

irk *(v.)* अर्क– to irritate, vex, or annoy कष्ट देना, खिझाना It *irks* me to go outside in summer.

iron *(n.)* आइरन्– 1. a hard metal that is used to make steel लोहा I want to buy an *iron* almirah.

2. *(v.)* to smooth (clothes or fabric) by removing (creases or wrinkles) using a heated iron; press इस्तरी करना Why din't you *iron* your shirt?

ironic *(adj.)* आइरॉनिक– of, characterized by, or using irony व्यंग्यात्मक It is *ironic* that Azharuddin was indulged in match-fixing.

irony *(n.)* आयरनी– the humorous or mildly sarcastic use of words to imply the opposite of what they normally mean व्यंग्य, व्यंग्योक्ति You will find *irony* in his statements.

irrational *(adj.)* इरैशनल– inconsistent with reason or logic; illogical; absurd अनुचित, तर्कहीन It is *irrational* to fear from spiders.

irregular *(adj.)* इरेग्यलर्–1. lacking uniformity or symmetry; uneven in shape, position, arrangement, etc. बेक़ायदा, अवैध Make sure that you don't follow any *irregular* procedure.

2. not occurring at expected or equal intervals अनियमित Why are you so *irregular* to school?

irregularity *(n.)* इरेगयलैरटी– the state or quality of being irregular अनियमितता Your *irregularity* will make you loose your image.

irrelevant *(adj.)* इरेलवन्ट– not relating or pertinent to the matter at hand; not important असंबद्ध, विसंगत, अप्रासंगिक Whatever you said was *irrelevant* to the subject.

irresistible *(adj.)* इरिज़िसटॅबल– not able to be resisted or refused; overpowering इतना प्रबल कि दबाया न जा सके, अप्रतिरोध्य I felt an *irresistible* urge to beat the thief.

irrigate *(v.)* इरिगेट– to supply (land) with water by means of artificial canals, ditches, etc., esp to promote the growth of food crops फ़सल को सींचना, पानी देना The farmer was *irrigating* in his field.

irritate *(v.)* इरिटेट–1. to annoy or anger (someone) चिढ़ाना, उत्तेजित करना, गुस्सा दिलाना Don't *irritate* the teacher with your funny questions.

2. to cause (a bodily organ or part) to become excessively stimulated, resulting in inflammation, tenderness, etc. दाह या जलन उत्पन्न करना My new shoes *irritate* my toes.

irritating *(adj.)* इरिटेटिंग— causing annoyance or anger क्रोध दिलाने वाला, चिड़चिड़ापन Oh God! she is so *irritating.*

islam *(n.)* इस्लाम— the religion of Muslims, having the Koran as its sacred scripture and teaching that there is only one God and that Mohammed is his prophet; Mohammedanism मुसलमानों का धर्म There are many followers of *Islam* in Finland.

island *(n.)* आइलैंड— a mass of land that is surrounded by water and is smaller than a continent द्वीप, टापू He found that it was a floating *island.*

isolated *(adj.)* आइसलेटिड— 1. placed or set apart; alone or caused to be alone अलग-थलग The child suffering from chickenpox was kept in an *isolated* room.

2. *(v.)* to place apart; cause to be alone अलग करना या रखना The child suffering from chickenpox was *isolated* from other children.

isolation *(n.)* आइसोलेशन— the act of isolating or the condition of being isolated अलगाव, पार्थक्य She wants to live in complete *isolation* from the outside world.

issue *(v.)* इशू—1. to publish or deliver (a newspaper, magazine, etc.) जारी करना, प्रकाशित करना I have not read the last *issue* published by your company.

2. *(n.)* the descendants of a person; offspring; progeny सन्तान Is she without an *issue*?

3. a topic of interest or discussion वाद विषय What is the main *issue* in your discussion?

italics *(n.)* इटैलिक्स— italic type or print तिरछे अक्षर Type the headings of the book in *italics.*

it *(pron.)* इट— refers to a nonhuman, animal, plant, or inanimate thing, or sometimes to a small baby यह, वह (निर्जीव एवं छोटी वस्तुओं एवं जानवरों आदि के लिए इस्तेमाल किया जाता है) *It* is so good to be with you.

itch *(n.)* इच—1. an irritation or tickling sensation of the skin causing a desire to scratch खुजली, खाज He scratched himself continuously unable to bear the *itch* on his back.

2. *(v.)* a restless desire बेचैन होना I am *itching* to go on a hill station.

3. to scratch (the skin) खुजली होना, खुजलाना Some plants can cause the skin to *itch.*

item *(n.)* आइटम—1. a thing or unit, esp included in a list or collection वस्तु, सूची में एक वस्तु Where are the other *items*?

2. a piece of information, detail, or note विषय What is the next *item* on the agenda?

3. a piece of information, detail, or note समाचार Did you read this *item* about a parrot that talks in English?

itself *(pron.)* इटसेल्फ़— the reflexive form of it स्वयं को, अपने को Money *itself* cannot buy everything.

ivory *(n.)* आइवरी— a hard smooth creamy white variety of dentine that makes up a major part of the tusks of elephants, walruses, and similar animals हाथीदांत Are these ornaments made of *ivory*?

Jj

Jj *(n.)* जे– अंग्रेज़ी वर्णमाला का दसवां अक्षर The tenth letter of the English alphabet. Jar begins with 'J'.

jab *(v.)* जैब– 1. to poke, inject चुभोना, कोंचना I grimaced in pain when the doctor *jabbed* a needle into my arm.
2. *(n.)* a sudden strong hit एकाएक ज़ोरदार धक्का The boy gave me a *jab* with his umbrella.

jack *(n.)* जैक–1. a device for lifting heavy object such as a motor vehicle (ज़मीन से गाड़ी आदि उठाने का उपकरण) जैक We changed the tire of the car with the help of *jack*.
2. a playing card bearing a picture of knave ताश में गुलाम का पत्ता *Jack* is a Court Card in a pack of playing cards.

jackal *(n.)* जैकल– a long-legged wild dog with pointed ears and muzzle of Africa and Southern Asia. गीदड़, सियार The *jackal* in the story fell into a tank of paint.

jacket *(n.)* जैकेट– a short coat extending either to the waist or the hips and has a front opening जाकेट, मिरजई आवरण Please iron my *jacket.*

jackfruit *(n.)* जैकफ्रूट– a tropical Asian tree bearing a large fruit कटहल Mother bought *jackfruit* from the market.

jackpot *(n.)* जैकपॉट– a large prize in cash or kind दांव पर लगी राशि, बड़ी इनाम राशि He got the *jackpot* in gambling.

jade *(n.)* जेड– a semiprecious, typically green stone used for making ornaments संगयशब She is wearing a *jade* necklace.

jaded *(adj.)* जेडिड– physically exhausted or tired थका-मांदा, क्लांत He looked *jaded* after working all week.

jagged *(adj.)* जैगेड– 1. sharp edges, pointed दाँतेदार, काँटेदार Be careful; this saw has a *jagged* edge.
2. rough, pointed खुरदरा और नुकीला We can see *jagged* rocks on the sea coast.

jaggery *(n.)* जैगरी– coarse brown sugar made from the sap of palm trees गुड I love to eat roasted grams with *jaggery.*

jaguar *(n.)* जैग्युअर– a large feline mammal of Central and South America that has a yellowish-brown coat with black spots similar to the leopard अमरीका के जंगलों में पाया जाने वाला चीते जैसा जानवर, जागुआर The *jaguar* is found in Central and South America.

jail *(n.)* जेल– 1. a place for the confinement of people accused or convicted of a crime क़ैदख़ाना, कारागृह, कारागार How far is the local *jail* from here?
2. *(v.)* to confine in prison जेल में डालना, कैद करना You can be *jailed* for rash driving.

Jain *(n.)* जैन– an adherent of Jainism जैन-धर्म का उपासक, जैनी Mahavir Swami is the founder of the *Jain* religion in India.

jam *(n.)* जैम– 1. a flavoured jelly sweet in taste मुरब्बा I want to buy a jar of apple *jam*.
2. a crowd or congestion in a confined space भीड़ Ram somehow managed to reach the station in time despite facing a major traffic-*jam*.

jamboree *(n.)* जैमूबॅरी– a large and often international gathering of Scouts मेला, समारोह The scouts held a *jamboree* on New Year Day.

jangle *(v.)* जैंगल– to make or cause to make a ringing metallic sound खड़खड़ाना, झनझनाना He *jangled* his keys to distract my attention.

January *(n.)* जैनूयुअरी– the first month of the year (वर्ष का प्रथम माह), जनवरी We celebrate Republic day on 26th of *January.*

jar *(n.)* जार्– 1. a wide-mouthed container usually cylindrical and without handles मर्तबान Please give me a *jar* of face cream.

2. an unpleasant or disturbing sound कानों को बुरी लगने वाली ध्वनि You should oil this door to stop its *jarring* sound.

3. *(v.)* a jolt or shock धक्का लगाना I was badly *jarred* when my bicycle struck the fence.

jargon *(n.)* जार्गन– specialized language or vocabulary concerned with a particular subject, culture, or profession खास बोली, विशिष्ट शब्दावली We should avoid using technical *jargon* when speaking to arts students.

jaundice *(n.)* जॉण्डिस– a disease resulting into yellowness of the skin पीलिया रोग Hepatitis B is one of the common causes of *jaundice* and affects the liver.

jaunt *(n.)* जॉण्ट– a short journey made for pleasure सैर-सपाटा, भ्रमण We went for a *jaunt* late in the night.

jaw *(n.)* जॉ– the upper and lower bony structures of the mouth जबड़ा I heard you had fallen and dislocated your *jaw*.

jealous *(adj.)* जेलस– resentful against someone or their achievements ईर्ष्यालु Don't be *jealous* of someone's achievements.

jealousy *(n.)* जेलसी– feeling or showing an envious resentment ईर्ष्या, डाह Salma felt a sharp pang of *jealousy* when she saw Salim with Arjun.

jeans *(n.)* जीन्स– informal trousers for casual wear, made esp of denim जीन्स की पैंट I went to buy a low waist *jeans*.

jeep *(n.)* जीप– a small, sturdy motor vehicle with four-wheel drive एक मज़बूत गाड़ी, जीप He likes to travel by *jeep*.

jeer *(n.)* जिअर्– 1. a rude and mocking remark उपहास, ताना The daughter-in-law started crying as she was unable to tolerate the *jeers* of her mother-in-law.

2. *(v.)* to laugh or scoff at sb फ़बती कसना, खिल्ली उड़ाना If you want to be a good speaker, you must not be afraid of being *jeered* at.

jelly *(n.)* जेली– a fruit flavoured dessert made from geletin जेली, अवलेह My wife has set up a small unit for making jams and *jellies*.

jeopardize (ise) *(v.)* जेपडाइज़्– to put in danger किसी को ख़तरे में डालना, हानि पहुंचाना He will never do anything to *jeopardize* her married life.

jerk *(n.)* जर्क– 1. a quick, sharp, sudden movement झटका, झकझोरा When I heard a sound near my bed, I got up with a *jerk*.

2. *(v.)* to move or cause to move with a jerk झटकना, झटका देना Don't *jerk* the steering wheel.

jest *(v.)* जेस्ट– 1. to act or speak in a joking way हँसी-मज़ाक़ करना Don't *jest* on every occasion, be serious sometimes.

2. *(n.)* a thing said or done for amusement; a joke मज़ाक़, दिल्लगी, मसख़री Please don't mind what I said in *jest*.

jet *(n.)* जेट– a modernized aircraft एक आधुनिक जेट विमान Mukesh Ambani gifted a *jet* plane to his wife on her birthday.

jet-black *(adj.)* जेट-ब्लेक– deep glossy black काला-स्याह, गहरा काला His father gave him a *jet-black* t-shirt.

jetty *(n.)* जेटी– a landing stage; dock पोतघाट, घाट Sanjay looked across the *jetty* where there was a glowing light.

jew *(n.)* जू– a person whose religion is Judaism यहूदी *Jews* believe that they are chosen for suffering from the God.

jewel *(n.)* जूअल– a precious stone or gem रत्न, जवाहर What is this *jewel* in your ring?

jewellery *(n.)* जूअलरि– ornaments, such as necklaces, made from jewels and precious metal रत्न या

आभूषण A big robbery took place in *jewellery* shop.

jib *(v.)* जिब– to be unwilling to do or accept something कोई बात मानने से इंकार करना She *jibbed* spending more money on interior designing.

jig *(v.)* जिग– to jerk or cause to jerk up and down rapidly उछलकूद करना या नाचना She was *jigging* her baby up and down on her knees.

jigsaw *(n.)* जिग्सॉ– a saw एक पतला छोटा आरा I Have never seen a *jigsaw*

jingle *(n.)* जिंगल– 1. a sound of metal छनक, खनक We heard the *jingle* of bells.
2. *(v.)* to make or cause to make a light metallic ringing sound छनकना, छनकाना, खनकना The young boy *jingled* the coins in his pocket.

jingling *(adj.)* जिंगलिंग– a catchy and rhythmic metallic ringing sound खनखनाती घंटियों की सुहानी आवाज़ The *jingling* sound in the street made the children run out of their home.

jinx *(n.)* जिंक्स– bad luck मनूहस, दुर्भाग्य, अशुभ He broke the *jinx* of not starting a new work on Saturday.

jinxed *(adj.)* जिंक्सड– an unlucky or malevolent force, person, or thing अभागा, मनहूस आदमी या वस्तु When the family lost their third child, they thought the house was *jinxed.*

job *(n.)* जॉब– an individual piece of work or task नौकरी, काम, कार्य Did you get the *job* for which you had applied?

jobless *(adj.)* जॉबलस– unemployed, without a job बेरोज़गार His brother is *jobless* since last few months.

jockey *(n.)* जॉकि– a person who rides horses in races घुड़दौड़ में घोड़े की सवारी करने वाला व्यक्ति, घुड़सवार Some countries have *jockey* clubs.

jocular *(adj.)* जाक्यूलर– characterized by joking; humorous or playful मज़ाकिया, विनोदपूर्ण Rahul made a *jocular* comment on his friend.

jog *(n.)* जॉग्– 1. a slow run हलकी दौड़, धीमी दौड़ I go for a *jog* every morning.
2. *(v.)* to run slowly धीरे-धीरे दौड़ना *Jogging* for half an hour every morning is a healthy exercise.
3. to nudge or knock slightly झटका देना, हल्का धक्का देना You *jogged* my elbow.

join *(v.)* जॉइन–1. to become a member of शामिल होना, भाग लेना Would you like to *join* our party?
2. to link; connect मिल जाना, जुड़ जाना Does this lane *join* the main road?
3. to unite to form one जोड़ना, मिलाना, एकत्र/संबद्ध करना Please *join* the two ends of the string.

joinery *(n.)* जाइनरी– a skill or craft of making finished woodwork बढ़ईगिरी Raheem is famous in the field of *joinery.*

joint *(n.)* जॉइंट– 1. combined together सम्मिलित, संयुक्त I opened a *joint* account with my father.
2. a junction of two or more parts or objects जोड़, गाँठ Roma's mother is suffering from *joint* pain.

joke *(n.)* जोक– 1. something that is said or done for fun; prank दिल्लगी, मज़ाक़ If you tell good *jokes,* you will be popular at parties.
2. *(v.)* to make fun of मज़ाक़ करना Please stop *joking* and be serious for a while.

jolly *(adj.)* जॉली– happy and cheerful प्रसन्न, आनंदित, गिलनसार Arun was liked by all because of his *jolly* nature.

jolt *(n.)* जोल्ट– 1. an abrupt rough or violent movement धक्का, झटका Passengers got a severe *jolt* when the bus stopped suddenly.
2. *(v.)* to push or shake (someone or something) झटका देना या लगाना The news of my friend's accident *jolted* me badly.

jostle *(v.)* जॉसल– to push roughly धक्का मारना या देना He *jostled* me against an old man in the bus.

jot *(v.)* जॉट– 1. to make a quick short note (संक्षेप में) लिख देना Have you *jotted* down the points of the speech you are going to make?
2. *(n.)* least part of something बिंदु, कण We don't care a *jot* for what you say.

journal *(n.)* जर्नल– newspaper or other periodical पत्र, अख़बार, पत्रिका Many reputed companies publish their monthly house *journals*.

journalism *(n.)* जर्नलिज़्म– work of writing for newspaper magazines, etc. पत्रकारिता, अख़बारनवीसी She is going to take admission in *journalism*.

journalist *(n.)* जर्नलिस्ट– a person engaged in journalism पत्रकार Vir Sanghvi is a well-known *journalist* in print media.

journey *(n.)* जर्नी– 1. travelling from one place to another यात्रा, सफ़र I am going on a long *journey*.
2. *(v.)* to travel सफ़र करना, यात्रा करना The pilgrims *journeyed* on foot from Delhi to Haridwar.

jovial *(adj.)* जोविअल– cheerful and friendly प्रसन्नचित्त He was in a *jovial* mood yesterday.

joy *(n.)* जॉय– the emotion of great delight and happiness आनंद, हर्ष The children while watching the magic show were full of *joy*.

joyful *(adj.)* जॉयफुल– filled with joy, very happy आनंदति, हर्षित Amit returned from the picnic in a *joyful* mood.

joyless *(adj.)* जॉयलस– without joy or pleasure आनंदरहित, नीरस We attended a *joyless* marriage last Sunday.

jubilation *(n.)* जूबिलेशन– act of rejoicing or jubilating हर्षोल्लास, आनंदोत्सव Christmas was celebrated with great joy and *jubilation*.

jubilee *(n.)* जुबिली– a special anniversary of an event जयंती महोत्सव They invited all their friends for the silver *jubilee* party of their marriage.

judaism *(n.)* जूडेइज़्म– the monotheistic religion of the Jews यहूदी धर्म *Judaism* is one of the first foreign religions of India.

judge *(n.)* जॅज– 1. a public official with authority to hear and decide cases in a court of law न्यायाधीश, न्यायकर्ता My uncle is a *judge* in the High Court.
2. *(v.)* form an opinion or conclusion about आंकना, अनुमान लगाना Never *judge* a man by his clothes.

judgement/judgment *(n.)* जजमेण्ट– decision फ़ैसला, निर्णय The *judgement* was passed against him.

judicial *(adj.)* जूडिशियल– of or by a court of justice न्यायिक, अदालती There will be a *judicial* enquiry against this crime.

judiciary *(n.)* जूडिशियरि– the system of courts of justice in a country न्यायतंत्र, न्यायपालिका She lost faith in *judiciary* when the court released her son's killer.

judicious *(adj.)* जुडिशस– showing or having good sense विवेकपूर्ण, विवेकी *Judicious* use of words will make your essay more interesting.

jug *(n.)* जॅग– a deep vessel with a handle and lip, a small pitcher सुराही, घड़ा, जग Please bring some cold water in a *jug*.

juggler *(n.)* जॅगलर्– a person who fraudulently manipulates facts or figures बाज़ीगर The *juggler* did a trick by tossing five knives together.

juice *(n.)* जूस– the liquid obtained from or present in fruit or vegetables रस Would you like some orange-*juice*?

juicy *(adj.)* जूसी– containing much juice रसदार There were two kg *juicy* oranges in the basket.

July *(n.)* जुलाई– seventh month of the year वर्ष का सातवां महीना, जुलाई Rita will come to Delhi in *July*.

jumble *(v.)* जॅम्बल– 1. to mix up in a confused way अस्त-व्यस्त/गड्डमड्ड कर देना Ramesh quickly wrote the correct sentence from the *jumbled* up words.

2. *(n.)* an untidy collection or pile of things मिश्रण, गड्डमड्ड Human mind is a *jumble* of ideas.

jumbo *(adj.)* जम्बो– unusually large भारी-भरकम, विशाल We brought a *jumbo* pack of potato chips.

jump *(n.)* जॅम्प– 1. an act of jumping कूद, छलाँग I won a prize in high *jump*.
2. *(v.)* to pass over छलांग लगाना, कूदना Don't *jump* to false conclusions.

jumpy *(adj.)* जम्पि– anxious and uneasy बेचैन, परेशान Why do you look so *jumpy* today?

junction *(n.)* जंक्शन– 1. joining or being joint संगम, मिलन Be careful while driving through a *junction* of the main road with a lane.
2. place where roads, railway lines meet जंक्शन Our train halted for half an hour at Mathura *junction*.

juncture *(n.)* जंक्चर– a specific point of time events, etc. विशिष्ट क्षण या परिस्थिति The matter has reached a *juncture*, and a decision must be taken.

June *(n.)* जून– sixth month of the year वर्ष का छठा महीना, जून *June* is named after the Roman goddess Juno.

jungle *(n.)* जंगल– forest land covered with tree जंगल, वन My native place is a village on the edge of the *jungle*.

junior *(adj.)* जूनिअर्– younger, lower in rank छोटा By how many years is your brother *junior* to you?

junk *(n.)* जंक– old, discarded things of little or no value कूड़ा-करकट, कबाड़ There were a lot of *junk* mails from an insurance company.

jurisdiction *(n.)* जुरिसडिक्शन– the right, power or authority to administer justice क्षेत्राधिकार, अधिकार-क्षेत्र It is under Supreme Court's *jurisdiction* to solve electricity dispute between two states.

jury *(n.)* जूरी– a body of persons who swear to give a true decision निर्णायकगण, जूरी The *jury* was alleged to be partial.

just *(adj.)* जॅस्ट– 1. no more than; merely; only मात्र, भर, मुश्किल से The poor man had *just* enough money to buy a loaf of bread.
2. fair न्यायपूर्ण, वैध, उचित The employer's decision to reward the laborious workers was *just*.
3. *(adv.)* at this moment, now अभी, तुरंत They are *just* going.
4. exactly; precisely वैसा ही, ठीक वैसी You are *just as* intelligent as your sister.
5. by a small margin; barely लगभग, क़रीब-क़रीब I was *just about* to tell you when you entered in the room.
6. simply; only; no more than यकायक, अकस्मात् He walked out in the street *just* like that.
7. at this very moment इस समय, इसी समय She is very busy *just* now.

justice *(n.)* जस्टिस– the quality of being right and fair न्याय, इंसाफ My father is known for his sense of *justice*.

justification *(n.)* जस्टिफ़िकेशन– the action of showing something to be right or reasonable औचित्य, प्रतिवाद, समर्थन There is no *justification* for holding my brother in jail.

justify *(v.)* जस्टिफ़ाई– to show that a person, statement or act is right सफ़ाई देना The captain *justified* his decision to bat first.

jut *(v.)* जॅट– extend out, over, or beyond the main body बाहर निकला हुआ होना Hammer that nail *jutting* out from the chair.

jute *(n.)* जूट– a fibre from the outer skin of certain plants जूट He carried the onions in a *jute* bag.

juvenile *(adj.)* जुवनाइल– young, youthful, or immature तरुण, किशोर You are now too old for such *juvenile* behaviour.

juxtapose *(v.)* जक्स्टपोज़– to place side by side अगल-बग़ल रखना, सटाना The traditional Ganesh idols were *juxtaposed* with Shiv idols in pandals.

Kk

Kk *(n.)* के–अंग्रेज़ी वर्णमाला का ग्यारहवां अक्षर The eleventh letter of the English alphabet. Kangaroo begins with 'K'.

kaleidoscope *(n.)* कलाइडस्कोप्– any complex pattern of frequently changing shapes and colours बहुमूर्तिदर्शी We saw changing patterns of colours in *kaleidoscope*.

kangaroo *(n.)* कैंगरू– a large Australian animal, having large powerful hind legs, used for leaping and a long thick tail (ऑस्ट्रेलिया देश का जानवर) कंगारू There were no *kangaroo* in the zoo this time.

karate *(n.)* कराटे– a traditional Japanese system of unarmed combat, employing smashes, chops, kicks, etc. made with the hands, feet, elbows, or legs (जापानी पद्धति जिसमें हाथ-पैर से लड़ा जाता है) कराटे I will join *karate* classes in the vacations.

kayak *(n.)* काइऐक– a small light canoe-like boat used by the Inuit, consisting of a light frame covered with watertight animal skins छोटी नाव People use a *kayak* in the village to cross the river.

keen *(adj.)* कीन–1. eager or enthusiastic उत्सुक, उत्साही I am very *keen* to spend my vacations in Goa.

2. having a sharp cutting edge or point तीक्ष्ण, पैना, तेज़ Do you have a knife with a *keen* edge?

keep *(n.)* कीप–1. living or support निर्वाह, भरण-पोषण How much do you pay for your *keep*?

2. *(v.)* to have or retain possession of रखना, पास रखना Can I *keep* this book for some days.

3. to have temporary possession or charge of ध्यान रखना *Keep* an eye on the child.

4. begins चलाना, चलना *Keep* to the left of the road.

5. to remain or cause to remain in a specified state or condition पूरा करना, निबाहना Once you make a promise, you must *keep* it up.

6. to have or take charge or care of देख-रेख करना Who *keeps* the house for you?

7. to remain or cause to remain in a specified state or condition ठीक रहना, नहीं बिगड़ना Can we *keep* these bananas for a couple of days?

8. to continue or cause to continue जारी रखना, निरंतर करते रहना *Keep* smiling.

➢ **keep away**– to refrain or prevent from coming (near) दूर रहना, पास न जाना, (किसी के), Please *keep away* from that dog.

➢ **keep back**– to refuse to reveal or disclose कुछ छिपाना, She was unable to *keep back* her tears.

➢ **keep down**– to repress; hold in submission दबाव या नियंत्रण में रखना, *Keep* the fan *down.*

➢ **keep off**– to stay or cause to stay at a distance (from) किसी चीज़ से दूर या अलग रहना, *Keep off* the sweets from my sight.

➢ **keep on**– to continue or persist in (doing something) जारी रहना, *Keep on* fanning me.

➢ **keep out**– to remain or cause to remain outside प्रवेश न करने देना, बचते रहना, Sona said, "Please *keep* this bulldog *out.*"

➢ **keep under**– to remain or cause to remain below दबाकर रखना, वश में रखना, She *keeps* her children *under* control.

keeper *(n.)* कीपर– a person in charge of animals, esp in a zoo

रक्षक Ramesh is a *keeper* of lions in the zoo.

keeping *(n.)* कीपिंग– being taken care of by sb रक्षा, देखरेख, The documents are in *keeping* of my lawyer.

keepsake *(n.)* कीपसेक– a gift that evokes memories of a person or event with which it is associated, memento यादगार, स्मृतिचिह्न This book will surely become a *keepsake.*

kennel *(n.)* केनल– a hutlike shelter for a dog कुत्ताघर, कुत्ताखाना When we go out, we put our dog in the *kennel.*

kerb *(n.)* कर्ब– a line of stone or concrete forming an edge between a pavement and a roadway सड़क का किनारा All the beggers were sitting near the *kerb.*

kernel *(n.)* कर्नल– the edible central part of a seed, nut, or fruit within the shell or stone गिरी, गरी, मींगी Almond *kernels* are good both for the brain and the eyes.

kerosene *(n.)* केरसीन– An oil that is made from petroleum मिट्टी का तेल, किरासिन Do you cook on a *kerosene* stove?

ketchup *(n.)* any of various piquant sauces containing vinegar टमाटर की चटनी French fries tastes yummy with *ketchup.*

kettle *(n.)* केटल– a metal or plastic container with a handle and spout for boiling water केतली, देगची I use an electric *kettle* for making tea.

key *(n.)* की– a metal instrument, usually of a specifically contoured shape, that is made to fit a lock and, when rotated, operates the lock's mechanism कुंजी, चाबी Where have you kept the *key* of the safe?

keyboard *(n.)* कीबॉर्ड– a complete set of keys, usually hand-operated, as on a piano, organ, typewriter, or typesetting machine कुंजीपटल I am going to get this *keyboard* replaced.

keynote *(n.)* कीनोट– a central or determining principle in a speech, literary work, etc. मुख्य स्वर या विचार This is the *keynote* of the writer's work.

keyword *(n.)* कीवर्ड– a word used as a key to a code कम्प्यूटर निर्देशक शब्द Try to search with other *keywords* also.

kick *(v.)* किक–1. to hit with the foot or feet लात या ठोकर मारना Please be careful, this horse *kicks.*

2. *(n.)* a thrust or blow with the foot दुलत्ती, ठोकर, लात He gave me a *kick* on the rump.

3. a stimulating or exciting quality or effect उमंग, जोश She gets her *kicks* by playing music.

➢ **kick yourself** *(v.)*– ashamed of oneself अपनी मूर्खता पर नाराज़ होना, You'll *kick yourself* when I tell you the answer.

➢ **kick-out** *(v.)*– to eject or dismiss निकाल बाहर करना, Smitha was *kicked out* of the tennis club.

➢ **kick-start** *(n.)*– an action or event resulting in the reactivation of something किसी काम को शुरू करने का विशेष प्रयत्न, Motivation is the *kick-start* you need to succeed at work.

kid *(n.)* किड– 1. a child; the young of a goat or of a related animal, such as an antelope बच्चा; मेमना Tell the *kids* not to play in street.

2. *(v.)* to tease or deceive for fun मज़ाक करना, चिढ़ाना She is always in *kidding* mood.

kidnap *(v.)* किडनैप– to carry off and hold (a person), usually for ransom अपहरण करना The child was *kidnapped* for money.

kidney *(n.)* किड्नी– either of two bean-shaped organs at the back of the abdominal cavity in man, one on each side of the spinal column गुर्दा, वृक्क My doctor is treating me for some *kidney* trouble.

kill *(v.)* किल–1. to cause the death of (a person or animal) मार डालना, हत्या करना He killed all the insects in the room.
2. to put an end to; destroy नष्ट करना, बंद करना The cold winter has *killed* the flowers in my garden.

killer *(n.)* किलर– a person or animal that kills, esp habitually हत्यारा, घातक The *killer* should be sentenced to death.

killing *(n.)* किलिंग– the act of causing death; slaying वध, हत्या There have been a number of *killings* of innocent people by the terrorists.

kilogram *(n.)* किलॅग्रैम– one thousand grams किलोग्राम I need 10 *kilograms* of sugar.

kilometre *(n.)* किलॅमीटर– one thousand metres, किलोमीटर, लंबाई की एक माप How many *kilometers* did you cover today?

kind *(n.)* काइन्ड–1. a class or group having characteristics in common; sort; type वर्ग, जाति I saw all *kinds* of people at the function.
2. essential nature or character किस्म, प्रकार What *kind* of fabric is this?
3. *(adj.)* having a friendly or generous nature or attitude कृपालु It was very *kind* of you to help me.

kindergarten *(n.)* किंडगार्टन– a class or small school for young children, usually between the ages of four and six to prepare them for primary education शिशु-पाठशाला, बालविहार, किंडरगार्टन Her daughter is studying in *kindergarten* now.

kind-hearted *(adj.)* काइंड-हर्टेड– characterized by kindness; sympathetic उदार हृदय वाला, दयालु Gurpreet is a very *kind-hearted* teacher.

kindle *(v.)* किण्डल–1.to set alight or start to burn सुलगाना *Kindle* the fire; it's so cold.
2. to arouse or be aroused रुचि उत्पन्न करना She *kindled* my interest in photography.

kindly *(adj.)* काइंडली–1. having a sympathetic or warm-hearted nature दयालु, कृपालु She is a *kindly* lady.
2. motivated by warm and sympathetic feelings कृपा करके, दया भाव से The doctor smiled *kindly*.

kindness *(n.)* काइंडनस– the practice or quality of being kind दयालुता She always shows the *kindness* to the poor people.

king *(n.)* किंग– a male sovereign prince who is the official ruler of an independent state राजा The child wished to play the role of the *king*.

kingdom *(n.)* किंग्डम– a territory, state, people, or community ruled or reigned over by a king or queen साम्राज्य, राज्य People were happy in the *kingdom* of Emperor Akbar.

king-size *(adj.)* किंग-साइज़– larger or longer than a standard size शाही, बड़ा I have brought a *king-size* bed for my room.

kink *(n.)* किंक– a sharp twist or bend in a wire, rope, hair, etc. esp one caused when it is pulled tight ऐंठन, बल The water tank had a *kink* in it.

kinship *(n.)* किनशिप– blood relationship ख़ून का रिश्ता, सगोत्रता I must break such *kinships* for it may harm me.

kiosk *(n.)* कीऑस्क– a small sometimes movable booth from which cigarettes, newspapers, light refreshments, etc. are sold खोका Get a newspaper from the nearby *kiosk*.

kiss *(v.)* किस– 1. to touch with the lips or press the lips against as an expression of love, greeting, respect, etc. चुम्बन करना The mother *kissed* her weeping child.
2. *(n.)* the act of kissing चुम्बन The mother gave the child a toffee and a *kiss*.

kit *(n.)* किट-- a set of tools, supplies, construction materials, etc. for use together or for a purpose किट, सामान, औज़ार Please pick up my *kit* before leaving home.

kitchen *(n.)* किचिन– a room or part of a building equipped for preparing and cooking food रसोईघर I am going to clean my whole *kitchen* today.

kite *(n.)* काइट–1. a light frame covered with a thin material flown in the wind at the end of a length of string पतंग Do you know how to fly a *kite*?
2. any diurnal bird of prey having a long forked tail and long broad wings and usually preying on small mammals and insects चील I saw a *kite* high up in the sky.

kitten *(n.)* किटन– a young cat बिलौटा There were so many *kittens* in the garden.

kitty *(n.)* किटी– any shared fund of money, etc. जमा पूंजी She has some good projects in her *kitty.*

kiwi *(n.)* किवी–1. New Zealand bird having a long beak, stout legs, and weakly barbed feathers (न्यूज़ीलैंड की चिड़िया) कीवी *Kiwis* are flightless birds found in New Zealand.
2. the edible oval fruit of the kiwi plant, grown extensively in New Zealand; it has a brown fuzzy skin and pale green flesh भूरे छिलके वाला एक फल *Kiwi* fruits are rich in many vitamins and minerals.

knack *(n.)* नैक्– a skilful, ingenious, or resourceful way of doing something योग्यता, दक्षता, कौशल She has a *knack* for writing poetry.

knead *(v.)* नीड– to work and press (a soft substance, such as bread dough) into a uniform mixture with the hands गूँथना, माँड़ना Please *knead* the dough well.

knee *(n.)* नी– the joint of the human leg connecting the tibia and fibula with the femur and protected in front by the patella घुटना My left *knee* was injured in a fall.

kneel *(v.)* नील– to rest, fall, or support oneself on one's knees घुटने टेकना Let us *kneel* in prayer.

knickers *(n.)* निकर्ज़– an undergarment for women covering the lower trunk and sometimes the thighs and having separate legs or leg-holes महिलाओं की निकर, जांघिया Savita bought a pair of *knickers* for her sister.

knife *(n.)* नाइफ़– a cutting instrument consisting of a sharp-edged often pointed blade of metal fitted into a handle or onto a machine चाकू, छुरी I can't work with sharp edged *knife.*

knight (n.) नाइट्– a person who served his lord as a mounted and heavily armed soldier घुड़सवार योद्धा Every girl has an image of her *knight* in shining armour in her mind.

knit *(v.)* निट– to make (a garment, etc.) by looping and entwining (yarn, esp wool) by hand by means of long eyeless needles बुनना My mom is *knitting* a sweater for me.

knob *(n.)* नॉब– a rounded projection from a surface, such as a lump on a tree trunk गुमटा, मूठ, दस्ता We saw decorative *knobs* on all the doors in the royal palace.

knock *(v.)* नॉक–1. to rap sharply with the knuckles, a hard object, etc. esp to capture attention खटखटाना I am *knocking* the door since half an hour.
2. to give a blow or push to; strike प्रहार करना, ठोंकना The champion boxer *knocked* down his opponent very easily.
3. *(n.)* a blow, push, or rap खटखटाहट My sister opened the door at the first *knock.*

knot *(n.)* नॉट–1. any of various fastenings formed by looping and tying a piece of rope, cord, etc. in upon itself, to another piece of rope, or to another object गाँठ, उलझन, ग्रंथि Please untie this *knot.*
2. a small cluster or huddled group समूह, पुंज Why have these people gathered in *knots*?
3. a tangle गाँठ, ग्रंथि This piece of wood is full of *knots.*

know *(v.)* नो–1. to be or feel certain of the truth or accuracy of (a fact, etc.) जानना I don't *know* how much you scored.
2. to have a familiarity or grasp of, as through study or experience ज्ञान होना Do you *know* geometry?
3. to be acquainted or familiar with परिचित होना I *know* Sudhir because he was my classmate.

➤ **know-how** ingenuity, aptitude, or skill; knack जानकारी, ख़ैरियत, Please send me your *know-how* about your family.

knowingly *(adv.)* नोइंगली– deliberately; intentionally जान-बूझकर How can you do this *knowingly?*

known *(n.)* नोन– a fact or entity known जाना हुआ, विदित, ज्ञात Jenny is no stranger but *known* to me.

knowledge *(n.)* नॉलेज़– the state of knowing ज्ञान, जानकारी I can't say anything as I don't have any *knowledge* about it.

knowledgeable *(adj.)* नॉलिज़्बल– possessing or indicating much knowledge जानकार, सुविज्ञ, मेधावी Poonam is very *knowledgeable.*

knuckle *(n.)* नक्ल्– a joint of a finger, esp that connecting a finger to the hand उंगली की गांठ, पोर I knocked at the door with my *knuckles.*

ಐ☙

Ll

Ll *(n.)* एल–अंग्रेज़ी वर्णमाला का बारहवां अक्षर The twelfth letter of the English alphabet. Lion begins with 'L'.

label *(n.)* लेबल– 1. a piece of paper, card, or other material attached to an object to identify it or give instructions or details concerning its ownership, use, nature, destination, etc; tag लेबल, परचा, नामपत्र I can't see any *label* on this bottle.

2. *(v.)* to fasten a label to लेबल/परचा लगाना या चिपकाना Have you *labelled* all the packets?

laboratory *(n.)* लबॉरट्री– a building or room equipped for conducting scientific research or for teaching practical science प्रयोगशाला Does your school have a well-equipped science *laboratory*?

laborious *(adj.)* लबॉरिअस– involving great exertion or long effort परिश्रमी, मेहनती I need only *laborious* workers for this job.

laboriously *(adv.)* लॅबरिअसली– in such a way as to involve great exertion or long effort श्रमसाध्य रीति से A beetle began to crawl *laboriously* up his leg.

labour *(n.)* लेबर्–1. productive work, esp physical toil done for wages श्रम, परिश्रम, मेहनत Gandhiji taught us the dignity of *labour*.

2. the people, class, or workers involved in this, esp in contrast to management, capital, etc. श्रमिक (वर्ग), मज़दूर I heard you had some *labour* trouble in your factory.

3. *(v.)* to strive or work hard (for something) मेहनत/मज़दूरी करना The farmer *labours* in the fields to feed the countrymen.

laboured *(adj.)* लेबर्ड– (of breathing) performed with difficulty कठिन, प्रयासपूर्ण He has a *laboured* style of speaking.

labourer *(n.)* लेबरर्– a person engaged in physical work, esp of an unskilled kind मज़दूर, श्रमिक, श्रमजीवी If you need a *labourer*, you should go to the labour market.

lace *(n.)* लेस्–1. a delicate decorative fabric made from cotton, silk, etc. woven in an open web of different symmetrical patterns and figures जालीदार कपड़ा She bought a very nice *lace* dress for the party.

2. a cord or string drawn through holes or eyelets or around hooks to fasten a shoe or garment फ़ीता I can't see the *laces* for my shoe.

3. *(v.)* to fasten (shoes, etc.) with a lace फ़ीता कसना *Lace up* your shoes.

lack *(n.)* लैक– 1. an insufficiency, shortage, or absence of something required or desired कमी, अभाव We always suffer from a *lack* of water in summer.

2. *(v.)* to be deficient (in) or have need (of) आवश्यकता से कम होना The dish *lacked* salt.

lacking *(adj.)* लैकिंग– missing or absent कमी, अभाव I told him there is something *lacking* in my life.

lacklustre *(adj.)* लैकलस्टर– lacking force, brilliance, or vitality निर्जीव, भावशून्य Namita gave a *lacklustre* performance on the stage.

laconic *(adj.)* लकॉनिक– (of a person's speech) using few words; terse नपा-तुला, अति संक्षिप्त He gave a *laconic* reply to me.

lactate *(v.)* लैकटेट– (of mammals) to produce or secrete milk दूध पिलाना The cat was *lactating* its kitten.

lacy *(adj.)* लेसी– made of or resembling lace जालीदार She has brought a red coloured *lacy* underwear.

lad *(n.)* लैड– a boy or young man लड़का, युवक Your son has grown into a fine young *lad.*

ladder *(n.)* लेडर्– a portable framework of wood, metal, rope, etc. in the form of two long parallel members connected by several parallel rungs or steps fixed to them at right angles, for climbing up or down सीढ़ी I am scared of climbing on *ladder.*

laden *(adj.)* लेडन– weighed down with a load; loaded लदा हुआ The auto-rickshaw was *laden* with so many boxes and bags.

ladle *(n.)* लेडल– a long-handled spoon having a deep bowl for serving or transferring liquids चमचा, कलछी I took more curry with a *ladle.*

lady *(n.)* लेडी– a polite name for a woman महिला This young *lady* has won everyone's heart.

ladybird *(n.)* लेडिबर्ड– a small flying insect which has red with black spots सोनपंखी The garden was full of *ladybirds* in rainy season.

lady's finger *(adj.)* लेडीज़-फिंगर– a green vegetable भिंडी *Lady's finger* is one of my favourite vegetable.

lag *(v.)* लैग– to hang (back) or fall (behind) in movement, progress, development, etc. पिछड़ना, पीछे रह जाना I don't want you to *lag* behind anyone.

lagoon *(n.)* लगून– a body of water cut off from the open sea by coral reefs or sand bars समुद्रताल, खारे पानी की झील Chilka Lake is a brackish water *lagoon* on the east coast of India.

laid-back *(adj.)* लैड-बैक– relaxed in style, character, or behaviour; easy-going and unhurried निश्चिंत एवं तनावमुक्त She is famous for her *laid-back* attitude.

laissez-faire *(adj.)* the doctrine of unrestricted freedom in commerce, esp for private interests अहस्तक्षेप His parents have a *laissez-faire* approach to bringing him up.

lake *(n.)* लेक– a large area of water entirely surrounded by land and unconnected to the sea except by rivers or streams झील, सरोवर Let's go for a nightwalk near the *lake.*

lamb *(n.)* लैम– the young of a sheep मेमना I saw a *lamb* when I went on my educational trip.

lame *(adj.)* लेम–1. disabled or crippled in the legs or feet लंगड़ा, पंगु One should always help the *lame* man while crossing the road.

2. weak; unconvincing आश्वस्त न करने वाला, बहाना, कमज़ोर Don't give me *lame* excuses if you don't want to work.

lament *(v.)* लॅमेण्ट– 1. to feel or express sorrow, remorse, or regret (for or over) विलाप एवं शोक करना The child *laments* for milk.

2. *(n.) an expression of sorrow* विलाप, दुःख का प्रदर्शन This song is a *lament* for those who were killed in battle.

laminated *(adj.)* लैमिनेटिड– covered with a thin protective layer of plastic or synthetic resin प्लास्टिक की परत चढ़ा हुआ Get these documents *laminated* fast.

lamp *(n.)* लैम्प– any of a number of devices that produce illumination बत्ती, चिराग As the electricity failed, I lit a *lamp.*

land *(n.)* लैण्ड– 1. the solid part of the surface of the earth as distinct from seas, lakes, etc. भूमि, ज़मीन I want to buy a piece of *land* near your area.

2. *(v.)* to come down or bring (something) down to earth after a flight or jump पहुँचना, (ज़मीन पर) उतरना By what time will you be able to *land* in delhi.

3. to win or obtain कुछ पाने में सफल हो जाना The company just *landed* ten million rupees contract.

landing *(n.)* लैंडिंग– the act of coming to land, esp after a flight or sea voyage ज़मीन पर उतरने की क्रिया The space travellers made a safe *landing* on the moon.

landlady *(n.)* लैंडलेडि– a woman who owns and leases property मकान-मालकिन My *landlady* is really so cruel.

landlord *(n.)* लैंडलॉर्ड– a man who owns and leases property मकान-मालिक My *landlord* asked me to leave this house as soon as possible.

landmark *(n.)* लैंडमार्क–1. a prominent or well-known object in or feature of a particular landscape पहचान-चिह्न Tell me some *landmark* so that I find the way to your place easily.
2. an important or unique decision, event, fact, discovery, etc. कोई महत्त्वपूर्ण घटना The Revolt of 1857 was a *landmark* in Indian history.

landowner *(n.)* लैंडओनर– a person who owns land ज़मींदार, भूस्वामी He is a wealthy *landowner* and has property in my village.

landscape *(n.)* लैंडस्केप– an extensive area of land regarded as being visually distinct प्राकृतिक दृश्य, दृश्यावली I love to paint *landscapes* on my canvas.

landslide *(n.)* लैंडस्लाइड– the sliding of a large mass of rock material, soil, etc. down the side of a mountain or cliff भू-स्खलन *Landslides* occur in the hilly terrains of India.

lane *(n.)* लेन– a narrow road or way between buildings, hedges, fences, etc. गली, पथ Till where does this *lane* go?

language *(n.)* लैंग्वेज– a system for the expression of thoughts, feelings, etc. by the use of spoken sounds or conventional symbols भाषा How many *languages* can you speak?

languish *(v.)* लैंग्विश– to lose or diminish in strength or energy बहुत अधिक दीन अवस्था में रहने वाला He continued to *languish* in Tihar jail for fifteen years.

lanky *(adj.)* लैंकी– tall, thin, and loose-jointed छरहरा, बहुत दुबला, पतला और लंबा Her husband is a *lanky* young man but a very good human being.

lantern *(n.)* लैंटर्न– a light with a transparent or translucent protective case लालटेन Don't go out into the dark of night without a *lantern*.

lap *(n.)* लैप–1. the area formed by the upper surface of the thighs of a seated person गोद, अंचल The baby felt asleep the moment I took him in my *lap*.
2. *(v.)* to scoop (a liquid) into the mouth with the tongue चाटना, लप-लप पीना I put some milk in the saucer for my cat to *lap* up.

lapse *(n.)* लैप्स–1. a drop in standard of an isolated or temporary nature भूल, ग़लती, अवनति I am sorry for this *lapse* on my part.
2. a break in occurrence, usage, etc. अंतराल She returned to her hometown after a *lapse* of fifteen years.
3. *(v.)* to decline gradually or fall in status, condition, etc. बीत जाना, समाप्त होना How much time has *lapsed* since we met last?

large *(adj.)* लार्ज– having a relatively great size, quantity, extent, etc.; big बड़ा, प्रचुर, विस्तृत I want a *large* size in this shirt.

largely *(adv.)* लार्जली– principally; to a great extent मुख्य रूप से Her failure was *largely* due to her depression.

large-scale *(adj.)* लार्ज-स्केल– wide-ranging or extensive बड़े पैमाने पर, व्यापक The industrialisation in Jharkhand on a *large-scale* will increase the wealth of poor people.

lash *(v.)* लैश–1. to hit sb with a whip, rope, stick, etc. कोड़े लगाना The tonga-driver was *lashing* his horse cruelly.

2. to bind or secure with rope, string, etc. बाँधना People usually *lash* their dogs at their house's entrance.

3. to flick or wave sharply to and fro घुमाना My cat *lashed* its tail in excitement when I threw up the ball.

4. *(n.)* a forceful beating or impact, as of wind, rain, or waves against something कोड़ा, कोड़े की मार The thief was sentenced fifty *lashes* on his back.

5. any one of the short curved hairs that grow from the edge of the eyelids बरौनी Sheela has long eye-*lashes.*

lass *(n.)* लैस– a girl or young woman लड़की, किशोरी She is a very industrious young *lass.*

last *(v.)* लास्ट–1. to continue to exist टिकना, बने रहना How long will the function *last*?

2. *(adj.)* being or occurring just before the present; most recent पिछला, गत What were you doing *last* night?

3. least suitable, appropriate, or likely अन्त, अन्तिम, आख़िरी You are the *last* to speak.

➢ **last attempt**– to make a last effort (to do something) or to achieve (something); try अंतिम प्रयास, His *last attempt* was appreciated by the audience.

➢ **last moment**– the last short indefinite period of time अंतिम क्षण, He changed his plan at the *last moment.*

lastly *(adv.)* लास्टली– at the end or at the last point अंततः, आख़िर में *Lastly,* I would like to thank you.

lasting *(adj.)* लास्टिंग– permanent or enduring स्थायी, टिकाऊ I believe in long *lasting* relationship.

latch *(v.)* लैच– 1. to fasten, fit, or be fitted with or as if with a latch सिटकनी/अर्गला लगाना Always *latch* the door from inside at night.

2. *(n.)* a fastening for a gate or door that consists of a bar that may be slide or lowered into a groove, hole, etc. साँकल, सिटकनी The door could not be closed properly because of the faulty *latch.*

late *(adj.)* लेट–1. occurring or arriving after the correct or expected time देर से, विलम्ब से Sorry! I got up *late* in the morning today.

2. having died, esp recently दिवंगत Did you know the *late* Mr. Kapoor?

3. *(adv.)* after the correct or expected time देर करके, उचित समय के बाद I came *late* last night.

latecomer *(n.)* लेटकमर– a person or thing that comes late देर से आने वाला व्यक्ति All the *latecomers* stand in the different line.

lately *(v.)* लेट्ली– in recent times; of late हाल में Have you seen Mohan *lately*?

latent *(adj.)* लेटंट– (esp of an infectious disease) not yet revealed or manifest छिपा हुआ, गुप्त Cancer is always *latent* in its early stage.

lateral *(adj.)* लैटरल– of or relating to the side or sides पार्श्विक, पार्श्व, बाज़ू का I found brilliant solution of my problem due to *lateral* thinking.

latest *(adj.)* लेटेस्ट– most recent, modern, or new नवीनतम Are you aware of the *latest* news?

lather *(n.)* लैदर– foam or froth formed by the action of soap or a detergent in water झाग, फेन Shampoo produces very poor *lather* in hard water.

latin *(n.)* लैटिन– the language of ancient Rome and the Roman Empire and of the educated in medieval Europe, which achieved its classical form during the 1st century BC रोम की प्राचीन भाषा Some English words are taken from *Latin* language.

latrine *(n.)* लॅट्रीन– a lavatory, as in a barracks, camp, etc. पाख़ाना, संडास You must clean the *latrine* every day.

latter *(adj.)* लैटर्– denoting the second or second mentioned of two distinguished from former बाद का, पिछला Between Anil and Sunil, I found the *latter* more intelligent.

lattice *(n.)* लैटिस– an open framework of strips of wood, metal, etc. arranged to form an ornamental pattern लकड़ी की जाली, टटिया I have a *lattice* which is used in fencing the lawn.

laugh *(v.)* लाफ़– 1. to express or manifest emotion, esp mirth or amusement हँसना We should not *laugh* at others.
2. *(n.)* the act or an instance of laughing हँसी, हँसी की बात We all had a good *laugh* when our father told us a story.

laughable *(adj.)* लाफ़बल– producing scorn; ludicrous हास्यजनक, हँसने योग्य We couldn't believe what she said. It was just *laughable*.

laughter *(n.)* लाफ़टर– the action of or noise produced by laughing हँसी, ठहाका, क़हक़हा *Laughter* is the best medicine.

launch *(n.)* लॉंच– 1. a motor driven boat used chiefly as a transport boat लॉंच, मोटर से चलने वाली किश्ती We were taken round the harbour in a *launch*.
2. *(v.)* to start off or set in motion आरंभ कर देना This store will be *launched* may be within this week.

laundry *(n.)* लॉण्ड्री– a place where clothes and linen are washed and ironed धोबीखाना, धुलाईघर Send all these dirty clothes to the *laundry*.

lavatory *(n.)* लैवट्री– a sanitary installation for receiving and disposing of urine and faeces, शौचघर Where is the *lavatory* in this theatre?

lavish *(n.)* लैविश– 1. prolific, abundant, or profuse ख़र्चीला They threw a *lavish* party at their wedding.
2. *(v.)* to give, expend, or apply abundantly, generously, or in profusion खुलकर ख़र्च करना He *lavished* expensive gifts on his wife on her birthday.

law *(n.)* लॉ– a rule or set of rules, enforceable by the courts, regulating the government of a state, क़ानून, विधि Don't try to break the *law*.

law-abiding *(adj.)* लॉ-अबाइडिंग– adhering more or less strictly to the laws क़ानून का पालन करने वाला We are the *law-abiding* citizens.

lawbreaker *(n.)* लॉब्रेकर– a person who breaks the law क़ानून को तोड़ने वाला व्यक्ति The *lawbreakers* are punished badly in Saudi Arabia.

law court *(n.)* लॉ-कोर्ट– a body which adjudicates legal disputes and attempts to administer justice in accordance with the law कचहरी, न्यायालय She dragged the case to the *law court*.

lawful *(adj.)* लॉफुल– allowed, recognized, or sanctioned by law; legal क़ानूनी Being the only daughter, she is the *lawful* owner of her father's property.

lawless *(adj.)* लॉलेस– without law अराजक, विधि-विहीन Women are not safe in a *lawless* society.

lawmaking *(n.)* लॉमेकिंग– the process of legislating or making laws विधि निर्माण, क़ानून बनाना *Law making* is carried out by Parliament.

lawn *(n.)* लॉन– a flat and usually level area of mown and cultivated grass मैदान, लॉन This *lawn* has been maintained so well.

lawyer *(n.)* लॉयर– a member of the legal profession, esp a solicitor वकील, क़ानूनदां I am going to hire a *lawyer* for my case.

lay *(v.)* ले–1. to put in a low or horizontal position; cause to lie रखना, बिछाना, लेटना I need to *lay* down on this bed for sometime.

2. (of birds, esp the domestic hen) to produce (eggs) (अण्डे) देना Our hen has *laid* an egg.

➢ **lay aside**– to abandon or reject त्याग देना, टालना She had to *lay* her work *aside*.

➢ **lay down**–1. to place on the ground, etc. मर मिटना, प्राण न्यौछावर करना, She was even prepared to *lay down* her life for her friend.

2. to formulate (a rule, principle, etc.) स्थापित करना, You can *lay down* some conditions.

➢ **lay in**– to accumulate and store भंडार करना, एकत्र करना, I like to *lay in* a few special dresses for the festival.

➢ **lay off**– to suspend (workers) from employment with the intention of re-employing them at a later date कुछ समय के लिए काम से हटा देना, They *laid off* 20 workers from their factory.

➢ **lay on**– to provide or supply कुछ उपलब्ध कराना, A car has been *laid on* to take you in the party.

➢ **lay out**– to arrange or spread out व्यवस्थित करना, All the food items were *laid out* on the dining table.

layabout *(n.)* लेअबाउट– a lazy person; loafer आवारा, आलसी व्यक्ति I have not seen any *layabout* like you before.

layer *(n.)* लेअर्– a thickness of some homogeneous substance, such as a stratum or a coating on a surface परत I saw a thin *layer* of frost on my car.

layman *(n.)* लेमैन– a man who is not a member of the clergy सामान्यजन, अविशेषज्ञ He is a complete *layman* in the field of computers.

laze *(v.)* लेज़– to be indolent or lazy आलसी होना, ख़ाली बैठना I spent the afternoon *lazing* in my room.

laziness *(n.)* लेज़िनस– idleness सुस्ती, आलस *Laziness* is a temptation for all.

lazy *(adj.)* लेजी– not inclined to work or exertion आलसी, सुस्त How can you be *so lazy*? Please get up fast and start your work.

lead *(v.)* लीड–1. to show the way to (an individual or a group) by going with or ahead ले चलना, मार्गदर्शन करना Where are you *leading* me?

2. to guide or be guided by holding, pulling, etc. नेतृत्व करना I am going to *lead* the students' educational trip to Goa.

3. to pass or spend बिताना The old couple *led* a quiet life.

4. to place, put, or be in a particular state or position किसी को विशेष स्थिति पर रखना She *laid* the child gently down on the sofa.

5. to place or dispose in the proper position किसी वस्तु को उपयोग के लिए तैयार करना Can you *lay* the chair please?

6. *(n.)* the first, foremost, or most prominent place मुख्य भूमिका She played the *lead* in the new movie.

7. anything that guides or directs; indication; clue सुराग़, सूत्र The police is trying their best to find all possible *leads*.

8. *(adj.)* graphite or a mixture containing graphite, clay, etc. used for drawing सिक्के की Please get me a *lead* pencil.

leader *(n.)* लीडर– a person who rules, guides, or inspires others; head नेता, मार्गदर्शक, सरदार Who will be the *leader* in this game?

leadership *(n.)* लीडरशिप– the position or function of a leader नेतृत्व, नेतागिरी The success of the party depends on the strong *leadership.*

leading *(adj.)* लीडिंग– principal or primary प्रमुख, नामी, सबसे अधिक महत्त्वपूर्ण Who is leading the team?

leaf *(n.)* लीफ़–1. the main organ of photosynthesis and transpiration in higher plants, usually consisting of a flat green blade attached to the stem directly or by stalk पत्ता, पर्ण A dry *leaf* was lying near my window.

2. one of the sheets of paper in a book पृष्ठ, पन्ना Don't tear any *leaf* out of your exercise-book.

league *(n.)* लीग– an association or union of persons, nations, etc. formed to promote the interests of its members संघ, दल, संगठन The All-India Muslim *League* was founded in 1906.

leak *(v.)* लीक– 1. to enter or escape or allow to enter or escape through a crack, hole, etc. चूना, टपकना Rain-water *leaked* through the ceiling and spoilt the furniture.

2. *(n.)* a crack, hole, etc. that allows the accidental escape or entrance of fluid, light, etc. दरार, छेद, सुराख़ We must repair the *leak* in the pipe before summer.

leakage *(n.)* लीकेज़– something that escapes or enters by a leak रिसाव There is a *leakage* of water above my seat.

lean *(v.)* लीन–1. to rest or cause to rest against a support झुकना, टेकना I was so tired that I *leaned* against the wall.

2. to be dependant on निर्भर होना, आश्रित होना Try to be self-reliant, don't *lean* on others every time.

3. *(adj.)* having no surplus flesh or bulk; not fat or plump दुबला-पतला, कृश, क्षीण She was so *lean*. Isn't it?

leaning *(adj.)* लीनिंग– a tendency or inclination झुकाव, नति *Leaning* Tower of Pisa is in Italy.

leap *(n.)* लीप–1. the act of jumping उछाल, कुदान He crossed the ditch in one long *leap*.

2. *(v.)* to jump suddenly from one place to another ऊंची छलांग लगाना How high can you *leap*?

3. to move or react quickly झपाटे से कुछ करना She *leaps* back when the milk boiled.

leap year *(n.)* लीप इअर– a calendar year of 366 days, February 29 (leap day) being the additional day, that occurs every four years अधिवर्ष, जिस वर्ष में फरवरी 29 दिन का होता है *Leap year* comes after every four years.

learn *(v.)* लर्न–1. to gain knowledge of (something) or acquire skill in (some art or practice) सीखना, अध्ययन करना I have to *learn* the whole subject before my exams.

2. to become informed; know पता चलना I *learned* that you are going abroad.

learned *(adj.)* लर्नेड– having great knowledge or erudition ज्ञानी, विद्वान, पंडित The Principal of my school is a very *learned* man.

learner *(n.)* लर्नर– someone who is learning something; beginner नौसिखिया, शिक्षार्थी He is still a *learner* so what if he did this mistake.

learning *(n.)* लर्निंग– knowledge gained by study; instruction or scholarship

ज्ञान, विद्या-प्राप्ति *Learning* is a process that never ends.

lease *(n.)* लीस– a contract by which property is conveyed to a person for a specified period, usually for rent ठेका, पट्टे पर उठायी गयी भूमि या जायदाद They have given their flat on *lease.*

least *(adj.)* लीस्ट–1. of very little importance or rank अल्पतम, लघुतम This is the *least* I could do for you.

2. at the minimum कम से कम Please reach the venue at *least* half an hour before.

leather *(n.)* लेदर्– a material consisting of the skin of an animal made smooth and flexible by tanning, removing the hair, etc. चमड़ा I bought a new *leather* wallet.

leave *(v.)* लीव–1. to go or depart (from a person or place) चला जाना, प्रस्थान करना When can I *leave* sir?

2. to cause to be or remain in a specified state छोड़ना, रहने देना Please *leave* me alone.

3. *(n.)* permission to do something इजाज़त, अनुमति Who took my book without my *leave*?

4. permission to be absent, as from a place of work or duty छुट्टी, अवकाश I have applied for a month's *leave.*

5. the plural of leaf पत्तियां The *leaves* of this tree are long and pointed.

lecture *(v.)* लैक्चर्– 1. to give or read a lecture (to an audience or class) व्याख्यान देना Every day my father *lectures* me on the merits of yoga.

2. *(n.)* a discourse on a particular subject given or read to an audience व्याख्यान Today's *lecture* was so boring. isn't it?

lecturer *(n.)* लेक्चरर्– a teacher in higher education without professorial status प्राध्यापक, व्याख्याता Is she our new *lecturer?*

leech *(n.)* लीच– a small worm which have a sucker at each end of the body and feed on the blood or tissues of other animals जोंक, जलौका *Leech* sucks the blood of animals.

left *(adj.)* लेफ्ट– 1. a left side, direction, position, area, or part related adjectives sinister sinistral बायाँ, बाईं My *left* hand got injured last night.

2. *(adv.)* of or designating the side of something or someone that faces west when the front is turned towards the north बाईं ओर Turn *left* from here.

left-handed *(adj., adv.)* लेफ्ट-हेंडड– using the left hand with greater ease than the right बायाँहत्था वामहस्तिक Saurav Ganguly is a *left-handed* batsman.

leg *(n.)* ले'ग–1. either of the two lower limbs, including the bones and fleshy covering टाँग, पैर I lost my *leg* in the accident.

2. something similar to a leg in appearance or function, such as one of the four supporting members of a chair पाया Call a carpenter to repair the *legs* of this table.

legacy *(n.)* लेगसी– a gift by will, esp of money or personal property विरासत, जायदाद, पैतृक संपत्ति Ashok's grandmother left him a generous *legacy* after her death.

legal *(adj.)* लीगल्–1. established by or founded upon law; lawful क़ानूनी Please keep me away from these *legel* matters.

legality *(n.)* लीगैलटि– the state or quality of being legal or lawful वैधता, औचित्य You cannot challenge the *legality* of my property.

legalize *(v.)* लीगलाइज़– to make lawful or legal उचित ठहराना, वैध बनाना You should *legalize* your marriage.

legally *(adv.)* लीगलि– in a manner allowable or required by law क़ानूनी रूप से Ramesh was *legally* entitled to inherit his father's property.

legend *(n.)* लेजण्ड– a popular story handed down from earlier times whose truth has not been ascertained किंवदंती, दंतकथा As per the *legend,* Krishna killed many demons.

legendary *(adj.)* लेजेण्डरी– of or relating to legend कीर्तिशाली, काफ़ी मशहूर Lata Mangeshkar is a *legendary* singer.

legible *(adj.)* लेजिबल– (of handwriting, print, etc) able to be read or deciphered सुपाठ्य, पढ़ने में आसान Use a *legible* ink to write your letter.

legibility *(n.)* लेजिबिलटी– the state or quality of being able to be read or deciphered पढ़ने में बहुत आसान, सुवाच्यता There was a *legibility* in her signature.

legislation *(n.)* लेजिस्लेशन– the act or process of making laws; enactment विधि-निर्माण, विधान, कानून One should understand the intricacies of *legislation.*

legitimate *(adj.)* लैजिटिमट– born in lawful wedlock; enjoying full filial rights न्यायसंगत, यथार्थ Do you have a *legitimate* reason for taking a leave today?

leisure *(n.)* लेश़र्– time or opportunity for ease, relaxation, etc. अवकाश, फ़ुरसत I seldom have the *leisure* to watch television.

leisurely *(adj.)* लेश़र्ली– unhurried; relaxed धीमी चाल, मंद गति I always walk *leisurely* after the dinner.

lemon *(n.)* लेमन– a small Asian evergreen tree, Citrus limon, having pale green glossy leaves and edible fruits नींबू Prices of *lemon* are increasing day by day.

lemonade *(n.)* लेमनेड– a drink made from lemon juice, sugar, and water or from carbonated water, citric acid, etc. शिकंजी A glass of *lemonade* makes me feel fresh.

lend *(v.)* लेन्ड– to provide (money) temporarily, often at interest उधार देना Would you *lend* me ten rupees?

length *(n.)* लेन्थ्– the linear extent or measurement of something from end to end, usually being the longest dimension or, for something fixed, the longest horizontal dimension लंबाई What is the *length* of your skirt?

- **at length**– in depth; fully विस्तारपूर्वक She narrated her love story *at length.*
- **at great length**– to work excessively hard to gain somthing कुछ पाने के लिए जरूरत से ज्यादा प्रयत्न करना, Shehla would go *to great lengths* to fulfil her ambition.
- **the length and breadth of**– the essential points or facts किसी वस्तु के सब हिस्सों में, The police searched *the length and breadth of* the area.

lengthen *(v.)* लैंगथन– to make or become longer लंबा करना The tailor *lengthened* my shirt.

lengthways *(adv.)* लैंगथवेज़– in, according to, or along the direction of length लंबाई में Please fold my dress *lengthwise.*

lengthy *(adj.)* लैंगथी– of relatively great or tiresome extent or duration बहुत लंबा-चौड़ा The paper was very *lengthy.* isn't it?

lenient *(adj.)* लीनिअन्ट– showing or characterized by mercy or tolerance नरम, सौम्य She is a *lenient* teacher and avoids punishing her students.

lentil *(n.)* लेन्टल– a seed that is dried and used in cooking मसूर

दाल We used to cook *lentil* soup in summer.

leopard *(n.)* लेपर्ड– a large animal of the cat family, that has yellowish-brown fur with black spots तेंदुआ *Leopards* live in Africa and Southern Asia.

leprosy *(n.)* लेप्रसी– a chronic infectious disease characterized by the formation of painful inflamed nodules beneath the skin and disfigurement and wasting of affected parts कोढ़/कुष्ठ रोग She is a *leprosy* patient.

lesbian *(n.)* लेज़बिअन– a female homosexual समलिंगी कामुक स्त्री These girls are notorious for their *lesbian* relationship.

less *(pron., adv.)* लैस– the comparative of little कम You must eat *less* if you want to become slim.

lessen *(v.)* लेसन– to make or become less कम कर देना The indigestion has *lessened* my appetite.

lesson *(n.)* लेसन–1. a unit, or single period of instruction in a subject पाठ, अध्याय How many *lessons* have you covered?

2. censure or punish चेतावनी, सीख, सबक़ Let this mistake teach you a *lesson.*

let *(v.)* ले'ट–1. to permit; allow अनुमति देना *Let* me accompany you.

2. to allow the occupation of (accommodation) in return for rent किराये पर देना, भाड़े पर उठाना I want to *let* a three-room flat. If this flat is to *let,* please *let* it to me.

3. to allow or cause the movement of (something) in a specified direction रहने देना, दख़ल नहीं देना *Let* him stay alone.

- **let go**– to relax one's hold (on); release छोड़ देना, Please don't *let* her *go.*
- **let down**– to fail to fulfil the expectations of (a person); disappoint विफलता, असफ़लता, Her struggle for rights was a big *let down.*
- **let loose**– to set free बंधन से मुक्त करना, That dog, if *let loose* can harm.
- **let out**– to come to an end समाप्त होना The meeting/movie has just *let out.*

lethal *(adj.)* लीथल– able to cause or causing death प्राणघातक, हानिकारक She was about to take a *lethal* dose of poison.

lethargic *(adj.)* लेथार्जिक– lacking energy or enthusiasm आलसी, निष्चेष्ट Don't be so *lethargic.* Get up now

lethargy *(n.)* लेथार्जी– sluggishness, slowness, or dullness आलस्य, सुस्ती You should shed off your *lethargy* to become successful in life.

letter *(n.)* लेटर्–1. any of a set of conventional symbols used in writing or printing a language, each symbol being associated with a group of phonetic values in the language; character of the alphabet पत्र, खत How many *letters* have you learnt till now?

2. a written or printed communication addressed to a person, company, etc. usually sent by post in an envelope पत्र खत I will write you a *letter* once I reach there.

level *(n.)* लेवल–1. a horizontal datum line or plane तल Shimla is 2213 metres above the sea *level.*

2. position or status in a scale of values स्तर What is the general *level* of the students in your class?

3. *(adj.)* having a surface of completely equal height समतल The surface of this table is not quite *level.*

4. *(v.)* to make (a surface) horizontal, level, or even समतल करना He *levelled* the soil.

5. to make sth equal, as in position or status बराबर करना Her goal *levelled* the scores of the two teams.

lever *(n.)* लीवर्– a rigid bar pivoted about a fulcrum, used to transfer a force to a load and usually to provide a mechanical advantage उत्तोलक Would you please help me pull the *lever*?

leverage *(n.)* लीवरेज– power to accomplish something; strategic advantage ताक़त, प्रभाव Wealth has given him enormous *leverage* in society.

liability *(n.)* लाइअबिलटी– the state of being legally responsible for sth उत्तरदायित्व, जिम्मेदारी I cannot accept *liability* for any damage.

liable *(adj.)* लायबल– legally responsible for sth उत्तरदायी, जिम्मेदार The company will be *Liable* for any damage.

liberal *(adj.)* लिबरल– tolerant of other people दानी, उदार Try to be little *liberal* while giving marks to your students.

liberality *(n.)* लिबरैलिटी– generosity; bounty उदारता, विशाल हृदयता King Akbar was known for his *liberality* in religion.

liberate *(v.)* लिबरेट to give liberty to; make free स्वतंत्र करना, मुक्त करना These appliances have *liberatod* the housewifes.

liberty *(n.)* लिबर्टी–1. the power of choosing, thinking, and acting for oneself; freedom from control or restriction स्वतंत्रता, आजादी, मुक्ति You are now at *liberty* to go home.

2. a social action regarded as being familiar, forward, or improper स्वच्छंदता I have the *liberty* to come late at night.

library *(n.)* लाइब्ररी– a room or set of rooms where books and other literary materials are kept पुस्तकालय I got this book from the *library*.

licence *(n.)* लाइसन्स– a certificate, tag, document, etc. giving official permission to do something लाइसेंस, अनुमति पत्र, अनुज्ञापत्र Do you have a *licence* to drive a heavy vehicle?

license *(v.)* लाइसन्स– to grant or give a licence for (something, such as the sale of alcohol) अनुज्ञा/लाइसेंस प्रदान करना He is *licensed* to sell alcohol.

lick *(v.)* लिक– to pass the tongue over, esp in order to taste or consume चाटना I like it when the puppy *lick* my leg.

lid *(n.)* लिड– a cover, usually removable or hinged, for a receptacle ढक्कन I want a box with a *lid* on it.

lie *(n.)* लाइ–1. an untrue or deceptive statement deliberately used to mislead झूठ, असत्य Anyone who tells a *lie* is a liar.

2. *(v.)* to speak untruthfully with intent to mislead or deceive झूठ बोलना Don't *lie* to me.

3. to place oneself or be in a prostrate position, horizontal to the ground लेटना, लेट जाना Please *lie* on the bed.

4. to rest or weigh पड़ा रहना I saw all his books *lying* on the floor.

5. to be situated, esp on a horizontal surface स्थित होना In which continent does India *lie*?

- **lie behind**– to hide something due to the situation परिस्थितिवश किसी बात को गुप्त रखना, I do not know what *lay behind* his decision to go abroad.
- **lie down**– to place oneself or be in a prostrate position in order to rest or sleep पड़े रहना, लेट कर आराम करना, I *laid down* after a long walk.

- **lie low**– to keep or be concealed or quiet चुपचाप रहना, She decided to *lie low* for a while.
- **white lie** *(n.)*– a minor or unimportant lie, esp one uttered in the interests of tact or politeness सफ़ेद झूठ, He was telling a *white lie* to her wife.

lieutenant *(n.)* लेफ़्टेनन्ट– a military officer holding commissioned rank immediately junior to a captain लेफ़्टिनेंट, सेना अधिकारी He is promoted to the post of *lieutenant.*

life *(n.)* लाइफ़–1. the period between birth and death जीवन Live *life* king size.

2. liveliness or high spirits ज़िंदादिली She is full of *life.*

3. a characteristic state or mode of existence किसी वस्तु के बने रहने की अवधि Mishandling reduces the *life* of the machine.

- **life-and-death** *(adj.)* vitally or gravely serious; possibly resulting in death बहुत गंभीर, जीवन-मरण का प्रश्न, It was a matter of *life and death* for her.

lifebelt *(n.)* लाइफ़बेल्ट– a ring filled with buoyant material or air, used to keep a person afloat when in danger of drowning जीवन रक्षा-पेटी Don't forget to wear your *lifebelt* while swimming.

lifeboat *(n.)* लाइफ़बोट– a boat, propelled by oars or a motor, used for rescuing people at sea, escaping from a sinking ship, etc. जीवन रक्षा-नौका We need some more *lifeboats* urgently.

lifeless *(adj.)* लाइफ़लस– without life; inanimate; dead मृत, निर्जीव, जीवनरहित Mars is a *lifeless* planet.

lifelike *(adj.)* लाइफ़लाइक– letter जीता-जागता, सजीव This statue is made of stone but looks very *lifelike.*

lifelong *(adj.)* लाइफ़लॉन्ग– lasting for or as if for a lifetime आजीवन, जीवनभर साथ देने वाला Education is a *lifelong* process.

lifespan *(n.)* लाइफ़स्पैन– the period of time during which a human being, animal, plant, etc. may be expected to live or function under normal conditions जीवनकाल, अवधि The average *lifespan* of a horse is not more than 40 years.

lifestyle *(n.)* लाइफ़स्टाइल– a set of attitudes, habits, or possessions associated with a particular person or group जीवनशैली Her *lifestyle* is different from ours.

lifetime *(n.)* लाइफ़टाइम– the length of time a person or animal is alive सारी उम्र, जीवन-काल This is going to be my *lifetime* achievement.

lift *(v.)* लिफ़्ट–1. to rise or cause to rise upwards from the ground or another support to a higher place उठाना I can't *lift* this box for long. It's so heavy.

2. *(n.)* the act or an instance of lifting लिफ़्ट, उत्थापक The *lift* in this building is out of order.

light *(n.)* लाइट–1. the medium of illumination that makes sight possible बत्ती, दीपक Where is the switch to this *light?*

2. electromagnetic radiation that is capable of causing a visual sensation प्रकाश, रोशनी In the *light* of the lamp, I read his letter.

3. *(adj.)* full having relatively low density मन्द, हल्का, फीका I like fabrics of *light* colours.

4. not heavy; weighing relatively little हलका I can carry this *light* box.

5. *(v.)* to ignite or cause to ignite जलाना, सुलगाना Please *light* a candle.

lighten *(v.)* लाइटन–1. to become or make light भार हलका कर देना या हो जाना I *lightened* my suitcase by taking out several pairs of shoes.

2. to shine; glow अधिक रोशनी कर देना, प्रकाशमय करना The white ceiling *lightened* the room.

lightly *(adv.)* लाइटली– in a gentle manner धीरे से, हलके से Why do you always take these issues so *lightly*?

lightning *(n.)* लाइटनिंग– a flash of light in the sky, occurring during a thunderstorm and caused by a discharge of electricity, बिजली, तड़ित There was a sudden flash of *lightning*.

lightweight *(n.)* लाइटवेट– a person or animal of a relatively light weight हलकी, कम भार की I am looking for some *lightweight* shoes.

like *(v.)* लाइक–1. to find (something) enjoyable or agreeable or find it enjoyable or agreeable (to do something) पसन्द करना Hey! I *like* your dress.

2. *(conj.)* similar to; similarly to; in the manner of समान, सदृश I bought a pen *like* yours.

likeable *(adj.)* लाइकबल– easy to like; pleasing प्रिय, पसंद किये जाने वाला You are very *likeable* to me.

likelihood *(n.)* लाइकलिहुड– the condition of being likely or probablo; probability संभावना There is very little *likclihood* of his success in the exams.

likely *(adj.)* लाइकली– an infinitive tending or inclined; apt संभवतः, कदाचित् Are you *likely* to go to Mumbai next week?

like-minded *(adj.)* लाइकमाइंडड्– agreeing in opinions, goals, etc. एक-सी रुचि या विचार रखने वाला They are *like-minded* friends.

likeness *(n.)* लाइकनस– the condition of being alike; similarity समानता The *likeness* of her voice with that of her mother often confuses me.

likewise *(adv.)* लाइकवाइज़– in like manner; similarly वैसा ही, वही Anil pushed the crowd and Harish did *likewise*.

liking *(n.)* लाइकिंग– the feeling of a person who likes; fondness पसंद, रुचि Coincidently our *likings* match.

limb *(n.)* लिम्ब–1. an arm or leg, or the analogous part on an animal, such as a wing अंग, अवयव I hope none of your *limbs* was injured in the accident.

2. any of the main branches of a tree शाखा I watched the squirrel run up a *limb* of the tree.

lime *(n.)* लाइम– a small round or oval greenish fruits नींबू *Lime* water in the morning makes your skin glow.

limelight *(n.)* लाइमलाइट– a position of public attention or notice लोक-प्रसिद्धि Sridevi is now no more in *limelight*.

limit *n.)* लिमिट– 1. the ultimate extent, degree, or amount of something सीमा, हद There is a *limit* to the powers of the Prime Minister.

2. (v.) to restrict or confine, as to area, extent, time, etc. सीमित करना, प्रतिबंध लगाना One must try to *limit* one's own expenditure.

limitation *(n.)* लिमिटेशन– something that limits a quality or achievement प्रतिबंध, सीमा, हद I know my own *limitations* while dealing with you.

limited *(adj.)* लिमिटेड– having a limit; restricted; confined सीमित I have only *limited* interest in classical music.

limp *(v.)* लिम्प–1. to walk with an uneven step, esp with a weak or injured leg लँगड़ाना Why are you *limping*?

2. an uneven walk or progress लँगड़ापन A young man walked with a slight *limp.*

3. *(adj.)* not energetic or vital शिथिल, निर्जीव These flowers have become *limp.*

line *(n.)* लाइन–1. a narrow continuous mark, as one made by a pencil, pen, or brush across a surface रेखा, लकीर Try to draw a staright *line* on your own.

2. a straight or curved continuous trace having no breadth that is produced by a moving point क़तार, ताँता Sit in a *line,* all of you.

3. *(v.)* to place in or form a row, series, or alignment क़तार लगाना People *lined* up to cast their vote.

➢ **line up**– to produce, organize, and assemble व्यवस्थित करना, I *lined up* all the meetings together.

linen *(n.)* लिनेन– a hard-wearing fabric woven from the spun fibres of flax सन का बना वस्त्र, लिनन Give this dirty *linen* to the washer-man.

linger *(v.)* लिन्गर्– to delay or prolong departure ठहर जाना, देर तक ठहरना, देर लगाना Why are you *lingering* here though the show is over?

linguist *(n.)* लिंग्विष्ट– a person who has the capacity to learn and speak foreign languages भाषाविज्ञानी, भाषाविद् Professor Kumar is a good *linguist.*

lining *(n.)* लाइनिंग– material used to line a garment, curtain, etc. अस्तर She tore the *lining* of her skirt.

link *(n.)* लिन्क– 1. any of the separate rings, loops, or pieces that connect or make up a chain कड़ी Are all the *links* in this chain equally strong?

2. *(v.)* to connect or be connected with or as if with links संबंध, संबद्ध करना, जोड़ देना Let us *link* hands to dance around the tree.

lint *(n.)* लिण्ट– an absorbent cotton or linen fabric with the nap raised on one side, used to dress wounds, etc. फाहा, घाव ढकने का नरम कपड़ा Get some *lint* to dress the wound.

lion *(n.)* लॉइअन– a large powerful animal of the cat family having a tawny yellow coat and, in the male, a shaggy mane शेर, सिंह I did not see any *lion* in the zoo.

lip *(n.)* लिप्–1. either of the two fleshy folds surrounding the mouth, playing an important role in the production of speech sounds, retaining food in the mouth, etc. होंठ, अधर How come your *lips* are so cracked?

2. any structure resembling a lip, such as the rim of a crater, the margin of a gastropod shell, etc. किनारा, धार The *lip* of this cup is not clean.

lip-read *(v.)* लिप-रिड– to interpret (words) by lip-reading होठों की हरकत को देखकर बोलते हुए शब्दों को समझना I can *lip-read* people.

lipservice *(n.)* लिपसर्विस– insincere support or respect expressed but not put into practice दिखावटी बातें Paying *lipservice* costs only a few words.

liquid *(adj.)* लिक्विड– 1. of, concerned with, or being a liquid or having the characteristic state of liquids द्रव, प्रवाही, (जो ठोस न हो) I am on *liquid* diet for two days.

2. *(n.)* a substance in a physical state in which it does not resist change of shape but does resist change of size तरल पदार्थ What is the golden-coloured *liquid* in that glass?

liquor *(n.)* लिकर्– any alcoholic drink, esp spirits, or such drinks collectively तेज़ शराब, मदिरा This area is full *of liquor* shop.

lisp *(n.)* लिस्प– the habit or speech defect of pronouncing s and z in this manner तुतलाहट The child has a *lisp* in his voice.

list *(n.)* लिस्ट– an item-by-item record of names or things, usually written or printed one under the other सूची, तालिका Is your *list* ready?

listen *(v.)* लिसन–1. to concentrate on hearing something सुनना Students were *listening* attentively to the teacher's talk.

2. to take heed; pay attention किसी बात पर ध्यान देना एवं उसे मानना Please *listen* to me.

listener *(n.)* लिसनर– someone who listens to something or someone श्रोता You should be a good *listener* to win this game.

listless *(adj.)* लिस्टलस– having no interest in what is going on about one, as a result of illness, weariness, dejection, etc.; spiritless; languid सुस्त, थका, ढीला, निर्जीव The disease has left her *listless.*

literally *(adv.)* लिटरली– actually; in fact अक्षरशः They were *literally* on the roads after their father's accident.

literary *(adj.)* लिटररी– of, having the nature of, or dealing with literature साहित्यिक Mahadevi Varma was a great *literary* figure.

literate *(adj.)* लिटरट– able to read and write शिक्षित, साक्षर My maid-servant is *literate* and can also read a newspaper.

literature *(n.)* लिट्रेचर– all writings in prose or verse, esp. those of an imaginative or critical character, without regard to their excellence साहित्य How much did you scored in *literature?*

litigation *(n.)* लिटिगेशन– the act or process of carrying on a lawsuit मुक़दमेबाज़ी, मुकदमा Her property dispute is still in *litigation.*

litre *(n.)* लीटर– the basic unit of volume or capacity in the metric system (किसी भी द्रव की एक माप-तोल लीटर) This tank can contain atlest 10 *litres* of water.

litter *(v.)* लिटर्– 1. to make messy with things scattered about कूड़ा-कचरा बिखराना His room was *littered* with old newspapers and magazines.

2. *(n.)* things lying about in disorder, esp., bits of rubbish scattered about कूड़ा Dump the *litter* in the dustbin.

little *(adj.)* लिटल–1. small in size; not big, large, or great छोटा, लघु This is a *little* house

2. small in force, intensity, etc.; weak किंचित् I feel a *little* unwell today.

3. short in duration or distance; brief; not long थोड़ा, कुछ ही I have *little* time to waste.

live *(v.)* लिव–1. to stay रहना, निवास करना How do you *live* here?

2. to be alive; have life जीना, जीवित होना Is your grandfather still *living*?

➢ **live by**– to live by trickery or craftiness रोज़ी-रोटी कमाना, They *live by* hunting and fishing.

➢ **live down**– to live in such a way as to wipe out the memory or shame of (some fault, misdeed, etc.) किसी की ग़लती को भुला देना I can never *live* that *down.*

➢ **live for**– to live for a reson किसी को अपने जीवन का मक़सद बनाना, He *lives for* the day when he would have his own house.

➢ **live it up**– to have a joyful, hilarious time जीवन का भरपूर मज़ा लेना, शान से रहना, Faris *lives it up* in San Francisco.

➢ **live off**– depend on as a source of income or support किसी व्यक्ति या वस्तु पर निर्भर रहना, Her family used to *live off* the interest from their savings.

➢ **live on**– to continue to live अस्तित्व का बना रहना, Mohd. Rafi is dead but his voice *lives on.*

➢ **live through**– to bear, to face झेलना, भोगना She *lived through* her nightmare.

➢ **live up**– to like something more than expected अपेक्षा से अधिक अच्छा होना, The film has certainly *lived up* to our expectations.

➢ **live with**– live together साथ रहना, My mother-in-law came to *live with* us.

livelihood *(n.)* लाइवलिहुड– means of living or of supporting life; subsistence रोज़ी, जीविका It's difficult to earn a *livelihood* as a poet.

lively *(adj.)* लाइवली– full of life; active; vigorous जिंदादिली, सजीव, प्रसन्न Her *lively* nature makes her everyone's favourite.

liver *(n.)* लिवर्– the largest glandular organ in vertebrate animals, located in the upper or anterior part of the abdomen जिगर, यकृत The *liver* is the largest solid organ in the body.

living *(n.)* लिविंग–1. the state of being alive जीविका How do you earn your *living*?

2. *(adj.)* alive; having life; not dead जीवित She has no *living* relatives.

lizard *(n.)* लिज़र्ड– a small reptile having tail, scaly skin and four legs छिपकली I can't tolerate any *lizard* around me.

load *(n.)* लोड–1. something carried or to be carried at one time or in one trip; burden; cargo भार, बोझ I can't carry this much *load* on myself.

2. *(v.)* to put something to be carried into or upon; esp., to fill or cover with as much as can be carried लादना Have they *loaded* all our household items in the truck?

3. to put into or upon a carrier भरना Have you *loaded* your gun?

loaf *(n.)* लोफ़– 1. a portion of bread baked in one piece डबल रोटी Go to the bakery and buy a *loaf* of bread.

2. *(v.)* to spend time idly; loiter or lounge about; idle, dawdle, etc. आवारागर्दी में समय ख़राब करना You do nothing but *loaf* in the streets.

loan *(n.)* लोन– the act of lending, esp. to use for a short time उधार, क़र्ज़ I will buy this car on *loan*.

loathe *(v.)* लोद– to feel intense dislike, disgust, or hatred for; abhor; detest घृणा/नफ़रत करना I *loathe* the very sight of him.

loath *(adj.)* लोथ– reluctant or unwilling अनिच्छुक, ख़ुशी से नहीं She seems *loath* to lend me her bag.

lobby *(n.)* लॉबी– a room or corridor used as an entrance hall, vestibule, etc. लॉबी, प्रतीक्षा-कक्ष There is a big *lobby* area in that house.

lobster *(n.)* लॉब्स्टर– a sea creature with a hard shell and a long body झींगा We fry and eat *lobster*.

local *(adj.)* लोकल–1. characteristic of or associated with a particular locality or area स्थानीय Where is the *local* bus stop?

2. *(n.)* an inhabitant of a specified locality स्थान विशेष में रहने वाला व्यक्ति We asked one of the *locals* to recommend a good hotel.

localize (ise) *(v.)* लोकलाइज़– to make or become local in attitude, behaviour, etc. स्थानीय बना देना या बन जाना We cannot *localize* the spreading diseases.

locally *(adv.)* लोकली– within a particular area or place स्थानीय रूप से Is this electric kettle *locally* made?

locate *(v.)* लोकेट– 1. to discover the position, situation, or whereabouts of; find स्थापित ठिकाने का पता लगाना Have you been able to *locate* the lost book?

2. *(adj.)* to situate or place स्थित Where is your house *located?*

location *(n.)* लोकेशन– a site or position; situation जगह, स्थान What is the exact *location* of your new house?

lock *(v.)* लॉक– 1. to fasten (a door, gate, etc.) or (of a door, etc.) to become fastened with a lock, bolt, etc. so as to prevent entry or exit ताला लगाना Have you *locked* the room properly?

2. *(n.)* a device fitted to a gate, door, drawer, lid, etc. to keep it firmly closed and often to prevent access by unauthorized persons ताला I bought a new *lock* for my cupboard.

locker *(n.)* लॉकर– a small compartment or drawer that may be locked, as one of several in a gymnasium, etc. for clothes and valuables ताले वाली अलमारी I can't see any *locker* here.

locket *(n.)* लॉकेट– a small ornamental case, usually on a necklace or chain, that holds a picture, keepsake, etc. लटकन, गले में पहनने का लाकिट He gave me a gold *locket* on my birthday.

lock-up *(n.)* लॉक-अप– a jail or block of cells हवालात The police put the thief in a *lock-up.*

locomotive *(n.)* लोकमोटिव– a self-propelled engine driven by steam, electricity, or diesel power and used for drawing trains along railway tracks इंजन Does our country export *locomotives*?

locust *(n.)* लोकस्ट– any of numerous orthopterous insects of the genera Locusta टिड्डी The *locusts* destroyed the whole crop.

lodge *(v.)* लॉज– 1. to live temporarily, esp in rented accommodation रहना, ठहरना I am planning to *lodge* here only.

2. *(n.)* a small house at the entrance to the grounds of a country mansion, झोंपड़ी, छोटा घर When I go for hunting, I stay in a *lodge* in the forest.

lodging *(n.)* लॉजिंग– a temporary residence रहने की जगह, अस्थायी निवास-स्थल They found *lodging* in the Mathura Road.

lofty *(adj.)* लॉफ़्टी–1. of majestic or imposing height ऊँचा, उत्तुंग Our old mansion has a *lofty* ceiling.

2. elevated, eminent, or superior उच्च, उत्कृष्ट I appreciate your *lofty* ideals.

log *(n.)* लॉग– a section of the trunk or a main branch of a tree, when stripped of branches लट्ठा, कुन्दा Put a *log* in the fire.

logic *(n.)* लॉजिक– the system and principles of reasoning used in a specific field of study तर्क I can't see any *logic* in your project.

logical *(adj.)* लॉजिकल– relating to, used in, or characteristic of logic तर्कसंगत, तार्किक His answer was completely *logical.*

logo *(n.)* लोगो– a trademark, company emblem, or similar device लोगो I think our *logo* should be catchy and different from others.

loiter *(v.)* लॉइटर्– to stand or act aimlessly or idly मटरग़श्ती करना He spends all his day *loitering* around the college campus.

lollipop *(n.)* लॉलिपॉप– a boiled sweet or toffee stuck on a small wooden stick एक चूसने की मिठाई I gave him a pack of *lollipops.*

lonely *(adj.)* लोनली– unhappy as a result of being without the companionship of others अकेला और उदास Please come back. I am feeling so *lonely.*

loner *(n.)* लोनर्– a person or animal who avoids the company of others or prefers to be alone एकांतप्रिय He is an eccentric *loner* and never meets anyone.

long *(adj.)* लॉन्ग–1. having relatively great extent in space on a horizontal plane लम्बा Draw a four inches *long* line.

2. *(v.)* to have a strong desire तरसना, लालायित होना I *long* to go on a holiday.

3. *(adv.)* for or lasting a long time देर तक How *long* will you be away?

4. for a certain time or period दीर्घकालीन I have not seen you for a *long* time.

➢ **long ago**– in the distant past: बहुत समय पहले, It happened *long ago.*

➢ **long before**– a long period बहुत पहले, We got married *long before.*

➢ **long-distance** *(adj.)* travelling or operating between distant places: लम्बी दूरी वाला, Our's is a relaxing car for a *long distance* drive.

➢ **long lasting** *(adj.)*– enduring or having endured for a long period of time लम्बे समय से, They have a *long lasting* relationship.

➢ **as long as**– during the whole time that जब तक, I shall do it *as long as* it is possible.

longevity *(n.)* लॉन्जेवटी– long life: लम्बी उम्र, दीर्घ आयु She wished me for my health and *longevity.*

longing *(n.)* लॉगिंग– a yearning desire: लालसा, चाहत She died with a *longing* to see her son.

long-life *(adj.)* लॉन्ग-लाइफ़– (of a product) able to continue working for longer than others of the same kind लम्बी उम्र They are giving you the *long-life* battery with this torch.

long-lived *(adj.)* लॉन्ग-लिव्ड– living or lasting a long time: दीर्घकालीन There is a *long-lived* dispute between them.

long-term *(adj.)* लॉन्ग-टर्म– occurring over or relating to a long period of time दीर्घकालीन I believe in *long-term* relationships.

long-time *(adj.)* लॉन्ग-टाइम– having had a specified role or identity for a long time: काफ़ी पुरानी Ours is a *long-time* friendship.

look *(n.)* लुक–1. an act of directing one's gaze in order to see someone or something दृष्टि, नज़र, निगाह There was a *look* of surprise on his face.

2. *(v.)* direct one's gaze in a specified direction दृष्टि डालना, देखना *Look* at this picture.

3. to search or seek खोजना Are you *looking* for someone?

4. to accord in appearance with (something) प्रतीत होना, लगना Sushila *looked* charming at the party.

➢ **look after**– to take care of; be responsible for देखभाल करना, The lady *looks after* her old mother-in-law.

➢ **look back**– to cast one's mind to the past पीछे मुड़कर देखना, Do not *look back* to your past life.

➢ **look before**– think before doing anythng समझबूझकर किसी काम में हाथ डालना, *Look before* you leap.

➢ **look down**– regard (someone) with a feeling of superiority घृणा करना, नीचा समझना, Never *look down* upon poor people.

➢ **look for**– attempt to find: उत्सुकता से प्रतीक्षा करना, I am *looking for* an improvement in his behaviour.

➢ **look forward**– await eagerly: आशा लगाना/होना, Reena was *looking forward* to the event.

➢ **look into**– investigate जांच-पड़ताल करना, He *looked into* my eyes to know the fact.

➢ **look round**– walk round (a place or building) in order to view any interesting features चारों तरफ़ देखना,

Uma *looked around* but could not see him.

➢ **look through**– to examine, esp cursorily एक नज़र से देख जाना, The writer *looked through* her book before giving it for printing.

➢ **look up**– to discover (something required to be known) by resorting to a work of reference, such as a dictionary खोजना, पता लगना, What are you *looking up* in the book?

➢ **look upon**– to be a spectator at an event or incident देखना, I *look upon* this matter as a disgrace.

loom *(n.)* लूम– 1. an apparatus, worked by hand (hand loom) or mechanically (power loom), for weaving yarn into a textile करघा Is this hand-*loom* cloth?

2. *(v.)* to come into view indistinctly with an enlarged and often threatening aspect अस्पष्ट या धुँधला दिखाई देना As we sat on the seashore, a ship *loomed* into sight.

loony *(adj.)* लूनी– crazy or foolish झक्की, सनकी She always gives a *loony* idea.

loop *(n.)* लूप– the round or oval shape formed by a line, string, etc. that curves around to cross itself फंदा, छल्ला She made a *loop* in a rope.

loophole *(n.)* लूपहोल– an ambiguity, omission, etc. as in a law, by which one can avoid a penalty or responsibility बचाव का रास्ता There isn't any *loophole* in this case now.

loose *(adj.)* लूज़–1. not firmly fixed ढीला, शिथिल This knot is very *loose,* please tighten it.

2. not fitted or fitting closely अलग One of my teeth is getting *loose.*

loose fitting *(adj.)* लूज़फिटिंग– not tight आरामदेह The doctor is wearing a *loose fitting* apron.

loosen *(v.)* लूज़न– to make or become less tight, fixed, etc. ढीला हो जाना या कर देना The sewing machine is not working properly as its screw has *loosened.*

loose-tongued *(adj.)* लूज़-टंगड– careless or irresponsible in talking बकवादी, बक-बक करने वाला He is a *loose-tongued* man.

loot *(v.)* लूट– 1. to steal (money or goods), esp during pillaging लूटना The robbers *looted* all the money from the house.

2. *(n.)* the act of looting or plundering लूटमार What was the extent of their *loot?*

lop *(v.)* लॉप– to sever (parts) from a tree, body, etc. esp with swift strokes कांट-छांट करना *Lop* off that old tree.

lopsided *(adj.)* लॉपसाइडिड– leaning or inclined to one side एकतरफ़ा, असंतुलित This story presents a somewhat *lopsided* view of incidents.

lord *(n.)* लॉर्ड–1. a title used to refer to God प्रभु, भगवान The *Lord* helps those who help themselves.

2. a feudal superior शासक The *lord* was excessively drunk.

3. a male member of the nobility स्वामी An Indian wife keeps fast for the long life of her *lord* husband.

lorry *(v.)* लॉरी– a large motor vehicle designed to carry heavy loads, esp one with a flat platform लारी, ट्रक We hired a *lorry* to move our things to the new house.

lose *(v.)* लूज़–1. to cease to have or possess खोना, खो देना I don't want to *lose.*

2. to fail to keep or maintain हार जाना Did you *lose* the match?

3. to fail to get or make use of नहीं (देख, सुन, समझ, पकड़) पाना If you do not hurry, you will *lose* the train.

4. to wander from so as to be unable to find भटक जाना Have you *lost* your way?

loser *(n.)* लूज़र– a person or thing that loses असफ़ल व्यक्ति She's a born *loser.*

loss *(n.)* लॉस– the act or an instance of losing नुक़सान I can't bear this *loss.*

lost *(adj.)* लॉस्ट– unable to be found or recovered चकराया हुआ He is *lost* in his own world.

lot *(n.)* लॉट–1. a great number or quantity ढेर The whole *lot* of garments was rejected.
2. *(adv.)* to a considerable extent, degree, or amount; very much बहुत अधिक She danced a *lot* at the party.
3. *(det.)* a great number or quantity ढेर सारा There are a *lot* of mistakes in your drawing.

lotion *(n.)* लोशन– a liquid preparation having a soothing, cleansing, or antiseptic action, applied to the skin, eyes, etc. लोशन Please give me some *lotion* for the boils on my skin.

lottery *(n.)* लॉटरी– a method of raising money by selling numbered tickets and giving a proportion of the money raised to holders of numbers drawn at random लॉटरी I bought this *lottery* ticket for 10 rupess.

loud *(adj.)* लाउड–1. (of sound) relatively great in volume ऊँचा, तीव्र Do not speak in a *loud* voice.
2. clamorous, insistent, and emphatic चटकीला I do not like *loud* colours.

loudly *(adv.)* लाउडली– in a loud way ऊँची आवाज़ में, प्रबलता से Say *loudly* I can't hear you.

loudspeaker *(n.)* लाउडस्पीकर– a device for converting audio-frequency signals into the equivalent sound waves by means of a vibrating conical diaphragm ध्वनि विस्तारक यंत्र The *loudspeaker* of my radio is not working.

lounge *(n.)* लाउन्ज– to sit, lie, walk, or stand in a relaxed manner बैठकखाना, विश्राम-कक्ष We sat in the *lounge* of the hotel.

louse *(n.)* लाउज़– a wingless bloodsucking insect that lives on the bodies of human and animals जूँ, चीलर She does not wash her hairs properly and has many *louses.*

lousy *(adj.)* लाउज़ी– inferior or bad बहुत बुरा It was a *lousy* dinner.

lout *(n.)* लाउट– a crude or oafish person; boor बेवकूफ़, गंवार Hari behaves like a *lout* in office.

lovable *(adj.)* लवबल– attracting or deserving affection प्यारा लगने वाला Bunty is such a little *lovable* boy.

love *(v.)* लव–1. to have a great attachment to and affection for प्रेम या प्यार करना I *love* my children.
2. to be in love (में) रुचि होना I *love* music.
3. to like or desire (to do something) very much चाहना, अच्छा समझना Do you *love* me, master?
4. *(n.)* an intense emotion of affection, warmth, fondness, and regard towards a person or thing स्नेह, प्रेम *Love* is immortal.
5. a beloved person: used esp as an endearment प्रेमी, प्रेमिका He is an old *love* of my sister.

love-affair *(n.)* लव-अफ़ेयर– a great enthusiasm or liking for something प्रेम-प्रसंग Kareena has a *love affair* with Saif since five years.

lovely *(adj.)* लवली– very attractive or beautiful सुंदर, प्यारा She was looking *lovely* today.

lover *(n.)* लवर–1. someone who loves a specified person or thing शौकीन Menaka Gandhi is an animal *lover.*

2. a person, now esp a man, who has an extramarital or premarital sexual relationship with another person प्रेमी, आशिक़ She said that he was her *lover.*

loving *(adj.)* लविंग– feeling, showing, or indicating love and affection प्यारा My room-mate is a fun *loving* girl.

low *(adj.)* लो–1. having little or no money अल्प Why have you kept the price of this shirt so *low*?

2. with a hushed tone; quiet or soft निम्न, धीमा Please speak in a *low* voice.

3. situated at a relatively short distance above the ground, sea level, the horizon, or other reference position निचला, नीचा Do not build your house on a *low* ground.

lower *(adj.)* लोअर– being below one or more other things निचला I want that book which is kept on that *lower* shelf.

lowland *(n.)* लोलैंड– relatively low ground नीची ज़मीन Asian farmers plant rice in *lowland* areas.

low-pitched *(adj.)* लो-पिचूड– pitched low in tone नीचा, निम्न She was gossiping in a *low-pitched* voice.

loyal *(adj.)* लॉइअल– having or showing continuing allegiance ईमानदार, वफ़ादार Our servant is very *loyal.*

loyalty *(n.)* लॉइअलटी– the state or quality of being loyal निष्ठा, वफ़ादारी His *loyalty* gave him this reward.

lubricate *(v.)* लूब्रिकेट– to cover or treat with an oily or greasy substance so as to lessen friction चिकना करना You must *lubricate* the engine of your car regularly.

lubrication *(n.)* लूब्रिकेशन– the act of lubricating something चिकनाई डालने की क्रिया This machine needs *lubrication.*

lucid *(adj.)* लूसिड– readily understood; clear सरल और सुबोध The book is written in a *lucid* style.

luck *(n.)* लक– events that are beyond control and seem subject to chance; fortune भाग्य, सौभाग्य This all depends upon your *luck.*

lucky *(adj.)* लकी– having or bringing good fortune भाग्यवान, ख़ुशक़िस्मत I am so *lucky* that I got to see you.

lucrative *(adj.)* लूक्रटिव– producing a profit; profitable; remunerative लाभप्रद He got a *lucrative* offer from the rival company.

ludicrous *(adj.)* लूडिक्रस– absurd or incongruous to the point of provoking ridicule or laughter बेतुका, हास्यास्पद You always give a *ludicrous* idea.

luggage *(n.)* लॅगेज– suitcases, trunks, etc. containing personal belongings for a journey; baggage सामान, असबाब Keep your *luggage* next to you.

lug *(v.)* लग– to carry or drag (something heavy) with great effort ज़ोर लगाकर खींचना, घसीटना The servant was *lugging* my heavy suitcase up the stairs.

lukewarm *(adj.)* लूकवॉर्म– (esp of water) moderately warm; tepid गुनगुना You need to gargle with *lukewarm* water.

lull *(v.)* लल-1. to soothe (a person or animal) by soft sounds or motions गाकर सुलाना, लोरी सुनाना My sister *lulled* her baby to sleep.

2. to calm (someone or someone's fears, suspicions, etc.) शांत करना He finally *lulled* him.

3. a short period of calm or diminished activity बेहोशी The drug had pect him a *lull.*

lullaby *(n.)* लॅलबाइ– a quiet song to lull a child to sleep लोरी I sang a *lullaby* to put my child to sleep.

lumber *(n.)* लम्बर– 1. logs; sawn timber काठ-कबाड़ The store room was full of *lumbers.*
2. *(v.)* to fill up or encumber with useless household articles फ़ालतू बेकार सामान से भरना His bedroom *lumbered* up with junk.

luminous *(adj.)* लूमिनस– radiating or reflecting light; shining; glowing प्रकाशमान My wrist-watch has *luminous* hands.

lump *(n.)* लॅम्प–1. a small solid mass without definite shape ढेला, पिण्ड, डला I put *lumps* of earth into the flower pot.
2. any small swelling or tumour सूजन What is this *lump* on your arm?

lump sum *(n.)* लॅम्प-सम– a relatively large sum of money, paid at one time, esp in cash एकमुश्त राशि He gave me *lump sum* for writing a book.

lumpy *(adj.)* लम्पी– full of or having lumps मोटा, ढेलेदार I have a green colour *lumpy* mattress.

lunacy *(n.)* लूनसी– foolishness or a foolish act पागलपन It is *lunacy* to drive fast.

lunar *(adj.)* लूनर– of or relating to the moon चंद्रमा से संबंधित Hijri is a *lunar* year of the Muslims.

lunatic *(n.)* लूनटिक– 1. a person who is insane पागल, बावला व्यक्ति A great loss in business turned the businessman into a *lunatic.*
2. *(adj.)* foolish; eccentric; crazy पागल We have a *lunatic* asylum in this town.

lunch *(n.)* लॅन्च– 1. a meal eaten during the middle of the day मध्याह्न-भोजन When will you have your *lunch* today?
2. *(v.) to eat lunch* दोपहर का भोजन करना या कराना I will have my *lunch* at 4 p.m.

lunch hour *(n.)* लॅन्चऑर– a break in the middle of the working day, usually of one hour, during which lunch may be eaten दोपहर के खाने का अवकाश He takes a nap in his *lunch hour.*

lunchtime *(n.)* लंचटाइम्– the time at which lunch is usually eaten भोजन का समय What is your *lunchtime* in the office?

lung *(n.)* लॅन्ग– either one of a pair of spongy saclike respiratory organs within the thorax of higher vertebrates, which oxygenate the blood and remove its carbon dioxide फेफड़ा Too much smoking would damage your *lungs.*

lunge *(v.)* लन्ज– to move or cause to move with a lunge झपटना, वार करना The man *lunged* towards him with a knife in hand.

lurch *(v.)* लर्च– to lean or pitch suddenly to one side डगमगाना, लड़खड़ाना The crowded bus suddenly *lurched* to the right side.

lure *(v.)* लुअर– 1. to tempt or attract by the promise of some type of reward फुसलाना, प्रलोभन देना The bright lights of the city *lured* her away from home.
2. *(n.)* a person or thing that lures लालच, प्रलोभन The *lure* of his mother's good cooking brought him back home.

lurid *(adj.)* लुअरिड– vivid in shocking detail; sensational सनसनीख़ेज़ The reporter gave *lurid* headlines for the newspaper.

lurk *(v.)* लर्क– to move stealthily or be concealed, esp for evil purposes छिपकर बैठना, घात लगाना A man was *lurking* around outside my house.

luscious *(adj.)* लशस्– extremely pleasurable, esp to the taste or smell अत्यंत स्वादिष्ट It is a very *luscious* and fragrant dessert wine.

lush *(adj.)* लॅश– (of vegetation) abounding in lavish growth हरा-भरा The bungalow was surrounded by *lush* green farms.

lust *(n.)* लस्ट– 1. a strong desire for sexual gratification कामुकता, लालसा

His affair was driven by pure *lust.* 2. *(v.)* to have a lust (for) कामातुर होना The man *lusted* for a woman

lustful *(adj.)* लस्टफुल– driven by lust कामुक She ignored his *lustful* glance.

lusture *(n.)* लस्टर– radiance or brilliance of light चमक, रौनक़ We saw *lusture* on the saint's face.

lusty *(n.)* लस्टी– having or characterized by robust health हृष्ट-पुष्ट, स्वस्थ एवं पुष्ट You cannot even push him, he is a *lusty* fellow.

luxurious *(adj.)* लग्श़ूअरियस– characterized by luxury आरामदायक, सुख-सुविधाओं से सम्पन्न He is leading a *luxurious* life.

luxury *(n.)* लक्श़री– indulgence in and enjoyment of rich, comfortable, and sumptuous living विलासिता, बहुत आरामदेह I have never seen this kind a *luxury* in my life.

lymph *(n.)* लिम्फ़– the almost colourless fluid, containing chiefly white blood cells, that is collected from the tissues of the body and transported in the lymphatic system लसीका Her *lymph* nodes have no sign of malignancy.

lyrical *(adj.)* लिरिकल– enthusiastic; effusive गीतात्मक, गीतमय After a long time I heard a *lyrical* melody.

lyrics *(n.)* लिरिक्स– the words of a popular song किसी गीत के बोल Did you notice the *lyrics* of that song?

lyricist *(n.)* लिरिसिस्ट– a person who writes the words for a song, opera, or musical play प्रगीतकार, गीतों के बोल लिखने वाला व्यक्ति Javed Akhtar is a famous *lyricist.*

ഇൽ

Mm

Mm *(n.)* एम्—अंग्रेज़ी वर्णमाला का तेरहवां अक्षर The thirteenth letter of the English alphabet. Monkey begins with 'M'.

ma'am *(n.)* मैम्— short for madam महोदया, मेमसाहब Hello *Ma'am*! How are you?

macabre *(adj.)* मकाब्र— gruesome; ghastly; grim ख़ौफ़नाक, डरावना The man told a real *macabre* tale of his village.

macaroni *(n.)* मैकरोनी— pasta tubes made from wheat flour इटली का एक व्यंजन जो मेवे को गूंथकर नलियों के आकार में बनाया जाता है, मैकरोनी I had yummy *macaroni* in my dinner yesterday.

mace *(n.)* मेस—1. a club, usually having a spiked metal head, used esp in the Middle Ages गदा The *mace* of Bhima was very strong.

2. a ceremonial staff of office carried by certain officials राजदण्ड The Mayors do not carry a *mace* now.

3. a spice made from the dried aril round the nutmeg seed जावित्री *Mace* is used to give flavour to Mughlai chicken.

machine *(n.)* मशीन्— an assembly of interconnected components arranged to transmit or modify force in order to perform useful work यन्त्र, मशीन Is this a printing *machine*?

machine-gun *(n.)* मशीन-गन— a rapid-firing automatic gun, usually mounted, from which small-arms ammunition is discharged (लगातार गोली छोड़ने वाली बंदूक़) मशीन-गन Terrorists used *machine-guns* to kill people.

machinery *(n.)* मशीनरी— machines, machine parts, or machine systems collectively पुरज़े, यंत्र, मशीनरी, यंत्रावली We need to have some good *machinery* for our new factory.

machinist *(n.)* मशीनिस्ट्— a person who operates machines to cut or process materials मशीन चालक His brother-in-law is a *machinist* in Delhi Cloth Mills.

macho *(adj.)* मैचो— denoting or exhibiting pride in characteristics believed to be typically masculine, such as physical strength, sexual appetite, etc. मर्द आदमी Sundar is too *macho* to admit his mistakes.

mackintosh *(n.)* मैकिन्टाश— a waterproof raincoat made of rubberized cloth बरसाती, मोमजामा His servant use *mackintosh* when he goes out in the rain.

mad *(adj.)* मैड्—1. mentally deranged; insane पागल, विक्षिप्त Has she gone *mad*?

2. angry; resentful उत्तेजित, क्रुद्ध She felt *mad* when her servant burnt her favourite sari.

3. senseless; foolish मूर्खतापूर्ण The idea of leaving your house for ever is really *mad.*

4. extremely excited or confused; frantic बेक़ाबू, उत्तेजित I went *mad* when I saw him.

madam *(n.)* मैडम्— a polite term of address for a woman, esp one considered to be of relatively high social status महोदया, भद्रे Hello *Madam!* How are you?

maddening *(adj.)* मैड्निंग— serving to send mad पागल या क्रुद्ध करने वाली Kiran has some *maddening* habits.

madly *(adv.)* मैड्लि—1. extremely or excessively बेतहाशा, अत्यधिक She is *madly* in love with him.

2. with great speed and energy अंधाधुंध They were rushing about *madly*.

madness *(n.)* मैड्नस्– insanity; lunacy पागलपन The *madness* displayed by the crowd was condemned by all.

maestro *(n.)* माइस्ट्रो– a distinguished music teacher, conductor, or musician संगीताचार्य, संगीतज्ञ Jagjit Singh is a great ghazal *maestro.*

mafia *(n.)* मॉफ़िआ– . an international secret organization founded in Sicily, probably in opposition to tyranny अपराधियों की अंतर्राष्ट्रीय संस्था The American *mafia* is involved in many criminal activities.

magazine *(n.)* मैग्ज़ीन्– a periodical paperback publication containing articles, fiction, photographs, etc. पत्रिका I love reading *magazines*.

magenta *(adj.)* मॅजेंटा– a deep purplish red that is the complementary colour of green and, with yellow and cyan, forms a set of primary colours गहरा लाल रंग I want to buy a *megenta* lehnga for my wedding.

magic *(n.)* मैजिक्–1. the art that, by use of spells, supposedly invokes supernatural powers to influence events; sorcery जादू, जादूगरी I have never seen this kind of *magic* before.

2. any mysterious or extraordinary quality or power जादू भरा Yesterday I took my children to a *magic* show.

magical *(adj.)* मैजिकल्– possessing or considered to possess mysterious powers जादू-टोने से संबंधित, मायावी, चमत्कारपूर्ण Bright colour sari and heavy make up produced a *magical* change in her looks.

magician *(n.)* मैजिशियन्– a person who practises magic जादूगर, बाज़ीगर Who is the *magician* in his show?

magistrate *(n.)* मैजिस्ट्रेट– a public officer concerned with the administration of law दण्डनायक, दण्डाधिकारी I was summoned to the *magistrate's* court to give evidence.

magnanimous *(adj.)* मैगनैनिमस– generous and noble उदार, उदारचेता You should be rich and *magnanimous* towards detractors.

magnate *(n.)* मैग्नेट– a person of power and rank in any sphere, esp in industry प्रभावशाली/धनी व्यक्ति Dhirubhai Ambani was an old *magnate*.

magnet *(n.)* मैग्नेट्– a body that can attract certain substances, such as iron or steel, as a result of a magnetic field; a piece of ferromagnetic substance चुंबक Her eyes are attractive as a *magnet.*

magnetic *(adj.)* मैग्नेटिक्– of, producing, or operated by means of magnetism चुंबकीय She has got *magnetic* features.

magnetism *(n.)* मैग्नटिज़्म्– the property of attraction displayed by magnets चुंबकीय आकर्षण She has some *magnetism* in her personality.

magnetize (ise) *(v.)* मैग्नटाइज़्– to attract strongly आकर्षित करना, मोहना Her dark brown eyes seemed to *magnetize* him.

magnificent *(adj.)* मैग्निफ़िसन्ट्– splendid or impressive in appearance शानदार What a *magnificent* view of sea! isn't it?

magnify *(v.)* मैग्निफ़ाइ–1. to increase, cause to increase, or be increased in apparent size, as through the action of a lens, microscope, etc. आवर्धन करना This lens *magnifies* the object fifty times.

2. to exaggerate or become exaggerated in importance बढ़ा-चढ़ा कर कहना She was *magnifying* her problem.

magnifying glass *(n.)* मैग्निफ़ाइंग ग्लास– a convex lens used to produce an enlarged image of an object आवर्धक लैंस Look at this small insect through a *magnifying glass*.

Mahatma *(n.)* महात्मा– a Brahman sage एक आध्यात्मिक व्यक्ति He is the man of *Mahatma*.

mahogany *(n.)* महॉगनी– reddish-brown wood of a tropical tree, used for making furniture लाल भूरे रंग की लकड़ी *Mahogany* is used for making furnitures.

maid *(n.)* मेड्– a female servant नौकरानी, कुमारी Our house-*maid* is honest and industrious.

maiden *(n.)* मेड्न्– a young unmarried girl, esp when a virgin अविवाहित स्त्री, कुमारी Sushmita Sen is still a *maiden*.

mail *(n.)* मेल्– letters, packages, etc. that are transported and delivered by the post office डाक I received a *mail* yesterday.

mailbox *(n.)* मेल्बॉक्स्– a private box into which letters, etc. are delivered ई-मेल का मेलबॉक्स My *mailbox* was full of his mails.

maim *(v.)* मेम– to mutilate, cripple, or disable a part of the body of (a person or animal) लंगड़ा-लूला कर देना, अपंग बना देना Many soldiers were *maimed* in the world war.

main *(adj.)* मेन– 1. chief or principal in rank, importance, size, etc. मुख्य, प्रमुख The chief guest was the *main* speaker at the school function.

2. Does this lane join the *main* road?

mainframe *(n.)* मेन्फ्रेम्– a high-speed general-purpose computer, usually with a large storage capacity एक बड़ा शक्ति-शाली कंप्यूटर, मेनफ्रेम Please link the main wire with the *mainframe*.

mainland *(n.)* मेनलैंड्– the main part of a land mass as opposed to an island or peninsula महाद्वीप Some tribal people migrate to the *mainland* during winters.

mainly *(adv.)* मेनली– for the most part; to the greatest extent; principally मुख्यत: Kanpur is *mainly* populated by people from adjoinging districts.

mainstream *(n.)* मेनस्ट्रीम– the main current (of a river, cultural trend, etc.) मुख्यधारा Muslims should join the *mainstream* of Indian culture for communal harmony.

maintain *(v.)* मेन्टेन–1. to continue or retain; keep in existence बनाए रखना, कायम रखना *Maintaining* any relationship is not that easy.

2. to defend against contradiction; uphold दावा करना Do you still *maintain* that you were right?

3. to keep in proper or good condition (मरम्मत करके) ठीक-ठीक बनाए रखना The old house costs a great deal to *maintain*.

maintenance *(n.)* मेण्टनन्स–1. a means of support; livelihood गुज़ारा-भत्ता The divorced wife could not claim for her *maintenance*.

2. the act of maintaining or the state of being maintained रखरखाव My car needs a lot of *maintenance*.

maize *(n.)* मेज़– a tall annual grass, Zea mays, cultivated for its yellow edible grains, which develop on a spike मक्का *Maize* is good for health.

majestic *(adj.)* मजेस्टिक्– having or displaying majesty or great dignity; grand; lofty राजसी, तेजस्वी His village is surrounded by *majestic* mountain scenery.

majesty *(n.)* मैजस्टी– 1. great dignity of bearing; loftiness; grandeur आकर्षकता, वैभवता The *majesty* of Himalayas is unparallaled.

2. supreme power or authority राजा या रानी की उपाधि Her *Majesty* the Queen of England visited India.

major *(adj.)* मेजर्– 1. an officer immediately junior to a lieutenant colonel मुख्य, बड़ा The soldier spent *major* portion of his life in guarding the country's frontiers.

2. *(n.)* a person who has reached the age of legal majority वयस्क, बालिग़ Is your brother a *major* now?

majority *(adj.)* मजॉरिटी– the greater number or part of something बहुमत The *majority* says that she was right.

make *(n.)* मेक्–1. brand, type, or style बनावट, गठन I din't like the *make* of this car.

2. *(v.)* to bring into being by shaping, changing, or combining materials, ideas, etc.; form or fashion; create बनाना Please *make* me a cup of tea.

3. to draw up, establish, or form निर्माण करना My shirt is *made* of cotton.

4. to cause, compel, or induce मजबूर करना Please don't *make* me go there.

5. to deliver or pronounce करना, देना I have to *make* a speech tomorrow.

6. to cause to seem or represent as being मनोभाव उत्पन्न करना The end of the movie *made* me cry.

➢ **make-believe**– a fantasy, pretence, or unreallty ढोंग, छल, Sonam seems to be living in a world of *make-believe.*

➢ **make do with**– t. to manage with whatever is available जो मिले उससे काम चलाना, If you can't get Coca Cola, you 'll have to *make do with* cold water.

➢ **make for**– to make towards, esp in haste की ओर बढ़ना, When the train reached the station, everyone *made for* the tea stall.

➢ **make it**– to be successful in doing something सफ़लता प्राप्त करना, She could not *make it* as a dancer.

➢ **make it up**– to settle (differences) amicably अपनी ग़लती मानना, I *made it up* with my friend and now we are friends again.

➢ **make off**– to go or run away in haste निकल भागना, The girl *made off* when I called her name.

➢ **make out**– to understand sth समझ पाना, I could not *make out* what he said to me.

➢ **make over**– to transfer the title or possession of (property, etc.) सौंप देना, Mr Dixit has *made over* half of his property to his younger son.

➢ **make up**– to devise, construct, or compose, sometimes with the intent to deceive बनाना, कुछ गढ़ना, Don't *make up* a lame excuse.

➢ **make up one's mind**– to decide (about something or to do something) दिमाग़ बनाना, I have *made up* my mind to leave him forever.

maker *(n.)* मेकर्– a person who makes (something); fabricator; constructor निर्माता, बनाने वाला व्यक्ति Mahesh Bhatt is a famous film *maker* of horror movies.

makeshift *(adj.)* मेक-शिफ़्ट्– serving as a temporary or expedient means, esp during an emergency कामचलाऊ It is a *makeshift* shelter for these poor people.

make-up *(n.)* मेकअप्–1. cosmetics, such as powder, lipstick, etc. applied to the face to improve its appearance शृंगार, रूपसज्जा My skin is allergic to *make-up.*

2. the manner of arrangement of the parts or qualities of someone or something चरित्र तथा स्वभाव Politeness has always been an important part of his *make-up.*

making *(n.)* मेकिंग्– the act of a person or thing that makes or the process of being made कुछ बनने की

क्रिया I want to see the *making* of this dish.

maladjusted *(adj)* मैलजस्टेड्– badly adjusted अव्यवस्थित There is a school of *maladjusted* boys near my house.

malady *(n.)* मैलडी– any disease or illness गंभीर रोग Thyroid is a life long *malady.*

malaria *(n.)* मलेअरिआ– an infectious disease characterized by recurring attacks of chills and fever, caused by the bite of an anopheles mosquito infected with any of four protozoans of the genus मलेरिआ, शीतज्वर I was down with *malaria* last month.

male *(n.)* मेल– 1. of, relating to, or characteristic of a man; masculine नर Head of the family is usually a *male* person.

2. *(adj.)* of, relating to, or designating the sex producing gametes (spermatozoa) that can fertilize female gametes (ova) नर-संबंधी पुरुष There was a seperate line for *males* and females.

malice *(n.)* मैलिस्– the desire to do harm or mischief दुर्भावना, द्वेष She intends no *malice* to anyone, but her language is bad.

malign *(adj.)* मलाइन्– evil in influence, intention, or effect अहितकर, हानिकारक Her gloomy house has a *malign* influence on me.

malignant *(adj.)* मलिगनेंट– having or showing desire to harm others घातक, ख़तरनाक Fortunately the cyst of her breast was not *malignant.*

malleable *(adj.)* मैलिअबल्– (esp of metal) able to be worked, hammered, or shaped under pressure or blows without breaking पिटवाँ, आघातवर्ध्य *Brass* is a *malleable* metal.

malnutrition *(n.)* मैलन्यूट्रिशन्– lack of adequate nutrition resulting from insufficient food, unbalanced diet, or defective assimilation कुपोषण His child is suffering from *malnutrition* since long.

malodorous *(adj.)* मैलओडरस– having a bad smell बदबूदार The drains of janta colony are *malodorous.*

malpractice *(n.)* मैलप्रैक्टिस– immoral, illegal, or unethical professional conduct or neglect of professional duty कदाचार The doctor was sent to jail due to his *malpractice.*

maltreat *(v.)* मैलट्रीट– to treat badly, cruelly, or inconsiderately दुर्व्यवहार करना We should not *maltreat* servants and maids.

mammal *(n.)* मैमल– animal that gives birth to live babies, not eggs. स्तनधारी प्राणी Cows, dogs and cats are *mammals.*

mammoth *(adj.)* मैमथ– of gigantic size or importance विशाल, विशालकाय Yesterday I attended a *mammoth* public meeting.

man *(n.)* मैन–1. a human being regardless of sex or age, considered as a representative of mankind; a person मानव, इंसान All *men* are mortal.

2. an adult male human being, as distinguished from a woman नर, पुरुष Do you know that *man*?

manage *(v.)* मैनेज–1. to be in charge (of); administer देखरेख करना, संभालना I can't *manage* this business.

2. to succeed in being able (to do something) despite obstacles; contrive सफ़ल होना, युक्ति निकालना Can you *manage* to come early?

3. to exercise control or domination over, often in a tactful or guileful manner वश में रखना Yes, I can easily *manage* him.

manageable *(adj.)* मैनेजबल्– able to be managed or controlled जिसे संभाला जा सके, नियंत्रणीय, वश्य These things are quite *manageable* if we do it properly.

management *(n.)* मैनेजमेंट– the members of the executive or administration of an organization or business प्रबंध, व्यवस्था There is a problem with the *management* of my company.

manager *(n.)* मैनेजर– a person who directs or manages an organization, industry, shop, etc. प्रबंधक, संचालक Who is the HR *manager* in your company?

mandate *(n.)* मैनडेट्– an official or authoritative instruction or command जनादेश This victory gave me a clear *mandate* to go ahead.

mandatory *(adj.)* मैन्डेटरी– having the nature or powers of a mandate अनिवार्य It is *mandatory* to submit the original documents.

mandible *(n.)* मैनडिबल्– the lower jawbone in vertebrates जबड़ा Kala has a pain in her left *mandible.*

mane *(n.)* मेन– the long coarse hair that grows from the crest of the neck in such mammals as the lion and horse अयाल, (घोड़े या शेर के लंबे बाल) The lion's *mane* was shining in the sun.

manganese *(n.)* मैंगनीज़्– a brittle grey white metallic element, used in making glass and steel भूरे रंग की एक भुरभुरी धातु, मैंगनीज *Manganese* is much produced in India.

mangle *(v.)* मैंगल्– to mutilate, disfigure, or destroy by cutting, crushing, or tearing बुरी तरह शक्ल बिगाड़ देना The dead body of a girl was *mangled* after the murder.

manhole *(n.)* मैनूहोल– a shaft with a removable cover that leads down to a sewer or drain मैनहोल, (सड़क पर बना एक बड़ा ढक्कनदार गड्ढा) The child fell into the *manhole* while playing.

mango *(n.)* मैंगो– a tropical fruit with yellow skin and soft flesh and a large seed inside आम *Mango* is my favourite fruit.

mania *(n.)* मेनिआ– a mental disorder characterized by great excitement and occasionally violent behaviour उन्माद, अति-उत्साह The IPL *mania* came to an end with Rajasthan Royals taking away the trophy.

maniac *(n.)* मैनिऐक– a wild disorderly person उन्मादी, सनकी He is a car *maniac.*

manicure *(n.)* मैनिक्युअर– care of the hands and fingernails, involving shaping the nails, removing cuticles, etc. नख-प्रसाधन My beauty package does'nt include *manicure* services.

manifest *(v.)* मैनिफ़ेस्ट– to show plainly; reveal or display व्यक्त/प्रकट करना God always *manifests* Himself in human forms.

manifesto *(n.)* मैनिफ़ेस्टो– a public declaration of intent, policy, aims, etc. as issued by a political party, government, or movement घोषणा-पत्र The communist party released its *manifesto.*

manifold *(adj.)* मैनिफोल्ड– of several different kinds; multiple कई गुना Your beauty has increased *manifold.*

manipulate *(v.)* मनिप्युलेट– to negotiate, control, or influence (something or someone) cleverly, skilfully, or deviously छल/चालबाजी करना Be staright-forward. Don't try to *manipulate.*

mankind *(n.)* मैनूकाइण्ड– human beings collectively; humanity मानव-जाति Pollution is harmful to the whole *mankind.*

manly *(adj.)* मैनली– possessing qualities, such as vigour or courage, generally regarded as appropriate to or typical of a man; masculine मर्दाना, पुरुषोचित His looks and voice are very *manly.*

man-made *(adj.)* मैन-मेड– made or produced by man; artificial मानव-निर्मित I went to see the exhibition of *man-made* fibres.

mannequin *(n.)* मैनिक्विन– a woman who wears the clothes displayed at a fashion show; model पुतला That dress on *mannequin* was better than their stock.

manner *(n.)* मैनर्– 1. a way of doing or being ढंग, रीति, प्रकार Please do it in a proper *manner.*
2. a person's bearing and behaviour शिष्टाचार Your polished *manners* ensure a welcome for you everywhere.

manoeuvre *(n.)* मैन्युवर–1. a contrived, complicated, and possibly deceptive plan or action युक्ति, तिकड़म, चाल A rapid *manoeuvre* by me prevented an accident.
2. a movement or action requiring dexterity and skill चालबाज़ी He tried to obtain an agreement by political *manoeuvre.*

manor *(n.)* मैनर्– (in medieval Europe) the manor house of a lord and the lands attached to it सामंत-भवन We have a huge *manor* in our native village.

manpower *(n.)* मैन्पाउअर्– power supplied by men मानव-शक्ति The strength of our company is the skilled *manpower.*

mansion *(n.)* मैन्शन– a large and imposing house हवेली, कोठी, भवन We live in an old *mansion* built by our grandfather.

manual *(adj.)* मैनूयुअल्– 1. of or relating to a hand or hands हस्त-चरित This is a *manual* job I don't need any computer for this.
2. *(n.)* a book that tells you how to operate sth परिचालन-निर्देशपुस्तिका This *manual* will teach you different recipes of cheese.

manufacture *(v.)* मैन्युफ़ैक्चर्– to process or make (a product) from a raw material, esp as a large-scale operation using machinery उत्पादन करना, कुछ बनाना What articles do you *manufacture* in your factory?

manure *(n.)* मेन्युअर्– animal excreta, usually with straw, used to fertilize land खाद The farmer added *manure* to the soil to make it more fertile.

manuscript *(n.)* मैन्युस्क्रिप्ट– a book or other document written by hand पाण्डुलिपि, हस्तलिखित I would like to see the whole *manuscript* before finalizing it.

many *(adj.)* मेनि– a large number of अनेक, बहुत से Wow! there are so *many* birds in this garden.

map *(n.)* मैप– a diagrammatic representation of the earth's surface or part of it, showing the geographical distributions, positions, etc. of natural or artificial features such as roads, towns, relief, rainfall, etc. नक़्शा, मानचित्र I want to buy a *map* of India.

marble *(n.)* मार्बल–1. a hard crystalline metamorphic rock resulting from the recrystallization of a limestone: takes a high polish and is used for building and sculpture संगमरमर I got the *marbel* flooring in my house this year.
2. a small round glass or stone ball used in playing marbles गोली, कंचा My son plays *marbles* with his friends.

march *(v.)* मार्च–1. to walk or proceed with stately or regular steps, usually in a procession or military formation प्रयाण करना, कूच करना We stood by the side of the road as the soldiers *marched* past.
2. to traverse or cover by marching जुलूस बनाकर चलना The protestors *marched* through the parliament.
3. *(n.)* a distance or route covered by marching पदयात्रा, प्रयाण The police barricaded the road to stop the agitationist's *march.*

4. the third month of the year, consisting of 31 days मार्च, वर्ष का तीसरा महीना I joined this company in *March* 2013.

mare *(n.)* मेअर्– the adult female of a horse or zebra घोड़ी The *mare* was decorated for the wedding.

margarine *(n.)* मार्जरीन– a substitute for butter, prepared from vegetable and animal fats by emulsifying them with water and adding small amounts of milk, salt, vitamins, colouring matter, etc. कृत्रिम मक्खन *Margarine* is made out of vegetable fats.

margin *(n.)* मार्जिन– an edge or rim, and the area immediately adjacent to it; border हाशिया, किनारा, गुंजाइश There was'nt any *margin* left for the rough work.

marinate *(v.)* मैरिनेट– to soak in marinade सिरके आदि में डुबाकर एवं मिलाकर रखना The cook *marinated* the fish before deep-frying.

marine *(adj.)* मरीन्– of, found in, or relating to the sea समुद्री Oil slick is a threat to *marine* animals.

marionette *(n.)* मैरीअनेट– a puppet or doll whose jointed limbs are moved by strings कठपुतली *Marionettes* are moved on strings.

marital *(adj.)* मैरिटल– of or relating to marriage विवाह-संबंधी She is into an extra *marital* affair.

maritime *(adj.)* मैरिटाइम– of or relating to navigation, shipping, etc.; seafaring समुद्री The travelers will explore the lovely coast of the *maritime* provinces.

mark *(n.)* मार्क–1. a letter, number, or percentage used to grade academic work अंक, नंबर How many *marks* did you score in your exams?

2. a sign, symbol, or other indication that distinguishes something निशान, चिह्न We walked straight till we came to a *mark* indicating right turn.

3. a visible impression, stain, etc. on a surface, such as a spot or scratch धब्बा, निशान There is a dirty *mark* on your shirt.

4. *(v.)* to characterize or distinguish मूल्यांकन करना Vikas and Sonia were *marked* absent.

market *(n.)* मार्केट्–1. an event or occasion, usually held at regular intervals, at which people meet for the purpose of buying and selling merchandise बाज़ार The *market* is closed today.

2. a place, such as an open space in a town, at which a market is held बाज़ार, मण्डी, ख़रीदारों की पर्याप्त संख्या His company is planning to expand its business into the European *Market.*

3. *(v.)* to offer or produce for sale विज्ञापन द्वारा माल बेचना Our company *markets* electrical appliances.

marketable *(adj.)* मार्केटबूल्– being in good demand; saleable विक्रेय, बेचने योग्य These are not *marketable* goods.

marketing *(n.)* मार्केटिंग– the provision of goods or services to meet customer or consumer needs बिक्री कला Our new product requires a heavy *marketing.*

market price *(n.)* मार्केट प्राइज्– the prevailing price, as determined by supply and demand, at which goods, services, etc. may be bought or sold अंकित मूल्य The *market price* of this property is increasing day by day.

market value *(n.)* मार्केट वैल्यू– the amount obtainable on the open market for the sale of property, financial assets, or goods and services सम्पत्ति का बाज़ार भाव The *market value* of your car is not more than one lakh.

marking *(n.)* मार्किंग– a sign, symbol, or other indication that distinguishes something अंकन, चिह्न *Marking* is always very hard in the UP Board.

maroon *(adj.)* मरून्–1. dark brownish red in colour गहरा भूरा लाल *Maroon* is one of my favourite colour.
2. *(n.)* left ashore and abandoned, esp on an island किसी निर्जन स्थान पर असहाय या अकेला छोड़ देना He was *marooned* on a barren island.

marriage *(n.)* मैरियेज– the state or relationship of living together in a legal partnership विवाह, शादी *Marriage* is a relationship of two hearts.

married *(adj.)* मैरिड्– having a husband or wife विवाहित, शादीशुदा Is this couple *married*?

marry *(v.)* मैरी– to take (someone as one's partner) in marriage विवाह करना या कराना Will you *marry* me?

marsh *(n.)* मार्श– low poorly drained land that is sometimes flooded and often lies at the edge of lakes, streams, etc. दलदल, कच्छ An old man could not cross the *marsh.*

martial *(adj.)* मार्शल– of, relating to, or characteristic of war, soldiers, or the military life युद्ध-संबंधी He is a professional in *martial* arts.

martyr *(n.)* मार्टर्–1. a person who suffers death rather than renounce his religious beliefs शहीद, बलिदानी Have you visited the *martyrs'* memorial in Kolkata?
2. a person who feigns suffering to gain sympathy, help, etc. कष्टभोगी, यातनाग्रस्त In my opinion Karan rather relishes the role of *martyr.*

marvel *(n.)* मार्वल– 1. something that causes wonder चमत्कार, अद्भुत वस्तु Your house is full of *marvels* of technology.
2. *(v.)* to be filled with surprise or wonder आश्चर्य करना We *marvel* at the way you help your friends.

marvellous *(adj.)* मार्वलस– causing great wonder, surprise, etc.; extraordinary अद्भुत, अति उत्तम, बढ़िया What a *marvellous* job you did this time!

marxism *(n.)* मार्कसिज़्म– the economic and political theory and practice originated by Karl Marx कार्ल मार्क्स के सिद्धांतों से संबंधित, मार्क्सवाद Some political parties are influenced by *marxism.*

mascara *(n.)* मैस्कारा– a cosmetic substance for darkening, colouring, and thickening the eyelashes, applied with a brush or rod अंजन *Mascara* doesn't suit my eyes.

masculine *(adj.)* मैस्क्युलिन्– possessing qualities or characteristics considered typical of or appropriate to a man; manly पुरुषोचित, मरदाना You have a deep, *masculine* voice.

mash *(v.)* मैश– to beat or crush into a soft mass कुचलना *Mash* the potatoes properly for the parathas.

mask *(n.)* मास्क– any covering for the whole or a part of the face worn for amusement, protection, disguise, etc. मुखौटा The child frightened his friend by wearing a devil *mask.*

masochism *(n.)* मैसकिज़्म्– a tendency to take sexual pleasure from one's own suffering परपीड़ित-कामुकता *Masochism* is not entertained anymore.

mason *(n.)* मेसन– a person skilled in building with stone राजमिस्त्री We shall have to call a *mason* to repair this wall.

masquerade *(n.)* मैस्क्वरेड– a pretence or disguise छद्मवेश, छल-कपट She really loved him, but she kept up the *masquerade* for the sake of her family.

mass *(n.)* मास– 1. a large coherent body of matter without a definite shape ढेर, राशि Look at the *mass* of dark clouds, it is about to rain.

2. a large amount or number, such as a great body of people जनसमूह, भीड़ Your speeches have the power to move the *masses.*

massacre *(n.)* मैसकर्– the wanton or savage killing of large numbers of people, as in battle हत्याकांड, सामूहिक हत्या No Indian would ever forget the Jallianwala *massacre* of 1919.

massage *(n.)* मसाज– 1. the act of kneading, rubbing, etc. parts of the body to promote circulation, suppleness, or relaxation मालिश I need a body *massage* this weekend.

2. *(v.)* to give a massage to मालिश करना *Massage* your hair well.

massive *(adj.)* मैसिव– (of objects) large in mass; bulky, heavy, and usually solid भारी, विशाल What is this *massive* machine supposed to do?

master *(n.)* मास्टर्–1. the man in authority, such as the head of a household, the employer of servants, or the owner of slaves or animals मालिक, अधिकारी Where is your *master?*

2. a person with exceptional skill at a certain thing पुरुष शिक्षक He is a biology *master.*

3. *(v.)* to become thoroughly proficient in अच्छे ढंग से सीखना या करना Have you *mastered* this subject?

4. to rule or control as master वश में कर लेना I have learned to *master* my fear of heights.

mastermind *(n.)* मास्टरमाइंड्– an intelligent person who plans and directs (a complex undertaking) शातिर दिमाग़, चतुराई से योजना बनाने वाला व्यक्ति He is a *mastermind.*

masterpiece *(n.)* मास्टर्पीस– an outstanding work, achievement, or performance अतिश्रेष्ठ रचना Wow! What a *masterpiece.*

mastery *(n.)* मास्टरी– full command or understanding of a subject पूर्ण ज्ञान, किसी काम में दक्षता Now she has gained *mastery* in her subject.

mat *(n.)* मैट– a thick flat piece of fabric used as a floor covering, a place to wipe one's shoes, etc. चटाई, पायदान We should get a new *mat* for our room.

match *(n.)* मैच–1. a thin strip of wood or cardboard tipped with a chemical that ignites by friction when rubbed on a rough surface or a surface coated with a suitable chemical दियासलाई I will require atlest 2 *match* sticks for this.

2. a formal game or sports event in which people, teams, etc. compete to win मैच, प्रतियोगिता Will you accompany me to the cricket *match*?

3. *(adj.)* of the same colour or design जोड़, जोड़ीदार You are dressed in *matching* colours.

4. *(v.)* tto resemble, harmonize with, correspond to, or equal (one another or something else) मेल मिलाना These colours do not *match.*

5. to arrange a competition between मुक़ाबला करना, सामना करना He is ready to *match* his strength with him.

mate *(n.)* मेट–1. an associate, colleague, fellow sharer, etc. साथी, सखा Anil is my class-*mate.*

2. a marriage partner पति-पत्नी, जोड़ा We want a *mate* for our parrot.

material *(n.)* मटिअरिअल–1. things to be used सामान, माल What all *material* will be required for this painting?

2. cloth or fabric कपड़ा Will you please show me some good-quality dress *material*?

materialize (ise) *(v.)* मटिअरिअलाइज़– to become fact; actually happen वास्तविक बनाना We could not *materialize* our plans.

materialism *(n.)* मटिअरिअलिज़्म– interest in and desire for money, possessions, etc. rather than spiritual or ethical values भौतिकतावाद, सांसारिकता *Materialism* is the main cause of social unrest.

maternal *(adj.)* मेटर्नल– of, relating to, derived from, or characteristic of a mother मातृत्व-विषयक She was taken over by *maternal* instincts and refused to send her child to the hostel.

maternity *(adj.)* मट्रनटी– relating to pregnant women or women at the time of childbirth मातृत्व She was on the *maternity* leave for 2 months.

mathematical *(adj.)* मैथमैटिकल– of, used in, or relating to mathematics गणितीय He was doing mistakes in *mathematical* calculations.

mathematics *(n.)* मैथमैटिक्स्– a group of related sciences, including algebra, geometry, and calculus, concerned with the study of number, quantity, shape, and space and their interrelationships by using a specialized notation गणित *Mathematics* is her weakest subject.

matinee *(n.)* मैटिनी– a daytime, esp afternoon, performance of a play, concert, etc. किसी फिल्म आदि का दोपहर का प्रदर्शन We saw the *matinee* show of the movie.

matrimonial *(adj.)* मैट्रिमोनिअल– relating to marriage वैवाहिक Please refer to our *matrimonial* site for more details.

matrimony *(n.)* मेट्रिमनी– the state or condition of being married दांपत्यावस्था, वैवाहिक जीवन They decided to join together in holy *matrimony*.

matron *(n.)* मेट्रन– a married woman regarded as staid or dignified, esp a middle-aged woman with children मेट्रन, प्रधान नर्स The *matron* scolded the hostellers who arrived late in the night.

matter *(v.)* मैटर्–1. to be of consequence or importance महत्त्वपूर्ण होना It *matters* a great deal.

2. *(n.)* thing; affair; concern; question विषय Let me discuss this *matter* first.

3. that which makes up something, esp a physical object; material भौतिक पदार्थ Liquid is a *matter.*

4. the content of written or verbal material as distinct from its style or form विषय-वस्तु (पुस्तक आदि का) What is the *subject matter* of this book?

➢ **a matter of course**– as a natural or normal consequence, mode of action, or event स्वाभाविक, After brilliant work, my success was *a matter of course.*

➢ **a matter of life and death**– a matter of extreme urgency अत्यधिक महत्त्वपूर्ण विषय, It's really *a matter of life and death* for me.

➢ **a matter of opinion**– a point open to question अपनी-अपनी राय, The Congress party is doing well, is *a matter of opinion.*

➢ **a different matter**– partly or completely unlike कुछ गंभीर बात होना, I can speak Urdu, bur writing is quite *a different matter.*

➢ **as a matter of fact**– in reality or actuality वास्तव में सच तो यह है कि, She likes him very much, *as a matter of fact.*

➢ **no matter**– regardless of; irrespective of चाहे जो भी हो जाए, I would ask him *no matter* what he says.

mattress *(n.)* मैट्रेस– a large flat pad with a strong cover, filled with straw, foam rubber, etc. and often incorporating coiled springs, used as a bed or as part of a bed गद्दा, तोशक I think we should buy a new *mattress.*

mature *(adj.)* मच्युअर्– relatively advanced physically, mentally, emotionally, etc.; grown-up परिपक्व She is *mature* enough to solve this problem at her end.

maverick *(n.)* मैवरिक्– a person of independent or unorthodox views स्वतंत्रचेता व्यक्ति, अपने ढंग से सोचने वाला Vijay Tendulkar was a *maverick* in the field of Indian theatre.

maxim *(n.)* मैक्सिम्– a brief expression of a general truth, principle, or rule of conduct सूत्र, सूक्ति, नीति-वचन Follow the *maxim* – boss is always right.

maximum *(adj.)* मैक्सिमम्– the greatest possible amount, degree, etc. अधिकतम What was the *maximum* strength of students last year?

may *(v.)* मे–1. to indicate that permission is requested by or granted to someone अनुमति प्राप्त करना *May* I have your number please?
2. to indicate possibility संभव होना I *may* go to Mumbai next month.
3. to express a strong wish (आशीर्वाद अर्थ में) शुभकामना प्रदान करने के लिए *May* he live long!
4. to indicate possibility दो चीज़ों में समानता या विरोध दिखाने हेतु She *may* be clever but she is not capable for this job.
5. *(n.)* the fifth month of the year, consisting of 31 days वर्ष का पांचवां महीना, मई She will come to meet us in the month of *may*.

may be *(adv.)* मे बी– a clause introduced by but that may be so शायद *May be* I'll go to his house.

Mayor *(n.)* मेअर्– the chairman and civic head of a municipal corporation in many countries महापौर He defeated the old *Mayor* by just a few votes.

maze *(n.)* मेज़– a complex network of paths or passages, esp one with high hedges in a garden, designed to puzzle those walking through it भूल-भुलैया I am caught up in the *maze* of my own problems.

me *(pron.)* मी– refers to the speaker or writer मुझे, मुझको Let *me* know if you have anything in your mind.

meagre *(adj.)* मीगर्– deficient in amount, quality, or extent स्वल्प, बहुत थोड़ा Why did you agree to work for such a *meagre* amount?

meal *(n.)* मील– any of the regular occasions, such as breakfast, lunch, dinner, etc. when food is served and eaten भोजन What will you have in your *meal* today?

mealtime *(n.)* मीलटाइम– any of the regular times when food is served and eaten भोजन का समय I will come to meet you in your *mealtime.*

mean *(v.)* मीन–1. to say or do in all seriousness अर्थ होना या रखना What do you *mean* by this?
2. intend अभिप्राय होना Tell me what these words *mean* in Sanskrit.
3. to foretell; portend संकल्प करना, निश्चय करना She *meant* to succeed.
4. *(n.)* a statistic obtained by multiplying each possible value of a variable by its probability and then taking the sum or integral over the range of the variable माध्य औसत The *mean* quantity between 2 and 8 is 5.
5. the middle point, state, or course between limits or extremes बीच का रास्ता She adopted a *mean* to be successful.
6. *(adj.)* miserly, ungenerous, or petty स्वार्थी, कंजूस She is so *mean* that she never spends on her friends.

meanness *(n.)* मीन्नेस– the quality of being cruel or nasty नीच प्रवृत्ति His *meanness* is very painful for his family members.

➢ **mean-minded**– the quality of being narrow-minded or selfish

मतलबी, ख़ुदग़र्ज़, Never be *mean-minded.*

meaning *(n.)* मीनिंग–1. the sense or significance of a word, sentence, symbol, etc.; import; semantic or lexical content अर्थ I did not undersatnd the *meaning* of this line.

2. the purpose underlying or intended by speech, action, etc. किसी अनुभव का प्रयोजन या महत्त्व Theatre gives *meaning* to my life.

meaningful *(adj.)* 1. मीनिंगफ़ुल– having great meaning or validity अर्थपूर्ण He looked at me with *meaningful* eyes.

2. eloquent, expressive उपयोगी, सार्थक We should keep *meaningful* relationships with others.

meaningless *(adj.)* मीनिंगलस– futile or empty of meaning तर्कहीन, अर्थहीन His speech is *meaningless* to me.

meanly *(adv.)* मीनली– in a miserly, ungenerous, or petty manner नीचता से, कमीनेपन से He behaves *meanly* with everyone.

means *(n.)* मीन्ज़–1. resources or income सम्पत्ति, आय You are a man of various *means.*

2. the medium, method, or instrument used to obtain a result or achieve an end उपाय, साधन By what *means* did he climb the wall?

meantime *(n.)* मीन्टाइम्– the intervening time or period, as between events इस बीच My brother ran for a doctor in the *meantime* I stayed at home.

meanwhile *(adj.)* मीन्वाइल्– at the same time, esp in another place इसी बीच, इतने में You write the letter, *meanwhile* I will get a stamp.

measles *(n.)* मीज़ल्ज़्– a highly contagious viral disease common in children, characterized by fever, profuse nasal discharge of mucus, conjunctivitis, and a rash of small red spots spreading from the forehead down to the limbs ख़सरा I looked ugly when I was suffering from *measles.*

measurable *(adj.)* मेश़रबल्– able to be measured; perceptible or significant स्पष्ट दिखाई पड़ने वाला There's been a *measurable* improvement in her life.

measure *(v.)* मेश़र–1. to determine the size, amount, etc. of by measurement माप का होना, मापना Please *measure* the length and breadth of this sheet.

2. to adjust or choose ध्यानपूर्वक एवं सावधानी से विचार करना She is a woman who *measures* her words.

3. *(n.)* degree or exten उपाय New *measures* have been taken to prevent theft and cheating.

4. a standard used in a system of measurements कसौटी, मानदंड Her appreciation is a *measure* of her hardwork.

measurement *(n.)* मेश़रमेण्ट– the act or process of measuring नाप, माप Can I have your *measurements* for the suit length?

meat *(n.)* मीट– the flesh of mammals used as food, as distinguished from that of birds and fish मांस, गोश्त Go to the butcher's shop and buy some *meat.*

Mecca *(n.)* मक्का– a city in W Saudi Arabia, joint capital (with Riyadh) of Saudi Arabia, birthplace of Mohammed; the holiest city of Islam, containing the Kaaba. इस्लाम धर्म का केन्द्रस्थल, मक्का *Mecca* is a place in Saudi Arabia where Muslims go for pilgrimage.

mechanic *(n.)* मकैनिक्– a person skilled in maintaining or operating machinery, motors, etc. मिस्त्री, मैकेनिक All the *mechanic* are on leave today?

mechanical *(adj.)* मकैनिकल–1. made, performed, or operated by or as if by a machine or machinery मशीनी, यांत्रिक We are becoming more and more dependent on *mechanical* objects.
2. (of a gesture, etc.) automatic; lacking thought, feeling, etc. मशीनों के समान In modern times life has become highly *mechanical.*

mechanism *(n.)* मैकैनिज़म– a system or structure of moving parts that performs some function, esp in a machine यंत्र-विन्यास, कलपुर्ज़े Manoj is interested to learn the *mechanism* of television.

mechanize (ise) *(v.)* मेकनाइज़– to equip (a factory, industry, etc.) with machinery यंत्रों या मशीनों से काम लेना Would it be feasible to *mechanize* entire production system?

medal *(n.)* मेडल– a small flat piece of metal bearing an inscription or image, given as an award or commemoration of some outstanding action, event, etc. पदक I won a gold *medal* in my race.

medallist *(n.)* मेडलिस्ट– a winner or recipient of a medal or medals पदक या तमग़ा पाने वाला, पदक विजेता He is a gold *medallist.*

meddle *(n.)* मेडल– to interfere officiously or annoyingly दख़लअन्दाज़ी करना We should not *meddle* in other people's affairs.

media *(n.)* मीडिआ– the means of communication that reach large numbers of people, such as television, newspapers, and radio जनसंचार माध्यम I don't want *media* to know about this mess.

median *(adj.)* मीडिअन– of, relating to, situated in, or directed towards the middle माध्यिका, औसत Mona always goes to the extreme, never remains to the *median* point.

mediate *(v.)* मीडिएट– to intervene (between parties or in a dispute) in order to bring about agreement मध्यस्थता करना The manager was asked to *mediate* in the dispute.

medical *(adj.)* मेडिकल– of or relating to the science of medicine or to the treatment of patients by drugs, etc. as opposed to surgery चिकित्सा-संबंधी You need to undergo some *medical* treatment for sure.

medicine *(n.)* मेडसन–1. any drug or remedy for use in treating, preventing, or alleviating the symptoms of disease दवा, औषधि Have you taken your *medicine?*
2. the science of preventing, diagnosing, alleviating, or curing disease चिकित्सा शास्त्र How much did you score in *medicine?*

medieval *(adj.)* मेडिईवल– of, relating to, or in the style of the Middle Ages मध्यकालीन Jahangir was a great *medieval* emperor.

mediocre *(adj.)* मीडिओकर्– average or ordinary in quality औसत, साधारण, सामान्य We do not want *mediocre* performers in our team.

meditate *(v.)* मेडिटेट– to think about something deeply चिंतन करना He has been *meditating* upon a workable solution over the past one week.

medium *(adj.)* मीडिअम– 1. midway between extremes; average औसत I have *medium*-length hair.
2. *(n.)* an intermediate or middle state, degree, or condition; mean माध्यम News channels are a faster *medium* than newspapers.

medley *(n.)* मेड्ली– a mixture of various types or elements घालमेल, गड्डमड्ड They all performed a very nice *medley.*

meek *(adj.)* मीक– patient, long-suffering, or submissive in disposition or nature; humble नम्र,

विनीत, दब्बू You cannot forge ahead if you are too *meek*.

meet *(v.)* मीट–1. to come together (with), either by design or by accident; encounter मिलना, भेंट होना Where shall we *meet* tomorrow?

2. to come into or be in conjunction or contact with (something or each other) मिलना, एकत्र हो जाना, जुड़ना Does this lane *meet* the main road?

3. to pay sth चुकाना Can you not *meet* my bill until next month?

meeting *(n.)* मीटिंग–1. an assembly or gathering सभा, बैठक When is your *meeting?*

2. an act of coming together; encounter मुलाक़ात It was nice *meeting* with you.

mega *(adj.)* मेगा– extremely good, great, or successful बहुत बड़ा The song was a *mega* hit last year.

megaphone *(n.)* मेगाफ़ोन– a funnel-shaped instrument used to amplify the voice भोंपू The director stood around *megaphone.*

melancholy *(adj.)* मेलन्कलि– a constitutional tendency to gloominess or depression उदास, दुःखी Why are you in such a *melancholy* mood?

melee *(n.)* मेले– a noisy riotous fight or brawl भीड़-भड़क्का, धक्कामुक्की There was a scuffle and I lost my bag in the *melee.*

mellow *(v.)* मैलो– 1. to make or become soften; mature विनम्र होना, मधुर होना Age *mellowed* her mother's attitude.

2. *(adj.) (esp of fruits)* full-flavoured; sweet; ripe मीठा तथा पका हुआ You can have these oranges, they are very *mellow.*

melodious *(adj.)* मलोडिअस– having a tune that is pleasant to the ear सुरीला, मधुर I love hearing her *melodious* voice.

melodramatic *(adj.)* मैलड्रमैटिक– involving the overdramatization of a situation by someone अतिनाटकीय, भावुकतापूर्ण The Hamlet of Shakespeare has a *melodramatic* ending.

melody *(n.)* मेलडी–1. a succession of notes forming a distinctive sequence; tune लय, राग I shall now sing you an Indian classical *melody.*

2. sounds that are pleasant because of tone or arrangement, esp words of poetry स्वरमाधुर्य We hear the *melody* of singing birds in the morning.

melon *(n.)* मेलन– a large fruit with yellow skin, sweet flesh and a lot of seeds ख़रबूज़ा We should take a lot of *melons* in summer.

➢ **watermelons** *(n.)*– a large fruit with dark green skin, red flesh and black seeds तरबूज़, *Watermelons* are good to reduce blood-pressure.

melt *(v.)* मेल्ट– 1. to melt (metal scrap) for reuse गलना, गलाना, द्रवित होना The hot metal *melted* the wax.

2. to liquefy (a solid) or (of a solid) to become liquefied, as a result of the action of heat पिघलाना या पिघलना The snow *melted* when the sun came out.

3. to make or become emotional or sentimental; soften पसीजना Richard gave her a smile which *melted* her heart.

➢ **melt away**– to disappear; fade ग़ायब हो जाना, चले जाना, His anger *melted away* to see me.

melting-point *(n.)* मेल्टिंग-पाइंट– the temperature at which a solid turns into a liquid. It is equal to the freezing point गलनांक (किसी ठोस पदार्थ के पिघलने का तापमान) Every substance has a different *melting point.*

member *(n.)* मेम्बर– a person who belongs to a club, political party, etc. सदस्य, सभासद Will you become a *member* of our club?

membership *(n.)* मेम्बरशिप– the members of an organization collectively सदस्यता Have you renewed your club *membership*?

membrane *(n.)* मेम्ब्रेन– any thin pliable sheet of material झिल्ली The *membrane* of the plant was so thin.

memento *(n.)* ममेंटो– something that reminds one of past events; souvenir स्मृति-चिह्न, यादगार, निशानी The chief guest was presented a *memento* at the function.

memo *(n.)* मेमो– short for memorandum ज्ञापन He was issued a *memo* for arriving late in the office every day.

memoirs *(n.)* मैमवार्ज़– a collection of reminiscences about a period, series of events, etc. written from personal experience or special sources आत्मचरित, जीवनवृत्त The *memoirs* of the expedition were enlightening.

memorandum *(n.)* मेमरेण्डम– a written statement, record, or communication such as within an office ज्ञापन-पत्र, विज्ञप्ति He gave a *memorandum* to the officer.

memorial *(n.)* मेमॉरिअल– something serving as a remembrance स्मारक, यादगार The Qutab Minar is a very grand *memorial* of medieval period.

memorize (ise) *(v.)* मेमराइज़– to commit to memory; learn so as to remember अच्छी तरह याद कर लेना He *memorized* thousands of verses.

memory *(n.)* मेमरी–1. the ability of the mind to store and recall past sensations, thoughts, knowledge, etc. स्मरण–शक्ति, याददाश्त She has a sharp *memory*.

2. the sum of everything retained by the mind स्मृति, याद I have happy *memories* of my first visit to America.

menace *(n.)* मेनस–1. a threat or the act of threatening ख़तरा, जोखिम Don't drive in such a way that you become a *menace* to pedestrians.

2. something menacing; a source of danger धमकी I felt an air of *menace* in his voice.

3. *(v.)* to threaten with violence, danger, etc. धमकी देना, डराना It is *menacing* to cross a highway amid speeding trucks.

mend *(v.)* मेन्ड–1. to repair (something broken or unserviceable) ठीक कर देना Workmen were *mending* faulty cabling

2. to heal or recover मरम्मत करना Foot injuries can take months to *mend*.

3. to improve or undergo improvement; reform सुधार करना या होना *Mend* your ways if you want to improve your financial condition.

menial *(adj.)* मीनिअल– consisting of or occupied with work requiring little skill, esp domestic duties such as cleaning छोटे स्तर का No one likes to do the *menial* jobs, but some people just don't have a choice.

menses *(n.)* मेन्सीज़– the period of time, usually from three to five days, during which menstruation occurs मासिक-धर्म, रजोधर्म She always gets pain at the time of *menses*.

menstrual *(adj.)* मेन्स्ट्रुअल– of or relating to menstruation or the menses मासिक- धर्म संबंधी Consult a doctor for your *menstrual* irregularity.

mental *(adj.)* मेंटल–1. affected by mental illness मानसिक, दिमागी, पागल Is there a *mental*-hospital in your city?

2. of or involving the mind or an intellectual process मनोभाव, मनोवृत्ति, मन का By *mental* effort, we can remember the details of past happenings.

mentality *(n.)* मेण्टैलिटी– the state or quality of mental or intellectual ability मनोवृत्ति, स्वभाव You have an unusual *mentality* if you do not like any game.

mentally *(adv.)* मेनूटली– as regards the mind दिमाग़ी तौर से, मन से Soldiers become physically and *mentally* exhausted.

mention *(n.)* मेन्शन– 1. a slight reference or allusion उल्लेख, ज़िक्र There was *mention* of poor boy's bravery in the article.
2. *(v.)* to acknowledge or honour ज़िक्र करना, चर्चा करना, कहना I haven't *mentioned* it to William yet.

mentor *(n.)* मेन्टॉर्– a wise or trusted adviser or guide अनुभवी परामर्शदाता He is my *mentor* in singing.

menu *(n.)* मे'न्यू– a list of dishes served at a meal or that can be ordered in a restaurant व्यंजन-सूची Waiter, please bring the *menu.*

mercenary *(adj.)* मर्सनरी– influenced by greed or desire for gain धनलोलुप She's nothing but a *mercenary* little gold-digger.

merchandise *(n.)* मॅर्चण्डाइज़– commercial goods; commodities माल, सौदा The *merchandise* for export were lost at sea.

merchant *(n.)* मॅर्चण्ट– a person engaged in the purchase and sale of commodities for profit, esp on international markets; trader व्यापारी, दुकानदार My uncle is a wholesale grain *merchant.*

merciful *(adj.)* मर्सिफुल– showing or giving mercy; compassionate दयालु, उदार William did not believe in being *merciful.*

merciless *(adj.)* मर्सिलस– without mercy; pitiless, cruel, or heartless दयाहीन A *merciless* attack with a blunt instrument.

mercilessly *(adv.)* मर्सिलसली– in way which is without mercy; pitilessly, cruelly, or heartlessly; unrelentingly बेरहमी से, कठोरतापूर्वक The thief was *mercilessly* beaten by the police.

mercury *(n.)* मर्क्यरि–1. the second smallest planet and the nearest to the sun. बुध ग्रह *Mercury* is a planet.
2. a heavy silvery-white toxic liquid metallic element occurring principally in cinnabar: used in thermometers, barometers, mercury-vapour lamps, and dental amalgams. पारा *Mercury* is used in thermometers and barometers.

mercy *(n.)* मर्सि– compassionate treatment of or attitude towards an offender, adversary, etc. who is in one's power or care; clemency; pity दया, करुणा Oh God, have *mercy* on us!

mere *(adj.)* मिअर्– being nothing more than something specified निरा, मात्र The city is a *mere* 20 minutes from some countryside.

merely *(adv.)* मिअर्ली– only; nothing more than केवल, मात्र, सिर्फ़ I *merely* want to give her a little advice.

merge *(v.)* मर्ज– to meet and join or cause to meet and join विलीन हो जाना The merchant bank *merged* with another broker.

merit *(n.)* मेरिट– worth or superior quality; excellence ख़ूबी, गुण The admission in this course will be strictly on *merit* basis.

meritorious *(adj.)* मेरिटॉरिअस– praiseworthy; showing merit सराहनीय, प्रशंसनीय He won a medal for his *meritorious* conduct.

mermaid *(n.)* मर्मेड– an imaginary sea creature fabled to have a woman's head and upper body and a fish's tail जलपरी The child bought the book 'The Little *Mermaid*'.

merry *(adj.)* मेरि–1. cheerful; jolly आनन्दित, प्रमुदित He wished me a *merry* Christmas.

2. very funny; hilarious प्रसन्नचित्त, ज़िन्दादिल The streets were dense with *merry* throngs of students.

mesmerize (ise) *(v.)* मेज़मराइज़– to hold (someone) as if spellbound सम्मोहित करना The child was *mesmerized* by the television screen.

mess *(n.)* मेस्–1. a state of confusion or untidiness, esp if dirty or unpleasant गड़बड़ी, घोटाला, गंदगी You will have to clear up this *mess* before you leave from here.

2. a place where service personnel eat or take recreation भोजनालय Do you take your food from a *mess*?

message *(n.)* मेसेज– a communication, usually brief, from one person or group to another संदेश Please give him this *message.*

messenger *(n.)* मेसेंजर– a person who takes messages from one person or group to another or others दूत A *messenger* brought the news of his accident.

Messiah *(n.)* मसाइआ– the awaited redeemer of the Jews, to be sent by God to free them मसीहा He really proved to be a *Messiah* for us in the middle of that chaos.

messy *(adj.)* मेसी– dirty, confused, or untidy अस्त-व्यस्त, गंदा Stripping wallpaper can be a *messy,* time-consuming job.

metal *(n.)* मेटल– any of a number of chemical elements, such as iron or copper, that are often lustrous ductile solids, have basic oxides, form positive ions, and are good conductors of heat and electricity धातु Of what *metal* are these articles made?

metallic *(adj.)* मटैलिक– of, concerned with, or consisting of metal or a metal धातु का, धात्विक The blade locked into place with a heavy *metallic* clunk.

metaphor *(n.)* मेटफ़र- a figure of speech in which a word or phrase is applied to an object or action that it does not literally denote in order to imply a resemblance रूपक He is a stone-hearted man. (Stone is a *metaphor.*)

meteoric *(adj.)* मीटिअरिक– of, formed by, or relating to meteors अति तीव्र Pushpa enjoyed a *meteoric* rise to fame.

meteorology *(n.)* मीटिअरालजी– the study of the earth's atmosphere, esp of weather-forming processes and weather forecasting मौसम-विज्ञान She wants to do a course in *meteorology.*

method *(n.)* मेथड– a way of proceeding or doing something, esp a systematic or regular one ढंग, तरीक़ा, रीति Which *method* are you applying to this formula?

methodical *(adj.)* मेथॉडिकल– characterized by method or orderliness; systematic सुव्यवस्थित, क्रमबद्ध She was so *methodical,* she kept everything documented.

methodology *(n.)* मथाडॉलजि– the system of methods and principles used in a particular discipline प्रणाली-विज्ञान His teacher doesn't know the teaching *methodologies* of English language.

meticulous *(adj.)* मटिक्युलस– very precise about details, even trivial ones; painstaking अत्यंत सतर्क/सावधान He gave a *meticulous* description of an incident.

metre *(n.)* मीटर– a metric unit of length equal to approximately 1.094 yards लंबाई की एक माप Please give me three *metres* of plain white lace.

metro *(n.)* मेट्रो–1. an underground, or largely underground, railway system in certain cities भूमिगत रेल सेवा My friends mostly travel by *metro.*

metropolitan *(adj.)* मेट्रोपॉलिटन्– constituting a city and its suburbs महानगरीय Mumbai, Madras are *metropolitan* cities.

mew *(v.)* म्यू– to make a characteristic high-pitched cry म्याउँ करना He heard *mewing* somewhere near the house

microbe *(n.)* माइक्रोब– any microscopic organism, esp a disease-causing bacterium जीवाणु, रोगाणु *Microbe* can only be seen with the help of microscope.

micro-organism *(n.)* माइक्रो-ऑर्गनिज़्म– any organism, such as a bacterium, protozoan, or virus, of microscopic size सूक्ष्म जीव All *micro-organisms* are not harmful.

microphone *(n.)* माइक्रोफ़ोन्– a device used in sound-reproduction systems for converting sound into electrical energy, usually by means of a ribbon or diaphragm set into motion by the sound waves माइक, ध्वनिग्राहक We could not hear your speech, as the *microphone* was not working properly.

microscope *(n.)* माइक्रोस्कोप्– an optical instrument that uses a lens or combination of lenses to produce a magnified image of a small, close object. सूक्ष्मदर्शी I could inspect the tiny insect only through a *microscope.*

microwave *(n.)* माइक्रोवेव– an oven that cooks or heats food quickly. (भोजन पकाने या गर्म करने के लिए एक बक्स की शक्ल की अंगीठी) माइक्रोवेव ओवन A cheesecake was defrosting in the *microwave.*

midday *(n.)* मिड्डे– the middle of the day; noon मध्याह्न, दोपहर I'll finish this work by *midday.*

middle *(n.)* मिडल्–1. मध्य, दरमियान Don't disturb me in the *middle* of my work.

2. an area or point equal in distance from the ends or periphery or in time between the early and late parts बीच में There was a pillar in the *middle* of the room.

3. *(adj.)* intermediate in status, situation, etc. अधेड़ The woman was in her middle forties.

middle class *(adj.)* मिडल् क्लास– of, relating to, or characteristic of the middle class मध्यम-वर्गीय Prem Singh belongs from a *middle class* family.

Middle East *(n.)* मिडल् ईस्ट– the area around the E Mediterranean, esp Israel and the Arab countries from Turkey to North Africa and eastwards to Iran पश्चिम एशिया Many Indians are earning in the *Middle East.*

middleman *(n.)* मिडलमैन– an intermediary बिचौलिया Prakash is a *middleman* between these two parties.

midget *(n.)* मिजेट्– a dwarf whose skeleton and features are of normal proportions बौना आदमी या औरत A *midget* was giving an interview on T.V.

midnight *(n.)* मिडनाइट्– the middle of the night; 12 o'clock at night आधी रात, अर्धरात्रि We had to leave at *midnight* for the airport.

midst *(n.)* मिडस्ट्– surrounded or enveloped by; at a point during, esp a climactic one के बीच A tall man was standing in the *midst* of the crowd.

midsummer *(n.)* मिडसमर्– the middle or height of the summer मध्य ग्रीष्मकाल She was with me on a beautiful *midsummer's* evening.

midway *(adj., adv.)* मिडवे– in or at the middle of the distance; halfway बीचोंबीच Peter came to a halt *midway* down the street.

midwife *(n.)* मिडवाइफ़– a person qualified to deliver babies and to care for women before, during, and after childbirth दाई, धात्री An ill-tempered *midwife* assisted at the birth of a child.

might *(n.)* माइट–1. power, force, or vigour, esp of a great or supreme kind शक्ति, सामर्थ्य I tried with all my *might* to move the heavy load.

2. the past tense or subjunctive mood of may (May का भूतकाल) किसी बात की संभावना के अर्थ में He *might* have returned home.

3. to indicate ability or capacity, esp in questions ग़ुस्से में दूसरे को नसीहत देने के अर्थ में He *might* at least call me.

mighty *(adj.)* माइटी– having or indicating might; powerful or strong बहुत शक्तिशाली Harsha Vardhana was the *mighty* king of Northern India.

migraine *(n.)* माइग्रेन– a throbbing headache usually affecting only one side of the head and commonly accompanied by nausea and visual disturbances सिर का तेज़ दर्द, माइग्रेन Hansa suffers from *migraine* when she drives.

migrant *(n.)* माइग्रण्ट– a person or animal that moves from one region, place, or country to another प्रवासी There are a number of *migrants* from Bangladesh in India.

migrate *(v.)* माइग्रेट– to go from one region, country, or place of abode to settle in another, esp in a foreign country प्रवास करना, परदेश जाकर बसना Rural populations have *migrated* to urban areas.

migration *(n.)* माइग्रेशन– the act or an instance of migrating प्रवास Sarala needed a *migration* certificate for admission to another university.

migratory *(adj.)* माइग्रटरि– nomadic; itinerant प्रवासी (पशु-पक्षी या व्यक्ति जो एक भाग से दूसरे भाग में प्रवास करते हैं) Flamingoes are the *migratory* birds.

mild *(adj.)* माइल्ड–1. gentle or temperate in character, climate, behaviour, etc. कोमल, सौम्य, नरम You always speak in a *mild* manner.

2. not extreme; moderate सुहावना The weather is *mild* today.

3. feeble; unassertive हल्का It was the first offence of that woman, so she was given a *mild* sentence.

mildly *(adv.)* माइल्डली– in a way which is not severe or extreme; moderately; slightly नरमी से 'Don't be childish,' he reproved *mildly*.

mile *(n.)* माइल– a unit of length used in the UK, the US, and certain other countries, equal to 1760 yards. 1 mile is equivalent to 1.609 34 kilometres मील I walk a couple of *miles* every morning.

mileage *(n.)* माइलिज– a distance expressed in miles मील, दूरी, माइलेज I checked the *mileage* before buying a second-hand car.

militant *(n.)* मिलिटण्ट– 1. a militant person उग्रवादी Many *militants* were killed in Kashmir.

2. *(adj.)* aggressive or vigorous, esp in the support of a cause लड़ाकू, झगड़ालू The army are in conflict with *militant* groups.

military *(adj.)* मिलट्री– 1. of or relating to the armed forces (esp the army), warlike matters, etc. सैनिक, फ़ौजी Do you get *military* training in your school?

2. *(n.)* the armed services (esp the army) सेना, फ़ौज Strict discipline is followed in the *military*.

milk *(n.)* मिल्क– an opaque white fluid rich in fat and protein, secreted by female mammals for the nourishment of their young दूध, दुग्ध I take a glass of *milk* every morning.

milkman *(n.)* मिल्कमन– a man who delivers or sells milk ग्वाला, दूधवाला

The name of my *milkman* is Hari, who comes from Haryana.

milkshake *(n.)* मिल्कशेक– a sweet drink made with milk and fruit, flavourings or ice cream (दूध में आम, चीनी आदि मिलाकर बनाया गया पेय पदार्थ) मिल्कशेक *Milkshake* is good for health.

milky *(adj.)* मिल्की– resembling milk, esp in colour or cloudiness दूध जैसा, दूधिया Not a blemish marred her *milky* skin.

milky way *(n.)* मिल्की वे– the diffuse band of light stretching across the night sky that consists of millions of faint stars, nebulae, etc. within our Galaxy आकाश गंगा I could see the *milky way* in the midnight.

mill *(n.)* मिल– a building in which grain is crushed and ground to make flour चक्की, कारख़ाना, मिल How many textile *mills* are there in your city?

millennium *(n.)* मिलेनिअम– a period or cycle of one thousand years सहस्राब्दी Amitabh Bachchan was awarded with the title of the star of the *millennium.*

millet *(n.)* मिलेट– a cereal grass, cultivated for grain and animal fodder बाजरा *Millet* was scattered at different places in the field.

milligram *(n.)* मिलिग्रैम– one thousandth of a gram भार तोलने की इकाई, मिलीग्राम There are 1000 *milligrams* in a gram.

millilitre *(n.)* मिलीलीटर– one thousandth of a litre ml द्रव नापने की इकाई, मिलीलीटर There are 1000 *millilitres* in a litre.

million *(adj.)* मिल्यन– amounting to a million दस लाख, दशलक्ष I've got *millions* of beer bottles in my cellar.

millionaire *(n.)* मिलयनेअर– a person whose assets are worth at least a million of the standard monetary units of his country करोड़पति I learn your guest is a *millionaire.*

mince *(v.)* मिन्स– to chop, grind, or cut into very small pieces क़ीमा करना, काटकर टुकड़े-टुकड़े करना I want to buy half a kilogram of *minced* meat.

mind *(v.)* माइण्ड–1. to pay attention to (something); heed; notice (पर) ध्यान देना, बुरा मानना Never *mind* the opinion polls.

2. to take care of; have charge of देखरेख करना We left our husbands to *mind* the children while we went out.

3. to take offence at आपत्ति करना, आपत्ति होना Would you *mind* if I smoke?

4. *(n.)* the human faculty to which are ascribed thought, feeling, etc; often regarded as an immaterial part of a person मन, चित्त Is your *mind* in your work?

5. attention or thoughts इरादा, विचार I thought I would return the same day but now I have changed my *mind.*

- **mind your own business**– refrain from meddling in other people's affairs. अपने काम से काम रखना, Please don't interfere and *mind your own business.*
- **come in mind**–एकाएक कोई बात याद आ जाना, An idea suddenly *came to* my *mind.*
- **in mind**–याद रखना, विचार करना, I will keep your suggestion *in mind.*
- **make up your mind**– to decide (about something or to do something) किसी बात के लिए अपना दिमाग़ बनाना, You have to *make up your mind* to go abroad.
- **out of mind**– बहुत चिंतित होना, She was going *out of* her *mind* when her daughter did not reach home on time.
- **presence of mind**– the ability to remain calm and act constructively during times of crisis हाज़िरजवाबी,

His *presence of mind* is very appreciating.

minded *(adj.)* माइंडिड– having a mind, inclination, intention, etc. as specified मनवाला, मस्तिष्कवाला I'm not scientifically *minded.*

mindful *(adj.)* माइंडफुल– keeping aware; heedful सतर्क, जागरूक Be *mindful* of your responsibilities, you are an elder son.

mindfully *(adv.)* माइंडफुल्ली– with awareness of what one is doing ध्यानपूर्वक Discharge your duties *mindfully.*

mindless *(adj.)* माइंडलस– stupid or careless लापरवाह A generation of *mindless* vandals.

mine *(pron.)* माइन– 1. something or someone belonging to or associated with me मेरा, मेरी That book is yours, this one is *mine.*
2. *(n.)* a system of excavations made for the extraction of minerals, esp coal, ores, or precious stones खान, खदान The antiquity of gold *mines* in Karnataka is quite impressive.

mineral *(n.)* मिनरल– any of a class of naturally occurring solid inorganic substances with a characteristic crystalline form and a homogeneous chemical composition खनिज पदार्थ India is rich in *minerals.*

mingle *(v.)* मिन्गल–1. to come into close association मिलाना या मिलना The sound of voices *mingled* with a scraping of chairs.
2. to mix or cause to mix घुलमिल जाना I like to *mingle* with all sorts of people.

miniature *(n.)* मिनएचर्– a model, copy, or similar representation on a very small scale लघुचित्र She made a *miniature* of Hawa Mahal.

minibus *(n.)* मिनिबस– a small bus able to carry approximately ten passengers छोटी बस The school hired the *minibus* for a small trip.

minimal *(adj.)* मिनिमल– of the least possible; minimum or smallest न्यूनतम The aircraft suffered *minimal* damage

minimize (ise) *(v.)* मिनिमाइज़– to reduce to or estimate at the least possible degree or amount न्यूनतम करना, कम कर देना The aim is to *minimize* costs.

minimum *(adj.)* मिनिमम– 1. of or relating to a minimum or minimums कम से कम, अल्पतम The trade union demanded an increase in the *minimum* wages. Who promises to give the maximum value at the *minimum* price?
2. *(adv.)* the least possible amount, degree, or quantity न्यूनतम रूप से She'll need Rs. 500 *minimum* for expenses.

minister *(n.)* मिनिस्टर्– a person appointed to head a government department मंत्री A close friend of mine has now become a *minister* in the cabinet.

ministry *(n.)* मिनिस्ट्री– the profession or duties of a minister of religion मंत्रालय, मंत्री का कार्यालय The *ministry* of Home Affairs is responsible for all the matters of the country.

minor *(adj.)* माइनर्– 1. lesser or secondary in amount, extent, importance, or degree छोटा, गौण She requested a number of *minor* alterations.
2. *(n.)* a person below the age of legal majority नाबालिग़, अल्पवयस्क, अवयस्क My son can't vote, as he is still a *minor.*

minority *(n.)* माइनॉरिटी– a group that is different racially, politically, etc. from a larger group of which it is a part अल्पसंख्यक Muslims are the largest *minority* community in India.

mint *(n.)* मिन्ट–1. a plant with dark green leaves, used in cooking as a herb पुदीना I use *mint* to flavour food in summer.

2. a place where money is coined by governmental authority टकसाल, (जहां सिक्के ढलते हैं) These coins are issued by the *mint* located in Nagpur.

minus *(n.)* माइनस–1. something detrimental or negative ऋण, ऋणात्मक Arithmetic begins with plus and *minus.*

2. *(prep.)* deprived of; lacking सिवाय, बिना Why have you come *minus* your cap?

minute *(n.)* मिनूइट–1. a period of time equal to 60 seconds; one sixtieth of an hour मिनिट/माइन्यूट–मिनट, क्षण I can do this job in ten *minutes.*

2. *(adj.)* very small; diminutive; tiny सूक्ष्म, अति लघु I did not notice the *minute* particles of dust on my specs.

minutely *(adv.)* माइन्यूटली– in great detail सूक्ष्म रीति से, बारीकी से The advocate studied the case *minutely.*

miracle *(n.)* मिरकल– any amazing or wonderful event चमत्कार, करामात As a *miracle,* most of the passengers were saved when their bus fell into a gorge.

miraculous *(adj.)* मिरैक्युलस्– of, like, or caused by a miracle; marvellous आश्चर्य- जनक, चमत्कारी I felt amazed and grateful for our *miraculous* escape.

mirage *(n.)* मिराज– an image of a distant object or sheet of water, often inverted or distorted, caused by atmospheric refraction by hot air मरीचिका, भ्रामक वस्तु The surface of the road ahead rippled in the heat *mirages.*

mirror *(n.)* मिरर्– a surface, such as polished metal or glass coated with a metal film, that reflects light without diffusion and produces an image of an object placed in front of it आईना, शीशा Who broke the *mirror?*

mirth *(n.)* मर्थ– laughter, gaiety, or merriment मनोरंजन There was an atmosphere of *mirth* in the house.

misapprehension *(n.)* मिस्ऐप्रिहेंशन– a failure to understand fully; misconception ग़लतफ़हमी He had this *misapprehension* that the house belonged to Mrs. Reynolds.

misappropriate *(v.)* मिस्अप्रोप्रिएट– to appropriate for a wrong or dishonest use; embezzle or steal धन का दुरुपयोग करना The report revealed that officials had *misappropriated* funds.

misbehave *(v.)* मिस्बिहेव– to behave (oneself) badly दुर्व्यवहार करना Josh *misbehaved,* pushing his food off the table.

miscalculate *(v.)* मिसकैलक्युलेट– to calculate wrongly गणना करने में भूल करना The shopkeeper *miscalculated* the amount of money given to him.

miscarriage *(n.)* मिस्कैरिएज–1. spontaneous expulsion of a fetus from the womb, esp prior to the 20th week of pregnancy गर्भपात She was crying from the severe pain of *miscarriage.*

2. an act of mismanagement or failure घोर अन्याय Sending an innocent boy to prison is a clear *miscarriage* of justice.

miscellaneous *(adj.)* मिसलेनिअस– composed of or containing a variety of things; mixed; varied विविध He picked up the *miscellaneous* papers in his in tray.

mischief *(n.)* मिस्चिफ़–1. wayward but not malicious behaviour, usually of children, that causes trouble, irritation, etc. शरारत, नटखटपन My youngest son is always up to some *mischief.*

2. injury or harm caused by a person or thing हानि You are too late, the *mischief* is done.

mischievous *(adj.)* मिस्चिवस– inclined to acts of mischief शैतान, नटखट, शरारती A *mischievous* boy drew a cartoon on the blackboard.

misconception *(n.)* मिस्कन्सेप्शन– a false or mistaken view, opinion, or attitude ग़लतफ़हमी Why do you have *misconception* about him?

misconduct *(n.)* मिस्कण्डक्ट– behaviour, such as adultery or professional negligence, that is regarded as immoral or unethical बुरा व्यवहार या आचरण He was punished for his *misconduct* with his neighbour.

misdirect *(v.)* मिस्डरेक्ट–1. to give (a person) wrong directions or instructions ग़लत सूचना देना, ग़लत निर्देश देना Voters were *misdirected* to the wrong polling station.
2. to address (a letter, parcel, etc.) wrongly ग़लत पता लिखना This courier was *misdirected* to the wrong street.

miser *(n.)* माइज़र्– a person who hoards money or possessions, often living miserably कंजूस, कृपण Some rich poeple behave like *misers.*

miserable *(adj.)* मिज़रबल–1. causing misery, discomfort, etc. बहुत दयनीय Their happiness made Anne feel even more *miserable.*
2. sordid or squalid बहुत खिन्न कर देने वाला It is a *miserable* cold day.

miserly *(adj.)* माइज़र्ली– of or resembling a miser; avaricious कंजूस His *miserly* great-uncle proved to be worth nearly £1 million.

misery *(n.)* मिज़्रि– intense unhappiness, discomfort, or suffering; wretchedness दुर्दशा, विपत्ति, दुःख I have seen people live in great *misery* because of poverty.

misfit *(n.)* मिस्फ़िट– a person not suited in behaviour or attitude to a particular social environment अनुपयुक्त व्यक्ति Being the youngest one, she often felt she was a *misfit* in the organisation.

misfortune *(n.)* मिस्फॉर्चून– evil fortune; bad luck बदनसीबी Tabassum has faced a series of *misfortunes* since last few years.

misguide *(v.)* मिस्गाइड–1. to guide or direct wrongly or badly गुमराह करना, बहकाना A long survey that can only *misguide* the general reader.

misguided *(adj.)* मिस्गाइडिड– foolish or unreasonable, esp in action or behaviour पथभ्रष्ट, विभ्रांत Their *misguided* belief that they were defending their country.

mishap *(n.)* मिस्हैप्– an unfortunate accident मामूली दुर्घटना The *mishap* had changed her life completely.

misinterpret *(v.)* मिसिंटर्प्रिट– to interpret badly, misleadingly, or incorrectly गलत समझना, गलत अर्थ लेना I think you're *misinterpreting* the situation.

misjudge *(v.)* मिस्जज– to judge (a person or persons) wrongly or unfairly ग़लत निर्णय लेना I've *misjudged* Doris—she hasn't told anyone.

mislead *(v.)* मिस्लीड्– to give false or misleading information to भ्रमित करना The government *misled* the public about the road's environmental impact.

misleading *(adj.)* मिस्लीडिंग– tending to confuse or mislead; deceptive गुमराह The advertisements of fairness creams are highly *misleading.*

mismanage *(v.)* मिस्मैनिज– to manage badly or wrongly कुप्रबंध करना He was accused of *mismanaging* the economy.

mismatch *(n.)* मिस्मैच– a bad or inappropriate match बेमेल जोड़ Their marriage was a *mismatch.*

misogynist *(n.)* मिसॉजिनिस्ट– a person who hates women स्त्रियों से

घृणा करने वाला व्यक्ति, नारी-द्वेषी Suhail is a *misogynist* and it would be worthless to argue with him.

misplace *(v.)* मिस्प्लेस– to put (something) in the wrong place, esp to lose (something) temporarily by forgetting where it was placed; mislay ग़लत स्थान पर रखना, खो देना She *misplaced* my book.

misplaced *(adj.)* मिसप्लेसड– (of trust, loyalty, etc) that has been bestowed inappropriately on someone or something (ग़लत व्यक्ति को विश्वासपात्र समझ लेना) अनुचित, गलत I realized that my trust in him was *misplaced.*

misprint *(n.)* मिस्प्रिंट– an error in printing, made through damaged type, careless reading, etc. मुद्रण-दोष The document was full of *misprints.*

miss *(v.)* मिस–1. to fail to attend or be present for चूकना, न मिलना Mandy *missed* the catch, and flung the ball back crossly.

2. to discover or regret the loss or absence of अभाव का अनुभव करना We shall all *miss* you when you go away.

3. to fail to see, hear, understand, or perceive न कर, सुन या देख पाना The villa is impossible to *miss*—it's right by the road.

4. to fail to reach, hit, meet, find, or attain (some specified or implied aim, goal, target, etc.) अभाव मालूम हो जाना, गुम होना One of my books is *missing.*

5. *(n.)* an unmarried woman or girl, esp a schoolgirl कुमारी What is your name, *miss*?

missile *(n.)* मिसाइल– any object or weapon that is thrown at a target or shot from an engine, gun, etc. मिसाइल, प्रक्षेपास्त्र The nuclear *missile* destroyed the whole city.

mission *(n.)* मिशन–1. a specific task or duty assigned to a person or group of people लक्ष्य, मिशन, दूतावास Are you working with the poor Indian *mission* in the USA?

2. errand, delegation दूतकार्य, शिष्टमंडल I was sent on a *mission* to Sri Lanka.

3. a person's vocation जीवन-लक्ष्य Spreading education among the poor is the *mission* of my life.

missionary *(n.)* मिशनरि– a member of a religious mission धर्म-प्रचारक, मिशनरी The school was founded by some Christian *missionaries.*

mist *(n.)* मिस्ट– a thin fog resulting from condensation in the air near the earth's surface कुहरा I did not go for my morning walk because of the *mist.*

mistake *(n.)* मिस्टेक–1. an error or blunder in action, opinion, or judgment भूल, ग़लती You have made a *mistake* in this sentence.

2. a misconception or misunderstanding ग़लती से I took your book by *mistake.*

3. *(v.)* to misunderstand; misinterpret दूसरा समझना I *mistook* you for your younger brother.

mistaken *(adj.)* मिस्टेकन– wrong in opinion, judgment, etc. ग़लत, भ्रमपूर्ण She wondered whether she'd been *mistaken* about his intentions.

mistreat *(v.)* मिस्ट्रीट– to treat badly बुरा व्यवहार करना, (के प्रति) निर्दय होना It is a moving tale about how the white man *mistreated* Indians.

mistrust *(v.)* मिस्ट्रस्ट्– to have doubts or suspicions about (someone or something) अविश्वास करना, यक़ीन न करना She always *mistrusts* strangers.

misunderstand *(v.)* मिसअंडर्स्टेंड– to fail to understand properly (किसी व्यक्ति या वस्तु को) समझने में ग़लती करना He had *misunderstood* the police officer's hand signals.

misuse *(n.)* मिसूयूज़– 1. erroneous, improper, or unorthodox use दुरुपयोग It was a clear case of *misuse* of power.
2. *(v.)* to use wrongly दुरुपयोग करना, ग़लत इस्तेमाल करना He was accused of *misusing* the funds of the company.

mite *(n.)* माइट– any of numerous small free-living or parasitic arachnids of the order Acarina (or Acari) that can occur in terrestrial or aquatic habitats कुटकी, एक छोटा कीड़ा She sprayed the insecticide to kill the *mites.*

mitigate *(v.)* मिटिगेट– to make or become less severe or harsh; moderate किसी बुरे प्रभाव को कम कर देना Drainage schemes have helped to mitigate this problem.

mix *(v.)* मिक्स–1. to combine or blend (ingredients, liquids, objects, etc.) together into one mass मिश्रण करना, मिलाना Sita *mixed* some water in orange squash to make a cold drink.
2. to come or cause to come into association socially मिलना-जुलना You are good at *mixing* with people.

mixed *(adj.)* मिक्स्ड–1. मिली-जुली (अच्छी और बुरी दोनों तरह की) Why do you have *mixed* feelings for him?
2. in a state of mental confusion; perplexed उलझन में You are all *mixed*-up.

mixture *(n.)* मिक्सचर– something mixed; a result of mixing मिश्रण, मेल Water is a *mixture* of hydrogen and oxygen.

moan *(v.)* मोन– 1. to utter (words) in a low mournful manner कराहना Are you in pain? You were *moaning* in your sleep.
2. *(n.)* a low prolonged mournful sound expressive of suffering or pleading विलाप, कराह, हाय-हाय The wounded man's *moans* could be heard all night.

mob *(n.)* मॉब– 1. a riotous or disorderly crowd of people; rabble उत्तेजित भीड़, जनसाधारण From my window, I saw the police firing in the air to disperse the riotous *mob.*
2. *(v.)* to surround, esp in order to acclaim मिलकर घेर लेना, तंग करना As we stood outside the theatre, we saw the popular film star being *mobbed* by his fans.

mobile *(adj.)* मोबाइल– able to move freely and quickly to any given area चलता-फिरता, गतिशील We have a *mobile* post office in our city.

mobilize (ise) *(v.)* मोबिलाइज़– to put into motion, circulation, or use गति प्रदान करना The government *mobilized* regular forces, and militia.

mock *(v.)* मॉक– 1. to imitate, esp in fun; mimic उपहास करना, हँसी उड़ाना Opposition MPs *mocked* the government's decision.
2. *(adj.)* serving as an imitation or substitute, esp for practice purposes नक़ली, दिखावटी Have you ever participated in a *mock* Parliament?

mockery *(n.)* मॉकरी– an imitation or pretence, esp a derisive one उपहास, हँसी, उपहासपात्र Johney Lever does a good *mockery* of many actors.

mode *(n.)* मोड–1. a manner or way of doing, acting, or existing प्रणाली, तरीक़ा My cell remains on silent *mode* during office hours.
2. the current fashion or style चलन, रिवाज, फ़ैशन She keeps up herself with prevailing *mode.*

model *(adj.)* मॉडल–1. a representation, usually on a smaller scale, of a device, structure, etc. नमूना I bought a *model* aeroplane for my son. Please show me the *model* of the proposed hospital building.
2. (as modifier) आदर्श Your son is a *model* student.

3. *(n.)* a person who poses for a sculptor, painter, or photographer मॉडल I learn your daughter is working as a *model.*

4. *(v.)* a representative form, style, or pattern (किसी व्यक्ति का) अनुकरण करना She is *modelling* herself on her aunt.

moderate *(v.)* मॉडरट/मोडरेट–1. to act as an external moderator of the overall standards and marks for कम/मन्द करना, संयत करना I shall not *moderate* my criticism.

2. to become or cause to become less extreme or violent कम होना Now the storm is *moderating.*

3. *(adj.)* not violent; mild or temperate मन्द, नरम I like the *moderate* weather of your town.

modern *(adj.)* मॉडर्न– of, involving, or befitting the present or a recent time; contemporary आधुनिक, आजकल का The pace of *modern* life.

modernity *(n.)* मॉडर्नटी– the quality or state of being modern आधुनिकता, नवीनता There was a touch of *modernity* in their new flat.

modernize (ise) *(v.)* मॉडर्नाइज़– to make modern in appearance or style आधुनिक बनाना He *modernized* the health service.

modest *(adj.)* मॉडिस्ट–1. having or expressing a humble opinion of oneself or one's accomplishments or abilities विनीत, विनयशील The *modest* behaviour of Sushila impressed everyone at the party.

2. decorous or decent मर्यादित I paid a *modest* price for this embroidered table-cloth.

modify *(v.)* मॉडिफ़ाई–1. to change the structure, character, intent, etc. of कुछ-कुछ बदलना, परिवर्तन करना She may be prepared to *modify* her views.

2. to change (a vowel) by umlaut सुधार करना, नम्र बनाना You should *modify* your tone.

moist *(adj.)* मॉइस्ट– slightly damp or wet गीला, भीगा हुआ Dry your *moist* hands with this towel.

moisture *(n.)* मॉइस्चर– water or other liquid diffused as vapour or condensed on or in objects नमी I could feel the *moisture* in the air.

moisturize (ise) *(v.)* मॉइस्चराइज़– to add or restore moisture to (the air, the skin, etc.) गीला करना, नमी प्रदान करना You should *moisturize* your dry skin with good lotion.

molar *(n.)* मोलर– any of the 12 broad-faced grinding teeth in man दाढ़ She was having pain in her left *molar.*

mole *(n.)* मोल– any congenital growth or pigmented blemish on the skin; birthmark त्वचा पर तिल Zara has a *mole* on her left arm.

molest *(v.)* मोलैस्ट– to disturb or annoy by malevolent interference (कामुकतापूर्ण) छेड़खानी करना, छेड़छाड़ करना He was charged with *molesting* of a ten-year-old boy.

moment *(n.)* मोमेण्ट– a short indefinite period of time क्षण, पल Getting the Nobel Prize is the happiest *moment* of any scientist. Our friend should be here any *moment.*

momentary *(adj.)* मोमन्ट्रि– lasting for only a moment; temporary क्षणिक A *momentary* lapse of concentration.

monarch *(n.)* मोनार्क– a sovereign head of state, esp a king, queen, or emperor, who rules usually by hereditary right राजा, बादशाह, शासक The *monarch* was wearing a golden *crown.*

monastery *(n.)* मॉनस्ट्री– the residence of a religious community, esp of monks, living in seclusion from secular society and bound by religious vows मठ, विहार, संघाराम The monks were resting in the *monastery.*

Monday *(n.)* मॅन्डे– the second day of the week; first day of the working week सोमवार The physiotherapist called her mother every *Monday.*

monetary *(adj.)* मॉनिटरी– of or relating to money or currency वित्तीय, मौद्रिक I have documents with little or no *monetary* value.

money *(n.)* मनी– the official currency, in the form of banknotes, coins, etc. issued by a government or other authority रुपया-पैसा, धन Can you lend me some *money*?

mongoose *(n.)* माँगूज़– a small animal with fur that kills rats, snakes, etc. नेवला, नकुल I watched the deadly fight between the snake and the *mongoose.*

monitor *(n.)* मॉनिटर्–1. a person or piece of equipment that warns, checks, controls, or keeps a continuous record of something छात्रनायक, कक्षा-नायक My son has been made the *monitor* of his class.
2. a television screen used to display certain kinds of information in a television studio, airport, etc. टेलीविज़न के समान पर्दे पर चित्र दिखाने वाली मशीन You should wear specs while sitting in front of the *monitor.*

monk *(n.)* मॉङ्क– a male member of a religious community bound by vows of poverty, chastity, and obedience संन्यासी, मठवासी The *monks* helped the wounded man they found.

monkey *(n.)* मंकी– an animal with a long tail, that climbs tree बंदर, वानर A big *monkey* caused much terror in the city.

monogamy *(n.)* मनॉगमी– the state or practice of having only one husband or wife over a period of time एक विवाह-प्रथा Many religious leaders insist men to follow *monogamy.*

monopoly *(n.)* मनॉपली– exclusive control of the market supply of a product or service एकाधिकार The company has a *monopoly* in garment making.

monotonous *(adj.)* मनॉटनस– dull and tedious, esp because of repetition एकरस, नीरस, उबाऊ Her slurred *monotonous* speech.

monotony *(n.)* मनॉटनी– wearisome routine; dullness नीरसता The atmosphere in a call centre is shrouded with *monotony.*

monsoon *(n.)* मॉन्सून– a seasonal wind that blows from the southwest in summer, bringing heavy rains, and from the northeast in winter वर्षा-ऋतु Now that the *monsoon* is near, we must repair our leaking roof.

monster *(n.)* मॉन्स्टर– a cruel, wicked, or inhuman person शैतान These kids are little *monsters.*

monstrous *(adj.)* मॉन्स्ट्रस–1. outrageous, atrocious, or shocking अस्वीकार्य, बेतुकापन Its really a *monstrous* act to pay men more than women for the same job.
2. abnormal, hideous, or unnatural in size, character, etc. राक्षसी, ख़ौफ़नाक, डरावना We saw a *monstrous* spider in the museum.

month *(n.)* मन्थ– one of the twelve divisions (calendar months) of the calendar year महीना, मास I have not come to you for a *month.*

monthly *(adj.)* मंथली– occurring, done, appearing, payable, etc. once every month हर महीने The Council held *monthly* meetings.

monument *(n.)* मॉन्युमेण्ट– an obelisk, statue, building, etc. erected in commemoration of a person or event or in celebration of something स्मारक, कीर्तिस्तम्भ Have you seen all the old *monuments* in Delhi?

mood *(n.)* मूड–1. a temporary state of mind or temper मनोदशा, चित्तवृत्ति

The boss seems to be in a happy *mood* today.

2. a prevailing atmosphere or feeling मिज़ाज, तबियत I want to speak to him when he is in a better *mood*.

moody *(adj.)* मूडी– sullen, sulky, or gloomy अस्थिर मनोदशा वाला, तुनकमिज़ाज Pallavi is a *moody* girl and suddenly becomes violent.

moon *(n.)* मून– the natural satellite of the planet. चन्द्रमा, शशि Look at the full *moon*!

moonlight *(n.)* मूनलाइट– light from the sun received on earth after reflection by the moon चांदनी The Taj Mahal looked beautiful in the *moonlight*.

moor *(n.)* मुअर– 1. a tract of unenclosed ground, usually having peaty soil covered with heather, coarse grass, bracken, and moss दलदलयुक्त बंजर भूमि The shepherds walked with their sheeps across the *moor*.

2. *(v.)* to secure (a ship, boat, etc.) with cables or ropes लंगर डालकर खड़ा करना The fishings boats were *moored* alongside the pier.

mop *(n.)* मॉप– 1. an implement with a wooden handle and a head made of twists of cotton or a piece of synthetic sponge, used for polishing or washing floors, or washing dishes झाड़न Ask the maid-servant to clean the floor with a *mop*.

2. (v.) to clean or soak up with or as if with a mop पोंछा लगाना, पोंछना She was *mopping* the floor.

mope *(v.)* मोप– to be gloomy or apathetic उदास होकर बैठे रहना You spend too much time *moping* about the house.

moral *(adj.)* मॉरल– 1. concerned with or relating to human behaviour, esp the distinction between good and bad or right and wrong behaviour नैतिक, सदाचारी They have a *moral* obligation to pay the money back.

2. *(n.)* the lesson to be obtained from a fable or event शिक्षा, सीख What is the *moral* of this story?

morale *(n.)* मोराल– the degree of mental or moral confidence of a person or group; spirit of optimism मनोदशा, मनोबल The defeat never broke the players' *morale.*

morality *(n.)* मरैलटी– the quality of being moral आचार नीति, नैतिकता We should teach the lesson of *morality* to our children.

morally *(adv.)* मॉरली– in accordance with a code of morals नैतिक दृष्टि से Theories which assert that all inequality is *morally* wrong.

more *(adj.)* मोर्–1. additional; further अधिक, ज्यादा Put *more* milk in this cup.

2. *(adv.)* to a greater degree than sth else (तुलनात्मक रूप में प्रयुक्त) अन्य से ज्यादा You are *more* intelligent than your sister.

moreover *(adv.)* मोरओवर– in addition to what has already been said; furthermore साथ ही, इसके अतिरिक्त *Moreover*, statistics show that competition for places is growing.

morning *(n.)* मॉर्निंग– sunrise; daybreak; dawn प्रभात, सवेरा At what time do you get up in the *morning*?

moron *(n.)* मॉरॉन– a foolish or stupid person बुद्धू, मूर्ख व्यक्ति She treats her husband like a *moron*.

morose *(adj.)* मॉरोस– ill-tempered or gloomy बदमिज़ाज, चिड़चिड़ा Why do she look *morose* today?

morphine *(n.)* मॉर्फ़ीन– an alkaloid extracted from opium: used in medicine as an analgesic and sedative, although repeated use causes addiction दर्दनिवारक The injection of *morphine* was given to her for reducing pain.

morsel *(n.)* मॉर्सल– a small slice or mouthful of food ग्रास, कौर I pitied the beggar entreating everyone for a *morsel* of food.

mortal *(adj.)* मॉर्टल–1. (of living beings, esp human beings) subject to death नश्वर, मरणशील All men are *mortal.*
2. a person मानव, मनुष्य No *mortal* can expect to live longer than a hundred years.

mortality *(n.)* मॉरटैलटी– the number of deaths in a given period मरने वालों की संख्या The infant *mortality* rate is so high in US compared to other countries.

mortgage *(n.)* मॉर्गिज्– an agreement under which a person borrows money to buy property, esp a house, and the lender may take possession of the property if the borrower fails to repay the money बंधक, गिरवी They *mortgaged* their house to send their son abroad.

mortify *(v.)* मॉर्टिफ़ाई– to humiliate or cause to feel shame लज्जित करना, नीचा दिखाना We should not *mortify* anyone.

mortuary *(n.)* मौर्चुऐरी– a building where dead bodies are kept before cremation or burial मुर्दाघर, शवगृह His body was sent to *mortuary* after his accidental death.

mosaic *(n.)* मोज़ेइक– a design or decoration made up of small pieces of coloured glass, stone, etc. पच्चीकारी, चित्रकारी Look at that *mosaic* painting. Isn't it beautiful?

mosque *(n.)* मॉस्क्– a Muslim place of worship, मस्जिद The *mosque* was beautifully decorated on Eid.

mosquito *(n.)* मस्कीटो– a flying insect that bites humans and spread malaria, dengue, etc. मच्छर I can't sit here anymore, there are so many *mosquitoes.*

moss *(n.)* मॉस– any bryophyte of the phylum Bryophyta, typically growing in dense mats on trees, rocks, moist ground, etc. काई Don't swim in that lake, it is full of *moss.*

most *(adv.)* मोस्ट– 1. the superlative of much सबसे अधिक, अत्यधिक Whick book do you find the *most* interesting?
2. *(adj.)* a great majority of; nearly all अधिकांश, ज़्यादातर *Most* of my friends are science students.

mostly *(adv.)* मोस्टली– almost entirely; chiefly ज़्यादातर Salim comes *mostly* at this time.

motel *(n.)* मोटेल– a roadside hotel for motorists, usually having direct access from each room or chalet to a parking space or garage (सड़क के किनारे बना छोटा होटल) ढाबा We stayed in a *motel* to take rest from a long journey.

moth *(n.)* मॉथ– a flying insect like a butterfly, attracted to bright light पतंगा, शलभ These naphthalene balls will protect your clothes from *moths.*

mother *(n.)* मदर्– a female who has given birth to offspring माता The *mother* picked up the child in her arms.

mother-in-law *(n.)* मदर्-इन-लॉ– the mother of one's wife or husband सास My *mother-in-law* is quite unwell these days.

motherland *(n.)* मदरलैंड– a person's native country मातृभूमि I love my mother and my *motherland.*

motherly *(adj.)* मदर्ली– of or resembling a mother, esp in warmth, or protectiveness माता के जैसा, मातृ-सुलभ She held both her arms wide in a gesture of *motherly* love.

mother-tongue *(n.)* मदर-टंग– the language first learned by a child मातृभाषा What is your *mother-tongue*?

motif *(n.)* मोटिफ़– a distinctive idea, esp a theme elaborated on in a piece of music, literature, etc अभिप्राय, मूलभाव The colourful hand-painted *motifs* which adorn narrowboats.

motion *(n.)* मोशन–1. the process of continual change in the physical position of an object; movement गति, चाल You must not open the door of the compartment while the train is in *motion.*

2. a formal proposal to be discussed and voted on in a debate, meeting, etc. प्रस्ताव Was your *motion* carried in the meeting?

motionless *(adj.)* मोशनलस्– not moving; absolutely still निश्चल, गतिहीन The students remained *motionless* when ordered to keep quite.

motivate *(v.)* मोटिवेट– to give incentive to प्रेरणा देना, प्रेरित करना He was primarily *motivated* by the desire for profit.

motivated *(adj.)* मोटिवेटड– inspired by a desire to achieve something अभिप्रेरित They are highly *motivated* students.

motive *(n.)* मोटिव– the reason for a certain course of action, whether conscious or unconscious मक़सद, प्रयोजन What was your *motive* in telling me a lie?

motor *(n.)* मोटर्– the engine, esp an internal-combustion engine, of a vehicle गति प्रदान करने का यंत्र Different kinds of electronic devices have *motors* which produce movement.

motorbike *(n.)* मोटरबाइक– a two-wheeled vehicle, that is driven by a petrol engine मोटरसाइकिल He bought a new *motorbike* for his son.

motorboat *(n.)*– a fast torpedo boat used by the navy इंजन से चलने वाली छोटी नाव Sailing in a *motorboat* was the fantastic experience of my life.

motorcycle *(n.)* मोटरसाइकल्– a two-wheeled vehicle, having a stronger frame than a bicycle, that is driven by a petrol engine मोटर-साइकिल He is taking part in a *motorcycle* race.

motorized (ise) *(adj.)* मोटराइज़्ड– to equip with a motor मोटर या इंजन में लगा हुआ, इंजन-चलित He is using a *motorized* wheelchair after an accident.

motorway *(n.)* मोटर्वे– a main road for fast-moving traffic, having limited access चौड़ा मार्ग *Motorways* are called Expressways, which are used for fast traffic.

motto *(n.)* मॉटो– a short saying expressing the guiding maxim or ideal of a family, organization, etc. esp when part of a coat of arms ध्येय वाक्य The *motto* of my life is – You can if you think you can.

mould *(v.)* मोल्ड–1. to make in a mould गढ़ना, साँचे में ढालना The smith would pour the molten metal into the shaped *mould.*

2. *(n.)* a shaped cavity used to give a definite form to fluid or plastic material साँचा, ढाँचा Get me the star-shaped *mould*; I'll prepare cookies.

3. a coating or discoloration caused by various saprotrophic fungi that develop in a damp atmosphere on the surface of stored food, fabrics, wallpaper, etc. फफूंदी Don't eat that bread, it is full of *mould.*

mound *(v.)* माउन्ड– a large pile of earth or stones; heap टीला Basmati rice was *mounded* on our plates.

mount *(v.)* माउन्ट–1. to go up (a hill, stairs, etc.); climb चढ़ना, सवारी करना Can you *mount* a horse?

2. to fix onto a backing, setting, or support फ्रेम चढ़ाना Please *mount* my photographs with silver frames.

3. to increase; accumulate राशि या आकार बढ़ना या बढ़ाना Don't you

think that your debts are *mounting* up?

mountain *(n.)* माउन्‌टिन– a natural upward projection of the earth's surface, higher and steeper than a hill and often having a rocky summit पर्वत, पहाड़ Next summer, I shall go trekking in the *mountains.*

mountaineer *(n.)* माउनटेनिअर– a person who climbs mountains पर्वतारोही Bachendri Pal is the first Indian woman *mountaineer* who climbed Mount Everest.

mountaineering *(n.)* माउनटेनिअरिंग– the act or hobby of climbing mountains पर्वतारोहण This place is ideal for sking and *mountaineering* in the winter.

mountainous *(adj.)* माउनटेनस–1. of or relating to mountains अनेक पर्वतों वाला, पहाड़ी Nepal is a *mountainous* country.

2. like a mountain, esp in size or impressiveness विशाल, भीमकाय A small boat was struggling with *mountainous* waves.

mounted *(adj.)* माउंटेड– equipped with or riding horses घोड़े पर सवार *Mounted* police was on duty day and night.

mourn *(v.)* मॉर्न– to feel or express sadness for the death or loss of (someone or something) शोक/विलाप करना We all *mourned* the death of our kind neighbour.

mournful *(adj.)* मॉर्नफुल– evoking grief; sorrowful दुःखी, मातमी Neha was listening to a *mournful* song.

mouse *(n.)* माउस– any of numerous small long-tailed rodents that are similar to but smaller than rats चुहिया I want to buy a *mouse*-trap.

moustache *(n.)* मस्टाश– the unshaved growth of hair on the upper lip, and sometimes down the sides of the mouth मूंछ He had long and bushy *moustache* like that of Veerappan.

mouth *(n.)* माउथ–1. the opening through which men and animals take in food and issue vocal sounds मुंह, मुख Always keep your *mouth* clean.

2. the point where a river issues into a sea or lake मुहाना We went on a trip in a launch up to the *mouth* of the river.

mouthful *(n.)* माउथफुल–1. a small quantity, as of food निवाला, कौर, ग्रास I am not hungry, only a *mouthful* would be enough.

2. a long word or phrase that is difficult to say उच्चारण में कठिन His name was a bit of a *mouthful* so we used to call him Raja.

mouth-watering *(adj.)* माउथवाटरिंग– whetting the appetite, as from smell, appearance, or description मुँह में पानी लाने वाला A *mouth-watering* mixture of French and English cuisine.

movable *(adj.)* मूवबल्– able to be moved or rearranged; not fixed (जो हिलाया या चलाया जा सके) चल, जंगम I have a *movable* cupboard in my bedroom.

move *(v.)* मूव–1. to go or take from one place to another; change in location or position हटाना, हिलाना She *moved* to the door.

2. to be or cause to be in motion; stir आना-जाना, चलना-फिरना From my seat, I watched the guests *moving* about the hall.

3. to change (one's dwelling, place of business, etc.) घर या जगह बदलना We *moved* from Mumbai to Delhi many years ago.

4. to arouse affection, pity, or compassion in; touch प्रभावित करना, प्रेरित करना We were *moved* to tears by his sad story.

movement *(n.)* मूवमेण्ट–1. the act, process, or result of moving हरकत, गति, हिलना-डुलना Loose clothes give me freedom of *movement* and easiness.

2. an instance of moving स्थान परिवर्तन The clouds have slow *movement* in the sky.

3. a group of people with a common ideology, esp a political or religious one आंदोलन The *movement* against Sati Pratha was led by Raja Ram Mohan Rai.

4. a change in the market price of a security or commodity बाज़ार में मंदी, गिरावट या तेज़ी There is an upward *movement* in the price of petrol.

movie *(n.)* मूवी– a form of entertainment, information, etc. composed of such a sequence of images and shown in a cinema, etc फ़िल्म Let's go out for a *movie.*

moving *(adj.)* मूविंग– arousing or touching the emotions हृदयस्पर्शी An unforgettable and *moving* book.

mow *(v.)* मो– to cut down (grass, crops, etc.) with a hand implement or machine काटना, कतरकर हल्का करना Roger *mowed* the lawn.

much *(pron.)* 1. मॅच– a great quantity or degree of बहुत अधिक, ज्यादा (मात्रा में) How *much* did you pay for this pen?

2. *(adj.)* enough बड़ी सीमा तक, काफ़ी Is there *much* water in the jug?

3. *(adv.)* extreme अत्यधिक Thank you very *much!*

muck *(n.)* मक– farmyard dung or decaying vegetable matter कीचड़, कूड़ा-करकट Please don't spread *muck* here.

mucus *(n.)* म्यूकस– the slimy protective secretion of the mucous membranes, consisting mainly of mucin बलग़म, कफ़ The *mucus* was coming out from his nose and throat.

mud *(n.)* मॅड– a fine-grained soft wet deposit that occurs on the ground after rain, at the bottom of ponds, lakes, etc. कीचड़ Take care Rakesh, lest you would fall in the *mud.*

muddle *(n.)* मॅडल– 1. a state of physical or mental confusion गड़बड़ी, अव्यवस्था, अस्त-व्यस्तता Everything in the house was in a *muddle.*

2. *(v.)* to confuse उलझना या उलझाना If your mind is *muddled,* you cannot think clearly.

muddy *(adj.)* मडी– covered or filled with mud कीचड़ से भरा हुआ They changed their *muddy* boots.

muffin *(n.)* मफ़िन– a thick round baked yeast roll, usually toasted and served with butter एक प्रकार का छोटा गोल केक We like to have *muffins* with tea.

muffle *(v.)* मफ़ल– to deaden (a sound or noise), esp by wrapping आवाज धीमी कर देना My sister *muffled* the sound of TV.

muffled *(adj.)* मफ़्लड– something that muffles दबी हुई मन्द आवाज़ His voice was *muffled.*

muffler *(n.)* मफ़्लर– a thick scarf, collar, etc. गुलूबन्द We use *mufflers* in the chilled winter season.

Mufti *(n.)* मफ़्टी– civilian dress, esp as worn by a person who normally wears a military uniform सादी पोशाक, सादे कपड़े The chief minister visited his native place in *Mufti.*

mug *(n.)* मॅग– a drinking vessel with a handle, usually cylindrical and made of earthenware प्याला I like to drink coffee from a *mug.*

muggy *(adj.)* मगी– (of weather, air, etc.) unpleasantly warm and humid उमस एवं घुटनभरा It was a hot, very *muggy* evening.

mulberry *(n.)* मलबरी– a tree with dark green leaves having edible blackberry-like fruit शहतूत The silk worms can be seen on *mulberry* leaves.

mulch *(n.)* मल्च– half-rotten vegetable matter, peat, etc. used to prevent soil erosion or enrich the soil घास-पात, पतवार We covered the root of the new plant with *mulch*.

mule *(n.)* म्यूल–1. the sterile offspring of a male donkey and a female horse, used as a beast of burden खच्चर A *mule* was carrying heavy iron boxes on his back.

2. an obstinate or stubborn person जिद्दी या हठी आदमी, अड़ियल टट्टू Arun is stubborn as a *mule*.

multicultural *(adj.)* मल्टिकल्चरल्– consisting of, relating to, or designed for the cultures of several different races बहु- सांस्कृतिक India is known for its *multicultural* society.

multinational *(adj.)* मलूटिनैशनल– (of a large business company) operating in several countries बहुराष्ट्रीय कम्पनी 1,500 troops were sent to join the *multinational* force.

multiple *(adj.)* मलूटिपल– having or involving more than one part, individual, etc. अनेक, विविध, बहुविध *Multiple* choice question was asked in my exam.

multiplication *(n.)* मल्टिप्लिकेशन– an arithmetical operation, defined initially in terms of repeated addition गुणा, गुणन Have you learnt *multiplication*?

multiply *(v.)* मलूटिप्लाइ–1. to combine (two numbers or quantities) by multiplication गुणा करना *Multiply* fourteen by nineteen.

2. to increase in number by reproduction बढ़ना, बढ़ाना Flies *multiply* fast.

multi-purpose *(adj.)* मलूटि-परपज़– able to be used for many purposes बहु-प्रयोजनीय Two tools may do a better job than one *multipurpose* tool.

multitude *(n.)* मलूटिट्यूड– a large gathering of people भीड़, जनसाधारण I was impressed by the *multitude* of people at yesterday's public meeting.

mum *(adj.)* मम्– keeping information to oneself; silent चुप, शांत Keep *mum* about this issue.

mumble *(v.)* मम्बल– to utter indistinctly, as with the mouth partly closed; mutter गुनगुनाना, फुसफुसाना He *mumbled* something she didn't catch.

mummy *(n.)* ममी–1. a female who has given birth to offspring मां, माता Her *mummy* is calling me.

2. an embalmed or preserved body, esp as prepared for burial in ancient Egypt कपड़े में लिपटा सुरक्षित शव A two thousand year old *mummy* was found in Egypt.

munch *(v.)* मंच– to chew (food) steadily, esp with a crunching noise आवाज़ करते हुए खाना We watched the movie *munching* on popcorn.

mundane *(adj.)* मण्डेन्– everyday, ordinary, or banal मामूली Stop musing over these *mundane* issues.

municipal *(adj.)* म्यूनिसिपल्– of or relating to a town, city, or borough or its local government नगर, नगरपालिका-संबंधी Are you a candidate for the coming *municipal* elections?

murder *(v.)* मर्डर्– 1. to kill (someone) unlawfully with premeditation or during the commission of a crime हत्या करना, खून होना He was accused of *murdering* his wife's lover.

2. *(n.)* the unlawful premeditated killing of one human being by another हत्या, क़त्ल She was charged to commit *murder*. Who was accused of the *murder*?

murderer *(n.)* मर्डरर्– a person who commits a murder हत्यारा, क़ातिल Has the police caught the *murderer*?

murderous *(adj.)* मर्डरस– intending, capable of, or guilty of murder हिंसक Mark gave him a *murderous* look.

murmur *(n.)* मर्मर्– 1. a continuous low indistinct sound, as of distant

voices फुसफुसाना, भुनभुनाना When I entered the room, the *murmur* of conversation stopped.
2. *(v.) to utter (something) in a murmur* मंद स्वर में कुछ कहना She *murmured* but no one heard what she said.

muscle *(n.)* मसल– a tissue composed of bundles of elongated cells capable of contraction and relaxation to produce movement in an organ or part मांसपेशी, बाहुबल We should work manually to strengthen our *muscles.*

muscular *(adj.)* मसक्युलर–1. of, relating to, or consisting of muscle मांसपेशियों से संबंधित Energy is needed for *muscular* activity.
2. whaving well-developed muscles; brawny हट्टा-कट्टा Stallone has a *muscular* body.

museum *(n.)* म्यूज़िअम– a place or building where objects of historical, artistic, or scientific interest are exhibited, preserved, or studied संग्रहालय, अजायबघर Have you seen the Salar Jang *museum* of Hyderabad?

mushroom *(n.)* मशरूम– a fungus with a round flat head and short stem कुकुरमुत्ता, खुंबी *Mushrooms* are cultivated in the backyard of his house.

music *(n.)* म्यूज़िक– an art form consisting of sequences of sounds in time, esp tones of definite pitch organized melodically, harmonically, rhythmically and according to tone colour संगीत I love *music* very much but I am not skilled in it.

musical *(adj.)* म्यूज़िकल– of, relating to, or used in music मधुर, संगीतमय They shared similar *musical* tastes

musician *(n.)* म्यूज़िशन– a person who plays or composes music, esp as a profession संगीतकार Ravi Shankar is a famous Indian *musician.*

muslim *(n.)* मुस्लिम– a follower of the religion of Islam मुसलमान, इस्लाम धर्म का अनुयायी *Muslims* follow Islamic laws and traditions.

muslin *(n.)* मॅज़लिन– a fine plain-weave cotton fabric मलमल Is your frock made of *muslin*?

must *(v.)* मॅस्ट– 1. used as an auxiliary to indicate necessity आवश्यक है, जरूरी है You *must* show your ID card.
2. *(n.)* an essential or necessary thing (परामर्श हेतु) अनिवार्य, परमावश्यक This book is a *must* for every student of history.

mustard *(n.)* मस्टर्ड– a small plant having yellow or white flowers and slender pods, grown for its seeds that are crushed to make mustard सरसों They use *mustard* oil for cooking food.

muster *(v.)* मस्टर– to call together (numbers of men) for duty, inspection, etc. or (of men) to assemble in this way जुटाना, बटोरना 17,000 men had been *mustered* on Haldon Hill.

musty *(adj.)* मस्टी– smelling or tasting old, stale, or mouldy सीलनभरा, बासी Sohan could not sit in the *musty* room.

mutate *(v.)* म्यूटेट– to undergo or cause to undergo mutation नवीन रूप धारण करना, बदलना Blues *mutated* into rock and roll.

mute *(adj.)* म्यूट– not giving out sound or speech; silent मूक, गूंगा He is *mute* by birth.

muted *(adj.)* म्यूटेड– (of a sound or colour) softened कोमल, अप्रबल The *muted* hum of the distant traffic.

mutiny *(n.)* म्यूटनी– open rebellion against constituted authority, esp by seamen or soldiers against their officers ग़दर The Revolt of 1857 was dismissed by the British as a sepoy *mutiny.*

mutter *(v.)* मॅटर्– to utter (something) in a low and indistinct tone बुदबुदाना,

फुसफुसाना He *muttered* something under his breath.

mutton *(n.)* मॅटन– the flesh of sheep, esp of mature sheep, used as food भेड़ का मांस Karim went to the butcher's shop to buy some *mutton.*

mutual *(adj.)* म्यूचुअल– experienced or expressed by each of two or more people or groups about the other; reciprocal आपसी, पारस्परिक *Mutual* understanding is necessary to keep a relationship alive.

muzzle *(v.)* मज़ल–1. to prevent from being heard or noticed मुँह पर जाली लगाना You should *muzzle* your ferocious dog.

2. to put a muzzle on (an animal) दबा देना, नियंत्रण करना How can democracy survive when the Press is *muzzled*?

3. *(n.)* the front end of a gun barrel नालमुख Be careful while cleaning the *muzzle* of the gun.

mysterious *(adj.)* मिस्टीरिअस– characterized by or indicative of mystery रहस्यमय His colleague had vanished in *mysterious* circumstances.

mystery *(n.)* मिस्टरि– an unexplained or inexplicable event, phenomenon, etc. रहस्य, भेद The *mysteries* of outer space.

mystic *(n.)* मिस्टिक– a person who achieves mystical experience or an apprehension of divine mysteries आत्मसमर्पण और ईश्वर में लीन होने का इच्छुक व्यक्ति Kabir was a *mystic* poet.

mystical *(adj.)* मिस्टिकल– relating to or characteristic of mysticism अद्‌भुत She has a pair of *mystical* eyes.

mystique *(n.)* मिस्टीक– an aura of mystery, power, and awe that surrounds a person or thing रहस्यात्मकता There is a certain *mystique* about eating oysters.

myth *(n.)* मिथ– a story about superhuman beings of an earlier age taken by preliterate society to be a true account, usually of how natural phenomena, social customs, etc. came into existence काल्पनिक विचार Some consider the story of Lord Rama a *myth.*

mythical *(adj.)* मिथिकल– imaginary or fictitious काल्पनिक, मनगढ़ंत Bakasura was a *mythical* demon with a crane's body.

mythological *(adj.)* माईथलॉजिकल– of or relating to mythology पौराणिक, पुराणों पर आधारित The tree of life is one of the oldest of all *mythological* symbols.

mythology *(n.)* माईथोलॉजी– a body of myths, esp one associated with a particular culture, institution, person, etc. पौराणिक कथाएं, देवी-देवताओं की कहानियां The Hindu *mythology* talks about numerous gods and goddesses.

Nn

Nn *(n.)* एन–अंग्रेज़ी वर्णमाला का चौदहवां अक्षर The fourteenth letter of the English alphabet. Nano begis with 'N'.

nab *(v.)* नैब– to catch (someone) in wrongdoing रंगे हाथों पकड़ना The Feds *nabbed* a suspected terrorist.

nadir *(n.)* नेडिअर– the lowest or worst moment पतन की चरमावस्था, सबसे बुरा समय Mohan is at the *nadir* of his career.

nag *(v.)* नैग– to scold or annoy constantly सिर खाना, तंग करना She constantly *nags* her daughter about getting married.

nail *(v.)* नेल–1. to attach with or as if with nails कील ठोंकना, कील से जड़ना *Nail* a new board on the wall.

2. *(n.)* a fastening device usually made from round or oval wire, having a point at one end and a head at the other कील Hang this picture on that *nail*.

3. the horny plate covering part of the dorsal surface of the fingers or toes नाख़ून, नख Always keep your *nails* clean.

> **nail down**– to extort a definite promise or consent from किसी को वचनबद्ध कर लेना, You can't *nail* her *down* to her promise.

nail-biting *(adj.)* नेल बाइटिंग– the act or habit of biting one's fingernails नाख़ून चबाना *Nail-biting* is a bad habit.

nail file *(n.)* नेल फ़ाइल– a small file used to shape the fingernails नाख़ून चिकना करने की रेती, नख-रेती She uses *nail file* while watching TV.

nail polish *(n.)* नेल पॉलिश– a quick-drying lacquer applied to colour the nails or make them shiny or esp both नख-पॉलिश *Nail polish* art designs are latest in fashion.

naive *(adj.)* नाईव– having or expressing innocence and credulity; ingenuous भोला-भाला Don't be so *naive* to work for free.

naivety *(n.)* नाईवटी– the state or quality of being naive; ingenuousness; simplicity भोलापन, निष्कपटता They laughed at her *naivety*.

naked *(adj.)* नेकेड–1. having the body completely unclothed; undressed नंगा, निर्वस्त्र I pitied the *naked* child in the arms of the beggar.

2. having no covering; bare; exposed खुला, अनावृत Was the fire caused by the *naked* electric wires?

name *(v.)* नेम–1. to give a name to; call by a name नाम रखना Hundreds of diseases had not yet been isolated or *named*.

2. *(n.)* a word or term by which a person or thing is commonly and distinctively known ख्याति, नाम I am sure your son will make a *name* for himself.

> **by name**– to have heard of without having met नाम से, I know him only *by name*.

> **in the name of**– using as a name के नाम पर, He took loan *in the name of* his company.

> **make a name for**– to gain name and fame नाम कमाना, Prabha *made a name for* herself as a writer.

nameless *(adj.)* नेमलस– without a name; anonymous अज्ञात, बिना नाम का Some pictures were taken by a *nameless* photographer.

namely *(adv.)* नेमली– that is to say अर्थात्, यानि The menu makes good use of Scottish produce, *namely* game and seafood.

namesake *(n.)* नेमसेक– a person or thing named after another समनाम,

एकनाम She is my *namesake* but we are very different in nature.

naming *(n.)* नेमिंग– act of giving a name to a thing or a person नामकरण *Naming* ceremony of his child will be held on coming Sunday.

nanny *(n.)* नैनी– a nurse or nursemaid for children आया, दायी, नर्स Her *nanny* is a very educated lady.

nap *(n.)* नैप– a short light sleep; snooze झपकी Do you take a *nap* after lunch?

nape *(n.)* नेप– the back of the neck गर्दन का पिछला हिस्सा, घाटिका, गद्दी Hari has a boil on his *nape*.

naphthalene *(n.)* नैफ़्थलीन– a white crystalline volatile solid with a characteristic penetrating odour: फ़िनाइल की गोलियां I put some *naphthalene* balls in the woollens to protect them from insects.

napkin *(n.)* नैपूकिन– a usually square piece of cloth or paper used while eating to protect the clothes, wipe the mouth, etc.; serviette नैपकिन Please keep some *napkins* on the dining table.

nappy *(n.)* नैपी– a piece of soft material, esp towelling or a disposable material, wrapped around a baby in order to absorb its urine and excrement पोतड़ा, लंगोट Don't you use disposable *nappies* for your baby?

narcotic *(n.)* नारकोटिक– anything that relieves pain or induces sleep, mental numbness, etc. मूर्च्छाकार, तेज़ नशीला पदार्थ Opium is a *narcotic* substance.

narrate *(v.)* नरेट– to tell (a story); relate वर्णन करना the story is *narrated* by the heroine.

narrator *(n.)* नरेटर– a person who tells a story or gives an account of something वर्णनकर्ता, वाचक Sohan is a first person *narrator* of the story.

narrow *(adj.)* नैरो– small in breadth, esp in comparison to length तंग, संकीर्ण Can our car pass through a *narrow* lane?

narrowly *(adv.)* नैरोली– very little difference बहुत थोड़े अंतर से The party was *narrowly* defeated in the elections.

narrow escape *(n.)* नैरो-स्केप– to get away or break free from (confinements, captors, etc.) बाल-बाल बचना She had a *narrow escape* in the road accident.

narrow-minded *(adj.)* नैरो-माइंडिड– having a biased or illiberal viewpoint; bigoted, intolerant, or prejudiced संकुचित विचारों वाला Bina could not move in a cultured society, hence she is very *narrow-minded.*

nasal *(adj.)* नेज़ल– of or relating to the nose नाक का I have a cold, please give me some *nasal* drops.

nastily *(adv.)* नॉस्टिली– in a way which is unpleasant, offensive, or repugnant फूहड़ ढंग से, बहुत बुरा Don't behave so *nastily.*

nasty *(adj.)* नास्टी–1. unpleasant, offensive, or repugnant गन्दा, अप्रिय This chemical has a *nasty* smell.
2. (of an experience, condition, etc.) unpleasant, dangerous, or painful ख़तरनाक There is a *nasty* bend in the road.

nation *(n.)* नेशन– an aggregation of people or peoples of one or more cultures, races, etc., organized into a single state राष्ट्र, क़ौम The world's leading industrialized *nations.*

national *(adj.)* नैशनल–1. of, involving, or relating to a nation as a whole राष्ट्रीय, पूरे राष्ट्र से संबंधित Congress is a *national* party.
2. a citizen or subject (एक राष्ट्र विशेष का) नागरिक I think you are acting in an anti-*national* manner.

nationalist *(n.)* नैशनलिस्ट– someone who favours a sentiment based on common cultural characteristics that binds a population and often produces a policy of national independence or separatism देशभक्त, राष्ट्रीयतावादी A meeting was organised by *nationalists.*

nationalistic *(adj.)* नैशनलिस्टिक– of or relating to loyalty or devotion to one's country; patriotic राष्ट्रवादी He was fiercely *nationalistic.*

nationality *(n.)* नैशनैलटी– the state or fact of being a citizen of a particular nation किसी देश का नागरिक होना He lives in Dubai but has American *nationality.*

nationalize (ise) *(v.)* नैशनलाइज़– to put (an industry, resources, etc.) under state control or ownership राष्ट्रीयकरण करना The Bank of England was *nationalized* in the winter of 1946-7.

native *(n.)* नेटिव– 1. a person born in a particular place मूल निवासी I am a *native* of India.
2. *(adj.)* relating or belonging to a person or thing by virtue of conditions existing at the time of birth जन्म-स्थान से संबंधित Hindi is the *native* language of northern India.

natural *(adj.)* नैचरल– of, existing in, or produced by nature स्वाभाविक, नैसर्गिक It is *natural* for the parents to feel concerned when their child is ill.

naturalize (ise) *(v.)* नैचरलाइज़– to give citizenship to (a person of foreign birth) किसी विदेशी को नागरिकता देना Eucalyptus trees are native to Australia but have become *naturalized* in many countries.

naturally *(adv.)* नैचुरली– in a natural or normal way स्वाभाविक रूप से, अपने आप The thought came to my mind *naturally.*

nature *(n.)* नेचर्– the fundamental qualities of a person or thing; identity or essential character स्वभाव, प्रकृति Have you seen the beauty of *nature* in the hills?

naughty *(adj.)* नॉटी– mildly indecent; titillating नटखट, शरारती You've been a really *naughty* boy.

nausea *(n.)* नॉज़िआ–1. the sensation that precedes vomiting उबकाई, मतली A wave of *nausea* swept over me when I saw an accidental death.
2. a feeling of disgust or revulsion अत्यधिक घृणा, अरुचि I am filled with *nausea* after eating stale food.

naval *(adj.)* नैवल– of, relating to, characteristic of, or having a navy नौसेना संबंधी, जहाज़ी Her father was a *naval* officer.

navel *(n.)* नेवल– the scar in the centre of the abdomen, usually forming a slight depression, where the umbilical cord was attached नाभि Some girls wear a silver and turquoise ring in the *navel.*

navigate *(v.)* नैविगेट–1. to plan, direct, or plot the path or position of (a ship, an aircraft, etc.) मानचित्र आदि का प्रयोग करना We'll go in my car—you can *navigate.*
2. to voyage in a ship; sail जहाज़ चलाना, नौ-चालन करना The river was too dangerous to *navigate.*

navy *(n.)* नेवि– the warships and auxiliary vessels of a nation or ruler नौसेना Manoj wants to join the *navy.*

near *(adj.)* निअर्–1. at or in a place not far away समीप, निकट Who was the man sitting *near* you at the party?
2. close पास, कम दूरी पर My school is *near* Birla Mandir.
3. not far away in time; imminent निकटवर्ती नज़दीक Holi is drawing *near.*
4. closely connected or intimate पास आ जाना, पहुंचना I am *nearing* the end of my work.

nearby *(adj.)* निअर्बाई– not far away; close at hand थोड़ी दूरी पर, पास ही He slung his jacket over a *nearby* chair.

nearly *(adv.)* निर्अली– not quite; almost; practically प्रायः, लगभग My job is *nearly* finished.

neat *(adj.)* नीट– clean, tidy, and orderly साफ़-सुथरा, सुव्यवस्थित His room is very *neat.*

neatly *(adv.)* नीटली– in a tidy and orderly way सफ़ाई से, अच्छे से She *neatly* sidestepped the question.

necessarily *(adv.)* नेससरलि– as an inevitable or natural consequence आवश्यक रूप से The number of seats in the class were *necessarily* limited.

necessary *(adj.)* नेससरी– needed to achieve a certain desired effect or result; required आवश्यक, ज़रूरी It's not *necessary* for you to be here.

necessity *(n.)* नसेसटी– something needed for a desired result; prerequisite आवश्यकता, जरूरत *Necessity* is the mother of invention.

neck *(n.)* नेक– the part of an organism connecting the head with the rest of the body गर्दन She has a beautiful long *neck.*

necklace नेकलस– a chain, band, or cord, often bearing beads, pearls, jewels, etc, worn around the neck as an ornament, esp by women हार This *necklace* will look more beautiful on a long neck.

nectar *(n.)* नेक्टर– a sugary fluid produced in the nectaries of plants and collected by bees and other animals पराग The honeybees collect *nectar* from flowers.

nectarine *(n.)* नेक्टरीन– a variety of peach tree, शफ़तालू (एक फल) *Nectarine* is a wonderful source of nutrients, anti-oxidants, minerals and vitamins.

need *(n.)* नीड्–1. a requirement आवश्यकता, ज़रूरत There was a great *need* of field workers in my office.
2. *(v.)* to require or be required of necessity आवश्यकता/ज़रूरत होना I *need* somebody's help in this matter.

needle *(n.)* नीडल–1. a pointed slender piece of metal, usually steel, with a hole or eye in it through which thread is passed for sewing कपड़ा सिलने की सुई Bring a *needle* and thread to stitch this button.
2. any slender pointer for indicating the reading on the scale of a measuring instrument घड़ी आदि उपकरणों की सुई The *needle* of this meter is not working.

needless *(adj.)* नीडलस– not required or desired; unnecessary ग़ैरज़रूरी I deplore *needless* waste.

needy *(adj.)* नीडी– in need of practical or emotional support; distressed ज़रूरतमंद The *needy* should apply for help.

negative *(adj.)* नेगटिव– 1. expressing or meaning a refusal or denial नकारात्मक I have received a *negative* reply to my proposal.
2. *(n.)* a statement or act of denial, refusal, or negation निगेटिव, प्रतिचित्र Can you develop this *negative*?

neglect *(v.)* निग्लेक्ट– to fail to give due care, attention, or time to ध्यान नहीं देना, ख़्याल न रखना The old churchyard has been sadly *neglected.*
2. to ignore or disregard उपेक्षा His old house is in a state of *neglect.*

negligence *(n.)* नेगलिजन्स– the state or quality of being negligent लापरवाही You will be dismissed for your *negligence.*

negotiable *(adj.)* नेगोशिएबल– 1. able to be negotiated मोल-भाव करने वाले, बदले जाने योग्य The prices of all the items in the shop are *negotiable.*

2. *(v.)* (of a bill of exchange, promissory note, etc.) legally transferable in title from one party to another सौदा करना, तय करना She *negotiated* the price of the jewellery.

negotiation *(n.)* निगोशिएशन– a discussion set up or intended to produce a settlement or agreement आपस में समझौता एवं बातचीत, वार्ता The demands of the workers are still under *negotiation.*

negro *(n.)* नीग्रो– a member of any of the dark-skinned indigenous peoples of Africa and their descendants elsewhere हब्शी, काला आदमी Kavish has a *Negro* classmate.

neigh *(n.)* ने– the high-pitched cry of a horse; whinny घोड़े की हिनहिनाहट I heard the *neigh* of the horse.

neighbour *(n.)* नेबर्– a person who lives near or next to another पड़ोसी Our *neighbour* is a very friendly person.

neighbouring *(adj.)* नेबरिंग– Neighbouring places or things are near other things of the same kind पड़ोस का, समीपवर्ती Pakistan is our *neighbouring* country.

neither *(adv.)* नाइदर्–1. not one nor the other (of two); not either दोनों में से कोई नहीं I *neither* saw nor heard you coming.

nephew *(n.)* नेफ़्यू– a son of one's sister or brother भतीजा, भानजा I have one *nephew* and two nieces.

nepotism *(n.)* नेपटिज़्म– favouritism shown to relatives or close friends by those with power or influence कुनबापरस्ती, भाई- भतीजावाद *Nepotism* is prevalent in some of the famous universities.

nerve *(n.)* नर्व– any of the cordlike bundles of fibres that conduct sensory or motor impulses between the brain or spinal cord and another part of the body स्नायु, धैर्य You are a man of strong *nerves.*

nervous *(adj.)* नर्वस–1. apprehensive or worried व्यग्र, उत्तेजित Staying in the house on her own made her *nervous.*

2. of, relating to, or containing nerves; neural स्नायु-संबंधी The patient was suffering from a *nervous* breakdown.

nervousness *(n.)* नर्वसनस– apprehension or worry भय, चिंता *Nervousness* gripped me when I went for an interview.

nervous breakdown *(n.)* नर्वस ब्रेकडाउन– any mental illness not primarily of organic origin in which the patient ceases to function properly तनाव आदि के कारण होने वाला रोग, शिथिलता She suffers from a *nervous breakdown* after getting divorced.

nervous system *(n.)* नर्वस सिस्टम– the sensory and control apparatus of all multicellular animals above the level of sponges, consisting of a network of nerve cells स्नायु-तंत्र The brain is an important part that controls the *nervous system.*

nest *(v.)* नेस्ट– 1. to make or inhabit a nest घोंसला बनाना The owls often *nest* in barns.

2. *(n.)* a place or structure in which birds, insects, reptiles, mice, etc., lay eggs or give birth to young घोंसला The tree in our garden is full of *nests.*

net *(n.)* नेट– an openwork fabric of string, rope, wire, etc.; mesh जाल Do you use a hair-*net*?

network *(n.)* नेटवर्क– an interconnected group or system जाल, तंत्र India has the largest *network* of railways.

neurologist *(n.)* न्युअरालजिस्ट– a specialist or expert in neurology तंत्रिका-विज्ञानी, नाड़ी संबंधित विशेषज्ञ We consulted a *neurologist* for his brain injury.

neurotic *(adj.)* न्युअराटिक– of, relating to, or afflicted by neurosis मानसिक रोगी He seemed a *neurotic*, self-obsessed character.

neutral *(adj.)* न्यूट्रल–1. not siding with any party to a war or dispute तटस्थ I always remain *neutral* when two people quarrel.
2. having zero charge or potential हलका, मंद His voice remained *neutral* as he spoke.

never *(adv.)* नेवर्– at no time; not ever कभी नहीं I have *never* seen such a strange animal before.

nevertheless *(adv.)* नेवरद़लस– in spite of that; however; yet तो भी, तथापि Statements which, although literally true, are *nevertheless* misleading.

new *(adj.)* न्यू–1. recently made or brought into being नया When did you buy this *new* car?
2. recently introduced (to); inexperienced (in) or unaccustomed (to) अनजान, अनभिज्ञ I am not *new* to this city.

newly *(adv.)* न्यूली– recently; lately or just हाल ही में A *newly* acquired hi-fi system.

news *(n.)* न्यूज़– current events; important or interesting recent happenings समाचार, ख़बर You can read the *news* in the daily papers.

news agency *(n.)* न्यूज़ एजेंसी– an organization that collects news reports for newspapers, periodicals, etc. समाचार एकत्र करने वाली संस्था, समाचार-पत्र-एजेंसी PTI is a *news agency* located in New Delhi.

newspaper *(n.)* न्यूज़पेपर– a weekly or daily publication consisting of folded sheets and containing articles on the news, features, reviews and advertisements समाचार-पत्र, अख़बार Where is today's *newspaper*?

newsreader *(n.)* न्यूज़रीडर– a news announcer on radio or television समाचार-वाचक Mahima wants to become a *newsreader* on the TV.

New Year *(n.)* न्यू'इअर– the first day or days of the year in various calendars, usually celebrated as a holiday **नववर्ष My** friends go out on *New Year's* eve.

next *(adj.)* ने'क्स्ट–1. immediately following अगला, आगामी We'll go to Corfu *next* year.

next door *(adj.)* नेक्स्टडोर– at, in, or to the adjacent house, flat, building, etc. ठीक बग़लवाला, बाज़ूवाला Raveena is our *next door* neighbour.

next of kin *(n.)* नेक्स्ट ऑफ किन– a person's closest relative or relatives निकटतम संबंधी Her brother is her *next of kin.*

next to *(prep.)* नेक्स्ट टू– adjacent to; at or on one side of से अगला, बग़ल में He was sitting *next to* me.

nibble *(v.)* निबल– (esp of animals, such as mice) to take small repeated bites (of) कुतरना He *nibbled* a biscuit.

nice *(adj.)* नाइस–1. pleasant or commendable सुंदर, मनोहर You look *nice* in this dress.
2. good or satisfactory रुचिकर This restaurant serves *nice* food.

niche *(n.)* निच–1. a position particularly suitable for the person occupying it विशिष्ट स्थान By doing selected roles, Konkona Sen has carved a *niche* for herself in the film industry.
2. a recess in a wall, esp one that contains a statue ताख़, आला You can put that statue in the *niche.*

nickname *(n.)* निक्नेम– a familiar, pet, or derisory name given to a person, animal, or place उपनाम My son Vikram's *nickname* is Bittu.

nicotine *(n.)* निकटीन– a colourless oily acrid toxic liquid that turns yellowish-brown in air and light: एक नशीला पदार्थ, निकोटीन *Nicotine* is an addictive substance found in cigarette.

niece *(n.)* नीस– a daughter of one's sister or brother भतीजी, भानजी My *niece* came to stay with us during her holidays.

niggle *(v.)* निगल–1. to irritate; worry चिंतित एवं परेशान करना Doreen wanted to discuss matters that *niggled* at her mind.

2. to be preoccupied with details; fuss ग़ैर-ज़रूरी बातों पर बहस करना You should stop *niggling* and go back to work.

night *(n.)* नाइट– the period of darkness each 24 hours between sunset and sunrise, as distinct from day रात, रात्रि What were you doing last *night*?

nightingale *(n.)* नाइटिंगेल– a brownish European songbird, well known for its musical song, usually heard at night बुलबुल Lata Mangeshkar is known as a *nightingale* of India.

nightmare *(n.)* नाइटमेअर– a terrifying or deeply distressing dream भयानक स्वप्न, दुःस्वप्न I had *nightmares* after watching the horror movie.

night-time *(n.)* नाइट-टाइम– the time from sunset to sunrise; night as distinct from day रात का समय He does not drive during *night-time*.

nimble *(adj.)* निम्बल– agile, quick, and neat in movement फुर्तीला Her mind was so *nimble* and she was so quick to learn.

nine *(n.)* नाइन– the cardinal number that is the sum of one and eight नौ There are *nine* mangoes in the basket.

nineteenth *(n./adv.)* नाइनटींथ– coming after the eighteenth in numbering or counting order, position, time, etc, being the ordinal number of nineteen उन्नीसवां She is celebrating her *nineteenth* birthday.

ninetieth *(n., det, adv.)* नाइनटिअथ– being the ordinal number of ninety in numbering or counting order, position, time, etc. नब्बेवां His name was on the *ninetieth* number in the list.

nip *(v.)* निप्– to remove by clipping, biting, etc. फुरती से काटना The child *nipped* on the biscuit.

nitrogen *(n.)* नाइट्रोजन– a colourless odourless relatively unreactive gaseous element एक प्रकार की रंगहीन तथा गंधहीन गैस *Nitrogen* forms about 80% of the air around the earth.

no *(det.)* नो– 1. an answer or vote of no नहीं, कोई नहीं Have you *no* money to lend me?

2. *(adv.)* used to express denial, disagreement, refusal, disapproval, disbelief, or acknowledgment of negative statements बिल्कुल नहीं When he asked me if I could accompany him, my answer was *'no'*.

nobility *(n.)* नोबिलटी–1. the state or quality of being morally or spiritually good; dignity कुलीनता, उदारता They showed great *nobility* in the marriage ceremony.

2. the class of people holding the titles of dukes, marquesses, earls, viscounts, or barons and their feminine equivalents collectively; peerage उच्चता, श्रेष्ठता She is famous for her *nobility*.

noble *(adj.)* नोबल–1. of or characterized by high moral qualities; magnanimous कुलीन, अभिजात, महान The Duchess of Kent and several other *noble* ladies.

2. having dignity or eminence; illustrious परोपकारी You have indeed done a *noble* deed.

3. of superior quality or kind; excellent उदार, नीतिवान I appreciate your *noble* sentiments.

nobleman *(n.)* नोबलमन– a man of noble rank, title, or status; peer;

aristocrat कुलीन व्यक्ति, उच्च कुल वाला My grandfather was a *nobleman.*

nobody *(n.)* नोबडी– no person; no-one कोई नहीं They went from *nobodies* to superstars.

nod *(n.)* नॉड–1. a quick down-and-up movement of the head, as in assent, command, etc. सिर हिलाना, सहमति प्रकट करना Give me a *nod* when you need a glass of water.
2. *(v.)* to let the head fall forward through drowsiness; be almost asleep ऊँघना, झपकी लेना The old lady was *nodding* in her chair.
3. to lower and raise (the head) briefly, as to indicate agreement, invitation, etc. स्वीकृति देने हेतु थोड़ा सिर झुकाना If you agree with me, just *nod* your head.

node *(n.)* नोड– a knot, swelling, or knob गांठ, गिलटी There was a *node* on the stem of a plant.

noise *(n.)* नॉइज़– loud shouting; clamour; din शोर, कोलाहल No *noise,* please!

noiseless *(adj.)* नॉइज़लस– making little or no sound; silent चुपचाप, शांत The cycle is a *noiseless* form of transport.

noisily *(adv.)* नॉइज़िली– in such a way as to make a loud or constant noise शोर मचाते हुए The children were playing *noisily.*

noisy *(adj.)* नॉइज़ि– making a loud or constant noise ऊधमी, शोरगुल से भरा There was a *noisy* traffic near the hospital.

nomad *(n.)* नोमैड– a member of a people or tribe who move from place to place to find pasture and food ख़ानाबदोश The *nomads* were looking for a suitable place to spend the night.

nominal *(adj.)* नॉमिनल– minimal in comparison with real worth or what is expected; token सामान्य से कम, नाममात्र, नाम को The shopkeeper gave the dress to me in a *nominal* price.

nominate *(v.)* नॉमिनेट– to propose as a candidate, esp for an elective office नामांकन/नामज़द करना The film was *nominated* for several Oscars.

nomination *(n.)* नॉमिनेशन– the act of nominating or state of being nominated, esp as an election candidate नामांकन, नामज़दगी He opposed her *nomination* to the post of Editor.

nominee *(n.)* नॉमिनी– a person who is nominated to an office or as a candidate मनोनीत या नामज़द व्यक्ति Renu is the only *nominee* of her parents.

non-alcoholic *(adj.)* नॉन-एल्कोहॉलिक– not containing alcohol मदिरारहित, अल्कोहलरहित He was thinking to have a non-*alcoholic* drink.

none *(prep.)* नॅन– no-one; nobody कोई (भी) नहीं *None* of my friends stays in Mumbai.

nonetheless *(adv.)* ननद्लेस– despite that; however; nevertheless फिर भी, तो भी, इसके बावजूद भी The movie was too long, but, *nonetheless* most entertaining.

non-existent *(adj.)* नॉन-एग्ज़िस्टंट– not having being or existence अस्तित्त्वहीन She pretended to tie a *non-existent* shoelace.

nonsense *(n.)* नॉन्सन्स– something that has or makes no sense; unintelligible language; drivel अनापशनाप, मूर्खता Don't talk *nonsense!*

non-stop *(adj., adv.)* नॉन-स्टॉप– done without pause or interruption सीधे, बिना रुके We had two days of almost *non-stop* rain.

non-violence *(n.)* नॉन-वॉइअलंस– abstention from the use of physical force to achieve goals अहिंसा Gandhiji had a firm belief in *non-violence.*

nook *(n.)* नुक– a corner or narrow recess, as in a room एक कोना, एकांत स्थान I like to sit in a *nook* of my garden.

noon *(n.)* नून– the middle of the day; 12 o'clock in the daytime or the time or point at which the sun crosses the local meridian दोपहर, दिन के 12 बजे का समय I shall return by *noon.*

norm *(n.)* नॉर्म– a standard of achievement or behaviour that is required, desired, or designated as normal मानदंड, मानक India has her own cultural and political *norms.*

normal *(adj.)* नॉर्मल– 1. usual; regular; common; typical साधारण The *normal* weather in December is chilly and cold.

2. *(n.)* the usual, average, or typical state, degree, form, etc. सामान्य, औसत Today my temperature has come down to *normal.*

normalize (ise) *(v.)* नॉर्मलाइज़– to bring or make into the normal state सामान्य हो जाना या बनाना The two countries *normalized* diplomatic relations in 1995.

normally *(adv.)* नॉर्मलि– in a normal manner सामान्यतः *Normally*, it takes three or four years to complete the training.

north *(adj.)* नॉर्थ– in or towards the north उत्तरी, उत्तर Finland is in *north* of Russia.

northerly *(adj.)* नॉर्दर्ली– of, relating to, or situated in the north उत्तर की ओर, उत्तर में We should keep going in a *northerly* direction.

northern *(adj.)* नॉर्दर्न– situated in or towards the north उत्तरी The cliff protects the bay from the *northern* winds.

nose *(v.)* नोज़– 1. to move or cause to move forwards slowly and carefully सावधानी से आगे बढ़ना The rickshaw *nosed* its way along the street.

2. *(n.)* the organ of smell and entrance to the respiratory tract, consisting of a prominent structure divided into two hair-lined air passages by a median septum नाक You have a very sharp *nose.*

➢ **poke your nose**– to pry into or interfere in दूसरों के मामले में टांग अड़ाना, Don't *poke your nose* in his matters.

➢ **turn your nose up**– to behave disdainfully towards (something) नाक-भौं सिकोड़ना, Why did you *turn your nose up* to see him?

nosy *(adj.)* नोज़ि– prying or inquisitive ताक-झांक करने वाला, जिज्ञासु Stop being so *nosy*!

not *(adv.)* नॉट– used to negate the sentence, phrase, or word that it modifies नहीं He has been warned *not* to touch.

notable *(adj.)* नॅटिबल–1. worthy of being noted or remembered; remarkable; distinguished उल्लेखनीय, असाधारण The results, with one *notable* exception, have been superb.

2. a notable person महत्त्वपूर्ण, नामी The function was attended by *notable* leaders of the area.

note *(n.)* नोट–1. a brief letter, usually of an informal nature नोट, पत्र Please give him this *note* when he comes.

2. a promissory note issued by a central bank, serving as money नोट Do you have a ten-rupee *note*?

3. a distinctive vocal sound, as of a species of bird or animal स्वर Can you play all the *notes* on this musical instrument?

4. *(v.)* to notice; perceive नोट कर लेना, ध्यान देना Please *note* the contents of this letter carefully.

notebook *(n.)* नोटबुक– a book for recording notes or memoranda कापी I have a small *notebook* to keep records of the work.

noted *(adj.)* नोटिड– distinguished; celebrated; famous नामी, प्रसिद्ध A *noted* patron of the arts.

noteworthy *(adj.)* नोटवर्दी– worthy of notice; notable उल्लेखनीय Indira Gandhi was a *noteworthy* Prime Minister of India.

nothing *(n.)* नथिंग– no thing; not anything, as of an implied or specified class of things कुछ नहीं I have *nothing* to give you.

notice *(n.)* नोटिस–1. information about a future event; warning; announcement सूचना, नोटिस Did you not read the *notice* saying that parking is not allowed here?

2. the act of perceiving; observation; attention ध्यान I smiled at Hari but he took no *notice.*

3. *(v.)* to recognize or acknowledge (an acquaintance) देख लेना I *noticed* that you had left the door open.

noticeable *(adj.)* नोटिसबल– easily seen or detected; perceptible ध्यान देने योग्य It's a *noticeable* increase in staff motivation.

noticeboard *(n.)* नोटिसबोर्ड– a board to which notices can be attached सूचनापट्ट A list of elected candidates was stuck on the *noticeboard.*

notion *(n.)* नोशन– a vague idea; impression धारणा, विचार, मत You seem to have no *notion* about how to tackle this job.

notorious *(adj.)* नोटॉरिअस्– well-known for some bad or unfavourable quality, deed, etc.; infamous बदनाम He was a *notorious* drinker and womanizer.

notwithstanding *(prep.)* नॉटविद्स्टैंडिंग – in spite of; despite के बावजूद (भी) She danced, *notwithstanding* they laughed.

noun *(n.)* नाउन– a word or group of words that refers to a person, place, or thing or any syntactically similar word संज्ञा A *noun* is a name of a person, place or thing.

nourish *(v.)* नॅरिश– to provide with the materials necessary for life and growth पोषित करना I was doing everything I could to *nourish* and protect the baby.

nourishing *(adj.)* नरिशिंग– providing substantial nourishment to a living thing पोषक I like a simple but *nourishing* meal.

novel *(n.)* नॉवल–1. an extended work in prose, either fictitious or partly so, dealing with character, action, thought, etc., esp in the form of a story उपन्यास Do you like to read *novels*?

2. *(adj.)* of a kind not seen before; fresh; new; original अभिनव, नया Your idea is indeed *novel.*

novelty *(n.)* नॉवलटी– the quality of being new and fresh and interesting नवीनता, अनोखापन The *novelty* in his ideas is appreciating.

November *(n.)* नवेम्बर– the eleventh month of the year, consisting of 30 days वर्ष का ग्यारहवां महीना, नवंबर In *November,* weather is so cool and pleasant.

novice *(n.)* नॉविस– a person who is new to or inexperienced in a certain task, situation, etc.; beginner; tyro नौसिखिया Be carefull You are a *novice* in swimming.

now *(adv.)* नाउ– at or for the present time or moment अब, इस समय, अभी Where are you living *now*?

nowadays *(adv.)* नाउअडेज़– in these times आजकल Road accidents are increasing *nowadays.*

nowhere *(adv.)* नोवेअर्–1. in, at, or to no place; not anywhere कहीं (भी) नहीं I looked for you but could find you *nowhere.*

2. a nonexistent or insignificant place किसी स्थान पर भी नहीं The book was *nowhere* to be found.

nuclear *(adj.)* न्यूक्लियर– of, concerned with, or involving the nucleus of an atom नाभिकीय India has a *nuclear* power station in Jaitapur (Maharashtra).

nucleus *(n.)* न्यूक्लिअस– a central or fundamental part or thing around which others are grouped; core केन्द्र, केंद्रक Could the doctor locate the *nucleus* of the pain?

nudge *(v.)* नॅज– to push or poke (someone) gently, esp with the elbow, to get attention; jog कोहनी से धक्का देना, टहोका देना People were *nudging* each other and pointing at me.

nuisance *(n.)* न्यूसन्स– a person or thing that causes annoyance or bother उपद्रव, कण्टक It's such a *nuisance* waiting for someone all alone.

numb *(adj.)* नम– deprived of feeling through cold, shock, etc. सुन्न My feet were *numb* with cold.

number *(n.)* नम्बर्–1. a concept of quantity that is or can be derived from a single unit, the sum of a collection of units, or zero. संख्या, अंक, नंबर Write down some *numbers* on this sheet of paper.

2. a group or band of people, esp an exclusive group समूह, बहुत से I met a *number* of old friends at the meeting.

3. *(v.)* to assign a number to संख्या देना या लगाना Gita *numbers* Rita among her best friends.

4. to list (items) one by one; enumerate to list (items) one by one; enumerate गिनना, गिनती लगाना Have you *numbered* the pages of your manuscript?

numeral *(n.)* न्यूमरल– a symbol or group of symbols used to express a number: for example, 6 अंक, संख्यात्मक Roman *numerals* are mostly used in books and magazines.

numerous *(adj.)* न्यूमरस– being many बहुत सारे, अनेक She had complained to the council on *numerous* occasions.

nun *(n.)* नन– a female member of a religious order साध्वी, ईसाई भिक्षुणी *Nuns* live in the convent nearby my house.

nurse *(n.)* नर्स– 1. a person who tends the sick, injured, or infirm नर्स, परिचारिका A team of doctors and *nurses* came to see her.

2. *(v.)* to tend (the sick) सेवा-शुश्रूषा करना, देखरेख करना He was gradually *nursed* back to health.

nursery *(n.)* नर्सरी– a room in a house set apart for use by children शिशु-सदन, बालकक्ष The new-born baby was kept in a *nursery* for few days.

nursing *(n.)* नर्सिंग– the practice or profession of caring for the sick and injured नर्स के रूप में काम करना She would love to go into *nursing*.

nursing home *(n.)* नर्सिंग होम– a private hospital or residence staffed and equipped to care for aged or infirm persons छोटा निजी अस्पताल We shifted the patient into a private *nursing home*.

nurture *(v.)* नर्चर्–1. to feed or support देखभाल करना Jarrett was *nurtured* by his parents in a close-knit family.

2. to educate or train विकसित करना It is important to *nurture* a good work environment.

nut *(n.)* नॅट–1. a dry one-seeded indehiscent fruit that usually possesses a woody wall अखरोट Can you break this *nut* with your teeth?

2. a small square or hexagonal block, usu. metal, with a threaded hole through the middle for screwing on the end of a bolt ढिबरी Bring some *nuts* and screws for repairing this door.

nutrition *(n.)* न्यूट्रिशन– a process in animals and plants involving the intake of nutrient materials and their subsequent assimilation into the tissues पोषाहार Read this book daily. It's a guide to good *nutrition*.

nutritional *(adj.)* न्यूट्रिशनल– of or relating to a process in animals and plants involving the intake of nutrient materials and their subsequent assimilation into the tissues पोषण संबंधी Milk has high *nutritional* value.

nutritious *(adj.)* न्यूट्रिशियस– nourishing, sometimes to a high degree पौष्टिक Home-cooked burgers make a *nutritious* meal.

nuts *(n.)* नट्स– extremely fond (of) or enthusiastic (about) अति उत्सुक Are you *nuts*?

nuzzle *(v.)* नज़ल– to push or rub gently against the nose or snout नाक रगड़ना, नाक छूना या लगाना He *nuzzled* her hair.

nylon *(n.)* नाइलॉन्– a class of synthetic polyamide materials used for making clothes, rope, etc. नाइलोन Socks made of *nylon* last longer.

ഇൽ

Oo

Oo *(n.)* ओ–अंग्रेज़ी वर्णमाला का पंद्रहवां अक्षर The fifteenth letter of the English alphabet. Owl begins with 'O'.

oaf *(n.)* ओफ़– a stupid or loutish person फूहड़, गंवार An *oaf* man came to my house yesterday.

oak *(n.)* ओक– any deciduous or evergreen tree or shrub having acorns as fruits and lobed leaves शाहबलूत की लकड़ी (पेड़) We were sitting under an old *oak* tree.

oar *(n.)* ऑर्– a long shaft of wood for propelling a boat by rowing, having a broad blade that is dipped into and pulled against the water. चप्पू I rowed the boat with a pair of *oars.*

oasis *(n.)* ओएसिस– a fertile patch in a desert occurring where the water table approaches or reaches the ground surface मरूद्यान, नखलिस्तान The caravans stay in the *oasis* for taking rest.

oath *(v.)* ओथ– a solemn pronouncement to affirm the truth of a statement or to pledge a person to some course of action, often involving a sacred being or object as witness शपथ, सौगन्ध They took an *oath* of allegiance to the king.

obedience *(n.)* ओबिडिअन्स– the act or an instance of obeying; dutiful or submissive behaviour आज्ञापालन, अनुसरण We shall act in *obedience* to our manager's orders.

obedient *(adj.)* ओबिडिअन्ट– obeying or willing to obey आज्ञाकारी She was totally *obedient* to him.

obese *(adj.)* ओबीस्– excessively fat or fleshy; corpulent मोटा, स्थूलकाय She was an *obese* child.

obey *(v.)* ओबे– to carry out (instructions or orders); comply with (demands) आज्ञा मानना I always *obey* my father.

obituary *(n.)* ओबिचुअरी– a published announcement of a death, often accompanied by a short biography of the dead person शोक-समाचार I read the *obituary* of my relative in a newspaper.

object *(n.)* ऑबूजे'क्ट–1. an aim, purpose, or objective उद्देश्य, लक्ष्य What is the *object* of your foreign tour?

2. a tangible and visible thing पदार्थ, चीज़ What is that *object* floating in the lake?

3. *(v.)* to state as an objection आपत्ति/एतराज़ करना I *object* to your rude remarks.

objection *(n.)* ऑब्जेक्शन– an expression, statement, or feeling of opposition or dislike एतराज़ They have raised no *objections* to the latest plans.

objectionable *(adj.)* ऑब्जेक्शनबल– unpleasant, offensive, or repugnant आपत्तिजनक I find his theory *objectionable* in its racist undertones.

objective *(n.)* ऑब्जेक्टिव– the object of one's endeavours; goal; aim लक्ष्य, उद्देश्य She is working hard to achieve her *objective*.

obligation *(n.)* ऑब्लिगेशन– a moral or legal requirement; duty बंधन, वचनबद्धता Ahmad imposed many *obligations* on his wife.

obligatory *(adj.)* ऑब्लिगटरी– required to be done, obtained, possessed, etc. अनिवार्य, बाध्यकर Use of seat belts in cars is now *obligatory*.

oblige *(v.)* ओब्लाइज–1. to bind or constrain (someone to do something) by legal, moral, or physical means आभारी बनाना, उपकृत करना Dinesh *obliged* his friends with dinner party.

2. to do a service or favour to (someone) बाध्य या विवश करना Do not *oblige* me to accompany you.

3. to make indebted or grateful (to someone) by doing a favour or service दबाव डालना My duties *oblige* me to work late.

oblivion *(n.)* ऑब्लिविअन– the condition of being forgotten or disregarded गुमनामी His name will fade into *oblivion.*

oblivious *(adj.)* अब्लिवियस– unaware or forgetful बेख़बर, विस्मरण She became absorbed, *oblivious* to the passage of time.

obnoxious *(adj.)* अब्नॉक्शस– extremely unpleasant घिनौना, अप्रिय, घृणित The worms inside the garden were *obnoxious.*

obscene *(adj.)* ऑबसीन– offensive or outrageous to accepted standards of decency or modesty अश्लील Few scenes were considered *obscene* by the censor board.

obscure *(v.)* ॲब्स्क्युअर्– 1. to make unclear, vague, or hidden ढक जाना, दिखाई न देना Grey clouds *obscure* the sun.

2. *(adj.)* unclear or abstruse अस्पष्ट, दुर्बोध Your motive in writing such a letter is *obscure* to me.

3. indistinct, vague, or indefinite अज्ञात This poem was composed by an *obscure* poet.

observance *(n.)* अब्ज़र्वन्स– recognition of or compliance with a law, custom, practice, etc. अनुपालन Sheela was fined for non-*observance* of traffic rules.

observation *(n.)* अब्ज़र्वेशन–1. detailed examination of phenomena prior to analysis, diagnosis, or interpretation निरीक्षण She was brought into hospital for *observation.*

2. a comment or remark टीका-टिप्पणी, अवलोकन He made some *observations* about the role of the hero.

observe *(v.)* ॲब्ज़र्व्–1. to see; perceive; notice देखना, अवलोकन करना She *observed* that all the chairs were already occupied.

2. to obey rules, laws etc. नियमों और निर्देशों का पालन करना All good players *observe* rules of fair play.

3. to make a comment or remark अपनी राय देना My friend *observed* that I should not attend the club meeting.

observer *(n.)* अब्ज़र्वर– a person or thing that observes प्रेक्षक, पर्यवेक्षक Siddhartha was a good political *observer.*

obsess *(v.)* अब्सेस्– to preoccupy completely; haunt किसी बात का मन में पूर्णतया ग्रस्त हो जाना He was *obsessed* with the idea of revenge.

obsession *(n.)* अबसेशन्– a persistent preoccupation, idea, or feeling धुन, मनोग्रस्तता Her daughter has an *obsession* of media.

obsessive *(adj.)* अबसेसिव्– motivated by a persistent overriding idea or impulse, often associated with anxiety and mental illness वहमी, ख़बती, मनोग्रस्त व्यक्ति She became *obsessive* about her school work.

obsolete *(adj.)* ऑब्सलीट्– out of date; unfashionable or outmoded अप्रचलित, पुराना Please dispose the old and *obsolete* machinery.

obstacle *(n.)* ऑब्स्टकल– a person or thing that opposes or hinders something बाधा, अड़चन Is there any *obstacle* in your taking a holiday tomorrow?

obstetrician *(n.)* ऑबस्टट्रिशन– a physician who specializes in obstetrics प्रसूति विशेषज्ञ Dr Shanta is a well-qualified *obstetrician.*

obstinacy *(n.)* ऑब्स्टिनसी– the state or quality of being obstinate हठ, ज़िद Sometimes he shows great *obstinacy.*

obstinate *(adj.)* ऑब्स्टिनेट– self-willed or headstrong ज़िद्दी, दुराग्रही Her *obstinate* determination to pursue a career in radio.

obstruct *(v.)* ऑब्स्ट्रक्ट– to block (a road, passageway, etc.) with an obstacle बाधा डालना She was *obstructing* the entrance.

obstruction *(n.)* ऑब्स्ट्रक्शन– the act or an instance of obstructing रुकावट, बाधा, अड़चन Illiteracy is a great *obstruction* in the path of progress.

obstructive *(adj.)* ऑब्स्ट्रक्टिव– if you say that someone is being obstructive, you think that they are deliberately causing difficulties for other people बाधक, अवरोधक Her *obstructive* behaviour is very much irritating to me.

obtain *(v.)* ऑब्टेन– to gain possession of; acquire; get पाना, प्राप्त करना Adequate insurance cover is difficult to *obtain.*

obtuse *(adj.)* अबट्यूज़– mentally slow or emotionally insensitive मंदबुद्धि, मूढ़, मोटी अक्ल He wondered if the doctor was being deliberately *obtuse.*

obvious *(adj.)* ऑब्विअस–1. exhibiting motives, feelings, intentions, etc., clearly or without subtlety स्पष्ट, ज़ाहिर It was *obvious* that he had been badly treated.

2. easy to see or understand; evident जो साफ़ दिखाई दे, प्रत्यक्ष Uma's angry looks made it *obvious* that she was displeased with Rekha.

occasion *(n.)* ॲकेश़न– 1. the time of a particular happening or event अवसर, सुयोग, घटना, मौक़ा We gave a party on the *occasion* of our son's first birthday.

2. a special event, time, or celebration कोई ख़ास कार्यक्रम That party was a happy *occasion.*

3. an opportunity (to do something); chance सही समय She will tell me when the *occasion* arises.

occasional *(adj.)* ॲकेश़नल– taking place from time to time; not frequent or regular सामयिक, कभी-कभी होने वाला He paid an *occasional* visit to his village.

occasionally *(adv.)* अकेश़नली– from time to time कभी-कभी, यदा-कदा We met up *occasionally* for a drink.

occult *(adj.)* ऑकल्ट– of or characteristic of magical, mystical, or supernatural arts, phenomena, or influences जादू-टोना, तंत्र-मंत्र Suresh indulges in witchcraft and the *occult* practices.

occupation *(n.)* ऑक्युपेशन– a person's regular work or profession; job or principal activity व्यवसाय What is your father's *occupation*?

occupational *(adj.)* ऑक्युपेशनल– of, relating to, or caused by an occupation व्यावसायिक Explosions are *occupational* hazard for coal miners.

occupier *(n.)* ऑक्युपाइअर– a person who is in possession or occupation of a house or land क़ाबिज़, निवासी, दखलदार Rehan is a legal *occupier* of the house.

occupy *(v.)* ऑक्युपाइ–1. to live or be established in (a house, flat, office, etc.) रहना, निवास करना The rented flat she *occupies* in Hampstead.

2. to take and hold possession of, esp as a demonstration कब्ज़ा करना The landlord was fighting a case in the court against the tenants who had *occupied* his house.

3. to keep (a person) busy or engrossed; engage the attention of व्यस्त रखना How do you *occupy* yourself during the holidays?

occur *(v.)* ॲकर्–1. to happen; take place; come about घटित होना The accident *occurred* at about 3.30 p.m.

2. to be found पाया जाना Sugar *occurs* in fruits.

occurrence *(n.)* ऑकरन्स– something that occurs; a happening; event घटना Vandalism used to be a rare *occurrence.*

ocean *(n.)* ओशन– a very large stretch of sea, esp one of the five oceans of the world, the Atlantic, Pacific, Indian, Arctic, and Antarctic सागर They scramble across the beach to the *ocean.*

o'clock *(n.)* ॲ'क्लोक– used after a number from one to twelve to indicate the hour of the day or night बजे It's 6 *o'clock* already and she is still not here.

octagon *(n.)* ऑक्टगन– a polygon having eight sides अष्टभुज The child was making an *octagon* on his drawing copy.

October *(n.)* ऑक्टोबर– the tenth month of the year, consisting of 31 days अक्टूबर, साल का दसवां महीना I won't be able to come in the month of *October.*

octopus *(n.)* ऑक्टपस– a sea creature having a soft oval body with eight long suckered tentacles अष्टभुजी जलकीट, ऑक्टोपस An *octopus* was crawling on the beach.

odd *(adj.)* ऑड–1. unusual or peculiar in appearance, character, etc. विलक्षण The neighbours thought him very *odd.*

2. out-of-the-way or secluded असाधारण It is really *odd* that you should be here at this hour.

3. not divisible by two विषम संख्या (1, 3, 5 आदि) I asked the students to write down some *odd* numbers.

4. occasional, incidental, or random बीच-बीच का (काम), फुटकर (स्थायी नहीं) They need a person to do *odd* jobs in the factory.

oddity *(n.)* ऑडटी– an odd quality or characteristic अनोखापन, विचित्रता Is there any *oddity* in my flat?

odds *(n.)* ऑड्ज़– the probability, expressed as a ratio, that a certain event will take place अनुकूल या प्रतिकूल स्थिति The *odds* are in your favour.

➢ **against all odds**– to face the difficult situations बड़ी कठिनाइयों से भिड़ना एवं उनका सामना करना, *Against all the odds* she recovered from her terrible injury.

ode *(n.)* ओड– a lyric poem, typically addressed to a particular subject, with lines of varying lengths and complex rhythms गीति-काव्य '*Ode* to a Nightingale' is a famous poem by John Keats.

odious *(adj.)* ओडिअस– offensive; repugnant घिनौना, घृणित She is a pretty *odious* character.

odour *(n.)* ओडर्– the property of a substance that gives it a characteristic scent or smell गन्ध, बू, वास, महक I can't tolerate the *odour* of cigarette smoke.

of *(prep.)* ऑफ– used with a verbal noun or gerund to link it with a following noun that is either the subject or the object of the verb embedded in the gerund का, के, की He is a famous leader *of* the party.

off *(adv., prep.)* ऑफ़–1. so as to be removed from, esp as a reduction अलग, पृथक He took his jacket *off.*

2. so as to be deactivated or disengaged बंद कर देना Please turn *off* the light.

3. out of the present location दूर, परे He is not so far *off.*

4. unsatisfactory or disappointing धीमा, सुस्त His business is *off* this year.

5. *(adj.)* begins उखड़ा हुआ My father is rather *off* with my sister today.

➢ **on and off**– intermittently; from time to time कभी-कभी, एक-एक कर, It rained *on and off* all day.

➢ **off-day**– a day on which sb is allowed not to come into work ढीला-ढाला दिन, Saturday was always an *off-day* for me.

➢ **well-off**– financially well provided for; moderately rich अमीर, सम्पन्न, Sarita is born in a *well-off* family.

➢ **offshore**– from, away from, or at some distance from the shore तट से थोड़ी दूर, He is trying to get an *offshore* job.

offence *(n.)* अफ़ेन्स– a violation or breach of a law, custom, rule, crime etc., crime ग़ैरकानूनी काम, अपराध He commited a new *offence* of obtaining property by deception.

offend *(v.)* अफ़ेण्ड– to hurt the feelings, sense of dignity, etc, of (a person) नाराज़ करना, अपमान करना I hope I have not *offended* you by my plain speaking.

offender *(n.)* अफ़ेण्डर– a person who has committed a crime अपराधी, मुजरिम The young *offender* should not be severely punished.

offensive *(adj.)* अफ़ेन्सिव– 1. causing anger or annoyance; insulting अपमानजनक The allegations made are deeply *offensive* to us.

2. *(n.)* an assault, attack, or military initiative, esp a strategic one चढ़ाई, आक्रमण The major *offensive* was launched on July 15.

offer *(n.)* ऑफ़र्– 1. something, such as a proposal or bid, that is offered प्रस्ताव I regret to inform you that your *offer* is not acceptable to me.

2. *(v.)* to present or proffer (something, someone, oneself, etc.) for acceptance or rejection प्रस्ताव करना/रखना, सामने रखना I was *offered* a job on the spot.

offering *(n.)* ऑफ़रिंग– something that is offered चढ़ावा, दान A big *offering* was made to Mata ka Mandir.

offhand *(adj.)* ऑफ़हैण्ड– 1. without care, thought, or consideration; sometimes, brusque or ungracious बिना विचार किये जाने वाला, लापरवाही भरा You were a bit *offhand* with her this afternoon.

2. *(adv.)* without preparation or warning; impromptu एकदम, बिना तैयारी के I don't know *offhand* how much we made last year.

office *(n.)* ऑफ़िस–1. a room or set of rooms in which business, professional duties, clerical work, etc., are carried out दफ़्तर I have to go to my *office* tomorrow.

2. a commercial or professional business आधिकारिक पद He is holding the *office* of foreign affairs.

officer *(n.)* ऑफ़िसर– a person in the armed services who holds a position of responsibility, authority, and duty, esp one who holds a commission अधिकारी, अफ़सर He is also a serving *officer* in the army.

official *(adj.)* ऑफ़िशियल– 1. of or relating to an office, its administration, or its duration सरकारी English is an *official* language of India.

2. *(n.)* a person who holds a position in an organization, government department, etc., esp a subordinate position अधिकारी, अफ़सर The meeting was attended by high *officials*.

officially *(adv.)* ऑफ़िशियली– in a formal or authoritative manner बाक़ायदा, आधिकारिक रूप से It was *officially* acknowledged that the economy was in recession.

officious *(adj.)* अफ़िशियस– unnecessarily or obtrusively ready to offer advice or services, self-important ज़बरदस्ती बीच में टांग अड़ाकर अपनी सलाह देने वाला Bharti is an *officious* warden of the girls hostel.

offload *(v.)* ऑफ़लोड– to get rid of (something unpleasant or burdensome), as by delegation to another सामान उतारना, बोझ उतारना

Please *offload* the luggage from the taxi.

offset *(v.)* ऑफ़सेट– to counterbalance or compensate for बराबर करना, कमी पूरी करना Donations to charities can be *offset* against tax.

offspring *(n.)* ऑफ़स्प्रिंग– the immediate descendant or descendants of a person, animal, etc.; progeny संतान She has two *offsprings* from her first marriage.

often *(adv.)* ऑफ़न– frequently or repeatedly; much of the time अक्सर, प्रायः He *often* goes for long walks by himself.

ogre *(n.)* ओगर– (in folklore) a giant, usually given to eating human flesh नर-भक्षी दानव, दैत्य The children got scared to hear the story about *ogre*.

oil *(n.)* ऑइल– any of a number of viscous liquids with a smooth sticky feel. तेल The sewing machine needs *oil*.

oily *(adj.)* ऑइलि– soaked in or smeared with oil or grease चिकना, तैलीय Taramasalata and hummus are both *oily* and rich.

ointment *(n.)* ऑइंटमन्ट– a fatty or oily medicated formulation applied to the skin to heal or protect मरहम He rubbed some *ointment* on his leg.

okay *(adv.)* ओके– in good or satisfactory condition ठीक-ठाक, अच्छा She looks *okay* now.

old *(adj.)* ओल्ड–1. age of उमर का How *old* is your father?

2. having lived or existed for a relatively long time बूढ़ा, वृद्ध My father is a very *old* man.

3. worn with age or use पुराना (फटने को तैयार) My shoes are getting *old*.

old age *(n.)* ओल्ड एज– very old or of long duration; ancient बुढ़ापा We should enjoy life in our *old age*.

old-fashioned *(adj.)* ओल्ड-फैशंड– belonging to, characteristic of, or favoured by former times; outdated दक़ियानूसी, पुराना Why did you get this *old-fashioned* kitchen range?

olive *(n.)* ऑलिव– an evergreen oleaceous tree, Olea europaea, having white fragrant flowers, and edible shiny black fruits ज़ैतून *Olive* oil is used in salad to make it tasty.

omelette *(n.)* ऑमलट– a savoury or sweet dish of beaten eggs cooked in fat (अंडे से बना) आमलेट Please make two *omelettes* for me.

omen *(n.)* ओमन– a phenomenon or occurrence regarded as a sign of future happiness or disaster शकुन, सगुन Throbbing of the right arm of men is considered a good *omen*.

ominous *(adj.)* ऑमिनस– foreboding evil अपशकुनी There were *ominous* dark clouds gathering overhead.

omission *(n.)* ओमिशन– something that has been omitted or neglected छूट, भूल, चूक There were few *omissions* of names from the list.

omit *(v.)* ओमिट–1. to neglect to do or include छोड़ देना Do not *omit* Amitabh's name from the list of invitees.

2. to fail (to do something) न जोड़ना, नहीं करना We read the play *omitting* the last two scenes.

omniscient *(adj.)* ऑमनिसिअंट– having infinite knowledge or understanding सर्वज्ञ, सब जानने वाला A third-person *omniscient* narrator.

omnivorous *(adj.)* ऑमनिवरस– eating food of both animal and vegetable origin, or any type of food indiscriminately सर्वभक्षक, सर्वाहारी The domestic pigs are *omnivorous*.

on *(prep.)* ऑन–1. in contact or connection with the surface of; at the upper surface of पर, के ऊपर The pen is lying *on* the table.

2. in the position or state required for the commencement or sustained continuation, as of a mechanical operation काम करते हुए, प्रयुक्त होते हुए All the lights were *on*.

once *(adv.)* वन्स–1. one time; on one occasion or in one case एक बार They deliver *once* a week.

2. at some past time; formerly किसी समय, कभी *Once* upon a time, there lived a great king.

> **once again**– a few times एक बार फिर, *Once again* I reached late.

> **once in a blue moon**– very rarely; almost never बहुत कम, She visits me *once in a blue moon.*

> **once in a while**– occasionally; now and then कभी-कभी, He visits me *once in a while.*

> **once upon a time**– used to begin fairy tales and children's stories बहुत पहले, एक समय, *Once upon a time* there lived a little girl called Alice.

> **at once**– immediately फ़ौरन, तुरंत, Go there *at once!*

oncoming *(adj.)* ऑनकमिंग– coming nearer in space or time; approaching आगामी, पास आने वाला She walked into the path of an *oncoming* car.

one *(pron., n.,det.)* वन– 1. single; lone; not two or more एक There's only room for *one* person.

2. a certain, indefinite, or unspecified (time); some किसी We will go to meet them *one* day.

> **one after another** *(pron.)*– turn by turn बारी-बारी से, *One after another* they were called for an interview.

> **one by one** *(pron.)*– one at a time एक-एक करके, They reached in the party *one by one.*

one another *(pron.)*– वन अनअदर the reflexive form of plural pronouns when the action, attribution, etc., is reciprocal परस्पर, They exchange their views with *one another.*

one-off *(adj.)*– something that is carried out or made only once एकबारगी, सिर्फ़ एक बार, They gave me a *one-off* payment for writing the book.

onerous *(adj.)* ऑनरस– laborious or oppressive कठिन, कष्टसाध्य He found his duties increasingly *onerous.*

oneself *(pron.)* वनसेल्फ़– one's normal or usual self स्वयं, ख़ुद One cannot think only of *oneself.*

one-sided *(adj.)* वन-साइडिड– considering or favouring only one side of a matter, problem, etc. एकतरफ़ा, असंतुलित It was a *one-sided* battle.

one-way *(adj.)* वन-वे– moving or allowing travel in one direction only एक ओर का, एक तरफ़ का We were driving to a *one-way* street.

ongoing *(adj.)* ऑनगोइंग– actually in progress जारी, चालू There was an *ongoing* programme of research.

onion *(n.)* अनयन– a vegetable with many layers inside, have a strong smell प्याज़ She was crying while cutting *onions.*

onlooker *(n.)* ऑनलुकर– a person who observes without taking part दर्शक, प्रेक्षक A crowd of *onlookers* had gathered around the dead body.

only *(adv.)* ओन्लि–1. without anyone or anything else being included; alone केवल There are *only* a limited number of tickets available.

2. merely or just सिर्फ़ I came to the party *only* because you were coming.

3. *(adj.)* (of a child) having no siblings अकेला, इकलौता Sunil is the *only* boy who can solve this problem.

4. unique by virtue of being superior to anything else; peerless एकमात्र This bus is *only* for ladies.

5. incomparable; unique सर्वश्रेष्ठ She is the *only* suitable candidate for this post.

only child *(n.)* ओन्ली चाइल्ड– a person who has no siblings इकलौती औलाद Shahjahan was the *only child* of Emperor Akbar.

onset *(n.)* ऑनसेट्– a start; beginning (किसी अप्रिय स्थिति का) आरंभ This seems to be the *onset* of typhoid.

onslaught *(n.)* ऑनस्लॉट– a violent attack भीषण विरोध या आक्रमण They faced an *onslaught* from tribal people.

onto *(prep.)* ऑनटु– to a position that is on किसी वस्तु के ऊपर Stick this paper *onto* the cardboard.

onwards *(adv.)* ऑनवर्ड्ज़– at or towards a point or position ahead, in advance, etc. समय विशेष के बाद, आगे You start this book from 10th page *onwards*.

ooze *(v.)* ऊज़– to flow or leak out slowly, as through pores or very small holes रिसना, चूना Blood was *oozing* from a wound in his scalp.

opaque *(adj.)* ओपेक–1. not transmitting light; not transparent or translucent अपारदर्शी Bottles filled with a pale *opaque* liquid.

2. hard to understand; unintelligible गहन, मुश्किल से समझ में आने वाला, गूढ़ Your report seems to be *opaque*.

open *(v.)* ओपन–1. to move or cause to move from a closed or fastened position खोलना, प्रकट करना Please *open* the door.

2. to extend or unfold or cause to extend or unfold खोलना (पुस्तक, टिन, मुंह आदि) Please *open* the book (the tin/the mouth, etc.)

3. *(adj.)* free to all to join, enter, use, visit, etc. सार्वजनिक It was an *open* mango eating competition in which we contested.

4. unobstructed by buildings, trees, etc. खुला, मुक्त You should take a walk in the *open* air.

5. ready to entertain new ideas; not biased or prejudiced खुला, उदार Have an *open* mind when you argue with others.

opener *(n.)* ओपनर– an instrument used to open sealed containers such as tins or bottles ढक्कन खोलने वाला यंत्र Please bring a tin *opener*.

opening *(n.)* ओपनिंग–1. a vacant or unobstructed space, esp one that will serve as a passageway; gap सुराख, छेद There was an *opening* in the wall.

2. the first performance of something, esp a theatrical production शुभारंभ The film is famous for its dramatic *opening*.

3. an opportunity or chance, esp for employment or promotion in a business concern नौकरी के लिए ख़ाली जगह There is an *opening* in the sales division.

openly *(adv.)* ओपनली– in such a way as to be exposed to view; blatantly खुलेआम, खुल्लमखुल्ला You can discuss your feelings *openly* with me.

open-minded *(adj.)* ओपन-माइंडिड– having a mind receptive to new ideas, arguments, etc.; unprejudiced खुले विचारों वाला Our leaders should be *open-minded* on political issues.

open-mouthed *(adj.)* ओपन-माउथ्ड– having an open mouth, esp in surprise हक्का-बक्का, चकित Taken aback, she could only stare at him *open-mouthed*.

openness *(n.)* ओपननस– the quality or state of being ready to entertain new ideas or of not being biased or prejudiced स्पष्टवादिता, खुलापन I was surprised by her *openness* about her private life.

opera *(n.)* ऑपरा– an extended dramatic work in which music constitutes a dominating feature, either consisting of separate recitatives, areas, and choruses, or having a continuous musical structure संगीतमय नाटक, ओपेरा An *opera* house is nearby my house.

operate *(v.)* ऑपरेट– to function or cause to function चलाना, परिचालित करना या होना The Prime Minister *operates* a system of divide and rule.

operation *(n.)* ऑपरेशन–1. the act, process, or manner of operating ऑपरेशन, शल्य-क्रिया The surgeon took two hours to perform the *operation.*
2. a process, method, or series of acts, esp of a practical or mechanical nature संचालन, क्रिया, व्यापार The boys watched with interest the *operation* of the huge machine.

operative *(adj.)* ऑपरटिव– in force, effect, or operation लागू हुआ The mining ban would remain *operative.*

opinion *(n.)* अपिन्यन–1. judgment or belief not founded on certainty or proof मत, जनमत What are your political *opinions*?
2. evaluation, impression, or estimation of the value or worth of a person or thing विचार, राय Ask an expert to give his *opinion* on the feasibility of your plan.

opponent *(n.)* अपोनन्ट– a person who opposes another in a contest, battle, etc. प्रतिपक्षी, विरोधी, प्रतिद्वंद्वी We defeated our *opponents* in the cricket match.

opportunist *(n.)* ऑपर्च्यूनिस्ट– a person who adapts his actions, responses, etc., to take advantage of opportunities, circumstances, etc. मौक़ापरस्त, अवसरवादी She is an *opportunist*, she avails herself of every opportunity.

opportunity *(n.)* ऑपर्च्यूनिटी– a favourable, appropriate, or advantageous combination of circumstances मौक़ा, अवसर I would like to have an *opportunity* to visit Kashmir.

oppose *(v.)* अपोज़– to fight against, counter, or resist strongly विरोध/सामना करना A majority of the electorate *opposed* EC membership.

opposed *(adj.)* अपोज़्ड– against; not in favour of विरुद्ध, विपरीत His views have always been *opposed* to me.

opposite *(adv.)* ऑपज़िट–1. on opposite sides सम्मुख, सामने A crowd gathered on the *opposite* side of the street.
2. *(adj.)* diametrically different in character, tendency, belief, etc. विपरीत, उल्टा You are an *opposite* of your brother in temperament.

opposition *(n.)* ऑपज़िशन– the act of opposing or the state of being opposed असहमति, विरोध He went abroad in *opposition* to his parent's wishes.

oppress *(v.)* अप्रेस– keep (someone) in subjection and hardship अत्याचार करना He was *oppressed* by some secret worry.

oppressive *(adj.)* अप्रेसिव– inflicting harsh and authoritarian treatment कष्टप्रद, दमनात्मक The Indians opposed the *oppressive* British policies.

opt *(v.)* ऑप्ट– to make a choice from a range of possibilities चयन करना Consumers will *opt* for low-priced goods.

optician *(n.)* आप्टिशन्– a person qualified to prescribe and dispense glasses and contact lenses, and to detect eye diseases आंखों की जांच करने वाला व्यक्ति, चश्मासाज I'll go to an *optician* to get my eyes tested.

optimist *(n.)* ऑप्टिमिस्ट– someone who is generally hopeful or who always expects the best आशावादी I am an *optimist* and always hope that things will change for the better.

option *(n.)* ऑप्शन्– a thing that is or may be chosen विकल्प I had no *option* but to stay back.

optional *(adj.)* ऑप्शनल– available to be chosen but not obligatory जो आवश्यक न हो, वैकल्पिक A wide range of *optional* excursions is offered.

or *(conj.)* ऑर– used to link alternatives अन्यथा, वरना, अथवा Are you interested to go *or* not?

oral *(adj.)* ऑरल– spoken rather than written; verbal मौखिक, ज़बानी How did you fare in your *oral* examination?

orally *(adv.)* ऑरली– by way of or using speech मौखिक रूप से The students gave their responses *orally.*

orator *(n.)* ऑरटर्– a public speaker, especially one who is eloquent or skilled वक्ता, व्याख्यान करने वाला व्यक्ति A political leader has to be a good *orator.*

orange *(n.)* ऑरिंज–1. a large round juicy citrus fruit with a tough bright reddish-yellow rind संतरा, नारंगी *Orange* is grown in plenty in Nagpur.
2. reddish yellow colour नारंगी रंग She wore an *orange* sari.

orbit *(n.)* ऑर्बिट– 1. the regularly repeated elliptical course of a celestial object or spacecraft about a star or planet ग्रह-उपग्रह का परिक्रमण-पथ The planets revolve around the sun in their fixed *orbits.*
2. *(v.)* (of a celestial object or spacecraft) to move in orbit round (a star or planet) परिक्रमा करना The planets *orbit* the sun.

orchard *(n.)* ऑर्चर्ड– a piece of enclosed land planted with fruit trees फलों का बाग, फलोद्यान I have brought some apples for you from my *orchard.*

orchestra *(n.)* ऑकिस्ट्रा– a group of instrumentalists, especially one combining string, woodwind, brass, and percussion sections and playing classical music ऑर्केस्ट्रा The *orchestra* was playing Italian music.

ordeal *(n.)* ऑडील– a very unpleasant and prolonged experience अग्नि-परीक्षा Working in shifts is really an *ordeal.*

order *(v.)* ऑर्डर्–1. to give an authoritative instruction to do something आदेश/आज्ञा देना She *ordered* me to leave.
2. [with object] request (something) to be made, supplied, or served मँगाना, मंगवाना My father has *ordered* a new sofa set from the furniture shop.
3. *(n.)* the arrangement or disposition of people or things in relation to each other according to a particular sequence, pattern, or method क्रम, अनुक्रम Arrange these words in an alphabetical *order.*
> **in working order**– in usable condition चालू हालत में, This printer is *in working order.*
> **out of order**– not working ठप्प ख़राब, The motor of the pump is *out of order.*

orderly *(adj.)* ऑर्डर्ली– neatly and methodically arranged सुव्यवस्थित ढंग से The crowd was quiet and *orderly.*

ordinance *(n.)* ऑर्डिनन्स– an authoritative order अधिनियम, अध्यादेश An *ordinance* was enacted by the President.

ordinary *(adj.)* ऑर्डिनरी– with no special or distinctive features; normal: साधारण, सामान्य, मामूली He sets out to depict *ordinary* people.

ordinarily *(adv.)* ऑर्डिनर्लि– in a normal way साधारण रूप से, प्रायः *Ordinarily,* we spend our evenings in Connaught Place.

ore *(n.)* ऑर– a naturally occurring solid material from which a metal or valuable mineral can be extracted profitably कच्ची धातु *Ore* is found in Jharkhand and Orissa.

organ *(n.)* ऑर्गन–1. a part of an organism which is typically self-contained and has a specific vital function अंग, अवयव Heart and liver are vital *organs* of our body.
2. a large musical instrument having rows of pipes supplied with air from bellows वाद्ययंत्र He is expert in playing a mouth *organ*.

organic *(adj.)* ऑर्गेनिक–1. produced or involving production without the use of chemical fertilizers, pesticides, or other artificial chemical प्राकृतिक सामग्री का प्रयोग करने वाला खाद्य पदार्थ (जिसमें रासायनिक खाद्य का प्रयोग नहीं होता), जैव The farmers improve the soil by adding *organic* matter.
2. relating to or derived from living matter जैविक, जीव-संबंधी *Organic* remains are found in rocks.

organize (ise) *(v.)* ऑर्गनाइज़–1. to make arrangements or preparations for (an event or activity) आयोजित करना *Organize* lessons in a planned way.
2. to arrange systematically; order संगठित करना You need to *organize* your work.

organized *(adj.)* ऑर्गनाइज़्ड–1. able to plan one's activities efficiently सुव्यवस्थित, सुसंगठित She used to be so *organized.*
2. arranged in a systematic way, especially on a large scale योजनाबद्ध, व्यवस्थित ढंग से I planned a well *organized* trip to Nainital.

organization *(n.)* ऑर्गनाइज़ेशन– an organized group of people with a particular purpose, such as a business or government department: संगठन He is the president of an international *organization.*

oriented *(adj.)* ऑरिएन्टिड– align or position relative to the points of a compass or other specified positions केंद्रित Her approach is always result *oriented.*

origin *(n.)* ऑरिजिन– the point or place where something begins, arises, or is derived उद्‌भव, आरंभ Has the doctor found out the *origin* of your illness?

original *(n.)* अरिजनल– 1. the earliest form of something, from which copies may be made मूल Is this picture *original* or is it a copy?
2. *(adj.)* present or existing from the beginning; first or earliest प्रारंभिक, आद्य The *original* way of travelling was on foot, now we travel by train.

originality *(n.)* अरिजनैलटी– the ability to think independently and creatively मौलिकता, नयापन Please show some *originality* in your expressions.

originally *(adv.)* अरिजनली– from or in the beginning; at first मूल रूप से, प्रारंभ में Katrina Kaif is *originally* from Kashmir.

originate *(v.)* अरिजिनेट– to happen for the first time शुरू करना या होना, उत्पन्न होना The Ganga *originates* from the Himalayas.

ornament *(n.)* ऑर्नमेण्ट– a thing used or serving to make something look more attractive but usually having no practical purpose आभूषण, गहना It is in the nature of women to like *ornaments.*

orphan *(n.)* ऑर्फ़न– a child whose parents are dead अनाथ, यतीम This little boy is an *orphan,* he lost his parents in an accident.

orphanage *(n.)* ऑर्फ़निज़– a residential institution for the care and education of orphans अनाथालय *Orphanages* need financial help.

orthodox *(adj.)* ऑर्थडॉक्स– following or conforming to the traditional or generally accepted rules or beliefs of a religion, philosophy, or practice

रूढ़िवादी She belongs to an *orthodox* family.

orthopaedics *(adj.)* ऑथपीडिक्स– the branch of medicine dealing with the correction of deformities of bones or muscles विकलांग विज्ञान My younger sister wants to become an *orthopaedics* doctor.

ostentatious *(adj.)* ऑस्टेन्टेशस– characterized by pretentious or showy display; designed to impress आडंबरपूर्ण, दिखावटी No one likes her *ostentatious* behaviour.

ostracize (ise) *(v.)* ऑस्ट्रसाइज़– exclude from a society or group बहिष्कृत करना, हुक्का-पानी बंद कर देना, मिलना-जुलना बंद कर देना She was afraid that if she spoke up the truth, her friends and colleagues would *ostracize* her.

ostrich *(n.)* ऑसट्रिच– a flightless swift-running African bird with a long neck, long legs, and two toes on each foot शुतुरमुर्ग *Ostrich* is the fastest runner bird but cannot fly.

other *(pron., adj.)* ॲदर्–1. used to refer to a person or thing that is different or distinct from one already mentioned or known about दूसरा, अतिरिक्त This room is my office, the *other* one is the library.

2. those remaining in a group; those not already mentioned अन्य, भिन्न Some people like milk, *others* do not.

3. recently हाल में I met Prakash the *other* day.

otherwise *(adv.)* अदर्वाइज़– in circumstances different from those present or considered; or else अन्यथा, वर्ना Mind your language *otherwise* I will call the police.

ought to *(v.)* ऑट् टू– used to indicate duty or correctness, typically when criticizing someone's actions चाहिए Students *ought to* respect their teachers.

ounce *(n.)* आउन्स– a unit for measuring weight, one sixteenth of a pound (equal 28.35 grams) तौल की माप, आउन्स An *ounce* of medicine recovered her from illness.

our *(det.)* अवर– belonging to or associated with the speaker and one or more other people previously mentioned or easily identified हमारा, हमारे *Our* business is going up.

ours *(pron.)* अवर्ज़– used to refer to a thing or things belonging to or associated with the speaker and one or more other people previously mentioned or easily identified हमारा Her house is very similar to *ours.*

ourselves *(pron.)* ऑवर्सेल्वज़–1. used as the object of a verb or preposition when this is the same as the subject of the clause and the subject is the speaker and one or more other people considered together स्वयं, अपने आप We can go there by *ourselves.*

2. we or us personally बिना किसी सहायता के We should enjoy *ourselves.*

out *(adv.)* आउट्–1. moving or appearing to move away from a particular place, बाहर Do not go *out* in the rain.

2. so as to be extinguished or no longer burning बुझी हुई The lights suddenly went *out.*

3. so as to be revealed or known रहस्य न रहना The results of the election are *out* at last.

4. out of fashion or treand फ़ैशन से बाहर Trousers are *out* this season.

5. to halt रोक लग जाना, बाहर हो जाना He will be *out* of the team until he recovers from his injury.

outbreak *(n.)* आउट्ब्रेक– a sudden occurrence of something unwelcome, such as war or disease आरंभ, प्रकोप The cyclone may lead to an *outbreak* of water-borne diseases.

outburst *(n.)* आउट्ब्रस्ट– a sudden release of strong emotion भड़ास, विस्फोट When the match go over, there was an *outburst* of cheers and applause.

outcome *(n.)* आउट्कम्– the way a thing turns out; a consequence फल, नतीजा, परिणाम She refused to comment on the *outcome* of the election.

outdated *(adj.)* आउट्डेटेड– out of date; obsolete प्रचलन से बाहर, पुराना This machine has become *outdated.*

outdoor *(adj.)* आउट्डोर– done, situated, or used out of doors घर से बाहर का Hockey is an *outdoor* game.

outer *(adj.)* आउट्र– outside; external बाहरी They pasted a poster on the *outer* wall of my house.

outermost *(adj.)* आउट्रमोस्ट– furthest from the centre बहुत दूर Fatehpur Sikri is situated in the *outermost* corner of Agra.

outfit *(n.)* आउट्फिट्– a set of clothes worn together, especially for a particular occasion or purpose ख़ास अवसर पर पहनने वाला परिधान I am going to buy a new *outfit* for wedding.

outgoing *(adj.)* आउट्गोइंग–1. friendly, sociable मिलनसार, मित्रतापूर्ण She is liked for her *outgoing* personality.
2. going out or away from a particular place निर्गामी, बाहर जाने वाली Please note down all the incoming and *outgoing* calls.

outing *(n.)* आउटिंग– a trip taken for pleasure, especially one lasting a day or less भ्रमण Let's go for an *outing.*

outlandish *(adj.)* आउट्लैंडिश– looking or sounding bizarre or unfamiliar अजीब, फूहड़, गंवारू, विदेशी She has an *outlandish* dressing sense.

outlast *(v.)* आउट्लास्ट– to live or last longer than दूसरे के मुक़ाबले देर तक रहना A leather bag will usually *outlast* a cloth one.

outlaw *(n.)* आउट्लॉ– a person who has broken the law, especially one who remains at large or is a fugitive भगोड़ा Daud Ibrahim is the world famous *outlaw.*

outlay *(n.)* आउट्ले– an amount of money spent on something ख़र्च, लागत They have spent a large *outlay* on scientific research.

outlet *(n.)* आउट्लेट– a commercial establishment retailing the goods of a particular producer or wholesaler विशेष प्रकार का सामान बेचने वाली दुकान There are many *outlets* of branded shoes near my house.

outline *(n.)* आउट्लाइन– the important features of an argument, theory, work, etc. रूपरेखा, ख़ाका What is the *outline* of your story?

outlook *(n.)* आउट्लुक– a mental attitude or point of view दृष्टिकोण Mahi has a pessimistic *outlook* on life.

out of *(prep.)* आउट् ऑफ़–1. not or no longer having any of (a substance, material, etc.) बाहर, परे She is *out of* danger now.
2. away from; not in अनुपस्थित He is *out of* the country.

➢ **out-of-date** *(adj.)*– no longer valid, current, or fashionable; outmoded पुराना, अप्रचलित, Why are you wearing *out-of-date* clothes?

output *(n.)* आउट्पुट– the act of production or manufacture उत्पादन, पैदावार The *output* of Nano car is 100 vehicles per day.

outrageous *(adj.)* आउट्रेजस– grossly offensive to decency, authority, etc. अत्याचारपूर्ण, नृशंस Her *outrageous* behaviour makes me annoyed.

outright *(n.)* आउट्राइट– straightforward; direct साफ़-साफ़ I gave her my *outright* decision.

outside *(adj.)* आउट्साइड–1. on or to the exterior of बाहर का, बाहर की ओर का They were painting the *outside* walls of the building.

2. *(adv.)* outside a specified thing or place; out of doors बाहर It is bitter cold *outside*.

3. *(n.)* the external side or surface किसी वस्तु की बाहरी सतह All the ingredients are written on the *outside* of the bottle.

outspoken *(adj.)* आउट्स्पोकन– candid or bold in speech मुंहफट, खरा बोलने वाला Sabia made an *outspoken* remark.

outstanding *(adj.)* आउट्स्टैंडिंग– superior; excellent; distinguished ख़ास, प्रमुख, उत्कृष्ट Reema was appreciated for her *outstanding* performance in dance competition.

outstretched *(adj.)* आउट्स्ट्रैच्ड– extended or expanded; stretched out फैला हुआ, फैलाये हुए My mother came towards me with her *outstretched* arms.

outward *(adj.)* आउट्वर्ड– of or relating to the outside of the body बाहरी, बाह्य The *outward* appearance of the building is not good.

outwards *(adv.)* आउट्वर्ड्ज़– towards the outside; out वहां से दूर, बाहर की ओर The door of the hotel opens *outwards*.

outwit *(v.)* आउट्विट– to get the better of by cunning or ingenuity चतुराई में मात देना, बुद्धि में उससे बढ़कर होना A fox had *outwitted* hunters for many days.

oval *(adj., n.)* ओवल–1. having the shape of an ellipse or ellipsoid अंडाकार I have an *oval*-shaped mirror in my room.

2. anything that is oval in shape, such as a sports ground अंडवक्र It is an *oval* race course not round.

ovation *(n.)* ओवेशन– an enthusiastic reception, esp one of prolonged applause अभिनंदन She received a standing *ovation* for her performance.

oven *(n.)* ॲवन– an enclosed heated compartment or receptacle for baking or roasting food चूल्हा, तंदूर My wife has bought an electric *oven*.

over *(prep.)* ओवर्–1. directly above; on the top of; via the top or upper surface of ऊपर, पार The boys climbed *over* the fence.

2. above; in preference to ऊपर, पर (अधिकार में) I always sleep with the blanket *over* my face. Who is *over* in your department?

3. *(adj.)* remaining; surplus (often in the phrase left over) ख़त्म, समाप्त When will the show be *over*?

4. once more फिर Please go through the sum *over* and *over* again.

5. more than अधिक, अतिरिक्त *Over* five hundred people attended the function.

overall *(adj.)* ओवर्ऑल– 1. from one end to the other कुल, सब दृष्टियों से What is the *overall* measurement of the stadium?

2. *(adv.)* in general; on the whole सामान्यतः, कुल मिलाकर How much will it cost *overall* for this work?

3. *(n.)* a protective work garment usually worn over ordinary clothes वस्त्रों के ऊपर पहना जाने वाला कपड़ा The lawyer was wearing a black *overall*.

overbearing *(adj.)* ओवर्बिअरिंग– domineering or dictatorial in manner or action दबंग, रोबीला Dr. Khan has an *overbearing* personality in his office.

overcharge *(v.)* ओवर्चार्ज–1. to charge too much बहुत अधिक दाम वसूलना The shopkeeper is *overcharging* for the shampoo.

2. to make greater, more noticeable, etc., than usual बढ़ा-चढ़ाकर कहना She was trying to *overcharge* importance of her matter.

overcoat *(n.)* ओवरकोट– a warm heavy coat worn over the outer clothes in cold weather ओवरकोट The detective was wearing a black *overcoat* in the movie.

overcome *(v.)* ओवरकम– to get the better of in a conflict (पर) विजयी होना I *overcame* my grief by engaging in work.

overcrowded *(adj.)* ओवरक्राउडेड– (of a room, vehicle, city, etc.) filled with more people or things than is desirable ठसाठस भरा The theatre was *overcrowded* on Sunday.

overdose *(n.)* ओवरडोज़– (esp of drugs) an excessive dose ख़ुराक की काफ़ी अधिक मात्रा, अतिमात्रा Nurse gave an *overdose* to the patient.

overdue *(adj.)* ओवर्ड्यू– past the time specified, required, or preferred for arrival, occurrence, payment, etc. अवधि बीतने पर भी जो चुकाया न गया हो The payment was *overdue* on him since long.

overflow *(v.)* ओवरफ़्लो–1. to fill or be filled beyond capacity so as to spill or run over लबालब भर जाना, बह निकलना The water was *overflowing* from the bucket.

2. to be filled with happiness, tears, etc. उमड़ना, बरबस बाहर आ जाना My heart was *overflowing* with gratitude.

3. to flow or run over (a limit, brim, bank, etc.) बहुत अधिक भर जाने से बाहर तक आ जाना The hospital was *overflowing* with victims of the bomb blast.

overgrown *(adj.)* ओवर्ग्रोन– to grow over or across (an area, path, lawn, etc.) फैला हुआ, ढका हुआ *Overgrown* plants should be trimmed in my garden.

overhead *(adv.)* ओवर्हेड– over or above head height, esp in the sky आसमान में An aeroplane was flying *overhead.*

overjoyed *(adj.)* ओवर्जॉइड– delighted; excessively happy प्रफुल्लित, बहुत ज्यादा ख़ुश Vinita was *overjoyed* at her selection in the dance competition.

overlap *(v.)* ओवर्लैप– to cover and extend beyond (something) ढक लेना, अतिव्याप्त होना A fish scales were *overlapping* eachother.

overload *(v.)* ओवर्लोड– to put too large a load on or in अधिक बोझ डालना He is *overloaded* with work.

overlook *(v.)* ओवर्लुक– to fail to notice or take into account नज़रअंदाज़ करना, ध्यान न देना Her mother *overlooked* her first fault.

overnight *(adj.)* ओवर्नाइट–1. for the duration of the night रात की They did an *overnight* journey to Lucknow.

2. in or as if in the course of one night; suddenly रातोंरात, बहुत शीघ्र Megha became a star *overnight.*

overpower *(v.)* ओवरपॉवर– to conquer or subdue by superior force पराजित करना Police managed to *overpower* the gunmen.

overseas *(adj.)* ओवरसीज़– of, to, in, from, or situated in countries beyond the sea समुद्रपार Masood has an *overseas* business in London.

overshadow *(v.)* ओवर्शैडो–1. to render insignificant or less important in comparison किसी की अहमियत घटाना, प्रमुखता कम करना He is always *overshadowed* by his brother.

2. to cast a shadow or gloom over किसी अवसर की प्रसन्नता को कम करना The game was *overshadowed* by violence.

oversleep *(v.)* ओवरस्लीप– to sleep beyond the intended time for getting up बहुत देर तक सोते रहना She *overslept* and could not go to office.

overt *(adj.)* ओवर्ट– open to view; observable प्रत्यक्ष, खुला The Prime Minister made an *overt* statement about the petrol prices.

overtime *(n.)* ओवर्‌टाइम– work at a regular job done in addition to regular working hours (कार्य के लिए निर्धारित समय से अधिक समय) अधिसमय They are not paid for their *overtime*.

overturn *(v.)* ओवर्‌टर्न– to turn or cause to turn from an upright or normal position उलटना, उलट जाना The bus *overturned* and fell into the ditch.

overweight *(adj.)* ओवरवेट– weighing more than is usual, allowed, or healthy बहुत भारी, मोटा, भारी-भरकम She could not get married as she was *over-weighted*.

overwhelming *(adj.)* ओवर्‌वेल्मिंग– overpowering in effect, number, or force तीव्र भावना, सशक्त रूप, ज़ोरदार I felt an *overwhelming* desire to get up and leave.

owe *(v.)* ओ –1. to be under an obligation to pay (someone) to the amount of ऋणी/देनदार होना When can you repay the money you *owe* me?

2. to feel the need or obligation to do, give, etc. आभारी होना I *owe* my present position in life to the guidance of my father.

owing *(adj.)* ओइंग– owed; due ऋणी/देनदार *Owing* to circumstances, the programme is cancelled.

owl *(n.)* आउल– a nocturnal bird of prey having large front-facing eyes, a small hooked bill, soft feathers, and a short neck उल्लू An *owl* can only see at night.

own *(v.)* ओन– 1. to have as one's possession मालिक/स्वामी होना My father *owns* this house.

2. *(adj.)* on behalf of oneself or in relation to oneself अपना, निजी I make my *own* breakfast.

owner *(n.)* ओनर– a person who owns; legal possessor मालिक, स्वामी Rohan is the *owner* of the house.

ownership *(n.)* ओनरशिप– the state or fact of being an owner स्वामित्व There is no quarrel over the *ownership* of this house.

ox *(n.)* ऑक्स– an adult castrated male of any domesticated species of cattle, used for pulling farm equipment, etc. बैल The farmer ploughed the land with the help of an *ox*.

oxygen *(n.)* ऑक्सिजन– a colourless odourless highly reactive gaseous element the most abundant element in the earth's crust (पेड़-पौधों से मिलने वाली गैस जो जीवन देती है) ऑक्सीजन All living things need *oxygen* to live.

ozone *(n.)* ओज़ोन– a poisonous gas with a strong smell that is a form of oxygen ओज़ोन *Ozone* is like oxygen and pleasant to breathe.

Pp

Pp *(n.)* पी–अंग्रेज़ी वर्णमाला का सोलहवां अक्षर The sixteenth letter of the English alphabet. Pen begins with 'P'.

pace *(v.)* पेस– 1. to set or determine the pace for, as in a race टहलना, क़दम-क़दम जाना I *paced* up and down the room.
2. *(n.)* a single step in walking क़दम, पग He worked at a quick *pace*.

pacify *(v.)* पैसिफ़ाई– to calm the anger or agitation of; mollify शांत करना, संतुष्ट करना The little girl was *pacified* only when we offered her a bar of chocolate.

pacific *(adj.)* पैसिफ़िक– not aggressive; peaceful opposed to the use of force शान्तिप्रिय, शांतिकर It's hard to *pacify* a baby.

pack *(n.)* पैक– 1. a bundle or load, esp one carried on the back गठरी, पोटली, डिब्बा How much tea does this *pack* contain?
2. *(v.)* to place or arrange (articles) in (a container), such as clothes in a suitcase बांधना, पैक करना Have you *packed* all your things?

> **pack in**– to carry (something) to base camp, etc. by pack खचाखच भर देना, We were *packed* into a mini bus.

> **pack off**– चलता करना, They *packed* Kishan *off* to his village.

> **pack up**– to give up (an attempt) or stop doing (something) कोई काम पूरा कर डालना, I want to *pack up* this work at the end of the day.

package *(n.)* पैकेज–1. any wrapped or boxed object or group of objects पेटी, संदूक, गठरी The coolie was putting the *package* on his head.
2. a complete unit consisting of a number of component parts sold separately पैकेज The company is offering holiday *package* for couples.

packed *(a.)* पैक्ड– completely filled; full खचाखच भरा हुआ The conference hall was fully *packed* with the delegates.

packet *(n.)* पैकेट– a small or medium-sized container of cardboard, paper, etc. often together with its contents डिब्बा, थैली The *packet* was too small to fill it with all the goods.

packing *(n.)* पैकिंग– material used to cushion packed goods सामान बांधने की क्रिया I have finished my *packing* .

pact *(n.)* पैक्ट– an agreement or compact between two or more parties, nations, etc. for mutual advantage समझौता A new peace *pact* was made between India and Pakistan.

pad *(n.)* पैड– a number of sheets of paper fastened together along one edge लिखने के लिए एक-से कटे क़ागजों का संग्रह I want to buy a letter *pad.*

paddle *(n.)* पैडल–1. a paddle wheel साईकिल का पैडल The *paddle* of my cycle is broken.
2. a short light oar with a flat blade at one or both ends, used without a rowlock to propel a canoe or small boat चप्पू, डॉंड It was difficult to hold the *paddle* of the boat.
3. *(v.)* to propel (a canoe, small boat, etc.) with a paddle नाव खेना The child was not able to *paddle* the boat.

padlock *(n.)* पैडलॉक– a detachable lock having a hinged or sliding shackle, बड़ा ताला The door to the farmhouse requires a big *padlock.*

Padma Bhushan *(n.)* पद्म भूषण– a distinctive award किसी .क्षेत्र में राष्ट्र की विशिष्ट सेवा के लिए प्रदान किए जाने वाली उपाधि Azim Premji got *Padma*

Bhushan in 2011 for Trade and Industry.

Padma Shri *(n.)* पद्म श्री– a distinctive award किसी विशिष्ट नागरिक को दी जाने वाली उपाधि Kajol was awarded *Padma Shri* in 2011 in the field of cinema.

Padma Vibhushan *(n.)* पद्म-विभूषण– a distinctive award भारत रत्न के बाद दी जाने वाली उपाधि The *Padma Vibhushan* is the second highest civilian award in the Republic of India.

paediatrician *(n.)* पीडिअट्रिशन– a medical practitioner who specializes in paediatrics बाल-चिकित्सक Vaccination for a new born baby was given by a good *paediatrician.*

paddy *(n.)* पैडी– a field planted with rice धान Our train travelled through *paddy* fields.

pagan *(n.)* पेगन– a member of a group professing a polytheistic religion or any religion other than Christianity, Judaism, or Islam विधर्मी, काफ़िर, मूर्तिपूजक He wanted to help all the *pagan* people.

page *(n.)* पेज– one side of one of the leaves of a book, newspaper, letter, etc. or the written or printed matter it bears पृष्ठ This book is a *page* turner.

pageant *(n.)* पैजेण्ट– an elaborate colourful parade or display portraying scenes from history, esp one involving rich costume झाँकी, प्रदर्शन, समारोह The magician showed a *pageant* to entertain the people in the circus.

pager *(n.)* पेजर– a small electronic device, capable of receiving short messages; usually carried by people who need to be contacted urgently (e.g. doctors) संदेश प्राप्त करने का एक उपकरण I have a *pager.*

pail *(n.)* पेल– a bucket, esp one made of wood or metal बाल्टी, डोल I filled the *pail* with water from the tap.

pain *(v.)* पेन– 1. to cause (a person) distress, hurt, grief, anxiety, etc. पीड़ा देना Your misbehaviour *pained* me greatly.
2. *(n.)* the sensation of acute physical hurt or discomfort caused by injury, illness, etc. दर्द, पीड़ा, तकलीफ़, व्यथा The doctor gave me a tablet to relieve the *pain* in my stomach.

painful *(adj.)* पेनफुल– causing pain; distressing पीड़ादायक, तकलीफ़देह The accident was a *painful* experience.

painkiller *(n.)* पेनकिलर– an analgesic drug or agent दर्द कम करने वाली दवा, पीड़ानाशक The doctor gave me a *painkiller* for my back pain.

painless *(adj.)* पेनलस– not causing pain or distress पीड़ारहित He got a slow and *painless* death.

painstaking *(adj.)* पैनज़टेकिंग– extremely careful, thorough अति सावधानी एवं परिश्रम द्वारा किया हुआ He cannot handle *painstaking* work.

paint *(v.)* पेण्ट– 1. to make (a picture) of (a figure, landscape, etc.) with paint applied to a surface such as canvas चित्र बनाना, रंगना Do you know how to *paint*?
2. *(n.)* the solid pigment of a paint before it is suspended in liquid रंगलेप What *paint* would you like for the walls of your room?

painter *(n.)* पेण्टर– a person who paints surfaces as a trade चित्रकार M.F. Hussain is a world famous *painter.*

painting *(n.)* पेन्टिंग– the art or process of applying paints to a surface such as canvas, to make a picture or other artistic composition रंगीन चित्र, चित्रकला We are going to buy *paintings.*

pair *(n.)* पेअर्– two identical or similar things matched for use together जोड़ा They work best as a *pair.*

pal *(n.)* पाल– a close friend; comrade दोस्त, मित्र, साथी An old *pal* met me on the way.

palace *(n.)* पैलस– the official residence of a reigning monarch or member of a royal family राजभवन, प्रासाद, महल The Queen of England lives in Buckingham *Palace.*

palaeontology *(n.)* पैलिआनटालॉजि– the study of fossils to determine the structure and evolution of extinct animals and plants and the age and conditions of deposition of the rock strata in which they are found जीवाश्म विज्ञान The *palaeontology* is the study of prehistoric life on earth.

palanquin *(n.)* पैलनक्विन– covered litter, formerly used in the Orient, carried on the shoulders of four men पालकी The *palanquin* was beautifully decorated.

palate *(n.)* पैलट– the roof of the mouth, separating the oral and nasal cavities तालू The *palate* is a great help while painting.

pale *(adj.)* पेल– lacking brightness of colour; whitish विवर्ण, फीका, निस्तेज Your face looks so *pale.*

pall *(v.)* पॉल– to become or appear boring, insipid, or tiresome (to) ऊबाउ हो जाना, कम रोचक हो जाना The work began to *pall* after a few years.

palm *(n.)* पाम–1. the inner part of the hand from the wrist to the base of the fingers हथेली, करतल Can you read a *palm*?
2. a straight tree with long leaves at the top ताड़, ताल वृक्ष Kerala is a land of *palm* trees.

palmistry *(n.)* पॉमिस्ट्री– the process or art of interpreting character, telling fortunes, etc. by the configuration of lines, marks, and bumps on a person's hand हस्तरेखा शास्त्र Sheena has firm belief in *palmistry.*

palpitate *(v.)* पैलपिटेट्– (of the heart) to beat with abnormal rapidity धड़कना, धक-धक करना My heart started *palpitating* on seeing the lion.

paltry *(adj.)* पॉल्ट्री– insignificant; meagre तुच्छ, नगण्य I was offered a *paltry* amount of money to do that work.

pamper *(v.)* पैम्पर्– to treat with affectionate and usually excessive indulgence; coddle; spoil बहुत लाड़-प्यार करना She has been *pampered* a lot.

pamphlet *(n.)* पैम्फ्लेट– a brief publication generally having a paper cover; booklet पुस्तिका, पैम्फलेट Our party has brought out a *pamphlet* on its aims and objectives.

pan *(n.)* पैन्– a wide metal vessel used in cooking तवा, कड़ाही Make an omelette in the *pan.*

panacea *(n.)* पैनसिआ– a remedy for all diseases or ills रामबाण, सर्वरोगहर There's no *panacea* to turn an idiot into an intelligent being.

Panchayat *(n.)* पंचायत– a village council in India भारत में गांव की एक प्रशासनिक इकाई His property dispute was solved in *Panchayat.*

pancreas *(n.)* पैंक्रिअस– a large elongated glandular organ, situated behind the stomach, that secretes insulin and pancreatic juice पाचन-ग्रंथि The *pancreas* is a small organ, around six inches long, located in the upper abdomen, and adjacent to the small intestine.

panda *(n.)* पाण्डा– a large black-and-white herbivorous bearlike mammal, inhabiting the high mountain bamboo forests of China पंडा, सफ़ेद रंग का चीनी भालू The pure giant *panda* is a native animal of China.

pane *(n.)* पेन– a sheet of glass in a window or door शीशा There are a lot of scratches on the window *pane.*

panel *(n.)* पैनल–1. a flat section of a wall, door, etc. खिड़की का शीशा The child broke the glass *panel.*

2. a public discussion by such a group मंडल The *panel* of judges declared them the clear winners.

pang *(n.)* पैंग– a sudden brief sharp feeling, as of loneliness, physical pain, or hunger कसक, टीस I felt a *pang* of pain while climbing the stairs.

panic *(n.)* पैनिक– 1. a sudden overwhelming feeling of terror or anxiety, आतंक, भगदड़, तहलका, संत्रस्त I feel a moment of sheer *panic* whenever I do some urgent work.

2. *(v.)* to feel or cause to feel *panic* आतंकित होना, घबरा जाना I *panicked* when I couldn't find my wallet.

panorama *(n.)* पैनरामा– an extensive unbroken view, as of a landscape, in all directions दृश्यपटल, चित्रावली There was an excellent *panorama* from the China Peak in Nainital.

pant *(v.)* पैण्ट– to breathe with noisy deep gasps, as when out of breath from exertion or excitement हाँफ़ना I was *panting* while exercising

panther *(n.)* पैन्थर– another name for the leopard, esp the black variety, which is known as the black panther तेंदुआ *Panther* is found in the forest of Karnataka.

pantry *(n.)* पैंट्री– a small room or cupboard in which provisions, cooking utensils, etc. are kept; larder रसोई-भंडार The *pantry* looked very dirty.

pants *(n.)* पैण्ट्स– an undergarment reaching from the waist to the thighs or knees पैंट I bought a new pair of *pants* yesterday.

papaya *(n.)* पपाइआ– a tropical fruit with yellow and green skin, sweet flesh and round black seeds पपीता *Papaya* is a wonderful fruit with many health benefits.

paper *(n.)* पेपर्–1. a substance made from cellulose fibres derived from rags, wood, etc. often with other additives, and formed into flat thin sheets suitable for writing on, decorating walls, wrapping, etc. काग़ज़ Give me a piece of *paper.*

2. a single piece of such material, esp if written or printed on अख़बार Where is today's *paper*?

3. a set of written examination questions प्रश्न-पत्र Yesterday's question *paper* was very difficult to answer.

4. a short essay, as by a student निबंध The professor read out a *paper* on atomic energy.

5. official documents relating to the ownership काग़ज़ात, प्रमाण This building is mine, I have the *papers* to prove it.

➢ **on paper**– b. in theory, as opposed to fact लिखित रूप में, I need to get some of my ideas down *on paper.*

paperback *(n.)* पेपरबैक– a book or edition with covers made of flexible card, sold relatively cheaply काग़ज़ के जिल्द की बनी पुस्तक The book was not available in *paperback*

paperweight *(n.)* पेपरवेट– a small heavy object placed on loose papers to prevent them from scattering काग़ज़ को दबाकर रखने वाली भारी वस्तु, पेपरवेट This is a rather light *paperweight.*

paperwork *(n.)* पेपरवर्क– clerical work, such as the completion of forms or the writing of reports or letters काग़ज़ी कार्य I have to finish all my *paperwork.*

par *(n.)* पार– a state of equality गुणवत्ता का स्तर She is a writer *par* excellence.

parable *(n.)* पैरबल– a short story that uses familiar events to illustrate a religious or ethical point नीतिकथा,

दृष्टांत The *parables* of Panchatantra are still as fresh as they were ages ago.

parachute *(n.)* पैरशूट– a device used to retard the fall of a man or package from an aircraft, consisting of a large fabric canopy connected to a harness पैराशूट, हवाई छतरी The *parachute* didn't deploy on time.

parade *(n.)* परेड–1 an ordered, esp ceremonial, march, assembly, or procession, as of troops being reviewed परेड, क़वायद, जलूस The *parade* will take place on the *parade* ground.
2. a visible show or display सैन्य-प्रदर्शन Thousands of people watch the Republic Day *Parade.*
3. *(v.)* to walk or march, esp in a procession (through) परेड करना The army will *parade* at dawn.

paradise *(n.)* पैरडाइस– heaven as the ultimate abode or state of the righteous स्वर्ग, आनंदधाम He is always dreaming of a *paradise.*

paradox *(n.)* पैरडॉक्स– a seemingly absurd or self-contradictory statement that is or may be true विरोधाभास There are a lot of *paradoxes* in everybody's life.

paragraph *(n.)* पैरग्राफ़– (in a piece of writing) one of a series of subsections each usually devoted to one idea and each usually marked by the beginning of a new line, indentation, increased interlinear space, etc. पैरा, अनुच्छेद He won the *paragraph* writing competition

parakeet *(n.)* पैरकीट– any of numerous small usually brightly coloured long-tailed parrots, लंबी पूंछ वाला तोता A *parakeet* can live 12 to 15 years or more.

parallel *(adv.)* पैरलेल– 1. separated by an equal distance at every point; never touching or intersecting समानांतर This is a *parallel* connection.
2. *(n.)* an exact likeness सादृश्य His quality of work is without *parallel.*

paralyze (se) *(v.)* पैरलाइज़– to render (a part of the body) insensitive to pain, touch, etc. esp by injection of an anaesthetic लक़वा मार जाना, हिलने-डुलने में असमर्थ हो जाना I was *paralyzed* with fear to see two armed men in the house.

parameter *(n.)* पैरमीटर– any constant or limiting factor मापदंड There are various *parameters* to judge the success of a person.

paramilitary *(adj.)* पैरमिलटरी– denoting or relating to a group of personnel with military structure functioning either as a civil force or in support of military forces अर्द्धसैनिक बल He called the *paramilitary* forces at once.

paramount *(adj.)* पैरमाउन्ट– of the greatest importance or significance; pre-eminent सर्वोपरि, सबसे ज़्यादा Helping his friend was of *paramount* importance to him.

paranoid *(adj.)* पैरनॉइड– of, characterized by, or resembling paranoia संभ्रांति He is *paranoid* about black cats.

paraphrasing *(n.)* पैरफ्रेज़िंग– an expression of a statement or text in other words, esp in order to clarify भावार्थ, व्याख्या This is not the correct *paraphrasing* of this article.

parasite *(n.)* पैरसाइट– an animal or plant that lives in or on another (the host) from which it obtains nourishment परजीवी, (दूसरों के सहारे जीवित रहने वाला) Beggers are *parasites* of our society.

parboil *(v.)* पार्बॉईल– to boil until partially cooked, often before further cooking थोड़ा पकने तक उबालना, उसनना, पकाना Mother *parboiled* the rice.

parcel *(n.)* पार्सल– something wrapped up; package पार्सल The *parcel* arrived on time.

parched *(adj.)* पार्च्ट– dried up as a result of being deprived of water सूखा, भुना हुआ The desert was completely *parched.*

pardon *(n.)* पार्डन–1. forgiveness क्षमा, माफ़ी I beg your *pardon.*

2. release from punishment for an offence क्षमादान का दस्तावेज़ The thief asked the judge for *pardon.*

3. *(v.)* to excuse or forgive (a person) for (an offence, mistake, etc.) क्षमा करना Many prisoners were *pardoned* on the eve of the king's birthday.

parents *(n.)* पे'अरन्ट्स– a father or mother माँ-बाप *Parents* are the greatest asset to a child

parentage *(n.)* पेअरनटिज– ancestry जनकता, जाति, कुल, वंश Karam Singh has a royal *parentage.*

parental *(adj.)* परेण्टल– of or relating to a parent or parenthood माता या पिता की He needs *parental* advise.

park *(n.)* पार्क–1. a large area of land preserved in a natural state for recreational use by the public उपवन, उद्यान We go to the *park* every evening.

2. a piece of open land in a town with public amenities मोटरगाड़ी खड़ी करने का स्थान *Parking* is not allowed here.

3. *(v.)* to stand in a specific place (a motor vehicle) खड़ा करना May I *park* my motor cycle here while I visit the market?

Parliament *(n.)* पार्लमेंट– an assembly of the representatives of a political nation or people, often the supreme legislative authority संसद, लोकसभा The *Parliament* is now in session.

parlour *(n.)* पार्लर– a living room, esp one kept tidy for the reception of visitors बैठक, अतिथि-कक्ष An old lady was sitting in a beauty *parlour.*

parody *(n.)* पैरडी– mimicry of someone's individual manner in a humorous or satirical way अनुकरण, नक़ल The *parody* was very hilarious.

parrot *(n.)* पैरट– a tropical bird having a short hooked bill, compact body, bright plumage, and an ability to mimic sounds तोता There are roughly 370 known species of *parrot.*

Parsee *(n.)* पारसी– an adherent of a monotheistic religion of Zoroastrian origin, the practitioners of which were driven out of Persia by the Muslims in the eighth century ad. जरथ्रुस्त धर्म का अनुयायी *Parsees* arrived in India from Persia.

part *(n.)* पार्ट–1. a piece or portion of a whole भाग, हिस्सा This book is divided into three *parts.*

2. a person's proper role or duty भूमिका I have a major *part* in the play to be put up by our club.

3. support someone in an argument पक्षपात, पक्ष पोषण We thank you for taking our *part.*

4. *(v.)* to divide or separate from one another; take or come apart अलग करना या होना The two friends were sad when they *parted* to go in different directions.

partake *(v.)* पार्टेक– to have a share; participate भाग लेना, शिरकत करना He did not *partake* in our business.

partial *(adj.)* पार्शल–1. relating to only a part; not general or complete आंशिक, अपूर्ण I am only in *partial* agreement with what you say.

2. biased पक्षपाती Parents are naturally *partial* to their children.

partiality *(n.)* पार्शऐलटी– favourable prejudice or bias पक्षपात, तरफ़दारी The boss was not *partiality* to anyone in the office.

partially *(adv.)* पार्शइलि– to some extent, partly आंशिक रूप से, अंशतः The work has been *partially* completed.

participate *(v.)* पार्टिसिपेट– to take part, be or become actively involved, or share (in) भाग लेना Will you *participate* in the dance competition?

particle *(n.)* पार्टिकल– an extremely small piece of matter; speck कण Some *particles* of dust are sticking to your shirt.

particular *(adj.)* पर्टिक्यलर्–1. exceptional or marked विशिष्ट, ख़ास, अमुक There are many pictures in this art gallery, but I want to look at this *particular* one.

2. exacting or difficult to please, esp in details; fussy सख़्त, नियमित, विशेष, सावधान Ramesh is very *particular* about his food.

3. of or belonging to a single or specific person, thing, category, etc. specific; special विवरण Please give *particulars* of all your achievements.

particularly *(adv.)* पर्टिक्युलरली– very much; exceptionally ख़ासकर, विशेषतः Be *particularly* careful while writing the examinations.

partition *(n.)* पार्टिशन– 1. a division into parts; separation विभाजन, बंटवारा, We divided our sitting room into two parts with a *partition.*

2. *(v.)* to separate or apportion into sections विभाजित करना, बंटवारा करना The two brothers *partitioned* their house.

partly *(adv.)* पार्टलि– to some extent; not completely कुछ अंशों में The work has been *partly* finished

partner *(n.)* पार्टनर्– a member of a partnership भागी, साझेदार I need a *partner* for dancing.

partnership *(n.)* पार्टनरशिप– a contractual relationship between two or more persons carrying on a joint business venture with a view to profit, each incurring liability for losses and the right to share in the profits भागीदारी, साझा Jawed has *partnership* in the business of his uncle.

partridge *(n.)* पर्ट्रिज– a brown bird with a short tail and round body तीतर *Partridges* are middle-sized non-migratory birds.

party *(n.)* पार्टी–1. a group of people associated in some activity दल, पार्टी Which political *party* do you belong to?

2. a social gathering for pleasure, often held as a celebration गोष्ठी, प्रीतिभोज Yesterday I was invited to a tea *party.*

3. a person, esp one who participates in some activity such as entering into a contract समर्थक, भाग लेने वाला व्यक्ति My brother was never a *party* to the fraud.

pass *(n.)* पास–1. an official document that shows, one has right to enter a place प्रवेश-पत्र Please show your entry *pass* before you go in.

2. *(v.)* to gain or cause to gain an adequate or required mark, grade, or rating in (an examination, course, etc.) उत्तीर्ण होना Has your son *passed* his final examination?

3. to move or cause to move onwards or over बीतना The days are *passing* very quickly.

4. to pronounce or deliver (judgment, findings, etc.) निर्णय देना The judge *passed* sentence.

5. to transfer or exchange or be transferred or exchanged हस्तान्तरित करना Please *pass* the salt.

6. (से) गुजरना, पार जाना Will you *pass* a bookshop on your way to office?

➢ **pass away**– to loose one's breath मर जाना, He *passed away* last night.

- **pass by**– to go or move past गुज़रना, He *passed by* my house last night.
- **pass down**– to give or teach sth to people or children एक पीढ़ी से दूसरी पीढ़ी तक पहुंचना, Knowledge *passes down* over the centuries.
- **pass into**– to become a part of sth धीरे-धीरे बदल जाना, A criminal *passed into* a noble man.
- **pass off** *(v.)* to come to a gradual end; disappear लुप्त होना, ग़ायब होना, Has your toothache *passed off?*

passable *(adj.)* पासएबल– adequate, fair, or acceptable संतोषजनक, कामचलाऊ This work is not *passable.* It has to be done by you.

passage *(n.)* पैसिज–1. a way, as in a hall or lobby गलियारा My room is at the end of the *passage.*
2. a section of a written work, speech, etc. esp one of moderate length परिच्छेद, उद्धरण Please read out to me any *passage* from your article.

passbook *(n.)* पासबुक– a book for keeping a record of withdrawals from and payments into a building society पासबुक, लेखा-पुस्तिका I'm going to the bank to update my *passbook.*

passenger *(n.)* पैसिन्जर्– a person travelling in a car, train, boat, etc. not driven by him यात्री, मुसाफ़िर The *passenger* had a lot of complaints.

passer-by *(n.)* पासर-बाई– a person that is passing or going by, esp on foot राहगीर, पथिक There were many *passers-by* on the footpath.

passing *(adj.)* पासिंग– transitory or momentary बीतता हुआ, गुजरता हुआ Meghna watched the *passing* cars.

passion *(n.)* पैश़न– ardent love or affection भावावेश, मनोवेग, अनुराग He has a great *passion* for reading.

passionate *(n.)* पैश़नट– capable of, revealing, or characterized by intense emotion भावुक His writings make me very *passionate.*

passive *(adj.)* पैसिव– not active or not participating perceptibly in an activity, organization, etc. निष्क्रिय He was very *passive* during the entire discussion.

passport *(n.)* पासपोर्ट– an official document issued by a government, identifying an individual, granting him permission to travel abroad, and requesting the protection of other governments for him पासपोर्ट, पारपत्र Have you obtained your *passport* for your proposed foreign tour?

past *(adj.)* पास्ट–1. completed, finished, and no longer in existence बीता हुआ Our *past* mistakes proved to be a learning experience.
2. *(prep.)* beyond in time बजकर (समय बताने के लिए प्रयुक्त) I'll see you at half *past* ten.
3. *(adv.)* on or onwards किसी वस्तु या व्यक्ति को पार करके She walked *past* me without even looking at me.
4. *(n.)* an earlier period of someone's life अतीत We often try to forget our *past,* but it haunts us always.

paste *(n.)* पेस्ट– 1. a mixture or material of a soft or malleable consistency, such as toothpaste पेस्ट, लेई I want to buy a tube of tooth-*paste.*
2. *(v.)* to attach by or as if by using paste चिपकाना A notice was *pasted* on the wall.

pastel *(adj.)* पैस्टल– soft colour फीका रंग, हल्का रंग He likes coloring with *pastel colours.*

pasteurized (ised) *(adj.)* पास्चराइज़्ड– subjected to pasteurization जीवाणुरहित *Pasteurized* milk destroys microorganisms that can cause illness.

pastime *(n.)* पास्टाइम्– an activity or entertainment which makes time pass pleasantly मनोरंजन, मन-बहलाव His favourite *pastime* is watching the television.

pastry *(n.)* पेस्ट्री– baked foods, such as tarts, made with this dough एक छोटा केक, पेस्ट्री Sarah likes to have chocolate *pastry* with coffee.

pasture *(n.)* पास्चर्– land covered with grass or herbage and grazed by or suitable for grazing by livestock गोचर भूमि We strolled around the green *pastures.*

pat *(v.)* पैट– 1. to hit (something) lightly with the palm of the hand or some other flat surface थपथपाना, शाबाशी देना I *patted* the boy on the back. 2. *(n.)* a light blow with something flat थपकी My teacher's *pat* on my back encouraged me to do better.

patch *(n.)* पैच–1. a piece of material used to mend a garment or to make patchwork, a sewn-on pocket, etc. थिगली, पैबन्द, फाहा I repaired the puncture in my bicycle with a *patch* of rubber.

2. any discoloured area on the skin, mucous membranes, etc. usually being one sign of a specific disorder धब्बा, चित्ती What are these *patches* on your arm?

patchwork *(n.)* पैचवर्क– needlework done by sewing pieces of different materials together पैबंदकारी *Patchwork* suits are common in fashion.

patch up *(v.)* पैच अप– मरम्मत करना, दुबारा जोड़ना Both of them are trying hard to *patch up.*

patent *(adj.)* पैटंट– open or available for inspection साफ़, स्पष्ट I knew that he was telling a *patent* lie.

paternal *(adj.)* पेटर्नल– inherited or derived from the male parent पैतृक, पित्रीय He is staying with his *paternal* grandparents.

path *(n.)* पाथ– a road or way, esp a narrow trodden track पथ, रास्ता The *path* towards school was long and messy.

pathetic *(adj.)* पथेटिक– evoking or expressing pity, sympathy, etc. करुणाजनक, भावपूर्ण The movie was *pathetic.*

pathologist *(n.)* पथालजिस्ट– someone who studies the branch of medicine concerned with the cause, origin, and nature of disease, including the changes occurring as a result of disease रोग विज्ञानी Arshi is working as a *pathologist* in a government hospital.

pathology *(n.)* पथालजी– the branch of medicine concerned with the cause, origin, and nature of disease, रोग विज्ञान He is doing research in *pathology.*

patience *(n.)* पेशन्स– tolerant and even-tempered perseverance धैर्य, सहनशीलता He is running out of *patience.*

patient *(n.)* पेशण्ट– 1. a person who is receiving medical care रोगी, मरीज़ The *patient* needs serious medical attention.

2. *(adj.)* enduring trying circumstances with even temper धैर्यवान, सहनशील Be *patient,* you will also be served food.

patiently *(adv.)* पेशण्टली– in such a way as to endure trying circumstances with even temper धीरज के साथ My dog waited *patiently* for me to return.

patricide *(n.)* पैट्रिसाइड– the act of killing one's father पिता की हत्या It's a sin to commit *patricide.*

patriot *(n.)* पैट्रिअट– a person who vigorously supports his country and its way of life देशभक्त Subhash Chandra Bose was a great *patriot.*

patron *(n.)* पेट्रन– a person, esp a man, who sponsors or aids artists, charities, etc. protector or benefactor संरक्षक He is a great *patron* of arts and literature.

patronage *(n.)* पेट्रनेज– the support given or custom brought by a patron or patroness संरक्षण A fair under the *patronage* of the leader was organised.

patronize (ise) *(v.)* पैट्रनाइज़– to behave or treat in a condescending way संरक्षक की तरह व्यवहार करना You should not *patronize* her.

patter *(n.)* पैटर्– a quick succession of light tapping sounds, as of feet पटपट करना, लगातार बोलना There was a lot of *pattering* in the class.

pattern *(n.)* पैटर्न–1. an arrangement of repeated or corresponding parts, decorative motifs, etc. नमूना, पैटर्न Meena used a paper *pattern* to make her new dress.
2. a model worthy of imitation आदर्श Your behaviour should be a *pattern* for others.
3. *(v.)* to model ढालना Children often *pattern* their personality after that of their parents.

pauper *(n.)* पॉपर्– a person who is extremely poor कंगाल, गरीब Her husband died a *pauper.*

pause *(v.)* पॉज़– 1. to cease an action temporarily; stop ठहर जाना, रुकना The speaker *paused* for a minute and took a sip of water.
2. *(n.)* a temporary stop or rest, esp in speech or action; short break विराम, ठहराव, विश्राम After a brief *pause,* he spoke again.

pavement *(n.)* पेवमेण्ट– a hard-surfaced path for pedestrians alongside and a little higher than a road पटरी He hit the *pavement* hard and died.

pavilion *(n.)* पविलिअन– a building at a sports ground, esp a cricket pitch, in which players change पैविलियन After being caught by Ricky Ponting, Sehwag went back to the *pavilion.*

paw *(n.)* पॉ– any of the feet of a four-legged mammal, bearing claws or nails पंजा, चंगुल Lions fight with their *paws.*

pawn *(n.)* पॉन– 1. a person or thing that is held as a security, esp a hostage मोहरा, कठपुतली The servant was used as a *pawn* by the rich industrialist in the murder case.
2. *(v.)* to deposit (an article) as security for the repayment of a loan, esp from a pawnbroker दांव पर लगाना The servant was *pawned* by the rich industrialist in the murder case.

pay *(n.)* पे–1. money given in return for work or services; a salary or wage वेतन, तनख़्वाह Have you received this month's *pay*?
2. *(v.)* to discharge (a debt, obligation, etc.) by giving or doing something चुकाना, अदा करना, दाम चुकाना What did you *pay* for this pen?
3. to make (a visit or call) (मिलने) जाना I hope to *pay* you a visit this week.

payable *(adj.)* पेअबल– to be paid देय What is the amount *payable* to me now?

payment *(n.)* पेमेण्ट– a sum of money paid भुगतान I have not received my full *payment.*

payroll *(n.)* पेरोल– a list of employees, specifying the salary or wage of each वेतन-चिट्ठा The workers were hired on a *payroll.*

pea *(n.)* पी– a climbing plant with small white flowers and long green pods containing edible green seeds मटर There is a great nutritional values and health benefits of eating green *peas.*

peace *(n.)* पीस– the state existing during the absence of war शांति It is getting difficult to imagine *peace* in this world.

peaceful *(adj.)* पीसफुल– inclined towards peace शांतिपूर्ण, शांतिमय I liked to do my writing in a *peaceful* atmosphere.

peacekeeping *(adj.)* पीसकीपिंग– the maintenance of peace, esp the prevention of further fighting between hostile forces in an area शान्ति बनाए हुए *Peacekeeping* troops were expected to move into the area by the start of the month.

peach *(n.)* पीच– a round edible fruit with soft red and yellow skin and a large seed inside आड़ू *Peach* is high in nutrition and reduces the cholesterol level in the body.

peacock *(n.)* पीकॉक– a male peafowl, having a crested head and a very large fanlike tail marked with blue and green eyeiike spots मोर The *peacock* dances in the rain.

peak *(n.)* पीक– the pointed summit of a mountain चोटी, शिखर He is at the *peak* of his career.

peaked *(adj.)* पीकड– having a peak; pointed नुकीला, चोटीदार One of my friends always wears a *peaked* cap.

peal *(n.)* पील–1. a loud prolonged usually reverberating sound, as of bells, thunder, or laughter घंटानाद As we approached the temple, we could hear the *peal* of the temple bells.
2. the set of bells in a belfry गड़गड़ाहट There was a *peal* of thunder and then the rain started.

peanut *(n.)* पीनट–1. the edible nutlike seed मूंगफली We enjoyed roasted *peanuts* while basking in the sun.
2. a trifling amount of money बहुत ही थोड़ी रक़म Why are you working for *peanuts* when you have so much of talent?

pear *(n.)* पेअर्– a yellow or green fruit which has a globular base and tapers towards the apex नाशपाती The mother sliced the *pears* for the child.

pearl *(n.)* पर्ल– a hard smooth lustrous typically rounded structure occurring on the inner surface of the shell of a clam or oyster मोती I bought a necklace of *pearls* as a present for my wife.

peasant *(n.)* पेज़ण्ट– a member of a class of low social status that depends on either cottage industry or agricultural labour as a means of subsistence किसान In the olden days the *peasants* were tread roughly.

pebble *(n.)* पेबल्– a small smooth rounded stone, esp one worn by the action of water कंकड़, रोड़ा The children are playing with *pebbles.*

peck *(v.)* पैक– to strike with the beak or with a pointed instrument चोंच मारना The sparrows *pecked* at the grains on the floor.

peckish *(adj.)* पेकिश– slightly hungry; having an appetite थोड़ा भूखा The old beggar looked *peckish.*

peculiar *(adj.)* पिक्यूलिअर्– strange or unusual; odd विलक्षण There is a *peculiar* smell in the air.

peculiarity *(n.)* पिक्यूलिऐरटि– a strange or unusual habit or characteristic विशिष्टता, विशेषता Cautious driving is a *peculiarity* of educated women.

pedal *(n.)* पेडल्– any foot-operated lever or other device, esp one of the two levers that drive the chain wheel of a bicycle, the foot brake, clutch control, or accelerator of a car, पेडल One of the *pedals* of my bicycle is broken.

peddle *(v.)* पेडल– to go from place to place selling (goods, esp small articles) फेरी लगाना, घूम-घूमकर सौदा बेचना Ganesh *peddles* fruits and mangoes in small streets.

pedestrian *(n.)* पडेस्ट्रिअन– a person travelling on foot; walker पदगामी, पैदल

There are a lot of *pedestrians* in the morning hours.

pediatrician *(n.)* पीडिअट्रिशियन– a medical practitioner who specializes in paediatrics बच्चों का डाक्टर, बाल-रोग विशेषज्ञ Dr. Shakdhar is a well-reputed and qualified *pediatrician.*

pedlar *(n.)* पेड्लर्– a person who peddles; hawker फेरीवाला I bought this brush from a *pedlar* at the door.

pee *(n.)* पी– to urinate पेशाब करना I need to *pee.*

peek *(v.)* पीक्– to glance quickly or furtively; peep छिपकर देखना The children were *peeking* in the other room.

peel *(v.)* पील– 1. to remove (the skin, rind, outer covering, etc.) of a fruit, egg, etc. छीलना, छिलका उतारना I like to help my mother to *peel* potatoes. 2. *(n.)* the skin or rind of a fruit, etc. छिलका Throw the *peels* in the dustbin.

peep *(v.)* पीप– to look furtively or secretly, as through a small aperture or from a hidden place झाँकना I *peeped* into the room to see if there was anyone inside.

peer *(v.)* पिअर्– to look intently with or as if with difficulty ताकना The boy was *peering* the girl.

peer group *(n.)* पिअर ग्रुप– a social group composed of individuals of approximately the same age समकक्ष व्यक्तियों का समूह The children like to be with the *peer group* most of the time.

peevish *(adj.)* पीविश– fretful or irritable चिड़चिड़ा He remains *peevish* throughout the day

peg *(n.)* पे'ग– a small cylindrical pin or dowel, sometimes slightly tapered, used to join two parts together खूंटी The *peg* is broken.

pelt *(v.)* पेल्ट– to throw (missiles) at (a person) फेंककर मारना The protestors *pelted* stones at the authorities

pen *(n.)* पे'न– an implement for writing or drawing using ink, formerly consisting of a sharpened and split quill, and now of a metal nib attached to a holder क़लम, लेखनी I bought a *pen* for my son as a birthday gift.

penal *(adj.)* पीनल– of, relating to, constituting, or prescribing punishment दंड-विषयक, दंडात्मक The accused was punished by the *penal* system.

penalty *(n.)* पेनल्टि– a legal or official punishment, such as a term of imprisonment दंड, सजा, जुर्माना In this library, you have to pay a *penalty* for returning the book late.

penance *(n.)* पेनन्स– voluntary self-punishment to atone for a sin, crime, etc. तपस्या, तप Monks perform *penance* for almost their entire life.

pencil *(n.)* पेन्सिल– a thin cylindrical instrument used for writing, drawing, etc. consisting of a rod of graphite पेंसिल Have you sharpened your *pencil*?

pendant *(n.)* पेनडन्ट– an ornament that hangs from a piece of jewellery गले में लटकता हुआ एक सुंदर आभूषण, लटकन My mother has a beautiful diamond *pendant.*

pending *(adj.)* पेण्डिंग– not yet decided, confirmed, or finished विचाराधीन, लंबित There is a lot of *pending* work.

pendulum *(n.)* पेण्ड्युलम– a body mounted so that it can swing freely under the influence of gravity. लोलक, पेंडुलम I have a wall clock which contains *pendulum.*

penetrate *(v.)* पेनिट्रेट– to find or force a way into or through (something); pierce; enter छेदना, बेधना It's difficult to *penetrate* their circle of friends.

penetrating *(adj.)* पेनिट्रेटिंग–1. tending to or able to penetrate तेज़, उग्र

कर्णभेदी (आवाज़) She suffers from the *penetrating* noise in her neighbourhood.

2. tending to or able to penetrate पैनी, (मन के भावों को पढ़ने वाला) He was looking to me with his *penetrating* green eyes.

penfriend *(n.)* पेनफ्रेण्ड– a person with whom one regularly exchanges letters, often a person in another country whom one has not met पत्रमित्र Ayub was her *penfriend* when she was in hostel.

penguin *(n.)* पेन्ग्विन– a black and white bird that cannot fly and lives in Antarctica, (अंटार्कटिका क्षेत्र की एक समुद्री चिड़िया) पेंग्विन *Penguins* live in Antarctica.

peninsula *(n.)* पनिनसुला– a narrow strip of land projecting into a sea or lake from the mainland प्रायद्वीप Iraqi prisoners of war were assembled on the Al-Faw *peninsula.*

penitent *(adj.)* पेनिटण्ट– feeling regret for one's sins; repentant अनुतापी, पश्चात्ताप करने वाला He was not *penitent* about his mistake.

penknife *(n.)* पेन्नाइफ़– a small knife with one or more blades that fold into the handle; pocketknife चाकू I sharpened my pencil with a *penknife.*

penniless *(adj.)* पेनिलस– very poor; almost totally without money कंगाल, दरिद्र He became *penniless* after a very long time .

penny *(n.)* पेनि– a bronze coin having a value equal to one hundredth of a pound अंग्रेज़ी सिक्का, एक पैसा He started saving every single *penny.*

pension *(n.)* पेन्शन– a regular payment made by the state to people over a certain age to enable them to subsist without having to work पेंशन, निवृत्ति-वेतन How much *pension* does your father get?

pentagon *(n.)* पेण्टगन– a polygon having five sides पंचभुज It seems that the love square has now become a *pentagon.*

people *(n.)* पीपल्–1. persons collectively or in general लोग The railway platform was full of *people.*

2. a group of persons considered together जनसाधारण *People* say that we shall have a cold winter this year.

peon *(n.)* पीअन– farm labourer or unskilled worker चपरासी The *peon* is cleaning the office floor.

pepper *(n.)* पे'पर्– a woody climbing plant, Piper nigrum, of the East Indies, having small black berry-like fruits, used to give a hot flavour to food काली मिर्च The dish became tastier with a tinge of *pepper.*

peppermint *(n.)* पे'पर्मिण्ट– a temperate mint plant with purple or white flowers, used to give flavour to food (एक प्राकृतिक पदार्थ पिपटमिंट जो ज़ायक़ा देता है) पिपरमिंट *Peppermint* is mostly used in sweets.

per *(prep.)* पर– by; through के अनुसार, प्रति The work has been done as *per* your instruction.

per capita *(adj.)* पर-कैपिटा– of or for each person प्रतिवर्ष, प्रतिव्यक्ति The *per capita* income of the country has been on a decline.

perceive *(v.)* परसीव–1. to become aware of (something) through the senses, देखना, जानना How do you *perceive* this problem?

2. to come to comprehend; grasp विशेष दृष्टि से समझना एवं सोचना I could *perceive* from his appearance that he was a foreigner.

3. to notice पता चलना, बोध होना I *perceived* a drastic change in her behaviour.

per cent *(n.)* a percentage or proportion प्रतिशत They carried out their plan 100 *per cent. (adj.)* in or for every hundred % प्रति सैकड़ा का एक भाग In India, 84 *per cent* have a television and 80 *per cent* own a mobile phone.

percentage *(n.)* परसेंटिज– proportion or rate per hundred parts प्रतिशतता She scored a high *percentage* of marks in the examinations.

perceptible *(adj.)* परसेपटबल– able to be perceived; noticeable or recognizable दिखाई देने वाला, गोचर The change in his behavior was quite *perceptible*.

perception *(n.)* परसेप्शन– insight or intuition gained by perceiving प्रत्यक्ष ज्ञान, बोध His *perception* about life changed after the accident.

perceptive *(adj.)* परसेपटिव– quick at perceiving; observant ज्ञान-विषयक, बोधगम्य The lawyer made a *perceptive* comment in the court which was appreciated by all.

perch *(v.)* पर्च– 1. to alight, rest, or cause to rest on or as if on a perch टिकना, बैठना The cuckoo *perched* on a tree branch and sang melodiously.
2. *(n.)* a pole, branch, or other resting place above ground on which a bird roosts or alights शाखा, पक्षी के बैठने का स्थान The bird sang sweetly from its *perch* on the tree.

perennial *(adj.)* पेरेनिअल– lasting throughout the year or through many years स्थायी, सदा रहने वाला, बारहमासी I saw that there was a *perennial* problem of water shortage in her village.

perfect *(adj.)* परफ़ेक्ट– having all essential elements आदर्श, सही Can you make a *perfect* copy of this design?

perfection *(n.)* परफ़ेक्शन– the act of perfecting or the state or quality of being perfect परिपूर्णता, पराकाष्ठा The actor Aamir Khan achieves *perfection* in all his roles.

perfectly *(adv.)* परफेक्टलि– completely, utterly, or absolutely पूर्णतः, पूरी तरह से Gita is *perfectly* well now.

perforate *(v.)* परफ़रेट– to make a hole or holes in (something); penetrate छेद कर देना, पैठना, घुसना The banking collapse *perforated* the economies of many countries.

perform *(v.)* परफ़ॉर्म–1. to carry out or do (an action) पालन करना, पूरा करना I always *perform* my duties sincerely.
2. to present or enact (a play, concert, etc.) before or otherwise entertain an audience अभिनय करना All the actors *performed* their roles remarkably in the play.

performance *(n.)* परफ़ॉर्मेन्स–1. the act, process, or art of performing अभिनय, प्रदर्शन My son was appreciated for his good *performance* in the school play.
2. manner or quality of functioning कार्य, क्रिया, निष्पत्ति What is the country's economic *performance*?

performer *(n.)* परफ़ॉर्मर– a person who performs a musical or dramatic piece or another form of entertainment in front of others अदाकार, प्रदर्शक The script requires a good stage *performer*.

perfume *(n.)* परफ़्यूम– 1. a mixture of alcohol and fragrant essential oils extracted from flowers, spices, etc. or made synthetically इत्र, इतर, सुगन्ध, खुशबू She wears a very pleasing *perfume*.
2. *(v.)* to impart a *perfume* to इतर लगाना, खुशबू लगाना She *perfumed* her hanky before putting it in the purse.

perhaps *(adv.)* पर्हैप्स– possibly; maybe शायद, कदाचित् *Perhaps* there might be another angle to the story.

peril *(n.)* पेरिल– exposure to risk or harm; danger or jeopardy जोखिम, ख़तरा You will go down this path at your *peril* .

perimeter *(n.)* पेरिमिटर– the curve or line enclosing a plane area घेरा, परिधि, परिमाप Please find out the *perimeter* of this ground.

period *(n.)* पीरिअड्–1. a portion of time of indefinable length अवधि, मुद्दत We lived for a short *period* in Agra before shifting to Delhi.
2. a portion of time specified in some way युग, काल The *period* of Chandragupta Maurya was the golden age of Indian history.
3. a division of time, esp of the academic day घंटा My son has seven *periods* in school.

periodic *(adj.)* पीरिऑडिक– happening or recurring at intervals; intermittent नियतकालिक, मियादी The sales of his company are periodic.

periodical *(n.)* पीरिऑडिकल– a publication issued at regular intervals, usually monthly or weekly पत्रिका He is the publisher of *TIME*–a periodical magazine.

peripheral *(adj.)* परिफ़रल– not relating to the most important part of something; incidental, minor, or superficial गौण, कम महत्त्व का Parents should not give *peripheral* vision to their children.

perish *(v.)* पेरिश– to be destroyed or die, esp in an untimely way नष्ट हो जाना, मर जाना Every passenger *perished* in the plane crash.

perishable *(adj.)* पेरिशबल– liable to rot or wither नाशवान, नश्वर, खराब होने वाला, बिगड़ने वाला Canned juices are *perishable*.

perjury *(n.)* परजरी– the offence committed by a witness in judicial proceedings who, having been lawfully sworn or having affirmed, wilfully gives false evidence झूठी गवाही The witness committed *perjury* in the court.

perk *(n.)* पर्क– pert; brisk; lively नियत वेतन के अतिरिक्त प्राप्त अन्य लाभ *Perks* offered to him by the company include a bike and free health insurance.

permanent *(adj.)* पर्मनन्ट–1. not expected to change for an indefinite time; not temporary स्थायी Have you been made *permanent* in your job?
2. existing or intended to exist for an indefinite period काफ़ी अर्से तक चलने वाला Is this temporary arrangement or a *permanent* one?

permanently *(adv.)* पर्मनेंट्ली– for ever सदा के लिए, स्थायी रूप से The job has been finished per*manently*.

permissible *(adj.)* परमिसिबल– permitted; allowable स्वीकार्य, उचित The evidence is *permissible* in the court.

permission *(n.)* परमिशन– authorization to do something इजाज़त, अनुमति, आज्ञा Do I have *permission* to use your pen?

permissive *(adj.)* परमिसिव– tolerant; lenient ज़रूरत से ज़्यादा स्वीकृति या छूट Her parents are too *permissive*.

permit *(v.)* परमिट– o grant permission to do something अनुमति देना Please *permit* me to go home early.

peroxide *(n.)* पराक्साइड– short for hydrogen peroxide, esp when used for bleaching hair एक रंगहीन द्रव She used *peroxide* to bleach her hair.

perpendicular *(adj.)* पर्पनडिक्यलर– at right angles to a horizontal plane लंब, अभिलंब The Maths teacher told students to draw a *perpendicular* line.

perpetrate *(v.)* पर्पिट्रेट– to perform or be responsible for (a deception, crime, etc.) ग़लत काम करना They *perpetrate* a crime against women

perpetual *(adj.)* पर्पेचुअल– eternal; permanent अविरल, अनन्त, नित्य There was a *perpetual* smile on her lips.

perplexed *(adj.)* पर्प्लेक्स्ड– confused and worried हतबुद्धि, व्याकुल The problem *perplexed* everyone.

per se *(adv.)* पर से– by or in itself; intrinsically स्वतः, अपने आप The theme of the novel was interesting *per se,* but the language was bad.

persecute *(v.)* पर्सिक्यूट– to oppress, harass, or maltreat, esp because of race, religion, etc. सताना, अत्याचार करना Hitler *persecuted* Jews mercilessly during the Second World War.

persecution *(n.)* पर्सिक्यूशन– the act of persecuting or the state of being persecuted अत्याचार, उत्पीड़न Religious *persecution* was common all over the world in the past.

perseverance *(n.)* पर्सिविअरन्स– continued steady belief or efforts, withstanding discouragement or difficulty; persistence निरंतर परिश्रम, दृढ़ता He succeeded through sheer *perseverance.*

persevere *(v.)* पर्सिविअर्– to show perseverance दृढ़ रहना, करते रहना Soldiers always *persevere* during wars.

persist *(v.)* पर्सिस्ट– to continue steadfastly or obstinately despite opposition or difficulty अड़ जाना, करते रहना The pain in my head *persists* even after taking medication.

persistent *(adj.)* पर्सिसटन्ट– incessantly repeated; unrelenting जिद्दी, दृढ़, अटल, कृतसंकल्प He was *persistent* about going to the movies.

person *(n.)* पर्सन–1. an individual human being व्यक्ति When I reached the office, two *persons* were waiting for me.

➢ **in person**– actually present स्वयं उपस्थित, आमने- सामने, I came *in person* to attend to this important matter.

personal *(adj.)* पर्सनल– of or relating to the private aspects of a person's life व्यक्तिगत, निजी The fight between them is due to some *personal* reasons.

personalize (ise) *(v.)* पर्सनलाइज़– to endow with personal or individual qualities or characteristics व्यक्तिगत बना लेना This towel is *personalized* with her initials.

personality *(n.)* पर्सनैलिटी–1. the distinctive character of a person that makes him socially attractive व्यक्तित्व He has a charming *personality.* 2. a well-known person in a certain field, such as sport or entertainment प्रसिद्ध व्यक्ति Tagore was an unmatched *personality.*

personally *(adv.)* पर्सनली– without the help or intervention of others स्वयं, निजी रूप से *Personally* I don't care if you win or lose.

personify *(v.)* पर्सनिफ़ाइ– to attribute human characteristics to (a thing or abstraction) मानवीकरण करना In Hinduism, Ganga is *personified* as a goddess.

personnel *(n.)* पर्सनेल– the people employed in an organization or for a service or undertaking कर्मचारीगण We need some more technical *personnel* in the department.

perspective *(n.)* पर्स्पेक्टिव– a way of regarding situations, facts, etc, and judging their relative importance दृष्टिकोण, मत A problem should be analyzed from his *perspective* as well.

perspiration *(n.)* पर्स्पिरेशन– the act or process of insensibly eliminating fluid through the pores of the skin, which evaporates immediately पसीना

Beads of *perspiration* rolled down the labourer's face.

perspire *(v.)* पर्स्पाइअर– to secrete or exude (perspiration) through the pores of the skin पसीना आना Why are you *perspiring* in cold weather?

persuade *(v.)* पर्स्वेड– to induce, urge, or prevail upon successfully समझाना, राज़ी करना I'm trying to *persuade* him to stop drinking.

persuasion *(n.)* परस्वेशन–1. an established creed or belief, esp a religious one धारणा, मत People of different religious *persuasions* live in India.

2. Pthe act of persuading or of trying to persuade समझाव-बुझाव, मनाने की क्रिया It took a lot of *persuasion* to get Mohini to agree.

persuasive *(adj.)* पर्स्वेसिव– having the power or ability to persuade; tending to persuade प्रभावपूर्ण, प्रत्यायी Some people are *persuasive* in nature.

pertinent *(adj.)* पर्टिनन्ट– relating to the matter at hand; relevant प्रासंगिक She had raised a *pertinent* question in her article.

perturb *(v.)* पर्टर्ब– to disturb the composure of; trouble चिंतित होना We were very *perturbed* because of his injury.

peruse *(v.)* परूज़– to read or examine with care; study अवलोकन करना *Peruse* the story well to detect the errors.

pervade *(v.)* पर्वेड्– to spread through or throughout, esp subtly or gradually; permeate व्याप्त होना God *pervades* everywhere.

perverse *(adj.)* पर्वर्स्– deliberately deviating from what is regarded as normal, good, or proper पथभ्रष्ट, पतित, दुष्ट Neha is a *perverse* child and takes pleasure in upsetting her parents.

perversion *(n.)* परवर्शन्– the act of perverting or the state of being perverted विकृत प्रवृत्ति, विकृति, विकृत रूप She gave a *perversion* of the truth to her mother.

pervert *(v.)* पर्वर्ट्– to lead into deviant or perverted beliefs or behaviour; corrupt भ्रष्ट कर देना My father believes that watching TV can *pervert* the minds of children.

pessimist *(n.)* पेसिमिस्ट– one who always expects bad things to happen निराशावादी He was a *pessimist* in his entire life

pest *(n.)* पे'स्ट्–1. any organism that damages crops, injures or irritates livestock or man, or reduces the fertility of land कीट, पशु, पक्षी आदि The farmer sprayed the pesticides to kill the *pests*.

2. a person or thing that annoys, esp by imposing itself when it is not wanted; nuisance चिढ़ पैदा करने वाला व्यक्ति Her son is quite a *pest*.

pester *(v.)* पे'स्टर्– to annoy or nag continually परेशान करना The children *pestered* the teacher with a lot of questions.

pesticide *(n.)* पेसटिसाइड– a chemical used for killing pests, esp insects and rodents कीटनाशक पदार्थ *Pesticides* are very important for agricultural sustainability.

pet *(n.)* पे'ट– a tame animal kept in a household for companionship, amusement, etc. पालतू पशु We have two *pets*, a dog and a cat.

petal *(n.)* पे'टल– any of the separate parts of the corolla of a flower: often brightly coloured पंखुड़ी In the flower show, I saw roses with big *petals*.

petition *(n.)* पेटिशन– a written document signed by a large number of people demanding some form of action from a government or other authority आवेदन, याचिका, अर्ज़ी The people of the locality sent a *petition* to the mayor asking for adequate supply of drinking water.

petrified *(adj.)* पेट्रिफ़ाइड्– stunned or dazed with horror, fear, etc. अत्यधिक भयभीत I was *petrified* when I saw a snake.

petrol *(n.)* पेट्रोल– any one of various volatile flammable liquid mixtures of hydrocarbons, mainly hexane, heptane, and octane, obtained from petroleum and used as a solvent and a fuel for internal-combustion engines पेट्रोल Do you have enough *petrol* in your car for a long trip?

petroleum *(n.)* पेट्रोलियम– a dark-coloured thick flammable crude oil खनिज तेल *Petroleum* is a source of various important fuels.

pet subject *(n.)* पेट-सब्जेक्ट– particularly cherished; favourite प्रिय विषय English Literature is my *pet subject.*

petticoat *(n.)* पेटिकोट– a woman's light undergarment in the form of an underskirt or including a bodice supported by shoulder straps साया, लहँगा, घाघरा His mother wears lacy *petticoats.*

pettish *(adj.)* पैटइश– peevish; petulant बदमिज़ाज, चिड़चिड़ा Small children are very *pettish* in nature.

petty *(adj.)* पैटि–1. of lesser importance क्षुद्र, तुच्छ Why are you quarrelling over such a *petty* thing?
2. minor or subordinate in rank छोटे स्तर का, मामूली Pramod is a *petty* shopkeeper.

phantom *(n.)* फ़ैण्टम– the visible representation of something abstract, esp as appearing in a dream or hallucination भूत-प्रेत I don't believe in the existence of *phantoms.*

pharmaceutical *(adj.)* फ़ार्मस्यूटिकल– of or relating to drugs or pharmacy औषधि निर्माण संबंधी Mankind is an emerging *pharmaceutical* company of India.

pharmacy *(n.)* फ़ार्मसी– a dispensary औषधालय Every hospital has a *pharmacy.*

phase *(n.)* फेज़– any distinct or characteristic period or stage in a sequence of events or chain of development (किसी वस्तु के विकास की) अवस्था या चरण Their relationship was going through a bad *phase.*

phenomenal *(adj.)* फ़नॉमिनल्– extraordinary; outstanding; remarkable असाधारण, चमत्कारिक She played a *phenomenal* role in taking the company to new heights.

phenomenon *(n.)* फ़नॉमिनन्– anything that can be perceived as an occurrence or fact by the senses प्राकृतिक या सामाजिक घटना The arrival of monsoon is a natural *phenomenon.*

philanthropist *(n.)* फ़िलैनथ्रपिस्ट– someone who freely gives help and money to people who need it परोपकारी व्यक्ति Michael Jackson was not only a singer but a great *philanthropist.*

philosopher *(n.)* फ़लासफ़र– a person who establishes the ideology of a cult or movement दार्शनिक Dr. Radhakrishnan was a noted *philosopher.*

philosophy *(n.)* फ़'लॉसफ़ी– the critical study of the basic principles and concepts of a discipline तत्त्वज्ञान, दर्शन (शास्त्र) I was a student of *philosophy* in college.

phlegm *(n.)* फ़्लेम– the viscid mucus secreted by the walls of the respiratory tract कफ़, बलग़म She has got severe cold and is coughing up *phlegm.*

phlegmatic *(adj.)* फ़्लेगमैटिक– having a stolid or unemotional disposition

शांत, स्थिरबुद्धि Rita has a *phlegmatic* temperament.

phobia *(n.)* फ़ोबिआ– an abnormal intense and irrational fear of a given situation, organism, or object (किसी वस्तु के प्रति अत्यधिक) भय He has *a phobia* of spiders.

phone *(n.)* फ़ोन– an electrical device for transmitting speech, consisting of a microphone and receiver mounted on a handset फ़ोन Can I use your *phone*?

phonetic *(adj.)* फ़ोनेटिक– of or relating to phonetics ध्वन्यात्मक Sanskrit has *phonetic* spellings unlike English.

photocopy *(n.)* फ़ोटोकॉपी– a photographic reproduction of written, printed, or graphic work प्रतिलिपि The *photocopy* of your documents is not clear enough.

photograph *(n.)* फ़ोटोग्राफ़– an image of an object, person, scene, etc. फ़ोटो I lost all my *photographs* of the trip we took together.

photographer *(n.)* फ़ोटोग्राफ़र– a person who takes photographs, either as a hobby or a profession छाया चित्रकार Prem is a *photographer* by profession.

photographic *(adj.)* फ़ोटग्रैफ़िक– of or relating to photography फोटोग्राफ़ संबंधी A *photographic* contest took place recently in my city.

photography *(n.)* फ़ोटोग्रैफ़ी– the art, practice, or occupation of taking and printing photographs, making cine films, etc. छाया चित्रकारी Roohi is good at *photography*.

phrase *(n.)* फ़्रेज़– a group of words forming an immediate syntactic constituent of a clause वाक्यांश He is fond of using idiomatic *phrases* in his speeches.

physical *(adj.)* फ़िज़िकल– of or relating to the body, as distinguished from the mind or spirit शारीरिक His *physical* fitness was always questionable.

physically *(adv.)* फ़िज़िकली– in a way that involves the body rather than the mind शारीरिक दृष्टि से The girl was *physically* handicapped.

physician *(n.)* फ़िज़िशन– a person legally qualified to practise medicine, esp one specializing in areas of treatment other than surgery; doctor of medicine वैद्य, डॉक्टर Is there a *physician* nearby?

physics *(n.)* फ़िज़िक्स– the branch of science concerned with the properties of matter and energy and the relationships between them भौतिक-विज्ञान Naheed is a lecturer in *physics*.

physiology *(n.)* फ़िज़िआलजी– the branch of science concerned with the functioning of organisms शरीर-विज्ञान *Physiology* is concerned with the study of the functions of the human body.

physiotherapist *(n.)* फ़िज़िओथेरपिस्ट– प्राकृतिक- someone who is trained in the therapeutic use of physical agents or means, such as massage, exercises, etc. चिकित्सा विशेषज्ञ The doctor advised me to consult a *physiotherapist* for cervical pain.

physiotherapy *(n.)* फ़िज़िओथेरपी– the therapeutic use of physical agents or means, such as massage, exercises, etc. व्यायाम, ताप एवं बिजली द्वारा की जाने वाली चिकित्सा *Physiotherapy* is good for physical disability.

physique *(n.)* फ़िज़ीक– the general appearance of the body with regard to size, shape, muscular development, etc. शरीर का गठन, डील-डौल A good *physique* always enhances a person's look.

pianist *(n.)* पिअनिस्ट– a person who plays the piano पियानो बजाने वाला

Arthur Rubinstein is a world famous *pianist.*

pick *(v.)* पिक–1. to remove loose particles from उठाना Please *pick* up those pieces of paper.

2. to choose (something) deliberately or carefully, from or as if from a group or number; select चुनना Please *pick* a good book for me.

- **pick a fight**– to persuade a fight intentionally जानबूझ कर लड़ना- झगड़ना, लड़ाई मोल लेना, He was trying to *pick a fight* with his neighbour.
- **pick a lock**– bleach बिना चाबी के ताला खोलना, It is not easy to *pick the lock* on my car door.
- **pick and choose**– to select fastidiously, fussily, etc. मनपसंद चीज़ें चुनना, You can *pick and choose* from this shop.
- **pick-pocket**– a person who steals from the pockets or handbags of others in public places किसी की जेब काटना, पैसे चुराना, An ugly man *pickedpocket* my purse in the bus.
- **pick your way**– to raise (oneself) after a fall or setback सावधानी से क़दम रखना, He *picked his way* down the slippery staircase.

pickle *(n.)* पिकल्– vegetables, such as cauliflowers, onions, etc. preserved in vinegar, brine, etc. अचार Indian *pickles* have become popular abroad.

pickpocket *(n.)* पिकपॉकेट– a person who steals from the pockets or handbags of others in public places जेबकतरा Today, I saw a *pickpocket* in the bus.

picky *(adj.)* पिकी– fussy; finicky; choosy नख़रेबाज़, मीनमेख़ वाला He is very *picky* about his projects.

picnic *(n.)* पिकनिक–1. a trip or excursion to the country, seaside, etc. on which people bring food to be eaten in the open air वनभोज, वनविहार Our class went on a *picnic* last Sunday.

picture *(n.)* पिक्चर्–1. a visual representation of something, such as a person or scene, produced on a surface, as in a photograph, painting, etc. चित्र, तस्वीर His drawing room is decorated with beautiful *pictures.*

2. *(v.)* to visualize or imagine छवि बनाना Try to *picture* the clouds in the empty sky.

picturesque *(adj.)* पिक्चरेस्क– visually pleasing, esp in being striking or vivid आकर्षक Kashmir has *picturesque* mountains.

piece *(n.)* पीस– an amount or portion forming a separate mass or structure; bit टुकड़ा, अंश The dress was torn into small little *pieces.*

pierce *(n.)* पिअर्स– to form or cut (a hole) in (something) with or as if with a sharp instrument छेदना, भेदना These days, many girls have their noses *pierced* so that they may wear nose-rings.

piercing *(adj.)* पिअर्सिंग– (of a sound) sharp and shrill ज़ोरदार, तेज़ I heard a *piercing* cry outside my house.

piety *(n.)* पायअटी– dutiful devotion to God and observance of religious principles श्रद्धा, भक्ति *Piety* is the virtue of a saint.

pig *(n.)* पिग– an animal with a broad nose, brown skin, short legs and a short tail सूअर There are some *pigs* sleeping in the sty.

pigeon *(n.)* पिजिन– a grey and white bird with short legs and long pointed wings कबूतर *Pigeon* is the symbol of peace.

piggy bank *(n.)* पिगी बैंक– a child's coin bank shaped like a pig with a slot for coins बच्चों की गोलक The child dropped the one-rupee coin in the *piggy bank.*

pigheaded *(adj.)* पिग-हेडिड– obstinate, stubborn अड़ियल The child was *pigheaded* enough not to acknowledge his mistake.

pigmentation *(n.)* पिगमेंटेशन– colouration in plants, animals, or man caused by the presence of pigments रंजकता, वर्णकता Few girls have acne and *pigmentation* on their face.

pigtail *(n.)* पिगटेल– a bunch of hair or one of two bunches on either side of the face, worn loose or plaited लंबी चोटी The girl has one swinging *pigtail* on her head.

pile *(n.)* पाइल– 1. a collection of objects laid on top of one another or of other material stacked vertically; heap; mound ढेर, राशि Please give this *pile* of dirty clothes to the washerman.
2. *(v.)* to collect or be collected into or as if into a pile ढेर लगाना She *piled* up all her clothes on the bed before packing them.

pilgrim *(n.)* पिलग्रिम– a person who undertakes a journey to a sacred place as an act of religious devotion तीर्थयात्री During my trip to Amarnath, I saw many *pilgrims* making the journey to the holy cave barefoot.

pilgrimage *(n.)* पिलग्रिमेज– a journey to a shrine or other sacred place तीर्थयात्रा The *pilgrimage* to Makkah (Mecca) is considered to be very tough.

pill *(n.)* पिल– a small spherical mass of a medicinal substance, intended to be swallowed whole गोली Nowadays there is a *pill* for almost every ailment.

pillar *(n.)* पिलर्– an upright structure of stone, brick, metal, etc. that supports a superstructure or is used for ornamentation खम्भा The *pillar* has rusted and is in dire need of maintenance.

pillow *(n.)* पिलो– a cloth case stuffed with feathers, foam rubber, etc. used to support the head, esp during sleep तकिया I need two *pillows* to sleep.

pillowcase *(n.)* पिलोकेस– a removable washable cover of cotton, linen, nylon, etc. for a pillow तकिया का ग़िलाफ़ I brought two pairs of satin *pillowcases.*

pilot *(n.)* पाइलट– 1. a person who is qualified to operate an aircraft or spacecraft in flight विमान-चालक, पायलट My son is a *pilot* in the Indian Airlines.
2. *(v.)* to act as pilot of जहाज़ चलाना He *piloted* the ship very carefully through the storm.

pimple *(n.)* पिंपल– a small round usually inflamed swelling of the skin मुँहासा She fumed over the *pimple* she got on her face.

pin *(n.)* पिन्– 1. abbreviation for personal identification number; PIN number पिन नंबर Specify the *PIN* code on the letter.
2. *(v.)* पिन– to attach, hold, or fasten with or as if with a pin or pins पिन लगाना, नत्थी करना Please *pin* these sheets of paper together.
3. *(n.)* a spring wire clasp with a covering catch, made so as to shield the point when closed and to prevent accidental unfastening धातु का पिन I need a safety *pin.*

pincer *(n.)* पिनसर– (also ***pincers***) one of a pair of jointed grasping appendages in lobsters and certain other arthropods चिमटी, संडसी Indian women cook breads with the help of a *pincer.*

pinch *(v.)* पिंच– 1. to press (something, esp flesh) tightly between two surfaces, esp between a finger and the thumb चिकोटी काटना I cried out in pain when he *pinched* my arm.
2. *(n.)* a very small quantity चुटकीभर Please put a *pinch* of salt in this curry.

pine *(n.)* a tree with leaves like needles चीड़, देवदारु, देवदार I saw *pine* forests in Nainital.

pineapple *(n.)* पाइनूऐपल– a tropical fruit with thick skin and sweet yellow flesh अनन्नास का फल *Pineapple* is a juicy fruit which has thick covering.

ping *(n.)* पिंग– a short high-pitched resonant sound, as of a bullet striking metal or a sonar echo पटाक, तड़-तड़ की आवाज़ The cooker went *ping* when the food was ready.

pinnacle *(n.)* पिनकल– the highest point or level, esp of fame, success, etc. शिखर, चोटी Ronita is at the *pinnacle* of her career.

pink *(adj.)* पिंक– any of a group of colours with a reddish hue that are of low to moderate saturation and can usually reflect or transmit a large amount of light; a pale reddish tint गुलाबी Jaipur is called the *Pink* City.

pinpoint *(v.)* पिनूपॉइन्ट– to locate or identify exactly किसी बात का सही-सही निरूपण करना Everyone in the room was trying to *pinpoint* the problem

pioneer *(n.)* पाइअनिअर्– a colonist, explorer, or settler of a new land, region, etc. अगुआ, अग्रसर Every industry has a *pioneer* who leads the change.

pious *(adj.)* पाइअस– having or expressing reverence for a God or gods; religious; devout धर्मपरायण My grandmother is a very *pious* lady.

pipe *(n.)* पाइप–1. a long tube of metal, plastic, etc. used to convey water, oil, gas, etc. नल, नली Even in olden days, water was carried through underground *pipes.*

2. an object made in any of various shapes and sizes, consisting of a small bowl with an attached tubular stem, in which tobacco or other substances are smoked चिलम Do you smoke a *pipe*?

pipeline *(n.)* पाइपलाइन– a long pipe, esp underground, used to transport oil, natural gas, etc. over long distances ज़मीन के अंदर बिछी हुई नलियां या पाइप Gas *pipelines* pass through 8 Indian states for industrial and domestic applications.

piping *(adj.)* पाइपिंग– making a shrill sound चिंघाड़, तेज़ चीख़ निकालने वाला A *piping* voice of a beaten child irritates me a lot.

piping hot *(adj.)* extremely hot बहुत गर्म, गरमागरम I was drinking a *piping hot* coffee.

piracy *(n.)* पाइरसी– the unauthorized use or appropriation of patented or copyrighted material, ideas, etc. साहित्यिक चोरी *Piracy* is illegal and punishable by law.

pirate *(n.)* पाइरेट– a person who commits piracy साहित्य की चोरी करने वाला व्यक्ति The *pirate* video cassettes are commonly available in the market.

piss *(v.)* पिस– to urinate पेशाब करना Babies *piss* in the diapers.

pistol *(n.)* पिसटल– a short-barrelled handgun तमंचा *Pistols* are now old-fashioned for criminals.

piston *(n.)* पिसटन– a disc or cylindrical part that slides to and fro in a hollow cylinder पिस्टन, मुषली The *piston* while moving up and down causes other parts of the engine to move.

pit *(n.)* पिट– a large, usually deep opening in the ground गड्ढा There was a huge *pit* in the middle of the jungle.

pitch *(n.)* पिच–1. (in many sports) the field of play खेल-पट्टी The rains dampened the cricket *pitch.*

2. the auditory property of a note that is conditioned by its frequency relative to other notes स्वर की ऊंचाई

का स्तर The children were shouting at a high *pitch*.

pitch-black *(adj.)* पिच-ब्लैक– extremely dark; unlit गहरा काला, एकदम गुप अँधेरा There was a *pitch-black* room in his house which frightened me.

pitcher *(n.)* पिचर्– a large jug, घड़ा, सुराही Do you have some water in that *pitcher*?

piteous *(adj.)* पिटिअस– exciting or deserving pity दयनीय Beggars on the street are always in *piteous* condition.

pitfall *(n.)* पिटफ़ाल– an unsuspected difficulty or danger झमेला, ख़तरा The *pitfalls* of pursuing this project are grave.

pith *(n.)* पिथ– the soft fibrous tissue lining the inside of the rind in fruits such as the orange and grapefruit फ़ल का गूदा The *pith* of watermelon was lying on the road.

pitiful *(adj.)* पिटिफुल– arousing or deserving pity करुणाजनक Hearing the *pitiful* groans of a wounded soldier, she fainted immediately.

pitiless *(adj.)* पिटिलस– having or showing little or no pity or mercy निर्दयी, बेरहम A *pitiless* killer remained 34 years in jail after savage murder of kids in UK.

pittance *(adj.)* पिटन्स– a small amount or portion, esp a meagre allowance of money अल्पवेतन She raised her children on *pittance*.

pity *(n.)* पिटि– sympathy or sorrow felt for the sufferings of another करुणा, दया He felt *pity* on the sick children.

pivot *(n.)* पिवट– a short shaft or pin supporting something that turns; fulcrum धुरी, चूल Ahmedabad is the *pivot* of the cotton trade in India.

placard *(n.)* प्लैकार्ड– a printed or written notice for public display; poster इश्तहार, विज्ञापन "We want justice" read the *placard* in the woman's hand.

place *(v.)* प्लेस– 1. to put or set in a particular or appropriate place रख देना *Place* the box in this corner.
2. *(n.)* a geographical point, such as a town, city, etc. स्थान, जगह Is there any quiet *place* where we can talk?

➢ **in place**– bat appropriate place सही स्थान पर, Dinner is ready, and everything is *in place*.

➢ **in place of**-- bin exchange for बजाय, Please give me new chair *in place of* the old chair.

➢ **out of place**– at a wrong place ग़लत स्थान पर, Nothing was *out of place* in her kitchen.

➢ **take place**– to happen or occur घटित होना, The First World War *took place* between 1914-1919.

placid *(adj.)* प्लेसिड– having a calm appearance or nature शांत, गंभीर His *placid* mind makes him more energetic.

plagiarism *(n.)* प्लेजरिज़म– something plagiarized साहित्यिक चोरी The author was alleged of *plagiarism*.

plague *(n.)* प्लेग्– any widespread and usually highly contagious disease with a high fatality rate महामारी, ताऊन, प्लेग Many people in Surat died of *plague*.

plain *(n.)* प्लेन– 1. a level or almost level tract of country, esp an extensive treeless region मैदान A fierce battle was fought on this *plain* once upon a time.
2. *(adj.)* not complicated; clear सरस, सुस्पष्ट My instructions to you were quite *plain*.
3. without pattern or of simple untwilled weave सादा My wife likes to wear a *plain* white dress.
4. not attractive असुन्दर, कुरूप Our neighbour's wife is rather *plain-looking*.

plainly *(adv.)* प्लेनली– you use 'plainly' to indicate that something is easily seen, noticed, or recognized साफ़-साफ़ He *plainly* refused to help the needy.

plaintiff *(n.)* प्लेनटिफ़– a person who brings a civil action in a court of law मुद्दई, वादी The landlord is the *plaintiff*.

plaintive *(adj.)* प्लेनटिव– expressing melancholy; mournful दुखी, करुण We heard her *plaintive* voice.

plait *(n.)* प्लैट– a length of hair, ribbon, etc. that has been plaited बालों की चोटी She always ties her hair in two *plaits*.

plan *(n.)* प्लान–1. a detailed scheme, method, etc. for attaining an objective योजना What are your *plans* for the summer holidays?
2. an outline, sketch, etc. नक़्शा Have you submitted the *plan* of your proposed house to the municipality?
3. *(v.)* to form a plan (for) or make plans (for) योजना बनाना, इरादा करना When are you *planning* to get married?

plane *(n.)* प्लेन–1. a wing or supporting surface of an aircraft or hydroplane विमान I went to Mumbai by *plane*.
2. a tool with a blade, used for making the surface of wood smooth रन्दा A carpenter cannot work without a *plane*.

planet *(n.)* प्लैनिट– any of the eight celestial bodies, Mercury, Venus, Earth, Mars, Jupiter, Saturn, Uranus, and Neptune, that revolve around the Sun ग्रह The Earth is one of the *planets* in the solar system.

plank *(n.)* प्लैंक– a stout length of sawn timber तख़्ता, पटरा The army built a *plank* to cross the river.

planner *(n.)* प्लैनर– a chart for recording future appointments, tasks, goals, etc. तिथियों वाली पुस्तकनुमा डायरी A diary *planner* was distributed to every employee in the office.

plant *(v.)* प्लाण्ट– 1. to set (seeds, crops, etc.) into (ground) to grow पौधा लगाना, रोपना Which flower trees have you *planted* in your garden?
2. *(n.)* any living organism that typically synthesizes its food from inorganic substances, possesses cellulose cell walls, responds slowly and often permanently to a stimulus पौधा, वनस्पति This is an evergreen *plant*.

plantation *(n.)* प्लानटेशन– a group of cultivated trees or plants बाग़ान, वृक्ष-वाटिका During our trip to Darjeeling, we visited a tea *plantation*.

plaster *(n.)* प्लास्टर्– 1. a mixture of lime, sand, and water, sometimes stiffened with hair or other fibres, that is applied to the surface of a wall or ceiling as a soft paste that hardens when dry पलस्तर The *plaster* of the wall was chipped.
2. *(v.)* to apply like plaster (टूटी हड्डी पर) पलस्तर चढ़ाना The doctor *plastered* his broken leg.

plastic *(n.)* प्लास्टिक– any one of a large number of synthetic usually organic materials that have a polymeric structure and can be moulded when soft and then set प्लास्टिक Many household articles are made of *plastic*.

plastic surgery *(n.)* प्लास्टिक् सर्जरी– the branch of surgery concerned with therapeutic or cosmetic repair or reformation of missing, injured, or malformed tissues or parts शरीर के कुरूप भाग को सही रूप देने की शल्य-क्रिया She wanted to undergo *plastic surgery* of her face after the accident.

plate *(n.)* प्लेट–1. a shallow usually circular dish made of porcelain, earthenware, glass, etc. on which food is served or from which food is eaten थाली, रकाबी He brought some sweets in a *plate*.

2. *(v.)* to coat (a surface, usually metal) with a thin layer of other metal by electrolysis, chemical reaction, etc. मुलम्मा चढ़ाना My wrist-watch is gold-*plated*.

plateau *(n.)* प्लैटो– a wide mainly level area of elevated land पठार, समतल भूमि The Deccan *Plateau* is a large plateau in India.

platform *(n.)* प्लैटफ़ॉर्म– a raised area at a railway station, from which passengers have access to the trains प्लेटफ़ार्म The train will arrive on *platform* number.

platinum *(n.)* प्लैटिनम– a ductile malleable silvery-white metallic element, very resistant to heat and chemicals. (सफ़ेद रंग की कीमती धातु जिसमें आभूषण बनते हैं) प्लैटिनम Rajesh gave a *platinum* ring to his wife on her birthday.

platonic *(adj.)* प्लटॉनिक– free from physical desire कामनारहित, निष्काम They say that their love is *platonic*.

platoon *(n.)* प्लटून– a subunit of a company usually comprising three sections of ten to twelve men: commanded by a lieutenant सैनिक टुकड़ी, पलटन The General was instructed to train a *platoon* of men.

plausible *(adj.)* पलॉज़बल– apparently reasonable, valid, truthful, etc. तर्कसंगत We were all waiting for him to give us a *plausible* explanation.

play *(n.)* प्ले–1. a dramatic composition written for performance by actors on a stage, on television, etc. drama नाटक, तमाशा I have acted in many *plays*.

2. *(v.)* to occupy oneself in (a sport or diversion); amuse oneself in (a game) खेल खेलना What games do you like to *play*?

3. to perform or act the part (of) in or as in a dramatic production; assume or simulate the role (of) बजाना Can you *play* the piano?

> **play at**– to use recklessly; squander or waste बिना रुचि के कुछ करना, She is only *playing at* studies.

> **play down**– to make little or light of; minimize the importance of महत्त्व को कम करके दिखाना या महत्त्व न देना, Rahul *played down* the damage of his cycle.

> **play off against**– अपने लाभ के लिए लोगों को एक-दूसरे से भिड़ा देना, She is *playing* me *off against* her friend.

> **play on**– to exploit or impose upon (the feelings or weakness of another) to one's own advantage भय या दुर्बलता से लाभ उठाना, The coach of the team told them to *play on*.

> **play up**– to hurt; give (one) pain or trouble परेशान करना, तकलीफ़ पहुंचाना, The children were *playing up* their teacher.

playboy *(n.)* प्लेबॉइ– a man, esp one of private means, who devotes himself to the pleasures of nightclubs, expensive holiday resorts, female company, etc. रसिक, मौज-मस्ती में रहने वाला धनी व्यक्ति Salman Khan played a role of *playboy* in the movie.

player *(n.)* प्लेअर– a person who participates in or is skilled at some game or sport खिलाड़ी A sports *player* has to train very hard.

playful *(adj.)* प्लेफ़ुल– full of high spirits and fun मज़ाकिया, अगंभीर It was a *playful* remark on him.

playground *(n.)* प्लेग्राउण्ड– a place or region particularly popular as a sports or holiday resort खेल का मैदान A huge *playground* is attached to this complex.

playhouse *(n.)* प्लेहाउस– a theatre where live dramatic performances are given नाट्यशाला There is a *playhouse* in my neighbourhood.

play-off *(n.)* an extra contest to decide the winner when two or more competitors are tied निर्णायक मैच या खेल The *play-off* between India and Australia was postponed due to the rains.

plaything *(n.)* प्लेथिंग– a person regarded or treated as a toy खिलौने की तरह प्रयुक्त She is like a *plaything* for her husband.

playtime *(n.)* प्लेटाइम– a time for play or recreation, esp the school break पढ़ाई के बीच खेलने का समय The *playtime* starts from 11:30 am.

playwright *(n.)* प्लेराइट– a person who writes plays नाटककार Habib Tanvir was a veteran *playwright* for theatre.

plea *(n.)* प्ली– an earnest entreaty or request याचना, निवेदन The judge agreed to listen to his *pleas.*

plead *(v.)* प्लीड– to appeal earnestly or humbly (to) याचना करना, निवेदन करना She *pleaded* guilty of stealing from her friends.

pleasant *(adj.)* प्लेज़ण्ट– giving or affording pleasure; enjoyable सुहाना The weather has been very *pleasant* for the last couple of days.

pleasantly *(adv.)* प्लेज़ण्टली– in a way that gives or affords pleasure मनोहर, प्यारा They were *pleasantly* surprised by his action.

please *(v.)* प्लीज़–1. used in making polite requests and in pleading, asking for a favour, etc. कृपया *Please* take a seat.
2. to give satisfaction, pleasure, or contentment to (a person); make or cause (a person) to be glad अच्छा लगना The new servant's hardworking nature *pleased* the master.

➢ **please onself**– to do as one likes जो चाहे सो करो, अपनी मन मर्ज़ी करना, *Please yourself!* I won't interfere you.

pleasing *(adj.)* प्लीज़िंग– giving pleasure; likable or gratifying मनोहर, प्यारा She has *pleasing* features.

pleasure *(n.)* प्लेश़र– an agreeable or enjoyable sensation or emotion मज़ा, आनंद It gives me great *pleasure* to play with children.

pledge *(v.)* प्लेज– 1. to promise formally or solemnly प्रतिज्ञा करना, वचन देना Our government has *pledged* to eradicate poverty from the country.
2. *(n.)* formal or solemn promise or agreement, esp to do or refrain from doing something वचन, सहमति It's my *pledge* to help you whenever you need me.

plenty *(n.)* प्लेण्टी– 1. a great number, amount, or quantity; lots प्रचुरता, यथेष्टता There is *plenty* of time left to finish the work.
2. *(adj.)* very many; ample बहुत मात्रा में, अधिक Apples are *plentiful* in Kashmir.

pliable *(adj.)* प्लाइअबल– easily moulded, bent, influenced, or altered लचीला Children have a *pliable* mind.

pliers *(n.)* प्लाइअर्ज़– a gripping tool consisting of two hinged arms with usually serrated jaws that close on the workpiece चिमटी, चिमटा The electrician pulled the cables by *pliers.*

plight *(n.)* प्लाइट– a condition of extreme hardship, danger, etc. दुर्दशा The *plight* of the flood victims moved me.

plod *(v.)* प्लॉड– to make (one's way) or walk along (a path, road, etc.) with heavy usually slow steps भारी क़दमों से धीरे-धीरे चलना The old woman *ploded* slowly along the path.

plop *(v.)* प्लॉप– to fall or cause to fall with the sound of a plop छप-छप

की आवाज़ करना The children were *plopping* in the rain water.

plot *(n.)* प्लॉट–1. a small piece of land भूखण्ड I have recently bought a *plot* of land.

2. the story or plan of a play, novel, etc. कथानक This story has an interesting *plot.*

3. *(v.)* to plan secretly (something illegal, revolutionary, etc.); conspire षड्यन्त्र करना The army general *plotted* to overthrow the government.

plough *(v.)* प्लाउ– 1. to till (the soil) with a plough हल चलाना, खेत जोतना The farmer *ploughed* his field before sowing the seeds.

2. *(n.)* an agricultural implement with sharp blades हल, लांगल Our farmers should use mechanised *ploughs.*

pluck *(v.)* प्लॅक– 1. to pull off (flowers, fruit, etc.) from (a tree, etc.) तोड़ना, बीनना Do not *pluck* flowers.

2. *(n.)* courage, usually in the face of difficulties or hardship हिम्मत, साहस The little boy was full of *pluck.*

plug *(v.)* प्लग– 1. to stop up or secure (a hole, gap, etc.) with or as if with a plug किसी वस्तु से छेद को भरना She *plugged* her ears on listening to the minister's speech.

2. *(n.)* a device having one or more pins to which an electric cable is attached: used to make an electrical connection when inserted into a socket बिजली का प्लग Get a new *plug* for the television cable.

plum *(n.)* प्लॅम्– an edible oval fruit that is purple, yellow, or green and contains an oval stone आलूबुख़ारा These *plums* are rotten.

plumage *(n.)* प्लूमिज– the layer of feathers covering the body of a bird पक्षियों के पर The pigeon had a thick *plumage.*

plumber *(n.)* प्लम्बर– a person who installs and repairs pipes, fixtures, etc. for water, drainage, and gas नलसाज़, नल का मिस्त्री The *plumber* fixed the leak in the taps.

plumbing *(n.)* प्लम्बिंग– the trade or work of a *plumber* नल, टोंटियां आदि लगाने का काम The *plumbing* was not adequate enough to hold the water.

plume *(n.)* प्लूम– a feather, esp one that is large or ornamental पर, बड़े पंख The peacock has beautiful *plumes.*

plump *(adj.)* प्लम्प– well filled out or rounded; fleshy or chubby गोलमटोल She is rather *plump,* isn't she?

plunder *(v.)* प्लण्डर्– 1. to steal (valuables, goods, sacred items, etc.) from (a town, church, etc.) by force, esp in time of war; loot लूटना, लूटमार करना The dacoits *plundered* the rich man's mansion.

2. *(n.)* anything taken by plundering or theft; booty लूट, लूटपाट का सामान They loaded the *plunder* in a truck and drove away.

plunge *(v.)* प्लॅन्ज– 1. to thrust or throw (something, oneself, etc.) ग़ोता या डुबकी लगाना I *plunged* into the water to save the drowning child.

2. *(n.)* a leap or dive as into water छलांग, डुबकी A careless *plunge* into the water can be harmful.

plural *(n.)* प्लुअरल– denoting a word indicating that more than one referent is being referred to or described बहुवचन रूप The *plural* of 'goat' is 'goats'.

plus *(prep.)* प्लस– increased by the addition of धन; और, मिलाकर Three *plus* three is equal to six.

plush *(adj.)* प्लश्– lavishly appointed; rich; costly विलासतापूर्ण He purchased a *plush* house in the heart of the city.

ply *(v.)* प्लाइ– to provide (with) or subject (to) repeatedly or persistently सड़कों

पर सेवा उपलब्ध कराना The man was *plying* rickshaw on the road.

plywood *(n.)* प्लाइवुड– a structural board consisting of an odd number of thin layers of wood glued together under pressure, with the grain of one layer at right angles to the grain of the adjoining layer लकड़ी का मोटा बोर्ड A carpenter was making a *plywood* table.

pneumonia *(n.)* न्यूमोनिआ– inflammation of one or both lungs, in which the air sacs (alveoli) become filled with liquid, which renders them useless for breathing निमोनिया, फेफड़ों की बीमारी *Pneumonia* has been spreading rapidly throughout the city.

poach *(v.)* पोच– to catch (game, fish, etc.) illegally by trespassing on private property गैर-कानूनी ढंग से पशुओं का शिकार करना *Poaching* is banned by the governments of most of the countries.

pocket *(v.)* पॉकिट– 1. to put into one's pocket जेब में रखना He *pocketed* the note after reading it.

2. *(n.)* a small bag or pouch in a garment for carrying small articles, money, etc. जेब My *pockets* are always full of odds and ends.

pocketbook *(n.)* पॉकिटबुक– a small bag or case for money, papers, etc. carried by a handle or in the pocket नोटबुक She keeps a *pocketbook* in her bag.

pocketmoney *(n.)* पॉकिटमनी– a small weekly sum of money given to children by parents as an allowance जेबख़र्च Samreen spends half of her *pocketmoney* on buying cosmetics.

pod *(n.)* पॉड– the fruit of any leguminous plant, consisting of a long two-valved case that contains seeds and splits along both sides when ripe फली (सेम, मटर आदि) We keep *pods* in cool place.

podium *(n.)* पोडिअम– a small raised platform used by lecturers, orchestra conductors, etc; dais छोटा मंच, चबूतरा The principal addressed the students through the *podium.*

poem *(n.)* पोइम– a literary composition that is not in verse but exhibits the intensity of imagination and language common to it कविता The Rhine of the Ancient Mariner is an amazing *poem.*

poet *(n.)* पोइट– a person who writes poetry कवि Wordsworth was a great nature *poet.*

poetic *(adj.)* पोएटिक– characteristic of poetry, as in being elevated, sublime, etc. काव्यात्मक Rajendra Prasad has written plays in *poetic* form.

poetry *(n.)* पोअट्री– literature in metrical form; verse कविता She has been writing *poetry* since she was a child.

poignant *(adj.)* पॉइन्यण्ट्– sharply distressing or painful to the feelings मार्मिक It was a *poignant* tale of an orphaned girl.

point *(v.)* पॉइंट–1. to indicate the location or direction of by or as by extending (a finger or other pointed object) towards it दिखलाना Can you *point* out the man who spoke to you?

2. *(n.)* the sharp tapered end of a pin, knife, etc. नोक He pricked me with the *point* of his pencil.

3. an important or fundamental reason, aim, etc. विषय There are several *points* in your article which I wish to discuss with you.

- **point of view** *(n.)*– a position from which someone or something is observed दृष्टिकोण, I cannot accept it from my *point of view.*
- **point out** *(v.)* to indicate or specify संकेत करना, बात स्पष्ट करना, Thank you for *pointing* this *out* to me.

pointed *(adj.)* पॉइण्टेड– having a point नुकीला Birds have a *pointed* nose.

pointer *(n.)* पाइन्टर– a helpful piece of information or advice सुझाव He gave me some useful *pointers* to tackle my problem.

pointless *(adj.)* पॉइण्टलेस– without meaning, relevance, or force व्यर्थ, बेकार It's *pointless* to continue working on this problem.

poise *(n.)* पॉइज़– composure or dignity of manner आत्मविश्वासपूर्ण आचरण She delivered her speech with *poise* and confidence.

poison *(v.)* 1. to give poison to (a person or animal) esp with intent to kill ज़हर देना Socrates was *poisoned* to death.
2. *(n.)* पॉइज़न– any substance that can impair function, cause structural damage or otherwise injure the body विष, ज़हर Potassium cyanide is a deadly *poison.*

poisoning *(n.)* पॉइज़निंग– the act of killing someone using a poisonous substance विषाक्तीकरण He got food *poisoning* from eating out.

poisonous *(adj.)* पॉइज़नस–1. having the effects or qualities of a poison घातक, विषाक्त, जहरीला Many people died from the leakage of *poisonous* gas in Bhopal.
2. capable of killing or inflicting injury; venomous ज़हरीला करने वाला Not all snakes are *poisonous.*
3. corruptive or malicious (किसी के मन में) ज़हर भर देने वाला, अशांत He wrote a *poisonous* letter criticizing her behaviour.

poke *(v.)* पोक्– to jab or prod, as with the elbow, the finger, a stick, etc. खरोंचना, कुरेदना He was constantly *poking* in affairs not concerning him.

poker *(n.)* पोकर– a card game of bluff and skill in which bets are made on the hands dealt, the highest-ranking hand winning the pool ताश का एक खेल *Poker* is played with playing cards by two people.

polar *(n.)* पोलर– situated at or near, coming from, or relating to either of the earth's poles or the area inside the Arctic or Antarctic Circles ध्रुवीय *Polar* zones are very cold.

pole *(n.)* पोल–1. either of two points or regions in a piece of material, system, etc. at which there are opposite electric charges, as at the two terminals of a battery बल्ला, डंडा There is a telephone *pole* just opposite our house.
2. either of the two antipodal points where the earth's axis of rotation meets the earth's surface ध्रुव The explorers went up to the North *Pole.*

police *(n.)* पोलिस्– an official organization esp in regard to the enforcement of law, the prevention of crime, etc. पुलिस The *police* arrived on time to stop the robbery.

police officer *(n.)* a member of a police force, esp a constable; policeman a member of a police force, esp a constable; policeman पुलिस अधिकारी The life of a *police officer* is filled with many struggles.

policy *(n.)* पॉलसी– a plan of action adopted or pursued by an individual, government, party, business, etc. नीति The company has a *policy* of declaring annual dividends.

polio *(n.)* पोलिओ– an acute infectious viral disease, esp affecting children. In its paralytic form (acute anterior poliomyelitis) the brain and spinal cord are involved, causing weakness, paralysis, and wasting of muscle फ़ालिज, पोलियो The World Health Organisation is trying hard to make India *polio*-free.

polish *(v.)* पॉलिश– 1. to make or become smooth and shiny by

rubbing, esp with wax or an abrasive पॉलिश करना, चमकाना His shoes were not *polished* and looked dirty.
2. *(n.)* a finish or gloss पालिश, चमक I want some *polish* for my car.

polished *(adj.)* पॉलिशड– impeccably or professionally done उच्च स्तर का He is a *polished* gentleman.

polite *(adj.)* पलाइट– showing regard for others, in manners, speech, behaviour, etc. courteous शिष्ट, भद्र His behavior has always been *polite*.

politeness *(n.)* पलाइटनस– the quality of being polite नम्रता *Politeness* costs nothing.

political *(adj.)* पलिटिकल– of or relating to the state, government, the body politic, public administration, policy-making, etc. राजनीतिक I have participated in *political* activities since my school days.

politically *(adv.)* पलिटिकली– with regard to the way that power is achieved and used in a country or society (through government, policy-making, etc.) राजनीतिक रूप से Bangladesh is a *politically* weak nation.

politician *(n.)* पॉलटिशन– a person actively engaged in politics, esp a full-time professional member of a deliberative assembly राजनीतिज्ञ Madhav Rao Sclndla was an honest *politician*.

politics *(n.)* पॉलटिक्स– the practice or study of the art and science of forming, directing, and administrating states and other political units राजनीति *Politics* has never been of great interest to women.

poll *(n.)* पोल्– the casting, recording, or counting of votes in an election; a voting मतदान We might have a mid-term *poll* very soon.

pollinate *(v.)* पालनेट– to transfer pollen from the anthers to the stigma of (a flower) पराग (फूलों का रस) खींचना Bees *pollinate* pollens from flowers.

polling *(n.)* पोलिंग– the casting or registering of votes at an election मतदान The *polling* was disturbed in some areas due to anti social elements.

polling-station *(n.)* पोलिंग-स्टेशन– a building, such as a school, designated as the place to which voters go during an election to cast their votes मतदान-केन्द्र We went to *polling station* after 3 p.m.

pollute *(v.)* प्लूट– to contaminate, as with poisonous or harmful substances गंदा करना, प्रदूषित करना The water has been *polluted* with toxic waste from the factories.

pollution *(n.)* पलूशन– harmful or poisonous substances introduced into an environment वायु-प्रदूषण CNG reduced the levels of environmental *pollution*.

polo *(n.)* पोलो– a game similar to hockey played on horseback using long-handled mallets (**polo** sticks) and a wooden ball चौगान का खेल *Polo* is an ancient game of India.

polyester *(n.)* पॉलिएसटर– any of a large class of synthetic materials that are polymers containing recurring -COO- groups: used as plastics, textile fibres, and adhesives कपड़ा बनाने के लिए एक प्रकार की कृत्रिम सामग्री We should not wear *polyester* clothes while cooking.

polygamy *(n.)* पलिगमी– the practice of having more than one wife or husband at the same time बहुविवाहवाद *Polygamy* is practiced in the Arab countries.

polythene *(n.)* पालिथीन– any one of various light thermoplastic materials made from ethylene with properties depending on the molecular weight of the polymer हलका एवं महीन प्लास्टिक (जो थैलियां बनाने में प्रयोग होता है) Please do not use *polythene* bags because its garbage is most toxic.

pomegranate *(n.)* पॉमिग्रैनेट्– a round edible fruit with red flesh full of seeds अनार There was a *pomegranate* tree in the village.

pomp *(n.)* पॉम्प– stately or magnificent display; ceremonial splendour तड़क-भड़क, धूमधाम There was a *pomp* celebration on his birthday.

pompous *(adj.)* पामपस– exaggeratedly or ostentatiously dignified or self-important आडंबरी, आडंबरपूर्ण Her *pompous* nature is disliked by everyone in the class.

pond *(n.)* पॉन्ड– a pool of still water, often artificially created तालाब, सरोवर There is a small *pond* outside our village where we go for a swim.

ponder *(v.)* पॉन्डर्– to give thorough or deep consideration (to); meditate (upon) चिन्तन करना The think tank *pondered* on all the possible solutions.

pony *(n.)* पोनी– any of various breeds of small horse, usually under 14.2 hands टट्टू (घोड़े का बच्चा) We rode on a *pony* in Nainital.

poodle *(n.)* पूडल– a breed of dog, with varieties of different sizes, having curly hair घुंघराले बालों वाला कुत्ता A child was playing with *poodle*.

pool *(n.)* पूल– 1. a small body of still water, usually fresh; small pond तालाब I go to the swimming *pool* every evening.

2. *(v.)* to collect money resources, funds, etc. लोगों से धन, विचार आदि एकत्रित करना We shall *pool* in some money for dinner.

poor *(adj.)* पॉर्–1. lacking financial or other means of subsistence; needy दरिद्र, निर्धन, गरीब India is a *poor* country.

2. deserving of pity; unlucky बेचारा, अभागा The *poor* dog had injured its paw.

3. lacking in quality; inferior घटिया, निकृष्ट This cloth is of *poor* quality.

poorly *(adv.)* पुअरली– 1. in a poor way or manner; badly बहुत ख़राब She is doing a *poorly* paid job.

2. *(adj.)* in poor health; rather ill बीमार, अस्वस्थ He seems to be a *poorly* student.

pop *(v.)* पॉप– to make or cause to make a light sharp explosive sound फटना, फट-सी आवाज़ करना He *popped* the bottle of champagne to start the bottle.

popcorn *(n.)* पॉपकार्न– **popcorn** मकई We treated ourselves with *popcorns* and pepsi in the theatre.

Pope *(n.)* पोप– the bishop of Rome as head of the Roman Catholic Church ईसाई धर्म गुरु, पोप *Pope* John Paul II was the second-longest serving *Pope* in history.

poplar *(n.)* पॉप्युलर– any tree of the salicaceous genus Populus, of N temperate regions, having triangular leaves, flowers borne in catkins, and light soft wood पहाड़ी पीपल का पेड़ *Poplar* trees are mostly grown in Uttarakhand.

popular *(adj.)* पॉप्युलर– connected with, representing, or prevailing among the general public; common लोकप्रिय Shah Rukh Khan is a *popular* actor among the masses.

popularity *(n.)* पॉप्युलैरटी– the quality of being well-liked लोकप्रियता, जनप्रियता He was elected due to his *popularity* in the area.

popularize (ise) *(v.)* पॉप्युलराइज़– to make popular; make attractive to the general public लोकप्रिय बनाना The film Bandit Queen *popularized* the story of Phoolan Devi.

popularly *(adv.)* पॉप्युलरली– by the public as a whole; generally or widely आमतौर से, सामान्यतया Kareena Kapoor is *popularly* known as Bebo.

population *(n.)* पॉप्युलेशन– all the persons inhabiting a country, city, or other specified place जनसंख्या, आबादी The *population* of China is the largest in the world.

porch *(n.)* पॉर्च– a low structure projecting from the doorway of a house and forming a covered entrance द्वारमंडप I halted the car in the *porch* of the house.

pore *(n.)* पॉर्–) any small opening in the skin or outer surface of an animal रोमकूप, छिद्र Regular bathing keeps the *pores* of our skin clean.

pork *(n.)* पॉर्क– the flesh of pigs used as food सुअर का मांस This restaurant serves roasted *pork.*

pornography *(n.)* पॉर्नाग्रफ़ी– writings, pictures, films, etc. designed to stimulate sexual excitement अश्लील साहित्य Nowadays *pornography* is very common in society.

porpoise *(n.)* पॉर्पस– any of various small cetacean mammals of the genus Phocaena and related genera, having a blunt snout and many teeth सूंस (थूथनदार लम्बा काला समुद्री जन्तु) We saw a group of *porpoise* in a film.

porridge *(n.)* पॉरिज– a dish made from oatmeal or another cereal, cooked in water or milk to a thick consistency दलिया *Porridge* is good for health.

port *(n.)* पोर्ट– a town or place alongside navigable water with facilities for the loading and unloading of ships बन्दरगाह Mumbai has the biggest *port* in India.

portable *(adj.)* पार्टबल– able to be carried or moved easily, esp by hand उठौआं, आसानी से हिलने एवं उठने वाला I just purchased a *portable* chair.

porter *(n.)* पॉर्टर– a person employed to carry luggage, parcels, supplies, etc. esp at a railway station or hotel पल्लेदार, कुली The *porter* put my luggage in the train.

portfolio *(n.)* पॉर्टफ़ोलिओ– a flat case, esp of leather, used for carrying maps, drawings, etc. छायाचित्र, आरेख, कागज़ात आदि का संग्रह He had an impressive *portfolio* of assets.

portion *(n.)* पॉर्शन– a part of a whole; fraction भाग, हिस्सा Everyone took a small *portion* of the pie.

portrait *(n.)* पोट्रेट– a painting, drawing, sculpture, photograph, or other likeness of an individual, esp of the face चित्र, प्रतिकृति He asked a well-known artist to paint a *portrait* of his father.

pose *(v.)* पोज़– to puzzle or baffle परेशानी उत्पन्न करना Pollution *poses* a major threat to the environment. *(n.)* a particular position in which sb sits or stands मुद्रा, भंगिमा She was dedicated to *pose* for her next shot.

posh *(adj.)* पॉश– upper-class or genteel समाज के उच्च वर्ग से संबंधित They live in a *posh* colony.

position *(n.)* पोज़िशन–1. the place, situation, or location of a person or thing स्थिति Who has moved my writing table from its original *position*?
2. a post of employment; job पद My brother has got a *position* as a lecturer.
3. the arrangement or disposition of the body or a part of the body अवस्था You should stand in an upright *position.*
4. the manner in which a person or thing is placed; arrangement परिस्थिति In my present *position,* I cannot help you.

positive *(adj.)* पॉज़िटिव– characterized by or expressing certainty or affirmation निश्चित: Are you *positive* that this contract has no secret clause?

positively *(adv.)* पॉज़िटिवलि– in a positive manner निश्चित रूप से They are coming tomorrow, *positively.*

possess *(v.)* पज़ेस– to have as one's property; own मालिक होना He *possess* a big threat to our organization

possession *(n.)* पज़ेशन– anything that is owned or *possessed* अधिकार, क़ब्ज़ा He has full *possession* over our assets.

possessive *(adj.)* पज़ेसिव– having or showing an excessive desire to possess, control, or dominate अपने ही क़ब्ज़े में रखने का इच्छुक Vandana is very *possessive* about her boyfriend.

possessiveness *(n.)* पज़ेसिवनस– having or showing an excessive desire to possess, control, or dominate स्वत्वबोधकता Her *possessiveness* is quite *irritating* for her husband.

possibility *(n.)* पासबिलटी– the state or condition of being possible संभावना There is a high *possibility* that we may lose the client

possible *(adj.)* पॉसिबल–1. capable of existing, taking place, or proving true without contravention of any natural law मुमकिन, किसी बात के होने की संभावना Is it *possible* to leave for Mumbai immediately? If *possible,* come back before the nightfall.

possibly *(adj.)* पॉसबली– perhaps or maybe यथासंभव, शायद I may *possibly* meet you in Kolkata.

post *(v.)* पोस्ट–1. to send by post डाक से भेजना Please *post* this letter.

2. *(n.)* letters, packages, etc. that are transported and delivered by the Post Office; mail डाक Send this letter by *post.*

3. a position to which a person is appointed or elected; appointment; job पद, नौकरी I am trying for a *post* in this office.

4. a length of wood, metal, etc. fixed upright in the ground to serve as a support, marker, point of attachment, etc. खम्भा The fence was made of wooden *posts.*

postage *(n.)* पोस्टिज– the charge for delivering a piece of mail डाक-शुल्क How much *postage* has to be paid for this letter?

postal *(adj.)* पोस्टल– of or relating to a Post Office or to the mail-delivery service डाक-संबंधी The postal address on this letter is wrong.

poster *(n.)* पोस्टर– a placard or bill posted in a public place as an advertisement इश्तहार, विज्ञापन During election time, *posters* appear everywhere.

posterity *(n.)* पॉस्टेरटी– future or succeeding generations भावी पीढ़ियां, संतति We must make some investments for the good of our *posterity.*

posthumous *(adj.)* पॉस्ट्युमस्– happening or continuing after one's death मरणोपरांत The general received the *posthumous* medal for bravery.

posting *(n.)* पोस्टिंग– an appointment to a *position* or post, usually in another town or country पदस्थता It is time to declare the *posting* of new officers.

postman *(n.)* पोस्टमन– a person who carries and delivers mail as a profession चिट्ठी बांटने वाला, डाकिया The name of my *postman* is Ramlal.

post-mortem *(n.)* पोस्ट-मार्टम– a medical analysis or study of a dead person in order to find out how they died शव-परीक्षा The *post-mortem* should reveal the real cause of the death.

post-natal *(adj.)* पोस्ट-नेटल– existing or taking place after giving birth प्रसवोत्तर She went into the *post-natal* depression after the delivery.

postpone *(v.)* पोस्पोन– to put off or delay until a future time स्थगित करना Our trip was *postponed* due to bad weather.

posture *(n.)* पॉस्चर्– a position or attitude of the limbs or body बैठने, खड़े होने, चलने की मुद्रा One needs to maintain a correct *posture* during exercises.

pot *(n.)* पॉट– a container made of earthenware, glass, or similar material; usually round and deep, often having a handle and lid, used for cooking and other domestic purposes पात्र, बर्तन My wife uses stainless steel *pots* for cooking.

potato *(n.)* पटेटो– a round white vegetable with a brown skin that grows underground आलू The *potato* is best known for its carbohydrate content.

potent *(adj.)* पोटेण्ट– possessing great strength; powerful सशक्त, मैथुन-समर्थ The doctor gave a *potent* drug to the patient.

potential *(adj.)* पटेन्शियल– 1. possible but not yet actual संभाव्य, संभावित A good salesman must know tricks of attracting the *potential* buyers.
2. *(n.)* latent but unrealized ability or capacity व्यक्ति या वस्तु में विद्यमान गुण She has a great *potential* as a dancer.

pottery *(n.)* पॉटरी– articles, vessels, etc. made from earthenware and dried and baked in a kiln मिट्टी के बर्तन Khurja is famous for its *pottery*.

pouch *(n.)* पाउच्–1. a saclike structure in any of various animals, such as the abdominal receptacle marsupium in marsupials or the cheek fold in rodents कुछ मादा पशुओं में बच्चा रखने की थैली A baby kangaroo remains in its mother's *pouch* for some time.
2. a small flexible baglike container चमड़े की छोटी थैली I have a beautiful *pouch* in my bag.

pounce *(v.)* पाउन्स्– to spring or swoop, as in capturing prey झपट्टा मारना The Lion *pounced* on its prey.

poultry *(n.)* पोल्ट्रि– domestic fowls collectively मुर्ग़ा, मुर्ग़ी I get fresh eggs every day from my friend's *poultry* farm.

pound *(v.)* पाउण्ड्– to beat to a pulp; pulverize दिल का ऊंची आवाज़ में धड़कना My heart was *pounding* with fear.

pour *(v.)* पॉर्– to flow or cause to flow in a stream उँड़ेलना Please *pour* me a drink.

➢ **pour down**– to rain heavily मूसलाधार वर्षा होना, पानी बरसना, The rain *poured down* whole night.

poverty *(n.)* पॉवर्टी– the condition of being without adequate food, money, etc. निर्धनता, ग़रीबी Many people live in *poverty*.

powder *(n.)* पाउडर्– a solid substance in the form of tiny loose particles पाउडर, चूर्ण Please give me a pack of face *powder*.

powdered *(adj.)* पाउडर्ड– a powdered substance is one which is in the form of a powder although it can come in a different form चूर्णित, सूखा हुआ She prepared tea for me with *powdered* milk.

power *(n.)* पाउअर्–1. a specific ability, capacity, or faculty बल, अधिकार The police have the *power* to arrest people.
2. ability or capacity to do something शक्ति I shall do everything in my *power* to help you.

powerful *(adj.)* पाउअर्फुल– having great power, force, potency, or effect

प्रभावशाली, शक्तिशाली Only the *powerful* and mighty can rule the world.

powerless *(adj.)* पाउअलस– without power or authority निर्बल, लाचार I felt *powerless* before my parents.

power station *(n.)* पावर स्टेशन– an electrical generating station बिजलीघर India is doing a great progress in generating electricity in nuclear *power station.*

practicable *(adj.)* प्रैक्टिकबल– capable of being done; feasible व्यावहारिक, साध्य His suggestion is just not *practicable.*

practical *(adj.)* प्रैक्टिकल– of, involving, or concerned with experience or actual use; not theoretical प्रयोगात्मक The company provided us with a *practical* solution to our problems.

practice *(n.)* प्रैक्टिस– a usual or customary action or proceeding आदत, प्रथा, रिवाज It is a dangerous *practice* to get off a moving bus.

practise *(v.)* प्रैक्टिस– to do or cause to do repeatedly in order to gain skill आदत डालना, अभ्यास करना *Practise* makes a man perfect.

practitioner *(n.)* प्रैक्टिशनर– a person who practises a profession or art दंत-चिकित्सक Dr. Lal is a general *practitioner* but not a specialist.

pragmatic *(adj.)* प्रैगमैटिक– advocating behaviour that is dictated more by practical consequences than by theory or dogma यथार्थवादी Sushil applied *pragmatic* approach to manage his problem.

praise *(v.)* प्रेज़– 1. to express commendation, admiration, etc. for प्रशंसा करना My son's teacher *praised* him for his good marks.

2. *(n.)* the act of expressing commendation, admiration, etc. प्रशंसा He is unaffected by *praise* or blame.

praiseworthy *(adj.)* प्रेज़वर्दी– deserving of praise; commendable प्रशंसा के योग्य His performance was *praiseworthy* in the play.

prance *(v.)* प्रान्स– to swagger or strut इतराना, ख़ुशी से इठलाना The children were *prancing* around the strange.

prawn *(n.)* प्रान– any of various small edible fish having a slender flattened body with a long tail and two pairs of pincers झींगा मछली They saw a large *prawn* in the sea.

pray *(v.)* प्रे– to utter prayers प्रार्थना करना We *pray* to God to help us.

prayer *(n.)* प्रेअर– a form of spiritual communion with a deity प्रार्थना People from all communities used to attend Gandhiji's samadhi for *prayer* meetings on October 2.

preach *(v.)* प्रीच– to make known (religious truth) or give religious or moral instruction or exhortation in (sermons प्रवचन या उपदेश देना Gandhiji *preached* truthfulness and continence.

preacher *(n.)* प्रीचर– a person who has the calling and function of preaching the Christian Gospel, esp a Protestant clergyman धर्म-उपदेशक, प्रवचन देने वाला Mahatma Gandhi was the *preacher* of non-violence.

preamble *(n.)* प्रीऐमबल– a preliminary or introductory conference, event, fact, etc. भूमिका, प्रस्तावना The *Preamble* highlights the salient features of the Constitution of India.

precarious *(n.)* प्रिकेअरिअस– liable to failure or catastrophe; insecure; perilous ख़तरनाक, जोखिमभरा His position on the top of the hill was *precarious.*

precaution *(n.)* प्रिकॉशन– an action taken to avoid a dangerous or undesirable event सतर्कता She takes great *precautions* while driving.

precede *(v.)* प्रिसीड– to go or be before (someone or something) in time, place, rank, etc. से पहले आना या

घटित होना Please follow me, I shall *precede* you.

precious *(adj.)* प्रेशस– beloved; dear; cherished बहुमूल्य Children are always *precious* to their parents.

precipitate *(adj.)* प्रिसिपिटेट–1. sudden and brief बिना सोचे समझे, जल्दबाज़ी में किया गया काम He is regretting the *precipitate* decision of his resignation.
2. *(v.)* done rashly or with undue haste जल्दबाज़ी करके संकट पैदा कर देना One small error can *precipitate* the big problem.
3. to throw or fall from or as from a height किसी को किसी विषम स्थिति में धकेल देना या पटक देना The drug treatment *precipitated* him into a severe constipation.

precis *(n.)* प्रेसी– a summary of the essentials of a text; abstract संक्षेप, सारांश Write the *precis* of this paragraph.

precise *(adj.)* प्रीसाइस्– strictly correct in amount or value यथार्थ, सही Please give a brief *precis* of the problem.

precisely *(adv.)* प्रिसाइसली– in a precise manner बिलकुल ठीक, सही-सही Please describe the incident *precisely.*

precision *(n.)* प्रिसिश्नन– the quality of being precise; accuracy शुद्धता His writings lacked a lot of *precision* which was expected from him.

preclude *(v.)* प्रिक्लूड– to make impossible, esp beforehand असंभव बना देना, कोई कार्य करने न देना Government should *preclude* those officials from their jobs who take bribe.

preconceive *(v.)* प्रीकनसीव– to form an idea of beforehand; conceive of ahead in time किसी चीज़ की धारणा पहले से बनाना, पूर्वधारणा बनाना Every person has *preconceived* notions about marriage.

preconceived *(adj.)* प्रीकनसीवड– formed beforehand before you have enough information about something or knowledge of it, पूर्व-कल्पित I went to meet them with no *preconceived* ideas.

preconception *(v.)* प्रीकनसेपशन– an idea or opinion formed beforehand पूर्व धारणा This book will challenge your *preconceptions* about Muslims.

precondition *(n.)* प्रीकण्डीशन– a necessary or required condition; prerequisite पूर्व शर्त Two years contract was a *precondition* for that job.

predator *(n.)* प्रीडटर– any carnivorous animal परजीव भक्षी, शिकारी What do you understand by the relationship between *predator* and prey?

predecessor *(n.)* प्रीडिसेसर्– a person who precedes another, as in an office पूर्वाधिकारी The *predecessor* of the current CEO had a better grasp on the job.

predicament *(n.)* प्रिडिकमेंट– a perplexing, embarrassing, or difficult situation अप्रिय स्थिति The *predicament* of the parents at the loss of their son was unimaginable.

predict *(v.)* प्रेडिक्ट– to state or make a declaration about in advance, esp on a reasoned basis; foretell भविष्यवाणी करना No one can *predict* the future.

prediction *(n.)* प्रेडिक्शन– something predicted; a forecast, prophecy, etc. भविष्यवाणी His *predictions* proved false.

predominance *(n.)* प्रिडॉमिनन्स– the quality or state of having superiority in power, influence, importance, etc. over others of the same type आधिपत्य, प्रधानता There is a *predominance* of the rich over the poor in our society.

preen *(v.)* प्रीन– in a healthy condition by arrangement, cleaning, and other contact सँवारना, ठीक करना She spent an hour *preening* herself in front of the mirror.

preface *(n.)* a statement written as an introduction to a literary or other work, typically explaining its scope, intention, method, etc. foreword भूमिका, प्राक्कथन I requested the minister to write a *preface* for my book.

prefer *(v.)* प्रि'फ़र्– to like better or value more highly (अधिक) पसंद करना I *prefer* to travel to the United States rather than Australia.

preferable *(adj.)* प्रेफ़रबल– preferred or more desirable बेहतर, वरीय Butterscotch ice-cream is *preferable* to vanilla ice-cream.

preference *(n.)* प्रेफ़रन्स– something or someone preferred प्राथमिकता, वरीयता What is your *preference* tea or coffee?

pregnancy *(n.)* प्रेगननूसी– the period from conception to childbirth गर्भावस्था She never travelled during her *pregnancy.*

pregnant *(adj.)* प्रेगनेंट– carrying a fetus or fetuses within the womb गर्भवती Anandi is seven months *pregnant.*

prehistoric *(adj.)* प्रीहिस्टारिक– of or relating to man's development before the appearance of the written word पूर्व-ऐतिहासिक The dinosaur is a *prehistoric* beast.

prejudice *(v.)* प्रेजुडिस– 1. to cause to be prejudiced पूर्वाग्रहित करना, पूर्वाग्रह रखना The newspaper gossip *prejudiced* her against him.
2. *(n.)* an opinion formed beforehand, esp an unfavourable one based on inadequate facts पूर्वाग्रह, पूर्वधारण He seems to have a *prejudice* against me.

preliminary *(adj.)* प्रिलिमिनरी– occurring before or in preparation; introductory प्राथमिक The finalists will be selected after the *preliminary* round.

premature *(adj.)* प्रेमचुअर– occurring or existing before the normal or expected time असामयिक, समय से पूर्व I was shocked to hear of her *premature* death.

premier *(adj.)* प्रेमिअर्– first in importance, rank, etc. सर्वोत्तम, प्रधान, प्रमुख It is a *premier* hotel in the city.

premiere *(n.)* प्रेमिअर्– the first public performance of a film, play, opera, etc. (नाटक या फ़िल्म का) प्रथम प्रदर्शन The actress was hounded by media at the *premiere.*

premises *(n.)* प्रेमिसिज़– a piece of land together with its buildings, esp considered as a place of business भवन, परिसर He built a wall around his *premises.*

premium *(n.)* प्रीमिअम– an amount paid in addition to a standard rate, price, wage, etc. bonus बीमे की क़िश्त I deposit yearly *premium* of my insurance policy in the first week of April.

preoccupied *(adj.)* प्रिऑक्युपाइड– engrossed or absorbed in something, esp one's own thoughts तल्लीन, निमग्न I'm *preoccupied* with a lot of work.

preparation *(n.)* प्रेपरेशन– the state of being prepared; readiness तैयारी Have you done all the *preparations* for the examinations?

preparatory *(adj.)* प्रिपैरटरी– introductory or preliminary प्रारंभिक All the members of the party attended the *preparatory* meeting of the election.

prepare *(v.)* प्रिपेअर्–1. to make ready or suitable in advance for a particular purpose or for some use, event, etc. बनाना What sweet dish have you *prepared* today?

2. to be willing and able (to do something) तैयार होना He is not *prepared* to help me.

preponderance *(n.)* प्रिपॉनडरन्स– the quality of being greater in weight, force, influence, etc. महत्ता, प्रचुरता There is a *preponderance* of girls students in the music department.

preposition *(n.)* प्रेपज़िशन– a word or group of words used before a noun or pronoun to relate it grammatically or semantically to some other constituent of a sentence पूर्वसर्ग A *preposition* is used before a noun or pronoun and is an important part of speech.

preposterous *(adj.)* प्रिपॉसटरस– contrary to nature, reason, or sense; absurd; ridiculous बेवकूफ़ी भरा, बेतुका These allegations on him are totally *preposterous.*

prescribe *(v.)* प्रिस्क्राइब– to recommend or order the use of (a drug or other remedy) नुसख़ा लिखना The doctor *prescribed* an effective medicine.

presence *(n.)* प्रेज़न्स– the state or fact of being present उपस्थिति, सुधबुध We should apply our *presence* of mind in difficult situations.

present *(v.)* प्रेज़ेन्ट–1. to give or award देना, प्रदान करना The guest of honour *presented* a trophy to the school.

2. *(n.)* anything that is presented; a gift उपहार, भेंट I received many *presents* on my birthday.

3. *(adj.)* in existence at the moment in time at which an utterance is spoken or written उपस्थित Were you *present* when the fire broke out?

4. denoting a tense of verbs used when the action or event described is occurring at the time of utterance or when the speaker does not wish to make any explicit temporal reference वर्तमानकालिक Our *present* teacher is very good.

presentation *(n.)* प्रेज़नटेशन– the manner of presenting, esp the organization of visual details to create an overall impression प्रस्तुतीकरण The *presentation* lacked some basic points.

presently *(adv.)* प्रेज़नटली– at the moment इन दिनों, आजकल She is *presently* working in a multinational company.

preservation *(n.)* प्रिज़र्वेशन– the act or an instance of protecting an abstract noun from decay or dissolution; maintain संरक्षण, परिरक्षण Food *preservation* is a growing industry.

preserve *(v.)* प्रिज़र्व– to keep safe from danger or harm; protect बचाना, सुरक्षित रखना *Preserve* this document carefully.

preside *(v.)* प्रिसाइड– to sit in or hold a position of authority, as over a meeting संचालन करना, सभापति होना The Managing Director *presided* over the meeting

president *(n.)* प्रेज़िडेण्ट– the chief executive or head of state of a republic राष्ट्रपति The US *President* is considered to be the most powerful man of the world.

press *(v.)* प्रेस–1. to apply or exert weight, force, or steady pressure on दबाव डालना Please do not *press* me to eat more.

2. to squeeze or compress so as to alter in shape or form दबाना I *pressed* the button of the door bell.

3. *(n.)* any of various machines used for printing मुद्रणालय, छापाख़ाना In which *press* was this book printed?

4. the opinions and reviews in the newspapers, etc. समाचार-पत्र, अख़बार I often write letters to the *press.*

press conference *(n.)* प्रेस कॉन्फरेन्स an interview for press and television reporters given by a politician, film star, etc. सम्मेलन The actor called the *press conference* for the controversy of his new movie.

pressure *(n.)* प्रेशर– the pressure exerted by the blood on the inner walls of the arteries. दबाव Her mother is having a high blood *pressure*.

➢ **under pressure** *(n.)* a moral force that compels दबाव में, किसी बोझ से परेशान एवं चिंतित, Children remain *under pressure* due to their board exams.

pressurize (ise) *(v.)* प्रेशराइज़– to increase pressure on दबाव डालना He was *pressurized* to pursue science for his education.

prestige *(n.)* प्रेस्टीज– high status or reputation achieved through success, influence, wealth, etc. renown प्रतिष्ठा, इज़्ज़त She could not marry the clerk. Afterall it was a matter of *prestige*.

prestigious *(adj.)* प्रेस्टिजस– having status or glamour; impressive or influential प्रतिष्ठित This is the most *prestigious* school in the city.

presume *(v.)* प्रिज़्यूम– to rely or depend अटकलें लगाना Don't *presume* his consent to work with us.

pretend *(v.)* प्रिटेण्ड– to claim or allege (something untrue) ढोंग रचना, बहाना बनाना He likes to *pretend* that he is a rich man.

pretext *(n.)* प्रीटेक्स्ट– a fictitious reason given in order to conceal the real one बहाना She left the job on the *pretext* of getting married.

pretty *(adj.)* प्रिटि– 1. pleasing or appealing in a delicate or graceful way रमणीय, सुंदर She is a *pretty* girl. 2. *(adv.)* fairly or moderately; somewhat बहुत, काफ़ी I'm *pretty* sure that he'll bring gift for me.

prevail *(v.)* प्रिवेल–1. to prove superior; gain mastery सफ़ल होना After a hard struggle, we *prevailed* over the opposite team.
2. to succeed in persuading or inducing राज़ी करना Can I *prevail* on you to have dinner with us?

prevailing *(adj.)* प्रिवेलिंग– generally accepted; widespread व्याप्त, प्रबल, हावी The *prevailing* conditions in the market are not healthy for the investors.

prevalent *(adj.)* प्रेवलण्ट– superior in force or power; predominant प्रचलित Sati Pratha was *prevalent* in our society.

prevent *(v.)* प्रिवेण्ट– to keep from happening, esp by taking precautionary action रोकना He was able to *prevent* an unmitigated disaster.

prevention *(n.)* प्रिवेन्शन– a hindrance, obstacle, or impediment रोकथाम, परहेज़ *Prevention* is better than cure.

preview *(n.)* प्रीव्यू– an advance or preliminary view or sight पूर्व समीक्षा, अग्रप्रदर्शन (किसी नाटक फ़िल्म आदि का) The *preview* of the film gave an idea of the story.

previous *(adj.)* प्रिविअस– existing or coming before something else in time or position; prior पिछला, पहले का Have you read the *previous* page?

prey *(v.)* प्रे– 1. to hunt or seize food by killing other animals शिकार करना, लूटना Leopards *prey* on deer.
2. *(n.)* an animal hunted or captured by another for food शिकार This forest is full of birds of *prey*.

price *(n.)* प्राइस–1. the sum in money or goods for which anything is or may be bought or sold भाव, दाम What is the *price* of this TV set?
2. the cost at which anything is obtained मूल्य This ancient work of art is *price*less.

prick *(v.)* प्रिक– to make (a small hole) in (something) by piercing lightly with a sharp point छेदना, चुभाना It's surprising how a small *prick* can cause a lot of pain.

prickle *(v.)* प्रिकल– 1. to feel or cause to feel a stinging sensation चुभन पैदा होना, चुभोना A cold breeze *prickled* my face.

2. *(n.)* a pointed process arising from the outer layer of a stem, leaf, etc. and containing no woody or conducting tissue कांटा *Prickles* can be seen on the stems of rose plant.

prickly *(adj.)* प्रिकली–1. having or covered with prickles कांटेदार He planted *prickly* bushes at the fence of his garden.

2. full of difficulties; knotty त्वचा में चुभन पैदा करने वाला My skin feels *prickly* in the sun.

3. bad-tempered or irritable जल्दी क्रोधित होने वाला As he got older, he became more *prickly* and forgetful.

pride *(n.)* प्राइड– a feeling of honour and self-respect; a sense of personal worth अभिमान, अहंकार There was *pride* on his face when he was declared employee of the month.

priest *(n.)* प्रीस्ट– a person ordained to act as a mediator between God and man in administering the sacraments, preaching, blessing, guiding, etc. पादरी The temple *priest* bathed deities in the morning.

primarily *(adv.)* प्राइमरिली– principally; chiefly; mainly मूलतः, मुख्य रूप से He is *primarily* an engineer.

primary *(adj.)* प्राइमरी–1. fundamental; basic प्राथमिक I have admitted my son to a *primary* school.

2. first in importance, degree, rank, etc. मूल, मूलभूत My *primary* intention in coming here was to meet you.

prime *(adj.)* प्राइम– first in quality or value; first-rate प्रधान, मुख्य The *prime* aim of the company this year is to restore the profit.

primitive *(adj.)* प्रिमटिव– characteristic of an early state, esp in being crude or uncivilized प्राचीन, आदिकालीन Some tribes still follow *primitive* customs and traditions in India.

prince *(n.)* प्रिन्स– the son or grandson of the ruler राजकुमार The *prince* punished the culprit.

princess *(n.)* प्रिनसेस– a daughter of the sovereign or of one of the sovereign's sons राजकुमारी *Princess* Diana was a very beautiful lady.

principal *(n.)* प्रिन्सिपल– 1. the head of a school or other educational institution प्राचार्य, प्रिंसिपल Who is the *principal* of your college?

2. *(adj.)* first in importance, rank, value, etc. chief मुख्य, प्रधान The *principal* item, we sell, is cosmetics.

principle *(n.)* प्रिन्सिपल–1. a standard or rule of personal conduct सिद्धांत He is a man of noble *principles.*

2. a rule or law concerning a natural phenomenon or the behaviour of a system आधारभूत तत्त्व Have you understood the *principle* of this law of Physics?

print *(n.)* प्रिण्ट– 1. printed matter such as newsprint मुहर, छाप My book is at present under *print.*

2. *(v.)* to reproduce (text, pictures, etc.), esp in large numbers, by applying ink to paper or other material by one of various processes छापना We *print* books of high standard.

printing press *(n.)* प्रिंटिंग-प्रैस– any of various machines used for printing छापा-ख़ाना, प्रेस The *printing press* suddenly caught fire.

prior *(adj.)* प्राइअर्– previous; preceding पूर्व, पूर्ववर्ती *Prior* to our meeting I had an interesting discussion with the directors.

prioritize (ise) *(v.)* प्राइऑरटाइज़– to arrange (items to be attended to) in order of their relative importance

(किसी को) अधिक महत्त्व देना You need to start *prioritizing* your work.

priority *(n.)* प्राइऑरटि– something given specified attention प्राथमिकता I give first *priority* to my family.

prison *(n.)* प्रिज़न– a public building used to house convicted criminals and accused persons remanded in custody and awaiting trial क़ैदखाना, कारागार, बंदीगृह The *prison* warden is an awful person.

prisoner *(n.)* प्रिज़नर– a person confined by any of various restraints क़ैदी, बंदी The government released the *prisoner* after five years.

privacy *(n.)* प्रिवसी–1. the condition of being private or withdrawn; seclusion गोपनीयता We needed *privacy* to discuss terms and conditions of the contract.

2. the condition of being necessarily restricted to a single person एकांतता, एकांत She doesn't want to disturb her *privacy*.

private *(adj.)* प्राइवेट– not widely or publicly known निजी Please don't interfere in my *private* life.

privately *(adv.)* प्राइवेटली– confidentially; secretly व्यक्तिगत रूप से, गुप्त रूप से May I speak to you *privately*?

privilege *(n.)* प्रिवलिज– a benefit, immunity, etc, granted under certain conditions सौभाग्य, विशेषाधिकार It is my *privilege* to join you for the movie.

privileged *(adj.)* प्रिवलिज्ड– enjoying or granted as a privilege or privileges विशेष-सुविधा-प्राप्त He is from a *privileged* family.

prize *(n.)* प्राइज़– a reward or honour for victory or for having won a contest, competition, etc. पुरस्कार, इनाम Who won the first *prize* in the music contest?

pro *(prep.)* प्रो–1. in favour of हिमायती, समर्थक I am *pro*-Indian.

2. professional practitioner पेशेवर खिलाड़ी Andrew is a golf *pro*.

probability *(n.)* प्रॉबबिलटी– an event or other thing that is probable संभावना, अनुमान There is a huge *probability* that we might succeed in our efforts.

probable *(adj.)* प्रॉबबल– likely to be or to happen but not necessarily so संभावित It's hard to find a *probable* cause of the murder.

probably *(adv.)* प्रॉबबली– in all likelihood or probability संभवतः, कदाचित Seema will *probably* call me tomorrow evening.

probation *(n.)* प्रबेशन– a system of dealing with offenders by placing them under the supervision of a probation officer परिवीक्षा-काल He violated his *probation* period.

probe *(n.)* प्रोब– to search into or question closely जाँच, तहकीकात The *probe* into the investigation revealed some shocking results.

problem *(n.)* प्रॉब्लम– any thing, matter, person, etc. that is difficult to deal with, solve, or overcome समस्या He had developed a drinking *problem*.

problematic *(adj.)* प्रॉबलमैटिक– having the nature or appearance of a problem; questionable जटिल, समस्यात्मक We have an argument on a *problematic* issue.

procedure *(n.)* प्रोसीजर– a way of acting or progressing in a course of action, esp an established method कार्यपद्धति, प्रक्रिया Manoj was asking the *procedure* to change the subject.

proceed *(v.)* प्रसीड–1. to undertake and continue (something or to do something) आगे बढ़ाना After a short rest, we *proceeded* on our way.

2. to advance or carry on करने लगना After taking a cup of tea, mother *proceeded* to cook the dinner.

proceeding *(n.)* प्रोसीडिंग– any step taken in a legal action क़ानूनी कार्यवाही The court *proceedings* moved at a very slow pace.

process *(n.)* प्रोसेस– a series of actions that produce a change or development प्रक्रिया, कार्यवाही Though a failure, the project proved to be a learning *process* for us.

processed *(adj.)* प्रोसेस्ड– treated or prepared by a special method, esp in order to preserve it कृत्रिम क्रिया द्वारा तैयार, संसाधित It is better to avoid *processed* food to stay healthy.

procession *(n.)* प्रोसेशन– a group of people or things moving forwards in an orderly, regular, or ceremonial manner जुलूस A large *procession* was blocking the traffic.

proclaim *(v.)* प्रोक्लेम– to announce publicly घोषित करना A man went round the market *proclaiming* the news.

procrastinate *(v.)* प्रोक्रैस्टिनेट– to put off or defer (an action) until a later time; delay टालमटोल करना, जान-बूझकर देर लगाना He always *procrastinates* his work.

procure *(v.)* प्रोक्युअर्– to obtain or acquire; secure प्राप्त करना He was able to *procure* the goods on time

prodigal *(adj.)* प्रॉडिगल– recklessly wasteful or extravagant, as in disposing of goods or money फ़िज़ूलख़र्च, ख़र्चीला No one knew that she was *prodigal* during shopping.

produce *(v.)* प्र'ड्यूस्–1. to bring (something) into existence; yield उत्पन्न करना, पैदा करना The magician *produced* a rabbit from his hat.
2. to manufacture (a commodity) रचाना, बनाना Where is this car *produced*?
3. *(n.)* anything that is produced; product माल, पैदावार, उपज The farmers brought their *produce* to the market.

producer *(n.)* प्रड्यूसर–1. a person or thing that produces उत्पादक Saudi Arab is a major *producer* of petrol.
2. a person responsible for the artistic direction of a play, including interpretation of the script, preparation of the actors, and overall design निर्माता Jon Landau is the *producer* of the movie Titanic.

product *(n.)* प्रॉडक्ट– something produced by effort, or some mechanical or industrial process पैदावार, उत्पाद The final *product* is not up to the required standards.

production *(n.)* प्रडक्शन– anything that is produced; product उत्पादन There is a mass *production* of agriculture in India in the last few years.

productive *(adj.)* प्रडक्टिव– producing or having the power to produce; fertile फलप्रद, उपयोगी His advise has always proved to be very *productive* for me.

profess *(v.)* प्रफ़ेस– to affirm or announce (something, such as faith); acknowledge मनोभाव व्यक्त करना In the end he *professed* to the crime.

profession *(n.)* प्रफ़ेशन–1. an occupation requiring special training in the liberal arts or sciences, esp one of the three learned professions, law, theology, or medicine व्यवसाय, पेशा I am a lawyer by *prefession.*
2. the act of professing; avowal; declaration घोषणा It is foolish to believe his *professions.*

professional *(adj.)* प्रफ़ेशनल– of, relating to, suitable for, or engaged in as a profession पेशेवर, व्यावसायिक You can be very successful by being highly *professional.*

professionally *(adv.)* प्रफ़ेशनली– in such a way as to be of, relating to, suitable for, or engaged in as a profession or an occupation requiring special training in the liberal arts or sciences व्यावसायिक रूप से *Professionally* she is a writer.

professor *(n.)* प्रफ़ेसर– the principal lecturer or teacher in a field of learning at a university or college; a holder of a university chair विश्वविद्यालय का शिक्षक Naseem is *a professor* of English at Aligarh University.

proficient *(adj.)* प्रफ़िशन्ट– having great facility (in an art, occupation, etc.); skilled दक्ष, प्रवीण, निपुण He is *proficient* in six languages.

profile *(n.)* प्रोफ़ाइल– a short biographical sketch of a subject ख़ाका, रूपरेखा, संक्षिप्त चरित्र-चित्रण He created a *profile* of the serial killer for the police.

profit *(v.)* प्रॉफ़िट– 1. to gain or cause to gain profit लाभ कमाना/पहुंचाना He *profited* by the sale of his car.
2. *(n.)* excess of revenues over outlays and expenses in a business enterprise over a given period of time, usually a year नफ़ा, लाभ, फायदा He sold his goods at a big *profit.*

profitable *(adj.)* प्रोफ़िटबल– affording gain, benefit, or profit फायदेमंद, लाभदायक The business is doing well if it is *profitable.*

pro forma *(adj.)* प्रोफ़ार्मा– prescribing a set form or procedure निदर्शन-पत्र, दस्तावेज़ Please prepare a *pro forma* of instructions and show it to me.

profound *(adj.)* प्रफ़ाउन्ड– penetrating deeply into subjects or ideas अत्यंत गहरा Sachin Tendulkar had a *profound* influence on young cricketers.

programme *(n.)* प्रोग्रैम– a written or printed list of the events, performers, etc. in a public performance कार्यक्रम, योजना Have you chalked out your *programme* for the vacation?

progress *(v.)* प्रोग्रेस्– 1. to move forwards or onwards, as towards a place or objective आगे बढ़ना How far have you *progressed* with the book you are writing?
2. *(n.)* satisfactory development, growth, or advance प्रगति, उन्नति My teacher was pleased with my *progress.*

progressive *(adj.)* प्रोग्रेसिव– of or relating to progress प्रगामी, उन्नति एवं प्रगति करने वाला Vijay is a man of *progressive* thoughts.

progressively *(adv.)* प्रोग्रेसिवली– in a way that proceeds or progresses by steps or degrees लगातार, धीरे-धीरे The students' performance was *progressively* worse in the class.

prohibit *(v.)* प्रहिबिट– to forbid by law or other authority मना करना Drinking is *prohibited* till the age of 25.

prohibition *(n.)* प्रोइबिशन– the act of prohibiting or state of being prohibited मनाही, निषेध There is a *prohibition* of smoking in public places.

project *(n.)* प्रोजेक्ट– 1. a proposal, scheme, or design परियोजना Have you prepared a *project* report for the industry you want to set up?
2. *(v.)* to predict; estimate; extrapolate अनुमान लगाना This company is trying to *project* a new image in the market.

projector *(n.)* प्रोजेक्टर– an optical instrument that projects an enlarged image of individual slides onto a screen or wall प्रक्षेपण-यंत्र, प्रक्षेपक The farmers saw a documentary film on *projector.*

prolific *(adj.)* प्रलिफ़िक– producing fruit, offspring, etc. in abundance बहुफलदायक A R Rahman is a *prolific* composer.

prologue *(n.)* प्रोलॉग– the prefatory lines introducing a play or speech भूमिका, प्रस्तावना She wrote a *prologue* of this chapter.

prolong *(v.)* प्रलॉन्ग– to lengthen in duration or space; extend लम्बा करना, बढ़ाना I would not like to *prolong* my stay in Kolkata.

prominent *(adj.)* प्रॉमिनेण्ट– widely known; eminent प्रमुख, मुख्य I was in the midst of *prominent* personalities.

promiscuous *(adj.)* प्रमिस्क्युअस– indulging in casual and indiscriminate sexual relationships व्यभिचारी *Promiscuous* persons are prone to AIDS.

promise *(n.)* प्रॉमिस–1. an undertaking or assurance given by one person to another agreeing or guaranteeing to do or give something, or not to do or give something, in the future वादा, वचन You should always keep your *promise.*

2. the thing of which an assurance is given विश्वास/आशा She shows *promise* as a singer.

3. *(v.)* to undertake to give (something to someone) वादा करना My mother *promised* to buy me a watch on my birthday.

promising *(adj.)* प्रॉमिसिंग– showing promise of favourable development or future success आशाजनक, होनहार His *promising* career came to an abrupt end because of the accident.

promote *(v.)* प्रमोट– to raise to a higher rank, status, degree, etc. आगे बढ़ाना, तरक्की देना My son has been *promoted* to the higher class.

promotion *(n.)* प्रमोशन– the act of raising to a higher rank, status, degree, etc. तरक्क़ी His *promotion* is being constantly blocked by the senior management.

prompt *(adj.)* प्रॉम्ट– performed or executed without delay तत्पर, उद्यत He always takes *prompt* action towards any problem.

promptly *(adv.)* प्रॉम्पट्ली– in such a way as to be quick or ready to act or respond तुरंत, तत्परता से, बिना रुके Sunil *promptly* accepted my invitation to dinner party.

prone *(adj.)* प्रोन– having an inclination to do something (किसी रोग या दुर्घटना की संभावना से) ग्रस्त, प्रवृत्त Small babies are easily *prone* to diseases.

pronoun *(n.)* प्रोनाउन्– one of a class of words that serves to replace a noun phrase that has already been or is about to be mentioned in the sentence or context सर्वनाम *Pronouns* make a sentence more constructive and precise.

pronounce *(v.)* प्रनाउन्स्– to utter or articulate (a sound or sequence of sounds) उच्चारित/उच्चारण करना Some words are very difficult to *pronounce.*

pronunciation *(n.)* प्रननूसिएशन– the supposedly correct manner of pronouncing sounds in a given language उच्चारण They speak English with the correct *pronunciation*

proof *(v.)* प्रूफ़– 1. to take a proof from (type matter, a plate, etc.) सबूत देना Can you *prove* that he committed the theft?

2. *(n.)* any evidence that establishes or helps to establish the truth, validity, quality, etc. of something सबूत, प्रमाण What is the *proof* that he committed the theft?

propaganda *(n.)* प्रॉपगैण्डा– the organized dissemination of information, allegations, etc. to assist or damage the cause of a government, movement, etc. प्रचार Despite the whole *propaganda,* the movie was a big flop.

propagate *(v.)* प्रॉपगेट– to move through, cause to move through, or transmit, esp in the form of a wave प्रचार करना, चारों ओर फैलाना Television serials *propagate* a false image of the ideal family.

proper *(adj.)* प्रॉपर्– appropriate or suited for some purpose ठीक, सही The *proper* procedure has to be followed while filling an application.

properly *(adv.)* प्रॉपर्ली– in a way that is necessary for some purpose सही तरीक़े से You are not dressed *properly.*

property *(n.)* प्रॉपर्टि– something of value, either tangible, such as land, or intangible, such as patents, copyrights, etc. ज़ायदाद, सम्पत्ति He owns residential *property* in Goa.

prophecy *(n.)* प्रॉफ़सी– a prediction or guess भविष्यवाणी The soothsayers *prophecy* for me came true.

prophet *(n.)* प्रॉफ़ेट– a person who supposedly speaks by divine inspiration, esp one through whom a divinity expresses his will पैग़म्बर *Prophet* Muhammad was the messenger of God.

propitiate *(v.)* प्रपिशिएट– to appease or make well disposed; conciliate राज़ी करना, मना लेना He *propitiated* her by presenting a bouquet of flowers.

proportion *(n.)* प्रपॉर्शन– the relationship between different things or parts with respect to comparative size, number, or degree; relative magnitude or extent; ratio अनुपात The *proportion* of men and women in the company is quite unequal.

proportionate *(adj.)* प्रपोर्शनट– being in proper proportion आनुपातिक, संतुलित The increase in price is *proportionate* to the increase in the cost of production.

proportionately *(adv.)* प्रपॉर्शनटली– in proportion यथानुपात, अनुपात में He divided the pizza *proportionately* into eight pieces.

propose *(v.)* प्रपोज़–1. to plan or intend (to do something) इरादा/विचार करना I *propose* to go abroad in the near future.
2. to make an offer of marriage (to someone) विवाह का प्रस्ताव करना I hear Madhav has *proposed* to Meena.

proposal *(n.)* प्रपोज़ल– something proposed, as a plan सुझाव, प्रस्ताव The board of directors accepted my *proposal* wholeheartedly .

proprietor *(n.)* प्रोप्राइअटर्– an owner of unincorporated business enterprise मालिक The *proprietor* of the hotel received me at the door.

prosecute *(v.)* प्रॉसिक्यूट– to bring a criminal action against (a person) for some offence मुक़दमा दायर करना, अभियोग लगाना Vansh was *prosecuted* by the counsel on a charge of robbery.

prosecution *(n.)* प्रॉसिक्यूशन– the act of prosecuting or the state of being prosecuted मुक़दमा, अभियोजन The evidence compelled the judge to bring a *prosecution* against him.

prospect *(n.)* प्रॉस्पेक्ट–1. a vision of the future; what is foreseen; expectation संभावना The *prospect* of losing this fight is unimaginable
2. a probability or chance for future success, esp as based on present work or aptitude प्रत्याशा I look forward to the *prospect* of seeing you.

prospectus *(n.)* प्रॉस्पेक्टस– a pamphlet or brochure giving details of courses, as at a college or school विवरण-पत्रिका, विवरण-पत्र The college issued a *prospectus* for admission of the students.

prosper *(v.)* प्रास्पर्– to thrive, succeed, etc. or cause to thrive, succeed, etc. in a healthy way फलना-फूलना, उन्नति करना His life *prospered* after his marriage.

prosperity *(n.)* प्रॉस्पेरटी– the condition of prospering; success or wealth

समृद्धि, खुशहाली May God give you good health and *prosperity!*

prosperous *(adj.)* प्रॉसपरस– rich; affluent; wealthy खुशहाल, संपन्न Now he is very *prosperous.*

prostitute *(n.)* प्रॉसटिट्यूट– a woman who engages in sexual intercourse for money वेश्या *Prostitutes* are now called call-girls.

protagonist *(n.)* प्रोटैगनिस्ट– the principal character in a play, story, etc. प्रमुख, नायक It was difficult to decide who was the *protagonist* in the movie.

protect *(v.)* प्रोटेक्ट्– to defend from trouble, harm, attack, etc. रक्षा करना, बचाना Doctor made the effort to *protect* the patient

protection *(n.)* प्रोटेक्शन्– the act of protecting or the condition of being protected सुरक्षा The terrorist was brought under the strict police *protection* to the court.

protective *(adj.)* प्रोटेक्टिव– giving or capable of giving protection रक्षात्मक, बचावी Parents are *protective* for their children.

protein *(n.)* प्रोटीन्– any of a large group of nitrogenous compounds of high molecular weight that are essential constituents of all living organisms प्रोटीन Vitamin D is an essential *protein* for bones.

protest *(v.)* प्रोटेस्ट्– 1. to make a strong objection (to something, esp a supposed injustice or offence) विरोध करना, असहमति प्रकट करना The employees *protested* against the policy of the management.

2. *(n.)* an expression of disagreement or complaint विरोध The union organised a *protest* against low wages.

protocol *(n.)* प्रोटकाल्– the formal etiquette and code of behaviour, precedence, and procedure for state and diplomatic ceremonies नयाचार The guests are to be seated according to *protocol.*

protrude *(v.)* प्रोट्रूड– to thrust or cause to thrust forwards or outwards सतह से बाहर निकलना The branches of the tree were *protruding* from the old wall of the cave.

proud *(adj.)* प्राउड्–1. having an inordinately high opinion of oneself; arrogant or haughty अभिमान, गर्व Every mother is *proud* of her children.

2. feeling honoured or gratified by or as if by some distinction गौरवपूर्ण Abhinav Bindra's winning of Olympic gold medal was a *proud* moment for the whole nation.

prove *(v.)* प्रूव– to establish or demonstrate the truth or validity of; verify, esp by using an established sequence of procedures or statements प्रमाणित/सिद्ध करना Can you *prove* your charge of theft against this man?

proven *(adj.)* प्रोवन्– tried; tested प्रमाणित, सिद्ध किया हुआ The charges against her were *proven* in court.

proverb *(n.)* प्रॉवर्ब– a short, memorable, and often highly condensed saying embodying, esp with bold imagery, some commonplace fact or experience कहावत, लोकोक्ति 'Every rose has a thorn' is a *proverb.*

provide *(v.)* प्रोवाइड्–1. to put at the disposal of; furnish or supply देना, प्रबंध करना We *provided* the poor family with a shelter.

2. supply means of support (to), esp financially प्रबंध करना Wise people *provide* for their old age.

provided *(conj.)* प्रोवाइडेड्– if you say that something will happen provided or provided that something else happens, you mean that the first thing will happen only if the second thing also happens इस शर्त पर कि, बशर्ते कि *Provided* that I complete the project on time, I might get a promotion.

province *(n.)* प्रॉविन्स्– a territory governed as a unit of a country or empire प्रान्त, सूबा, प्रदेश Fighting is still going on in the eastern *province* of Afghanistan.

provision *(n.)* प्रोविश़न्– the act of supplying or providing food, etc. प्रावधान There is no *provision* of tea in his office.

provisional *(adj.)* प्रोविश़नल– arranged but not yet definite अस्थायी I had a *provisional* driving licence while learning to drive.

provocative *(adj.)* प्रोवाकेटिव– acting as a stimulus or incitement, esp to anger or sexual desire; provoking भड़काऊ His *provocative* remarks always pinch me.

provoke *(v.)* प्रवोक– to promote (certain feelings, esp anger, indignation, etc.) in a person उकसाना, उत्तेजित करना Do not *provoke* him, it might not be good for you.

proximity *(n.)* प्रॉक्सिमिटी– nearness in space or time समीपता, निकटता I don't like close *proximity* of people that I don't know.

prudent *(adj.)* प्रूडण्ट– practical and careful in providing for the future विवेकपूर्ण *Prudent* use of electricity would contribute in conservation of power.

pry *(v.)* प्राई– to make an impertinent or uninvited inquiry (about a private matter, topic, etc.) ताक-झांक करना It is wrong to *pry* in other peoples personal matters.

psychiatrist *(n.)* साइकाइअट्रिस्ट– a doctor who treats people suffering from mental illness मनोरोग चिकित्सक A *psychiatrist* does the psychoanalysis of depressed beings.

psychic *(adj.)* साइकिक्– mental as opposed to physical; psychogenic मानसिक He is a spiritual man with *psychic* powers.

psychological *(adj.)* साइकलॉजिकल्– of or relating to the mind or mental activity मनोवैज्ञानिक Love and care give *psychological* development of a child.

psychology *(n.)* साइकॉलजी– the scientific study of all forms of human and animal behaviour, sometimes concerned with the methods through which behaviour can be modified मनोविज्ञान We should understand the *psychology* of children very well.

pub *(n.)* पब्– a building with a bar and one or more public rooms licensed for the sale and consumption of alcoholic drink, often also providing light meals मधुशाला We had an exciting time in the *pub* last night.

puberty *(n.)* प्यूबर्टी– the period at the beginning of adolescence when the sex glands become functional and the secondary sexual characteristics emerge यौवनारंभ, तारुण्य Natasha has reached at the age of *puberty*.

public *(n.)* पब्लिक– 1. well-known or familiar to people in general जनता, जनसाधारण Is this a *public* thoroughfare?
2. *(adj.)* of, relating to, or concerning the people as a whole, open or accessible to all सार्वजनिक, खुलेआम, प्रकट रूप से There are certain things that I cannot say in *public*. A restaurant is a *public* place.

publication *(n.)* पब्लिकेशन– the act or process of publishing a printed work प्रकाशन Pustak Mahal is a reputed *publication* house of books.

publicity *(n.)* पब्लिसिटी– the technique or process of attracting public attention to people, products, etc, as by the use of the mass media प्रचार, ख्याति Film actors engage in a lot of *publicity* during the launch of their movie.

public relations *(n.)* पब्लिक रिलेशन्स– the practice of creating, promoting, or maintaining goodwill and a favourable image among the public towards an institution, public body, etc. जनसंपर्क Vaibhav works as a *public relations* manager.

public service *(n.)* government employment जनसेवा, लोकसेवा She has applied for the job in union *public service* commission.

public transport *(n.)* पब्लिक ट्रान्सपोर्ट– a system of buses, trains, etc. running on fixed routes, on which the public may travel सार्वजनिक यातायात We travelled to our hometown by *public transport.*

publish *(v.)* पब्लिश– to produce and issue (printed or electronic matter) for distribution and sale प्रकाशित करना It is getting to get a book *published* these days.

publisher *(n.)* पब्लिशर– a company or person engaged in publishing periodicals, books, music, etc. प्रकाशक This *publisher* pays a good royalty to the authors.

puddle *(n.)* पडल्– a small pool of water, esp of rain छोटे-छोटे पानी भरे गड्ढे During the rainy season the roads are filled with *puddles.*

puff *(n.)* पफ़– a short quick draught, gust, or emission, as of wind, smoke, air, etc. esp a forceful one कश, फूंक Would you like to take a *puff* on a cigarette?

puffed *(adj.)* पफ्ड– breathing with difficulty because you have been using a lot of energy हांफता हुआ, सांस फूला हुआ Madhu was *puffed* after climbing the stairs.

puffy *(adj.)* पफ़ी– swollen or bloated सूजा हुआ Her eyes looks *puffy.* She might have been crying.

puke *(v.)* प्यूक– to vomit उलटी करना, कै करना She *puked* all the way because she drank too much alcohol.

pull *(v.)* पुल– to exert force on (an object) so as to draw it towards the source of the force खींचना Please *pull* down the curtain.

- **pull apart**– to criticize harshly आलोचना करना, The selection committee *pulled* him *apart.*
- **pull down**– to destroy or demolish किसी इमारत को ढहाना, My old house was *pulled down.*
- **pull leg**– a practical joke or mild deception मज़ाक़ बनाना, Why are you *pulling* my leg?
- **pull off**– to succeed in performing (a difficult feat) किसी काम में सफल होना, The bowler *pulled off* two wickets in the end.

pulp *(n.)* पल्प– soft or fleshy plant tissue, such as the succulent part of a fleshy fruit गूदा, लुगदी She made a thick *pulp* of tomatoes.

pulsate *(v.)* पलसेट– to expand and contract with a rhythmic beat; throb धड़कना, कांपना, फड़कना His heartbeat *pulsated* on seeing his girlfriend.

pulse *(n.)* पल्स– the rhythmic contraction and expansion of an artery at each beat of the heart, often discernible to the touch at points such as the wrists नाड़ी The doctor felt my *pulse.*

pump *(v.)* पम्प– 1. to raise or drive (air, liquid, etc. esp into or from something) with a pump or similar device पम्प करना, हवा भरना I *pumped* air into the tube.

2. *(n.)* any device for compressing, driving, raising, or reducing the

pressure of a fluid, esp by means of a piston or set of rotating impellers पम्प I have purchased a new water *pump.*

pumpkin *(n.)* पम्पकिन– the large round fruit of any of these plants, which has a thick orange rind, pulpy flesh, and numerous seeds कद्दू *Pumpkin* is a rich source of nutrients and antioxidants that fights cancer.

punch *(v.)* पन्च– 1. to strike blows (at), esp with a clenched fist घूंसा मारना, मुक्का मारना The boxer *punched* on his nose.

2. *(n.)* a blow with the fist घूंसा, मुक्का Sachin gave him a hard *punch* on his face.

punctual *(adj.)* पन्क्चुअल– arriving or taking place at an arranged time; not late पाबन्द, समयनिष्ठ He has been reliable and *punctual.*

punctuation *(n.)* पन्क्चुएशन– the use of symbols not belonging to the alphabet of a writing system to indicate aspects of the intonation and meaning not otherwise conveyed in the written language विराम-चिह्न विधान He used wrong *punctuation* in the paragraph making it incorrect.

puncture *(v.)* पंक्चर– 1. to pierce (a hole) in (something) with a sharp object पंचर होना या करना A nail *punctured* my car tube.

2. *(n.)* a small hole made by a sharp object ट्यूब में होने वाला छेद, पंचर I got a *puncture* in my car tube last night.

punish *(v.)* पनिश– to force (someone) to undergo a penalty or sanction, such as imprisonment, fines, death, etc. for some crime or misdemeanour दंड देना, सज़ा देना The police *punished* the criminals severely.

punishable *(adj.)* पनिशबल– liable to be *punished* or deserving of punishment दंडनीय, सज़ा के योग्य Piracy is *punishable* by law all over the world.

punishment *(n.)* पनिशमन्ट– a penalty or sanction given for any crime or offence सज़ा, दण्ड The teacher gave the students strict *punishment* over their mistakes.

pupil *(n.)* प्यूपिल्–1. a student who is taught by a teacher, esp a young student शिष्य, छात्र He has been my *pupil* since he was a child.

2. the dark circular aperture at the centre of the iris of the eye, through which light enters आँख की पुतली A cat's *pupils* are dilated in the dark.

puppet *(n.)* पपेट–1. a small doll or figure of a person or animal moved by strings attached to its limbs or by the hand inserted in its cloth body कठपुतली We enjoyed watching the *puppet* show.

2. a person, group, state, etc.that appears independent but is in fact controlled by another किसी और के इशारों पर चलने वाला व्यक्ति Stop being a *puppet* in his hands.

puppy *(n.)* पपी– a young dog; pup पिल्ला The little girl pampered the *puppy.*

purchase *(v.)* पर्चेज़– 1. to obtain (goods, etc.) by payment खरीदना For how much did you *purchase* this tape recorder?

2. *(n.)* something that is purchased, esp an article bought with money ख़रीद She put all her *purchases* in a bag.

pure *(adj.)* प्युअर्–1. free from tainting or polluting matter; clean; wholesome शुद्ध We should always drink *pure* water.

2. free from moral taint or defilement निरा He laughed with *pure* joy.

purify *(v.)* प्युअरिफ़ाइ– to free (something) of extraneous, contaminating, or debasing matter शुद्ध करना, साफ़ करना People should consume only *purified* water.

purity *(n.)* प्युअरटि– the state or quality of being pure पवित्रता, शुद्धता, पाकीज़गी The Ganges river is a symbol of *purity.*

purple *(n.)* पर्पल– any of various colours with a hue lying between red and blue and often highly saturated; a nonspectral colour बैंगनी Rajesh became *purple* with rage.

purpose *(n.)* पर्पस्– the reason for which anything is done, created, or exists उद्देश्य What is the *purpose* of your visit?

purposeful *(adj.)* पर्पसफुल– having a definite purpose in view उद्देश्यपूर्ण His brother joined in defence services with a *purposeful* mind.

purposely *(adj.)* पर्पसली– for a definite reason; on purpose किसी ख़ास उद्देश्य से He committed the crime *purposely.*

purse *(n.)* पर्स– a small bag or pouch, often made of soft leather, for carrying money, esp coins बटुआ, थैली His *purse* is filled with money.

pursue *(v.)* पर्स्यू– to follow (a fugitive, etc.) in order to capture or overtake पीछा करना The investigator *pursued* the case vigorously and judiciously.

push *(v.)* पुश– 1. to apply steady force to (something) in order to move it धकेलना, धक्का देना I *pushed* the door open.

2. *(n.)* a part or device that is pressed to operate some mechanism धक्का We gave the heavy box a good *push* to move it.

put *(v.)* पुट–1. to cause to be (in a position or place) रखना Where have you *put* my spectacles?

➢ **put across**– to communicate in a comprehensible way अपनी बात साफ़ तरीके से कहना, Sheena was trying to *put across.*

➢ **put aside**– to ignore or disregard किसी बात को भूल जाना, He must *put aside* his pride.

➢ **put away**– to save वस्तुओं को संभाल कर रखना, The child *puts* his toys *away* every night.

➢ **put back**– to return to its former place वापस उसी जगह पर रखना, *Put* the plate *back* on the table.

➢ **put down**–1. to make a written record of कुछ लिखना, *Put down* your name and mobile no.

2. to repress बलपूर्वक दबा देना, The police *put down* a rebellion.

➢ **put in**– to devote (time, effort, etc.) to a task के अंदर रखना, She *puts* all her energy *in* her work.

➢ **put off**– to postpone or delay स्थगित करना, I cannot *put off* my visit to Mumbai.

➢ **put on**– to clothe oneself in पहनना, *Put on* your clothes quickly.

➢ **put out**– to extinguish or douse (a fire, light, etc.) बुझाना, Please *put out* the light.

➢ **put together**–1. कुल मिलाकर, He can't work out how to *put* this table *together.*

2. to consult together कुछ नई तरह की योजना बनाना, He is currently *putting together* a sales and marketing team.

➢ **put up**– to build; erect दीवार पर लगाना, Can I *put up* some posters here?

puzzle *(v.)* पज़ल– 1. to perplex or be perplexed उलझन में डालना Your actions *puzzle* me.

2. *(n.)* a problem that cannot be easily or readily solved पहेली, समस्या Can you solve this crossword *puzzle*?

puzzled *(adj.)* पज़ल्ड– confused or bewildered because you do not understand something भ्रांत, उलझनपूर्ण Everyone was clearly *puzzled* by the complexity of the problem.

pygmy *(v.)* पिगमी– an abnormally undersized person बौना Sunil is a *pygmy* as compared to other classmates.

pyjamas *(n.)* पजामज़– loose-fitting night clothes comprising a jacket or top and trousers पायजामा *Pyjamas* are the attire of sleeping in the night.

pyramid *(n.)* पिरमिड– a huge masonry construction that has a square base and, four sloping triangular sides सूची-स्तंभ, पिरामिड There is a lot of mystery surrounding the existence and purpose of *pyramids.*

pyre *(n.)* पाइअर्– a heap or pile of wood or other combustible material, esp one used for cremating a corpse चिता The body was burnt on the *pyre.*

python *(n.)* पाइथन– any large nonvenomous snake of the family Pythonidae अजगर The *python* is a large snake but it is not poisonous.

ꕥ

Qq

Qq *(n.)* क्यू–अंग्रेज़ी वर्णमाला का सत्रहवां अक्षर The seventeenth letter of the English alphabet. Quality begins with 'Q'.

quack *(n.)* क्वैक–1. an unqualified person who claims medical knowledge or other skills नीम-हकीम, कठवैद्य Do not ever visit that doctor. He is a *quack* and does not hold a medical degree.

2. the sound of a duck (बतख़ की आवाज़) काँ-काँ I could hear the *quacks* of the ducks from a distance.

3. *(v.)* to make a noise like a duck काँ-काँ करना He was *quaking* because of the cold weather.

quadrangle *(n.)* क्वॉडरैंगल– a plane figure consisting of four points connected by four lines. चतुर्भुजीय खुला स्थान, चतुष्कोण There was a yard in the shape of a *quadrangle*.

quadruped *(n.)* क्वाड्रुपेड– an animal, esp a mammal, that has all four limbs specialized for walking चौपाया A cow is a *quadruped* animal.

quail *(v.)* क्वेल– 1. to shrink back with fear; cower डर से काँपना The convict *quailed* when he was sentenced.

2. *(n.)* a brown bird whose meat and eggs are used for food बटेर I saw a *quail* yesterday.

quaint *(adj.)* क्वेंट–1. attractively unusual, esp in an old-fashioned style निराला, अनोखा The old man's house was old and *quaint*.

2. odd, peculiar, or inappropriate अजीब I saw a *quaint* old lady.

quake *(v.)* क्वेक– to shake or tremble with or as with fear काँपना You are *quaking* with cold.

qualification *(n.)* क्वॉलिफ़िकेशन– an official record of achievement awarded on the successful completion of a course of training or passing of an exam योग्यता, अर्हता Your *qualifications* are good enough for this job.

qualified *(adj.)* क्वॉलिफ़ाइड– having the abilities, qualities, attributes, etc. necessary to perform a particular job or task योग्य, अनुभवी You are not *qualified* for this job.

qualify *(v.)* क्वॉलिफ़ाइ– to attribute a quality to; characterize योग्य होना You do not *qualify* for this post.

qualitative *(adj.)* क्वॉलिटटिव– involving or relating to distinctions based on quality or qualities गुणात्मक, गुणों से संबंधित A *qualitative* analysis is required to complete this project.

quality *(n.)* क्वॉलटी–1. a distinguishing characteristic, property, or attribute क़िस्म, कोटि This tea is of a bad *quality*.

2. having or showing excellence or superiority गुण Honesty is one of the *qualities* of an ideal businessman.

qualm *(n.)* क्वाम– a sudden sensation of misgiving or unease आशंका, संशय I have no *qualms* about going to his place again and again.

quantitative *(adj.)* क्वॉनटिटटिव– capable of being measured परिमाणात्मक, मात्रिक Please convert all this data into *quantitative* form.

quantity *(n.)* क्वॉन्टटी–1. the aspect or property of anything that can be measured, weighed, counted, etc. मात्रा, परिमाण Pearls are found in large *quantities* in this part of the sea.

2. a specified or definite amount, weight, number, etc. निश्चित मात्रा, संख्या Just add a small *quantity* of water to the medicine.

quarantine *(n.)* क्वॉरन्टीन– a period of isolation or detention, esp of persons or animals arriving from abroad, to prevent the spread of disease, रोक, प्रतिबंध (संक्रामक रोगियों को दूसरों से मिलने-जुलने पर रोक देने की अवधि) We may not see Umesh because he is in *quarantine.*

quarrel *(v.)* क्वॉरल– 1. to engage in a disagreement or dispute; argue झगड़ा/कलह करना The children are *quarrelling* about who should have the red pen.

2. *(n.)* an angry disagreement; argument विवाद, लड़ाई-झगड़ा We don't know the cause of their *quarrel.*

quarrelsome *(adj.)* क्वॉरलसम– inclined to quarrel or disagree; belligerent झगड़ालू Mohan is a *quarrelsome* child.

quarry *(v.)* क्वॉरी–1. to extract (stone, slate, etc.) from or as if from a quarry निकालना, खोदना Large quantities of slate are *quarried* in Wales.

2. an open surface excavation for the extraction of building stone, slate, marble, etc. by drilling, blasting, or cutting खुली खान The *quarry* was polluting the atmosphere in the village.

3. *(n.)* an animal, bird, or fish that is hunted, esp by other animals; prey शिकार The hunter followed his *quarry* for several hours.

quart *(n.)* क्वॉर्ट– a unit of liquid measure equal to 2 pints or 1.14 litres क्वार्ट There are two pints in a *quart.*

quarter *(n.)* क्वॉर्टर्–1.one of four equal or nearly equal parts of an object, quantity, amount, etc. चौथाई, चतुर्थांश It is *quarter* to four.

2. the fraction equal to one divided by four (1⁄4) चौथाई भाग Would you like to have a *quarter* of bread?

3. a region or district of a town or city मुहल्ला, बस्ती We went to all the *quarters* of Rohtak district.

quarterly *(adv.)* क्वॉटर्ली– occurring, done, paid, etc. at intervals of three months तिमाही, हर तीसरे महीने You may pay your instalments *quarterly.*

quartz *(n.)* क्वॉर्ट्स्– a colourless mineral often tinted by impurities, found in igneous, sedimentary, and metamorphic rocks. काँचमणि, स्फटिक Sometimes gold is found in *quartz.*

quash *(v.)* क्वॉश– to subdue forcefully and completely; put down; suppress दबाना या कुचल देना India *quashed* Pakistan in the cricket finals.

queen *(n.)* क्वीन–1.a female sovereign who is the official ruler or head of state महारानी King Dashratha had three *queens.*

2. a playing card with the picture of a queen on it बेगम I played a *queen* and won the trick.

queenly *(adj.)* क्वीनली– resembling or appropriate to a queen रानी-सदृश She has *queenly* manners.

queer *(adj.)* क्विअर्–1. differing from the normal or usual in a way regarded as odd or strange विचित्र, अनोखा Ahmad is a *queer* man. He talks to nobody.

2. faint, giddy, or queasy अस्वस्थ Rishi felt a little *queer* after taking rice.

3. suspicious, dubious, or shady संदिग्ध, संदेहशील We should not trust the *queer* characters.

quell *(v.)* क्वे'ल– to suppress or beat down (rebellion, disorder, etc.); subdue दमन करना, कुचलना The fighting was *quelled* by the police.

quench *(v.)* क्वें'च– to put out (a fire, flame, etc.); extinguish आग बुझाना, शमन करना He *quenched* his thirst with a glass of water.

query *(n.)* क्वे'री– 1. a question, esp one expressing doubt, uncertainty, or an objection प्रश्न, संदेह Please solve my *queries* marked in this book.

2. *(v.)* to express uncertainty, doubt, or an objection concerning (something) संदेह करना I would like to *query* these facts.

quest *(n.)* क्वे'स्ट– the act or an instance of looking for or seeking; search खोज He is on a *quest* to complete the mission.

question *(n.)* क्वे'स्चन–1. a form of words addressed to a person in order to elicit information or evoke a response; interrogative sentence प्रश्न, सवाल I request you to answer my *questions.*

2. a point at issue विचारणीय बात The *question* is, how to beat the competitors.

3. a difficulty or uncertainty; doubtful point संदेह, संशय Please accept my proposal without any *question.*

4. *(v.)* to put a question or questions to (a person); interrogate सवाल करना I would like to *question* you.

questionable *(adj.)* क्वेसचनबल– (esp of a person's morality or honesty) admitting of some doubt; dubious संदेहयुक्त, शंकास्पद His recent actions have been very *questionable.*

questionnaire *(n.)* क्वेसचनेअर– a set of questions on a form, submitted to a number of people in order to collect statistical information प्रश्नावली, प्रश्नमाला A *questionnaire* was given to the applicant by the research investigator.

queue *(n.)* क्यू–1. a line of people, vehicles, etc. waiting for something पंक्ति, कतार Please stand in a *queue.*

2. a list in which entries are stored in a specific order एक विशेष क्रम में बनाई गई सूची Please take your place in the *queue.*

3. *(v.)* to form or remain in a line while waiting पंक्ति/कतार में लगना या लगाना People *queue* at the bus-stop.

quick *(adj.)* क्विक–1 (of an action, movement, etc.) performed or occurring during a comparatively short time तेज़, शीघ्र We should take *quick* decisions.

2. characterized by rapidity of movement; swift or fast फुर्तीला, शीघ्रगामी Rishi Raj has a very *quick* mind.

quicken *(v.)* क्विकन– to make or become faster; accelerate गति बढ़ाना, फुर्ती करना She *quickened* her pace as she was getting late for the meeting.

quickly *(adv.)* क्विक्लि– with great speed; fast, rapidly शीघ्रता से, जल्दी से Please talk slowly not *quickly.*

quickness *(n.)* क्विकनस– the state of being fast तीव्रता, शीघ्रता, जल्दी *Quickness* helps in saving time and money.

quicksand *(n.)* क्विकसैण्ड– a deep mass of loose wet sand that submerges anything on top of it बलुआ दलदल His vehicle was burried in the *quicksand.*

quiet *(adj.)* क्वाइअट–1. pacify or become peaceful चुप, मौन, शांत Be *quiet,* please.

2. characterized by an absence or near absence of noise शांत, जहां शोरगुल न हो Some people like a *quiet* life.

3. *(n.)* the state of being silent, peaceful, or untroubled बहुत कम शोरगुल, शांति I love the peace and *quiet* of the countryside.

quieten *(v.)* क्वाइअटन– to make or become calm, silent, etc.; pacify or become peaceful चुप/शांत कराना Try to *quieten* the child.

quietly *(adv.)* क्वाइअटली– in a quiet manner शांतिपूर्वक, ख़ामोशी से Please move *quietly.*

quill *(n.)* क्विल– any of the large stiff feathers of the wing or tail of a bird पक्षी का पंख In olden times, people used to write with *quill.*

quilt *(n.)* क्विल्ट– a thick warm cover for a bed, consisting of a soft filling sewn between two layers of material, usually with crisscross seams रज़ाई, लिहाफ़ He uses two *quilts* in the winters to warm himself.

quirk *(n.)* क्वर्क– an individual peculiarity of character or behaviour चरित्र या व्यवहार की विशेषता I loathe his *quirk* nature.

quit *(v.)* क्विट–1. to depart from; leave खाली करना, चले जाना *"Quit* the hall at once", ordered the teacher.
2. to resign; give up (a job) छोड़ना, चले जाना We wanted to *quit* the place as fast as we could.

quite *(adv.)* क्वाइट–1. to the greatest extent; completely or absolutely बिलकुल The orange was *quite* nice in taste.
2. in actuality; truly पूर्णरूप से Are you *quite* certain that you will pass?

quiver *(v.)* क्विवर्– 1. to shake with a rapid tremulous movement; tremble कम्पन होना, काँपना, धीरे से फड़फड़ाना The leaves of the tree *quivered* in the wind.
2. *(n.)* a case for carrying arrows तरकस, तूणीर There are three arrows in my *quiver.*

quivering *(adj.)* क्विवरिंग– shaking with a rapid tremulous movement; trembling कंपन He was *quivering* with fear.

quiz *(n.)* क्विज़– any set of quick questions designed to test knowledge प्रश्नोत्तरी Let us try to answer this poetry *quiz.*

quizzical *(adj.)* क्विज़िकल– questioning and mocking or supercilious प्रश्नभरी, आश्चर्यभरा He gave me such a *quizzical* look that I got surprised.

quota *(n.)* क्वोटा– the proportional share or part of a whole that is due from, due to, or allocated to a person or group कोटा, अभ्यंश, यथांश The mail messages in my inbox exceeded the *quota.*

quotation *(n.)* क्वोटेशन– a phrase or passage from a book, poem, play, etc. remembered and spoken, esp to illustrate succinctly or support a point or an argument उद्धरण, वाक्यांश Ram copied a *quotation* from Rabindranath Tagore's writings.

quote *(v.)* क्वोट–1.to recite a quotation (from a book, play, poem, etc.), esp as a means of illustrating or supporting a statement उद्धृत करना The people often *quote* Shakespeare.
2. to state (a current market price) of (a security or commodity) मूल्य बताना Ask Mr. Gopal to *quote* a price for his TV set.

quotient *(n.)* क्वोशण्ट– the result of the division of one number or quantity by another भागफल The teacher taught calculating *quotient* in division.

Rr

Rr *(n.)* आर–अंग्रेज़ी वर्णमाला का अठारहवां अक्षर The eighteenth letter of the English alphabet. Rabbit begins with 'R'.

rabbit *(n.)* रैबिट– any of various common gregarious burrowing leporid mammals खरगोश, खरहा *Rabbits* like to eat carrotsn.

rabble *(n.)* रैबल– a disorderly crowd; mob कोलाहलपूर्ण भीड़ She gave a speech which appealed to the *rabble.*

rabies *(n.)* रेबीज़– an acute infectious viral disease of the nervous system transmitted by the saliva of infected animals, esp dogs. रैबीज़ (खतरनाक छूत का रोग जो पागल कुत्ते के काटने पर होता है) The dog bites me and I got infected with *rabies.*

race *(n.)* रेस–1. a group of people of common ancestry, distinguished from others by physical characteristics जाति, वंश We all belong to the human *race.*

2. a contest of speed, as in running, swimming, driving, riding, etc. दौड़ Suresh came first in the 3 kilometre *race.*

3. *(v.)* to move or go as fast as possible तेज़ चलना या तेज़ चलाकर ले जाना Let us *race* to the next door.

4. to engage (oneself or one's representative) in a race, esp as a profession or pastime दौड़ लगाना या लगवाना Hamid *races* his pigeons every day.

racial *(adj.)* रेशियल– denoting or relating to the division of the human species into races on grounds of physical characteristics प्रजातीय There is *racial* discrimination against whites in South Africa.

racing *(n.)* रेसिंग– a contest of speed, as in running, swimming, driving, riding, etc. दौड़ प्रतियोगिता He won the *racing* competition with a small margin

rack *(n.)* रैक– 1. a framework for holding, carrying, or displaying a specific load or object रैक, टाँड़ Put these books in the *rack.*

2. *(v.)* to cause great stress or suffering to दुखना After working in the field the whole day, his body *racked* with pain.

racket *(n.)* रैकेट–1. a noisy disturbance or loud commotion; clamour; din शोर, कोलाहल, गुलगपाड़ा What a *racket* the children are creating!

2. a bat consisting of an open network of nylon or other strings stretched in an oval frame with a handle, used to strike the ball in tennis, badminton, etc. रैकिट We use a *racket* while playing badminton.

racy *(adj.)* रेसी– (of a person's manner, literary style, etc.) having a distinctively lively and spirited quality; fresh उत्तेजक, अश्लील His personality is very *racy* in some matters.

radar *(n.)* रेडार्– a method for detecting the position and velocity of a distant object, such as an aircraft यात्रा में दिशा ज्ञात करने के लिए प्रयोग किया जाने वाला रेडियो-यंत्र, रडार The flight suddenly disappeared from the *radar.* Everyone was surprised.

radiant *(adj.)* रेडिअंट्–1. characterized by health, intense joy, happiness, etc. प्रसन्नमुख, प्रफुल्लित Asha was *radiant* when she learnt that she had stood first in the class.

2. sending out rays of light; bright; shining चमकता हुआ The morning sun was *radiant.* It made everything look bright.

radiate *(v.)* रेडिएट्– to emit (heat, light, or some other form of radiation) or (of heat, light, etc.) to be emitted as radiation प्रसारित करना, केन्द्र से किरणें या गर्मी आदि बाहर फेंकना There was a positive feel *radiating* from him as he entered the room.

radiation *(n.)* रेडिएशन– the emission or transfer of radiant energy as particles, electromagnetic waves, sound, etc. विकिरण, ख़तरनाक किरणें Sun creams are useful as they block harmful ultraviolet *radiation.*

radiator *(n.)* रेडिएटर– a device for heating a room, building, etc, consisting of a series of pipes through which hot water or steam passes प्रसारक, रेडिएटर The room is heated by electric *radiators.*

radical *(adj.)* रैडिकल– of, relating to, or characteristic of the basic or inherent constitution of a person or thing; fundamental मौलिक, मूलभूत Over the years his personality has changed *radically.*

radio *(n.)* रेडियो–1. the use of electromagnetic waves, lying in the radio-frequency range, for broadcasting, two-way communications, etc. आकाशवाणी, प्रसार केन्द्र My father works in All India *Radio,* New Delhi.

2. an electronic device designed to receive, demodulate, and amplify radio signals from sound broadcasting stations, etc. रेडियो (सेट) We bought a new *radio* set.

3. *(v.)* to transmit (a message) to (a person, radio station, etc.) by means of radio waves बेतार-यंत्र द्वारा सूचना देना Ships in danger *radio* for help.

radish रैडिश– a white root vegetable with a strong taste, eaten raw in salads मूली We can buy a bunch of *radishes* at the green-grocer's.

radium *(n.)* रेडियम– a highly radioactive luminescent white element of the alkaline earth group of metals. (एक बहुमूल्य धातु) रेडियम *Radium* is used in the treatment of many diseases.

radius *(n.)* रेडिअस्–1. a straight line joining the centre of a circle or sphere to any point on the circumference or surface व्यासार्ध, त्रिज्या The teacher asked the students to draw a circle with a *radius* of 5 centimetres.

2. a circular area of a size indicated by the length of its radius घेरा This job is not within the *radius* of our expertise.

raft *(n.)* राफ़्ट– a buoyant platform of logs, planks, etc. used as a vessel or moored platform बेड़ा (लकड़ी के लट्ठों का तैरता हुआ गट्ठा) The *raft* had many small pores in it.

rag *(n.)* रैग– 1. a fragmentary piece of any material; scrap; shred चीथड़ा, लत्ता The beggar's clothes were in *rags.*

2. *(v.)* to play rough practical jokes on सताना, चिढ़ाना, तंग करना The senior students of the medical college *ragged* the first year students.

rage *(n.)* रेज– 1. intense anger; fury क्रोध या रोष Sultana could not control her *rage* when Rashid broke her toy.

2. *(v.)* to feel or exhibit intense anger बहुत अधिक क्रोध करना His father *raged* about the room as if he were mad.

3. (esp of storms, fires, etc.) to move or surge with great violence उग्र होना, ज़ोर पकड़ना A storm was *raging* all night long.

ragged *(adj.)* रैगिड–1. (of clothes) worn to rags; tattered फटे-पुराने The poor man was wearing *ragged* clothes.

2. (of a person) dressed in shabby tattered clothes फटीचर That street boy is *ragged* and dirty.

3. not smooth, straight or even ऊबड़-खाबड़, खुरदरा We were passing from a *ragged* coastline.

raid *(v.)* रेड– 1. to make a raid against (a person, thing, etc.) छापा मारना, धावा बोलना The police *raided* an illicit liquor distillery.
2. *(n.)* a sudden surprise attack धावा, छापा Many areas were destroyed in the air *raids.*

raider *(n.)* रेडर– a person who carries out a raid छापामार The *raiders* raided the village in the middle of the night.

rail *(n.)* रेल–1. a horizontal bar of wood, metal, etc. supported by vertical posts, functioning as a fence, barrier, handrail, etc. छड़, पटरी, बाड़ा, घेरा, जंगला When you come down the stairs, keep your hand on the *rail.*
2. a permanent track composed of a line of parallel metal rails fixed to sleepers, for transport of passengers and goods in trains रेलवे These parcels should be sent by *rail.* My cousin works in the railways.

railing *(n.)* रेलिंग– a horizontal bar of wood, metal, etc. supported by vertical posts, functioning as a fence, barrier, handrail, etc. जंगला, लोहे की छड़ों से बनी बाड़ The iron *railing* has rusted and is need of serious maintenance.

railway *(n.)* रेलवे– a permanent track composed of a line of parallel metal rails fixed to sleepers, for transport of passengers and goods in trains रेलमार्ग A *railway* engine was running well on the track.

rain *(v.)* रेन– 1. to be the case that rain is falling वर्षा होना, बौछार होना It's *raining* quite heavily, so it's best to stay indoors.
2. *(n.)* a fall of rain; shower बरसात, वर्षा Don't go out in the *rain.*

rainbow *(n.)* रेनबो– a bow-shaped display in the sky of the colours of the spectrum, caused by the refraction and reflection of the sun's rays through rain or mist इन्द्रधनुष A *rainbow* has seven colours.

raincoat *(n.)* रेनकोट– a coat made of a waterproof material बरसाती She has lost her *raincoat* in the bus.

rainfall *(n.)* रेनफ़ाल– precipitation in the form of raindrops वर्षा के जल की मात्रा Rajasthan has had a low *rainfall* this year.

rainwater *(n.)* रेनवाटर– water from rain (as distinguished from spring water, tap water, etc.) बरसात का पानी *Rainwater* harvesting is a excellent technique to utilize rain water.

rainy *(adj.)* रेनी– wet or showery; bearing rain वर्षा-ऋतु *Rainy* season runs from June end to September all over India.

raise *(v.)* रेज़–1. to set or place in an upright position उठाना, खड़ा करना She *raised* her arms above her head.
2. to increase in amount, size, value, etc. बढ़ाना, वेतन वृद्धि करना The manager agreed to *raise* her wages from the next month.
3. to obtain (money, funds, capital, etc.) इकट्ठा करना We should *raise* enough funds to buy a new TV set for our school.
4. to cause to be heard or known; utter or express ऊँचा बोलना Please *raise* your voice so that we may be able to hear you.
5. *(n.)* to advance in rank or status; promote बढ़ोतरी, बढ़ती I asked my boss for a *raise.*

raisin *(n.)* रेज़िन– a dried grape किशमिश (सुखाये हुए अंगूर) *Raisins* added that extra flavour which was needed in the cake.

rake *(v.)* रेक–1. to scrape, gather, or remove (leaves, refuse, etc.) with or as if with a rake एकत्र करना The farmers were *raking* up the hay.

2. to search or examine carefully छानबीन करना We *raked* among the heap but could not find the bracelet.
3. *(n.)* a hand implement consisting of a row of teeth set in a headpiece attached to a long shaft and used for gathering hay, straw, leaves, etc. or for smoothing loose earth पांचा (एक दांतों वाला औज़ार जो कुछ बटोरने या खुरचने के काम आता है) I need a *rake* to gather the hay.

rally *(n.)* रैली– 1. a large gathering of people for a common purpose, जमघट The leader addressed a youth *rally.*
2. *(v.)* to bring (a group, unit, etc.) into order, as after dispersal, or (of such a group) to reform and come to order (आदेश पालन करने के लिए) इकट्ठा होना The young students *rallied* around their leader.

ram *(n.)* रैम्– 1. an uncastrated adult sheep मेढ़ा A male sheep is called *ram.*
2. *(v.)* to stuff or cram (something into a hole, etc.) ठूँसना I hastily *rammed* my papers into my bag.
3. (of a moving object) to crash with force (against another object) or (of two moving objects) to collide in this way टक्कर मारना The steamer *rammed* our boat in the dark night.

ramble *(v.)* रैमबल्– 1. to stroll about freely, as for relaxation, with no particular direction सैर-सपाटा करना I used to *ramble* through my village with my friend.
2. *(n.)* a leisurely stroll, esp in the countryside सैर, भ्रमण Let us have a *ramble* through the jungle.

rambler *(n.)* रैमबलर्– a person who rambles, esp one who takes country walks सैर-सपाटा करने वाला, घुमक्कड़ You will find many *ramblers* on the beach in the evening.

rambling *(adj.)* रैम्ब्लिंग्– of speech or writing) lacking a coherent plan; diffuse and disconnected असंबद्ध His constant *rambling* about his problem put me off.

ramp *(n.)* रैम्प्– a sloping floor, path, etc. that joins two surfaces at different levels ढाल, ढलान Fashion models train very hard to walk on fashion *ramps.*

rampage *(v.)* रैम्पेज्– to rush about in an angry, violent, or agitated fashion आवेश या गुस्से में इधर-उधर भागना The pack of elephant went on a *rampage* in the entire jungle.

ramshackle *(adj.)* रैमशैकल– (esp of buildings) badly constructed or maintained; rickety, shaky, or derelict जर्जर, टूटा-फूटा The *ramshackle* building made me quiver with fear.

random *(n.)* रैंडम– 1. in a purposeless fashion; not following any prearranged order निरुद्देश्य, बिना किसी निश्चित उद्देश्य के The enemy fired at *random.*
2. *(adj.)* lacking any definite plan or prearranged order; haphazard बिना सोचे-विचारे You should not mind his *random* remarks.

range *(n.)* रेंज़–1. a large stove with burners and one or more ovens, usually heated by solid fuel चूल्हा Dinner was cooked on the kitchen *range.*
2. the maximum effective distance of a projectile fired from a weapon फैलाव, क्षेत्र This gun has a *range* of twenty-five miles.
3. the total products of a manufacturer, designer, or stockist एक ही प्रकार की विभिन्न वस्तुएं Try our new *range* of beauty products.
4. the limits within which any fluctuation takes place सीमा Temperatures are expected to be in the *range* of 35 to 45 degrees.

rangoli *(n.)* रंगोली– a traditional Indian art form using coloured sand or powder to decorate a floor, courtyard, or other flat surface ज़मीन पर फूलों या रंगों की आकृति She won the *rangoli* making competition.

rank *(n.)* रैंक–1. a position, esp an official one, within a social organization, esp the armed forces पंक्ति The boys stood in a *rank*.

2. high social or other standing; status स्तर, रुतबा, कोटि Is he an artist of a high *rank*?

3. *(v.)* to accord or be accorded a specific position in an organization, society, or group दर्जा रखना, किसी ख़ास श्रेणी में आना An admiral *ranks* higher than a captain.

4. to arrange (people or things) in rows or lines; range गिनना, श्रेणीबद्ध करना Do you not *rank* me among your intimate friends?

rankle *(v.)* रैंकल– to cause severe and continuous irritation, anger, or bitterness; fester चुभना, दुख पहुंचाना His *rankle* opinions about my work angered me.

ransack *(v.)* रैन्सैक–1. to plunder; pillage लूटना The burglars *ransacked* the house and took away some valuables.

2. to search through every part of (a house, box, etc.); examine thoroughly छान मारना, खोजबीन करना My wife *ransacked* the suitcase but she could not find her wrist watch.

ransom *(v.)* रैन्सम–1. to pay money to sb that the price demanded or stipulated for such a release फिरौती देना The ruler was *ransomed* by the capitalists.

2. *(n.)* the release of captured prisoners, property, etc. on payment of a stipulated price फिरौती The kidnappers demanded a large *ransom* for the child they had kidnapped.

rant *(v.)* रैण्ट– to utter (something) in loud, violent, or bombastic tones चीख़-चिल्लाकर दोषारोपण करना, गला फाड़ना Her constant *ranting* woke up the neighbours.

rap *(v.)* रैप– 1. to strike (a fist, stick, etc) against (something) with a sharp quick blow; knock खटखट करना, ठकठक करना I *rapped* on the door but nobody opened it.

2. *(n.)* a sharp quick blow or the sound produced by such a blow ठकठक, खटखट Give a *rap* on the door.

rape *(v.)* रेप– 1. to commit rape upon (a person) बलात्कार करना The police man *raped* a minor girl.

2. *(n.)* the offence of forcing a person, esp a woman, to submit to sexual intercourse against that person's will बलात्कार *Rape* cases are increasing rapidly in India.

rapid *(adj.)* रैपिड– (of an action or movement) performed or occurring during a short interval of time; quick तेज़, शीघ्रगामी Society can only progress if there are *rapid* changed in technology.

rapport *(n.)* रैपॉर– a sympathetic relationship or understanding संबंध, घनिष्ठता I have to built a good *rapport* with my seniors to succeed.

rapt *(adj.)* रैप्ट– totally absorbed; engrossed; spellbound, esp through or as if through emotion मग्न, तल्लीन I listened to her with *rapt* attention.

rapture *(n.)* रैप्चर्– the state of mind resulting from feelings of high emotion; joyous ecstasy हर्षोन्माद She was into *raptures* to stand first in the whole university.

rare *(adj.)* रे'अर्–1. not widely known; not frequently used or experienced; uncommon or unusual दुर्लभ I have got some *rare* stamps in my collection.

2. occurring seldom कभी-कभी Ganesh lives far away from his parents, so he pays *rare* visits to them.

rarely *(adj.)* रेअरली– hardly ever; seldom बहुत कम, असाधारणतः I have *rarely* seen him make a mistake at work.

raring *(adj.)* रेअरिंग– enthusiastic (esp in the phrase raring to go) अति उत्साहित He was *raring* to enter the competition.

rarity *(n.)* रेअरटी– a rare person or thing, esp something interesting or valued because it is uncommon दुर्लभता Due to its *rarity*, the gem was very expensive.

rascal *(n.)* रास्कल–1. a disreputable person; villain धूर्त, दुर्जन He is a *rascal,* don't trust him.

2. an affectionate or mildly reproving term for a child or old man शैतान लड़का The little *rascal* has finished the whole packet of biscuits.

rash *(adj.)* रैश– 1. acting without due consideration or thought; impetuous उतावला Don't be *rash* in taking a decision.

2. *(n.)* any skin eruption (त्वचा पर निकली लाल-लाल फुंसियाँ) ददोरा When we saw the *rash,* we came to know that the young boy had chicken-pox.

raspberry *(n.)* राज़बरी– a small dark red fruit that grows on bushes रसभरी I love eating *raspberries* in the summer season.

rat *(n.)* रैट– a long-tailed small animal that looks like large mouse बड़ा चूहा, मूषक The thief was caught like a *rat* in a trap.

rate *(v.)* रेट–1. to estimate the value of; evaluate दर, मूल्य निर्धारित करना They *rated* their flat quite high.

2. to consider; regard मानना, समझना Don't *rate* your chances of success highly.

3. to assign or receive a position on a scale of relative values; rank सम्मान करना, स्थान निर्धारित करना Indian's *rate* Kalidasa as one of the greatest poets of the world.

4. to be worthy of; deserve क़द्र करना I *rate* him high.

5. *(n.)* a charge made per unit for a commodity, service, etc. दाम, मूल्य Please tell us your *rates.*

6. relative quality; class or grade अनुपात, स्तर This is a first-*rate* TV set.

7. a quantity or amount considered in relation to or measured against another quantity or amount गति The cycle was moving at the *rate* of ten miles an hour.

8. the relative speed of progress or change of something variable; pace दर The *rate* of interest for home loans has risen.

> **at any rate**– a. in any case; at all events; anyway किसी भी हालत में, I can not marry her *at any rate.*

rather *(adv.)* रादर्–1. relatively or fairly; somewhat थोड़ा-सा My mother is feeling *rather* ill today.

2. to a significant or noticeable extent; quite बल्कि (अथवा अधिक ठीक कहें तो) The rising sun is golden, *rather* red.

3. to a limited extent or degree कुछ हद तक Your brother's behaviour is *rather* foolish.

ratify *(v.)* रैटिफ़ाइ– to give formal approval or consent to औपचारिक रूप से पुष्टि करना The draft to the select committee had to be *ratified* over and over again.

rating *(n.)* रेटिंग– a classification according to order or grade; ranking श्रेणी निर्धारण, मूल्यांकन The *rating* agencies played a pivotal role in the recession.

ratio *(n.)* रेशिओ– a measure of the relative size of two classes expressible as a proportion अनुपात The sex *ratio* of men to women is falling in our country.

ration *(v.)* रैशन– 1. to restrict the distribution or consumption of (a commodity) by (people) वस्तु के कम होने पर सीमित मात्रा में वितरण करना Grain was *rationed.*

2. *(n.)* a fixed allowance of food, provisions, etc. esp a statutory one for civilians in time of scarcity or soldiers in time of war रसद–खाद्य पदार्थ की निश्चित मात्रा There was shortage of grain in the country, so each family received a *ration* every week.

rational *(adj.)* रैशनल्– using reason or logic in thinking out a problem तर्कसंगत He gave a *rational* and logical explanation for his actions.

rationale *(n.)* रैशनाल्– a reasoned exposition, esp one defining the fundamental reasons for a course of action, belief, etc. तर्काधार, मूलाधार The sales representative explained the *rationale* behind the new product.

rattle *(v.)* रैटल–1. to make or cause to make a rapid succession of short sharp sounds खड़खड़ाना The storm makes windows and doors *rattle* noisily.

2. sharp sounds, as of loose pellets colliding when shaken in a container खनखनाना, बजाना The child *rattled* the coins in the tin box.

3. *(n.)* a rapid succession of short sharp sounds खड़खड़ाहट The *rattle* of empty bottles was being heard from a junk dealer.

rattlesnake *(n.)* रैटलस्नेक– a poisonous American snake that makes noise like a rattle एक ज़हरीला सांप (जिसकी पूंछ झुनझुने की तरह खड़खड़ाती है) Most of the *rattlesnakes* are found in the desert.

ravage *(v.)* रैविज– to cause extensive damage to नष्ट कर देना, तहस-नहस करना He was *ravaged* by the death of his friend.

rave *(v.)* रेव–1. to utter (something) in a wild or incoherent manner बड़बड़ाना She *raved* in her sleep when she had a nightmare.

2. to utter (something) in a wild or incoherent manner, as when mad or delirious मूर्खता-भरी बातें करना The young lady *raved* about the film stars.

ravenous *(adj.)* रैवनस– very hungry; starving बहुत भूखा, भुक्खड़ The child looked *ravenous.*

raw *(adj.)* रॉ–1. an unfinished, natural, or unrefined state; not treated by manufacturing or other processes कच्चा (सामान) All the *raw* materials for building the house have been acquired.

2. (of food) not cooked बिना पकाया हुआ We prefer *raw* vegetables.

ray *(n.)* रे– a narrow beam of light; gleam किरण His idea provided all of us with a *ray* of hope.

raze *(v.)* रेज़– to demolish (a town, buildings, etc.) completely; level (esp in the phrase raze to the ground) पूरी तरह ध्वस्त कर देना, ढाना The building was completely *razed* in a bomb blast.

razor *(n.)* रेज़र्– a sharp implement used esp by men for shaving the face उस्तरा The barber uses the *razor* to shave.

re *(pre.)* रि– indicating repetition of an action दुबारा

➢ **reappear**– to appear again (परीक्षा में) दुबारा बैठना, His brother *reappeared* in the B.A. examination.

➢ **recall** *(v.)*– to bring back to mind; recollect; remember याद करना, स्मरण करना, We can *recall* the days of our childhood.

➢ **reconstruct** *(v.)*– to construct or form again; rebuild दुबारा निर्माण करना, The shop destroyed in the fire has been *reconstructed.*

➢ **reopen** *(v.)*– to open or cause to open again दुबारा खुलना, Our school closes on Saturday evening and *reopens* on Monday morning.

> **rewrite** *(v.)*– to write (written material) again, esp changing the words or form दुबारा लिखना, Your story is badly written. Please *rewrite* it.

recount *(n.)* रिकाउण्ट– 1. a second or further count, esp of votes in a closely contested election पुनः गणना The defeated candidate requested a *recount* of votes in the election.
2. *(v.)* to count (votes, etc.) again दुबारा गिनना, वर्णन करना, He *recounted* how he had shot the lion.

reach *(v.)* रीच–1. to arrive at or get to (a place, person, etc.) in the course of movement or action पहुँचना We hope to *reach* Delhi tomorrow morning.
2. to pass or give (something to a person) with the outstretched hand हाथ या बांह बढ़ाना (कुछ छूने के लिए) Will you *reach* me that bag please?
3. to extend as far as (a point or place) (तक) बनना The labourers are making a new road, but it hasn't *reached* Shahdara yet.
4. to come to (a certain condition, stage, or situation) पहुँचना, आयु का होना When I *reach* the age of sixty, I shall reduce my working hours.
5. *(n.)* the extent or distance of reaching पहुँच, पकड़ Dry fruits are out of *reach* of a common man.

react *(v.)* रिएक्ट– (of a person or thing) to act in response to another person, a stimulus, etc. or (of two people or things) to act together in a certain way प्रतिक्रिया करना He did not *react* when he was arrested for fraud.

reaction *(n.)* रिऐक्शन– a response to some foregoing action or stimulus प्रतिक्रिया The interviewer tried to get a *reaction* from his panel of speakers

reactionary *(adj.)* रिएक्शनरी– of, relating to, or characterized by reaction, esp against radical political or social change प्रतिक्रियात्मक Some *reactionary* steps have been taken to bring change in our social system.

reactivate *(v.)* रिऐकटिवेट– to make (something) active or functional again फिर से सक्रिय करना He has *reactivated* all his past connections.

read *(v.)* रीड–1. to comprehend the meaning of (something written or printed) by looking at and interpreting the written or printed characters पढ़ना We should not *read* lying down on the bed.
2. to look at, interpret, and speak aloud (something written or printed) पढ़कर सुनाना Now please *read* me the story of Rama. The boy will *read* this letter to his grandmother.
3. to interpret the significance or meaning of through scrutiny and recognition आशय समझना You cannot *read* my thoughts.

> **read into**– to discern in or infer from a statement (meanings not intended by the speaker or writer) कुछ का कुछ समझ लेना, Why are you *reading* too much *into* my comment?

> **read on**– बिना रुके पढ़ते रहना, Don't stop, *read on* the story.

> **read out**– to read (something) aloud लोगों को पढ़कर सुनाना, Why don't you *read out* the name of the winner?

> **read through**– ग़लती ढूंढ़ने के लिए पढ़ना, I *read through* my article a few times before printing it.

> **read up**– to acquire information about (a subject) by reading intensively किसी विषय का ढंग से अध्ययन करना, I *read up* on the history of the place I visited.

readable *(adj.)* रीडबल्–1. (of style of writing) interesting, easy, or pleasant to read पढ़ने में रोचक एवं सुगम

This book is quiet informative and highly *readable*.

2. (of handwriting, etc.) able to be read or deciphered; legible पठनीय, पढ़ने लायक Sometimes doctor's handwriting is not *readable.*

reader *(n.)* रीडर्– a person who reads पाठक Hundreds of *readers* come there every day.

readily *(adv.)* रेडिली– promptly; eagerly; willingly तुरन्त ही, शीघ्र ही The students *readily* agreed for a two day picnic.

readiness *(n.)* रेडिनस्– the state of being ready or prepared, as for use or action शीघ्रता, मुस्तैदी Rashmi has learnt everything in *readiness.*

reading *(n.)* रीडिंग्–1. any matter that can be read; written or printed text पठन-पाठन The Delhi Public Library has a big *reading* room.

2. the act of a person who reads पठन, पढ़ना *Reading* and writing are her hobbies.

3. an interpretation, as of a piece of music, a situation, or something said or written विशेष विचार, व्याख्या What is your *reading* of his response to his crisis?

readjust *(v.)* रीअडजस्ट्– to adjust or adapt (oneself or something) again, esp after an initial failure परिस्थिति के अनुसार बनना या बन जाना After divorce, she took a lot of time to *readjust* herself to being single.

ready *(adj.)* रे'डि–1. in a state of completion or preparedness, as for use or action तैयार Please come soon. Breakfast is *ready.*

2. prompt or rapid तुरन्त, शीघ्र Be *ready* to do anything for your country.

3. quick in perceiving; intelligent उद्यत, (पहले से) तैयार Amitabh always has a *ready* answer.

4. willing or eager कुछ करने के लिए इच्छुक या उत्सुक I am *ready* to go to Shimla.

real *(adj.)* रिअल–1. not artificial or simulated; genuine असली Are these pearls *real*?

2. true; actual; not false प्राकृतिक, कृत्रिम Yes, these are *real* pearls.

real estate *(n.)* immovable property, esp land and buildings, including proprietary rights over land, such as mineral rights अचल सम्पत्ति (ज़मीन-जायदाद) Dinesh has fifty acres of *real estate.*

realist *(n.)* रीअलिस्ट– a person who is aware of and accepts the physical universe, events, etc. as they are; pragmatist यथार्थवादी, असलियत को स्वीकारने वाला It is difficult to find people these who are *realist.*

realistic *(adj.)* रीअलिसटिक– practical or pragmatic rather than ideal or moral यथार्थवादी Her *realistic* approach inspires me a lot.

reality *(n.)* रिऐलटी– pthe state of things as they are or appear to be, rather than as one might wish them to be यथार्थ, वास्तविकता, असलियत He is far from *reality.* Someone needs to tell him the truth.

realize (ise) *(v.)* रिअलाइज़– to become conscious or aware of (something) एहसास होना He quickly *realized* that his method of working was incorrect.

really *(adv.)* रिअली– truly; genuinely सचमुच में, वास्तव में Are the rumours surrounding you *really* true?

realm *(v.)* रि'अल्म– a royal domain; kingdom राज्य, क्षेत्र You cannot work beyond your *realm.*

reap *(v.)* रीप– to cut or harvest (a crop), esp corn, from (a field or tract of land) फ़सल काटना As you sow so shall you *reap.*

reappear *(v.)* रीअपिअर– to appear again फिर से दिखाई पड़ना The sun *reappeared* after the rain.

rear *(n.)* रिअर्– 1. the area or position that lies at the back पृष्ठ भाग, पिछला हिस्सा We want to sit in the *rear* of the bus. There was a garden at the *rear* of the palace.

2. *(v.)* to raise itself on its back legs (चौपाया का) पिछले पाँवों पर खड़ा होना When horses take fright, they *rear.*

3. to care for animals and young children देखभाल करना The farmer *rears* milch animals.

rearrange *(v.)* रीअरेंज– to put (something) back in its original order after it has been displaced फिर से व्यवस्थित करना The surgeons had to *rearrange* his face due to the accident.

reason *(n.)* रीज़न–1. a cause or an explanation कारण, हेतु Do you know the *reason* of her absence?

2. argument तर्क, दलील He was foolish for he refused to listen to *reason.*

3. *(v.)* to argue तर्क करना When the teacher *reasoned* with the naughty pupil, he begged his pardon.

reasonable *(adj.)* रीज़नबल– moderate in price; not expensive विवेकपूर्ण, उचित The firm charged with us a *reasonable* amount for their services.

reasoning *(n.)* रीज़निंग– the act or process of drawing conclusions from facts, evidence, etc. तर्क, बहस What is the *reasoning* behind this sudden change in programme?

reassure *(v.)* रीअशॉर्– to relieve (someone) of anxieties; restore confidence to आश्वासन देना The management *reassured* their employees of their jobs.

rebel *(v.)* रे'बल– 1. to show repugnance (towards) विद्रोह करना Students *rebel* against the rules of their school.

2. *(n.)* a person who rebels सत्ता-विरोधी, राजद्रोही All the *rebel* candidates in the election fray were expelled by their parties.

3. a person who dissents from some accepted moral code or convention of behaviour, dress, etc. विद्रोही, बाग़ी The district is swarming with *rebels.*

rebellion *(n.)* रिबेलियन– organized resistance or opposition to a government or other authority बग़ावत, विद्रोह There is a *rebellion* against the convention.

rebellious *(adj.)* रिबेलयस– showing a tendency towards rebellion अक्खड़, अवज्ञापूर्ण, विद्रोही Teenagers are often *rebellious* against their parents.

rebound *(v.)* रिबाउन्ड– to spring back, as from a sudden impact टकराकर फिर से वापस लौटना He scored the point via a *rebound.*

rebuke *(v.)* रिब्यूक– 1. to scold or reprimand (someone) भर्त्सना करना, डाँटना Our father often *rebuked* us for not speaking the truth.

2. *(n.)* a reprimand or scolding डांट-फटकार The *rebuke* chastened us.

recapture *(v.)* रीकैप्चर– to recover, renew, or repeat (a lost or former ability, sensation, etc.) स्मरण करना The king was able to *recapture* his land from his enemies.

recede *(v.)* रिसीड– to become more distant ओझल होना His *receding* hairline caused him a great worry.

receive *(v.)* रिसीव–1. to take (something offered) into one's hand or possession प्राप्त करना We hope to *receive* a letter from our father.

2. to greet or welcome (visitors or guests), esp in formal style स्वागत करना, (घर में आये व्यक्ति का) आदर-सत्कार करना The lady *received* her guests.

receipt *(n.)* रिसीट– a written acknowledgment by a receiver of money, goods, etc. that payment or delivery has been made रसीद Do not forget to collect the *receipts* of your deposits.

recent *(adj.)* रीसण्ट– having appeared, happened, or been made not long ago; modern, fresh, or new हाल ही The *recent* events have left her quite insane.

recently *(adv.)* रीसण्टलि– if you have done something recently or if something happened recently, it happened only a short time ago हाल ही में I *recently* came to know that you got married.

reception *(n.)* रिसे'प्शन–1. an area in an office, hotel, etc. where visitors or guests are received and appointments or reservations dealt with स्वागत-कक्ष The manager is busy, please sit at the *reception*.
2. the act of receiving or state of being received आदर, सत्कार, स्वागत My aunt gave a warm *reception* when I went to see her.
3. a formal party for guests, such as one after a wedding स्वागत-समारोह Most of the guests have been personally invited to the wedding *reception*.

receptionist *(n.)* रिसेपशनिस्ट– a person employed in an office, hotel, doctor's surgery, etc. to receive clients, guests, or patients, answer the telephone, arrange appointments, etc. स्वागतकर्ता Rekha is working as a *receptionist* in a five star hotel.

recess *(n.)* रिसे'स– a break between classes at a school मध्यावकाश, अल्पावकाश The students were eagerly waiting for the *recess*.

recession *(n.)* रिसेशन– a temporary depression in economic activity or prosperity मंदी का दौर In America, the economy falls back into *rocossion*.

recharge *(v.)* रीचार्ज– to cause (an accumulator, capacitor, etc.) to take up and store electricity again पुनः सक्रिय करना Please *recharge* the battery of cell phone.

recipe *(n.)* रेसिपि– a list of ingredients and directions for making something, esp a food preparation भोजन बनाने की विधि Mother gave us the *recipe* for making a masala dosa.

reciprocate *(v.)* रे'सिप्रकेट्– to give or feel in return आदान-प्रदान करना She *reciprocated* his smile with a frown.

recitation *(n.)* रेसिटेशन– the act of reciting from memory, or a formal reading of verse before an audience सस्वर पाठ, पठन There was a *recitation* competition in the school.

recite *(v.)* रिसाइट– to repeat (a poem, passage, etc.) aloud from memory before an audience, teacher, etc. कविता-पाठ करना He can *recite* the entire Hanuman Chalisa in one go.

reckless *(adj.)* रे'कलस– having or showing no regard for danger or consequences; heedless; rash अंधाधुंध, लापरवाह The accident was caused due to *reckless* driving.

reckon *(v.)* रे'कन–1. to calculate or ascertain by calculating; compute हिसाब करना, गिनना The price was *reckoned* high.
2. to consider or regard सोचना, मानना I *reckon* Premchand among our best writers.
3. to think or suppose; be of the opinion भरोसा रखना, अवलम्बित होना Can you *reckon* on her help?

reckoning *(n.)* रेकनिंग– settlement of an account or bill कुल देय खर्च There will be a heavy *reckoning* to pay his expenses.

recognize (ise) *(v.)* रेकगनाइज़–1. to perceive (a person, creature, or thing) to be the same as or belong to the same class as something previously seen or known; know again पहचानना We can easily *recognize* our neighbour in this picture.

2. to accept or be aware of (a fact, duty, problem, etc.) स्वीकार करना, मान्यता देना Gita *recognizes* that Rama is a better singer than she (Gita) is.

recognition *(n.)* रेकगनिशन– acceptance or acknowledgment of a claim, duty, fact, truth, etc. पहचान He was always searching for *recognition* in his entire life.

recoil *(v.)* रिकॉइल– to jerk back, as from an impact or violent thrust अप्रिय वस्तु से पीछे हटना The snake *recoiled* after its first attack.

recollect *(v.)* रे'कलेक्ट– to recall from memory; remember बीती हुई घटना या बात याद होना We all are trying to *recollect* what the teacher said in the class.

recollection *(n.)* रेकलेकशन– the act of recalling something from memory; the ability to remember अनुस्मरण, याद The *recollection* of my past fills me with many sweet memories.

recommend *(v.)* रे'कमेंड–1. to advise as the best course or choice; counsel परामर्श देना This motorcycle is defective. I would *recommend* purchasing another.

2. to praise or commend सिफ़ारिश/ संस्तुति करना Can you *recommend* her for the job?

3. to entrust (a person or thing) to someone else's care; commend स्वीकृति होना This book has been *recommended* for the tenth class by the Central Board of Secondary Education.

recommendation *(n.)* रेकमेनडेशन– the act of recommending सिफ़ारिश, अनुशंसा, संस्तुति He got the top job via my *recommendation*.

recompense *(n.)* रेकमपेन्स– compensation for loss, injury, etc. क्षतिपूर्ति She did not take any *recompense* for the damage of her vehicle.

reconcile *(v.)* रेकन्साइल–1. to make (oneself or another) no longer opposed; cause to acquiesce in something unpleasant झगड़ा मिटाना, मेल मिलाप करना Amitabh was glad to be *reconciled* to his cousin after they quarrelled.

2. to become friendly with (someone) after estrangement कलह के बाद मित्र बनना After both the parties had apologised, the two became *reconciled*.

3. to settle (a quarrel or difference समझौता कर लेना I have learnt to *reconcile* with my fate.

reconsider *(v.)* रीकनसिडर– to consider (something) again, with a view to changing one's policy or course of action पुनः विचार करना He gave him another chance to *reconsider* his offer.

reconstruct *(v.)* रीकनस्ट्रक्ट– to construct or form again; rebuild पुनः निर्माण करना The police *reconstructed* the entire crime scene to solve the case.

record *(n.)* रेकॉर्ड–1. an account in permanent form, esp in writing, preserving knowledge or information about facts or events रिकार्ड, विवरण, हिसाब, लेखा Has she a good *record*?

2. anything serving as evidence or as a memorial कीर्तिमान, रिकार्ड Salim has broken the *record* for the high jump.

3. a written account of some transaction that serves as legal evidence of the transaction प्रमाण, लिखित तथ्य It is on *record* that I have

done this work and not she, though she may claim credit for it.

4. *(v.)* to make a recording of (music, speech, etc.) अंकित करना, टेप करना Father's voice has been *recorded* on the tape.

record-breaking *(adj.)* कीर्तिमान- a record-breaking success, result, or performance is one that beats the previous best success, result, or performance स्थापक The temperature reached a *record-breaking* 46 degree yesterday.

recording *(n.)* रिकॉर्डिंग– the act or process of making a record, esp of sound on a gramophone record or magnetic tape टेप पर रिकार्ड करना The *recording* on the disc has been corrupted.

recount *(v.)* रिकाउंट– to tell the story or details of; narrate किसी के बारे में बताना या विवरण देना I can't *recount* as to how many people were there in the room.

recover *(v.)* रि'कवर्–1. to find again or obtain the return of (something lost) खोई हुई वस्तु प्राप्त करना I *recovered* my bag which I had lost in the market.

2. (of a person) to regain (health, spirits, composure, etc.), as after illness, a setback, or a shock, etc. स्वास्थ्य लाभ करना Has she *recovered* from her illness?

recovery *(n.)* रिकवरी–1. restoration to a former or better condition, recuperation पुनर्लाभ, स्वास्थ्यलाभ We are delighted to learn about her *recovery* from pneumonia.

2. an action of getting sth back वसूली He came for the *recovery* of his old debts.

recreation *(n.)* रे'क्रिएशन–1. refreshment of health or spirits by relaxation and enjoyment मनबहलाव My favourite *recreation* is playing cards.

2. an activity or pastime that promotes this मनोरंजन का साधन Gardening is a good source of *recreation.*

recruit *(n.)* रिक्रूट– 1. a newly joined member of a military service रंगरूट Many *recruits* will join the police force.

2. *(v.)* to enlist (men) for military service भरती करना The object is to *recruit* 500 policemen a month.

rectify *(v.)* रेक्टिफ़ाइ– to put right; correct; remedy संशोधन करना, सुधारना, शुद्ध करना He did not *rectify* his mistake and repeated it again.

rectangle *(n.)* रेकटैंगल– a parallelogram having four right angles आयत A *rectangle* is longer than it is wide.

recur *(v.)* रिकर्– to happen again, esp at regular intervals पुनरावृत्ति होना The imagery of fire *recurs* throughout the novel.

recycle *(v.)* रीसाइकल– to pass (a substance) through a system again for further treatment or use पुनर्चक्रण होना या करना To protect the environment we must use *recycled* products.

red *(n.)* रैड–1. red is the complementary colour of cyan and forms a set of primary colours with blue and green लाल I have a *red* colour carpet.

2. in debit; owing money घाटे में The strike put his business in the *red.*

redden *(v.)* रे'डन– to flush with embarrassment, anger, etc.; blush लाल होना The young girl *reddened* when the principal shouted at her.

reddish *(adj.)* रेडिश– somewhat red कुछ-कुछ लाल, रक्तिम Her hair was painted in a *reddish* colour.

redeem *(v.)* रिडीम– to recover possession or ownership of by payment of a price or service; regain उद्धार करना, मुक्ति दिलाना She *redeemed* the blunder by apologizing and rectifying the mistake.

redemption *(n.)* रिडेम्पशन– the act or process of redeeming छुटकारा, मुक्ति

He was looking for *redemption* from his colleagues.

redevelop *(v.)* रीडेवेलप– to rebuild or replan (a building, area, etc.) पुनः विकसित करना The entire floor was *redeveloped* to accommodate the new staff.

red-handed *(n.)* रैड-हैंडड– in the act of committing a crime or doing something wrong or shameful रंगेहाथों He was caught *red-handed* while stealing.

redistribute *(v.)* रीडिस्ट्रिब्यूट– to distribute (something) again or differently पुनः बांटना He *redistributed* the gifts.

redo *(v.)* रीडू– to do sth again कोई काम दुबारा करना He was advised to *redo* his entire work.

reduce *(v.)* रिड्यूस–1. to bring down the price of (a commodity) कम होना, क़ीमत आदि का घटना या घट जाना Has the price of wheat been *reduced*?
2. to make or become slimmer; lose or cause to lose excess weight कम करना, घटाना You seem to have *reduced* quite a lot of weight

reduction *(n.)* रिडक्शन– the act or process or an instance of reducing घटाव, कमी, कटौती There has been no *reduction* in the price of oil.

redundant *(adj.)* रिडनडंट– surplus to requirements; unnecessary or superfluous ग़ैर-जरूरी, फालतू, व्यर्थ This technology has become obsolete and *redundant.*

reed *(n.)* रीड– any of various widely distributed tall grasses that grow in swamps and shallow water and have jointed hollow stalks सरकंडा *Reeds* are used for thatching.

reek *(n.)* रीक– a strong offensive smell; stink बदबू, दुर्गन्ध The *reek* of diesel smoke proved claustrophobic.

reel *(n.)* रील–1. a roll of celluloid exhibiting a sequence of photographs to be projected कैमरे की रील Have you got a *reel* of film for your camera?
2. to whirl about or have the feeling of whirling about (दृश्य का) घूम जाना The scene *reeled* before my eyes.

refer *(v.)* रिफ़र्–1. to direct the attention of (someone) for information, facts, etc. के पास भेजना, सुपुर्द करना The matter was *referred* to the Headmaster for settlement.
2. to seek information (from) नई जानकारी के लिए उलटना-पलटना I have to *refer* to this book of general knowledge.
3. to make mention (of) उल्लेख करना When I talk about corruption, I am not *referring* to anyone here.

referee *(n.)* रे'फ़री– a person to whom reference is made, esp for an opinion, information, or a decision निर्णायक The *referee* behaved in an impartial manner in the match.

reference *(n.)* रेफ़रन्स– the act or an instance of referring संदर्भ, हवाला He gave me two *reference* books of English.

referendum *(n.)* रेफ़रेनडम– submission of an issue of public importance to the direct vote of the electorate मत-संग्रह जनमतसंग्रह Many problems of our nation can be solved by *referendum.*

refill *(v.)* रीफ़िल– to fill (something) again दुबारा भरना Please *refill* our drinks quickly.

refine *(v.)* रिफ़ाइन–1. to make or become free from impurities, sediment, or other foreign matter; purify साफ़ करना *Refining* oil is a tedious process.
2. to make or become free from coarse characteristics; make or become elegant or polished शुद्ध करना Toy makers are constantly *refining* their designs.

refined *(adj)* रिफ़ाइन्ड्– not coarse or vulgar; genteel, elegant, or polite सुसंस्कृत, शिष्ट Sudha is quite *refined* in her behaviour.

refinement *(n.)* रिफ़ाइनमेण्ट– the act of refining or the state of being refined शोधन, परिष्कार *Refinement* of sugar is necessary for health.

refinery *(n.)* रिफ़ाइनरी– a factory for the purification of some crude material, such as ore, sugar, oil, etc. परिष्करण-शाला Kamal works in a sugar *refinery.*

reflect *(v.)* रिफ़्ले'क्ट–1. to think, meditate, or ponder चिन्तन करना *Reflect* before you make a decision.

2. to show or express प्रतिबिंबित होना, परछाईं डालना A mirror *reflects* light.

reflection *(n.)* रिफ़्लेक्शन– something reflected or the image so produced, as by a mirror प्रतिबिंब, परछाईं The water was so clear that I could almost see my *reflection* in it.

reform *(v.)* रिफ़ॉर्म– 1. to improve (an existing institution, law, practice, etc.) by alteration or correction of abuses सुधार करना The new principal has greatly *reformed* the administration of the school.

2. *(n.)* an improvement or change for the better, esp as a result of correction of legal or political abuses or malpractices सुधार People are pleased with the new manager's *reforms* of the bonus rules.

reformer *(n.)* रिफ़ार्मर– someone who improves (an existing institution, law, practice, etc.) by alteration or correction of abuses समाज-सुधारक Swami Vivekanand was a great *reformer* of India.

refrain *(v.)* रिफ़्रेन–1. to abstain (from action); forbear न करना, बाज़ आना, बचना We must *refrain* from spitting on the floor.

2. ख़ुद को रोकना People must *refrain* from talking in the cinema hall.

3. *(n.)* a regularly recurring melody, such as the chorus of a song गाने की बार-बार दोहरायी जाने वाली लाइनें All the students should join in singing the *refrain* of this song.

refresh *(v.)* रिफ़्रेश–1. to make or become fresh or vigorous, as through rest, drink, or food; revive or reinvigorate नई शक्ति प्रदान करना (या प्राप्त होना) Sleep *refreshes* us when we feel tired.

2. to enliven ताज़ा करना या होना I looked at the road map to *refresh* my memory of the route.

refreshing *(adj.)* रिफ्रेशिंग– able to or tending to refresh; invigorating स्फूर्तिदायक When you are tired, a cup of tea is very *refreshing.*

refreshment *(n.)* रिफ्रेशमेण्ट–1. snacks and drinks served as a light meal अल्पाहार, हल्का-फुल्का नाश्ता, जलपान *Refreshments* were provided after the meeting.

2. the act of refreshing or the state of being refreshed ताज़गी, तरोताज़ा The sightseeing was like a *refreshment* activity to me.

refrigerator *(n.)* रिफ्रिजरेटर्– a chamber in which food, drink, etc. are kept cool रेफ्रिजरेटर, प्रशीतित्र The *refrigerator* stopped working because the power went out.

refuge *(n.)* रिफ्यूज– shelter or protection, as from the weather or danger शरण, आश्रय We took *refuge* under a tree from the scorching sun.

refugee *(n.)* रेफ़्यू'जी– a person who has fled from some danger or problem, esp political persecution शरणार्थी Delhi was crowded with *refugees* following the partition of India.

refund *(v.)* रिफ़न्ड– to return of money to a purchaser or the amount so returned लौटाना, वापस करना My security hasn't been *refunded* to me yet.

refusal *(n.)* रिफ़्यूजल– the act or an instance of refusing इनकार Her *refusal* disappointed me.

refuse *(v.)* रिफ़्यूज़– 1. to decline to give or grant (something) to (a person, organization, etc.) अस्वीकार करना I asked her for help, but she *refused.*

2. *(n.)* anything thrown away; waste; rubbish कूड़ा-करकट The industrial *refuse* should be disposed off properly.

regain *(v.)* रिगेन– to take or get back; recover फिर से प्राप्त करना It is difficult to say when will he *regain* his memory.

regal *(adj.)* रीगल्– of, relating to, or befitting a king or queen; royal राजसी, शाही He was not a king, but his robes were *regal.*

regard *(v.)* रिगार्ड–1. to hold (a person or thing) in respect, admiration, or affection आदर देना, सम्मान करना I *regard* Pratibha as my best friend.

2. to look upon or consider in a specified way ध्यान देना Why don't you *regard* your parent's advice?

3. *(n.)* esteem, affection, or respect आदर-भाव I have great *regard* for Pratibha.

4. good wishes or greetings शुभ कामनाएं Please give my best *regards* to your mother.

5. reference, relation, or connection विषय (में) As *regards* Sudha, I will write to you at once.

regarding *(prep.)* रिगार्डिंग– in respect of; on the subject of के विषय में He never told me anything *regarding* his financial matters.

regardless *(adv.)* रिगार्डलस– taking no regard or heed; heedless जैसे भी हो, चाहे जो हो *Regardless* of what his parents, she did the exact opposite.

regime *(n.)* रेजीम– a system of government or a particular administration शासन-व्यवस्था Free trade is not permissible under the present *regime.*

regiment *(v.)* रेजिमेण्ट–1. to form into organized groups अनुशासित होना The tourists *regimented* into large parties for sightseeing.

2. *(n.)* a military formation varying in size from a battalion to a number of battalions सैन्यदल There were many *regiments* in the I.N.A.

region *(n.)* रीजन– an area considered as a unit for geographical, functional, social, or cultural reasons भाग, प्रदेश In India, there are many *regions.*

regional *(adj.)* रीजनल– of, characteristic of, or limited to a region क्षेत्रीय, प्रादेशिक There are many *regional* languages in India.

register *(v.)* रे'जिस्टर्– 1. to enter or cause someone to enter (an event, person's name, ownership, etc.) on a register; formally record पंजीकरण करना You have to *register* your case with the police.

2. *(n.)* an official or formal list recording names, events, or transactions रजिस्टर, पंजिका The teacher checked the attendance *register* thoroughly.

registered *(adj.)* रेजिस्टर्ड– officially entered on a register or list; formally recorded पंजीकृत I sent you certificates by *registered* post.

registrar *(n.)* रेजिस्ट्रार– a person who keeps official records पंजीकरण अधिकारी Hussain is the *registrar* of Aligarh University.

registration *(n.)* रेजिस्ट्रेशन– the act of registering or state of being registered पंजीकरण Half of the class hasn't done its *registration* for the program yet.

registry office *(n.)* रजिस्ट्री ऑफ़िस– a government office where civil marriages are performed and births, marriages, and deaths are recorded पंजीकरण कार्यालय He went to the *registry office* to take death certificate of his grandfather.

regressive *(adj.)* रिग्रेसिव– regressing or tending to regress प्रतिगामी, अधोगामी The theme of the movie seemed to be *regressive.*

regret *(v.)* रिग्रे'ट–1. to feel sorry, repentant, or upset about पश्चात्ताप करना, पछतावा होना I *regret* being so late for the meeting.

2. to bemoan or grieve the death or loss of दुखी होना I *regret* to tell you my mother-in-law is ill.

3. *(n.)* a sense of loss or grief शोक, दुख There was great *regret* in the town at the minister's death.

4. a sense of repentance, guilt, or sorrow, as over some wrong done or an unfulfilled ambition खेद, पश्चात्ताप Yes, I failed but I have no *regrets.*

regular *(adj.)* रे'ग्युलर्–1. according to a uniform principle, arrangement, or order नियमित, नियम में Our *regular* working hours at the office are 10 to 5:30.

2. occurring at fixed or prearranged intervals समयानुसार Try to be *regular* in your office.

regularity *(n.)* रैगयुलैरटी– frequency; the characteristic of doing something regularly or as a custom नियमितता The key to his constant *success* is his regularity.

regularly *(adv.)* रेगयुलरलि– frequently; in such a way as to do something regularly or as a custom नियमित समय पर These days trains run *regularly.*

regulate *(v.)* रेग्युलेट– to adjust (the amount of heat, sound, etc. of something) as required; control नियंत्रित करना This valve *regulates* the flow of water.

regulation *(n.)* रेग्युलेशन– a rule, principle, or condition that governs procedure or behaviour नियम या क़ानून The new *regulations* clearly defined the duties of the workers.

regurgitate *(v.)* रिगर्जिटेट– to vomit forth (partially digested food) खाया हुआ भोजन उगलना I saw the bird was *regurgitating* half-digested worm to feed its young ones.

rehabilitate *(v.)* रीहैबिलिटेट– to restore to a former position or rank पुनर्वासित करना The government is trying to *rehabilitate* the flood effected victims.

rehearsal *(n.)* रिहर्सल– a session of practising a play, concert, speech etc. in preparation for public performance the act of reciting पूर्वाभ्यास We need to conduct a dress *rehearsal* for the play.

rehearse *(v.)* रिहर्स– to practise (a play, concert, etc.), in preparation for public performance पूर्वाभ्यास करना You need to *rehearse* your part again.

reign *(v.)* रेन– 1. to exercise the power and authority of a sovereign शासन करना The English rulers *reigned* over India for about one hundred and fifty years.

2. *(n.)* the period during which a monarch is the official ruler of a country राजकाल, शासन The queen introduced many reforms during her *reign* of forty-five years.

reimburse *(v.)* रीइमबर्स– to repay or compensate (someone) for (money already spent, losses, damages, etc.) चुकाना, अदा करना The company will *reimburse* him for travel expenses.

rein *(n.)* रेन– one of a pair of long straps, usually connected together and made of leather, used to control a horse, बागडोर When the *reins* were pulled tightly, the horse reared.

reindeer *(n.)* रेनडियर– a large deer with long antlers बारहसिंगा *Reindeers* are used for transporting goods in Arctic regions.

reinforce *(v.)* रीइन्'फ़ॉर्स–1. to give added strength or support to कुमुक भेजना, बढ़ाना, सुदृढ़ करना When China attacked our country, our army was *reinforced.*

2. to give added emphasis to; stress, support, or increase प्रभावशाली बनाना, मज़बूत करना You should *reinforce* your arguments by giving more logic.

3. to give added support to (a military force) by providing more men, supplies, etc. अधिक शक्तिशाली बनाना The army would be *reinforced* to meet enemy attacks.

reinforcement *(n.)* रीइनफ़ार्समेण्ट्– the act of giving added strength or support to प्रबलन Without timely *reinforcements* we would lost the battle.

reinstatement *(n.)* रीइनस्टेट्मेण्ट्– the act or an instance of bringing back or restoring (something), esp officially बहाली She got *reinstatement* after suspension of one year.

reject *(v.)* रिजे'क्ट–1. to refuse to accept, अस्वीकार करना I was foolish to *reject* Indra's offer of help.

2. to refuse to accept, acknowledge, use, believe, etc. रद्द करना, नामंज़ूर करना His proposal was *rejected* by the governing body of the committee.

3. to throw out as useless or worthless; discard काम में न लाना, ठुकरा देना The lady *rejected* a cup in the crockery shop because it was cracked.

rejoice *(v.)* रिजॉइस–1. to feel or express great joy or happiness प्रसन्न होना, आनंदित होना The family *rejoiced* when the son returned home from a foreign trip.

2. to cause to feel joy रंगरलियां मनाना India *rejoiced* at its victory in the World Cup Cricket 2011.

rejoicing *(n.)* रिजॉइसिंग– the act of feeling or expressing great joy or happiness हर्षोल्लास There was great *rejoicing* among the cricketers when they won the match.

rejoin *(v.)* रिजॉइन– to put or join together again; reunite फिर से मिल जाना I have got an offer to *rejoin* my previous company.

rejuvenate *(v.)* रिजूवनेट– to give new youth, restored vitality, or youthful appearance to पुनः युवा बनाना, कायाकल्प कर देना After an hour in the spa I felt *rejuvenated* .

relate *(v.)* रिलेट–1. to tell or narrate (a story, information, etc.) कहानी कहना, कथा सुनाना The hunter *related* some of his adventures in the forest.

2. to establish association (between two or more things) or (of something) to have relation or reference (to something else) संबंध जोड़ना, मेल करना The two incidents might be *related* to each other.

related *(adj.)* रिलेटेड– connected; associated संबद्ध He is not *related* to me in any way.

relation *(n.)* रिलेशन–1. connection by blood or marriage; kinship रिश्ता, नातेदारी I have many uncles, cousins, nieces and other *relations* in Delhi.

2. the position, association, connection, or status of one person or thing with regard to another or others व्यावहारिक संबंध *Relations* between teachers and students in our school are very good.

relationship *(n.)* रिलेशनशिप– the mutual dealings, connections, or feelings that exist between two parties, countries, people, etc. संबंध, नाता There *relationship* is going strong since last five years.

relative *(n.)* रिलेटिव– a person who is related by blood or marriage; relation रिश्तेदार Rohan is my close *relative.*

relatively *(adv.)* रिलेटिवली– in comparison or relation to something else; not absolutely in comparison or relation to something else; not absolutely अपेक्षाकृत Portuguese is *relatively* similar to the Spanish language.

relax *(v.)* रिलैक्स–1. to take rest or recreation, as from work or effort आराम करना After the test, we *relaxed.*

2. to make (muscles, a grip, etc.) less tense or rigid or (of muscles, a grip, etc.) to become looser or less rigid ढीला करना *Relax* your grip on my arm, you are hurting me.

relaxation *(n.)* रिलैक्सेशन– rest or refreshment, as after work or effort; recreation आराम, विश्राम After a week's hard work we need *relaxation.*

relaxed *(adj)* रिलैक्सड– calm and not worried or tense बेफ़िक्र Go and talk to him. He looks in a *relaxed* mood.

relaxing *(adj.)* रिलैक्सिंग– that is relaxing is pleasant and helps you to feel calm and less tense आरामदेह, सुखद He is *relaxing* after a long time so don't disturb him.

relay *(v.)* रिले– to carry or spread (something, such as news or information) by relays सह-प्रसारण करना Please *relay* this message to my parents as soon as possible.

release *(v.)* रिलीज़–1. to free (a person, animal, etc.) from captivity or imprisonment छोड़ना The judge ordered the police to *release* the innocent boy.

2. to free (someone) from obligation or duty मुक्त करना, रिहा करना Nelson Mandela was *released* from the prison after 27 years.

3. *(n.)* the act of issuing for sale or publication विमोचन, प्रकाशन The book won't go on *release* until August.

relent *(v.)* रिलेन्ट– to change one's mind about some decided course, esp a harsh one; become more mild or amenable नरम पड़ जाना After denying for long, she *relented* and agreed to come for the excursion.

relevant *(adj.)* रेलवन्ट– having direct bearing on the matter in hand; pertinent संगत, संबद्ध Please state only the *relevant* facts in your article.

reliable *(adj.)* रिलाइअबल– able to be trusted; predictable or dependable भरोसेमंद Are you sure that this information is from a *reliable* source?.

relief *(n.)* रिलीफ़–1. deliverance from or alleviation of anxiety, pain, distress, etc. आराम, राहत Father got *relief* from headache after I rubbed some balm on his forehead.

2. help or assistance, as to the poor, needy, or distressed सहायता The timely *relief* sent for the refugees saved their lives.

relieve *(v.)* रिलीव– to bring alleviation of (pain, distress, etc.) to (someone) राहत देना, चैन पहुंचाना When he took one tablet of Asprin, his headache was immediately *relieved.*

relieved *(adj.)* रिलीव्ड– experiencing relief, esp from worry or anxiety चिंतामुक्त The children were *relieved* when they finally got their results.

religion *(n.)* रिलिजन– belief in, worship of, or obedience to a supernatural power or powers considered to be divine or to have control of human destiny धर्म, सम्प्रदाय, मत We should not discriminate on the basis of *religion*.

religious *(adj.)* रिलिजस– pious; devout; godly धार्मिक, धर्मनिष्ठ Arvind Ghosh was a *religious* man.

religiously *(adv.)* रिलिजसली– with regard to the belief in a God or gods and the activities that are connected with this belief कर्तव्यनिष्ठा से Her mother follows all the rituals *religiously*.

relish *(v.)* रेलिश– 1. to anticipate eagerly; look forward to किसी बात की उत्सुकता से प्रतीक्षा करना She *relished* the idea of going abroad.
2. *(n.)* liking or enjoyment अत्यंत आनंद The child ate the chocolate with great *relish*.

reluctance *(n.)* रिलॅकटन्स– lack of eagerness or willingness; disinclination अनिच्छा, हिचक I show *reluctance* to share my room with anybody.

reluctant *(adj.)* रिलॅकटन्ट– not eager; unwilling; disinclined अनिच्छुक Vivek is usually *reluctant* to take sweets.

reluctantly *(adv.)* रिलॅकटन्टली– in a reluctant manner हिचकते हुए, अनिच्छा से He *reluctantly* came with us on the trip.

rely *(v.)* रिलाइ– to be dependent (on) विश्वास करना, भरोसा करना I can always *rely* on her for help.

remain *(v.)* रिमेन–1. to continue to be बने रहना The weather *remained* very hot on Monday.
2. *(n.)* to be left, as after use, consumption, the passage of time, etc. शेष, बाकी After dining, the *remains* should be collected for the birds.

remainder *(n.)* रिमेण्डर– a part or portion that is left, as after use, subtraction, expenditure, the passage of time, etc. शेष, बाक़ी Take 4 from 13, and what is the *remainder*?

remand *(v.)* रिमाण्ड– to send back फिर हिरासत में भेजना Bhagat was *remanded* on bail.

remark *(v.)* रिमार्क– 1. to pass a casual comment (about); reflect in informal speech or writing राय प्रकट करना, टिप्पणी देना The chief guest *remarked* favourably about the arrangements made by us.
2. *(n.)* a brief casually expressed thought or opinion; observation टिप्पणी I wish to make a few *remarks* about the elections.

remarkable *(adj.)* रिमार्कबल– unusual, striking, or extraordinary विशिष्ट, ख़ास His performance in the match was truly *remarkable*.

remedial *(adj.)* रिमीडिअल– affording a remedy; curative उपचारात्मक (मंदबुद्धि बच्चों के लिए सहायक) The poor children were sent for the *remedial* English classes.

remedy *(n.)* रे'मडी–1. any drug or agent that cures a disease or controls its symptoms दवा The physician suggested the patient a *remedy* for his fever.
2. anything that serves to put a fault to rights, cure defects, improve conditions, etc. उपाय No *remedy* is left to correct this situation.

remember *(v.)* रिमेम्बर– to retain (an idea, intention, etc.) in one's conscious mind (ज़बानी) याद करना, रटना He finds it difficult to *remember* as to what he did yesterday.

remembrance *(n.)* रिमेमब्रन्स– the act of honouring some past event, person, etc. स्मरण, याद, स्मरणशक्ति This charity is in the dear *remembrance* of my father.

remind *(v.)* रिमाइंड– to cause (a person) to remember (something or to do something); make (someone) aware (of something he may have forgotten) स्मरण कराना, याद दिलाना Please *remind* me about it when you come again.

reminder *(n.)* रिमांइडर– a note to remind a person of something not done स्मरण पत्र The company sent the *reminders* to all its members.

reminisce *(v.)* रेमिनिस्– to talk or write about old times, past experiences, etc. बीती हुई घटनाएं याद करना She was *reminiscing* her days at school.

reminiscence *(n.)* रेमिनिसन्स– the act of recalling or narrating past experiences संस्मरण, पुरानी यादें The book is a collection of *reminiscences* of her days at school.

remit *(v.)* रिमिट– to cancel or refrain from exacting (a penalty or punishment) कर्ज़ या सज़ा माफ़ करना The child requested to *remit* the fine charged by the teacher.

remnant *(n.)* रेमूनेंट– a part left over after use, processing, etc. बचा हुआ अंश, शेष The *remnant* of the building was finally destroyed after a long time.

remorse *(n.)* रिमॉर्स– a sense of deep regret and guilt for some misdeed पछतावा, पश्चात्ताप The criminal expressed his *remorse* for his crimes.

remote *(adj.)* रिमोट– distant in time बहुत पहले Many Buddhist monuments were built in the *remote* past.

remotely *(adv.)* रिमोटली– use remotely with a negative statement to emphasize the statement; slightly बहुत कम She is *remotely* interested in domestic problems.

removable *(adj.)* रिमूवबल– a removable part of something is a part that can easily be moved from its place or position स्थानांतरणीय, जिसे हटाया जा सके Sharon has a *removable* dressing table.

removal *(n.)* रिमूवल– the act of removing or state of being removed निष्कासन, बरखास्तगी His *removal* from the company can cause serious repercussions.

remove *(v.)* रिमूव– 1. to take away and place elsewhere दूर करना, परे करना Please *remove* your shoes when you enter the temple.

2. to cause (dirt, stains, or anything unwanted) to disappear; get rid of हटाना Will you *remove* the stain from my shirt?

3. to displace (someone) from office; dismiss बर्ख़ास्त करना She has been *removed* from her service.

render *(v.)* रे'न्डर–1. to give or provide (aid, charity, a service, etc.) देना, अर्पित करना Doctors *rendered* their services free of charge at the charitable health check-up camp.

2. to help किसी की मदद करना We hope to *render* certain services to your company.

rendezvous *(n.)* रॉण्डेवोज़– a meeting or appointment to meet at a specified time and place (मिलने की पहले से तयशुदा जगह) मिलन-स्थल We will *rendezvous* here again at 6 o'clock.

renew *(v.)* रिन्यू–1. to restate or reaffirm नया करना, नवीकरण करना We should *renew* our library membership for one more year.

2. to begin (an activity) again; recommence कोई काम दुबारा करना We must *renew* the decorations of our shop.

renewal *(n.)* रिन्यूअल– the act of renewing or state of being renewed नवीनीकरण The *renewal* of their contract gave them much satisfaction.

renewable *(adj.)* रिन्यूअबल– renewable resources are natural ones such as wind, water, and sunlight which are always available जिसका नवीनीकरण

संभव हो Scientists are working hard to find new sources of *renewable* energy.

renounce *(v.)* रिनाउन्स– to give up (a claim or right), esp by formal announcement त्याग देना Rabindra Nath Tagore *renounced* his title because of the British oppression.

renovate *(v.)* रिनवेट्– to restore (something) to good condition मरम्मत करना, नया कर देना He did *renovate* his house.

renown *(n.)* रिनाउन– widespread reputation, esp of a good kind; fame प्रसिद्धि He is a doctor of great *renown.*

renowned *(adj.)* रिनाउण्ड– having a widespread, esp good, reputation; famous प्रसिद्ध, विख्यात Ashoka was a *renowned* king of India.

rent *(n.)* रे'ण्ट– 1. a payment made periodically by a tenant to a landlord किराया How much *rent* do you pay for your shop?

2. *(v.)* to grant (a person) the right to use one's property in return for periodic payments किराये पर देना Will you *rent* this house?

3. to occupy or use (property) in return for periodic payments किराये पर लेना I *rented* this house two years ago.

renunciation *(n.)* रिननसिएशन– a formal declaration renouncing something त्याग, सन्यास He is planning for the *renunciation* of worldly pleasures.

reorganize (ise) *(v.)* रिऑर्गनाइज़– to change the way (something) is organized फिर से गठन करना She *reorganized* my entire work space and schedule.

repair *(v.)* रिपेअर्–1. to restore (something damaged or broken) to good condition or working order मरम्मत करना Has your TV been *repaired*?

2. to heal (a breach or division) in (something) सुधारना, ठीक करना The cobbler will *repair* our shoes.

3. *(n.)* the act, task, or process of repairing मरम्मत The house is under *repair.*

4. a part that has been repaired सुधार Your watch is beyond *repair,* you must buy a new one.

repay *(v.)* रिपे–1. to pay back (money) to (a person); refund or reimburse (राशि या कोई अन्य वस्तु) चुकाना, लौटाना Have you enough money to *repay* your debts?

2. to make a return for (something) by way of compensation बदला चुकाना We can never *repay* our mother for her kindness and affection.

repayment *(n.)* रिपेमेंट– an amount of money which you pay at regular intervals to a person or organization in order to repay a debt वापसी, चुकौती He has failed again in the *repayment* of his loan.

repeat *(v.)* रिपीट–1. to say or write (something) again, either once or several times; restate or reiterate दुबारा कहना Her mother was almost deaf so I had to *repeat* my question.

2. to do or experience (something) again once or several times दोहराना Can you *repeat* what you said?

repeated *(adj.)* रिपीटिड– done, made, or said again and again; continual or incessant बारम्बार किया जाने वाला I made *repeated* attempts to see you.

repeatedly *(adv.)* रिपीटिडली– many or several times; frequently; continually बार-बार A thief had been stabbed *repeatedly* in the stomach.

repel *(v.)* रिपेल–1. to force or drive back (something or somebody, esp an attacker) मार भगाना, पीछे धकेलना The enemy's attack was *repelled.*

2. to produce a feeling of aversion or distaste in (someone or something); be disgusting (to) बुरा लगना The way he ate with dirty hands and licked his finger *repelled* everybody.

repent *(v.)* रिपे'ण्ट– to feel remorse (for); be contrite (about); show penitence (for) पछताना He *repented* about his sins on his deathbed.

repentance *(n.)* रिपेन्टअन्स– remorse or contrition for one's past actions or sins पश्चात्ताप, पछतावा Is your *repentance* sincere?

repercussion *(n.)* रीपर्कशन– a recoil after impact; a rebound प्रतिघात, प्रतिक्रिया The collapse of the company will have serious *repercussions* on the employees.

repetition *(n.)* रेपटिशन– a thing, word, action, etc. that is repeated पुनरावृत्ति There was a lot of *repetition* of the same idea in his essay.

replace *(v.)* रिप्लेस–1. to substitute a person or thing for (another which has ceased to fulfil its function); put in place of बदलना, बदलकर देना These cells are defective, kindly *replace* them.

2. to put back or return; restore to its rightful place लौटाना, (पहले वाली जगह पर) लाना या रखना We can take the magazine down from the shelf, but after reading we must *replace* it.

3. to take the place of; supersede (की जगह पर) लेना Hamid is unwell, so he has been *replaced* with Majid in the team.

replacement *(n.)* रिप्लेसमण्ट– a person or thing that replaces another प्रतिस्थापन We need to find a *replacement* for our maid quickly.

replay *(n.)* रीप्ले– a showing again of a sequence of action दुबारा खेला जाने वाला खेल The *replay* showed that the batsman was out of his crease.

replenish *(v.)* रिप्लेनिश– to make full or complete again by supplying what has been used up or is lacking फिर से भरना, पुनर्भरण करना Scientists are working hard to *replenish* the natural resources on our planet.

replete *(adj.)* रिप्लीट– copiously supplied (with); abounding (in) परिपूर्ण The book is *replete* with pictures.

replica *(n.)* रेपलिका– an exact copy or reproduction, esp on a smaller scale प्रतिकृति This book seems to be a *replica* of a famous novel.

replicate *(v.)* रेपलिकेट– to make or be a copy of; reproduce हूबहू नक़ल करना I have successfully *replicated* your results.

reply *(v.)* रिप्लाइ– 1. to make answer (to) in words or writing or by an action; respond मौखिक या लिखकर उत्तर देना The judge asked repeatedly, but the thief did not *reply*.

2. *(n.)* an answer made in words or writing or through an action; response जवाब, उत्तर I received no *reply* from my parents.

report *(v.)* रिपॉर्ट–1. to give an account (of); describe विवरण देना The occurrence was *reported* in the Hindustan Times.

2. to complain about (a person), esp to a superior शिकायत करना, विरोध में सूचना देना He was *reported* to the police for trespassing.

3. to present oneself or be present at an appointed place or for a specific purpose (बहुधा अपने से वरिष्ठ अधिकारी को) मिलकर सूचित करना I have been ordered to *report* for duty.

4. *(n.)* an account of the deliberations of a committee, body, etc. विवरण Have you got the *report* of the meeting?

reportedly *(adv.)* रिपॉटिडली– according to rumour or report लोगों के कहने के अनुसार She *reportedly* remained his mistress for many years.

repose *(n.)* रिपोज़– a state of quiet restfulness; peace or tranquillity विश्राम, नींद After a day's *repose,* I shall try to join my night duty.

represent *(v.)* रेप्रिज़ेण्ट– to stand as an equivalent of; correspond to प्रतिनिधित्व करना When you go to for the meeting you will be *representing* the firm.

representation *(n.)* रेपरिज़ेनटेशन– anything that represents, suchas a verbal or pictorial portrait प्रतिनिधित्व There was a poor *representation* of women in UP Assembly.

representative *(n.)* रेपरिज़ेनटटिव– a person or thing that represents another or others प्रतिनिधि We need to hire a new sales *representative* for the north district.

repress *(v.)* रिप्रेस– to keep (feelings, etc.) under control; suppress or restrain दमन करना She somehow *repressed* her desire to go on a holiday.

repressed *(adj.)* रिप्रेसड– (of a person) repressing feelings, instincts, desires, etc. दमित, दबाया हुआ She has *repressed* many sad memories of her past.

repressive *(adj.)* रिप्रेसिव– acting to control, suppress, or restrain दमन करने वाली The British had formed a *repressive* government in India.

reprimand *(v.)* रे'प्रिमाण्ड– to admonish or rebuke, esp formally; reprove फटकारना The principal *reprimanded* the student on his poor performance.

reproduce *(v.)* रिप्रॉड्यूस– to make a copy, representation, or imitation of; duplicate चित्रण करना, प्रतिलिपि तैयार करना He was able to *reproduce* the previous year's results.

reproduction *(n.)* रीप्रडक्शन– any of various processes, either sexual or asexual, by which an animal or plant produces one or more individuals similar to itself पुनरुत्पादन, पुनरुत्पत्ति Did you study *reproduction* in plants?

reproof *(n.)* रिप्रूफ़– an act or expression of rebuke or censure फटकार Aastha received a mild *reproof* from her mother.

reptile *(n.)* रेप्टाइल– any of the cold-blooded vertebrates, characterized by lungs, an outer covering of horny scales or plates, and young produced in amniotic eggs रेंगने वाला जन्तु, सरीसृप A snake is a *reptile.*

republic *(n.)* रिपब्लिक– a form of government in which the people or their elected representatives possess the supreme power गणराज्य, गणतंत्र India is a *republic* while Britain is a kingdom.

repugnant *(adj.)* रिपगनण्ट– repellent to the senses; causing aversion प्रतिकूल, अप्रिय I don't like the *repugnant* smell of rotten eggs.

repulsive *(adj.)* रिपल्सिव– causing or occasioning repugnance; loathsome; disgusting or distasteful घृणास्पद, अरुचिकर His heinous crimes made us fell *repulsive.*

reputable *(adj.)* रेप्युटबल– having a good reputation; honoured, trustworthy, or respectable प्रतिष्ठित, आदरणीय Namita is doing a *reputable* job.

reputation *(n.)* रेप्युटेशन–1. a high opinion generally held about a person or thing; esteem प्रतिष्ठा, ख्याति, मान Your father lived up to his *reputation.*

2. notoriety or fame, esp for some specified characteristic नेकनामी या बदनामी If you do anything wrong, your *reputation* will suffer.

request *(v.)* रिक्वे'स्ट– 1. to express a desire for, esp politely; ask for or demand प्रार्थना करना, निवेदन करना

You are *requested* not to talk loudly.
2. *(n.)* the act or an instance of requesting, अनुरोध The candidate made a *request* to the voters to vote for him.

require *(v.)* रिक्वायर–1. to have need of; depend upon; want ज़रूरत होना The hungry man *requires* food.
2. to make formal request (for); insist upon or demand, esp as an obligation माँग करना या कोई आदेश देना, के लिए आवश्यक होना I *require* you to be here now.

requirement *(n.)* रिक्वायरमेंट– something demanded or imposed as an obligation जरूरत, आवश्यकता Does this order fulfill all your *requirements?*

rescue *(v.)* रेस्क्यू– 1. to bring (someone or something) out of danger, attack, harm, etc. deliver or save रक्षा/बचाव करना The coast guard came to the *rescue* of the divers.
2. *(n.)* the act or an instance of rescuing बचाव, उद्धार My friend always comes to my *rescue* when I need him.

research *(n.)* रिसर्च– 1. systematic investigation to establish facts or principles or to collect information on a subject खोज The scientists conducted many *researches.*
2. *(adj.)* to carry out investigations into (a subject, problem, etc.) खोज करने वाला She has been deputed as *research* adviser.

resemblance *(n.)* रिज़ेमब्लन्स– the state or quality of resembling; likeness or similarity in nature, appearance, etc. समानता, समरूपता I do not share any sort of physical *resemblance* with my brother.

resemble *(v.)* रिज़े'म्बल– to possess some similarity to; be like शक्ल मिलना, आकृति का मेल होना You *resemble* your father closely.

resent *(v.)* रि'ज़ेंट– to feel bitter, indignant, or aggrieved at क्रुद्ध होना, नाराज़ होना She *resented* his rude remarks about her character.

resentment *(n.)* रिज़े'न्टमेंट– anger, bitterness, or ill will नाराज़गी Though her brother treated her badly, Pramila didn't feel any *resentment.*

reservation *(n.)* रेज़र्वेशन– something reserved, esp hotel accommodation, a seat on an aeroplane, in a theatre, etc. आरक्षण I have got a *reservation* on the 6:15 flight to Mumbai.

reserve *(v.)* रिज़र्व–1. to keep back or set aside, esp for future use or contingency; withhold बचाकर रखना I always *reserve* some money for the weekend.
2. to keep for oneself; retain सुरक्षित रखना The best fruits are *reserved* for the loving child.
3. *(n.)* something kept back or set aside, esp for future use or contingency बचाकर रखा हुआ धन, निधि, संचय You should spend some money and keep the rest in *reserve.*

reside *(v.)* रिज़ाइड– to live permanently or for a considerable time (in a place); have one's home (in) रहना, वास करना Could you please tell me where you *reside?*

residence *(n.)* रेज़िडन्स– the place in which one resides; abode or home रिहाइस, निवास-स्थान 43, Laxmi Nagar is my friend's *residence.*

resident *(n.)* रज़िडण्ट– a person who resides in a place निवासी Shakeel is an American *resident* but his family lives in India.

residential *(n.)* रेज़िडेनशल– relating to or having residence रिहायशी, आवासी What is your *residential* address?

residual *(adj.)* रेज़िडुअल– of, relating to, or designating a residue or remainder; remaining; left over

अवशेष The company was dumping the *residual* waste in the river.

residue *(n.)* रेज़िड्यू– matter remaining after something has been removed अंश, अवशेष The *residue* left after the distillation of the petroleum is used to make paraffin wax.

resign *(v.)* रिज़ाइन– to give up tenure of (a job, office, etc.) त्यागपत्र देना The Prime Minister asked the minister facing corruption charges to *resign* from the cabinet.

resignation *(n.)* रेज़िगनेशन– a formal document stating one's intention to resign इस्तीफ़ा, त्यागपत्र The management has accepted my *resignation* from the company.

resist *(v.)* रिज़िस्ट– to stand firm (against); not yield (to); fight (against) प्रतिरोध करना, सामना करना The society always *resists* change of any sort in the beginning.

resistance *(n.)* रेज़िसटन्स– the act or an instance of resisting विरोध, प्रतिरोध The company's plan to cut salaries was met with heavy *resistance*.

resolute *(adj.)* रेज़लूट्– firm in purpose or belief; steadfast दृढ़संकल्प, अटल Kanchan remained *resolute* in her belief that the situation would improve.

resolve *(v.)* रिज़ॉल्व–1. to decide or determine firmly संकल्प करना We should *resolve* not to tell a lie.

2. to express (an opinion) formally, esp (of a public meeting) one agreed by a vote प्रस्ताव पास करना It is *resolved* to re-elect the president.

3. *(n.)* firmness of purpose; determination संकल्प It's my *resolve* not to tell a lie.

resonant *(adj.)* रेज़नेंट– (of sound) resounding or re-echoing गुंजायमान I heard a deep *resonant* voice from the house. The house was still *resonant* with memories of his childhood.

resort *(v.)* रिज़ॉर्ट– 1. to have recourse (to) for help, use, etc. शरण या सहारा लेना He *resorted* to smuggling because he was not satisfied with his honest earnings.

2. *(n.)* the last possible course of action open to one आख़री चारा या रास्ता As a last *resort*, I'll have to borrow some money.

3. a place to which many people go for recreation, rest, etc. अवकाश बिताने की जगह We stayed in a good *resort*.

resource *(n.)* रिसॉर्स– a means of doing something; expedient साधन, उपाय I'm running out of *resources* to help you.

resourceful *(adj.)* रिसॉर्सफुल– ingenious, capable, and full of initiative, esp in dealing with difficult situations सक्षम एवं चतुर Only a *resourceful* person can survive in today's business.

respect *(v.)* रिस्पेक्ट– 1. to have an attitude of esteem towards; show or have respect for सम्मान करना We should *respect* our elders and never be rude to them.

2. *(n.)* an attitude of deference, admiration, or esteem; regard आदर, सम्मान We show *respect* to our uncle whenever he pays a visit to us.

3. a detail, point, or characteristic; particular (कुछ) हद तक, (कुछ) अंश तक I may agree with her in some *respects*, but on the whole I think she is not right.

respectable *(adj.)* रिस्पेक्टबल– 1. having or deserving the respect of other people; estimable; worthy आदरणीय, सम्माननीय Shahla is doing a *respectable* job.

2. relatively or fairly good; considerable ठीक-ठाक, अच्छा-ख़ासा He is getting a *respectable* salary.

respective *(adj.)* रिस्पेक्टिव– belonging or relating separately to each of several people or things; several अलग-अलग, निजी The students were asked to sit on their *respective* seats.

respectively *(adv.)* रिस्पेक्टिवली– (in listing a number of items or attributes that refer to another list) separately in the order given क्रम के अनुसार Sahil and Sameer were given 30 and 45 marks *respectively.*

respiration *(n.)* रेसपरेशन– the process in living organisms of taking in oxygen from the surroundings and giving out carbon dioxide (सांस लेना एवं छोड़ना) श्वसन The *respiration* in plants is continuous day and night.

respond *(v.)* रिस्पॉण्ड– to act in reply; react उत्तर देना, प्रतिक्रिया दिखाना The police *responded* to the distress call quickly.

response *(n.)* रिस्पॉन्स– the act of responding; reply or reaction प्रतिक्रिया The patient's *response* to the medicine is quite good.

responsibility *(n.)* रिस्पॉन्सबिलटी– a person or thing for which one is responsible ज़िम्मेदारी The *responsibility* of timely completion of this task rests with you.

responsible *(adj.)* रिस्पॉन्सिबल्– being accountable for one's actions and decisions (to) उत्तरदायी, ज़िम्मेदार We are not *responsible* for the losses you suffer.

responsibly *(adv.)* रिस्पॉन्सबली– in a responsible and sensible way पूरी ज़िम्मेदारी से Megha discharged her duty *responsibly.*

responsive *(adj.)* रिस्पॉन्सिव–1. reacting or replying quickly or favourably, as to a suggestion, initiative, etc. उत्तरदायी She is appreciated for her *responsive* nature.
2. reacting to a stimulus संवेदनशील He was addressing a *responsive* class.

rest *(v.)* रेस्ट– 1. place or position (oneself, etc) for rest or relaxation विश्राम करना They *rested* under a big tree.
2. *(n.)* relaxation from exertion or labour विश्राम, आराम Please take *rest* for a while.

➢ **come to rest** *(n.)* . to slow down and stop रुक जाना, ठहर जाना, My eyes *came to rest* on a photograph of a handsome man.

restaurant *(n.)* रेसट्रॉण्ट– a commercial establishment where meals are prepared and served to customers खाने का होटल Delhi has many *restaurants* which serve excellent food.

restless *(adj.)* रेस्टलस– unable to stay still or quiet बेचैन, अशांत Do not get *restless* regarding your result

restore *(v.)* रिस्टॉर्–1. to return (something lost, stolen, etc.) to its owner लौटाना The police *restored* all the stolen articles to its owner.
2. to return (something, esp a work of art or building) to an original or former condition नया बनाना The old picture was cleaned and *restored.*

restrain *(v.)* रिस्ट्रेन– to hold (someone) back from some action, esp by force रोकना, नियंत्रण में रखना *Restrain* your dog from attacking people.

restraint *(n.)* रिस्ट्रेण्ट– the ability to control or moderate one's impulses, passions, etc. रोक, नियंत्रण, प्रतिबंध Saints keep their passions under *restraint.*

restrict *(v.)* रिस्ट्रिक्ट– to limit the size, range or amount of sth सीमित करना, रोक लगाना My outings have been *restricted* by my parents.

restriction *(n.)* रिस्ट्रिकशन– something that restricts; a restrictive measure, law, etc. रोक, पाबंदी There are no *restrictions* on walking here.

result *(n.)* रिज़ॅल्ट– 1. something that ensues from an action, policy, course of events, etc. outcome; consequence परिणाम The *result* of the hockey match was a draw.
2. *(v.) to issue or terminate (in a specified way, state, etc.); end* घटित होना The accident *resulted* in a fracture in Abdulla's leg.
3. to be the outcome or consequence (of) परिणाम निकलना Her negligence *resulted* in a heavy loss in business.

resume *(v.)* रिज़्यूम– to begin again or go on with (something adjourned or interrupted) आरंभ करना, दुबारा शुरू करना We need to *resume* our work as soon as possible.

resumption *(n.)* रिज़म्पशन– the act of resuming or beginning again पुनरारंभ Both parties are now hoping for a quick *resumption* of harmonial relations.

resurrect *(v.)* रेज़रेक्ट– to rise or raise from the dead; bring or be brought back to life पुनः जीवित करना या होना The government have *resurrected* plans to build a new prison just outside the capital.

retail *(n.)* रीटेल– the sale of goods individually or in small quantities to consumers परचून, खुदरा Usually the shopkeepers buy goods in large quantities and sell in *retail* to make profit.

retailer *(n.)* रिटेलर– a person or business that sells goods to the public फुटकर विक्रेता Wal-Mart Stores Inc are the world's largest *retailer.*

retain *(v.)* रिटेन– to keep in one's possession रख लेना, रोक लेना As per our agreement I would *retain* half of the land.

retarded *(adj.)* रिटार्डेड– underdeveloped, esp mentally पिछड़ा, मंदबुद्धि Mentally *retarded* children need special core.

rethink *(v.)* रीथिंक– to think about (something) again, esp with a view to changing one's tactics or opinions पुनः सोच-विचार करना We all need to *rethink* our strategy before moving forward.

retire *(v.)* रिटायर– to give up or to cause (a person) to give up his work, a post, etc. esp on reaching pensionable age सेवानिवृत्त होना My father *retired* at the age of sixty-two.

retirement *(n.)* रिटायरमेंट– the act of retiring from one's work, office, etc. सेवानिवृत्ति He is now living in *retirement.*

retort *(v.)* रिटॉर्ट– 1. to utter (something) quickly, sharply, wittily, or angrily, in response (गुस्से से) रूखा उत्तर देना The clerk *retorted* with anger when he was questioned by the manager.
2. *(n.)* a sharp, angry, or witty reply खीझ भरा उत्तर He gave a good *retort* to him and left the house.

retract *(v.)* रिट्रैक्ट– to withdraw (a statement, opinion, charge, etc.) as invalid or unjustified अपनी बात से पीछे हटना, मुकरना He *retracted* from his earlier statement and made a fool of himself.

retreat *(v.)* रिट्रीट– 1. to withdraw or retire in the face of or from action with an enemy, either due to defeat or in order to adopt a more favourable position शत्रु के सामने होने पर पीछे लौटना The general commanded his troops to *retreat.*
2. *(n.)* a withdrawal or retirement in the face of the enemy वापसी, पीछे हटना Their *retreat* was carried out very quietly.
3. a place, such as a sanatorium or monastery, to which one may retire for refuge, quiet, etc. एकांत स्थान The holiday *retreat* was fun.

retrieve *(v.)* रिट्रीव– to get or fetch back again; recover पुनः प्राप्त करना The army was able *to retrieve* the body from under the debris.

retrospect *(n.)* रेट्रोस्पेक्ट– the act of surveying things past आत्मावलोकन In *retrospect* some of the decision I took were not of a wise person.

retrospective *(adj.)* रेट्रास्पेक्टिव– looking or directed backwards, esp in time; characterized by retrospection पूर्व प्रभावी The scheme was introduced with *retrospective* effect.

retrospectively *(adv.)* रेट्रास्पेक्टिवली– at a later point in time पूर्व प्रभाव से She wrote *retrospectively* about her personal life.

return *(v.)* रिटर्न–1. to give, take, or carry back; replace or restore लौटाना You must *return* the pen she lent you.

2. to come back वापस आना, लौटना We *returned* to Mumbai by the Frontier Mail.

3. to get selected, elected लोकसभा आदि में चुना जाना Mr. A.B. Vajpayee was *returned* by a good majority to the parliament.

returnable *(adj.)* रिटर्नबल– able to be taken, given, or sent back वापस करने योग्य The application forms are *returnable* not later than 5th June.

reunion *(n.)* रीयूनिअन्– 1. the act or process of coming together again पुनर्मिलन पार्टी All the old students were invited for the college *reunion.*

2. a gathering of relatives, friends, or former associates मित्र-समागम् There was a family *reunion* after twenty-five years.

reveal *(v.)* रिवील– 1. to disclose (a secret); divulge गुप्त बात प्रकट करना या होना The truth was *revealed at last.*

2. *(n.)* expose to view or show (something concealed) प्रदर्शित, प्रकट I promised Amitabh that I would never *reveal* his secrets.

revealing *(adj.)* रिवीलिंग– of significance or import छुपी हुई बात को प्रकट करने वाला This book provides me a *revealing* insight into the world of cinema.

revenge *(n.)* रिवेंज–1. the act of retaliating for wrongs or injury received; vengeance बदला, प्रतिरोध He swore to take a *revenge* on his enemies.

2. something done as a means of vengeance प्रतिशोध *Revenge* is not a remedy to establish peace on earth.

3. *(v.)* to inflict equivalent injury or damage for (injury received); retaliate in return for बदला लेना Mohit *revenged* his brother's death.

revenue *(n.)* रेवन्यू–1. the income accruing from taxation to a government during a specified period of time, usually a year राजस्व Income tax is one of the major sources of *revenue* for the government.

2. the gross income from a business enterprise, investment, property, etc. आमदनी का ज़रिया They get more than a crore *revenue* every year from their land.

reverberate *(v.)* रिवर्बरेट– to resound or re-echo ध्वनि का गूंजना The sound of her voice *reverberated* loudly in the mountains

revere *(v.)* रिविअर्– to be in awe of and respect deeply; venerate आदर करना The society must always *revere* their elders.

reverse *(v.)* रिवर्स– 1. to turn or set in an opposite direction, order, or position विपरीत कर देना, उलटा कर देना Writing is *reversed* in the mirror.

2. *(n.)* the back or rear side of something विपरीत दिशा में, पीछे का What is there at the *reverse* of the painting?

3. *(adj.)* opposite or contrary in direction, position, order, nature, etc.; turned backwards विपरीत, उसके

प्रतिकूल The new policy had the *reverse* effect of what was expected.

reversible *(adj.)* रिवर्सबल– capable of being reversed उलटा करने योग्य, पलटवाँ This chemical reaction is not *reversible.*

revert *(v.)* रिवर्ट– to go back to a former practice, condition, belief, etc. वापस आना Please *revert* back to your superiors as soon as you finish your work.

review *(v.)* रिव्यू–1. to look at or examine again समीक्षा करना The movie was favourably *reviewed* in the newspapers.

2. to look back upon (a period of time, sequence of events, etc.); remember पुनरावलोकन करना The company *reviewed* the progress over the past one year.

3. *(n.)* a general survey or report समालोचना The movie got good *reviews* in newspapers.

4. a formal or official inspection सर्वेक्षण The company decided to hold an annual *review* of the progress.

revise *(v.)* रिवाइज़– to reread (a subject or notes on it) so as to memorize it, esp in preparation for an examination दोहराना, फिर से पढ़ना Please *revise* the second chapter.

revision *(n.)* रिविज़न– the act or process of revising सुधार, संशोधन Your essay needs *revision.*

revival *(n.)* रिवाइवल– a renewed use, acceptance of, or interest in (past customs, styles, etc.) पुनर्जीवन, पुनरुद्धार The consultancy firm is working hard towards the *revival* of the company.

revive *(v.)* रिवाइव–1. to bring or be brought back to life, consciousness, or strength; resuscitate or be resuscitated पुनर्जीवित होना The doctors were able to *revive* the patient in the nick of time.

revolt *(v.)* रिवोल्ट– 1. to rise up in rebellion against authority विद्रोह करना The peasants *revolted* against their landlords.

2. *(n.)* a rebellion or uprising against authority बग़ावत, विद्रोह The peasants' *revolt* was badly crushed.

revolution *(n.)* रेवलूशन– the overthrow or repudiation of a regime or political system by the governed क्रान्ति The French *Revolution* was a period of radical, social and political upheaval.

revolutionary *(adj.)* रेवलूशनरी– relating to or characteristic of a revolution क्रान्तिकारी Chandrashekhar Azad was the *revolutionary* leader of India.

revolve *(v.)* रिवॉल्व–1. to move or cause to move around a centre or axis; rotate घूमना, (चारों ओर) चक्कर लगाना The moon *revolves* round the earth, and earth *revolves* round the sun.

2. to be centred or focused (upon) गहराई से विचार करना, किसी महत्त्वपूर्ण चीज पर केन्द्रित होना Several ideas *revolve* in my mind.

revolver *(n.)* रिवॉल्वर– a pistol having a revolving multichambered cylinder that allows several shots to be discharged without reloading छोटी बंदूक़ It is illegal to keep a *revolver* without a valid license .

reward *(v.)* रिवॉर्ड– 1. to give (something) to (someone), esp in gratitude for a service rendered; recompense इनाम देना, पुरस्कार देना The boy who saved the little girls was *rewarded* for his bravery.

2. *(n.)* something given or received in return for a deed or service rendered इनाम, पुरस्कार The conductor of the D.T.C. bus, who found the gentleman's purse, was given a *reward* for returning it.

rewarding *(adj.)* रिवार्डिंग– giving personal satisfaction; gratifying लाभप्रद The project which they undertook was quite *rewarding* for them.

rewrite *(v.)* रीराइट– to write (written material) again, esp changing the words or form दोबारा लिखना My son was *rewriting* his entire essay.

rhyme *(n.)* राइम– identity of the terminal sounds in lines of verse or in words तुकान्त गीत या कविता The sign of a good poem is that it has many *rhyming* words.

rhythm *(n.)* रिद्म– the arrangement of the relative durations of and accents on the notes of a melody, usually laid out into regular groups (bars) of beats लय, ताल, सामंजस्य He suddenly started singing out of *rhythm.*

rib *(n.)* रिब्– any of the 24 curved elastic arches of bone that together form the chest wall in man पसली Eve was said to be born from Adam's *rib.*

ribbon *(n.)* रिबन– a narrow strip of fine material, esp silk, used for trimming, tying, etc. पट्टी, फीता The hair of the girl was tied with a *ribbon.*

rice *(n.)* राइस– white or brown grain grown on wet land चावल *Rice* is a staple dish in India.

rich *(adj.)* रिच–1. well supplied with wealth, property, etc.; owning much संपन्न, धनी Hard work made him a *rich* man.

2. having an abundance of natural resources, minerals, etc. भारी, गरिष्ठ I cannot digest *rich* food. It makes me feel ill.

richly *(adv.)* रिचली– fully and appropriately पूर्णरूप से Her dress was *richly* decorated with heavy embroidery.

rickety *(adj.)* रिकटी– (of a structure, piece of furniture, etc.) likely to collapse or break; shaky कमज़ोर, जर्जर The pillars supporting the floor seemed to be *rickety* .

rickshaw *(n.)* रिक्शॉ– a small two-wheeled passenger vehicle drawn by one or two men, साइकिल रिक्शा A foreigner was sitting in a *rickshaw* near Lal Quila.

rid *(v.)* रिड– to relieve or deliver from something disagreeable or undesirable; make free (of) मुक्त करना We need to get *rid* of the rat in the house.

riddle *(n.)* रिडल– a question, puzzle, or verse so phrased that ingenuity is required for elucidation of the answer or meaning; conundrum पहेली The answer to the *riddle* was very difficult

ride *(v.)* राइड– 1. to sit on and propel (a bicycle or similar vehicle) चढ़ाना, सवारी करना Can you *ride* a motorcycle?

2. *(n.)* a journey or outing on horseback or in a vehicle सवारी से की गई यात्रा We had a pleasant *ride.*

rider *(n.)* राइडर– a person or thing that rides, esp a person who rides a horse, a bicycle, or a motorcycle सवार The *rider* performed breathtaking stunts on his bike.

ridiculous *(adj.)* रिडिकुलस– worthy of or exciting ridicule; absurd, preposterous, laughable, or contemptible बेतुका, हास्यास्पद You look *ridiculous* in this long gown.

rifle *(n.)* राइफ़ल– 1. a firearm having a long barrel with a spirally grooved interior, which imparts to the bullet spinning motion and thus greater accuracy over a longer range बन्दूक़ I went out armed with a *rifle.*

2. *(v.)* to search (a house, safe, etc.) and steal from it; ransack लूटने की दृष्टि से खोजना The whole house has been *rifled.*

rift *(n.)* रिफ्ट– a break in friendly relations between people, nations, etc. दरार The *rift* between them kept on widening because of their different views.

right *(adj.)* राइट–1. in accordance with accepted standards of moral or legal behaviour, justice, etc. उचित It was not *right* of you to help my opponent.

2. worn on a right hand, foot, etc. दायाँ (हाथ या ओर) We write with our *right* hand. Is it not the *right* way to write?

3. indicating or designating the correct time ठीक Is your watch *right*?

4. *(n.)* any claim, title, etc. that is morally just or legally granted as allowable or due to a person अधिकार You have no *right* to shout at me.

right away *(adj.)* राईट-अवे– without delay; immediately or promptly तत्काल, तुरंत They want it sent *right away*.

righteous *(adj.)* राइचस– characterized by, proceeding from, or in accordance with accepted standards of morality, justice, or uprightness; virtuous नेक, ईमानदार He is a *righteous* man and shall go to heaven.

right-hand *(adj.)* for use by the right hand; right-handed दाहिने ओर का Sachin Tendulkar is *right-handed* batsman.

right-handed *(adj.)* using the right hand with greater skill or ease than the left दाहिने हाथ से सब काम करने वाला Imran Nazir is a *right-handed* batsman of the Pakistan cricket team.

rightly *(adv.)*–1. in accordance with the facts; correctly पूरी तरह से Somebody has *rightly* remarked that truth always wins.

2. in accordance with principles of justice or morality सही ढंग से Mahak is not capable to decide the matter *rightly*.

3. with good reason; justifiably वास्तव में I am not *rightly* sure.

rigid *(adj.)* रिजिड्– not bending; physically inflexible or stiff सख़्त, कठोर He is a *rigid* old man, and does not welcome changes.

rigidity *(adj.)* रिजिडटि– unbending; rigorously strict; severe सख़्ती, कठोरता The *rigidity* of his nature caused harm to everyone at home.

rigorous *(adj.)* रिगरस– characterized by or proceeding from rigour; harsh, strict, or severe सख्त, कठोर The training in the army is very tough and *rigorous*.

rim *(n.)* रिम्– the raised edge of an object, esp of something more or less circular such as a cup or crater किसी गोलाकार वस्तु का किनारा, घेरा The *rim* of her spectacles was golden in colour.

ring *(n.)* रिंग– 1. a circular band usually of a precious metal, esp gold, often set with gems and worn upon the finger as an adornment or as a token of engagement or marriage अंगूठी The bride wears three *rings* on her fingers.

2. *(v.)* to emit or cause to emit a sonorous or resonant sound, characteristic of certain metals when struck बजाना The peon will *ring* the bell.

ringleader *(n.)* रिंगलीडर– a person who leads others in any kind of unlawful or mischievous activity सरदार, सरगना He was the *ringleader* of his gang in the last riots.

ringworm *(n.)* रिंगवम– any of various fungal infections of the skin (esp the scalp) or nails, often appearing as itching circular patches दाद She has *ringworms* on her feet.

rinse *(v.)* रिन्स– to remove soap from (clothes, etc) by applying clean water in the final stage in washing साफ़ करना, धोना, खँगालना Mother *rinses* woollen sweaters in warm water.

riot *(n.)* राइअट– 1. a disturbance made by an unruly mob or (in law) three or more persons; tumult or uproar दंगा, कोलाहल, हंगामा The rebels who took part in the *riot* broke many articles in the shop.

2. *(v.)* to take part in a riot हंगामा करना, क़ाबू के बाहर होना They *rioted* the streets also.

rip *(v.)* रिप्– 1. to tear or be torn violently or roughly; split or be rent चीरना, एकदम से फाड़ डालना I *ripped* my dress.

2. *(n.)* the place where something is torn; a tear or split चीरा, छेद There was a big *rip* in my dress.

ripe *(adj.)* राइप–1. (of fruit, grain, etc.) mature and ready to be eaten or used; fully developed परिपक्व, पका हुआ We should eat *ripe* fruits.

2. fully developed in mind or body परिपक्व (अवस्था) I have reached the *ripe* age of 42.

ripple *(n.)* रिपल्– a slight wave or undulation on the surface of water छोटी लहर The earthquake caused massive *ripples* in the oceans.

rise *(v.)* राइज़्–1. to get out of bed, esp to begin one's day उठना, उदय होना The sun *rises* in the morning and sets in the evening.

2. to get up from a lying, sitting, kneeling, or prone position विद्रोह करना, (विरुद्ध) उठ खड़े होना Some day, the exploited people will *rise* against the cruel ruler.

3. *(n.)* an increase in rank, status, or position बढ़ोतरी, वृद्धि There has been a *rise* in the prices of some essential commodities.

risk *(v.)* रिस्क– 1. to expose to danger or loss; hazard जोखिम उठाना, दाँव पर लगाना Vinayak *risked* his life to save a child from drowning.

2. *(n.)* the possibility of incurring misfortune or loss; hazard ख़तरा You are taking a *risk* of displeasing your boss if you just stay away from work.

risky *(adj.)* रिस्की– involving danger; perilous ख़तरनाक, जोखिमभरा Driving on roads without proper training is very *risky*.

rite *(n.)* राइट– a formal act or procedure prescribed or customary in religious ceremonies रीति, विधि They performed the funeral *rites* immediately after the death.

ritual *(n.)* रिचुअल्– the prescribed or established form of a religious or other ceremony कर्मकांड, रीति-रिवाज His last *rituals* were performed in Haridwar.

rival *(n.)* राइवल– a person, organization, team, etc. that competes with another for the same object or in the same field प्रतिद्वन्द्वी The two *rival* gangs caused a lot of problems for the local community.

rivalry *(n.)* राइवल्री– the act of rivalling; competition प्रतिस्पर्धा The India Pakistan cricket *rivalry* will never die down.

river *(n.)* रिवर–1. a large natural stream of fresh water flowing along a definite course, usually into the sea, being fed by tributary streams नदी Ganga and Yamuna are holy *rivers.*

2. any abundant stream or flow दरिया We can see boats sailing on the *river.*

riverside *(n.)* रिवर्साइड– नदी तट They had a picnic by the *riverside.*

rivet *(v.)* रिवेट– to cause to be fixed or held firmly, as in fascinated attention, horror, etc. रुचि को बनाए रखना, जकड़ना We all were *riveted* by her story.

road *(n.)* रोड–1. an open way, usually surfaced with asphalt or concrete, providing passage from one place to another सड़क Rama is driving a car along the *road*.

2. a way, path, or course सड़क मार्ग से Many people like to go by *road.*

3. a street मार्ग, सड़क Is this the *road* to India Gate?

roadside *(n.)* रोडसाइड़– the area at the edge of a road सड़क के किनारे There are many stones lying on the *roadside.*

roam *(v.)* रॉम– to travel or walk about with no fixed purpose or direction; wander घूमना, भटकना We were *roaming* aimlessly on the roads.

roar *(n.)* रोर्– 1. a loud deep cry, uttered by a person or crowd, esp in anger or triumph ध्वनि, गर्जना, शोर The tiger sprang up towards me with a *roar.*

2. *(v.)* to utter characteristic loud growling cries ध्वनि करना, शोर मचाना The listener *roared* with laughter at my story.

roaring *(adj.)* रॉरिंग– very brisk and profitable ज़ोरदार The coaching institute boast of *roaring* success every year.

roast *(v.)* रोस्ट– to cook (meat or other food) by dry heat, usually with added fat and esp in an oven भूनना The cook *roasted* the chicken.

rob *(v.)* रॉब– to take something from (someone) illegally, as by force or threat of violence लूटना He was *robbed* at gunpoint in broad daylight.

robbery *(n.)* रॉबरी– the stealing of property from a person by using or threatening to use force लूटमार The *robbery* was foiled by the security guard.

robe *(n.)* रोब– any loose flowing garment, esp the official vestment of a peer, judge, or academic लबादा, गाउन The girl was dressed in an attractive *robe.*

robin *(n.)* रॉबिन– a small European songbird गाने वाली छोटी चिड़िया *Robin* is a beautiful European bird.

robot *(n.)* रोबॉट– any automated machine programmed to perform specific mechanical functions in the manner of a man यंत्र-मानव It seems in future, all the work would be done by the *robots.*

robust *(adj.)* रोबस्ट– strong in constitution; hardy; vigorous हृष्ट-पुष्ट, हट्टा-कट्टा The company boasted of *robust* growth in the next quarter.

rock *(n.)* रॉक्– 1. any aggregate of minerals that makes up part of the earth's crust. चट्टान There are many big *rocks* in the sea.

2. *(v.)* to move or cause to move from side to side or backwards and forwards हिलाना, झुलाना She *rocked* her baby and sang a lullaby to put him to sleep.

rock and roll *(n.)* a type of pop music originating in the 1950s as a blend of rhythm and blues and country and western तेज़ गति वाला संगीत *Rock and roll* is a popular music which originated in the US in late 1940s.

rock climbing *(n.)* the technique and sport of climbing on steep rock faces, usually with ropes and other equipment and as part of a team or pair पहाड़ों पर चढ़ने का खेल *Rock climbing* has become a professional sport in the recent years.

rocket *(n.)* रॉकेट– a self-propelling device, esp a cylinder containing a mixture of solid explosives, used as a firework, distress signal, line carrier, etc. राकेट, यान The designs for the *rocket* are still not perfect.

rocky *(adj.)* रॉकी– consisting of or abounding in rocks चट्टानों से भरा हुआ It was difficult for me to walk on a *rocky* road.

rod *(n.)* रॉड– a slim cylinder of metal, wood, etc. stick or shaft छड़ Carry the fishing *rod* with you.

rodent *(n.)* रोडण्ट– any of the relatively small placental mammals that constitute the order Rodentia, having constantly growing incisor teeth specialized for gnawing. मज़बूत और तेज़ दांतों से कुतरने वाला जन्तु (चूहा, गिलहरी आदि) All *rodents* have strong sharp front teeth.

rogue *(n.)* रोग– a dishonest or unprincipled person, esp a man; rascal; scoundrel दुष्ट, दुर्जन, बदमाश The *rogue* trader bought down the whole company.

role *(n.)* रोल–1. a part or character in a play, film, etc. to be played by an actor or actress भूमिका What will be my *role* in this campaign?
2. usual or customary function नाटक या फ़िल्म में निभाया गया पात्र She played the *role* of a widowed mother in the play.

roll *(v.)* रोल– 1. move or cause to move along by turning over and over लुढ़कना, ढुलकना The baby is about to *roll* down the bed.
2. *(n.)* an official list or register, esp of names नामों की सूची I will call the *roll* now.
3. a trilling sound; trill गड़गड़ाहट, गर्जन Suddenly, the sky became dark and they heard a *roll* of thunder.

roller *(n.)* रोलर– a cylinder having an absorbent surface and a handle, बेलन The captain the ground staff to use a big *roller* on the pitch.

Roman *(n.)* रोमन– a citizen or inhabitant of ancient or modern Rome रोमवासी The *Romans* believed in many different gods and goddesses.

romance *(n.)* रोमैन्स–1. a love affair, esp an intense and happy but short-lived affair involving young people साहस और प्रेम की कहानी, प्रेम कथा Modern young girls mostly read nothing but books of *romance.*
2. love, esp romantic love idealized for its purity or beauty प्रेम-प्रसंग It was a beautiful *romance*, but it didn't last.

romantic *(n.)* रोमैंटिक– a person who is romantic, as in being idealistic, amorous, or soulful भावुक, काल्पनिक She is very fond of reading *romantic* novels.

romp *(v.)* रॉम्प– to play or run about wildly, boisterously, or joyfully उछल-कूद करना Children were having a *romp* in the break-time.

roof *(n.)* रूफ़– a structure that covers or forms the top of a building छत (का ऊपरी भाग) The *roof* has been made rock solid .

rooftop *(n.)* रूफ़टॉप– the outside part of the roof of a building घर की छतों का सबसे ऊपरी हिस्सा We looked down over the *rooftop* of our house.

room *(n.)* रूम–1. space or extent, esp unoccupied or unobstructed space for a particular purpose स्थान, जगह Is there *room* for me in the compartment?
2. an area within a building enclosed by a floor, a ceiling, and walls or partitions कमरा There is enough space in the *room.*
3. opportunity or scope अवसर, मौक़ा There is *room* for improvement in this situation.

room-mate *(n.)* रूम-मेट– a person with whom one shares a room or lodging संगी, कमरा-साथी My *room-mate* is giving me a very hard time.

roost *(n.)* रूस्ट– a place, perch, branch, etc. where birds, esp domestic fowl, rest or sleep पक्षियों का अड्डा, बसेरा There was a big *roost* on a Neem tree near my house.

root *(n.)* रूट– 1. the organ of a higher plant that anchors the rest of the plant in the ground, absorbs water and mineral salts from the soil, and does not bear leaves or buds जड़ (वृक्ष या पौधों की) The *roots* keep the plant steady, and help it to grow.

2. *(v.)* to search vigorously but unsystematically खोज करना The family doctor is trying to get to the *root* of my mother's illness.

rope *(n.)* रोप– 1. a fairly thick cord made of twisted and intertwined hemp or other fibres or of wire or other strong material रस्सी The cows were tied with strong *ropes.*

2. *(v.)* to bind or fasten with or as if with a rope रस्सी से बाँधना The traveller *roped* his horse to the tree and lay down to take rest.

rosary *(n.)* रोज़री– a series of prayers counted on a string of beads सुमिरनी, माला The *rosary* was filled with fresh and new flowers.

rose *(n.)* रोज़– a flower with sweet smell with thorns गुलाब My garden is full of a large variety of *roses.*

rostrum *(n.)* रॉसट्रम– any platform, stage, or dais on which public speakers stand to address an audience चबूतरा, मंच Boys have made a big *rostrum* for prize distribution programme.

rosy *(adj.)* रोज़ी– of the colour rose or pink गुलाबी The young girl had *rosy* cheeks.

rot *(v.)* रॉट– to decay or cause to decay as a result of bacterial or fungal action सड़-गल जाना, खराब करना Too many chocolates will *rot* your teeth.

rotate *(v.)* रोटेट्– to turn or cause to turn around an axis, line, or point; revolve or spin धुरी पर घूमना Apart from revolving around the sun, the planets also *rotate* on their own axis.

rotation *(n.)* रोटेशन– a regular cycle of events in a set order or sequence घुमाव, चक्कर One *rotation* of the earth completes 4 minutes less than 24 hours.

rotten *(adj.)* रॉटन–1. affected with rot; decomposing, decaying, or putrid सड़ा-गला The basket is full of *rotten* mangoes.

rough *(adj.)* रॅफ़–1.) not smooth; uneven or irregular सस्ता, खुरदरा I need some *rough* cloth.

2. rude, coarse, ill mannered, inconsiderate, or violent कठोर, कर्कश Don't be *rough* with women and babies.

3. harsh or sharp रूखा, अशिष्ट Father was angry and spoke in a *rough* voice.

4. not polished or perfected in any detail; जल्दी-जल्दी तैयार किया हुआ, कच्चे रंग से तैयार किया हुआ This is a *rough* drawing.

roughage *(n.)* रफ़ेज– the coarse indigestible constituents of food or fodder, which provide bulk to the diet and promote normal bowel function मोटा चारा The human body requires requires a lot of *roughage.*

roughly *(adv.)* रफ़लि–1. without being exact or fully authenticated; approximately लगभग, अंदाज़न There were *roughly* thirty persons in the gathering.

2. in a crude or primitive manner बुरे ढंग से, दुर्व्यवहारपूर्वक The policeman *roughly* pushed the prisoner into the cell.

round *(n.)* राउण्ड–1. a series of calls, esp in a set order घटनाओं का दौर The company is considering a fresh *round* of interviews from next week.

2. the usual activities of one's day फेरा The director is on his daily *round.*

3. a stage of a competition प्रतियोगिता का एक चक्र या दौर Australia has qualified for the next *round.*

4. a general outburst of applause, cheering, etc प्रशंसा-प्रक्रिया He was welcomed with a huge *round* of applause.

5. *(v.)* to end समाप्त करना He *rounded* his speech with a quotation.
6. in rotation or revolution चक्कर लगाना His car was *rounding* the whole city.
7. *(adj.)* having a flat circular shape, as a disc or hoop गोलाकार The table was *round* in shape.
8. *(adv.)* in all directions from a point of reference किसी वस्तु के चारों ओर The dog went *round* and round the car.

roundabout *(adj.)* राउण्डबाउट– 1. indirect or circuitous; devious घुमाव-फिराव का, लंबा We took a *roundabout* route to reach the station.
2. *(n.)* a revolving circular platform provided with wooden animals, seats, etc., on which people ride for amusement; merry-go-round गोल चक्कर We turned left at the first *roundabout.*

rouse *(v.)* राउज़्– to bring (oneself or another person) out of sleep, unconsciousness, etc. or (of a person) to come to consciousness in this way जगाना, जागना I was *roused* by the voice of the crying baby.

route *(n.)* रूट्– the choice of roads taken to get to a place मार्ग, रास्ता We deliberately took the longer *route.*

routine *(n.)* रूटीन– a usual or regular method of procedure, esp one that is unvarying दिनचर्या, दैनिक कार्य Shouting and swearing is *routine* in his line of work.

rove *(v.)* रोव– to wander about (a place) with no fixed direction; roam घूमना, भटकना You spent all day *roving* through the jungle.

row *(n.)* रो– 1. an arrangement of persons or things in a line पंक्ति, कतार The people were standing in a *row* near the ration shop.
2. *(v.)* to propel (a boat) by using oars चप्पू चलाना, नाव चलाना The boatmen *row* their boats, they make the boats travel through the water.

rowdy *(adj.)* राउडी– tending to create noisy disturbances; rough, loud, or disorderly उपद्रवी The police finally arrested all the *rowdy* boys from the street.

royal *(adj.)* रॉइअल– of, relating to, or befitting a king, queen, or other monarch; regal शाही He gave all his guests a *royal* treatment.

royalty *(n.)* रॉइअल्टी– a percentage of the revenue from the sale of a book, performance of a theatrical work, use of a patented invention or of land, etc. paid to the author, inventor, or proprietor रॉयल्टी, स्वत्व-शुल्क Nobody knows this but he belongs to *royalty.*

rub *(v.)* रॅब– to apply pressure and friction to (something) with a circular or backward and forward motion रगड़ना Don't *rub* harder, your shoes are already shining.

- **rub down**– to make or become smooth by rubbing घिसाई करना, रगड़ना You have to *rub down* the walls well before painting.
- **rub in**– to spread with pressure, esp in order to cause to be absorbed क्रीम आदि मलना Please *rub in* iodex on my back.
- **rub it in**– to harp on (something distasteful to a person, of which he or she does not wish to be reminded) किसी को अप्रिय बात याद दिलाना There is no need to *rub it in* the stupid mistake.
- **rub off**– to remove or be removed by rubbing मल कर निकाल देना She *rubbed* the stain *off* his shirt.
- **rub out**– to remove or be removed with a rubber मिटा देना *Rub out* what you have drawn.
- **rub shoulder with**– to mix with socially or associate with बड़े लोगों से मिलना-जुलना या सम्पर्क में आना, The journalist is *rubbing* his *shoulders with* leaders all the time.

➢ **rub up**– to refresh one's memory (of) अचानक कहीं मुलाक़ात हो जाना He *rubbed up* the old woman.

rubber *(n.)* रबर–1. a cream to dark brown elastic material obtained by coagulating and drying the latex रबड़ She wears *rubber* gloves while washing utensils.

2. a piece of rubber or felt used for erasing something written, typed, etc.; eraser पेंसिल के लिखे को मिटाने वाला रबड़ Please give me a *rubber* to *rub* pencil-marks.

rubbish *(n.)* रॅबिश–1. worthless, useless, or unwanted matter कूड़ा-करकट We must thrown our *rubbish* in the dustbin.

2. foolish words or speech; nonsense ऊल-जलूल, निरर्थक She is talking *rubbish.* Really she knows nothing about it.

rubble *(n.)* रबल– any fragmented solid material, esp the debris from ruined buildings मलबा There was a lot of *rubble* collected after the building collapsed.

ruby *(n.)* रूबी– a deep red transparent precious variety of corundum मानिक, लाल क़ीमती पत्थर She was wearing a ring studded with *ruby.*

rudder *(n.)* रडर– a pivoted vertical vane that projects into the water at the stern of a vessel and can be controlled by a tiller, wheel, or other apparatus to steer the vessel पतवार The *rudder* of the boat broke half way through the journey.

rude *(adj.)* रूड–1. insulting or uncivil; discourteous; impolite अशिष्ट, अभद्र Amita is a polite girl. She is not *rude.*

2. lacking refinement; coarse or uncouth असभ्य It is *rude* to speak with your mouthfull.

rudeness *(n.)* रूडनेस्– insulting or uncivil behaviour; discourtesy; impoliteness अशिष्टता, अभद्रता His parents scolded him on his *rudeness* towards fellow students.

ruffle *(v.)* रफ़ल– to make into a ruffle; pleat अस्त-व्यस्त करना, शिकन पड़ना The *ruffled* look works best for him.

ruffian *(n.)* रॅफ़ियन– a violent or lawless person; hoodlum or villain गुंडा, बदमाश The landlord was attacked by a gang of *ruffians.*

rug *(n.)* रॅग–1. a blanket, esp one used as a wrap or lap robe for travellers कम्बल Our cat likes to sit on the *rug.*

2. a floor covering, smaller than a carpet and made of thick wool or of other material, such as an animal skin क़ालीन We have a *rug* in the car.

rugged *(adj.)* रगेड– having an uneven or jagged surface ऊबड़-खाबड़ The police man could not catch the thief as the land was very *rugged.*

ruin *(v.)* रुइन– 1. to bring to ruin; destroy नाश होना, धराशायी होना A severe earthquake totally *ruined* the big city.

2. *(n.)* destroyed or decayed building or town तबाही, विनाश We visited the *ruin* of an old palace.

rule *(n.)* रूल– 1. an authoritative regulation or direction concerning method or procedure, as for a court of law, legislative body, game, or other human institution or activity नियम You will be disqualified for disobeying the *rules* of the club.

2. *(v.)* to exercise governing or controlling authority over (a people, political unit, individual, etc.) शासन करना Aurangzeb, the mighty Mughal emperor, *ruled* India for many years.

ruler *(n.)* रूलर– a person who rules or commands शासक Alexander was a great *ruler* of his time.

ruling *(adj.)* रूलिंग– controlling or exercising authority शासनिक, प्रबल

The court gave its *ruling* regarding the case .

rum *(n.)* रम– spirit made from sugar cane, either coloured brownish-red by the addition of caramel or by maturation in oak containers, or left white शराब They were drinking *rum* with roasted chicken.

rumble *(v.)* रमबल– to make or cause to make a deep resonant sound भूख से गड़गड़ करना The *rumbling* in my stomach stopped after I ate something.

rumbling *(n.)* रमबलिंग– a widespread murmur of discontent असंतोषसूचक There has been a lot of *rumbling* in the office today.

ruminant *(n.)* रूमिनेंट– any animal that chews the cud, such as a camel जुगाली Buffalows and cows are both *ruminants.*

rumour *(n.)* रयूमर्– information, often a mixture of truth and untruth, passed around verbally अफ़वाह, उड़ती ख़बर There are a lot of *rumours* in the air regarding your relationship.

run *(v.)* रॅन–1. to move on foot at a rapid pace so that both feet are off the ground together for part of each stride भागना The policeman is *running* after the thief.

2. to run in a race as specified, esp for a particular reason उम्मीदवार के रूप में लोकसभा आदि के लिए चुनाव में खड़ा होना। He is *running* for parliament.

3. to cause or allow (liquids) to flow or (of liquids) to flow, esp in a manner specified बहना The Ganges *runs* through a thick valley.

4. taking care of/working on to keep its existence संचालन करना Who is *running* the business?

➢ **run across**– to meet unexpectedly; encounter by chance संयोग से किसी से मुलाक़ात हो जाना, I *ran across* my old friend in a party.

➢ **run after**– to pursue (anything) persistently के पीछे पड़ा रहना, Why are you *running after* him?

➢ **run away**– to go away; depart घर से भाग जाना, Damini *ran away* from home.

➢ **run down**– to hit and knock to the ground with a moving vehicle कुचल देना, Anjali was *run down* by a truck.

➢ **run over**– to examine hastily or make a rapid survey of सरसरी दृष्टि से, The child was *running over* his poem.

➢ **run with**– to associate with habitually बहते पानी या किसी द्रव से सन जाना, My face was *running with* sweat.

runaway *(adj.)* रनअवे्– A runaway vehicle or animal is moving forward quickly, and its driver or rider has lost control of it बेक़ाबू The bull suddenly became a *runaway* .

runner *(n.)* –रनर्– a person who runs, esp an athlete दौड़ाक, दौड़ने वाले The batsman called a *runner* to run for him.

runner-up *(n.)* रनर-अप्– a contestant finishing a race or competition in second place उपविजेता He was happy to be in the *runners-up* position

running *(n.)* रनिंग्– an act, instance, or period of running धावन, दौड़ He was tired because of *running* for long hours.

runway *(n.)* रनवे– a hard level roadway or other surface from which aircraft take off and on which they land धावन-पथ The plane was landing on the *runway.*

rupee *(n.)* रुपी– the standard monetary unit रुपया My father made me understand the value of a *rupee* in life.

rupture *(n.)* रपचर्– the act of breaking or bursting or the state of being broken or burst दरार, फटन His windpipe was *ruptured* because of the accident.

rural *(adj.)* रूरल– of, relating to, or characteristic of the country or country life ग्रामीण *Rural* India needs utmost attention from the central government.

rush *(v.)* रॅश–1. to hurry or cause to hurry; hasten दौड़ना, जल्दी करना You are very late. You should *rush* to the office.

2. to proceed or approach in a reckless manner तेज़ी से कहीं पहुंचना After the accident, the injured were *rushed* to the hospital.

3. *(n.)* a sudden surge towards someone or something भीड़ There was a great *rush* at the main gate of the cinema hall.

rush hour *(n.)* रॅश-आर– a period at the beginning and end of the working day when large numbers of people are travelling to or from work व्यस्त समय It's foolish to drive during a *rush-hour.*

rust *(n.)* रॅस्ट– 1. a reddish-brown oxide coating formed on iron or steel by the action of oxygen and moisture ज़ंग There were patches of *rust* on the motorbike.

2. *(v.)* to become or cause to become coated with a layer of rust ज़ंग लग जाना Some parts of the motorbike had *rusted.*

rustic *(adj.)* रस्टिक– having qualities ascribed to country life or people; simple; unsophisticated देहाती, गँवारू He has a very *rustic* personality.

rustle *(v.)* रसल– to move swiftly and energetically सरसराना, फड़-फड़ करना I heard she *rustled* the papers on her desk.

rusty *(adj.)* रस्टी– covered with, affected by, or consisting of rust ज़ंग लगा हुआ His music skills have become very *rusty* for the last two years.

ruthless *(adj.)* रूथलेस– feeling or showing no mercy; hardhearted कठोर, बेरहम Wrestlers must have *ruthless* aggression to win a competition.

Ss

Ss *(n.)* एस—अंग्रेज़ी वर्णमाला का उन्नीसवां अक्षर The nineteenth letter of the English alphabet. Sister begins with 'S'.

sabotage *(v.)* सैबटाज— to damage or destroy sth deliberately जानबूझकर तोड़-फोड़ करना The enemy *subotaged* our car.

sachet *(n.)* सैशे— a small sealed envelope, usually made of plastic or paper, for containing sugar, salt, shampoo, etc. प्लास्टिक या कागज़ का छोटा पैकेट, थैली Get a *sachet* of coffee from the nearby shop.

sack *(n.)* सैक्— 1. a large bag made of coarse cloth, thick paper, etc. used as a container बोरा She filled up the *sack* with potatoes. She got the *sack* for stealing.

2. *(v.)* to dismiss from a job नौकरी से बर्ख़ास्त करना He was *sacked* from the job because of bad behaviour.

sacred *(adj.)* सेक्रिड— exclusively devoted to a deity or to some religious ceremony or use; holy; consecrated पवित्र, पावन, धार्मिक The Gita is a *sacred* book of the Hindus.

sacrifice *(v.)* सेक्रिफ़ाइस— 1. to make a sacrifice (of); give up, surrender, or destroy (a person, thing, etc.) त्याग करना Those who *sacrifice* their personal interests for a great cause never fail.

2. *(n.)* a surrender of something of value as a means of gaining something more desirable or of preventing some evil त्याग, बलिदान, कुरबानी His *sacrifices* for the country will always be remembered.

sacrilege *(n.)* सैक्रिलिज— the misuse or desecration of anything regarded as sacred or as worthy of extreme respect अपवित्रीकरण It would be *sacrilege* to tear the holy book from the mosque.

sad *(adj.)* सैड— feeling sorrow; unhappy दुखी, उदास Why are you so *sad* today?

sadden *(v.)* सैडन— to make or become sad दुखी होना या करना We were all *saddened* by his sudden death.

saddle *(n.)* सैडल— 1. a seat for a rider, usually made of leather, placed on a horse's back and secured with a girth under the belly ज़ीन, काठी The rider put the *saddle* on his horse's back.

2. *(v.)* to put a saddle on (a horse) ज़ीन या काठी को कसना We *saddled* our horses and got ready to march.

sadism *(n.)* सेडिज़म— the gaining of pleasure or sexual gratification from the infliction of pain and mental suffering on another person परपीड़न-कामुकता *Sadism* was a part of his sexual life.

sadist *(n.)* सेडिस्ट— someone who gains pleasure or sexual gratification from the infliction of pain and mental suffering on another person परपीड़नकामी A *sadist* obtains pleasure from inflicting pain on others.

sadly *(adv.)* सैडली— in an unhappy or sad manner मुंह लटकाए, दुखद ढंग से He went away *sadly* without talking to me.

sadness *(n.)* सैडनस— the quality or state of feeling sorrow; unhappiness दुःख, उदासी I cannot understand the reason of your *sadness*.

safe *(adj.)* सेफ़— 1. affording security or protection from harm सुरक्षित Is it *safe* driving in this area?

2. *(n.)* a strong container, usually of metal and provided with a secure lock, for storing money or valuables अलमारी या तिजोरी Keep the money in the *safe*.

safeguard *(n.)* सेफ़गार्ड– a person or thing that ensures protection against danger, damage, injury, etc. संभावित ख़तरों से सुरक्षा देने वाली वस्तु He promised to *safeguard* our interests in the deal.

safety *(n.)* सेफ़टी– the quality of being safe सुरक्षा She was worried about the *safety* of her children.

saffron *(adj.)* सैफ़रन्– a bright yellow powder made from crocus flowers केसरिया, ज़ाफ़रानी She was wearing a *saffron*-coloured sari.

sag *(v.)* सैग– to hang unevenly; droop लटक जाना The skin on her arms was *sagging*.

saga *(n.)* सागा– any of several medieval prose narratives written in Iceland and recounting the exploits of a hero or a family वीर गाथा Her grandfather always sang the *saga* of freedom movement.

sage *(n.)* सेज– 1. a man revered for his profound wisdom पंडित, संत A true *sage* is he who has the deepest love for mankind.

2. *(adj.)* wise, esp one has a lot of experience विवेकी His *sage* advice saved my life.

sail *(n.)* सेल– 1. an area of fabric, usually Terylene or nylon (formerly canvas), with fittings for holding it in any suitable position to catch the wind, used for propelling certain kinds of vessels, esp over water पाल, जलयात्रा Jack put up the *sail* of the ship.

2. *(v.)* to travel in a boat or ship जल में यात्रा करना (नाव या जहाज़ से) He will not *sail* until all dangers are over.

sailing *(n.)* सेलिंग– the practice, art, or technique of sailing a vessel नौका चलाने वाला खेल, नौ-चालन, जलयात्रा Sohan took three *sailings* from one side to other.

sailor *(n.)* सेलर– any member of a ship's crew, esp one below the rank of officer नाविक Fa-hien was a great *sailor* who travelled to India in 339 AD.

saint *(n.)* सेंट– a person of exceptional holiness or goodness धर्मात्मा, संत Many people claim to be *saints*, but very few of them are true.

sake *(n.)* सेक–1. benefit or interest कारण, हेतु She will help for our mother's *sake*.

2. the purpose of obtaining or achieving के कारण, के लिए You should go for a walk for the *sake* of your health.

salad *(n.)* सैलड– a dish of raw vegetables, such as lettuce, tomatoes, etc. served as a separate course with cold meat, eggs, etc. or as part of a main course सलाद She preferred to have *salad* over a heavy meal.

salary *(n.)* सैलॅरि– a fixed regular payment made by an employer, often monthly, for professional or office work as opposed to manual work वेतन I receive a good *salary* as a manager in the firm.

sale *(n.)* सेल–1. the exchange of goods, property, or services for an agreed sum of money or credit बिक्री, विक्रय He made a good profit on the *sale* of his car.

2. an auction नीलाम, बोली देकर बेचना Furniture is put up for *sale* at this shop every Sunday.

3. an event at which goods are sold at reduced prices, usually to clear old stocks सस्ते में बेचना I purchased my shoes at a reduction *sale*.

salesman *(n.)* सेलज़मन– a person who sells merchandise or services either in a shop or by canvassing in a designated area विक्रेता Rajan is working as a *salesman* in my uncle's company.

salesperson *(n.)* सेल्ज़पर्सन– a person who sells merchandise or services either in a shop or directly to customers on behalf of a company सामान बेचने के लिए दुकान पर रखा आदमी Many *salesperson* are looking for the job.

salient *(adj.)* सेलिअण्ट– prominent, conspicuous, or striking प्रमुख What are the *salient* features of this book?

saliva *(n.)* सलाइवा– the secretion of salivary glands, consisting of a clear usually slightly acid aqueous fluid of variable composition लार *Saliva* helps in swallowing the food in the mouth.

salon *(n.)* सैलॉन– a commercial establishment in which hairdressers, beauticians, etc. carry on their businesses सैलून She went to a beauty *salon* to get her hair cut.

salt *(n.)* साल्ट–1. a white powder or colourless crystalline solid, consisting mainly of sodium chloride and used for seasoning and preserving food नमक We add *salt* to make our food tasty.

2. preserved in, flooded with, containing, or growing in salt or salty water लवण There is *salt* in the sea water.

salty *(adj.)* साल्टी– of, tasting of, or containing salt खारा, नमकीन The sea water is *salty.*

salute *(v.)* सैल्यूट– 1. to address or welcome with friendly words or gestures of respect, such as bowing or lifting the hat; greet सलामी देना An English man *salutes* a lady by raising his hat.

2. *(n.)* a formal military gesture of respect अभिवादन Soldiers must greet their officers with a *salute.*

salvation *(n.)* सैल्वेशन– a person or thing that is the means of preserving from harm मुक्ति Buddha showed the path of *salvation* to man.

same *(pron., adv., adj.)* सेम–1. identical वही (उसी) Luv and Kush were born on the *same* day.

2. in an identical manner समान (एक से रूप आकार वाला) Her twin daughters look the *same* in height and appearance.

3. unchanged in character or nature पूर्णतया समान Whether you come to me or I come to you, is all the *same* to me.

➢ **at the same time** *(adj.)* simultaneously एक ही समय पर, Both Roohi and I went to stay in hostel *at the same time.*

sample *(n.)* सैम्पल– 1. a small part of anything, intended as representative of the whole; specimen नमूना By a small *sample* we may judge the whole piece.

2. *(v.)* to take a sample or samples of चखना, स्वाद या क़िस्म जानने के लिए खाना Mother allowed us to *sample* the Diwali sweets which she had prepared.

sanatorium *(n.)* सैनटॉरिअम– an institution for the medical care and recuperation of persons who are chronically ill स्वास्थ्य निवास Bhowali is famous for its T.B. *sanatorium* which was established in 1912.

sanction *(v.)* सैंक्शन– to give authority to; permit स्वीकृति देना The officer refused to *sanction* my leave.

sanctuary *(n.)* सैंक्चुअरी– a place, protected by law, where animals, esp birds, can live and breed without interference अभ्यारण्य, मृगवन There is a bird *sanctuary* in Bharatpur.

sand *(n.)* सैंड– loose material consisting of rock or mineral grains, esp rounded grains रेत They took the children to play on the *sands.*

sandal *(n.)* सैंडल– a light shoe consisting of a sole held on the foot by thongs, straps, etc. सैंडिल, खड़ाऊँ The child put on his *sandals* before going to the market.

sandalwood *(n.)* सैंडलवुड– any of several evergreen hemiparasitic trees of the genus Santalum, having hard light-coloured heartwood चंदन The perfume had the fragrance of *sandalwood.*

sandcastle *(n.)* सैंडकासल्– a mass of sand moulded into a castle-like shape, esp as made by a child on the seashore रेत का घरौंदा The kids made a *sandcastle* at the beach.

sandstorm *(n.)* सैंडस्टॉर्म– a strong wind that whips up clouds of sand, esp in a desert रेतीली आंधी The *sandstorm* blinded our vision.

sandwich *(n.)* सैंडविच– two or more slices of bread, usually buttered, with a filling of meat, cheese, etc. सैंडविच Do you like jam *sandwiches*?

sandy *(adj.)* सैण्डी– consisting of, containing, or covered with sand रेतीला The children were playing on a *sandy* beach.

sane *(adj.)* सेन– sound in mind; free from mental disturbance स्वस्थचित्त, समझदार You should take a decision in a *sane* state of mind.

sanely *(adv.)* सेनली– in a sane manner समझदारी से We must behave *sanely* in times of stress and strain.

sanitary *(adj.)* सैनिटरी– of or relating to health and measures for the protection of health स्वास्थ्यपरक, स्वच्छता संबंधी The *sanitary* condition of her house was not good.

sanitation *(n.)* सैनिटेशन– the study and use of practical measures for the preservation of public health स्वच्छता, सफ़ाई There was proper *sanitation* in the hotel premises.

sanity *(n.)* सैनटी– the state of being sane स्वस्थचित्तता, मानसिक संतुलन Seema keeps her *sanity* by singing and listening songs.

sapphire *(n.)* सैफ़ाइअर्– any precious corundum gemstone that is not red, esp the highly valued transparent blue variety. नीलम The astrologer advised her to wear a *sapphire.*

sarcastic *(adj.)* सार्कैस्टिक– characterized by sarcasm व्यंग्यपूर्ण, तीखा He made a *sarcastic* comment on her looks.

sarcastically *(adv.)* सार्कैस्टिकली– in a manner characterized by sarcasm व्यंग्यपूर्वक She laughed *sarcastically* at her.

sarcasm *(n.)* सार्कैज़्म– mocking, contemptuous, or ironic language intended to convey scorn or insult कटाक्ष *Sarcasm* was dissolved in his words.

sash *(n.)* सैश– a long piece of ribbon, silk, etc. worn around the waist like a belt or over one shoulder, as a symbol of rank दुपट्टा, कमरबंद, पेटी Village-girls put on coloured and decorated *sashes.*

Satan *(n.)* सेटन– the devil, adversary of God, and tempter of mankind: sometimes identified with Lucifer शैतान *Satan* beguiled Eve to eat the apple.

satellite *(n.)* सैटलाइट– a celestial body orbiting around a planet or star उपग्रह The moon is a *satellite* of the earth.

satire *(n.)* सैटाइअर्– a novel, play, entertainment, etc. in which topical issues, folly, or evil are held up to scorn by means of ridicule and irony व्यंग्य That author is good at writing *satire.*

satisfaction *(n.)* सैटिसफ़ैक्शन– the act of satisfying or state of being satisfied संतुष्टि, संतोष Good shopkeepers aim at the *satisfaction* of their customers.

satisfactory *(adj.)* सैटिसफ़ैक्टरि– adequate or suitable; acceptable संतोषजनक Your work is not *satisfactory.*

satisfied *(adj.)* सैटिसफ़ाइड– if you are satisfied with something, you are happy because you have got what you wanted or needed संतुष्ट Maid was *satisfied* with her salary.

satisfy *(v.)* सैटिस्फ़ाइ– to fulfil the desires or needs of (a person) संतुष्ट करना, संतोष देना It is difficult to *satisfy* a greedy person.

saturate *(v.)* सैचरेट–1. to soak or wet totally भिगो देना, तरबतर कर देना The continuous downpour *saturated* the grass of my lawn.

2. to fill sth completely भर देना, लाद देना The market is *saturated* with cheap used cars.

Saturday *(v.)* सैटडे– the seventh and last day of the week शनिवार I watch English movies on *Saturday* night.

sauce *(n.)* सॉस– any liquid or semiliquid preparation eaten with food to enhance its flavour चटनी Tomato *sauce* is eaten with bread pakoras.

saucer *(n.)* सॉसर्– a small round dish on which a cup is set (कप के साथ की) प्लेट, तश्तरी He put the cup on the *saucer.*

sausage *(n.)* सॉसिज– finely minced meat, esp pork or beef, mixed with fat, cereal or bread, and seasonings (sausage meat), and packed into a tube-shaped animal intestine or synthetic casing गुलमा We had liver *sausage* with soft drinks.

savage *(n.)* सैविज– 1. a member of a nonliterate society, esp one regarded as primitive बर्बर, हिंसक Is man not still a *savage*?

2. *(adj.)* wild; untamed जंगली, वहशी Everybody hates his *savage* behaviour.

save *(n.)* सेव– 1. the act of saving a goal बचाव, बचत *Save* something for tomorrow.

2. *(v.)* to rescue, preserve, or guard (a person or thing) from danger or harm सुरक्षित करना, संकट से बचाना She was *saved* from drowning by a life-guard.

3. to avoid the spending, waste, or loss of (money, possessions, etc.) नष्ट होने से बचाना You must *save* time by cycling to work.

saving *(n.)* सेविंग– preservation or redemption, esp from loss or danger बचत He invested all his *savings* to save his mother's life.

saw *(n.)* सॉ– 1. any of various hand tools for cutting wood, metal, etc. having a blade with teeth along one edge आरी The carpenter cuts the wood with his *saw.*

2. *(v.)* to cut with a saw आरी से काटना He is *sawing* the wood.

sawdust *(n.)* सॉडस्ट– particles of wood formed by sawing लकड़ी का बुरादा *Sawdust* is still used as a fuel in many villages.

say *(v.)* से– to speak, pronounce, or utter कहना Listen to what others *say* and do what you ought to do.

saying *(n.)* सेइंग– a maxim, adage, or proverb कहावत *Saying* and doing are two different things.

scab *(n.)* स्कैब– the dried crusty surface of a healing skin wound or sore खुरंड, पपड़ी Her wound was now covered with the *scab.*

scald *(v.)* स्काल्ड–1. to burn or be burnt with or as if with hot liquid or steam झुलसना, जलाना या जलना (गर्म पानी से) Don't *scald* your tongue in other people's broth.

2. to subject to the action of boiling water, esp so as to sterilize (गरम पानी से) साफ़ करना या होना A cat who is *scalded* once fears even cold water.

scabies *(n.)* स्केबीज़– a contagious skin infection caused by the mite, characterized by intense itching खुजली There are many home remedies for *scabies.*

scale *(v.)* स्केल–1. thin plates of hard material that cover the skin of fish छिलका Scrape the *scales* off the fish before cooking it.

2. measure, amount, quantity परिमाण, मात्रा At present, we grow vegetables and fruits on a small *scale* only.

3. an instrument that is used for measuring पैमाना, फुटा Have you a *scale* for measurements?

4. *(v.)* to climb to the top of (a height) by or as if by a ladder चढ़कर पार करना You cannot *scale* the wall unless someone lifts you.

scalp *(n.)* स्कैल्प– the skin and subcutaneous tissue covering the top of the head सिर की खाल, शिरोवल्क She massaged her *scalp* with oil.

scam *(n.)* स्कैम– a stratagem for gain; a swindle घोटाला The minister was badly caught in the *scam.*

scamper *(v.)* स्कैम्पॅर्– to run about playfully दौड़ना, उछल-कूद करना The children *scampered* round the playground.

scan *(v.)* स्कैन– to scrutinize minutely ध्यान से देखना, बारीकी से देखना You should *scan* this page to see if there are any spelling mistakes.

scandal *(n.)* स्कैण्डल–1. censure or outrage arising from an action or event कलंक, बुराई, निंदा A lie has no legs, but a *scandal* has wings.

2. malicious talk, esp gossip about the private lives of other people बदनामी का क़िस्सा, लोकापवाद Never listen to *scandals.*

scandalous *(adj.)* स्कैण्डलस– disgraceful; causing a scandal बदनामीभरा, लज्जास्पद There has never been a *scandalous* tale without some foundation.

scanty *(adj.)* स्कैण्टी–1. insufficient; inadequate बहुत थोड़ा, कम He had given me *scanty* details of her life.

scar *(n.)* स्कार्– a permanent change in a person's character resulting from emotional distress धब्बा, दाग़, कलंक God will not look you over for medals, but for *scars*!

scarce *(adj.)* स्केअर्स–1. rarely encountered दुर्लभ, विरल Some animals are becoming *scarce* in India.

2. insufficient to meet the demand बहुत कम Strawberries are *scarce* this year.

scarcely *(adv.)* स्केअर्सली– hardly at all; only just मुश्किल से, न के बराबर I had *scarcely* sat down when the bell rang.

scare *(n.)* स्केअर्–1. a sudden attack of fear or alarm डर, भय, आतंक A good *scare* is worth more to a man than good advice.

2. a sudden feeling of fear भय, डर The crows got a *scare* when they saw a *scare*-crow.

3. *(v.)* to fill or be filled with fear or alarm डराना, भयभीत करना The scare-crow *scares* away the crows.

scared *(adj.)* स्केअर्ड– frightened or nervous भयभीत Everyone was *scared* of the darkness.

scarf *(n.)* स्कार्फ़– a rectangular, triangular, or long narrow piece of cloth worn around the head, neck, or shoulders for warmth or decoration स्कार्फ़ She wore a *scarf* to protect herself from cold.

scarlet *(adj.)* स्कॉर्लट– of the colour scarlet सिंदूरी रंग Her dress was *scarlet* in colour.

scary *(adj.)* स्केअरी– causing fear or alarm; frightening डरावना It was a bit *scary* ghost story.

scatter *(v.)* स्कैटर्– to separate and move or cause to separate and move in various directions; disperse छितराना The string broke and all the pearls *scattered* on the floor.

scavenger *(n.)* स्कैवेंजर– a person or animal that scavenges झाड़ू-बरदार, झाड़ूवाला I saw a documentary film on *scavengers.*

scenario *(n.)* सनारिओ– a summary of the plot of a play, etc. including information about its characters, scenes, etc. दृश्य-लेख, दृश्य-विधान, योजना The worst *scenario* would be backing out from the competition.

scene *(n.)* सीन–1. the setting for the action of a play, novel, etc. (नाटक का) दृश्य The curtain was lowered at the end of each *scene.*

2. an incident or situation, real or imaginary, esp as described or represented (आँखों के आगे का) दृश्य They were charmed by the beautiful *scene.*

scenery *(n.)* सीनरी– the natural features of a landscape प्राकृतिक दृश्य The *scenery* was very beautiful.

scent *(n.)* सेंट–1. fragrance गंध, महक I like the *scent* of roses.

2. a distinctive smell, esp a pleasant one सुगंध, ख़ुशबू The sweet *scent* of lavender filled the garden.

3. *(v.)* to fill with odour or fragrance सुगंधित करना The air was *scented* with honeysuckle.

sceptic *(n.)* स्केपटिक– a person who habitually doubts the authenticity of accepted beliefs संशयवादी Rahul is very *sceptic* but I will try to convince him more.

schedule *(v.)* शेड्यूल– 1. to make a schedule of or place in a schedule योजना बनाना, कार्यक्रम बनाना The bus is *scheduled* to arrive at 8.15 a.m.

2. *(n.)* a plan of procedure for a project, allotting the work to be done and the time for it कार्य-योजना This *schedule* allows you one week to finish the work.

scheme *(n.)* स्कीम– 1. a systematic plan for a course of action योजना His *scheme* to fake certificates got him into trouble.

2. *(v.)* to form intrigues (for) in an underhand manner षड्यंत्र करना The prime minister *schemed* to dethrone the king.

schizophrenia *(n.)* स्किटसफ्रीनिआ– a mental illness characterized by progressive deterioration of the personality, withdrawal from reality, hallucinations, delusions, social apathy, emotional instability, etc. मनोविदलता 'Sadma' was a good movie on *schizophrenia.*

schizophrenic *(adj.)* स्किटसफ्रीनिक– experiencing or maintaining contradictory attitudes, emotions, etc. मनोविदलित Kareena plays a *schizophrenic* role in the movie 'Heroine'.

scholar *(n.)* स्कॉलर्– a learned person, esp in the humanitie विद्वान He is really a *scholar* and knows a lot about different things.

scholarly *(adj.)* स्कॉलर्ली– A scholarly person spends a lot of time studying and knows a lot about academic subjects बौद्धिक, अध्ययनशील, विद्वतापूर्ण She is always busy in her *scholarly* activities.

scholarship *(n.)* स्कॉलर्शिप– academic achievement; erudition; learning छात्रवृत्ति Her sister is receiving *scholarship* of Rs 5000 p.m. for research study.

school *(n.)* स्कूल– an institution or building at which children and young people usually under 19 receive education विद्यालय, स्कूल We learn different lessons in the *school.*

schooling *(n.)* स्कूलिंग– education, esp when received at school स्कूल की शिक्षा Reema did her *schooling* from DPS.

schoolmate *(n.)* स्कूलमेट– a companion at school; fellow pupil सहपाठी Her *schoolmate* is very cooperative by nature.

science *(n.)* साइंस– the systematic study of the nature and behaviour of the material and physical universe, based on observation, experiment, and measurement विज्ञान *Science* increases our power of observation.

scientific *(adj.)* साइन्‌टिफ़िक– of, relating to, derived from, or used in science वैज्ञानिक The laboratory is full of *scientific* instruments.

scientist *(n.)* साइन्‌टिस्ट– a person who studies or practises any of the sciences or who uses scientific methods वैज्ञानिक Former Indian President APJ Abdul Kalam is a notable *scientist.*

scissors *(n.)* सिज़र्ज– a cutting instrument used for cloth, hair, etc. having two crossed pivoted blades that cut by a shearing action, with ring-shaped handles at one end कैंची (बहुवचनांत संज्ञा) Lila cut out the picture with a pair of *scissors.* These *scissors* are very sharp.

scoff *(v.)* स्कॉफ़– to speak contemptuously (about); express derision (for); mock ताना मारना We should not *scoff* at anyone.

scold *(v.)* स्कोल्ड– to find fault with or reprimand (a person) harshly; chide डाँटना, झिड़कना I was *scolded* for coming home very late.

scolding *(n.)* स्कोल्डिंग– the act of scolding or being scolded झिड़की, डाँट-डपट You'll get a *scolding* from mother for breaking the dish.

scooter *(n.)* स्कूटर्– a vehicle consisting of a low footboard on wheels, steered by handlebars स्कूटर Do you own a *scooter*?

scope *(n.)* स्कोप–1.opportunity for exercising the faculties or abilities; capacity for action गुंजाइश There is no *scope* for originality in this job.

2. range of view, perception, or grasp; outlook कार्य-क्षेत्र What is the *scope* of work in this project?

scorch *(v.)* स्कॉर्च– to burn or become burnt, so as to affect the colour, taste, etc, or to cause or feel pain झुलसाना The iron was very hot. It *scorched* the cloth.

scorching *(adj.)* स्कॉर्चिंग– very hot झुलसाने वाला The farmer worked under the *scorching* sun.

score *(v.)* स्कॉर्–1. to gain (a point or points) in a game or contest खेल में अंक बनाना The captain *scored* two goals for his team.

2. to make a total score of अंक लेना Has Vishwa Nath *scored* yet?

3. *(n.)* the total number of points made by a side or individual in a game or match बनाए हुए अंक, प्राप्तांक The *score* at the end of the game was two hundred for five.

scorn *(n.)* स्कॉर्न– open contempt or disdain for a person or thing; derision अवज्ञा, अनादर, तिरस्कार Silence is the most perfect expression of *scorn.*

scornful *(adj.)* स्कॉर्नफुल– expressing or feeling scorn तिरस्कारभरा He gave a *scornful* look to the beggar.

scorpion *(n.)* स्कॉर्पिअन– a small creature with six legs, two front claws, a curved tail terminating in a venomous sting बिच्छू *Scorpions* of desert region are very dangerous.

scotch *(n.)* स्कॉच– whisky distilled esp from fermented malted barley and made in Scotland स्कॉटलैंड की ह्विस्की He brought a bottle of *scotch* to his house.

scoundrel *(n.)* स्काउण्ड्रल– a worthless or villainous person बदमाश, दुष्ट This *scoundrel* stole my pen.

scour *(v.)* स्काउअर– to clean or polish (a surface) by washing and rubbing, as with an abrasive cloth माँजना,

रगड़कर साफ़ करना She was *scouring* out a saucepan.

scourge *(n.)* स्कज– a person who harasses, punishes, or causes destruction संकट, बला, विपत्ति Undoubtedly, Sachin Tendulkar was the *scourge* of the Pakistani bowlers.

scout *(n.)* स्काउट– a person, ship, or aircraft sent out to gain information बालचर, स्काउट A *scout* is supposed to do a good deed every day.

scowl *(v.)* स्काउल– to contract the brows in a threatening or angry manner त्यौरी चढ़ाना The old man *scowled* at her when she abused him.

scrabble *(v.)* स्क्रैबल– to struggle to gain possession, esp in a disorderly manner टटोलना I *scrabbled* my purse for some loose change.

scraggy *(adj.)* स्क्रैगि– lean or scrawny दुबला-पतला Why do you look so *scraggy* today?

scramble *(v.)* स्क्रेम्बल– to climb or crawl, esp by using the hands to aid movement (हाथ पैर के बल) चलना The monkey *scrambled* up the trees.

scrap *(v.)* स्क्रैप– a small piece of something larger; fragment टुकड़ा Throw away these *scraps* of paper.

scrapbook *(n.)* स्क्रैपबुक– a book or album of blank pages in which to mount newspaper cuttings, pictures, etc. रजिस्टर (जिसमें अख़बार आदि की कतरन चिपकाई जाती है) She was sticking the cuttings of newspaper in her *scrapbook*.

scrape *(n.)* स्क्रेप– a difficult situation मुसीबत, उलझन You are so mischievous that you often get into a *scrape*.

scrappy *(adj.)* स्क्रेपी– fragmentary; disjointed भद्दा, बेतरतीब He has written a very *scrappy* essay.

scratch *(v.)* स्क्रैच–1. to mark or cut (the surface of something) with a rough or sharp instrument खरोंचना, नोचना Who *scratched* the paint off this almirah?

2. to scrape (the surface of the skin) with the nails, as to relieve itching ख़राश आना My legs were *scratched* by thorns.

3. *(n.)* a slight grating sound चीख Her hands were covered with *scratches* from the thorns.

scrawl *(v.)* स्क्राल– to write or draw (signs, words, etc.) carelessly or hastily; scribble घसीट मारकर लिखना The teacher *scrawled* the chapter's name hastily on the blackboard.

scream *(v.)* स्क्रीम– 1. to utter or emit (a sharp piercing cry or similar sound or sounds), esp as of fear, pain, etc. चीख़ मारना, चिल्लाना The child *screamed* loudly when she saw a dog.

2. *(n.)* a sharp piercing cry or sound, esp one denoting fear or pain चीख़ The girl let out a sudden *scream* when she was frightened.

screech *(v.)* स्क्रीच– to utter with or produce a screech ज़ोर से चीखना, चिल्लाना Why are you *screeching* at her?

screen *(n.)* स्क्रीन– 1. flat surface at the front of a TV, cinema, etc. to shelter, protect, or conceal टीवी या सिनेमा का पर्दा My father writes stories for the *screen*.

2. *(v.)* to project (a film) onto a screen, esp for public viewing चित्रपट पर दिखाना All the feature films are *screened* only after they are certified by the Censor Board.

screw *(v.)* स्क्रू– 1. to rotate (a screw or bolt) so as to drive it into or draw it out of a material पेंच कसना The carpenter *screwed* down the lid of the box.

2. *(n.)* a device used for fastening materials together, consisting of a threaded and usually tapered shank that has a slotted head by which it may be rotated पेंच, स्क्रू I need some nails and *screws* to repair this table.

scribble *(v.)* स्क्रिबल– to write or draw in a hasty or illegible manner घसीट में लिखना, घसीटना If you *scribble* your homework, the teacher will make you rewrite it properly.

script *(n.)* स्क्रिप्ट–1. handwriting as distinguished from print, esp cursive writing लिखावट, लिपि Your *script* is altogether illegible.
2. written copy for the use of performers in films and plays पटकथा Have you reviewed the *script* of Shekhar's play?

scripture *(n.)* स्क्रिप्चर्– a sacred, solemn, or authoritative book or piece of writing धर्मग्रंथ The Hindu *scriptures* teach various ways to reach the God.

scroll *(v.)* स्क्रॉल– to roll up like a scroll ऊपर-नीचे घुमाना या चलाना Use the arrow keys to *scroll* down to the bottom of the document.

scrub *(v.)* स्क्रॅब– to rub (a surface) hard, with or as if with a brush, soap, and water, in order to clean it पानी और ब्रश से साफ़ करना Please *scrub* the kitchen floor.

scruffy *(adj.)* स्क्रफ़ि– dirty or shabby गंदा एवं मैला He was wearing a *scruffy* jeans today.

scruples *(n.)* स्क्रूपलूज़– doubts or hesitation as to what is morally right in a certain situation हिचक, संकोच Kamala had no *scruples* in asking money at anyone's house in the neighbourhood.

scrutiny *(n.)* स्क्रूटनी– close or minute examination सूक्ष्म-परीक्षण Her work was under close *scrutiny.*

scuffle *(n.)* स्कफ़ल– a short fight or struggle हाथापाई There was a *scuffle* between the tenant and the landlord.

sculpture *(n.)* स्कल्पचर्– the art of making figures or designs in relief or the round by carving wood, moulding plaster, etc. or casting metals, etc. मूर्तिकला The exhibition was filled with fine pieces of *sculpture.*

scurry *(v.)* स्करी– to move about or proceed hurriedly जल्दबाज़ी से आगे बढ़ना Monika said good bye to me and *scurried* back to her home.

scuttle *(v.)* 1.– to run or move about with short hasty steps दौड़ जाना, भागना A frightened rabbit *scuttled* into the hole as I passed by the field.
2. to cause (a vessel) to sink by opening the seacocks or making holes in the bottom डुबा देना The enemy was trying to capture the ship, but the captain *scuttled* it.

sea *(n.)* सी–1. one of the smaller areas of ocean समुद्र Oil has been found under the *sea.*
2. anything resembling the sea in size or apparent limitlessness समुद्र की स्थिति, लहरों की गति There was a stormy *sea* running that day.

seafood *(n.)* सीफूड– edible saltwater fish or shellfish समुद्री भोजन (मछली, झींगा आदि) *Seafood* is good for diabetics.

seal *(n.)* सील–1. a device impressed on a piece of wax, moist clay, etc., fixed to a letter, document, etc. as a mark of authentication मुद्रा, मुहर Put the office *seal* on this letter.
2. a sea animal that is aquatic but come on shore to breed सील मछली *Seals* live in the sea.
3. *(v.)* to enclose (a place) with a fence, wall, etc. पूरी तरह से बंद करना The police *sealed* the room so that it could be examined later.

sea level *(n.)* सी लेवल– the level of the surface of the sea with respect to the land, taken to be the mean level between high and low tide, and used as a standard base for measuring heights and depths समुद्रतल Shimla is situated at an altitude of 2213 metres above *sea level.*

seam *(n.)* सीम– 1. the line along which pieces of fabric are joined, esp by stitching सीवन The tailor sewed the *seam* carefully.
2. *(v.)* to join or sew together by or as if by a seam दो टुकड़ों को एक साथ सीना She carefully *seamed* the two pieces of the old cloth together.

search *(v.)* सर्च–1. to look through (a place, records, etc.) thoroughly in order to find someone or something खोज करना, तलाशना *Search* others for their virtues, and yourself for your vices.
2. to examine (a person) for concealed objects by running one's hands over the clothing तलाशी लेना, छानबीन करना The police *searched* the house of the suspected person but found nothing.
3. *(n.)* the act or an instance of searching तलाश, खोज You can make a *search* for your lost book.

searching *(adj.)* सर्चिंग– keenly penetrating खोज में सहायक A *searching* investigation was carried on for a few weeks.

searchlight *(n.)* सर्चलाइट– a device, consisting of a light source and a reflecting surface behind it, that projects a powerful beam of light in a particular direction घूमने वाली तेज़ रोशनी का लैंप The vehicle was carrying a powerful *searchlight* on its front.

search warrant *(n.)* सर्च-वारंट– a written order issued by a justice of the peace authorizing a constable or other officer to enter and search premises for stolen goods, drugs, etc. तलाशी अधिपत्र The police officer entered the building with a *search warrant.*

seashore *(n.)* सीशॉर– land bordering on the sea समुद्रतट Soon after the barrier was built, plants began to grow on the former *seashore.*

seasick *(adj.)* सीसिक– suffering from nausea and dizziness caused by the motion of a ship at sea जलयात्रा से बीमार होने वाला We were all *seasick* except father.

seasickness *(n.)* सीसिकनस– nausea and dizziness caused by the motion of a ship at sea जलयात्रा के दौरान होने वाली मतली Please take some tablets for *seasickness.*

seaside *(n.)* सीसाइड– any area bordering on the sea, esp one regarded as a resort समुद्रतट They stayed at a highly romantic *seaside* resort.

season *(n.)* सीज़न– one of the four equal periods into which the year is divided by the equinoxes and solstices, resulting from the apparent movement of the sun north and south of the equator during the course of the earth's orbit around it. ऋतु, मौसम There are six *seasons* in a year in India.

seasonal *(adj.)* सीज़नल– of, relating to, or occurring at a certain season or certain seasons of the year मौसमी This work is *seasonal,* not permanent.

seasoned *(adj.)* सीज़न्ड्– experienced अति अनुभवी He is a *seasoned* writer and has written a number of books.

seat *(v.)* सीट–1. to bring to or place on a seat; cause to sit down आसन या कुर्सी लगाना, सीटें लगाना This cinema hall *seats* about a thousand people.
2. to provide with seats बैठाना, आसीन करना Please be *seated.* He is just coming.
3. *(n.)* a piece of furniture designed for sitting on, such as a chair or sofa कुर्सी आदि की सीट, आसन, पीढ़ा Let me bring you a *seat.*

seating *(n.)* सीटिंग– the act of providing with a seat or seats आसन व्यवस्था The *seating* arrangement in the wedding hall was not sufficient.

seaweed *(n.)* सीवीड– any of numerous multicellular marine algae that grow on the seashore, in salt marshes, in brackish water, or submerged in the ocean समुद्री शैवाल There were different types of *seaweeds* on the shore.

secluded *(adj.)* सिक्लूडेड– kept apart from the company of others निर्जन We enjoyed a few quiet moments at a *secluded* beach.

second *(n.)* सेकंड–1. 1/60 of a minute of time मिनट का साठवाँ भाग How many *seconds* are there in a minute?
2. *(adj.)* corning directly after the first in numbering or counting order, position, time, etc.; being the ordinal number of two दूसरा Monday is the *second* day of the week.

secondary *(adj.)* सेकण्डरी–1. one grade or step after the first; not primary गौण, द्वितीयक The gift was of *secondary* importance for her.
2. of or relating to the education of young people between the ages of 11 and 18 माध्यमिक After the primary school, students go to the *secondary* school.

second-best *(adj.)* सेकंड-बेस्ट– not as good as the best, an acceptable alternative सर्वोत्तम के बाद का The sari is my *second-best* option for the party.

second-class *(adj.)* सेकंड-क्लास– of the class or grade next to the best in quality, etc. द्वितीय श्रेणी का, घटिया They were travelling to Mumbai in a *second-class* compartment.

second-degree *(adj.)* सेकंड डिग्री– less serious than first-degree crimes, जलने में गंभीरतम प्रकार परंतु गंभीर श्रेणी का नहीं *Second-degree* burns caused by friction.

second-floor *(n.)* सेकंड फ़्लोर– the storey of a building immediately above the first and two floors up from the ground दूसरी मंजिल We live on the *second-floor* of the building.

second-hand *(adj.)* सेकंड-हैण्ड–1. previously owned or used पुराना I shall buy a *second-hand* typewriter.
2. not from an original source or experience सुनी-सुनाई जानकारी He brought a *second-hand* information.

secondly *(adv.)* सेकण्डलि– another word for second, usually used to precede the second item in a list of topics दूसरे Firstly we must clean the kitchen, *secondly* we must cook some food.

second-rate *(adj.)* सेकंड रेट– not of the highest quality; mediocre घटिया, मामूली क़िस्म का Why were you talking with a *second-rate* poet?

secrecy *(n.)* सीक्रसी– the state of keeping something secret गोपनीयता This is a matter of utmost *secrecy.*

secret *(n.)* सीक्रट– 1. something unrevealed; mystery गुप्त भेद, रहस्य He who confides his *secrets* in a servant makes him his master.
2. *(adv.)* kept hidden or separate from the knowledge of others गुप्त, रहस्यपूर्ण The robbers made a *secret* plan to rob the bank.

secret agent *(n.)* सीक्रट एजेन्ट– a person employed in espionage गुप्तचर He was playing a role of *secret agent* in the movie.

secretarial *(adj.)* सेक्रटेअरिअल– of or relating to a secretary सचिवीय She was appointed for *secretarial* work.

secretariat *(n.)* सेक्रटेअरिअट– an office responsible for the secretarial, clerical, and administrative affairs of a legislative body, executive council, or international organization सचिवालय The President's *secretariat* is located at Rashtrapati Bhavan, New Delhi.

secretary *(n.)* सेक्रटरी– a person who handles correspondence, keeps records, and does general clerical work for an individual, organization, etc. सचिव We can telephone his *secretary* if we need to see him earlier.

secretary General *(n.)* से'क्रटरी जनरल the chief administrator of an organization महासचिव The *Secretary-General* of the United Nations is the head of the Secretariat of the UN.

secrete *(v.)* सिक्रीट– (of a cell, organ, etc.) to synthesize and release (a secretion) द्रव निकलना Saliva is *secreted* by glands in the mouth.

secretive *(adj.)* सीक्रेटिव– inclined to secrecy; reticent गोपनशील, छिपाऊ Why should we be so *secretive* about our plans?

sect *(n.)* सेक्ट– a subdivision of a larger religious group (esp the Christian Church as a whole) the members of which have to some extent diverged from the rest by developing deviating beliefs, practices, etc. पंथ, संप्रदाय, मत John belongs to a Christian *sect.*

section *(n.)* सेक्शन–1. a part cut off or separated from the main body of something भाग, अंश, खंड, हिस्सा How many *sections* are there in this catalogue?
2. a distinct part or subdivision of a country, community, etc. विभाग My brother is a *section*-officer in the Law Ministry.

sector *(n.)* सेक्टर्– a part or subdivision, esp of a society or an economy कार्यक्षेत्र The new budget provided some relief to the service *sector.*

secular *(adj.)* सेक्युलर्– not concerned with or related to religion धर्म-निरपेक्ष India is a *secular* country.

secure *(adj.)* सिक्युअर्–1. free from danger, damage, etc. सुरक्षित The baby is *secure* in her pram.
2. not likely to fail, become loose, etc. निश्चित Your victory is *secure.*
3. *(v.)* to obtain or get possession of प्राप्त करना My son *secured* sixty-six percent marks.

securely *(adv.)* सिक्युअरली– firmly मज़बूती से Please do this work *securely*, otherwise you might lose the balance.

security *(n.)* सेक्यूरिटी– the state of being secure सुरक्षा-व्यवस्था A great *security* was provided to the officer.

sedate *(adj.)* सिडेट– habitually calm and composed in manner; serene गंभीर एवं शांत Rohan's mother is a *sedate* old lady.

sedative *(n.)* सेडटिव– having a soothing or calming effect राहत एवं आराम पहुंचाने वाला, शामक The nurse gave a *sedative* injection to the patient.

sedentary *(adj.)* सेडनटरी– tending to sit about without taking much exercise बहुत कम चलने वाला, जो सक्रिय न हो These workers are leading a *sedentary* life in their office.

sedimentary *(adj.)* सेडिमेंटरी– characteristic of, resembling, or containing sediment तलछटी, अवसादी The *sedimentary* rocks can be found deep in the earth

seditious *(adj.)* सिडिशस– of, like, or causing sedition राजद्रोहात्मक, राजद्रोही He was indulged in a *seditious* conspiracy.

seduce *(v.)* सिड्यूस– to lead astray, as from the right action बहकाना, फुसलाना Politicians always *seduce* innocent people.

seductive *(adj.)* सिडक्टिव– tending to seduce or capable of seducing; enticing; alluring बहकाने वाला, सम्मोहक He gave a *seductive* opinion to her but failed.

see *(v.)* सी–1. to perceive with the eyes देखना We *see* the moon.

2. to perceive (an idea) mentally; understand (किसी बात को) समझना, महसूस करना A wise man *sees* as much as he ought to, not as much as he can.

➢ **see about**– to take care of; look after काम निपटाना, She will *see about* everything.

➢ **see eye to eye**– to agree (with) किसी से सहमत होना, We never *see eye to eye* on emotional matters.

➢ **see off**– to be present at the departure of (a person making a journey) विदा करना या देना, They will come to *see* me *off* tonight.

➢ **see through**– to perceive the true nature of सच को भांप जाना, The pupil could *see through* his guru very well.

➢ **see you later**– an expression of farewell अलविदा कहने के लिए प्रयुक्त, He told me, "I will *see you later*."

seed *(n.)* सीड– a mature fertilized plant ovule, consisting of an embryo and its food store surrounded by a protective seed coat बीज Most plants grow from a *seed.*

seedling *(n.)* सीडलिंग– a very young plant produced from a seed छोटा नया पौधा, पौध No matter how long you garden for, spring time is always exciting to see *seedlings* pushing through.

seek *(v.)* सीक– to try to find by searching; look for ढूँढ़ना *Seek* and you shall find.

seem *(v.)* सीम– to give the impression of existing; appear to be दिखाई देना You *seem* to be sick. What's the matter?

seeming *(adj.)* सीमिंग– apparent but not actual or genuine प्रतीत होता हुआ *Seeming* contradictions came along later.

see-saw *(n.)* सी-सॉ– a plank balanced in the middle so that two people seated on the ends can ride up and down by pushing on the ground with their feet झूमा-झूमी खेल (लकड़ी का बना ढाँचा जो ऊपर-नीचे होता है) The *see-saw* moves up and down.

segment *(n.)* सेगमेण्ट्– one of several parts or sections into which an object is divided; portion भाग He put a *segment* of orange in my mouth.

segregate *(v.)* सेग्रिगेट– to set or be set apart from others or from the main group अलग करना We should not *segregate* people by race, religion, creed, ideology or physical condition.

seize *(v.)* सीज़– to take hold of quickly; grab घेरा डालकर पकड़ लेना The smuggled goods were *seized* by the customs officers.

seldom *(adv.)* सेल्डम– not often; rarely कभी-कभी Barking dogs *seldom* bite.

select *(v.)* सिलेक्ट– to choose (someone or something) in preference to another or others चुनना I *selected* one banana out of three.

selection *(n.)* सिलेक्शन– the act or an instance of selecting or the state of being selected चयन Were not you a member of the *selection* board?

selector *(n.)* सिलेक्टर– a person or thing that selects चयनकर्ता The *selectors* of the party-candidates will meet tomorrow morning.

self *(n.)* सेल्फ़– the distinct individuality or identity of a person or thing व्यक्ति का अपना स्वभाव या गुण आदि The best victory is to conquer one's own *self. (prefix)* myself, yourself, etc. आत्म, स्वयं, स्वतः, अपने से अपना (उपसर्ग की भांति प्रयोग) She has given me a *self*-addressed envelop.

self-centred *(adj.)* सेल्फ़-सेंटर्ड– totally preoccupied with one's own concerns आत्म-केंद्रित Geeta is such a *self-centred* girl of her class.

self-confident *(adj.)* सेल्फ़-कॉन्फीडेंट– 1. having confidence in your own powers, judgment, etc. आत्मविश्वासी Aman is a very *self-confident* child and always succeeds.
2. *(n.)* confidence in one's own powers, judgment, etc. आत्मविश्वास Lack of *self-confidence* is found very commonly in depressed women.

self-control *(n.)* सेल्फ़-कंट्रोल– the ability to exercise restraint or control over one's feelings, emotions, reactions, etc. आत्मनियंत्रण *Self-control* is the best form of discipline.

self-defence *(n.)* सेल्फ़-डिफेंस– the act of defending oneself, one's actions, ideas, etc. आत्मरक्षा Honey learnt judo and karate for *self-defence*.

self-discipline *(n.)* सेल्फ़-डिसिप्लिन– the act of disciplining or power to discipline one's own feelings, desires, etc.esp with the intention of improving oneself आत्मानुशासन The teacher encouraged *self-discipline* in all students by giving them guidelines.

self-employed *(adj.)* सेल्फ़-एंप्लॉयड– earning one's living in one's own business or through freelance work, rather than as the employee of another स्व-रोजगार करने वाला *Self-employed* people use their talent for their own benefits.

self-esteem *(n.)* सेल्फ़-एसटीम– respect for or a favourable opinion of oneself आत्मसम्मान It was a matter of my *self-esteem*.

self-evident *(n.)* सेल्फ़-एविडेंट– containing its own evidence or proof without need of further demonstration स्वयंसिद्ध, स्वयं-प्रमाण It is *self-evident* that all men are created equal.

self-explanatory *(adj.)* सेल्फ़-एक्सप्लेनेटरि– understandable without explanation; self-evident स्वतः स्पष्ट The contents of the book should be quite *self-explanatory*.

self-importance *(adj.)* सेल्फ़-इंपॉर्टेंस– the quality of having or showing an unduly high opinion of your own abilities, importance, etc. अहंकार, अभिमान Dr. Sharma is a man of arrogance and *self-importance*.

self-interest *(adj.)* सेल्फ़-इंटरेस्ट– one's personal interest or advantage स्वार्थ He was motivated purely by *self-interest*.

selfish *(adj.)* सेल्फ़िश– chiefly concerned with one's own interest, advantage, etc. esp to the total exclusion of the interests of others स्वार्थी Don't be too *selfish*.

selfishness *(n.)* सेल्फ़िशनस– the quality of being chiefly concerned with your own interest, advantage, etc. esp to the total exclusion of the interests of others स्वार्थपरता *Selfishness* is the root of all evils.

self-respect *(n.)* सेल्फ़-रेस्पेक्ट– a proper sense of one's own dignity and integrity आत्मसम्मान *Self-respect* is the virtue of a man of character.

self-restraint *(n.)* सेल्फ़-रेस्ट्रेंट– restraint imposed by oneself on one's own feelings, desires, etc. आत्मसंयम People should exercise *self-restraint* in everyday life.

self-righteous *(adj.)* सेल्फ़-राइटिअस– having or showing an exaggerated awareness of one's own virtuousness or rights दंभी, स्वयं को सही मानने वाला Some people who are so *self-righteous* will make you sick.

self-satisfied *(adj.)* सेल्फ़-सैटिस्फाइड– having or showing a complacent satisfaction with oneself, one's own actions, behaviour, etc. आत्म-संतुष्ट Muneer is very *self-satisfied* with his professional life.

self-sufficient *(adj.)* सेल्फ़-सफीशंट– able to provide for or support oneself without the help of others

आत्मनिर्भर India is now *self-sufficient* in latest technologies.

sell *(v.)* सेल्– to dispose of or transfer or be disposed of or transferred to a purchaser in exchange for money or other consideration; put or be on sale बेचना What does the baker *sell*?

➢ **sell-off**– the act or an instance of selling something, esp an industry owned by the state, or a company's shares किसी वस्तु को सस्ता बेचना, The shops *sell* their winter clothes *off* in the summer sales.

➢ **see out of**– if a shop is sold out of something, it has sold all of it that it had सारा माल बिक जाना, He had *sold out of* milk.

seller *(n.)* सेलर– a person who sells विक्रेता Kamal is a greedy *seller*, I don't buy anything from him.

semester *(n.)* सेमिस्टर्– (in some universities) either of two divisions of the academic year, ranging from 15 to 18 weeks अध्ययन-सत्र The course is divided into four *semesters*.

semi *(pre.)* सेमि– partially, partly, not completely, or almost आधा, अर्ध, आंशिक My brother is employed in a *semi*-government concern.

semicircle *(n.)* सेमिसर्कल– one half of a circle अर्द्धवृत्त The chairs were arranged in a *semicircle* for the audience.

semi-final *(n.)* सेमि-फ़ाइनल– the round before the final in a competition आख़री मैच से पहले खेले जाने वाला मैच India won the *semi-final* match.

seminar *(n.)* सेमिनार– a small group of students meeting regularly under the guidance of a tutor, professor, etc. to exchange information, discuss theories, etc. संगोष्ठी I will leave for the *seminar* tomorrow.

semi-skilled *(adj.)* सेमि-स्किल्ड्– partly skilled or trained but not sufficiently so to perform specialized work अर्द्धकुशल, कारीगर Raju is a *semi-skilled* machine operator.

send *(v.)* सेंड–1. to cause or order (a person or thing) to be taken, directed, or transmitted to another place भेजना He wants to *send* a parcel to his son.

2. to direct or cause to go to a place or point स्थिति विशेष में पहुंचाना My mother is ill. She must be *sent* for the doctor.

3. to cause to happen or come भिजवाना Mr. Agarwal *sends* us his good wishes.

sender *(n.)* सेंडर– someone who sends something, esp a letter by post प्रेषक Who is the *sender* of this letter?

senile *(adj.)* सीनाइल– mentally or physically weak or infirm on account of old age सनकी, सठियाना Her mother is going *senile* due to her old age.

senior *(adj.)* सीनिअर्– 1. older in years बड़ा, ज्येष्ठ Vagish is the *senior* of the two brothers.

2. *(n.)* higher in rank or length of service वरिष्ठ, उच्च पद पर प्रतिष्ठित We must consult our *seniors*.

senior citizen *(n.)* सीनिअर् सिटीज़न– an old age pensioner वरिष्ठ नागरिक, बुजुर्ग Indian Airlines provides 50 per cent *senior citizen* discount for all domestic flights.

seniority *(n.)* सीनिऑरटी– precedence in rank, etc. due to senior status वरिष्ठता, ज्येष्ठता The promotion should be based on *seniority* level.

sensation *(n.)* सेन्सेशन– a state of widespread public excitement संवेदन, अनुभूति The news created a lot of *sensation* among the masses.

sensational *(adj.)* सेन्सेशनल– causing or intended to cause intense feelings, esp of curiosity, horror, etc. सनसनीख़ेज The news channels feature only *sensational* stories these days.

sense *(n.)* सें'स–1. any of the faculties by which the mind receives information about the external world or about the state of the body. ज्ञानेन्द्रिय, जानने या पहचानने की क्षमता We have five *senses,* a *sense* of smell, touch, hearing, seeing and taste.
2. sound practical judgment or intelligence परख, समझ, बुद्धि No man in his *senses* behaves in a silly manner.

senseless *(adj.)* सेन्सलस– 1. lacking in sense; foolish बेतुका, ऊटपटाँग It is a *senseless* idea to run after a bus which is left.
2. *(n.)* lacking in feeling; unconscious बेहोश, बेसुध A man was lying *senseless* on the footpath.

sensibility *(n.)* सेन्सबिलटी– the capacity for responding to emotion, impression, etc. संवेदनशीलता, समझदारी Tabassum is known for her *sensibility* and caring attitude.

sensible *(adj.)* सेन्सिबल– having or showing good sense or judgment समझदार, तार्किक No *sensible* person would disagree with you.

sensitive *(adj.)* सेनसटिव– having the power of sensation नाजुक मिजाज, भावुक Zehra is such a *sensitive* child that when scolded she starts crying.

sensual *(adj.)* सेनशुअल tending to arouse the bodily appetites, esp the sexual appetite कामुक Aishwarya Rai has *sensual* eyes and lips.

sentence *(n.)* सेन्टे'न्स–1. a sequence of words capable of standing alone to make an assertion, ask a question, or give a command, usually consisting of a subject and a predicate containing a finite verb वाक्य The best *sentence* is the shortest one.
2. any short passage of scripture employed in liturgical use उम्र-क़ैद, दंड The murderer was given the death *sentence.*
3. *(v.)* to pronounce sentence on (a convicted person) in a court of law दण्ड देना The thief was *sentenced* to one month's imprisonment.

sentiment *(n.)* सेंटिमेंट– susceptibility to tender, delicate, or romantic emotion मनोभाव, भाव What were her *sentiments* about you?

sentimental *(adj.)* सेंटिमेंटल– tending to indulge the emotions excessively भावुक I heard a *sentimental* song of Lata Mangeshkar.

sentry *(n.)* सेनटि– a soldier who guards or prevents unauthorized access to a place, keeps watch for danger, etc. पहरेदार, संतरी Sudesh is a very honest *sentry.*

separate *(v.)* सेपरेट– 1. to act as a barrier between पृथक करना *Separate* the good mangoes from the bad ones.
2. *(adj.)* set apart from the main body or mass पृथक I cut the apple into two *separate* parts.

separately *(adj.)* सेपरेटली– at different times; individually अलग-अलग They came into the room *separately.*

separation *(n.)* सेपरेशन– the act of separating or state of being separated अलगाव *Separation* is not always bad.

September *(n.)* सेपटेमबर– the ninth month of the year, consisting of 30 days सितंबर My birthday falls on 24th of *September.*

septic *(adj.)* से'प्टिक– of, relating to, or caused by sepsis विषाक्त A *septic* wound takes a longer time to heal than a normal wound.

sequel *(n.)* सीक्वल– anything that follows from something else; development उत्तरकथा The director is planning to make a *sequel* to the movie.

sequence *(n.)* सीक्वन्स्– an arrangement of two or more things in a successive order क्रम The editor ensures that the scenes of the movie are in correct *sequence*.

serene *(adj.)* सेरीन– peaceful or tranquil; calm शांत, गंभीर The lake was *serene* and still in the night.

sergeant *(n.)* सार्जण्ट– a noncommissioned officer in certain armed forces, usually ranking above a corporal सार्जेन्ट My uncle was a *sergeant* in the army.

serial *(adj.)* सीरीअल– of, relating to, or resembling a series क्रमिक, क्रम संख्या What is your *serial* number?

series *(n.)* सीरीज़– a group or connected succession of similar or related things, usually arranged in order माला, शृंखला, सिलसिला My favourite publisher is coming up with a new *series* of romantic novels.

serious *(adj.)* सीरिअस–1. grave in nature or disposition; thoughtful गंभीर One must be *serious* about one's career.
2. concerned with important matters महत्त्वपूर्ण This is a *serious* issue and requires immediate action.

seriously *(adv.)* सीरिअसली– in a serious manner or to a serious degree गंभीरता-पूर्वक Most men *seriously* believe that women wear make-up to attract them.

sermon *(n.)* सर्मन– an address of religious instruction or exhortation, often based on a passage from the Bible, esp one delivered during a church service धर्मोपदेश, प्रवचन A religious *sermon* changed his life completely.

serpent *(n.)* सर्पण्ट– a snake, esp large one साँप *Serpent* is the name given to a snake in a religious or mythological context.

serrated *(adj.)* सरेटिड– having a notched or sawlike edge दाँतेदार Use a knife with a *serrated* edge.

servant *(n.)* सर्वण्ट– a person employed to work for another, esp one who performs household duties नौकर He is our faithful *servant*.

serve *(v.)* सर्व–1. to render or be of service to (a person, cause, etc.); help सेवा करना, सहायता करना We should *serve* our nation selflessly.
2. to provide with a regular supply of जनता के हित में कुछ करना, सेवा उपलब्ध कराना My uncle *served* the country as a soldier for fifteen years.
3. to provide (guests, customers, etc.) with food, drink, etc. परोसना The dinner was *served* to each and every member of the family.

service *(n.)* 1. सर्विस– an act of help or assistance सेवा, नौकरी Dear, I am at your *service*.
2. the act or manner of serving guests, customers, etc. in a shop, hotel, restaurant, etc. परोसने का कार्य एवं ढंग We enjoyed the food but the *service* of the restaurant was not good.
3. *(v.)* to make fit for use जाँच एवं मरम्मत करना AC should be *serviced* regularly.

servile *(adj.)* सर्वाइल– obsequious or fawning in attitude or behaviour; submissive ख़ुशामदी, चापलूस Harish has a *servile* attitude.

servility *(n.)* सर्वाइलिटी– the state of being obsequious or fawning in attitude or behaviour; submissiveness चापलूसी He is leading a life of *servility* under a cruel master.

session *(n.)* से'शन– the meeting of a court, legislature, judicial body, etc. for the execution of its function or the transaction of business अधिवेशन, बैठक, सत्र In the next *session,* we shall do an advance course.

set *(n.)* से'ट– 1. a piece of equipment for receiving radio or TV signals (रेडियो) सेट आदि Have you purchased a radio *set*?

2. *(v.)* to go down below the horizon अस्त होना The sun has *set.*
3. to arrange sth व्यवस्थित करना The manager *set* the clerks to work and went to see the owner.

➢ **set aside**– to move sth to one side एक तरफ़ रख देना I told the shopkeeper to *set aside* some embroidery suits.

➢ **set back**– to delay the progress of sth/sb किसी बात में विलम्ब आ जाना The bad weather has *set back* our plan for picnic.

➢ **set eyes on**– to see continuously towards sth किसी पर आंखें गड़ाये देखना She *set her eyes on* the furniture of my house.

➢ **set forth**– to start a journey यात्रा आरंभ करना They were *setting forth* for Banaras next week.

➢ **set off**– to start a process तुरंत आरंभ करना All the players *set off* at the whistle.

➢ **set out**– to depart रवाना होना His family *set out* for Mumbai.

➢ **set up**– to arrange for sth to happen स्थापित करना, लगाना, Aruna is going to *set up* a boutique.

➢ **set upon**– to bring on किसी बात पर अचानक हमला करना, उकसाकर पीछे लगाना He *sets* his dog *upon* a stranger.

setback *(n.)* सैटबैक– a hitch; something that reverses progress, hinders, or thwarts धक्का, आघात Sheena suffered a major *setback* when her boyfriend left her.

settee *(n.)* सेटी– a seat, for two or more people, with a back and usually with arms लंबा बेंचनुमा सोफ़ा I brought a red-coloured *settee* for my living room.

setting *(n.)* सेटिंग– the surroundings in which something is set; scene वातावरण The *setting* around the school was satisfactory.

settle *(v.)* से'टल–1. to put in order; arrange in a desired state or condition फ़ैसला करना The two parties *settled* the dispute.
2. to take up or cause to take up residence बस जाना Our forefathers had *settled* in West Punjab.

settle down *(v.)* सेटल डाउन– 1. to make or become quiet and orderly आरामदायक स्थिति में बैठना Please *settle down* all of you. I am going to narrate a story.
2. to adopt an orderly and routine way of life, take up a permanent post, etc. esp after marriage स्थायी रूप से बस जाना या रहना They *settled down* in Jaipur.

settlement *(n.)* सेटलमेण्ट– the act or state of settling or being settled समाधान, समझौता We came to a *settlement* with one another.

settler *(n.)* सेटलर– a person who settles in a new country or a colony उपनिवेशी Our forefathers were among the first *settlers* in Fiji.

seven *(n.,det.)* से'वन– the cardinal number that is the sum of six and one and is a prime number सात There are *seven* days in a week.

seventh *(adj.)* सेवन्थ– coming after the sixth and before the eighth in numbering or counting order, position, time, etc. being the ordinal number of seven, often written 7th सातवाँ July is the *seventh* month of a year.

seventeenth *(adv.)* सेवनटीन्थ– coming after the sixteenth in numbering or counting order, position, time, etc. being the ordinal number of seventeen often written 17th सत्रहवां Today is her *seventeenth* birthday.

sever *(v.)* सेवर– to put or be put apart; separate काटना, दो भागों में बांटना This river *severs* the city into two parts.

several *(adj.)* से'वूरल–1. various; separate कई, अनेक I requested you *several* times but you did not care.

2. distinct; different विभिन्न या पृथक The workers had put forth *several* demands but none of them was fulfilled.

severe *(adj.)* सिविअर्–1. rigorous or harsh in the treatment of others; strict सख्त, कड़ा, कठोर The burn caused me *severe* pain.

2. critical or dangerous कष्टप्रद, गंभीर My father is just recovering from a *severe* illness.

severely *(adv.)* सिविअरली– you use severely to emphasize the intensity or extremity of sth bad or undesirable अत्यधिक, सख़्ती से He may be punished *severely*.

sew *(v.)* सो–1. to join or decorate (pieces of fabric, etc.) by means of a thread repeatedly passed through with a needle or similar implement सीना Mother can *sew* expertly.

2. to attach, fasten, or close by sewing दो चीज़ों को सीकर जोड़ना She *sews* up the buttons on Gita's coat.

sewage *(n.)* सूइज– waste matter from domestic or industrial establishments that is carried away in sewers or drains for dumping or conversion into a form that is not toxic मैला, कूड़ा-कचरा *Sewage* from the factories pollute the city.

sewer *(n.)* सीवर– a drain or pipe, esp one that is underground, used to carry away surface water or sewage नाला There was an elaborate and well-developed sanitary *sewer* system in Mohenjodaro.

sex *(n.)* से'क्स–1. either of male and female that distinguish organisms on the basis of their reproductive function लिंग (नर एवं स्त्री वर्ग) Every citizen of India enjoys equal rights irrespective of his/her *sex*.

2. feelings or behaviour resulting from the urge to gratify the sexual instinct कामावेग, यौन-क्रियाकलाप Modern movies are full of *sex* and violence.

sexual *(adj.)* सेक्शुअल– of, relating to, or characterized by sex or sexuality यौन-संबंधी His *sexual* behaviour is not permissible.

sexuality *(n.)* सेक्शुऐलटी– the state or quality of being sexual काम भाव, काम वासना Meeta is confused about her *sexuality*.

sexually *(adv.)* सेक्शुएली– in a manner involving the act of sex or sexual activity काम भावना से She was *sexually* harassed.

sexy *(adj.)* सेक्सी– provoking or intended to provoke sexual interest कामोत्तेजक She was wearing a very *sexy* dress at the party.

shabby *(adj.)* शैबि–1. wearing worn and dirty clothes; seedy फटा-पुराना, जीर्ण-शीर्ण My skirt is *shabby*. I want to buy a new one.

2. mean, despicable, or unworthy दुर्व्यवहार Vivek's treatment of his friends is very *shabby*.

shackle *(n.)* शैकल–1. a metal ring or fastening, usually part of a pair used to secure a person's wrists or ankles; fetter हथकड़ी, बेड़ी The *shackles* could not be removed.

2. a U-shaped bracket, the open end of which is closed by a bolt (shackle pin), used for securing ropes, chains, etc. कुंडी A *shackle* is used to shut the door.

shade *(n.)* शेड–1. relative darkness produced by the blocking out of light छाया The cow is lying in the *shade* of a tree.

2. a colour that varies slightly from a standard colour due to a difference in hue, saturation, or luminosity थोड़ा अंतर, रंग के प्रकार There were many *shades* of opinion among the friends.

3. a slight amount एक विशेष प्रकार का रंग, आभा Give me a lighter *shade* of blue.

shadow *(n.)* शैडो– 1. a dark image or shape cast on a surface by the interception of light rays by an opaque body परछाईं *Shadows* grow longer towards evening.

2. *(v.)* to follow or trail secretly पीछा करना The fugitives were *shadowed* by the police.

shaft *(n.)* शाफ़्ट– a long, narrow passage in a building, allowing air in or out कूपक, निकास (कुएं जैसा एक रास्ता जो हवा और रोशनी के लिए छोड़ा जाता है) There is a ventilation *shaft* in each room of my house.

shaggy *(adj.)* शैगी– having or covered with rough unkempt fur, hair, wool, etc. झबरा Manek has *shaggy* beard and hair.

shake *(v.)* शेक–1. to move or cause to move up and down or back and forth with short quick movements; vibrate हिलाना, झिंझोड़ना If you don't wake up, I shall *shake* you up.

2. to bring or come to a specified condition by or as if by shaking झकझोरना, हिल उठना The earthquake has *shaken* the foundations of the houses.

shaky *(adj.)* शेकी–1. tending to shake or tremble काँपता हुआ Her legs were *shaky* because of fear.

2. liable to prove defective; unreliable डावाँडोल, कमज़ोर I feel *shaky* today.

shall *(v.)* शैल– used as an auxiliary to make the future tense भविष्यकाल की सूचक क्रिया I *shall* overcome someday from my worries.

shallow *(adj.)* शैलो– having little depth उथला, छिछला This pond is too *shallow* to swim in. We can't swim in *shallow* water.

sham *(n.)* शैम– 1. anything that is not what it purports or appears to be झूठा, असत्य His illness is merely a *sham,* he is quite well.

2. *(v.)* to falsely assume the appearance of (something); counterfeit ढोंग या पाखण्ड करना She was not hurt, she was only *shamming.*

shame *(n.)* शेम– a painful emotion resulting from an awareness of having done something dishonourable, unworthy, degrading, etc. लज्जा, शर्म, हया *Shame* is worse than death.

shameful *(adj.)* शेमफुल– causing or deserving shame; scandalous शर्मनाक It was one of the most *shameful* episodes of British rule in India.

shameless *(adj.)* शेमलस– having no sense of shame; brazen बेशर्म He is a *shameless* servant, he may harm you one day.

shampoo *(v.)* शैम्पू– 1. to wash (the hair, etc.) with such a preparation शैम्पू करना, बाल साफ़ करना You must *shampoo* your hair, they look dirty.

2. *(n.)* a liquid or cream preparation of soap or detergent to wash the hair (बालों को धोने का एक तरल पदार्थ) शैम्पू I shall buy a good *shampoo* for you.

shape *(n.)* शेप– 1. the outward form of an object defined by outline रूप, आकृति What is the *shape* of his radio set?

2. *(v.)* to receive or cause to receive shape or form आकृति देना I am *shaping* clay into a ball.

shapeless *(adj.)* शेपलस– lacking a symmetrical or aesthetically pleasing shape भद्दा, बेढंगा She comes to school in a *shapeless* uniform.

share *(v.)* शेअर्– 1. to divide or apportion, esp equally हिस्सा बाँटना, मिलकर बाँटना Let us *share* the cake among us.

2. *(n.)* a part or portion of something owned, allotted to, or contributed by a person or group हिस्सा, अंश Where is my *share* of the sweets?

shareholder *(n.)* शेअरहोल्डर– the owner of one or more shares in a company हिस्सेदार, अंशधारी A meeting of the *shareholders* was organised on Monday.

shark *(n.)* शार्क– a large sea fish with a long body, two dorsal fins, rows of sharp teeth, and between five and seven gill slits on each side of the head शार्क मछली Have you ever seen a *shark*?

sharp *(adj.)* शार्प–1. having a keen edge suitable for cutting तेज, तीक्ष्ण Is your knife *sharp*? I heard a *sharp* cry of pain.
2. moving, acting, or reacting quickly, efficiently, etc. तीव्र, (गति में), तेज़ His memory is very *sharp*.

sharpen *(v.)* शार्पन– to make or become sharp or sharper तेज़ करना *Sharpen* your pencil with a sharpener.

shatter *(v.)* शैटर्– to break or be broken into many small pieces टूटकर टुकड़े-टुकड़े होना The looking glass fell to the ground and was *shattered.*

shattered *(adj.)* शैटर्ड– tired out or exhausted थककर चकनाचूर होना, परेशान होना I was absolutely *shattered* after a long journey.

shave *(v.)* शेव– to remove (the beard, hair, etc.) from the face, head, or body by scraping the skin with a razor हजामत बनाना I *shave* off my moustache every morning.

shawl *(n.)* शॉल– a piece of fabric or knitted or crocheted material worn around the shoulders by women or wrapped around a baby गर्म कपड़े की शाल, दुशाला Put on your *shawl* before you go out.

she *(pron.)* शी– 1. refers to a female person or animal वह (स्त्रीलिंग) *She* is a lovely woman.
2. *(n.)* a female person or animal (मादा प्राणी) बकरी I have two he-goats and four *she*-goats.

sheaf *(n.)* शीफ़– a bundle of reaped but unthreshed corn tied with one or two bonds गट्ठा, गट्ठर What does this *sheaf* contain?

shear *(v.)* शिअर्– to remove (the fleece or hair) of sheep, etc. by cutting or clipping कैंची से काटना Sheep are *sheared* once a year.

sheath *(n.)* शीथ– a case or covering for the blade of a knife, sword, etc. म्यान, आवरण He put his sword in its *sheath.*

shed *(v.)* शे'ड–1. to separate or divide off (some farm animals) from the remainder of a group झड़ना, गिराना In autumn, the trees *shed* their leaves.
2. to pour forth or cause to pour forth आँसू बहाना The young girl *shed* tears when her mother went out.

sheen *(n.)* शीन्– a gleaming or glistening brightness; shine चमक In summers, the skin loses its *sheen.*

sheep *(n.)* शीप– an animal with a thick coat of wool, kept on farms for its meat भेड़ (भेड़ें) A *sheep* is an animal that has a coat of wool.

sheepish *(adj.)* शीपिश– abashed or embarrassed, esp through looking foolish or being in the wrong शर्म एवं संकोचभरा She looked *sheepish* when caught copying in exams.

sheer *(adj.)* शिअर्– perpendicular; very steep एकदम ढालू, खड़ा Over the edge of the cliff was a *sheer* drop.

sheet *(n.)* शीट– a rectangular piece of paper for writing or printing on पन्ना How many *sheets* of paper do you need?

shelf *(n.)* शे'ल्फ़– a thin flat plank of wood, metal, etc. fixed horizontally against a wall, etc. for the purpose of supporting objects अलमारी का एक खाना, ताक The baby's toys are on the *shelf.* Our *shelves* are full of books.

shell *(n.)* शे'ल— 1. the protective calcareous or membranous outer layer of an egg, esp a bird's egg आवरण, छिलका, ऊपरी परत A *shell* is the outside of anything.
2. *(v.)* to separate or be separated from an ear, husk, cob, etc. छिलका उतारना I have to *shell* peas.

shelter *(v.)* शे'ल्टर्— 1. to provide with or protect by a shelter शरण लेना, आश्रय उपलब्ध कराना The children *sheltered* under a tree until it stopped raining.
2. *(n.)* something that provides cover or protection, as from weather or danger; place of refuge शरण, आश्रय, पनाह We took *shelter* in a house until the storm was over.

shelves *(n.)* शेल्वज़्— the plural of shelf बहुत से ताक़ There were many *shelves* in that old building.

shepherd *(n.)* शे'पर्ड— a person employed to tend sheep गड़रिया The *shepherd* secured his sheep from the wolf.

shield *(v.)* शील्ड— 1. to protect, hide, or conceal (something) from danger or harm बचाना How can I tell a lie to *shield* you from punishment?
2. *(n.)* any protection used to intercept blows, missiles, etc. such as a tough piece of armour carried on the arm ढाल, कवच The soldier came out armed with a sword and a *shield*.

shift *(n.)* शिफ़्ट— 1. a group of workers who work for a specific period पाली One week he works the day *shift* and the next week the night *shift*.
2. *(v.)* to move or cause to move from one place or position to another उठाना, खिसकाना, हटाना Who has *shifted* my chair?

shiftless *(adj.)* शिफ़्टलस— lacking in ambition or initiative उत्साहहीन My servant is a *shiftless* person. He does not work willingly.

shifty *(adj.)* शिफ्टी— furtive in character or appearance चालबाज़ Beware of him. He is a *shifty* fellow. He can't be trusted.

shimmer *(v.)* शिमर्— to shine with a glistening or tremulous light झिलमिलाना The waves in the river were *shimmering* in the sunlight.

shine *(v.)* शाइन—1. to emit light चमकना Make hay while the sun *shines.*
2. to glow or be bright with reflected light चमकाना Have you *shined* your shoes today?

ship *(n.)* शिप— a vessel propelled by engines or sails for navigating on the water, esp a large vessel that cannot be carried aboard another, as distinguished from a boat जहाज़, पोत A *ship* is a large vessel for carriage of passengers and goods by sea.

shipment *(n.)* शिपमेण्ट— goods shipped together as part of the same lot नौभार, लदान The bags of grains were ready for *shipment.*

shipping *(n.)* शिपिंग— the business of transporting freight, esp by ship नौपरिवहन, पोत-परिवहन He is an officer in a *shipping* corporation.

shipwreck *(n.)* शिपरेक— the partial or total destruction of a ship at sea पोत-ध्वंस Titanic was the world's greatest *shipwreck* in 1912.

shirk *(v.)* शर्क—1. to avoid discharging (work, a duty, etc.); evade (काम से) जी चुराना Lazy men *shirk* work.

shirt *(n.)* शर्ट— a garment worn on the upper part of the body, esp by men, usually of light material and typically having a collar and sleeves and buttoning up the front कमीज़ I bought three readymade *shirts.*

shiver *(v.)* शिवर्— 1. to shake or tremble, as from cold or fear (सर्दी, भय या उत्तेजना से) काँपना, सिहरना, ठिठुरना He is *shivering* with cold.

2. *(n.)* the act of shivering; a tremulous motion सिहरन, कँपकँपी A *shiver* ran through him when someone touched him in the dark.

shock *(n.)* शॉक– 1. a sudden and violent jarring blow or impact धक्का, सदमा The news of my friend's death came as a great *shock* to me.

2. *(v.)* to experience or cause to experience extreme horror, disgust, surprise, etc. आघात पहुंचाना, सदमा पहुंचाना I was *shocked* when my best friend cheated me.

shocking *(adj.)* शॉकिंग– causing shock, horror, or disgust मानसिक आघात, झटका His sudden death was a *shocking* news for me.

shoe *(n.)* शू– one of a matching pair of coverings shaped to fit the foot, esp one ending below the ankle, having an upper of leather, plastic, etc. on a sole and heel of heavier leather, rubber, or synthetic material जूता I want to buy a new pair of *shoes.*

shoelace *(n.)* शूलेस– a cord or lace for fastening shoes तसमा, जूते का फ़ीता Please tie up your *shoelaces.*

➢ **on a shoestring**– a very small or petty amount of money बहुत कम पैसों के सहारे, They are living *on a shoestring.*

shoo *(v.)* शू– to drive away by or as if by crying "shoo." हाथ हिलाते हुए पशु-पक्षियों को भगाना She *shooed* the cat out of the kitchen.

shoot *(v.)* शूट– 1. to hit, wound, damage, or kill with a missile discharged from a weapon गोली दागना The farmer *shoots* the fox that kills his chickens.

2. *(n.)* the action or motion of something that is shot बंदूक़ का धमाका How many *shots* did you hear?

3. any new growth of a plant, such as a bud, young branch, etc. अंकुर/नई कोपल We saw a lot of new *shoots* on the plant.

shop *(n.)* शॉप– a place, esp a small building, for the retail sale of goods and services दुकान, हाट *Shops* were closed on Sunday.

shopkeeper *(n.)* शॉपकीपर– a person who owns or manages a shop or small store दुकानदार This *shopkeeper* is skilled in business.

shoplifter *(n.)* शॉपलिफ़्टर– a person who steals goods from a shop during shopping hours उचक्का, उठाईगीरा The *shoplifter* was prosecuted.

shopping *(n.)* शॉपिंग– the act or an instance of making purchases ख़रीदारी She likes to go for window *shopping* every Saturday.

shore *(n.)* शॉर्–1. the land along the edge of a sea, lake, or wide river related adjective littoral किनारा (समुद्र का) We can find many shells on the sea-*shore.*

2. land, as opposed to water (esp in the phrase on shore) तट The children walked along the *shore* picking up pebbles.

short *(adj.)* शॉर्ट– 1. of little length; not long छोटा, अल्प, थोड़ा *Short* prayers reach heaven.

2. *(v.)* To cut short छोटा होना या कर देना Wherever you can *shorten* a sentence, do so.

shortage *(n.)* शॉर्टिज– a deficiency or lack in the amount needed, expected, or due; deficit कमी, अभाव There was a *shortage* of trained teachers in the school.

short circuit *(n.)* शॉर्ट-सर्किट– a faulty or accidental connection between two points of different potential in an electric circuit, bypassing the load and establishing a path of low resistance through which an excessive current can flow लघु परिपथ The wires had burnt out because of *short circuit.*

shortcoming *(n.)* शॉर्टकमिंग– a failing, defect, or deficiency दोष, कमी Everyone has *shortcomings.*

short cut *(n.)* शॉर्टकट– a route that is shorter than the usual one सरल रास्ता, सुगम उपाय We took a *short cut* to reach home early.

shorthand *(n.)* शॉर्टहैण्ड– a system of rapid handwriting employing simple strokes and other symbols to represent words or phrases आशुलिपि Her secretary knows typing and *shorthand.*

shortlist *(v.)* शॉर्टलिस्ट– to put on a shortlist संक्षिप्त सूची में नाम रखना, छाँटना Five candidates were *shortlisted* for the interview.

shortlived *(adj.)* शॉटलिव्ड– living or lasting only for a short time अल्पजीवी My happiness was *shortlived.*

shortly *(adv.)* शॉटली– in a short time; soon शीघ्र A post of senior editor will *shortly* be vacant in his office.

short-sighted *(adj.)* शॉर्ट-साइटिड– 1. relating to or suffering from myopia (निकट की वस्तुओं को देखने में असमर्थ) निकटदर्शी My mother wears glasses because she is *short-sighted.* 2. lacking foresight अदूरदर्शी I am fed up with her *short-sighted* attitude.

short story *(n.)* शॉर्ट स्टोरी– a prose narrative of shorter length than the novel, esp one that concentrates on a single theme लघुकथा, छोटी कहानी R.K. Narayan is a famous *short story* writer of India.

short-term *(adj.)* शॉर्ट टर्म– of, for, or extending over a limited period अल्पकालीन Vinod took a *short-term* loan from his office.

shot *(n.)* शॉट– the act or an instance of discharging a projectile बंदूक़ से निशाना The police man fired a *shot* into the criminal.

should *(aux. v.)* शुड– used as an auxiliary verb to indicate that an action is considered by the speaker to be obligatory चाहिए We *should* respect our elders.

shoulder *(n.)* शोल्डर्– 1. the part of the vertebrate body where the arm or a corresponding forelimb joins the trunk; the pectoral girdle and associated structures कंधा The labourer carried the luggage on his *shoulders.* 2. *(v.)* to bear or carry (a burden, responsibility, etc.) as if on one's shoulders ज़िम्मेदारी लेना I can happily *shoulder* all the responsibilities.

shout *(v.)* शाउट– 1. to utter (something) in a loud cry; yell चिल्लाना Am I deaf? Why are you *shouting* at me? 2. *(n.)* a loud cry, esp to convey emotion or a command चीख़, चिल्लाहट Your *shouts* could be heard from outside.

shove *(n.)* शव– 1. the act or an instance of shoving ज़ोर का धक्का This weak man should not go in the crowd, he may get a *shove.* 2. *(v.)* to give a thrust or push to (a person or thing) जोर से धक्का देना The children were *shoving* each other in the street.

show *(v.)* शो–1. to make, be, or become visible or noticeable दिखाना *Show* me the man who did this. 2. to instruct by demonstration बताना, समझाना Please *show* me how to do this job. 3. to exhibit or present (oneself or itself) in a specific character ज्ञात होना, सिद्ध होना Her face *showed* how happy she was. 4. *(n.)* a theatre performance, exhibit प्रदर्शन Are you going to the film-*show*?

showdown *(n.)* शोडाउन– an action that brings matters to a head or acts as a conclusion or point of decision झगड़ा There was a huge *showdown* in the Parliament.

shower *(n.)* शॉउअर्– a brief period of rain, hail, sleet, or snow बौछार, बारिश Rakhi and Rina have been caught in a *shower* in the rain.

show-off *(n.)* शो-ऑफ़– a person who makes a vain display of himself दिखावा करने वाला व्यक्ति She is such a *show-off,* I don't like her.

shred *(n.)* श्रे'ड–1. a long narrow strip or fragment torn or cut off चीथड़ा, धज्जी In the scuffle, his shirt was torn to *shreds.*
2. a very small piece or amount; scrap लेशमात्र, कण There was not a *shred* of truth in his report.

shrewd *(adj.)* श्रूड– astute and penetrating, often with regard to business चुस्त-चालाक, तीक्ष्ण बुद्धि A *shrewd* businessman would never say such a thing.

shriek *(v.)* श्रीक– a shrill and piercing cry चीख़ना The kids *shrieked* with joy.

shrill *(adj.)* श्रिल– sharp and high-pitched in quality तेज़ और अप्रिय आवाज़ She has a *shrill* voice.

shrine *(n.)* श्राइन– a place of worship hallowed by association with a sacred person or object समाधि, मंदिर Many foreigners visit the *shrine* of Swami Vivekananda.

shrink *(v.)* श्रिंक–1. to contract or cause to contract as from wetness, heat, cold, etc. सिकुड़ना Your sweater may *shrink* if you wash it.
2. to feel great reluctance (at) संकोच करना, मुंह मोड़ना Some persons *shrink* from meeting a stranger.

shrivel *(v.)* श्रिवल– to make or become shrunken and withered मुरझा जाना Excessive heat of summer *shrivelled* up the plants of my garden.

shroud *(n.)* श्राउड– 1. a garment or piece of cloth used to wrap a dead body कफ़न The dead body was wrapped in a *shroud.*
2. *(v.)* to cover, envelop, or hide ढकना, छिपाना Silence was *shrouding* the atmosphere.

shrub *(n.)* श्रब– a woody perennial plant, smaller than a tree, with several major branches arising from near the base of the main stem झाड़ी The rose *shrub* in the garden looks beautiful.

shrug *(v.)* श्रग– 1. to draw up and drop (the shoulders) abruptly in a gesture expressing indifference, contempt, ignorance, etc. कंधा उचकाना (यह दिखाना कि उसे मालूम नहीं या कोई परवाह नहीं है) The shopkeeper simply *shrugged* when I told him that his prices were very high.
2. *(n.)* the gesture so made कंधों को चढ़ाने की मुद्रा Mother answered with a *shrug.*

shudder *(v.)* शॅडर्– 1. to shake or tremble suddenly and violently, as from horror, fear, aversion, etc. कांप उठना, थरथराना, रोंगटे खड़े होना The terrible thought made her *shudder.*
2. *(n.)* the act of shuddering; convulsive shiver भय या ठंड से उत्पन्न हुई कंपकंपी A *shudder* passed through me when I looked at the dead body.

shuffle *(v.)* शफ़ल– to mix up (cards in a pack) to change their order ताश के पत्ते फेंटना She *shuffled* the cards well.

shun *(v.)* शॅन– to avoid deliberately; keep away from (से) दूर रहना, (से) बचना, टालना We should *shun* cheats.

shunt *(v.)* शॅन्ट–1. to turn or cause to turn to one side; move or be moved aside छकड़े आदि को बग़ल की पटरी या रेल पर लाना Our carriage was *shunted* aside until the Toofan Express had passed.
2. to transfer (rolling stock) from track to track एक स्थान से दूसरे स्थान पर जाना They can't just *shunt* patients off to other hospital.

shut *(v.)* शॅट–1. to move (something) so as to cover an aperture; close बंद करना *Shut* all the doors and windows.
2. to close (something) by bringing together the parts मीचना *Shut* your eyes.

3. to cease to talk or make a noise or cause to cease to talk or make a noise: often used in commands चुप रहो! *Shut* up! Keep quiet.

4. to prevent (a business, etc.) from operating बंद होना (काम समाप्त होना) The concern was *shut down* because it was running in loss.

5. to close or lock the doors of प्रवेश न करने देना, अंदर आने से रोकना If you come late to the hotel, you will be *shut out*.

shy *(adj.)* शाइ– 1. not at ease in the company of others संकोची, शर्मीला Don't feel *shy* before the interview-board.

2. *(v.)* to draw back; recoil जी चुराना He always *shies* away from work.

shyly *(adv.)* शाइली– in a way that shows you are not at ease in the company of others संकोचपूर्वक, लज्जा से Why do you answer *shyly* when you are asked a question?

sibling *(n.)* सिबलिंग– a person's brother or sister सगे भाई-बहन How many *siblings* do you have?

sick *(adj.)* सिक–1. suffering from ill health अस्वस्थ, बीमार, रोग-ग्रस्त It is very difficult for a *sick* man to move briskly.

2. mentally, psychologically, or spiritually disturbed किसी बात से नाराज या विक्षुब्ध हो जाना He felt *sick* at the sight of his brother.

sickle *(n.)* सिकल– an implement for cutting grass, corn, etc. having a curved blade and a short handle हँसिया The man was cutting the grass using a *sickle*.

sickly *(adj.)*–1. सिकली– disposed to frequent ailments; not healthy; weak अस्वस्थ, रोगी They have a *sickly* child.

2. (of a smell, taste, etc.) causing revulsion or nausea दूषित A *sickly* smell of rotten fruits was coming from her neighbourhood.

sickness *(n.)* सिकनस– an illness or disease बीमारी, रोग The child was absent in the class because of *sickness*.

side *(n.)* साइड–1. a line or surface that borders anything किनारे Sonia was riding by the *side* of the road.

2. either of the two surfaces of a flat object एक तरफ़ When you prepare a manuscript, don't write on both *sides* of the paper.

3. the area immediately next to a person or thing पास You must stand by my *side*.

4. a district, point, or direction within an area identified by reference to a central point दिशा People gathered from all *sides* of the area.

5. being on one side; lateral पक्ष Is she on your *side* or Amitabh's?

side effect *(n.)* साइड-इफ़ेक्ट– any unwanted nontherapeutic effect caused by a drug दूषित प्रभाव All drugs have *side-effects*.

side road *(n.)* साइड-रोड– a minor or subsidiary road, especially one leading off a main road उपमार्ग We should not travel through the *side-road* during night time.

sideways *(adv.)* साइडवेज़– moving, facing, or inclining towards one side एक तरफ़ Please turn the table *sideways*.

sleve *(n.)* सीव– a device for separating lumps from powdered material, straining liquids, grading particles, etc. consisting of a container with a mesh or perforated bottom through which the material is shaken or poured छलनी, चालनी These seeds will grow better if the soil is *sieved* before they are sown.

sift *(v.)* सिफ़्ट–1. to sieve (sand, flour, etc.) in order to remove the coarser particles छानना We must *sift* the flour before baking.

2. to examine minutely छानबीन करना The magistrate tried to *sift* the truth from the murderer's story.

sigh *(v.)* साइ– 1. to draw in and exhale audibly a deep breath as an expression of weariness, despair, relief, etc. आह भरना, ठंडी साँस लेना It is better not to *sigh* for days that are gone.
2. *(n.)* the act or sound of sighing ठंडी साँस She heaved a *sigh* of relief when the loan was paid back.

sight *(n.)* साइट–1. the power or faculty of seeing; perception by the eyes; vision नज़र, दृष्टि, नज़ारा Her uncle lost his *sight* in an accident.
2. a glimpse or view नज़ारा, दर्शनीय स्थान We went for *sight*-seeing.

sign *(v.)* साइन– 1. to write (one's name) as a signature to (a document, etc.) in attestation, confirmation, ratification, etc. हस्ताक्षर करना Never forget to *sign* a letter before you post it.
2. *(n.)* something that indicates or acts as a token of a fact, condition, etc. that is not immediately or outwardly observable चिन्ह् There was no *sign* of life in the patient.

signal *(v.)* सिग्नल–1. to communicate (a message, etc.) to (a person) संकेत करना The referee *signalled* the players to begin.
2. used to give or act as a signal सिग्नल देना The driver of the bus *signals* when he wants to stop it.
3. *(n.)* anything that acts as an incitement to action रेलवे सिग्नल A red *signal* is a *signal* of danger.
4. any sign, gesture, token, etc. that serves to communicate information संकेत सूचक The bell gives the *signal* for a new period.

signature *(n.)* सिग्नेचर्– the name of a person or a mark or sign representing his name, marked by himself or by an authorized deputy हस्ताक्षर Please put your *signature* on the cheque. Is this your usual *signature*?

signify *(v.)* सिग्निफ़ाइ– to indicate, show, or suggest सूचित करना, अभिप्राय प्रकट करना We put up our hands to *signify* that we agreed with the speaker.

significance *(n.)* सिग्‌निफ़िकन्स्– consequence or importance अभिप्राय, महत्त्वपूर्ण We must understand the *significance* of the Prime Minister's speech.

sikh *(n.)* सिख– of or relating to the Sikhs or their religious beliefs and customs सिख धर्म का अनुयायी Giani Zail Singh was the first *Sikh* President of India.

silence *(n.)* साइलन्स–1. the state or quality of being silent शान्ति, ख़ामोशी *Silence* is wisdom, when speech is folly.
2. a period of time without noise मौन *Silence* is a friend that will never betray.

silent *(adj.)* साइलेण्ट– characterized by an absence or near absence of noise or sound चुप रहने वाला, मौन *Silent* men are deep and dangerous.

silk *(n.)* सिल्क– the very fine soft lustrous fibre produced by a silkworm to make its cocoon रेशम My shirt is made of *silk.*

silken *(adj.)* सिल्कन– made of silk रेशमी I usually wear *silken* clothes.

silky *(adj.)* सिल्की– resembling silk in texture; glossy कोमल एवं रेशम जैसा Rakhi has *silky* hair.

silly *(adj.)* सिली–1. lacking in good sense; absurd मूढ़ता, बेवकूफ़ी भरा We must not say *silly* things.
2. frivolous, trivial, or superficial निरर्थक, उपहासास्पद The clown does *silly* things to make us laugh.

silt *(n.)* सिल्ट– a fine deposit of mud, clay, etc. esp one in a river or lake

कीचड़, गाद The drain was choked up with *silt.*

silver *(n.)* सिल्वर्–1. a very ductile malleable brilliant greyish-white element having the highest electrical and thermal conductivity of any metal चाँदी Some coins are made of *silver.*

2. well-articulated रजत His wife has a *silver* ring.

silver wedding *(n.)* सिल्वर् वेडिन्ग– the 25th anniversary of a married couple's wedding पच्चीसवीं सालगिरह Roohi is celebrating her *silver wedding* in a hotel.

similar *(adj.)* सिमिलर्– showing resemblance in qualities, characteristics, or appearance; alike but not identical समान My pen is *similar* to yours.

similarity *(n.)* सिमलैरिटी– if there is a similarity between two or more things, they are similar to each other समानता There is a great *similarity* between you and me.

simmer *(v.)* सिमर्– to cook (food) gently at or just below the boiling point धीमी आँच पर पकना Let the gravy *simmer* for a while.

simple *(adj.)* सिम्पल–1. not involved or complicated; easy to understand or do सादा, सरल A *simple* life has its own reward.

2. plain; unadorned साधारण, सजावट से रहित The greatest truths are the *simplest,* and so are the greatest men.

simplicity *(n.)* सिमप्लिसटी– the quality or condition of being simple सादगी Sania is known for her *simplicity.*

simplify *(v.)* सिमप्लिफ़ाइ– to make less complicated, clearer, or easier सरल बनाना I shall teach you how to *simplify* a fraction.

simply *(adv.)* सिम्पली– in a simple manner बिलकुल, एकदम Explain it as *simply* as you can.

simultaneous *(adj.)* साइमल्टेनिअस– occurring, existing, or operating at the same time; concurrent सहकालिक Several *simultaneous* blasts took place in the city.

sin *(n.)* सिन– transgression of God's known will or any principle or law regarded as embodying this पाप The recognition of *sin* is the beginning of happiness.

since *(adv.)* सिन्स– since that time तब से अब तक She came to Delhi two years ago and ever *since* she has been living here.

sincere *(adj.)* सिन्सिअर्– not hypocritical or deceitful; open; genuine ईमानदार Ramesh is a *sincere* man.

sinful *(adj.)* सिनफुल– having committed or tending to commit sin अधर्मी, अनैतिक, पापी She will repent for her *sinful* act.

sing *(v.)* सिंग– to produce or articulate (sounds, words, a song, etc.) with definite and usually specific musical intonation गाना I shall *sing* a song for you.

singe *(v.)* सिन्ज्– to burn or be burnt superficially; scorch झुलसना, झुलसाना I *singed* my eyebrows while bending over the flame.

singer *(n.)* सिंगर– a person who sings, esp one who earns a living by singing गायक We gave the poor *singer* some money.

single *(adj.)* सिंगल–1. existing alone; solitary अविवाहित Are you still *single*?

2. (of a flower) having only one set or whorl of petals एकमात्र The bush has a *single* flower.

➢ **single-handed** *(adj.)*– unaided or working alone अपने बलबूते पर, कृतसंकल्प She did all this *single-handedly.*

➢ **single-minded** *(adj.)*– having but one aim or purpose; dedicated

एकनिष्ठ Veena is very *single-minded* about her career.

singly *(adv.)* सिंगलि– apart from others; separately; alone अकेले ही Do you sell these packets *singly*?

singular *(n.)* सिंगुलर्– 1. unusual; odd एकवचन Do you know the *singular* of 'children'?

2. *(adj.)* remarkable; exceptional; extraordinary असाधारण Rita's rescuing of the young child from drowning was a deed of *singular* bravery.

sinister *(adj.)* सिनिस्टर्– threatening or suggesting evil or harm; ominous अमंगलसूचक He looks *sinister* to me.

sink *(v.)* सिंक–1. to descend or cause to descend, esp beneath the surface of a liquid or soft substance डूबना The ship *sank* in the storm.

2. to slope downwards; dip डुबाना Our warship *sank* one of the enemy's ships.

3. to make or become lower in volume, pitch, etc. (आवाज़) खो जाना Your voice *sank* amidst the loud noise and we could hardly hear you.

4. *(n.)* a fixed basin, esp in a kitchen, made of stone, earthenware, metal, etc. used for washing हौज़, बरतन धोने का सिंक I have a *sink* made of steel in my kitchen.

sip *(n.)* सिप्– 1. a small quantity of a liquid taken into the mouth and swallowed छोटा घूंट, चुस्की You must take small *sips.*

2. *(v.)* to drink (a liquid) by taking small mouthfuls; drink gingerly or delicately चुस्की भरना या लेना, घूंट भरना I *sipped* my coffee slowly because it was very hot.

sir *(n.)* सर–1. a formal or polite term of address for a man उपाधि *Sir* Francis Drake was a great English seaman.

2. a gentleman of high social status श्रीमान Follow me, *sir.*

siren *(n.)* साइरन– a device for emitting a loud wailing sound, esp as a warning or signal, typically consisting of a rotating perforated metal drum through which air or steam is passed under pressure (संकट के साथ) चेतावनी के रूप में The ship's *siren* sounded when the fog came down.

sister *(n.)* सिस्टर्–1. a female person having the same parents as another person बहन My *sister* works in Ahmedabad.

2. a nun or a title given to a nun अस्पताल की नर्स The *sister* nursed the patient in the hospital.

sister-in-law *(n.)* ननद या साली the sister of one's husband or wife (पति या पत्नी की बहन) Her *sister-in-law* is running her own school.

sit *(v.)* सिट–1. to adopt or rest in a posture in which the body is supported on the buttocks and thighs and the torso is more or less upright बैठना Please *sit* down for a while.

2. (of a bird) to perch or roost अंडे देना The hen has been *sitting* on eggs for five days.

site *(n.)* साइट– the piece of land where something was, is, or is intended to be located (मौके की) जगह This is a good *site* for the shop.

situated *(adj.)* सिचुएटिड– located; placed स्थित Her house is *situated* at the end of the street.

situation *(n.)* सिचुएशन–1. state of affairs; combination of circumstances स्थिति The *situation* is now under control.

2. a position of employment; post नौकरी, काम Uncle obtained a *situation* as a clerk.

six *(n.,det.)* सिक्स– a numeral, 6, VI, etc. representing this number छह Her daughter is *six* years old.

sixth *(n.)* सिक्सथ– one of six equal or nearly equal parts of an object, quantity, measurement, etc. छठा This is my *sixth* cup of tea.

sixty *(n.)* सिक्स्टी– a numeral, 60, LX, etc. representing sixty साठ My mother is *sixty* years old.

size *(n.)* साइज़– the dimensions, proportions, amount, or extent of something आकार, नाप What is the *size* of your shirt?

sizzle *(v.)* सिज़ल– to make the hissing sound characteristic of frying fat कड़कड़ाना Sausages were *sizzling* in the frying pan.

skate *(n.)* स्केट–1. the steel blade or runner of an ice skate बर्फ़ पर फिसलने में सहायता करने के लिए पहिये लगी चप्पल Have you got a new pair of *skates*?

2. to glide swiftly over ice on ice skates बर्फ़ पर फिसलने की क्रिया *Skating* is a good fun.

3. a boot having a steel blade fitted to the sole to enable the wearer to glide swiftly over ice बर्फ़ पर जूते पहनकर फिसलने का एक खेल Have you ever gone for *skating*?

skeleton *(n.)* स्केलिट्न्–1. a hard framework consisting of inorganic material that supports and protects the soft parts of an animal's body and provides attachment for muscles हड्डियों का ढाँचा Have you ever seen the *skeleton* of an animal in the museum?

2. the essential framework of any structure, such as a building or leaf, that supports or determines the shape of the rest of the structure प्रारंभिक ढाँचा I'll prepare a *skeleton* for the next year's programmes.

sketch *(n.)* स्केच– a rapid drawing or painting, often a study for subsequent elaboration रेखाचित्र The artist drew a pencil *sketch.*

ski *(v.)* स्की– 1. one of a pair of wood, metal, or plastic runners that are used for gliding over snow. बर्फ़ पर फिसलने के लिए लकड़ी का पतला लम्बा और तिरछा पटड़ा Is the snow firm enough for us to *ski*?

2. *(v.)* to travel on skis बर्फ़ पर चलना या फ़िसलना One who *skies* is a *skier.*

skid *(v.)* स्किड– to cause (a vehicle) to slide sideways or (of a vehicle) to slide sideways while in motion, esp out of control फिसलकर नियंत्रण से बाहर होना The motorcycle *skidded* on the wet road.

skilful *(adj.)* स्किलफुल– possessing or displaying accomplishment or skill कुशल Rahul Gandhi is a very *skilful* politician.

skill *(n.)* स्किल– special ability in a task, sport, etc. esp ability acquired by training दक्षता, कौशल, कारीगरी The mechanic maintained his *skill* in repairing sewing machines.

skilled *(adj.)* स्किल्ड– possessing or demonstrating accomplishment, skill, or special training निपुण दक्षता-प्राप्त He was a *skilled* workman.

skim *(v.)* स्किम– 1. to remove floating material from the surface of (a liquid), as with a spoon ऊपर आई मलाई, झाग या गंदगी को धीरे से हटाना Mother *skimmed* the milk before drinking it.

2. to glide smoothly or lightly over (a surface) ऊपरी सतह या हवा में हल्के से तैरना Seagulls *skim* the water in search of fish.

skin *(n.)* स्किन–1. the tissue forming the outer covering of the vertebrate body खाल, त्वचा Our body is covered with *skin.*

2. outer layer of some fruits and vegetables छाल, छिलका Peel off the *skin* before you eat the orange.

skinny *(adj.)* स्किनी– lacking in flesh; thin अत्यंत दुबला-पतला Girls want to look *skinny* and slim.

skintight *(adj.)* स्किनटाइट– (of garments) fitting tightly over the body; clinging तंग, कसी हुई Savita was wearing a *skintight* jeans.

skip *(v.)* स्किप– to omit (intervening matter), as in passing from one part or subject to another (बीच में) छोड़ जाना These two pages are too difficult. You can *skip* them.

skirmish *(n.)* स्कर्मिश– any brisk clash or encounter, usually of a minor nature झड़प, भिडंत, वाद-विवाद One of our soldiers was lost in a *skirmish* with the enemy.

skirt *(n.)* स्कर्ट– a garment hanging from the waist, worn chiefly by women and girls घाघरा, स्त्रियों का लहँगा The poor woman's *skirt* was covered with dust.

skit *(n.)* स्किट– a brief satirical theatrical sketch प्रहसन, छोटा व्यंग्यात्मक नाटक Shankar was taking part in a *skit.*

skull *(n.)* स्कॅल– the bony skeleton of the head of vertebrates खोपड़ी, कपाल The motor-cyclist fractured his *skull* in the accident.

sky *(n.)* स्काइ– outer space, as seen from the earth आकाश, आसमान Birds fly in the *sky* and chirp cheerfully.

skyscraper *(n.)* स्काइस्क्रैपर– a very tall multistorey building गगनचुंबी इमारत The Burj Al Arab is the most famous *skyscraper* of Dubai.

slab *(n.)* स्लैब– a broad flat thick piece of wood, stone, or other material पटिया We have granite stone *slabs* in our kitchen.

slack *(adj.)* स्लैक– not busy मंदा Trade is very *slack* these days.

slacken *(v.)* स्लैकन– to make or become looser ढीला कर देना He *slackened* his belt and sat down on the chair.

slacks *(n.)* स्लैक्स– informal trousers worn by both sexes ढीली-ढाली पतलून She bought a pair of *slacks* for me.

slake *(v.)* स्लेक– to satisfy (thirst, desire, etc.) बुझाना I *slaked* my thirst with cold drink.

slam *(v.)* स्लैम– to cause (a door or window) to close noisily and with force or (of a door, etc.) to close in this way (दरवाजे आदि को) ज़ोर से बंद करना, ज़ोर से मारना Don't *slam* the door as you go out, or the noise will awaken the baby.

slander *(n.)* स्लैण्डर– 1. defamation in some transient form, as by spoken words, gestures, etc. निंदा, बुराई It is a *slander* against her good reputation. 2. *(v.)* to utter or circulate slander (about) झूठी निंदा करना या बुराई करना To *slander* a friend behind her back is a sin.

slang *(n.)* स्लैंग– vocabulary, idiom, etc. that is not appropriate to the standard form of a language or to formal contexts, may be restricted as to social status or distribution गंवारू बोली, अपभाषा 'Shut up' is the *slang* for 'be quiet'.

slant *(n.)* स्लाण्ट– to incline or be inclined at an oblique or sloping angle तिरछी ढाल वाला The top roof of my house is *slant.*

slap *(v.)* स्लैप– to hit sb with four open hand थप्पड़ मारना Was it not wrong of you to *slap* the baby?

slash *(n.)* स्लैश– a sharp, sweeping stroke, as with a sword or whip चीरा The razor left a *slash* on his cheek. *(v.)* to cut or lay about (a person or thing) with sharp sweeping strokes, as with a sword, knife, etc. झटके से चीर या काट डालना He *slashed* his cheek while shaving.

slate *(n.)* स्लेट– 1. a compact fine-grained metamorphic rock formed by the effects of heat and pressure on shale. पत्थर का समतल भाग, स्लेट Children used to do their sums on the *slates.*

2. *(v.)* to cover (a roof) with slates स्लेट-पत्थर लगाना The roof of the old house has just been *slated.*

slaughter *(v.)* स्लॉटर्– 1. to kill (animals), esp for food हत्या करना Animals are *slaughtered* for food.

2. *(n.)* massacre; the killing of animals, esp for food नरसंहार, पशुसंहार There was a great *slaughter* in the battle.

slave *(n.)* स्लेव– a person legally owned by another and having no freedom of action or right to property दास, ग़ुलाम In the 19th century, there were *slaves* in America.

slavery *(n.)* स्लेवरी– the state or condition of being a slave; a civil relationship whereby one person has absolute power over another and controls his life, liberty, and fortune गुलामी, दासता Abraham Lincoln considered *slavery* illegal.

slay *(v.)* स्ले–1. to kill, esp violently मार डालना, हत्या कर देना Hunters *slay* many animals while hunting.

2. to strike काट डालना Has the butcher *slain* two cocks?

sleazy *(n.)* स्लीज़ी– sordid; disreputable घटिया, मामूली There is a *sleazy* bar house near his office.

sleek *(adj.)* स्लीक– smooth and shiny; polished चिकना और आकर्षक The ipod was very *sleek*.

sleep *(n.)* स्लीप– 1. a periodic state of physiological rest during which consciousness is suspended and metabolic rate is decreased नींद, निद्रा, सुस्ती Seven to eight hours *sleep* is essential for human beings.

2. *(v.)* to be in or as in the state of sleep नींद आना, सोना The baby is *sleeping* in the cradle.

sleeper *(n.)* स्लीपर्–1. a person, animal, or thing that sleeps सोने वाला Some people are light *sleepers*, others are heavy *sleepers*.

2. a railway sleeping car or compartment (रेलगाड़ी में) शयनयान I reserved a *sleeper* on the train to Mumbai.

sleepless *(adj.)* स्लीपलस– without sleep or rest निद्राहीन, निद्रारहित I passed a *sleepless* night due to backache.

sleepy *(adj.)* स्लीपि– inclined to or needing sleep; drowsy निद्रालु, सोता हुआ If you feel *sleepy*, please lay down on bed.

sleeve *(n.)* स्लीव– the part of a garment covering the arm (बाज़ू के भाग को ढकने वाला कपड़ा) आस्तीन I tore the *sleeve* of my shirt.

slender *(adj.)* स्लेण्डर– of small width relative to length or height पतला या पतली Sony has beautiful hands with long *slender* fingers.

slice *(n.)* स्लाइस– 1. a thin flat piece cut from something having bulk फाँक Can I have a *slice* of bread?

2. *(v.)* to divide or cut (something) into parts or slices फाँक काटना, क़तला करना She *sliced* the apple.

slide *(v.)* स्लाइड–1. to move or cause to move smoothly along a surface in continual contact with it सुगमता से सरकना (बिना अटके) The window *slides* up and down very easily.

2. to move (an object) unobtrusively or (of an object) to move in this way चुपके से खिसकना The children love to *slide* on ice.

3. *(n.)* a small piece of glass that sth Is placed on so that it can be looked at under a microscope शीशे की पट्टी, स्लाइड Children prepared *slides* for their experiments in the science class.

slight *(adj.)* स्लाइट–1. small in quantity or extent थोड़ा, मामूली I saw a *slight* change in him.

2. of small importance; trifling बिलकुल भी नहीं I am not in the *slightest* hurry.

3. slim and delicate दुबला-पतला A *slight* young woman entered in his room.

slightly *(adv.)* स्लाइटलि– in small measure or degree बहुत मामूली-सा,

कुछ-कुछ Are you not *slightly* better today than yesterday?

slim *(v.)* स्लिम– 1. to reduce or decrease or cause to be reduced or decreased पतला होने का प्रयत्न करना Some people *slim* down by avoiding heavy meals.

2. *(n.)* small in amount or quality क्षीण She has *slim* hopes of getting what she wants.

slime *(n.)* स्लाइम्– soft thin runny mud or filth कीचड़ *Slime* deposited on the walls in the rainy season.

slimy *(adj.)* स्लाइमि– characterized by, covered with, containing, secreting, or resembling slime कीचड़ से भरा, गंदा The pond was very *slimy.*

sling *(n.)* स्लिंग– 1. a simple weapon consisting of a loop of leather, etc. in which a stone is whirled and then let fly, catapult गुलेल His fractured arm was put in a *sling.*

2. *(v.)* to throw sth somewhere फेंकना, उछालना Tell the children not to *sling* stones at the puppy.

slip *(n.)* स्लिप– 1. a small mistake छोटी-सी ग़लती You have made a *slip* in the bill.

2. *(v.)* to move or cause to move smoothly and easily गिरना (फिसलकर) The looking-glass *slipped* through my fingers and was broken.

slipper *(n.)* स्लिपर– a light shoe of some soft material, for wearing around the house पहनने का खुला जूता, स्लीपर, चट्टी Mother will buy a pair of *slippers* for me today.

slippery *(adj.)* स्लिपरी– causing or tending to cause objects to slip फिसलन से भरा हुआ The heavy rain has made the ground *slippery.*

slipshod *(adj.)* स्लिपशॉड– (of an action) negligent; **careless** असावधानी से भरा हुआ, लापरवाही से He was writing in a *slipshod* manner.

slit *(v.)* स्लिट– 1. to make a straight long incision in; split open चीरना I received an envelope and *slit* it open with a knife.

2. *(n.)* a long narrow cut चीर, दरार The boys watched the football match through a *slit* in the fence.

slob *(n.)* स्लॉब– a slovenly, unattractive, and lazy person बेहद आलसी एवं फूहड़ व्यक्ति Maybe you'd rather be trying to become the laziest *slob* in your house?

slog *(v.)* स्लॉग–1. to work hard; toil कठिन काम ज़्यादा देर तक करना She has been *slogging* away her homework for hours.

2. to move with difficulty; plod बहुत कठिनाई के साथ एक दिशा में चलना I was *slogging* up in the dark with difficulty.

slogan *(n.)* स्लोगन– a distinctive or topical phrase used in politics, advertising, etc. नारा, घोष She won the first prize in the *slogan* writing contest.

slope *(n.)* स्लोप– an inclined portion of ground ढाल, उतराई It is very difficult to walk up the *slope* of the hill.

sloppy *(adj.)* स्लॉपि– careless; untidy लापरवाह Mohan is a *sloppy* worker of his factory.

slot *(n.)* स्लॉट– an elongated aperture or groove, such as one in a vending machine for inserting a coin झिरी, छेद Put the 5 Rs coin in the *slot* of the donation box.

slovenly *(adj.)* स्लवनली– negligent and careless; slipshod सुस्त एवं लापरवाह Ratna is the most *slovenly* teacher in the school.

slow *(adj.)* स्लो–1. taking a long time धीमा The clock is *slow.* It is showing incorrect time. My work is making a *slow* progress.

2. not readily responsive to stimulation; intellectually unreceptive मोटी बुद्धि का, भौंदू She is very *slow* to understand anything.

3. *(v.)* to decrease or cause to decrease in speed, efficiency, etc. धीरे चलना (या चलाना) *Slow* down before reaching the stop signal.

slowly *(adv.)* स्लोली– in a slow manner धीरे-धीरे He walked *slowly* to his house.

slow motion *(n.)* action that is made to appear slower than normal by passing the film through the taking camera at a faster rate than normal or by replaying a video tape recording more slowly मंदगति Every shot of Sachin Tendulkar was shown in a *slow motion* on the TV.

sludge *(n.)* स्लज– soft mud, snow, etc. कीचड़भरा, तलछट It was difficult to walk as the road was full of *sludge.*

sluggish *(adj.)* स्लगिश– lacking energy; inactive; slow-moving सुस्त एवं मंद He was having a *sluggish* heartbeat after the attack.

slum *(n.)* स्लम– a squalid overcrowded house, etc. झुग्गी-झोंपड़ी There are *slums* close to that colony.

slumber *(n.)* स्लॅम्बर्– to sleep, esp peacefully गहरी नींद सोना The family was in a deep *slumber* when the thieves came.

slump *(n.)* स्लम्प– a sudden or marked decline or failure, as in progress or achievement; collapse मंदी, गिरावट There is a *slump* in the property business.

slur *(n.)* स्लर– a slighting remark; aspersion कलंक, लांछन It is a *slur* on her character.

slurp *(v.)* स्लर्प– to eat or drink (something) noisily आवाज़ करते हुए खाना-पीना करना She was *slurping* the mango shake.

sly *(adj.)* स्लाइ– playfully mischievous; roguish कपटपूर्ण, बेईमान, अविश्वसनीय The shopkeeper is *sly.* He speaks politely but sells inferior things.

smack *(n.)* स्मैक– a sharp resounding slap or blow with something flat, or the sound of such a blow तमाचा, थप्पड़ I gave him a tight *smack* on his cheek.

small *(adj.)* स्मॉल–1. comparatively little; limited in size, number, importance, etc. थोड़ा, लघु, अल्प, कम *Small* courtesies matter a lot in life.

2. of little importance or on a minor scale साधारण Don't worry. It is a *small* quarrel, it will be over soon.

smallpox *(n.)* स्मॉलपॉक्स– an acute highly contagious viral disease characterized by high fever, and a pinkish rash changing in form from papules to pustules, चेचक *Smallpox* has left scars on her body.

small-scale *(adj.)* स्मॉल-स्केल– of limited size or scope लघु, छोटा He is running a *small-scale* business.

smart *(adj.)* स्मार्ट–1. astute, as in business; clever or bright चुस्त, चाकचौबंद Do you want a *smart* worker for your office?

2. quick witty and often impertinent in speech चालाक, बुद्धिमान Really you are very *smart.*

3. well-kept; neat देखने में साफ़-सुथरा The soldiers were praised for their *smart* appearance.

4. *(v.)* to feel, cause, or be the source of a sharp stinging physical pain or keen mental distress दुखना, पीड़ा करना The thick smoke from the bonfire made my eyes *smart.*

smash *(v.)* स्मैश– to break into pieces violently and usually noisily चूर-चूर हो जाना The furniture *smashed* into pieces.

smashing *(adj.)* स्मैशिंग– excellent or first-rate; wonderful अति उत्तम, उत्कृष्ट She gave a *smashing* answer to her colleague.

smear *(v.)* स्मिअर– to be daub or cover with oil, grease, etc. गन्दा करना, मैला करना Please don't *smear* the page with your dirty hands.

smell *(v.)* स्मे'ल–1. to perceive the scent or odour of (a substance) by means of the olfactory nerves सूँघना We *smell* with our nose.
2. to have a specified smell; appear to the sense of smell to be गंध देना Roses *smell* sweet.
3. *(n.)* anything detected by the sense of smell; odour; scent गंध, बू, वास, महक All are attracted by the sweet *smell* of flowers.

smile *(v.)* स्माइल– 1. to look (at) with a kindly or amused expression मुस्कराना *Smile* is the language of love.
2. *(n.)* an expression that one has on your face when he or she is happy, amused, etc. मुस्कराहट, मुस्कान A face that does not carry a *smile* is never pretty.

smith *(n.)* स्मिथ– a person who works in metal, esp one who shapes metal by hammering धातुकर्मी The black*smith* works with iron, he makes horse shoes.

smoke *(n.)* स्मोक– 1. the product of combustion, consisting of fine particles of carbon carried by hot gases and air धुआँ Where there is *smoke,* there is fire.
2. *(v.)* to emit smoke or the like, sometimes excessively or in the wrong place सिगरेट पीना, धूम्रपान करना *Smoking* is prohibited. Please don't *smoke* here.

smoky *(adj.)* स्मोकी– emitting, containing, or resembling smoke धूम्रमय, धूमिल Samina has *smoky* eyes.

smooth *(adj.)* स्मूद– silky to the touch कोमल, मृदु, सरल, अच्छा *Smooth* words make *smooth* ways.

smother *(n.)* स्मॅदर्– anything, such as a cloud of smoke, that stifles (से) भर देना, भरा होना, लिप्त होना The player returned home from the playground *smothered* in mud.

smoothly *(adv.)* स्मूदली– without obstructions or difficulties; easily आसानी से, सहज में Things were not going on *smoothly* with me last year.

smoulder *(v.)* स्मोल्डर्– to burn slowly without flame, usually emitting smoke धीरे-धीरे जलना, सुलगना The fire has not gone out. It is *smouldering.*

smudge *(v.)* स्मॅज्– to smear, blur, or soil or cause to do so धब्बा डालना Water *smudged* the kohl of her eyes.

smuggle *(v.)* स्मॅगल– to import or export (prohibited or dutiable goods) secretly तस्करी करना In olden days, smugglers brought wines. Nowadays some people *smuggle* watches and jewellery.

snack *(n.)* स्नैक– a light quick meal eaten between or in place of main meals अल्पाहार We ordered tea and *snacks.*

snake *(n.)* स्नेक– a reptile having a scaly cylindrical limbless body, fused eyelids, and a jaw modified for swallowing large prey साँप, सर्प All *snakes* are not poisonous.

snail *(n.)* स्नेल– any of numerous terrestrial or freshwater gastropod molluscs with a spirally coiled shell, esp any of the family घोंघा He walks like a *snail.*

snap *(v.)* स्नैप–1. to break or cause to break suddenly, esp with a sharp sound दाँत गड़ाना Do not tease the dog. It may *snap* at your hand.
2. to seize something suddenly or quickly जल्दी से फ़ोटो खींचना He *snapped* you as you were coming round the corner.

snarl *(v.)* स्नार्ल–1. (of an animal) to growl viciously, baring the teeth गुर्राना Her dog *snarls* at the visitors.
2. to speak or express (something) viciously or angrily रूखे और कठोर स्वर

में कहना The angry mother *snarled,* "Why didn't you bring your book."

snatch *(v.)* स्नैच–1. to seize or grasp (something) suddenly or peremptorily छीनना, झपटना The thief *snatched* the girl's chain and ran away.

2. to take hurriedly भकोसना, जल्दी-जल्दी खाना I want only five minutes to *snatch* some food.

sneak *(v.)* स्नीक– to move furtively आँख बचाकर निकलना I saw the thief *sneak* down the stairs and out of the shop.

sneer *(v.)* स्निअर्– to say or utter (something) in a scornful or contemptuous manner खिल्ली उड़ाना, उपहास करना He is only a beginner at tennis, so we should not *sneer* at him for missing easy shots.

sneeze *(v.)* स्नीज़– 1. to expel air and nasal secretions from the nose involuntarily, esp as the result of irritation of the nasal mucous membrane छींकना You are catching a cold. You have *sneezed* many times today.

2. *(n.)* the act or sound of sneezing छींक Mostly *sneezing* is a sign of cold.

snide *(adj.)* स्नाइड– (of a remark, etc.) maliciously derogatory; supercilious व्यंग्यात्मक He made a *snide* remark on her performance.

sniff *(v.)* स्निफ़– 1. to perceive or attempt to perceive (a smell) by inhaling through the nose (नाक) सुड़कना, सूँ-सूँ करना Please don't *sniff,* use your handkerchief.

2. *(n.)* a smell perceived by sniffing, esp a faint scent सुड़क, सूँ-सूँ I took a *sniff* of this perfume.

snippet *(n.)* स्निपेट– a small scrap or fragment छोटा टुकड़ा, कतरन I threw a *snippet* of waste cloth in the dustbin.

snob *(n.)* स्नॉब्– a person who strives to associate with those of higher social status and who behaves condescendingly to others घमंडी She is a big *snob.*

snobbery *(n.)* स्नॉबरी– attitudes and behaviour that are typical of a snob घमंड, गुमान, दंभ *Snobbery* is a sign of decay.

snoop *(v.)* स्नूप– to pry into the private business of others ताक-झाँक करना Sushma always *snoops* on her neighbours.

snooty *(adj.)* स्नूटि– aloof or supercilious नकचढ़ा, अकड़ू Geeta is a *snooty* girl, she never mixes with her classmates.

snooze *(n.)* स्नूज़– 1. a nap झपकी The labourers had a *snooze* after lunch.

2. *(v.)* to take a brief light sleep झपकी लेना The labourers *snoozed* after lunch.

snore *(n.)* स्नॉर्– 1. the act or sound of snoring ख़र्राटे I was disturbed the whole night by my brother's *snores.*

2. *(v.)* to breathe through the mouth and nose while asleep with snorting sounds caused by vibrations of the soft palate ख़र्राटे लेना Your *snoring* is intolerable.

snout *(n.)* स्नाउट– the part of the head of a vertebrate, esp a mammal, consisting of the nose, jaws, and surrounding region, esp when elongated थूथन I could see the *snout* of crocodile above the water.

snow *(v.)* स्नो– 1. precipitation from clouds in the form of flakes of ice crystals formed in the upper atmosphere हिमपात होना, बर्फ़ पड़ना It started *snowing* in the hills.

2. *(n.)* a layer of snowflakes on the ground बर्फ़, हिम The *snow* was falling from the sky.

snowfall *(n.)* स्नोफ़ॉल– the amount of snow received in a specified place and time हिमपात, बर्फ़बारी There was a heavy *snowfall* in Shimla.

snowy *(adj.)* स्नोइ– covered with or abounding in snow बर्फ़ीला There was a *snowy* weather outside the lodge.

snub *(v.)* स्नॅब्– to insult (someone) deliberately रूखा बरताव करना She *snubbed* him badly for entering the room without asking for permission.

snuffle *(v.)* स्नफ़ल– to breathe noisily or with difficulty नाक से सूँ-सूँ की आवाज़ करना The dog was *snuffling* when he came to me.

so *(adv.,conj.)* सो–1. to such an extent बहुत It was *so* embarrassing for me.

2. in an equative comparison to the same extent as भी, और भी I like dancing and *so* does Huma.

soak *(v.)* सोक–1. to make, become, or be thoroughly wet or saturated, esp by immersion in a liquid भींगना You have been out in the rain and are *soaked.*

2. (of a liquid) to penetrate or permeate भिगोना *Soak* the raisins in water for two hours.

so-and-so *(n.)* a person whose name is forgotten or ignored फलाँ-फलाँ, अमुक I suppose, Mrs *so and so* will join our office on Monday.

soap *(n.)* सोप– 1. a cleaning or emulsifying agent made by reacting animal or vegetable fats or oils with potassium or sodium hydroxide साबुन Which *soap* do you use?

2. *(v.)* to apply soap to साबुन लगाना He *soaped* himself well to clean the dirt.

soar *(v.)* सॉर्–1. to rise or fly upwards into the air ऊँचा चढ़ना Don't *soar* too high to fall, but stoop to rise.

2. to rise or increase in volume, size, etc. तेज़ी से बढ़ना Last year, the prices of foodgrains *soared* up very high.

sob *(v.)* सॉब– 1. to weep with convulsive gasps सिसकना The baby was *sobbing.*

2. *(n.)* a convulsive gasp made in weeping सिसकी Her *sobs* could be heard clearly from outside.

sober *(adj.)* सोबर–1. sedate and rational तर्कपूर्ण, शांत-गंभीर Pay heed to your teacher's *sober* advice.

2. not given to excessive indulgence in drink or any other activity नशा त्यागने वाला, नशे में नहीं होना We'll talk about this tomorrow, when you're *sober.*

so-called *(adj.)* सो-काल्ड– designated or styled by the name or word mentioned, esp (in the speaker's opinion) incorrectly तथाकथित You could call your *so-called* friend to help you in trouble.

social *(adj.)* सोशल– living or preferring to live in a community rather than alone सामाजिक Shobha De is not only a writer but also a *social* figure.

socially *(adv.)* सोशली– in a manner that relates to society or the way society is organized सामाजिक रूप से Your mother is a *socially* renowned woman.

socialist *(adj.)* सोशलिस्ट– of, characteristic of, implementing, or relating to socialism समाजवादी India is a *socialist* country.

social science *(n.)* सोशल-साइंस– the study of society and of the relationship of individual members within society, including economics, history, political science, psychology, anthropology, and sociology सामाजिक विज्ञान *Social science* is a good subject to understand the society.

social work *(n.)* सोशल् वर्क– any of various social services designed to alleviate the conditions of the poor and aged and to increase the welfare of children समाज सेवा Hasan wants to do *social work* after his retirement.

society *(n.)* ससायटी–1. the totality of social relationships among organized groups of human beings or animals समाज, सोसाइटी *Society* doesn't love its critics.

2. those with whom one has companionship दूसरों के साथ मित्रता We like the *society* of interesting people.

sociology *(n.)* सोशिऑलजी– the study of the development, organization, functioning, and classification of human societies समाजशास्त्र *Sociology* is a scientific study of society and social relations.

sock *(n.)* सॉक– a cloth covering for the foot, reaching to between the ankle and knee and worn inside a shoe जुर्राब, मोज़ा I bought a pair of *socks.*

soda *(n.)* सोडा–1. any of a number of simple inorganic compounds of sodium, such as sodium carbonate (washing soda), sodium bicarbonate (baking soda), and sodium hydroxide (caustic soda) क्षार, सज्जी *Soda* bicarbonate is used in baking.

2. an effervescent beverage made by charging water with carbon dioxide under pressure खारा पानी, सोडा वाटर In small towns, people enjoy *soda*-water.

sofa *(n.)* सोफ़ा– an upholstered seat with back and arms for two or more people सोफा, बैठने का आरामदेह आसन Father bought a new *sofa*-set from the market.

soft *(adj.)* सॉफ़्ट– fine, light, smooth, or fluffy to the touch कोमल, नरम, मुलायम Wool is *soft* to touch.

soften *(v.)* सॉफ़्टन– to make or become soft or softer कोमल बनाना A lotion has *softened* her skin.

soft-hearted *(adj.) easily moved to pity* कोमल हृदय, दयालु Open your eyes and you will be less *soft-hearted* toward him.

softness *(n.)* the quality or an instance of being soft कोमलता, मृदुता Her *softness* in nature is liked by everyone.

soft-spoken *(adj.)* speaking or said with a soft gentle voice मृदुभाषी She was always *soft-spoken* to everyone.

soggy *(adj.)* सॉगी– soaked with liquid बहुत गीला और नरम The sandwiches became *soggy* when left in open.

soil *(v.)* सॉइल– 1. to make or become dirty or stained मैला करना She will *soil* her dress if she sits on the muddy grass.

2. *(n.)* the top layer of the land surface of the earth that is composed of disintegrated rock particles, humus, water, and air मिट्टी This *soil* is very fertile.

solace *(n.)* सॉलेस– something that gives comfort or consolation सांत्वना After travelling to so many places, I found *solace* in my own home.

solar *(adj.)* सोलर्– of or relating to the sun सौर, सूर्य-संबंधी The earth is a part of the *solar* system. It revolves round the sun.

soldier *(n.)* सोल्जर–1. a person who serves or has served in an army योद्धा *Soldiers* fight and kings become heroes.

2. a noncommissioned member of an army as opposed to a commissioned officer सैनिक, फ़ौजी There are many *soldiers* in an army.

sole *(adj.)* सोल– 1. being the only one; only अकेला, एकमात्र She was the *sole* child of her parents.

2. *(n.)* the underside of the foot पैर का तलुआ, जूते का तल्ला Please show me a shoe with a rubber *sole.*

solemn *(adj.)* सॉलम– characterized or marked by seriousness or sincerity गंभीर The manager had a *solemn* manner when he addressed the staff.

solemnly *(adv.)* सॉलमली– seriously, glumly, or pompously विधिवत् He listened to his statement *solemnly.*

solicit *(v.)* सलिसिट– to make a request, application, or entreaty to (a person for business, support, etc.) धन मांगना, याचना करना The poor man was *soliciting* help from a famous business man.

solid *(adj.)* सॉलिड– of, concerned with, or being a substance in a physical state in which it resists changes in size and shape ठोस, सख़्त The patient cannot take *solid* food. He can only take tea or milk.

solidarity *(n.)* सॉलिडैरटी– unity of interests, sympathies, etc. as among members of the same class एकजुटता, पूर्ण एकता, हमदर्दी They expressed their *solidarity* with her opinion.

solitary *(adj.)* सॉलिटरी– following or enjoying a life of solitude एकांत, निर्जन Few people like to live in *solitary* places.

solitude *(n.)* सॉलिट्यूड– the state of being solitary or secluded अकेलापन, एकाकीपन Saints live in *solitude.*

solo *(n.)* सोलो– a musical composition for one performer with or without accompaniment एकल गायन/वादन/प्रदर्शन Reema sang a *solo* at the concert.

solution *(n.)* सल्यूशन, सलूशन–1. a specific answer to or way of answering a problem समाधान, समस्या का हल Provide me a *solution* to this problem.

2. the state of being dissolved घोल, मिश्रण The *solution* of these two chemicals can be explosive.

solve *(v.)* सॉल्व–1. to find the explanation for or solution to (a mystery, problem, etc.) किसी प्रश्नमाला आदि का सही उत्तर मालूम करना Let me help you *solve* that crossword puzzle.

2. to work out the answer to (a problem) समाधान करना, हल करना *Solve* your problems yourself.

sombre *(adj.)* सॉम्बर्– dim, gloomy, or shadowy अंधकारपूर्ण और विषादयुक्त The graveyard was shrouded with a *sombre* darkness.

some *(pron. & adj.)* सॅम–1. indicating a group of a specified number of members कुछ, थोड़े से (लोग या वस्तु आदि) *Some* are born great, *some* achieve greatness.

2. certain unknown or unspecified कुछ, कोई, कई *Some* children are playing in the playground.

somebody *(pron.)* समबडी– some person; someone कोई भी *Somebody* is waiting for me outside the gate.

somehow *(adv.)* समहाउ– in some unspecified way किसी भी तरह से Don't worry, I will do your work *somehow.*

something *(pron.)* समथिंग– an unspecified or unknown thing; some thing कोई भी वस्तु Do you want *something* to drink?

sometimes *(adv.)* समटाइम्ज़–1. now and then; from time to time; occasionally कभी-कभी We *sometimes* watch television in the night.

2. formerly; sometime कुछ अवसरों पर *Sometimes* a half is better than the whole.

somewhere *(adv.)* समवेअर– in, to, or at some unknown or unspecified place or point कहीं, किसी जगह I saw her *somewhere*, but I can't remember where.

son *(n.)* सॅन– a male offspring; a boy or man in relation to his parents

पुत्र, संतान We all are the *sons* and daughters of Mother India.

song *(n.)* सॉन्ग्– a piece of music, usually employing a verbal text, composed for the voice, esp one intended for performance by a soloist गीत Which is your favourite *song* in the album?

soon *(adv.)* सून– in or after a short time; in a little while; before long शीघ्र ही, जल्दी, तुरंत Don't worry, we shall *soon* be back.

sooner *(adv.)* सूनर– rather; in preference आज नहीं तो कल, कभी न कभी *Sooner* or later, the strong need the help of the weak.

soot *(n.)* सूट– finely divided carbon deposited from flames during the incomplete combustion of organic substances such as coal कालिख, काजल Clouds of *soot* rose from the chimney.

soothe *(v.)* सूद– to make calm or tranquil सांत्वना देना, ढाँढ़स बंधाना The boy was very excited but his sister *soothed* him and made him calm.

sophisticated *(adj.)* सफ़िस्टिकेटेड– having refined or cultured tastes and habits अनुभवी और सयाना She is a smart and *sophisticated* lady.

soppy *(adj.)* सॉपि– silly or sentimental भावुक We saw a *soppy* romantic film last night.

sorcery *(n.)* सॉर्सरी– the art, practices, or spells of magic, esp black magic जादू-टोना, झाड़-फूंक He saved the child with his power of *sorcery*.

sore *(adj.)* सॉर– 1. (esp of a wound, injury, etc.) painfully sensitive; tender दुखता हुआ My eyes are *sore* from reading too much.

2. *(n.)* resentful; irked दुखते घाव, ज़ख़्म My *sores* have healed.

sordid *(n.)* सॉडिड– dirty, foul, or squalid हेय, घिनौना, भ्रष्ट I was shocked to hear about her *sordid* past.

sorrow *(n.)* सॉरो–1. the characteristic feeling of sadness, grief, or regret associated with loss, bereavement, sympathy for another's suffering, for an injury done, etc. दुःख, उदासी, शोक *Sorrow* will pay no debts.

2. a particular cause or source of regret, grief, etc. व्यथा, दुखद घटना, दुख का कारण *Sorrows* are our best educators.

sorry *(adj.)* सॉरी–1. feeling or expressing pity, sympathy, remorse, grief, or regret दुख, खेद I am *sorry* I shall not be able to come.

2. pitiful, wretched, or deplorable (किसी भी बीमारी आदि पर दुःख प्रकट करना) दुःखपूर्ण, दुःखी I am *sorry* to know that your mother is ill.

sort *(n.)* सॉर्ट– 1. a class, group, kind, etc. as distinguished by some common quality or characteristic क़िस्म, प्रकार What *sort* of sweets do you like most?

2. *(v.)* to arrange according to class, type, etc. चुनना *Sort* out these letters quickly.

so-so *(adj.)* सो-सो– 1. neither good nor bad ठीक-ठाक, कामचलाऊ The day was *so-so.*

2. *(adv.)* कामचलाऊ ढंग से She did *so-so* in her exams.

soul *(n.)* सोल–1. the spirit or immaterial part of man, the seat of human personality, intellect, will, and emotions, regarded as an entity that survives the body after death आत्मा I must put my heart and *soul* into my studies.

2. a person; individual (कोई) व्यक्ति There is not even a single *soul* in the house.

sound *(n.)* साउंड–1. a periodic disturbance in the pressure or density of a fluid or in the elastic strain of a solid, produced by a vibrating object ध्वनि Listen! What *sounds* can you hear?

2. anything that can be heard आवाज़ Did you hear the *sound* of a shot?

3. *(v.)* to pronounce distinctly or audibly आवाज़ निकालना, सुनाई देना How does it *sound*?

4. *(adj.)* free from damage, injury, decay, etc. अच्छी दशा में She has reached safe and *sound.*

5. in good condition स्वस्थ, अच्छा A *sound* body has a *sound* mind.

sound effect *(n.)* साउंड इफ़ेक्ट– any sound artificially produced, reproduced from a recording, etc. to create a theatrical effect, such as the bringing together of two halves of a hollow coconut shell to simulate a horse's gallop; used in plays, films, etc. कृत्रिम रूप से उत्पन्न की गई ध्वनि The *sound effect* of the computer game was not matching.

soundly *(adv.)* साउण्डली– if you sleep soundly, you sleep deeply and do not wake during your sleep अच्छी तरह His baby was sleeping *soundly.*

soundproof *(adj.) not penetrable by sound* ध्वनिरोधी We visited a *soundproof* studio.

soup *(n.)* सूप– a liquid food made by boiling or simmering meat, fish, vegetables, etc. usually served hot at the beginning of a meal शोरबा, रसा You must start your lunch with a bowl of chicken *soup.*

sour *(adj.)* साउअर्– having or denoting a sharp biting taste like that of lemon juice or vinegar खट्टा, अम्ल Lemons taste *sour,* grapes are sweet.

sourly *(adv.)* साउरली– in a bad-tempered and unfriendly manner खट्टेपन के साथ, कटुता लिए हुए The manager replied very *sourly* because he was unhappy.

source *(n.)* सोर्स–1. the point or place from which something originates स्रोत, उद्गम The *source* of the Ganges is a spring in the Himalayas.

2. anything, such as a story or work of art, that provides a model or inspiration for a later work मूल कारण, आधार His friendship is a *source* of great pleasure to us.

south *(n.)* साउथ– one of the four cardinal points of the compass, at 180° from north and 90° clockwise from east and anticlockwise from west दक्षिण दिशा The *south* is on our right at sunrise.

southern *(adj.)* सदर्न– situated in or towards the south दक्षिणी Chennai is in the *southern* part of India.

south-east *(n.)* The south-eastern part of a region or the point of the horizon midway between south and east दक्षिण-पूर्व The culture of *South-east* Asian nations is diverse.

south-west *(n.)* The south-western part of a region or the point of the horizon midway between south and west दक्षिण-पश्चिम The *south-west* direction is considered very inauspicious in Vastu Shastra.

sovereign *(adj.)* सॉव्रिन–1. supreme in rank or authority प्रभुसत्ता सम्पन्न A *sovereign* nation is a nation which has the freedom and power to rule itself.

2. of, relating to, or characteristic of a sovereign स्वतंत्र, आज़ाद India, which was once ruled by the British, is now a *sovereign* state.

sow *(v.)* सो–1. to scatter or place (seed, a crop, etc.) in or on (a piece of ground, field, etc.) so that it may grow बोना, बुआई करना *Sow* good work and you will reap satisfaction.

2. to implant or introduce रोपना, छितरना The farmers *sowed* the seeds after they had ploughed the fields.

soyabean *(n.)* an Asian bean plant, cultivated for its nutritious seeds, for forage, and to improve the soil सोयाबीन, एक विशेष प्रकार की फली *Soyabean* oil is widely used oil and is called vegetable oil.

spa *(n.)* स्पा– a place where people can relax and improve their health व्यायाम और सौंदर्य उपचार का स्थान I will go to a health *spa* this weekend.

space *(n.)* स्पेस–1. a blank portion or area दूरी, अंतर Leave proper *space* between words.

2. the region beyond the earth's atmosphere containing the other planets of the solar system, stars, galaxies, etc.; universe अंतरिक्ष, आकाश Kalpana Chawla was the first Indian woman to go into *space*.

spaceship *(n.)* स्पेसशिप– a manned spacecraft अंतरिक्ष यान Man can travel into space in a *spaceship*.

spacious *(adj.)* स्पेशस– having a large capacity or area लम्बा-चौड़ा, विस्तृत Our library hall is quite *spacious*.

spade *(n.)* स्पेड– a tool for digging, typically consisting of a flat rectangular steel blade attached to a long wooden handle फावड़ा Labourers were using *spades* for digging the land.

span *(n.)* स्पैन– the interval, space, or distance between two points, such as the ends of a bridge or arch चौड़ाई, फैलाव, विस्तार The railway bridge across the canal has a *span* of fifty yards.

spank *(n.)* स्पैन्क– 1. a slap or series of slaps with the flat of the hand (थप्पड़ की) मार, पिटाई The boy who teases cats and puppies deserves a good *spanking*.

2. *(v.)* to slap or smack with the open hand, esp on the buttocks थप्पड़ बरसाना The teacher *spanked* the students who had disobeyed him.

spanner *(n.)* स्पैनर्– a steel hand tool with a handle carrying jaws or a hole of particular shape designed to grip a nut or bolt head (पेंच कसने का औज़ार,) रेंच, पाना The electrician tightened the nuts with a *spanner*.

spare *(v.)* स्पेअर्– 1. to refrain from using दे सकना I can *spare* a little money, if you want.

2. *(adj.)* in excess of what is needed; additional अतिरिक्त, फ़ालतू Come and stay with us, we have a *spare* room.

spark *(n.)* स्पार्क– a fiery particle thrown out or left by burning material or caused by the friction of two hard surfaces चिंगारी, स्फुलिंग *Sparks* flew from the fire.

sparkle *(v.)* स्पार्कल– to issue or reflect or cause to issue or reflect bright points of light चमकना, झिलमिलाना Diamonds *sparkle*, and so do stars in the sky.

sparkling *(adj.)* स्पार्कलिंग– clear and bright and shining with a lot of very small points of light जगमग, चमचमाता हुआ I was amazed to see her *sparkling* blue eyes.

sparrow *(n.)* स्पैरो– a small bird having a brown or grey plumage and feeding on seeds or insects चिड़िया, गौरैया A *sparrow* built a nest in the tree.

sparse *(adj.)* स्पार्स– scattered or scanty; not dense बिखरा, छितरा The population in Ladakh is quite *sparse*.

spasm *(n.)* स्पैज़्म– an involuntary muscular contraction, esp one resulting in cramp or convulsion मरोड़, ऐंठन He had a muscle *spasm* while exercising.

speak *(v.)* स्पीक– to make (verbal utterances); utter (words) बोलना, कहना Think before you *speak*. Read before you think.

speaker *(n.)* स्पीकर– a person who speaks, esp at a formal occasion वक्ता The *speaker* remained undisturbed even when the audience started hooting.

spear *(n.)* स्पिअर्– a weapon consisting of a long shaft with a sharp pointed end of metal, stone, or wood that may be thrown or thrust बरछा, भाला Caveman used *spear* to hunt.

spearmint *(n.)* स्पिअरमिण्ट– a type of mint, cultivated for its leaves, which yield an oil used for flavouring पुदीना *Spearmint* tea helps to control excessive hair growth in women.

special *(adj.)* स्पेशल– distinguished, set apart from, or excelling others of its kind विशेष, विशिष्ट This is my father's *special* pen. No one else may write with it.

specialist *(n.)* स्पेशलिस्ट– a person who specializes in or devotes himself to a particular area of activity, field of research, etc. विशेषज्ञ Today she will go to consult an eye *specialist.*

specially *(adv.)* स्पेशली– for a particular person or purpose ख़ासकर, विशेष रूप से This cake is *specially* available for the invitees.

species *(n.)* स्पीशीज़– a group into which a genus is divided, the members of which are capable of interbreeding, often containing subspecies, varieties, or races प्रजाति, वर्ग Give me the list of endangered *species* of India.

specific *(adj.)* स्पे'सिफ़िक– explicit, particular, or definite विशेष, विशिष्ट What was the *specific* reason behind the fight?

specification *(n.)* स्पेसिफ़िकेशन– the act or an instance of specifying विशेष विवरण, पूरा ब्यौरा I had to provide him the proper *specifications* of the problem before we could proceed to solve it.

specify *(v.)* स्पेसिफ़ाइ– to refer to or state specifically ब्यौरा देना, विशेष रूप से उल्लेख करना *Specify* the area else you might be confused.

specimen *(n.)* स्पे'सिमन– an individual, object, or part regarded as typical of the group or class to which it belongs नमूना, बानगी Please give us some *specimens* of your new publications.

speck *(n.)* स्पे'क्– a very small mark or spot दाग़, धब्बा Now the ship was a mere *speck* on the horizon.

spectacle(s) *(n.)* स्पे'क्टेकल(ज़)–1. a public display or performance, esp a showy or ceremonial one समारोह Our annual procession was a very fine *spectacle.*
2. a pair of glasses for correcting defective vision चश्मा Please lend me your *spectacles.*

spectator *(n.)* स्पे'क्ट्टेटर्– a person viewing anything; onlooker; observer दर्शक Many *spectators* stood round the field to watch the hockey match.

speculate *(v.)* स्पेक्युलेट– to conjecture without knowing the complete facts अंदाज/अटकल लगाना Scientists *speculated* about the possibility of life on Mars.

speech *(n.)* स्पीच–1. the act or faculty of speaking, esp as possessed by persons वाणी, कथन, भाषा *Speech* is the gift of all, but thought of few.
2. a person's characteristic manner of speaking वाक्शक्ति, उक्ति *Speech* is silver, silence is golden.
3. a national or regional language or dialect भाषण His *speech* was impressive.

speechless *(adj.)* स्पीचलस– not able to speak मूक She stood *speechless* with surprise.

speed *(v.)* स्पीड– 1. to move or go or cause to move or go quickly तेज़ी से चलना If we *speed* up our work, we shall be able to finish it before Sunday.
2. *(n.)* to move or go or cause to move or go quickly गति, रफ़्तार, चाल Your *speed* of working is not satisfactory.

speed limit *(n.)* स्पीड लिमिट– the maximum permitted speed at which a vehicle may travel on certain roads गति-सीमा Traffic police stopped him to see the *speed limit* of his car.

speedy *(adj.)* स्पीडी– characterized by speed of motion तेज़ गति से, शीघ्रतापूर्वक Mahima got a *speedy* recovery from her disease.

spell *(v.)* स्पे'ल– 1. to write or name in correct order the letters that comprise the conventionally accepted form of (a word or part of a word) हिज्जे करना Can you *spell* my name?
2. *(n.)* a verbal formula considered as having magical force जादू The fairy cast a *spell* on the little boy and turned him into a young ox.

spelling *(n.)* स्पेलिंग– the act or process of writing words by using the letters conventionally accepted for their formation; orthography वर्तनी, वर्णविन्यास He is very bad at *spellings.*

spend *(v.)* स्पेन्ड–1. to concentrate (time, effort, thought, etc.) upon an object, activity, etc. बिताना, गुज़ारना I have *spent* the whole week in my research.
2. to pay out (money, wealth, etc.) ख़र्च करना How much money did you *spend* on your new TV set?

spendthrift *(n.)* स्पेन्डथ्रिफ्ट– a person who spends money in an extravagant manner फ़िज़ूलख़र्च, अपव्ययी My brother is a *spendthrift.* He spent all the money he had.

spending *(n.)* स्पेनडिंग– the action of paying out money खर्च की गई धनराशि Purchasing lots of suits and shoes is not a wise *spending.*

sperm *(n.)* स्पर्म– a male reproductive cell; male gamete शुक्राणु The doctor adviced him for *sperm* test.

sphere *(n.)* स्फ़िअर्–1. particular field of activity; environment कार्य-क्षेत्र This work is beyond my *sphere* of specialisation.
2. a three-dimensional closed surface such that every point on the surface is equidistant from a given point, the centre गोला, गोल Learn how to compute the surface area of a *sphere.*

spherical *(adj.)* स्फे़रिकल– shaped like a sphere गोल आकार का Most of the celestial bodies are *spherical* in shape.

spice *(n.)* स्पाइस–1. any of a variety of aromatic vegetable substances, such as ginger, cinnamon, nutmeg, used as flavourings मसाला Addition of *spices* made the food tastier.
2. something that represents or introduces zest, charm, or gusto दिलचस्पी Media added *spice* to the whole incident.

spider *(n.)* स्पाइडर्– a small creature, having four pairs of legs and a rounded unsegmented body मकड़ी *Spiders* spin webs in which they catch insects.

spill *(v.)* स्पिल–1. to fall or cause to fall from or as from a container, esp unintentionally छलकाना, छलकना You will *spill* the milk if you do not hold the jug straight.
2. to disgorge (contents, occupants, etc.) or (of contents, occupants, etc.) to be disgorged झटके से इधर-उधर छलक जाना या बिखर जाना The milk was *spilt* out due to my carelessness.

spin *(v.)* स्पिन– 1. to rotate or cause to rotate rapidly, as on an axis बुनना, कातना In the village, the old lady was *spinning* wool.
2. *(n.)* a swift rotating motion; instance of spinning चक्रण, घुमाव I have been in a *spin* since I came to this place.

spinach *(n.)* स्पिनिच– a vegetable with large dark green leaves पालक *Spinach* is very good for health.

spine *(n.)* स्पाइन– the spinal column रीढ़, मेरुदंड She has some defect in her *spine.*

spineless *(adj.)* स्पाइनलस– lacking strength of character, resolution, or courage डरपोक, दब्बू A *spineless* man let his wife make all the decisions.

spinster *(n.)* स्पिनस्टर– an unmarried woman regarded as being beyond the age of marriage अविवाहित स्त्री, कुमारी She wanted to pass her life as a *spinster.*

spire *(n.)* स्पाइअर्– a tall structure that tapers upwards to a point, esp one on a tower or roof or one that forms the upper part of a steeple मीनार, लाट The *spire* of Salisbury Cathedral is one of the highest in the world.

spirit *(n.)* स्पिरिट–1. liveliness; mettle उत्साह Roma was a girl of *spirit.* She knew what she wanted to do and no one could stop her from doing that.
2. the force or principle of life that animates the body of living things आत्मा Some people believe that the *spirits* of the dead exist in this world.

spiritual *(adj.)* स्पिरिचुअल– relating to the spirit or soul and not to physical nature or matter; intangible आत्मिक The modern civilization lacks *spiritual* values.

spit *(v.)* स्पिट– 1. to expel saliva from the mouth; expectorate थूकना Don't *spit* on the floor.
2. *(n.)* a pointed rod on which meat is skewered and roasted before or over an open fire मांस पकाने की लोहे की सीख The chicken was roasted on the *spit.*

spite *(n.)* स्पाइट– 1. maliciousness involving the desire to harm another; venomous ill will हानि पहुँचाने की इच्छा Don't tear his exercise-book out of *spite.*
2. *(v.)* to annoy in order to vent spite ईर्ष्या करना, द्वेष करना Never *spite* others.

spiteful *(adj.)* स्पाइटफुल– full of or motivated by spite; vindictive ईर्ष्यालु, द्वेषपूर्ण No one likes *spiteful* people.

splash *(v.)* स्प्लैश– to scatter (liquid) about in blobs; spatter छिड़कना She *splashed* some water on her face.

splatter *(v.)* स्प्लैटर्– to splash with small blobs; spatter छलकाना She *splattered* water all over the room.

spleen *(n.)* स्प्लीन– a spongy highly vascular organ situated near the stomach in man तिल्ली, प्लीहा The *spleen* acts primarily as a blood filter.

splendid *(adj.)* स्प्ले'न्डिड– brilliant or fine, esp in appearance भव्य, शानदार, गौरवपूर्ण, उत्कृष्ट The prince lived in a *splendid* palace.

splendidly *(adv.)* स्प्लेण्डिडली– impressively or magnificently भव्य रूप से, शान से Lila sang *splendidly* at the concert.

splendour *(n.)* स्प्लेण्डर– the state or quality of being splendid वैभव, गौरव The rich man lived in great *splendour* in his newly built palace.

splinter *(n.)* स्प्लिण्टर– 1. a very small sharp piece of wood, glass, metal, etc. characteristically long and thin, broken off from a whole छोटा-सा टुकड़ा, किरच The soldier was severely wounded by a shell *splinter.*
2. *(v.)* to break or be broken off in small sharp fragments टुकड़े-टुकड़े होना The wooden cup crashed to the floor and *splintered.*

split *(v.)* स्प्लिट–1. to divide or be divided among two or more persons आपस में बाँटना The friends *split* the bill and paid Rs. 50 each.
2. to break or cause to break, esp forcibly, by cleaving into separate pieces, often into two roughly equal pieces समूहों या दलों में बंट जाना Differences of opinion *split* the association.

spoil *(v.)* स्पॉइल– to cause damage to (something), in regard to its value, beauty, usefulness, etc. बिगाड़ना, सिर चढ़ाना Don't *spoil* my time with your foolish talk.

spoilt *(adj.)* स्पॉइल्ट– a past tense and past participle of spoil पूरी तरह नष्ट या ख़राब A *spoilt* child never cares for his parents.

spoke *(n.)* स्पोक– a radial member of a wheel, joining the hub to the rim अर, आरा The hub of a wheel is connected with *spokes* to the rim.

spokesperson *(n.)* स्पोक्सपर्सन– a person authorized to speak on behalf of another person, group of people, or organization किसी संस्था का प्रवक्ता Manish Tiwari is a congress *spokesperson.*

sponge *(n.)* स्पन्ज– a piece of the light porous highly absorbent elastic skeleton of certain sponges, used in bathing, cleaning स्पंज Have you a *sponge* to clean the slate?

sponsor *(n.)* स्पॉनसर– a commercial organization that pays all or part of the cost of putting on a concert, sporting event, etc. प्रायोजक He refused to be his *sponsor.*

spontaneous *(adj.)* स्पॉण्टेनिअस– occurring, produced, or performed through natural processes without external influence अनायास His comic acts evoke a *spontaneous* laughter.

spooky *(adj.)* स्पूकी– ghostly or eerie डरावना Going inside the deserted bungalow was a *spooky* experience.

spoon *(n.)* स्पून– a metal, wooden, or plastic utensil having a shallow concave part, usually elliptical in shape, attached to a handle, used in eating or serving food, stirring, etc. चम्मच Stir the gravy with a wooden *spoon.*

sport *(n.)* स्पॉर्ट– an individual or group activity pursued for exercise or pleasure, often involving the testing of physical capabilities and taking the form of a competitive game such as football, tennis, etc. मनोरंजन, मनबहलाव Wrestling in one of the international *sports.*

sportsmanlike *(adj.)* स्पॉर्टसमनलाइक– exhibiting the qualities highly regarded in sport, such as fairness, generosity, observance of the rules, and good humour when losing उदार एवं शिष्ट आचरण वाला The coach of the team has a *sportsmanlike* attitude.

sportsmanship *(n.)* स्पॉर्टसमनृशिप– the practice of the ideals of sport, such as fairness, generosity, observance of the rules, and good humour when losing खिलाड़ीपन, क्रीड़ा-कौशल He showed *sportsmanship* in acknowledging defeat in the game.

spot *(n.)* स्पॉट– 1. a location स्थान, जगह Please find a quiet *spot* where we can discuss the matter.

2. a small mark on a surface, such as a circular patch or stain, differing in colour or texture from its surroundings धब्बा, दाग़ How can I remove an ink *spot*?

spotless *(adj.)* स्पॉटलस– free from stains; immaculate बेदाग़, बिना धब्बे का My clothes are *spotless.*

spotted *(adj.)* स्पॉटिड– characterized by spots or marks, esp in having a pattern of spots चित्तीदार, धब्बेदार She wore a *spotted* dress.

spout *(n.)* स्पाउट–1. a tube, pipe, etc. allowing the passage or pouring of liquids, grain, etc. टोंटी Our teapot lost its *spout.*

2. *(v.)* to discharge (a liquid) in a continuous jet or in spurts, esp through a narrow gap or under pressure, or (of a liquid) to gush

thus जोड़ से निकलना Tea *spouted* from the broken teapot.

sprain *(n.)* स्प्रेन– 1. the resulting injury to such a joint, characterized by swelling and temporary disability मोच It was a bad *sprain*.
2. *(v.)* to injure (a joint) by a sudden twisting or wrenching of its ligaments मोच आना She fell and *sprained* her toe.

spray *(v.)* स्प्रे– to scatter (liquid) in the form of fine particles छिड़कना, फुहारना, छिड़काव करना He *sprayed* fresh paint on his motorcycle.

spread *(v.)* स्प्रे'ड–1. to extend or unfold or be extended or unfolded to the fullest width खोलकर बिछाना, फैलाना Please *spread* a cloth on the table.
2. to extend or cause to extend over a larger expanse of space or time फैलाना The parrot *spread* its wings and flew away.
3. *(n.)* the act or process of spreading; diffusion, dispersal, expansion, etc. फैलाव Doctors try to prevent the *spread* of contagious diseases.

spring *(n.)* स्प्रिंग–1. the season of the year between winter and summer, when plants begin to grow वसंत ऋतु In *spring*, flowers begin to grow.
2. a twisted piece of metal स्प्रिंग-पुर्जा, छल्ला The *spring* of your watch is broken, so it stopped.
3. *(v.)* to move or cause to move suddenly upwards or forwards in a single motion उछलना The little lambs *spring* about in the field.

springy *(adj.)* स्प्रिंगई– possessing or characterized by resilience or bounce लोचदार, लचीला We were lying on the soft *springy* bed.

sprinkle *(v.)* स्प्रिंकल– to scatter (liquid, powder, etc.) in tiny particles or droplets over (something) (कम मात्रा में) छिड़कना, बुरकना Please *sprinkle* some salt on the salad.

sprint *(n.)* स्प्रिंट– 1. a fast finishing speed at the end of a longer race, as in running or cycling, etc. थोड़ी-सी तेज़ दौड़ We cheered when our friend won the *sprint*.
2. *(v.)* to go at top speed, as in running, cycling, etc. थोड़ी दूरी तक तेज़ दौड़ना *Sprint* along the road and catch the train.

sprout *(n.)* स्प्राउट– 1. a newly grown shoot or bud अंकुर, अँखुआ I had *sprouts* for breakfast.
2. *(v.)* (of a plant, seed, etc.) to produce (new leaves, shoots, etc.) पौधे का अंकुरित होना The seeds *sprouted* at the appropriate time.

spur *(n.)* स्पर– 1. anything serving to urge or encourage, motivation प्रेरणा The performer thought of a wonderful trick at the *spur* of the moment.
2. *(v.)* to goad or urge with or as if with spurs प्रेरित एवं प्रोत्साहित करना Hunger *spurred* the poor man to seek work.

spurt *(v.)* स्पर्ट– to gush or cause to gush forth in a sudden stream or jet निकल पड़ना Water *spurted* out of the broken pipe.

spy *(n.)* स्पाइ– a person employed by a state or institution to obtain secret information from rival countries, organizations, companies, etc. गुप्तचर Isn't it a dangerous thing to be a *spy*?

squabble *(v.)* स्क्वॉबल– 1. to quarrel over a small matter टंटा मचाना, तू-तू मैं-मैं करना Never *squabble* with your relations.
2. *(n.)* a petty quarrel छोटी-मोटी बात का झगड़ा, तू-तू मैं-मैं We never like to *squabble* about petty things.

squadron *(n.)* स्क्वॉड्रन– a subdivision of a naval fleet detached for a particular task सैनिक टुकड़ी The commander ordered his *squadron* to attack.

squall *(v.)* स्क्वॉल– 1. to cry loudly चीख़ मारना Don't *squall*, I shall not hurt you.

2. *(n.)* a sudden strong wind or brief turbulent storm तूफ़ान, अंधड़ The boat was overturned in a *squall.*

squander *(v.)* स्क्वॉण्डर– to spend wastefully or extravagantly; dissipate पैसा बरबाद करना She *squandered* a lot of money on shopping.

square *(n.)* स्क्वेअर्–1. plane geometric figure having four equal sides and four right angles चतुर्भुज, चतुष्कोण A *square* has four equal sides.

2. *(adj.)* fair and honest सच्चा, ईमानदार We give every customer a *square* deal.

3. complete and sufficient पूर्ण, संतोषजनक I could not have a *square* meal for a week.

4. *(v.)* to make into a square or similar shape चतुष्कोण बनाना *Square* the corners of this wood.

squash *(v.)* स्क्वॉश– 1. to press or squeeze or be pressed or squeezed in or down so as to crush, distort, or pulp कुचलकर भुरता बनाना She *squashed* the boiled tomatoes to make the soup.

2. *(n.)* a drink made from fruit juice or fruit syrup diluted with water फलों के रस से बना एक पेय, शरबत Please give me a chilled glass of orange *squash.*

squat *(v.)* स्क्वॉट– to rest in a crouching position with the knees bent and the weight on the feet उकड़ूं बैठना Monkeys were *squatting* on the tree.

squatter *(n.)* स्क्वॉटर– person who occupies property or land to which he has no legal title अनाधिकार ज़मीन पर कब्ज़ा जमा लेने वाला व्यक्ति Many *squatters* have settled in the government land.

squeak *(n.)* स्क्वीक– 1. a short shrill cry or high-pitched sound चूँ-चूँ, चीं-चीं की आवाज़ I heard a faint *squeak* from the bedroom.

2. *(v.)* to make or cause to make a squeak चूँ-चूँ करना, चरमराना The old stool *squeaked* as Ram climbed on it.

squeal *(v.)* स्क्वील– 1. to make a long or high sound चिल्लाना, किलकारी मारना The children *squealed* with joy when the dancing monkey entered the stage.

2. *(n.)* a high shrill yelp, as of pain चीख़, किलकारियाँ The children's *squeals* could be heard from a long distance.

squeeze *(v.)* स्क्वीज़–1. to grip or press firmly, esp so as to crush or distort; compress निचोड़ना *Squeeze* two lemons together in the glass.

2. to apply gentle pressure to, as in affection or reassurance दबाना Don't *squeeze* my hand.

squint *(n.)* स्क्विंट– 1. the act or an instance of squinting; glimpse भेंगापन She was born with a *squint.*

2. *(v.)* to cross or partly close (the eyes) अधखुली आंखों से देखना We *squinted* in the bright sunlight.

squirrel *(n.)* स्क्विरल– a small animal with a long bushy tail गिलहरी A *squirrel* lives in a tree. It has a long bushy tail.

stab *(v.)* स्टैब– 1. to pierce or injure with a sharp pointed instrument छुरा घोंपना A robber *stabbed* him in the neck.

2. *(n.)* the act or an instance of stabbing प्रहार, छुरा घोंपने से हुआ घाव There were two *stab* wounds on the body.

stability *(n.)* स्टेबिलिटी– the quality of being stable स्थिरता Ashok can provide financial *stability* to his family.

stabilize (ise) *(v.)* स्टेबलाइज़– to make or become stable or more stable स्थायी बनाना, मज़बूत होना The patient's condition was *stabilized* after the injection.

stable *(n.)* स्टेबल– 1. a building, usually consisting of stalls, for the lodging

of horses or other livestock घुड़साल, अस्तबल Jesus was born in a *stable*.
2. *(v.)* to put, keep, or be kept in a stable अस्तबल में रखना Can we *stable* our horses in this shed?
3. *(adj.)* steady in position or balance; firm अचल, स्थिर, टिकाऊ Was the provincial government not *stable*?

stack *(n.)* स्टैक– 1. a pile or heap ढेरी, अंबार Get the red book from the *stack*.
2. *(v.)* to place in a stack; pile ढेरी बनाना, चट्टा लगा देना *Stack* the books well on the shelf.

stadium *(n.)* स्टेडिअम– a sports arena with tiered seats for spectators मैदान, स्टेडियम We saw the hockey match in the National *Stadium*.

staff *(n.)* स्टॉफ़–1. a group of people employed by a company, individual, etc. for executive, clerical, sales work, etc. कर्मचारीगण Have you not recently joined the *staff* of this office?
2. a stick with some special use, such as a walking stick or an emblem of authority छड़ी The old man walked with the help of a long wooden *staff*.
3. *(v.)* to provide with a staff कर्मचारीगण रखना Our office is *staffed* by seven employees.

stag *(n.)* स्टैग– the adult male of a deer, esp a red deer हिरन, मृग The *stag* was caught by its horns in a thorny bush.

stage *(n.)* स्टेज–1. a raised area or platform मंच, पाड़ Would you like to go on the *stage*?
2. phase मंजिल, पड़ाव Her cancer is on the final *stage*.
3. *(v.)* to perform (a play), esp on a stage अभिनीत होना The play had been *staged*.

stagger *(v.)* स्टैगर्– 1. to astound or overwhelm, as with shock विचलित करना या होना I was simply *staggered* by the dance performance.
2. to walk or cause to walk unsteadily as if about to fall लड़खड़ाना He *staggered* as he got up suddenly.

stagnant *(adj.)* स्टैग्नन्ट– (of water, etc.) standing still; without flow or current स्थिर, निश्चल *Stagnant* water is a cause of various diseases.

stain *(n.)* स्टेन– 1. a dirty mark on sth धब्बा या दाग The ink fell and left a *stain* on the table.
2. *(v.)* to mark or discolour with patches of something that dirties दाग लगाना, धब्बा डालना Her fingers were *stained* with blue ink.

stainless steel *(n.)* स्टेन्लस स्टील– a type of steel resistant to corrosion as a result of the presence of large amounts of chromium ज़ंगरहीत स्टील She always uses a *stainless steel* pan for making tea.

stair *(n.)* स्टेअर्– one of a flight of stairs सीढ़ी, सोपान Is there a toilet at the top of the *stairs*?

staircase *(n.)* स्टेअर्केस– a flight of stairs, its supporting framework, and, usually, a handrail or banisters ज़ीना, सीढ़ी All the stairs together are called a *staircase*.

stake *(n.)* स्टेक– 1. the money or valuables that a player must hazard in order to buy into a gambling game or make a bet दाँव, बाज़ी If we lose this contract, we will lose our credibility. *Stakes* are very high.
2. *(v.)* to invest in or support by supplying with money, etc. दाँव पर लगाना Why are you *staking* your future by getting involved in this issue?

stale *(adj.)* स्टेल–1. (esp of food) hard, musty, or dry from being kept too long बासी The meal is *stale*. It is not fit to be eaten.
2. no longer new पुरानी ख़बर, नीरस, उबाऊ This joke is *stale*. There is nothing new or fresh about it.

stalk *(n.)* स्टॉक– 1. the main stem of a herbaceous plant डंठल This rose has a long *stalk.*
2. *(v.)* to follow or approach (game, prey, etc.) stealthily and quietly छिपकर पीछा करना Our party *stalked* the tiger in the jungle.

stall *(n.)* स्टॉल– 1. a compartment in a stable or shed for confining or feeding a single animal छोटी दुकान, स्टॉल Delhi station has many book*stalls.*
2. *(v.)* to cause (a motor vehicle or its engine) to stop, usually by incorrect use of the clutch or incorrect adjustment of the fuel mixture, or (of an engine or motor vehicle) to stop, usually for these reasons अचानक रुक जाना The engine of my car *stalled,* so I had to push the car to the side of the road.

stamina *(n.)* स्टैमिना– enduring energy, strength, and resilience दमख़ाम, (शारीरिक-मानसिक) शक्ति He can play cricket all day. He has a lot of *stamina.*

stammer *(v.)* स्टैमर्– 1. to speak or say (something) in a hesitant way, esp as a result of a speech disorder or through fear, stress, etc. अटक-अटक कर बोलना, तुतलाना, हकलाना When a man *stammers,* the listeners laugh.
2. *(n.)* a speech disorder characterized by involuntary repetitions and hesitations हकलाहट, तुतलाहट He speaks with a slight *stammer.*

stamp *(n.)* स्टैम्प–1. a printed paper label with a gummed back for attaching to mail as an official indication that the required postage has been paid डाक टिकट Some children like to collect postage *stamps.*
2. a tool for printing the date, etc. used for commercial or trading purposes मुहर Have you brought a rubber-*stamp* and an ink pad?
3. *(v.)* to distinguish or reveal सिद्ध करना This action *stamps* him as rogue.

stampede *(n.)* स्टैम्पीड– any sudden large-scale movement or other action, such as a rush of people to support a candidate भगदड़ A sudden explosion of bomb lead to *stampede* in the theatre.

stand *(n.)* स्टैण्ड–1. a place where a person or thing stands (बस या गाड़ी रुकने की जगह) अड्डा Where is the cycle-*stand?* I want to *stand* my bike.
2. *(v.)* to be or cause to be in an erect or upright position खड़ा होना Can you *stand* on your head?
3. to be or exist in a specified state or condition किसी विशेष अवस्था में खड़े होना Everyone *stood* up when the President came in.
4. to remain in force or continue in effect सहना I cannot *stand* all this noise.

➢ **stand aside**– to stand on a corner एक तरफ़ खड़े हो जाना, You should *stand aside* to let the people pass.

➢ **stand back**– to stand on the back side पीछे हटना, They told me to *stand back* from the pillar.

➢ **stand for**– to represent or mean किसी का संक्षिप्त रूप होना, What does WWF *stand for*?

➢ **stand out**– to be distinctive or conspicuous विशिष्ट होना, Four topics *stand out* as being more important than the rest.

➢ **stand up**– to rise to the feet सीधा खड़ा होना, Children *stood up* when the teacher entered in the class.

standard *(n.)* स्टैण्डर्ड– an accepted or approved example of something against which others are judged or measured स्तर, कोटि, मानदंड His work does not reach the required *standard.*

standard of living *(n.)* स्टैण्डर्ड ऑफ लिविंग a level of subsistence or material welfare of a community, class, or person जीवन स्तर The *standard of living* in the villages is very low.

standby *(n.)* स्टैण्डबाइ– something that is useful or reliable when needed स्थानापन्न, ज़रूरत के समय मौजूद होना An ambulance was on *standby* outside the gate of a hospital.

standing *(n.)* स्टैनडिंग– social or financial position, status, or reputation प्रतिष्ठा, हैसियत What is the *standing* position of his property?

standpoint *(n.)* स्टैण्डपॉइन्ट– a physical or mental position from which things are viewed दृष्टिकोण His *standpoint* is totally different from me.

standstill *(n.)* स्टैण्ड्स्टिल– a complete cessation of movement; stop; halt ठहराव The economy of the country came to a *standstill* after the war.

stanza *(n.)* स्टैण्ज़ा– a fixed number of verse lines arranged in a definite metrical pattern, forming a unit of a poem छंद Do you remember the second *stanza* of the song?

staple *(v.)* स्टेपल– to secure (papers, wire, etc.) with a staple or staples कागज़ों को बांधना या जोड़ना You have to *staple* the zerox copy of your identity card to the application form.

star *(n.)* स्टार्– any of a vast number of celestial objects that are visible in the clear night sky as points of light सितारा, तारा *Stars* twinkle at night.

starch *(n.)* स्टार्च– 1. a white substance found in rice, potatoes etc. used for making clothes, etc. मांड, कलफ़ *Starch* is an important part of our diet. 2. *(v.)* to stiffen with or soak in starch कलफ़ देना *Starch* the collar of this shirt. That will keep its shape better.

stardom *(n.)* स्टार्डम– the fame and prestige of being a star in films, sport, etc. प्रसिद्धि She reached international *stardom* in a Karan Johar film.

stare *(v.)* स्टेअर्– 1. to look or gaze fixedly, often with hostility or rudeness आँखें फाड़कर देखना, ताकना I *stared* with surprise at the strange snake.
2. *(n.)* the act or an instance of staring टकटकी, ताक It was difficult to face his angry *stare.*

stark *(adj.)* स्टार्क– devoid of any elaboration; blunt कठोर और अनिवार्य The book explores the *stark* realities of life.

starry *(adj.)* स्टारी– (of the sky) filled, covered with, or illuminated by stars तारों से भरा हुआ The sky was *starry,* and there was no moon.

start *(v.)* स्टार्ट– 1. to begin or cause to begin (something or to do something); come or cause to come into being, operation, etc. आरंभ करना We must *start* our work today.
2. *(n.)* the first or first part of a series of actions or operations, a journey, etc. शुरुआत, आरंभ करने की प्रक्रिया Remember to take your medicine before making a *start* in the morning.

starting point *(n.)* स्टार्टिंग पॉइंट– the place from which you start आरंभ-बिंदु या स्थान I think this should be the *starting point* of our journey.

startle *(v.)* स्टार्टल– to be or cause to be surprised or frightened, esp so as to start involuntarily चौंकना या चौंकाना We were *startled* to see him in this state.

starvation *(n.)* स्टार्वेशन– the act or an instance of starving or state of being starved भुखमरी Many died of *starvation* during the floods last year.

starve *(v.)* स्टार्व– to die or cause to die from lack of food भूखों मरना It is a sin to waste food when a large number of people are *starving* in our country.

state *(n.)* स्टेट–1. a sovereign political power or community राज्य, सरकार India is divided into many *states.*
2. any mode of existence दशा The house was in a poor *state.*
3. *(v.)* to articulate in words; utter प्रकट करना It is *stated* that all people injured in the accident are safe.

statement *(n.)* स्टेट्मेंट– something that is stated, esp a formal prepared announcement or reply कथन, वक्तव्य The prisoner's *statement* was found to be a false one.

static *(adj.)* स्टैटिक– not active or moving; stationary स्थिर, अपरिवर्तनशील Prices on the stock market can never be *static.*

station *(n.)* स्टेशन–1. a place along a route or line at which a bus, train, etc. stops for fuel or to pick up or let off passengers or goods, esp one with ancillary buildings and services केन्द्र, स्थान, ठिकाना, स्टेशन All workers should remain at their *stations* for the next twenty-four hours.
2. *(v.)* to place in or assign to a station ठहराना, तैनात करना The soldiers were *stationed* to Solan.

stationary *(adj.)* स्टेशनरी– not moving; standing still स्थिर, अचल I don't know how you'll manage to drive into a *stationary* vehicle.

stationer *(n.)* स्टेशनर्– a person who sells stationery or a shop where stationery is sold लेखन-सामग्री-विक्रेता My uncle is a well-known *stationer.*

stationery *(n.)* स्टेशनरि– any writing materials, such as paper, envelopes, pens, ink, rulers, etc. लेखन-सामग्री Our address must be printed on all our *stationery.*

statistics *(n.)* स्टटिसटिक्स– quantitative data on any subject, esp data comparing the distribution of some quantity for different subclasses of the population आँकड़े We check the growth of population with the help of *statistics.*

statuary *(n.)* स्टैचूअरी– statues collectively मूर्ति-संग्रह The *statuary* in this museum is remarkable.

statue *(n.)* स्टैचू– a wooden, stone, metal, plaster, or other kind of sculpture of a human or animal figure, usually life-size or larger बुत, मूर्ति, प्रतिमा The *statue* of Mahatma Gandhi, the Father of Nation, stands in the middle of the municipal park.

stature *(n.)* स्टैचर्– the height of something, esp a person or animal when standing क़द, लंबाई His physical *stature* makes him a remarkable man.

status *(n.)* स्टेटस–1. a social or professional position, condition, or standing to which varying degrees of responsibility, privilege, and esteem are attached स्थिति, महत्त्व Please mention your marital *status* here.
2. a high position or standing; prestige प्रतिष्ठा The job offered him good *status* apart from a good salary.

status symbol *(n.)* स्टेटस सिम्बल– a possession which is regarded as proof of the owner's social position, wealth, prestige, etc. प्रतिष्ठा का प्रतीक Imported cars are the latest *status symbol* of modern times.

statutory *(n.)* स्टैचटरि– subject to a punishment or penalty prescribed by statute वैधानिक, क़ानूनी There was a *statutory* warning to hoarders

staunch (adj.) स्टाँच– loyal, firm, and dependable स्वामिभक्त, निष्ठावान, पक्का He is a *staunch* follower of Buddhism.

stay *(v.)* स्टे– 1. to continue or remain in a certain place, position, etc.

ठहरना, रुकना The train does not *stay* for long at the station.

2. *(n.)* the act of staying or sojourning in a place or the period during which one stays ठहराव, निवास I had a pleasant *stay* in Ooty last summer.

steadfast *(adj.)* स्टेडफ़ास्ट– (esp of a person's gaze) fixed in intensity or direction; steady अटल, निश्चयबद्ध Karan remained *steadfast* in his mission to bring the criminals to the police station.

steadily *(adv.)* स्टेडिलि– regularly नियमित गति से, निरंतर, अनवरत I work *steadily* all day.

steady *(adj.)* स्टेडी– not able to be moved or disturbed easily; stable स्थिर, स्थायी, अटल Slow and *steady* wins the race.

steal *(v.)* स्टील– to take (something) from someone, etc. without permission or unlawfully, esp in a secret manner चुराना, चोरी करना Our maid-servant *stole* some money from my mother's purse.

stealth *(n.)* स्टेल्थ– the act or characteristic of moving with extreme care and quietness, esp so as to avoid detection छिपाव, दुराव Amit took away Anuj's calculator by *stealth.*

stealthily *(adv.)* स्टेलथिली– very quietly, so as to escape detection गुप्त ढंग से, चोरी से, चुपके से He entered in the kitchen *stealthily.*

steam *(n.)* स्टीम– 1. the gas or vapour into which water is changed when boiled भाप, वाष्प Some engines are driven by *steam.*

2. *(v.)* to emit or be emitted as steam धीरे-धीरे भाप निकालना I like to watch the trains *steam* out of the station.

steel *(n.)* स्टील– any of various alloys based on iron containing carbon and often small quantities of other elements such as phosphorus, sulphur, manganese, chromium, and nickel. इस्पात, फौलाद The cap of my fountain pen is made of *steel.*

steep *(adj.)* स्टीप– having or being a slope or gradient approaching the perpendicular खड़ी (चट्टान, ढलान) The hill is very *steep.* It is almost straight up.

steer *(v.)* स्टीअर्– to direct the course of (a vehicle or vessel) with a steering wheel, rudder, etc. परिचालन करना, चलाना The seamen *steered* east in the hope of finding land.

steering *(adj.)* स्टिअरिंग– the mechanical parts that make it possible to steer a car स्टिअरिंग, चालन-चक्का Please tighten the *steering*-wheel of the car.

stem *(n.)* स्टे'म– 1. the main axis of a plant, which bears the leaves, axillary buds, and flowers and contains a hollow cylinder of vascular tissue तना This tree has a very big *stem.*

2. *(v.)* to make headway against (a tide, wind, etc.) रोकना We should try to *stem* the flood by putting down sandbags.

stench *(n.)* स्टेंच– a strong and extremely offensive odour; stink दुर्गंध, बदबू The rotten eggs left an unbearable *stench.*

step *(n.)* स्टे'प–1. the act of motion brought about by raising the foot and setting it down again in coordination with the transference of the weight of the body कदम, पग The baby moved towards the mother with small *steps.*

2. one of a sequence of separate consecutive stages in the progression towards some goal प्रक्रिया का चरण The discovery of radium was a great *step* forward in the science of healing.

3. *(v.)* to move by raising the foot and then setting it down in a different position, transferring the weight of the body to this foot and

repeating the process with the other foot क़दम रखना We should *step* out together.

4. *(adj.)* indicating relationship through the previous marriage of a spouse or parent rather than by blood सौतेला (सौतेली) Lila is Renu's *step*-mother. Renu is the *step*-daughter of Lila.

➢ **step by step** *(n.)*– with care and deliberation; gradually एक-एक करके, He was giving *step by step* instructions.

stereo *(n.)* स्टेरिओ– a stereophonic record player, tape recorder, etc. स्टीरियो सिस्टम, दो स्पीकरों वाला यंत्र The *stereo* in my car is not working properly.

stereotype *(n.)* स्टेरिअटाइप्– 1. a set of inaccurate, simplistic generalizations about a group that allows others to categorize them and treat them accordingly घिसा-पिटा रूप The women have broken the *stereotype* of being the housewives.

2. *(v.)* to make a stereotype of घिसा-पिटा रूप देना, पुराने सांचे में ढालना Serials *stereotype* the relationship between a mother-in-law and a daughter-in-law.

sterile *(adj.)* स्टेराइल– unable to produce offspring; infertile बाँझ, वन्ध्या She can never give birth to a baby because she is a *sterile* woman.

sterilize (ise) *(v.)* स्टरलाइज़्– to render sterile; make infertile or barren जीवाणुरहित बनाना, बाँझ बनाना The doctors should always *sterilize* their surgical instruments.

stern *(adj.)* स्टर्न–1. showing uncompromising or inflexible resolve; firm, strict, or authoritarian कठोर, निर्दयी The Principal of our college was very *stern.*

2. having an austere or forbidding appearance or nature अनुशासनप्रिय, सख्त Soldiers follow *stern* discipline.

sternly *(adv.)* स्टर्नली– firmly or strictly सख़्ती के साथ The captain *sternly* ordered the soldiers to fight the enemy.

stew *(v.)* स्ट्यू– 1. to cook or cause to cook by long slow simmering सिझाना, सीझना I'll *stew* some vegetables for dinner.

2. *(n.)* a dish of meat, fish, or other food, cooked by stewing दमपुख्त I had some *stew* for dinner.

steward *(n.)* स्ट्यूअर्ड– a person who administers the property, house, finances, etc. of another प्रबंधक, कारिन्दा After the death of her father, Alka made her uncle the *steward* of her property.

stick *(v.)* स्टिक–1. to fasten or be fastened by or as if by an adhesive substance लगाना, चिपकाना Did you *stick* the stamp to the envelope?

2. to pierce or stab with or as if with something pointed चुभाना Don't *stick* a fork into the fruit.

3. *(n.)* any long thin piece of wood छड़ी My old grandfather uses a walking-*stick.*

➢ **stick in** *(v.)* in a difficult position अटक जाना, My car was *stuck in* the mud.

sticker *(n.)* स्टिकर– an adhesive label, poster, or paper चिपकने वाला चित्र She covered her cupboard with colourful *stickers.*

sticky *(adj.)* स्टिकी– covered or daubed with an adhesive or viscous substance चिपकने वाला पदार्थ There was a *sticky* substance lying on the floor.

stiff *(adj.)* स्टिफ़–1. not easily bent; rigid; inflexible कठोर, कड़ा You have a *stiff* manner. You are not a good friend.

stifle *(v.)* स्टाइफ़ल– to feel or cause to feel discomfort and difficulty in breathing दम घोंटना I was almost *stifled* by the stale air in the room.

stigma *(n.)* स्टिगमा– a distinguishing mark of social disgrace कलंक There is still a social *stigma* attached to single women.

stile *(n.)* स्टाइल– a set of steps or rungs in a wall or fence to allow people, but not animals, to pass over सीढ़ी, ज़ीना Help the old man over the *stile.*

still *(adv.)* स्टिल– 1. continuing now or in the future as in the past अब भी Vagish is *still* sitting. He has not moved up till now.
2. *(adj.)* motionless; stationary स्थिर *Still* waters run deep.

stimulate *(v.)* स्टिमुलेट– to fill (a person) with ideas or enthusiasm प्रेरित करना, प्रेरणा देना Jai Prakash Narayan's kind words *stimulated* the dacoits and smugglers to give up their bad ways of living.

sting *(n.)* स्टिंग– 1. sharp pointed part of an insect or creature डंक A wasp can hurt us with its *sting.*
2. *(v.)* (of certain animals and plants) to inflict a wound on (an organism) by the injection of poison डंक मारना A bee *stung* me in my face.

stingy *(adj.)* स्टिंजी– unwilling to spend or give कंजूस, मक्खीचूस Some people are quite *stingy* in their ways.

stink *(v.)* स्टिंक– to emit a foul smell बदबू मारना His clothes were *stinking.*

stipend *(n.)* स्टाइपेण्ड– a fixed or regular amount of money paid as a salary or allowance वृत्ति, वज़ीफ़ा He was getting a *stipend* of Rs. 2000 while working as an intern.

stir *(v.)* स्टर्–1. to move an implement such as a spoon around in (a liquid) so as to mix up the constituents हिलना-डुलना Nobody *stirred* when a dacoit came into the house.
2. to mix briskly or vigorously मिलाना, चम्मच से चलाना या हिलाना *Stir* the solution.

stitch *(n.)* स्टिच– 1. a link made by drawing a thread through material by means of a needle टाँका A *stitch* in time saves nine.
2. *(v.)* to sew, fasten, etc. with stitches सीना, टाँकना The tailor *stitches* the shirt.

stock *(v.)* स्टॉक– 1. to keep (goods) for sale संचय करना, संग्रह करना Do you *stock* toothpaste and toothbrushes?
2. *(n.)* the total goods or raw material kept on the premises of a shop or business भंडार, संग्रह, बिक्री का माल We are sorry we have no grain in our *stock.*

stock exchange *(n.)* a highly organized market facilitating the purchase and sale of securities and operated by professional stockbrokers and market makers according to fixed rules शेयर बाज़ार The Mumbai Stock Exchange is Asia's oldest *stock exchange.*

stocking *(n.)* स्टॉकिंग– one of a pair of close-fitting garments made of knitted yarn to cover the foot and part or all of the leg मोज़ा, जुर्राब The policeman wears a pair of black *stockings.*

stoic *(adj.)* स्टोइक– a person who maintains stoical qualities शांत एवं गंभीर, उदास While others were quite broken by the tragedy, her *stoic* appearance was appreciated by all.

stoke *(v.)* स्टोक– to feed, stir, and tend (a fire, furnace, etc.) कोयला झोंकना, आग भड़काना The man was *stoking* up a fire with more coal.

stomach *(n.)* स्टॅमक– (in vertebrates) the enlarged muscular saclike part of the alimentary canal in which food is stored until it has been partially digested and rendered into chyme आमाशय, उदर, पेट The patient had a weak *stomach* and could not digest solid food.

stomach ache *(n.)* स्टॅमक एक– pain in the stomach or abdominal region, as from acute indigestion पेट का दर्द,

उदरशूल If we eat food so quickly, we shall get *stomach ache.*

stone *(v.)* स्टोन– 1. to throw stones at, esp to kill पत्थर मारना The rioters *stoned* the speaker in the public meeting. 2. *(n.)* the hard compact nonmetallic material of which rocks are made पत्थर There was a heap of *stones* on the ground.

stone-hearted *(adj.)* स्टोनहार्टेड– unfeeling; hardhearted पत्थर दिल इंसान, निर्दयी Ganesh is a *stone-hearted* man.

stonemason *(n.)* स्टोनमेसन– a person who is skilled in preparing stone for building संगतराश The *stonemasons* in the middle ages had great importance.

stony *(adj.)* स्टोनी– of or resembling stone पथरीला It was difficult to walk for the pedestrians on the *stony* road.

stool *(n.)* स्टूल–1. a backless seat or footrest consisting of a small flat piece of wood, etc. resting on three or four legs, a pedestal, etc. बिना पीठ की कुर्सी, स्टूल She sat on the four-legged *stool.*

2. waste matter evacuated from the bowels पाखाना, मल The doctor examined the report of the urine and *stool* of thc patient.

stop *(v.)* स्टॉप–1. to cease from doing or being (something); discontinue किसी क्रिया, गाड़ी आदि को रोकना Usually we *stop* our work at 5.30 p.m.

2. to prevent the continuance or completion of बंद करना Please *stop* talking now.

3. *(n.)* a place where something halts or pauses गाड़ी आदि के रुकने की जगह Where is the bus-*stop*?

stopover *(n.)* स्टॉपओवर– a stopping place on a journey पड़ाव Sameer had a two days *stopover* in Delhi on his way to Finland.

stoppage *(n.)* स्टॉपिज– something that stops or blocks रुकावट, बाधा There was a two days *stoppage* in production because of the strike.

storage *(n.)* स्टोरज– space or area reserved for storing भंडार-गृह, संचयन The upper room of the house is being used for *storage.*

store *(n.)* स्टॉर–1. a large supply or stock kept for future use भंडार, गोदाम We have a lot of goods in *store* for the bad weather.

2. a large amount or quantity संचय Have you a good *store* of hay for your cow?

3. a storage place such as a warehouse or depository घर के सामान की जगह We put our broken pieces of furniture in our *store.*

4. *(v.)* to keep, set aside, or accumulate for future use संग्रह करना Never *store* more than you need.

storey *(n.)* स्टॉरी– a floor or level of a building तल्ला, मंज़िल In large cities, some buildings have more than twenty *storeys.*

stork *(n.)* स्टॉर्क– a large black and white bird with long legs, beak and neck that lives near water लकलक, सारस A *stork* is a large bird that usually lives near pools.

storm *(n.)* स्टॉर्म– 1. a violent weather condition of strong winds, rain, hail, thunder, lightning, blowing sand, snow, etc. आँधी The *storm* raged all day. 2. *(v.)* to attack or capture (something) suddenly and violently हमला करना The army was ordered to *storm* the town at midnight.

stormy *(adj.)* स्टार्मी– with strong winds, heavy rain or snow तूफ़ानी We postponed our programme because of the *stormy* weather.

story *(n.)* स्टॉरी–1. a narration of a chain of events told or written in prose or verse कथा, कहानी The old man told us the *story* of his journeys.

2. an account of past events अतीत की घटनाओं का वर्णन Would you tell me the *story* of your life?

stout *(adj.)* स्टाउट– solidly built or corpulent हृष्ट-पुष्ट Vivek looks *stout* but he lacks stamina. Rakesh has a *stout* body.

stove *(n.)* स्टोव– any heating apparatus, such as a kiln चूल्हा She uses the gas *stove* to cook food.

straddle *(v.)* स्ट्रेडल– to have one leg, part, or support on each side of दोनों ओर टाँगें फैलाकर बैठना She *straddles* her legs on the bench.

straggle *(v.)* स्ट्रैगल– 1. to go, come, or spread in a rambling or irregular way; stray बिछड़ जाना, अलग हो जाना After completing education I *straggled* from my group.

2. to linger behind or wander from a main line or part भटक जाना Aman *straggled* behind, carrying the shopping bags.

straight *(adv.)* स्ट्रेट– 1. not curved or crooked; continuing in the same direction without deviating सीधे This road goes *straight* to Rohtak.

2. *(adj.)* straightforward, outright, or candid सीधा-सच्चा, बिना मोड़े-तोड़े, सरल I want a *straight* answer from you.

straightforward *(adj.)* स्ट्रेट-फ़ावर्ड– (of a person) honest, frank, or simple ईमानदारी से, सरल ढंग से Tell us the story in a *straightforward* way.

strain *(v.)* स्ट्रेन– 1. to draw or be drawn taut; stretch tight पूरी शक्ति लगाकर सुनना, देखना आदि They *strained* their ears to hear what the speaker was saying.

2. *(n.)* an intense physical or mental effort दबाव, तनाव In the fast life of metropolitan cities, people work under great *strain.*

strained *(adj.)* स्ट्रैण्ड– (of an atmosphere, relationship, etc.) not relaxed; tense तनावपूर्ण Akash looks tired and *strained* today.

strainer *(n.)* स्ट्रेनर– a sieve used for straining sauces, vegetables, tea, etc. छलनी, चलनी, छन्ना We use *strainer* to put the tea in the cup.

straits *(n.)* स्ट्रेट्स– very difficult situation, esp because of lack of money तंगी, संकट We were in dire *straits* when we lost all our money.

stranded *(adj.)* स्ट्रैनडिड– left helpless, as without transport असहाय, मुसीबत में He left her *stranded* on the way.

strange *(adj.)* स्ट्रेंज–1. odd, unusual, or extraordinary in appearance, effect, manner, etc.; peculiar आश्चर्य (की बात) It is *strange* that he is not here. He always comes at this time.

2. not known, seen, or experienced before; unfamiliar अपरिचित The new boy is still *strange* to the school.

3. not easily explained अजीब, विचित्र This handwriting is *strange* to me. I don't know who has written this.

strangely *(adv.)* स्ट्रेंजलि– oddly or peculiarly अजीब ढंग से She behaved *strangely.*

stranger *(n.)* स्ट्रेंजर– any person whom one does not know अजनबी, अपरिचित He was a *stranger* to me but I trusted him.

strangle *(v.)* स्ट्रैंगल– to kill by compressing the windpipe; throttle गला घोंटकर मारना The victim was *strangled* to death.

strap *(v.)* स्ट्रैप– to fasten sth, using a strap or straps फ़ीता बाँधना *Strap* the two packets together. I want to carry them in one hand.

strategy *(n.)* स्ट्रैटजी– the art or science of the planning and conduct of a war; generalship रणनीति What will be our new marketing *strategy*?

straw *(n.)* स्ट्रॉ–1. stalks of threshed grain, esp of wheat, rye, oats, or barley, used in plaiting hats, baskets, etc. or as fodder तिनका, तृण *Straw* is used for making mats.

2. a long thin hollow paper or plastic tube or stem of a plant, used for sucking up liquids into the mouth ठंडा पीने का पाइप Bring me a *straw* to drink Coca Cola.

strawberry *(n.)* स्ट्रॉबरि– a red fruit with small yellow seeds स्ट्रॉबेरी *Strawberries* contain a broad range of beneficial nutrients, including vitamin C, folate and fiber.

stray *(adj.)* स्ट्रे– 1. scattered, random, or haphazard आवारा, भटका हुआ *Stray* animals are causing serious traffic problems these days.

2. *(v.)* to wander away, as from the correct path or from a given area आवारा भटकना We *strayed* from the road and lost our way.

streak *(n.)* स्ट्रीक– 1. a long thin mark, stripe, or trace of some contrasting colour धारी A *streak* of lightning flashed in the dark sky.

2. *(v.)* to move rapidly in a straight line तेज़ी से चलना The racing cars were *streaking* on the track.

streaked *(adj.)* स्ट्रीक्ड– marked or daubed with (something) अलग-अलग रंग की, धारीदार Stella has brown hair *streaked* with golden colour.

stream *(n.)* स्ट्रीम–1. any of several parallel classes of schoolchildren, or divisions of children within a class, grouped together because of similar ability ताँता अर्थात् भीड़ I saw a *stream* of people coming out of the cinema house.

2. a small river; brook झरना Hundreds of *streams* flow down the Himalayas.

3. *(v.)* to emit or be emitted in a continuous flow (धारा) बहना Tears *streamed* down his cheeks.

streamline *(v.)* स्ट्रीमलाइन– to make streamlined आधुनिक तरीक़े से सरल एवं उपयोगी बनाना We must *streamline* the production procedure of our company.

street *(n.)* स्ट्रीट– name a public road that is usually lined with buildings, esp in a town सड़क, गली Take care when you cross the *street.*

strength *(n.)* स्ट्रै'न्थ–1. the state or quality of being physically or mentally strong शक्ति, ताक़त I have no *strength* to lift this heavy load.

2. the ability to withstand or exert great force, stress, or pressure. एक परिमित सैन्य संख्या, सैनिक शक्ति We equalled the enemy in *strength.*

strengthen *(v.)* स्ट्रैंगथॅन– to make or become stronger बलशाली बनाना, ताक़त बढ़ाना Yoga exercises can *strengthen* your knees and legs.

strenuous *(adj.)* स्ट्रैन्युअस– requiring or involving the use of great energy or effort श्रमसाध्य Preparing the database of all the customers was a *strenuous* job.

stress *(n.)* स्ट्रे'स–1. mental, emotional, or physical strain or tension दबाव, बोझ, भार, बल Can you bear the *stress* of working late?

2. special emphasis or significance attached to something विशेष बल या ध्यान In prayer, we lay *stress* on making a relation with the God.

3. *(v.)* to give emphasis or prominence to ज़ोर देना, दबाव डालना Father *stressed* the need for special care.

stressful *(adj.)* स्ट्रेसफुल– causing stress चिंता एवं दबाव डालने वाला Seema is doing such a *stressful* job.

stretch *(n.)* स्ट्रे'च– 1. extent in time, length, area, etc. विस्तार, फैलाव Can you work for six hours at a *stretch*?

2. *(v.)* to draw out or extend or be drawn out or extended in length, area, etc. फैलाना *Stretch* your arms full length.

stretcher *(n.)* स्ट्रे'चर्– a device for transporting the ill, wounded, or dead, consisting of a frame covered by canvas or other material रोगी को उठाकर लाने का पटरा, स्ट्रेचर The patient was carried on a *stretcher.*

strict *(adj.)* स्ट्रिक्ट– adhering closely to specified rules, ordinances, etc. अनुशासनप्रिय, कठोर His father is very *strict* with his children.

strictly *(adv.)* स्ट्रिक्टली– stringently; rigorously कठोरतापूर्वक Kamal *strictly* deals with her.

stride *(v.)* स्ट्राइड– 1. to walk with long regular or measured paces, as in haste, etc. लंबे-लंबे डग भरना He *strode* out of the room.

2. *(n.)* a long step or pace लंबे कदम She crossed the road in three long *strides.*

strident *(adj.)* स्ट्राइडण्ट– (of a shout, voice, etc.) having or making a loud or harsh sound कर्णभेदी, तीक्ष्ण Western music is always *strident* to my mother's ears.

strife *(n.)* स्ट्राइफ़– angry or violent struggle; conflict विवाद, झगड़ा The *strife* between the two parties ended after the election.

strike *(v.)* स्ट्राइक–1. to deliver (a blow or stroke) to (a person) बजाना When the clock *struck* five, the office was closed.

2. to come or cause to come into sudden or violent contact (with) टकराना The ship *struck* a large rock.

3. to make an attack on मारना The naughty boy *struck* the donkey with a stick.

4. *(n.)* an act or instance of striking, a cessation of work by workers in a factory, industry, etc. as a protest against working conditions or low pay हड़ताल The mill workers are on *strike* these days.

striking *(adj.)* स्ट्राइकिंग– attracting attention; fine; impressive उल्लेखनीय, बहुत स्पष्ट There is a *striking* resemblance between the two sisters.

string *(n.)* स्ट्रिंग–1. a thin length of cord, twine, fibre, or similar material used for tying, hanging, binding, etc. धागा, सुतली I need a *string* to make a garland of flowers.

2. a group of objects threaded on a single strand वस्तुओं या व्यक्तियों की पंक्ति, कतार A *string* of people waited in front of the ration shop.

strip *(v.)* स्ट्रिप–1. to denude or empty completely एकदम खाली करना The bungalow was *stripped* of everything of value by the robbers.

2. to take or pull (the covering, clothes, etc.) off (oneself, another person, or thing) कपड़े उतारना, नंगा होना The men *stripped* of their clothes and dived into the river.

strive *(v.)* स्ट्राइव– to make a great and tenacious effort प्रयास करना I *strove* hard to reach the peak of the mountain.

stroke *(n.)* स्ट्रोक–1. the act or an instance of striking; a blow, knock, or hit प्रहार, आघात The cat killed a number of mice in a single *stroke.*

2. a sudden action, movement, or occurrence क्रिकेट या गोल्फ़ में मार The batsman made a good *stroke* at the ball.

3. *(v.)* to touch, brush, or caress lightly or gently सहलाना She *stroked* her pet dog affectionately as it sat in her lap.

stroll *(v.)* स्ट्रोल– 1. to walk about in a leisurely manner चहलक़दमी/मटरगश्ती करना We were *strolling* in the garden when you saw us.

2. *(n.)* a leisurely walk सैर, टहल We went out for a *stroll* in the garden.

strong *(adj.)* स्ट्राँग–1. involving or possessing physical or mental strength बलिष्ठ, ताक़तवर The king sent a *strong* army to fight against the enemy.

2. intense in quality; not faint or feeble हृष्ट-पुष्ट Rakesh is very *strong.* He can carry a heavy load.

3. solid or robust in construction; not easily broken or injured पुख़्ता, पक्का This fence is *strong* enough to keep out the animals.

4. containing or having a specified number कड़ा, तेज़ Don't you like *strong* tea?

strongly *(adv.)* स्ट्राँगली– solidly or robustly ज़ोर से The principal *strongly* delivered the speech.

strong-smelling *(n.)* स्ट्राँग-स्मैलिंग– with strong ordour तेज़ गंध This is a very *strong-smelling* perfume.

strong-minded *(adj.)* स्ट्राँग-माइन्डड– having strength of mind; firm, resolute, and determined दृढ़निश्चयी I have never seen such a *strong-minded* lady.

structure *(n.)* स्ट्रॅक्चर्–1. a complex construction or entity ढाँचा (भवन आदि का) This *structure* cost me five lakhs nine thousand rupees.

2. the way in which a mineral, rock, rock mass or stratum, etc. is made up of its component parts बनावट This cinema has a weak *structure.*

struggle *(v.)* स्ट्रॅगल– 1. to exert strength, energy, and force; work or strive संघर्ष करना The people *struggled* to get out of the burning house.

2. *(n.)* a fight or battle संघर्ष, लड़ाई You will be able to beat off your attackers after a hand-to-hand *struggle.*

stubble *(n.)* स्टॅबल– the stubs of stalks left in a field where a crop has been cut and harvested ठूँठ, ठूँठी He looks *stubbles* in a field.

stubborn *(adj.)* स्टॅबर्न– refusing to comply, agree, or give in; obstinate अड़ियल, ज़िद्दी, हठी, अटल I see that you are too *stubborn* to change your mind.

stubbornly *(adv.)* स्टॅबर्नली– in such a way as to refuse to comply, agree, or give in; obstinately हठधर्मी से He refused to move from that place *stubbornly.*

stuck *(adj.)* स्टक– to come or cause to come to a standstill अटका हुआ, रुका हुआ My father was *stuck* in traffic for many hours.

student *(n.)* स्टूयूडण्ट– a person following a course of study, as in a school, college, university, etc. छात्र, विद्यार्थी Sanjana is a brilliant *student* of her class.

studio *(n.)* स्टूडिओ– a room in which an artist, photographer, or musician works कार्यशाला, स्टूडियो It was a recording *studio* which was sound-proof.

studious *(adj.)* स्टूडिअस– of a serious, thoughtful, and hard-working character अध्ययनशील Ten out of forty students are *studious* in a class of government school.

study *(v.)* स्टॅडि– 1. to apply the mind to the learning or understanding of (a subject), esp by reading अध्ययन करना We *studied* the case very carefully and made a report.

2. *(n.)* the act or process of studying अध्ययन, पढ़ाई Your *study* of marine life has enabled you to know much about their habits.

3. a room used for studying, reading, writing, etc. अध्ययन-कक्ष The late Prime Minister Nehru's *study* had bookcases on every wall.

stuff *(n.)* स्टॅफ़–1. any general or unspecified substance or accumulation of objects सामान, माल You have a lot of *stuff* in your house that must be thrown away.

2. any thing, material चीज़, सामान What sort of *stuff* do you put in the cushions?

3. *(v.)* to pack or fill completely; cram (रद्दी माल) ठूँसना She *stuffed* her doll with rags.

stuffed *(adj.)* स्टफ्ड– filled with something, esp (of poultry and other food) filled with stuffing भरा हुआ In the museum, we can see *stuffed* animals which almost look alive.

stumble *(v.)* स्टम्बल–1. to trip or fall while walking or running लड़खड़ाना The old beggar *stumbled* while crossing the road.
2. to come (across) by accident संयोग से पता लगना At last, we *stumbled* on the explanation.

stump *(n.)* स्टम्प–1. the base part of a tree trunk left standing after the tree has been felled or has fallen ठूँठ We sat on a tree-*stump* to rest.
2. the part of something, किसी वस्तु का टुकड़ा I took the *stump* of pencil and wrote down her address.

stun *(v.)* स्टन– to surprise or shock sb so much that he cannot think or speak हक्का-बक्का/स्तब्ध करना The old man was *stunned* when he learnt of his only son's death.

stunning *(adj.)* स्टनिंग– very attractive, impressive, astonishing, etc. अत्यंत आकर्षक, मुग्धकारी What a *stunning* beauty she is!

stunt *(n.)* स्टण्ट–1. the act or an instance of stunting करतब, कलाबाज़ी The actor performs all his *stunts* himself.
2. an acrobatic, dangerous, or spectacular action इश्तहारबाज़ी The whole affair was merely a publicity *stunt*.
3. *(v.)* to prevent or impede the growth or development of (a plant, animal, etc.) विकसित होने से रोक देना Irregular rains *stunted* the growth of plants.

stupid *(adj.)* स्ट्युपिड– lacking in common sense, perception, or normal intelligence मूर्ख, बेवकूफ़ Only a *stupid* person walks in the middle of a road.

stupidity *(n.)* स्टयुपिडिटी– a stupid act, remark, etc. मूर्खता I am ashamed of my *stupidity*.

stupidly *(adv.)* स्टयुपिडलि– in a way that is lacking in common sense, perception, or normal intelligence मूर्खता से The servant behaved very *stupidly* infront of the guests.

sturdy *(adj.)* स्टर्डी– healthy, strong, and vigorous तगड़ा, मज़बूत Don't worry, you are quite *sturdy* and will soon recover from measles.

style *(n.)* स्टाइल– a form of appearance, design, or production; type or make शैली, ढंग, रीति, तरीका I did not like your *style* of dress.

stylish *(adj.)* स्टाइलिश– having style; smart; fashionable फ़ैशन के अनुसार, आकर्षक Vagish has bought a *stylish* pair of shoes.

suave *(adj.)* स्वाव– (esp of a man) displaying smoothness and sophistication in manner or attitude; urbane आत्मविश्वासी और शिष्ट Her performance was *suave* as always.

subconscious *(adj.)* सबकॉनशस– acting or existing without one's awareness अवचेतन The memories are lying in my *subconscious* mind.

subcontinent *(n.)* सबकॉनटिनन्ट– a large land mass that is a distinct part of a continent, such as India is of Asia उपमहाद्वीप Bangladesh, Pakistan and Sri Lanka are Indian *subcontinents*.

subdivide *(v.)* सबडिवाइड– to divide (something) resulting from an earlier division उपविभाजन करना, हिस्सों में बांटना India is *subdivided* into twenty eight states and seven union territories.

subdue *(v.)* सबड्यू–1. to establish ascendancy over by force, to defeat हराना, विजय प्राप्त करना We shall fight our enemies until we *subdue* them.

2. to overcome and bring under control, as by intimidation or persuasion शांत करना The baby's cries gradually *subdued.*

subject *(n.)* सब्जे'क्ट–1. the predominant theme or topic, as of a book, discussion, etc. विषय We have to learn eleven *subjects* simultaneously.
2. a person who lives under the rule of a monarch, government, etc. प्रजा The king must be kind to his *subjects.*
3. *(v.)* to bring under the control or authority (of) अधीन करना The poor girl is *subjected* to her step-mother.

subjective *(adj.)* सबजेकटिव– belonging to, proceeding from, or relating to the mind of the thinking subject and not the nature of the object being considered व्यक्तिपरक, व्यक्तिनिष्ठ No one liked his highly *subjective* point of view.

sublime *(adj.)* सब्लाइम–1. inspiring deep veneration, awe, or uplifting emotion because of its beauty, nobility, grandeur, or immensity भव्य, उत्कृष्ट Wordsworth felt the *sublime* presence of God in Nature.
2. of high moral, aesthetic, intellectual, or spiritual value; noble; exalted शानदार, अति प्रशंसा के योग्य The bravery of the Rani of Jhansi was *sublime.*

submarine *(n.)* सबूमरीन– 1. a vessel, esp one designed for warfare, capable of operating for protracted periods below the surface of the sea पनडुब्बी The *submarine* surfaced after an hour.
2. *(adj.)* occurring or situated below the surface of the sea समुद्र के भीतर के, समुद्री Sea-anemones are *submarine* creatures.

submerge *(v.)* सबूमर्ज– to plunge, sink, or dive or cause to plunge, sink, or dive below the surface of water, etc डुबकी या गोता लगाना The submarine *submerged* after it left the port.

submission *(n.)* सबमिशन– something submitted; a proposal, argument, etc. पेशी, स्वीकरण What is the last date for the *submission* of form?

submissive *(adj.)* सबमिसिव– of, tending towards, or indicating submission, humility, or servility दब्बू, झुकने वाली प्रवृत्ति वाला Her husband acts like a *submissive* servant.

submit *(v.)* सबूमिट–1. to subject or be voluntarily subjected (to analysis, treatment, etc.) समर्पण करना The general agreed to *submit* to the enemy.
2. to state, contend, or propose deferentially प्रस्तुत करना I shall *submit* my plan for a new hospital to the council.

subordinate *(adj.)* सबॉर्डिनेट– 1. of lesser order or importance गौण, अधीन, आश्रित In many places in India, women are still considered *subordinate* to men.
2. *(v.)* to put in a lower rank or position (than) अधीनस्थ बनाना The quality was *subordinated* to quantity.
3. *(n.)* a person or thing that is subordinate अधीनस्थ व्यक्ति You should treat your *subordinates* well to gain respect from them.

subscribe *(v.)* सब्सक्राइब–1. to pay or promise to pay (a sum of money) as a contribution (to a fund or charity, for a magazine, etc.), esp at regular intervals चंदा देना Did you *subscribe* to the Lions Club?
2. to give support or approval समर्थन/मंजूर करना I don't *subscribe* to your views.

subscription *(n.)* सबस्क्रिपशन– a payment or promise of payment for consecutive issues of a magazine, newspaper, book, etc. over a specified period of time चंदा, शुल्क Have you paid your half-yearly *subscription*?

subsequent *(adj.)* सॅब्सिक्वन्ट– occurring after; succeeding उत्तरवर्ती, बाद का His first and all the *subsequent* visits were kept secret.

subsequently *(adv.)* सॅब्सिक्वेण्टली– after something else बाद में, तदनन्तर *Subsequently,* all the Indians settled in Ghana came back to India.

subservient *(adj.)* सबसर्विअण्ट– obsequious in behaviour or attitude चापलूस, ज़ीहुज़ूरी करने वाला He was accused of being *subservient* to the leader.

subside *(v.)* सबसाइड– to become less loud, excited, violent, etc; abate मंद पड़ना, उतरना His anger was gradually *subsided.*

subsidy *(n.)* सबसिडी– a financial aid supplied by a government, as to industry, for reasons of public welfare, the balance of payments, etc. इमदाद, आर्थिक सहायता The government announced to give agricultural *subsidies.*

substance *(n.)* सब्स्टन्स–1. a specific type of matter, esp a homogeneous material with a definite composition पदार्थ, वस्तु, द्रव्य Is not chalk a white *substance*?
2. the tangible matter of which a thing consists सार, तत्त्व There is some *substance* in what you say.

substantial *(adj.)* सबस्टैनशल– of a considerable size or value अच्छी-ख़ासी, पर्याप्त Raj is getting a *substantial* sum of money for this project.

substitute *(n.)* सब्स्टिट्यूट– 1. a person or thing that **serves** in place of another स्थानापन्न, **एवज़,** एवज़ी Soniya cannot play the violin today, so Sony will be her *substitute.*
2. *(v.)* to serve or cause to serve in place of another person or thing स्थानापन्न वस्तु या व्यक्ति की तरह प्रयुक्त करना Sony has been *substituted* for Soniya.

substitution *(n.)* सब्स्टिट्यूशन– the act of substituting or state of being substituted प्रतिस्थापन, स्थानापत्ति This *substitution* will serve the purpose.

subtle *(adj.)* सटल– difficult to detect or analyse, often through being delicate or highly refined सूक्ष्म, जटिल I could never understand her *subtle* ways.

subtract *(v.)* सबट्रेक्ट– to calculate the difference between (two numbers or quantities) by subtraction घटाना You had not *subtracted* the given amount.

suburb *(n.)* सॅबर्ब– a residential district situated on the outskirts of a city or town उपनगर We live in the *suburbs* of Delhi.

suburban *(adj.)* सबर्बन– of, relating to, situated in, or inhabiting a suburb or the suburbs उपनगरीय Every day I go to my shop by the *suburban* railway.

subway *(n.)* सबवे– an underground passage or tunnel enabling pedestrians to cross a road, railway, etc. भूमिगत पैदल पारपथ Let us go by the *subway;* there is a lot of traffic on the road.

succeed *(v.)* सक्सीड–1. to accomplish an aim, esp in the manner desired सफल होना If we do not *succeed* in the first attempt, we must try again.
2. to acquit oneself satisfactorily or do well, as in a specified field का स्थान लेना Mr. Prakash was *succeeded* as director by Mr. Mahajan.
3. to come into possession (of property, etc.); inherit विरासत में प्राप्त करना, उत्तराधिकारी होना The prince *succeeded* his father to the throne.

success *(n.)* 1. सक्सैस– the favourable outcome of something attempted सफ़लता, कामयाबी We wished him *success* in his new profession.

2. a person or thing that is successful एक अत्यधिक सफलता, सौभाग्य I passed my examination with great *success*.

successful *(adj.)* सक्सैसफुल– having succeeded in one's endeavours सफ़ल, कामयाब His son has become a *successful* doctor.

successfully *(adv.)* सक्सैसफुलि– in a manner that achieves what it was intended to achieve सफ़लतापूर्वक, कामयाबी के साथ She *successfully* completed her Ph.D.

successor *(n.)* सक्सैसर– a person or thing that follows, esp a person who succeeds another वारिस He was his father's *successor.*

succumb *(v.)* सकम्– to not be able to fight an illness, attack, etc. हार मान लेना He *succumbed* to a heart failure.

such *(adj.)* सॅच– 1. of the sort specified or understood इस तरह का *Such* behaviour will be disliked by everybody.

2. of this sort ऐसा Beware of flatterers, *such* men are dangerous.

3. so great; so much इतना बड़ा, इतना अधिक I had never seen *such* a huge monkey.

suck *(v.)* सॅक–1. to draw (a liquid or other substance) into the mouth by creating a partial vacuum in the mouth पीना, चुसकी लेना The children were *sucking* the cold drinks through straws.

2. to draw in (fluid, etc.) by or as if by a similar action चूसना Don't *suck* your thumb.

sudden *(adj.)* सॅडन– occurring or performed quickly and without warning आकस्मिक We heard a *sudden* cry but could not see anything in the dark.

suddenly *(adv.)* सॅडनलि– quickly and without warning; unexpectedly एकाएक, अचानक The train stopped *suddenly* and a young woman fell forward.

sue *(v.)* सू– to institute legal proceedings (against) मुक़दमा दायर करना The actress *sued* the journalists for libel.

suffer *(v.)* सॅफ़र्– to undergo or be subjected to (pain, punishment, etc.) पीड़ा या कष्ट सहना My father often *suffered* toothaches.

suffering *(n.)* सॅफ़रिंग– the pain, misery, or loss experienced by a person who suffers वेदना या व्यथा The kind man was moved by the *suffering* of the poor old woman.

suffice *(v.)* सफ़ाइस– to be adequate or satisfactory for (something) पर्याप्त या यथेष्ट होना A cover letter of minimum two pages should *suffice* for the interview.

sufficient *(adj.)* सफ़िशियण्ट– enough to meet a need or purpose; adequate पर्याप्त Don't worry, I have *sufficient* money for shopping.

sufficiently *(adv.)* सफ़िशियण्टली– in an adequate or sufficient manner पर्याप्त मात्रा में, यथेष्ट मात्रा How much money do you feel is necessary to live self-*sufficiently*.

suffocate *(v.)* सॅफ़केट– to kill or be killed by the deprivation of oxygen, as by obstruction of the air passage or inhalation of noxious gases दम घुटना I felt *suffocated* in that organisation.

sugar *(n.)* शुगर– a white crystalline sweet substance, found in many plants and extracted from sugar cane and sugar beet चीनी, खांड, शक्कर *Sugar* is made from a plant called *sugar*-cane.

suggest *(v.)* सजे'स्ट– to put forward (a plan, idea, etc.) for consideration सुझाव देना, प्रस्ताव करना The doctor *suggested* that she should take rest for one week.

suggestion *(n.)* सजेसचन– something that is suggested सुझाव He made this *suggestion* after a complete check-up.

suggestive *(adj.)* सजेसटिव– conveying a hint (of something) सांकेतिक The song is *suggestive* of cold winter nights.

suicidal *(adj.)* सूइसाइडल्– involving, indicating, or tending towards suicide आत्मघातक She is depressed and has *suicidal* tendencies.

suicide *(n.)* सूइसाइड– the act or an instance of killing oneself intentionally आत्महत्या, आत्मघात Why did the old lady commit *suicide*?

suit *(n.)* सूट– 1. any set of clothes of the same or similar material designed to be worn together, now usually (for men) a jacket with matching trousers or (for women) a jacket with matching or contrasting skirt or trousers पोशाक, वेश The tailor made a nice *suit* for me.

2. *(v.)* to make or be fit or appropriate for अनुकूल होना Tea does not *suit* me. I take milk.

3. to meet the requirements or standards (of) सुविधाजनक होना Will it *suit* you if we start at 7 o'clock?

suitable *(adj.)* सूटबल– appropriate; proper; fit उपयुक्त I think it will be *suitable*.

suitably *(adv.)* सूटब्ली– appropriately for the occasion उपयुक्त रूप से We must come to office *suitably* dressed.

suitcase *(n.)* सूटकेस– a portable rectangular travelling case, usually stiffened, for carrying clothing, etc. सूटकेस His *suitcases* were full of gifts.

suited *(adj.)* सूटेड– suitable for; appropriate for सही एवं उपयुक्त She is best *suited* to such a job.

sulk *(v.)* सॅल्क– to be silent and resentful because of a wrong done to one, esp in order to gain sympathy रूठना, नाराज़ या अप्रसन्न होना Never sit and *sulk* in a corner.

sullen *(adj.)* सॅलन– unwilling to talk or be sociable; sulky; morose रूखा, चिड़चिड़ा; उदास एवं आनंदरहित The atmosphere was *sullen* in the evening.

sulphur *(n.)* सलफ़र– a chemical element is a pale yellow substance used in medicine and industry गंधक *Sulphur* is used in chemical and paper industries.

sultry *(adj.)* सलट्री– (of weather or climate) oppressively hot and humid उमसभरा It was a *sultry* summer afternoon.

sum *(n.)* सॅम– 1. the result of the addition of numbers, quantities, objects, etc. जोड़, योगफल Yesterday she got all the three *sums* correct.

2. *(v.)* to add or form a total of (something) सार प्रस्तुत करना We can *sum* up all we have discussed.

summary *(n.)* सॅमरी– a brief account giving the main points of something सार-संक्षेप I don't have time to read the whole novel; just tell me its *summary*.

summer *(n.)* सॅमर्– the warmest season of the year, between spring and autumn ग्रीष्म We enjoyed the *summer* vacation very much.

summertime *(n.)* सॅमरटाइम– the period or season of summer ग्रीष्मकाल The centre will remain close in *summertime*.

summit *(n.)* समिट–1. the highest point or part, esp of a mountain or line of communication; top चोटी, शिखर, चरम बिन्दु It is very hard to climb the *summit* of Mount Everest.

2. an official meeting between two governments or leaders शीर्ष-सम्मेलन

At the *summit* meeting, the world leaders discussed ways to control nuclear arms.

summons *(n.)* सॅमॅन्स- 1. a call, signal, or order to do something, esp to appear in person or attend at a specified place or time तलबनामा, कचहरी का सम्मन/आदेश Have you received *summons* to attend the court day after tomorrow?

2. *(v.)* to take out a summons against (a person) सम्मन भेजना The General *summoned* his officers to discuss plans for the battle.

sumptuous *(adj.)* सम्पचुअस– expensive or extravagant बहुत क़ीमती The stones which were robbed were very *sumptuous*.

sun *(n.)* सॅन–1. the star at the centre of our solar system. सूर्य, सूरज The *sun* shines during the day. The moon shines at night.

2. the radiant energy, esp heat and light, received from the sun; sunshine धूप Oh, it is a very beautiful *sun*-lit room!

sunny *(adj.)* सनी–1. full of or exposed to sunlight उज्ज्वल, चमकीला We started on a *sunny* day.

2. radiating good humour प्रसन्नचित्त His *sunny* nature warms every heart.

sunburn *(n.)* सनबर्न– inflammation of the skin caused by overexposure to the sun धूप में होने वाली झुलसन He got *sunburns* while playing cricket.

Sunday *(n.)* सण्डे– the first day of the week and the Christian day of worship रविवार *Sunday* is the first day in a week.

sunflower *(n.)* सनफ़्लॉवर– a large yellow flower grown in gardens सूरजमुखी का फूल *Sunflower* oil is good for cooking food.

sunglasses *(n.)* सनग्लॉसेज़– glasses with darkened or polarizing lenses that protect the eyes from the sun's glare धूप का चश्मा We should use *sunglasses* to protect our eyes from the sun.

sunshine *(n.)* सनशाइन्– the light received directly from the sun सूरज की रोशनी, धूप They sat down in the *sunshine* and had coffee.

sunstroke *(n.)* सनस्ट्रोक– heatstroke caused by prolonged exposure to intensely hot sunlight लू, धूप आघात Dizziness, sweating, headache and high fever are the symptoms of *sunstroke*.

superb *(adj.)* सूपर्ब– surpassingly good; excellent शानदार, आलीशान Mahesh Bhupati is a *superb* tennis player.

superficial *(adj.)* सूपर्फ़िशल– involving only the surface area बाहरी, सतही, ऊपरी Don't worry, the wound is *superficial*.

superfluous *(adj.)* सूपर्फ्लुअस– exceeding what is sufficient or required फ़ालतू, अतिरिक्त Delete the *superfluous* words from your article.

superintendent *(n.)* सूपरिटेंडेंट– a person who directs and manages an organization, office, etc. अधीक्षक, संचालक The *superintendent* of police in our zone is a very intelligent person.

superior *(adj.)* सूपिरियर–1. of high or extraordinary worth, merit, etc. वरिष्ठ, अधिक उत्कृष्ट An editor is *superior* to a proofreader in the press.

2. higher in rank or status श्रेष्ठ, विशिष्ट Uncle has got a *superior* position in his office.

3. *(n.)* a person or thing of greater rank or quality वरिष्ठ अधिकारी Be respectful to your *superiors*.

superiority *(n.)* सूपिरियॉरटी– the quality of being better than sth or sb else प्रधानता, श्रेष्ठता There is a male *superiority* over women in Islam.

supernatural *(adj.)* सूपर्नैचरल– of or relating to things that cannot be explained according to natural laws अलौकिक, लोकोत्तर Stories about ghosts describe *supernatural* events.

superpower *(n.)* सूपर्पॉउअर– extremely high power, esp electrical or mechanical अत्यधिक शक्तिशाली एवं प्रभावशाली The United States of America is the number one *superpower* in the world.

superstar *(n.)* सूपर्स्टार– a popular singer, film star, etc. who is idolized by fans and elevated to a position of importance in the entertainment industry लोकप्रिय अभिनेता Shahrukh Khan is a *superstar* of Bollywood.

superstition *(n.)* सूपर्स्टिशन– irrational belief usually founded on ignorance or fear and characterized by obsessive reverence for omens, charms, etc. अन्धविश्वास There is a *superstition* which makes some people afraid of walking under a ladder.

supervise *(v.)* सूपर्वाइज़–1. to watch over so as to maintain order, etc. देखरेख करना Our mother *supervises* her domestic work every day.
2. to direct or oversee the performance or operation of निरीक्षण करना The Principal asked the teacher to *supervise* the examinees.

supervision *(n.)* सूपर्विश्‌न– the process of making sure that sb is doing a task or behaving correctly निगरानी, निरीक्षण All the teachers are busy in *supervision* during the exams.

supper *(n.)* सॅपर्– an evening meal, esp a light one रात का भोजन *Supper* is the last meal of a day. Have you had your *supper* or not?

supplement *(n.)* सपलिमेंट– an addition designed to complete, make up for a deficiency, etc. शेषपूर्ति, परिशिष्ट Fruits are the *supplement* of food.

supply *(v.)* सप्लाइ– 1. to furnish with something that is required (खाद्य सामग्री) आपूर्ति करना The milkman *supplies* us milk.
2. to make available or provide (something that is desired or lacking) मुहैया करना Some shopkeepers *supply* all we want.
3. *(n.)* an amount available for use; stock भंडार We have enough *supply* of provisions for this month.

support –*(v.)* सपोर्ट–1. to provide the necessities of life for (a family, person, etc.) सहायता पहुँचाना, मदद करना The kind rich man *supported* many poor students.
2. to give approval to (a cause, principle, etc.); subscribe to समर्थन देना Without the *support* of all its partners, the coalition government cannot function.
3. *(n.)* the act of supporting or the condition of being supported आश्रय, सहारा I couldn't have been successful without your *support*.

supporter *(n.)* सपोर्टर– a person who or thing that acts as a support समर्थक She must have at least twenty *supporters*.

supportive *(adj.)* सपोर्टिव– providing support, esp moral or emotional support कठिन काम में समर्थन देने वाला Zakir was very *supportive* when Tanveer lost his job.

suppose *(v.)* सपोज़–1. to presume (something) to be true without certain knowledge समझना, विचार होना, (की) She is *supposed* to be at home by 8 o'clock in the evening.
2. to imply the inference or assumption (of) अपेक्षा रखना I do not *suppose* we shall see each other again.
3. to consider as a possible suggestion for the sake of discussion, elucidation, etc; postulate कल्पना

करना The work was over earlier than we had *supposed.*

supposing *(conj.)* सपोज़िंग– to presume (something) to be true without certain knowledge अगर ऐसा हुआ तो *Supposing* it rains, what shall we do?

suppress *(v.)* सप्रेस– to put an end to; prohibit दबाना, दमन करना, रोकना The soldier *suppressed* his fear and went on fighting.

suppression *(n.)* सप्रेसन an act of suppressing sth अवरोध, रुकाव The people rose against the *suppression* of the tyrant ruler.

supremacy *(n.)* सूप्रीमसी– supreme power; authority श्रेष्ठता, प्रभुत्व We all know about Japan's *supremacy* in the field of electronics.

supreme *(adj.)* सुप्रीम–1. of highest status or power महान, वरिष्ठ King Mahendra was the *supreme* ruler of Nepal.

2. greatest in degree; extreme सर्वोच्च Have you ever seen the *Supreme* Court of India?

3. of highest quality, importance, etc. उच्चतम The army remained *supreme* in the country after the war.

sure *(adj.)* शॉर्– having no doubt, as of the occurrence of a future state or event आश्वस्त, विश्वस्त, निश्चित I am *sure* we have enough money for shopping.

surely *(adv.)* शॉरली– without doubt; assuredly अवश्य, निःसन्देह *Surely* she will come.

surety *(n.)* शुअरटी– a person who assumes legal responsibility for the fulfilment of another's debt or obligation and himself becomes liable if the other defaults ज़मानत Raju gave ₹ 5,000 as a *surety* for his friend.

surface *(v.)* सर्फ़ेस– 1. to rise or cause to rise to or as if to the surface (of water, etc.) सतह पर आना The submarine *surfaced* after an hour.

2. *(n.)* the exterior face of an object or one such face बाहरी सतह The *surface* of the teapot has been scratched.

surfing *(n.)* सर्फ़िंग– the sport of riding towards shore on the crest of a wave by standing or lying on a surfboard इंटरनेट पर कुछ रोचक खोज He was *surfing* the net for some information on Indian culture.

surgeon *(n.)* सर्जन– a medical practioner who specializes in surgery शल्य चिकित्सक, सर्जन, चीरफाड़ करने वाला डॉक्टर The *surgeon* performed the difficult operation skilfully.

surly *(adj.)* सरलि– sullenly ill-tempered or rude रूखा, चिड़चिड़ा She gave a *surly* expression to me.

surmount *(v.)* सरमाउन्ट– to prevail over; overcome किसी कठिनाई को पार करना I *surmounted* my problems bravely.

surname *(n.)* सर्नेम– a family name, nickname उपनाम My name is Seema Malik. Malik is my *surname.*

surpass *(v.)* सर्पास–1. to be greater than in degree, extent, etc. (से) बढ़कर होना Asha has *surpassed* Usha in English, but Usha is better in Sanskrit.

2. to overstep the limit or range of गात कर देना Your performance in the drama *surpassed* everybody else's.

3. to be superior to in achievement or excellence आशा से बढ़कर काम करना Rakesh was intelligent, but my brother soon *surpassed* him.

surplus *(n.)* सर्प्लस– a quantity or amount in excess of what is required बढ़ती, बचा हुआ (फ़ालतू) The farmers use as much grain as they need and sell the *surplus* to other villagers.

surprise *(v.)* सर्‌प्राइज़– 1. to cause to feel amazement or wonder अचरज में डालना, आश्चर्यचकित होना She will be *surprised* to see me.
2. *(n.)* the act or an instance of surprising; the act of taking unawares आश्चर्य, अचरज It was a great *surprise* to him when he was declared first in the university.

surprised *(adj.)* सरप्राइज़्ड– If you are surprised at something, you have a feeling of surprise, because it is unexpected or unusual आश्चर्यचकित I was very *surprised* at the news.

surprising *(adj.)* सरप्राइजिंग– causing surprise; unexpected or amazing आश्चर्यजनक His abrupt arrival was *surprising.*

surrender *(n.)* सरे'न्डर्– 1. the act or instance of surrendering आत्मसमर्पण, त्याग Has the general accepted the *surrender* of the enemy?
2. *(v.)* to relinquish to the control or possession of another under duress or on demand आत्मसमर्पण करना, त्यागना The enemy was so powerful that they made us *surrender* the fort.

surround *(v.)* सराउण्ड– 1. to encircle or enclose or cause to be encircled or enclosed घेरना, बाड़ा लगाना The bungalow is *surrounded* by gardens.
2. *(n.)* a border around the edge of sth किनारा, घेरा The *surround* of a sari is decorated.

survey *(v.)* सर्वे– 1. to view or consider in a comprehensive or general way सर्वेक्षण करना, भूमि की नाप-जोख करना Before we buy a plot, we ask a surveyor *to survey* the land.
2. *(n.)* a critical, detailed, and formal inspection सर्वेक्षण, अवलोकन The Principal gave us a *survey* of the year's work.

survive *(v.)* सर्वाइव–1. to live after the death of (another) जीवित रहना, मरने से बच जाना Only one hundred people in the village *survived* the epidemic.
2. to continue in existence or use after (a passage of time, an adversity, etc.) जीवित बने रहना The father is *survived* by two daughters and a son.

survivor *(n.)* सर्वाइवर– a person or thing that survives उत्तरजीवी The old woman was one of the *survivors* of the disaster.

suspect *(v.)* सस्पे'क्ट– 1. to believe guilty of a specified offence without proof संदेह करना, अविश्वास करना She *suspects* her husband to be a spy.
2. *(n.)* a person who is under suspicion संदिग्ध अपराधी The policeman caught all the *suspects.*

suspend *(v.)* सस्‌पेण्ड–1. to hang from above so as to permit free movement स्थगित करना The chairman suddenly fell ill during the meeting and we had to *suspend* it until the next week.
2. to cause to remain floating or hanging लटकाना Can you *suspend* the electric lamp from the middle of the ceilling?
3. to debar temporarily from privilege, office, etc. as a punishment निलंबित करना After the inquiry, the general manager was *suspended.*

suspense *(n.)* सस्‌पेन्स– the condition of being insecure or uncertain असमंजस, दुविधा He was creating *suspense* for all of us.

suspicion *(n.)* सस्पिशन– the act or an instance of suspecting; belief without sure proof, esp that something is wrong शंका, सन्देह *Suspicion* kept her awake all night.

suspicious *(adj.)* सस्पिशस– exciting or liable to excite suspicion; questionable शंकायुक्त We were too *suspicious* about her.

suspiciously *(adv.)* सस्पिशसली– in such a way as to indicate or express suspicion संदेहजनक He looked at me *suspiciously.*

sustain *(v.)* सस्टेन–1. to provide for or give support to, esp by supplying necessities भरण-पोषण करना During the famine, many people did not have enough food to *sustain* themselves.

2. to hold up under; withstand गुज़ारा करना, बने रहना During their long march, the men were *sustained* by tinned food.

sustenance *(adj.)* ससूटनन्स– means of sustaining health or life; nourishment आहार There is not much *sustenance* in a cup of milk.

swab *(n.)* स्वॉब–1. a small piece of cotton, gauze, etc. for use in applying medication, cleansing a wound, or obtaining a specimen of a secretion, etc. फाहा Nurse used the *swab* to clean the wound.

2. a mop for cleaning floors, decks, etc. झाड़न, पुचारा Her maid was using a *swab* for dusting and cleaning.

swallow *(n.)* स्वॉलो–1. a small bird, having long pointed wings, a forked tail and short legs, अबाबील पक्षी Many *swallows* gather and twitter in the sky at sunset.

2. *(v.)* to pass (food, drink, etc.) through the mouth to the stomach by means of the muscular action of the oesophagus निगलना You must chew your food thoroughly before you *swallow* it.

swamp *(v.)* स्वॉम्प– 1. to drench or submerge or be drenched or submerged समा लेना, जल से भर देना They were afraid that the huge waves would *swamp* their boat.

2. *(n.)* permanently waterlogged ground that is usually overgrown and sometimes partly forested दलदल There are many large *swamps* in Myanmar.

swan *(n.)* स्वॉन– a large white bird having a long neck and usually a white plumage राजहंस *Swan* is a very beautiful water bird.

swarm *(v.)* स्वॉर्म– 1. to move in or form a swarm भीड़ एवं झुंड में आना या घूमना After the show, the spectators *swarmed* on to the road.

2. *(n.)* a group of social insects, esp bees led by a queen, that has left the parent hive in order to start a new colony झुंड, भीड़ A *swarm* of honeybees attacked him when he disturbed the honeycomb.

swathe *(v.)* स्वेथ– to bandage (a wound, limb, etc.), esp completely पट्टियाँ बाँधना His hand was *swathed* in bandages.

sway *(v.)* स्वे– 1. to swing or cause to swing to and fro झूलना, डोलना The branches of the trees *sway* in the wind.

2. *(n.)* control; power शासन India was under the *sway* of British for over a hundred years.

swear *(v.)* स्वे'अर्–1. to declare or affirm (a statement) as true, esp by invoking a deity, etc. as witness शपथ लेना, क़सम खाना We *swear* we shall serve our nation. You must *swear* that you will speak only the truth.

2. to assert or affirm with great emphasis or earnestness गुस्से में बोलना The thief *swore* when he bumped his head against a pole in the dark.

sweat *(v.)* स्वेट्– 1. to secrete (sweat) through the pores of the skin, esp profusely पसीना आना You are *sweating.* You must change your shirt.

2. *(n.)* the secretion from the sweat glands, esp when profuse and visible, as during strenuous activity, from excessive heat, etc. पसीना His brow is wet with honest *sweat.*

sweaty *(adj.)* स्वेटी– covered with sweat; sweating पसीने का, पसीनेदार

He was tired and *sweaty* after the match.

sweep *(v.)* स्वीप–1. to clean or clear (a space, chimney, etc.) with a brush, broom, etc. झाड़ू लगाना, बुहारना The servant *sweeps* the room clean.

2. to convey, clear, or abolish, esp with strong or continuous movements जल्दी से घेर कर सब कुछ नष्ट करना The flood *swept* away the colonies on the banks of the river.

sweeper *(n.)* स्वीपर– a person employed to sweep, such as a road-sweeper बुहारनेवाला, सफ़ाईकर्मी I called a *sweeper* to clean my carpets.

sweeping *(adj.)* स्वीपिंग– comprehensive and wide-ranging व्यापक He made a *sweeping* statement.

sweet *(adj.)* स्वीट– 1. having or denoting a pleasant taste like that of sugar मीठा, मधुर, सुरीला Her voice was very *sweet.*

2. *(n.)* any of numerous kinds of confectionery consisting wholly or partly of sugar, esp of sugar boiled and crystallized मिठाई Eating too many *sweets* is not good for health.

sweetcorn *(n.)* स्वीटकॉर्न– a variety of maize, whose kernels are rich in sugar and eaten as a vegetable when young मकई She likes to eat boiled *sweetcorns.*

sweetheart *(n.)* स्वीटहार्ट– a person loved by another प्रेमिका या प्रेमी Once she was a *sweetheart* of her husband.

sweetly *(adv.)* स्वीटली–1. melodically, pleasantly, smoothly, and gently मधुर एवं आकर्षक ढंग से Anuradha sings *sweetly.*

2. in such a way as to be free from unpleasant odours सुनने एवं सुगंध में मधुर एवं आत्मीय A nightingale was singing *sweetly* in the tree.

sweet potato *(n.)* स्वीट पॅटाटो– a root vegetable that is yellow inside and tastes sweet शकरक़ंद Gobind likes to eat fried *sweet potatoes.*

sweet-smelling *(adj.)* स्वीट स्मैलिंग– having a pleasant smell अच्छी महक I liked the *sweet-smelling* gulabjamuns at the party.

swell *(v.)* स्वे'ल–1. to grow or cause to grow in size, esp as a result of internal pressure सूजना A bee has stung her hand. It is *swelling* up.

2. to expand or cause to expand at a particular point or above the surrounding level; protrude फूलना If we soak rice in water for half an hour, it *swells.*

swelling *(n.)* स्वेलिंग– the state of being or becoming swollen सूजन, फुलाव, बढ़ाव You had a *swelling* in your neck.

swelter *(v.)* स्वे'ल्टर्– to suffer under oppressive heat, esp to sweat and feel faint पसीने से तर-बतर होना With no shelter from the sun, we lay *sweltering* on the sand.

swerve *(v.)* स्वर्व– to turn or cause to turn aside, usually sharply or suddenly, from a course घूम जाना The ball *swerved* just as the batsman prepared to hit it.

swift *(adj.)* स्विफ़्ट– moving or able to move quickly; fast शीघ्रगामी, फुर्तीला P.T.Usha is a *swift* runner of India.

swiftly *(adv.)* स्विफ़्टली– in a quick movement; fast तेज़ी से Seeing the policemen, the thief *swiftly* ran round the corner.

swim *(v.)* स्विम– 1. to move along in water, etc. by means of movements of the body or parts of the body, esp the arms and legs, or (in the case of fish) tail and fins तैरना, तैरकर पार करना Can you *swim*?

2. *(n.)* the act, an instance, or period of swimming तैराकी I want to go for a *swim.*

swimmer *(n.)* स्विमर– a person who swims, esp for sport or pleasure तैराक I am a good *swimmer.* I used to go to the swimming-pool regularly.

swimsuit *(n.)* स्विमसूट– a woman's one-piece swimming garment that leaves the arms and legs bare तैराकी की पोशाक The *swimsuit* was very loose for her.

swindle *(v.)* स्विनडल– to cheat (someone) of money, etc. defraud ठगना, धोखेबाज़ी से ऐंठ लेना He *swindled* thousands of rupees out of her.

swine *(n.)* स्वाइन– pig सुअर The *swine* ate dirty things.

swing *(n.)* स्विंग–1. a seat for *swinging* on hung from above on ropes झूला, हिंडोला Girls were playing on the *swings.*
2. *(v.)* to move or cause to move rhythmically to and fro, as a free-hanging object; sway झुलाना, लटकना We *swing* our arms when we walk.

swirl *(v.)* स्वर्ल– to turn or cause to turn in a twisting spinning fashion चक्कर खाते हुए घूमना The leaves *swirled* in the wind.

swish *(v.)* स्विश– 1. to move with or make or cause to move with or make a whistling or hissing sound सरसराना He *swished* his stick through the air.
2. *(n.)* a hissing or rustling sound or movement सरसराहट The pony gave a *swish* of its tail.

switch *(v.)* स्विच–1. to shift, change, turn aside, or change the direction of (something) बटन दबाना *Switch* on the light for it is getting dark.
2. to exchange (places); replace (something by something else) फेरना, घुमाना I *switched* the conversation to another less painful subject.
3. *(n.)* a mechanical, electrical, electronic, or optical device for opening or closing a circuit or for diverting energy from one part of a circuit to another बटन Where is the *switch*-board in your house?

swollen *(adj.)* स्वॉलन– tumid or enlarged by or as if by swelling सूजा हुआ, फूला हुआ She was looking at him with *swollen* eyes.

swoop *(v.)* स्वूप– to sweep or pounce suddenly झपट्टा मारना We saw an owl *swooping* on a mouse.

sword *(n.)* सॉर्ड– a thrusting, striking, or cutting weapon with a long blade having one or two cutting edges, a hilt, and usually a crosspiece or guard तलवार The soldier drew his *sword* and rushed at the enemy.

swot *(v.)* स्वॉट– to study (a subject) intensively, as for an examination गहन अध्ययन करना John is *swotting* for his medical entrance exam.

syllabus *(n.)* सिलेबस– an outline of a course of studies, text, etc. पाठ्यक्रम CBSE *syllabus* is better than ICSE.

symbol *(n.)* सिम्बल– something that represents or stands for something else, usually by convention or association, esp a material object used to represent something abstract प्रतीक ₹ is the *symbol* for rupee.

symmetry *(n.)* सिमट्री– similarity, correspondence, or balance among systems or parts of a system समरूपता, समामिति There was perfect *symmetry* of the two flower pots kept on either side of the table.

sympathetic *(adj.)* सिम्पैथेटिक– characterized by, feeling, or showing sympathy; understanding सहानुभूतिशील We must feel *sympathetic* towards invalids.

sympathize (ise) *(v.)* सिम्पथाइज़– to feel or express compassion or sympathy (for); commiserate सहानुभूति रखना या प्रकट करना We must *sympathize* with the poor and the needy.

sympathy *(n.)* सिम्पथी– the sharing of another's emotions, esp of sorrow or anguish; pity; compassion सहानुभूति, हमदर्दी I have no *sympathy* for students who waste their time.

symptom *(n.)* सिम्पटम– any sensation or change in bodily function experienced by a patient that is associated with a particular disease (रोग का) लक्षण A gumboil is a *symptom* of decaying teeth.

syndicate *(n.)* सिंडिकेट– an association of business enterprises or individuals organized to undertake a joint project requiring considerable capital व्यवसाय-संघ Are you a member of New Era Writers' *syndicate*?

synonym *(n.)* सिननिम– a word that means the same or nearly the same as another word, such as bucket and pail पर्याय, समानार्थ Can you suggest a few *synonyms* for the word 'promise'?

synopsis *(n.)* सिनॉप्सिस्– a condensation or brief review of a subject; summary सारांश Send me the *synopsis* of the novel before sending the whole manuscript.

synthesis *(n.)* सिन्थसिस– the process of combining objects or ideas into a complex whole संयोजन, संश्लेषण His poetry is a *synthesis* of modern values.

synthetic *(n.)* सिनथेटिक– a synthetic substance or material कृत्रिम Nylon is a *synthetic* material.

syrup *(n.)* सिरप– a solution of sugar dissolved in water and often flavoured with fruit juice: used for sweetening fruit, etc. शर्बत, शीरा Would you prepare some sugar *syrup*?

system *(n.)* सिस्टम–1. a group or combination of interrelated, interdependent, or interacting elements forming a collective entity; a methodical or coordinated assemblage of parts, facts, concepts, etc. प्रणाली, पद्धति It is difficult to do a job well unless you have some *system.*

2. any scheme of classification or arrangement वस्तुओं या भागों का साथ जुड़ा हुआ समूह या परिवार Have you got any knowledge about the solar *system*?

systematic *(adj.)* सिस्टमैटिक– characterized by the use of order and planning; methodical व्यवस्थित, क्रमबद्ध We should do our work in a *systematic* way.

systematically *(adv.)* सिस्टमैटिकली– comprising or resembling a system व्यवस्थित रूप से I completed my work *systematically*.

Tt

Tt *(n.)* टी–अंग्रेज़ी वर्णमाला का बीसवां अक्षर The twentieth letter of the English alphabet. Tree begins with 'T'.

tab *(n.)* टैब– a small flap of material, घुंडी, टँगनी She has to pick up the *tab.*

table *(n.)* टेबल–1. a flat horizontal slab or board, usually supported by one or more legs, on which objects may be placed मेज़ Put the teapot on the *table.*

2. an arrangement of words, numbers, or signs, usually in parallel columns, to display data or relations तालिका Before we buy a book, we always look at the *table* of contents.

tablecloth *(n.)* टेबलक्लॉथ– a cloth for covering the top of a table, esp during meals मेज़पोश The *tablecloth* should match the colour of the plates.

tablet *(n.)* टैबलेट– a medicinal formulation made of a compressed powdered substance containing an active drug टिकिया, दवा की गोली I have to take three different *tablets* for my pain everyday.

taboo *(n.)* टबू– any prohibition resulting from social or other conventions वर्जित शब्द या कर्म, निषिद्ध Divorce is still considered a *taboo* in many Indian societies.

tabulate *(v.)* टैब्युलेट– to set out, arrange, or write in tabular form तालिका बनाना The clerk *tabulated* all the statements.

tack *(v.)* टैक–1. to sew (something) with long loose temporary stitches टाँकना If you *tack* the dress, I shall be able to try it on.

2. to steer (a sailing vessel) on alternate tacks हवा के विरुद्ध जहाज़ को चलाना We had to *tack* to reach the harbour.

3. to attach or append पतली कीलें जड़ना I *tack* the picture to the frame.

tackle *(v.)* टैकल– 1. to undertake (a task, problem, etc.) हाथ में लेना, में जुट जाना Aunt says she must *tackle* a lot of sewing today.

2. *(n.)* the equipment required for a particular occupation, etc. मछली पकड़ने का काँटा You can buy a fishing *tackle* at this shop.

3. a physical challenge to an opponent, as to prevent his progress with the ball फुटबॉल मैच में प्रतिपक्षी को रोकने की क्रिया That was a fine *tackle*!

tacky *(adj.)* टैकि– shabby or shoddy फ़ैशन के विपरीत, फूहड़ She wore a *tacky* outfit at the party.

tact *(n.)* टैक्ट– skill or judgment in handling difficult or delicate situations; diplomacy कला, व्यवहार-कौशल You have the *tact* of persuading the men to go back to work.

tactful *(adj.)* टैक्टफुल– demonstrating a sense of what is fitting and considerate in dealing with others or in handling difficult or delicate situations, so as to avoid giving offence or to win good will चतुर, व्यवहारकुशल My sister is *tactful* in dealing with quarrelsome people.

tactfully *(adv.)* टैक्टफुली– in such a way as to demonstrate a sense of what is fitting and considerate in dealing with others निपुणता से He handled the problem *tactfully.*

tactic *(n.)* टैक्टिक– a piece of tactics; tactical move युक्ति, उपाय The coach discussed *tactics* with the players.

tactical *(adj.)* टैक्टिकल– skilful or diplomatic योजनापूर्ण It is her *tactical* decision to marry a rich man.

tactically *(adv.)* टैक्टिकली– in a way that is intended to help someone achieve what they want to achieve in a particular situation योजनापूर्वक The enemy was *tactically* superior.

tactless *(adj.)* टैक्टलस– if you describe someone's behaviour or speech as tactless, you think that it is likely to offend other people अकुशल, बेशऊर You should not pass a *tactless* remark on her height.

tadpole *(n.)* टैड्पोल– the aquatic larva of frogs, toads, etc. छुछमछली (मेंढक का बच्चा) We caught a *tadpole* in the garden.

tag *(n.)* टैग– a piece or strip of paper, plastic, leather, etc. for attaching to something by one end as a mark or label लुपी, लेबल, लटकन The police secretly *tagged* all the ruffians in the crowd.

tail *(n.)* टेल–1. the region of the vertebrate body that is posterior to or above the anus and contains an elongation of the vertebral column पूँछ The monkey uses its *tail* when climbing trees.
2. anything resembling such an appendage in form or position; the bottom, lowest, or rear part दुम से मिलती-जुलती वस्तु, पुछल्ला I fastened a *tail* to my kite.

tailor *(n.)* टेलर्– a person who makes, repairs, or alters outer garments, esp menswear दरज़ी I need the best *tailor* in town to stitch my suit.

take *(v.)* टेक–1. to make, do, or perform (an action) ले जाना Father is going to *take* Hamid and Majid to the sea for fishing.
2. to use as a means of transport पकड़ना My father *takes* the 9 a.m. bus to go to his office.
3. to consume लगना It will *take* half an hour to reach there.
4. to give ले जाकर देना Please *take* this bag to your mother.
5. to rent or lease किराये पर लेना We have *taken* this room for a month.
6. to win विजय प्राप्त करना After heavy fighting, the army *took* control of the city.
7. to obtain interest लेना Do you *take* any interest in drawing?

- **take aback**– to astonish or disconcert चौंका देना या चकित कर देना, Sonam *took* everyone *aback*.
- **take after**– to resemble in appearance, character, behaviour, etc. परिवार के बड़े-बूढ़े जैसा आचरण करना या अनुरूप होना, The girl *takes after* her mother.
- **take apart**– to separate (something) into component parts पुर्ज़े खोलना, The mechanic has *taken apart* the machine but cannot repair it.
- **take aside**– to take on another side एक ओर या किनारे ले जाना, She *took* me *aside* and said something about him.
- **take away**– detract from दूर कर देना, This medicine will *take away* your pain.
- **take back**– to retract or withdraw (something said, written, promised, etc.) वापस लेना, I must *take back* my words.
- **take down**– to record in writing लिख देना, I am *taking down* what she is saying.
- **take from**– to reduce घटाना, कम करना, The child could not *take* two *from* eight.
- **take in**– to comprehend or understand झूठी बात पर यक़ीन करना, She is completely *taken in* by his words.
- **take off**– to remove or discard (a garment) निकाल देना या उतार देना, As the plane *took off* I felt a jerk in my stomach.
- **take on**– to agree to do; undertake कोई काम हाथ में लेना, Raheem has

taken on a new project but he cannot complete it.

- **take out**– to extract or remove अंदर से कुछ बाहर निकालना, Aunty *took out* her sari from the almirah.
- **take over**– to assume the control or management of पद या दायित्व संभालना, का भार लेना, Who will *take over* the charge of the company?
- **take to**– to form a liking for आदत डालना, को पसंद करने लगना, Anwar *took to* smoking last few years.
- **take up**– to adopt as a protégé; act as a patron to ज़िम्मेदारी लेना, She *takes up* her duties respectfully.
- **take up with**– to discuss with (someone); refer to कुछ पूछना या शिकायत करना, I decided to *take* the matter *up with* the chairman.

take-off *(n.)* टेक-ऑफ़– the act or process of making an aircraft airborne उड़ान भरना The plane was not ready for *take-off*.

takings *(n.)* टेकिंग्ज़– the income earned, taken or received by a shop, business, etc. (व्यापार में) प्राप्ति, आय His firm has good *takings* every week.

tale *(n.)* टेल–1. a report, narrative, or story कहानी, कथा, क़िस्सा The mother told the child a fairy *tale* before making her sleep.

2. a malicious or meddlesome rumour or piece of gossip विवरण, वृत्तांत The reporters told different *tales* about the accident.

talent *(n.)* टैलेण्ट– innate ability, aptitude, or faculty, esp when unspecified; above average ability प्रतिभा, योग्यता His *talent* was discovered at a very late stage of his mediocre career.

talented *(adj.)* टैलेण्टेड– having a special talent or above average ability, as in a certain skill, etc. प्रवीण, प्रतिभासंपन्न Children these days are very *talented* in some field.

talk *(v.)* टॉक–1. to communicate or exchange thoughts by mean of words through mouth बोलना The baby cannot *talk* yet; as she grows up, she will learn to *talk*.

2. to hold a conversation about; discuss महत्त्वपूर्ण विषय पर बातचीत करना Vagish often *talks* to his parents about his college.

3. *(n.)* idle chatter, gossip, or rumour वार्तालाप We had a long *talk* about going to Mumbai.

- **talk about**– used informally and often ironically to add emphasis to a statement परामर्श करना, What were you *talking about*?
- **talk away**– to gossip and chit-chat गपबाज़ी में समय बिताना, He is *talking away* all these days.
- **talk back**– to answer boldly or impudently (अशिष्टता से) जवाब देना, Kiran *talked back* to her mother.
- **talk down**– to override (a person or argument) by continuous or loud talking मुंह बंद कर देना, मौन करना, If she comes, he will *talk* her *down*.
- **talk over**– to persuade to one's opinion विचार-विमर्श करना, I have an important matter to *talk over* with you.

talkative *(adj.)* टॉकटिव– given to talking a great deal बातूनी This particular section is very *talkative* in the entire school.

talking *(n.)* टॉकिंग– the act of expressing your thoughts, feelings, or desires by means of words; speaking बातचीत Please stop *talking* and listen to me.

tall *(adj.)* टॉल–1. of more than average height लंबा Sony is a *tall* girl.

2. having a specified height ऊँचा There are some very *tall* buildings in Mumbai.

tamarind *(n.)* टमारिंड– a tropical evergreen tree, having brown pulpy pods इमली *Tamarind* chutney can be used as a sauce for numerous Indian snacks.

tambourine *(n.)* टैमबरीन– a percussion instrument consisting of a single drumhead of skin stretched over a circular wooden frame डफ़ली, खंजरी *Tambourine* is used in the folk dance of Punjab.

tame *(adj.)* टेम– 1. not fearful of human contact पालतू A cat is a *tame* animal. It is not wild.
2. *(v.)* to make tame; domesticate पालतू बनाना Coaches *tame* animals in circus.

tamper *(v.)* टैम्पर्– to interfere or meddle छेड़छाड़ करना Someone *tampered* with the evidence while it was in police custody

tan *(n.)* टैन्– 1. the brown colour produced by the skin after intensive exposure to ultraviolet rays, esp those of the sun धूप-ताम्रता Prolonged exposure to sun gave her skin a dusky *tan.*
2. *(v.)* to go brown or cause to go brown after exposure to ultraviolet rays धूप में फिरने से रंग का जल जाना Prolonged exposure to sun *tanned* her skin.

tangible *(adj.)* टैन्जिबल– capable of being clearly grasped by the mind; substantial rather than imaginary स्पष्ट He wrote some *tangible* opinions about the report.

tangle *(n.)* टैन्गल– 1. a confused or complicated mass of hairs, lines, fibres, etc. knotted or coiled together उलझन, गुत्थी Her hair is in a *tangle.*
2. *(v.)* to become or cause to become twisted together in a confused mass उलझना The kitten played with knitting wool and *tangled* it up.

tank *(n.)* टैंक–1. a large container or reservoir for the storage of liquids or gases तालाब, टंकी We have a *tank* for rainwater at our backdoor.
2. an armoured combat vehicle moving on tracks and armed with guns, etc., मिलिट्री टैंक *Tanks* are used in war. They are able to cross rough land.

tanker *(n.)* टैंकर– a ship, lorry, or aeroplane designed to carry liquid in bulk, such as oil टंकी, तेल ढोने वाला जहाज We need another water *tanker* for our house.

tantalize (ise) *(v.)* टैनटलाइज़– to tease or make frustrated, as by tormenting with the sight of something greatly desired but inaccessible ललचाना, तरसाना Some people *tantalize* their kids with false promises.

tantrum *(n.)* टैन्ट्रम– a childish fit of rage; outburst of bad temper चिड़चिड़ेपन का दौरा, आवेश I cannot tolerate her *tantrums* anymore.

tap *(n.)* टैप–1. a valve by which a fluid flow from a pipe नलका, टोंटी Who left the *tap* running?
2. a light blow or knock, or the sound made by it थपकी She felt a *tap* on her shoulder.

tap dance *(n.)* a step dance in which the performer wears shoes equipped with taps पैरों से ताल देने वाला एक मशहूर नृत्य The *tap dancing* of Michael Jackson can be seen in his album Thriller.

tape *(n.)* टेप–1. a long thin strip, made of cotton, linen, etc., used for binding, fastening, etc. फीता, माप-पट्टी The dress-maker uses a *tape* when he measures a man for a new dress.
2. the speech, music, etc., so recorded रिकार्ड की गई आवाज़ Have you heard Lata's latest *tape*?
3. *(v.)* to record (speech, music, etc.) आवाज़ रिकार्ड करना Did you *tape* Lata's new song?

tape measure *(n.)* टेप मेज़र– a tape or length of metal marked off in inches, centimetres, etc., used principally for measuring and fitting garments नापने का फ़ीता The tailor was using the *tape-measure* for the cloth.

tapeworm *(n.)* टेपवर्म– any parasitic ribbon-like flat worm that lives in intestines of human and animals फ़ीताकृमि Many *tapeworms* were found in his stomach.

tar *(n.)* टार्– any of various dark viscid substances obtained by the destructive distillation of organic matter such as coal, wood, or peat तारकोल, डामर *Tar* is commonly used in preparation of roads.

tardy *(adj.)* टार्डि– slow in progress, growth, etc. सुस्त, मंदगति He was very *tardy* and messy in his life.

target *(n.)* टार्गिट– any point or area aimed at लक्ष्य The sniper recognized its *target* in the crowd.

tariff *(n.)* टैरिफ़– a tax levied by a government on imports or occasionally exports for purposes of protection, support of the balance of payments, or the raising of revenue शुल्क दर The *tariff* at our hotel was hundred rupees for lunch and dinner.

tarnish *(v.)* टार्निश–1. to lose or cause to lose the shine बदरंग हो जाना, मटमैला होना Your silver glasses will be *tarnished* unless you polish them often.

2. to stain or become stained; taint or spoil कलुषित करना, दूषित करना Your bad behaviour will *tarnish* your name.

tarpaulin *(n.)* टार्पॉलिन्– a heavy hard-wearing waterproof fabric made of canvas or similar material coated with tar, wax, or paint, for outdoor use as a protective covering against moisture तिरपाल The luggage was packed on a lorry and covered with a large *tarpaulin.*

tart *(adj.)* टार्ट– having sour taste खट्टा This mango is very *tart.* It can't be eaten.

task *(n.)* टास्क– 1. a specific piece of work required to be done as a duty or chore काम, कर्तव्य One of my *tasks* is to teach my niece.

2. *(v.)* to subject to severe strain काम का अतिरिक्त बोझ लेना Never *task* your strength by carrying heavy loads.

tassel *(n.)* टैसल– a tuft of loose threads secured by a knot or ornamental knob, used to decorate soft furnishings, clothes, etc. फुँदना, फुंदा Long *tassels* were hanging from curtains.

taste *(n.)* टेस्ट–1. the sense by which the qualities and flavour of a substance are distinguished by the taste buds स्वाद, जायक़ा Lemons have a sour *taste.*

2. a preference or liking for something; inclination गुण एवं दोष का ज्ञान, रुचि My sister has a good *taste* for fashion.

3. *(v.)* to take a small amount of (a food, liquid, etc.) into the mouth, esp in order to test the quality स्वाद लेना, चखना The brave never *taste* defeat.

tasteful *(adj.)* टेस्टफ़ुल– indicating good taste स्वादिष्ट, सुरुचिपूर्ण It was a *tasteful* room decorations with fresh flowers.

tasteless *(adj.)* टेस्टलस– lacking in flavour; insipid निःस्वाद, फीका The dish that you prepared is very *tasteless.*

tasty *(adj.)* टेस्टि– having a pleasant flavour ज़ायक़ेदार These cookies are very *tasty.*

tattered *(adj.)* टैटर्ड्– ragged or worn फटा-पुराना The beggar covered himself with a *tattered* blanket on the cold winter night.

tattoo *(n.)* टैटू– a picture or design that is marked on a person's skin शरीर पर गोदा गया चित्र, टैटू I got a *tattoo* painted on my ankle.

tatty *(adj.)* टैटी– worn out, shabby, tawdry, or unkempt फटा-पुराना Her dress was looking very *tatty* and old

taunt *(n.)* टॉण्ट्– 1. a jeering remark कटाक्ष As a child, I often had to endure *taunts* for being fat.
2. *(v.)* to provoke or deride with mockery, contempt, or criticism व्यंग्य करना, ताना कसना As a child, I was *taunted* for being fat.

taut *(adj.)* टॉट्– tightly stretched; tense कसा हुआ In youth, the skin is *taut.* But in the old age, it begins to sag.

tax *(v.)* टैक्स– 1. to levy a tax on persons, companies, etc. or their incomes, etc.) कर या टैक्स लगाना The new law did not *tax* the people heavily.
2. *(n.)* a compulsory financial contribution imposed by a government to raise revenue, levied on the income or property of persons or organizations, कर, टैक्स *Taxes* are levied on property, income, profits and many other items.

taxable *(adj.)* टैक्सबल– capable of being taxed; able to bear tax कर लगाये जाने योग्य Your gains from gambling are also *taxable.*

taxation *(n.)* टैक्सशन– the act or principle of levying taxes or the condition of being taxed कराधान, करारोपण The rate of *taxation* is different for every income group.

tax-free *(adj.)* टैक्सफ्री– not needing to have tax paid on it कर से मुक्त Kuwait, Bahrain and Saudi Arabia are the *tax-free* countries.

taxi *(n.)* टैक्सी– a car, usually fitted with a taximeter, that may be hired, along with its driver किराये की गाड़ी (टैक्सी) Bring me a *taxi* for New Delhi railway-station.

taxonomy *(n.)* टैक्सॉनमी– the science or practice of classification वर्गीकरण-विज्ञान Naresh is a zoologist and has a good knowledge of *taxonomy.*

tea *(n.)* टी–1. dried leaves of the tea bush चाय Mother makes *tea.* She pours boiling water on *tea*-leaves, and mixes milk and sugar. Sometimes she uses *tea bags* in making *tea.*
2. the dried shredded leaves of this shrub, चाय की पत्ती Darjeeling *tea* is famous world over.

teach *(v.)* टीच–1. to help to learn; tell or show (how) शिक्षा देना The teachers *teach* us very efficiently.
2. to give instruction or lessons in (a subject) to (a person or animal) पढ़ाना We must *teach* the baby to talk properly.

teaching *(n.)* टीचिंग–1. the art or profession of a teacher शिक्षण *Teaching* is a respectable profession.
2. something taught; precept शिक्षाएं (उपदेश एवं सिद्धांत) The *teachings* of Mahatma Gandhi will always be remembered.

teak *(n.)* टीक– a large tree having white flowers and yielding a valuable dense wood सागौन की लकड़ी The doors of the house are made of *teak.*

team *(n.)* टीम– 1. a group of people organized to work together (एक साथ काम करने वाले लोगों का) दल या टोली Ravi is a member of the cricket *team* in his school.
2. *(v.)* to make or cause to make a team एक साथ मिलकर काम करना We should do our work with a *team* spirit.

teamwork *(n.)* टीमवर्क– the cooperative work done by a team सामूहिक सहयोग, प्रयास *Teamwork* is the key factor to attain success.

tear *(v.)* टिअर्– 1. to cause (material, paper, etc.) to come apart or (of ma-

terial, etc.) to come apart; rip फाड़ना, चीरना Rama has *torn* her frock.
2. *(n.)* a hole, cut, or split फटाव, चीर Her mother will mend the *tear.*
3. a drop of the secretion of the lacrimal glands आंसू When we cry, *tears* drop from our eyes. She was in *tears* to see her new doll broken.

➢ **tear away**– to persuade (oneself or someone else) to leave किसी चीज़ को बलपूर्वक अलग कर लेना, Why are you *tearing* yourself *away* from me?

➢ **tear down**– to destroy or demolish नष्ट कर देना, गिरा देना, We *tore down* our old house and built an apartment.

➢ **tear up**– to part in portions टुकड़े-टुकड़े कर देना, I was *tearing up* all his photographs.

tearful *(adj.)* टिअरफुल– tending to produce tears; sad दुखद Sonali saw me with her *tearful* eyes.

tease *(v.)* टीज़– to annoy (someone) by deliberately offering something with the intention of delaying or withdrawing the offer तंग करना, परेशान करना, चिढ़ाना, छेड़ना Don't *tease* animals.

technical *(adj.)* टेक्निकल–1. of, relating to, or specializing in industrial, practical, or mechanical arts and applied sciences तकनीकी Have you got a *technical* training to handle this kind to machinery?
2. relating to or characteristic of a particular field of activity प्राविधिक It is a *technical* error. Ordinary man can't judge it.

technicality *(n.)* टैक्निकैलटी– a petty formal point arising from a strict interpretation of rules, etc. प्राविधिक You should know the legal *technicalities* of this case.

technically *(adv.)* टैक्निकली– in relation to industrial, practical, or mechanical arts and applied sciences तकनीकी ज्ञान एवं व्यवहार की दृष्टि से Naseem is *technically* accomplished in his profession.

technician *(n.)* टैक्निशन– a person skilled in mechanical or industrial techniques or in a particular technical field तकनीशियन, मिस्त्री Rohan is a laboratary *technician.*

technique *(n.)* टेक्निक– proficiency in a practical or mechanical skill तकनीक, प्रविधि Now the industry needs a modern *technique.*

technology *(n.)* टेक्नॉलजी– the application of practical sciences to industry or commerce तकनीकी उपकरण Nowadays modern *technology* is very advance.

tedious *(adj.)* टीडिअस– causing fatigue or tedium; monotonous नीरस, थकानेवाला, उबानेवाला The speaker's speech became *tedious* after he had been talking for twenty minutes.

teem *(v.)* टीम– to be prolific or abundant (in); abound (in) भरा होना The road was *teeming* with various big and small vehicles.

teenage *(adj.)* टीनेज– of or relating to the time in a person's life between the ages of 13 and 19 inclusive किशोरावस्था का She is a mother of two *teenage* children.

teenager *(n.)* टीनेजर– a person between the ages of 13 and 19 inclusive किशोर, किशोरी *Teenagers* often find the advice of their parents rubbish.

teens *(n.)* टीन्स– the years of a person's life between the ages of 13 and 19 inclusive किशोरावस्था Harshita is still in her early *teens.*

teetotaller *(n.)* टीटोट्लर्– a person who abstains from alcoholic drink धूम्रपान और मदिरापान न करने वाला व्यक्ति, मद्यत्यागी When offered a drink, he politely refused and said that he was a *teetotaller.*

telecast *(v.)* टेलिकास्ट– to broadcast (a programme) by television प्रसारण करना Her programme will be *telecasted* on every channel.

telecommunications *(n.)* टेलिकम्यूनिकेशन्ज़ the science and technology of communications by telephony, radio, television, etc. दूरसंचार The government will invest more money in the industry of *telecommunications.*

telegraph *(n.)* टेलिग्राफ़– a device, system, or process by which information can be transmitted over a distance, esp using radio signals or coded electrical signals sent along a transmission line connected to a transmitting and a receiving instrument तार-यंत्र, तारप्रेक्षण, टेलीग्राफ The *Telegraph* was one of the initial steps towards telecommunications.

telepathy *(n.)* टेलेपथी– the communication between people of thoughts, feelings, desires, etc., involving mechanisms that cannot be understood in terms of known scientific laws अतींद्रिय बोध, दूरबोध, टेलीपैथी I was feeling that you would come today and you came. Was it a case of *telepathy*?

telephone *(v.)* टेलिफ़ोन– 1. to call or talk to (a person) by telephone दूरसंचार पर बात करना You can *telephone* from here. 2. *(n.)* an electrical device for transmitting speech, consisting of a microphone and receiver mounted on a handset दूरभाष, टेलीफ़ोन Never talk senselessly on *telephone.*

telesales *(n.)* टेलिसेल्ज़– the selling or attempted selling of a particular commodity or service by a salesman who makes his initial approach by telephone टेलीफ़ोन पर बेचने की प्रणाली Sangeeta works in *telesales.*

telescope *(n.)* टेलिस्कोप– an optical instrument for making distant objects appear larger and brighter by use of a combination of lenses (refracting telescope) or lenses and curved mirrors दूरबीन The scientists use *telescopes* to study the stars.

television *(n.)* टेलिविज़न– an electronic equipment with a screen on which one can watch programmes with moving pictures and sound दूरदर्शन *Television* has now become a necessity.

tell *(v.)* टेल–1. to let know or notify बताना, कहना, प्रकट करना Kindly *tell* the principal that I want to see him. 2. to comprehend, discover, or discern कल्पना करना It is difficult to *tell* the end of this struggle. 3. to order or instruct (someone to do something) आज्ञा देना I have *told* you many times that you must obey the rules of the institution.

➢ **tell off**– to reprimand; scold ग़लती पर ग़ुस्सा करना, The teacher *told* her *off* for not bringing her textbook.

➢ **tell on**– to exhaust थका देना या थकाना, If I go on foot it will *talk upon* me.

telling *(adj.)* टेलिंग– revealing सच्चाई दिखाने वाला It was a *telling* argument with him.

temper *(n.)* टेम्पर्– a frame of mind; mood or humour मिजाज़, मनोदशा, तबियत, प्रकृति My father is in a bad *temper* today because he is very angry with me.

temperament *(n.)* टे'म्प्रमेण्ट– an individual's character, disposition, and tendencies as revealed in his reactions प्रकृति, स्वभाव Rupa has a sad *temperament,* she is often unhappy.

temperate *(adj.)* टेम्परेट–1. moderate or mild in temperature न ठंडा न गरम, संतुलित Bangalore has a *temperate* climate.

2. mild in quality or character; exhibiting temperance संयमी, मिताचारी You are a very *temperate* man, for you neither eat nor drink more than what is good for you.

temperature *(n.)* टेम्प्रचर–1. the degree of hotness of a body, बुख़ार, ज्वर The girl had a high *temperature* yesterday, but now she is normal.

2. a measure of this degree of hotness, indicated on a scale that has one or more fixed reference points तापमान What was the maximum *temperature* yesterday?

tempest *(n.)* टेम्पस्ट– a violent wind or storm तूफ़ान, झंझावात The *tempest* destroyed the ships on the seashore.

tempestuous *(adj.)* टेमपेसचुअस– of or relating to a tempest तूफ़ानी, प्रचंड Our ship rolled heavily in the *tempestuous* sea.

template *(n.)* टेम्प्लेट्– a pattern, to help shape something accurately नमूना, साँचा I have prepared the *template* for you. Now prepare all the documents in the same style.

temple *(n.)* टेम्पल्– a building or place dedicated to the worship of a deity or deities मंदिर I visit the *temple* every morning.

tempo *(n.)* टेम्पो–1. the speed at which a piece or passage of music is meant to be played, गति, रफ़्तार The *tempo* in this song keeps on changing from slow to fast.

2. freighter सामान ढोने वाला तिपहिया वाहन Load the material in a *tempo.*

temporary *(adj.)* टेम्पॅररी–1. not permanent; provisional कामचलाऊ The church hall will be used as a *temporary* school until the new school is built.

2. lasting only a short time; transitory अस्थायी This post is quite *temporary.*

3. अल्पकालिक I want to get a *temporary* job because I am waiting for my appointment in the university.

temporarily *(adv.)* टेमपररली– not permanently; provisionally अस्थायी रूप से I have managed a room *temporarily.*

tempt *(v.)* टेम्पट्– 1. to attempt to persuade or entice to do something, लुभाना, बहकाना, लालच देना Do not *tempt* the little boy to eat too many sweets.

2. to allure, invite, or attract प्रेरित करना Can I *tempt* you to have some more of this cake?

temptation *(n.)* टेम्पटेशन– the act of tempting or the state of being tempted लालच, लोभ She has difficulty in resisting *temptation* for chocolates.

tempting *(adj.)* टेम्पटिंग– attractive or inviting लालच पैदा करने वाला, मोहक The job offer was very *tempting* for him.

ten *(n., pron.)* टेन– a numeral, 10, X, etc., representing this number दस He bought *ten* dozen bananas from the market.

tenacious *(adj.)* टनेशस– holding or grasping firmly; forceful दृढ़, ज़िद्दी, हठी Akash is quite *tenacious* in his decision to marry the same girl.

tenant *(n.)* टेनन्ट–1. a person who holds, occupies, or possesses land or property by any kind of right or title, esp from a landlord under a lease किरायेदार Every month the landlord collects the rent from his *tenants.*

2. a person who has the use of a house, flat, etc., subject to the payment of rent दख़लदार, क़ाबिज़ Our *tenant* is a very gentle fellow.

tend *(v.)* टेण्ड–1. to care for देखभाल करना Nurses *tend* sick people. They serve mankind.

2. to pay attention ध्यान देना, (का कारण उत्पन्न करना) Ranjana's accident will *tend* to make her more careful while crossing roads.

3. to have a general disposition (to do something); be inclined प्रवृत्त होना, की ओर झुकना Father *tends* to get tired in the evening.

tendency *(n.)* टेनडन्सि– an inclination, predisposition, propensity, or leaning रुझान, प्रवृत्ति He has a *tendency* to make mistakes on a regular basis.

tender *(adj.)* टेण्डर–1. gentle and delicate कोमल, मुलायम, नाज़ुक You have such *tender* skin that you get rashes after a short exposure to sun.

2. having or expressing warm and affectionate feelings सहृदय, स्नेहभरा, करुणामय Mother is *tender* with her baby.

3. young age छोटी उम्र This solid food is not suitable for the child at *tender* age.

4. *(n.)* to offer (money or goods) in settlement of a debt or claim टेंडर, ठेकेदार द्वारा प्रस्तुत होने वाले काम के लिए देय राशि का ब्यौरा (पहले से प्रस्तुत) The council has invited *tenders* for the building of a hall.

5. *(v.)* to give, present, or offer प्रस्तुत करना Have you *tendered* your resignation from the post of editor?

tenement *(n.)* टेनमेण्ट– a large building divided into separate flats (चाल की) कोठरी Two large houses have been divided into *tenements*.

tennis *(n.)* टेनिस– a racket game played between two players or pairs of players who hit a ball to and fro over a net on a rectangular court of grass, टेनिस नामक खेल *Tennis* is very popular in European countries.

tense *(adj.)* टेन्स– 1. stretched or stressed tightly; taut or rigid तनावयुक्त The whole audience was *tense* with excitement about the result of the music competition.

2. *(n.)* a category of the verb or verbal inflections, such as present, past, and future, काल There are three *tenses* in grammar – past *tense*, present *tense* and future *tense*.

tension *(n.)* टेनशन– mental or emotional strain; stress तनाव, खिंचाव There was a lot of *tension* between the couple.

tent *(n.)* टेण्ट– a portable shelter of canvas, plastic, or other waterproof material supported on poles and fastened to the ground by pegs and ropes तम्बू, खेमा, शिविर A *tent* is made of canvas. It is held in place by *tent*-pegs.

tentative *(adj.)* टेन्टटिव– provisional or experimental; conjectural अनिश्चित I have decided the name of my book, though it is still *tentative*.

tenth *(pron.)* टेन्थ– one of 10 equal divisions of a particular measurement, etc. दसवाँ भाग On the *tenth* of July she will come to meet me.

tenure *(n.)* टेन्यर्– the length of time an office, position, etc., lasts; term अवधि The firm extended his *tenure* to work because of his performance.

tepid *(adj.)* टेपिड– slightly warm; lukewarm गुनगुना, कुनकुना You have to take this tablet with *tepid* water.

term *(n.)* टर्म–1. any of the divisions of the academic year during which a school, college, etc., is in session शैक्षिक सत्र I was absent from college for the whole of the summer *term*.

2. conditions of an agreement शर्तें Find out the *terms* on which we can get a room for the holidays.

3. mutual relationship or standing समझौता If you are willing to sell your house, we can settle the *terms*.

4. a point in time determined for an event or for the end of a period अवधि, मियाद Her *term* in office ends in December.

terminal *(adj.)* टर्मिनल– of, being, or situated at an end, terminus, or boundary अंतिम (पड़ाव) From which *terminal* does your flight depart.

terminate *(v.)* टर्मिनेट– to form, be, or put an end (to); conclude समाप्त होना/करना, नौकरी से निकाल देना The firm *terminated* her because she did not adhere to the rules.

terminology *(n.)* टर्मिनॉलजी– the body of specialized words relating to a particular subject शब्दावली The business *terminology* gives definitions and resources for some business terms.

terminus *(n.)* टर्मिनस–1. the last or final part or point (रेल या बस का) अंतिम स्थल Wait for them at the bus *terminus.* 2. a boundary or boundary marker सीमा का सूचक खंभा या पत्थर All passengers must leave the lorry at the *terminus.*

termite *(n.)* टर्माइट– whitish ant-like insect that lives in organized groups of warm and tropical regions. दीमक The door was eaten up by the *termites.*

terrace *(n.)* टेरस– a horizontal flat area of ground, often one of a series in a slope चबूतरा, छज्जा, वेदिका Rachna and Minakshi had tea sitting on the *terrace.*

terrible *(adj.)* टेरबल–1. very serious or extreme भयानक, भीषण, प्रचण्ड There was a *terrible* storm in which many ships were wrecked.
2. of poor quality; unpleasant or bad बहुत बुरा I can't bear this *terrible* cold.

terribly *(adv.)* टेरिबली– in a terrible manner बहुत खराब She was *terribly* sorry for her conduct.

terrific *(adj.)* टरिफ़िक– very good; excellent बढ़िया, उत्कृष्ट He is a *terrific* singer.

terrified *(adj.)* टेरिफ़ाइड– very frightened भयभीत I am *terrified* of walking home at night.

terrify *(v.)* टेरिफ़ाइ– to inspire fear or dread in; frighten greatly भयभीत कर देना, दहलाना Our dog *terrified* us when it jumped into the pond.

territory *(n.)* टेरटरी– any tract of land; district क्षेत्र, प्रदेश There is a great deal of forest *territory* in India.

terror *(n.)* टे'रर्– great fear, panic, or dread त्रास, आतंक, दहशत Animals have a great *terror* of fire.

terrorism *(n.)* टेररिज़्म– systematic use of violence and intimidation to achieve some goal आतंकवाद *Terrorism* affects Muslims of India just like other Indians.

test *(v.)* टैस्ट– 1. to ascertain (the worth, capability, or endurance) of (a person or thing) by subjection to certain examinations; try परीक्षण करना, जांच करना Before we buy an equipment we should always *test* it.
2. *(n.)* a method, practice, or examination designed to test a person or thing परीक्षा, टैस्ट Her teacher gave her a *test* in spelling.

testament *(n.)* टे'सटमेण्ट– a proof, attestation, or tribute विधान The Old and New *Testaments* are the two parts that make up the Bible.

testify *(v.)* टेस्टिफ़ाइ– to state (something) formally as a declaration of fact गवाही या साक्ष्य देना, सिद्ध करना When I speak to the judge, we *testify* before him.

testimony *(n.)* टेसटिमनी– a thing that shows that sth is true साक्ष्य, प्रमाण What I say in my *testimony.*

tetanus *(n.)* टेटनस– an acute infectious disease in which sustained muscular spasm, contraction, and convulsion are caused by bacteria धनुषटंकार The doctor gave a *tetanus* injection to the injured patient.

tether *(v.)* टेदर्– to tie an animal to a post खूंटे पर बाँधना *Tether* your horse to this post while you go for shopping.

text *(n.)* टेक्स्ट– the main body of a printed or written work as distinct from commentary, notes, illustrations, etc. मूल पाठ, मूल विषय The *text* of a book does not include the picture.

textbook *(n.)* टेक्स्टबुक– a book used as a standard source of information on a particular subject पाठ्यपुस्तक We have a separate *textbook* for each subject in college.

textile *(n.)* टेक्स्टाइल– any fabric or cloth, esp woven कपड़ा, वस्त्र का उद्योग My friend works in a *textile* mill.

texture *(n.)* टेक्सचर– the surface of a material, esp as perceived by the sense of touch बुनावट, गठन, संरचना The *texture* of her silken sari was very smooth.

than *(conj.)* दैन– used to introduce the second element of a comparison (की) अपेक्षा A motorcycle can go faster *than* a bicycle.

thank *(v.)* थैन्क– to convey feelings of gratitude to धन्यवाद देना, शुक्रिया अदा करना You must *thank* your lucky stars that you were not in the house when the robbers attacked it.

thankful *(adj.)* थैंकफुल– grateful and appreciative कृतज्ञ, शुक्रगुज़ार I am *thankful* to you for your timely help.

thankfully *(adv.)* थैंकफुलि–1. showing gratitude or appreciation कृतज्ञता-पूर्वक He accepted my invitation *thankfully.*

2. fortunately *(conj.)* शुक्र है कि *Thankfully* it has stopped raining.

thankless *(adj.)* थैंकलस– receiving no thanks or appreciation बेकार, अप्रिय Amir did a *thankless* job for me.

that *(pron.)* दैट– 1. used preceding a noun that has been mentioned at some time or is understood वह, अर्थात्, यानी, जो This is the dog *that* bit the thief.

2. *(conj.)* used to introduce a noun clause कि I told Ramesh I hated him, and *that* he should leave the room immediately.

3. *(adv.)* used with adjectives or adverbs to reinforce the specification of a precise degree already mentioned यानि, इतना He is a cutler, *that* is to say, a man who sells knives and sharp tools.

4. *(adj.)* intensifier यह, वह, उस, इस This is the girl *that* lives in Lajpat Nagar.

thatch *(v.)* थैच– a roofing material that consists of straw, reed, etc. छप्पर The cottage had been newly *thatched.*

thatched *(adj.)* थैच्ड– covered with a roofing material that consists of straw, reed, etc. छप्पर, घास-फूँस की छत The farmer lived in a *thatched* hut.

thaw *(v.)* थॉ– 1. to melt or cause to melt from a solid frozen state पिघलना, पिघलाना The ice on the pond will *thaw* when the weather gets warmer.

2. *(n.)* the act or process of thawing द्रवण, गलन After the *thaw,* the streams flow fast.

the *(adj.)* द, दी– used before comparative adjectives or adverbs for emphasis वह, वही

- *The* moon is very cool. *The* sun is very hot.
- *The* man you met steals money.
- *The* shopkeeper you know is a dishonest man.
- I saw *the* fellow you had wanted.

- *The* sooner you go from this sad atmosphere, *the* better you will feel.
- I saw a cow on *the* road. *The* cow was grazing *the* grass.

theatre *(n.)* थीअॅटर्–1. a building designed for the performance of plays, operas, etc. रंगमंच, नाचघर, नाट्यशाला Had you gone to the *theatre* last night?

2. a room in a hospital or other medical centre equipped for surgical operations शल्यशाला The patient was moved to the operation *theatre.*

theft *(n.)* थेफ़्ट– the dishonest taking of property belonging to another person with the intention of depriving the owner permanently of its possession चोरी The police arrested a man for the *theft* of my bicycle.

their *(det.)* देअर– of, belonging to, or associated in some way with them उनका Did they finish *their* work?

theirs *(pron.)* देअरज़्– something or someone belonging to or associated in some way with them उनका, उनके My friends came to my home but I could not go *theirs.*

them *(pron.)* दैम– refers to things or people other than the speaker or people addressed उन्हें I explained *them* but no one believed me.

theme *(n.)* थीम– an idea or topic expanded in a discourse, discussion, etc. सार, संक्षेप, मूल विषय Please tell me the *theme* before narrating the whole story.

themselves *(pron.)* दमसेलव्ज़्– the reflexive form of they or them स्वयं They were discussing among *themselves.*

then *(adv.)* देन–1. at that time; over that period of time उस समय Come, let us go to him at about 9 p.m., he will be at home by *then.*

2. in that case; that being so तब We know it is wrong, *then* what is the alternative for it?

thence *(adv.)* दे'न्स– from that place उस स्थान से, तत्पश्चात् We went to Delhi and *thence* to Amritsar.

theory *(n.)* थिअरी–1. a system of rules, procedures, and assumptions used to produce a result सिद्धांत If anybody wants to study art properly, he should also learn the *theory* of it.

2. abstract knowledge or reasoning परिकल्पना, विचार-मात्र Old stories had been based on the false *theory* that the sun is revolving and the earth is stationary.

therapeutic *(adj.)* थेरप्यूटिक– of or relating to the treatment of disease; curative आरोग्यकर He gave a *therapeutic* drug to the patient.

therapy *(n.)* थेरपी– the treatment of physical, mental, or social disorders or disease चिकित्सा, रोगोपचार Aroma *therapy* is said to relieve tension and stress.

there *(adv.)* दे'अर्–1. in, at, or to that place, point, case, or respect वहाँ (उस स्थान या स्थिति में) Please do not go *there,* be seated.

2. who or which is in that place or position किसी स्थान के साथ पूरक रूप में *There* are fifteen students in the class.

3. that place इसी क्षण *There* is no money in my purse.

thereabouts *(adv.)* देअरबाउटस्– near that place, time, amount, etc. के आस-पास The Jain family lives in Sector 44 Gurgoan or *thereabouts.*

thereafter *(adv.)* देअरआफ़्टर– from that time on or after that time उसके बाद, फिर I reached office at 9 o'clock, Himani came *thereafter.*

therefore *(adv.)* दे'अर्फ़ॉर्– thus; hence, used to mark an inference on the speaker's part इसलिए, अतः, इस कारण से We are going to the cinema in the evening, *therefore* we will be home late.

therein *(adv.)* देअरइन– in or into that place, thing, etc. उसके भीतर या उसमें, वहां She lives alone, *therein* lies the cause of her sadness.

thereupon *(adv.)* देअरपॉन– immediately after that; at that point ठीक उसके बाद He abused her and *thereupon* they came to fight.

thermometer *(n.)* थर्मॉमीटर्– an instrument used to measure temperature तापमापी, थर्मामीटर A *thermometer* measures temperature.

thesaurus *(n.)* थिसॉरस– a book containing systematized lists of synonyms and related words पर्याय-कोश Consult a *Thesaurus* and tell me a better word for 'big'.

these *(pron.)* दीज़– the form of this used before a plural noun ये *These* children are very naughty.

thesis *(n.)* थिसिस– a dissertation resulting from original research, esp when submitted by a candidate for a degree or diploma शोध-प्रबंध I did my *thesis* on modern Indian literature.

they *(pron.)* दे– refers to people or things other than the speaker or people addressed वे, ये (लोग) There are your notebooks. *They* are on the table.

thick *(adj.)* थिक– of relatively great extent from one surface to the other; fat, broad, or deep घना, मोटा, गाढ़ा, गहरा It is hard to walk through the *thick* forest.

thicken *(v.)* थिकन– to make or become thick or thicker गाढ़ा करना, सघन करना The cook *thickened* the custard by adding corn flour.

thickness *(n.)* थिकनस– the dimension through an object, as opposed to length or width मोटाई, सघनता The *thickness* of a book doesn't mean that its good.

thicket *(n.)* थिकिट– a dense growth of small trees, shrubs, and similar plants झुरमुट, झाड़-झंखाड़ The robbers were hiding in the *thicket*.

thick-skinned *(adj.)* insensitive to criticism or hints; not easily upset or affected मोटी चमड़ी वाला, भावशून्य These reporters are pretty *thick-skinned*.

thief *(n.)* थीफ़– a person who steals something from another चोर, तस्कर People who steal things are called *thieves*.

thigh *(n.)* थाइ– the part of the leg between the hip and the knee in man जांघ, रान, जंघा Your *thighs* are need of surgery so as to stop the clot.

thin *(adj.)* थिन–1. weak; poor; insufficient पतला, दुर्बल, कमज़ोर If you do not eat your dinner well, you will grow *thin*.

2. slim or lean पतला, दुबला (जो मोटा नहीं होता) You are a *thin* girl but she is a fat.

3. of relatively small extent from one side or surface to the other; fine or narrow बारीक This needle is too *thin*. Please get me a thicker one.

4. having low density, usually insufficient to produce a satisfactory positive हलका रंग She was wearing a *thin* colour skirt.

thing *(n.)* थिंग–1. any inanimate object वस्तु, चीज़ Please give me some *thing* to eat.

2. an object or entity that cannot or need not be precisely named कोई गुण या दशा A *thing* of beauty is a joy for ever.

think *(v.)* थिंक–1. to consider, judge, or believe सोचना Look before you leap. *Think* before you speak.

2. to exercise the mind as in order to make a decision; ponder समझना Father *thinks* that Rajan is a nice man.

3. to be capable of conscious thought किसी दूसरे के विषय में सोचना We should never *think* of taking what belongs to others.

4. to consider; regard विचार या मत रखना I *think* you should see the doctor.

- **think better of**– to change one's course of action after reconsideration विचार बदल देना, She intended to go, but later *thought better of* it.
- **think over**– to ponder or consider विचार कर लेना, She *thought* it *over* and said yes.
- **think up**– to invent or devise नई चीज़ या योजना सोचना, I am *thinking up* new title of the book.

thinker *(n.)* थिंकर– a person who spends a lot of time thinking deeply about important things विचारक He is one the great *thinkers* of our time.

thinking *(n.)* थिंकिंग– 1. opinion or judgment चिंतन, सोच-विचार This incident changed my *thinking* about people.

2. *(adj.)* capable of using intelligent thought विवेकी, विचारशील She brought a *thinking* woman's magazine to home.

third *(det.)* थर्ड– coming after the second and preceding the fourth in numbering or counting order, position, time, etc.; तीसरा, तृतीय Vaibhav came *third* in the race competition.

third-degree *(adj.)* torture or bullying, esp used to extort confessions or information क़बूल कराने या कोई गुप्त सूचना प्राप्त करने के लिए पुलिस द्वारा दी जाने वाली प्रबल यातनाएं The cause of his death were *third-degree* burns all over his body.

thirdly *(adv.)* थर्डलि– in the third place तीसरी बार, तीसरे She has three qualities: first she is intelligent, secondly, well-educated and *thirdly*, very beautiful.

third party *(n.)* थर्डपार्टी– a person who is involved by chance or only incidentally in a legal proceeding, agreement, or other transaction, esp one against whom a defendant claims indemnity अन्य पक्ष He listened to the *third party*.

third person *(n.)* थर्ड पर्सन– a grammatical category of pronouns and verbs used when referring to objects or individuals other than the speaker or his addressee(s) अन्य पुरुष (जिसके विषय में बात की जा रही है) This book is written in the *third person* narrative.

thirst *(n.)* थर्स्ट–1. a craving to drink, accompanied by a feeling of dryness in the mouth and throat प्यास The traveller quenched his *thirst* at the well.

2. an eager longing, craving, or yearning लालसा, तीव्र इच्छा My son has a great *thirst* for knowledge.

thirsty *(adj.)* थर्स्टी– feeling a desire to drink प्यासा Jogging makes me very *thirsty*.

thirteenth *(det., adv.)* थर्टीन्थ– coming after the twelfth in numbering or counting order, position, time, etc. being the ordinal number of thirteen often written 13th तेरहवां They invited me for their *thirteenth* wedding anniversary.

this *(pron. & adj.)* दिस– used with adjectives and adverbs to specify a precise degree that is about to be mentioned यह, इस

- What is *this*?
- Would you rather have *this* pen or that one?
- Did you find *this* purse on the road?
- I intend to go to Kolkata *this* month.

thither *(adv.)* दिदर्– to or towards that place; in that direction परला He was running hither and *thither.*

thorn *(n.)* थॉर्न–1. a sharp pointed woody extension of a stem or leaf काँटा, कंटक Baby's balloon settled on a rose bush and was punctured by its *thorns.*
2. a source of irritation काँटोंभरी Life is full of *thorns.*

thorny *(adj.)* थॉर्नि– bearing or covered with thorns काँटेदार, कँटीला Roses are grown in *thorny* bushes.

thorough *(adj.)* थॅर– carried out completely and carefully सम्यक्, सम्पूर्ण You need a *thorough* check-up. Anant is confident and *thorough* in this subject.

thoroughly *(adv.)* थॅरली–1. completely and with great attention to detail पूरी तरह से Have you studied this subject *thoroughly*?
2. to the greatest possible extent or degree पूर्णतया, पूरा-पूरा Check the luggage *thoroughly.*

thoroughfare *(n.)* थॅरफ़ेअर्– a road from one place to another, esp a main road आम रास्ता This is not a *thoroughfare.*

though *(conj.)* दो–1. despite the fact that यद्यपि, भले ही, हालांकि The medicine will do you good, *though* you may not like the taste of it.
2. nevertheless; however किन्तु, परन्तु, लेकिन, मगर She walks as *though* her feet hurt her.

thought *(n.)* थॉट– a concept, opinion, or idea विचार, ख़्याल, धारणा He had a terrible *thought* about me.

thoughtful *(adj.)* थॉटफुल– showing careful thought विचारमग्न I became *thoughtful* for a moment.

thoughtless *(adj.)* थॉटलस– unable to think; not having the power of thought लापरवाह, बेलिहाज़ She is *thoughtless* in carrying out her domestic work.

thoughtlessly *(adv.)* थॉटलसली– inconsiderately विचारशून्य होकर, लापरवाही से He treats his parents *thoughtlessly.*

thoughtlessness *(n.)* थॉटलसनस– lack of consideration बेमुरौवती, स्वार्थीपन I am exceedingly mortified at this shameful piece of *thoughtlessness.*

thousand *(adj.)* थाउज़ॅन्ड– a numeral, 1000, 10^3, M, etc., representing this number हज़ार Ten hundreds make a *thousand.*

thrash *(v.)* थ्रैश– to beat or plunge about in a wild manner पीटना, मारना The mother will *thrash* the child if she catches him stealing the coins.

thrashing *(n.)* थ्रेशिंग– a physical assault; flogging पिटाई He needs a good *thrashing.*

thread *(v.)* थ्रे'ड– 1. to pass (thread, film, magnetic tape, etc.) through (something) धागा डालना I will *thread* the needle.
2. *(n.)* a fine strand, filament or fibre of some material धागा Have you a reel of black *thread*?

threat *(v.)* थ्रे'ट– 1. to be a threat to धमकी देना The teacher *threatened* to punish the whole class if there was any more noise.
2. *(n.)* a declaration of the intention to inflict harm, pain, or misery धमकी The gardener's *threat* to thrash the boys who steal the mangoes has frightened them away.

three *(adj.)* थ्री– a numeral, 3, III, (iii), representing this number तीन *Three* little pigs had a race. The black pig came third.

thresh *(v.)* थ्रेश– to beat or rub stalks of ripe corn or a similar crop either with a hand implement or a machine to separate the grain from the husks and straw अनाज को गाहना After harvesting, the crops were *threshed* to get the grains.

threshold *(n.)* थ्रे'शोल्ड– a sill, esp one made of stone or hardwood, placed at a doorway दहलीज़, द्वार As soon as we crossed the *threshold* of uncle's house, his dog barked loudly.

thrift *(n.)* थ्रिफ़्ट– wisdom and caution in the management of money मितव्ययिता, कमखर्ची By continuous *thrift*, Vagish saved enough money to buy a bike.

thrifty *(adj.)* थ्रिफ़्टी– showing thrift; economical or frugal मितव्ययी, किफ़ायती, कमखर्च Mother taught us all to be *thrifty*.

thrill *(n.)* थ्रिल– 1. a sudden sensation of excitement and pleasure रोमांच, पुलक I can't forget the *thrill* of winning my first prize.

2. *(v.)* to feel or cause to feel a thrill रोमांचित करना, पुलकित करना The news that she had won a prize *thrilled* her parents.

thrilling *(adj.)* थ्रिलिंग– very exciting or stimulating रोमांचकारी It was a *thrilling* moment when the mother found her lost baby.

thrive *(v.)* थ्राइव– to grow strongly and vigorously फलना-फूलना We *thrive* on fresh air and wholesome food.

throat *(n.)* थ्रोट–1. the front part of the neck गला, कंठ The *throat* is the front part of the neck.

2. that part of the alimentary and respiratory tracts extending from the back of the mouth to just below the larynx श्वास और आहार की नली Wear a scarf lest you should get a sore *throat*.

throb *(v.)* थ्रॉब– to pulsate or beat repeatedly, esp with increased force धड़कना If you run very fast, your heart will *throb* loudly.

throne *(n.)* थ्रोन– the ceremonial seat occupied by a monarch, bishop, etc. on occasions of state राजसिंहासन, राजगद्दी The English are loyal to the *throne*.

throng *(v.)* थ्रॉंग– to gather in or fill (a place) in large numbers; crowd भीड़ लगाना, भीड़ से भर जाना People *thronged* the roads.

throttle *(v.)* थ्रॉटल– to kill or injure by squeezing the throat गला घुटना या घोंटना The tight collar of my overcoat is *throttling* me.

through *(prep.)* थ्रू–1. going in or starting at one side and coming out or stopping at the other side of (के) आर-पार, (के) पार, (के) दौरान The sun shines *through* the day and moon shines *through* the night.

2. as a result of; by means of के कारण, की वजह से The accident happened *through* my own carelessness.

throughout *(adv., prep.)* थ्रूआउट–1. through the whole of some specified period or area सदा, पूरी अवधि में *Throughout* the day she had been typing.

2. right through; through the whole of (a place or a period of time) सब जगह, हर जगह The house was searched *throughout*.

throw *(v.)* थ्रो–1. to put or move suddenly, carelessly, or violently गिराना, पटकना The horse *threw* its rider off.

2. to project or cast (something) through the air, esp with a rapid motion of the arm and wrist फेंकना *Throw* me the ball, I will kick it.

3. to direct or cast (a shadow, light, etc.) डालना (रोशनी या छाया) This information may *throw* light upon the mystery of the rich man's death.

4. to cause to fall or be upset; dislodge फेरना, घुमाना She *threw* her head back.

5. to tip (dice) out onto a flat surface के ऊपर छोड़ना Samina *threw* herself at the mercy of court.

throwaway *(adj.)* थ्रोअवे– said or done incidentally, esp for rhetorical effect;

casual मज़ाक या बिना सोचे कही गई बात I became very upset at what to him was just a *throwaway* comment.

thrust *(v.)* थ्रस्ट– to push (someone or something) with force or sudden strength पेलना, ढकेलना Hari *thrust* his hand into his pocket to find out how many coins were there.

thud *(n.)* थड– a dull heavy sound धम, धमाका A ball hit him on his head and he fell with a *thud* on the ground.

thumb *(n.)* थॅम– 1. the first and usually shortest and thickest of the digits of the hand अँगूठा Illiterate persons put their *thumb* impressions as signature.

2. *(v.)* to touch, mark, or move with the thumb अँगूठे से जल्दी-जल्दी पन्ने पलटना I began *thumbing* through the pages of a reference book.

thump *(v.)* थम्प– to strike or beat heavily; pound मारना, ठोकना, प्रहार करना He will *thump* you if you say that again.

thunder *(n.)* थण्डर्– 1. any loud booming sound गर्जन, बादलों की गर्जन The lightning flashed and the *thunder* roared.

2. *(v.)* to make (a loud sound) or utter (words) in a manner suggesting thunder गड़गड़ाने की आवाज़ करना This engine came *thundering* along the rails.

3. to utter vehement threats or denunciation; rail क्रोध में भरकर बोलना, गरजना The manager *thundered* —"Get out of here at once."

thunderstorm *(n.)* थण्डरस्टॉर्म– a storm caused by strong rising air currents and characterized by thunder and lightning and usually heavy rain or hail गरज वाला तूफ़ान The state government has issued an *thunderstorm* warning.

Thursday *(n.)* थर्सडे– the fifth day of the week; fourth day of the working week बृहस्पतिवार *Thursday* comes after Wednesday.

thus *(adv.)* दॅस– in this manner इसलिए We knew that he was dishonest, *thus* we did not believe him.

thwart *(v.)* थ्वॉट– to oppose successfully or prevent; frustrate व्यर्थ/निष्फल The work pressure at office *thwarted* my vacation plans.

thyroid *(n.)* थाइरॉइड– of or relating to the thyroid gland अवटुग्रंथि One of the most important glands in our body is the *thyroid* gland.

tick *(v.)* टिक– to mark or check (something, such as a list) with a tick निशान लगाना The teacher *ticked* the name of the students who had entered the bus.

ticket *(v.)* टिकिट– a printed piece of paper that gives one the right to travel on a train, bus, etc. or to go into theatre, etc. टिकट Always buy a *ticket* when you travel by bus or train.

tickle *(n.)* टिकल्– to touch, stroke, or poke (a person, part of the body, etc.) so as to produce pleasure, laughter, or a twitching sensation गुदगुदाना The baby laughs when mother *tickles* his toes.

ticklish *(adj.)* टिकलिश– susceptible and sensitive to being tickled गुदगुदी His skin is very soft and *ticklish*.

tide *(n.)* टाइड– the cyclic rise and fall of sea level caused by the gravitational pull of the sun and moon ज्वार-भाटा At low *tide*, the sea falls and goes far out.

tidy *(v.)* टाइडि– 1. to put (things) in order; neaten साफ़-सुथरा रखना She is *tidying* her room.

2. *(adj.)* characterized by or indicating neatness and order सुव्यवस्थित, ठीक-ठाक Asha always keeps her room *tidy*.

tie *(v.)* टाइ– 1. to fasten or be fastened with string, thread, etc. बाँधना Mother, please *tie* my shoelaces.

2. *(n.)* a long narrow piece of material worn, esp by men, under the collar of a shirt, tied in a knot close to the throat with the ends hanging down the front टाई (गले में बाँधने का कपड़े का टुकड़ा) Father wears a *tie* round his neck.

tiger *(n.)* टाइगर्– a large wild animal having a tawny yellow coat with black stripes बाघ, व्याघ्र *Tiger* is a wild animal.

tight *(adj.)* टाइट– fitting or covering in a close manner तंग, वायु/जल-रोधी My new shoes are too *tight.*

tighten *(v.)* टाइटन– to make or become tight or tighter कसना या कस देना *Tighten* your belt and wear your coat.

tile *(n.)* टाइल– 1. a flat thin slab of fired clay, rubber, linoleum, etc., usually square or rectangular and sometimes ornamental, used with others to cover a roof, floor, wall, etc. खपड़ा, टाइल The bathroom *tiles* are of golden colour.

2. *(v.)* to cover with tiles टाइल लगाना या बिछाना The masons were *tiling* the kitchen.

till *(prep.)* टिल– 1. up to (a time) that (उस समय) तक The farmer works from morning *till* evening.

2. *(v.)* to cultivate and work (land) for the raising of crops (ज़मीन) जोतना, हल चलाना The cultivators *till* the soil.

3. *(n.)* a box, case, or drawer into which the money taken from customers is put, now usually part of a cash register दराज़, पैसा रखने की जगह While the cashier was out, someone robbed the *till.*

tilt *(v.)* टिल्ट– to incline or cause to incline at an angle एक तरफ़ झुकना या झुकाना The Leaning Tower of Pisa is slightly *tilted.*

timber *(n.)* टिम्बर– wood, esp when regarded as a construction material इमारती लकड़ी A huge forest of *timber* has been destroyed by fire.

time *(n.)* टाइम–1. a quantity measuring duration, समय We want to reach the office in *time.*

2. the continuous passage of existence in which events pass from a state of potentiality in the future, through the present, to a state of finality in the past सैकड़ों मिनटों, घण्टों, दिनों, महीनों या वर्षों का समय *Time* seemed to stand still.

3. an instance or occasion बार, दफ़ा, मर्तबा It is useless to repeat, I heard you the first *time* itself.

➢ **ahead of time**– before the deadline निश्चित समय से पहले, Her boss always expects everything *ahead of time.*

➢ **all the time**– continuously हर समय, सदा They were busy *all the time.*

➢ **at the same time**– simultaneously एक साथ, She has two projects *at the same time.*

➢ **at the time**– at specific period of time उस समय, तब He was agreed *at the time* but later changed her mind.

➢ **at times**– sometimes कभी-कभी, समय-समय पर *At times* I wish I would never eat junk food.

➢ **behind time**– later than was expected विलंब से, देर से They arrived *behind time.*

➢ **by this time**– by now अब तक He has not come *by this time.*

➢ **for the time being**– for the moment; temporarily फ़िलहाल, अस्थायी रूप से Be with me *for the time being.*

➢ **from time to time**– at intervals; occasionally कभी-कभी, जब तब His son has been coming to India *from time to time.*

➢ **in no time**– very quickly; almost instantaneously तुरंत, झटपट She completed my work *in no time.*

➢ **in time**– early or at the appointed time समय के अंदर Farha has come *in time* for the first time in her life.

➢ **time limit** a time or date before which a particular task must be completed अंतिम तिथि, समय सीमा, You have to set *time limit* for the game.

timely *(adj.)* टाइमली– at the right or an opportune or appropriate time मौक़े पर, यथासमय The *timely* intervention of the fireman stopped the fire from spreading.

timid *(adj.)* टिमिड– easily frightened or upset, esp by human contact; shy डरपोक, कायर Squirrels are *timid* creatures.

tin *(n.)* टिन– an airtight sealed container of thin sheet metal coated with tin, used for preserving and storing food or drink कनस्तर, डिब्बा, टीन We need two *tins* of vegetable oil.

tinge *(v.)* टिंज– 1. to colour or tint faintly (का) पुट देना, रंगत चढ़ाना The rays of the setting sun *tinge* the clouds pink.
2. *(n.)* a slight tint or colouring पुट, झलक, रंगत There is no *tinge* of regret in his voice.

tingle *(v.)* टिंगल– to feel or cause to feel a prickling, itching, or stinging sensation of the flesh, as from a cold plunge or electric shock झुनझुनी चढ़ना या होना Cold air makes my ears *tingle.*

tinkle *(v.)* टिंकल– to ring or cause to ring with a series of high tinny sounds, like a small bell टनटनाना The bells on the pony's harness *tinkle* as it trots along.

tint *(v.)* टिंट– 1. to colour or tinge हल्का रंग रंगना या रंग का छींटा देना You can *tint* the sky in your picture with some light blue paint.
2. *(n.)* a shade of a colour, esp a pale one रंगत, हल्का छींटा रंग का There were *tints* of yellow and gold in the morning sky.

tiny *(adj.)* टाइनी– very small; minute बहुत छोटा, नन्हा
• A *tiny* lamp was burning near the shrine.
• The *tiny* boy won the race.

tip *(v.)* टिप– 1. to tilt or cause to tilt झुकाना, तिरछा करना, उलटाना I *tipped* my glass over by mistake.
2. *(n.)* thin pointed end of sth नोक, नुकीला सिरा She touched the cat with the *tip* of her cane.

tiptoe *(n.)* टिप्टो– standing on the front part of one's foot पंजा (पंजों के बल) He *tiptoed* to his room so as to not wake everyone.

tire *(v.)* टाइर्– to reduce the energy of, esp by exertion; weary थकना, थकाना Climbing up that steep hill will *tire* you.

tired *(adj.)* टाइअर्ड– weary; fatigued थका हुआ, थका-माँदा, पस्त The long journey by bus has *tired* me.

tireless *(adj.)* टाइअलस– unable to be tired; indefatigable अथक (परिश्रम) His *tireless* labour will succeed at last.

tiresome *(adj.)* टाइअर्सम– boring and irritating; irksome उबाऊ, थकाऊ I did not like his *tiresome* speech.

tiring *(adj.)* टाइअरिंग– if you describe something as tiring, you mean that it makes you tired so that you want to rest or sleep थकाने वाला This was a very *tiring* journey.

tissue *(n.)* टिस्यू–टिश्यू– a part of an organism consisting of a large number of cells having a similar structure and function ऊतक The body is held together by muscular *tissues.*

titbit *(n.)* टिट्बिट्– a pleasing scrap of anything, such as scandal चटपटी और मज़ेदार खबर We always find him ready with jokes and funny *titbits.*

title *(n.)* टाइटल–1. the distinctive name of a work of art, musical or literary composition, etc. पुस्तक का नाम What is the *title* of your novel?
2. a name or epithet signifying rank, office, or function उपाधि, व्यक्ति के पद, व्यवसाय ओहदा प्रकट करने का विशेष नाम Some Indians were honoured with

the *title* 'Sir' for their services to the British during the latter's rule in India.

titter *(v.)* टिटर्– to snigger, esp derisively or in a suppressed way हीं-हीं करके हँसना, ठी-ठी करना Why are you *tittering* without any reason?

to *(prep.)* टु– 1. used to indicate the destination of the subject or object of an action को, की ओर The old lady is going *to* the market.

2. used to mark the indirect object of a verb in a sentence के लिए, अथवा संयुक्त क्रिया के प्रयोग में

- The old man is going *to* buy meat.
- Do you want *to* finish your job today?

toast *(v.)* टोस्ट–1. to brown under a grill or over a fire डबल रोटी को सेंकना Mother *toasts* bread for the family's breakfast.

2. to propose or drink a toast to (a person or thing) किसी व्यक्ति के स्वास्थ्य एवं शुभकामना के लिए कहे गए शब्दों के बाद मद्यपान करना Let us *toast* the newly weds.

3. *(n.)* sliced bread browned by exposure to heat, usually under a grill, over a fire, or in a toaster डबलरोटी का टुकड़ा, टोस्ट Would you like *toast* and coffee for breakfast?

tobacoo *(n.)* टबैको– dried leaves of the tobacco plant, used for making cigarottos or chewing. तम्बाकू Chewing or smoking *tobacco* is injurious to health.

today *(n.)* टुडे– 1. this day, as distinct from yesterday or tomorrow आज *Today* is a holiday.

2. *(adv.)* nowadays आजकल The scenario is different *today*.

toddle *(v.)* टॉडल– to walk with short unsteady steps, as a child does when learning to walk गिरते-पड़ते चलना The baby can't walk properly yet, but he can *toddle*.

toe *(n.)* टो– any one of the digits of the foot पैर की अँगुली We have five *toes* on each foot.

toffee टॉफ़ि– a sweet made from sugar or treacle boiled with butter, nuts, etc. टॉफ़ी (चीनी और क्रीम-चाकलेट के द्वारा बनाई गई मिठाई) The children like *toffee* very much.

together *(adv.)* टुगेदर्–1. closely, cohesively, or compactly united or held मिलकर, आपस में My brother and I had gone for a walk *together.*

2. with cooperation and interchange between constituent elements, members, etc. सभी (वस्तुओं) के साथ We gathered *together* our belongings and left.

togetherness *(n.)* टुगेदरनस– a feeling of closeness or affection from being united with other people मेलजोल की भावना We enjoyed the joy and *togetherness* of our annual congregational dinner in the hotel.

toil *(v.)* टॉइल– hard or exhausting work कठिन परिश्रम करना The farm-workers *toil* until late in the evening.

toilet *(n.)* टॉइलट– the act of dressing and preparing oneself शौचालय Every day Shanta spends minimum twenty minutes in her *toilet.*

token *(n.)* टोकन– an indication, warning, or sign of something चिह्न, प्रतीक, संकेत The enemy waved a white flag as a *token* of surrender.

tolerate *(v.)* टॉलरेट– to treat with indulgence, liberality, or forbearance सहन करना, सहना We have to *tolerate* in others what we permit in ourselves!

tolerable *(adj.)* टॉलरबल– able to be tolerated; endurable सहनीय, सहने लायक़ The pain in her decayed tooth was not *tolerable.*

tolerant *(adj.)* टॉलरेण्ट– able to withstand extremes, as of heat and cold सहनशील She is a very *tolerant* child and never demands for anything.

toll *(v.)* टौल– 1. to ring or cause to ring slowly and recurrently घंटा बजाना The bell ringers will *toll* the bell during the funeral service.

2. *(n.)* an amount of money levied, esp for the use of certain roads, bridges, etc., to cover the cost of maintenance मार्गशुल्क, राहदारी, महसूल In some countries, people pay a *toll* to use the motorways.

tomato *(n.)* टमाटो– a soft red fruit that is eaten as a vegetable either raw or cooked टमाटर *Tomato* is a vegetable.

tomb *(n.)* टूम्– a place, esp a vault beneath the ground, for the burial of a corpse क़ब्र, समाधि, मक़बरा Muslims bury a dead body in the ground and build a *tomb* over it.

tomboy *(n.)* टॉमबॉइ– a girl who acts or dresses in a boyish way, liking rough outdoor activities (लड़कों जैसी दिखने वाली) मरदानी लड़की Khushboo is a *tomboy* in the hostel.

tombstone *(n.)* टूमस्टोन– a stone marking a grave and usually inscribed with the name and dates of the person buried क़ब्र पर लगा पत्थर He put a *tombstone* on his father's grave.

tomorrow *(n.)* टुमॉरो–1. the day after today आने वाला कल (का दिन) *Tomorrow* is the day after today. If this is Monday, *tomorrow* will be Tuesday.

2. near future निकट भविष्य Do not put off till *tomorrow* what you can do today.

ton *(n.)* टन– a unit of weight equal to 2240 pounds or 1016.96 kilograms टन (तोल की एक माप) The rickshaw was carrying two *tons* weight of rice.

tone *(n.)* टोन–1. sound with reference to quality, pitch, or volume स्वर, ध्वनि, तान The piano has an excellent *tone.*

2. any of the pitch levels or pitch contours at which a syllable may be pronounced, such as high tone, falling tone, etc. लहजा, आवाज़ I knew by the angry *tone* of Vatsya's voice that he was annoyed.

3. *(v.)* to give greater firmness or strength to स्वास्थ्य बढ़ाना She has *toned* up her body by doing Yoga.

tongue *(n.)* टंग–1. a movable mass of muscular tissue attached to the floor of the mouth in most vertebrates ज़बान, जीभ We taste with our *tongue.* We also speak with it.

2. a manner of speaking बोलने का ढंग Be slow of *tongue* and quick of eye.

3. a language, भाषा What is your mother-*tongue*?

➢ **tongue-tied** *(adj.)* speechless, esp with embarrassment or shyness मुंहबंद, मुंहसिला, चुप्पीलगा (व्यक्ति) She was sitting *tongue-tied* and shy in front of him.

tonic *(n.)* टॉनिक– a medicinal preparation intended to improve and strengthen the functioning of the body or increase the feeling of wellbeing स्फूर्तिदायक पदार्थ Mother's milk is a *tonic* for infants.

tonight *(n.)* टुनाइट– the night or evening of this present day आज की रात They will come to meet us *tonight.*

tonsil *(n.)* टॉन्सिल– either of two small masses of lymphatic tissue situated one on each side of the back of the mouth गलतुंडिका, तुंडिका-शोथ If we open our mouth wide in front of a mirror, we shall be able to see our *tonsils.*

too *(adv.)* टू–1. as well; in addition; also इसके अतिरिक्त, भी, (आवश्यकता से अधिक) You can see a star. Can you see a fairy *too*?

2. in or to an excessive degree; अत्यधिक The patient is *too* weak to walk.

3. more than a fitting or desirable amount बहुत ज़्यादा Your shoes are *too* big for you.

tool *(n.)* टूल– an implement, such as a hammer, saw, or spade, that is used by hand औज़ार, हथियार The carpenter has gone to the market to fetch new tools.

toot *(v.)* टूट– to give or cause to give (a short blast, hoot, or whistle) सीटी या भोंपू बजाना You should *toot* your horn to see the crowd.

tooth *(n.)* टूथ–1. any of various bonelike structures set in the jaws of most vertebrates and modified, according to the species, for biting or chewing दाँत We chew with our *teeth.*

2. anything resembling a tooth in shape, prominence, or function दाँता My comb has lost three of its *teeth.*

toothpick *(n.)* टूथपिक– a small sharp sliver of wood, plastic, etc. used for extracting pieces of food from between the teeth दाँत कुरेदनी He always has a *toothpick* in his mouth.

top *(adj.)* टॉप– 1. the highest degree or point सर्वोच्च Please give *top* priority to this work.

2. *(n.)* a toy that is spun on its pointed base by a flick of the fingers, by pushing a handle at the top up and down, etc. लट्टू Can you spin the *top* round and round?

➢ **on top of**– in complete control of (a difficult situation, job, etc.) के ऊपर, सबसे ऊपर, The files were lying *on top of* the shelf.

topic *(n.)* टॉपिक–1. a subject or theme of a speech, essay, book, etc. विषय, प्रसंग, प्रकरण Fashion, films and politics are the *topics* on which people generally talk.

2. a subject of conversation; item of discussion शीर्षक What are the *topics* of today's discussion?

topical *(adj.)* टॉपिकल– of, relating to, or constituting current affairs सामयिक, प्रासंगिक The leaders did not discuss on any of the *topical* issues.

topmost *(adj.)* टॉपमोस्ट– highest; at or nearest the top उच्चतम, सर्वोच्च I gave *topmost* priority to his work.

topple *(v.)* टॉपल– to lean precariously or totter गिर पड़ना, गिरा देना The big pile of books *toppled* over.

top secret *(adj.)* टॉपसीक्रॅट– containing information whose disclosure would cause exceedingly grave damage परम गुप्त The army classified this mission *top secret.*

torch *(n.)* टॉर्च– a small portable electric lamp powered by one or more dry batteries मशाल, टार्च (सेलों वाली) My friend gave me a *torch* to see my way in the night.

torment *(v.)* टॉर्मेण्ट– 1. to afflict with great pain, suffering, or anguish; torture यातना देना, यंत्रणा देना Sudha was *tormented* by a toothache.

2. *(n.)* physical or mental pain यातना, पीड़ा The prisoner could not bear the *torment* in the cell and died.

tornado *(n.)* टॉर्नेडो– a small but violent squall or whirlwind, चक्रवात, तूफान The *tornado* caused massive destruction to both life and property.

torpedo *(v.)* टॉर्पीडो– to render ineffective; destroy or wreck प्रक्षेपास्त्र मारना, (जलयान को) बरबाद कर देना The ship sank within a few minutes of being *torpedoed.*

torrent *(n.)* टॉरण्ट– a fast, voluminous, or violent stream of water or other liquid प्रचण्ड धारा After the heavy rain, the stream became a *torrent.*

tortoise *(n.)* टॉर्टस– a reptile with round hard shell, it can pull its head and legs into its shell कछुआ Some *tortoises* live on land and the others in sea.

tortuous *(adj.)* टॉचुअस– twisted or winding टेढ़ी-मेढ़ी, चक्करदार I was driving on a narrow *tortuous* lane.

torture *(v.)* टॉर्चर्– 1. to cause extreme physical pain to, esp in order to extract information, break resistance, etc. यातना देना, यंत्रणा देना, उत्पीड़न देना The police *tortured* the thief to make him speak about the things stolen by him.
2. *(n.)* physical or mental anguish यातना, यंत्रणा, उत्पीड़न Political prisoners were put to *torture.*

toss *(v.)* टॉस– 1. to throw lightly or with a flourish, esp with the palm of the hand upwards सिक्का या गेंद उछालना *Toss* the ball over the wall.
2. *(n.)* the act or an instance of tossing सिक्का उछालने की क्रिया In cricket much depends on which team wins the *toss.*

total *(adj.)* टोटल– 1. complete; absolute पूर्ण, सम्पूर्ण, सारा, समूचा The ship struck the rock and became a *total* wreck.
2. *(v.)* to add up जोड़ करना Now you *total* up the bills and I shall check them.

totally *(adv.)* टोटली– completely पूरी तरह से He *totally* agreed to his point of view.

totter *(v.)* टॉटर्–1. to sway or shake as if about to fall लड़खड़ाना Young children *totter* about when they first try to walk.
2. to be failing, unstable, or precarious डगमगाना The old man *tottered* along and nearly fell once or twice.

touch *(n.)* टॅच–1. a gentle push, tap, or caress स्पर्श The nurse had a gentle *touch.*
2. act or an instance of something coming into contact with the body सम्पर्क में आना Are you in *touch* with Mr. Sanjay Pandit?
3. *(v.)* to tap, feel, or strike, esp with the hand स्पर्श करना I can barely *touch* the ceiling.
4. to affect; concern मर्महित करना, द्रवित करना/होना We were *touched* by her kindness.

touched *(adj.)* टच्ड्– moved to sympathy or emotion; affected भावुक, प्रभावित Sheela was deeply *touched* by his precious gift.

touching *(adj.)* टचिंग– evoking or eliciting tender feelings मर्मस्पर्शी, हृदयस्पर्शी He could not resist *touching* the painting.

touchy *(adj.)* टची– easily upset or irritated; oversensitive चिड़चिड़ा, तुनकमिज़ाज Reema is a bit *touchy* about her height.

tough *(adj.)* टफ़–1. strong or resilient; durable ठोस, कड़ा Meat that is *tough,* is difficult to cut and eat.
2. difficult or troublesome to do or deal with कठिन, सख़्त To succeed both in education and sports is really a *tough* job.

tour *(n.)* टुअर्– 1. an extended journey, usually taken for pleasure, visiting places of interest along the route दौरा, यात्रा, पर्यटन We made a *tour* of the city.
2. *(v.)* to make a tour of (a place) दौरा करना, घूमना We are *touring* the Himalayas this summer.

tourist *(n.)* टुअरिस्ट– a person who travels for pleasure, usually sightseeing and staying in hotels पर्यटक, सैलानी A lot *tourist* visit this shrine every year.

tournament *(n.)* टॉर्नमेण्ट– a sporting competition in which contestants play a series of games to determine an overall winner खेल-प्रतियोगिता What was the result of India-Australia cricket *tournament*?

tout *(v.)* टाउट्– to solicit (business, customers, etc.) or hawk (merchandise), esp in a brazen way दलाली

करना, ग्राहक जुटाना The product was *touted* as the best among its rivals.

tow *(v.)* टो– 1. to pull or drag (a vehicle, boat, etc.), esp by means of a rope or cable घसीटना, खींचना The lorry *towed* the battered car to the garage.

2. *(n.)* the act or an instance of towing खिंचाई A *tow* truck was to send for auction.

towards *(prep.)* टुवॉर्डज–1. in the direction or vicinity of की ओर Vagish walked *towards* the car.

2. with regard to के लिए, के प्रति The millionaire behaves generously *towards* all poor people.

towel *(n.)* टाउअल– 1. a square or rectangular piece of absorbent cloth or paper used for drying the body तौलिया We can wipe our wet hands on the *towel.*

2. *(v.)* to dry or wipe with a towel तौलिए से पोंछना, रगड़ना He was *towelling* his hair dry.

tower *(v.)* टाउअर्– 1. to be or rise like a tower; loom ऊँचा उठना The tall fir trees *tower* over the small house.

2. *(n.)* a tall, usually square or circular structure, sometimes part of a larger building and usually built for a specific purpose मीनार, लाट, बुर्ज We can hear the bells ringing in the clock-*tower.*

town *(n.)* टाउन– a densely populated urban area क़स्बा, छोटा शहर

- A *town* is a small city.
- There are streets and shops in a *town.*
- She would rather live in a village than in a *town.*

toxic *(adj.)* टॉक्सिक– of, relating to, or caused by a toxin or poison; poisonous ज़हरीला Vehicles release *toxic* gases in the air.

toxicity *(n.)* टॉक्सिसटी– the degree of strength of a poison विषैलापन, ज़हरीला Unfiltered water has a high level of *toxicity.*

toxin *(n.)* टॉक्सिन्– any other poisonous substance of plant or animal origin जीवविष, एक ज़हरीला पदार्थ Some poisonous mushrooms have *toxins* in them.

toy *(n.)* टॉय– 1. an object designed to be played with खिलौना Children play with their *toys.*

2. *(v.)* to play, fiddle, or flirt खेलना, खिलवाड़ करना All the time she talked, she was *toying* with her purse.

trace *(v.)* ट्रेस–1. to track down and find खोज निकालना The police are trying to *trace* the man who stole the van.

2. to copy (a design, map, etc.) by drawing over the lines visible through a superimposed sheet of transparent paper or other material अनुरेखित करना, खींचना You can *trace* a map from your atlas.

3. *(n.)* a very small amount of sth थोड़ी मात्रा, अल्प मात्रा The soup has a *trace* of onion in it.

track *(v.)* ट्रैक– 1. to follow the trail of (a person, animal, etc.) खोजना, पीछा करना Hunters *track* elephants by their footprints.

2. *(n.)* any road or path affording passage, esp a rough one पगडंडी, कच्चा रास्ता There was only a rough *track* across the ground.

traction *(n.)* ट्रैक्शन– the application of a steady pull on a part during healing of a fractured or dislocated bone, using a system of weights and pulleys or splints कर्षण, संकर्षण He went to the physio-therapist for *traction.*

tractor *(v.)* ट्रैक्टर्– a motor vehicle used to pull heavy loads, esp farm machinery such as a plough or harvester ट्रैक्टर *Tractors* are used by farmers for pulling the plough.

trade *(n.)* ट्रेड– 1. exchange of one thing for something else व्यवसाय, लेन-देन Speculation is the romance of *trade.*

2. *(v.) to buy and sell* व्यापार करना We *trade* in second-hand cars.

trademark *(n.)* ट्रेडमार्क– any distinctive sign or mark व्यापार-चिह्न Just Do It is Nike's best-known *trademark.*

tradition *(n.)* ट्रेडि'शन– the handing down from generation to generation of the same customs, beliefs, etc., esp by word of mouth परम्परा Everywhere the basis of principles is *tradition.*

traffic *(n.)* the vehicles coming and going in a street, town, etc. यातायात A big city like Delhi faces many *traffic* problems.

tragedy *(n.)* ट्रैजडी–1. a shocking or sad event; disaster त्रासदी, दुखांत घटना Life is a *tragedy* – we are its spectators.
2. the unfortunate aspect of something दारुण विपत्ति You cannot forget your personal *tragedy.*

tragic *(adj.)* ट्रैजिक– mournful or pitiable दुखांत, दुखद It was a *tragic* accident when he lost his legs.

trail *(n.)* ट्रेल– a print, mark, or marks made by a person, animal, or object पुछल्ला The aeroplane left a long *trail* of white smoke behind it.

train *(n.)* ट्रेन– 1. a line of coaches or wagons coupled together and drawn by a railway locomotive रेलगाड़ी, गाड़ी Some *trains* carry people. They are called passenger-*trains.* Some *trains* carry goods.They are called goods-*trains.*
2. *(v.)* to guide or teach (to do something), as by subjecting to various exercises or experiences सिखाना, प्रशिक्षण देना They *train* Nina well in household work.

trained *(adj.)* ट्रेण्ड– (of a person) having been prepared to do something, by being taught the relevant skills प्रशिक्षित Is she a *trained* teacher?

trainer *(n.)* ट्रेनर– a person who trains प्रशिक्षक He is a racehorse *trainer* who trains the horses for the circus.

training *(n.)* ट्रेनिंग– the process of bringing a person to an agreed standard of proficiency by practice and instruction प्रशिक्षण I am under *training.*

trait *(n.)* ट्रेट– a characteristic feature or quality distinguishing a particular person or thing विशेष गुण, लक्षण She has several good *traits* of character.

traitor *(n.)* ट्रेटर्– a person who is guilty of treason or treachery, in betraying friends, country, a cause or trust, etc. विश्वासघाती, देशद्रोही The rogue was condemned to death as a *traitor.*

tram *(n.)* ट्रैम– an electrically driven public transport vehicle that runs on rails let into the surface of the road, ट्राम (बिजली से पटरी पर चलने वाली गाड़ी) Buses in Delhi have been replaced by *Trams.*

tramp *(n.)* ट्रैम्प– 1. a person who travels about on foot पद-यात्रा We went for a *tramp* across the woods.
2. *(v.)* to wander about as a vagabond or tramp मारा-मारा फिरना, धब-धब करते चलना Don't *tramp* about the garden.

trample *(v.)* ट्रैम्पल– to stamp or walk roughly (on) रौंदना, कुचलना The kids *trampled* the grass.

trance *(n.)* ट्रान्स– any mental state in which a person is unaware or apparently unaware of the environment, सुषुप्ति की अवस्था, बेहोशी She was walking on the road in a state of *trance.*

tranquil *(adj.)* ट्रैन्क्विल– calm, peaceful or quiet शांत My mind was *tranquil* and at peace.

tranquilize (ise) *(v.)* ट्रैन्किवलाइज़्– to make or become calm or calmer शांत करना Nothing contributes so much to *tranquilize,* as soothing music.

transact *(v.)* ट्रैन्ज़ैक्ट– to do, conduct, or negotiate (business, a deal, etc.) पूरा करना, सम्पादित करना When my father *transacted* all his business, he left Bhagalpur.

transaction *(n.)* ट्रैनज़ैकशन– something that is transacted, esp a business deal or negotiation सौदा, लेन-देन He made many *transactions* in one day.

transcript *(n.)* ट्रैनस्क्रिप्ट– a written, typed, or printed copy or manuscript made by transcribing प्रतिलेख, प्रतिलिपि Where is the *transcript* of the interview?

transcription *(n.)* ट्रैनस्क्रिपृशन– a representation in writing of the actual pronunciation of a speech sound, word, or piece of continuous text प्रतिलेखन In the phonetic *transcription,* there were several errors.

transfer *(v.)* ट्रैन्स्फ़र–1. to change or go or cause to change or go from one thing, person, or point to another तबादला करना/स्थानांतरित करना The luggage was *transferred* from the station to the ship.
2. to displace (a drawing, design, etc.) from one surface to another दूसरी जगह ले जाना She *transferred* the almirah from one room to another.

transform *(v.)* ट्रैन्स्फ़ार्म– to alter or be altered radically in form, function, etc. एक रूप से दूसरे रूपाकार में बदलना The witch *transformed* the goat into a princess.

transfusion *(n.)* ट्रैन्सफ्यूज़न– the injection of blood, blood plasma, etc., into the blood vessels of a patient (किसी व्यक्ति को रोग के कारण दूषित रक्त के स्थान पर नया रक्त चढ़ाने की क्रिया), रक्त-संचरण Many patients have been saved because of blood *transfusion.*

transgress *(v.)* ट्रैन्स्ग्रेस– to go beyond or overstep (a limit) उल्लंघन करना, अतिक्रमण करना We must remember the promise not to *transgress* again.

transistor *(n.)* ट्रैनज़िसूटर– a transistor radio ट्रांज़िस्टर, रेडियो I'm not able to find a shop which would repair my *transistor.*

transit *(n.)* ट्रैनज़िट– the passage or conveyance of goods or people पारगमन, पारवहन He lost his baggage during *transit.*

transition *(n.)* ट्रैनज़िशन– change or passage from one state or stage to another संक्रांति काल Adolescence is a *transition* period from childhood to youth.

translate *(v.)* ट्रान्सलेट–1. to express in another language or dialect अनुवाद करना The New Testament was *translated* from Greek into English.
2. to transform or convert स्थानांतरित/बदली करना It is time to *translate* words into action.

translation *(n.)* ट्रैन्सलेशन– something that is or has been translated, esp a written text अनुवाद The art of *translation* requires a good knowledge of many languages.

translator *(n.)* ट्रैन्सलेटर– a person or machine that translates speech or writing अनुवादक Sonia is appointed as a *translator* in a publishing company.

transmission *(n.)* ट्रैन्समिशन– the act or process of transmitting संचारण, प्रसारण The *transmission* to the set top box was blocked by heavy rains.

transmit *(v.)* ट्रैन्समिट– to pass or cause to go from one place or person to another; transfer भेजना, संप्रेषित करना, स्थानांतरित करना That message was *transmitted* by telephone.

transparency *(n.)* ट्रैन्सपैरनसि– the state of being transparent पारदर्शिता We should maintain *transparency* in every relationship.

transparent *(adj.)* ट्रैंसपेअरन्ट– permitting the uninterrupted passage of light; clear पारदर्शी Glass is *transparent.*

transplant *(v.)* ट्रेन्सप्लांट– to transfer (an organ or tissue) from one part of the body to another or from one person or animal to another during a grafting or transplant operation (अंगों का) प्रत्यारोपण करना The kidney *transplant* was successful.

transport *(v.)* ट्रान्सपोर्ट– 1. to carry or cause to go from one place to another, esp over some distance ढोना, एक जगह से दूसरी जगह ले जाना Many ships are required to *transport* food across the oceans.
2. *(n.)* the business or system of transporting goods or people परिवहन The ships are used for *transport.*

trap *(n.)* ट्रैप–1. a mechanical device or enclosed place or pit in which something, esp an animal, is caught or penned पिंजरा, चूहेदानी Have you set a *trap* to catch the mice?
2. any device or plan for tricking a person or thing into being caught unawares जाल The army fell into a *trap,* as they found themselves between the sea and the enemy.

trapdoor *(n.)* ट्रैपडॉर– a door or flap flush with and covering an opening, esp in a ceiling चोर दरवाज़ा We built a *trapdoor* for the dog to enter the house.

trauma *(n.)* ट्रॉमा– a powerful shock that may have long-lasting effects मानसिक आघात, सदमा Manto's story Toba Tek Singh deals with the *trauma* of Partition.

travel *(v.)* ट्रैवल– 1. to go, move, or journey from one place to another यात्रा करना, भ्रमण करना We have been *travelling* for over a month now.
2. *(n.)* a tour or journey यात्रा, भ्रमण Air *travel* is quick but expensive.

traveller *(n.)* ट्रैवलर– a person who travels, esp habitually यात्री, मुसाफ़िर Ibn-e-battuta was a great Muslim *traveller* and scholar.

traverse *(v.)* ट्रैवर्स– to pass or go over or back and forth over (something); cross आर-पार जाना, पार करना It took us ten days to *traverse* the ocean.

trawl *(n.)* ट्रॉल– a search (something, such as information, or someone, such as a likely appointee) from a wide variety of sources छानबीन, खोज He got the job after the *trawl* through the newspaper.

tray *(n.)* ट्रे– a thin flat board or plate of metal, plastic, etc., usually with a raised edge, on which things can be carried ट्रे, रकाबी The mother brought tea in a *tray.*

treacherous *(adj.)* ट्रेचरस– betraying or likely to betray faith or confidence विश्वासघाती, बेईमान, अविश्वसनीय The *treacherous* scientist sold some of his country's secrets to the enemy.

treachery *(n.)* ट्रेचरी– the act or an instance of wilful betrayalधोखा, विश्वासघात His *treachery* will not go unanswered.

tread *(v.)* ट्रे'ड–1. to walk or trample in, on, over, or across (something) किसी चीज पर चलना Don't *tread* on the carpet with your muddy boots.
2. to do by walking or dancing पैर से दबाना या रखना Don't *tread* on the cat's tail.
3. to walk or trample in, on, over, or across (something) कुचल देना, रौंद देना The mob passing through these fields have *trodden* down the plants.

treadle *(n.)* ट्रे'डल– a rocking lever operated by the foot to drive a machine पांवों से चलाई जाने वाली मशीन Have you bought a *treadle* sewing machine from the agency?

treason *(n.)* ट्रीज़न– any treachery or betrayal देशद्रोह, राजद्रोह He was proved with the charge of *treason* against his country.

treasure *(v.)* ट्रेशर्– 1. to store up and save; hoard संजोये रखना, बहुत संभालकर रखना I *treasure* my gold watch. 2. *(n.)* wealth and riches, usually hoarded, esp in the form of money, precious metals, or gems खज़ाना Many *treasures* of gold and silver have been found in old castles.

treasurer *(n.)* ट्रैशरर– a person appointed to look after the funds of a society, company, city, or other governing body ख़ज़ांची Ram is an honest *treasurer* of the club.

treat *(v.)* ट्रीट–1. to apply treatment to इलाज करना Doctors *treat* their patients. 2. to deal with or regard in a certain manner व्यवहार करना, बर्ताव करना Old age needs to be *treated* gently in words as well as in deeds.

3. *(n.)* any delightful surprise or specially pleasant occasion आनन्ददायक वस्तु It was a *treat* to hear such good singing.

treatment *(n.)* ट्रीटमेंट–1. the application of medicines, surgery, psychotherapy, etc., to a patient or to a disease or symptom उपचार My uncle is under medical *treatment*.

2. the manner of handling or dealing with a person or thing, व्यवहार, बरताव I have no complaint about her *treatment*.

treaty *(n.)* ट्रीटी– a formal agreement or contract between two or more states, such as an alliance or trade arrangement संधि, समझौता Many peace *treaties* were signed after the second World War.

treble *(v.)* ट्रेबल– to make or become three times as much तिगुना हो जाना Prices on food items have *trebled* in the past few years.

tree *(n.)* ट्री– any large woody perennial plant with a distinct trunk giving rise to branches or leaves at some distance from the ground वृक्ष, पेड़ There are many *trees* in the woods.

trek *(n.)* ट्रेक– 1. a journey or stage of a journey, esp a migration by ox wagon पर्वतों की लंबी कठोर पैदल यात्रा They finally reached the top after a three-day *trek* across the mountains.

2. *(v.)* to make a trek लंबी पैदल यात्रा पर जाना Let's go *trekking* this summer.

tremble *(v.)* ट्रेम्बल– to vibrate with short slight movements; quiver कांपना We *tremble* when we are excited or full of fear.

tremendous *(adj.)* ट्रमेन्डस– vast; huge ज़बरदस्त, भयानक No one expected him to deliver such a *tremendous* presentation.

tremendously *(adv.)* ट्रमेनडसली– greatly; very much बहुत अधिक Nisha was missing her mother *tremendously*.

tremor *(n.)* ट्रेमर्– an involuntary shudder or vibration, as from illness, fear, shock, etc. कंपन Cold weather made a *tremor* run through her limbs.

trench *(n.)* ट्रेंच– a deep ditch or furrow खाई *Trenches* have been dug across the town to drain off the water.

trend *(n.)* ट्रेन्ड– fashion; mode नया फ़ैशन It is usually the movie stars who set the *trends* in fashion.

trendy *(adj.)* ट्रेनडि– consciously fashionable फ़ैशनेबल She loves to wear *trendy* clothes.

trespass *(v.)* ट्रेसपस– to go or intrude (on the property, privacy, or preserves of another) with no right or permission अतिक्रमण करना, बिना आज्ञा प्रवेश करना They were caught *trespassing* on government property.

trial *(n.)* ट्राइअल–1. process of testing the ability or quality परीक्षण, वस्तु की जांच The latest car model is having its *trial* this week.

2. the act or an instance of trying or proving; test or experiment परख Truth fears no *trial.*

triangle *(n.)* ट्राइऐन्गल– a three-sided polygon त्रिकोण, त्रिभुज Can you draw a *triangle*?

tribe *(n.)* ट्राइब– a social division of a people, esp of a preliterate people, defined in terms of common descent, territory, culture, etc. जनजाति There are many *tribes* in India.

tribunal *(n.)* ट्राइब्यूनल– a court of justice or any place where justice is administered विशेष अदालत, न्यायालय The Supreme Court is the highest *tribunal* in India.

tributary *(n.)* ट्रिब्यट्री– a stream, river, or glacier that feeds another larger one सहायक नदी The Yamuna is a *tributary* of the Ganga.

tribute *(n.)* ट्रिब्यूट– a gift or statement made in acknowledgment, gratitude, or admiration esp for a dead person श्रद्धांजलि, प्रशंसा The newly elected member of Parliament paid *tribute* to the voters who had voted for him in the elections.

trick *(n.)* ट्रिक– 1. a deceitful, cunning, or underhand action or plan युक्ति, दाँव-पेंच Every profession has its *tricks.*

2. *(v.)* to defraud, deceive, or cheat (someone), esp by means of a trick किसी से छल करना, धोखा करना We are bitter against those who *trick* us.

trickery *(n.)* ट्रिकरी– the practice or an instance of using tricks छल, धोखाधड़ी He got money from her by *trickery.*

trickle *(v.)* ट्रिकल– to run or cause to run in thin or slow streams बूंद-बूंद टपकना A tear *trickled* down her cheeks.

tricky *(adj.)* ट्रिकी– involving snags or difficulties पेंचीदा, जटिल I was caught in a *tricky* situation.

tricycle *(n.)* ट्राइसाइकल– a three-wheeled cycle, esp one driven by pedals तीन पहियों वाली साइकिल A *tricycle* runs on three wheels.

trident *(n.)* ट्रिडेण्ट– a weapon with three prongs त्रिशूल Lord Shiva has a *trident* in his right arm.

trifle *(n.)* ट्राइफ़ल–1. a thing of little or no value or significance छोटी-सी बात, ज़रा सी बात Mother told Raju not to cry over *trifles.*

trigger *(n.)* ट्रिगर्– a small projecting lever that activates the firing mechanism of a firearm बंदूक़ का घोड़ा, लिबलिबी The gunners pressed the *triggers* and the guns went off.

trillion *(n.)* ट्रिलियन– the number represented as one followed by twelve zeros; a million million एक लाख करोड़ *Trillion* is written by a unit and twelve zeroes.

trim *(v.)* ट्रिम– 1. to put in good order, esp by cutting or pruning काटना-छांटना, कतरना, सुव्यवस्थित करना I must *trim* the hedge because it looks so untidy.

2. *(adj.)* neat and spruce in appearance छरहरा एवं आकर्षक Himani has a *trim* figure.

trinket *(n.)* ट्रिंकिट– a trivial object; trifle सस्ता गहना I shopped for *trinkets* in the Tibetan market.

trio *(n.)* ट्रीओ– a group of three people or things तिकड़ी, तीन व्यक्तियों का समूह These comedians are a comical *trio.*

trip *(n.)* ट्रिप– 1. an outward and return journey, often for a specific purpose यात्रा, भ्रमण Uncle and aunt have gone for a *trip* to the sea.

2. *(v.)* to stumble or cause to stumble लड़खड़ाना, गिरना Tommy *tripped* over a loose stone.

triple *(v.)* ट्रिपल– to increase or become increased threefold; treble तिगुना करना/होना The world's population has *tripled* in last 72 years.

tripod *(n.)* ट्रिपॉड, ट्राइपॉड– a stand or table having three legs तिपाई, तीन पांवों वाला स्टूल (कैमरा सेट करने का) The photographer set up a *tripod* for taking some snapshots.

triumph *(n.)* ट्राइअंफ़– a success, victory or major achievement विजय, जीत, सफलता We were given a day's holiday to celebrate our *triumph* in the football cup.

triumphant *(adj.)* ट्राइअमेफ़न्ट– experiencing or displaying triumph विजय से उत्फुल्ल, सफ़ल He won a *triumphant* victory in the MCD election.

trivial *(adj.)* ट्रिविअल– of little importance; petty or frivolous तुच्छ, नगण्य, छोटी-सी I made only a *trivial* motoring offence.

trolley *(n.)* ट्रॉलि– a small vehicle with wheels, used for conveying food, drink, etc. छोटी छकड़ा गाड़ी, ठेला, ट्रॉली In the hospital, tea is served from a *trolley*.

troop *(n.)* ट्रूप–1. a large group or assembly; flock दल, टोली, मंडली A *troop* of school children marched along the pavement.

2. armed forces; soldiers सैन्यदल, सेना The *troop* galloped into battle.

trophy *(n.)* ट्रोफ़ी– a memento of success विजय स्मारक, पुरस्कार Vagish won a *trophy* in swimming.

trot *(n.)* ट्रॉट– 1. a gait of a horse or other quadruped, faster than a walk दुलकी चाल, तेज चाल This horse always keeps up a steady *trot*.

2. *(v.)* to move or cause to move at a trot उछल-उछलकर चलना The child *trotted* along beside his father.

trouble *(v.)* ट्रॅबल–1. to cause trouble to; upset, pain, or worry तंग करना Don't *trouble* your teacher by asking silly questions.

2.to cause inconvenience or discomfort to कष्ट देना I am sorry to *trouble* you.

3. *(n.)* effort or exertion taken to do something कठिनाई The *trouble* with opportunity is that it always comes in the disguise of hard work.

troublemaker *(n.)* ट्रबलमेकर– a person who makes trouble, esp between people उपद्रवी, झगड़ा पैदा कराने वाला व्यक्ति Sahil is a *troublemaker* for everyone.

troubleshoot *(v.)* ट्रबलशूट– to locate the cause of trouble and remove or treat it समस्याओं को दूर करना She likes to *troubleshoot* all the problems of her office.

troublesome *(adj.)* ट्रबलसम– causing a great deal of trouble; worrying, upsetting, or annoying दुख देने वाला, गड़बड़ी पैदा करने वाला, कष्टदायक Akshat was a *troublesome* child in his childhood.

trough *(n.)* ट्रॉफ़– a narrow open container, esp one in which food or water for animals is put नाँद (जानवरों को चारा आदि देने का खुला पात्र) The farmer poured the horses' food into the *trough*.

trousers *(n.)* ट्राउज़र्ज़– a garment shaped to cover the body from the waist to the ankles or knees with separate tube-shaped sections for both legs पाजामा, पतलून Do you want to make a new pair of *trousers*?

trout *(n.)* ट्राउट– a common fresh water fish, used for food एक छोटी मछली (जो नदी में मिलती है) Have you ever seen a *trout* in the river?

trowel *(n.)* ट्राउअल– any of various small hand tools having a flat metal blade attached to a handle

करनी The mason uses the *trowel* in construction work.

truant *(n.)* ट्रूअंट– a student who stays away from school without permission नाग़ा करने वाला विद्यार्थी Don't be a *truant.*

truck *(n.)* ट्रक–1. a vehicle for carrying heavy loads by road ट्रक Our transport company owned about fifty *trucks.*
2. an open railway vehicle designed to carry heavy loads, esp one with a flat platform दो पहियों की गाड़ी (जिसे रेलवे कुली हाथों से पकड़कर, रेलवे प्लेटफ़ार्म पर, उसके ऊपर सामान रखकर ढोते हैं) The railway porter piled our luggage on his *truck.*

trudge *(v.)* ट्रॅज– to walk or plod heavily or wearily पैर घसीटकर चलना We had to *trudge* more than 9 kilometres thrcugh a dust-storm.

true *(adj.)* ट्रू–1. not false, fictional, or illusory; factual or factually accurate; conforming with reality सच, सही Say what is *true.*
2. being of real or natural origin; genuine; not synthetic वास्तविक, असली, सच्चा The novel is base on a *true* story.

truly *(adv.)* ट्रुली– in a true, just, or faithful manner सचमुच If I was to speak *truly* then yes I have committed mistakes.

trump card *(n.)* ट्रम्पकार्ड– your trump card is something powerful that you can use or do, which gives you an advantage over someone तुरुप का पत्ता It is the best time to play *trump card.*

trumpet *(n.)* ट्रम्पेट– 1. a valved brass instrument of brilliant tone consisting of a narrow tube of cylindrical bore ending in a flared bell, normally pitched in B flat. तुरही, भोंपू My uncle plays the *trumpet* in a military band.
2. *(v.)* to proclaim or sound loudly घोषित करना, प्रचारित करना Netaji Subhash's praise was *trumpeted* throughout India.

trunk *(n.)* ट्रँक–1. the elongated prehensile nasal part of an elephant; proboscis सूँड़ An elephant has a *trunk.* It is his long nose.
2. the main stem of a tree, usually thick and upright, covered with bark and having branches at some distance from the ground वृक्ष का तना The stem of a tree is called a tree *trunk.*
3. a large strong case or box used to contain clothes and other personal effects when travelling and for storage लोहे का बक्सा We put our clothes in a *trunk.*

trunk road *(n.)* ट्रँक रोड– a main road, esp one that is suitable for heavy vehicles राजमार्ग, मुख्य मार्ग We travelled from Delhi to Lucknow by car on grand *trunk road.*

trust *(v.)* ट्रॅस्ट– 1. to place confidence in (someone to do something); have faith (in); rely (upon) विश्वास करना, भरोसा रखना Love all but *trust* a few.
2. *(n.)* treliance on and confidence in the truth, विश्वास, यक़ीन I will not betray your *trust.*
3. worth, reliability, etc., of a person or thing; faith आस्था Have *trust* in God.

trustee *(n.)* ट्रस्टी– a person to whom the legal title to property is entrusted to hold or use for another's benefit न्यासी (सम्पत्ति की देखभाल करने वाला) Mr. Chawla is a *trustee* of this hospital.

trusting *(adj.)* ट्रसटिंग– characterized by a tendency or readiness to trust others विश्वासी, दूसरों पर जल्दी यक़ीन करने वाला I have a *trusting* nature.

trustworthy *(adj.)* ट्रस्टवर्दी– worthy of being trusted; honest, reliable, or dependable भरोसेमंद Ramu is a *trustworthy* servant of my house.

truth *(n.)* ट्रुथ–1. the quality of being true, genuine, actual, or factual सच्चाई, सत्यता *Truth* wins in the end.
2. a proven or verified principle or statement; fact सत्य बात, सत्य कथन If you tell the *truth,* you don't have to remember anything.

truthful *(adj.)* ट्रुथफुल– realistic सत्यवादी, ईमानदार He has never been entirely *truthful* about his dealings with us.

try *(v.)* ट्राइ–1. to make an effort or attempt प्रयत्न करना, कोशिश करना Time is short, but I shall *try* to catch the bus.
2. to sample, test, or give experimental use to (something) in order to determine its quality, worth, etc. सिले हुए कपड़े को पहनकर नाप देखना You had better *try* on the coat before you buy it.
3. *(n.)* an experiment or trial प्रयत्न, प्रयास, कोशिश Come on, it is worth a *try.*

trying *(adj.)* ट्राइंग– upsetting, difficult, or annoying थकाऊ, कष्टसाध्य He is *trying* hard to rectify his mistakes.

tsunami *(n.)* सूनामी– a large, often destructive, sea wave produced by a submarine earthquake, subsidence, or volcanic eruption. विनाशकारी समुद्री लहरें *Tsunami* and earthquake hit Indonesia on 11 April, 2012.

tub *(n.)* टब–1. a low wide open container, typically round, made of plastic or wood and used esp for washing (पानी जमा करने का) टब, बाल्टी Mother stored water in a *tub.*
2. a bath, esp one not permanently fixed नाँद Father bought a bath *tub* for daily use.

tube *(n.)* ट्यूब–1. a long hollow and typically cylindrical object, used for the passage of fluids or as a container प्लास्टिक का ट्यूब The inner part of a bicycle tyre contains a rubber *tube.*
2. any hollow cylindrical structure नली, नलिका The water runs along a *tube* into the boiler.

tuberculosis *(n.)* ट्यूबर्क्युलोसिस– a communicable disease caused by infection with the tubercle bacillus, most frequently affecting the lungs तपेदिक, यक्ष्मा, टीबी The disease *tuberculosis* is spreading rapidly throughout the city

tuck *(n.)* टक– 1. a pleat or fold in a part of a garment, तह, परत, चुन्नट I shall *tuck* in your dress as it is too long for you.
2. *(v.)* to push or fold into a small confined space or concealed place or between two surfaces तह लगाना I *tucked* the napkin under my chin.

Tuesday *(n.)* ट्यूज़डे– the third day of the week; second day of the working week मंगलवार If this is Sunday, the day after tomorrow will be *Tuesday.*

tuft *(n.)* टॅफ़्ट– a bunch of feathers, grass, hair, etc., held together at the base गुच्छा, झाड़ी का एक हिस्सा There was sand and few *tufts* of coarse grass.

tug *(n.)* टॅग– 1. a boat with a powerful engine, used for towing barges, ships, etc. (एक छोटा जहाज़ जो बड़े जहाज़ों को बन्दरगाह की ओर खींचकर ले आता है) एक छोटा शक्तिशाली जहाज़ A *tug* Is a little ship. It helps to pull a big ship into dock.
2. *(v.)* to pull or drag with sharp or powerful movements ज़ोर से खींचना We shall *tug* the boat out of the water on to the river bank.

tuition *(n.)* ट्यूइशन– instruction, esp that received in a small group or individually ट्यूशन He seriously requires *tuition* for mathematics.

tulip *(n.)* ट्यूलिप– a brightly coloured spring flower, shaped like a cup (कप के आकार का) एक फूल, ट्यूलिप A *tulip* is a spring flower. We can grow *tulips* in many different colours.

tumble *(v.)* टॅम्बल्– to fall or cause to fall, esp awkwardly, precipitately, or violently गिर पड़ना, धड़ाम से गिरना, ढहना I slipped and *tumbled* down the stairs.

tumbler *(n.)* टॅम्बलर्– a flat-bottomed drinking glass with no handle or stem. कांच का गिलास The child broke the glass *tumbler.*

tumult *(n.)* ट्यूमॅल्ट– a loud confused noise, as of a crowd; commotion हंगामा, गुलगपाड़ा, शोरगुल I tried to make my voice heard above the *tumult,* but in vain.

tumour *(n.)* ट्यूमर– any abnormal swelling गांठ, रसौली Her mother has a brain *tumour.*

tune *(n.)* ट्यून– 1. a melody, esp one for which harmony is not essential धुन, राग, लय Can you play a *tune* on the piano?
2. *(v.)* to adjust a musical instrument to a certain pitch स्वर निकालना, सुर मिलाना I *tune* my violin before playing it.

tunic *(n.)* ट्यूनिक– any of various hip-length or knee-length garments, such as the loose sleeveless garb बिना बांह का कुरता या जाकेट She wore a jacket over her *tunic.*

tunnel *(n.)* टॅनल– an underground passageway, सुरंग This *tunnel* leads to a dead end.

turban *(n.)* टर्बन– a man's headdress, worn esp by Muslims, Hindus, and Sikhs, made by swathing a length of linen, silk, etc., around the head or around a caplike base पगड़ी, पाग In India, some people wear *turbans* on their heads.

turbulent *(adj.)* टर्ब्यलंट– wild or insubordinate; unruly उपद्रवी, उग्र Our flight was very *turbulent* and it scared everyone.

turf *(v.)* टर्फ़– to cover with pieces of turf ज़मीन पर छोटी-छोटी घास लगाना An old man was *turfing* the field.

turkey *(n.)* टर्की– a large bird of North America, having a bare wattled head and neck and a brownish iridescent plumage. अमरीकी चिड़िया A *turkey* is a big bird. The Americans like to eat it.

turmeric *(n.)* टर्मरिक– a yellow powder made from the root of a plant, used in cooking as a spice हल्दी *Turmeric* is one of nature's most powerful healers.

turmoil *(n.)* टर्मॉइल– violent or confused movement; agitation; tumult खलबली, हलचल The present central government is in a state of *turmoil* on various issues.

turn *(n.)* टर्न्– 1. a movement of complete or partial rotation बारी Gopal is having a ride on a horse. It will be my *turn* after him.
2. *(v.)* to move or cause to move around an axis घूमना, पलटना The horse will *turn* around when it comes to the fence.
3. to reverse or cause to reverse position उलटना Shyama likes *turning* over the pages in her storybook.

turning *(n.)* टर्निंग– a road, river, or path that turns off the main way मोड़, घुमाव The rotors of the boat are *turning* at a fast pace.

turning point *(n.)* टर्निंगपॉइंट a moment when the course of events is changed निर्णायक क्षण या मोड़ Now this is a *turning point* in her life.

turnip *(n.)* टर्निप– a round white and purple root vegetable शलजम (एक प्रकार की सब्जी) A *turnip* is a vegetable. Mother cooks *turnips* for dinner.

turn-off *(n.)* टर्न्ऑफ़– a road or other way branching off from the main thoroughfare शाखा मार्ग I missed the *turn-off* for the office.

turnout *(n.)* टर्न्आउट– attendance or crowd, as at a particular event

जमावड़ा The *turnout* to the concert was quite amazing.

turnover *(n.)* टर्नओवर– the amount of a company's business or sales in a financial year सकल आय The annual *turnover* of the company is in crores.

turpentine *(n.)* टर्पनटाइन– a liquid with a strong smell, used for making paint, thinner तारपीन का तेल *Turpentine* is frequently used in thinners and varnishes.

turret *(n.)* टरट– a small tower that projects from the wall of a building, esp a medieval castle कंगूरा, बुर्ज Pigeons were sitting on a *turret.*

tusk *(n.)* टस्क– a pointed elongated usually paired tooth in the elephant, हाथी दाँत, हाथी के बाहर निकले हुए दो दाँत Ivory is obtained from the *tusks* of elephants.

tussle *(n.)* टॅसल– a vigorous fight; scuffle; struggle हाथापाई, लड़ाई The police engaged in a *tussle* with the public.

tutor *(n.)* ट्यूटर्– a teacher, usually instructing individual pupils and often engaged privately शिक्षक Rabindra Nath was not willing to go to school, so he had to have a private *tutor.*

tweed *(n.)* ट्वीड– a thick woollen often knobbly cloth ऊनी कपड़ा Do you like to wear a *tweed* jacket?

tweezers *(n.)* ट्वीज़र्ज– a small pincer-like instrument for handling small objects, plucking out hairs, etc. चिमटी She was having a pair of *tweezers.*

twelve *(adj.)* ट्वेल्व– a numeral, 12, XII, etc., representing this number बारह The child can count up to *twelve.*

twelfth *(adj.)* ट्वेलफ़्थ– coming after the eleventh in number or counting order, position, time, etc.; being the ordinal number of twelve: often written 12th बारहवाँ The school education is over after *twelfth* standard.

twenty *(adv.)* टुवेंटी– a numeral, 20, XX, etc., representing this number बीस Two tens make *twenty.*

twice *(adv.)* ट्वाइस– two times; on two occasions or in two cases दो बार *Twice* he was reminded of the work but he still didn't do it.

twig *(n.)* ट्विग– any small branch or shoot of a tree or other woody plant टहनी, शाखा The birds were sitting on the *twigs* while singing.

twilight *(n.)* ट्वाइलाइट– the soft diffused light occurring when the sun is just below the horizon, esp following sunset सांध्य-प्रकाश, झुटपुटा (सूर्यास्त से पहले का समय) We must go for a walk in the *twilight.*

twin *(n.)* ट्विन– either of two persons or animals conceived at the same time जुड़वा (बच्चा) She has a *twin* sister who looks and acts just like her.

twinge *(n.)* टविन्ज– a sudden brief darting or stabbing pain टीस, दर्द She suddenly felt a *twinge* in her neck.

twinkle *(v.)* ट्विंकल–1. to emit or reflect light in a flickering manner; shine brightly and intermittently; sparkle टिमटिमाना The stars *twinkle* in the sky.

2. to sparkle, esp with amusement or delight (आँखें) खुशी से चमकना Your eyes *twinkled* with mischief.

3. *(n.)* an intermittent gleam of light; flickering brightness; sparkle or glimmer टिमटिमाहट, चमचमाहट In the dark, we could see the stars *twinkling.*

twirl *(v.)* ट्वर्ल– to move or cause to move around rapidly and repeatedly in a circle घुमाना, फिराना He *twirled* the pen in his hand.

twist *(v.)* ट्विस्ट–1. to wind or cause to wind; twine, coil, or intertwine बटना,

बल देना Rope is made by *twisting* lengths of cord together.

2. to cause (one end or part) to turn or (of one end or part) to turn in the opposite direction from another; coil or spin मोड़ा जाना या मुड़ जाना Mary *twisted* her ankle when she fell.

3. to revolve or cause to revolve; rotate ऐंठना, मरोड़ना *Twist* those strings together to make a strong rope.

twitch *(v.)* ट्विच– to move or cause to move in a jerky spasmodic way झटका देना, फड़काना She *twitched* her lips in amusement.

twitter *(v.)* ट्विटर्– (esp of a bird) to utter a succession of chirping sounds चहचहाना, चहकना, चीं चीं करना The birds *twitter* cheerfully in the trees.

two *(adj.)* टू– a numeral, 2, II, (ii), etc., representing this number दो One plus one make *two.*

two-faced *(adj.)* टूफ़ेस्ड– deceitful; insincere; hypocritical धोखेबाज़, बेईमान, कपटी Nobody realized that he was a *two-faced* personality.

two-way *(adj.)* टू वे– moving, permitting movement, or operating in either of two opposite directions दुतरफ़ा, द्विपथी The flyover is now open to *two-way* traffic.

tycoon *(n.)* टाइकून्– a business man of great wealth and power उद्योगपति He is a powerful business *tycoon.*

type *(n.)* टाइप– 1. a kind, class, or category, the constituents of which share similar characteristics प्रकार, क़िस्म, मुद्रण या टंकण का अक्षर We find several *types* of vegetables.

2. *(v.)* to write (copy) on a typewriter टाइप करना Please *type* fast!

typhoid *(n.)* टाइफ़ॉइड– an acute infectious disease characterized by high fever, आन्त्र-ज्वर *Typhoid* is often caused by eating and drinking impure food or drink.

typhoon *(n.)* टाइफून– a violent tropical storm or cyclone प्रचंड तूफान A *typhoon* is like a cyclone.

typical *(adj.)* टिपिकल– being or serving as a representative example of a particular type; characteristic प्रारूपी, प्रतीक स्वरूप His behaviour towards her was very *typical.*

typically *(adv.)* टिपिकली– you use typically to say that something usually happens in the way that you are describing विशिष्ट रूप से *Typically,* it was an old man who offered his help.

typist *(n.)* टाइपिस्ट– a person who types, esp for a living टाइपिस्ट, टंकक Please ask the *typist* to *type* carefully.

tyranny *(n.)* टिरनी– arbitrary, unreasonable, or despotic behaviour or use of authority अत्याचार, ज़ुल्म Indians refused to accept the *tyranny* of the British government.

tyrant *(n.)* टाइरण्ट– a person who governs oppressively, unjustly, and arbitrarily; despot तानाशाह, निरंकुश शासक He ran the company like a *tyrant.*

tyre (ire) *(n.)* टायर– a rubber ring placed over the rim of a wheel of a road vehicle to provide traction and reduce road shocks, esp a hollow inflated ring रबर के टायर My car has four *tyres.*

Uu

Uu *(n.)* यू–अंग्रेज़ी वर्णमाला का इक्कीसवाँ अक्षर The twenty-first letter of the English alphabet. Umbrella begins with 'U'.

ubiquitous *(adj.)* यूबिक्विटस– having or seeming to have the ability to be everywhere at once; omnipresent सर्वव्यापी, सर्वव्यापक Dilip Kumar is the *ubiquitous* movie star of Bollywood.

ugly *(adj.)* ॲग्लि– of unpleasant or unsightly appearance बदसूरत, कुरूप Cinderella had two *ugly* sisters. They were unkind to her.

ulterior *(adj.)* ॲल्टिअरिअर्– lying beneath or beyond what is revealed, evident, or supposed गुप्त, गूढ़, अव्यक्त He has some *ulterior* motive in helping me in my work.

ultimate *(adj.)* ॲल्टिमेट–1. the highest or most significant, final सर्वोत्तम, परम, अंतिम Serving our clients with honesty is the *ultimate* aim of this organisation.
2. *(n.)* the most significant, highest, furthest, or greatest thing सबसे बड़ा एवं उत्तम The movie was the *ultimate* in cinematography.

ultimately *adv.)* अलटिमटली– in the end; at last; finally आख़िरकार, अंत में *Ultimately* he had to bow down to the wishes of his parents.

ultimatum *(n.)* अल्टिमटम– any final or peremptory demand, offer, or proposal अंतिम निर्णय She issued an *ultimatum* — either he finds a job or they will get divorced.

ultrasound *(n.)* अलट्रासाउण्ड– a medical process that produces an image of what is inside your body (शरीर के अंदरूनी अंगों का चित्र प्रस्तुत करने वाली एक प्रक्रिया) अल्ट्रासाउंड *Ultrasound* shows that her baby is three months old.

ultraviolet *(adj.)* अलट्रावाइलट– of, relating to, or consisting of radiation lying in the ultraviolet पराबैंगनी (एक प्रकार का प्रकाश जो त्वचा के लिए घातक सिद्ध होता है) *Ultraviolet* rays are harmful for eyes and delicate skin.

umbrella *(n.)* अम्ब्रेला– a portable device used for protection against rain, snow, etc., and consisting of a light canopy supported on a collapsible metal frame mounted on a central rod छाता, छतरी An *umbrella* protects us from the rain or the sun.

umpire *(n.)* अम्पाइअर्– an official who rules on the playing of a game, as in cricket or baseball निर्णायक, रेफरी, अम्पायर The *umpire* declared that the batsman had been run out.

umpteen *(pron.)* अम्प्टीन– very many बहुत बार I can watch that movie *umpteen* number of times.

un *(pre.)* अन– रहित के अर्थ में Unkind, unlock, unfold, untidy.

unable *(adj.)* ॲनेबल्– lacking the necessary power, ability, or authority (to do something); not able अयोग्य, असमर्थ I shall be *unable* to attend the meeting tomorrow.

unacceptable *(adj.)* अनकसेप्टबल– not satisfactory; inadequate अस्वीकार्य Such behaviour was *unacceptable* to me.

unaccompanied *(adj.)* अनकम्पनीड– not accompanied अकेला, बिना किसी साथी के *Unaccompanied* girls were not allowed in the discotheque.

unaffected *(adj.)* ॲनअफ़ेक्टिड– unpretentious, natural, or sincere अप्रभा- वित He was totally *unaffected* by the loss.

unanimous *(adj.)* युनैनिमस्– in complete or absolute agreement एकमत, सर्वसम्मत The decision to appoint him as the CEO was *unanimous*.

unarmed *(adj.)* अनआर्म्ड– without weapons निरस्त्र, निहत्था The civilians were *unarmed* when they entered in the house.

unashamed *(adj.)* अनशेम्ड– feeling no shame or embarrassment लज्जाहीन, निर्लज्ज He is now *unashamed* to admit that he feels like a little boy who clings to his mother's hand.

unattached *(adj.)* अनटैच्ड– not connected with any specific thing, body, group, etc.; independent असंबद्ध, असंलग्न He goes for counselling because he is *unattached* to his feelings.

unattended *(adj.)* अनटेंडेड– not looked after or cared for उपेक्षित, बिना देखभाल के Never leave your precious things *unattended.*

unauthorized (ised) *(adj.)* अन-ऑथराइज़्ड– not having official permission अनधिकृत, अवैध They are living in an *unauthorized* building.

unavailable *(adj.)* अनवेलबल– not obtainable or accessible अलभ्य, अप्राप्य The doctor is *unavailable* for a couple of days.

unavoidable *(adj.)* अनवॉइडबल– unable to be avoided; inevitable अनिवार्य, अपरिहार्य It was an *unavoidable* delay from her.

unaware *(adj.)* अनवेअर– not aware or conscious (of) अनजान, बेख़बर Huma was *unaware* of all their problems.

unbearable *(adj.)* अनबेअरबल– not able to be borne or endured असहनीय, असह्य The noise of the loudspeaker was *unbearable* for the patient.

unbeatable *(adj.)* अनबीटबल– unable to be defeated or outclassed; surpassingly excellent अद्वितीय, अपराजेय Sony TV led for sale at *unbeatable* prices.

unbelievable *(adj.)* अनबिलीवबल– unable to be believed; incredible or astonishing अविश्वसनीय His progress is *unbelievable* to me.

unblock *(v.)* अनब्लॉक– to remove a blockage from (a pipe, etc.) साफ़ कर देना या खोल देना The four workers entered sewers to *unblock* the pipes.

unbreakable *(adj.)* अनब्रेकबल– not able to be broken न टूटने वाला, अखंडनीय The twins share an *unbreakable* bond between them.

unbroken *(adj.)* अनब्रोकन– undaunted in spirit अखंडित, अभग्न She could not get an *unbroken* sleep since her mother is ill.

uncertain *(adj.)* अनसर्टन– not able to be accurately known or predicted अनिश्चित, ढुलमुल I'm still *uncertain* that our plan will work or not.

unchanged *(adj.)* अनचेंजड– not altered or different in any way पहले जैसा, अपरिवर्तित My decision will remain *unchanged.*

unchecked *(adj.)* अनचेक्ड– not examined or inspected बिना जँचा हुआ, अनजाँचा You should not leave the gas pipes *unchecked.*

uncle *(n.)* अंकल– a brother of one's father or mother ताया, चाचा, मामा, फूफा, मौसा Father's brother is *Uncle* Gopal. Mother's brother is *Uncle* Lal.

unclean *(adj.)* अनक्लीन्– lacking moral, spiritual, ritual, or physical cleanliness मैला, गंदा, अपवित्र Anuj was wearing an *unclean* jacket.

uncomfortable *(adj.)* अनकम्फ़र्टबल– not comfortable कष्टदायक, असुविधाजनक I'm very *uncomfortable* with the tone of your voice.

uncompromising *(adj.)* अनकॉमप्र-माइज़िंग– not prepared to give ground or to compromise अड़ियल, हठधर्म, अटल How can I talk to someone who has an *uncompromising* attitude.

unconcerned *(adj.)* अनकनसंर्ड– not worried बेफिक्र, निश्चिंत He always remained *unconcerned* with his wife.

unconscious *(adj.)* अनकॉनशस– lacking normal sensory awareness of the environment; insensible बेहोश, बेसुध Kashish was found lying *unconscious* on her bed.

undecided *(adj.)* अनडिसाइडिड– not having made up one's mind अनिश्चत, अनिर्णीत It's still *undecided* as to where I will pursue my higher studies.

under *(prep.)* ॲन्डर्–1. directly below; on, to, or beneath the underside or base of नीचे से, किसी के नीचे The dog jumps over the fence. The pig crawls *under* it.
2. subject to the supervision, jurisdiction, control, or influence of के अधीन, के अंतर्गत I am working *under* the supervisor.

under-age *(adj.)* अनडॅरएज– a person who is under age is legally too young to do something, for example to drink alcohol, have sex, or vote नाबालिग, अवयस्क One in four *under-age* children have profiles on social networking sites.

underarm *(n.)* अनडॅरआर्म– a person's armpit काँख, बगल She went to the parlour for an *underarm* waxing.

undercover *(adj.)* अनडॅर्कवर– done or acting in secret गुप्त एवं जासूसी से किया हुआ She was working as an *undercover* agent.

underdeveloped *(adj.)* अण्डर्डेवेलप्ड– immature or undersized पिछड़ा हुआ, अल्पविकसित An international monetary help is given to *underdeveloped* countries.

underestimate *(v.)* अण्डरएसटिमेट– to make too low an estimate of वास्तविकता से कम आंकना Do not *underestimate* my power.

undergo *(v.)* अण्डर्गो– to experience, endure, or sustain सहना, झेलना The doctor says Asha will have to *undergo* an operation.

underground *(adj.)* अण्डर्ग्राउन्ड– occurring, situated, or used below ground level भूमिगत We found an *underground* passage leading from the temple to the palace.

undergrowth *(n.)* अण्डर्ग्रोथ– small trees, bushes, ferns, etc., growing beneath taller trees in a wood or forest झाड़-झंखाड़ The path to the small village goes through the dense *undergrowth.*

underline *(v.)* अण्डर्लाइन– to put a line under रेखांकित करना The teacher *underlined* the mistakes made by the students.

undermine *(v.)* अण्डर्माइन–1. to dig or excavate beneath the earth सुरंग खोदना, जड़ खोदना The earth has been *undermined* by archeologists.
2. to weaken gradually or insidiously नष्ट करना Don't *undermine* your health by getting up very late every day.

underneath *(adv.,prep.)* ॲन्डर्नीथ– under; beneath के नीचे The coin rolled *underneath* the table.

underpass *(n.)* ॲन्डर्पास– a section of a road that passes under another road, railway line, etc. तलमार्ग The bus was allowed to pass only through the *underpass.*

underprivileged *(adj.)* ॲन्डर्प्रिविलिज्ड– lacking the rights and advantages of other members of society; deprived शोषित, पददलित ST, SC are the most *underprivileged* sections of the society.

undersigned *(n.)* ॲन्डर्साइन्ड– having signed one's name at the foot of a document, statement, etc. अधोहस्ताक्षरी The *undersigned* is directed to inform you that your services are no longer required for the trust.

understand *(v.)* अँन्डर्स्टैन्ड–1. to know and comprehend the nature or meaning of समझना, जानना Mother seems to *understand* every word the baby says.

2. to realize or grasp (something) ज्ञान होना I *understand* how radio and television work.

understanding *(adj.)* अँन्डर्स्टैन्डिंग– possessing judgment and intelligence जानकारी, समझ He is a very *understanding* person.

undertake *(v.)* अँन्डर्टेक– to contract to or commit oneself to (something) or (to do something) उत्तरदायित्व लेना, (का) भार लेना Prof. Raman has *undertaken* to deliver a lecture once a week.

underwear *(n.)* अँन्डर्वेयर– clothing worn under the outer garments, usually next to the skin अंदर पहनने का कपड़ा, कच्छा, बनियान, जांघिया Have you washed your *underwear*?

undesirable *(adj.)* अन्डिज़ाइअरबल–1. not desirable or pleasant; objectionable आपत्तिजनक Your presence is *undesirable* here.

2. a person or thing that is considered undesirable अवांछनीय Rogues are *undesirable* persons, people do not want to be friendly with them.

undisputed *(adj.)* अनडिस्पयूटेड– not challenged or questioned; accepted अविवादित, निर्विवाद He had an *undisputed* claim on the property.

undisturbed *(adj.)* अनडिस्टर्बड– not disturbed; uninterrupted अविक्षुब्ध, शांत The house has been *undisturbed* since you left it .

undo *(v.)* अँन्डू–1. to reverse the effects of नष्ट करना, बिगाड़ना When the new manager is appointed, he usually *undoes* most of the work done previously.

2. to untie, unwrap, or open or become untied, unwrapped, etc. खोलना (गाँठ या बटन) We must *undo* all our buttons before taking off our shirt.

undoubtedly *(adv.)* अँन्डाउटिडली– certainly or definitely; unquestionably निस्सन्देह, निश्चयपूर्वक We shall *undoubtedly* reach Mumbai by next week.

undue *(adj.)* अँनड्यू– excessive or unwarranted अनुचित You should not take *undue* advantage of your friends.

uneasy *(adj.)* अँनूईज़ी–1. (of a person) anxious; apprehensive अस्थिर, डगमग I eventually fell into an *uneasy* sleep.

2. (of a thought, etc.) disturbing; disquieting चिंतित, फ़िक्रमंद Mother becomes *uneasy* if you come late.

uneducated *(n.)* अँनएजुकेटेड– not having been educated to a good standard अशिक्षित, निरक्षर I spend my spare time in teaching the *uneducated.*

unemployed *(adj.)* अँनिइम्प्लॉइड– without remunerative employment; out of work बेकार, बेरोज़गार It is vey frustrating to be *unemployed.*

unemployment *(n.)* अँनिइम्प्लॉइमन्ट– the condition of being unemployed बेरोज़गारी *Unemployment* is a great curse.

unequal *(adj.)* अँनूईक्वल–1. not equal in quantity, size, rank, value, etc. (के) अयोग्य The manager is *unequal* to his task.

2. (of character, quality, etc.) irregular; varying; inconsistent असमान Your quality of work is very *unequal,* sometimes it is fair, sometimes not.

unethical *(adj.)* अनएथिकल– not ethical; improper अनैतिक He resorted to *unethical* ways to earn money.

uneven *(adj.)* अनईवन– (of a surface, etc.) not level or flat ऊबड़-खाबड़, खुरदरा, असमतल His breathing was fast and *uneven.*

unexpected *(adj.)* अनिकस्पेकटिड– surprising or unforeseen अप्रत्याशित It was an *unexpected* delay from her side.

unfair *(adj.)* ऑनफ़ेअर्– characterized by inequality or injustice अन्यायपूर्ण, भेदभाव-पूर्ण No matter what others say, his decision was *unfair.*

unfairly *(adv.)* ऑनफ़ेअरलि– in an unjust manner अनुचित रूप से Julie was treated *unfairly* in the class because she was a negress.

unfaithful *(adj.)* अनफ़ेथफुल– not true to a promise, vow, etc. बेवफ़ा, निष्ठाहीन Her *unfaithful* husband deserted her.

unfamiliar *(adj.)* अनफ़मिलिअर– not known or experienced; strange अपरिचित, अनजान I'm totally *unfamiliar* with this scientific concept.

unfashionable *(adj.)* अनफ़ैशनबल– not fashionable अप्रचलित She always buys *unfashionable* clothes.

unfavourable *(adj.)* अनफ़ेवरबल– not favourable; adverse or inauspicious नापसंद Roohi can never be *unfavourable* to me.

unfinished *(adj.)* अनफ़िनिशड– incomplete or imperfect अपूर्ण, असमाप्त I never leave anything *unfinished.*

unfit *(adj.)* ऑनफ़िट– unqualified, incapable, or incompetent अयोग्य, अस्वस्थ You were *unfit* to play hockey because you had hurt your knees.

unfold *(v.)* ऑनफ़ोल्ड–1. to open or spread out or be opened or spread out from a folded state खोलना *Unfold* the letters and read it.

2. to develop or expand or be developed or expanded प्रकट होना A wonderful view of nature *unfolded* before us.

unforgettable *(adj.)* अनफ़र्गेटबल– impossible to forget; highly memorable अविस्मरणीय His wedding was an *unforgettable* moment of my life.

unfortunate *(adj.)* अनफ़ॉर्चनट– causing or attended by misfortune दुर्भाग्यशाली, अभागा It is *unfortunate* that people are still dying of starvation in India.

unfortunately *(adv.)* अनफॉर्चनटली– it is regrettable that; unluckily दुर्भाग्य से *Unfortunately,* I could not meet them.

unfriendly *(adj.)* अनफ्रेन्डली– not friendly; hostile अमैत्रीपूर्ण The old man was quite *unfriendly* towards them.

ungrateful *(adj.)* अनग्रेटफुल– not grateful or thankful अकृतज्ञ, एहसान-फ़रामोश Aadesh is the only *ungrateful* member in the family.

unhappiness *(n.)* अनहैपिनस– the quality of being sad or disappointed दुख The teacher expressed her *unhappiness* over the behaviour of the children.

unhappy *(adj.)* अनहैपि– not joyful; sad or depressed दुखभरा, दुखी The result made him very *unhappy.*

unhealthy *(adj.)* अनहेल्थी– characterized by ill-health; sick; unwell अस्वस्थ They are living in an *unhealthy* condition.

unicorn *(n.)* यूनिकॉन– an imaginary creature usually depicted as a white horse with one long spiralled horn growing from its forehead एकशृंग/एकशृंगी A *unicorn* is a lengendary animal from European folklore.

unidentified *(adj.)* अनआइडेन्टिफ़ाइड– not identified or recognized अज्ञात An *unidentified* body has been found on the railway track.

uniform *(n.)* यूनिफ़ॉर्म–1. a characteristic feature or fashion of some class or group एकरूप All the benches in our school are *uniform.*

2. identical; alike or like एक समान The legs of a chair are of *uniform* length.

3. the distinctive clothing worth by members of a organisation or body वर्दी Soldiers, policemen and firemen always wear their *uniforms.*

uniformity *(n.)* यूनिफ़ॉर्मटी– a state or condition in which everything is regular, homogeneous, or unvarying एकरूपता There is a great deal of *uniformity* required in the manufacturing process.

unimportant *(adj.)* अनइमपॉर्टेण्ट– lacking in significance or value महत्त्वहीन Don't discuss *unimportant* issues with me.

uninhabited *(adj.)* अनइनहैबिटेड– (of a place) not having inhabitants वीरान, ग़ैर-आबाद We came across an *uninhabited* island in our journey on the cruise.

uninterested *(adj.)* अन्इनट्रस्टेड– indifferent; unconcerned रुचिहीन, उदासीन Sahar seems to be *uninterested* in politics.

union *(n.)* यूनिअन–1. the condition of being united, the act of uniting, or a conjunction formed by such an act एकता, संयोग *Union* is strength.

2. an association, alliance, or confederation of individuals or groups for a common purpose, esp political संगठन, यूनियन A trade *union* is a group of workers in the same trade who join together to get fair wages and good conditions of work.

unique *(adj.)* यूनीक– being the only one of a particular type; single; sole अद्वितीय, अनुपम The Taj Mahal is a *unique* monument.

unisex *(adj.)* यूनिसेक्स– of or relating to clothing, a hairstyle, etc., that can be worn by either sex एकलिंगी There are many *unisex* salons in the town.

unison *(n.)* यूनिसन– complete agreement; harmony साथ-साथ, एकबद्ध होकर They said in *unison,* "We will go there."

unit *(n.)* यूनिट–1. a single undivided entity or whole समूह We work as a *unit* in the office.

2. having a value defined as one for the system इकाई Hectare is a *unit* of area.

unite *(v.)* युनाइट– to make or become an integrated whole or a unity; combine मिलाना, जोड़ देना The people of India are *united* with a common cultural heritage.

unity *(n.)* यूनटी– the state or quality of being one; oneness एकता There is *unity* in diversity in India.

universe *(n.)* यूनिवर्स– the aggregate of all existing matter, energy and space विश्व, जगत् The earth is only a part of the *universe.*

university *(n.)* यूनिवर्सटी– an institution of higher education having authority to award bachelors' and higher degrees, usually having research facilities विश्वविद्यालय I am in love with the *university* I study in.

unjust *(adj.)* अन्जस्ट– not in accordance with accepted standards of fairness or justice; unfair अनुचित It is *unjust* to punish an innocent man.

unkind *(adj.)* अन्काइण्ड– lacking kindness; unsympathetic or cruel रूखा, निष्ठुर Don't be so *unkind* to her.

unknown *(adj.)* ऑन्नोन– not known, understood, or recognized अज्ञात, अनाम He who can live *unknown* is really a gentleman.

unlawful *(adj.)* अन्लॉफुल– illegal ग़ैरक़ानूनी There is a slight chance that he may be involved in *unlawful* activities.

unless *(conj.)* ॲन्ले'स–1. except under the circumstances that; except on the condition that यदि.... नहीं You must not go out *unless* you have your shoes on.

unlike *(adj.)* ॲन्लाइक– not alike; dissimilar or unequal; different असमान, विपरीत Your appearance is quite *unlike* your brother's.

unlikely *(adj.)* ॲन्लाइकलि– not alike; dissimilar or unequal; different असंभावित It is *unlikely* that the work would be finished at the stipulated date.

unlimited *(adj.)* अन्लिमिटेड– not restricted, limited, or qualified असीम, अपरिचित I have got a package of free *unlimited* calls from idea to idea.

unlock *(v.)* अन्लॉक– to unfasten (a lock, door, etc.) चाबी से ताला खोलना I cannot *unlock* the door of her house.

unluckily *(adv.)* अन्लकिली– in an unfortunate manner दुर्भाग्यवश *Unluckily* she could not succeed.

unlucky *(adj.)* अनलकी– characterized by misfortune or failure बदक़िस्मत, अभागा She has always been *unlucky* in the matters of love.

unmanageable *(adj.)* अन्मैनेजबल– difficult or impossible to control, use, or manipulate अनियंत्रिणीय, बेकाबू It is difficult to deal with an *unmanageable* person.

unmarried *(adj.)* अन्मैरिड– not married अविवाहित, कुंआरा She wants to remain *unmarried* throughout her life.

unmistakable *(adj.)* अन्मिस्टेकबल– not mistakable; clear, obvious, or unambiguous सुस्पष्ट, बिना गलती का The voice I hear was *unmistakable,* because it could not be anyone else's but Rajendra's.

unnatural *(adj.)* अन्नैचरल– contrary to nature; abnormal अस्वाभाविक The world is facing many *unnatural* calamities.

unnaturally *(adv.)* अन्नैचरली– in a manner that is not typical or usual अस्वाभाविक रूप से Her lips were *unnaturally* red.

unnecessary *(adj.)* अन्नेससरी– not necessary अनावश्यक He likes to take *unnecessary* risks with his life.

unnoticed *(adj.)* अन्नोटिस्ड– not perceived or observed अनदेखा His wrongdoings somehow went *unnoticed* by everyone

unofficial *(adj.)* अन्फ़िशियल– not official or formal ग़ैर-सरकारी It was an *unofficial* visit of the leader to his constituency.

unpleasant *(adj.)* अन्प्लेज़न्ट– not pleasant or agreeable अप्रिय, अरुचिकर Abhay has an *unpleasant* personality.

unpredictable *(adj.)* अन्प्रिडिकटबल– not capable of being predicted; changeable भविष्यवाणी न करने योग्य, अपरिवर्तनीय His *unpredictable* nature makes him a very hard to read as a person.

unqualified *(adj.)* अन्क्वॉलिफ़ाइड– lacking the necessary qualifications अयोग्य He found her *unqualified* for the post.

unquestionable *(adj.)* अन्क्वेसचनबल– indubitable or indisputable निश्चित, असंदिग्ध Her truthfulness is *unquestionable* to all of us.

unrealistic *(adj.)* अन्रिअलिसटिक– not realistic अव्यावहारिक It is *unrealistic* to expect him to be able to solve all my problems.

unreasonable *(adj.)* अन्रीज़नबल– immoderate; excessive अनुचित The union was making *unreasonable* demands from the management.

unreliable *(adj.)* अन्रिलाइअबल– not reliable; untrustworthy अविश्वसनीय Her story is *unreliable.* You should not trust her.

unrest *(n.)* अनरेस्ट– a troubled or rebellious state of discontent असंतोष,

बेचैनी Greed breeds social *unrest* in India.

unrivalled *(adj.)* अन्राइवल्ड– having no equal; matchless बेजोड़, अद्वितीय His knowledge on Islam is *unrivalled.*

unruly *(adj.)* अनरूली– disposed to disobedience or indiscipline बेक़ाबू, बेलगाम Teenagers are *unruly* in this school.

unsafe *(adj.)* अन्सेफ़– not safe; perilous असुरक्षित It's quite *unsafe* for females to travel at night.

unsatisfactory *(adj.)* अन्सैटिसफ़ैकटरी– not adequate or suitable; unacceptable असंतोषजनक The performance of the team has remained highly *unsatisfactory.*

unsavoury *(adj.)* अन्सेवरी– objectionable or distasteful घृणित, बदनाम Ashmit has some rather *unsavoury* habits.

unseen *(adj.)* अनसीन– not observed or perceived; invisible अनदेखा Few people believe in *unseen* powers.

unselfish *(adj.)* अन्सेलफ़िश– not selfish or greedy; generous निःस्वार्थ I have *unselfish* devotion to my siblings.

unsettle *(v.)* अन्सेटल– to confuse or agitate (emotions, the mind, etc.) डाँवाँडोल/अस्थिर करना Their separation might *unsettle* the kids.

unsettled *(adj.)* अन्सेटल्ड– lacking order or stability बेचैन, अशांत The couple is still *unsettled* in their new flat.

unskilled *(adj.)* अन्स्किल्ड– not having or requiring any special skill or training अप्रशिक्षित The factory is need of *unskilled* labour .

unstable *(adj.)* अन्स्टेबल– not having or requiring any special skill or training अस्थिर, ढुलमुल Her condition is still *unstable* after the operation.

unsteady *(adj.)* अन्स्टडी– not securely fixed अस्थिर, लड़खड़ाता हुआ Asif is still *unsteady* on her knee after the operation.

unsuccessful *(adj.)* अन्सकसेसफ़ुल– not having succeeded असफ़ल His business venture proved to be very *unsuccessful.*

unsuccessfully *(adv.)* अन्सकसेसफ़ुली– in a manner that does not achieve what it was intended to achieve असफ़लतापूर्वक They climbed up to the China peak *unsuccessfully.*

unsuitable *(adj.)* अन्सूटबल– not appropriate, suitable, or fit अनुपयुक्त The film Murder 2 is *unsuitable* for young children.

unsympathetic *(adj.)* अन्सिमपथेटिक– not characterized by, feeling, or showing sympathy कठोर सहानुभूति His behaviour towards the poor is very *unsympathetic.*

unthinking *(adj.)* अन्थिंकिंग– lacking thoughtfulness; inconsiderate बिना सोचे-समझे हुए, लापरवाह Ashu is regretting badly for his *unthinking* comment on her friend.

untidily *(adv.)* ॲन्टाइडली– in a slovenly or not neat manner लापरवाही से, बेसिलसिले The woman is *untidily* dressed.

untidy *(adj.)* ॲन्टाइडी– not neat; slovenly अस्त-व्यस्त, बेढ़ंगा The students left the hall in a very *untidy* shape after the party.

untie *(v.)* अनटाइ– to unfasten or free (a knot or something that is tied) or (of a knot or something that is tied) to become unfastened गांठ खोलना Please *untie* your shoe laces.

until *(prep.)* ॲन्टिल– in or throughout the period before जब तक.... नहीं Asha will not go to bed *until* 9.30 p.m. *until* your parents arrive back we you will adhere to my rules.

untimely *(adj.)* अन्टाइमली– occurring before the expected, normal, or proper time असामयिक, बेमौका Their *untimely* arrival surprised us all.

untold *(adj.)* अनटोल्ड– incapable of description or expression अनकहा, अकथित, बेशुमार She is a woman of *untold* virtues.

untouchable *(n.)* अनूटचबल– unable to be touched अछूत, अस्पृश्य व्यक्ति More than 160 million people in India are considered *untouchable*.

untrue *(adj.)* अनूट्रू– incorrect or false मिथ्या, झूठा Her accusation is totally *untrue*.

unused *(adj.)* अनूयूस्ड– not being or never having been made use of अप्रयुक्त, अनभ्यस्त His set of skills have been *unused* properly by the firm.

unusual *(adj.)* अनूयूश़अल– out of the ordinary; uncommon; extraordinary अनोखा, ग़ैर-मामूली It is *unusual* for a teenage girl to drive a car.

unusually *(adv.)* अन्‌यूश़ुअली– in an uncommon and extraordinary manner असाधारण तरीक़े से *Unusually* I forgot their wedding anniversary.

unwanted *(adj.)* अनूवॉनटेड– not wanted or desired अवांछित, अनचाहा It was an *unwanted* gift for me.

unwell *(adj.)* ॲनूवे'ल– not well; ill अस्वस्थ She has been *unwell* for quite a number of days.

unwilling *(adj.)* अनूविलिंग– unfavourably inclined; reluctant अनिच्छुक She was *unwilling* to invest any money in business.

up *(adv.)* ॲप–1. to an upward, higher, or erect position, esp indicating readiness for an activity ऊपर Kamla and Vimla went *up* the hill.

2. over or completed पूरी तरह से I ate *up* all the bananas.

3. to increase or raise और ऊँचे Please speak *up*, I cannot hear you well.

- **up and down** *(n.)* alternating periods of good and bad fortune, high and low spirits, etc. उतार-चढ़ाव, Life is full of *ups and downs*.
- **climb up**– to go up or ascend (stairs, a mountain, etc.) चढ़ना, *Climb up* the tree for plucking mangoes.
- **get up**– to wake and rise from one's bed or cause to wake and rise from bed उठना, *Get up* early in the morning.
- **stand up**– to rise to the feet खड़े होना, *Stand up* when an elderly person comes to you.
- **wake *up***– an alert or intelligent person जागना, It is the time to *wake up*.

upbringing *(n.)* अपब्रिंगिंग– rearing पालन-पोषण, लालन-पालन His mental weakness is due to his strict *upbringing*.

update *(v.)* अपडेट– to bring up to date नवीनतम सूचना देना The doctor *updated* us on the condition of the patient.

uphold *(v.)* ॲपूहोल्ड– to maintain, affirm, or defend against opposition or challenge समर्थन करना In the end he *upheld* his promise towards me.

uplift *(v.)* अपलिफ़्ट– to raise morally, spiritually, culturally, etc. उन्नत करना, ऊँचा करना Indian government is doing a lot to *uplift* the deprived people.

upon *(prep.)* अपॉन– indicating a position reached by going up (के) ऊपर The birds are sitting *upon* the turret.

upper *(adj.)* ॲपर्– higher or highest in relation to physical position, wealth, rank, status, etc. (दो की तुलना में) ऊपर का, वरिष्ठ I live in the *upper* storey. Parliament has two houses – the *upper* house and the lower house.

uppermost *(adj.)* अपर्मोस्ट– highest in position, power, importance, etc. उच्चतम, सर्वोच्च There is a ripe guava on the *uppermost* branches of the tree.

upright *(adj.)* ॲपूराइट–1. vertical or erect सीधा, खड़ा Please stand *upright* while I measure your height.
2. honest, honourable, or just ईमानदार We can trust Ravi, for he has always been *upright* in his dealings with us.

uprising *(n.)* अपूराइजिंग– a revolt or rebellion विद्रोह, बग़ावत There was an *uprising* near the police station.

uproar *(n.)* ॲपरॉर्– a commotion or disturbance characterized by loud noise and confusion; turmoil होहल्ला, शोरगुल, कोलाहल, हंगामा The girls made such an *uproar* that the head-mistress had to come to quieten them.

upset *(adj.)* ॲप्से'ट– 1. emotionally or physically disturbed or distressedविचलित, परेशान Shanta was very much *upset* when she heard about her husband's accident.
2. *(v.)* to disturb mentally or emotionally चिंतित एवं परेशान कर देना, गड़बड़ा देना Never *upset* other people's programmes.

upside down *(adj.,adv.)* अपसाइड डाउन– turned over completely; inverted उलटा, औंधा The children are hanging *upside down* on the swings.

upstairs *(adv.)* अपस्टेअर्ज़– up the stairs; to or on an upper floor or level ऊपरी मंज़िल He carried my luggage *upstairs.*

up to date *(adj.)* अपटुडेट– having complete knowledge अद्यतन, आधुनिकतम Sohan has *up to date* knowledge about the technology.

upturned *(adj.)* अपटर्ंड– turned up at the end ऊपर की ओर उठा हुआ Madhuri has an *upturned* nose.

upward *(adj.)* अपवर्ड– directed or moving towards a higher point or level ऊपर की ओर जाने वाला The rocket shot in an *upward* direction.

urban *(adj.)* अर्बन– of, relating to, or constituting a city or town शहरी The *urban* population growth rate of the country is estimated at more than 5 per cent per year.

urbane *(adj.)* अर्बेन– characterized by elegance or sophistication सुसंस्कृत, सभ्य, शिष्ट He is a man of *urbane* manners.

urge *(n.)* अर्ज–1. a strong impulse, inner drive, or yearning लालसा, तीव्र इच्छा Anupam had an *urge* to eat ice-cream.
2. *(v.)* to entreat अनुनय-विनय करना Subhash Chandra Bose felt a great *urge* to achieve the freedom of our country from the British.

urgency *(n.)* अर्जन्सी– the condition of needing to be dealt with as soon as possible अत्यावश्यक The *urgency* of the message frightened my mother.

urgent *(adj.)* अर्जण्ट– requiring or compelling speedy action or attention बहुत आवश्यक The board of directors have convened an *urgent* meeting.

urinary *(adj.)* यूरिनरी– of or relating to urine or to the organs and structures that secrete and pass urine मूत्र-संबंधी His grand father has some *urinary* trouble.

usage *(adj.)* यूसेज– the act or a manner of using; use; employment शब्दों का प्रयोग, भाषा-प्रयोग, किसी वस्तु का प्रयोग She spoiled the laptop by rough *usage.*

use *(v.)* यूज़–1. to put into service or action; employ for a given purpose प्रयोग करना We *use* our cycles to ride.
2. *(n.)* usefulness; advantage लाभ, फायदा It is a great misfortune to be of no *use* to anybody.
3. the act of using or the state of being used प्रयोग, इस्तेमाल What is

the *use* of being a cross? It doesn't do any good.

useful *(adj.)* यूसफ़ुल– able to be used advantageously, beneficially, or for several purposes; helpful or serviceable उपयोगी A pin is a very *useful* thing.

useless *(n.)* यूसलेस– having no practical use or advantage बेकार, अनुपयोगी The report that you have submitted is totally *useless*.

usual *(adj.)* यूशुअल– of the most normal, frequent, or regular type; customary सामान्य, पहले के समान

1. Uncle has gone out for his *usual* morning walk.

2. Always go to school at the *usual* time.

usually *(adv.)* यूशअली– customarily; at most times; in the ordinary course of events सामान्यतः I *usually* go for long walks in the evening

utensil *(n.)* यूटे'नूसिल– an implement, tool, or container for practical use पात्र, बर्तन A pan is a cooking *utensil.*

utility *(n.)* यूटिलटी– the quality of practical use; usefulness; serviceability उपयोगिता This tool has no *utility* for me.

utilize (ise) *(v.)* यूटिलाइज़– to make practical or worthwhile use of उपयोग करना We should *utilize* natural resources.

utmost *(adj.)* अट्मोस्ट– of the greatest possible degree or amount चरम, अत्यधिक The project requires your *utmost* attention.

utter *(v.)* ॲटर्–1. to give audible expression to (something) कुछ कहना She *uttered* a few words in foreign language.

2. *(adj.)* sometimes निरा, निपट, पूरा He is an *utter* coward.

utterly *(adv.)* ॲटर्ली– completly पूर्णतया, पूरी तरह से Children are *utterly* dependent on their parents.

ୡ୦ଓ

Vv

Vv *(n.)* वी–अंग्रेज़ी वर्णमाला का बाइसवाँ अक्षर The twenty-second letter of the English alphabet. Violin begins with 'V'.

vacancy *(n.)* वेकनसी–1. the state or condition of being vacant or unoccupied; emptiness (नौकरी के लिए) ख़ाली जगह There is a *vacancy* of computer operator in his office.

2. an unoccupied room in a boarding house, hotel, etc. ख़ाली कमरा There is no *vacancy* in this hotel.

vacant *(adj.)* वेकण्ट– not being used, empty ख़ाली, रिक्त There was a *vacant* seat on the bus.

vacation *(n.)* वकेशन– a period of the year when the law courts or universities are closed अवकाश, (लंबी) छुट्‌टी We had been planning this *vacation* for a long time.

vaccinate *(v.)* वैक्सिनेट– to inoculate (a person) with a vaccine so as to produce immunity against a specific disease टीका लगाना The children are being *vaccinated.*

vaccination *(n.)* वैकसिनेशन– the act of vaccinating टीकाकरण *Vaccination* against contagious diseases is essential.

vaccinator *(n.)* वैकसिनेटर– someone who administers a vaccination टीका लगाने वाला व्यक्ति The *vaccinators* should take care of cleanliness.

vacuum *(n.)* वैक्युअ़म–1. a region containing no matter; free space शून्य, खाली जगह, निर्वात Tinned food is mostly *vacuum* packed.

2. of, containing, measuring, producing, or operated by a low gas pressure सफ़ाई करने वाला विद्युत उपकरण My brother brought a *vacuum* cleaner from London.

vagabond *(n.)* वैगबॉण्ड– a person with no fixed home आवारागर्द, आवारा, घुमक्कड़ We don't know about his whereabouts; he is a *vagabond.*

vagrant *(n.)* वेग्रण्ट– a person of no settled abode, income, or job; tramp आवारा The *vagrant* man saw a mobile on the bench.

vague *(adj.)* वेग– (of statements, meaning, etc.) not explicit; imprecise अस्पष्ट, धुंधला, अनिश्चित His answers to select committee were *vague* and feeble.

vaguely *(adv.)* वेगली– in a manner that is not precise or clear कुछ-कुछ, अस्पष्ट रूप से His face is *vaguely* familiar to me.

vagueness *(n.)* वेगनस– lack of clarity or precision अस्पष्टता I could not understand anything due to *vagueness* in her speech.

vain *(adj.)* वेन– 1. inordinately proud of one's appearance, possessions, or achievements व्यर्थ, बेकार Hari made a *vain* search for his pen. He couldn't find it anywhere.

2. *(adv.)* worthless बेकार ही He shouted in *vain* for help.

valentine *(n.)* वैलनटाइन– a card expressing love or affection प्रेम-पत्र Will you send a *valentine* to me?

valiant *(adj.)* वैलिअण्ट– courageous, intrepid, or stout-hearted; brave शूरवीर, साहसी He made a *valiant* effort to rescue the princess.

valiantly *(adv.)* वैलिअण्टली– in a valiant manner साहसपूर्वक The soldiers fought for their country *valiantly.*

valid *(adj.)* वैलिड– having some foundation; based on truth मान्य,

वैध, प्रामाणिक Your membership to the library is *valid* for only a month.

validate *(v.)* वैलिडेट– to confirm or corroborate सत्यापित करना, मान्य करना You have to *validate* your suspicion.

valley *(n.)* वैली– an area of low land between hills or mountains घाटी A *valley* is a place between two hills.

valuable *(adj.)* वैलयुअबल– having considerable monetary worth बहुत क़ीमती, बहुमूल्य These goods are very *valuable* and need to kept safely.

value *(v.)* वैल्यू–1. to assess or estimate the worth, merit, or desirability of; appraise मूल्य लगाना, मूल्य निर्धारित करना The automobile dealer had *valued* my old scooter at five thousand rupees.

2. to have a high regard for, esp in respect of worth, usefulness, merit, etc.; esteem or prize महत्त्व देना, मूल्यवान मानना I *value* the advice of my elders.

3. *(n.)* an amount, esp a material or monetary one, considered to be a fair exchange in return for a thing; assigned valuation मूल्य, क़ीमत The chief *value* of my motorcycle is that it lets me get about so quickly.

4. the desirability of a thing, often in respect of some property such as usefulness or exchangeability; worth, merit, or importance उपयोगी, महत्त्व Physical exercises are of great *value* for strengthening your muscles.

valve *(n.)* वैल्व–1. any device that shuts off, starts, regulates, or controls the flow of a fluid वाल्व, कपाट A *valve* prevents the air from leaking out of tyre.

2. a flaplike structure in a hollow organ, such as the heart, that controls the one-way passage of fluid through that organ हृदय का वाल्व A *valve* lets blood flow in one direction only.

vampire *(n.)* वैमपाइअर– a corpse that rises nightly from its grave to drink the blood of the living रक्त चूसने वाला भूत *Vampires* existed in the past.

van *(n.)* वैन–1. a covered motor vehicle for transporting goods, etc. by road गाड़ी, वैन A *van* is a car that is used for carrying load.

2. a closed railway wagon in which the guard travels, for transporting goods, mail, etc. बंद माल डिब्बा We put trunks in the luggage *van.*

vandal *(n.)* वैनडल– a person who deliberately causes damage or destruction to personal or public property कलाकृति-ध्वंसक A group of *vandals* caused a lot of commotion on the street.

vanilla *(n.)* वनिला– any tropical climbing orchid of the genus Vanilla, esp V. plonifolia, having spikes of large fragrant greenish-yellow flowers and long fleshy pods containing the seeds (beans) स्वादिष्ट बनाने वाला एक खाद्य पदार्थ, वनीला She likes *vanilla* ice cream.

vanish *(v.)* वैनिश– to disappear, esp suddenly or mysteriously लुप्त होना, ग़ायब होना When the sun rose, the mist *vanished.*

vanity *(n.)* वैनटि– the state or quality of being vain; excessive pride or conceit घमंड, ग़रूर I found *vanity* in her speech.

vanquish *(v.)* वैंकक्विश– to defeat or overcome in a battle, contest, etc.; conquer हराना, परास्त करना He *vanquished* his opponent in a contest.

vapour *(n.)* वेपर्– particles of moisture or other substance suspended in air and visible as clouds, smoke, etc. वाष्प, भाप *Vapour* rises from boiling water.

variable *(adj.)* वेअरिअबल– liable to or capable of change परिवर्तनशील Prices are *variable* in his shop.

variation *(n.)* वेअरिएशन– the act, process, condition, or result of changing or varying; diversity भिन्नता, परिवर्तन There is a slight *variation* in the weather.

variety *(n.)* वराइअटी– the quality or condition of being diversified or various विविधता, विभिन्न वस्तुओं का संग्रह She has different *variety* of clothes in her wardrobe.

various *(adj.)* वेअरिअस–1. of different kinds, though often within the same general category; diverse अनेक She left the job with *various* valid reasons.

2. displaying variety; many-sided विविध, नानारूप The police tried *various* ways to make the thief confess.

varnish *(v.)* वार्निश– 1. to give a smooth surface to, as if by painting with varnish रोग़न करना, चमकाना He painted the door and then *varnished* it.

2. *(n.)* a preparation consisting of a solvent, a drying oil, and usually resin, rubber, bitumen, etc., for application to a surface where it polymerizes to yield a hard glossy, usually transparent, coating लकड़ी चमकाने का एक रंगहीन द्रव पदार्थ The windows have been given a new coat of *varnish.*

vary *(v.)* वेरी–1. to undergo or cause to undergo change, alteration, or modification in appearance, character, form, attribute, etc. बदल जाना, बदल देना, रूपान्तरित करना The weather *varies* from day to day.

2. to be different or cause to be different; be subject to change भिन्न होना The size of the books *varied.* Some were large, others were small.

vase *(n.)* वाज़्– a vessel used as an ornament or for holding cut flowers फूलदान, गुलदान We put flowers in a *vase.* It is called a flower-*vase.*

vast *(adj.)* वास्ट– unusually large in size, extent, degree, or number; immense सुविस्तृत, विशाल, बड़ा He has a *vast* amount of information.

vault *(n.)* वॉल्ट– a strongroom for the safe-deposit and storage of valuables तहख़ाना, सुरक्षित स्थान Valuables are stored in a *vault* at the bank.

vegetable *(n.)* वेजिटेबल– any of various herbaceous plants having parts that are used as food, such as peas, beans, cabbage, potatoes, cauliflower, and onions शाक, भाजी, सब्ज़ी, तरकारी Potatoes, pumpkins, carrots, onions, turnips and beans are all *vegetables.* A farmer grow *vegetables* in the field.

vegetarian *(adj.)* वे'जिटेअरिअन– relating to, advocating, or practising vegetarianism शाकाहारी *Vegetarian* food is good for health.

vehicle *(n.)* वीअकल–1. any conveyance in or by which people or objects are transported, esp one fitted with wheels गाड़ी, सवारी, वाहन Motor cars, buses, trucks and carts are all *vehicles.*

2. a medium for the expression, communication, or achievement of ideas, information, power, etc. अभिव्यक्ति का माध्यम Language is a good *vehicle* for expressing our feelings.

veil *(v.)* वेल–1. to wear or put on a veil पर्दा करना, घूंघट करना Muslim women are always *veiled* when they go out of their homes.

2. to cover, conceal, or separate with or as if with a veil छिपाना, ढकना

Could you *veil* your disgust at his conduct?

3. *(n.)* a piece of more or less transparent material, usually attached to a hat or headdress, used to conceal or protect a woman's face and head नक़ाब, बुरक़ा The bride wore a colourful *veil.*

vein *(n.)* वेन– any of the tubular vessels that convey oxygen-depleted blood to the heart नस, रग He is so skinny that one can clearly see his *veins* on his hands.

velocity *(n.)* वलसिटी– speed of motion, action, or operation; rapidity; swiftness वेग, रफ़्तार The bullet struck him at a great *velocity.*

velvet *(n.)* वे'लवेट– a fabric of silk, cotton, nylon, etc, with a thick close soft usually lustrous pile मख़मल, रोयेंदार मुलायम कपड़ा *Velvet* is a soft cloth. It is smooth to touch.

vendor *(n.)* वेण्डर– a person who sells something, esp food, newspapers, etc. विक्रेता The vegetable *vendor* didn't show up today.

venerate *(v.)* वेनरेट– to hold in deep respect; revere श्रद्धा रखना, आदर करना The best way to *venerate* him is to show your undying respect.

venereal disease *(n.)* वेनेरिअल डिज़ीज़ any of various diseases, such as syphilis or gonorrhoea, transmitted by sexual intercourse यौन रोग Hakeem Hari Kishan is a well known specialist in *venereal diseases.*

vengeance *(n.)* वे'न्जन्स– the act of or desire for taking revenge; retributive punishment प्रतिशोध, बदला Nothing is more poisonous than *vengeance.* In fact, *vengeance* has no foresight.

venom *(n.)* वे'नम– a poisonous fluid secreted by such animals as certain snakes and scorpions and usually transmitted by a bite or sting विष, ज़हर The *venom* of a cobra is highly powerful and causes death quickly.

venomous *(adj.)* वेनमस– poisonous; secreting venom ज़हरीला He threw a *venomous* glance and left.

ventilate *(v.)* वेंटिलेट– to drive foul air out of (an enclosed area) वायु-संचार करना Father opened the window to *ventilate* the room.

ventilation *(n.)* वे'न्टिलेशन– the act or process of ventilating or the state of being ventilated वायु संचार There is a foul smell circulation through the *ventilation* system.

venture *(v.)* वे'नचर्– 1. to expose to danger; hazard जोखिम में डालना Do not *venture* into the woods on such a dark night.

2. *(n.)* an undertaking that is risky or of uncertain outcome जोखिम, साहसिक कार्य It is a risky *venture* to start a college in the village.

venue *(n.)* वेन्यू– the place in which a cause of action arises घटना-स्थल The *venue* of the wedding was changed.

veranda *(n.)* वरे'ण्डा– a porch or portico, sometimes partly enclosed, along the outside of a building बरांडा, बरामदा I like to sit in my *veranda* in the evenings to talk to my neighbours.

verb *(v.)* वर्ब– (in traditional grammar) any of a large class of words in a language that serve to indicate the occurrence or performance of an action, the existence of a state or condition, etc. क्रिया There are two kinds of *verbs* – transitive and intransitive.

verbal *(adj.)* वर्बल– of, relating to, or using words, esp as opposed to ideas, etc. शाब्दिक, ज़बानी He has given *verbal* instructions.

verbatim *(adv.)* वर्बेटिम– using exactly the same words; word for word शब्दश: She copied the article from Internet *verbatim.*

verdict *(n.)* वर्डिक्ट–1. any decision, judgment, or conclusio अभिनिर्णय, फ़ैसला Honour the *verdict* of the jury.
2. the findings of a jury on the issues of fact submitted to it for examination and trial; judgment बहुत सोच-विचार के बाद का निर्णय What is your *verdict* on the quality of this cloth?

verge *(n.)* वर्ज– an edge or rim; margin किनारा, सिरा, छोर, सीमा He was on the *verge* of losing his wealth.

verify *(v.)* वे'रिफ़ाइ– to prove to be true; confirm; substantiate प्रमाणित करना, सत्य सिद्ध करना Your statement must be *verified* by a witness.

veritable *(adj.)* वेरिटबल– genuine or true; proper खरा, वास्तविक I require a *veritable* proof.

vermilion *(n.)* वर्मिलिअन– mercuric sulphide, esp when used as a bright red pigment; cinnabar सिंदूर All married Hindu women put *vermilion* on the forehead and at the parting of the hair.

vermin *(n.)* वर्मिन– small animals collectively, esp insects and rodents, that are troublesome to man, domestic animals, etc. पीड़क जन्तु, कीड़े-मकोड़े Lice and fleas are considered to be *vermin.*

verminous *(adj.)* वर्मिनस– covered with vermin छोटे-मोटे कीड़ों से ग्रस्त Don't neglect the dog, otherwise it will be *verminous.*

vernacular *(n.)* वर्नैक्यूलर्– the language spoken in a specific area देशी भाषा या बोली In India, we have several *vernaculars.*

versatile *(n.)* वर्सटाइल– capable of or adapted for many different uses, skills, etc. बहुमुखी, सर्वतोमुखी Johnny Depp is a *versatile* actor.

verse *(n.)* वर्स– (not in technical usage) a stanza or other short subdivision of a poem कविता, पद्य A *verse* is a short piece of poetry.

version *(n.)* वर्शन– a film/movie, novel, etc. is in a differernt form, style or language from an earlier form रूपांतर The Tamil *version* of the novel is due for publication next year.

versus *(prep.)* वर्सस– (esp in a competition or lawsuit) against; in opposition to बनाम, प्रति Today's international match is Pakistan *versus* India.

vertebrate *(n.)* वर्टिब्रेट– any chordate animal of the subphylum Vertebrata, characterized by a bony or cartilaginous skeleton and a well-developed brain: the group contains fishes, amphibians, reptiles, birds, and mammals रीढ़ की हड्डी वाले जीव (पशु पक्षी आदि) Mammals, birds, fish, rodents, reptiles, amphibians and whales are *vertebrates.*

vertical *(adj.)* वर्टिकल– at right angles to the horizon; perpendicular; upright खड़ा, लंबवत् He rode the bike in an almost *vertical* position.

very *(adv.)* वे'री–1. (intensifier) used to add emphasis to adjectives that are able to be graded बहुत अधिक I am *very* fond of ice-cream.
2. *(adj.)* used with nouns preceded by a definite article or possessive determiner, in order to give emphasis to the significance, appropriateness or relevance of a noun in a particular context, or to give exaggerated intensity to certain nouns मात्रा, केवल The *very* idea of it makes me sad.

3. real or true; genuine यही, दूसरा नहीं He is the *very* person I sought to see.

vessel *(n.)* वे'सल–1. any object used as a container, esp for a liquid बर्तन, पात्र Empty *vessels* make the most noise.

2. a tubular structure that transports such body fluids as blood and lymph रुधिरवाही नलिका Our veins are blood-*vessels.* They carry blood throughout the body.

vest *(n.)* वे'स्ट–1. an undergarment covering the body from the shoulders to the hips, made of cotton, nylon, etc. वास्कट, फतूही, बंडी It is essential to wear a *vest* in winters.

2. *(v.)* to place or settle (power, rights, etc., in) निहित होना In India, power is *vested* usually in the Prime Minister and the cabinet.

vested Interest *(adv.)* वेसटिड इनट्रेस्ट– a strong personal concern in a state of affairs, system, etc., usually resulting in private gain निहित-स्वार्थ He has a *vested interest* in whatever he is doing for you.

vet *(n.)* वेट– a person suitably qualified and registered to practise veterinary medicine पशु-चिकित्सक I took my dog to the *vet.*

veteran *(n.)* वे'टरन– a person or thing that has given long service in some capacity अनुभवी व्यक्ति Sachin Tendulkar is a *veteran* cricketer and batsman.

veterinary *(n.)* वे'टनरी– of or relating to veterinary medicine पशु-चिकित्सा Our cow was ill, so we took it to the *veterinary* surgeon.

veto *(n.)* वीटो– the power to prevent legislation or action proposed by others; prohibition निषेधाधिकार The President used her *veto* power over the resolution.

vex *(v.)* वे'क्स– to anger or annoy चिढ़ाना, खिजाना, परेशान करना We will *vex* our teacher if we keep asking him silly questions.

vexed *(adj.)* वेक्स्ड– annoyed, confused, or agitated जटिल, विवादग्रस्त We live in *vexed* and troubled times.

via *(prep.)* वाइआ– by way of; by means of; through से होकर, के मार्ग से, द्वारा My flight came to Delhi *via* Bombay.

viable *(adj.)* वाइअबल– capable of becoming actual, useful, etc.; practicable व्यवहार्य Do you think this project is commercially *viable*?

vibrant *(adj.)* वाइब्रण्ट– characterized by or exhibiting vibration; pulsating or trembling जीवन्त, झंकृत करने वाला, उत्तेजक Uma showed *vibrant* enthusiasm in her new assignment.

vibrate *(v.)* वाइब्रेट– to move or cause to move back and forth rapidly; shake, quiver, or throb कांपना, कंपाना Father's voice *vibrated* with anger.

vibration *(n.)* वाइब्रेशन– the act or an instance of vibrating थर्राहट, कम्पन The *vibration* of the engine shook us.

vicar *(n.)* विकर्– a clergyman appointed to act as priest of a parish from which, formerly, he did not receive tithes but a stipend पादरी The *vicar* lives in a church.

vice *(n.)* वाइस– 1. an immoral, wicked, or evil habit, action, or trait व्यसन, दुर्गुण, दोष Gambling is a *vice* that leads to great unhappiness.

2. *(prefix.)* serving in the place of or as a deputy for उप, उप-प्रधानाचार्य Since you are the *Vice*-Captain, you will take the Captain's place when he is ill.

vice versa *(adv.)* वाइस वर्सा– with the order reversed; the other way around इसके विपरीत, जो अभी कहा उसका उलटा India trades with China and *vice versa.*

vicinity *(n.)* विसिनिटी– a surrounding, adjacent, or nearby area; neighbourhood निकटता, नज़दीकी There was a slum in the *vicinity* of our house.

vicious *(adj.)* विशस– wicked or cruel; villainous दुष्ट, निर्मम A *vicious* man attacked the nightclub.

victim *(n.)* विक्टिम– a person or thing that suffers harm, death, etc., from another or from some adverse act, circumstance, etc. शिकार, पीड़ित There are many *victims* of this road accident. Food is being collected for the *victims* of the floods.

victor *(n.)* विक्टर– a person, nation, etc., that has defeated an adversary in war, etc. विजेता Abha was the *victor* in the last race in the sports.

victorious *(adj.)* विकटॉरिअस– having defeated an adversary विजयी We welcomed the *victorious* hockey team at the airport.

victory *(n.)* विक्टरी–1. final and complete superiority in a war विजय, सफ़लता, जीत Our army won a great *victory* over Pakistan in the battle on the North-Western border.

2. the act of triumphing or state of having triumphed फ़तह, विजयश्री Everyone hankers after a *victory*.

video *(n.)* विडिओ– the visual elements of a television broadcast चित्रमुद्रण, वीडियो The entire conversation was *video* tapped secretly.

view *(n.)* व्यू–1. the act of seeing or observing; an inspection दृश्य We had a clear *view* from the top of the hill. Really, it was a lovely *view*.

2. *(v.)* to examine or inspect carefully देखना, निरीक्षण करना We can *view* the inside of the castle.

3. to consider in a specified manner किसी विषय में विशेष प्रकार से सोचना The local people *viewed* new comers with suspicion.

viewpoint *(n.)* व्यूपॉइण्ट– the mental attitude that determines a person's opinions or judgments; point of view दृष्टिकोण Consider this issue from my *viewpoint*.

vigil *(n.)* विजिल– a purposeful watch maintained, esp at night, to guard, observe, pray, etc. रात्रि-जागरण The watchman kept *vigil* all night.

vigilance *(n.)* विजिलन्स– the fact, quality, or condition of being vigilant सतर्कता, चौकसी There is a need of increasing police *vigilance* in the area.

vigilant *(adj.)* विजिलन्ट– keenly alert to or heedful of trouble or danger, as while others are sleeping or unsuspicious सतर्क, चौकस, सावधान The police was *vigilant* all the time and caught the thief in a few days.

vigour *(n.)* विगर्–1. exuberant and resilient strength of body or mind; vitality बल, ताक़त, तंदुरुस्ती We will not win many games unless we put more *vigour* into our play.

2. substantial effective energy or force जोश, उमंग, उत्साह The *vigour* with which you work is amazing.

vile *(adj.)* वाइल– abominably wicked; shameful or evil दुष्ट, चरित्रहीन, बहुत अप्रिय या ख़राब Do you think I'm capable of such *vile* conduct?

villa *(n.)* विला– a country house, usually consisting of farm buildings and residential quarters around a courtyard देहाती बंगला, ग्राम निवास My brother has a beautiful *villa* in a small town.

village *(n.)* विलेज– a small group of houses in a country area, larger than a hamlet गांव, ग्राम The thieves plundered the entire *village*

villager *(n.)* विलेजर– an inhabitant of a village ग्रामीण, देहाती Many *villagers* go to big cities for better livelihood.

villain *(n.)* विलन– a wicked or malevolent person दुष्ट, बदमाश,

खलनायक, शरारती In many plays, the *villain* meets a bad end.

villainous *(adj.)* विलॅनस– of, like, or appropriate to a villain दुष्ट, खल Rama killed Ravan for his *villainous* acts.

vindicate *(v.)* विण्डिकेट–1. to clear from guilt, accusation, blame, etc., as by evidence or argument दोष मुक्त करना The report *vindicated* him completely.
2. to uphold, maintain, or defend (a cause, etc.) वैध ठहराना, उचित ठहराना The decision to advertise has been *vindicated* by the fact that sales has grown.

vine *(n.)* वाइन– any of various plants, esp the grapevine, having long flexible stems that creep along the ground or climb by clinging to a support by means of tendrils, leafstalks, etc. अंगूर की बेल *Vine* is a creeping plant. Grapes grow on the grape *vine.*

vinegar *(n.)* विनगर्– a sour-tasting liquid consisting of impure dilute acetic acid, made by oxidation of the ethyl alcohol in beer, wine, or cider सिरका *Vinegar* is used as a preservative in pickles.

vintage *(adj.)* विनटेज– of lasting interest and importance; venerable; classic पुरानी और बढ़िया He has a collection of *vintage* cars in the garage.

violate *(v.)* वाइअलेट– to break, disregard, or infringe (a law, agreement, etc.) क़ानून का उल्लंघन करना We should not *violate* the rules and regulations of the road.

violence *(n.)* वाइअलन्स– an unjust, unwarranted, or unlawful display of force, esp such as tends to overawe or intimidate हिंसा *Violence* is not a way to settle an argument.

violent *(adj.)* वॉइअलण्ट– marked or caused by great physical force or violence तेज़, प्रबल, हिंसक The *violent* storm blew down the huts.

violently *(adv.)* वाइअलण्टली– in a way that uses or involves violence, especially in order to injure or intimidate others हिंसापूर्वक Why are you knocking *violently* on the window?

violet *(adj.)* वाइअलट–1. any of various temperate perennial herbaceous plants नीलपुष्प, बनफ्शा *Violet* is a flower. It is pale purple in colour.
2. any of a group of colours that vary in saturation but have the same purplish-blue hue. बैंगनी, नीललोहित *Violet* is also a colour. It is like the colour of the flower of the same name.

violin *(n.)* वाइअलिन– a bowed stringed instrument, hollow wooden body with waisted sides, and a sounding board connected to the back by means of a soundpost that also supports the bridge वायलिन He can play the *violin* very well

viper *(n.)* वाइपर्– a small venomous snake एक छोटा ज़हरीला साँप Have you ever seen a *viper*?

virgin *(n.)* वर्जिन– 1. a person, esp a woman, who has never had sexual intercourse कुमारी, कुँवारी लड़की Rima was married last year. Her sister Kusum still remains a *virgin.*
2. *(adj.)* pure and natural, uncorrupted, unsullied, or untouched अछूता, विशुद्ध, पवित्र *Virgin* soil of this forest is very fertile.

virginity *(n.)* वर्जिनिटी– the condition of being untouched, unsullied, etc. कौमार्य Girls should keep their *virginity* before marriage.

virtual *(adj.)* वर्चुअल– having the essence or effect but not the appearance or form of लगभग, तक़रीबन A *virtual* war always exists between India and Pakistan.

virtually *(adv.)* वर्चुअलि– in effect though not in fact; practically; nearly वस्तुतः He is *virtually* out of cash

virtue *(n.)* वर्चू–1. the quality or practice of moral excellence or righteousness सद्गुण, विशेषता, ख़ूबी No *virtue* is small.

2. any of the cardinal virtues (prudence, justice, fortitude, and temperance) or theological virtues (faith, hope, and charity) उच्च नैतिकता The *virtues* of society are vices of the saint.

virtuous *(adj.)* वर्चुअस– characterized by or possessing virtue or moral excellence; righteous; upright सदाचारी, नेक This woman is leading a *virtuous* life.

virulent *(adj.)* विरयलेण्ट– extremely poisonous, injurious, etc. बहुत ख़तरनाक एवं गंभीर Health officials were worried about a *virulent* outbreak of food-borne illness.

virus *(n.)* वाइरस– any of a group of submicroscopic entities consisting of a single nucleic acid chain surrounded by a protein coat and capable of replication only within the cells of living organisms: many are pathogenic विषाणु A highly contagious *virus* of AIDS is spreading very fast in China.

visa *(adj.)* वीज़ा– an endorsement in a passport or similar document, signifying that the document is in order and permitting its bearer to travel into or through the country of the government issuing it प्रवेश-पत्र Certain countries provide *visa* on arrival facility.

visibility *(n.)* विज़बिलटी– the condition or fact of being visible दृश्यता, स्पष्टता The *visibility* was poor in the fog.

visible *(adj.)* विज़िबल– capable of being perceived by the eye दृष्टिगोचर, स्पष्ट The ship is clearly *visible* from the beach.

vision *(n.)* विश़न–1. the act, faculty, or manner of perceiving with the eye; sight दृष्टि, नज़र He has to wear eye-glasses as his *vision* is poor.

2. the ability or an instance of great perception, esp of future developments मानसिक प्रतिबिंब, मनोरूप Writing needs men of *vision.*

visionary *(n.)* विश़नरी– 1. marked by vision or foresight दिव्यदर्शी Gautam Buddha was a great *visionary.*

2. *(adj.)* characterized by idealistic or radical ideas, esp impractical ones काल्पनिक, अव्यवहारिक Gautam Buddha was a *visionary* preacher.

visit *(v.)* विज़िट– 1. to go or come to see (a person, place, etc.) (से) मिलने जाना या आना My mother has gone to *visit* my grandmother.

2. *(n.)* the act or an instance of visiting भेंट, मुलाक़ात An old friend paid a *visit* to my father.

visual *(adj.)* विशुअल– of, relating to, done by, or used in seeing दृश्य, चाक्षुष The students have some *visual* aids such as maps and charts in their lessons.

vital *(adj.)* वाइटल–1. essential to maintain life अनिवार्य (जीवन के लिए) The *vital* signs of his body are constantly improving .

2. forceful, energetic, or lively ओजस्वी, तेजपूर्ण He has a *vital* personality.

3. indispensable or essential बहुत आवश्यक Getting good marks in the examination is *vital* to you.

vitamin *(n.)* विटमिन– any of a group of substances that are essential, in small quantities, for the normal functioning of metabolism in the body विटामिन Always take a balanced food enriched with multi-*vitamins.*

vivacious *(adj.)* विवेशस– (esp of a woman) having attractive personality आकर्षक, जीवंत She is known for her *vivacious* nature.

viva voce *(n.)* वाइवॅवोसी– by word of mouth मौखिक परीक्षा The date is still not fixed for *viva voce.*

vivid *(adj.)* विविड–1. (of a colour) very bright; having a very high saturation or purity; produced by a pure or almost pure colouring agent चमकीला, तेज़, उज्ज्वल A *vivid* lightning flash lit the sky.

2. (of a recollection, memory, etc.) remaining distinct in the mind सजीव, सुस्पष्ट She gave a *vivid* description of the sky.

vocabulary *(n.)* वकैबूयलरी–1. a listing, either selective or exhaustive, containing the words and phrases of a language, with meanings or translations into another language; glossary शब्द भण्डार, शब्द समूह We can improve our *vocabulary* by learning some new words everyday.

2. all the words contained in a language शब्दावली Your dictionary has a *vocabulary* of ten thousand words.

vocal *(adj.)* वोकल–1. of, relating to, or designed for the voice मौखिक, वाचिक She excels in *vocal* music.

2. eloquent or meaningful अपने विचारों को खुलकर प्रकट करते हुए You should be *vocal* about your grievances.

vocally *(adv.)* वोकली–1. in a vociferous way ऊंचे एवं गंभीर स्वर में The union leader protested *vocally.*

2. in a way that involves the voice मौखिक रूप से, ज़बानी Why don't you communicate with him *vocally*?

vocation *(n.)* वोकेशन– a specified occupation, profession, or trade व्यवसाय, पेशा, धंधा Finally, he has got into the *vocation* he likes.

vociferous *(adj.)* वसिफ़रस– characterized by vehemence, clamour, or noisiness चिल्लानेवाला, कोलाहलपूर्ण A *vociferous* group of protestors was on the road.

vogue *(n.)* वोग– the popular style at a specified time प्रचलन, रिवाज, चलन Gold jewellery is no longer in *vogue.*

voice *(n.)* वॉइस–1. written or spoken expression, as of feeling, opinion, etc. आवाज़ The poor cannot *voice* their opinions.

2. the musical sound of a singing voice, with respect to its quality or tone वाणी, कंठस्वर Lata has such a pleasant *voice* that everybody enjoys listening to her songs.

3. a category of the verb or verbal inflections that expresses whether the relation between the subject and the verb वाच्य A verb has two *voices* – active *voice* and passive *voice.*

void *(n.)* वॉइड– a feeling or condition of loneliness or deprivation रिक्ति, शून्य I often feel a *void* in my life.

volatile *(adj.)* वॉलटाइल–1. capable of readily changing from a solid or liquid form to a vapour; having a high vapour pressure and a low boiling point वाष्पशील Perfume is a *volatile* liquid.

2. disposed to caprice or inconstancy; fickle; mercurial अस्थिर She has a *volatile* nature.

volcano *(n.)* वॉल्केनो– an opening in the earth's crust from which molten lava, rock fragments, ashes, dust, and gases are ejected from below the earth's surface ज्वालामुखी In Kangra, there is a *volcano* which disgorges fire.

volley *(n.)* वॉली–1. the simultaneous discharge of several weapons, esp firearms (कुछ बंदूकों की एक साथ) बौछार,

(पत्थरों की) वर्षा A *volley* of missiles was fired to push the enemy back.

2. *(v.)* to strike or kick (a moving ball) before it hits the ground उड़ती गेंद को मारना In tennis, the players *volley* the ball.

voltage *(n.)* वोल्टेज– an electromotive force or potential difference expressed in volts विद्युत-शक्ति, वोल्टेज Switch off the light. The *voltage* is very high.

volume *(n.)* वॉल्यूम–1. a bound collection of printed or written pages; book पुस्तक, ग्रंथ This *volume* contains all of Sharat Chandra's writings.

2. fullness or intensity of tone or sound मात्रा The *volume* of sound coming from your transistor is too low.

voluminous *(adj.)* वलूमिनस– of great size, quantity, volume, or extent विस्तृत, बहुत बड़ा The Mahabharta is a *voluminous* epic.

voluntary *(adj.)* वॉलण्टरी–1. serving or acting in a specified function of one's own accord and without compulsion or promise of remuneration स्वैच्छिक, ऐच्छिक The members of Arya Samaj render many *voluntary* services.

2. performed, undertaken, or brought about by free choice, willingly, or without being asked स्वयंसेवी, बिना कोई पारिश्रमिक लिए This library has been running on *voluntary* contributions.

volunteer *(v.)* वालनटिअर– 1. to offer (oneself or one's services) for an undertaking by choice and without request or obligation स्वेच्छा से कोई काम करना The brave women *volunteered* themselves to go into the burning house.

2. *(n.)* a person who performs or offers to perform voluntary service स्वयंसेवक Many *volunteers* offered to help the victims of earthquake.

vomit *(v.)* वॉमिट–1. to eject (the contents of the stomach) through the mouth as the result of involuntary muscular spasms of the stomach and oesophagus उल्टी करना, कै करना She was seriously ill and began to *vomit.*

2. to eject or be ejected forcefully; spew forth वमन करना, बाहर की तरफ़ फेंकना The chimney of the mill *vomits* black smoke.

voracious *(adj.)* वरेशस– gluttonous; greedy पेटू, भुक्खड़, लालची He is a *voracious* eater.

vote *(v.)* वोट– 1. to give or register a vote मत देना, वोट देना None of his family members *voted* in the elections.

2. *(n.)* an indication of choice, opinion, or will on a question, such as the choosing of a candidate, by or as if by some recognized means, such as a ballot मतदान, मत, वोट *Vote* is the most important instrument of democracy.

vouch *(n.)* वाउच– the act of vouching; assertion or allegation किसी की ईमानदारी या भला होने का ज़िम्मा लेना I can certainly *vouch* for his honesty.

voucher *(n.)* वाउचर्– a document serving as evidence for some claimed transaction, as the receipt or expenditure of money ख़र्च का पर्चा, वाउचर He received a gift *voucher* on his purchase

vow *(n.)* वाउ– 1. a solemn promise made to a deity or saint, by which the promiser pledges himself to some future act, course of action, or way of life प्रतिज्ञा, वायदा A newly married man and woman take *vows* to love and cherish each other.

2. *(v.)* to make a promise to do sth वादा करना, क़सम खाना They *vowed* never to leave each other.

vowel *(n.)* वाउअल– a voiced speech sound whose articulation is characterized by the absence of friction-causing obstruction in the vocal tract, allowing the breath stream free passage. स्वर The English language has five *vowels* – a, e, i, o, u.

voyage *(v.)* वॉइएज– 1. to travel, esp in a ship समुद्री यात्रा करना I have an ambition to *voyage* around the world. 2. *(n.)* a journey, travel, or passage, esp one to a distant land or by sea or air समुद्री यात्रा We were seasick on the *voyage* around the world.

vulgar *(adj.)* वॅल्गर्– marked by lack of taste, culture, delicacy, manners, etc. असभ्य, अशिष्ट He was giving her very *vulgar* looks.

vulnerable *(adj.)* वलनरबल– open to temptation, persuasion, censure, etc. नाज़ुक, संवेदनशील, कमज़ोर She is a *vulnerable* girl and can catch any disease easily.

vulture *(n.)* वॅल्चर्– a person or thing that preys greedily and ruthlessly on others, esp the helpless गीध, गिद्ध, लोभी व्यक्ति *Vultures* feed on the dead bodies of animals.

ഇരു

Ww

Ww *(n.)* डबल्यू–अंग्रेज़ी वर्णमाला का तेईसवां अक्षर The twenty-third letter of the English alphabet. Woman begins with 'W'.

wacky *(adj.)* वैकि– eccentric, erratic, or unpredictable मसख़रा, मज़ाक़िया He has a *wacky* personality.

wad *(n.)* वॉड– a roll or bundle of something, esp of banknotes गड्डी He gave me a *wad* of ₹ 100 notes.

waddle *(v.)* वॉडल– to walk with short steps, rocking slightly from side to side, like a duck छोटे-छोटे क़दम बढ़ाते हुए चलना Very fat people often *waddle* as they walk along.

wade *(v.)* वेड– to walk with the feet immersed in (water, a stream, etc.) पानी में चलना, पार करना I like to *wade* in the river. You are not *wading* but having a swim.

wafer *(n.)* वेफ़र्– a thin crisp sweetened biscuit with different flavourings, served with ice cream, etc. पतला बिस्कुट Usually we take a *wafer* with an ice cream.

waffle *(v.)* वॉफ़ल– to speak or write in a vague and wordy manner गप्प लड़ाना, बेमतलब की बातें हांकना Why are you both *waffling*?

waft *(v.)* वॉफ़्ट– to carry or be carried gently on or as if on the air or water हवा में बहना या बिखरना The smell if the dead cat *wafted* inside our house.

wag *(n.)* वैग– 1. the act or an instance of wagging ठट्ठेबाज़, दिल्लगीबाज़ मसखरा Uncle Arora is quite a *wag.*

2. *(v.)* to move or cause to move rapidly and repeatedly from side to side or up and down हिलाना The puppy *wags* its tail when it is happy.

wage *(n.)* वेज–1. payment in return for work or services, esp that made to workmen on a daily, hourly, weekly, or piece-work basis वेतन या मज़दूरी की दर Harish's *wage* rate as a mason is 500 rupees a day.

2. recompense, return, or yield वेतन, मज़दूरी Give the labourer his *wages* before his perspiration be dry.

waggle *(v.)* वैगल– to move or cause to move with a rapid shaking or wobbling motion हिलना-डुलना या हिलाना-डुलाना The curtains of her room *waggled* in the wind.

waggon, wagon *(n.)* वैगन– any of various types of wheeled vehicles, ranging from carts to lorries, esp a vehicle with four wheels drawn by a horse, tractor, etc., and used for carrying crops, heavy loads, etc. छकड़ा, चौपहिया गाड़ी Usually every farmer has a *wagon* on his farms. He carries hay in the *wagon.*

waif *(n.)* वेफ़– a person, esp a child, who is homeless, friendless, or neglected लावारिस, अनाथ बच्चा He was sad because he was a *waif.*

wail *(v.)* वेल–1. to utter a prolonged high-pitched cry, as of grief or misery बिलखना, रोना-चिल्लाना, विलाप करना Don't *wail* over your lost money, for I am sure you will soon find it.

2. to lament, esp with mournful sounds साँय-साँय करना The wind *wailed* in the chimney.

3. *(n.)* a prolonged high-pitched mournful cry or sound विलाप, चीख़, चिल्लाहट The *wails* of the aircrash victims' relatives could be heard in the hospital.

waist *(n.)* वेस्ट– the constricted part of the trunk between the ribs and hips कमर, कटि, मध्यभाग The size of your *waist* is increasing at an alarming rate.

waistband *(n.)* वेस्ट्बैंड– an encircling band of material to finish and strengthen a skirt or trousers at the waist कटिबंध, पेटी I like to wear a *waistband.*

waistcoat *(n.)* वेसकोट– a sleeveless waist-length garment with buttons at the front, often worn under a suit jacket वास्कट, फतूही *Waistcoats* were fashionable in the olden days.

waistline *(n.)* वेस्ट्लाइन– a line or indentation around the body at the narrowest part of the waist कमर का माप या घेरा What is your *waistline*?

wait *(n.)* वेट– 1. a period of waiting प्रतीक्षा, इंतजार I had a long *wait* for the train.

2. *(v.)* to stay in one place or remain inactive in expectation (of something); hold oneself in readiness (for something) प्रतीक्षा करना, बाट जोहना *Wait* here until I come back.

> **wait for**– do not act before the proper moment घात में रहना, The lion is *waiting for* its prey.

> **wait in**– watching for an enemy or potential victim and preparing to attack them किसी के आने की आशा में प्रतीक्षा करना, He has to *wait in* for the electrician.

> **wait on**– await the convenience of: फल या परिणाम होना, We're *waiting on* the blood test reports.

> **wait up**– not go to bed until someone arrives or something happens किसी की प्रतीक्षा में जागते रहना, Don't *wait up* for me; I may be late.

waiter *(n.)* वेटर– a man whose occupation is to serve at table, as in a restaurant बैरा Nadeem is a *waiter* in a restaurant.

waiting *(n.)* वेटइंग– Ethe act of staying in one place or remaining inactive in expectation of something प्रतीक्षा, इंतजार We have been *waiting* for our turn for a long time.

waiting list *(n.)* वेटिंग-लिस्ट– a list of people waiting to obtain some object, treatment, status, etc. प्रतीक्षा-सूची She was expecting her name on the *waiting list.*

waiting room *(n.)* वेटिंगरूम– a room in which people may wait, as at a railway station, doctor's or dentist's office, etc. प्रतीक्षालय They were sitting in the *waiting room.*

waive *(v.)* वेव– to refrain from enforcing (a claim) or applying (a law, penalty, etc.) स्वेच्छापूर्वक अपना दावा या अधिकार छोड़ देना She *waived* her claim on her father's property.

wake *(n.)* वेक–1. to rouse or become roused from sleep जगाना, जागना Please *wake* me up whenever you want.

2. to rouse or become roused from inactivity सचेत हो जाना, सक्रिय हो उठना I usually *wake* up at six o'clock in the morning.

> **wake up to**– to be fully alert to (a person, thing, action, etc.) किसी खतरा या बात का एहसास हो जाना, It's time you *wake up to* the fact that life is not a bed of roses.

walk *(v.)* वॉक–1. to move along or travel on foot at a moderate rate चलना, टहलना I *walk* to the office every day.

2. *(n.)* the act or an instance of walking भ्रमण Let us go for a morning *walk.*

3. a place set aside for walking; promenade रास्ता, सड़क The *walk* to the beach took us through a small forest.

> **walk off with**– steal चुरा ले जाना, She *walked off with* all the Jewellery.

- **walk out of**– to leave without explanation, esp in anger अचानक गुस्सा होकर चले जाना, He *walked out of* the room this morning.
- **walk over**– an easy or unopposed victory आसानी से बाज़ी मार लेना, They *walked over* their opposite team.

walk stick *(n.)* वॉक-स्टिक– a stick or cane carried in the hand to assist walking छड़ी Her grandfather uses *walk stick.*

wall *(n.)* वॉल– a vertical construction made of stone, brick, wood, etc., with a length and height much greater than its thickness, used to enclose, divide, or support भित्ति, दीवार The investigation suddenly ran into a *wall.*

wallet *(n.)* वॉलेट– a small folding case, usually of leather, for holding paper money, documents, etc. बटुआ Always keep your all-route bus pass in your *wallet.*

wallop *(v.)* वॉलप– to beat soundly; strike hard जमकर पिटाई करना India *walloped* Pakistan in the Cricket World Cup.

wallow *(v.)* वॉलो– (esp of certain animals) to roll about in mud, water, etc., for pleasure लोट लगाना, मौज-मस्ती करना Buffaloes were *wallowing* in the river.

wallpaper *(n.)* वालपेपर्– paper usually printed or embossed with designs for pasting onto walls and ceilings दीवार पर लगाने वाला काग़ज़, भित्तिपत्र *Wallpaper* is used for decorating the *walls.*

walnut *(n.)* वॉलनट– brown nut of the walnut tree. अख़रोट The wood of the *walnut* tree is used for making fine furniture.

walrus *(n.)* वॉलरस– an animal like a large seal, having a tough thick skin, upper canine teeth enlarged as tusks, and coarse whiskers and feeding mainly on shellfish (सील की तरह का समुद्री जीव) वालरस A *walrus* is a large sea animal which looks like a seal.

waltz *(n.)* वॉल्स– 1. a piece of music composed for or in the rhythm of this dance एक सुंदर नाच के साथ बजने वाला संगीत The couple is very proficient in the *waltz.*
2. *(v.)* to dance or lead (someone) in or as in a waltz नाचना, वॉल्स नृत्य करना He *waltzed* you round and round.

wan *(adj.)* वॉन– unnaturally pale esp from sickness, grief, etc. पीला, विवर्ण, फीका, हल्का, मंद He was ill for many days so his face was pale and *wan.*

wand *(n.)* वॉण्ड– a slender supple stick or twig छड़ी In a fairy tale, the fairy always waves her magic *wand* to make dreams come true.

wander *(v.)* वॉण्डर्– to move or travel about, in, or through (a place) without any definite purpose or destination भटकना, घूमना He *wandered* alone in the woods.

wane *(v.)* वेन– 1. to decrease gradually in size, strength, power, etc. कम होना, घटना As time passed, my hopes of getting money *waned.*
2. *(n.)* a decrease, as in size, strength, power, etc. घटाव, ह्रास From today, the moon will be on the *wane.*

wangle *(v.)* वैंगल– to use devious or illicit methods to get or achieve (something) for (oneself or another) तिकड़म रचना, चापलूसी से कुछ गाँठ लेना He *wangled* a way out of the problem.

want *(n.)* वॉण्ट–1. anything that is needed, desired, or lacked अभाव, कमी Poor people are in *want* of food.
2. *(v.)* to wish, need, or desire (something or to do something)

चाहना, इच्छा करना Do you *want* more money?

wanting *(adj.)* वाँटिंग– lacking or absent; missing गायब, अनुपस्थित She has been *wanting* to go to the concert for a long time.

wanton *(adj.)* वॉनटन–1. dissolute, licentious, or immoral खिलवाड़ करने वाला, बेलगाम Her work is pending because she always remains in a *wanton* mood.

2. maliciously and unnecessarily cruel or destructive विद्वेषपूर्ण, क्रूरता It was an act of *wanton* aggression.

war *(n.)* वॉर्– open armed conflict between two or more parties, nations, or states युद्ध, संग्राम, लड़ाई, शत्रुता Soldiers win *wars* and generals get the credit.

ward *(n.)* वॉर्ड–1. a person who is under the protection or in the custody of another प्रतिपाल्य, आश्रित Since his parents died he has been the *ward* of his grandfather.

2. a room in a hospital, esp one for patients requiring similar kinds of care वार्ड, रोगी-कक्ष She was in the children's *ward.*

3. *(v.)* to guard or protect रक्षा एवं निगरानी करना A warden *wards* his area and looks after his patients.

warden *(n.)* वॉर्डन–1. a person who has the charge or care of something, esp a building, or someone छात्रपाल The *warden* in our boarding school was very kind.

2. any of various public officials, esp one responsible for the enforcement of certain regulations अभिरक्षक, अध्यक्ष Were you not a traffic *warden* at the time of your retirement?

warder *(n.)* वॉर्डर्– an officer in charge of prisoners in a jail जेलर, वार्डर, जेलख़ाने का इंचार्ज The *warder* of our jail was a very cruel man.

wardrobe *(n.)* वार्डरोब–1. a tall closet or cupboard, with a rail or hooks on which to hang clothes कपड़े रखने की जगह, अलमारी Is your *wardrobe* not out of fashion?

2. the total collection of articles of clothing belonging to one person परिधान-कक्ष, वस्त्र-कक्ष Bring my suit from the *wardrobe.*

wards *(suffix.)* वॉर्ड्स– indicating direction towards (के) प्रति, (की) ओर Is the Chinese language written down*wards*?

ware *(n.)* वेअर– articles of the same kind or material माल, सौदा A painter was selling his *wares* to tourist.

warehouse *(n.)* वेअर्हाउस– a place where goods are stored prior to their use, distribution, or sale गोदाम, मालगोदाम The *warehouse* needs to expanded to store more goods.

warfare *(n.)* वॉरफ़ेअर– conflict, struggle, or strife सशस्त्र संघर्ष, संग्राम The art of *warfare* has changed over centuries

warily *(adj.)* वेअरिली– cautiously सावधानी से Please walk *warily* lest you should fall.

warlike *(adj.)* वारलाइक– of, relating to, or used in war युद्ध-संबंधी, सामरिक The Kargil conflict created a *warlike* situation.

warm *(adj.)* वॉर्म–1. characterized by or having a moderate degree of heat; moderately hot गर्म, ऊष्ण It is a *warm* day.

2. having or showing ready affection, kindliness, etc. हार्दिक, मैत्रीपूर्ण They gave us a *warm* welcome.

3. maintaining or imparting heat गुनगुना, कुनकुना In western countries, people use *warm* water for bathing.

4. *(v.)* to raise or be raised in temperature; make or become warm or warmer गर्म करना Please *warm* some water for me.

5. to give a caning to तपाना, सेंकना *Warm* your palms on the heater.

➢ **warm up** *(v.)*– to get ready for something important; prepare किसी काम को करने की तैयारी करना, He *warmed up* before the dance.

warm-blooded *(adj.)* वार्म-ब्लडएड– ardent, impetuous, or passionate जिसके रक्त में जोश और गर्मी ज़्यादा हो Birds and mammals are the *warm-blooded* animals.

warm-hearted *(adj.)* वॉर्म-हॉर्टेड– kindly, generous, forgiving, or readily sympathetic नरम दिल वाला, दयालु He is a very *warm-hearted* person.

warmly *(adv.)* वॉर्मली– cordially स्नेह भाव से We talked in a *warmly* manner.

warmonger *(n.)* वॉरमंगर– a person who fosters warlike ideas or advocates war जंगख़ोर Militants are *warmongers*.

warmth *(n.)* वॉर्मृथ–1. affection or cordiality प्यार एवं उत्साह I was very much pleased with the *warmth* of their welcome.

2. the state, quality, or sensation of being warm गरमाहट, उष्णता It is good to feel the *warmth* of the sun in winter season.

warn *(v.)* वॉर्न–1. to notify or make (someone) aware of danger, harm, etc. चेतावनी देना The manager *warned* the clerk about his repeated negligence.

2. to advise or admonish (someone) as to action, conduct, etc. सचेत करना I *warned* him not to skate on thin ice.

warning *(n.)* वार्निंग– a hint, intimation, threat, etc., of harm or danger चेतावनी Your failure in the monthly tests is a kind of *warning* to you.

warp *(v.)* वॉर्प– to twist or cause to twist out of shape, as from heat, damp, etc. टेढ़ा हो जाना या मुड़ जाना The small plant began to *warp*.

warrant *(n.)* वॉरण्ट–1. an authorization issued by a magistrate or other official allowing a constable or other officer to search or seize property, arrest a person, or perform some other specified act (गिरफ़्तारी) वारंट, परवाना A policeman will not search your house unless he has a *warrant* from a magistrate.

2. anything that gives authority for an action or decision; authorization; sanction आज्ञा-पत्र Can you pay my bill until you get a *warrant* from the treasurer?

warranty *(n.)* वॉरण्टी– an express or implied term in a contract, such as an undertaking that goods contracted to be sold shall meet specified requirements as to quality, etc. लिखित गारंटी The *warranty* for my iPod has expired.

warrior *(n.)* वॉरिअर– a person engaged in, experienced in, or devoted to war योद्धा, सैनिक, सिपाही Alexander was a great Greek *warrior.*

wart *(n.)* वार्ट– any firm abnormal elevation of the skin caused by a virus मस्सा She has a *wart* on her left shoulder.

wartime *(n.)* वार्टाइम– a period or time of war युद्धकाल, युद्धकालीन He is fond of reading *wartime* novels.

wary *(adj.)* वेरी– watchful, cautious, or alert सावधान, चौकस, चौकन्ना, सतर्क Be *wary* of the dog, for it is very fierce.

wash *(n.)* वॉश– 1. the act or process of washing; ablution स्नान, प्रक्षालन Daily *wash* is essential for good health.

2. *(v.)* to apply water or other liq-

uid, usually with soap, to (oneself, clothes, etc.) in order to cleanse धोना, स्नान करना We should *wash* ourselves regularly to remain clean.

> **wash away**– erosion of the earth's surface by the action of running water बहा ले जाना The waves *washed away* the footprints on the sand.

> **wash off**– to wash (the inside of something) so as to remove (dirt) साफ़ करना, मिटाना It is difficult to *wash off* the stains of ink.

> **wash one's hands of** *(v.) . to have nothing more to do with* ज़िम्मेदारी से हाथ खींच लेना या छोड़ देना She *washed her hands of* the household activities.

> **wash out**– to wash (the inside of something) so as to remove (dirt) अंदर से धोकर साफ़ करना Don't you ever *wash out* your tea pot?

> **wash up**– to wash one's face and hands मुंह-हाथ धोना Please *wash up* your face and hands.

washable *(adj.)* वॉशबल–(esp of fabrics or clothes) capable of being washed without deteriorating धोने लायक़, धुलाई-सह Is this silk kurta *washable*?

washbasin *(n.)* वॉशबेसन– a basin or bowl for washing the face and hands वाशबेसिन, चिलमची There is no water in the *washbasin.*

washed out *(adj.)* वाशड-आउट– exhausted, esp when being pale in appearance थका माँदा, लस्त-पस्त Rajat feels *washed out* today.

washerman *(n.)* वाशरमॅन– a person who washes clothes for a living धोबी A *washerman* was carrying a bundle of clothes.

washing *(n.)* वाशिंग– articles that have been or are to be washed together on a single occasion धुलाई All our clothes are cleaned in the *washing* machine.

washing up *(n.)* वाशिंग अप– the washing of dishes, cutlery, etc., after a meal बर्तनों की धुलाई My maid will do the *washing up.*

washroom *(n.)* वाशरूम– a room, esp in a factory or office block, in which lavatories, washbasins, etc., are situated शौचालय, शौचघर Can I go to the *washroom*?

wasp *(n.)* वॉस्प– a black-and-yellow flying insect that can sting ततैया, भिड़, बर्र A *wasp* can sting. It has black and yellow stripes on its body.

wastage *(n.)* वेसटिज– anything lost by wear or waste बर्बादी, अपव्यय There has been a lot of *wastage* of raw materials.

waste *(v.)* वेस्ट–1. to fail to take advantage of व्यर्थ गंवाना, बरबाद करना We must not *waste* food.

2. to use, consume, or expend thoughtlessly, carelessly, or to no avail लापरवाही से ख़र्च करना, अपव्यय करना Don't *waste* your money in buying things you don't need.

3. *(n.)* anything or anyone rejected as useless, worthless, or in excess of what is required बर्बादी Haste makes *waste.*

4. a land or region that is wild or uncultivated बंजर भूभाग, निर्जन There is a *waste* and outside the house.

wasted *(adj.)* वेसटिड– not exploited or taken advantage of व्यर्थ, फ़ालतू, बेकार A lot of time has been *wasted* over this work.

wasteful *(adj.)* वेस्टफुल– tending to waste or squander; extravagant खर्चीला, फ़िज़ूलख़र्च Young girls have generally *wasteful* habits.

wasteland *(n.)* वेस्टलैण्ड– a barren or desolate area of land, not or no longer used for cultivation or building बंजर ज़मीन Approximately 68.35

million hectares area of the land is lying as *wastelands* in India.

watch *(n.)* वॉच– 1. a small portable timepiece, usually worn strapped to the wrist (a wristwatch) or in a waistcoat pocket जेब या हाथ की घड़ी Father had a pocket *watch.* Mother wore a *watch* round her wrist.

2. *(v.)* to look at or observe closely or attentively देखना, रखवाली करना We *watched* for our friend coming home at night.

➢ **watchout**– the act of watching out for something सावधान रहना, You'll meet an accident if you don't *watch out.*

watchful *(adj.)* वाचफुल– vigilant or alert सतर्क, जागरूक He is under the *watchful* eyes of the guard.

watchman *(n.)* वाचमैन– a person employed to guard buildings or property चौकीदार A *watchman* is a man who watches the building during the night.

water *(v.)* वॉटर्–1. to sprinkle, moisten, or soak with water पानी छिड़कना You should *water* the lawn every day in dry weather.

2. to sprinkle, moisten, or soak with water पानी देना, जल से सींचना Every morning, I *water* my potted plants.

3. (of the eyes) to fill with tears आँखों से पानी बहना Chopping onions makes my eyes *water.*

4. *(n.)* a clear colourless tasteless odourless liquid that is essential for plant and animal life and constitutes, in impure form, rain, oceans, rivers, lakes, etc. पानी, जल We drink *water* when we are thirsty.

➢ **water down**– to dilute or weaken with water कमज़ोर या परोक्ष बना देना, (रिपोर्ट, कथन आदि), The report of the investigation had been *watered down.*

water-borne *(adj.)* वाटर्बॉर्न– floating or travelling on water जलवाहित, Jaundice is a *water-borne* disease.

watercolour *(n.)* वाटर्कलर– water-soluble pigment, applied in transparent washes and without the admixture of white pigment in the lighter tones पानी में घुलने वाला रंग She loves painting with *watercolours.*

waterfall *(n.)* वाटर्फॉल– a cascade of falling water where there is a vertical or almost vertical step in a river झरना Jog Falls is the highest *waterfall* in India.

waterlogged *(adj.)* वाटर्लॉग्ड– (of a vessel still afloat) having taken in so much water as to be unmanageable जलाक्रांत The children could not play because the playground was *waterlogged.*

watermelon *(n.)* वॉटर्मेलन– a type of large melon with dark green skin तरबूज़ He loves to eat *watermelons* in summers.

waterproof *(adj.)* वॉटरप्रूफ– not penetrable by water जलसह, वाटरप्रूफ़ He bought a *waterproof* bag to the school.

watertight *(adj.)* वॉटरटाइट– not permitting the passage of water either in or out जलरोधी There was a sale of *watertight* containers.

water vapour *(n.)* वॉटरवेपर– water in the gaseous state, esp when due to evaporation at a temperature below the boiling point वाष्प, भाप *Water vapour* is extremely important to the weather and climate.

watery *(adj.)* वाटरि– relating to, consisting of, containing, or resembling water पनीला, पतला I didn't like the *watery* tomato soup.

watt *(n.)* वॉट– the derived SI unit of power, वाट This is a 100-*watt* bulb.

wave *(v.)* वेव–1. to move or cause to move freely to and fro लहराना, हवा में हिलाना *Wave* your hand to us as you leave.

2. to signal or signify by or as if by waving something फहराना When the guard *waved* his green flag, the train steamed off.

3. *(n.)* any undulation on or at the edge of a surface reminiscent of such a wave लहर, तरंग, हिलोर A *wave* turned their boat over.

4. air around the sea शीत लहर How long is this cold *wave* going to last?

wavelength *(n.)* वेवलेंथ– distance between two similar points on a wave of energy, such as light or sound तरंग-दैर्घ्य The distance between two sound waves is called a *wavelength*.

waver *(v.)* वेवर्– to become unsteady डाँवाँडोल होना, अस्थिर होना Don't *waver* too long about buying the almirah, otherwise someone else may buy it.

wavy *(adj.)* वेवी– having curves or full of waves घुँघराला Sanjana has long and *wavy* hair.

wax *(v.)* वैक्स– 1. to become larger, more powerful, etc. बढ़ना The new moon will *wax* until it is full.

2. *(n.)* any of various viscous or solid materials of natural origin, characteristically lustrous, insoluble in water, and having a low softening temperature, they consist largely of esters of fatty acids मोम *Wax* is used for making candles.

way *(n.)* वे–1. a street in or leading out of a town मार्ग, रास्ता The little child lost his *way*. He could not find his *way* back home.

2. a means or line of passage, such as a path or track सड़क Which is the *way* to the interstate bus stand?

3. a route or direction दिशा, ओर, तरफ़ Always look at both the *ways* before crossing the road.

4. a manner, method, or means विधि, तरीक़ा, प्रकार, उपाय This book tells you the *way* to use words in sentences.

5. distance, usually distance in general दूरी Will you meet me half *way*?

6. *(adv.)* at a considerable distance or extent बहुत दूर She finally found my name *way* down at the end of the list.

- **anyway**– in any case; at any rate; nevertheless; anyhow बहरहाल, *Anyway*, I am not going to the market.
- **by the way**– in passing or incidentally ऐसे ही, वैसे ही, प्रसंगवश, *By the way* if she meets you, ask her to come.
- **give way**– to collapse or break down झुक जाना He suddenly *gave way* and fell.
- **have your own way**– to use own thought and mind अपनी बात मनवाना You should *have your own way*.
- **in any way**– no matter what; anyhow किसी भी तरह से *In any way* I cannot work in a small office.
- **underway**– having started moving or making progress शुरू होकर आगे बढ़ना एवं उन्नति करना Discussions between them are now *underway*.

wayward *(adj.)* वेवर्ड– wanting to have one's own way regardless of the wishes or good of others अड़ियल, ज़िद्दी Ankur is a *wayward* child of a rich family.

we *(pron.)* वी– refers to the speaker or writer and another person or other people हम, हम लोग *We* are going for a picnic.

weak *(adj.)* वीक्–1. lacking in physical or mental strength or force; frail or feeble दुर्बल, कमज़ोर, निर्बल (व्यक्ति) She is feeling *weak* after her illness.
2. lacking in resolution or firmness of character कम हिम्मत, डरपोक He is very *weak* spirited.
3. lacking strength, power, or intensity क्षीण, धीमा She spoke to him in a very *weak* voice.
4. lacking the usual, full, or desirable strength of flavour पतला, हलका He prepared a *weak* coffee.

weaken *(v.)* वीकन– to become or cause to become weak or weaker कमज़ोर या दुर्बल कर देना His heart was *weakened* by his death.

weakness *(n.)* वीकनेस– a deficiency or failing, as in a person's character कमज़ोरी, कमी, अवगुण We all have *weaknesses.*

wealth *(n.)* वे'ल्थ– a large amount of money and valuable material possessions सम्पत्ति, धन-संपदा The rich man gave away all his *wealth* to build a hospital for the poor people.

wealthy *(adj.)* वेल्थी– possessing wealth; affluent; rich धनवान, अमीर, धनी She comes from a very *wealthy* family.

weapon *(n.)* वेपन– an object or instrument used in fighting हथियार Swords, shields, spears and guns are *weapons.*

wear *(n.)* वेअर्–1. anything designed to be worn पहनावा, लिबास In readymade clothes shop, you can find children's *wear* also.
2. *(v.)* to carry or have (a garment, etc.) on one's person as clothing, ornament, etc. पहनना, धारण करना The poor lady is *wearing* an old dress.
3. to carry or have on one's person habitually लगातार या बराबर पहनना She always *wears* the same dress.
4. to have in one's aspect चेहरे पर भाव प्रकट करना That beautiful girl always *wears* a happy smile.

➢ **wear away**–1. pressure जीर्ण हो जाना, His coat has *worn away.*
2. pressure मिट जाना या मिटा देना (बार-बार छूकर), The inscriptions on the pillars had *worn away.*

➢ **wear down**– to consume or be consumed by long or constant wearing, rubbing, etc. घिस जाना या घिस डालना, The heels of her sandle are *wearing down.*

➢ **wear off**– to decrease in intensity gradually धीरे-धीरे समाप्त या लुप्त हो जाना, The attraction of new relationship will soon *wear off.*

➢ **wear out**– to make or become unfit or useless through wear तेज़ी से घिस जाना, Cheap materials soon *wear out.*

➢ **wear and tear** *(n.)*– damage, depreciation, or loss resulting from ordinary use टूट-फूट, छीलन, Keep 20 per cent for the *wear and tear* of your machine.

wearily *(adv.)* विअरली– in a tired way बहुत थककर We walked the last two kilometres *wearily.*

weariness *(n.)* विअरिनेस– tiredness थकान, थकावट He couldn't attend the party because of his *weariness.*

wearisome *(adj.)* विअरिसम– causing fatigue or annoyance; tedious थकाऊ, उबाने वाला He has given a *wearisome* task to me.

weary *(adj.)* विअरी–1. tired or exhausted थका-माँदा, निढाल Are you not *weary* after the day's work?
2. *(v.)* to make or become weary थकाना या थक जाना Please don't *weary* me with your silly talk.

3. causing fatigue or exhaustion ऊब जाना, उकता जाना You *weary* me with your silly arguments.

weather *(n.)* वे'दर्–1. the day-to-day meteorological conditions, esp temperature, cloudiness, and rainfall, affecting a specific place ऋतु A change in the *weather* is enough to renew the world and ourselves.

2. relating to the forecasting of weather मौसम When two people meet, their talk usually begins with a discussion on *weather*.

weather forecast *(n.)* a statement saying what the weather will be like the next day, or the next few days मौसम का हाल एवं जानकारी The news reporter gave the wrong *weather forecast*.

weave *(n.)* वीव–1. the method or pattern of weaving or the structure of a woven fabric बुनावट Do you prefer a loose *weave* for your sweater?

2. *(v.)* to form (a fabric) by interlacing (yarn, etc), esp on a loom कपड़ा बुनना They spend most of their time *weaving*.

3. to create (a way, etc) by moving from side to side टेढ़े-मेढ़े चलना The motorcyclist *weaved* in and out of the traffic.

weaver *(n.)* वीवर– a person who weaves, esp as a means of livelihood जुलाहा, बुनकर The *weaver* made quite a beautiful sweater for me.

web *(n.)* वे'ब– any structure, construction, fabric, etc., formed by or as if by weaving or interweaving जाल He entangled us all in a *web* of his lies.

webbed *(adj.)* वेब्ड– (of the feet of certain animals) having the digits connected by a thin fold of skin जालपाद, झिल्लीवाला Animals like ducks, swans, geese and turtles have *webbed* feet.

wed *(v.)* वेड– to take (a person of the opposite sex) as a husband or wife; marry विवाह करना, शादी करना They *wedded* in May last year.

wedding *(n.)* वे'डिंग–1. the act of marrying or the celebration of a marriage विवाह, शादी Have you got Ramesh's *wedding* card?

2. the anniversary of a marriage विवाह समारोह How many guests have you invited to the *wedding*?

wedge *(v.)* वे'ज–1. to secure with or as if with a wedge खूंटा लगाना, ठोकना Please *wedge* the door open.

2. to squeeze or be squeezed like a wedge into a narrow space कसना या पकड़ना The cutter *wedged* the log.

3. *(n.)* a block of solid material, esp wood or metal, that is shaped like a narrow V in cross section and can be pushed or driven between two objects पच्चर, फ़न्नी Take out the *wedge* from the log.

Wednesday *(n.)* वे'न्ज़्डे– the fourth day of the week; third day of the working week बुधवार I'll not come to the office on *Wednesday*.

weed *(n.)* वीड– 1. any plant that grows wild and profusely, esp one that grows among cultivated plants, depriving them of space, food, etc. फ़ालतू उगने वाली घास-पात, अपतृण A *weed* is a wild plant.

2. *(v.)* to remove (useless or troublesome plants) from (a garden, etc.) घास-पात उखाड़ना The gardener is *weeding* the field.

➢ **weed out** *(v.)*– to separate out, remove, or eliminate (anything unwanted) छांटना, बेकार लोगों को बाहर फेंकना, She *weeded out* all the inexperienced workers.

weedy *(adj.)* वीडी– thin or weakly in appearance कमज़ोर एवं ठिगना A small *weedy* man was crossing the road.

week *(n.)* वीक–1. period of seven consecutive days, esp one beginning with Sunday सप्ताह, हफ़्ता There are seven days in a *week* and fifty-two *weeks* in a year.

2. the period of time within a week devoted to work काम के दिन Every day of the *week* is *week*-day except Saturday and Sunday.

weekend *(n.)* वीकएण्ड– the end of the week, esp the period from Friday night until the end of Sunday सप्ताहांत Lets party hard this *weekend.*

weekly *(adj.)*– 1. happening or taking place once a week or every week साप्ताहिक She is a *weekly* reporter.

2. *(adv.)* once a week or every week हर सप्ताह, प्रति सप्ताह She is paid *weekly.*

3. *(n.)* a newspaper or magazine issued every week साप्ताहिक पत्र या पत्रिका Entertainment is a *weekly* American magazine.

weep *(v.)* वीप्– to shed (tears) as an expression of grief or unhappiness रोना, आँसू बहाना We all were *weeping* for the loss of our friend.

weigh *(v.)* वे– to measure the weight of वज़न करना, मूल्यांकन करना How much do you *weigh*?

➢ **weigh against**– to be contrary to (principles or beliefs) ख़िलाफ़ चला जाना, प्रतिकूल होना, Her past records *weighed against* her.

➢ **weigh down**–1. to press (a person) down by or as if by weight दब जाना, झुकाना, The blackmailer is *weighed down* with guilt.

➢ **weigh in (out)**– pressure वज़न करना या तोलना, Please *weigh out* one kg of onions.

➢ **weigh on**– to make worried or anxious परेशान करना, The household responsibilities are *weighing on* her.

➢ **weigh up**– to make an assessment of (a person, situation, etc.); judge किसी बात पर सावधानी से विचार करना, She needs to *weigh up* her decision.

weight *(n.)* वेट– a measure of the heaviness of an object; the amount anything weighs भार, वज़न Do you know your exact *weight*?

weightless *(adj.)* वेटलस– (of a body) having no actual weight भारहीन, गुरुत्वहीन Your *weightless* training program is scheduled for tomorrow.

weightlifting *(n.)* वेटलिफ़टिंग– the sport of lifting barbells of specified weights in a prescribed manner for competition or exercise भारो-त्तोलन A ten-year-old girl broke the World *Weightlifting* Record in Texas, USA.

weighty *(adj.)* वेटि– important or momentous महत्त्वपूर्ण एवं वज़नी He raised a *weighty* question in the meeting.

weird *(adj.)* विअर्ड– suggestive of or relating to the supernatural; eerie विचित्र, अलौकिक, असामान्य He talks with a *weird* accent when he is around us

welcome *(n.)* वेल्कम– 1. gladly and cordially received or admitted स्वागत They gave us a warm *welcome.*

2. *(v.)* to greet the arrival of (visitors, guests, etc.) cordially or gladly स्वागत करना Aunt *welcomed* us warmly.

3. *(inter.)* an expression of cordial greeting, esp to a person whose arrival is desired or pleasing आपका स्वागत *Welcome* everybody.

weld *(v.)* वे'ल्ड–1. to unite (pieces of metal or plastic) together, as by softening with heat and hammering or by fusion टाँक कर जोड़ना, झलाई करना A welder *welds* pieces of metal by heat and pressure.

2. to bring or admit of being brought into close association or union जोड़ना, एक करना Standing by each

other in the times of need has *welded* our friendship.

welfare *(n.)* वे'ल्फ़ेअर्– health, happiness, prosperity, and well-being in general कल्याण, ख़ैरियत The government should look after the *welfare* of the society.

well *(n.)* वे'ल–1. a hole or shaft that is excavated, drilled, bored, or cut into the earth so as to tap a supply of water, oil, gas, etc. कुआँ The *well* is full of water.

2. *(adv.)* satisfactory, agreeable, or pleasing अच्छी तरह से, बख़ूबी He is doing very *well* in business. I know him very *well.*

3. an expression of surprise, indignation, or reproof शाबाश *Well* done!

4. *(adv.)* prudent; advisable मशहूर Indian cine artistes are quite *well* known in Russia.

5. *(adj.)* pressure अच्छा, स्वस्थ I am not *well.*

6. satisfactory, agreeable, or pleasing सन्तोषजनक All is *well* that ends *well.*

7. fortunate or happy भाग्यशाली It was *well* for us that we were not inside the auditorium when a fire broke out there.

8. *(inter.)* an expression of surprise, indignation, or reproof ओह, अच्छा *Well,* I am not sure.

- **as well**– in addition; too न चाहते हुए भी, I will *as well* tell you the truth.
- **as well as**– in addition to के अतिरिक्त, भी, साथ ही, She is an editor *as well as* a columnist.
- **do well**– moderately wealthy सफ़ल होना, She has *done well* at college.

well-adjusted *(adj.)* वेल एडजस्टड्– mentally and emotionally stable घुलमिल जाना, रम जाना Bobby is *well-adjusted* in her new environment.

well balanced *(adj.)* वेल बैलंस्ड्– having good balance or proportions संतुलित We should take a *well balanced* diet.

well behaved *(adj.)* वेल बिहेव्ड्– conducting oneself in a satisfactory manner शिष्ट, व्यवहारशील His children are very *well behaved.*

well-being *(n.)* वेल बीइंग– the condition of being contented, healthy, or successful; welfare कल्याण, भलाई I'm really concerned about your *well-being.*

well-defined *(adj.)* वेल डिफ़ाइन्ड– clearly delineated, described, or determined सुपरिभाषित Everything was *well-defined* in the memorandum.

well-developed *(adj.)* वेल डेवलप्ड– carefully or extensively elaborated or evolved सुविकसित, पूर्ण विकसित Her senses are *well-developed* at this tender age.

well dressed *(adj.)* वेल ड्रेस्ड– neatly, expensively, or fashionably attired बना-ठना, सजा-धजा All of you must come *well dressed* for the party.

well earned *(adj.)* वेल अर्न्ड– fully deserved स्वर्जित You deserve a *well earned* rest after this hectic work.

well established *(adj.)* वेल इस्टैबलिश्ड– having permanence or security in a certain place, condition, job, etc. सुप्रतिष्ठित They are *well-established* in Rampur.

well fed *(adj.)* वेल फ़ेड– having a nutritious diet; well nourished अच्छी खुराक लेने वाला Eshan has a *well fed* pet dog.

well informed *(adj.)* वेल इन्फ़ॉर्म्ड– having knowledge about a great variety of subjects जानकार, बहुत कुछ जानने वाला The guide was *well informed* about the monument.

well known *(adj.)* वेल नोन्– widely known; famous; celebrated सुप्रसिद्ध,

मशहूर He is a *well known* surgeon in the city.

well off *(adj.)* वेल ऑफ़– in a comfortable or favourable position or state, rich सुसंपन्न, धनाढ्य They belong from a *well off* family.

well-ordered *(adj.)* वेल ऑर्डरड्– arranged, well-organised सुव्यवस्थित I keep everything *well-ordered* in my house.

well-planned *(adj.)* वेल प्लांड– (of an event, project, etc.) suitably devised or drafted in advance to ensure success सुनियोजित It was a *well-planned* murder.

well-read *(adj.)* वेल रैड– having read widely and intelligently; erudite बहु-पठित Siraj Muneer is a *well-read* scholar and critic.

well-to-do *(adj.)* वेल टू डू– moderately wealthy धनी, संपन्न, अमीर She is married into a *well-to-do* family.

well-wisher *(adj.)* वेल विशर– a person who shows benevolence or sympathy towards a person, cause, etc. शुभचिंतक, हितैषी The caller on the phone claimed to be my *well-wisher*.

west *(n.)* वेस्ट– 1. the direction towards the point of the horizon where the sun sets at the equinoxes पश्चिम, मग़रिब Can the east and the *west* meet?
2. *(adj.)* situated in, moving towards, or facing the west पश्चिमी The *west* wind always brings us rain.
3. *(adv.)* in, to, or towards the west पश्चिम की ओर This building faces *west*.

westbound *(adj.)* वेस्टबाउण्ड– going or leading towards the west पश्चिम की तरफ़ जाने वाला The *Westbound* educational services give opportunities to study abroad.

westerly *(adj.)* वेस्टर्ली– of, relating to, or situated in the west पछवाँ, पश्चिमी The ship was travelling in a *westerly* direction.

western *(adj.)* वेस्टर्न– 1. situated in or towards or facing the west पश्चिम में, पश्चिमी *Western* India consists of the states of Goa, Gujarat and Maharashtra along with the Union Territories.
2. going or directed to or towards the west पश्चिमी भाग Do you like to visit the *western* part of the country?

westerner *(n.)* वेस्टर्नर– a native or inhabitant of the west of any specific region, esp of the western states of the US or of the western hemisphere पश्चिमवासी, यूरोपवासी Why do *Westerners* think that India is a poor country?

westernize (ise) *(v.)* वेसटर्नाइज़– to influence or make familiar with the customs, practices, etc., of the West पाश्चात्य रंग में रंगा होना या रंग देना He was on a crusade to *westernize* his office.

westward *(adj.)* वेस्टवर्ड– moving, facing, or situated in the west पश्चिमी His kite was flying in a *westward* direction.

westwards *(adv.)* वेस्टवर्ड्ज़– towards the west पश्चिम की ओर We should proceed *westwards* to reach our destination.

wet *(adj.)* वैट– 1. moistened, covered, saturated, etc., with water or some other liquid गीला, तर, भीगा It is raining. It is a *wet* day.
2. *(v.)* to make or become wet भिगोना, गीला करना Please *wet* the towel and wash the table-glass.

wetland *(n.)* वेटलैण्ड– an area of swampy or marshy land, esp considered as part of an ecological system दलदल The *wetlands* are home to a wide variety of birds.

whack *(v.)* वैक– 1. to strike with a sharp resounding blow तड़ाक से मारना या प्रहार करना A police man *whacked* the thief with a stick.
2. *(n.)* a sharp resounding blow or the noise made by such a blow तड़ाक से किया हुआ प्रहार, मार He gave the horse a *whack* across the back with his stick.

whale *(n.)* व्हेल– any of the larger cetacean mammals, excluding dolphins, porpoises, and narwhals. व्हेल मछली I was lucky enough to see a *whale* with my own eyes.

wharf *(n.)* वॉर्फ़– 1. a platform of timber, stone, concrete, etc., built parallel to the waterfront at a harbour or navigable river for the docking, loading, and unloading of ships घाट, जहाज़ घाट A ship was unloaded at the *wharf.*
2. *(v.)* to moor or dock at a wharf घाट पर लगाना The captain ordered his men to *wharf* the ship.

what *(pron.)* वॉट–1. used with a noun in requesting further information about the identity or categorization of something क्या (प्रश्नवाची) *What* is the time by your watch?
2. (used in indirect questions) क्या, जो I have finished replies to *what* letters were left.
3. in what respect? to what degree? विस्मयादिबोधक अर्थ में *What* nonsense!

whatever *(det.,pron.,adv.)* वॉटएवर्– everything or anything that जो भी, जो कुछ, कुछ भी *Whatever* you do, do not call him in the evening.

whatsoever *(adj.)* वॉटसोएवर्– at all: used as an intensifier with indefinite pronouns and determiners such as none, any, no one, anybody, etc. कुछ भी, किसी भी तरह *Whatsoever* she did, she did for her satisfaction.

wheat *(n.)* वीट– a plant grown for its grain that is used to produce the flour for bread गेहूँ *Wheat* is the major harvest of northern India.

wheel *(n.)* वील– 1. a solid disc, or a circular rim joined to a hub by radial or tangential spokes, that is mounted on a shaft about which it can turn, as in vehicles and machines पहिया, चक्कर A car has four *wheels.* My uncle has a two-*wheeler.* A rickshaw has three *wheels.*
2. *(v.)* to turn or cause to turn on or as if on an axis आगे बढ़ना, पहिया का चलना His car *wheeled* along the highway.

wheelchair *(n.)* वीलचेअर– a special chair mounted on large wheels, for use by invalids or others for whom walking is impossible or temporarily inadvisable पहिएदार कुर्सी He is forced to used a *wheelchair* after the accident.

wheeze *(v.)* वीज़– to breathe or utter (something) with a rasping or whistling sound कष्ट से सांस लेना She started *wheezing* while climbing the stairs.

when *(adv., conj.)* वेन–1. at what time? over what period? कब (प्रश्नवाची) *When* are you going to Mumbai?
2. at a time at which; at the time at which; just as; after जब, तब, कब (जब के अर्थ में) How can I tell *when* he will be able to come? You will see me next Sunday *when* I shall attend a meeting of the welfare association.

whence *(adv.)* वेन्स– from what place, cause, or origin? जहां (से) कहां (से) She returned *whence* she came.

whenever *(adv.)* वेनएवर– from what place, cause, or origin? जब भी, जब चाहें तब You can call me *whenever* you need my help.

where *(adv.)* वेअर्–1. in, at, or to what place, point, or position? कहां, कौन-सी जगह *Where* does the king live? The king lives in a palace. Masoodpur is the village *where* I live.

whereabouts *(n.)* वेअर्अबाउट्स– the place, esp the approximate place, where a person or thing is अता-पता, पता-ठिकाना The police can't determine the *whereabouts* of the fraudster

whereas *(conj.)* वेअर्ऐज़– about or concerning which जबकि She is good at studies *whereas* he is good at sports.

whereby *(adv.)* वेअर्बाइ– by or because of which जिससे, जिसके द्वारा There is a law *whereby* small children cannot work in a factory.

whereupon *(n.)* वेअर्पॉन– at which; at which point; upon which जिसके बाद, जिस पर I demanded my money from her *whereupon* she stopped talking to me.

wherever *(conj., adv.)* वेअर्एवर–1. at, in, or to every place or point which; where कहीं भी, जहां भी You may go *wherever* you like.

2. in, to, or at whatever place जहाँ, जिस जगह My friends follow me *wherever* I go.

whet *(v.)* वे'ट्– to increase or enhance (the appetite, desire, etc.); stimulate किसी वस्तु की चाह को और बढ़ाना A really good cover can also *whet* readers' appetite for reading.

whether *(conj.)* वे'दर्–1. used to introduce an indirect question or a clause after a verb expressing or implying doubt or choice in order to indicate two or more alternatives (मुझे संदेह है कि) या, दो में से एक, यदि I have not yet decided *whether* to go out or to stay in.

2. used to introduce any indirect questionयदि (है कि नहीं) The child asked the mother *whether* there was any more milk left.

which *(adj.)* विच–1. used with a noun in requesting that its referent be further specified, identified, or distinguished from the other members of a class जो, जिसने, जो कोई Try to find out *which* man stole my sewing machine.

2. (used in indirect questions) कौन-सा Mother asked Harish *which* pen he had selected.

3. *(pron.)* (as pronoun) कौन, कौन-सा (सही चुनने के लिए प्रयुक्त) *Which* of these lanes shall we prefer?

4. used in relative clauses with inanimate antecedents जो, जो कि The book *which* I bought is on the shelf.

5. as; and that: used in relative clauses with verb phrases or sentences as their antecedents यह, जो This is the bookshop *which* also sells magazines.

whichever विचएवर– any (one, two, etc., out of several) चाहें कोई, जो, कोई भी, जो भी *Whichever* of you will solve the problem will get a prize.

whiff *(n.)* विफ़– a passing odour गंध, हल्की बदबू Did you not notice a *whiff* of cigar smoke as you entered the room?

while *(n.)* वाइल–1. a period or interval of time समय, अरसा Father will worry if you do not get home in a short *while.*

2. a period or interval of time थोड़ी देर में I shall telephone you in a little *while.*

3. *(conj.)* whereas; and in contrast किन्तु, पर, जबकि Amit brought the milk, *while* Minakshi prepared the breakfast.

4. *(conj.)* in spite of the fact that जबकि Poonam is beautiful *while* her husband is ugly.

whim *(n.)* विम्– a sudden, passing, and often fanciful idea; impulsive or irrational thought सनक He lives in a world of his own *whims* and fancies.

whimper *(v.)* विम्पर्– to cry, sob, or whine softly or intermittently ठुनकना The baby *whimpered* for milk.

whine *(n.)* वाइन– a long high-pitched plaintive cry or moan चीखना, चिल्लाना, खीझना The baby was *whining* for no apparent reason.

whip *(v.)* विप– 1. to strike (a person or thing) with several strokes of a strap, rod, etc. कोड़ा मारना, चाबुक मारना The cartman is in a hurry and *whips* his bull.

2. *(n.)* a device consisting of a lash or flexible rod attached at one end to a stiff handle and used for driving animals, inflicting corporal punishment, etc. कोड़ा, चाबुक The tongawala has a long *whip.*

➢ **whip through**– to come, go, etc., in a rapid sudden manner तेज़ी से समाप्त करना, The leader *whipped through* customs in fifteen minutes.

➢ **whip up**– to excite; arouse उकसाना, भड़काना, The advertisements on TV *whip up* our excitement.

whirl *(v.)* वर्ल– 1. to spin, turn, or revolve or cause to spin, turn, or revolve तेज़ी से घुमाना या घूमना The strong wind *whirled* the dead leaves round and round in the garden.

2. *(n.)* the act or an instance of whirling; swift rotation or a rapid whirling movement हड़बड़ी, चक्कर, घुमाव Your mind is now in a *whirl.* Please think about your problem coolly later on.

whirlpool *(n.)* वर्लपूल– a powerful circular current or vortex of water, usually produced by conflicting tidal currents or by eddying at the foot of a waterfall भँवर, जलावर्त His son could not come out of the *whirlpool.*

whirlwind *(n.)* वर्लविण्ड– a column of air whirling around and towards a more or less vertical axis of low pressure, which moves along the land or ocean surface चक्रवात, तूफ़ानी बबूला His hut was destroyed by the *whirlwind.*

whirr *(v.)* वर– to make a continuous low sound or buzz, as of a motor working or wings flapping खड़खड़ाने की आवाज़ करना, खरखराना The noise of the *whirring* cooler did not let me sleep well.

whisk *(v.)* विस्क–1. to brush, sweep, or wipe off lightly झाड़ना, उड़ा देना The cow *whisks* flies with its long tail.

2. *(n.)* a light rapid sweeping movement or stroke फेंटनी, झाड़ *Whisk* the egg-onion mixture until smooth.

whisker *(n.)* विस्कर्– any of the stiff sensory hairs growing on the face of a cat, rat, or other mammal मूंछ-दाढ़ी, गलमुच्छा The cat was missing her *whiskers.*

whisky *(n.)* विस्की– a spirit made by distilling fermented cereals, which is matured and often blended ह्विस्की *Whisky* is an alcoholic drink made from grains.

whisper *(v.)* विस्पर्– 1. to speak or utter (something) in a soft hushed tone, esp without vibration of the vocal cords फुसफुसाना, कानाफूसी करना *Whisper* to mother so that no one else can hear.

2. *(n.)* a low soft voice फुसफुसाहट, खुसर-फुसर In the presence of the teacher, students spoke in *whispers.*

whistle *(v.)* विसल–1. to produce (shrill or flutelike musical sounds), as by passing breath through a narrow constriction most easily formed by the pursed lips सीटी बजाना The policeman *whistled* at the road.

2. *(n.)* a device for making a shrill high-pitched sound by means of air or steam under pressure सीटी

The guard blows a *whistle* to see the thief.

white *(adj.)* वाइट–1. having no hue due to the reflection of all or almost all incident light सफ़ेद, श्वेत The old lady's hair was completely *white.*

2. having a fair complexion; blond सफ़ेद, गोरा-चिट्टा Saira has a *white* complexion.

3. having pale-coloured or white skin, fur, or feathers पीला पड़ना, रंग उतरना Her face went *white.*

white-collar *(adj.)* वाइट-कॉलर– of, relating to, or designating nonmanual and usually salaried workers employed in professional and clerical occupations दफ़्तर का बाबू He is searching for a *white-collar* job

white elephant *(n.)* वाइट एलिफ़ंट– a rare albino or pale grey variety of the Indian elephant, regarded as sacred in parts of S Asia बहुत ख़र्चीला A *white elephant* is found in Myanmar.

white lie *(n.)* वाइट लाइ– a minor or unimportant lie, esp one uttered in the interests of tact or politeness सफ़ेद झूठ I knew that he was telling a *white lie* to me.

whiten *(v.)* वाइटन– to make or become white or whiter; bleach सफ़ेद बनना या बनाना The new toothpowder has *whitened* my teeth.

whitewash *(n.)* वाइटवॉश– 1. a substance used for whitening walls and other surfaces, consisting of a suspension of lime or whiting in water, often with other substances, such as size, added पुताई, क़लई Now my house needs *whitewash.*

2. *(v.)* to cover or whiten with whitewash पुताई करना, क़लई करना Tom was *whitewashing* the fence.

whither *(adv.)* विदर्– to what place? जहां कहीं We may go *whither* we wish.

whizz *(v.)* विज़्– to make or cause to make a loud humming or buzzing sound सनसनाना A racing car *whizzed* down the road.

who *(pron.)* हू–1. which person? what person? used in direct and indirect questions जो Minakshi is the girl *who* sang the song.

2. the one or ones who; whoever जिसे, जिन्हें Mr. Rai, *who* has a lot of teaching experience at primary level.

whoever *(pron.)* हूएवर– any person who; anyone that जो भी, जो कोई *Whoever* they are, tell them to wait.

whole *(adj.)* होल–1. containing all the component parts necessary to form a total; complete सम्पूर्ण योग The *whole* city was filled with rats.

2. constituting the full quantity, extent, etc. कुल I have spent the *whole* night coughing.

3. association पूरा समूचा I will spend the *whole* rainy season in Mumbai.

4. *(n.)* all the parts, elements, etc., of a thing समग्र We must sell our plot as a *whole.*

5. an assemblage of parts viewed together as a unit सब मिलाकर Had your father not kept the *whole* of his money in the bank?

wholefood *(n.)* होलफ़ूड– food that has been refined or processed as little as possible and is eaten in its natural state, such as brown rice, wholemeal flour, etc. स्वास्थ्यवर्धक आहार Kids need *wholefoods* to be healthy.

wholehearted *(adj.)* होलहार्टेड– done, acted, given, etc., with total sincerity, enthusiasm, or commitment

हार्दिक, सच्चा, एकनिष्ठ He gave me his *wholehearted* sympathy and support.

wholeheartedly *(adv.)* होलहार्टेडली– with total sincerity, enthusiasm, or commitment सच्चे हृदय से They welcomed me *wholeheartedly.*

wholesale *(adj.)* होलसेल– 1. made, done, etc., on a large scale or without discrimination थोक, थोक का We are selling these shoes at *wholesale* prices.

2. of, relating to, or engaged in such business थोक-व्यापार संबंधी They have *wholesale* business of ladies garments.

wholesome *(adj.)* होलसम– conducive to health or physical wellbeing पौष्टिक एवं स्वास्थ्यवर्द्धक There is *wholesome* food market near my house.

wholly *(adj.)* होललि– completely, totally, or entirely पूरी तरह, पूर्णतया We must not *wholly* believe what others say.

whom *(pron.)* हूम– the objective form of who, used when who is not the subject of its own clause जिसे, जिसको *Whom* do you want to meet?

whoosh *(n.)* हूश– a hissing or rushing sound सरसराहट (हवा की चाल की अवाज़) A *whoosh* of air inflamed everything.

whose *(pron.)* हूज़– of whom? belonging to whom? used in direct and indirect questions किसका, जिसका *Whose* book is this?

why *(adv.)* वाइ–1. for what reason, purpose, or cause? क्यों, किस समय *Why* do you think that I have no money?

2. (used in indirect questions) किसलिए, किस कारण से *Why* have you come to meet me?

3. for or because of which जिस कारण, जिसके लिए This is *why* I informed you about the matter very early.

wick *(n.)* विक– a cord or band of loosely twisted or woven fibres, as in a candle, cigarette lighter, etc., that supplies fuel to a flame by capillary action बत्ती, वर्तिका Before lighting the kerosene lamp, you must see that the *wick* is clean.

wicked *(adj.)* विकिड्– morally bad in principle or practice दुष्ट, पापी, बुरा, चरित्रहीन Man is not born *wicked,* he becomes so, as he becomes sick.

wickedness *(n.)* विकिड्नस– moral badness in principle or practice दुष्टता, बुराई To see and listen to the wicked is the beginning of *wickedness.*

wicker *(n.)* विकर्–1. a slender flexible twig or shoot, esp of willow लचीली टहनी Warn the child not to sit on a *wicker.*

2. made, consisting of, or constructed from wicker टोकरी बुनने के काम आने वाली तीली Do you not want to buy a *wicker* basket?

wicket *(n.)* विकिट– 1. either of two sets of three vertical sticks with pieces of wood lying across the top विकेट A *wicket* is one of the two sets of three sticks which are used in cricket.

2. *(adj.)* a small door or gate, esp one that is near to or part of a larger one आधा दरवाज़ा, छोटा फाटक As the main gate was closed, we entered the building through the *wicket* door.

wide *(adj.)* वाइड– 1. having a great extent from side to side चौड़ा, विस्तृत The door of the cow shed is *wide* open.

2. *(n.)* a wide space or extent विशाल, व्यापक For years, I have wandered far and *wide* in the deserts of life.

widen *(v.)* वाइडन– to make or become wide or wider विस्तृत होना, चौड़ा कर देना या हो जाना There is a *widening* gap between the rich and the poor in our society.

widespread *(adj.)* वाइडस्प्रेड– extending over a wide area व्याप्त, फैला हुआ The *widespread* northern plains in India are very rich and fertile.

widow *(n.)* विडो– a woman whose husband has died विधवा A rich *widow's* tears dry soon.

widower *(n.)* विडोअर्– a man whose wife has died and who has not remarried विधुर (पुरुष) A *widower* cannot forget his first wife even when he gets married again.

width *(n.)* विड्थ– the linear extent or measurement of something from side to side, usually being the shortest dimension or (for something fixed) the shortest horizontal dimension चौड़ाई The *width* of the door is five feet.

wield *(v.)* वील्ड– to handle or use (a weapon, tool, etc.) चलाना, संभालना, नियंत्रित करना The manager *wielded* his power very carefully.

wife *(n.)* वाइफ़– a man's partner in marriage; a married woman पत्नी, जोरू, गृहिणी Ascend a step to choose a friend, descend a step to choose a *wife*.

wig *(n.)* विग– an artificial head of hair, either human or synthetic, worn to disguise baldness, as part of a theatrical or ceremonial dress, as a disguise, or for adornment बालों की टोपी (असली या नक़ली बालों की बनी) In olden days, people used to wear *wigs* on their heads.

wiggle *(v.)* विगल– to move or cause to move with jerky movements, esp from side to side हिलना-डुलना The dog *wiggled* its tail on seeing its master.

wild *(adj.)* वाइल्ड–1. (of animals) living independently of man; not domesticated or tame हिंसक, जंगली Lions are *wild* animals.
2. of great violence or intensity तूफ़ानी, भयानक It was a *wild* night, with wind and heavy rain.
3. intensely enthusiastic or excited अत्यंत मदमस्त, चूरचूर I was *wild* with joy when I won the first-prize.
4. *(n.)* a desolate, uncultivated, or uninhabited region जंगल, निर्जन स्थान I saw a hunter hunting in the *wild*.

wilderness *(n.)* वाइल्डर्नस– a wild, uninhabited, and uncultivated region उजाड़, बंजर भूमि He was lost in the *wilderness* somewhere in the jungle.

wildlife *(n.)* वाइल्डलाइफ़– wild animals and plants collectively वन्य जीवन, जंगली जीव-जन्तु Living in the *wildlife* has its own experience.

wildly *(adv.)* वाइल्डली– to a very great degree; hugely; enormously उच्छृंखलपूर्वक They pushed the boy *wildly*.

wilful *(adj.)* विलफुल– intent on having one's own way; headstrong or obstinate जानबूझ कर किया गया The evidence shows that this damage is *wilful*.

will, would *(v.)* विल–1. used as an auxiliary to make the future tense भविष्य सूचक You *will* send me a letter, won't you? She *will* not attend the marriage, *will* she? I shall ask you the question you *would* not want to answer. My friend told me that he *would* not reach in time.
2. the declaration of a person's wishes regarding the disposal of his or her property after death अंतिम इच्छा के रूप में वसीयतनामा लिखना Shankar had *willed* all his property to his only daughter.
3. *(n.)* determined intention संकल्प, अभिप्राय You have no *will* of your own. Great men have the *will* to succeed.

4. used as an auxiliary to express compulsion, as in commands उत्तम पुरुष की भविष्यत्काल की क्रिया, जिसमें 'अवश्य' का बोध होता है Don't worry, I *will* reach there whatever happens.

5. used as an auxiliary to indicate willingness or desire इच्छाशक्ति, संकल्प शक्ति Character is a perfectly educated *will.*

willing *(adj.)* विलिंग– favourably disposed or inclined; ready राज़ी, इच्छुक He seems to be *willing* to help me in my work.

willingly *(adv.)* विलिंगली– freely, voluntarily स्वेच्छा से His servant did the work *willingly.*

willingness *(n.)* विलिंगनस– cheerfulness, enthusiasm or eager compliance इच्छा My friend showed his *willingness* to accompany me.

willpower *(n.)* विल पावर– the ability to control oneself and determine one's actions मनोबल, इच्छा-शक्ति His willpower is very low.

willow *(n.)* विलो– the wood of willow tree, used for making cricket bats क्रिकेट का बल्ला बनाने वाली लकड़ी *Willow* is mostly used for making cricket bats.

willy-nilly *(adv.)* विलि निलि– whether desired or not बिना सोचे-समझे, चाहे-अनचाहे Don't waste your time *willy-nilly.*

wilt *(v.)* विल्ट– to become or cause to become limp, flaccid, or drooping (पौधे का) मुरझाना, कुम्हलाना, सूख जाना The scorching sun made the flowers in our garden *wilt.*

wily *(adj.)* वाइलि– characterized by or proceeding from wiles; sly or crafty धूर्त, चालाक Beware of her, she is cunning and *wily.* He is a *wily* fellow, never trust him.

wimp *(n.)* विम्प– a feeble ineffective person मन से कमज़ोर He sometimes behaves like a *wimp.*

win *(v.)* विन– 1. to achieve first place in a competition जीत लेना, विजय पाना Who will *win* the race?

2. *(n.)* a success, victory, or triumph जीत, विजय Our team has had three *wins* and two losses in this year's cricket tournaments.

wince *(v.)* विन्स– to start slightly, as with sudden pain; flinch दर्द से मुंह पर शिकन आ जाना I *winced* in pain when he held my hand tightly.

wind *(n.)* विण्ड–1. विंड– a current of air as a result of natural forces पवन, हवा There was a strong *wind* yesterday and the leaves were blown off the trees.

2. the direction from which a wind blows, usually a cardinal point of the compass टेढ़े-मेढ़े चलना The streams *wind* their way through the wood.

3. to turn or coil (string, cotton, etc.) around some object or point or (of string, etc.) to be turned etc., around some object or point लपेटना *Wind* the wire round this stick.

➢ **wind down**– to lower or move down by cranking कड़ी मेहनत के बाद आराम करना, The government is *winding down* its nuclear testing programme.

➢ **wind up**– to bring to or reach a conclusion समापन करना, Please *wind up* the discussion.

windfall *(n.)* विण्डफ़ाल– a piece of unexpected good fortune, esp financial gain अप्रत्याशित लाभ Only *windfall* gains can save his company now.

winding *(adj.)* वाइंडिंग– curving; sinuous घुमावदार, घूमा हुआ There are many *winding* roads through the hills of Mussoorie.

window *(n.)* विंडो– a light framework, made of timber, metal, or plastic, that contains glass or glazed opening frames and is placed in a wall or roof to let in light or air or to see through खिड़की, झरोखा The *windows* were open when it rained. The *window*-panes were smashed by the storm.

window-shopping *(n.)* विंडो-शॉपिंग– the practice of looking at goods in shop windows without buying them दुकान में प्रदर्शित वस्तुओं को देखना परंतु ख़रीदने के लिए अंदर न जाना She is not satisfied by doing just *window-shopping.*

windpipe *(n.)* विण्डपाइप– the membranous tube with cartilaginous rings that conveys inhaled air from the larynx to the bronchi श्वासनली The child choked up the candy that was stuck in his *windpipe.*

windscreen *(n.)* विण्डस्क्रीन– the sheet of flat or curved glass that forms a window of a motor vehicle, esp the front window हवा रोकने वाला शीशा The *windscreen* wipers of my car are broken.

windsurf *(v.)* विण्डसर्फ़– to take part in the sport of windsurfing लकड़ी के फट्टे की मदद से पानी पर खड़े होकर फिसलना Most tourists come to *windsurfing.*

windy *(adj.)* विण्डी– of, characterized by, resembling, or relating to wind; stormy तूफ़ानी It was a *windy* night. We could not sleep well.

wine *(n.)* वाइन– an alcoholic drink produced by the fermenting of grapes with water and sugar अंगूरी शराब, मदिरा French *wines* are supposed to be very good.

wing *(n.)* विंग–1. either of the modified forelimbs of a bird that are covered with large feathers and specialized for flight in most species पंख, डैना A bird has two *wings.* It flies with its *wings.* An aeroplane has *wings.*

2. a part of a building that is subordinate to the main part खंड, भाग Students from the primary *wing* will be taken for a picnic.

3. *(v.)* to cause to fly or move swiftly उड़ना The summer was over and the swallows were *winging* their ways away.

wink *(v.)* विंक– 1. to close and open one eye quickly, deliberately, or in an exaggerated fashion to convey friendliness, etc. झपकाना, पलक मारना There is a time to *wink* as well as to see.

2. *(n.)* a winking movement, esp one conveying a signal, etc., or such a signal झपकी You have not slept a *wink* all day.

winner *(n.)* विनर– a person or thing that wins विजेता There can only be one *winner* of the contest.

winning *(adj.)* विनिंग– gaining victory विजयी The *winning* team was welcomed warmly.

winnow *(v.)* विनो– to separate (grain) from (chaff) by means of a wind or current of air अनाज ओसाना या पछारना, फटकना He was *winnowing* wheat.

winter *(n.)* विंटर्– the coldest season of the year, between autumn and spring शीत ऋतु, जाड़ा *Winter* is a cold season. It is the coldest season in the western countries.

wintertime *(n.)* विंटरटाइम– the winter season शीतऋतु The nights are longer in *wintertime.*

wipe *(v.)* वाइप– to rub (a surface or object) lightly, esp with (a cloth, hand, etc.), as in removing dust, water, grime, etc. पोंछना The table is wet, please *wipe* its top.

wire *(n.)* वाइअर्– 1. a slender flexible strand or rod of metal तार The copper *wire* was defected.

2. *(v.)* to send a telegram to (a person or place) तार देना *Wire* me to inform about the time of your arrival.

wireless *(n.)* वाइअरलॅस– communicating without connecting wires or other material contacts रेडियो You can send your message by *wireless.*

wiry *(n.)* वाइअरि– (of people or animals) slender but strong in constitution पतला-दुबला परंतु बलिष्ठ Her husband is a *wiry* little man.

wisdom *(n.)* विज़डम– the ability or result of an ability to think and act utilizing knowledge, experience, understanding, common sense, and insight विद्वता, ज्ञान Gandhiji was a man of great *wisdom.*

wise *(adj.)* वाइज–1. prudent; sensible बुद्धिमान We must listen to her advice, for she is a *wise* lady.

2. aware, informed, or knowing सचेत, होशियार It was *wise* of the mother to keep her child indoors while he had a cold.

wish *(n.)* विश्–1. want or desire (something, often that which cannot be or is not the case) इच्छा, कामना If a man could have half his *wishes,* he would double his troubles.

2. to desire or prefer to be as specified इच्छापूर्ति, कामना, मन्नत If *wishes* were horses, beggars might ride.

3. *(v.)* to feel or express a desire or hope concerning the future or fortune of इच्छा करना, कामना करना I *wish* I were a king!

wispy *(adj.)* विस्पी– wisplike; delicate, faint, light, etc. नरम लटवाली James was tall and handsome with a *wispy* beard.

wistful *(adj.)* विस्टफुल– sadly pensive, esp about something yearned for उदासीभरा The writer gave a *wistful* sigh on getting the rejection letter.

wit *(n.)* विट्– a person possessing, showing, or noted for such an ability, esp in repartee बुद्धि, समझ, हाज़िरजवाबी *Wit* without employment is a disease.

witch *(n.)* विच– historically, in mythology and fiction, a woman believed to practise magic or sorcery, esp black magic डायन, जादूगरनी In fairy tales, *witches* have very important roles.

witchcraft *(n.)* विचक्राफ़्ट– the art or power of bringing magical or preternatural power to bear or the act or practice of attempting to do so टोना-टोटका, जादू-टोना *Witchcraft* and superstitions are the two darksides of India.

with *(prep.)* विद–1. accompanying; in the company of के साथ Bring your brother *with* you.

2. caused or prompted by के कारण, के फलस्वरूप He is suffering *with* cold and fever.

3. possessing; having सहित, के पास We saw a policeman *with* a rod in his hand.

4. in a manner characterized by के अन्दर, के Never find faults *with* others.

withdraw *(v.)* विदड्रॉ– to take or draw back or away; remove निकालना, वापस लेना *Withdraw* a sum of ₹ 5000 from the bank next week.

withdrawal *(n.)* विदड्रॉअल– an act or process of withdrawing; retreat, removal, or detachment आहरण, वापसी Her *withdrawal* from life and activities was a matter of concern for all.

wither *(v.)* विदर्– (esp of a plant) to droop, wilt, or shrivel up पौधों का मुरझा जाना The leaves *withered* away in autumn.

withhold *(v.)* विदहोल्ड– to keep back; refrain from giving रोक रखना, देने से इंकार करना He *withheld* information from the police.

within *(prep.)* विदिन– 1. in; inside; enclosed or encased by समयावधि की सीमा के अंदर He was back *within* an hour.

2. *(adv.)* inside; internally व्यक्ति या वस्तु के भीतर All the blessings were coming from deep *within* her.

without *(n.)* विदाउट– not having बिना Had you not gone out *without* your shoes?

withstand *(v.)* विदस्टैन्ड– to stand up to forcefully; resist बरदाश्त कर लेना, सहन करना I could not *withstand* the pain.

witness *(n.)* विट्नस– 1. a person who has seen or can give first-hand evidence of some event गवाह She is the only *witness* who has seen the accident.

2. *(v.)* to give or serve as evidence (of) गवाही देना, साक्षी होना I have really *witnessed* many odd things in my life.

witty *(adj.)* विटी– characterized by clever humour or wit हाजिर जवाब, विनोदपूर्ण Lalu Prasad Yadav delivered a very *witty* speech.

wizard *(n.)* विज़र्ड–1. a person who is outstandingly clever in some specified field; expert जादूगर Do you still believe in witches and *wizards*?

2. a male witch or a man who practises or professes to practise magic or sorcery प्रतिभाशाली, चमत्कारी पुरुष I have a great regard for Kalidasa, he was a *wizard* indeed.

wobble *(v.)* वॉबल– to move, rock, or sway unsteadily डगमगाना, लड़खड़ाना Stop *wobbling* the chair. I can't sit properly.

woe *(n.)* वो– intense grief or misery शोक, विषाद, उदासीन, संकट The villagers told many tales of *woe* that befell them when the river flooded their houses.

wolf *(n.)* वुल्फ़–1. a large wild animal of the dog family भेड़िया One day, a *wolf* attacked me in the woods.

2. *(v.)* to gulp (down) गटकना, भकोसना The hungry beggar greedily *wolfed* down the food.

woman *(n.)* वुमन– an adult female human being महिला, नारी, औरत Baby is little girl. When she grows up she will be a *woman.*

womanhood *(n.)* वुमनहुड– the state or quality of being a woman or being womanly औरतपन, नारीत्व Some people think that beauty contests are degrading *womanhood.*

womanish *(adj.)* वुमनिश– having qualities or characteristics regarded as unsuitable to a strong character of either sex, esp a man ज़नाना, स्त्री-सदृश Bobby talks in a *womanish* manner.

wonder *(v.)* वंड्र्–1. to be amazed (at something) आश्चर्य करना I *wonder* where Sarla has gone.

2. to indulge in speculative inquiry, often accompanied by an element of doubt (concerning something) जिज्ञासा होना, कुतूहल होना How I *wonder* what you are!

3. *(n.)* the feeling excited by something strange; a mixture of surprise, curiosity, and sometimes awe अचरज, अचम्भा, विस्मय As knowledge increases, *wonder* deepens.

wonderful *(adj.)* वनडर्फुल– exciting a feeling of wonder; marvellous or strange अद्भुत, आश्चर्यजनक The new teacher came up with a *wonderful* idea.

wood *(n.)* वुड–1. an area of trees smaller than a forest जंगल, वन There are many trees in the *woods.*

2. the trunks of trees that have been cut and prepared for use as a building material लकड़ी, जलाने की लकड़ी We get *wood* from trees. This table is made of *wood.*

woodcutter *(n.)* वुडकटर– a person who fells trees or chops wood लकड़हारा A poor *woodcutter* lived in a village.

wooden *(adj.)* वुडन– made from or consisting of wood लकड़ी से निर्मित *Wooden* furniture is long lasting.

woodpecker *(n.)* वुडपेकर– any climbing bird typically having a brightly coloured plumage and strong chisel-like bill with which they bore into trees for insects कठफोड़वा *Woodpeckers* has a long beak and is found worldwide.

woodwork *(n.)* वुडवर्क– the art, craft, or skill of making things in wood; carpentry काष्ठकर्म, लकड़ी का काम The *woodwork* frame needs painting.

woof *(n.)* वुफ़– the crosswise yarns that fill the warp yarns in weaving; weft कुत्ते के भौंकने या ग़ुर्राने की आवाज़ We heard a *woof* from the backyard.

wool *(n.)* वूल– yarn spun from the coat of sheep, etc., used in weaving, knitting, etc. ऊन My mother bought some *wool* to knit a sweater for me. Bring a ball of *wool* from the almirah.

woollen *(adj.)* वुलन– relating to or consisting partly or wholly of wool ऊनी Have you got a *woollen* jersey?

word *(v.)* वर्ड–1. to write or say sth using words शब्दों में कहना How shall I *word* this story?

2. *(n.)* an undertaking or promise प्रतिज्ञा, वचन, आश्वासन Give me your *word* that you will pay me a visit next Sunday.

3. a verbal signal for action; command संकेत, संदेश Send me a *word* when you hear from Rachna.

4. one of the units of speech or writing that native speakers of a language usually regard as the smallest isolable meaningful element of the language शब्द He who does not know the force of *words* can't know a man.

5. news or information शब्द-प्रति-शब्द, शब्दशः This is the *word for word* message he gave me.

➢ **have a word**– to communicate संक्षिप्त वार्तालाप करना, I'll *have a word* with her and see if she'll help.

➢ **by word of mouth**– orally rather than by written means ज़बानी, मौखिक रूप से, This information is picked up *by word of mouth* from an old colleague.

➢ **man of words**– person who keeps his/her words बात का धनी, My father is a *man of words.*

wording *(n.)* वर्डिंग– the way in which words are used to express a statement, report, etc., esp a written one शब्दचयन He checked every single *wording* of the document.

work *(v.)* वर्क–1. to exert effort in order to do, make, or perform something काम करना, परिश्रम करना Everybody is *working.* Daddy *works* in the office. Mother *works* in the kitchen. Brother *works* in the garden.

2. *(n.)* physical or mental effort directed towards doing or making something काम, कार्य I have some urgent *work* to do in the office.

3. a duty, task, or undertaking काम, कर्तव्य An ounce of *work* is worth many pounds of words.

4. paid employment at a job or a trade, occupation, or profession परिश्रम *Work* is worship.

Workout 1. to solve or find out by reasoning or calculation हिसाब लगाना They *worked out* their shares of profit in business.

2. to understand the real nature of किसी को समझाना I am not able to *work* her *out.*

➢ **work up to**– to move or cause to move gradually upwards उन्नति करना, The music *worked up to* a rousing finale.

workable *(adj.)* वर्कबल– practicable or feasible व्यावहारिक The firm is still trying to find a *workable* solution with the client.

workaholic *(n.)* वर्कहॉलिक– a person obsessively addicted to work काम के प्रति मोहग्रस्त People call me *workaholic.*

worker *(n.)* वर्कर– a person or thing that works, usually at a specific job कार्यकर्ता The *workers* of his factory went on strike for their demands.

working *(adj.)* वर्किंग– concerned with, used in, or suitable for work चालू हालत में He has stopped *working* hard as he used to.

workmanship *(n.)* वर्कमनशिप– the art or skill with which something is made or executed कारीगरी We are God's *workmanship.*

workshop *(n.)* वर्कशॉप– a room or building in which manufacturing or other forms of manual work are carried on कारख़ाना, कार्यशिविर His *workshop* is situated very far from his house.

world *(n.)* वर्ल्ड–1. the earth as a planet, esp including its inhabitants संसार, दुनिया, लोक The *world* is the place we live in.

2. the universe or cosmos; everything in existence जगत् The *world* is nothing but an endless seesaw.

3. a complex united whole regarded as resembling the universe सृष्टि, ब्रह्मांड The *world* is a net; the more we stir in it, the more we are entangled.

world-famous *(adj.)* वर्ल्ड-फ़ेमस– known around the world विश्वप्रसिद्ध Mona Lisa is the *world-famous* painting.

worldly *(adj.)* वर्ल्डली– not spiritual; mundane or temporal लौकिक, सांसारिक Saints give up *worldly* needs and wants to start their path.

worldwide *(adv.)* वर्ल्डवाइड– applying or extending throughout the world; universal दुनियावी, विश्वव्यापक The Presidents interview will be telecasted *worldwide.*

worm *(n.)* वर्म– a long thin creature with no bones and legs, lives in soil कीड़ा, केंचुआ A *worm* is a small creature that lives in the ground. It creeps like a snake.

worn-out *(adj.)* वॉर्न आउट–1. extremely tired थका-हारा, थककर चूर-चूर He was badly *worn-out* and went to bed.

2. used so much to the point of no longer being usable फ़टा-पुराना, जीर्ण His dress was completely *worn-out.*

worried *(adj.)* वरिड– feeling uneasy about a situation or thing; anxious फ़िक्रमंद, चिंतित, परेशान I'm *worried* about the quality of your work.

worry *(v.)* वॅ'री–1.to be or cause to be anxious or uneasy, esp about something uncertain or potentially dangerous चिंता करना, फिक्र करना Mother *worries* about Raju's cought.

2. *(n.)* an act of worrying चिंता, फ़िक्र It is a *worry* for her.

3. a state or feeling of anxiety समस्या, परेशानी My life is full of *worries.*

worse *(adj.)* वर्स– 1. the comparative of bad बहुत ख़राब, बदतर The performance of Indian football team is *worse* than that of other country.

2. *(adv.)* in a more severe or unpleasant manner पहले से भी अधिक ख़राब It's hot *worse* than ever.

worsen *(v.)* वर्सन– to grow or cause to grow worse और अधिक बुरा हो जाना, बदतर होना Relations between India and Pakistan have *worsened.*

worship *(n.)* वर्शिप– 1. religious adoration or devotion पूजा, आराधना, इबादत He goes to the temple everyday to worship.

2. *(v.)* to be devoted to and full of admiration for पूजना, आराधना करना For your happiness *worship* God.

worst *(adj.)* वर्स्ट– 1. the superlative of bad सबसे बुरा, बदतरीन The team did not expect the *worst* performance in finals.

2. *(pron.)* in the most extreme or bad manner or degree सबसे बुरी बात या स्थिति His behaviour is at its *worst* when he is with strangers.

worth *(adj.)* वर्थ– 1. worthy of; meriting or justifying (के) योग्य, (के) लायक This book is *worth* five hundred rupees.

2. *(n.)* high quality; excellence कीमत, मूल्य The *worth* of this gem is unknown.

worthless *(adj.)* वर्थलस–1. without practical value or usefulness किसी काम का नहीं, व्यर्थ These goods are *worthless* for me.

2. without merit; good-for-nothing निकम्मा, बेकार Such *worthless* person can never be believable.

worthwhile *(adj.)* वर्थवाइल– sufficiently important, rewarding, or valuable to justify time or effort spent करने योग्य, उपयोगी This investment turned out to be quite *worthwhile*.

worthy *(adj.)* वर्दी– 1. having sufficient value (for something or someone specified); deserving आदरणीय She is *worthy* of respect from all of them.

2. having worth, value, or merit श्रेष्ठ, योग्य Akbar was a *worthy* ruler of Medieval India.

3. a person of distinguished character, merit, or importance अच्छा, सुयोग्य, के योग्य Your work is *worthy* of reward.

would *(v.)* वुड– Past of will! भूतकाल में प्रयुक्त modal verb; Would you like come with me to work tomorrow?

wound *(v.)* वून्ड– 1. to inflict a wound or wounds upon (someone or something) घायल करना, चोट मारना Uncle Sharma was *wounded* in the war.

2. *(n.)* any break in the skin or an organ or part as the result of violence or a surgical incision घाव, ज़ख़्म, चोट His *wounds* were not serious.

wow *(inter)* वाउ– an exclamation of admiration, amazement, etc. वाह-वाह (प्रशंसा एवं आश्चर्य प्रकट करने के लिए) *Wow*! What a beautiful dress!

wrangle *(v)* रैंगल– to argue, esp noisily or angrily झगड़ा करना, नोक-झोंक करना The board of directors started to *wrangle* with each other.

wrap *(v.)* रैप–1. to fold or wind (paper, cloth, etc.) around (a person or thing) so as to cover लपेटना, चादर ओढ़ना Please *wrap* this book by paper.

2. a garment worn wrapped around the body, esp the shoulders, such as a shawl or cloak कम्बल, शाल, आवरण I covered my head with a *wrap*.

wrapper *(n.)* रैपर्– the cover, usually of paper or cellophane, in which something is wrapped आवरण, रैपर The child ate the candy and threw away the *wrapper*.

wrapping *(n)* रैपिंग– the material used to wrap something लपेटन, बेठन The *wrapping* paper was of good quality.

wrath *(n.)* रॉथ– angry, violent, or stern indignation क्रोध, रोष I could not control my *wrath* at his foolish action.

wreath *(n.)* रीथ– a band of flowers or foliage intertwined into a ring, usually placed on a grave as a memorial or worn on the head as a garland or a mark of honour माला, हार, गजरा The people showed respect to their dead leader with the *wreaths* of flowers.

wreck *(n.)* रे'क– 1. the accidental destruction of a ship at sea बरबाद

जहाज़, नष्ट-भ्रष्ट पोत Nothing could be saved from the *wreck.*

2. *(v.)* to involve in or suffer disaster or destruction बरबाद होना, नष्ट-भ्रष्ट होना The bogey ran off the rail-track and was *wrecked.*

wreckage *(n)* रेकेज– the remains of something that has been destroyed मलबा It was difficult to find clues in all the *wreckage.*

wrench *(n.)* रे'न्च–1. a parting that is difficult or painful to make दुःख, मानसिक पीड़ा I felt a *wrench* when my younger brother left home.

2. a forceful twist or pull कसने का यंत्र Use your *wrench* and tighten the screws of my bike.

3. *(v.)* to give (something) a sudden or violent twist or pull esp so as to remove (something) from that to which it is attached मरोड़ना *Wrench* the screw of your pressure cooker with this small instrument.

wrestle *(v.)* रे'सल– to fight (another person) by holding, throwing, etc., without punching with the closed fist कुश्ती लड़ना, मल्लयुद्ध करना The physical training instructor taught his pupils how to box and *wrestle.*

wrestling *(n.)* रेसलिंग– any of certain sports in which the contestants fight each other according to various rules governing holds and usually forbidding blows with the closed fist कुश्ती, पहलवानी *Wrestling* is very popular in Japan.

wretch *(n.)* रे'च–1. a person pitied for his misfortune अभागा, ग़रीब उदास इंसान The poor *wretch* looked so distressed that I felt sorry for him.

2. a despicable person नीच, कमीना The man who stole the money from the poor widow was a wicked *wretch.*

wretched *(adj.)*–1.in poor or pitiful circumstances नीच, घृणास्पद His brother is a *wretched* little miser.

2. (intensifier qualifying something undesirable) घटिया क़िस्म का, बहुत ख़राब Today is a *wretched* weather. I can't go out.

3. characterized by or causing misery अभागा, बदनसीब, दुखी They are living a *wretched* life.

wriggle *(v.)* रिगल– to manoeuvre oneself by clever or devious means कुलबुलाना, तड़पना The patient was *wriggling* in pain .

wring *(v.)* रिंग–1. to twist and compress to squeeze (a liquid) from (cloth, etc.) मरोड़ना, निचोड़ना, ऐंठना *Wring* the wet shirt to get the water out of it.

2. to obtain by or as if by forceful means यत्नपूर्वक निकालना At last, the policemen *wrung* the truth from the thief.

wrinkle *(n.)* रिंकल– 1. a slight ridge in the smoothness of a surface, such as a crease in the skin as a result of age झुर्री, शिकन The old man has *wrinkles* on his forehead.

2. *(v.)* to make or become wrinkled, as by crumpling, creasing, or puckering चेहरे पर शिकन डालना या लाना The baby *wrinkled* its face and began to cry.

wrist *(n.)* रिस्ट– the joint between the forearm and the hand कलाई, मणिबंध My *wrist* was broken in the accident.

wrist watch *(n.)* रिस्ट वाच्– a watch worn strapped around the wrist कलाई-घड़ी Have you got your *wrist-watch* back?

writ *(n)* रिट– a document under seal, issued in the name of the Crown or a court, commanding the person to whom it is addressed to do or refrain from doing some specified act याचिका, आदेश She can file a *writ* in the High Court.

write *(v.)* राइट– 1. to draw or mark (symbols, words, etc.) on a surface, usually paper, with a pen, pencil, or other instrument लिखना, लेखन कार्य करना I can read the words you *write.*
2. *(n.)* the activity or skill of writing: लिखाई Your *writing* is not clear.

- **write back**– to reply back उत्तर देना, I will *write* her *back.*
- **write down**– to set down in writing क़लमबंद करना, I *wrote down* important notes of the project.
- **write in**– to insert in (a document, form, etc.) in writing लिखकर जोड़ना, सम्मिलित कर लेना, I *wrote in* all his valuable suggestions.
- **write off**– an act of officially stating that someone does not need to pay back money owed लिख भेजना, I have to *write off* an article for the magazine.

writer *(n.)* राइटर– a person who writes books, articles, etc., esp as an occupation लेखक He is a prolific *writer* of poetry.

wrong *(adj.)* रॉन्ग–1. not correct or truthful ग़लत, अनुचित It is *wrong* to tell a lie.
2. not working properly; amiss ख़राबी What is *wrong* with this radio-set? It is *wrong* to steal.
3. *(n.)* a bad, immoral, or unjust thing or action पाप, अधर्म The remedy for *wrongs* is to forget them.

wrongdoing *(adj)* रांगडुइंग– the act or an instance of doing something immoral or illegal अवैध कार्य, ग़ैर-क़ानूनी काम He was punished severely for his *wrongdoings* .

wrongly *(adv)* रांगली– unjustly, illegally, or unfairly ग़लत ढंग से, अनुचित रीति से The lawyer claimed that his client has been *wrongly* accused.

Xx

Xx *(n.)* ऐक्स–अंग्रेज़ी वर्णमाला का चौबीसवाँ अक्षर The twenty-fourth letter of the English alphabet. X-ray begins with '*X*'.

xanthippe *(n.)* जैनूथिपि– any nagging, peevish, or irritable woman कर्कश/लड़ाका स्त्री Day by day She is becoming a *xanthippe.*

xenophobia *(n.)* ज़नॉफ़ोबिऑ– hatred or fear of foreigners or strangers विदेशियों के प्रति घृणा, विदेशी-द्वेष There is still a feeling of *xenophobia* is certain sections of the western society.

xerox *(n.)* ज़ेरॉक्स– 1. a xerographic copying process छायाप्रति, प्रतिलिपि This is a *xerox* of the original document. 2. *(v.)* to produce a copy of (a document, illustration, etc.) by this process प्रतिलिपि कराना या करना Get this document *xeroxed.*

xmas *(n.)* क्रिसमस्– short for Christmas बड़ा दिन, ईसा का जन्मदिवस, 25 दिसम्बर Sometimes we spell Christmas as *Xmas. Xmas* is an important festival of Christians.

x-rated *(adj.)* अक्स्रेटेड– (esp of a film or movie) considered suitable for viewing by adults only ऐसी फिल्म (जिन्हें अठारह बरस से कम उम्र के लोग न देख सकते हों) *X-rated* movies are not allowed in Indian theatres.

x-ray *(n.)* एक्स-रे– electromagnetic radiation that can pass through objects and make it possible to see inside them एक्सरे *X-ray* was a very important discovery in the field of medicine.

xylography *(n.)* ज़ाइलॉग्राफ़ी– the art, craft, or process of printing from wooden blocks काष्ठ-चित्रकला *Xylography* is becoming a dying art.

xylophone *(n.)* ज़ाइलफ़ोन– a musical instrument consisting of a set of wooden bars of graduated length. काष्ठतरंग, एक वाद्ययंत्र We need to find someone who can play the *xylophone* with their eyes closed.

ഇര

Yy

Yy *(n.)* वाइ–अंग्रेज़ी वर्णमाला का पच्चीसवाँ अक्षर
The twenty-fifth letter of the English alphabet. Yard begins with 'Y'.

yacht *(n.)* यॉट– a vessel propelled by sail or power, used esp for pleasure cruising, racing, etc. छोटी नौका, डोंगी Millionaires own big expensive *yachtes.*

yachting *(n.)* याटिंग– the sport or practice of navigating a yacht नौका-विहार *Yachting* is a well-organized and recognized winter sport.

yak *(n.)* यैक– an animal of the cow family with long horns याक, तिब्बती साँड़, चमर *Yak* is found throughout the Himalayan region of south Central Asia, and the Tibetan Plateau.

yam *(n.)* यैम–1. the root of a tropical plant used as a vegetable रतालू, घुइयाँ, अरबी *Yam* is a favourite vegetable of many people.

yank *(v.)* यैंक– to pull, jerk, or move with a sharp movement; tug झटके से खींचना, झटका देना He *yanked* the door.

yard *(n.)* यार्ड–1. a unit of length equal to 3 feet and defined in 1963 as exactly 0.9144 metre गज Three feet make one *yard.*
2. an enclosed area outside a building अहाता, बाड़ा There is a fence round the *yard.*

yardstick *(n.)* यार्डस्टिक– a measure or standard used for comparison मानदंड What would be the *yardstick* to judge the performance?

yarn *(n.)* यार्न–1. a continuous twisted strand of natural or synthetic fibres, used in weaving, knitting, etc. सूत, धागा There was a shortage of *yarn,* so the weavers had to face unemployment.
2. a long story usually telling of incredible or fantastic events कहानी The old sailor told his children an interesting *yarn.*

yashmak *(n.)* यैश्मैक– the face veil worn by Muslim women when in public बुरक़ा According to Muslim texts, Women must wear *yashmaks.*

yawn *(v.)* यॉन– 1. to open the mouth wide and take in air deeply, often as in involuntary reaction to tiredness, sleepiness, or boredom उबासी लेना, जँभाई लेना She *yawned* and put down the book she was reading.
2. *(n.)* the act or an instance of yawning जँभाई, उबासी "I'm feeling sleepy," she said with a *yawn.*

yaw *(v.)* यॉ– (of a ship or plane) to turn to one side and away from a right course (जहाज का) विचलना, सही मार्ग से अलग होना In a voyage, the ship had *yawed*

year *(n.)* यिअर्–1. a period of twelve months from any specified date, such as one based on the four seasons वर्ष, साल A *year* has twelve months and fifty-two weeks.
2. age, time of life आयु You look young for your *years.*

yearly *(adv.)* यिअर्ली– occurring, done, appearing, etc. once a year or every year; annual वार्षिक, सालाना The *yearly* performance review of employees will be declared soon.

yearn *(v.)* यर्न–1. to have an intense desire or longing (for) ललकना, लालायित होना Abha is *yearning* for a bicycle.

yearning *(n.)* यर्निंग– a strong desire लालसा, ललक, उत्कंठा The mother had no great *yearning* to see her lost son.

yeast *(n.)* यीस्ट– a fungus used in making bread, beer, etc. ख़मीर *Yeast* is an important ingredient to make bread.

yell *(n.)* ये'ल– 1. a cry of words or syllables, used in cheering in unison चीख, चिल्लाहट, अट्टाहास, किलकारी The speaker was greeted with *yells* of challenge.

2. *(v.)* to shout, scream, cheer, or utter in a loud or piercing way चीख़ना, चिल्लाना, किलकारना I saw the dog *yelling* with pain.

yellow *(adj.)* ये'लो– 1. of the colour yellow पीला, पीत Monkey eats *yellow* bananas.

2. yellowish in colour पीला रंग He was dressed in *yellow.*

3. cowardly or afraid कायर, डरपोक A *yellow* fellow lives in my neighbourhood.

yellowish *(adj.)* येलोइश– tending towards yellow; somewhat yellow आपीत, पीला-सा This document has a *yellowish* tinge because it is so old.

yellow journalism *(n.)* सनसनीख़ेज़, the type of journalism that relies on sensationalism and lurid exaggeration to attract readers पत्रकारिता *Yellow journalism* has become a mainstay in today's world.

yelp *(v.)* येल्प– (esp of a dog) to utter a sharp or high-pitched cry or bark, often indicating pain चीख़ना The dog *yelped* when somebody stepped on its tail.

yes *(inter.)* ये'स–1. used to express acknowledgment, affirmation, consent, agreement, or approval or to answer when one is addressed जी हां, अवश्य, सचमुच If you can do something, you must say – *Yes,* I can.

2. an answer or vote of yes हां, ठीक है I want a straight *yes* or no from you.

yesterday *(n.)* ये'स्टर्डे– 1. the day immediately preceding today बीता हुआ कल *Yesterday* is the day before today.

2. *(adv.)* on the day before today कुछ समय पहले, कल Have you got *yesterday's* newspaper?

yet *(adv.)* ये'ट–1. so far; up until then or now अभी तक Has the manager not come *yet*? Sorry, he is not here *yet.*

2. *(conj.)* nevertheless; still; in spite of that तो भी The work is very hard, *yet* it is worth trying.

3. even; still के होते हुए भी, के बावजूद She wasn't well, *yet* she managed to appear for the examination.

➢ **yet again**– another or second time; once more; anew दूसरी बार, एक बार फिर, Prices of petrol are increased *yet again.*

➢ **yet to do**– still to work upon जिस काम को करना या लेना हो, The final decision has *yet to* be taken.

➢ **as yet**– . up to now; so far अभी भी या अभी तक, *As yet*, Karim is silent on this matter.

➢ **not yet**– not at present अभी नहीं, The work is *not yet* done.

yield *(v.)* यील्ड–1. to give forth or supply (a product, result, etc.;), esp by cultivation, labour, etc.; produce or bear उत्पन्न करना, पैदा करना Your efforts will definitely *yield* success.

2. to surrender or relinquish, esp as a result of force, persuasion, etc. पराजय स्वीकार करना, घुटने टेकना Though the warrior was defeated, he refused to *yield* the post.

3. *(n.)* the result, product, or amount yielded उपज We have an excellent *yield* of mangoes this year.

yoga *(n.)* योगा– a Hindu system of philosophy aiming at the mystical union of the self with the Supreme Being in a state of complete awareness and tranquillity through certain physical and mental exercises योग, शारीरिक व्यायाम *Yoga* helps in achieving peace of mind.

yoghurt *(n.)* योगर्ट– a thick custard-like food prepared from milk that has been curdled by bacteria, often sweetened and flavoured with fruit, chocolate, etc. दही His dinner is incomplete without *yoghurt*.

yoke *(n.)* योक– 1. a wooden frame, usually consisting of a bar with an oxbow or similar collar-like piece at either end, for attaching to the necks of a pair of draught animals, esp oxen, जुआ, जूआ A farmer ploughed fields by *yoke*.

2. *(v.)* to join or be joined by means of a yoke; couple, unite, or link जोतना *Yoke* your bulls to the carts.

yolk *(n.)* योक– the yellow part in the middle of an egg ज़रदी, अंडे का पीला भाग The *yolk* of an egg is rich in protein.

you *(pron.)* यू– refers to the person addressed or to more than one person including the person or persons addressed but not including the speaker तुम, आप *You* are indispensible to the company.

young *(adj.)* यंग–1. having lived, existed, or been made or known for a relatively short time छोटा, कम उम्र का A *young* child is called a baby.

2. of or relating to youth युवा, जवान The old know what they want, the *young* are bewildered.

3. *(n.)* offspring, esp young animals जानवरों के बच्चे A *young* tiger is called a cub. A *young* sheep is called a lamb. A *young* goat is called a kid.

youngish *(adj.)* यंगिश– fairly young युवा-सा, जवान-सा Bill Clinton was the third *youngish* president of America.

youngster *(n.)* यंगस्टर्– a young person; child or youth किशोर The target audience for the movie were *youngsters*.

your *(det., pron. & adj.)* यॉर– of, belonging to, or associated with you तुम्हारा, आपका *Your* family owes me a lot of money.

yours *(pron.)* यॉर्ज़– something or someone belonging to or associated in some way with you तुम्हारा, भवदीय Is this bag *yours*?

yourself *(pron.)* यॉर्सेल्फ़– the reflexive form of you तुम स्वयं, तुम ख़ुद Just act *yourself* in the interview and everything will be fine.

youth *(n.)* यूथ–1. the quality or condition of being young, immature, or inexperienced किशोरावस्था The use of tobacco among *youth* and young adults is of growing concern.

2. the period between childhood and maturity, esp adolescence and early adulthood जवानी, युवावस्था, यौवन In *youth,* we run into difficulties; in old age, difficulties run into us.

3. young people collectively युवा, नवयुवक समूह Many *youths* participated in the movement.

youthful *(adj.)* यूथफुल– of, relating to, possessing, or characteristic of youth युवा, जवान Gambhir is a *youthful* player of the Indian cricket team.

yuck *(exclamation.)* यक– an exclamation indicating contempt, dislike, or disgust छिः! ऊँह! *Yuck*! I don't like it.

yummy *(adj.)* यमी– delicious, very good to eat ज़ायक़ेदार, स्वादिष्ट The dishes served in dinner were very *yummy*.

Zz

Zz *(n.)* ज़ेड–अंग्रेज़ी वर्णमाला का छब्बीसवाँ और अंतिम अक्षर The tweny-sixth and last letter of the English alphabet. Zoo begins with '*Z*'.

zany *(adj.)* ज़ेनि– comical in an endearing way; imaginatively funny or comical, esp in behaviour मसखरा, विदूषक, मज़ाक़िया The Hindi film industry does not have *zany* comedians these days.

zap *(v.)* ज़ैप– to attack, kill, or destroy, as with a sudden bombardment जान से मारना, प्रहार करना The soldiers *zapped* theirs enemies instantly.

zeal *(n.)* ज़ील– fervent or enthusiastic devotion, often extreme or fanatical in nature, as to a religious movement, political cause, ideal, or aspiration उत्साह, जोश, सरगर्मी He has a great *zeal* for work. *Zeal* without knowledge is like an expedition in the dark.

zealot *(n.)* जीलट– an immoderate, fanatical, or extremely zealous adherent to a cause, esp a religious one कट्टरपंथी या उन्मादी व्यक्ति A *zealot* is a narrow-minded person.

zealous *(adj.)* ज़ीलस– filled with or inspired by intense enthusiasm or zeal; ardent; fervent उत्साही, जोशीला Youth is always *zealous.*

zebra *(n.)* ज़ेब्रा– an african wild animal like a horse with black and white stripes on its body जेबरा A *zebra* has white and black stripes on its body.

zebra Crossing *(n.)* ज़ेब्रा-क्रासिंग– a pedestrian crossing marked on a road by broad alternate black and white stripes. चौराहे पर सफ़ेद और काली धारियों वाला भाग (जहाँ पैदल चलने वालों को सड़क पार करने का अधिकार होता है) Vehicles must stop at the *zebra crossing* to allow the pedestrians to cross the road safely.

zenith *(n.)* ज़ेनिथ– the highest point; peak; acme चरमसीमा, पराकाष्ठा, शीर्ष बिंदु The climbers celebrated at the *zenith* of the mountain.

zero *(n.)* ज़िअरो–1. the symbol 0, indicating an absence of quantity or magnitude; nought सिफ़र, शून्य Water freezes at *zero* degrees.
2. nothing; nil कुछ नहीं, अंडा, शून्यांक He got *zero* marks in Mathematics.

zest *(n.)* ज़ेस्ट– invigorating or keen excitement or enjoyment उत्साह की भावना His *zest* for knowledge does not decrease.

zigzag *(adj.)* ज़िगज़ैग– 1. formed in or proceeding in a zigzag टेढ़ा-मेढ़ा, सर्पिल Draw a *zigzag* line to represent rivers.
2. *(v.) to proceed or cause to proceed in a zigzag* टेढ़ा-मेढ़ा आगे बढ़ना The boat had to *zigzag* to avoid being struck by big rocks.

zinc *(n.)* ज़िंक– a brittle bluish-white metallic element that becomes coated with a corrosion-resistant layer in moist air and occurs chiefly in sphalerite and smithsonite. जस्ता *Zinc* is a hard white metal.

zip *(n.)* ज़िप– 1. a fastening device operating by means of two parallel rows of metal or plastic teeth on either side of a closure that are interlocked by a sliding tab ज़िप Undo the *zip* of the bag.
2. *(v.)* to fasten (clothing, a bag,

etc.) with a zip ज़िप खोलना या बंद करना *Zip* the bag properly.

zip code *(n.)* ज़िप कोड– a code of letters and digits used as part of a postal address to aid the sorting of mail ज़िपकोड–पते के अंत में लिखे जाने वाले अंक, पिनकोड Write the *zip code* in your address.

zodiac *(n.)* ज़ोडिऐक– an imaginary area in the sky which contains the 12 zodiacal constellations and within which the moon and planets appear to move राशि चिह्न My *zodiac* sign is Cancer.

zone *(n.)* ज़ोन– a region, area, or section characterized by some distinctive feature or quality क्षेत्र, मंडल During the war, the nearby villages were declared as a danger *zone*.

zoo *(n.)* ज़ू– a place where live animals are kept, studied, bred, and exhibited to the public चिड़ियाघर Many wild animals and birds are kept in the *zoo*.

zoological *(adj.)* जोअलॉजिकल– of or relating to zoology प्राणिविज्ञान (संबंधी) National *Zoological* Park of Delhi provides a natural habitat for a variety of animals and birds.

zoology *(n.)* ज़ोऑलजि– the study of animals, including their classification, structure, physiology, and history प्राणिविज्ञान The study of *Zoology* helps students of veterinary science.

zoom *(v.)* ज़ूम–1. to move very rapidly; rush (गरजते हुए) तेज़ी से गुज़रना The aeroplane *zoomed* into the air.
2. to increase quickly अचानक बढ़ जाना onion prices have *zoomed* up this year.

zoroastrian *(n.)* ज़ोरोस्ट्रियन– a follower of Zoroaster or adherent of Zoroastrianism; in modern times a Parsee पारसी धर्म का अनुयायी A small community of *zoroastrians* exists mostly in Mumbai.

CLASSIFIED VOCABULARY

Earth co-ordinate system

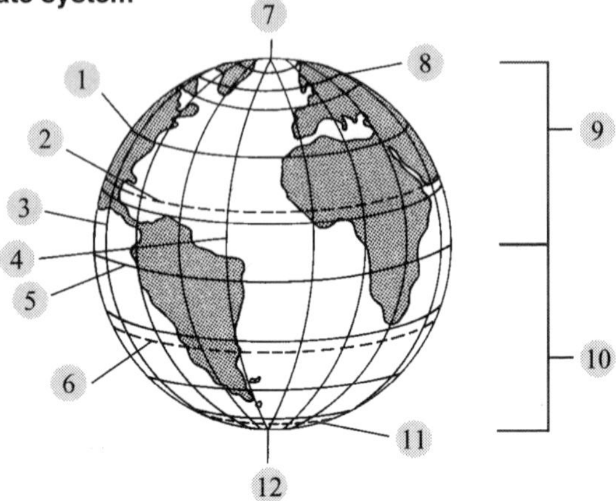

Celestial co-ordinate system

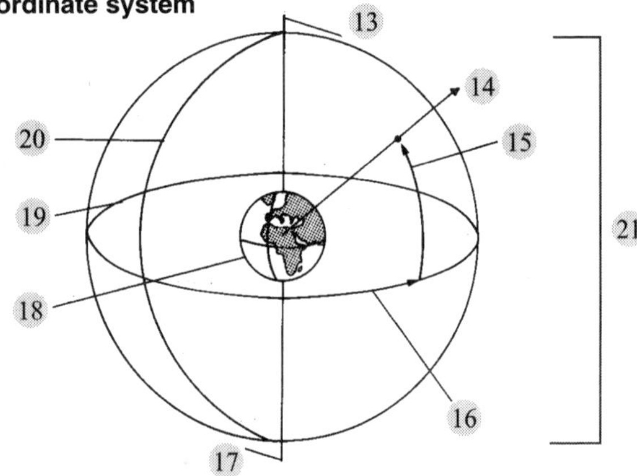

Seasons of the year

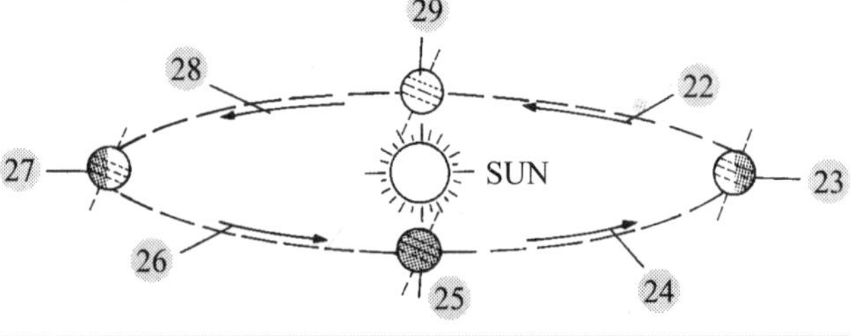

1.	Latitude	2.	Tropic of cancer	3.	Longitude	4.	Meridian
5	Equator	6.	Tropic of capricorn	7.	North pole	8.	Arctic circle
9.	Northern hemisphere	10.	Southern hemisphere	11.	Antarctic circle	12.	South pole
13.	North celestial pole	14.	North celestial pole	15.	Declination	16.	Right ascension
17.	South celestial pole	18.	Terrestrial sphere	19.	Celestial equator	20.	Celestial meridian
21.	Celestial sphere	22	Winter	23.	Winter solstice	24.	Autumn
25.	Autumnal equinox	26.	Summer	27.	Summer slostice 28. Spring	29.	Vernal equinox

Profile of the earth's atmosphere

Space achievements

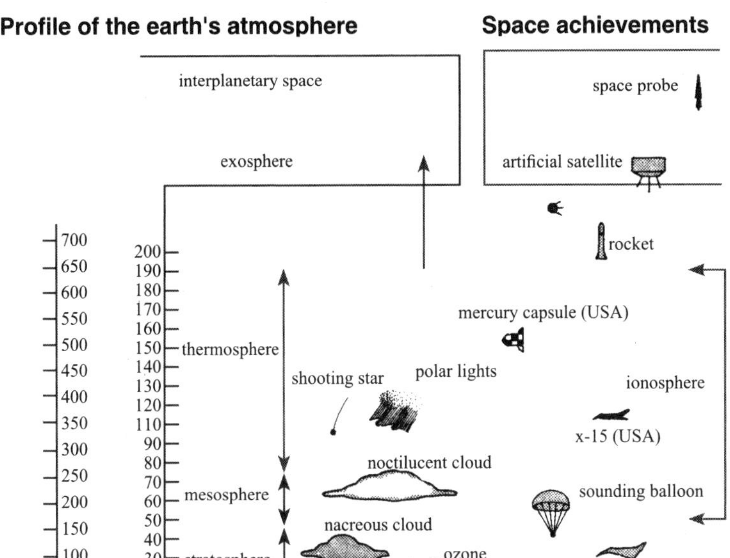

Configuration of the continents

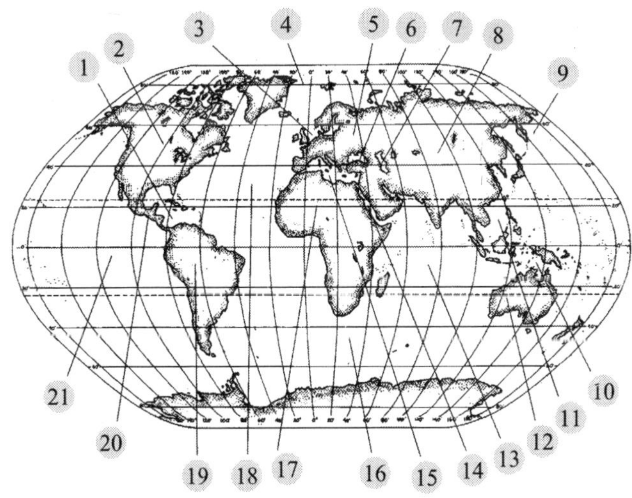

1.	Caribbean Sea	2.	North America	3.	North Sea	4.	Arctic Ocean
5	Europe	6.	Black Sea	7.	Caspian Sea	8.	Asia
9.	Bering Sea	10.	Oceania	11.	China Sea	12.	Australia
13.	Indian Ocean	14.	Red Sea	15.	Mediterranean Sea	16.	Antarctic Ocean
17.	Africa	18.	Atlantic Ocean	19.	South America	20.	Central America
21.	Pacific Ocean						

Major types of stone fruits

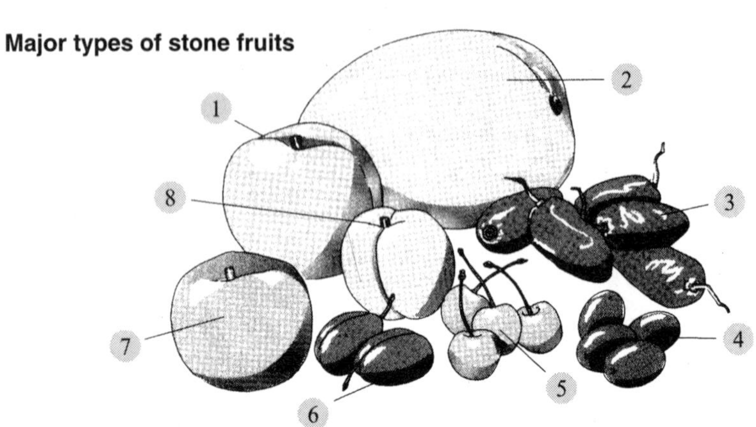

Principal types of pome fruits

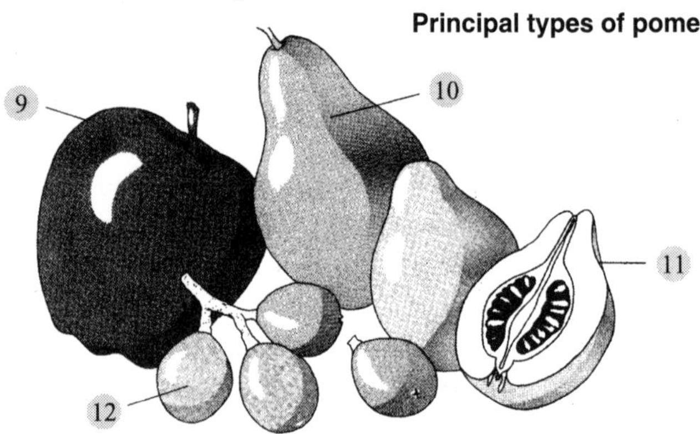

Major types of citrus fruits

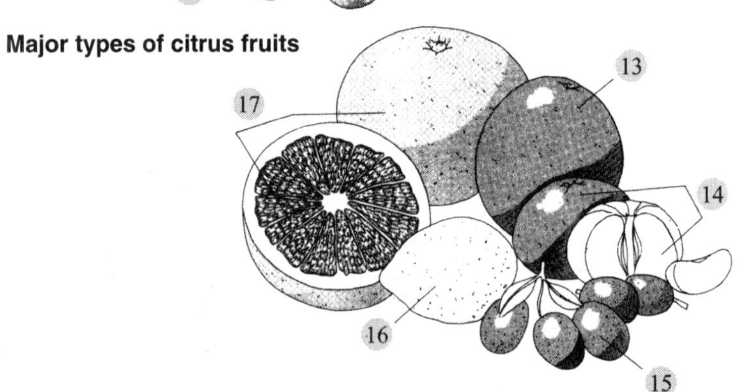

1. Peach	2. Mango	3. Date	4. Olive
5 Cherry	6. Plum	7. Nectarine	8. Apricot
9. Apple	10. Pear	11. Quince	12. Japan plum
13. Orange	14. Mandarin	15. Kumquat	16. Lemon
17. Grapefruit			

Tropical fruits

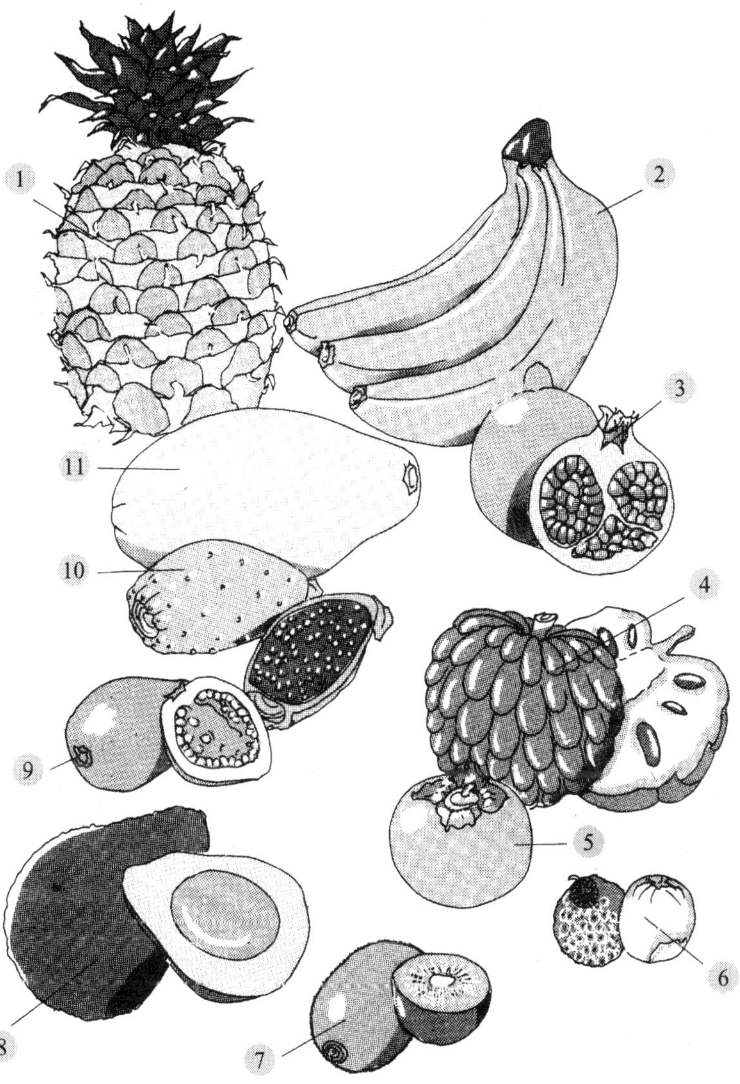

1. Pineapple	2. Banana	3. Pomegranate	4. Cherimoya
5 Japanese persimmon	6. Litchi	7. Kiwi	8. Avocado
9. Guava	10. Indian fig	11. Papaya	

Vegetables

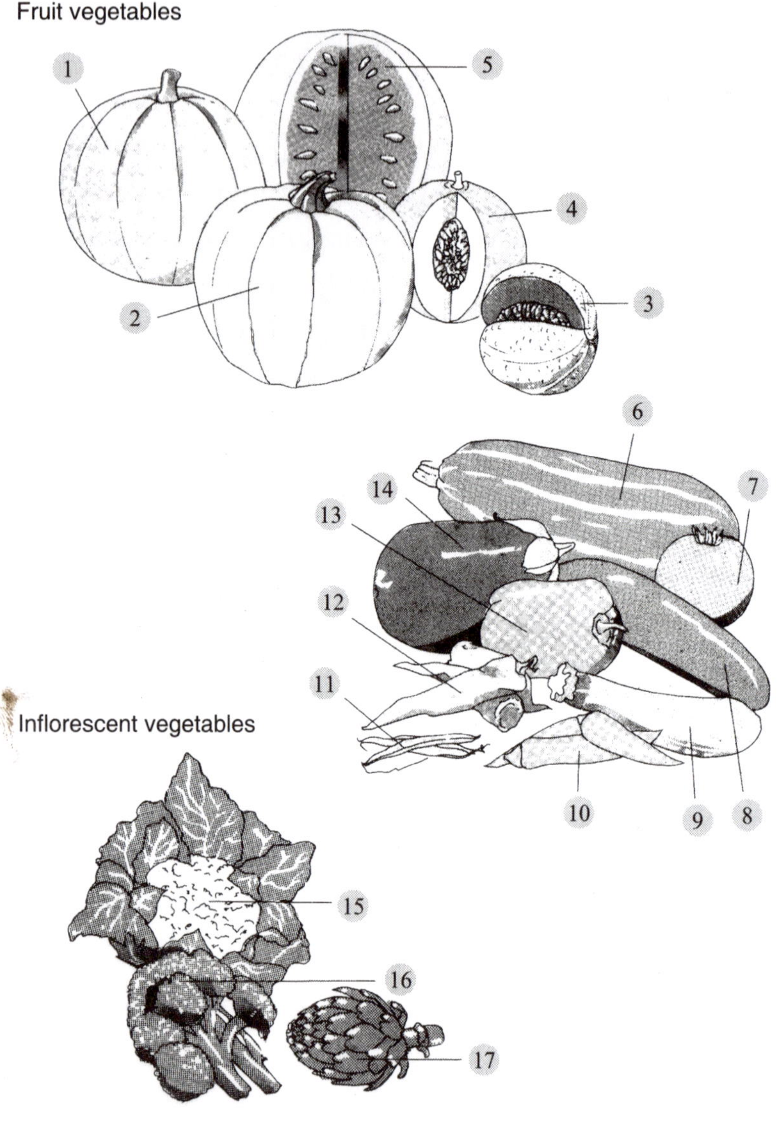

1. Autumn squash
2. Pumpkin
3. Cantaloupe
4. Muskmelon
5 Watermelon
6. Marrow
7. Tomato
8. Cucumber
9. Courgette
10. Okra
11. Grean bean
12. Chilli pepper
13. Sweet pepper
14. Aubergine
15. Cauliflower
16. Broccoli
17. Artichoke

Animal Kingdom

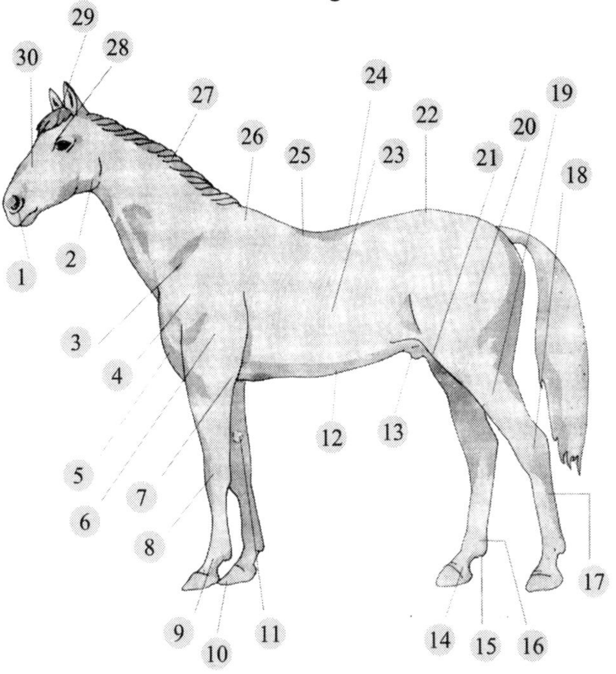

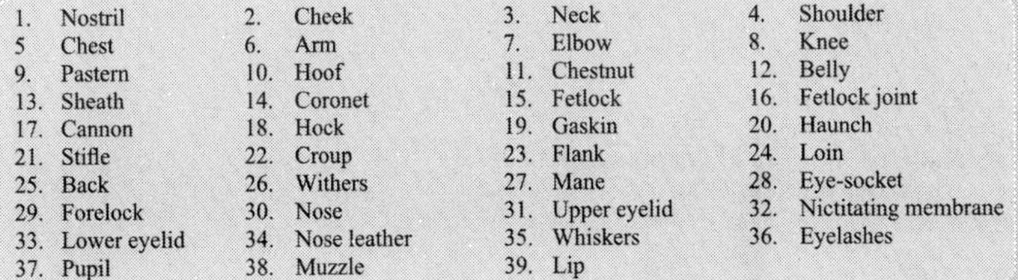

1.	Nostril	2.	Cheek	3.	Neck	4.	Shoulder
5	Chest	6.	Arm	7.	Elbow	8.	Knee
9.	Pastern	10.	Hoof	11.	Chestnut	12.	Belly
13.	Sheath	14.	Coronet	15.	Fetlock	16.	Fetlock joint
17.	Cannon	18.	Hock	19.	Gaskin	20.	Haunch
21.	Stifle	22.	Croup	23.	Flank	24.	Loin
25.	Back	26.	Withers	27.	Mane	28.	Eye-socket
29.	Forelock	30.	Nose	31.	Upper eyelid	32.	Nictitating membrane
33.	Lower eyelid	34.	Nose leather	35.	Whiskers	36.	Eyelashes
37.	Pupil	38.	Muzzle	39.	Lip		

Human body

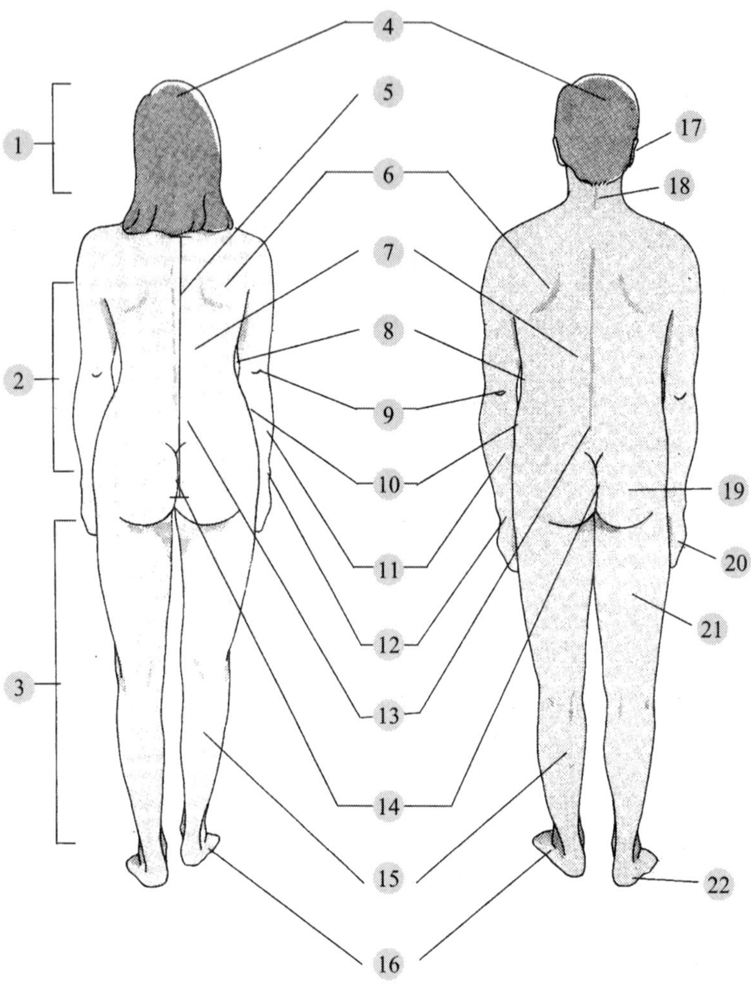

1. Head	2. Arm	3. Leg	4. Hair
5 Trunk	6. Shoulder blade	7. Back	8. Waist
9. Elbow	10. Hip	11. Forearm	12. Wrist
13. Loin	14. Posterior rugae	15. Calf	16. Foot
17. Ear	18. Nape	19. Buttock	20. Hand
21. Thigh	22. Heel		

Buildings

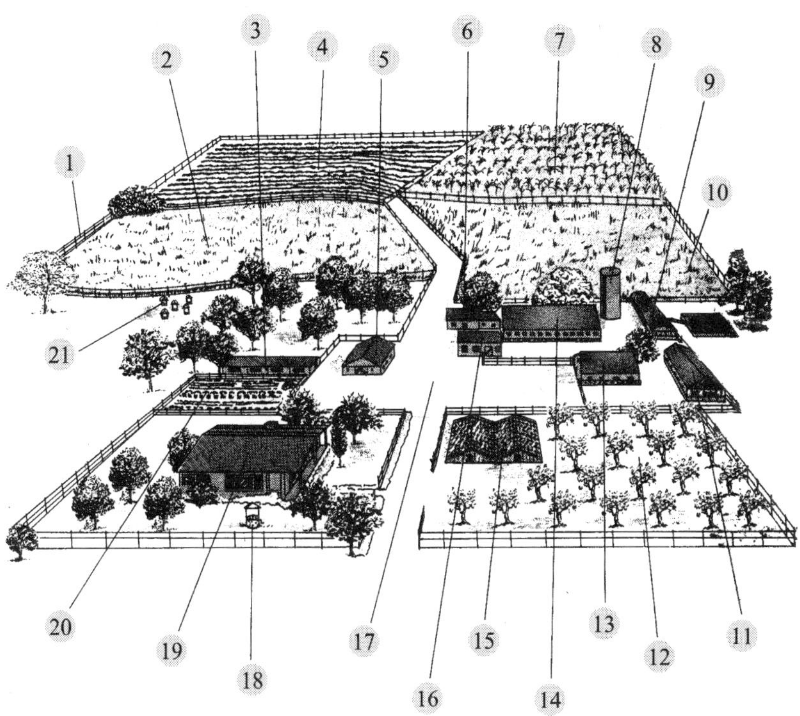

1. Electrified fence
2. Permanent pasture
3. Poultry house
4. Ploughed land
5 Barn
6. Milking parlour and dairy
7. Wheat
8. Tower silo
9. Silage bunker
10. Grass ley
11. Machinery store
12. Orchard
13. Piggery
14. Cowshed
15. Greenhouse
16. Loose boxes
17. Farmyard
18. Well
19. Farmhouse
20. Vegetable garden
21. Beehive

Urban scene

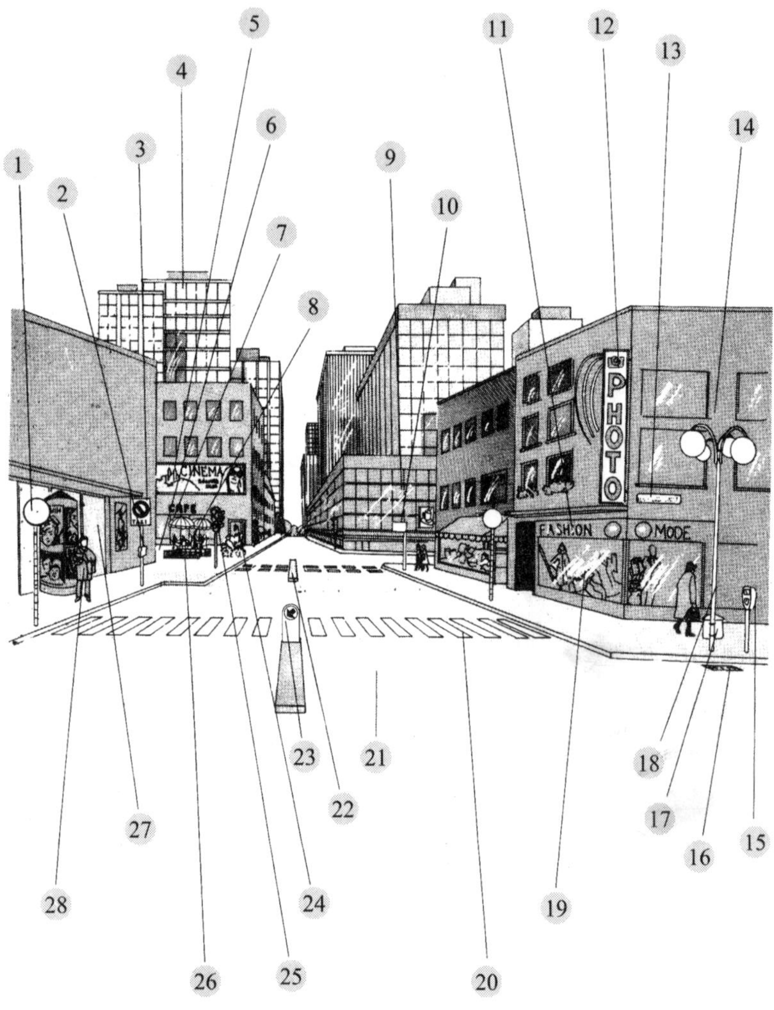

1. Belisha beacon	2. Taxi telephone	3. Taxi rank	4. High-rise office building
5 Hoarding	6. Pedestrian precinct	7. Street cafe	8. Terrace
9. Department store	10. Bus stop	11. Shop sign	12. Neon sign
13. Street sign	14. Street light	15. Parking meter	16. Drain
17. Litter bin	18. Lamp-post	19. Shop window	20. Pedestrian crossing
21. High street	22. Traffic island	23. Keep-left sign	24. Telephone box
25. Traffic lights	26. Subway entrance	27. Cinema	28. Newspaper vendor

House Styles

Exterior of a house

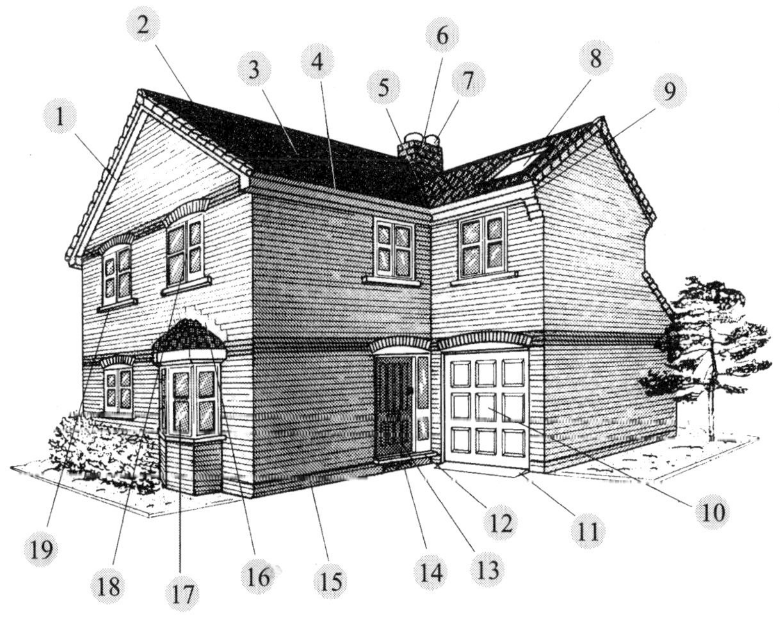

1.	Eaves	2.	Ridge tile	3.	Root	4.	Gutter
5	Valley	6.	Chimney stack	7.	Chimney pot	8.	Skylight
9.	Cornice	10.	Garage	11.	Ramp	12.	Doorstep
13.	Front door	14.	Airbrick	15.	Damp proof course	16.	Flashing
17.	Bay window	18.	Window frame	19.	Window sill		

Chairs and couches

Principal types

1. Three-seater settee	2. Récamier	3. Director's chair	4. Two-seater settee
5 Club chair	6. Chesterfield	7. Meridienne	8. Rockin chair

Kitchen utensils

Baking utensils

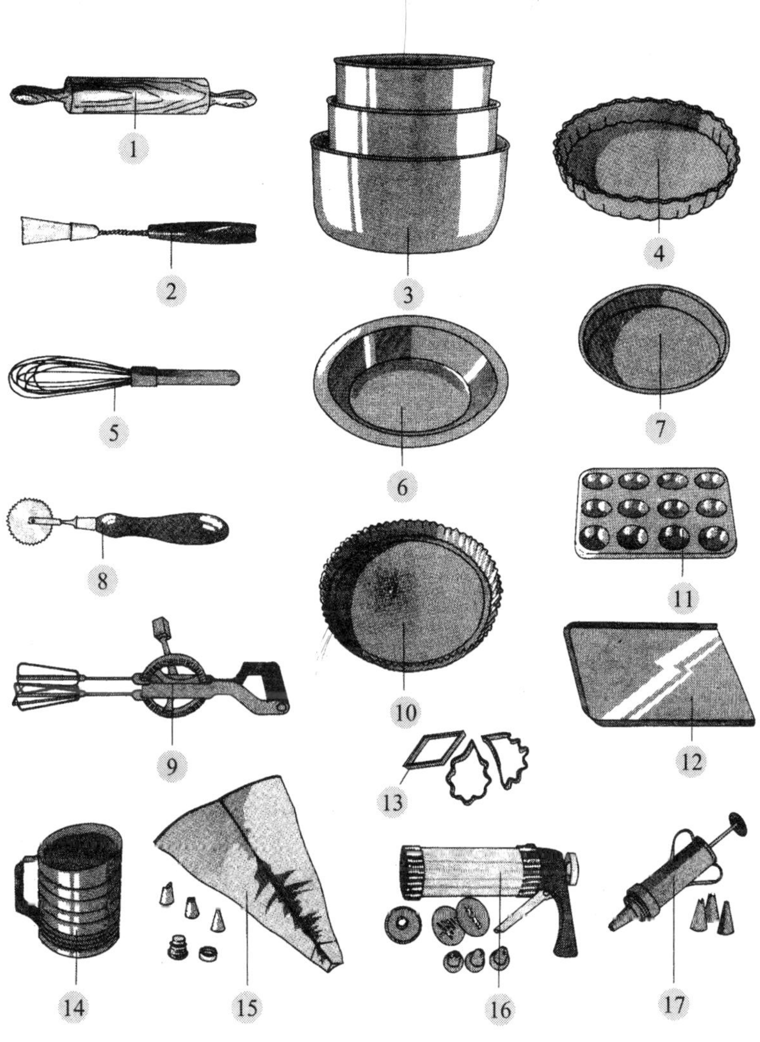

1.	Rolling pin	2.	Pastry brush	3.	Mixing bowls	4.	Quiche tin
5	Whisk	6.	Pie tin	7.	Cake tin	8.	Pastry cutting wheel
9.	Egg beater	10.	Flat tin	11.	Individual bun tin	12.	Baking sheet
13.	Biscuit cutters	14.	Sifter	15.	Savoy bag and nozzles	16.	Buiscuit press
17.	Icing syringe						

Kitchen utensils

Miscellaneous utensils

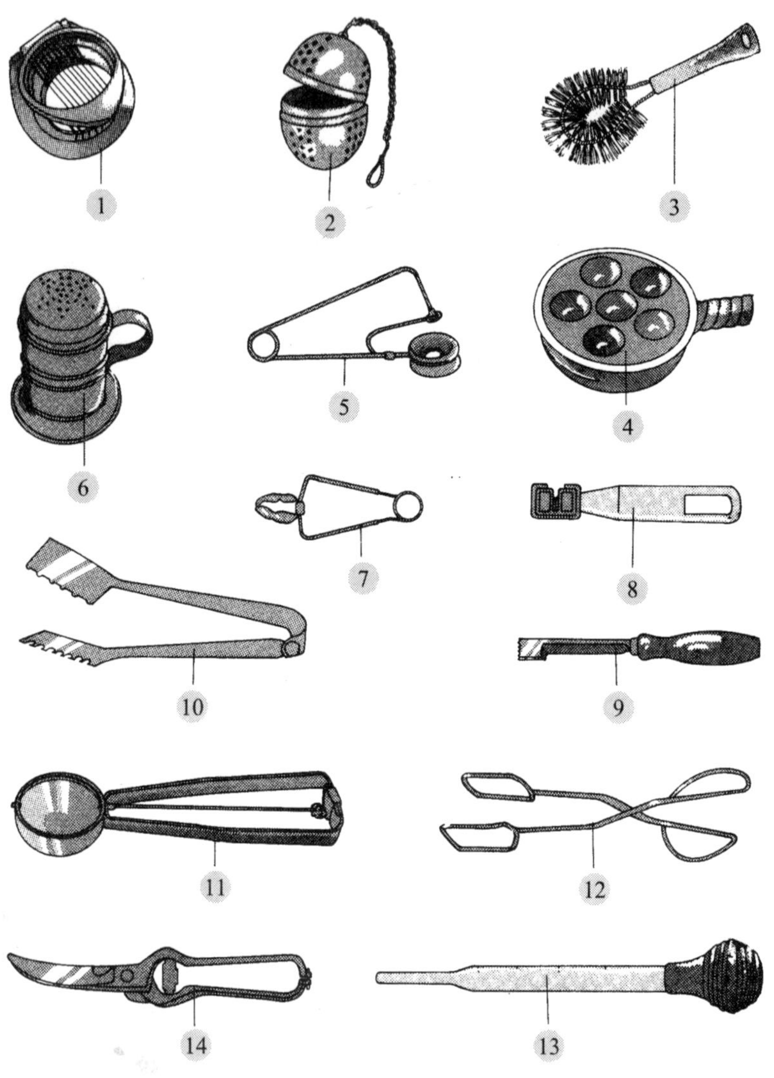

1. Egg slicer	2. Tea infuser	3. Vegetable brush	4. Snail dish
5 Stoner	6. Shaker	7. Snail tongs	8. Knife sharperner
9. Corer	10. Spaghetti tongs	11. Ice cream scoop	12. Tongs
13. Baster	14. Poultry shears		

Tools and equipment

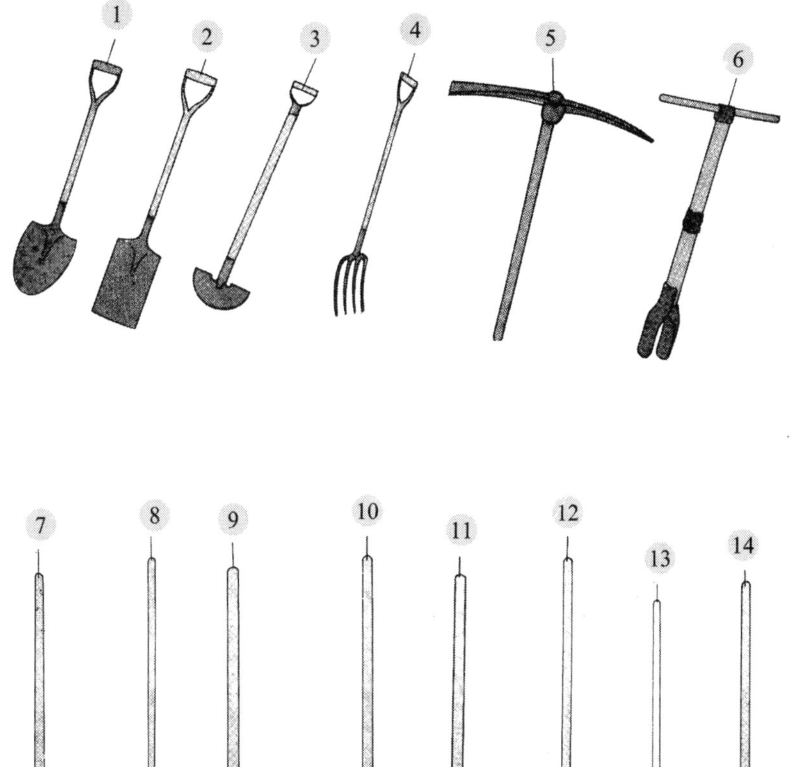

1. Shovel	2. Spade	3. Lawn edger	4. Digging fork
5 Pick	6. Post-hole digger	7. Rake	8. Lawn rake
9. Spreading fork	10. Dutch hoe	11. Ridging hoe	12. Draw hoe
13. Weeding hoe	14. Grubbing hoe		

Tools and equipment

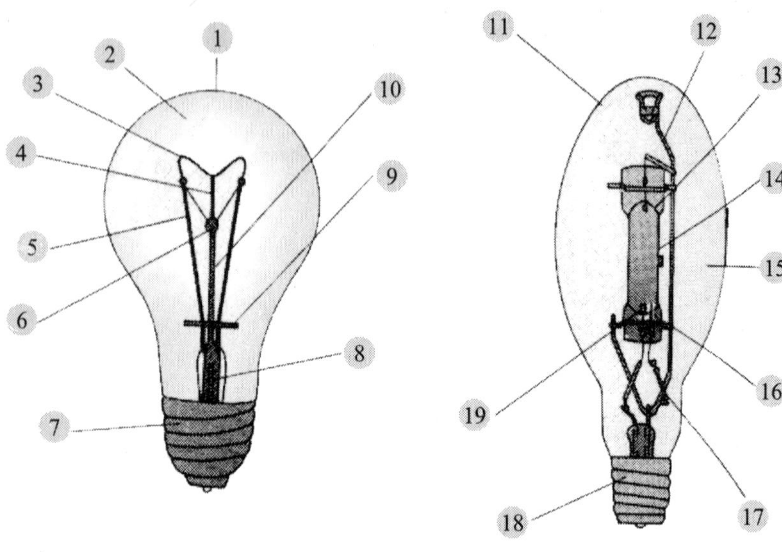

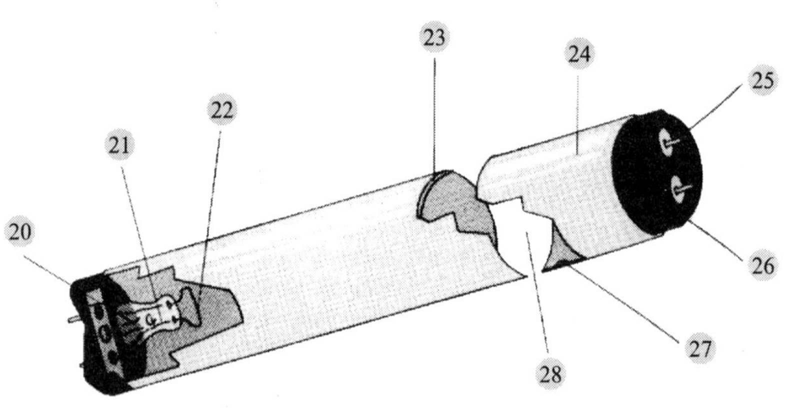

1. Bulb	2. Inert gas	3. Filament	4. Support
5 Lead-in wire	6. Button	7. Screw base	8. Exhaust tube
9. Heat deflecting disc	10. Stem	11. Bulb	12. Arc tube mount structure
13. Reflector	14. Arc tube	15. Nitrogen	16. Starting electrode
17. Starting resistor	18. Screw base	19. Main Electrode	20. Exhaust tube
21. Lead-in wire	22. Electrode	23. Phosphor coating	24. Bulb
25 Pin	26. Cap	27. Mercury	28. Gas

Personal Articles

Haircutting scissors

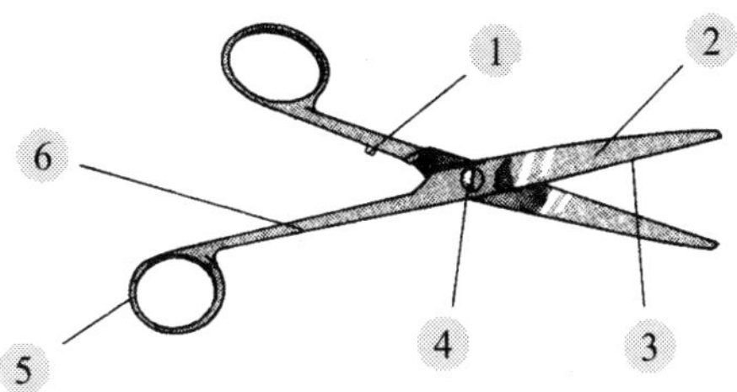

Notched double-edged thinning scissors

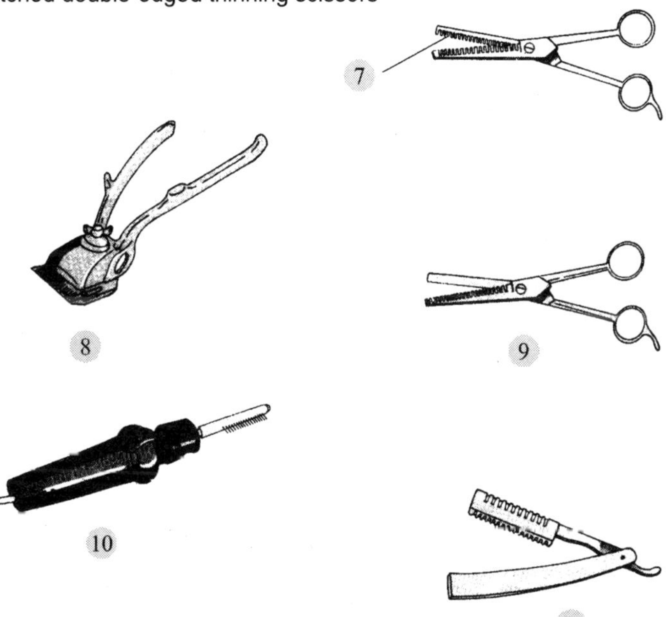

1. Blade close stop	2. Blade	3. Cutting edge	4. Pivot
5 Ferrule	6. Shank	7. Tooth	8. Clippers
9. Notched single-edged thinning scissors	10. Warm-air comb	11. Thinning razor	

Personal Articles

Hairbrushes

Combs

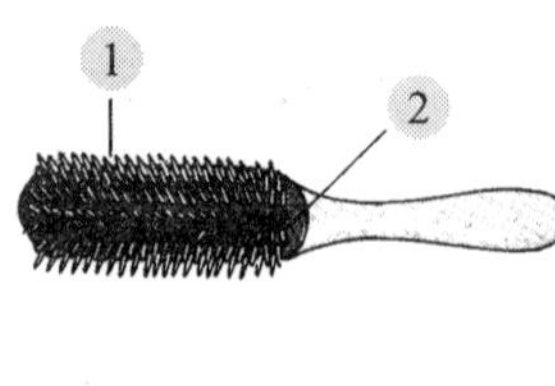

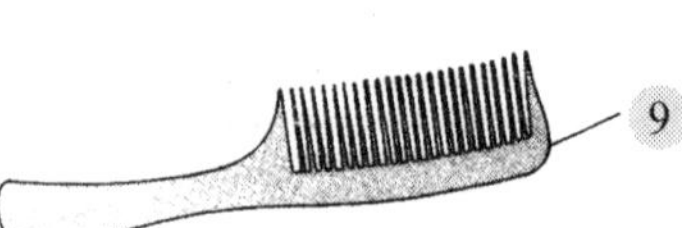

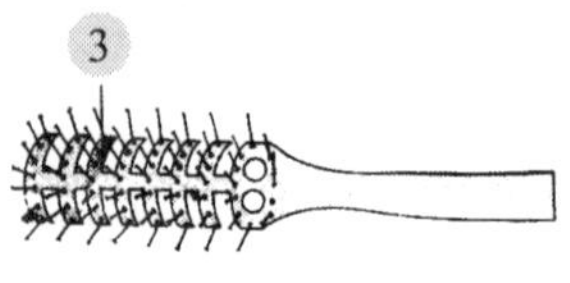

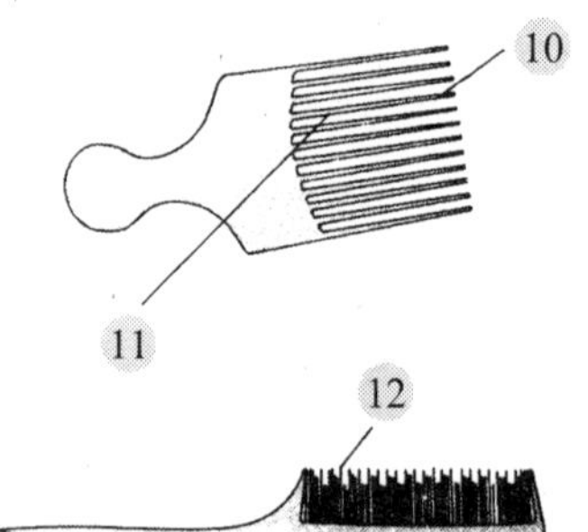

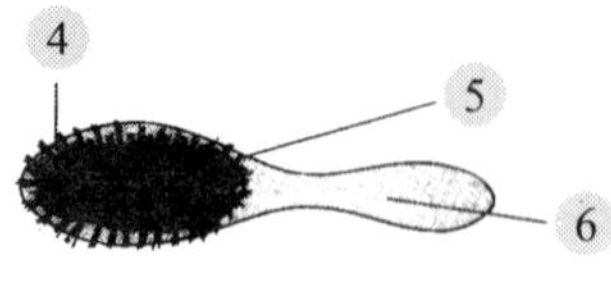

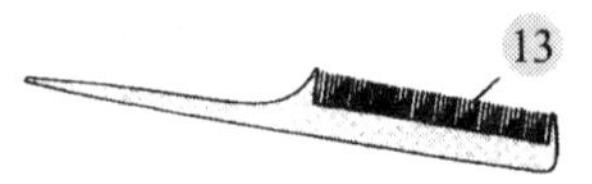

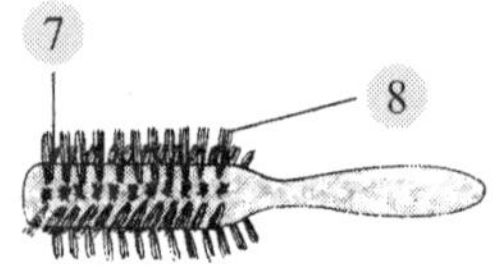

1. Quill brush	2. Row	3. Vent brush	4. Flat-back brush
5 Rubber base	6. Handle	7. Round brush	8. Bristle
9. Rake comb	10. Afro comb	11. Tooth	12. Teaser comb
13. Tail comb	14. Barber comb	15. Pitchfork comb	

Car

Front view

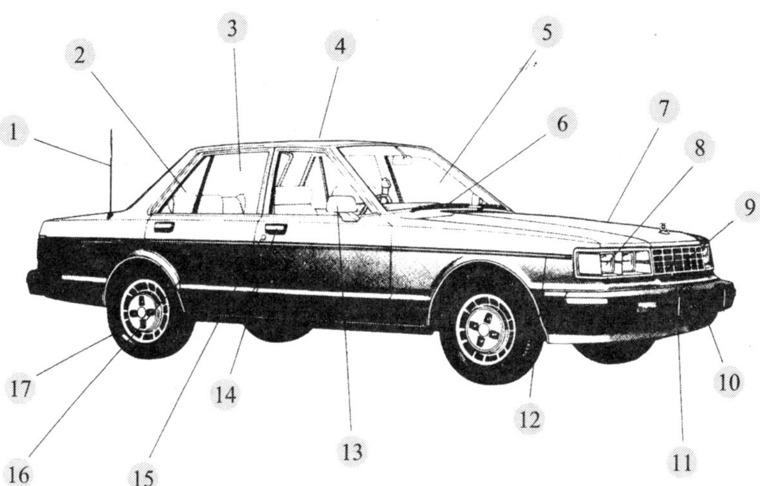

Rear view

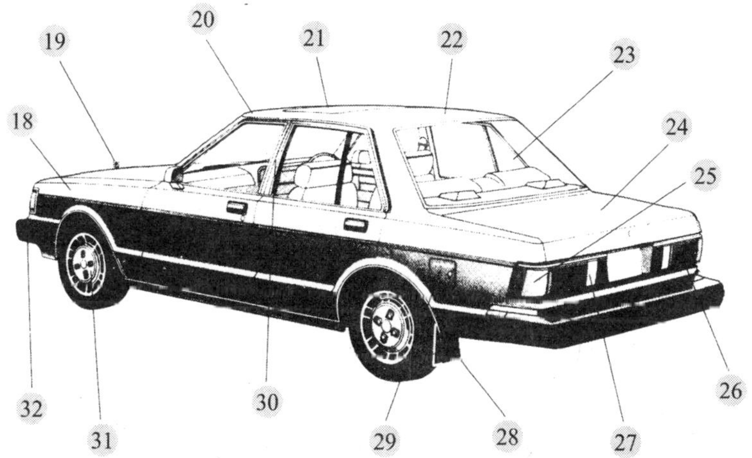

1. Aerial	2. Quarter window	3. Window	4. Root
5 Windscreen	6. Scuttle panel	7. Bonnet	8. Headlight
9. Grille	10. Bumper	11. Overrider	12. Side panel
13. Door mirror	14. Door handle	15. Door lock	16. door
17. Wheel	18. Wing	19. Emblem	20. Drip moulding
21. Sun roof	22. Rear window frame	23. Rear window	24. Boat
25. Indicator light	26. Rear light	27. Reversing light	28. Mud flap
29. Petrol flap	30. Door pillar	31. Hubcap	32. Front bumper

Bicycle

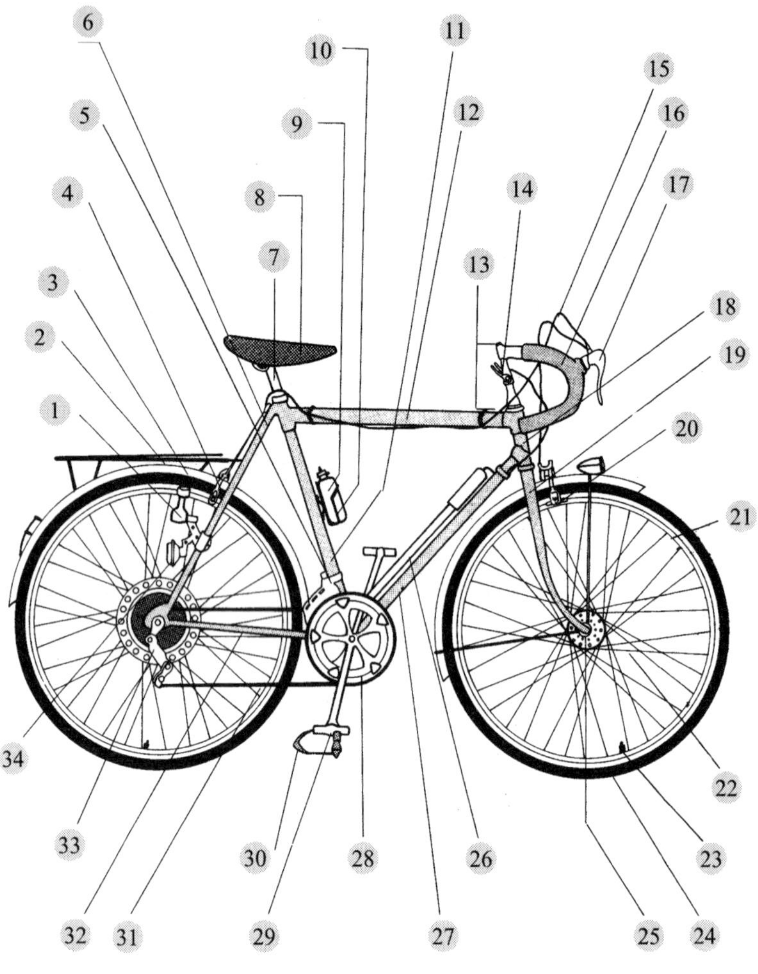

1.	Dynamo	2.	Carrier	3.	Mudguard	4.	Rear brake
5	Front derailleur	6.	Seat stay	7.	Seat post	8.	Saddle
9.	Water bottle	10.	Water bottle clip	11.	Seat tube	12.	Crossbar
13.	Stem	14.	Gear selector	15.	Brake cable	16.	Handlebars
17.	Brake lever	18.	Head tube	19.	Fork	20.	Front brake
21.	Rim	22.	Spoke	23.	Tyre valve	24.	Tyre
25.	Hub	26.	Tyre pump	27.	Down tube	28.	Chain wheel
29.	Pedal	30.	Toe clip	31.	Drive chain	32.	Chain stay
33.	Rear derailleur	34.	Rear light				

Passenger liner

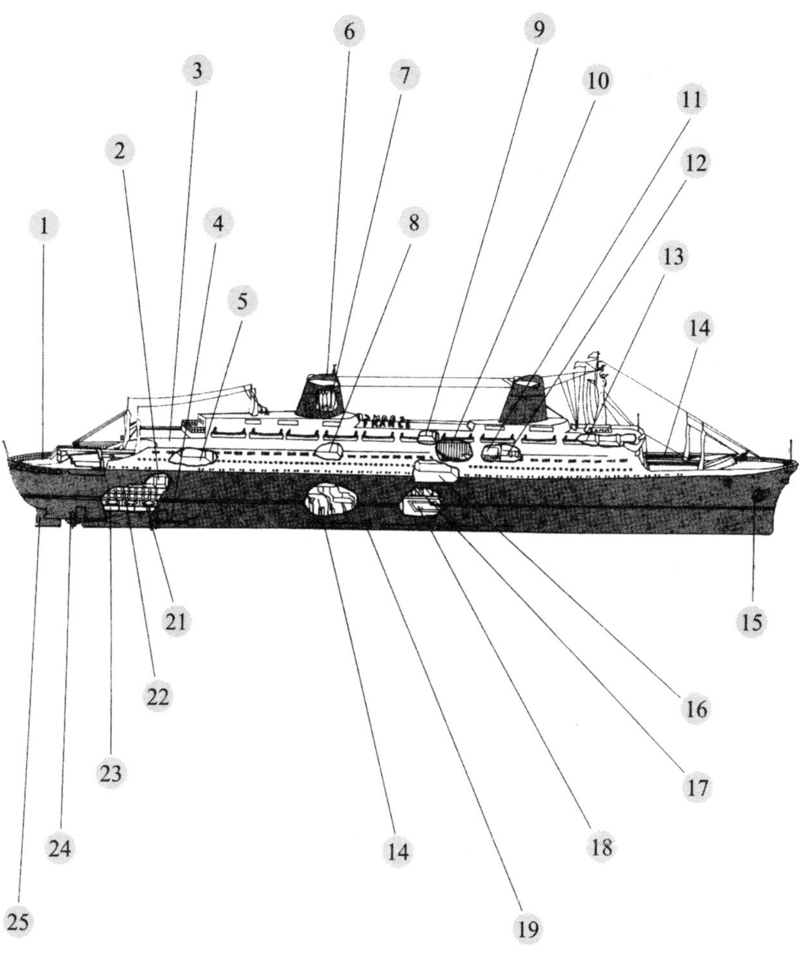

1.	Sundeck	2.	Tourist-class cabin	3.	Boat deck	4.	Propeller shaft
5	Hall	6.	Funnel aileron	7.	Smoke filter	8.	Lounge
9.	Deluxe suite	10.	Theatre	11.	Chapel	12.	Play room
13.	Captain's quarters	14.	Cargo hatch	15.	Anchor-windlass room	16.	Dining room
17.	Wine cellar	18.	Swimming pool	19.	Aft stabilizer fin	20.	Boiler room
21.	Garage	22.	Crew quarters	23.	Cargo hold	24.	Propeller
25.	Rudder						

Long-range aircraft

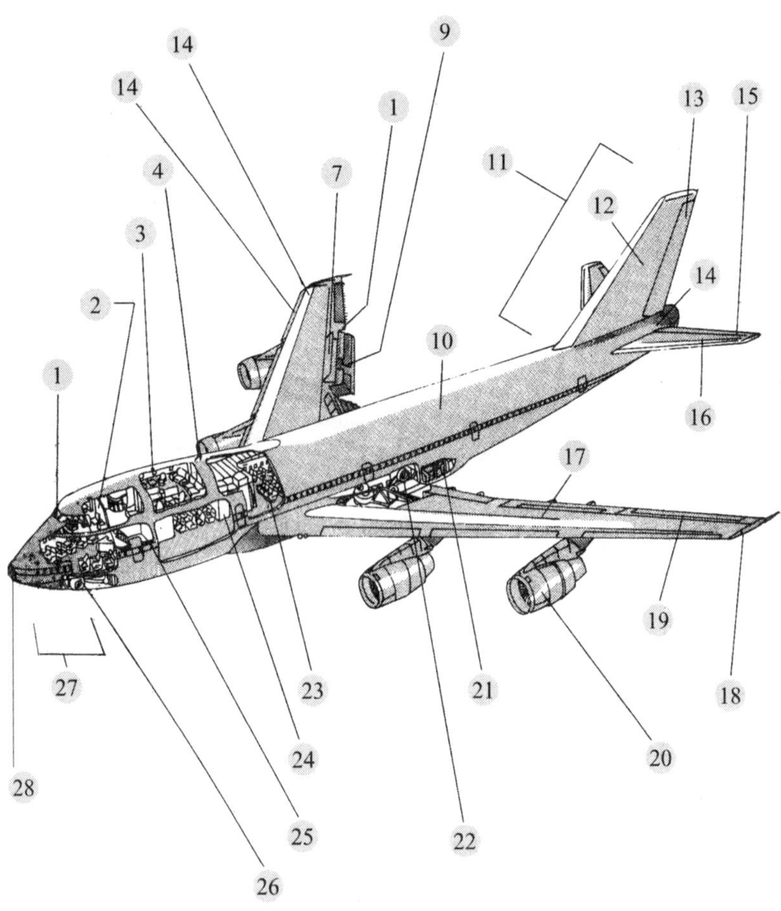

1. Windshield	2. Flight deck	3. Anti-collision light	4. Antenna
5 Leading edge	6. Leding edge flap	7. Spoiler	8. Trailing edge
9. Trailing edge flap	10. Fuselage	11. Tail assembly	12. Fin
13. Rudder	14. Tail	15. Elevator	16. Tail plane
17. Wing	18. Navigation light	19. Aileron	20. Turbofan jet engine
21. Freight hold	22. Main undercarriage	23. Passenger cabin	24. Gallery
25. Window	26. Nose wheel	27. Nose	28. Weather radar

Stationery

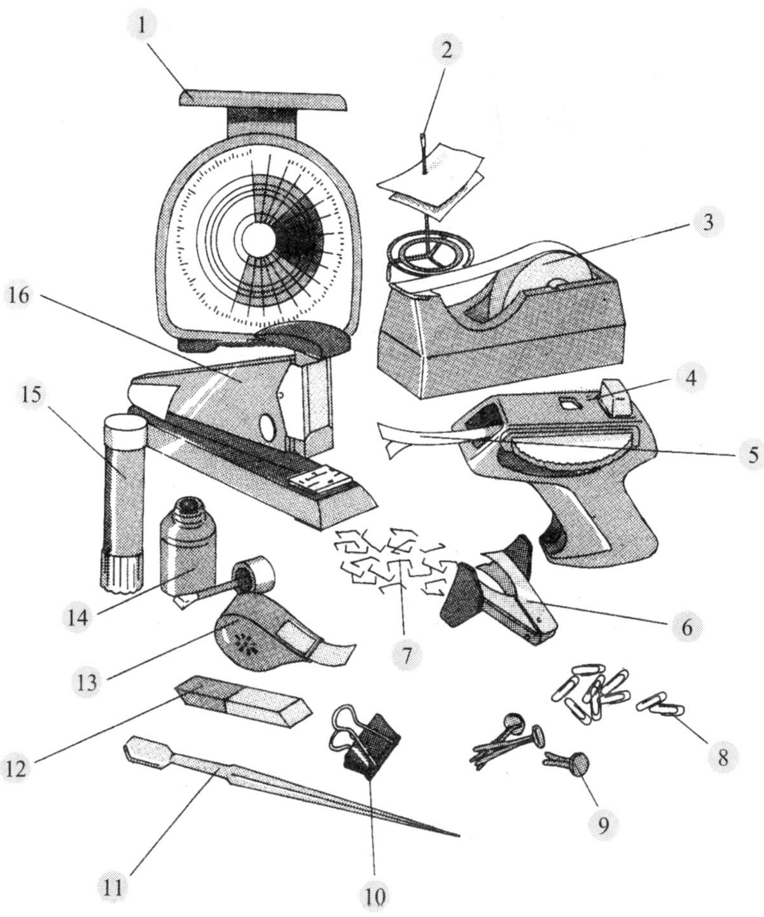

1. Letter scales
2. Spike file
3. Tape dispenser
4. Label maker
5 Tape
6. Staple remover
7. Staples
8. Paper clips
9. Paper fasteners
10. Foldback clip
11. Letter opener
12. Eraser
13. Correction paper
14. Correction fluid
15. Glue stick
16. Stapler

Stationery

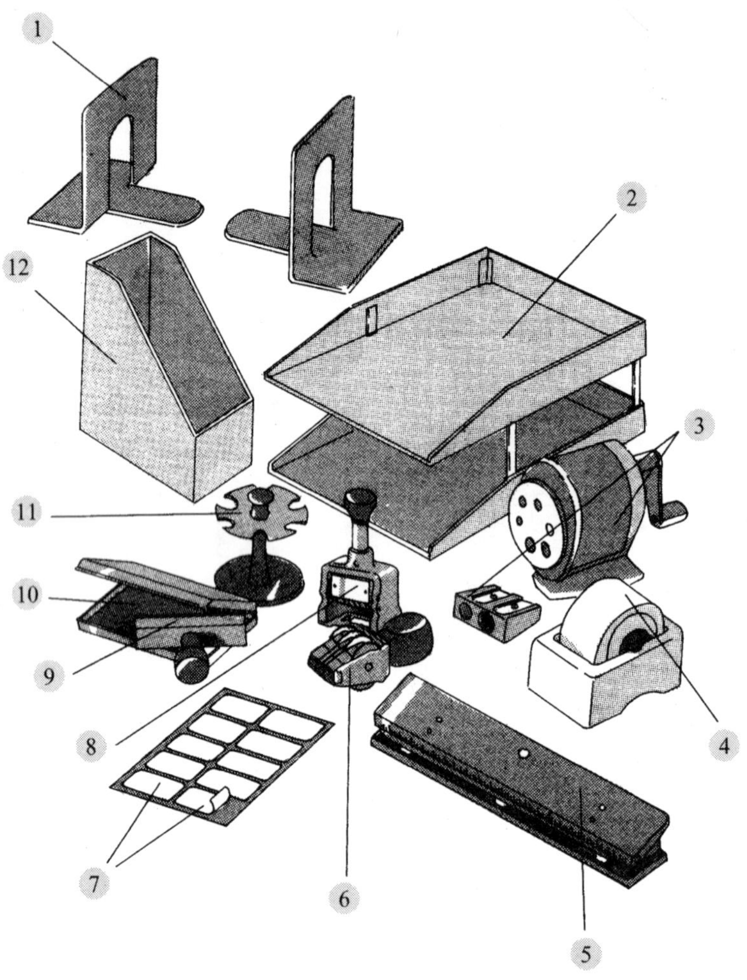

1. Book end	2. Desk tray	3. Pencil sharpeners	4. Moistener
5 paper punch	6. Dater	7. Self-adhesive lables	8. Numbering machine
9. Rubber stamp	10. Stamp pad	11. Stamp rack	12. Fitting box